Merging with Siva, fo
Siva, is the epitome c
ward realizations anc
manity and especially for followers of Hindu Dharma. Swamiji has presented a lucid exposition of the life divine in its manifold aspects, recognizing and responding to the many doubts and queries that spiritual aspirants are beset with. It is a veritable compendium, teaching about the soul's gradual evolution into a perfect state of full absorption into Siva (Sivavilaya). The program of daily spiritual contemplation and living is systematically laid out in a practical way, enabling seekers to cultivate their *sadhana.* Swamiji has revealed a vast fund of knowledge of Hindu philosophy and yoga psychology and spirituality, mainly on the basis of the southern school of Saiva Siddhanta, of which Swamiji is a living *acharya.* The entire trilogy seems to be Swamiji's personal offering to Parasiva, his dear Lord!

Dr. Mahesh Mehta, author, editor and professor of Religious Studies and Oriental Studies, University of Windsor; Ontario, Canada

Satguru Sivaya Subramuniyaswami has brought out this extraordinary book, *Merging with Siva,* presenting 365 daily lessons for Hindu families and their children to build character, understand the mind and strive for God Realization. It is stated how wisdom, or the burst of knowledge, begins to unfold and express itself. Such a burst of knowledge can happen only in the lives of those who strive hard to tread the spiritual path. Those who seek the path of enlightenment will surely be benefitted by these 365 daily lessons. The spiritual experiences narrated in this book will perhaps change one's life forever. *Merging with Siva* will no doubt serve the cause of Global Hindu Renaissance.

H.H. Jagadguru Sri Balagangadharanatha Swamiji, President, Sri Adichunchanagiri Mahasamsthana Mutt; Bangalore, India

Fortunate will be those who read and practice the principles of metaphysics explained and simplified in this unique book, *Merging with Siva*, based on the 50 years of practical experience and *sadhana* of Jagadacharya Satguru Sivaya Sri Subramuniyaswamigal of Kauai Aadheenam. In my opinion, this is God's boon for modern society living in complexity and confusion. This book is a guiding light which illuminates the path to peace, prosperity and happiness by integration and harmony of mind, body and soul to lead towards the ultimate purpose and goal of human life. I highly recommend the precious work, *Merging with Siva,* to every serious-minded person.

H.H. Sri Sri Swami Bua Maharaj, Centenarian, Founder and Head of Indo-American Yoga-Vedanta Society; New York

Merging with Śiva

शिवे विलयम्

சிவனோடு ஒன்றுகூடுதல்

First Edition

 Designed, typeset and illustrated by the *sannyāsin swāmīs* of the Śaiva Siddhānta Yoga Order and published by Himalayan Academy, 107 Kaholalele Road, Kapaa, Hawaii, 96746-9304, USA.

Published by
Himalayan Academy
India • USA

PRINTED IN USA

Library of Congress Catalog Card Number 98-73075

ISBN 0-945497-74-1

www.hindu.org/ashram/

Merging with Śiva

Hinduism's Contemporary Metaphysics

शिवे विलयम्

सनातनधर्मस्य सहवर्तिन्यः अतिविज्ञानविद्याः

சிவனோடு ஒன்றுகூடுதல்

இந்து சமயத்தின் தற்கால மெய்ஞ்ஞானம்

Satguru Sivaya
Subramuniyaswami

Indra Sharma
1958

ഉ

Dedication

Samarpaṇam

समर्पणम्

TO WHOM SHALL WE DEDICATE *MERGING WITH ŚIVA*? TO ŚIVA HIMSELF? WELL, ŚIVA IS WITHIN EVERYONE. ACTUALLY, IT IS NOT POSSIBLE FOR Him to withdraw Himself from us. So, *Merging with Śiva* truly must be dedicated to Sadāśiva, in the form of my *satguru*, Śiva Yogaswāmī of Sri Lanka, and to all whom I have encountered on the path through this and my many past lives. This dedication honors those mature souls who have guided me into what to do, how to live, think and feel, and those not-so-evolved souls who have taught me by their example, words and actions how not to live for a productive, joyous life. Yes, "All are our teachers—some teach us what to do. Others teach us what not to do." The decision as to which of these two paths to follow is ours and ours alone. It is to all who have influenced my life that *Merging with Śiva* is dedicated, especially to my *satguru*, 161st preceptor of the Nandinātha Sampradāya's Kailāsa Paramparā. He and his mystical followers lived the extraordinary story of unfoldment you are about to read. ¶In this birth, I have experienced a rare time on Earth. I wouldn't have missed it for anything. All in a few decades, the age of the farmer merged into the age of the technician, then into the age of space exploration, and now the information age. We have seen religion give way to science and now science giving way to religion—just a little, but it's a good omen. Hopefully, a new breed of souls will mature on this planet who, inspired by the eternal Vedic truths, will blend the best of science with the best of religion.

Contents

Vishayasūchī

विषयसूची

PART ONE: Dancing in the Light

PART TWO: Living in the Now

PART THREE: Merging in the All

PART FOUR: Cognizantability
The Conquest of the Mind

Author's Introduction

Granthakāra Bhūmikā

ग्रन्थकारभूमिका

THE PAST CENTURY HAS BROUGHT AN OVERWHELMING INFLUX OF FAR EASTERN THOUGHT TO THE WESTERN COUNTRIES. THERE, NEEDless to say, have been innumerable approaches made to psychology, philosophy and the *yogic* science from all states of consciousness. Some excellent, highly recommended works have been published, written by the illuminati, those rare beings inspired by the superconscious mind. Others have compiled comparative intellectual studies, and still others have written purely instinctively. Inspired, perhaps, by brief flashes from the great beyond, they write only to clarify their own minds on various points relative to the unfoldment of the mind and spirit.

It is of the greatest importance to note from what state of consciousness an author has written his works. This is an easy task for the "old timer," but exceedingly difficult for the beginner, who finds himself faced with an array of books to choose from. Though eager to know himself and unfold into deeper realms of thought, the problem of knowing what to choose and how to study what has been chosen is a great one.

Merging with Śiva is a collection of a lifetime of realization. *Realization* is knowing, the aftermath of experience, having proven to oneself from the inside of oneself the deeper knowing. It also means "what has been seen." This no one can take away, change or alter. If you are as I am, liking to peruse a book from the back to the front, *Merging with Śiva* is just that book for you. The end is the beginning, and the beginning is the end.

It all started in 1949 when I had certain great realizations of "Truth," "Self," "Paraśiva," "Absolute Reality," in the Caves of Jalani in Sri Lanka, followed by meeting my *satguru,* receiving initiation into the order of *sannyāsa* and returning to America. That was a long time ago. It was in 1950 that the *jñāna,* wisdom, bursts of knowledge, began to happen; in speaking out from the "inner skies," the *vak* or unrehearsed knowing, was released. As the five states of mind began to unfold in all their intricate variations, aphorisms were spoken and then immediately written before forgotten, not unlike the *sūtras* or *ślokas* of olden Vedic times.

These aphorisms and their commentaries, or *bhāshyas,* mystically written seven years later, make up Part Four of *Merging with Śiva,* called "Cognizantability," which was published separately in 1958, 1962, 1966 and 1970, and under the title *Rāja Yoga* in 1973. This took place many years ago, when I was first beginning the mighty mission my *satguru* gave to me, to build a bridge between the East and West, to erect temples, to feed thousands and roar like a lion around the world. From deep inside, these profound aphorisms emerged to be quickly written down. Coming as they did, from the deep inner mind, they explain the structure of the mind itself. *Merging with Śiva's* lessons are based on a few of these many aphorisms that eventually comprised the first book to be published when I began my first formal teaching ministry, in 1957. This is the foundation of *Merging with Śiva's* 52 chapters, comprising 365 daily lessons. So, we can see that the end is the beginning.

It may be of interest to relate how the commentaries came about. It was in Denver, Colorado—the mile-high city in the Rocky Mountains—that the commentaries were written, seven years after the aphorisms were revealed. My external mind was learning to fully accept superconscious knowing, and the deeper inner mind was actively making itself the knower of the known. Oddly enough, one day the inner said to the outer mind to number each aphorism, which are now Sections One and Two of "Cognizantability," and place them all face down on the floor. I obediently did this. Then, one after another, the commentaries were revealed, three words at a time with a significant pause between. The superconscious would dictate word by word to the conscious mind to be written down. Amazingly, it proceeded to dictate the commentary to number seven, then number fourteen and so on. When all were done, the natural impulse urged me to turn over the aphorisms that were still face down on the floor with a number on the back to see if the commentary matched the aphorism. It did! They all did! Truly, I became a more dedicated believer in the *jñāna mārga*, the aftermath of experiencing the beyond of the beyond of the beyond, which we call Paraśiva, the fulfillment of the *yoga mārga.* As the years passed by one after another, this procedure of bringing unrehearsed wisdom through from the higher mind to the external became a natural part of my daily life—"one of the tools of the trade," I have often said. These psychic powers sometimes take years to develop. But under the right circumstances those ones carried over from a previous incarnation come immediately, of course, and are as much available as the ability to speak, listen and feel.

What you are about to study will be a progressive, mind-changing experience in 365 daily lessons. Read and reread them as a book. Or, as a *sādhana,* take one lesson a day and contemplate it as a beautiful gem. The discourses or inspired talks which make up the lessons have been brought together in this remarkable collection from half a century of teaching and guiding devotees. In assembling *Merging with Śiva,* I personally reviewed each word, sentence and paragraph from the original texts. You may be assured that you now hold in your hands a lifetime of realization and transformation which should stimulate you into pursuing some of the same realizations. Many of these inspired talks were given and recorded twenty, thirty or forty years ago. I endeavored to keep with the original wording as much as possible, often taking subsequently published versions back to their earlier form, while making virtually no, or only slight, changes when I felt such changes were needed to be effective in the present era. Hence they maintain their conversational style, which I call "Talkenese," having not been reedited in a more book-like manner. (You will enjoy the special inspired talks chronology on page 1307). I say this to avoid any possible disputes in the future that might arise: "I read aloud, edited and revalidated every word in this treasure-trove, during a three-year retreat from 1996 to 1999, making a mature evaluation, at age 72, of what stands as true and trustworthy, rock solid, worthy to pass on to the future." There is much power in these words because of the combined *brahmacharya* force, the divine spiritual energy of the *tapas* and *sādhana,* of our Nandinātha order of *āchāryas, swāmīs, yogīs* and *sādhakas.*

Merging with Śiva is a book that has your potential woven into it. It is not the typical book expounding the techniques of *yoga* or various methods of improving the physical body. It does not offer six dozen kinds of breath control or 108 postures. Instead, it reveals the *yoga* of life, *jñāna yoga,* of self-understanding and relationship, of who you are deep inside. This is the *yoga* of change, of unfolding new perspectives. It is, indeed, the discovery of your own true, divine identity—the I Am, the Being within, the Watcher, the Seer. Discover various areas of your inner and outer mind through carefully observing your reactions to intuitive flashes as you read. You may find yourself thinking, "I have always known that," or "Yes, that is truly what I have experienced." Then mentally build on the acknowledgment of these tiny realizations, and the bigger ones will naturally come at the right time and in the right way.

How to Study this Book

To study *Merging with Śiva,* it is important to read through the entire book at least once. Then go through the daily lessons day after day just before sleep. Read the lesson of the day to the family, to friends and send it to loved ones on e-mail. The 365 lessons are divided into three parts: "Dancing in the Light," "Living in the Divine" and "Merging in the All," organized as to the three seasons we follow at Kauai Aadheenam. Thus, Part One corresponds with the season that begins April 14. Part Two begins on August 15, and Part Three begins on December 15. Serious seekers will choose one of these mystical times to commence the *sādhana* of reading the daily lessons around the year. Look back over the year, and you will clearly view your spiritual unfoldment as to how you have changed in belief, attitude and have been transformed a little in various departments of your life.

Each lesson is to be absorbed into the subconscious mind, to be experienced, sometimes immediately, such as the lessons on affirmation and the numerous lessons on awareness flowing through the mind as a traveler journeys from city to city. This anyone of any background can experience. Inner light is also described in many lessons. It has been experienced by many, many—the light within a darkened room shining within the body. You do not have to be a saint, sage, philosopher or anything but an ordinary person to experience inner light. This experience makes you an extraordinary person.

Read and absorb each chapter as a complete concept. Don't belabor each point. This is not a rigorous philosophical treatise, but a free-flowing *upadeśa* of a *guru* seeing things as they are and responding to questions of devotees at the time, explaining situations that had arisen in the group around him, from an inner perspective. These spontaneous spoken essays describe the strivings of tens of thousands of seekers over a period of fifty years. Their questions are, no doubt, your questions, and my answers given here would no doubt be your answers, because these eternal matters don't change all that much through the millennia. This is not an intellectual study.

Remember that there are two books that precede *Merging with Śiva* for a full and deepening transformation. They are *Dancing with Śiva* and *Living with Śiva*. Both envision a complete change in philosophy and lifestyle. *Dancing with Śiva, Living with Śiva* and *Merging with Śiva* form a trilogy, my legacy. In philosophical terms relating to the path of attainment: the *charyā mārga* is *Dancing with Śiva*, the *kriyā mārga* is *Living with Śiva* and *Merging with Śiva* outlines the *yoga* and *jñāna mārga*. Here, in our trilogy, we have a complete study for a lifetime, or two, or possibly more?

Part Four of *Merging with Śiva* is "Cognizantability," the thought-provoking *rāja yoga* aphorisms and their commentaries. The Resource Section is rich and searching, beginning with "There Can Be Only One Final Conclusion," which explores monism and pluralism in Śaiva Siddhānta. Then follows a brief synopsis of Śaivism and its holy lineages. Resource Three is Swāmī Vivekānanda's little-known poem "Song of the *Sannyāsin*," extolling the ideals of renunciation upheld by today's three million Hindu monastics. This is followed by a "Key to the Astral Colors" and "Charts: Cosmology, Chakras and Tattvas." All this is the fruit of a lifetime of meditation.

The quotations on the title page of each chapter are verses from the *Tirumantiram*, the Nandinātha Sampradāya's oldest Tamil scripture; written ca 200 BCE by Ṛishi Tirumular. It is a vast storehouse of esoteric *yogic* and *tantric* knowledge, the first book of the *Tirumurai*, which is a collection of celebrated Tamil scriptures by the South Indian saints of Śaiva Siddhānta. The *Tirumantiram's* 3,047 verses contain the mystical essence of *rāja yoga* and *siddha yoga*, and the fundamental doctrines of the twenty-eight *Śaiva Siddhānta Āga-*

mas, which along with the *Vedas* form the basis of our tradition.

Ṛishi Tirumular was a pre-eminent theologian of our Śaiva faith, but not merely a theologian. He was also a *siddhar,* an accomplished *yogī.* His *satguru* was Mahāṛishi Nandinātha who had eight disciples. Some were sent to China and others elsewhere. It was Tirumular who was sent to South India to teach monistic Śaiva Siddhānta and resolve the Monism-Pluralism problem, which was present even then. Ṛishi Tirumular was the *guru* of the *guru* who initiated the *guru* who became the *guru* who trained the *guru* who, when the succession had passed through two thousand years, eventually ordained my *satguru,* who initiated me, and then I trained for three decades my three well-qualified successors, following the same pattern as set in the long, long ago. Our Hindu scriptures come from such great men, men who have attained to the deepest realizations through their *sādhana* and their devotion. Their awareness dwells in the superconscious states resident in all men but penetrated intentionally by only a few, and when they speak out from that state, we consider that it is not man himself who has thus spoken, but the Divine through man. Ṛishi Tirumular was such a knower of the Unknowable, who held Truth in the palm of his hand, and his words are valued as a divine message for mankind.

The Hindu View of Liberation

Merging with Śiva is all about liberation, the earning of freedom from the body, mind and emotions through union with the Divine, ultimately in total inextricable merger of the soul in God. Having lived many lives, each soul seeks release from mortality, experiences the Divine directly through Self Realization and ultimately attains *moksha,* liberation from the round of births and deaths.

The religions of India are unique in their knowledge of the soul's spiritual evolution through a multitude of physical incarnations. Scripture tells us this evolution culminates in Self Realization, which, once sufficient *karma* is resolved, confers *moksha*, release from the cycle of birth and death.

Moksha, from the root *much* or *moksh,* has many connotations: to loose, to free, release, let loose, let go and thus also to spare, to let live, to allow to depart, to dispatch, to dismiss and even to relax, to spend, bestow, give away and open. Thus it means "release from worldly existence or transmigration; final or eternal emancipation."

Moksha is not a state of extinction of the soul, nor of nonexistence, nor of nonconsciousness. It is perfect freedom, an indescribable state of nondifferentiation, a proximity to the Divine within. *Moksha* marks an end to the Earthly sojourn, but it may also be understood as a beginning, not unlike graduation from the university. *Kaivalya* is another apt term for this ineffable condition of perfect detachment, freedom and oneness.

To reach this emancipation beyond all joy and sorrow, all difference and decay, the soul must remove, in order, the three fetters: *karma,* which is "the power of cause and effect, action and reaction;" *māyā,* which is "the power of manifestation" sometimes called illusion; and *āṇava,* "the power of egoity or veil of duality." Once freed by God's grace from these bonds—which do not cease to exist, but no longer have the power to bind—the soul experiences *nirvikalpa samādhi.* This is the realization of the Self, Atattva Parabrahman—timeless, formless, spaceless—a oneness beyond all change or diversity. Self Realization is man's natural state, which each soul eventually comes to. While the ultimate goal of earthly life is the experience (or more precisely the nonexperience) of Self Realization, the by-product of that realization is *moksha.* These two are not synonymous.

While some sects of Hinduism teach that liberation

comes only upon death, most embrace the state of *jīvanmukti,* liberation in which the advanced soul unfolds its inherent perfection while alive. It is said of such a great one that "He died before he died," indicating the totally real, not merely symbolic, demise of the ego.

It is possible to realize the Self and still not reach the emancipated state. If this happens, the soul would return and in its next birth easily become a *jīvanmukta* by virtue of the past realization. What distinguishes the *mukta* from the nonliberated is his total freedom from all selfishness and attachments, his permanent abidance in the all-pervading Divine Presence, his lucid, witnessing consciousness and his *jñāna,* revealed in spontaneous utterances.

To attain liberation while living, the realization of the Self has to be brought through into every aspect of life, every atom of one's body. This occurs after many encounters with *nirvikalpa samādhi.* Through harnessing the power of *sādhana* and *tapas,* the adept advances his evolution, moving ahead ten lives or more. Only great *tapasvins* achieve *jīvanmukti,* for to catalyze the death of the astral body and then revive the life forces, one must be proficient in *brahmacharya, yoga, prāṇāyāma* and the varied *sādhanas.* It is a grace, made possible by guidance of a living *satguru,* attained by single-minded and strong-willed efforts of *yoga,* worship, detachment and purification. Non-*yogīs* may be freed at death, provided all *karmas* have been worked out and the Self is realized as the body is released.

Even having attained perfect liberation, a soul may consciously choose to be reborn to help others on the path. Such a one is called an *upadeśī*—exemplified by the benevolent *satguru*—as distinguished from a *nirvāṇī,* the silent ascetic who abides at the pinnacle of consciousness, shunning all worldly involvement. The concept of *moksha* for every Hindu sect is informed and modified by its understanding of the soul and its relationship to God. Most Hindus believe that after release from birth and death the soul will exist in the higher regions of the inner worlds where the Gods and mature beings live. Some sects contend the soul continues to evolve in these realms until it attains perfect union and merger with God. Others teach that the highest end is to abide eternally and separately in God's glorious presence. Four distinct views are explored below.

Smārta Hinduism

Smārtism is an ancient *brāhmanical* tradition reformed by Ādi Śaṅkara in the ninth century. Worshiping six forms of God, this liberal Hindu path is monistic, nonsectarian, meditative and philosophical. Īśvara and man are in reality Absolute Brahman. Within *māyā,* the soul and Īśvara appear as two. *Jñāna,* spiritual wisdom, dispels the illusion.

Most Smārtas believe that *moksha* is achieved through *jñāna yoga* alone—defined as an intellectual and meditative but non-*kuṇḍalinī yoga* path. Guided by a realized *guru* and avowed to the unreality of the world, the initiate meditates on himself as Brahman to break through the illusion of *māyā.* The ultimate goal of Smārtas is to realize oneself as Brahman—the Absolute and only Reality. For this, one must conquer the state of *avidyā,* or ignorance, which causes the world to appear as real. All illusion has vanished for the realized being, *jīvanmukta,* even as he lives out life in the physical body. If the sun were cold or the moon hot or fire burned downward, he would show no wonder. The *jīvanmukta* teaches, blesses and sets an example for the welfare of the world. At death, his inner and outer bodies are extinguished. Brahman alone exists and he is That forever, all in All.

Liberation depends on self-culture, which leads to spiritual insight. It does not come from the recitation of hymns, sacrificial worship or a hundred fasts. Man is liberated not by effort, not by *yoga,* not by any self-transformation, but only by the knowledge gained from scripture and self-reflection that he himself is Brahman. *Jñāna yoga's* progressive stages are scriptural study *(śravaṇa)*, reflection *(manana)* and sustained meditation *(dhyāna)*. Devotees may also choose from three other nonsuccessive paths to cultivate devotion, accrue good *karma* and purify the mind. These are *bhakti yoga, karma yoga* and *rāja yoga,* which Smārtas teach can also bring enlightenment.

Scripture teaches, "For the great-souled, the surest way to liberation is the conviction that 'I am Brahman'" *(Śukla Yajur Veda, Paiṅgala Upanishad* 4.19 UPR). Śrī Jayendra Saraswathi of Kañchi Peedam, Tamil Nadu, India, affirms, "That state where one transcends all feelings is liberation. Nothing affects this state of being. You may call it 'transcendental bliss,' purified intuition that enables one to see the Supreme as one's own Self. One attains to Brahman, utterly liberated."

Vaishṇava Hinduism

The primary goal of Vaishṇavites is *videhamukti,* disembodied liberation—attainable only after death—when the small self realizes union with God Vishṇu's body as a part of Him, yet maintains its pure individual personality. God's transcendent Being is a celestial form residing in the city of Vaikuṇṭha, the home of all eternal values and perfection, where the soul joins Him when liberated. Souls do not share in God's all-pervasiveness or power to create.

Most Vaishṇavites believe that religion is the performance of *bhakti sādhanas,* and that man can communicate with and receive the grace of Lord Vishṇu who manifests through the temple Deity, or idol. The path of *karma yoga* and *jnāna yoga* leads to *bhakti yoga.* Through total self-surrender, called *prapatti,* to Lord Vishṇu, liberation from *samsāra* is attained. Vaishṇavites consider the *moksha* of the *advaita* philosophies a lesser attainment, preferring instead the bliss of eternal devotion. There are differing categories of souls which attain to different levels of permanent release, called *sālokya*, "sharing the world" of God; *sāmīpya*, "nearness" to God; *sārūpya*, "likeness" to God; and *sāyujya*, "union" with God. *Jīvanmukti* exists only in the case of great souls who leave their place in heaven to take a human birth and later return.

There is one school of Vaishṇavism, founded by Vallabhāchārya, which takes an entirely different view of *moksha*. It teaches that, upon liberation, the soul, through its insight into truth revealed by virtue of perfect devotion, recovers divine qualities suppressed previously and becomes one with God, in identical essence, though the soul remains a part, and God the whole. This is described by the analogy of sparks issuing from a fire.

Swāmī Prākāśanand Saraswati of the International Society of Divine Love, Texas, offers a Vaishṇava view, "Liberation from *māyā* and the *karmas* is only possible after the divine vision of God. Thus, sincere longing for His vision is the only way to receive His grace and liberation."

Śākta Hinduism

Śāktas believe the soul is one with God Śiva. Emphasis is given to the Feminine Manifest by which the Masculine Unmanifest is ultimately reached. The Divine Mother, Śakti, is mediatrix, bestowing this *advaitic moksha* on those who worship Her. *Moksha* is complete identification with the transcendent God Śiva, achieved when the *kuṇḍalinī śakti* power is raised through the *sushumṇā* current of the spine to the top of the head to unite with Śiva. Alternatively, *moksha* may be conceived of as union with Devī, or with Brahman. The spiritual practices in Śāktism are similar to those in Śaivism, though there is more emphasis in Śāktism on God's Power as opposed to Being, on *mantras* and *yantras*, and on embracing apparent opposites: male-female, absolute-relative, pleasure-pain, cause-effect, mind-body. Shamanistic Śāktism employs magic, trance mediumship, firewalking and animal sacrifice for healing, fertility, prophecy and power. "Left hand" *tantric* rites transcend traditional ethical codes.

The state of *jīvanmukti* in Śāktism is called *kulāchāra,* "the divine way of life," attained through *sādhana* and grace. The liberated soul is known as *kaula,* to whom wood and gold, life and death are the same. The *kaula* can move about in the world at will, even returning to earthly duties such as kingship, but nevertheless remaining liberated from rebirth, as his actions can no longer bind him.

The Goddess, Devī, gives both *mukti* and *bhukti*—liberation and worldly enjoyment. Dr. S. Rādhākṛishṇan explained one view, "The *jīva* under the influence of *māyā* looks upon itself as an independent agent and enjoyer until release is gained. Knowledge of Śakti is the road to salvation, which is dissolution in the bliss effulgence of the Supreme." Śrī Śrī Śrī Śivarātnapūri Swāmī of Kailās Āshram, Bangalore, India, declares, "My message to mankind is 'Right thought, right living and unremitting devotion to the Divine Mother.' Faith is the most important thing that you should cultivate. By faith does one obtain knowledge."

Śaivite Hinduism

The path for Śaivites is divided into four progressive stages of belief and practice called *charyā, kriyā, yoga* and *jñāna.* The soul evolves through *karma* and reincarnation from the instinctive-intellectual sphere into virtuous and moral living, then into temple worship and devotion, followed by internalized worship or *yoga* and its meditative disciplines. Union with God Śiva comes through the grace of the *satguru* and culminates in the soul's maturity in the state of *jñāna,* or wisdom. Śaivism values both *bhakti* and *yoga*, devotional and contemplative *sādhanas. Moksha* is defined differently in Śaivism's six schools.

Pāśupata Śaivism emphasizes Śiva as supreme cause and

personal ruler of the soul and world. It teaches that the liberated soul retains its individuality in a state of complete union with Śiva.

Vīra Śaivism holds that after liberation the soul experiences a true union and identity of Śiva and soul, called Liṅga and *aṅga.* The soul ultimately merges in a state of Śūnya, or Nothingness, which is not an empty void.

Kashmīr Śaivism teaches that liberation comes through a sustained recognition, called *pratyabhijñā,* of one's true Self as nothing but Śiva. After liberation, the soul has no merger in God, as God and soul are eternally nondifferent.

In Gorakhnāth Śaivism, or Siddha Siddhānta, *moksha* leads to a complete sameness of Śiva and soul, described as "bubbles arising and returning to water."

In Śiva Advaita, liberation leads to the "*ākāśa* within the heart." Upon death, the soul goes to Śiva along the path of the Gods, continuing to exist on the spiritual plane, enjoying the bliss of knowing all as Śiva, and attaining all powers except creation.

Śaiva Siddhānta has two sub-sects. Meykandar's pluralistic realism teaches that God, soul and world are eternally coexistent. Liberation leads to a state of oneness with Śiva, in which the soul retains its individuality, like salt added to water. Tirumular's monistic theism, or Advaita Īśvaravāda, reflected in *Merging with Śiva,* holds that evolution continues after earthly births until *jīva* becomes Śiva, the soul merges in perfect oneness with God, like a drop of water returning to the sea. Scriptures teach, "Having realized the Self, the *ṛishis,* perfected souls, satisfied with their knowledge, passion-free, tranquil—those wise beings, having attained the Omnipresent on all sides—enter into the All itself *(Atharva Veda, Muṇḍaka Upanishad* 3.2.5 BO UPH)."

Monistic Śaiva Siddhānta

The primary goal of this form of monistic Śaivism is realizing one's identity with God Śiva, in perfect union and non-differentiation. This is termed *nirvikalpa samādhi*, Self Realization, and may be attained in this life, granting *moksha*, permanent liberation from the cycles of birth and death. A secondary goal is *savikalpa samādhi*, the realization of *Satchidānanda*, a unitive experience within superconsciousness in which perfect Truth, knowledge and bliss are known.

Moksha does not mean death, as some misunderstand it. It means freedom from rebirth before or after death, after which souls continue evolving in the Antarloka and Śivaloka, and finally merge with Lord Śiva as does river water when returning to the ocean. *Moksha* comes when all earthly *karmas* have been fully resolved. The *Vedas* promise, "If here one is able to realize Him before the death of the body, he will be liberated from the bondage of the world." All embodied souls—whatever be their faith or convictions, Hindu or not—are destined to achieve *moksha*, but not necessarily in this life. Śaivites know this and do not delude themselves that this life is the last. Old souls renounce worldly ambitions and take up *sannyāsa* in quest of Paraśiva even at a young age. Younger souls desire to seek lessons from the experiences of worldly life which is rewarded by many, many births on Earth. After *moksha* has been attained—and it is an attainment resulting from much *sādhana*, self-reflection and realization—subtle *karmas* are made and swiftly resolved, like writing on water. Finally, at the end of each soul's evolution comes *viśvagrāsa*, total absorption in *Śiva*. "The Self cannot be attained by the weak, nor by the careless, nor through aimless disciplines. But if one who knows strives by right means, his soul enters the abode of God *(Atharva Veda, Muṇḍaka Upanishad* 3.2.4 BO UPM)."

"But who is Śiva?" one might well ask. Our Hindu Catechism, *Dancing with Śiva,* explains, "God Śiva is all and in all, one without a second, the Supreme Being and only Absolute Reality. He is Pati, our Lord, immanent and transcendent. To create, preserve, destroy, conceal and reveal are His five powers. Aum. God Śiva is a one being, yet we understand Him in three perfections: Absolute Reality, Pure Consciousness and Primal Soul. As Absolute Reality, Śiva is unmanifest, unchanging and transcendent, the Self God, timeless, formless and spaceless. As Pure Consciousness, Śiva is the manifest primal substance, pure love and light flowing through all form, existing everywhere in time and space as infinite intelligence and power. As Primal Soul, Śiva is the five-fold manifestation: Brahmā, the Creator; Vishṇu, the Preserver; Rudra, the Destroyer; Maheśvara, the Veiling Lord, and Sadāśiva, the Revealer. He is our personal Lord, source of all three worlds. Our divine Father-Mother protects, nurtures and guides us, veiling Truth as we evolve, revealing it when we are mature enough to receive God's bountiful grace. God Śiva is all and in all, great beyond our conception, a sacred mystery that can be known in direct communion. Yea, when Śiva is known, all is known. The *Vedas* state: 'That part of Him which is characterized by *tamas* is called Rudra. That part of Him which belongs to *rajas* is Brahmā. That part of Him which belongs to *sattva* is Vishṇu' (*Kṛishṇa Yajur Veda, Maitreya Upanishad* 5.2 BO UPH)."

Nine Ways of Merging with Śiva

Merger—that is what this book, the third book in the trilogy of *Dancing with Śiva, Living with Śiva* and *Merging with Śiva,* is all about. Some of the big questions about something as wonderful as becoming one with the universe or with God are: Is merger something to accomplish in this lifetime, or shall we put it off to another round? Is merger something that can be achieved even in future lives, or should we consider that it might never happen, or that it just might happen unexpectedly? Is merger with Śiva complete annihilation, an undesirable nothingness that we should delay as long as possible? Shall we cease all striving for realization and wait for *mahāpralaya,* the end of the universe, the Great Dissolution commanded by Lord Śiva, when every soul, young or old, merges in the All of the All—no exceptions, no one left behind, the ultimate perk of the Divine Cosmic Drama, the guarantee of final merger of every soul? Fortunately, the next Big Bang may happen after Śiva gets lonely dancing by Himself and starts His creation all over again.

Merger on the great inner path described in this book is already happening in your life and in the life of every soul on the planet, in the natural course of evolution. In Sanskṛit, we translate "Merging with Śiva" as *Śive Vilayam,* "dissolution, melting, disappearing in the Divine." Nine progressive ways of merging with Śiva are possible today—in fact impossible to avoid. Shall we now explore these nine ways—the wonderful ways of merging with Śiva as we walk the San Mārga—the straight path of *dharma?*

A *jīva,* or soul, merges with his potential mother who gives a physical body to which his astral body is attached. This is the first merger. Then, when his first *guru,* the parents, train him to quell the instinctive mind and become a producing member of the family and the social and global communities, the second merger occurs. Why should these two developments be related to merging with the Supreme? It is because Śiva is the life of our lives, as the venerable saints teach. Śiva is the life of the life of all sentient and insentient beings, the sea of *prāṇa,* ever emanating, mysteriously, from the All of the Allness of His mystery Being, by which all life exists and all happenings happen. Therefore to merge energies with all other humans without making differences is to find Śivaness in all and within all.

Having merged with the biological and social worlds, it then is for the young *jīva,* embodied soul, to be introduced by the parents to the family *guru* for spiritual training. Obedience and devotion to the *guru* is again another merger into Śivaness, for the *satguru* is Sadāśiva, or Śiva in form, having realized Śiva in Formlessness. It is from the *satguru's* constant, silent emanation that the *śishya* thrives, as do flowering trees, bushes and vines thrive and grow from the sun's silent rays and the occasional showers of rain. No words need be spoken, for both *śishya* and *guru* know the same—the *śishya* having had his training in scripture, divine inspiration of song, meaning and dance from his first *guru,* the parents.

Having walked the San Mārga through the *charyā* and *kriyā mārgas,* and having disciplined mind and emotions, the *śishya* is ready for the fourth merger into Śivaness. This is accomplished through art, calligraphy, drawing divine forms, writing out scripture in one's own hand and depicting through drama, by learning and playing music, by having all bodily currents move into the rhythm of the sounds of nature, for nature is *nāda* in the external. It has its own choreography, and this merger is with Naṭarāja, Lord of the Dance. It is also the merger with knowledge of all kinds, of language and mathematics, of the many sciences and arts.

The fifth merger is deeper: endeavoring to penetrate the intuitive world, communing with nature, encountering the many dreams, visions and other mystical experiences that await the seeker of Truth. It is merger with the selfless life, of seeing oneself in others, and others in oneself, of losing the barriers that divide one from another, and the internal world from the external world. It is living a harmonious life with a heart filled with love, trust and understanding for all, desiring to give rather than wanting only to receive.

The light that lights each thought picture when traced to its source is the sixth merger—the *yoga* of detaching awareness from that which it is aware of and being the light that lights the thoughts, rather than claiming identity as being the thoughts, then tracing this light of the mind out of the mind into the beyond of the beyond. Yea, this is the sixth way we merge into the Divine. The Lord of the Dance emanates His own lighting effects, does His own choreography, creates His own music and enjoys, as the audience, His own performance.

The seventh merger is into the *nāda-nāḍī śākti,* that unrelenting sound heard as an inexplainable eeeee, of a thousand *vīṇās* being played simultaneously by Vīṇādhāra, another form of Lord Śiva, the maker of sound, the composer of the symphony. The *nāda* is traced to its source, deep within the within, the city of a thousand lights and sounds, for sound is light and light is sound in this sphere of Satchidānanda, all-pervasive oneness with all form, the Self flowing through the mind, untouched by it, yet sustaining it in a mightily mysterious way.

The eighth merger with Śiva is Paraśiva. Becoming and being timeless, formless, spaceless is the total transformation of the soul body, the mental body, the astral body, the *prāṇic* body and the physical body. It is the breaking of seals which subsequently makes changes never to be repaired. A new, an entirely new, process begins. It is the ultimate healing of all *karmas,* the ultimate knowing of *dharma.*

And now, lastly, once soul the soul evolves out of the physical, *prāṇic,* emotional, mental and causal sheaths—*annamaya, prāṇamaya, manomaya, vijñānamaya* and *ānandamaya kośas*—and they are needed no more, it evolves into *viśvagrāsa,* the ninth and final merger with Śiva, as an infant effortlessly becomes a child, a child a youth and a youth an adult. Yes, the soul, *jīva,* encased in five bodies, is indeed merged into the emanator, preserver and absorber of the inner and outer universes as simply as a drop of water merges into the ocean, never to be found again. This is the timeless path the holy *Vedas* of the Sanātana Dharma proclaim.

As a seed becomes a bud, and a bud becomes a flower, these nine steps of spiritual unfoldment are inevitable for all humankind.

Autobiography of an Unfinished Life

Having been orphaned in 1938 at eleven years of age and raised by a family friend who had lived five or more years as a guest of the Mahārāja of Mysore, where she explored Indian art, dance and culture, it was in the path of my natural evolution to come to know Śiva Naṭarāja, the God of the Dance. During those early days I was taught to drape a *dhotī,* wrap a turban, dance the *tāṇḍava* of Lord Śiva, and much more. Indian culture was no stranger then, nor is it now.

In the teenage years, I was much exposed to Swāmī Vivekānanda's writings and lectures by other *swāmīs* who preached the Smārta philosophy. Everything was there for me, except for one philosophical glitch. That was Paraśiva or Parabrahman, the timeless, spaceless, causeless Śivam. Knowledge about this aspect of philosophy must have been a carry-over from a past life, for it came up ever so strong in my mind at the time.

More exposure to the Smārta sect followed near the end of the 1930s when the *Bhagavad Gītā* was introduced to the West as the Holy Bible of the Hindus. The metaphysical and philosophical circles and intelligentsia in America could not believe that an excerpted episode of the *Mahābhārata* preaching violence could be anything but detrimental to future generations in the West. This has proven to be true in many, some bitter, contests, right up to the Supreme Court level. The *swāmīs* in those early years tried to justify God Kṛishṇa's urging his devotee to kill his relatives and his *guru,* that all would be well in the end because the soul never dies, and those who were killed would reincarnate. Western people were at that time, and still are, innocent and believing—having never been taught the notion of divine deception, or a manner of writing where one thing actually means another (they were of the opinion that it was to duty of the wise to make themselves clear)—when Lord Kṛishṇa was seen to tell the warrior Arjuna to fight and slay his own clan and then have a good night's sleep, free from conscience, that did not go over well at all. Contemporary *swāmīs* made fruitless efforts to philosophically justify the *Gītā,* but their arguments and explanations were not convincing. This was before the West experienced the Second World War, when people were still very religious, moral and thoughtful about these matters. Eventually, the *Gītā* was rejected for the lofty *Upanishads* of the *Vedas* which scholars discovered and made available in English.

Yet, in this century the Smārtas, along with many Vaishṇavas, have taken the *Bhagavad Gītā* as their prime scripture, a text which is not a revealed scripture at all. It is *smṛiti,* specifically Itihāsa, meaning history, a poem excerpted from the *Mahābhārata* epic. Whereas, the *Vedas*—the four divinely revealed and most revered scriptures, *śruti,* of all Hindus, the most ancient of all books in the world, the bible of the Sanātana Dharma—promoted *ahiṁsā,* nonviolence, the *Gītā* condoned war and has thus been critically called *kolai nul* by eminent *swāmīs,* "the book of carnage," a book that gives divine sanction to violence.

At age twenty-one I arrived in India, off the ship that had carried me across the seas, walking through the massive Gateway to India, in Mumbai, which was Bombay in those days. Later I would travel South, to Madras, now Chennai, finally coming to Colombo in Sri Lanka. It was the Śaivite elders and *pandits* of Jaffna, Sri Lanka—one of whom adopted me into his extended family of the Chettiar caste and initiated me into temple worship—who augmented my already mature knowledge of Vedānta. I was happy to find a complete culture that accepted the monistic *advaita* of Vedānta and yet cherished and practiced the many other dimensions of life, celebrated festivals, valued the great *yoga* called *bhakti,* honored those who performed *sādhanas,* understood the way of *kuṇḍalinī yoga,* knew the mysteries of penance or *prāyaśchitta,* including rolling around the temple in the hot noonday sun, and lost itself—or should I say found itself?—in the chambers of the hallowed temples where *darshan* was sought out and the Gods were seen and felt as real beings when invoked by the magical priests to enter the temple at the height of the ceremony.

So, then, not long after I had discovered this richness, Śaiva Siddhānta—a happy, contented blend of Siddhānta (worship) and Vedānta (philosophical teachings)—became a vital part of my daily life. After this I became aware of a problem within Śaiva Siddhānta, which was loosely translated to mean "the final conclusions of the *Vedas* and *Āgamas.*" The problem was monism and pluralism, which had been a subject of popular debate for about two thousand years, I was told. It seemed strange to me that it persisted that long and still was not satisfactorily concluded. Of course, I was in my early twenties and had a lot to learn about the way of *pandits* and their conundrums.

I first became involved in this ongoing debate in 1948 while staying and performing *sādhana* in Jaffna, living with my adopted family in a humble mud hut, prior to my initiation from the great sage, Jñānaguru Yogaswāmī. I learned that pluralist adherents in the village were not at all pleased with this modern mystic's monistic statements and conclusions. At my very first meeting with this extraordinary Nātha *siddha,* whom I had traveled halfway around the world to seek out, Satguru Yogaswāmī tested me by asking, "What do you think about monism and pluralism? Explain it to me." He obviously knew I had been exposed to both sides of the debate through village discussions with elders and *pandits.* I said, "Swāmī, both are true. It is totally dependent upon how one is looking at the mountain. The pluralist looks at the mountain from the foothills and feels separate from its lofty peak. The monist sits in oneness on that lofty peak." He smiled, nodded and was pleased.

In my life, the issue again came into prominence in the early '80s after my recognition by the world community of Śaivites and all of the other three Hindu denominations as Guru Mahāsannidhānam of Kauai Aadheenam and 162nd Jagadāchāryā of the Nandinātha Sampradāya's Kailāsa Paramparā. By that time, our small but dynamic Hindu church had distributed thousands of copies of our Hindu Catechism, *Dancing with Śiva*, boldly proclaiming the monistic truths of Śaiva Siddhānta and bravely claiming the term as our own. This did not go unnoticed by pluralist scholars and *pandits*, who for generations had faced little opposition to their claim that Śaiva Siddhānta is pluralistic by definition. I was challenged and rose to the occasion, thinking that if the debate had not been settled for two or more thousand years, then giving it a little fire and a few challenges might, just might, make a difference, and it did.

The debate goes on even to this day and will continue into the future of futures because, honestly, in every denomination there is this dichotomy, this discussion of how man and God and world relate. Each generation will confront the matter, and each way of looking at the Ultimate is from where the the perceiver is sitting, at the bottom of the mountain or at the top. If you are interested in the "ins and outs" of the discussion, turn to Resource One of this book and ascertain for yourself how it finally concluded. Or did it?

Having lived a fairly long time on planet Earth—through the '30s financial crash, orphaned at eleven, through World War II, through an international emergency ending in incarceration in Algeria with guns at our back when we innocently arrived in 1968 in a nation in turmoil, through innumerable earthquakes in California, three devastating hurricanes on my beloved island of Kauai, several riots in India, an ethnic war in Sri Lanka, the economic roller coaster of America including 1987 Black Monday, winter snowstorms in Nevada and freezing days in Russia with Gorbachev and 2,500 political and spiritual leaders and media huddled in the Kremlin chanting "Aum" three times together, through the banning of our magazine, HINDUISM TODAY, in Malaysia, the 1993 Parliament of World's Religions in Chicago, elected one among 23 religious presidents, the 1995 controversial incident of the Great Last Papers of Gandhi in the UK, through a million phone calls from every corner of the Earth on every issue known to mankind, through the opposition of great men and the support of greater men, having been honored and paraded six miles on chariots in Kilinochi, Sri Lanka, pulled by old men and young boys, the showering of baskets of flowers tossed from the rooftops of the town of Tuticorin in South India, received at airports with music and songs and garlands from the crowds as they had received Swāmī Vivekānanda nearly a century before, in Madurai at the Mīnākshī Sundaram Temple paraded with five elephants, umbrellas, several camels in holy processions, the guest of the governments, meeting with Presidents, Prime Ministers, Ministers and religious leaders of all faiths and leaders in all walks of life, establishing temples in the USA, Fiji, Mauritius, Canada, Denmark, Germany, England, Switzerland and several other countries, often by establishing Lord Gaṇeśa icons to begin the worship, and later presiding over the completion of some of them, then to endure the issues of the '80s and the '90s—yes, having gone through all this and more, I was prepared for the challenges of guiding several hundred families in missions in eight countries and, not the least of it, raising and training 30 *āchāryas, swāmīs, yogīs* and *sādhakas* from six nations and being there for the flood of visitors and pilgrims to our remote island from all parts of the world, not to mention the struggle to unite all of the world's Hindus through our international magazine, HINDUISM TODAY, a monthly effort that reaches to all corners of the Earth, teaching the core Vedic philosophy accepted by all four of the denominations of Sanātana Dharma. Why did all this happen to me? Well, it was from three words from my *satguru:* "Follow inner orders." I thought the orders would never stop, and indeed they continue until this day. Have I been through it all? You might say that! But, it's not over yet!

When I decided to launch HINDUISM TODAY in 1979, my thinking was: to make Śaivism strong, we have to make all the other three main denominations strong. Because our philosophy is being devoted to Śiva in everyone, we support every Hindu sect equally. Our strength is in having oneness with all the Hindus around the world, even though our philosophical, doctrinal and cultural approaches may differ somewhat. This is for the benefit of the overall Hindu renaissance, which is gaining in power as the century turns, for as each becomes strong, that strength benefits the overall body of Hinduism, giving pride, stability and courage to proceed with confidence. This is Hindu solidarity, one of our heartfelt commitments. The other is monistic theism—Advaita Īśvaravāda—of Śaiva Siddhānta.

Now that uniting all the Hindus is being accomplished through HINDUISM TODAY, at the simultaneous turn of the century and the millennium, new challenges are to be faced. The experiences and accomplishments of the past are the foundation for the accomplishments of the future. Having lived this long in this life, and having had many, many lives preceding it, especially at this time on our planet, when controversy, distrust and intrigue are marketable commodities, I can truly say without any dissembling, "I would not have wanted to miss this birth for anything. It has been a fun time, but it would not have been without home base, 'the Self,' as you shall discover and come to know and love and become as you read on in *Merging with Śiva.*"

Self Realization

When the knowledge of the Self first became commonly planted into English and other European languages at the turn of the century, brought by the Vedic *Upanishads,* it was an event of the time. Mystically inclined people were enthralled and elated. All began striving for the high goal before even preparing for the lower ones that lead up to it. No one thought much about their nonattainment at that time, but went on into other "-isms" and "-asms," such as Druidism, which was big at that time.

Then came Theosophy and the various sciences of the mind. It was not until the 1960s, after two world wars, that the search for the Self became popular in the mass consciousness. It was talked about, sought for and even touched into by various striving souls. Psychedelic drugs promised 'the Self' with a capital *S.* But alas, these drugs wreaked havoc and became illegal, and there was no way in promoting chemical Self Realization any more. So, the spelling changed. The *S,* in caps, became lower case *s.* This psychological seeking caught on like a wildfire. "Find your self;" "Explore your ego (with the small *e* of course);" "Discover your identity;" "Be your own person;" "Realize your highest potential"—these were the mottos then, and this has carried into the '90s.

Well, that is not all that happened in the European-based languages, which began to expand to encompass the myriad terms of Earth's peoples for the highest of the high. The Buddhists have their interpretation of the Self, as do the native American Indian tribes. African tribal religions have theirs, as do the ever-more-popular Pagans of Europe, and even the existentialists and materialists have theirs.

The *Self*—known in Vedic Sanskṛit as *ātman,* Parabrahman and Paraśiva—meant one thing to the *yogīs* of India and soon meant many things to the uninitiated. *Self Real-*

ization can, and does today, have a conscribed meaning of realizing sexuality through *tantra,* or independence from parents and authority figures. It is, in fact, still a money-making proposition, having a small *s* or a big *S,* widely sold on the open market as a highly viable product.

But back to the beginning—the Self is all-pervasive energy within and through all creation, and transcends even that as being timeless, formless and spaceless. This cannot be sold, bought or mass-produced. Vedically speaking, it is for those souls who have prepared for the journey and is attained only at the cost of egolessness. Nevertheless, it is also sold in many other *s*'s: symposiums, seminars, *sādhanas,* secret *mantras,* seclusive initiations and seductive sex *tantras.*

In today's world there are many institutions and teachers presenting *kuṇḍalinī yoga* as an elixir of life. True, it can be stimulated upward, but it then goes downward because of the lack of control of the emotions, lower instinctive nature and lack of philosophical background. As a thermometer reacts to heat and cold, so does the *kuṇḍalinī* when tampered with by the novice under the guidance of commercialization. It is an age where money is a product. It is an age where very little is sacred if it can be sold. The wear and tear on the vital forces of physical, astral and mental bodies is severe when *kuṇḍalinī,* the holy of holies, is stimulated in the unholy of unholies, those who lack remorse and do not seek penance, those who see themselves as the beginning and end of all, those who are devoid of conscience, who anger and jealously retort, who are self-centered, taking care of me, mine and I first. They are in the lower-nature *chakras.* In today's world, some are even paying multi-money for the "*kuṇḍalinī* experience."

Some groups, like Transcendental Meditation, have given out techniques too freely to those who are unprepared and unsuited to sustain the consequences of the disciplines. If the lower is not closed off, no one should be introduced into deep meditation, intense *prāṇāyāma* and occult arts such as Reiki. These are well-known examples of digression from established protocols for the metaphysical teachings.

At the turn of the century, *yogīs* came to America and taught so much, all high-powered teachings and techniques, without traditional preparations, that they put many, impressionable women especially, into our mental institutions. During my early ministry I visited mental institutions and released back to their families a few such people who had gone over the edge because of occult practices. In those days when one went into a mental institution he often never came out. A man whose wife began practicing *yoga* would have her committed. This cycle is repeating itself. The problem is that certain *siddhis* arise which are just a by-product of the practices, not a development of *sādhana,* and the repercussions could be disastrous as far as society is concerned.

Śrī Chinmoy, Bengali mystic and *yogī,* world renowned expert on *kuṇḍalinī yoga* and United Nations peace emissary, has this to say about enlightenment in his book, *Samādhi and Siddhi*: "To realize the highest Absolute as one's very own and to constantly feel that this realization is not something you have actually achieved, but something you eternally are—that is called realization.... *Nirvikalpa samādhi* and the other *samādhis* are all high stages. But there is a stage which is superior to *nirvikalpa samādhi.* That is the stage of divine transformation, absolute transformation. You can be in *samādhi,* but *samādhi* does not give you transformation. While you are in your trance, you become exalted, for you are one with God. But when you come back into the material plane, you become an ordinary man. But if you have transformed your outer and inner consciousness, then you are no more affected by the ignorance of the world.... To reach liberation is no easy matter. It is very, very difficult to become freed from ignorance. Out of the millions and billions of human beings on Earth, there may be ten or twenty or even a hundred liberated souls. But God alone knows how many realized souls exist."

There are many concepts as to what happens to the soul after Self Realization and many concepts as to what Self Realization is. There are many concepts as to eventual attainment, and there are many concepts as to whether it is an intellectual understanding that means the end or the goal of the path, and there is nothing beyond that, or experiencing all-pervasiveness, and that is the end of the path, and there is nothing beyond that, or experiencing the void, becoming nothing, and there is nothing beyond that. These concepts are spin-offs of the realizations of various masters who have attained and explained to their disciples the results of their attainments. But actually, realization by understanding the *Vedas* is basically an intellectual realization of the Self, based on reason, memory, deduction and certain internal perceptions of what this experience must be like. It is, in fact, a realization, and probably a very great one before the days of science and technology. But it is not Self Realization in the truest sense, for there is no transformation as an aftermath. The person is the same person before and after, with the same desires, outlook on life, motivations, temptations, trepidations, stress levels and day-to-day habits.

The experience of Satchidānanda, the all-pervasive essence of *prāṇa,* can be had through *bhakti yoga,* total *prapatti.* In prostrating the physical body before the icons of God, Gods and *guru,* energy goes into the head. It goes up from the *mūlādhāra.* It goes up from the soles of the feet. That is total surrender, and in the aftermath one feels a oneness with the universe. Oneness is a captivation of the soul. The same experience can be had through an opposite force. The husband or wife leaves, moves out of the house or dies, or disaster strikes the family, the house burns down, all possessions are destroyed—the soul turns to God and experiences oneness; temporarily becomes as a renunciate. The soul seeks something more than attachments to people, places and things, and when released from people, places and things through inharmonious disasters becomes its own essence, its all-pervasiveness. This, truly, is a superconscious realization of a superconscious identity, often called the Self, just as an intellectual understanding of what others say the Self is is often called the realization of the Self.

Our scriptures tell us the Self is timeless, causeless, spaceless, beyond mind, form and causation. It is what it is, to be realized to be known. It is the fullness of everything and the absence of nothing. Therefore, it is not a void. Therefore, it is not an intellectual understanding, and therefore it is not all-pervasive, for there is nothing to pervade.

Five, six, eight thousand years ago, Indian society developed over long centuries to a maturity sufficient to bring forth from the inner of the inner, the core of knowledge itself, the *Vedas,* four in number, called *śruti,* meaning revealed by God, not composed by man. Meditate upon the following verse and revel in its deep, deep meaning: "He who knows God as the Life of life, the Eye of the eye, the Ear of the ear, the Mind of the mind—he indeed comprehends fully the Cause of all causes" *(Śukla Yajur Veda, Bṛihadāraṇyaka Upanishad* 4.4.18 UPP). Yet another verse explains closeness leading to merging into oneness. Need we say more? It was already said in the so long ago and is alive and potent today as it was then. "As water poured into water, milk poured into milk, *ghee* into *ghee* become one without differentiation, even so the individual soul and the Supreme Self become one" *(Śukla Yajur Veda, Paiṅgala Upanishad* 4.10 UPR).

On the *rāja* and *jñāna yoga* path, in attempts to realize Paraśiva, we go to the brink of the Absolute, hover there like a hummingbird over a flower, listening to the *nāda,* at the brink of where the *nāda* comes from, being the light at the brink of where the light that lights the images of the mind comes from, and this is all we can do—our one step. The Self realizes you—its nine steps. This is why Śaiva Siddhānta is so great—you move toward God; God moves toward you. You look at God; God looks toward you more graciously, more intently. The Divine comes quickly when the carnal is transmuted into its essence. His *darshan* of you. You take one step toward God, and He immediately, in the flash of a blink, takes nine toward you. In Śaiva Siddhānta, God is the devotee, and He experiences Himself within Himself in His devotee. The devotee is the devotee of Śiva, endeavoring to experience himself in his God. This process is called *yoga, rāja yoga,* of which *jñāna yoga* is a by-product of the results and accomplishments along the way.

This is to explain that the mind cannot realize the Self. Awareness cannot realize the Self. Consciousness cannot realize the Self. There can be no name for the Self. To name it is to disqualify it into form. This is why in the incomparable Shum language it has no name, only *emkaef,* awareness aware of itself dissolving. Like any other realization, it does have its aftermath and impact on all five states of the mind.

Love and blessings ever flowing to you
from this and inner worlds,

Satguru Sivaya Subramuniyaswami
162nd Jagadāchārya of the Nandinātha
Sampradāya's Kailāsa Paramparā,
Guru Mahāsannidhānam,
Kauai Aadheenam, Hawaii, USA
73rd Jayanthi, 50th Anniversary of Ministry
Hindu year 5100, January 5, 1999

The Self God

Paraśivaḥ

परशिवः

ON OCTOBER, 3, 1959, AT OUR TEMPLE IN SAN FRANCISCO, JUST BEFORE FLYING TO THE ISLAND OF OAHU IN HAWAII, I SAT WITH A SMALL group of initiates in a discussion of the mind and the mind's essence. We attempted to penetrate in consciousness the realms attained when an individual leaves the actinodic causal body, becoming a pure state of consciousness, a pure state of actinicity, and finally merging into the Absolute, the Self God. And though no one has been able to explain adequately this experience, which is beyond the mind, I was overly inspired to explain the unexplainable. It is just as fresh and relevant today. Inner truths never change. On the following pages, you will find *The Self God* in my own hand.

From this inspired explanation, we learn that man is not man, man is God, and that the inherent nature of his soul is divine, existing in perfect oneness with God. This identity of the soul with God always exists and awaits man's awakening into realization. In the years that followed, tens of thousands of copies of the little booklet called *The Self God* were printed in America and in Asia and have been widely distributed. To show just how widely, one day our car experienced a flat tire on a road outside a remote village in South India. As it was being repaired, we wandered about. People were passing by now and again. After a while, an elderly villager noticed us and inquired as to our "native place." I handed him a little pamphlet to be polite. He looked at us, refused my offer and pulled a little booklet from his shirt pocket, saying, "I am in need of nothing more. I have all I need right here." He held up my *The Self God* booklet. Having made his point to these strangers, he walked on, not knowing he had been speaking to the author. In India and Śrī Lanka it is often referred to as "the little gem," and is highly regarded as an explanation of the inexplicable *nirvikalpa samādhi.*

As you read this inspired talk, don't think about it, feel it. Try to feel the vibration of the room in which it was given. Try to feel it in the innermost depths of your being.

This inspired talk has not been edited. You will find it simple and direct, clear and to the point. You will find it deep within yourself. Read it many times. Ponder it. It tells you about your true nature. It gives you hope, it gives you new life. It points the way. It proves to you that God is within man, and man is not man; man is God. It shows you that it is possible for you to realize God. But you and you alone must ponder this work deeply. Let each word that you read vibrate every atom of your being, and you will find that you will begin to know what is meant by the statement: "The Self cannot be explained; the mind knows of its existence. The Self God is within man; you are that Self. All else is illusion of the mind's creation, the mind that creates, preserves and destroys."

The Self God

The Self
You can't explain It
You can sense its existence
Through the refined state
of your senses,
but you cannot explain It
To know It,
you have to experience It
And the best you can say
about It is that It is
the depth of your Being,
the very core of you
It is you.
If you visualize
above you - nothing
below you - nothing;
to the right of you - nothing;
to the left of you - nothing;
If you visualize

in front of you—nothing;
in back of you—nothing;
and dissolve yourself
into that nothingness,
that would be the best way
you could explain
the realization of the Self
And yet that nothingness
would not be
the absence of something,
like the nothingness
on the inside of an empty box,
which would be like a void
That nothingness
is the fullness of everything.
the power, the sustaining power,
of the existence
of what appears to be everything
After you realize the Self
you see the mind for what it is

the self-created principle
That is the mind
ever creating itself
The mind is form
ever creating forms,
preserving form,
creating new forms
and destroying old forms.
That is the mind, the illusion,
the great unreality,
the part of you
that in your thinking mind
you dare to think is real.
What gives the mind that power?
Does the mind have power
if it is unreal?
What difference whether it
has power or hasn't power,
or the very words
that I am saying when

The Self exists because of itself?.
You could live in the dream
and become disturbed by it.
You can seek and desire
with a burning desire
to cognize reality
and be blissful because of it.
Man's destiny leads him
back to himself.
Man's destiny leads him into
the cognition of his own Being
leads him further
into the realization
of his True Being
They say you must
step on the spiritual path
to realize the Self
You only step
on the spiritual path
when you and you alone

are ready,
when what appears real to you
loses its appearance of reality
Then and only then
are you able
to detach yourself enough
to seek to find a new
and more permanent reality
Have you ever noticed
that something you think
is permanent,
you and you alone
give permanence to that thing
through your protection of it?
Have you ever stopped
to even think and get
a clear intellectual concept
that the Spirit within you
is the only permanent thing?
That everything else is changing?

That everything else
has a direct wire
connecting it to the realms
of joy and sorrow?
That is the mind.
As the Self,
your Effulgent Being,
comes to life in you,
joy and sorrow
become a study to you.
You do not have to think
to tell yourself
that each in its own place
is unreal.
You know
from the innermost depths
of your being
that form itself is not real
The subtlety of the joys
that you experience

As you come into
your Effulgent Being
cannot be described.
They can only be projected to you
if you are refined enough
to pick up
the subtlety of vibration
If you are in harmony enough,
you can sense the great joy,
the subtlety of the bliss
that you will feel
as you come closer and closer
to your Real Self.
If you strive to find your Self
by using your mind,
you will strive and strive in vain,
because the mind
cannot give you truth;
a lie cannot give you the truth.
A lie can only

entangle you in a web of deceit
But if you sensitize yourself,
awaken your true,
fine, beautiful qualities
that all of you have,
then you become a channel,
a chalice in which
your Effulgent Being
will begin to shine.
You will first think
that a light is shining
within you.
You will seek to find that light
You will seek to hold it,
like you cherish and hold
a beautiful gem,
You will later find
that the light
that you found within you
is in every pore,

every cell of your being
You will later find that
that light permeates
every atom of the universe
You will later find
that you are that light,
and what it permeates
is the unreal illusion
created by the mind.
How strong you must be
to find this Truth.
You must become very, very strong
How do you become strong?
Exercise.
You must exercise every muscle
and sinew of your nature
by obeying
the dictates of the law,
of the spiritual laws
It will be very difficult.

A weak muscle
is very difficult to make strong
but if you exercise
over a period of time
and do what you should do,
it will respond.
Your nature will respond, too.
But you must work at it.
You must try.
You must try.
You must try very, very hard.
Very diligently
How often?
Ten minutes a day?
No.
Two hours a day?
No.
Twenty-four hours a day!.
Every day!
You must try very, very hard.

Preparing you for the
realization of the Self is
like tuning up a violin, like
tightening up each string
so it harmonizes
with every other string.
The more sensitive
you are to tone,
the better you can tune a violin,
and the better the violin is tuned,
the better the music.
The stronger you are
in your nature,
the more you can bring through
your real nature;
the more you can
enjoy the bliss
of your True Being.
It is well worth working for.
It is well worth craving for

It is well worth denying yourself
many, many things for
to curb your nature.
It is well worth struggling
with your mind,
to bring your mind
under the dominion of your will.
Those of you who have
experienced contemplation
know the clarity
from which I am speaking.
You have had a taste
of your true Self.
It has tasted like
nothing that you have ever
come in contact with before.
It has filled and thrilled
and permeated your whole being
even if you have only
remained in that state

of contemplation
not longer than sixty seconds
Out of it you have gained
a great knowing,
a knowing that you could
refer back to,
a knowing that will bear
the fruit of wisdom
if you relate
future life experiences
to that knowing.
a knowing greater
than you could acquire
at any university
or institute of higher learning.
Can you only try to gain a clear
intellectual concept of realizing
this Self that you felt
permeating through you
and through all form

in your state of contemplation?
That is your next step.
Those of you who are wrestling
with the mind
in your many endeavors to try
to concentrate the mind,
to try to meditate
to try to become quiet,
to try to relax,
keep trying
Every positive effort
that you make
is not in vain
Every single brick
added to a temple made of brick
brings that temple
closer to completion.
So keep trying
and one day,
all of a sudden,

you will pierce
the lower realms of your mind
and enter into contemplation.
And you will be able to say:
"Yes, I know,
I have seen.
Now I know fully
the path that I am on!"
Keep trying.
You have to start somewhere.
The Self you cannot speak of.
You can only
try to think about it,
if you care to,
in one way:
feel your mind,
body and emotions.
and know that you are
the Spirit
permeating through mind,

which is all form,
body, which you inhabit;
and emotions which you either
control or are controlled by
Think on that,
ponder on that,
and you will find
you are the light
within your eyes.
You are the feel
within your fingers.
"You are more radiant
than the sun,
purer than the snow,
more subtle than the ether"
Keep trying.
Each time you try
you are one step closer
to your true
Effulgent Being.

MANIVEL...

Śiva's Cosmic Dance

Śivānanda Tāṇḍavaḥ

शिवानन्द ताण्डवः

THE COSMIC DANCE OF ŚIVA NAṬARĀJA IS BOTH SYMBOL AND REALITY. IT IS THE MOVEMENT OF CREATION, PRESERVATION AND DISSOLUTION, the triad which taken together is the principle of *māyā*, God's endless impulse, taking place within each of us, within every atom of the universe. We are all dancing with Śiva this very moment and He with us. In the midst of His agitated dance, God Śiva's HEAD is balanced and still, His EXPRESSION serene and calm, in perfect equipoise as the unmoved Mover. His right EARRING, made of a snake, is masculine. His left, a large discus, is feminine. Together they symbolize the fact that Śiva is neither male nor female, but transcends both. God Śiva's THIRD EYE is the eye of fire and symbolizes higher perception, extending throughout past, present and future. God Śiva's HAIR is in the long untended locks of the ascetic, flying out energetically. On His hair are: the SERPENT ŚEŚANĀGA, representing the cycle of years; a SKULL, symbolizing Śiva's power of destruction; the fifth-day CRESCENT MOON, symbolizing His creative power; and the GODDESS GAṄGĀ, India's most sacred river, symbol of descending grace. God Śiva's BACK LEFT HAND holds a blazing flame, the fire God Agni, symbolizing His power of destruction, *saṁhāra*, by which the universe is reabsorbed at the end of each cycle of creation, only to be recreated again by God Śiva. This hand represents **Na** in the Pañchākshara Mantra, **Na-Ma-Śi-Vā-Ya**. His PLANTED FOOT stands for the syllable **Ma** and symbolizes His concealing grace, *tirodhāna śakti*, which limits consciousness, allowing souls to mature through experience.

Śiva dances upon the figure known as APASMĀRA, "forgetful or heedless," who represents the soul bound by *āṇava mala*, the individuating veil of duality, source of separation from God. Apasmāra looks up serenely at Lord Śiva's raised foot, the ultimate refuge, release and destiny of all souls without exception. Lord Śiva's LEFT FRONT HAND, representing the syllable **Vā**, held in the elephant trunk pose, *gajahasta*, points to His left foot, source of revealing grace, *anugraha śakti*, by which souls return to Him. Left and right back arms are balanced, as are creation and destruction. Śiva's BACK RIGHT HAND, standing for the syllable **Śi**, holds the thin-waisted rattle drum, *damaru*, symbol of creation, which begins with soundless sound, Paranāda, from which arises the *mantra Aum*. The FRONT RIGHT HAND is raised in the gesture *abhaya*, "fear not," symbolizing Śiva's power of *sṛishṭi*, preservation and protection, and standing for the syllable **Ya**. Lord Śiva's RAISED FOOT symbolizes His revealing grace, *anugraha śakti*, by which the soul ultimately transcends the bonds of *āṇava*, *karma* and *māyā* and realizes its identity with Him. Lord Śiva's SKIN is a pinkish color. His body is smeared with white HOLY ASH, *vibhūti*, symbol of purity. The BLUE THROAT represents His compassion in swallowing the deadly *hālāhala* poison to protect mankind. He wears a SKULL NECKLACE, symbolizing the perpetual revolution of ages. The SERPENT JAHNUWI adorns His body, symbol of His identity with the *kuṇḍalinī* power, the normally dormant spiritual force within man coiled at the base of the spine. Raised through *yoga*, this force propels man into God Realization. Śiva wears a TIGER SKIN, symbol of nature's power. His SASH, *kaṭibhandha*, is blown to one side by His rapid movement. The ARCH OF FLAMES, *prabhāvali*, in which Śiva dances is the Hall of Consciousness. Each flame has three sub-flames, symbolizing fire on Earth, in the atmosphere and in the sky. At the top of the arch is MAHĀKĀLA, "Great time." Mahākāla is God Śiva Himself who creates, transcends and ends time. Śiva

Naṭarāja dances within the state of timeless transcendence. The double lotus PEDESTAL, *mahāmbujapīṭha*, symbolizes manifestation. From this base springs the cosmos.

The four sacred *Vedas*, mankind's oldest scriptures, intone, "To Rudra [Śiva], Lord of sacrifice, of hymns and balmy medicines, we pray for joy and health and strength. He shines in splendor like the sun, refulgent as bright gold is He, the good, the best among the Gods (*Ṛig Veda* 1.43.4-5)." "He is God, hidden in all beings, their inmost soul who is in all. He watches the works of creation, lives in all things, watches all things. He is pure consciousness, beyond the three conditions of nature (*Yajur Veda, Svetāśvatara Upanishad* 6.11 UPM)." "There the eye goes not, nor words, nor mind. We know not. We cannot understand how He can be explained. He is above the known, and He is above the unknown (*Sama Veda, Kena Upanishad* 1.3 UPM)." "Fire is His head, the sun and moon His eyes, space His ears, the *Vedas* His speech, the wind His breath, the universe His heart. From His feet the Earth has originated. Verily, He is the inner Self of all beings (*Atharva Veda, Muṇḍaka Upanishad* 2.1.4 EH)."

Jyotishi Nartanam

ज्योतिषि नर्तनम्

Part One

Dancing In the Light

Śivadarśanaṁ Katham

शिवदर्शनं कथम्

How to Realize God

Bereft of distracting thoughts, ascending the way of *kuṇḍalinī*, seeking the Creator that created all, Him that is beauteous light, reaching the mystic moon in union, he becomes one with the Uncreated Being. That, in truth, is *samādhi's* tranquility.

TIRUMANTIRAM 628

Monday
LESSON 1
Paraśiva, Life's Ultimate Goal

Never have there been so many people living on the planet wondering, "What is the real goal, the final purpose, of life?" However, man is blinded by his ignorance and his concern with the externalities of the world. He is caught, enthralled, bound by *karma.* The ultimate realizations available are beyond his understanding and remain to him obscure, even intellectually. Man's ultimate quest, the final evolutionary frontier, is within man himself. It is the Truth spoken by Vedic *ṛishis* as the Self within man, attainable through control of the mind and purification. ¶It is *karma* that keeps us from knowing of and reaching life's final goal, yet it is wrong to even call it a goal. It is what is known by the knower to have always existed. It is not a matter of becoming the Self, but of realizing that you never were not the Self. And what is that Self? It is Paraśiva. It is God. It is That which is beyond the mind, beyond thought, feeling and emotion, beyond time, form and space. That is what all men are seeking, looking for, longing for. When *karma* is controlled through *yoga* and *dharma* well performed, and the energies are transmuted to their ultimate state, the Vedic Truth of life discovered by the *ṛishis* so long ago becomes obvious. ¶That goal is to realize God Śiva in His absolute, or transcendent, state, which when realized is your own ultimate state—timeless, formless, spaceless Truth. That Truth lies beyond the thinking mind, beyond the feeling nature, beyond action or any movement of the *vṛittis,* the waves of the mind. Being, seeing, this Truth then gives the correct perspective, brings the external realities into perspective. They then are seen as truly unrealities, yet not discarded as such. ¶This intimate experience must be experienced while in the physical body. One comes back and back again into flesh simply to realize Paraśiva. Nothing more. Yet, the Self, or Paraśiva, is an experience only after it has been experienced. Yet, it is not an experience at all, but the only possible nonexperience, which registers in its aftermath upon the mind of man. Prior to that, it is a goal. After realization, one thing is lost, the desire for the Self.

Tuesday
LESSON 2
Like a Child's Self-Discovery

Look at a child standing before a mirror for the first time, feeling its nose and ears, eyes and mouth, looking at itself reflected in the glass. Feeling and seeing what has always been there is a discovery in experience. Paraśiva is the same. It is always there in each and every human being on the planet. But involvement in the externalities of material existence inhibits their turning inward. The clouding of the mirror of the mind—that reflective pond of awareness which when calm sees clearly—or the ripples of disturbance on the mind's surface distort seeing and confuse understanding. Without a clear mirror, the child lacks the seeing of what has always been there—its own face. Paraśiva is an experience that can be likened to the hand feeling and the eyes seeing one's own face for the first time. But it is not experience of one thing discovering another, as in the discovery of one's face. It is the Self experiencing itself. Experience, experienced and experiencer are one and the same. This is why it is only registered on the external mind in retrospect. ¶Most people try to experience God through other people. Disciples see a *guru* as God. Wives see their husband as God. Devotees see the Deity in the temple as God. But all the time, behind the eyes of their seeing, is God. The Self, Paraśiva, can be realized only when the devotee turns away from the world and enters the cave within as a way of life through initiation and under vows. We know the Self within ourself only when we fully turn into ourselves through concentration, meditation and contemplation and then sustain the resulting *samādhi* of Satchidānanda, pure consciousness, in hopes of finding—determined to find—That which cannot be described, That which was spoken about by the *ṛishis,* Paraśiva, beyond a stilled mind, Paraśiva that has stopped time, transcended space and dissolved all form.

Wednesday
LESSON 3
Defining the Destination

How can we know when we're ready to know the Self? How do we know when the soul is spiritually mature? When we begin a journey and clearly define our destination, then we must begin from where we are, not elsewhere. Clearly defining our destination requires knowing where we are, requires determining whether or not we want to go there at this time. We must ask whether we have the means, the willpower, to get there. Are we ready to leave the world, or must we fulfill further obligations in the world and to the world? Have we paid all of our debts? We cannot leave the world with *karmas* still unresolved. Perhaps we desire something more, some further human fulfillment of affection, creativity, wealth, professional accomplishment, name and fame. In other words, do we still have worldly involvements and attachments? Are we ready for the final journey life has to offer? Are we prepared to endure the hardships of *sādhana,* to suffer the death of the ego? Or would we prefer more pleasures in the world of "I" and "mine"? It is a matter of evolution, of what stage of life we have entered in this incarnation—is it *charyā, kriyā, yoga* or *jñāna?* When the soul is spiritually mature, we know when we're ready to know the Self. ¶When one is bound down by his past *karma*s, unhappy, confused and not performing with enthusiasm his *dharma*—be it born or chosen—making new *karmas* as a result, his lethargy results in despair. The camel walks slower with a heavy burden and stops if the burden is still heavier. The burdened have no sense of urgency, no expression of joy. They have stopped. They are standing on the path holding their troubles in their hands, unwilling and unable to let go. ¶Worship of Lord Gaṇeśa sets the path of *dharma.* Go to His Feet. He alone can perform this miracle for you. He will release the mental and emotional obstructions to spiritual progress. He will remove the burdens of worldliness. To live the perfect life of the *gṛihastha dharma,* of family life, brings as its fulfillment the all-knowing bliss of Satchidānanda, realizing ourself not as formless Paraśiva but as the pure consciousness that sustains and pervades all forms in the universe. Yes, there is a sense of urgency on the path of enlightenment, but only when we are unburdened of *karma,* only when we are walking the path of *dharma.* Only then can true *yoga* be practiced and perfected. ¶All Hindus without exception believe in reincarnation. In each birth we must fulfill more goals leading to the one ultimate goal which after many births well lived will loom before us as the only goal worthy of striving for in this lifetime. All other desires, all other aims and ambitions pale under the brilliance of even the thought of realization of Satchidānanda and Paraśiva. ¶In fulfillment of our duties to parents, relations and the community at large, become a good householder, be a good citizen, live a rewarding physical, emotional and intellectual existence. These are the natural goals of many. Once this is accomplished in a lifetime, it is easy in future lives to perpetuate this pattern and evolve toward more refined and more difficult goals, such as gaining a clear intellectual knowledge of the truths of the *Āgamas* and *Vedas,* most especially the *Upanishads,* and establishing a personal contact with Lord Śiva within His great temples through the fervor of worship.

Thursday
LESSON 4
Harnessing the Energies

Still other goals must be met: quieting the energies, the *prāṇas,* through *prāṇāyāma,* purifying or refining mind and emotion, quelling the ever-constant movement of the restless, external mind and its immediate subconscious, where memories are stored, preserved memories which give rise to fear, anger, hatred and jealousy. It is our past that colors and conditions, actually creates, the future. We purge the past in the present, and we fashion the future in the present. ¶All of these emotions are the powerful force that bursts the seals of the psychic *chakras,* four, five, six and seven. Once harnessed, turned inward and transmuted, this life force drives the spiritual process forward. Ours is the path of not only endeavoring to awaken the higher nature, but at the same time and toward the same end dealing positively and consciously with the remnants of the lower nature, replacing charity for greed and dealing with, rather than merely suppressing, jealousy, hatred and anger. ¶Most people do not understand that they have a mind, that they have a body and emotions, that what they are is something far more lasting and profound. They think they are a mind, they presume they are a body and they feel they are a given set of emotions, positive and negative. To progress on the spiritual path, they must learn they are not these things but are, in fact, a radiant, conscious soul that never dies, that can control the mind and directs the emotion toward fulfillment of *dharma* and resolution of *karma.* While living in a normal agitated state of fears, worries and doubts, seeing the deeper truths is impossible. To such a person there is no doubt about it: "I am fearful. I am worried. I am confused. I am sick." He says such things daily, thinking of himself in a very limited way. ¶This wrong identification of who we are must be unlearned. Before we actually begin serious *sādhana,* we must understand ourselves better, understand the three phases of the mind: instinctive, intellectual and superconscious. This takes time, meditation and study—study that must culminate in actual experience of the instinctive mind, the intellectual mind and the transcendent subsuperconscious state of the mind. ¶Seeing the mind in its totality convinces the seeker that he is something else, he is the witness who observes the mind and cannot, therefore, be the mind itself. Then we realize that the mind in its superconsciousness is pure. We do not have to purify it, except to carry out its native purity into life, into the intellect by obtaining right knowledge and transmuting the instinctive or animal qualities. This is accomplished from within out. It is not as difficult as it may seem.

Friday
LESSON 5
Preparations For True Yoga

We must live in the now to follow the path to enlightenment. In the lower realms of the mind, where time and space seem very real, we are worried about the past or concerned about the future. These two intermingle and limit conscious awareness. Living in the past or the future obstructs us in this way: the past by reliving old experiences—mainly the negative ones, for they are vividly remembered—clouds our vision of the future. Living in the future overactivates the intellect, the emotion and the desires. The future is little more than another form of mental fantasy. Past and future are equally unreal and a hindrance to spiritual unfoldment. A person functioning in the now is in control of his own mind. He is naturally happier, more successful. He is performing every task with his fullest attention, and the rewards are to be seen equally in the quality of his work and the radiance of his face. He cannot be bored with anything he does, however simple or mundane. Everything is interesting, challenging, fulfilling. A person living fully in the now is a content person. ¶To attain even the permission to perform *yoga* one must have the grace of Lord Gaṇeśa and the grace of Lord Muruga. Lord Muruga is the God of the *kuṇḍalinī,* of the advanced *yogic* practices. Unfoldment all happens within the *kuṇḍalinī* and the *chakras* within our subtle bodies. Once a profound relationship is developed with Lord Muruga, then with the *guru's* permission and guidance, true *yoga* may commence. Otherwise, no matter how long one sits in meditation, no matter how hard one tries, it is just sitting, it is just trying. There is no fire there, no *śakti,* no power, no change.

It is the Gods who control the fire and at this stage help the devotee immensely, bringing him closer and closer to the supreme God, Śiva. Quite often the *yogī* in his deep internalized state may see in vision the feet or form of God Śiva before he begins to blend into the mind of God Śiva, called Satchidānanda. It is God and Gods in form that help us to find the formless God.

Saturday
LESSON 6
The Perspective Of the Knower

Most people have not realized that they are and were Śiva before they search for Śiva. They are confined to their own individual *āṇava,* their personal ego and ignorance. When we realize that we have come from Śiva, the way back to Śiva is clearly defined. That is half the battle, to realize we came from Śiva, live in Śiva and are returning to Śiva. Knowing only this much makes the path clear and impels us to return to Him, to our Source, to our Self. We only see opposites when our vision is limited, when we have not experienced totally. There is a point of view which resolves all contradictions and answers all questions. Yet to be experienced is yet to be understood. Once experienced and understood, the Quiet comes. ¶The only change that occurs is the awakening of the *sahasrāra chakra* and the perspective that a mind has which has undone itself, transcended itself in formless Being and Non-Being, and then returned to the experiences of form. The experiences are all still there, but never again are they binding. The fire or life energy which rises in the normal person high enough to merely digest the food eaten, rises to the top of the enlightened man's head, burns through a seal there, and his consciousness has gone with it. He is definitely different from an ordinary person. He died. He was reborn. He is able and capable of knowing many things without having to read books or listen to others speak their knowledge at him. His perceptions are correct, unclouded and clear. His thoughts manifest properly in all planes of consciousness—instinctive, intellectual and superconscious or spiritual. He lives now, fully present in all he does. ¶The internal difference that makes a soul a *jñānī* is that he knows who he is and who you are. He knows Truth, and he knows the lie. Another difference is that he knows his way around within the inner workings of the mind. He can travel here and there with his own 747, without extraneous external conveyances. He knows the goings-on in far-off places. He is consciously conscious of his own *karma*, *dharma* and that of others. For him there is no apartness, due to his attainment within the *chakras* previously described. His only gift to others, to the world, would be blessings, an outpouring of energy to all beings from the higher planes where he resides. It is the *jñānī*, the enlightened being who sees beyond duality and knows the oneness of all. He is the illumined one, filled with light, filled with love. He sees God everywhere, in all men. He is the one who simply is and who sees no differences. That is his difference.

Sunday
LESSON 7
A Path Of Love

We have been walking through the path of the many Śaiva saints on our garden temple lands. Together we have looked back through history and seen real people, living real lives, doing pragmatic things, sometimes foolish things—some even hurtful. There were workers among them, royalty, housewives, *yogīs*, businessmen—a spiritual community divided by caste, but with one thing only in common. They all loved Śiva. That is their heritage. That is their message—that there is hope for all of us on this path to Śiva, hope of attaining His grace. These men and women will be remembered as they were for thousands of years. On this path, you don't have to be a great *ṛishi* or a highly trained *yogī*. You don't have to be a great philosopher. You don't have to know Sanskṛit. Just love God, which is the Life of the life within everyone. And to realize that God is the Light of the light within everyone, you have to be very simple, very uncomplicated, so that obvious realization can manifest through your conscious mind, through your subconscious mind, through your superconscious mind. ¶It's very simple: the energy within our body is the same energy that pervades the universe, and it's all emanating right out of Lord Śiva. It's very simple: the light that lights our thoughts—that light doesn't care—it has no preferences—whether it's a good thought or not a good thought. That light is illuminating every thought. Take away the thoughts, and you realize that you are just light. ¶The path of Śaiva Siddhānta, as you all know, is a very simple path. It's the path of love, a path of devotion, which makes you want to be self-disciplined, because to maintain a feeling of love all the time, you have to be self-disciplined. You don't discipline yourself to attain the feeling of love. You attain the feeling of love and then you want to discipline yourself because you love the discipline, because it brings more love. ¶The path of Śaiva Siddhānta is worshiping God on the outside and realizing God on the inside, and when the two come together—transformation! That means that you're different than you were. You have different desires. You have different motivations, different goals in life, because you've been transformed. You look at your previous life and you say, "That's another person." Why? Because you have found something real on the inside of you. Thoughts on the inside of you—they're not real, they're always changing. Feelings on the inside of you—they're not real, they're always changing. Śiva on the inside of you is right there—never changes. Those of you who hear the *nāda,* it's the same inner sound, morning, noon and night, 365 days a year. The light that lights your thoughts, 365 days a year, twenty-four hours a day, is the same. It lights up your dreams also. And the energy of your body—all coming from Śiva. ¶Śiva is so close to you. The Nayanars, the saints of Tamil Śaivism, teach us a great lesson. They did so much wrong, but they survived with just the love of Śiva, and maintained that love without anything getting in the way of it. Of course if you love Śiva, obviously you have to love everyone else. Love brings forgiveness. Love brings understanding. Love brings feeling. ¶I thought the great *guru* Satya Sai Baba had something very insightful to say to his disciples, "If each one of you love me, then you all love each other." All Śaivites of the world love Śiva. They all love each other, and they love the Vaishṇavites, the Śāktas, the Smārtas, the tribal Hindus and everyone in the world, because Śiva's energy is working through everyone in the entire world—plants, trees, animals, fish, birds. It's so simple. The object of the lesson is to make yourself a very simple, uncomplicated person. Aum Namaḥ Śivāya.

Sarvajñastvadantareva Vidyate

सर्वज्ञस्त्वदन्तरेव विद्यते

All Knowing Is Within You

The *māyā* we seek to understand envelops the soul, inside and out. The hypnosis it creates baffles thought and word. When you are freed from it, your knowledge becomes purified. Transmuted into the bliss called Śivānanda, it becomes a protective roof over you.

TIRUMANTIRAM 2275

Monday
LESSON 8
The Immortal Body of the Soul

As soon as we start on the path to enlightenment, we begin to wonder about our own personal life, and that becomes very important to us even to the point where sometimes it could make an aspirant rather selfish, because he becomes more interested in himself, his own personal life, than people around him. ¶This is one of the things on the path that really should be avoided, and again, a complete change of perspective is needed. We have to change our perspective and begin to realize that beautiful body of the soul which has been growing through the many, many lifetimes that we have spent on the Earth. It's an indestructible body, and each lifetime it grows a little bit stronger in its inner nerve system. That is called the soul, or the psyche. ¶This body has been in existence for some thousand years or more on this planet, through the reincarnation process, and it is rather mature when the individual asks for the realization of the Self. It has lived so many lifetimes and gone through so many different experiences that in its maturity it wants its last experience on this Earth, that of Self Realization. ¶So, therefore, our individual existence, our individual life, should be identified with the immortal body, not with the physical body, not with the emotional body, not with the intellectual body, not with the astral body, which of course, is the instinctive-intellectual body, but with the body of the soul that has come along and had one body after another. It's come along on the physical plane and had a physical body. Then it was overshadowed by an astral body. Then it was overshadowed by another physical body. Then it was overshadowed by an astral body. Then it was overshadowed by a physical body. And the layers went onto the body of the soul—the instinctive, the intellectual, the physical. And now, in its maturity, the layers are coming off again. ¶We drop off the intellect. We drop off the instinctive actions and reactions. The only thing we want to keep is the physical body and the body of the soul. And that is the path that we are on. And when this begins to happen, when the beautiful, refined body of light and the physical body merge as one, we see light all the way through the physical body, right into the feet, into the hands, through the head, through the torso, through the spine. We're just walking in a sea of light. ¶This inner light is so beautiful. All day long my head has been filled with light. It feels that if I were to reach up and put both hands around the top of my head, there wouldn't be a head there. It feels like there is nothing there. It just goes on and on and on into endless space, as I look back up within the head. When I look into the back of my neck, I see an array of, they look like, wires, and these, of course, are the nerve currents that run through the spinal cord. They're all bright and active and scintillating, drawing energy from the central source of energy. And, of course, if you looked into the central source of energy, what would you see? You would see light coming out of nothing. That's what it looks like, light coming out of nothing.

Tuesday
LESSON 9
Everything Is Within You

The Self God is within all of this. It is beyond all bodies. It is beyond all form. It is beyond all intellect, beyond time, beyond space. That is the big realization on this planet, the thing that should be yearned for, sought for; all desires should be pointed in that direction. And then, once realized, you live out the life of the physical body and do what you can do in service to fellow man who is also coming along the same path that you have walked on before. ¶All knowing also is right within you. This body of light of the soul is the body of the superconscious mind. It is all-knowing. We have to approach it through the physical brain, and it takes a little time to draw forth inspiration and knowing, but the more refined the physical body becomes, the more like this soul body, the knowing is there superconsciously. It's a beautiful thing to think about, that all knowing is within man. Everything that has been brought through—all books, all systems, all religions, all philosophies—have come through man, but not always through the intellectual man or the instinctive man, but through the man whose body of his soul and his physical body have merged as one. ¶There are other things that are within us, too. Even the devil that they talk about, it's also right within us. That's the instinctive mind. That's also the intellectual mind, the doubter that says, "I don't know if I should be on the path to enlightenment. Maybe I should be doing something else." That's the area of the mind that causes us to argue with ourselves, or have a mental argument with a friend of ours. That's the antagonistic force of the instinctive area of the mind, as well as the intellectual area of the mind.

Wednesday
LESSON 10
Handling each Experience

And while this is going on, what does the body of the soul, the real body of you, what does it do? It's about its business, working, learning, studying on inner planes of consciousness and waiting for the instinctive and intellectual and physical elements to grow up a little bit and merge, for life is just a tremendously great experience. Each lifetime has been a great experience for the soul. ¶The more experiences we can have during a lifetime and approach those experiences in a positive way, the more we begin to crush out the instinctive elements, the more we begin to mold the intellect so it is like the superconscious mind rather than being like the instinctive area of the mind, the more we can begin to mold the physical atoms so that they become closer attuned to the spiritual forces emanating from the soul body. The more experiences we can have and face those experiences positively, the faster we evolve. The fewer experiences we have, the slower we evolve. ¶The knowing of how to handle each experience that comes to us in our lifetime comes from the soul. It's our superconscious self. ¶The instinctive mind will want to run after certain experiences and be repelled by other experiences. It is the area of duality, of likes and dislikes. The instinctive mind will react and resent experiences of a certain nature. The intellectual mind will rationalize other types of experiences that happen to us during a lifetime, argue them out and try to find out reasons why. The superconscious mind of the soul will know the reason why. It will come in an intuitive flash. If it doesn't, it doesn't matter anyway. ¶The spiritual body of you, which is permanent, has always remained constant. It has always been constant because it's directly in tune with the constant central source of all energy of the universe. This one source of energy feeds through your spiritual body and out through the intellectual sheath, the astral or emotional sheath, and the physical body. So identify yourself as the inner being. Never see yourself as an outer being. Then experience won't be reacted to. It will be understood from a mountaintop consciousness. Then experience won't be sought for for the enjoyment of the experience. The Self will be sought for, and the experience will be part of the path to you.

Thursday
LESSON 11
No Good, No Bad

Each experience that we have is a good experience because it molds us. It shapes us, just like an artist would mold a piece of clay. From an ugly hunk of clay can emerge a divine being, molded by the artist. In that same way, the experiences of life, even those that boomerang back on us and those we think are terrible, mold us. But they only mold us quickly and benefit us tremendously if we hold our perspective as the inner man, the timeless man, the immortal being. Only in this way can this happen. That's the attitude, the thoughts we must have, as we go along on the path of enlightenment. ¶The mere fact that you want Self Realization in this life means that you have been through hundreds of thousands of experiences. You have been nearly everything that there is to be on this planet. And now, in your last lifetime, you are finishing up the experiential patterns that you didn't handle in a life prior. ¶Life is a series of experiences, one after another. Each experience can be looked at as a classroom in the big university of life if we only approach it that way. Who is going to these classrooms? Who is the member of this university of life? It's not your instinctive mind. It's not your intellectual mind. It's the body of your soul, your superconscious self, that wonderful body of light. It's maturing under the stress and strain, as the intellect gives back its power to the soul, as the instinct gives back its power to the soul, as the physical elements give back their power to the soul and all merge into a beautiful oneness. In this way, the beings of the New Age are going to walk on Earth. Each one will have light flowing through his whole body and he will inwardly see his body glowing in light, even in the darkest night. ¶The good-and-bad concept should be thrown out with a lot of other things, including the up-and-down concept. There is no good; there is no bad. You don't raise your consciousness, nor do you lower it. These are just concepts that have come in by various philosophers who tried to explain these deeper teachings the very best that they could. What is bad is good, and what is good is good. And a higher state of consciousness and a lower state of consciousness, they don't exist at all. We simply hold a certain perspective of awareness, and we look out, and we go in.

Friday
LESSON 12
Inner States, Outer States

When you look out through the eyes of your soul, it's like a great executive in a large building's penthouse office. His desk is right in the middle of that office, and he looks out and he sees the people working around him. Then he looks farther out, and he sees the vast panes of windows. Then he looks farther out, and he sees the city below, and he sees the sky, he sees the traffic. Then he looks back into himself. He sees his subconscious mind, with thoughts about his home life and other things that do not involve his immediate surroundings in this grand office. He looks deeper into himself and he has an intuitive flash. Something has come to him, how he can help his enterprise be moved and motivated in a more dynamic way. He looks deeper within himself for the source of where that intuitive flash comes from, begins to see light within his head, light within his body. Again he becomes conscious of people working around him. Again he becomes conscious of the panes of the windows. He has to leave this office. He goes down in an elevator. He walks out onto the street. He is the same being. His perspective is an inner perspective. He doesn't go up and down in consciousness. ¶The mystic does not go up and down in consciousness. It only seems like that. But that is not actually what happens. It makes it very difficult when we hold the up-and-down and good-and-bad concepts, because they work in time sequences. If we are bad, it takes a certain amount of time before we can become good. And if we are good, there is a great possibility that we might be bad during a certain period of our life. If we are in a high state of consciousness, percentages have it that we may be in a low state of consciousness. It's going to take a lot of time to climb up high, and we might fall down, so what's the use? We have all of these semantic connotations with the words *good* and *bad* and *up* and *down,* and therefore we throw them out of our mystical vocabulary and the connotations that go along with them. We say we go within, deep within. We say we come out, into outer consciousness. We say there is no good, there is no bad, there is just experience, and within each experience there is a lesson. Some experiences might make our nervous system react so strongly that it may take hours to pull ourselves together. ¶But once we pull ourselves together, that exercise evolves the body of the soul that much more. We have transmuted tremendous instinctive and intellectual energies into this body of the soul. We have fed it. We have given it a good meal. And we never face that same experience again, nor react the same way.

Saturday
LESSON 13
Experience Without Reacting

The next time the same experiential pattern appears, we approach it from a mountaintop consciousness, because we have conquered those instinctive elements. Our intellect has been trained by family and friends, schoolteachers and business acquaintances. We have to build a new intellect, an intellect from the soul, out into the intellectual mind rather than from the instinctive area of the mind into the intellect to be successful on the path of enlightenment. ¶If we look at the past and we look at the future as both a series of dreams, and the only thing that we are concerned with is our immediate reactions and what we carry with us now—we see that the past is there to test us and the future is there to challenge us. We cannot change the past, but we can change how we react to what has happened to us in the past, and we can change the future anytime we want to. ¶The soul builds a body around us in this life. That's what's happened to all of us. This body goes through the same experiences year after year, the emotions go through the same experiences year after year, until we build up strong enough within ourself to face the experience without reaction to the experience. Then we go into a new series of experiences. ¶Give yourself a test to prove this out. Go to a movie, one that will make you laugh and make you cry and make you suffer right along with the players. And that's how we live our life. We laugh, we cry, we suffer, we have joy, we have peace, like actors on a great stage. Then go to the same movie the next day and go through the same emotions again—another cycle in the same life pattern. Then go to the movie the day following that, and go through the same emotions. Then go the next day, and you will find you will go through the same emotions, but not quite as well. Then go the next day. You will find your mind begins to wander into how the film was produced, just where the cameraman was standing when he filmed this emotional shot. You're becoming mystical. That is how the mystic faces his experiences. "How was this produced? Where was the cameraman?" Go the next day and you will again be distracted, and may wonder about the voltage that runs the carbon arc light that penetrates the film! Then go the next day. You won't be involved in the picture at all, or the emotion. You could care less. You had that experience, you lived it through, and you lived it out. It was neither good nor bad. It was neither high nor low. But you're completely involved in the cameraman, the actors, the personalities of the actors. You begin to get perceptive, and you see that a particular actor was saying something and going through something but thinking about something entirely different. You didn't catch that the first time. You were blinded by emotion.

Sunday
LESSON 14
Waiting for Intuitive Flashes

Go again and again and again, and finally you would become deeply involved with yourself and the people around you, and you will start having a new set of experiences. Someone's eating popcorn on the left side and someone's smoking on the right side, and you get up and move. The very first time you went to see the movie, you were not even conscious of anyone around you. ¶And finally, after going to this same movie for two weeks, you sit down and you start breathing and going within yourself, and you are not conscious of someone on the left side or someone on the right side, or the film or the light penetrating the film or what is on the film. You are breathing and going within yourself, and you begin to enjoy the bliss of your own being. That is what a mystic does in life. That's a wonderful meditation. If you don't want to go to the same film two or three weeks, night after night after night, well then just pretend that you do. Meditate on it and in the course of a short meditation you will see how a mystic lives his life. Now, of course, one film and its nerve-wracking experiences conquered, there's always another film being played in town, and you could start right over again—the same thing we do in our experiences. We go through one set of experiences. We react to them. We go within ourselves. We lose consciousness of the experience itself because we know how it was created. We studied it out so well. It has come to us in intuitive flashes. Then we go into the next movie, the next scene. ¶Now, when the mystic wants to understand his series of experiences, he does not analyze himself. He doesn't go through the emotion of "Why did this happen to me?" "What did I do to deserve that?" "What did this experience come to me for? I want to know the reason, and only when I know the reason can I go on." This binds him to the intellectual area of the mind. He lives his experiences in the consciousness of the eternity of the moment, and if an intuitive flash, a mountaintop consciousness, comes to him where he can see how he fit into the experiential pattern, he accepts it and he knows it's right, because it permeates him so dramatically, from the top of his head right through his entire body. ¶The mystic waits for these intuitive flashes, and he links one up with another. But he doesn't flow his awareness through the intellectual mind and spend time in that area to try to analyze each happening or each reaction to try to justify it, to excuse it or to find out why it has happened. He doesn't do that. Why? Because the soul, the superconscious mind, doesn't work that way.

Jīvanasya Prayojanam

जीवनस्य प्रयोजनम्

The Purpose of Life

The great souls that realize Śiva who is the Self within will seek forth Śiva in the Self. Those who do not reach Śiva in the Self will never reach Śiva. Do not lament that you know Him not. Follow the proper way and you shall meet Him. He who creates all as the twin lights, Śiva-Śakti, is united in my heart as one light.

TIRUMANTIRAM 2349-2350

Monday
LESSON 15
Find the Core Of Your Being

The superconscious mind and the body of the soul have been around a long time. This immortal body of yours has been around a long time, and it's seen many lives come and go, many experiences pass by the windows of its eyes. Some need no explanation, because they are the playing out of vibrations. Others do need an explanation, the explanation that would come and impress you intellectually from your superconscious, would give you power maybe to face an experience that was yet to come. So, don't analyze every nuance of a reaction or try to anticipate the next series of experiential patterns, for life is a series of experiences. They are all great experiences. ¶Hold your center. Find the place within you that has never ever changed, that's been the same for many lives, that feeling that has been the same within you since you were a little child up to this very time. Find that! Catch that vibration, and you've caught the vibration of the soul and identified it to your intellectual mind and your instinctive area of the mind. Then build on that. Work with that. Say to yourself, "There's something within me that never changes, no matter what happens." ¶Work on the analogy that if your foot hurts, your head doesn't hurt. If you have a pain in your stomach, it doesn't mean that you have a pain in your hand. In the very same way, if your emotions are upset and you're suffering, there's an area within you that's calm, peaceful, dynamic, vibrant, watching. That's the body of the soul. Work with that. Find that within you that has never changed, never will change, cannot change. All it can do is become more than what it is. This will give you understanding. This will allow you to innersearch, because you have an inner anchor which you're always trying to get into. You have identified the core of yourself very, very thoroughly. And each time you have unwound the emotional patterns and the intellectual patterns of an experience, you've graduated out of that classroom and you're on to greater and fuller experiences in this lifetime. If you would like to live a lifetime where you have no experiences at all, because you don't like experiences—you've had a lot of experiences that have been distasteful to you—you cannot do it on this planet. Lifetimes don't come about that way on this planet. But the core of you is the observer of all experience of the emotional, the instinctive, the intellectual areas of the mind.

Tuesday
LESSON 16
Awareness as A Lotus Flower

Be That which never changes. Then what happens? When we become this spiritual body and grasp that infinite intelligence of it, we're just in a state of pure consciousness and we come into the clear white light. We have a wonderful foundation, the only foundation necessary for Self Realization—at that point piercing the last veils of the mind, for even light is mind, and consciousness is, of course, the mind itself. And then we merge with the Self itself. ¶So, that is the path: experience, harnessing the reactions to experience, becoming the body of the soul, merging that body with the physical body after the instinctive and intellectual elements have been harmonized, coming into the clear white light, and then the realization of the Self. It's a beautiful path. It's a challenging path, and it's the path that you're on; otherwise you wouldn't be here listening to the story about the path. ¶See awareness as a lotus flower. The lotus flower goes through many, many experiences. A few weeks ago in Bangkok, on Innersearch, we drove out into the Thai countryside and we saw many, many lotus flowers growing wild. They're just beautiful. See awareness as a lotus flower. First awareness is a seed, and it's breaking out of the instinctive elements, the hard shell of the seed. But it's living right within the seed. It is dynamic life, at that very time, tuned in with the central source of energy. Then it breaks out and it becomes roots, and then awareness becomes a stem, becomes conscious of water all around it. Finally, the stem emerges above the water and awareness has leaves and a bud. It's still limited awareness, because it's not in its fullness. But as that awareness expands, it opens up into a beautiful lotus flower, then creates more seeds for more flowers. This is the path of awareness. Become acquainted with the awareness, that one beautiful, pure element of the soul, your superconscious body, which is easily found and easily discovered by simply closing your eyes and opening them and saying "I'm aware," not necessarily of what you are aware of. Close your eyes. Say, "I am aware." Awareness is closely identified to the realms of sight—hearing, of course, too, but more predominantly sight. As awareness expands and as awareness contracts, we find that we have power over awareness. It merely becomes a tool. The underlying power of awareness is the blissful state of the spiritual body of man, pure consciousness, the central source of all energies in its blissful, calm state. Meditate on awareness being like a lotus flower.

Wednesday
LESSON 17
The Path of Unfoldment

Meditate on man being like a lotus flower. He comes through the mud, his instinctive mind, and he's aware of the things of the instinctive mind: hate and greed and love and passion, and jealousy and sorrow, and happiness and joy and excitement. He comes into the intellectual mind. He becomes aware of ancient history and predictions about the future, politics, all sorts of systems, all sorts of organizations, institutions and opinions of other people. And this consumes and overshadows the soul, life after life after life, just as the desires and cravings of the instinctive mind overshadow the soul life after life after life after life. But all this time, the body of the soul is growing up. It's getting stronger. It's absorbing the reactions of each lifetime, drawing more energies from the central source of energy to build and absorb these reactions; and this is food for the soul. Then, finally, awareness comes into its bud state. It says, "Here I am, a bud, and I'm out of the mud, and I'm out of the water." We'll look at the mud as being the instinct, we'll look at the water as being the intellect and we'll look at the air as superconsciousness. "Now I want to unfold, and be of service to mankind and everyone else who is unfolding, I see them all down in the mud, caught in the mud like I was at one time. I want to help them out of the mud. Then I see hundreds of people caught in the intellect. They're all in the water. They think they're a stem, but I know I'm a bud." Then begins the process on the path of enlightenment for this bud unfolding and awareness expanding. First it becomes aware of the inner processes of the body and how breath controls thought. Then it becomes aware of the inner processes of the mind, how light moves through the body, how the mind of light begins to work, and it goes on unfolding and unfolding and unfolding through the ages. ¶If we look at the past as a catalog and the future as a planning book, and now as the only reality of time, we have dodged the past and we have dodged the future, because we have brought them both into the eternity of the moment. The mystic on the path of unfoldment doesn't allow his awareness to go into the past and flow though all the yesterdays and relive in his mind what formerly happened to him physically. The mystic doesn't go into the future and live emotionally experiences that may or may not happen to him. The mystic remains in the present, right now—using the catalog of the experiences of the past and a planning book for his future. This makes him wise, for intellect when it is correctly used at the right time is wisdom. ¶Holding the eternity of the moment feeling and the feeling of the being within that has never changed, finally you don't even say it's a being within. That in itself is duality. You just identify it as you, an immortal being who's lived for thousands of years, which never changes except it unfolds more, and it lives now. The past and the future are only intellectual concepts that we live with and have been developed by man himself in that particular area of the mind.

Thursday
LESSON 18
Making Wise Decisions

Life is a series of decisions also. One decision builds into another. To make a good decision, we have to again bring our total awareness to the eternity of the moment. If we project ourselves into the future to try to make a decision, we do not make a decision with wisdom. If we project ourselves into the past and in that way formulate our decisions, again they are not wise decisions, for they are decisions made through the powers of the intellectual or the instinctive area of the mind. The only good decisions come to us when we hold the consciousness of the eternity of the moment and go within ourself for the answer. ¶The best thing in making a decision is: when in doubt, do nothing. Have the subject matter so clearly in mind, so well thought out, that soon the answer will be self-evident to you. There will be just no other way to go. Good, positive decisions bring good, positive action and, of course, positive reactions. Decisions that are not well worked out—we jump into experiential patterns haphazardly or emotionally—bring reactions of an emotional nature that again have to be lived through until we cease to be aware of them and experience them emotionally. ¶Each time we have a decision to make, it's a marvelous test in this classroom of experience. We can make a good decision if we approach it in the eternity of the moment. And, of course, there are no bad decisions. If we make a decision that's different than what we would make in the eternity of the moment—we make it through the instinctive area of the mind or the intellectual area of the mind—we're not sure, totally, of ourself. We do not have enough information to make a good, positive decision. ¶So, when in doubt in making a decision that's the time to know we have to collect up more information, think about it more. Each decision is the foundation for the next series of experiences. When you are in a sequential series of experiential patterns, you are not making decisions at that time. Only when your experiential pattern has come to an end, and you're ready for a new set of experiences in certain areas of your life, those are the times when you make new decisions. Weigh carefully each decision, because that is the rudder that guides your ship through the whole pattern of life. ¶Think it over carefully. Go in for intuitive guidance. And nobody knows better than yourself, your own superconscious being, what is to be the next set of experiential patterns for you to go through in your quest for enlightenment. It's all based on decisions. Don't expect someone to make decisions for you. They are secondhand, not the best. Others maybe can give a little bit of advice or supply a different perspective or added information for you to make a better decision. But the decision you make yourself in any matter is the most positive, most powerful one, and should be the right one. Do it from the eternity of the moment. That is the state of awareness to hold.

Friday
LESSON 19
The Habit of Being Constant

There are several ways we can make decisions, and there are guidelines to help us. There are basic principles that we can follow in life that other people have followed which helped guide their decisions along. It worked out fairly well, so we can follow basic principles, too. And we'll go in after a while to outlining some of these basic principles that help us make good, positive decisions, for we can learn by observing other people, the decisions they have made, the reactions and experiential patterns that follow. We can learn by observing other people. ¶The first faculty of the expression of the inner being of your immortal soul is the great power of observation, to learn through observation, as your individual awareness detaches itself from that which it is aware of. You have tremendous powers of observation, for you are a free spirit. You're just here on this planet to observe. And through your powers of observation, you can go through the experiential patterns of other people, by observing what they're going through, without having to go through them yourself. Some mystics live several lifetimes in one in this way. ¶Living by basic principles keeps awareness clean-cut, pure, direct and positive, out of the areas of the mind that are confused, unwholesome, unhealthy, areas that react back upon the nerve system of the physical nature. When we are clean-cut, our perceptions are precise. We make our decisions from an up-down point of view, and our path through life is guided by each decision that we make. ¶When we make a decision, it has its reaction. If we do not make a decision, that has a reaction too, for then decisions are made for us by circumstance, other people, situations or confusion. The confusion becomes so intense that finally we're forced into a decision. When we become accustomed to making one decision after another from an up-down point of view, our lives are guided in a systematic, positive, clean-cut, beautiful way. Who does the guiding? You do, with your awakened perceptive faculties.

Saturday
LESSON 20
Are You Ready To Turn Inward?

Basic principles for a good foundation in our lives can be established through consistency. The consistency in approach to what you are doing, a good habit pattern in living our life—as we approach our inner life, the understanding of our inner life, the study of it and the experience of it—has to be on a day-to-day basis. To develop a contemplative lifestyle that is sensible, that is positively worked out, and program that into our complete pattern of daily life gives us a foundation strong enough to face decisions and the ensuing experiences and the reaction to those experiences in a way that they enhance our spiritual unfoldment. Remember, the lifestyle that we now have was programmed for you by mothers, fathers, religious leaders, teachers, people that we had just met along the way, and good friends. It's not a particularly good lifestyle in which to hold the perspective that we're an immortal being. It's a great lifestyle to hold the perspective that we're a temporal being, and we're only here a few years and then we die. ¶To develop a whole new lifestyle takes thought. Our desire has to be transmuted into doing that. In the ordinary lifestyle of human consciousness, our desires generally are for things, for emotional experiences, for intellectual knowing. And that's all good, but they're not organized. We have to organize the tremendous power of desire so that it's transmuted, and we desire the realization of the Self more than anything else. Then you'll have enough desire left over to get things, to get happiness and to get all the getting that humans want. ¶But the tremendous force of desire is transmuted. The perspective is changed. We see ourself as an immortal being, and we work consistently with our lifestyle day after day, week after week, month after month and year after year. Each decision that we make is an easier decision to make, and each reaction that we face, we face it joyfully. Each meditation that we hold is more profound than the last, and the spiritual being, the soul body, begins to merge with the physical body, as the elements of the instinct and the elements of the intellect that have been supreme life after life after life begin to give up and transmute their energies into the immortal body of the soul.

Sunday
LESSON 21
On Earth to Realize the Self

Look through your entire life and make a memo of each major experience in this life. Then surmise how many major experiences you have had for the last ten lives. All the accumulative experiences have brought you to the point where you are now, ready to turn inward and realize your infinite being. They have all been good experiences. The reactions to the experience has also been good. It brought you to the point where you are, ready to sit down and say to yourself, "Who am I? Where did I come from? Where am I going? What is the power of That which has never changed, which I am and can feel in every cell of my body? Where does the clear white light come from? What is the underlying power of pure consciousness out of which awareness emerges?" All of this and more, too, you will ask yourself and get answers from within yourself, as you, your awareness as the lotus flower begins to unfold. Always try to remember the reason why you are here. You're here to separate awareness from that which it is aware of and gain your own independence, your liberation, from the instinctive area of the mind. ¶When we're in it, we believe that everything we're going through is us. The intellectual area of the mind—when we're attached and in it strongly, we believe that that is us. When we're in the superconscious area of the mind, awareness is detached from that which it is aware of. We see ourselves as the traveler traveling through all areas of the mind, not getting stuck in any one area. Then we're here to go in, to take awareness off the surface of the Earth into outer space, or out of the instinctive and intellectual areas of the mind, into pure superconsciousness, into the clear white light, so it permeates every cell of the body. ¶We're here to realize the Self, have that one dramatic experience where everything that we thought was things is turned upside down, and our whole perspective afterwards changes. That is the purpose for living on this Earth. That is the purpose for being here this very moment. That is the purpose for my speaking to you in this way, to impress upon you very thoroughly that you are here for Self Realization, walking on this planet. Get it. Direct all your energies toward it, and then the tremendous power of desire will be for the one goal, not for the many goals toward which desires usually flow. When that happens, Self Realization will come to you. It'll be very easy. One day, you will be Self Realized.

Jīvana Nadī

जीवननदी

The River of Life

The black-footed Garuda bird flies across the sky;
a black-hued serpent dies in a deep well, all unseen.
So, stop bragging of your greatness, O heart! Be like
the river that merges into the wavy ocean.

TIRUMANTIRAM 2513

Monday
LESSON 22
The River, a Symbol of Life

You have all heard about the sacred river Ganges, but have you ever wondered why this river is sacred? Why has this river become personified among all the rivers of the world? Let us meditate on this and let the river tell its own story to us. The river is the esoteric symbol of life's force, and as it flows it tells us how those cosmic currents flow through the physical body, quieting the emotions and awakening the willpower so that we can keep the mind under our control. This all happens, of course, providing we are in tune and flow with that life force, that illimitable power within us. ¶The birth of this river high in the Himālayas we can liken to our own conception and entrance into physical consciousness. As the river flows to meet the sea, it drops off many disturbances, just as our life absorbs many of its hindrances. The rapids smooth out, the waterfalls become smaller, the mouth of the river broadens, and as the river flows into the ocean we can see this esoteric symbol of life ending its manifest physical form. ¶Let us relate that symbol to our own consciousness, holding it within our mind, the river as a symbol of life. Now look at yourself and see what stops that river from flowing. What stops you from flowing with cosmic forces and becoming one with life's ocean of eternal bliss? Is it not attachment that keeps us clinging to the bank of the river? Is it not fear that we are attached to? All of the personalities we know and the various material objects we are clinging to keep us holding tightly to the banks of life's cosmic river. The river still flows on, but we do not flow with it. We are fighting against life's currents when we allow ourselves to become attached. ¶Think today about the personal experiences in your lifetime and clearly view just how often you cling to the banks of life's river by attaching yourself to personalities and possessions. Have you ever stopped to think that we even become attached to things that we do not like and to the things that we have done against our better judgment? We are attached to objects, values, schedules, habits, memories, even likes and dislikes. We become attached because we do not stop to understand that each of those experiences that conceived the attachment was just a boulder, a waterfall or an old tree trunk blocking one of the little rivulets as it tried to merge with the great stream ever merging itself into the ocean.

Tuesday
LESSON 23
Affectionate Detachment

Meditate on a river. Follow it as a visual image from its source to the end where it merges into the sea. You can now clearly see where you have been clinging to the bank of life's river. You will plainly see just how long you have been clinging to various attachments by holding onto fears, worries, doubts of the future and regrets about the past. Looking at attachment, we see how it holds the mind down—how it submerges personality. Attachment is a stationary thing. Attachment creates the personality. The popular concept of the intellect at this point would be to say, "Well, then, according to this, we are not supposed to be attached to anything, or even have a personality." ¶But I take this one step farther and tell you, become affectionately detached, for by becoming affectionately detached you absorb all the power of the spiritual force within you. When you absorb the power of the spirit through the body, you will be able to feel it flowing through your most subtle nerves. This vibrant spiritual force within you, vibrating through every cell of the body, quieting the emotions and bringing the mind into effortless concentration, is born of affectionate detachment. ¶Affectionate detachment is stronger than any attachment could possibly be, because attachment is created through unfulfilled desire, salted and peppered with fear. Fear of loss, fear of the unexpected, fear that life may not have much more to offer than what has already been offered, fear of old age, fear of harm, fear of accident—these are the fears which salt and pepper the unfulfilled desires. This is attachment. ¶To be affectionately detached—that is a power. That is a wisdom. That is a love greater than any emotional love, a love born of understanding, a love that merges you into the river of life and allows actinic force to flow within you so that you realize God. ¶We all still have those little attachments—the good ones, the need for love, acceptance and security. These attachments form the positive aspects of the subconscious. We want to free ourselves of all negative attachments, then use the subconscious positively, as a powerhouse directed by our superconsciousness. ¶There is a great wisdom in cultivated affectionate detachment. Let go of the past. Let go of the future. Be a being right now. Being detached does not mean running away from life or being insensitive. It makes us extremely sensitive. When we have the ability to let go, we are warmer, more friendly, more wholesome, more human and closer to our family and friends.

Wednesday
LESSON 24
Subconscious Basement

I liken the subconscious mind to a basement. Those of you who have lived in the same house for a number of years have observed the following: as life progresses in the home, old things make way for the new, and the old things invariably are put into the basement. The basement is likened to the subconscious mind; the main floor, to the conscious mind. If one is putting too many things too fast into the basement and is too busy enjoying the new things passing through the conscious mind into the subconscious basement, there is no time to keep the basement in order. Suppose there is an earthquake, an emotional upheaval in life, and the entire house shakes. The lamp shades of the big lamps get mixed up with the shades of the small ones; the pillows of the old sofa get mixed up with the pillows of the armchairs. Should we enter the basement, it may take us several hours to find the articles we're looking for. That is the subconscious mind. It gets all mixed up if we do not look into ourselves constantly and put our subconscious basement in order. ¶Our subconscious basement is created first through association with our immediate friends and family and the interrelated strains, tensions, misunderstandings, joys, pleasures, happy memories and sorrows. In a lesser degree it is created in the outside world through the people to whom we have become attached. These attachments are reflections of what is already in the subconscious basement. In other words, we bring out of these people qualities similar to the qualities in our own subconscious. However, if every day at a certain time we meditate, go down into that basement and put a few things in order, pretty soon our basement is orderly and clean. We begin to understand the subconscious, seeing it as transparent, and we have no attachment to anything in it. We are not holding onto any old hates, fears or ancient misunderstandings within ourselves. ¶When we are not harboring negative attachments to anything that happened twenty or thirty years ago, thus creating tensions in our body and confusion in our mind, the subconscious becomes a powerhouse. The superconscious energies flood easily through you, bringing into your life an abundance of creativity, intuition, perception and bliss. The subconscious, in this pure state, is of great benefit to you both inwardly and outwardly when properly programmed.

Thursday
LESSON 25
"Nobody Understands Me"

In practicing affectionate detachment, we are learning to live in the here and now, right in the moment. We are awakening the power of direct cognition, the power that enables us to understand what happens, when it happens and why it happens. We are tuning into the river of life, the great actinic flow. This river flows directly from the essence of being through the subconscious basement and the conscious-mind main floor, creating life's experiences. Along the way, our cognition of these experiences completes the cycle of its continual flow. That is what we have to learn to tune into. All of our higher teachings give us that wisdom. It is a great step to learn it intellectually and to be able to talk about it, but once that step has been taken, it is not a great step anymore. ¶This wisdom must first be applied at home, then at work. Then it has to be applied among all of your acquaintances and friends. Everyone should understand you and about you, and if you feel there is someone close to you who does not understand you, that signifies that the part of yourself that this person represents does not understand what you think they do not understand. If someone who is close to you does not understand your inner nature, you do not understand your inner subconscious yourself. Why? Because you have only intellectually grasped certain things; you have not fully realized these concepts. They, the friend, as a reflection of yourself, therefore, will not quite grasp your studies or your concepts. As soon as you understand yourself, by having purified yourself, you can explain your realization to your friends in a way they will understand. ¶When explaining *yoga* teachings, use common examples like the following: "If you plant a seed and water it, you will eventually give birth to the flower." That is simple and complete. Anyone can understand it. Use little examples and stay away from big terms, mysterious words, for little examples of life are powerful. Talk about trees and how they grow. Talk about children and how they mature into adulthood. Talk about flowers and how they bloom, and relate these to the laws of life. Talk about the mind and how it can be opened up through *yoga* techniques of concentration and meditation, and you'll become a great missionary of Hindu Dharma and do much for yourself as well as others. ¶Those who say "Well, nobody understands me. I feel all alone on the path" are going through a period in which they have memorized everything but understand very little and therefore cannot explain or convince their fellow man of these great truths due to the fact that their subconscious basement is still full. When we only learn intellectually and have not put *dharma* into practice, our subconscious is still cluttered by uncognized memories.

Friday
LESSON 26
Be Like the River Water

You can plainly see that we have to go into the subconscious basement and straighten it out, if need be, by letting go and becoming free. That's easy to say. It's a little more difficult to do. Why? Because the basement took time to fill, and it takes time to clean. If we were to straighten out the subconscious basement too fast, that would not be good. It would be going against a natural law. It would be like pouring hot water on plants, as they do commercially, to make them bloom quickly. We must not force natural laws, so we take time in our spiritual unfoldment. The more time you are willing to take, the less pressure you have on yourself and the faster you will attain a permanent enlightenment. ¶Let's look again at the river of life as it flows into the sea, and again relate that to ourselves and see ourselves letting go of the river banks, merging ourselves into this river, flowing with it and realizing ourselves as the essence of life. Let us not worry about the past ever again. Do not even think about the past. Face everything that comes up in the light of the present, not in the darkness of the past. ¶Be like the river water. Water flows freely anywhere, easily finding its way around rocks and trees. Be pliable in your life, moving in rhythm with life. Let go of everything that blocks the river of life's energy. Watch your thinking and be careful of your thoughts. Judge every action that you make, judge every word you speak, with this law: "Is it true? Is it kind? Is it helpful? Is it necessary?" Become your own kind judge and make each second a day of judgment, for each second is really a day, if you live life fully. If you live completely each second, you will experience many days inside each twenty-four hours. ¶Be free from life's attachments and don't allow any more negative attachments to occur in your life. Loosen yourself—be free. Attachments bring all sorts of complications. Freedom brings no complications at all. So, that is what we have to do, recreate our lives each second. Become affectionately detached and manifest a greater love through action. Selfless service to mankind makes you free in the world of mortals. Measure yourself objectively with the river of life and merge with it into the sea of life. Let your service to mankind begin at home and radiate out to the world. Begin at home, with those closest to you, before venturing out among friends and strangers. Let your example be your first teaching. Be free from the past; abide in the present; detach yourself from the future; and live in the eternal now.

Saturday
LESSON 27
Performing Gaṅgā Sādhana

Close your eyes and visualize a river flowing into the sea, and see yourself holding on to the bank of the river, and the river flowing on past you. Now, let go of the bank of the river and flow down with the river and merge into the sea of life. Feel yourself, right at this instant, living in the here and now. Holding onto the river bank, we hold the consciousness of time and space. Holding on to the banks of the river of life is to recreate within you fear, worry, doubt, anxiety and nervousness. Detach yourself from the banks of the river and again be free. Love the banks as you pass, with a love born of understanding, and if you have no understanding of the bank, study your attachments until you do.

¶Learn to concentrate the mind so that you can study, not from books, but from observation, which is the first awakening of the soul. Learn to study by practice. Learn to study by application. Become a student of life and live life fully, and as you merge into the sea of actinic life, you will realize that you are not your mind, your body or your emotions. You will realize that you are the complete master of your mind, your body and your emotions. ¶There is a sacred practice you should perform to keep flowing beautifully with the river of life. It will be a challenge to discipline yourself to set aside the time, but it will benefit you. You must sit by a rolling river and listen to the river saying "Aum Namaḥ Śivāya, Śivāya Namaḥ Aum," as its water runs over the rocks. Listen closely to the water connecting to the rocks, and you will hear the sacred *mantra* of life, "Aum Namaḥ Śivāya." Relax into the sounds the river is chanting and try to be in tune with the perfect universe. The cosmos is perfect, you know. Its laws are divine, its timing flawless, its design unique. ¶While you are sitting alone by the side of the river being one with the perfect universe—the earth, the air, the fire, the water and the *ākāśa,* the mind—when a thought arises from your subconscious, something about your daily life, a problem or difficulty, pluck a leaf from a tree or bush, mentally put the problem into the leaf and place it into the river. The river will carry the leaf away along with the thought you placed into it. Then pluck a flower and humbly offer it into the river with both hands in loving appreciation for doing this great service for you. Perform this Gaṅgā Sādhana each month, and you will advance on the spiritual path.

Sunday
LESSON 28
Śiva's Perfect Universe

Slowly, slowly, by performing Gaṅgā Sādhana you will blend your external consciousness with our most perfect universal consciousness. While sitting by the river, close enough to touch the water, on a rock or tree limb, you are truly uninvolved with everything but yourself. You are now in tune with nature itself. Earth is there. Water is there. Fire is there. Air is there. *Ākāśa* is there. All the five elements are there. They are outside of you to see and feel, as well as inside of you to see and feel. The goal is to release that part of your subconscious mind that doesn't blend the within of you with that which is outside of you. You perform this blending by listening to the river murmur, "Aum Namaḥ Śivaya, Śivāya Namaḥ Aum," the sounds of Śiva's perfect universe. ¶Now the challenge. This will not be an easy task. The quiet of the noise of nature will release thought after thought from your subconscious mind. So, when each new thought arises—a mental argument or something which has not been settled in your past, an appointment missed or an image of a loved one—gather up the *prāṇic* energy of the thought and put its vibrations into a leaf. To do this, hold the leaf in your right hand and project your *prāṇa* into it along with the thought form that distracted you. Then release the leaf and with it the thought patterns into the river. Let the river take them away, while you listen to "Aum Namaḥ Śivāya, Śivāya Namaḥ Aum" of the river as it does. Each time this happens, thank the river by humbly offering a flower with the right hand into the river in appreciation of its having absorbed the worldly thought. To show appreciation is a quality of the soul, something not to be ignored, and, therefore, a vital part of this *sādhana.* ❡*Sādhana* is performing the same discipline over and over and over again. Just as we methodically exercise the physical body to build up its muscles, we perform spiritual disciplines over and over again to strengthen our spiritual, inner bodies. Perform Gaṅgā Sādhana time and time again. You will rapidly advance. Remember, the outer river is symbolically representing the inner river of your own nerve system, life force and consciousness that flows through you night and day. So, even as you sit on this rock and look upon the water, in a mystical way, see it as your own superconscious energies taking away these problems, worries, doubts, ill-conceived and unresolved experiences of the past. Flow with the river of life and merge in Śiva's ocean of oneness.

Sākshikathā

साक्षिकथा

The Story of Awareness

Coursing the *śakti kuṇḍalinī*, transcend the successive gates of awareness. Reduce the perishable body to its elemental constituents and then discard them. Then do you enter the grace of the Holy One, and there you abide and adore. That, indeed, is the fitting worship of Sadāśiva.

TIRUMANTIRAM 1854

Monday
LESSON 29
Awareness, a Ball of Light

The average person who is not a mystic lives two-thirds in the external area of the mind and one-third within himself. The within of himself can be and sometimes is very foreboding. He doesn't understand it. He is a little afraid of it, and prefers to involve himself with external things. Possibly he's had some inner experiences, some emotional unhappinesses, and he shuns anything that is inner. The mystic lives, and is taught to live, two-thirds within himself and only one-third in the external. In learning how to do this, the mystic is taught to become consciously conscious, or aware that he is aware. He learns to separate awareness from that which he is aware of. The person who is not a mystic, living two-thirds in the external mind, he says, "I am happy," meaning, "I am aware of a state of mind called happiness, and I am in that state, so that is me." Or, "I am unhappy. Unhappiness is me." The mystic living two-thirds within says to himself, "I am flowing through the area of the mind that's always unhappy." He doesn't change; he is a pure state of awareness. ¶Visualize a little ball of light. We'll call that man's individual awareness, and that light is shining right out from his eyes, and this little ball of light is going through the mind. It's going through the area of the mind that's always unhappy. It's going through the area of the mind that's always dreaming, the area of the mind that's delightfully happy, the area of the mind that's in absolute bliss, the area of the mind that's absolutely in jealousy all the time, the area that's in fear all the time—many people live in this area of the mind; it's quite crowded with lots of balls of light there. This ball of light flows through the area of the mind that's in resentment. It's like a churning ocean. It's a delightful place to be in, especially if you're a little ball. You get bounced all around. Then there's the area of the mind that is completely peaceful and has always been peaceful. No mood or emotion has ever been in it to ruffle it, because that's the peaceful area of the mind. The one who meditates seeks out this area to become aware in. ¶Man's individual awareness is just like this little ball of light, and it's like a camera. It photographs. It registers. It understands. It's pure intelligence. Man knows where he is in the mind, but the first step in awakening on the path of enlightenment is to separate awareness from that which it is aware of.

Tuesday
LESSON 30
Claim the Being Of Yourself

We say, "I am sick," and in the English language that means my body is sick, or I am aware of this body not being in a perfect state of health. The mystic knows he is not this body. He can even remember dropping off the body many, many different times, getting new bodies through the process of reincarnation. We are not what we are aware of. We are separate from that which we are aware of. We are only flowing through these areas of the mind. If we live in San Francisco, we're not San Francisco. If we live in unhappiness, we're not unhappiness. That's only one of the cities of the mind. This is a great meditation. You can grasp this awakening in thirty seconds. You can grasp this awakening in thirty hours, or thirty minutes. You can grasp this awakening and have it come to you vibrantly in thirty weeks, thirty months, or thirty years or thirty lifetimes. It just depends upon your willpower. ¶As soon as we can understand awareness detached from that which it is aware of, we have a vibrant energy, a tremendous drive; a tremendous willpower is released from within us. And we live with the feeling that we can do anything that we want to do, almost as quickly as we want to do it. We want things to happen now, for we vividly see the area where they already exist within the force fields of the mind itself. ¶How do we live our life from this point? We begin to apply this philosophy in every department of our life. There are some habit patterns in our subconscious mind that have not caught up with this new perspective as yet. And you'll be running up against them. As soon as you find awareness totally identified with a subconscious area that has become conscious, immediately turn inward, detach awareness from that which it is aware of and just be pure energy. You can expect a beautiful life, a beautiful relationship with the being of yourself. Claim the being of yourself as you. You have enough knowledge now. You don't have to discover the being of yourself and keep looking for it. Just be the being of yourself and travel through the mind as the traveler travels around the globe. ¶The wonderful story of awareness, I could go on and on talking about it, because it is so very basic and so very, very important. This then makes an infinite intelligence and everyone the same. Only, they are living in different areas of the mind, or different houses.

Wednesday
LESSON 31
The Mechanics Of Attachment

Have you ever had people come to you and tell you all of their problems? What did they do? As a pure state of awareness, they came to you as a pure state of awareness. You were not identified in the area of the mind that they are living in. So, they came to you because they want to get out of the area of the mind that they're living in. They've been living in it so long, they think they are that area of the mind, like somebody that has lived in a house so long and is so attached to it that they would rather die than move from the house. So then they come to you and start telling all the problems. First they start with the little ones, and then they start with the big ones, and all their complaints, heartaches and everything that that area of the mind involves in. Now, you can do one of two things. You gently talk with them and bring them out of that area of the mind into your area of the mind, or they can move your awareness right into that area of the mind, too. And they go away and you are feeling terrible. You're feeling just awful. ¶You've gone to a movie. The movie screen is just a screen. The film is just film. And the light is just light. And yet, the combination of the three can move your awareness into areas of the mind that can upset your nerve system, make you cry, make you laugh, make you have bad dreams for a week, change your whole entire perspective of life—these three combinations of physical elements can do this, if they can attract your attention. ¶Now, if we are sitting in a movie, and we are realizing that we're going through moods and emotions but we are not the moods and emotions that we're going through—all we're doing is being entertained by our senses—then that's the mystic. He is enjoying life and what life has to offer. He's even remembering in past lives when he has had similar experiences that the players are portraying on the screen, and he has empathy with them. He's living a full and a vibrant life, and yet when he walks out of the movie house, he's forgotten the whole thing. He doesn't carry it with him. His awareness is immediately right where he is currently. That's the power of the great eternity of the moment.

Thursday
LESSON 32
Living Two-Thirds Within

Living two-thirds within oneself and one-third in the external world—how do we do it? As soon as we live within ourselves, we become conscious of all of our various secret thoughts, all of our various emotions, that we would just as soon be without. Therefore, we distract ourselves and endeavor to live two-thirds in the external world and only one-third within ourselves. As aspirants on the path, you have to live your life two-thirds within yourself. When you are conscious of the thoughts that you don't want to think, the emotions that you don't want to feel, go deep within where they don't exist. Take awareness to the central source of energy, right within the spine itself. Feel that energy flowing through the body, moving the muscles, enlivening the cells. Then you are two-thirds within yourself, and the world looks bright and cheery all the time; the sun is always shining. Immediately, when we begin to identify totally with our thoughts as being reality, then we begin to make mistakes. We're living two-thirds in the external world. ¶How to strike the balance? Regulate the breath throughout the day. Keep the spine always straight. Always sit up straight. As soon as the spine is bent, awareness is externalized. We're living two-thirds in the external area of the mind and only one-third in. As soon as the spine is straight, our awareness is internalized. We're living two-thirds within and only one-third out. ¶What's the biggest barrier? Fear. Afraid of our secret thoughts. Afraid of our secret feelings. What's the biggest escape from fear? Go to the center, where energy exists, the energy that moves the life through the body. The simplest way is move your spine back and forth. Feel the power that moves that spine. Feel the power that moves that spine back and forth. Feel that energy going out through the physical body. Open your eyes and look at the world again, and you'll see it bright and shiny. You're two-thirds in and one-third out in awareness. You're balanced. ¶"Be renewed by a change of your mind." Be renewed by releasing awareness from one area of the vast universe of the mind, drawing it back into its source and, releasing it again, sending it to another of the vast areas of the mind.

Friday
LESSON 33
The Great Study Of Awareness

The study of awareness is a great study. "I am aware." The key to this entire study is the discovery of who or what is the "I am." It is the key to the totality of your progress on the path of enlightenment. What is awareness? As you open your physical eyes, what is it that is aware of what you see? When you look within, deep within, and feel energy, you almost begin to see energy. A little more perception comes, and you do actually see energy as clearly as you see chairs and tables with your physical eyes open. ¶But what is it that is aware? When awareness moves through superconsciousness, it seems to expand, for it looks out into the vastness of superconsciousness from within and identifies with that vastness. This is what is meant by an expanded state of awareness. What is awareness? Discover that. Go deep within it. Make it a great study. You have to discover what awareness is before you can realize the Self God. Otherwise, realization of the Self God is only a philosophy to you.

It is a good philosophy, however, a satisfying and stable philosophy. But philosophies of life are not to be intellectually learned, memorized and repeated and nothing more. They are to be experienced step by step by step. Get acquainted with yourself as being awareness. Say to yourself, "I am awareness. I am aware. I am not the body. I am not the emotions. I am not the thinking mind. I am pure awareness." ¶It will help for us to make a mental picture. Let us now try to visualize awareness as a round, white ball of light, like one single eye. This ball is being propelled through many areas of the mind, inner and outer, and it is registering all the various pictures. It has, in fact, four eyes, one on each side of it. It is not reacting. The reaction comes when awareness is aware of the astral body and the physical body. It is in those bodies that reaction occurs. We are aware of the reactions in these bodies, for the physical body and the astral body are also part of the vast, vast universe of the mind. ¶Each individual awareness, ball of light, is encased in many bodies. The first and nearest encasement is the body of the soul. The second encasement is the astral, or intellectual-emotional, body. The third encasement is the physical body. The radiation from awareness, this ball of light, is the aura. ¶Awareness is an extension of *prāṇa* from the central source, issuing energy. Energy goes where awareness flows. When awareness focuses on relationships, relationships flow. When awareness focuses on philosophy, that unfolds itself. Ultimately, when awareness focuses on itself, it dissolves into its own essence. Energy flows where awareness goes. I was always taught that if one foot was injured, for example, to focus on the other foot and transfer the healthy *prāṇa* from that foot to the ailing foot.

Saturday
LESSON 34
Awareness and Consciousness

Consciousness and awareness are the same when awareness is totally identified with and attached to that which it is aware of. To separate the two is the artful practice of yoga. Naturally, the Shum-Tyaef language is needed to accomplish this. When awareness is detached from that which it is aware of, it flows freely in consciousness. A tree has consciousness. Awareness can flow into the tree and become aware of the consciousness of the tree. Consciousness and mind are totally equated as a one thing when awareness and consciousness are a one thing to the individual. But when awareness is detached from that which it is aware of, it can flow freely through all five states of mind and all areas of consciousness, such as plants and the Earth itself, elements and various other aspects of matter. Here we find awareness separate from consciousness and consciousness separate from the five states of mind attributed to the human being. In Sanskṛit we have the word *chaitanya* for consciousness, and for *awareness* it is *sākshin,* meaning witness, and for *mind* the word is *chitta.* Consciousness, mind, matter and awareness experience a oneness in being for those who think that they are their physical body, who are convinced that when the body ends, they end and are no more. ¶We have three eyes. We see with our physical eyes and then we think about what we have seen. Going into meditation, we see with our third eye our thoughts. Then we choose one or two of them and think about them and lose the value of the meditation. It is the control of the breath that controls the thoughts that emerge from the subconscious memory patterns. Once this is accomplished, and the *iḍā, piṅgalā* and *sushumṇā* merge, we are seeing with the third eye, which is the eye of awareness, wherever we travel through the mind, inside or outside of our own self. ¶The minute awareness is attached to that which it is aware of, we begin thinking about what we were aware of. Controlling the breath again detaches awareness, and it flows to another area of the mind, as directed by our innate intelligence—this intangible superconscious, intelligent being of ourselves that looks out through the eye of awareness in a similar way as do the two eyes of the physical body. This then divides what we are aware of and thinking of what we were aware of, or distinguishes the process of thinking from that of seeing during meditation. ¶Awareness travels into the wonderful strata of thought, where thought actually exists in all of its refined states. First in these strata of thought is an area where ideas are only in a partial, overall, conceptual stage. Deeper into this stratum, they, as concepts, become stronger and stronger until finally they almost take physical form. Finally, they do take physical form. But you are the pure individual awareness, the ball of seeing light that is seeing all of this occur within these strata of mind and not identifying too closely with them. The quest is to keep traveling through the mind to the ultimate goal, merging with Śiva. When you are conscious that you are awareness, you are a free awareness, a liberated soul. You can go anyplace in the mind that you wish. ¶The mission is: don't go anyplace. Turn awareness back in on itself and simply be aware that you are aware. Try to penetrate the core of existence. Become conscious of energy within the physical body and the inner bodies, flowing out through the nerve system and drawing forth energy from the central source of the universe itself. Now, try to throw awareness into this central source of energy and dive deeper and deeper in. Each time you become aware of something in the energy realm, be aware of being aware. Finally, you go beyond light. Finally, you go into the core of existence itself, the Self God, beyond the stillness of the inner areas of mind. That is the mission and that is what humanity is seeking—total Self-God Realization.

Sunday
LESSON 35
Awareness Finds A New Home

Needless to say, the Self does not mean the realization of your personality. Some people think that this is what Self Realization means. "I want Self Realization," they say, thinking all the time it means, "I want to realize that I am an individual and not dependent upon my parents. I want Self Realization." Other people feel it means, "I want to realize my artistic abilities and be able to create." It does not mean that at all. All this is of external consciousness, the intellectual area of the mind. It is a lesser form of self realization. Self Realization is finding That which is beyond even superconsciousness itself, beyond the mind—timeless, causeless, spaceless. ¶After Self Realization, awareness has a new home. It does not relate to the external mind anymore in the same way. It relates to the Self God, Paraśiva, as home base and flows out into the various layers of the mind, and in again. Before Self Realization, awareness was in the external mind trying to penetrate the inner depths. Then it would return to the external mind and again try to penetrate the within through the processes of meditation. After Self Realization, the whole process of the flow of awareness is reversed. ¶Mind and consciousness are synonymous. Awareness is man's individual spiritual being, the pure intelligence of his spiritual body, flowing through this vast universe of the mind. We want to be able to flow awareness through any area of the mind consciously, at will, as we go in and in and in toward our great realization of the Self God, which is beyond mind, beyond time, beyond consciousness, beyond all form. Yet, it is not an unconscious state. It is the essence of all being, the power which makes the electricity that flows through the wire that lights the light that illumines the room. When we sit, simply being aware of being aware, the currents of the body harmonized, the aura turns to streaks of light dashing out into the room, and we are sitting in our own perfect bliss, simply aware, intensely aware, of being aware. Awareness itself then turns in on itself enough to experience, to become, the Self God—That which everyone is seeking. ¶That is the sum total of the path. That is the path that you are on. That is the experience that if you keep striving you will have in this life, even if it is at the point of death. It is then you will reincarnate as a great teacher on the planet and help many others through to the same goal. For there is no death and there is no birth for the immortal body of the soul that you are, that pure intelligence that goes on and on and on and on and on and on. So go in and in and in and in and in and in. Arrive at the ultimate goal. Make it your journey, your quest. Want it more than life itself. ¶Generally our greatest fear is death. Why? Because it is the most dramatic experience we have ever had in any one lifetime. Therefore we fear it. We are in awe of death. It is so dramatic that we do not remember really what happened during part of the experience, though occasionally some people do. However, the body of the soul knows no birth, knows no death. It goes on and on and on, and its awareness goes in and in and in to its ultimate goal—awareness of itself turned so much in on itself that it dissolves in the very essence of Being, as it merges in Śiva. You cannot say anything more about the Self, because to describe the Self adequately there are no words. It is beyond time, form, cause, mind. And words only describe time, cause and mind consciousness, which is form. You have to experience It to know It. And by experiencing It, you do know It.

Prajñānapanthāḥ

प्रज्ञानपन्थाः

Wisdom's Path

They who have awareness see all worlds. They who have awareness know no sorrows. When they who have awareness are truly realized, they indeed have seen the Infinite.

TIRUMANTIRAM 1786

Monday
LESSON 36
The Purity Of Awareness

To the awakened mystic, there is only one mind. There is no "your mind" and "my mind," just one mind, finished, complete in all stages of manifestation. Man's individual awareness flows through the mind as the traveler treds the globe. Just as the free citizen moves from city to city and country to country, awareness moves through the multitude of forms in the mind. ¶Before we meditate, we view the cycles of our life and erroneously conclude that the mind changes, that it evolves. We view joy one moment, and despair the next and, because we feel so different in these states, assume we have changed. We grow up and look back on our childhood and again see the appearance of change. Through meditation, however, we observe that we have not changed at all. Awareness becomes our real identity, and it is pure and changeless. It was the same at seven years of age as it is today. It is the same in happiness as it is in sadness. Pure awareness cannot change. It is simply aware. Therefore, you are right now the totality of yourself. You never were different, and you never will be. You are perfect at this very moment. Change is only a seeming concept created through false identification with the experiences we have in various areas of the one mind. ¶Everything in the world and everything in the mind is as it should be—in a perfect state of evolution. Superconsciously, we can clearly see this through the eyes of our soul. When looking at it through the instinctive-intellectual mind, we don't see this perfection. It is as if we have blinders on both sides of our eyes, like a donkey. The carrot of desire dangles right in front of our nose when we are in the instinctive-intellectual mind, and we are going after it, step at a time, step at a time, with our blinders on. We have to go in and in and in and reach an expanded state of awareness and gain that mountaintop consciousness where we perceive that there is no injustice in the world. There is not one wrong thing. All is in perfect order and rhythm in Śiva's cosmic dance.

Tuesday
LESSON 37
The Mind Is Complete

Should we acquire the ability to identify as the experiencer instead of the experience, the true and valid nature of awareness and its patterns of movement in the mind become evident. We see the mind as a total manifestation, containing all of the past and future evolutions in the eternal now. The mind is vast in its combinations of time, space and form. It contains every vibration from subtle to gross. Awareness is free to travel in the mind according to our knowledge, our discipline and our ability to detach from the objects of awareness and see ourselves as the experience of awareness itself. This explains many of the so-called mysteries of life. ¶There are people with the ability to look back into the past and ahead to the future accurately and in detail. That feat is understood clearly in the light of awareness traveling through the mind. The entire mind exists right now—past and future included. These psychically talented individuals have trained their awareness to flow into areas of the mind that are unavailable to the average person. They go into the mind itself to view these phenomena. Similarly, ESP, mind-reading and other mystical wonders are illumined by the knowledge that there is only one mind, and all phases of it are open to the spiritually awakened person. ¶What we term states of mind are, therefore, areas of distinct vibration. On the Earth we have continents, nations, regions, states and cities. Each is distinct and unique. Denmark is different from Spain. Australia is different from China. Paris is not at all like Honolulu. So it is in the mind. We have five states of mind—conscious, subconscious, sub of the subconscious, subsuperconscious and superconscious—and within each are hundreds and thousands of cities. In the subconscious area, the traveler can encounter fear, hatred, love and good memories. In the conscious mind area he can experience business, human relationships and intellectual, social vibrations. In the superconscious area, there are even more regions, and he comes into visions, light, sound, overwhelming joy and peace.

Wednesday
LESSON 38
Remaining Free, Detached

As we move through the mind, the mind stays the same, just as the world stays the same as the traveler moves from city to city. Paris does not vanish when he enters New Delhi. It is still there. Others remain in the city, and he can return. Fear does not disappear from the mind when we are blissfully fearless. Others still experience it. Our awareness has simply moved to a more refined area. Therefore, the goal is to make awareness totally free by not getting too magnetically attached to only a few of the many areas. If the traveler enjoys Paris and settles down there, he will never know the other cities of the world. We on the spiritual path must work hard at keeping ourselves detached from friends, places, habits. Only then can we keep awareness free enough to travel uninhibitedly through the sublime, inner areas of the mind. ¶Work on that every day. Observe when awareness gets so involved that it identifies with an experience. Then consciously tell yourself, "I am not fear. I am awareness flowing in the area of fear, and I can move into other areas at will." Work at that. Strive for that simple ability to detach awareness from that which it is aware of. The rewards gained will be more than worth the effort. Be renewed by a change of your mind. Be renewed by releasing awareness from one area of the vast universe of the mind, drawing it back into its source and releasing it again, sending it to another of the vast areas of the mind.

Thursday
LESSON 39
The Power of Observation

Observation is the first faculty to appear in the awakening of the superconscious regions. Observation, when perceptively performed, is cultivated by abstinence from excessive talk. Talk dissipates the energies of the aura and of the vital body of man. A mystic generally does not talk very much, for his intuition works through reason, but does not use the processes of reason. Any intuitive breakthrough will be quite reasonable, but it does not use the processes of reason. Reason takes time. Superconsciousness acts in the now. All superconscious knowing comes in a flash out of the nowhere. Intuition is more direct than reason, and far more accurate. Therefore, the mystic does not ask many questions or enter into lengthy conversations. ¶Ponder over this and apply it to yourself. Take this into yourself and feel it is for you. Do not feel it is being shared with you to simply know more about the mind and its processes. Apply it to yourself, for you are on the spiritual path toward merger with Śiva. Begin to feel that observation is one of your finest faculties, one that you most cherish. It is the first faculty of the awakening of your superconscious. Mentally say to yourself many times, "I have good observation. Therefore, I am superconscious." This will help you to program your subconscious to accept the fact that, yes, you are a superconscious being, not a temporal being that is only on this planet a short span of years and then disappears forever. Remember, your powers of observation are cultivated by abstinence from excessive talk. That is all you have to do to begin with—be more silent and observing, not wasting or dissipating this most vital power. Some people on the spiritual path cannot wait to talk about their meditations even before they come out of them. They really should stop doing this. It lessens their vital energies and proves to perceptive people that they are not superconscious beings.

Friday
LESSON 40
Tapping into Your Intuition

Begin to feel that your intuition works rather rapidly and is generally very reasonable, but does not use the process of reason. When you really want to reason something out, it may take a lot of time, but when you get an intuitive flash, it's right there. Then if you want to prove it, you have to reason it out. You will find that reason and intuition agree. Intuition is more direct than reason. That is why you should always use intuition. Always go in and in and in and find answers from within yourself, rather than wasting time scurrying around in the externalities of the mind. ¶Take this teaching in and apply it to yourself, making every metaphysical and philosophical area work within you. Do not carry all of this around with you as knowledge in the intellect. It will burden your intellect, and soon you will have to forget it, because the subconscious will have more than it can handle of inner teaching. It takes a while to convince the subconscious that you are a spiritual being whose existence does not begin and end with this life. Therefore, this inner teaching must begin to be applied as soon as it has begun to be understood. ¶The superconscious mind is the most wonderful area of the mind there is, although awareness is not always in it. We are not always aware in the superconscious mind, because we are generally aware in the conscious mind, or aware of our own subconscious or that of another. But the more and more we detach awareness from subconscious binds and conscious-mind attachments, the more we become superconscious. When we feel as if we are living totally in the moment, as if there is no past and there never has been any past or future, we are becoming subconsciously certain we are an intense, vibrating entity of the eternal now. That is superconsciousness, and that is very real. More real than a table, a chair, an automobile or a person sitting next to you is this feeling of being an intense sheath of energy right in the eternal moment, with no past, no future. This is superconsciousness.

Saturday
LESSON 41
Superconscious Signposts

When your awareness is in superconsciousness, you see yourself as pure life force flowing through people, through trees, through everything. I have seen myself, in a certain state of *samādhi,* as pure life force flowing through a jungle, through trees, through plants, through water, through air. That is superconsciousness. It is so permanent. It is so real. Nothing could touch it. Nothing could hurt it. In this state we see the external world as a dream, and things begin to look transparent to us. People begin to look transparent. This is superconsciousness. When we look at a physical object and we begin to see it scintillating in light as it begins to become transparent, this is superconsciousness. It is a very beautiful and natural state to be in. ¶Occasionally, in deep meditation we see the head filled with an intense light, and we know that that is the natural state of man. This is superconsciousness: when we can look at another person and know what he is thinking and how he is feeling and how his subconscious is programmed. While we are looking at him, all of a sudden he can be seen in a past life, or in the future, or in the eternity of the moment. You are so naturally, without striving, in the superconscious area of the mind. No technique can give you these experiences that you unfold into as you walk the path toward merger. You come right into them, and the experience is how you are. Occasionally, when you close your eyes in meditation, you may see the face of your *guru* or some divine being that possibly once lived on Earth, and now just the shell of his subtle body remains vibrating in the ethers. You see superconscious beings while in the superconscious area of the mind. Occasionally, you clairaudiently hear voices singing, music playing, just as Beethoven heard his wonderful symphonies that he recorded like a scribe. It is the superconscious mind again, so near, so real, so vibrant. ¶And when you are in contemplation, so engrossed in the energies within you—within the physical body and the energy within that, and that within that—that you become totally engrossed in the peace of the central source of all energy, that too is superconsciousness. Being on the brink of Self Realization, having lost consciousness of the physical body and of being a mind, you are only conscious of a vast, bluish white light. You get into this through going into the clear white light and out through the other side of it. Then you come into pure consciousness. It is a vast, pure, pale bluish white light—endless, endless inner space. It is just on the brink of the Absolute, just on the brink of the fullness of Self Realization. When you are in this beautiful, blissful state of pure consciousness, you are barely conscious that you are there, because to have a consciousness of being conscious, you have to be conscious of another thing. ¶These are some of the wonderful signposts on the path, all within your immediate grasp in this life, just as the ability to play the *vīṇā* or the flute beautifully in this life is within your immediate grasp. It takes practice, following the rules and then more practice.

Sunday
LESSON 42
Maturity Of Being

Now we begin to see the vastness and yet the simplicity of the superconscious mind as awareness flows through it. Nothing is there for awareness to attach itself to. When aware of something other than itself, awareness is in its natural state in subsuperconsciousness. Occasionally in superconsciousness we can feel and actually inwardly see the inner body, the body of the soul, and we can feel this body inside the physical body. This is the body of light. Then we know through feeling and seeing that this body has existed and will exist forever and ever and ever, and we enjoy moving within the energies of this inner body. As we feel them, we become so quiet, so centered, that awareness is aware of itself so intently that we are right on the brink of the Absolute, ready to dissolve, to merge, into That which is man's heritage on Earth to realize, the maturity of his being, the Self God.

¶We grow up physically. We grow up emotionally. We acquire a lot of knowledge. We must acquire the best knowledge, the cream of all knowledge. This is the knowledge of the path to enlightenment. And then, as awareness soars within, we begin to experience the realms of superconsciousness, man's natural state. Then we have our ultimate experience, awareness dissolving into itself, beyond superconsciousness itself. ¶After Self Realization, you are looking at the film, the movie of the actors and actresses, including yourself, previously seen as real, being more subsuperconsciously conscious of the light projected on the back of the film than of the pictures displayed, which were seen as real before this awakening.

Saṅkalpaśaktiḥ

सङ्कल्पशक्तिः

Willpower

When you seek to reach the Lord and miss your goal, take it as the work of your past evil *karmas* and fervently persevere in your devotion. You shall, at last, reach the Primal Lord.

TIRUMANTIRAM 2668

Monday
LESSON 43
Finish What You Start

We are not always sitting down concentrating on a flower in the search for the Self. Once you have decided that Self Realization is the ultimate goal for you, go on living your normal life. Everything that you do in life can collectively be channeled toward the ultimate goal, for what you need is a dynamic will. You need a strong willpower. ¶Willpower is the channeling of all energies toward one given point for a given length of time. This will can be brought out from within in everything that we do through the day. It's a powerful will. It's available to everyone. It is channeling the rarefied energies of the body, of awareness itself, into attention and concentration upon everything that we do through the day. ¶How do we cultivate the willpower? What do we mean by will? Will means that if you're going to complete something, you complete it. Finish that which you begin. Finish it well, beyond your expectations, no matter how long it takes. If you are going to do something, do it well, no matter if it is a simple task or a complicated one. If you're going to read a book and intend to finish the book, then read the book, finish the book, and understand what it had to offer you, for that was the purpose for reading it.¶It is not developing a strong will by having a lot of half-finished jobs. It is not developing a strong will by starting out with a bang on a project and then fizzling out. These only attach awareness to that which it is aware of and lead us into the distraction of thinking the external mind is real. Then we forget our inner goal of Self Realization because the subconscious becomes too ramified with, basically, our being disappointed in ourselves, or the willpower being so diversified, or awareness being so divided in many different ways that whatever we want to do never works out because there is not enough will, or shove, or centralization of energy, or awareness is not at attention over the project enough, to make it come into completion. A tremendous will is needed on the path of Self Realization, of drawing the forces of energy together, of drawing awareness away from that which it is aware of constantly, of finishing each job that we begin in the material world, and doing it well, so that we are content within ourselves. Make everything that you do satisfy the inner scrutiny of your inner being. Do a little more than you think that you are able to do. That brings forth just a little more will.

Tuesday
LESSON 44
Willpower Is the Fuel

You need a tremendous, indomitable will to make a reality of your quest of realizing the Being within. Unfoldment doesn't take a lot of time. It just takes a lot of willpower. Someone can go along and sit at attention, and concentrate and meditate for years and years and years and, with a minimal amount of willpower, constantly be distracted, constantly be complaining and constantly be unsuccessful. Another person can have the exact same approach and over a short period of time be extremely successful, because he has will. The previous way he lived his life, the previous things that he did, he handled in such a way that that willpower was there, or his awareness is a manifestation of willpower, and he goes soaring within on this will. ¶Will is the fuel which carries awareness through all areas of the mind, that spirit, that spiritual quality, which makes all inner goals a reality. Unfoldment does not take time. It takes a tremendous will. That will has to be cultivated, just as you would cultivate a garden. It has to be cultivated. Those energies have to all be flowing through, in a sense, one channel, so that everything that you do is satisfying, is complete, beautiful. ¶Discover the will. Back to the spine. Feel the energy in the spine. There is no lack of it, is there? The more you use of it, the more you have to use of it. It is tuned right into the central source. When you become aware of the energy within your spine and within your head, you have separated awareness from that which it is aware of, for that is awareness itself, and that is will. We are playing with words a little. After awhile we will gain a new vocabulary for this kind of talk, but right now we are using our old-words' way of looking at it, because our subconscious mind is more familiar with these words. Energy, awareness and willpower are one and the same. When we are subconsciously conscious that we are a superconscious being, and the subconscious mind has accepted the new programming that energy, willpower and awareness are one and the same thing, when the subconscious mind has accepted the fact that the mind was all finished long ago in all its phases of manifestation, from the refined to the gross—then the subconscious begins working as a pure channel, so to speak, for superconsciousness. Awareness can then flow in a very positive, in a very direct, way. ¶You want awareness to be renewed. The first step is—don't try to go to the Self; you haven't realized it yet—go to the spine. Feel the spine. After you realize the Self, you go deeper than the spine, you go into the Self and come back. Before you realize the Self and have that *samādhi*—attention, concentration. Concentrate on the energy within the spine. Go in. Awareness, energy and will are all one. Come slowly out again and you have all the willpower you need to finish any job that you've ever started, to make decisions, to do and handle your external life in a very positive way, so that it does not capture awareness and hold it steadfast for a period of time, deterring you on the path of enlightenment.

Wednesday
LESSON 45
Realization Requires Will

Work with willpower, awareness and energy as three separate items first. Feel awareness and discover what it is. Use willpower and discover what it is. Feel energy and analyze energy and discover what it is. Then separate the three of them in your intellectual mind and experiential pattern. Then, after you've gotten that done, you will begin to see inside yourself that the three are one and the same. And it is actually the beautiful, pure intelligence of the immortal soul body, that body of light of you, on its path inward into its last phase of maturity on this planet. This inner body of light has been maturing through many, many different lives. ¶If you would like to know how it came along, for instance if you had ninety lives on this planet, each life the body of light matured one year. So your body of light would be ninety years old, so to speak. You can look at it that way. That's not quite the way it actually is, but looking at it that way gives you an idea of the maturing of this body of light. The pure intelligence of it is your awareness—which is energy and which is willpower—that life after life becomes stronger, more steadfast. Finally, in your last incarnation on the Earth, you merge into its final experience, that great *samādhi*, the Self, beyond the complete, still area of consciousness. You go in not knowing what you are getting into, and you come out wise. Your complete perspective is changed, and you only talk about it to those that are on the path of enlightenment, as they are the only ones steady enough or free enough to understand the depth of this realization. ¶Here are the ingredients: attention, concentration, meditation, contemplation, *samādhi.* Willpower is the fuel. It does not take time. Someone asked me, "Do you think I can have this *samādhi,* realize the Self, in ten years?" I said, "I certainly don't. I don't think you have enough willpower to realize it in a hundred years, because it doesn't take time. It takes will. If you had the will, you wouldn't add ten years on it. You would simply be telling me, 'I am going to have this realization.' And I would believe you because I would feel your will moving out of every atom of your body. But the mere fact that you take an intellectual approach, I have to say no, because whatever I did think wouldn't make any difference one way or the other. You are not going to get it with an attitude like that, because it's not something you go out and buy. It's not another getting, like 'I have a car. I have clothes. I have a little money. And now, after I get my television paid for, I think I'll get the Self, because that is the next thing to get. It's really great. I read about it. I heard about it. I heard a speaker speak about it. I'm all fired up to get this Self, and it's in next in the line of getting, so I'm going to get it!' It doesn't work like that. You don't get that which you have. You can't get that which you have. It's there. You have to give up the consciousness of the television, the money, the clothes, the people that you know, the personality that you thought you were, the physical body. You have to go into the elements of the physical body, into the elements of that, and into the energy of that, and into the vast inner space of that, and into the core of that, and into the that of that, and into the that of that, and finally you realize that you have realized the Self. And you've lost something. You lost your goal of Self Realization. And you come back into the fullness of everything, and you are no longer looking, and you are no longer asking, and you are no longer wanting. You just are." When you get tired of the external area of the mind that you are flowing through, you simply dive in again.

Thursday
LESSON 46
Progress Takes Discipline

When you go into a meditation, decide first what you are going to meditate upon and then stick with it. It is not advisable to habitually sit for meditation with no particular goal or direction, for we often end up walking in mental or subconscious circles. We have to avoid going into a meditation and then taking off into random or unintended directions, for this then can lend new vigor and strength to uncomely states of mind. You have to be very firm with yourself in meditation sessions. They are serious, not ponderous, but serious applications of life's force. They are moments of transformation and discovery, and the same care and earnestness of a mountain climber must be observed constantly if real progress and not mere entertainment is the goal. In the very same way, in the external world, if you begin something, you finish it. If you are working on a project creatively, you maintain your efforts until you bring it to a conclusion. It is such people who become truly successful in meditation. ¶You can learn to meditate extremely well, but will be unsuccessful if you don't approach it in an extremely positive way, if you allow yourself to get side-tracked on the inside once the inside opens up and you can really become aware of inner states. Care must be taken not to wander around in inner states of consciousness. You can wander in extraneous, unproductive areas for a long, long time. ¶So, you have to be very, very firm with yourself when you begin a meditation so that you stay with it the way you originally intended to do and perform each meditation the way you intended to perform it. This brings us into discipline. Undisciplined people are generally people whom nobody can tell what to do. They won't listen. They can't tell themselves what to do, and nobody else is going to tell them either! If you sincerely want to make headway in meditation and continue to do so year after year after year, you have to approach it in a very positive, systematic way. By not seeking or responding to discipline, you can learn to meditate fairly well, just as you can learn to play the *vīṇā* fairly well, but you will never go much farther than that.¶For many years I've seen hundreds and hundreds and hundreds of people come and go, each one firmly determined to go in and realize the Self, firmly determined to meditate and meditate well. Many did, up to a point. Then they lost interest, became involved in the next social fad or just reached the depth equal to their ability to be constant and well disciplined. They are not anyplace today, inside or outside, for they undoubtedly reached the same barriers in their next pursuit and were compelled to seek another and yet another. I want to impress on you if you start a meditation, stay with it. Attack it positively. Go on and on and in and in and in.

Friday
LESSON 47
Hold Awareness Firmly

Now, what do you do if during meditation the power becomes very strong and carries you into refined but unanticipated areas of superconsciousness? It is not unusual for a good meditator to go in a different direction when the inner forces or energies become so intense that awareness itself becomes all energy. That's fine. That's what you want. That's also part of your meditation. Go right in and become aware of being aware and enjoy that intensity of inner power. Hold it steady. It won't side-track you or disturb your meditation in the least, but you have to come right back when that power begins to wane to the original meditation that you intended to work with. Work with it in a very positive way. Stay with it and don't get side-tracked in another area, no matter how interesting it is. ¶Only in this way are you going to really go on past the point of being able to meditate only adequately well. Only in this way, once you are unfolded spiritually to a certain degree, can you go on with your unfoldment. This is a difficult practice, because you will go in for a very fine meditation and get into profound depths and burst into new and interesting areas. This will happen, and the side-track will be fascinating, perhaps much more than your meditation subject. That is the time you must hold awareness firmly and fulfill your original intent. ¶The potter is a good example. He is going to make a beautiful planter pot, and it turns out to be a milk pot instead, simply because he was side-tracked. Then he says, "Oh, an impulse told me I should make a milk pot, right in the middle of making a planter pot." This example tells you that you have to fulfill your original intent. Then you get confidence. You build a whole layer of subconscious confidence because you know where you are going to go on the inside. ¶Think about this and work with it, because it's very important to get a grip on awareness in all areas of the mind. Start out with a very firm foundation. This principle will carry through everything that you do. You will become more and more precise. Your physical body will become firm and energetic. Your personal habits will become precise. The way you handle your thinking will be precise. You will pay more attention to details. You won't assume so much, and you will follow intricate lines of thought through to their conclusion. ¶Someone who meditates well also thinks well. He can flow through that thinking area of the mind and work out things through the thought processes. Someone who meditates has confidence in all departments of life. You can build that confidence. If you sit down to meditate, meditate! Don't get sidetracked on anything else, no matter how attractive it may be. If the power builds within you, sit for a long time afterwards and let the energy absorb into the cells of your external body. Great energy is released from within. Don't get up after your meditation and immediately run off to do something. Sit in silent stillness until that power subsides in a gradual and refined way.

Saturday
LESSON 48
Don't Get Side-tracked

The mystic seeks to gain the conscious control of his own willpower, to awaken knowledge of the primal force through the direct experience of it and to claim conscious control of his own individual awareness. In the beginning stages on the path, you will surely experience your mind wandering—when awareness is totally identified with everything that it is aware of. This gives us the sense, the feeling, that we are the mind or that we are the emotion or the body. And, when sitting in meditation, myriad thoughts bounce through the brain and it becomes difficult to even concentrate upon what is supposed to be meditated upon, in some cases even to remember what it was. That is why the *sādhana* of the practices of *yoga* given in these lessons must be mastered to some extent in order to gain enough control over the willpower and sense organs to cause the meditation to become introverted rather than extroverted. The grace of the *guru* can cause this to happen, because he stabilizes the willpower, the awareness, within his devotees as a harmonious father and mother stabilize the home for their offspring. If one has no *guru* or has one and is only a part-time devotee, then he must struggle in his efforts as an orphan in the institution of external life. For the world is your *guru*. His name is Śrī Śrī Viśvaguru Mahā Mahārāj, the most august universal teacher, grand master and sovereign. ¶Even before we sit down to meditate, one of the first steps is to acquire a conscious mastery of awareness in the conscious mind itself. Learn attention and concentration. Apply them in everything that you do. As soon as we bring awareness to attention and train awareness in the art of concentration, the great power of observation comes to us naturally. We find that we are in a state of observation all the time. All awakened souls have keen observation. They do not miss very much that happens around them on the physical plane or on the inner planes. They are constantly in a state of observation. ¶For instance, we take a flower and begin to think only about the flower. We put it in front of us and look at it. This flower can now represent the conscious mind. Our physical eyes are also of the conscious mind. Examine the flower, become aware of the flower and cease being aware of all other things and thoughts. It is just the flower now and our awareness. The practice now is: each time we forget about the flower and become aware of something else, we use the power of our will to bring awareness right back to that little flower and think about it. Each time we become aware of any other thoughts, we excuse awareness from those thoughts. Gently, on the in-breath, we pull awareness back to the world of the flower. This is an initial step in unraveling awareness from the bondages of the conscious mind.

Sunday
LESSON 49
Gaining Self-Control

Perhaps the biggest battle in the beginning stages of practicing attention and concentration is the control of breath. The beginner will not want to sit long enough, or not be able to become quiet enough to have a deep, controlled flow of breath. After five minutes, the physical elements of the subconscious mind will become restless. He will want to squirm about. He will sit down to concentrate on the flower and begin thinking of many other things that he should be doing instead: "I should have done my washing first." "I may be staying here for a half an hour. What if I get hungry? Perhaps I should have eaten first." The telephone may ring, and he will wonder who is calling. "Maybe I should get up and answer it," he thinks and then mentally says, "Let it ring. I'm here to concentrate on the flower." If he does not succeed immediately, he will rationalize, "How important can breathing rhythmically be, anyway? I'm breathing all right. This is far too simple to be very important." He will go through all of this within himself, for this is how he has been accustomed to living in the conscious mind, jumping from one thing to the next. ¶When you sit at attention, view all of the distractions that come as you endeavor to concentrate on one single object, such as a flower. This will show you exactly how the conscious and subconscious mind operate. All of the same distractions come in everyday life. If you are a disciplined person, you handle them systematically through the day. If you are undisciplined, you are sporadic in your approach and allow your awareness to become distracted by them haphazardly instead of concentrating on one at a time. Such concerns have been there life after life, year after year. The habit of becoming constantly distracted makes it impossible for you to truly concentrate the mind or to realize anything other than distractions and the desires of the conscious mind itself. ¶Even the poor subconscious has a time keeping up with the new programming flowing into it from the experiences our awareness goes through as it travels quickly through the conscious mind in an undisciplined way. When the subconscious mind becomes overloaded in recording all that goes into it from the conscious mind, we experience frustration, anxiety, nervousness, insecurity and neuroses. These are some of the subconscious ailments that are so widespread in the world today. ¶There comes a time in man's life when he has to put an end to it all. He sits down. He begins to breathe, to ponder and be aware of only one pleasant thing. As he does this, he becomes dynamic and his will becomes strong. His concentration continues on that flow. As his breath becomes more and more regulated, his body becomes quiet and the one great faculty of the soul becomes predominant—observation—the first faculty of the unfoldment of the soul. ¶We as the soul see out through the physical eyes. As we look through the physical eyes at the flower and meditate deeply upon the flower, we tune into the soul's vast well of knowing and begin to observe previously unknown facts about the flower. We see where it came from. We see how one little flower has enough memory locked up within its tiny seed to come up again and again in the very same way. A rose does not forget and come up as a tulip. Nor does a tulip forget and come up as a lily. Nor does a lily forget and come up as a peach tree. There is enough memory resident in the genes of the seeds of each that they come up as the same species every season. As we observe this single law and pierce into the inner realms of the mind, we see the flower as large as a house, or as small as the point of a pin, because the eyes of the superconscious mind, the spiritual body, can magnify or diminish any object in order to study it and understand it. To know this, to experience this, is to develop willpower to transform oneself into the knower of what is to be known. Yes, willpower is the key, the must, the most needed faculty for spiritual unfoldment on this path. Work hard, strive to accomplish, strengthen the will by using the will. But remember, "With love in the will, the spirit is free." This means that willpower can be used wrongly without the binding softening of love, simple love. Say in your mind to everyone you meet, "I like you. You like me, I really do like you. I love you. I truly love you."

Prasanna Śukla Jyotiḥ

प्रसन्नशुक्लज्योतिः

The Clear White Light

The luminaries, fire, sun and moon, receive their luminosity by the grace of divine inner Light. The Light that gives light to those is a mighty effulgence. That Light, dispelling my darkness, stood within me, suffused in oneness.

TIRUMANTIRAM 2683

Monday
LESSON 50
Beyond Past And Future

Whenever man comes to the point in his evolution where he has sufficient mastery in the mind to produce "things," he suffers for the lack of peace, for in his activity on the mental spheres in conceiving, planning, gathering the forces together and finally viewing the outcome as a physical manifestation, he has exercised an intricate control over the nerve fibers of his mind. Thus caught in this pattern, he must go on producing to insure his mental security, for should he stop for a moment, the whiplash upon his senses as the generative functions ceased to be active would cause paranoiac depressions, at times almost beyond repair. ¶The man looking into the "where and when" of the future, blending his energies with those who are also striving to evolve into a more ramified state of mind, can suffer well if he keeps going, producing, acquiring and believing that materiality is reality. Evolution of the species takes its toll, for as man's mind evolves, he is no longer content projecting into the "where and when" of the material consciousness, and as he seeks some reward of peace for his efforts, he begins to look into the past for solutions, the "there and then" of it all. Thus, finding himself born into a cross-section of awareness between past and future, having experienced both of these tendencies of the mind, causes him to reflect. Philosophy holds few answers for him. Its congested mass of "shoulds" and "don'ts" he knows has proved more to the philosopher who cleared his mind on paper than to the reader who has yet to complement with inner knowing its indicated depths. ¶Occultism is intriguing to him, for it shows that there are possibilities of expression beyond the senses he has become well accustomed to using. But again, evolution rounding his vision causes him to discard the occult symbolism, laws and practices as another look into the past or future of the mind's depths. ¶The idea of *yoga*, union through perceptive control of the flow of thought, and of the generative processes of a perceptive idea before thought is formed, is most satisfying. The cognition of the actinic process of life currents intrigues him, and he looks further into the practice of *yoga* techniques and finds that peace is gained through a conscious government first of the life currents through the body and second of the realm of ideas as they flow into thought. And while remaining the observer of it all in the eternity of the here and now, the seeker fully realizes that time, space and causation are only indicated through holding an off-balanced consciousness of past and future.

Tuesday
LESSON 51
Capturing the Here and Now

The feeling and the realization of the here and now intensity of consciousness becomes intriguing to him, and he works daily on *yoga* techniques to strengthen psychic nerve fibers and perfect his artistry of maintaining this awareness. Many things fall away from him as he expands his consciousness through the classical practices of meditation. He loosens the odic bonds of family and former friends. Magnetic ties to possessions and places fade out, until he is alone, involved with the refined realms of mind and in the actinic flow of energies. Occasionally his awareness is brought out into a habit pattern or a concept of himself as he used to be, but viewed with his new stability in his recently found inner security of being whole, this too quickly fades.

¶Whenever darkness comes into the material world, this centered man is light. He sees light within his head and body as clearly as he did in former states of materialistic consciousness when looking at a glowing light bulb. While involved in innersearching some hidden laws of existence or unraveling the solution to a problem of the outer mind, he sits viewing the inner light, and the light shines through the knitted law of existence, clearly showing it in all its ramifications, as well as shining out upon the snarled problem, burning it back into proportionate component parts. ¶Thus becoming adept in using his newly found faculties, he begins to study the findings of others and compare them to his own. This educational play-back process elucidates to his still-doubting intellect the "all-rightness" of the happenings that occur within him. He finds that for six thousand years men have, from time to time, walked the classical *yoga* path and attained enlightenment, and he begins to see that he has yet far to go, as his light often is dimmed by the pulling he experiences of the past, by the exuberance he shares with the future and by the yet fawn-like instability of the "here and now eternity" he has most recently experienced. ¶Now, in the dawn of a new age, when many men are being drawn within, it is eminently easier to attain and maintain clarity of perception through the actinic light within the body. Through the classical *yoga* techniques, perfecting the conscious use of the actinic willpower, the energies can be drawn inward from the outer mind, and the awareness can bask in the actinic light, coming into the outer mind only at will, and positively. ¶Occasionally young aspirants burst into inner experience indicating a balance of intense light at a still-higher rate of vibration of here and now awareness than their almost daily experience of a moon-glow inner light—the dynamic vision of seeing the head, and at times the body, filled with a brilliant clear white light. When this intensity can be attained at will, more than often man will identify himself as actinic force flowing through the odic externalities of the outer mind and identify it as a force of life more real and infinitely more permanent than the external mind itself.

Wednesday
LESSON 52
Psychic Sounds

Occasionally, through his newly exercised extrasensory perception, he may hear the seven sounds he previously studied about in occult lore. The sounds of the atomic structure of his nerve system, his cells, register as voices singing, the *vīṇā* or *sitār*, *tambūra*, or as symphonies of music. Instruments to duplicate these sounds for the outer ears were carefully tooled by the *ṛishis* of classical *yoga* thousands of years ago, including the *mṛidaṅga* or *tabla*, and the flute. He will hear the shrill note, likened to a nightingale singing, as psychic centers in his cranium burst open, and then an inner voice indicating to his external consciousness—like a breath of air—direction, elucidation. This inner voice remains with him as a permanent *yoga* of the external, with the internal consciousness an ever-ready guide to the unraveling of complexities of daily life. ¶Occasionally, in a cross-section of the inner mind, when light merges into transcendental form, the young aspirant may view the golden actinic face of a master peering into his, kindly and all-knowing. He is looking at his own great potential. As the clear white light becomes more of a friend to his external mind than an experience or vision and can be basked in during contemplative periods of the day, the nourishment to the entirety of the nerve system, as ambrosia, bursts forth from the crown *chakra.* This is identified inadequately as "the peace that passeth understanding," for he who reaches this state can never seem to explain it. ¶The highly trained classical *yoga* adept intensifies, through techniques imparted to him from his *guru*, the clear white light to the brink of God Realization, the void. His entire body is faded into a sea of blue-white light, the *ākāśa,* where now, past and future are recorded in the linear depths or layers, sometimes seeing himself seated or standing on a lotus flower of shimmering light in an actinodic clear, transparent, neon, plastic-like-body outline as his consciousness touches, in tune with a heart's beat, into the Self, God Realization. ¶Keeping this continuity alive and not allowing the external consciousness to reign, the young aspirant lives daily in the clear white light, having occasionally more intense experiences as just described while meeting daily chores here and now, until he attains the maturity of the nerve fiber essential to burst his consciousness beyond itself into the pure nonconscious state, *nirvikalpa samādhi,* the Self. Only known and identified by him as an experience experienced. Only recognized by others as he maintains his point of reference: that mind is only illusion, ever changing and perpetuating itself by mingling concepts of past and future into the present; that the only reality is the timeless, formless, causeless, spaceless Self beyond the mind. He knows that the mind, which is made from a consciousness of time, creates, maintains and defabricates form, and exists in a relative concept of space. The Self is the only reality and is an intensity far greater than that of any phase of the mind.

Thursday
LESSON 53
A Few Cardinal Signposts

The young aspirant just becoming acquainted with the path to enlightenment may wonder where he is, how much he has achieved so far. There are a few cardinal signposts he may identify with to know he has touched into the inner realms of his mind. Should he ever have experienced a "here and now" consciousness, causing him to fight the "where and when" of the future and the "there and then" of the past afterwards, he can fully impart to himself an award of having achieved some attainment by striving even more diligently than before. The ability to see the external world as transparent, a game, a dream, encourages the aspirant to seek deeper. The moon-like light within the center of his head appears during his tries at meditation, sometimes giving him the perceptive ability to cognize the intricate workings of another's external and subconscious states of mind, as well as his own, intimately. The ability of the ardent soul to recognize his *guru* and identify himself in the actinic flow from whence the master infuses knowledge by causing inner doors to open is another signpost that the aspirant has become an experiencer and is touching in on the fringe or perimeter of transcendental states of mind. ¶Many on the path to enlightenment will be able to identify, through their personal experience, some of these signposts, and recall many happenings that occurred during their awakenings. But remember, the recall and the experience are quite different. The experience is "here and now;" the recall is "there and then." However, by identifying the experience and relating it to a solid intellectual knowledge, the ability will be awakened to utilize and live consciously in inner states of superconsciousness. After acquiring this ability to consciously live superconsciously comes the ability to work accurately and enthusiastically in the material world while holding the intensity of the inner light, giving perceptive awareness of its mechanical structure. There also comes the ability to work out quickly in meditation experiences of the external mind or worldly happenings through finding their "innerversity" aspects rather than being drawn out into the swirl of them. In doing so, the cause-and-effect *karmic* experiential patterns of the aspirant's life that tend to lower his consciousness into congested areas of the mind will clear up as, more and more, the actinic flow of superconsciousness is maintained as the bursts of clear white light become frequent.

Friday
LESSON 54
The Leaders Of Tomorrow

Those among the youth of today who have had some measure of attainment, of which there are many, will be the leaders, businessmen, politicians and educators of tomorrow. As the New Age comes more into fulfillment, they will be able to work effectively in all states of the mind, consciously identified with the overshadowing power of the clearness of perceptive vision of visible white light within the body and through the mind. Still others—disciplined beings of a vaster vision and more profound purpose—will become the mendicant *sannyāsin,* the sage, the catalyst teacher, the *pandit* philosopher, all working as individuals together to keep the teaching of the classical *yoga* path to enlightenment alive and vibrant on planet Earth yet another six thousand years. ¶Remember, when the seal is broken and clear white light has flooded the mind, there is no more a gap between the inner and the outer. Even uncomplimentary states of consciousness can be dissolved through meditation and seeking again the light. The aspirant can be aware that in having a newfound freedom internally and externally there will be a strong tendency for the mind to reconstruct for itself a new congested subconscious by reacting strongly to happenings during daily experiences. Even though one plays the game, having once seen it as a game, there is a tendency of the instinctive phases of nature to fall prey to the accumulative reactions caused by entering into the game. ¶Therefore, an experience of inner light is not a solution; one or two bursts of clear white light are only a door-opener to transcendental possibilities. The young aspirant must become the experiencer, not the one who has experienced and basks in the memory patterns it caused. This is where the not-too-sought-after word *discipline* enters into the life and vocabulary of this blooming flower, accounting for the reason why *ashrams* house students apart for a time. Under discipline, they become experiencers, fragmenting their entanglements before their vision daily while doing some mundane chore and mastering each test and task their *guru* sets before them. The *chela* is taught to dissolve his reactionary habit patterns in the clear white light each evening in contemplative states. Reactionary conditions that inevitably occur during the day he clears with actinic love and understanding so that they do not congest or condense in his subconscious mind, building a new set of confused, congested forces that would propel him into outer states of consciousness, leaving his vision of the clear white light as an experience in memory patterns retreating into the past. ¶The young aspirant can use this elementary classical *yoga* technique of going back over the day at the end of the day in an internal concentration period, holding the thought flow on just the current daily experience, not allowing unrelated thoughts from other days to enter. When a reactionary condition appears that was not resolved during the day with love and understanding, in turning to the inner light it will melt away, usually under the power of a perceptive flash of understanding.

Saturday
LESSON 55
Turning to the Inner Light

Thousands of young aspirants who have had bursts of inner light have evolved quickly. Assuredly, this has been their natural evolutionary flow. This oversensitization of their entire mind structure, so suddenly intensified into transcendental realms, caused the materialistic states to decentralize attachments to their present life-pattern, school interests and plans for the future. A springboard is needed. A new balance must be attained in relating to the materialistic world, for the physical body still must be cared for to unfold further into the human destiny of *nirvikalpa samādhi,* the realization of the Self beyond the states of mind. Enlightened seers are turning inward to unravel solutions in building new models to bring forth new knowledge from inner realms to creatively meet man's basic needs, and to bring through to the external spheres beauty and culture found only on inner planes—thus heralding the Golden Age of tomorrow and the illuminated beings of the future who, through the use of their disciplined third eye and other faculties, can remain "within" the clear white light while working accurately and enthusiastically in the obvious dream world. ¶Should he come out too far into materialism in consciousness, the inner voice may be falsely identified as an unseen master or a God talking into his right inner ear, but when in the clarity of white light, he knows that it is his very self. Realizing he is the force that propels him onward, the aspirant will welcome discipline as an intricate part of his internal government, so necessary to being clear white light. ¶It is a great new world of the mind that is entered into when first the clear white light dawns, birthing a new actinic race, immediately causing him to become the parent to his parents and forefathers. When living in an expanded inner state of mind, he must not expect those living in materialistic consciousness to understand him. On this new path of "the lonely one," wisdom must be invoked to cause him to be able to look through the eyes of those who believe the world is real, and see and relate to that limited world in playing the game as if it were real, thus maintaining the harmony so necessary for future unfoldments. To try to convince those imbedded in materialism of the inner realities only causes a breach in relationship, as it represents a positive threat to the security they have worked so hard to attain. ¶First we had the instinctive age, of valuing physical strength and manly prowess, followed by the intellectual age, facts for the sake of facts, resulting in the progress of science. Now we are in an age of new values, new governing laws, an actinic age, with new understanding of the world, the mind, but most of all, the Self. Understanding is preparation for travel, for it is an age of the mind, and in the mind, much more intense than the speed of light, exist spheres which seers are only willing to speak of to those who have the inner ear with which to listen. ¶The mind of man tends either toward light or toward darkness, expanded awareness or materialistic values. Depending upon the self-created condition of the mind, man lives either within the clear white light of the higher consciousness, or in the external mind structure which reflects darkness to his inner vision.

Sunday
LESSON 56
Springboard To Eternity

The uninitiated might ask: "What is it like to be in the clear white light?" The young aspirant may reply, "It is as simple as sitting in a darkened room, closing the eyes in deep concentration and finding the entire inside of the cranium turning into light." At first it may be only a dim, moon-like glow, a pale flicker of several different colors, but then it becomes as bright and intense as the radiance of the noonday sun, then crystal clear and white. It all depends upon the composition of the mind states of reactionary patterns as to how the light in the cranium will first appear. ¶Of course, clear white light is not absolute, for light invariably implies the existence of shadow. The shadows that sometimes fade out inner light are the instinctive functions that hold the physical body intact. These are represented as attributes in the external mind and character of man. ¶Attachment, for instance, holds our cells together; it is also the root of much suffering, for attachment to material objects or people keeps man's awareness externalized, incapable of expressing itself in full freedom. Man who is caught in the magnetic forces is prone to resentment. Not being able to cognize various fears as they occur, he stores them up into a conscious resentment of all threats to the false securities found in attachment. Resentment burrows deeply into the outer mind's layers, undermining much of a person's creative endeavor. The reactionary conditions resentment is capable of agitating are subconscious and cast many shadows over clarity of perception for long periods of time. ¶Those who resent are often jealous, another shadow or character weakness which stems from feelings of inferiority, a limited view of one's real Self. After one burst of clear white light has occurred, the force fields of attachment, resentment and jealousy are shattered. An increased control of the mind, an expanded consciousness, is maintained which frees man little by little from ever again generating the magnetic holds consuming his consciousness in these shadows. When man allows himself to routine his external thinking and action to settle into uncreative, static conditions, pressures of various sorts build up, and the undisciplined mind releases itself to the emotion of anger, a state of consciousness which renders a man blind to the existence of inner light in any degree. ¶Fear is another shadow which causes man to have an inability to face a critical moment, even in the intimacy of his deepest meditation. But fear is a protective process of the instinctive mind, allowing time to temporarily avoid what must later be faced. Fear, being an intense force in the mind's, as well as the body's, structure, must be handled positively, for when man thinks under the shadow of fear, he causes his fears to manifest. The flickering shadows of worry brought on by allowing mind to irrationally jump from one subject to another, never centralizing on any one point long enough to complete it, must be handled through disciplining the flow of thought force, for worry provokes a darker shadow—fear. Fear when disturbed causes anger, submerged anger, resentment, causing a jealous nature. Hence the constant play of the clear white light versus its shadows. ¶By becoming conscious of the way in which the mind operates in even a small degree, the young aspirant to light finds it easy to fold back the shadows into shafts of clear white light.

Hṛidayapadman

हृदयपद्मन्

The Lotus of the Heart

Pervading all nature, Śiva blesses all. But they know not the Truth and adore Him not. To them who adore Him Who is immanent, He is the golden stem of the lotus of the heart deep within.

TIRUMANTIRAM 1717

Monday
LESSON 57
Emanations From Within

Visualize within yourself a lotus. Have you ever seen a lotus flower? I am sure you have. Now visualize this lotus flower centered right within the center of your chest, right within your heart. You have read in the Hindu scriptures that the Self God dwells in the lotus within the heart. Let's think about that. We all know what the heart is, and we know what happens when the heart stops. Try to mentally feel and see the heart as a lotus flower right within you. Within the center of the lotus, try to see a small light. Doubtless you have read in the Hindu scriptures that the Self God within the heart looks like a brilliant light about the size of your thumb—just a small light. This light we shall call an emanation of your effulgent being. We could also call it your atomic power, the power that motivates, permeates, makes the mind self-luminous. It is dwelling right within. The Self God is deeper than that. The lotus is within the heart, and the Self God dwells deep within that lotus of light. ¶The subconscious area of the mind consumes many different things. Begin now to think about all the things that you own in your home and all of your personal possessions. The subconscious area of the mind is attached magnetically to each of them. They not only exist in the external world, they also exist, quite alive, within the subconscious area of your mind, along with all the ramifications connected to them. Each item that you own has a story attached to it which, of course, you remember. This story, too, dwells within the subconscious mind and is carried along with you all of the time. ¶But it is easy to rid yourself of the attachments to material things by going within, once you know how.

The light which emanates from the lotus of the heart knows nothing about what the subconscious area of the mind consumes, because the total area of the mind in which we are aware is a composite of many things.

Tuesday
LESSON 58
The Subtlety Within You

Everyone who functions in external and inner life lives in a slightly different area of the mind and consumes within his conscious and subconscious areas many thousands of concepts. No person is exactly the same as another in this respect. The Self within knows nothing of this, because it exists of itself. Wherever awareness flows through the totality of the mind, the Self is always the same. When individual awareness turns inward, it is possible to contact the light radiations within the lotus of the heart; it then is possible to fully realize Satchidānanda. It is useless to think about the Self, because it does not exist in the area of the mind where thoughts are. If you were to think about it, you would only become aware of concepts within the mind, and that would take you away from it. It is also useless to talk about the Self, really, in your efforts to realize it, because when you do, again you take awareness deep into the conceptual area of the mind, which is further away from your real, self-effulgent being. ¶The first step is to try to feel the subtlety within you. The light within the lotus of the heart comes from someplace, doesn't it? Let us think about it in this way. Each time you take a breath, you bring yourself a little closer, you turn yourself within just a little bit more and release a little bit of actinic energy emanating from the self-effulgent being residing within your heart. This energy is called life. We say, "This is my life." If you stop breathing, the life in your body stops. We have to use willpower to control the breath. When we do control the breath, we begin to have an immense control, and awareness begins to become detached from that which it is aware of. This means that we're consciously conscious of what we are aware of, that we are aware. We control our individual awareness more than we realize when we practice the regulation and control of breath. For instance, as we breathe, *prāṇāyāma,* in on nine counts, hold one, out on nine counts, hold one, we find that we begin to become more alert, more alive. Our awareness is more subtle and refined.

Wednesday
LESSON 59
The Evolution Of Awareness

The emanation of the light that wells from within the lotus of the heart is always there, regardless of what you do. You may not be aware of the existence of it, but it does exist. You may not care to realize it, but it still exists. When man does not wish to look for the Self God, it is only because his awareness is busy in other areas of the mind, concerned with desires, and he is on the road to fulfill them. The fulfillment of desires causes reactionary conditions within the subconscious mind itself and clouds vision. This causes what is known as the darkness of the mind. When man wishes and desires to find his true Self, his external desires fall in line with basic religious codes for living, and he then is on the path. He is able to realize the essence of each desire on the path of enlightenment, and is able to sense Reality within himself. ¶A beautiful practice is to try to sit quietly, visualizing within the lotus within the heart a light, a strong light emanating clearly, a light that is always there. This light is radiating at a higher vibration than any form with which you are familiar. Let us say, if you were to have this light in your hand and were able to use it in the external world, each form you turned it upon would disappear under the vibration of the light itself. That is as powerful as the effulgent light emanating from the Self, the Śivaness, which you will see within the lotus of the heart. ¶The mind, or consciousness, is form with intense vibrations and lesser vibrations, all interrelating. When we are happy and joyous, we are aware of the refined states of consciousness. But when we are not happy or joyous, we are living in the grosser, darker areas of consciousness. We have all lived in the gross area of consciousness, and we have all lived in the happy, joyous areas of consciousness. This is the evolution of man's individual awareness.

Thursday
LESSON 60
The Pendulum Of Emotion

Man, awareness, seeks happiness, and when he finds happiness, he often finds fault with it, and then he becomes aware in unhappy areas of the mind. This gives him the power to seek happiness again. Man finds fault with happiness and begins to look for something better. In looking for something better, he becomes selfish, greedy, unhappy, and finally he attains what he thinks will make him happy. He finds that it does not, and this makes him again unhappy, and he goes on through life like this. That is the cycle of awareness traveling through the instinctive-intellectual areas of the mind. Therefore, when you are unhappy, don't feel unhappy about it! And when you become happy, know that the pendulum of awareness will eventually swing to its counter side. This is the natural and the normal cycle of awareness. ¶When you are feeling unhappy and you feel unhappy because you are unhappy, and you feel rather ill all over, sit down and breathe deeply. Try to control your individual awareness and become aware of an area of the mind that is always buoyant and happy. Be gentle with your awareness. Realize that you are not the unhappy area of the mind that you are aware of. Whatever was the cause of your unhappiness doesn't really matter, because the powerful radiance within the lotus of the heart knows nothing of this unhappy area of the mind. You will be surprised at how quickly your awareness will move from the unhappy area of the mind, seemingly rejuvenate itself and become joyous again at the very thought of the Self God within the lotus of your heart.

Friday
LESSON 61
The Cycles of Experience

There are many things in life which endeavor to keep us away from our true being. These are the cycles of life. We must watch and be careful of these recurring cycles in our life. These joyous and sorrowful occurrences that awareness experiences, sometimes each day, sometimes each week, sometimes each month, are totally dependent upon the positive control that we have of awareness. But then there are greater experiences that have even longer cycles—perhaps a three-year cycle, a five-year cycle, a ten-year cycle or a fifteen-year cycle. ¶The subconscious area of the mind is something like the sacred cow of India. It relives what it takes in. The cow will take in grass and chew it, and then she will chew her food all over again at a later time. The subconscious area of the mind does the same thing. You will find yourself aware of reliving your life, or getting back into the same cycle of the same pattern of life that you experienced many years ago. This you want to avoid, naturally. It is easy. Ponder over what you are doing now, how you are living, and then go back and find out within yourself how that compares to a previous time in your life when you were living more or less in the same way. In this way, you will come to know what area of the mind you will become aware in next. ¶If something good happened to you after a series of events in the past, you can expect something good to happen to you again. If something happened that was not as good or joyous as you would like it to have been, then you can know that you will become aware in this area of the mind in the future. This you can avoid. You have the power to control your cause and effect.

Saturday
LESSON 62
The Diamond Of Light

How do you avoid unhappy states of mind? By consciously flowing awareness into the radiance, the light emanating from the self-effulgent being within the lotus of the heart. Direct awareness through controlled breathing. Remembering this basic principle, tell yourself that it is there, and soon you will begin to feel it. You will actually cause to grow within yourself a subtle nerve force that will turn awareness into the inner being so that consciously you can feel the Self God, your Śivaness, and its emanation that even now exists within you. In this way you can experience true bliss, true happiness—blissful happiness that does not cycle or fade. ¶One moment of contact with your inner being that resides within the lotus of the heart, that is always there—one moment will clear up a whole situation in the external area of the mind for you. It will give you clear insight into how you should live your life, how to meet your circumstances, how to avoid whatever you do not want to find yourself involved in as the cycles of your life begin to repeat themselves. ¶This self-luminous emanation is like a diamond that is filled with light. Think about it in that way. It is filled with light, this diamond that resides within the lotus of your heart. Try to visualize this clearly and precisely as you read. Visualization of inner things is the same as opening an inner door for awareness to flow through to gain the experience that is already there. Visualization helps to pinpoint awareness and hold awareness concentrated in one certain area of the mind and gently move it to another. With this shining diamond constantly within the body, how could you become aware of an unhappy area of the mind? How could you become selfish? How could you hold resentment? How would it be possible for you to dislike another? This diamond within the lotus is within others, too.

Sunday
LESSON 63
Ardent Striving On the Path

How are we going to master awareness so that it does not feel that it is what it is aware of? We have to pull awareness within, to the more refined areas of the mind. This is called going within yourself. You have to temporarily gain enough composure, enough control over awareness, so that in thirty seconds you can pull within yourself and, in a sense, light up because you become a little bit aware of the existence of the inner light. Now, of course, if we are pressured by desires that conflict with basic religious principles, it will be difficult even to become aware of or to even think about the inner light. It's easy, though, to find the darkness of the mind. ¶But if desires are flowing in accordance with the proper, basic action-and-reaction patterns of life, and one is living up to what he knows he should be living up to and allows the awareness to flow through unwholesome areas of the mind, he begins to hurt deeply on the inside. That is the so-called conscience hurting, because the light shines through the conscience, too, and makes the conscience self-luminous to us. We cannot see the light, but we can feel it. And when awareness flows into the consciousness of bliss and peace, you won't hurt anymore on the inside. The nerve system will be filled with a new energy, an actinic energy radiating out of the light from the lotus within the heart. Then you will be happy and joyous until awareness wanders again and brings up other emotional or desire temptations. Then you will hurt again. This is what is meant by the statement "constant striving on the path"—staying mentally healthy so that the conscience does not hurt. ¶The Self God is within you. The light emanating from your effulgent being is within you, too, within the lotus of your heart. The Self God is. It simply is. We do not have to awaken the light within the lotus of the heart because it is always there, always has been, and always will be. We just have to become aware of it. Then go in and in and in to it until awareness aware only of itself dissolves, and be the Self. Be That.

Tamaso Jyotiḥ Prati

तमसो ज्योतिः प्रति

From Darkness To Light

The Primal Lord blesses all inhabitants of Earth below and the heavens above. From the soul's blackest chamber, He dispels darkness by radiating from within the pure rays of His dazzling light.

TIRUMANTIRAM 435

Monday
LESSON 64
The Light of Understanding

People speak of the "light of understanding." Before the bright light of spiritual perception is experienced, the light of understanding must be laid as a foundation of philosophical training and appreciation—learning to understand life, for instance, through action rather than reaction. The purified, integrated mind, so perfected in its own understanding, lives in close communion with the soul radiance so that light becomes the constant experience of the mind. It is this to which the *yoga* student aspires. Living in the light, everything that formerly was hidden becomes revealed. Answers to questions that you had been pondering for many years become instantaneously unraveled in the light of the superconscious. But the mind has a way, in its instinctive, intellectual nature, of casting shadows over the natural radiance of the inner light. ¶Doubt is the by-product of the intellect's inability to cope with light. When a person depends upon memory or reason for meaningful answers, the mind will break down in doubt. Only when the higher elucidation of the intuition is sought is doubt dispelled. ¶When the instinctive mind becomes lifted into the light, a person is strong enough to be kind when he could have become angry. He generates enough spiritual power to be generous when he might have reacted selfishly. Disciplined periods of meditation nurture a magnanimous and benevolent nature. Such a being is naturally in the light of the supreme consciousness. His great strength is humility, a shock absorber for the malicious experiences in life. Humility makes one immune to resentment and places everything in proportion and balance within the mind.

A person lacking in humility does not give the appearance of being firmly rooted and poised within himself. At the other extreme, the arrogant person who lives in the shadows of the mind presents a pitiful picture of insecurity and incompleteness. ¶Seeking for God in the depths of one's being through control of the mind, control of one's thoughts, feelings and emotions, gives birth to the highest qualities of nature. This transformation begins to take place as the light of the soul becomes more and more apparent within the mind. ¶The spiritual path is a constant turning within, turning the light of the superconscious into the dark corners and recesses of the mind. "What is hidden shall be revealed," and so it is on this path as man reveals his Self to himself. As you sit in meditation in a darkened room, practice directing your consciousness inward, to the center of your brain. If you are able to perceive light within your body, you are on the path to immortality. But should darkness prevail, work diligently each day to clear out resentment, jealousy, fear, worry and doubt from your nature. Then you can sit in a darkened room and be a being of light. ¶The next time you are in a state of worldliness—jealous, angry or feeling sorry for yourself—sit down and seek for the light. If you cannot find it, visualize a light bulb within your head or a flashlight at the top of your head shining down into it. Flash the light on and off mentally, and when the flashlight does not go off, even if you have mentally turned off the switch, then you know that you have the inner light. You will watch awareness move out of the darker area of the mind. It's a wonderful feeling, and it's a basic practice of the contemplative life of living two-thirds within oneself and one-third in the external world. ¶I'm often asked, "Do I see light or do I just think that I am seeing light?" I reply, "If you were in a darkened room, you would see light within you just as you'd see on the outside if lights were on in the room or you were in broad daylight. This is because you are seeing with your inner eye, your third eye, which you actually use all of the time. You use your third eye, for example, when you study your subconscious mind and see the memories of your past. The light around the memories is the inner light. If it wasn't there, you could not see your memories. Take away the mental pictures, and the light alone is before you. You will learn to consciously use the inner eye to see with as you spiritually unfold. All of a sudden, one day you will realize that you are seeing light with your third eye at the same time you are seeing physical things with your two physical eyes. ¶The inner light is so beautiful. It is firm, like a plasma. It is sometimes fibrous and full of energy. And yet, it is quiet and full of colors. You begin to see color, and in that realm you can hear color at the same time that you see color. You can hear sound and see color all at the same time, and you have the faculty to turn hearing on and to turn hearing off, because you hear with an inner ear. This is, of course, very useful in daily life. When you listen to someone talking, you begin to know exactly what they are meaning because of your listening through your inner ear. When you look at someone, you know exactly where they are in consciousness, because you are looking at them with your inner eye.

Tuesday
LESSON 65
Disappointment, Discouragement

Another instinctive response to the ebb and flow of life force is disappointment, which intensified becomes discouragement, depression and despair. These three negative states are obstacles to all human endeavor, especially for the spiritual seeker, who must learn early to regulate, control and balance the emotional ups and downs so well that he never experiences discouragement, which is nothing more than an imbalance of force. ¶Life tests and retests our emotional maturity. Whether we meet those tests or fail is entirely up to us. On the Śaivite path, the *satguru* gives the tests in order to mold and strengthen the seeker's character. Great strength of character is required to attain spiritual goals, enormous courage and forbearance, and anyone who lacks that strength and stamina will cease striving long before full realization is attained. ¶Therefore, to bring out the natural strengths, the *guru* will offer challenges. He knows that we all fall short of our own expectations now and again, and that we react either positively by reaffirmation or negatively through discouragement. As the tests of life present themselves, the *satguru* will observe the seeker's response time and time again until his emotional body grows strong enough to combat negative reaction to what appears to be failure and later to absorb within itself all reaction to disappointment, the father of discouragement. ¶It is the day-to-day reactions to circumstance that indicate the attainment and not mere recorded knowledge about the path. When the aspirant is able to meet ordinary happenings and respond to them in the effortless wisdom born of detachment, that indicates that his striving is genuine. When he is able to encounter conditions that send ordinary people into states of disappointment or discouragement and when his emotional nature indicates mastery over these lesser states of consciousness, he is well on his way toward filling the gaps of a natural growth of the instinctive vehicles—body, emotions and intellect. ¶But to attain emotional stability, recognition of those vulnerable areas must be cultivated. It is quite natural to encounter circumstances that are potential sources of disappointment. The very recognition and admission are half of the necessary adjustments. As one set of conditions is resolved, another set of a more intense vibration arises naturally to be mastered. With disappointment reined in, the aspirant next faces tendencies of discouragement, then depression and finally despair, for they are all linked together in the instinctive nature of humankind. Once he recognizes these states as belonging to all men and ceases to identify them as personal tendencies, he is then able to cognize its source and convert it. In this way the emotional nature matures under the loving guidance of the spiritual teacher.

Wednesday
LESSON 66
Emotional Maturity

What is emotional maturity? It certainly is not to be equated with physical age. I know people who are well past middle life and are not yet emotionally mature. Even if the physical body is totally mature, the intellect, as well as the emotional unit, can remain childish and unstable. The mind may have been educated to the nth degree, and yet such a scholar remains vulnerable to depression and discouragement. The very first step toward emotional mastery is recognition coupled with admission that in some areas we are not yet perfect. Only through open admission can we devote ourselves to the *sādhana* that will balance and lessen the forces, allowing us to strive within ourselves to secure ourselves within ourselves. An emotionally mature man or woman is totally secure within and prepared to tap the greater realms of spiritual being. ¶We make very little progress when we strive to conquer these baser instincts in a good mood. However, vast strides are possible when we are miserable and work with ourselves to replace our misery with joy and understanding. Therefore, if you are ever disappointed or discouraged, count it a blessing, for you then have the opportunity to conquer the instinctive nature and really stabilize yourself dynamically on the spiritual path. ¶Often we are disappointed not only with ourselves and our circumstances but with other people as well. We can oversee this and other instinctive responses, such as mental criticism or jealousy, by looking at everyone and saying to ourselves, "I like you. I send you blessings." We cannot be discouraged or disappointed or jealous when we look our fellow man in the eye and say and simultaneously feel and believe through every atom of our being, "I like you. I send you blessings." Impossible! Love overcomes all instinctive barriers between people. ¶There may be certain people or a certain person to whom you can say, "I like you," but for whom this is hard to believe in your heart. If you look deeper into them, you may find they are emotionally immature, a 12-year-old emotional body walking around in a 35-year-old physical body. Are you going to dislike a person for that? No, of course not. You are going to understand him or her. I've seen people with 22-year-old bodies with the wisdom of an 80-year old and the emotional stability of a 40-year old. I've seen people walking around in a 60-year-old body with a 12-year-old emotional body. By learning to understand, we cease to be a personality leaning upon our fellow man and falling into disappointment when he lets us down. No, we must lean on no one but ourselves, our own spine, and not be the reactionary victims of the ups and downs of the world around us or the people around us. Then we will gain our freedom from the instinctive forces we were born into and attain sufficient emotional maturity to love and bless the world no matter what our circumstances may be.

Thursday
LESSON 67
Understanding Other People

Love is the source of understanding. You know intellectually that within you resides the potential, expressed or not, for all human emotion, thought and action. Yet, you no doubt meet or observe people occasionally whose life and actions are repellent or unacceptable to you. The absence of love has created a vacuum of understanding. For the meditating person, there should not be a single human being whose actions, habits, opinions or conduct lies beyond your ability to love and understand. ¶Try this. This week look at everyone you meet, and feel, from your finger tips right down to your toes, love welling up from your deepest resources and radiating out to them through every cell of your body and especially through your face. Say to yourself, "I like you"—and really feel it. There are many thousands of things that most people do not understand from their confused states of mind, and they therefore act in unseemly ways, due to the ignorance of past *karma*. Should their ignorance confuse you?

Should it cloud your own understanding? Certainly not! We do not love the flower and hate the muddy roots from which it grew, and we cannot hate the instinctive roots of mankind. ¶With understanding, a great thing happens—your life becomes even, balanced and sublime. The ups and downs within yourself level out, and you find yourself the same in every circumstance, find yourself big enough to overcome and small enough to understand. Then you can really begin to do something. When emotional ups and downs are allowed, what happens? Your poor nerve system is terribly strained in a constant state of frenzy and uncertainty. All of your energies are then devoted to coping with yourself, and not much is reserved to accomplish creative, productive projects. As your life evens out by using the great power of understanding, the emotional self of you heals and grows strong. Your nervous system, believe it or not, grows, and it grows strong if you feed it correctly by handling your mind. Understanding is the best nourishment for the emotional body. ¶You must have a basis for understanding your fellow man, and a very good basis is: "I perceive him with my two physical eyes. He appears to be forty years old, but I intuit him to be emotionally a little younger and mentally about sixty—a learned person. I know he is a being of pure awareness going through the experiences he needs to evolve further. Therefore, I shall understand him in this light and make allowances accordingly." This is not something to think about and appreciate philosophically. It must become as much a part of you as your hands and feet. It's an easy process if we apply it and a difficult process if we ignore its practice. ¶Understanding, loving and making allowances—these are the strengths of the soul awakened through *sādhana,* once the emotional ups and downs and the barriers of the instinctive influences of fear, jealousy, anger, deceit and disappointment are conquered. If you are creative, you will begin to truly create. If you are a mystic, you will have deeper and ever more fulfilling insights in your daily meditations. All of the mysteries of life will unfold before your inner vision once the instinctive mind is mastered in your life.

Friday
LESSON 68
Facing Up To Yourself

So, here we come to a very important state for spiritual unfoldment, and that is to face yourself. Have the courage to admit when you are right or the courage to admit when you are wrong. Have the intelligence to know that these are states of mind through which your awareness is passing and they have nothing to do with you at all, because you are pure spirit. The life force within you is pure spirit. It has nothing to do with the turmoil of the mind. And you have the intelligence to know that through the proper handling of your mind, you control your mind. ¶So, for example, you might face yourself and say, "All right, so I was wrong. I became angry, and for three days before I became angry, I was sort of angling for it, sort of creating the situation and antagonizing the situation to work myself up into that state. Now I don't perhaps know why I did that. Perhaps because things were too peaceful and I was bored. So I thought I would create the upset. Of course, I didn't know I would create such an upset and react and feel so badly, but at least it was a change. Things were too quiet and too peaceful, and the person I became angry at was too happy." When you begin to face your mind like that, you find out how you create every situation, whether you know it or not. ¶Mentally look back at the various states of mind through which you have passed. It is like taking a trip in your automobile. Each city and each state has its personality and its experience, and each state of mind through which consciousness has passed has its personality, too, and its experiences. And yet, that You is always the same—the You that lives a little bit behind the conscious mind in which you dwell each day. ¶You will have this power if you dedicate each Friday or Monday as a holy day. Work for the sake of work if you have to work on Friday or Monday, dedicating the fruits of your labor to the highest within you. Pray on Friday or Monday and dedicate the fruits of your prayers to the highest within you. Sing on Friday or Monday and dedicate your song to the spirit within you that gave you the power to open your mouth in the first place, and you will find that your consciousness will expand. You will be able to solve your problems from your expanded consciousness all through the week, intuitively. That is what the expanded consciousness brings you into, your intuitive mind, your intuitive, superconscious mind, which is much nearer to you than you think. The only barriers are the confusion of the subconscious and the state of mind which continues that confusion by not following spiritual principles.

Saturday
LESSON 69
The Yoga Break

The *yoga* break is a break in time in which one may penetrate the eternity of the moment. It is practiced in this way. If you find yourself nervous, upset, confused, drained of energy, lie down on the nearest flat, hard surface, not a bed or sofa, for they will not offer the proper support to your spine. Stretch out, preferably on the floor, take a deep breath and command your body and your mind to relax, to release, to let go of all thoughts and tensions of the moment. Don't bother trying to make your mind blank, but simply visualize yourself floating, relaxed on a cloud buoyed up in space, as it were, apart from all the problems and tensions of the Earth. Your eyes are closed, your hands are relaxed by your side, and as you inhale, gently lift the stomach muscles so that the lower part of the lungs fill with air before the upper part of the chest does. Visualize a powerful light flooding into your solar plexus as you breathe in, charging all the batteries of the nervous system, filling your body and mind with energy and positive will. As you exhale, feel this light energy diffusing into every part of your body, filtering down through the legs, through the arms, out through your fingers, up through the top of your head. As this light floods and fills your body while you breathe out, it expels ahead of it all the bothers and tensions of the day. After a few minutes, your breathing will have gained a deep rhythm. You will feel the life force within you build, and you will be regenerated through the lifting of the spiritual force within your own body. With the inrush of new energy you will feel inspiration returning to your mind, for as the body relaxes, so does the mind relax. If you are especially tense before you begin the *yoga* break, your muscles may relax quickly, and they will sometimes give a little jerk or twitch as the nervous system disentangles itself. By the time five minutes have passed in the prone position, with your mind solely occupied with the rhythm of your breath and the visualization of the physical body floating on a cloud—filling itself with light as it inhales, distributing the light throughout the body as it exhales—you may feel the inrush of energy flooding through you as if a hose had somewhere been opened. The *yoga* break gives perspective in the middle of the busy day, when your mind tends to become tensely narrowed by details.

Sunday
LESSON 70
Finding Time For a Break

People who live under tension all of the time are like a machine. They are a product of the material world. Only when they release that tension may they become creative again, products of the soul. In a relaxed state, happiness is found, and the qualities of the soul shine forth. Selfish, greedy people are tense, concerned, often inhibited. Tension breeds negative thinking. Relaxation gives birth to positive creations. If you have little or no control over your mind, it will be difficult for you to find even five minutes during your day in which to place your body in a prone position. Watch then the tendency of your mind to live over and recreate the circumstances that were occupying your mind before you began your *yoga* break. If you are going to relive the details of your day during your five-minute *yoga* break, neither your body nor your mind will relax enough to allow the inrush of spiritual energy that should be yours. And if you cannot take even five minutes out of your day to enjoy the relaxation of a *yoga* break, if you are so wound up and so busy, you may be headed for an illness of some kind. A nervous disorder may finally catch up with you as the years go by, because the physical forces cannot stand constant tension. ¶The best time to take a *yoga* break is when you feel that you have the least time. If your world were suddenly to fall down around you, leaving you standing alone with no one to lean on, no finances, no family, no friends, where would your power come from? You would have to, in that moment, reexperience the same power that you felt flooding through you as you lay concentrated and relaxed upon the floor. That effulgent, rejuvenating power is the Self, the real You, flowing through "your" mind and "your" body. ¶Freedom from worldly tensions is only achieved to the degree in which people are able to control the forces of their own mind. In this control they are able to lean upon the power of their own inner security, found in the eternity of the moment. In that moment, your inner strength is found. So, take your *yoga* break whenever you feel even a little tired physically, a little nervous, a little distraught. That is the time, not when you have time.

Dṛiḍhavākśaktiḥ

दृढवाक्शक्तिः

The Power of Affirmation

Let all your thoughts be thoughts of Śiva, and the Lord by His grace will reveal all. If your thoughts are Śiva-saturated, He will abide ever so closely in you.

TIRUMANTIRAM 1582

I WILL BE WHAT I WILL TO BE, I WILL DO WHAT I WILL TO DO. I WILL BE WHAT I WILL TO BE, I WILL DO WHAT I WILL TO DO.

Monday
LESSON 71
Affirmation Is a Power

The power of affirmation changes and remolds the putty-like substance that makes up the subconscious areas of the mind. For years we have repeated sayings and statements, attached meaning to them in our thoughts and through listening to ourselves speak. This has helped form our life as we know it today, for the subconscious brings into manifestation the impressions we put into it. Therefore, to change the subconscious pattern and increase the spinning velocity of it, we must remold with new ideas and new concepts its magnetic forces. This can be done through the power of affirmation. ¶Affirmation, when used in wisdom for spiritual reasons, is a power, and should be understood through meditation. Before beginning to work with an affirmation, we must understand completely from within what we are doing, being sure that when our subconscious has been remolded we can take the added responsibilities, the new adventures and challenges that will manifest as a result of breaking out of one force field and entering into another. Only when we face and accept fully the new effects of our effort should we proceed with an affirmation. First we must understand the nature of this power. ¶An affirmation is a series of positive words repeated time and time again in line with a visual concept. Such a statement can be repeated mentally or, preferably, verbally. Words in themselves, without a pictorial understanding, make a very poor affirmation. To choose the affirmation best suited to our needs, first we must realize what we do not want, and then we must take steps to change it, in the very same way we would discriminate in giving away or throwing away our possessions in order to purchase new ones. Whether one is dealing with home and possessions, thoughts and concepts, self-created inhibitions, or blocks and barriers of the subconscious, the principle is basically the same. If one feels, "I can't," he cannot. If he is always criticizing himself and lamenting over what he cannot do, then he has to reverse this pattern and change the flow of magnetic mental force, enliven its intensity by saying orally and feeling through all the pores of his body, "I can. I will. I am able to accomplish what I plan."

Tuesday
LESSON 72
Reprogramming Old Patterns

In applying this *tantra*, begin by repeating the affirmation fifty or a hundred times a day. In watching your reactions, you may find that the subconscious will not accept these three statements, "I can. I will. I am able." You may still have feelings of "I can't. I won't. I am not able." This then begins a period to live through where the mind's magnetic forces fight with one another, in a sense. The aggressive forces of your nature are trying to take over and reprogram the passive ones that have been in charge for so many years. Of course, the aggressive forces will win if you will persist with your verbal and visual affirmation. You must not give up saying, "I can. I will. I am able," until you find the subconscious structure actually creating situations for you in which you can and are able to be successful, happy and acquire what you need, be it temporal goods or unfoldment on the inner path. ¶Here is another positive affirmation that might be helpful for you: "I am the complete master of all my forces. My spiritual energies govern and control the force fields wherever I am for the highest good. Through understanding, being pure, full of spirited life, I am filled and thrilled with unlimited power, now and forever. I will be what I will to be. I will do what I will to do." Affirm this affirmation each day this week for seven days. Repeat it three times each morning, three times at noon and three times each evening. ¶You have perhaps often heard friends repeat the same complaint over and over again. They were not only making an affirmation, perhaps unknowingly, for their own subconscious mind, but for yours as well. Therefore, it behooves us always to be with positive people, spiritual, life-giving people, in order to be positive ourselves. It behooves us to listen to that with which we want to live, and to be the changer rather than the changed. The affirmations which violence sets up in the subconscious reactionary habit patterns in the minds of men cause them to fight and kill by spinning emotional force fields out of control. Fear then holds them in these brackets of mind as they react to what they have done. It takes great courage to go from one force field of the mind to another, for this means tearing up long-accustomed patterns and facing a period of adjustment while new subconscious patterns are recreated. It all has to do with changing the subconscious patterns. This is a power. You can change the patterns of your mind yourself. Try it. It is not too difficult.

Wednesday
LESSON 73
Availing the Higher Energies

Each day we make affirmations with our thoughts and our feelings—and the very words that we speak stabilize these patterns. But as the inner light begins to dawn its life-giving rays, a new, positive power comes into our words, our thoughts and the feelings that well up from the subconscious, making new manifest patterns in the force fields of the conscious world for us to meet and speedily experience. An affirmation can alter your life by creating mentally the patterns and moods of each day through which you will subsequently move. Here is one that can be used to dynamically begin each day. "I am now open to a flow of spiritual energy in which I perceive the most worthy course of action for this day. My service, being selfless, opens new doors of supply, making available all of the tools required so that my work will be beautiful, energetic and influential to the highest degree." The subconscious mind is like a piece of clay that can be impressed. These impressions go into the subconscious from the conscious mind and remain there vibrating until changed. The intuitive mind, which we call the superconscious, works through the subconscious when the channels of the subconscious are open. Hence, in impressing the subconscious mind, we must be very careful to create positive channels, and not to create a negative block. You can also write your own affirmation, but it must always be positive and carefully worded. ¶The power of thought is very strong, but only strong for a short time. It is the power of feeling that awakens the knowing consciousness. For example, suppose we repeat an affirmation such as this: "All my needs will always be met." And we repeat it again, "All my needs will always be met." In the initial stating of this affirmation, we understand something about it. However, unless we gain a conscious mental picture of what the words mean, they mean little more than nothing, for they do not reach deep enough to make contact with the limitless powers of your inner self. ¶Get into the rhythm of the affirmation. This causes strong feelings and impressions deep in the inner mind. Each word has a certain rate of vibration. Feeling is greater than visualization. Although each word of your affirmation may have a certain meaning to you intellectually, the rate of vibration of the word may not impress your mind in the exact same way in which you think it should to produce the result that you desire.

Thursday
LESSON 74
Utilizing the Power of Feeling

An antidote to this is to use affirmations in this way. Repeat the affirmation, "All my needs will always be met," and feel how it is to feel after all of your needs have been met. Until you find this feeling, you should not expect the affirmation to work. Every time that you have a need and that need is met, a certain feeling is then produced in you. That same feeling you have to feel the very instant you speak the affirmation. You then open a channel that instant to your own intuition through which all good comes. In this state of mind one has inspiration and will. It is from the intuition that, at the eleventh hour, fifty-ninth minute, fifty-ninth second, every need is met. ¶The next time you have complete feelings from the innermost sources of your being that your every need will be met, quietly repeat that affirmation over again: "All my needs will always be met." Simultaneously think, visualize and feel deeply with an inner, all-encompassing knowing that each need will be met. This is the esoteric secret of making an affirmation work. ¶People say affirmations work for them but sometimes they do not. Why do affirmations only work sometimes? It is because the subconscious is receiving the affirmation at a psychological moment, and a greater knowing, visualization and feeling has been awakened to some extent. However, at the times when an affirmation did not work, there was no knowing, no visualization or feeling attached to it. Just words. When affirmations are repeated over and over again without feeling or visualization, occasionally negative results are produced, as the vibrations of the words themselves may not register what is intended in the subconscious. ¶Here is another affirmation: "I am the master of my body." Sit and feel that you are the master of your body. Say to yourself over and over again, "I am the master of my body." Now, quietly, without thinking, feel and visualize that you are the master of your body. Really know that you are director of your physical vehicle. In repeating this next affirmation, "I am the master of my body, my mind and my emotions," feel and visualize exactly what these words mean. Then repeat time and time again, "I am the master of my body, my mind and my emotions," all the while visualizing and feeling exactly what you eventually want to be like, because what you cause now you cause in your future.

Friday
LESSON 75
All Your Needs Will Be Met

This ancient *tantra* is often used in gaining the material things of life. Affirmations do work in this respect, maybe even a little better than in gaining spiritual awakening, because the material desires are often stronger. If you need some material possession, and if it will do only good for yourself, your family and your friends, use the power of affirmation and see how quickly your need is manifested through one external channel or another. Distinguish carefully a material need from a desire. Desires are dangerous because it is easy to manifest material desires, but it is not as easy to assume responsibility for what the fulfillment of the desire might entail. That is why people sometimes do attract to themselves material possessions through affirmations and suffer the complications produced in their lives. This happened because they did not understand the full responsibility of having the desired possessions. ¶An example of a material need is having sufficient money for necessities. Generate the feeling and the picture that you now have sufficient sums of money to meet every human need, but not necessarily every human desire; just the needs. Then practice this affirmation: "I will always have sufficient money to meet all my needs." Repeat it once. Now stop affirming. Remain quiet, know, visualize and then feel how it is to be open to a sufficient flow of money to meet your every need. Get that feeling! It is a secure feeling, not a flamboyant, reckless feeling, not a feeling that now you can go out and have a good time. No, this is a quiet, secure feeling—born of being in a judicious state of mind. ¶Let us look closely at this feeling again: "I will always have sufficient money to meet all my needs." Now resolve to hold yourself open to ways and means by which you will have money to meet your every need for yourself and for your family. Be open to ways in which you can better budget the money you now have. Live by the ethic, "Waste not, want not." Soon you will find that you begin to become secure within yourself as the vibrations of your verbal, visual feeling of this affirmation ring through you entirely. Today you will begin handling the funds you have more judiciously, and soon you will begin attracting abundance from unexpected creative sources. Be open to new ideas, new people, new opportunities, expectant and ready to handle the wealth you have proclaimed as yours.

Saturday
LESSON 76
Consistency Is Essential

You can write many kinds of affirmations and use them for many different purposes, but remember, they are powerful. They should be carefully worded, and only used in a way which enhances your spiritual life. To be effective, they should be repeated regularly on schedule, five minutes in the morning, at noon and five minutes at night for seven days to begin with. You will surely benefit by the results you cause spiritually, emotionally and materially. The greatest emotional security is brought about through the affirmation, "I'm all right, right now," which quiets not only the conscious but also the subconscious instinctive fears, bringing forth an immediate influx of spiritual energy through the subconscious, giving peace and contentment to the entirety of the mind by expanding consciousness. As we expand our consciousness through the conscious control of spiritual energy, we become aware of new attributes and possibilities within our nature. Also, we become aware of the realms of knowledge within us that can be tapped during meditation, or the conscious use of the intuitive mind, to not only solve problems that confront us in our daily activity, but to derive creative solutions from the inner recesses of our own mind. ¶When you say to yourself, "I am all right, right now," you immediately bring the forces of the mind together. All fears, worries and doubts cease. An influx of spiritual energy fills the subconscious, and a sense of dynamic security permeates your being. "Tomorrow I shall wake up filled with energy, creatively alive and in tune with the universe." Say this several times to yourself and feel the spiritual force begin to move, the life force begin to move, within your body. You will wake up in the morning filled with creative energy, with a desire to be productive, to create. Answers to problems will be immediately unfolded from within yourself. You will experience finding solutions to questions that have been unanswered within your subconscious mind perhaps for years. A devotee having thus exercised this control over his mind to the point where when he commands the mind to be instantaneously creative, or puts a time limit on it—"Tomorrow I shall be creative, alive and in tune with the universe"—and his mind obeys, then has achieved a conscious control of the intuitive forces of mind. He is truly all right, in every now.

Sunday
LESSON 77
All Knowing Is within You

"I will be what I will to be. I will do what I will to do." You can repeat these two powerful affirmations over time and time again and thus rearrange, restructure, the forces of your subconscious mind and create a great inner peace within yourself. Become acquainted with the spiritual energies and bring the forces of superconsciousness through your subconscious. This creates feeling, a feeling that you are what you say you are—positive, direct, full of life and energy and creative power. Your intuitive mind proves this through your conscious mind, not only through feeling, but you will find yourself acting out the part in all kindness and security, exercising the positive will of "I will be what I will to be" and "I will do what I will to do." Feel the spiritual force permeating the entirety of your body. You are the security of your statement, and you accept it into your subconscious mind. As the days go by, you will become more creative and more consciously aware of your spiritual destiny. Find your spiritual destiny for this lifetime. ¶The greatest thing that a devotee must learn is that all knowing is within oneself. Therefore, go to the great superconscious school within you and bring forth knowledge. In order to do this, be confident within yourself. In order to be confident within yourself, have no fear. In order to have no fear, say to yourself, "I am all right, right now." This will quickly bring you into the here-and-now consciousness. You will feel spiritual force permeating your body, and your intuitive state of mind will be active. Go ahead in full confidence that you are the knower of all that is known. This does not mean that you know everything that is to be known about the material plane, the emotional world of people, or what goes on within their minds. This means that you are nearing the source of all sources, that you understand the ultimate destiny of all souls—to unequivocally merge with Śiva. ¶Spiritual destiny is manifested in the lives of those who stand out from the masses and actually do something, who live a creative life for the benefit of others. This last affirmation affirms an age-old truth and may be said several times before sleep and upon awakening: "I am not my body, mind or emotions. They are but shells of the infinite energy that flows through them all. I am this energy. I am its source. I am on my way to merge with Śiva."

Dhyāna Samārambhaṇam

ध्यानसमारम्भणम्

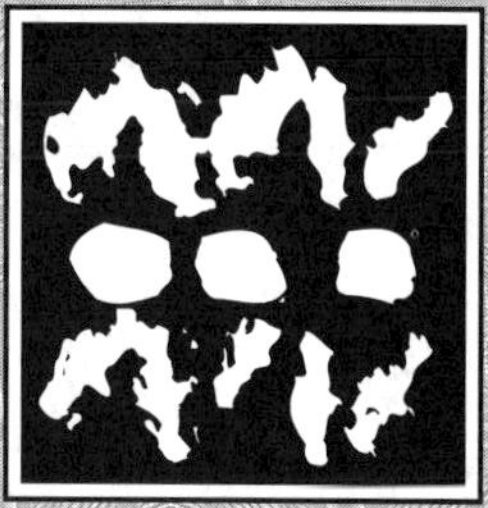

Beginning to Meditate

Let your awareness be unswerving, bound to the *mūlādhāra.* Through the spinal shaft within, gaze into the inner void. See and yet see not. Hear and yet hear not. Thus sit in meditation. That is the sure means to bar death's way. When *prāṇāyāma* is practiced in proper time-measure, breath retention will stand harmonized with *prāṇa.* In him who trains breath that is *prāṇa*, time and life remain inseparable.

TIRUMANTIRAM 591–592

Monday
LESSON 78
Unexpected Consequences

Desperate states of mind are disturbing many people these days. They are caught in emotional turmoil and entanglement, scarcely knowing how to get themselves out of it, or even fully realizing what state they are in. This condition, which often deteriorates as the years go by until nervous difficulties and mental illnesses set in, can be alleviated by the simple practice of meditation. Those who are content to live in a mesh of mental conflict, which is not only conscious but subconscious, will never get around to meditation or even the preliminary step: concentration. But a person who is wise enough to struggle with his own mind to try to gain the mastery of his mind will learn the vital practice of meditation. Just a few moments each morning or evening enables him to cut the entangled conditions that creep into the conscious mind during the day. The consistent practice of meditation allows him to live in higher states of consciousness with increasing awareness and perception as the years go by. ¶There are surprises, many of them, for the beginning meditator, as well as for those who are advanced—unexpected consequences that are often more than either bargained for, because on the road to enlightenment every part of one's nature has to be faced and reconciled. This can be difficult if the experiences of life have been unseemly, or relatively easy if the experiences have been mostly comfortable. What is it that meditation arouses to be dealt with? It is the reactions to life's happenings, recorded in the subconscious mind, both the memory of each experience and the emotion connected to it. Buried away, normally, waiting to burst forth in the next birth or the one to follow it, these *vāsanās,* or deep-seated impressions, often come forward at the most unexpected moments after serious meditation is begun. It is the *śakti* power of meditation that releases them. There can be no repressed secrets, no memories too woeful to confront for the serious meditator. These experiences can be scary if one is "in denial" about certain embarrassing or disturbing happenings. ¶When this upheaval occurs for you, and it will, combat the paper dragon with the deep, inner knowing that the energy of the body has its source in God, the light of the mind that makes thought pictures recognizable also has its source in God, and nothing can or has happened that is not of one's own creation in a past life or in this. Thus armed with Vedic wisdom, we are invincible to the emotions connected with the memory of formerly locked-away experiences. When they come rolling out, patiently write down the emotional impressions of hurt feelings and injustices of years gone by and burn the paper in an open fireplace. Seeing the fire consume the exposed *vāsanās,* the garbage of yesterday, is in itself a great release.

Tuesday
LESSON 79
Mastery of The Mind

The experienced meditator seeks out the unwholesome areas within himself, endeavoring to expose and rid himself of each knot of *karma.* The beginning meditator may be shocked and shrink from even continuing the practice of meditation, as his inner mind plays back unhappy thoughts that impose themselves upon his *śānti.* Many stop meditating altogether at this point and turn instead to the distractions of modern life for solace. ¶But true meditation happens because of soul evolution. We evolve into meditative practices from *bhak-*

ti, the *yoga* of devotion. The transition is earned through past good *karmas*, not chosen as an intellectual or recreational pastime. As the transition of external worship to internal worship is made, the devotee has to face all bad *karmas* cheerfully and honestly in order to resolve them and move forward. ¶Sitting in a state of real meditation, one must be more alive and alert than a tight-rope walker suspended without a net on a taut cable three hundred feet above the Earth. Do you suppose that this man is sleepy, that he allows his mind to wander? No, every muscle and sinew of his body, every thought, every feeling within him, is absolutely under his control. It is the only way he can maintain the balance which keeps him from plunging to the earth beneath. He must be the master of himself, all the while seeking to identify with his pure soul being, not allowing attention to be pulled here and there—to the physical body, to outside sounds, to thoughts of the past or to concerns about the future. ¶In meditation, you will feel the same intensity of purpose as the tight-rope walker. Every atom in your being must be alive, every emotion under control, every thought seeking to impose itself upon your mind set aside until your purpose is accomplished. If the man three hundred feet up in the air feels a gust of wind coming against him, he must exercise perhaps a hundred times more will and concentration to remain poised in his precarious condition. Likewise, in meditation your mind may be intensely concentrated upon a particular object or thought, and yet you find an opposing thought seeking to divert your attention. The opposing thought may simply be a wind from your subconscious. You must then put more effort into the object of your concentration so that the opposing thoughts will be set aside and not have power to topple your balance. ¶Upon entering a state of meditation, one may find that awareness is enmeshed in a struggle between two states of mind: the subconscious of the past and the conscious, external, waking state concerned with the present and future. The experienced meditator learns that he is the watcher, pure awareness. When concentration is sustained long enough, he dives into the superconscious, intuitive state of mind. It enables the meditator, in time, to unravel the mystery. An integrated, one-pointed state of being is the goal—a state of inner perception without vacillation, with the ability to move awareness through the mind's various states at will. To become the ruler of the mind is the goal. To then go beyond the mind into the Self is the destiny of all living on this planet, for most in a life to come.

Wednesday
LESSON 80
Odic and Actinic Forces

Meditation can be sustained only if one lives a wholesome life, free from emotional entanglements and *adharmic* deeds. Intensive, consistent meditation dispels the antagonistic, selfish, instinctive forces of the mind and converts those channels of energy into uplifted, creative action. The same force works to make either the saint or the sinner. The same force animates both love and hate. It is for the devotee to control and direct that one force so that it works through the highest channels of creative expression. When this soul force is awakened, the refined qualities of love, forgiveness, loyalty and generosity begin to unfold. In this ascended state of concentrated consciousness, the devotee will be able to look down on all the tense conditions and involvements within his own mind from a view far "above" them. As the activity of his thoughts subsides, he begins to feel at home in that pure state of Being, released from his identification with and bondage to lower states of mind. A profound feeling of complete freedom persists. ¶Meditation is similar to watching the play of light and pictures on television. Identify with the pictures, and emotion is experienced. Identify with the light, and peace is experienced. Both light and energy forms have their source in God. Begin this evening while watching the news on TV by keeping awareness more within the light than the pictures. By all means, begin this ancient, mystical art, but as you progress, don't be surprised when regrets, doubts, confusions and fears you hardly knew you remembered loom up one by one to be faced and resolved. Perform the *vāsanā daha tantra:* simply write down all the regrets, doubts, confusions and fears in as much detail as possible, then burn the paper in a fireplace or garbage can. Claim the release from the past impression that this *tantra* imparts. Begin searching within now. ¶There are two forces that we become conscious of when we begin to meditate: the odic force and the actinic force. Actinic force is pure life energy emanating from the central source of life itself. Odic force is magnetism that emanates out from our physical body, attracts and merges with the magnetism of other people. The odic force is what cities are made of, homes are made of. The actinic force, flowing through the physical body, out through the cells and through the skin, eventually becomes odic force. ¶As soon as we begin to meditate, we become conscious of these two forces and must be aware of how to deal with them. The odic forces are warm, sticky. The actinic forces are inspirational, clean, pure, true. We seek in meditation the actinic force.

Thursday
LESSON 81
Transmuting The Energies

When we begin to meditate, we have to transmute the energies of the physical body. By sitting up straight with the spine erect, the energies of the physical body are transmuted. The spine erect, the head balanced at the top of the spine, brings one into a positive mood. In a position such as this we cannot become worried, fretful or depressed or sleepy during our meditation. ¶Slump the shoulders forward and short-circuit the actinic forces that flow through the spine and out through the nerve system. In a position such as this it is easy to become depressed, to have mental arguments with oneself or another, or to experience unhappiness. With the spine erect and head balanced at the top of the spine, we are positive, dynamic. Thoughts race through the mind substance, and we are aware of many, many thoughts. Therefore, the next step is to transmute the energies from the intellectual area of the mind so that we move our awareness into an area of the mind which does not think but conceives, looks at the thinking area. ¶The force of the intellectual area of the mind is controlled and transmuted through the power of a regulated breath. A beginning *prāṇāyāma* is a method of breathing nine counts as we inhale, holding one; nine counts as we exhale, holding one count. Be very sure to maintain the same number of counts out as in, or that the breath is regulated to the same distance in as the same distance out. This will quickly allow you to become aware of an area of the mind that does not think but is intensely alive, peaceful, blissful, conceives the totality of a concept rather than thinking out the various parts. This perceptive area of the mind is where the actinic forces are most vibrant. *Sushumṇā,* the power of the spine, is felt dynamically, and we are then ready to begin meditation. ¶Meditate on awareness as an individual entity flowing through all areas of the mind, as the free citizen of the world travels through each country, each city, not attaching himself anywhere. ¶In meditation, awareness must be loosened and made free to move vibrantly and buoyantly into the inner depths where peace and bliss remain undisturbed for centuries, or out into the odic force fields of the material world where man is in conflict with his brother, or into the internal depths of the subconscious mind. Meditate, therefore, on awareness traveling freely through all areas of the mind. The dynamic willpower of the meditator in his ability to control his awareness as it flows into its inner depths eventually brings him to a state of bliss where awareness is simply aware of itself. This would be the next area to move into in a meditation. Simply sit, being totally aware that one is aware. New energies will flood the body, flowing out through the nerve system, out into the exterior world. The nature then becomes refined in meditating in this way.

Friday
LESSON 82
The Benefits Of Meditation

After one has finished a powerful meditation—and to meditate for even ten to fifteen minutes takes as much energy as one would use in running one mile—it fills and thrills one with an abundance of energy to be used creatively in the external world during the activities of daily life. After the meditation is over, work to refine every attribute of the external nature. Learn to give and to give freely without looking for a thank-you or a reward. Learn to work for work's sake, joyfully, for all work is good. Find the "thank-yous" from deep within yourself. Learn to be happy by seeking happiness, not from others, but from the depths of the mind that is happiness itself. ¶And when in daily life, observe the play of the forces, the odic force as it plays between people and people, and people and their things. When it is flowing nicely between people, it is called harmony. But when the odic force congests itself between people and tugs and pulls and causes unhappiness, it is called contention. And then when the odic force congests within oneself, we become aware of unhappy, fretful, disturbed states of the mind. The odic force then is called turbulence. It's the same force. The meditator learns to work with the odic forces of the world. He avoids shying away from them. The out-there and the within are his playground. ¶The finest times to meditate are before dawn, at noon, sunset and midnight. All four of these times could be used, or choose one. The meditation should be from fifteen minutes to one-half hour to begin with. What to meditate on? The transmutation of the odic forces back to their source, the actinic force. Through perfect posture, *āsana,* we transmute the physical forces and the emotional forces. Through the control of the breath, *prāṇāyāma,* we transmute the intellectual forces and move awareness out of the area of the mind that is always thinking—the great dream. ¶Then we become vibrant and confident in ourselves, feeling the power of our spine through which the actinic forces flow out through the nerve system. We learn to lean on our own spine more than on any other person, teacher, book, organization or system. Answers begin to become real and vibrant, hooked onto the end of each question. And these and many more are the dynamic rewards of the sincere aspirant who searches within through meditation.

Saturday
LESSON 83
Becoming Simple

When one begins to meditate, he should approach it dynamically, for it is becoming more alive. He is penetrating his awareness into the very source of life itself, for eventually he hopes to attain the ultimate goal, merger with Śiva, the experience of the Self beyond all time, beyond all form, beyond all cause. The experience of Paraśiva is attained only when one has become very simple, direct, uncomplicated. When a new nerve system has been built within this very body, strong enough to hold awareness within enough so that awareness itself can completely dissolve itself into its own essence, Satchidānanda and Paraśiva are experienced. ¶After that dynamic experience, man's heritage in this lifetime, one enters back into the mind which is all form—creating, preserving, destroying, completely finished in all areas of manifestation—and moves freely through the mind, seeing it for what it is. ¶Paraśiva is the ultimate goal in merging with Śiva, the realization of the Self in its totality. How does one know that one has experienced such an experience if you cannot speak of it, if it is beyond the mind, thought, cause, time and space? And yet one does know and vibrantly knows. There are various signposts. One is that one could go into Paraśiva an ignorant person and come out wise. Another: the urgency, the goal, the quest is over. He loses something—the desire for Self Realization. Another signpost is that the

Self, the very core of existence, is always his point of reference. He relates to the exterior world only as an adult relates to the children's toys. Paraśiva is to be sought for, worked for and finally attained. But a lot of work must be done first. ¶Choose a time for your meditation. Sit up so straight and strong and dynamic that you feel you are at that very moment the center of the universe. Regulate your breath so precisely that awareness flows freely out of the realm of thought into the perceptive areas of the mind. Then begin meditating on the two forces, odic and actinic. Be like the spaceman high above the surface of the Earth looking at the odic forces of the cities. Look then, too, at the odic forces, the magnetic forces, that motivate your life within yourself and between people and you and things. Feel the actinic force flooding out from the central source of energy itself. And then turn awareness in upon itself. Simply be aware of being aware. Sit in dynamic bliss. ¶And in coming out of this meditation, next feel the power of the spine, vibrant energy flooding out through the nerve system, the hands, the arms, the legs, the head. Enter back into life joyfully, joyously.

Sunday
LESSON 84
Discipline And Success

It is very important to decide exactly what you are going to meditate on before beginning. Then stay with the decision throughout the meditation and make every effort to avoid the tendency to become distracted and take off in a new direction. The Shum language as a tool for guiding the meditator is very helpful because the individual's awareness is precisely held within the chosen area. This is similar to how we must discipline ourselves to be successful in outer activities. To become distracted is unacceptable. Successful people finish what they begin. It is possible to learn to meditate extremely well but be unsuccessful in practicing it if the meditator allows himself to become sidetracked once the inside of the mind has opened. To be successful, one has to be very, very firm with oneself when beginning a meditation. Each meditation must be performed in the way it was intended to be performed when the meditation was begun. ¶To be successful in meditation, we have to bring the mind into a disciplined state. Undisciplined people can never be told what to do, because they will not listen. Their awareness is wafted around by every little fancy that comes along. Those who really want to make progress in meditation and continue to do so and better themselves year after year after year have to approach this art in an extremely positive and systematic way. Here, again, the Shum language can be a great help. ¶Thousands of devotees have come and gone since the beginning of my mission in 1949. Each one of them was determined to go deep within and realize the Self, but many gave up along the way. This was because at times the *śakti* power became very strong within them and their inner nerve system was not ready to receive the impact. Others were successful because they were more disciplined, and when their inner power came up, they enjoyed its intensity by holding it steady within the spine. They rested in the bliss of awareness aware only of itself. They then continued the meditation as planned after the power began to wane.

Paraśivadarśana Pādapañchakam

परशिवदर्शनपादपञ्चकम्

Five Steps to Enlightenment

Step by step, practice withdrawal of the mind and look inward. One by one, you will witness the myriad good things within. Now and here below, you may meet the Lord for whom the ancient *Veda* still searches everywhere.

TIRUMANTIRAM 578

Monday
LESSON 85
Step One: Attention

The grand old man of the East who ordained me, Jñānaguru Yoganāthan, Yogaswāmī of Jaffna, used to say time and time again, "It was all finished long ago." It's finished already. The whole mind is finished, all complete, in all stages of manifestation. Man's individual awareness flows through the mind as the traveler trods the globe. ¶Now we come to the real study, and this applies right to you and to you personally: the five steps on the path of enlightenment. What are they? Attention, concentration, meditation, contemplation and Self Realization. Those are the five steps that awareness has to flow through, almost gaining strength each time, on the path to enlightenment. When we first start, awareness is flowing through many areas of the mind. And if it is a mature awareness, we will say it's a great big ball of light, flowing through the mind. And if it's not a mature awareness, it's like a little ping-pong ball, bouncing around. The little ping-pong ball awareness is not going to walk the path of enlightenment, so to speak. It's going to bobble around in the instinctive mind, incarnation after incarnation, until it grows to a great big ball, like a great big beach ball. Then finally it will have enough experiences flowing through the mind to turn in on itself. When this happens, certain faculties come into being. One of them is willpower. And we learn to hold attention. We learn to hold awareness at attention. Awareness: attention! ¶What is attention? Attention is the first of the five steps on the path, that is, holding awareness steady, centralized in only one area of the mind, and the area that we choose it to be in, not the area that someone else has chosen it to be in. Our awareness is moved around by other people through the mind at such a fast rate that we think we are moving awareness ourself, so to speak. That's a funny way to talk because I'm saying we move awareness as if awareness is something else other than us. But awareness and energy and willpower are all the same thing. So, we will just call it awareness from here on out. When other people move awareness through one area or another, we call that distraction, or worldly distractions. The mission is to move awareness yourself. How do you learn to do that? Holding it at attention. ¶How does attention work? Attention is awareness poised like a hummingbird over a flower. It doesn't move. The flower doesn't move, and awareness becomes aware of the flower—poised. The entire nerve system of the physical body and the functions of breath have to be at a certain rhythm in order for awareness to remain poised like a hummingbird over a flower. Now, since the physical body and our breath have never really been disciplined in any way, we have to begin by breathing rhythmically and diaphragmatically, so that we breathe out the same number of counts as we breathe in. After we do this over a long period of time—and you can start now—then the body becomes trained, the external nerve system become trained, responds, and awareness is held at attention.

Tuesday
LESSON 86
Step Two: Concentration

Then we automatically move into the next step, concentration. The hummingbird poised over the flower held at attention, begins to look at the flower, to concentrate on it, to study it, to muse about it, not to be distracted by another flower—that is then awareness moving. Awareness distracted, here, is awareness simply moving to another flower, or moving to another area of the mind. ¶Give up the idea that thoughts come in and out of your mind, like visitors come in and out of your house. Hold to the idea that it is awareness that moves, rather than the thoughts that move. Look at awareness as a yo-yo at the end of a string. The string is hooked to the very core of energy itself, and awareness, flows out, and it flows in. Awareness might flow out toward a tree and in again, and then out toward a flower, and then in again, and down toward the ground and then in again. This wonderful yo-yo of awareness—that is a good concept to grasp in order to become more acquainted with awareness. Awareness held at attention can then come into the next vibratory rate and concentrate. ¶Take a flower and place it in front of you. Breathe deeply as you sit before it. Simply look at it. Don't stare at it and strain your eyes. But simply become aware of it. Each time awareness moves to some other area of the mind, with your willpower move awareness back and become aware of the flower again. Keep doing this until you are simply aware of the flower and not aware of your body or your breath. Then begin to concentrate on the flower. That is the second step. Think about the flower. Move into the area of the mind where all flowers exist in all phases of manifestation, and concentrate on the flower. Move from one area to another—to where all stems exist, to the stem of that particular flower, to the root that that particular flower came from, and to the seed. Concentrate, concentrate, concentrate on the flower. This is what concentration is—remaining in the thought area of the particular item that you are aware of and flowing through the different color and sound vibrations of the thoughts. How does it work? The powers of concentration—it is only a name. Actually, what is happening is you are flowing awareness through the area of the mind which contains the elements which actually made that particular flower, and you are perceiving how all those elements came together.

Wednesday
LESSON 87
Step Three: Meditation

After we are able to hold awareness hovering over that which we are concentrating upon, we come into great powers of observation. We are able to look into and almost through that which we are concentrating upon and observe its various parts and particles, its action and its reaction, because we are not distracted. Even observation in daily life, as a result of regular participation in the practice of concentration, comes naturally. We are able to see more, hear more, feel more. Our senses are more keen and alive. Observation is so necessary to cultivate, to bring awareness fully into the fullness of meditation. ¶This leads us then into our very next step, meditation. Meditation and concentration are practically the same thing, though meditation is simply a more intense state of concentration. The state of meditation is careful, close scrutiny of the individual elements and energies which make up that flower. You are scrutinizing the inner layers of the mind, of how a flower grows, how the seed is formed. You are observing it so keenly that you have forgotten that you are a physical body, that you are an emotional unit, that you are breathing. You are in the area of mind where that flower exists, and the bush that it came from, and the roots and the seed and all phases of manifestation, all at the same time. And you are seeing it as it actually is in that area of the mind, where the flower that you first put awareness at attention upon, then began to concentrate upon. Then you are meditating on the actual inner area of the mind where, in all stages of manifestation, that particular species actually is within the mind.

Thursday
LESSON 88
Step Four: Contemplation

Out of meditation we come into contemplation. Contemplation is concentrating so deeply in the inner areas of the mind in which that flower and the species of it and the seed of it and all exist. We go deeper, deeper, deeper within, into the energy and the life within the cells of the flower, and we find that the energy and the life within the cells of the flower is the same as the energy within us, and we are in contemplation upon energy itself. We see the energy as light. We might see the light within our head if we have a slight body consciousness. In a state of contemplation, we might not even be conscious of light itself, for you are only conscious of light if you have a slight consciousness of darkness. Otherwise, it is just your natural state, and you are in a deep reverie. In a state of contemplation, you are so intently alive, you can't move. That's why you sit so quietly. ¶Yogaswāmī once said, "I went in and in and in, and so deep within, that a bird was sitting on my head." That is the type of teaching he would give to cause people to think that the physical body was so quiet and quiet for so long that a bird was just sitting on his head, didn't even know it was a man sitting there—"I went in and in and in and in so deeply that a bird was sitting on my head." Go in and in and in and in so deeply that a bird could sit on your head, through the stages of attention, concentration, meditation and contemplation of the inner energies of the universe itself. ¶When you are in the mind of energy, in that rarefied consciousness, you are not conscious of the Earth or any planets. You are just conscious of the strata of energy that runs through Earth, space and planets. It's not even really energy. We are only conscious of energy when we are conscious of something that seems to be not energy. However, this is contemplation, the very source of that which is within and running through form.

Friday
LESSON 89
Step Five: Samādhi

This, then, leads to *samādhi,* the very deepest *samādhi,* in where we almost, in a sense, go within one atom of that energy and move into the primal source of all. There's really nothing that you can say about it, because you cannot cast that concept of the Self, or that depth of *samādhi,* you cannot cast it out in words. You cannot throw it out in a concept, because there are no areas of the mind in which the Self exists, and yet but for the Self the mind-consciousness would not exist. ¶You have to realize It to know It; and after you realize It, you know It; and before you realize It, you want It; and after you realize It, you don't want It. You have lost something. You have lost your goal for Self Realization, because you've got it. ¶I realized, went through that deep *samādhi,* right through these steps. I was taught these steps at a very young age: attention, concentration, meditation and contemplation, and then into the very deepest, deepest *samādhi.* After I went through that, I came out into contemplation, into meditation, into concentration, and thought, "How simple. Where was I, wandering around all this time, not to have been able to perceive and be the obvious?" ¶The *Çhāndogya*

Upanishad (7.25.1-3) expresses it so beautifully: "The Infinite is below, above, behind, before, to the right, to the left. I am all this. This Infinite is the Self. The Self is below, above, behind, before, to the right, to the left. I am all this. One who knows, meditates upon, and realizes the truth of the Self—such a one delights in the Self, revels in the Self, rejoices in the Self. He becomes master of himself, and master of all the worlds. Slaves are they who know not this truth. He who knows, meditates upon, and realizes this truth of the Self, finds that everything—primal energy, ether, fire, water and all the other elements—mind, will, speech, sacred hymns and scriptures—indeed the whole universe—issues forth from it."

Saturday
LESSON 90
Going In and Coming Out

The Self is so simple. You have to be so simple to realize the Self, not simple-minded, but so unattached. Awareness has to be able to move so nimbly through the mind, like a graceful deer going through the forest, so deftly through the mind, that none of the sticky substance of the mind, so to speak, sticks onto awareness and holds it steadfast for a period of time. And only with that agility can you move awareness in quickly to the Source, in on itself, until you come out having realized the Self. It is an experience you come out of more than go into. ¶If you were to explain Self Realization in another way, look at it in this way. Right out here we have a swimming pool. Beneath the surface of the water, we will call that the Self. The surface of the water, just the surface of it, we will call that the depths of contemplation, that pure consciousness, that most super-rarefied area of the mind, the most refined area of the mind of pure consciousness. And we are going to dive through pure consciousness into the Self. We will call the physical body awareness. It's a body of light, and it's going to dive into the Self, into the depths of *samādhi.* But to do that, it has to break the surface, has to break pure consciousness. ¶So, then, we make a preparation. Attention! We take all our clothes off. We put on a bathing suit and walk around the pool. We are getting ready for this great dive. Concentration! We pull our forces together, We don't quite know what is going to happen to us. Meditation! We look over the swimming pool. We look over the whole thing. We are studying out the philosophy of just what we are going to do. We even try to measure the depth of the Self. We talk to people about it and ask, "Have you jumped in there?" Some say, "No, but I intend to one day," and others will answer, "Yes." "Well, can you tell me something about it?" They say, "Uh-uh, no." Then you go into contemplation. You just stand. And you are completely aware of just standing there, right on the brink of the Absolute, and you are standing—so, so, so much conscious that you're there, you are just aware of being aware. And then you laugh, and then you jump in. As your hands and head go into the water, they disappear. As the body breaks the surface, it disappears. As the legs go in, they disappear. And we are all looking at the surface of the swimming pool and don't see you there anymore. You just disappeared, the whole body. ¶As you come out of that *samādhi,* first the hands and head come up and begin to appear again—then the chest, then the entire torso. Then, as you climb out from the pool, the legs reappear, and finally the feet appear again. You are just the same as you were before, but you are all clean on the inside. Awareness has a new center. The center is way down in the bottom of there, someplace that you can't even talk about. You have realized, when you come out, that you have realized the Self. ¶Before you went in, you knew all sorts of things about it. You could quote a thousand different things about the Self. You knew so much. And when you come out, you don't know anything about it at all. You know you have had a tremendous experience. You have had an inner bath. Then you go back into just enjoying the experience—contemplation. Then you begin to meditate, coming out again on the experience. And there is a vastness in you that awareness can no longer penetrate. It's a tremendous vastness; you just can't penetrate it anymore. You go in and in and in, and then all of a sudden you realize that you have realized the Self again. And you go in and in and in, and then all of a sudden you realize that you have realized the Self again. And everything is different. ¶You look at the world from the inside out. You look at people from the inside out. You look at a person, and immediately you see how they came along through life. You look at their face, and you see what their mother looks like. You look into their subconscious mind; you see what their home looked like. You see what they were like when they were ten years old, fourteen, twenty, twenty-five years old; now they are thirty. And at the same time you are seeing what they are going to look like when they are forty years old, and so forth. You see the whole sequence, all now. Then you really know, after that deep *samādhi*, that the mind, in all phases of manifestation, was all finished long ago. It's already complete. ¶Before that, you try to believe in that concept. And it's a vast concept to believe in, because at certain times, when awareness is flowing in the external areas of the mind, it certainly doesn't look that way at all. Our perspective is limited.

Sunday
LESSON 91
After Self Realization

After the deep *samādhi* of Self Realization, our perspective couldn't really be called vast; we simply see things the way they are. And it's as simple as that. We see things the way they are, and that is the way they are, from the inside out. You look at a tree. You see the energies of the tree all working within the tree. Then, after that, you see the leaves and the bark, and yet you see it all at the same time, all working together. That is Self Realization. ¶Those are the five steps on the path of enlightenment, five steps that you have to work with. The first one could be the most difficult—attention. It is making a strong, brave soldier that's going on a great mission out of awareness. By calling awareness to attention, awareness immediately has to detach itself from that which it was previously aware of. For when awareness is attached to that which it is aware of, it thinks it is that thing. It doesn't think it is that thing, but seemingly so. When we detach awareness from that which it is aware of, we can move freely through the mind, first in a limited area of the mind, then in a more and more vast area of the mind. ¶Then we learn to concentrate, which awakens the power of observation. If you have attention and concentration, the other stages come automatically. But for Self Realization, you have to really want it more than your life, for that deep *samādhi*, that's what it is, more than your life. The realization of the Self, beyond the rarefied areas of pure consciousness, is more than your life. You have to want it more than your life. ¶Memorize these five steps: attention, concentration, meditation, contemplation, *samādhi.* Now, there are various stages of *samādhi—savikalpa samādhi, nirvikalpa samādhi*—but when I use the word *samādhi,* I refer to Self Realization, the Totality, the Ultimate, which I just described. It is worth seeking for. It is worth striving for. It is worth making a mission of existence on this planet for. ¶We are not on this planet to become educated, to get things, to make money, to dress up the physical body, to acquire property, to feed ourselves. We are on this planet for the realization of the Self, for that one thing, to go within ourselves. That is why we have come to this planet, and we will keep coming back through the process of reincarnation, time and time and time again, until that awareness grows up into a great big ball, where it is strong enough to move through the rarefied areas of the mind—if we are comparing awareness to a ball, from a ping-pong ball, to a volleyball, to a beach ball—and finally, we are just there. Intellectually, we have to compare awareness to something in order to get the idea. Once we have the idea and have caught the vibration and have released awareness from that which it is aware of, we are on our way in our innersearch for the ultimate goal, inwardly.

Jīvanaṁ Mahānubhūtiḥ

जीवनं महानुभूतिः

Life, the Great Experience

Though they practice *yoga* for eight thousand years, still men do not see the Lord, sweet as ambrosia and delightful to the eye. But if, illumined, you seek Him within, He is there in you, as a reflection in a mirror.

TIRUMANTIRAM 603

Monday
LESSON 92
Establish Basic Principles

At one time or another in life, each of us has had similar experiences of temptation. There were times when we went against what we knew to be the better action, did things we knew we would be sorry for later. We knew because the actual knowing of the consequences of our actions or inactions is resident within us. Even the demons of ancient scripture are actually within us, for that is the lower, instinctive nature to which power is given when we go against what we know to be the best for us. Even the greatest souls have temptations. The souls who are the oldest and the strongest have the strongest temptations and desires. Do you often ask, "Why should this happen to me? What did I do to deserve this?" The experience was created and born of your own strength. Any lesser experience would have meant little more than nothing to you because no lesson would have been derived from it. ¶When we go to kindergarten, we are taught gently. When we go to the university, we are taught in the language of the university. The teachings only come to us from life in a way that we can best understand them, in a way that we can best call forth our inner strength. I have been in many situations and expected people to meet certain standards, but I have discovered that there are many basic things people just don't know. ¶If you check back through the pages recording various periods of your life, you will observe that knowing grew from certain experiences which you held memory of in your subconscious mind. You can also look within yourself and observe all that you do not know that you knew. For example, start with all those things you are not sure about. You must resolve all of these things through understanding before you can clear your subconscious mind. When you have cleared your subconscious mind through understanding the lessons from the experiences you are still reacting to, you will unfold the inner sight of your clear white light and begin to live in your true being. ¶The *yoga* student must establish basic principles in his life. He must try very hard to do this. The knowledge of interrelated action and reaction is within the consciousness of man. To understand the deeper experiences of life, we must analyze them. We must ask ourselves, "What does this experience mean? What lesson have I derived from it? Why did it happen?" ¶We can only find answers to these questions when we have established a foundation of *dharmic* principles, which are the mental laws governing action and reaction. On pages 194-195 are listed thirty-six contemporary *dharmic* principles that stabilize external forces so that a contemplative life may be fully lived. When practiced unrelentingly, they bring the understanding of the external and deeper experiences of life. ¶If you desire to find the answer to any question intently enough, you can find the answer within yourself, or you can find it in our holy scriptures or books of wisdom. Pick up one of these books, open it, and you will intuitively turn to the page which holds an answer to your question. You have had the experience at one time or another of recognizing your answer as confirmation that all knowing is within you.

Tuesday
LESSON 93
Seeking for Understanding

There is a state of mind in which the sifting-out process of action and reaction is not possible. This is when the subconscious mind is confused. Too many experiences have gone into the subconscious that have not been resolved through understanding. Balancing the subconscious mind is like keeping accounts or balancing books. ¶Suppose you have hurriedly put many figures on your ledger. Some of them are correct but a few are not, and others do not belong, so, the books don't balance. You may spend hours over these ledgers, but they won't balance because it is human nature that we do not see our own mistakes. It takes someone else to gently point them out to you. As you quietly sit in concentration over your books, trying to balance them with a deeper understanding, your *guru*, teacher or friend may walk in the door and in five minutes find the error. You correct it and, like magic, the darkness lifts, the books balance perfectly and you inwardly see your clear white light. The ledger is your subconscious mind, the figures are your experiences, and until you understand them you will remain in darkness, in a state of imbalance. You will not only feel this disharmony, you will be able to see it portrayed as darkness within your body. ¶For just as it is your experience which makes up your subconscious state of mind, so it is your subconscious which creates the physical body and makes it look as it does. There are some people skilled enough to look at your face and your body and thereby read what is in your subconscious mind. My spiritual master, Jñānaguru Yogaswāmī, could look at another's mind, see and understand the nature and intensity of the darkness or light. It is a science only a few are trained in accurately. He knew that the physical body is really created by the sum total of the conflicts and tranquilities within the subconscious state of mind. As man becomes

Thirty-Six Contemporary Dharmic Principles

1. Simplify life and serve others.
2. Live in spiritual company.
3. Seek fresh air and sunshine.
4. Drink pure water.
5. Eat simple, real foods, not animal flesh.
6. Live in harmony with nature.
7. Consume what you genuinely need rather than desire.
8. Revere the many forms of life.
9. Exercise thirty minutes every day.
10. Make peace, not noise.
11. Make a temple of your home.
12. Develop an art form or craft.
13. Make your own clothing and furniture.
14. Express joy through song and dance.
15. Grow your own food organically.
16. Plant twelve trees a year.
17. Purify your environment.
18. Leave beauty where you pass.
19. Realize God in this life.

20. Be one with your *guru.*
21. Be nonviolent in thought and action.
22. Love your fellow man.
23. Rely on the independent energy in the spine.
24. Observe the mind thinking.
25. Cultivate a contemplative nature by seeking the light.
26. Draw the lesson from each experience of life.
27. Detach awareness from its objects.
28. Identify with infinite intelligence, not body, mind or intellect.
29. Be aware in the eternal now, not in the past or the future.
30. Do not take advantage of trust or abuse credit.
31. Keep promises and confidences.
32. Restrain and direct desire.
33. Seek understanding through meditation.
34. Work with a spiritual discipline.
35. Think and speak only that which is true, kind, helpful or necessary.
36. Create a temple for the next generation by tithing.

enlightened through cognition, the conflict lessens, giving birth to the dawn after the darker hours. Hence the statement about the third eye, "When the eye becomes single, the whole body shall be filled with light."

Wednesday
LESSON 94
Experience Is A Classroom

Each experience is a classroom. When the subconscious mind has been fully reconciled to everything that has happened, when you have fully realized that everything you have gone through is nothing more and nothing less than an experience, and that each experience is really a classroom, you will receive from yourself your innerversity personal evaluation report and it will be covered with the highest grades, denoting excellent cognition. ¶Each of these higher grades is important, for when you put them together they will unfold a consciousness of understanding, making you eligible for your graduation certificate of visually seeing the clear white light within your head while sitting in a darkened room. Yet, if you have failed a class, or several classes, not only will the marks show, but it will also take you longer to graduate. If you haven't taken from each experience its sum of understanding, subconsciously you remain in the classroom reacting to the lesson you are learning, even though the experience may have occurred fifteen or twenty years ago. ¶So, we have to end each of these experiences in understanding. We have to be promoted to the next deeper grade of awareness so that, with the universal love born of understanding, we can close the classroom doors behind us and receive our diploma. When we receive this first diploma of the clear white light, we are given the greater knowledge and wisdom of what this great experience of life is all about.

How do we realize what life is all about? By having lived it fully we fully realize that the past is nothing more and nothing less than a dream, and a dream is comprised of pleasant experiences and nightmares. Both are just experiences, neither good nor bad, right nor wrong. ¶But you must remember that even the greatest souls have had nightmares, confusions, heartbreaks, disappointments, losses, desires that have been unfulfilled and experiences that they have not been able to cognize. And then they have come to a point in their lives when their inner being started pushing forward to the conscious plane. In other words, they have had just about all the experience necessary to graduate out of the instinctive-intellectual world, or consciousness. The great, intuitive superconscious nature begins pushing forward to the conscious plane, stirring up within the subconscious the remnants of the past. As those remnants come up, they have to be faced and cognized through meditation, thus creating the foundation for understanding the basic laws and principles of life. Then comes the dawn of the clear white light.

Thursday
LESSON 95
We Create Our Mind Each Instant

I always try to keep the approach to the study of life and the unfoldment of the inner Self very simple by giving examples of the flower that begins as the little seed and grows into a stem forming a bud. We know nothing of the blossom until the bud opens, and we know little of the bud after it has become a blossom. However, each process within that growth to maturity is an experience for the plant. The seed contains within itself its basic laws of growth. The stem will tell its own story as it grows. The bud contains many experiences and has contained within it a complete story of its own. As the blossom unfolds, it tells a radiant autobiography of beauty. ¶In the philosophies of the Orient, the inner mind is often depicted as the lotus flower. That is what the mind would look like if you could see the mind. We can look at things on the material plane. The ugly things tell us how ugly the mind can become. When we look at the beautiful creations of nature, we see how lovely the mind can be. ¶It is up to us to choose how we want to create the mind, conscious and subconscious. I say "how we want to create the mind" because we are creating our mind each instant. There is no past! That dream as it passes before our vision is right now. We call it the past because we say we remember, but as we are remembering, we are recreating what we are remembering in the present. There is no future! That is also a dream or a vision, just like the past, because when we think of the so-called future we are recreating it before our vision right now. Therefore, there is no past, there is no future. Now is the only apparent reality! ¶Now is the only apparent reality, and it is up to us to decide how we want to create our mind, because we do create our mind each instant. We can make basic decisions. "I would like to be nice to a certain friend of mine. That is the one who has not been too friendly to me lately." This is a basic decision. Go out today and if someone does harm to you, or your friend is not kind to you, show your love by doing something kind for him. It is up to us to decide how to face life, be it "Love your neighbor," or "An eye for an eye and a tooth for a tooth." It is up to us to fathom the reaction we are going to cause in ourselves and others by each of our decisions. Since each decision will bring its own reward, it is up to us to determine whether we want to suffer through a reaction as a result of an action that we have not duly considered in the light of *dharmic* principles. ¶Life is a series of decisions. Each instant, as we create the instant, we are creating the decision. We are facing the reaction we caused to come before us, and in facing it with the power of principle we are building the so-called future. So, a man has two paths, and every moment is a moment of judgment. Good judgment comes from concentration—directing the flow of thought. It does not always have to be difficult to choose.

Friday
LESSON 96
The Art of Being Constant

There is an art which you can learn which will make all of your decisions easier. It is the art of being constant. Consistency wins. Consistency is one of the most important qualities of a devotee. It is only through consistency in your daily life that you gain the awareness which enables you to cognize the experiences of life, taking from them their real lessons. It is only through consistency that you can avoid many of the boulders that lie in your way on the classical *yoga* path to enlightenment. ¶Practice the art of being constant and you will unfold your destiny, discover what you were born to do and learn how to accomplish it in this life. For in that security you will awaken and fulfill your destiny and realize the Self. Thus, having your feet planted firmly on the ground, your consciousness can dwell freely in the spirit born of Self Realization. ¶Study your approach to life today as you practice this exercise. Take some of the experiences from your subconscious state of mind. Add them up and see how well your life balances out. Visualize a scale before you. Put the total of the experiences understood and the lessons derived from them on one side. Put on the other side of the scale the total number of experiences that you do not fully understand and from which you can still reap lessons. See how they balance. If they balance evenly, you are well on your way to becoming steadfast and constant. If they overbalance on the reactionary side, you are on the right track because you now have the power to balance your scale—your subconscious. If they overbalance on the understanding side, you should consider dedicating your life to the service of others. ¶Sit quietly with your eyes closed. Look deep within and trace back to the peak experiences that have happened through your life from your earliest days. Quickly fan through the pages of your life and pinpoint each climax, and know that that climax was the sum total of many experiences, forming one great experience out of which one great lesson of life was born. ¶Take the experiences that you are not quite sure of—all the ones that you cannot form into a solid stone of understanding. Take those experiences and resolve to trace down each intuitively. Don't analyze. Just look at the sum total of the experiences, and after awhile you will get your clarification in a flash of intuition. This will be of great benefit to you. The great lessons that those experiences offer will become apparent as you progress in your practice of concentration. Do this and you will do much for yourself.

Saturday
LESSON 97
Awakening Willpower

This is why you were born. The one and only reason why you are existing in your material body is first to unfold into your clear white light, then penetrate deeper and deeper, touch into the Self, become a knower of the Self, Satchidānanda, and then deeper still into *nirvikalpa samādhi,* Self Realization, preparing for the next steps on the classical *yoga* path—*moksha,* freedom from rebirth, and *viśvagrāsa,* merging with Śiva. You will soon realize that you create the mind in any way that you want, that you are master of your mind. To become master of your mind, you must realize that understanding is fifty percent of control of the mind, and you have to work at it as an accountant would work to balance his books, as a musician has to work to master his instrument. ¶To know yourself is why you are on Earth. You were born to realize the Self. You are not here to make money, to clothe yourself or to entertain yourself. These are incidentals. You are here on this planet to realize the Self God, and the only way to experience Self Realization is to awaken within you a dynamic, indomitable, actinic will. To do this, the steps are: first, find out what and where the willpower is. Everyone has it. Willpower is that quietness within, that serenity that is likened to a light so bright that you cannot see it with the physical eyes. Second, learn to use this actinic will. Begin with little things that you do. Become satisfied with everything that you do. To you, it must be a work of art, even if it is just drying a dish, cleaning a floor or painting a picture. Your work must satisfy you, and if it does not satisfy the inner you one hundred percent, you must use your indomitable willpower and keep striving until it does. ¶You must become a perfectionist unto yourself, but first decide what your standard for perfection is. You must control the quality of your work. Take on no responsibility that you cannot handle. By doing this, you will find that you have much more control over the physical body and emotions than you ever thought possible. You will begin to demonstrate to yourself your powers of control over material creations, the physical body and the emotions of the instinctive area of the mind. Demonstration comes as you use your indomitable willpower.

Sunday
LESSON 98
To Live a Radiant Life

It is one thing to talk; it is another thing to demonstrate what is declared. Demonstration is a result of your awareness flowing through the superconscious area of the mind. The superconscious mind is actinic or radiant force, whereas the conscious and subconscious states of mind are manifestations of odic force, or magnetism. Excessive talk arises out of confused conscious and subconscious states of mind. ¶Find your actinic spiritual destiny in this life. Learn to live fully each instant, completely in the eternity of the moment. Become refined by constructive, rather than abusive practices. Become positive through the generation of good deeds, rather than those uncomplimentary experiences we react to and reenact. Yours is a new and positive destiny, one that is true, constant and free from want or dangers. Life ahead for you can only become one of fulfillment and radiance as you adjust to *dharmic* principles. Follow these thirty-six gentle guidelines for living and meditate regularly in the morning when you awaken and just before sleep each night. That is all that is needed by the beginner on the eternal path to those enlightened heights of superconsciousness to which the subtle, individual, intelligent awareness of man aspires. ¶On and on through the mind we travel daily, once awareness has become detached from the limited area of mind it has been trapped in. The journey seems endless! It is. Seek on, seek on. Look in, look in. And on that solid foundation of good character, move into that place in the mind and live there, seeing no difference between the inner and the outer states of fluctuating awareness. Be that now for which you have been striving. The search is within. Go within the mind. Go in and in and in and in and make fathomable the unfathomable depth of Being. You can do it. It has been done countless times over the past several thousand years. Give yourself the great benefit of believing in yourself and flow inward, inward—to the totality of it all.

Jīvanaparīkshā Abhi Kramaṇam

जीवनपरीक्षा अभि क्रमणम्

Facing Life's Tests

Purity, compassion, modest appetite, patience, forthrightness, truth and steadfastness—these he ardently cherishes. Killing, stealing and lusting he abhors. Thus stands the one who observes the ten virtues of *yama's* way. *Tapas, japa,* serenity, belief in God, charity, vows in the Śaiva way and Siddhānta learning, sacrificial offerings, Śiva *pūjā* and pure speech—with these ten, the one following *niyama* perfects his ways.

TIRUMANTIRAM 556-557

Monday
LESSON 99
Restraints and Observances

When we are children, we run freely, because we have no great subconscious burdens to carry. Very little has happened to us. Of course, our parents and religious institutions try to prepare us for life's tests. But because the conscious mind of a child doesn't know any better, it generally does not accept the preparation without experience, and life begins the waking up to the material world, creating situations about us—magnificent opportunities for failing these tests. If we do not fail, we know that wc havc at some prior time learned the lesson inherent in the experience. Experience gives us a bit of wisdom when we really face ourselves and discover the meaning of failure and success. Failure is just education. But you shouldn't fail once you know the law. ¶There have been many systems and principles of ethics and morality established by various world teachers down through the ages. All of these have had only one common goal—to provide for man living on the planet Earth a guidepost for his thought and action so that his consciousness, his awareness, may evolve to the realization of life's highest goals and purposes. The ancient *yoga* systems provided a few simple *yamas* and *niyamas* for religious observance, defining how all people should live. The *yamas,* or restraints, provided a basic system of discipline for the instinctive mind. The *niyamas,* or positive observances, are the affirming, life-giving actions and disciplines. From the holy *Vedas* we have assembled on pages 208-209 ten *yamas* and ten *niyamas,* a simple statement of the ancient and beautiful laws of life. ¶Life offers you an opportunity. As the Western theologian speaks of sins of omission as well as

The Ten *Yamas,* Restraints for Proper Conduct from the *Vedas*

1) Noninjury, *ahiṁsā:* Not harming others by thought, word, or deed.

2) Truthfulness, *satya:* Refraining from lying and betraying promises.

3) Nonstealing, *asteya:* Neither stealing, nor coveting nor entering into debt.

4) Divine conduct, *brahmacharya:* Controlling lust by remaining celibate when single, leading to faithfulness in marriage.

5) Patience, *kshamā:* Restraining intolerance with people and impatience with circumstances.

6) Steadfastness, *dhṛiti:* Overcoming nonperseverance, fear, indecision and changeableness.

7) Compassion, *dayā:* Conquering callous, cruel and insensitive feelings toward all beings.

8) Honesty, straightforwardness, *ārjava:* Renouncing deception and wrongdoing.

9) Moderate appetite, *mitāhāra:* Neither eating too much nor consuming meat, fish, fowl or eggs.

10) Purity, *śaucha:* Avoiding impurity in body, mind and speech.

The Ten *Niyamas,* Observances For Spiritual Life from the *Vedas*

1) Remorse, *hrī:* Being modest and showing shame for misdeeds.

2) Contentment, *santosha:* Seeking joy and serenity in life.

3) Giving, *dāna:* Tithing and giving generously without thought of reward.

4) Faith, *āstikya:* Believing firmly in God, Gods, *guru* and the path to enlightenment.

5) Worship of the Lord, *Īśvarapūjana:* The cultivation of devotion through daily worship and meditation.

6) Scriptural listening, *siddhānta śravaṇa:* Studying the teachings and listening to the wise of one's lineage.

7) Cognition, *mati:* Developing a spiritual will and intellect with the *guru's* guidance.

8) Sacred vows, *vrata:* Fulfilling religious vows, rules and observances faithfully.

9) Recitation, *japa:* Chanting *mantras* daily.

10) Austerity, *tapas:* Performing *sādhana,* penance, *tapas* and sacrifice.

sins of commission, so we find that life offers us an opportunity to break the law as indicated by the *yamas,* as well as to omit the observances of the *niyamas.* If we take the opportunity to live out of tune with Hindu *dharma,* reaction is built in the subconscious mind. This reaction stays with us and recreates the physical and astral body accordingly.

Tuesday
LESSON 100
Learning to Face Yourself

Have you ever known a friend who reacted terribly to an experience in life and as a result became so changed mentally and physically that you hardly recognized him? Our external conscious mind has a habit of not being able to take the meaning out of life's most evident lessons. ¶The basic laws of life are so simple that many people don't heed them. Why? Generally because the opportunities afforded us to fail these tests are so plentiful that we generate very good reasons for not paying attention to our lessons. Shall we say it is normal to fail some of these tests? Yes, isn't this like getting a failing grade on a report card in school, not passing some of the tests and having to take a course over again? We must learn from our experiences or find ourselves repeating them again and again. ¶It is our teaching not to react to life's experiences, but to understand them and in the understanding to free ourselves from the impact of these experiences, realizing the Self within. The true Self is only realized when you gain a subconscious control over your mind by ceasing to react to your experiences so that you can concentrate your mind fully, experience first meditation and contemplation, then *samādhi,* or Self Realization. First we must face our subconscious. ¶There are many amusing ways in which people go about facing themselves. Some sit down to think things over, turning out the light of understanding. They let their minds wander, accomplishing nothing. Let me suggest to you a better way. ¶In facing ourselves let us relate our actions, our thoughts and our feelings to the *yamas* and the *niyamas,* the wise restraints and observances of Hindu *dharma.* In aligning ourselves with these universal laws, we can soon see how clear or muddy is our own subconscious. Fulfilling the restraints first allows us to take the next step on the spiritual path, which is the fulfillment of the observances. As long as we are evading our taxes, it is difficult to live up to the ideal of honesty. As long as we are beating our children, it is difficult to adhere to nonviolence. As long as we are swearing, using *asura*-invoking, profane words in the home, it will be difficult to cultivate patience. As long as we indulge in pornography, a mental form of adultery, it will be difficult to practice purity. Yes, it will be difficult to cultivate a contemplative nature. All these and more will require serious penance, *prāyaśchitta* as it is known in Sanskṛit, to change the nature and bring it into harmony with the profound ideals of the ancient Indian sages and *yogīs.*

Wednesday
LESSON 101
Each Test Is An Opportunity

We carry with us in our instinctive nature basic tendencies to break these divine laws, to undergo the experiences that will create reactive conditions until we sit ourselves down and start to unravel the mess. If we are still reacting to our experiences, we are only starting on the *yoga* path to enlightenment. As soon as we cease to react, we have for the first time the vision of the inner light. ¶What do we mean by this word *light?* We mean light literally, not metaphysically or symbolically, but light, just as you see the light of the sun or a light emitted by a bulb. Even in the Abrahamic scripture, it is given, "When your eye becomes single, your whole body shall be filled with light." You will see light first at the top of the head, then throughout the body. An openness of mind occurs, and great peace. As a seeker gazes upon his inner light in contemplation, he continues the process of purifying the subconscious mind. As soon as that first *yoga* awakening comes to you, your whole nature begins to change. You have a foundation on which to continue. The *yamas* and the *niyamas* are the foundation. ¶On the spiritual path to enlightenment, each of your decisions is going to be a basic decision, based on your knowledge of the laws of the mind. You must be aware that if you have not been tested by life through breaking its laws, you will in the future be so tested. You have to be aware that each test is an opportunity for either failure or success, and it is all up to you. Circumstances will always present opportunities for failure, and your reasoning mind will always be able to say, "I could have done nothing else under the circumstances." ¶Often, even under the circumstances, advanced souls are able to take the more difficult course through the natural exercise of humility. Decisions of this nature direct the conscious mind to the recognition of natural inner security. When you fail one of life's tests, all you can fail is yourself, the Self within you.

Thursday
LESSON 102
On the Edge of The Mountain

Knowing the law puts you at a psychological disadvantage in a way. It is not quite as bad when you act for the first time out of ignorance, in any situation.

Suppose you are riding with a friend in a car and he passes through a red light and gets a ticket and a scolding from the officer. And you say to your friend, "Oh, that's all right, you didn't know. You haven't been driving long and your lesson may cost you some money." You are forgiving of your friend's error. Two months later, in riding with him again, he passes through another red light. And what do you know, he gets another ticket and a scolding, and you sit back and say, "There is no excuse for that; you knew better. You saw that red light, didn't you?" This time you are not lenient with your friend, because you know he is aware of the law. ¶You will behave with your own mind in the same way subconsciously if you depart from the spiritual law once you recognize its intrinsic value. Through concentration on life's basic principles, you will become subconsciously aware of these laws, and then it will be easy for you to maintain them without effort, and the example of your life will be a light to shine for the benefit of many others. ¶Have you ever stood right at the edge of a mountain cliff? You were very careful about falling over the edge, weren't you? But have you ever experienced that tendency in your nature that makes you a little shaky at the edge of the mountain, that makes you wonder what it might be like to be falling over the cliff, even if the first ledge, shall we say, is not too much of a drop? What is it that makes you want to experience falling over the edge? Some people say they experience this feeling. Others may not have. But let anyone stand on the edge of a mountain precipice and then say that there is not something occurring within them that makes them be quite careful. ¶If you deliberately fall, even a short distance, you could not climb back to the top without having some kind of scar or bruise on your physical form—maybe only a blow to your pride. But you would carry back with you the results of the fall. It is the same with the spiritual law. Once you are aware of its operation and you deliberately allow yourself to fall, you can return to the path with effort, scarred by the memory and strengthened with the influx of renewed energy as you again search for enlightenment, remembering that we only fail when we stop trying. ¶Concentrate each night upon the events of the day and see how close you have come, either consciously or subconsciously, to deviating from your newly established *yoga* principles. Your span of life here is only a short time, and it benefits you to live it the best way that you can.

Friday
LESSON 103
Transcending Our Pettiness

Your journey on this Earth has only one goal, Self Realization. You are here to attain the highest possible states of consciousness. You are not here to react to the petty incidents that occur in the valley of the subconscious. You are here to learn to control the mind and live on the mountaintop. If you fail yourself, you are the one who must suffer your failure. Often, in retelling their failures or their sufferings, people react to or re-enact the original experience all over again. But learning to extract the lesson from the experience is like walking through the rain without getting wet. ¶We have to hold a constant vigil and keep our feet firmly planted on the spiritual path at all times, knowing that we can fall off the path until we have attained full illumination, or Self Realization, in this or future lives. By taking a stand within yourself on small issues, you can always find a different way, a way which will open the door to new opportunity, selflessness and serenity. But, to the degree that we are unable to restrain the inclinations of our lower mind, to the degree that we find ourselves incapable of entering into positive observances, so do we open ourselves to inferiority complex, jealousy, hatred, self-indulgence, lust, fear, greed and all sorts of mental and physical ailments. Being aware of the laws of life allows an unhibited and natural unfoldment, just as a bud unfolds into a flower. ¶People sometimes say to me,"I am a little fearful of the path of classical *yoga* unfoldment, because I don't want to lose the way I am." Of course, these people are not really happy with the way they are. Look back at your baby pictures and you will see that most naturally you lost and left behind the form that was yours at that time, and assuredly this will happen in the future. As you unfold in *yoga*, you will lose the way you are. You will mature as a bud matures into a flower, fulfilling its evolution, but it must leave behind its original shape, and open. In this same way, through discipline, your mind will open up into its fullness. ¶Here is a visualization exercise. Bring before the vision of your inner eye the qualities and attributes which you would like to unfold in your nature. Visualize yourself being the kind of person you want to be, doing the kind of things that are going to benefit mankind most. Look back over your day and find out how close to the edge of the mountain you came. Train your subconscious mind to keep you away from the edge of the mountain. Make the *yamas* and *niyamas* meaningful habit patterns to your subconscious, as they were meaningful to your intellect.

Saturday
LESSON 104
Changing Your Circumstances

You change your own circumstances all the time, whether you know it or not. Even your mind is different today than it was a week ago. The various experiences you have brought to yourself have made it that way. The point to realize is that you can gain an intricate control of the various things that change in and about you. Lean the thoughts and feelings of your creation in the right direction, and discover how quickly your circumstances will change their direction. This is the secret of self-control. This is the practice of *yoga.* Try it, and lose the habit of concern, for concern is only a by-product of a part of the mind being out of control. ¶What does the world offer us but an opportunity for action? It is the reaction that we sometimes get surprised by. The circumstances of your life are either pushing you toward greater understanding, if you are aspiring to realize the real Self, or they are pushing you toward confusion, if you have a tendency to react animalistically, making the personal self predominant. When personal concerns become the most important things in life, you are bound to suffer under the emotion of resentment, and resentment is just a confused state of mind. ¶The unfortunate thing is, resentment tends to attract even more circumstances worthy of even more resentment. So don't bother to resent, because you are only making yourself inferior to the person or the circumstance that you hold resentment for. That is right. Resentment, in all its heaviness, places your consciousness beneath that of the person you feel is imposing on you. ¶Be equal to whatever you meet! That is a better way to react to life. It is accomplished simply by meeting everything in understanding, by demanding understanding from within yourself. And if you feel that everything happening to you is a play of universal love and you are able to maintain that consciousness of universal love in yourself, then you are beyond the happenings of the world. Lifted in consciousness, you can see through and enjoy all the states of consciousness. The circumstances of your life will reflect this change. ¶Watch for those small incidents that imperceptively get under your skin and create an eruption a few days later. Little things that do not contribute creatively to your life are an indication that there is some kind of subconscious disturbance that you have not resolved. Look your nature right in the face in meditation, without squirming, and you will discover what the little disturbances are, some issue over which you are rationalizing, a small resentment or worry that is keeping a part of your mind confused, and thus necessarily, most of your circumstances confused.

Sunday
LESSON 105
Learn to Assimilate

People always tend to identify, instinctively, freedom with abandon. But the type of abandon that seeks personal gratification always gets you "tied up in a knot." Abandon instead your personal fears and desires by bringing your mind under the dominion of concentration in everything you do, and you, the real you, will become freed, released from the bonds of your own mind. Concentrate your mind when you are feeling confused, and you will bring peace to its disturbed states. Peace is control, and control is freedom. ¶If everyone gave half as much thought to the digestive power of the mind as we do to our stomachs, there would be fewer asylums. Are you able to assimilate and understand everything you put into your mind? Or do you carry experiences with you for days, mulling over the past? Some of the things that you see, hear, read about or think about impress you deeply. Other things do not. What kind of impressions do you carve upon your mind? Turning our backs on everything that may be unpleasant to us is not the answer, but if you observe your reactions as they are taking place and then later, the same day, turn a calm, detached eye to your experience, you will reenter understanding through the controlled state of your meditation. Do not wait for muddy waters of the mind to settle down in their own good time when you feel confused. You will only hasten your evolution by making your mind silent and composed by using a dynamic willpower to restore order when you feel least disposed to do so. Draw upon your resources. ¶People like patterns. The subconscious has a natural tendency to resist change. It is slow to realize that life is constant change. That is why it is so easy to fall into a rut. It requires a daring, spirited nature to call forth unused resources, to step out of the routine into a fuller and freer life. It requires daring to leave behind confused states of mind and bring forth new knowledge or wisdom from a meditation. Control is always silent power. Emotion, confusion, lack of control is noisy weakness. ¶Learn to assimilate. When you are engaged in conversation, do as the wise men of India do—pause after a while and let your thoughts assimilate. Have a view of the direction in which your mind is going, and you will have a good control over the direction of your life's circumstance. Rely on the Self. Find the permanency within you that has never changed through the ages, and you will realize that change is only in the ever-changing mind. Control your mind to the nth degree and you will realize your own natural state of Being, beyond all circumstances—the Self. You will go through many different tests to prove your own realization to yourself. Face each test graciously. Welcome each test and welcome each temptation that shows you the strength of your will over the chaotic senses. You have only to quiet all things of the mind to realize your identity with the eternity of God Śiva, the Spirit, the eternal Self within you.

Kuśalyahaṁ Sāṁpratameva

कुशल्यहं सांप्रतमेव

I'm All Right Right Now

Faces drawn in distress, hearts stricken with grief, the *devas* all together rushed and cried, "Lord! We bow to You." Thus they prayed, prostrating low. And He of unsurpassing renown said, "Arise; fear not."

TIRUMANTIRAM 352

Monday
LESSON 106
Everything Is Perfect!

Nowadays meditation is becoming very popular. Everyone is talking about being centered. If you're right in the *center* of yourself, you don't hear any of the noise or activity. You're just peaceful within yourself. It's only when we come into the cross-section, the cross-fire of life, that we feel we're not all right. Then we begin living in the great lie of the universe, the great fear that if we die we might be gone forever. We forget all of the wonderful philosophy and beautiful teachings that we've been studying, and we're just not all right. ¶My *satguru,* Yogaswāmī, made the very bold statement once, "There is not even one thing in this world that is not perfect!" You have to take a master like that very seriously. He was *satguru* for over 50 years in a very orthodox area of the world. "There is not even one thing in this world that is not perfect," he said. Some of us look around at the world, and we find plenty of things that are wrong with it. I never have. I have always thought this is a wonderful planet—wouldn't have missed it for anything. It is a great time now to be alive, even though some of us don't think so, even though the planet is somewhat polluted, and some people have a myriad of complaints. ¶Meditation is not an escape from the exterior world. We have to straighten ourselves out in the exterior world first before meditation and inner life can really be successful. Sometimes we worry about our job, our business, our family or even that we are not living as spiritually as we think we should. ¶This is my advice: gain the perspective first that it is a wonderful world, that there is nothing wrong in the world at all. Then ask yourself this question: "Am I not all right, right now, right this instant?" And answer, "I'm all right, right now." Declare that. Then a minute later in another now ask again, "Am I all right, right now?" Just keep asking this one question for the rest of your life, and you will always feel positive, self-assured and fine. This attitude eliminates fear, worry and doubt. ¶I discovered this formula when I was seven years of age. It came to me from the inside one day when I was worried about missing my favorite radio program. We were on our way home in a snow storm at Lake Tahoe, and I was afraid we might get stuck and I'd miss the program. I saw my mind, awareness, go off into the future, and I brought it back by telling myself, "I'm all right, right now. It hasn't happened yet." As it turned out, we didn't get stuck in the snow and I did get to listen to Captain Midnight. After that, I would say to myself, "I'm all right, right now," every time something came up that stretched my imagination into the future, into worry, or into the past when something disturbing lingered in my memory patterns that I did yesterday that maybe I shouldn't have done. Each time that happened I would say, "I'm all right, right now, am I not?" And I would have to always answer, "Of course, yes." I started doing this at the age of seven, and still today I am convinced that I am all right, right now!

Tuesday
LESSON 107
Lean on Your Own Spine

How can we stabilize the path on those days when it's just plain rough? The first thing to do on the path is to change our perspective of looking at life. Initially, as we come onto the inner path, we look at the map of the journey—we read books. A book is a map. We then make up our mind whether or not we want to make a change in our lifestyle and our perspective. Once we decide that we do wish to go on, a good way to begin is to reprogram the clay-like subconscious mind. Reprogram the negative habit patterns by firmly believing that you're really all right. ¶The second thing to accomplish is to learn to lean on your own spine. Everyone nowadays wants to lean on someone else. We lean on our families until they push us out into the world. Then we lean on our friends until they can't help us anymore. But still we keep on leaning. Then we lean on our therapist until we run out of money. This attitude of leaning on another is not the foundation needed for the delicate states of deep meditation to be sustained. ¶We have to lean on our own spine. But first we have to claim our spiritual heritage and feel "I'm all right, right now." By saying this and believing it, we pull the energies in just a little and become centered again. When we ask ourselves point blank, "Am I all right, right now?" we have to come up with a "Yes." Lean on your own spine. Feel the power in the spine. Feel the energy in the spine. The energy in the spine is not concerned with any fear or worry or doubt—not at all. It is a pure, powerful, blissful energy. Lean on it, and you will go crashing through into inner states of meditation. Things in the world will also work out right for you. You will be in the flow of life. You will have perfect timing. Beautiful things will begin to happen to you in the exterior world. Opportunities will open up for you where there were no opportunities before. People will become nice to you who ordinarily would not. All this and more begins to happen because mentally you are leaning on yourself, and people in general like you to do this. ¶Don't lean on a philosophy.

Don't lean on a *guru.* Don't lean on a teacher. Lean on your own spine and that power within it. Then the *guru* can be some help to you, for you will obey his directions when he speaks. The philosophy begins to come alive in you, for you can complement it with your own inner knowing.

Wednesday
LESSON 108
Realization Is the Key

What does it mean to "get centered" and to "be centered"? Actually, what it means is to feel the primal source within, to feel so centered that you are the center. And we always are something of what we feel, our hands or our legs or our bodies or our emotions or our desires. Most people on the path have the desire to get rid of their desires. It's an impossible battle. Have you ever tried to get rid of your desires? If you would stop trying to get rid of your desires, then you would be centered, because you then take the energy out of desire. You take awareness away from that world of desire, and you get right in the primal source of the energy which flows through the physical body. It flows through the emotional network, right through the intellectual mind. That primal source of energy is flowing through the spine in each and every one of us this very moment. Feel it? ¶The entire spiritual unfoldment process, oddly enough, is designed to throw you off center so that you have to work to pull yourself on center. First life throws you off center. You have all kinds of experiences. You make mistakes and, with your indomitable will, have to control that fluctuating awareness to get it right on center and be all right, right now. Feel that powerful energy flowing through every nerve current and be that energy rather than the fluctuating nerve current. Then, one day, when you really get good at it, you find a *guru*. You are firmly on center, and he tries to throw you off. ¶My *guru*, Yogaswāmī, would always throw his disciples off center and set them spinning. They had to work hard with themselves to get on center again. That strengthens the sinews and the muscles of man's becoming himself, becoming totally aware that he is aware and then controlling his mind by not allowing his awareness to get caught up in the vast illusion of the externalities of the mind. How's that? That's a good one—the vast illusion of the externalities of the mind! ¶What is this center? Well, it's like the inside of an empty glass. You know something is there, and when you're aware of it, you know that you're aware inside that empty glass. However, when you're aware of the glass itself, that's something else. When you're aware of the outside of the glass, that's something else again. When you're aware of the table the glass is sitting on, again that's something else. Now imagine you are like the glass. Become aware of the space inside. That is the tangible intangible you have to grasp. ¶The best way to work this is a very simple way. Let's try it now. Just open and close your hands and feel the muscles and the bones. Now feel an intangible something, an intangible energy, which is that life force, and soon you will feel a force within that. That is your force of awareness that gives the command to the life forces, to the muscles and sinews which open and close your hand. So, be that intangible force rather than the hand. Be the commander who commands the muscles to relax and tense, to open and close. It's an intangible reality. This you realize. You don't think about it. Your intellect cannot give it to you. Your instinct and emotions cannot give it to you. It's something you have to realize. When you grasp it, you start to unfold and awaken spirituality. It comes from the deeper *chakras*, the higher *chakras*. And it's very easy. You either have grasped it or you haven't grasped it. So, work with that and grasp that. Then the unfoldment process begins. Finally you begin to see light within the head, light within the body. You begin to have beautiful, beautiful inner experiences. Everybody these days wants to have profound inner experiences without the use of drugs, or without the use of anything but their own positive willpower. That's the goal of the unfoldment of the people of all nations today, according to my own poll. And it is the right and mature goal.

Thursday
LESSON 109
The Meditative Perspective

Someone asked, "What happens in a person's daily life when he first starts to meditate?" Many things can and do happen to you when you first start to meditate. For instance, your friends may think that you're withdrawing from them. They'll say you're afraid of the world so you're trying to get away from it all by meditating. Other people will quickly congratulate you and say, "You're finally on the path. We've waited a long time for you to find the path." Then you're taken into a certain social group who are also on the path, who have long since stopped meditating but do appreciate it when you do! They will talk to you so much about the path, they will finally get you to stop meditating, too. All sorts of things will happen to you. ¶The best thing to do when you begin meditation is to live in a good environment, among good people. Meditate alone and don't talk about it to anyone except the person who is helping you on the path. Do it inconspicuously, privately. It's an inner process, so it should be performed alone. Then only inner things will happen to you, and your outer life will become better and better and better. You'll get into a blissful flow with life—a perfect timing in your outer life. You will find yourself standing in the right place at the right time, every day. You will be in the energy flow with life, guided by your intuition. All the wonderful things that you should be experiencing on this planet will begin to come to you. ¶By changing yourself, you don't necessarily outwardly alter world events. But you do find where the world is and that it is functioning just as it should be, in a perfect balance of adjusting forces. From his position at the pinnacle of consciousness, my *guru*, Yogaswāmī, saw the harmony of life. From the top of the mountain looking down, you see the natural role of a raging ocean and the steep cliffs below—they are beautiful. From the bottom of the mountain, the ocean can appear ominous and the cliffs treacherous. Yogaswāmī looked at the universe from the inside out and saw that there is not one thing out of place or wrong. You can gain that perspective through meditation, which releases the human concepts of right and wrong, good and bad, easy and difficult. This is the perspective you find on the inside of yourself. ¶Man is in a perfect state of being right now. The great sages and *ṛishis* found this truth. They were not more perfect than their contemporaries, just more aware. You are perfect this very moment. You are all that you will ever be. If you don't see it that way, then you live in a difficult state of affairs, striving toward perfection and being imperfect along the way.

Friday
LESSON 110
We Always Have a Choice

Awareness of perfection is attained by sitting down and arriving at the state of expanded cosmic consciousness inside yourself. It's there only to be discovered. You can do that in nine minutes, nine hours, nine days or nine years. Take as long as you like. The fact remains that deep inside you is perfection. So, you see, you have a choice. You can remain in the valley, live in fear of the stormy ocean of life and death, or you can scale the nearby mountain and see from the top how it is from that perspective. Either way, you and everyone in the world are all right in the now. ¶The mystic lives within himself and deals positively with the events and forces outside himself. He is always consciously striving to realize that limitless Reality within him. That is his practice. Yet, he welcomes the challenges of the world, not as a *karma* forced upon him against his will but as his own self-created *dharma.* If he is really a mystic, he doesn't run away from these challenges. He inwardly knows that life's daily difficulties bring forth his inner strength in response to them. He sees the underlying purpose of life. He accepts and doesn't reject. He searches for understanding, for the lesson that lies behind each experience instead of resenting the experience, which then creates another subconscious barrier for him. He knows that most problems are with man and the way he looks at things. So, the mystic doesn't need to retreat from the world. ¶The same process continues regardless of where he goes. He can be as peaceful or as disturbed in New York City as in a secluded Himālayan valley. It all depends on what goes on within him. Nor should he be emotionally concerned with the problems of the world in which he finds himself. A concert *sitārist* is doing himself and his fellow man no good by saying, "How can I play so beautifully when everyone else plays so poorly?" Similarly, the mystic cannot take the attitude, "How can I be peaceful and content when the world is in such a mess?" We need beautiful music and we need beautiful, peaceful beings. ¶Actually, the mystic sees the world as a conglomerate of adjusting forces, and through this perspective he is not emotionally involved in these forces. The world is a mirror of ourselves and is perfectly all right to the man who is content within himself. But you have to find this out for yourself, because unless you experience it, nothing I say will convince you that everything you have been through and are going through is wonderful and a fulfillment of the great pattern of your life.

Saturday
LESSON 111
Knowing Who Is the "I Am"

Even a great soul faces difficulties, but he does not take them personally. Generally people take problems too personally by identifying closely with them. When they experience anger, they are angry. When they experience bliss, they are blissful. The mystic identifies with the experiencer instead of the experience. He sees himself as pure awareness that travels in the mind. When he is in San Francisco, he is not San Francisco. Similarly, when he is in anger, he is not anger. He says to himself, "I am pure energy. I am the spiritual energy that floods through mind and body. I am not the body, the mind or the emotions. I am not the thoughts I think or the experiences I experience." Thus, he molds a new identity of himself as a free being who can travel anywhere in the mind. Such a person is always at the top of the mountain. ¶We have to examine this concept of who we are. When we begin to totally feel all right about ourself, the meaning of the word *I* begins to change. *I* no longer means the body of us. *I* means energy, awareness and willpower. Soon we gain the total truth that we are living in the body, but we are not the body we live in. Examine the word *I* and honestly see what it means to you. Does it mean the physical body? Does it mean the emotions? Does it mean the intellect? Does it mean the spiritual energy? ¶When we forget who we are, who we really are, we live in a consciousness of time and space, and we relate to the future, to the external us, to the past, and to our subconscious internal us. This can be rather confusing. Most people are therefore confused and seek to distract themselves in an effort to find peace. A conscious awareness of now only comes when we remember who we really are. This doesn't mean we cannot plan for the future or benefit ourselves by reviewing experiences of the past. It simply means that we always remember that we are the essence of all energy, the source. ¶Return to the source. Merge with Śiva. At the source there is always peace. The key to this entire practice is to become consciously aware of energy. In this constant remembering we have the feeling of being the center of the universe, with the whole world functioning around us. To be fully anchored in the knowledge of the source of our being, the eternal now can and must be a constant experience. It's easy to live in the now if you work with yourself a little every day and concentrate on what you are doing each moment.

Sunday
LESSON 112
Living in the Eternal Now

To begin to work toward establishing yourself in the eternal now, first limit time and space by not thinking about or discussing events that happened more than four days past or will happen more than four days in the future. This keeps awareness reined in, focused. Be aware. Ask yourself, "Am I fully aware of myself and what I'm doing right now?" ¶Once you have gained a little control of awareness in this way, try to sit quietly each day and just be. Don't think. Don't plan. Don't remember. Just sit and be in the now. That's not as simple as it sounds, for we are accustomed to novelty and constant activity in the mind and not to the simplicity of being. Just sit and be the energy in your spine and head. Feel the simplicity of this energy in every atom of yourself. Think energy. Don't think body. Don't think about yesterday or tomorrow. They don't exist, except in your ability to reconstruct the yesterdays and to create the tomorrows. Now is the only time. This simple exercise of sitting and being is a wonderful way to wash away the past, but it requires a little discipline. You have to discipline every fiber of your nerve system, work with yourself to keep the power of awareness expanded. Regular practice of meditation will bring you intensely into the eternity of the moment. Practice supersedes philosophy, advice, psychology and all pacifiers of the intellect. We have to practice to keep awareness here and now. If you find yourself disturbed, sit down and consciously quiet the forces in yourself. Don't get up until you have completely quieted your mind and emotions through regulating the breath, through looking out at a peaceful landscape, through seeking and finding understanding of the situation. This is the real work of meditation that is not written much about in books. If you can live in the eternity of now, your life will be one of peace and fulfillment. ¶Visualize yourself sitting on top of a mountain. There is no place to go except inside yourself. If you were to go down the northern side of the mountain, you would be going into the future and its ramifications, which are only conceptual. If you were to go down the southern side, you would be going into the past and its similar recorded ramifications. So, you stay where you are, at the pinnacle of consciousness, well balanced between past and future. Everything is in its rightful place in the master plan of evolution, so you sit, just watching, sensing the clarity of your own perfect being, learning to live in spiritual consciousness every day. That is your heritage on this Earth.

Ananta Vartamānam

अनन्तवर्तमानम्

The Eternal Now

They traverse the spheres of sun and moon, *piṅgalā* and *iḍā,* and see visions of past, present and future. And in that full moon day the nectar, *amṛita,* ripens. Until lowering into the external mind from *kuṇḍalinī* heights, time stands still.

TIRUMANTIRAM 875

Monday
LESSON 113
You Only Have a Minute

"You have only just a minute, only sixty seconds in it. Didn't want it, forced upon you, can't refuse it, didn't seek it, didn't choose it, it is up to you to use it. You must suffer if you lose it, give account if you abuse it. Just a tiny little minute, but eternity is in it. For not to love is not to live, and not to give is not to live." There is really very little to be said intellectually about the eternal now. You have to live in it, and in living in it you discover a higher state of consciousness than you have experienced in your life. Because the vibration of the eternal now is so very high, part of your mind and nature does not like to experience the security of the eternal now, which is really the height of security. It takes practice to maintain a continued experience of the eternal now. ¶Can you visualize yourself, right at this instant, balanced on the top of a tall tree? If the tree were to bend too far forward, you would fall to the ground, or down into time and thought. If it were to bend too far back, you would again fall. Balanced on the top of this tree, you can look out over the countryside and enjoy everything you see. But if you stop to think about one thing of the past, you would become so engrossed in what you are thinking about that you again fall to the ground. You find that you cannot live in a thinking consciousness balanced so high. Here you live in the eternal now, with great awareness of what is around you and within you, but with no thought on it. ¶Can you feel like this? Right now you are *here.* Right now nothing else matters. You are aware. You are alive, and you are in eternity. Finding the eternal now is a vibration even more powerful than that of sound or light, for you are in the consciousness of Being—being intensely aware, being very alive. In that state of consciousness you can see that when you begin to think, it is like climbing down the tree and walking along through the forest. On the ground you cannot see the forest for the trees. On top of the tree you can see the entire forest and enjoy it. In the eternal now you find awareness in every part of your body, every fiber of your consciousness. Your life depends upon your awareness! Here you can enjoy seeing the birds fly by, the waterfall, the countryside. ¶You can enjoy all that, but you dare not stop to think upon the flight of one bird, because you would become too engrossed in thought and fall into a lower state of consciousness. That bird might remind you of a pet bird you had at home, and the thinking mind would go on and on, landing you on the ground. When you become aware and start living in eternity, in the eternal now, you find that eternity is within you. Then you can see there is no life. Nor is there any death. You have transcended even the laws of reincarnation in that state, holding the consciousness of eternity, for you are beyond the soul which reincarnates and creates a new form around itself.

Tuesday
LESSON 114
Torn Between Past and Future

What is the instant? That is what we have to discover through a moment of concentration. What is the moment? We all know what the past is—many people live in the past, over and over again, and they never catch up with the present. Other people live in the future—but of course when they do, they are really only living in the past, too, and they never find the present either. ¶Just as an example, how many times have you gone to the temple without being fully there? Part of you was there, part of you was living in the past, part of you was trying to live in the future; and there you were, emoting over the things that happened that should never have happened, and fearful of things that might happen in the future, which probably won't happen unless you continue being fearful of their happening until you create them! ¶Do you know that the ability to live right now, in the instant, is a spiritual power, reflecting the awakening of the soul and requiring a subconscious control of the mind? Your soul is never bothered with the things that disturb the rest of the mind! The mind lives in the past, and the mind tries to live in the future. But when you quiet your mind, you live in the present. You are living within your soul, or the higher state of your mind which is undisturbed by the things of time. ¶Also, when you live in the present, you eliminate fears, worries and doubts. Of course, you might feel a little out of place for a while, as if you weren't anybody, if for years and years you have been accustomed to making fears, worries and doubts your cherished possessions—more important to you than anything. There are people who just wouldn't know who they were if you took away from them their fears, worries and doubts. But if you want to *be* somebody, something, a state of being, you want to live in the eternal now. ¶There is a simple formula for attaining the eternal now. If you can remember it, you can center yourself within yourself very quickly and experience living right this instant. Imagine yourself now, worried, bothered and disturbed, and in the midst of your disturbance say to yourself, "I am all right, right now. Just this instant, I am all right." What a shock to the disturbed part of your mind! It will not only be shocked, it will be shattered out of its disturbance when you declare the truth that you are all right in the eternal now.

Wednesday
LESSON 115
I Am All Right, Right Now

It is one thing to say "I am all right, right now," and it is another thing to feel it. Can you feel that you are all right, right now? Can you really believe it? Can you hold that feeling, so that this affirmation becomes permeated through your subconscious mind? Let this feeling permeate so deeply through your subconscious mind that it begins working within you, the same way your involuntary subconscious keeps your heart beating and the other processes of your body going. ¶"I'm all right, right now." Let the feeling of these words vibrate within you. Then every time you abide in the luxury of worry—and the luxury of worry is one luxury you cannot afford—say to yourself, "I'm all right, right now," and forget about where you are going, forget about where you have been and just be where you are, where your physical body is, in its immediate surroundings. ¶When you do that, you find that where you were going and what you were worried about has to do with the egotistical you—your pride and the various qualities that you hasten to rid yourself of when you think you should improve yourself. So, it is really very practical to live now and be all right in all the nows. But remember, since living in the eternal now lifts you into a higher state of consciousness than you have been accustomed to, you have to continue to feel that you are all right, right now. When you continue in the consciousness of the eternal now, something mysterious and wonderful begins to happen—your soul, your superconscious, begins to work out your spiritual destiny. When you quiet your mind, and only when you quiet your mind, you give your soul a chance. What difference does it make if you do have problems? They will work themselves out if you can keep the confusion of your lower states of mind out of the way. ¶Visualize your soul now as a shaft of light. Visualize your mind as various layers surrounding that soul, covering up the brilliancy of that light. If you live in the layers around the soul, which only cover up the brilliancy of the light, you add to the confusion around the soul. But you can live in that shaft of light. By realizing that you are all right this instant, that light of your soul has a chance to shine through the surrounding layers of the mind just a little, enough to calm your future. For your future is made in the present, in the eternal now.

Thursday
LESSON 116
Progress Takes Persistence

When you find yourself with your mind calmed, your future automatically works itself out. I have had so many people ask me questions, seeking advice. I very seldom give advice, because very few people really want it. The majority have already made up their own minds, and what they are looking for is permission to go ahead and do what they have already decided upon. But if a person asks a question three, four, five times, then you know they are seeking advice. It is a rare person, however, who can take that advice. ¶Often enough some people may bring to you their problems. They tell you all their troubles, and you tell them how to work them out, because you can see a little bit farther than they can due to the fact their minds are confused and yours is calm. But they end up by taking their problems right back again, and instead of working them out, they only add to the confusion. That is like going to a university, sitting in on a class, skipping the rest of the classes and expecting to pass the final exam when you have had only one lesson. It does not work there, and it doesn't work in spiritual life either. ¶There are those who run from one teacher to another, staying with each one only long enough to find enough fault with him or his organization to be able to avoid the teaching and to run on to another teacher. These people are far from the stability of living in the eternal now, for as soon as they find fault with themselves and face overcoming their problems, they have to blame it all on someone else and run away. ¶Spiritual unfoldment is not unlike a university in this sense: you have to go through with all it has to offer for a number of years. If you skip from one university to another and back again and expect to graduate, you find that you are always being set back before you can go ahead! It just does not work. ¶It takes the average person some time before he can bring his entire mind and all his actions into the focus of the eternal now. Just hearing about it is not going to give you a birth into that state of consciousness. You will have to struggle and strive to hold the eternal now. It will take constant practice of spiritual principles to permeate the grosser layers of the mind with the clarity of the eternal now.

Friday
LESSON 117
The Quest For Security

You have at one time or another watched yourself pick up a new idea: "I shall do this and this and this!" Then, because you had a reaction over something, your enthusiasm died; you forgot the idea and bounded off onto something else. This is the way the mind works. You forget when you reach a part of your mind that has no inclination to understand. That is a part of the instinctive mind. If you run up against a habit pattern that is too strong for your will, it is like going along in a straight line and suddenly ricocheting off in another direction. But while this happens for a long time, after a lot of study and constant self-discipline—without which the study does not do too much good—the principles of the spiritual life finally become permeated through your entire being, and you become close to your soul in the eternal now. ¶This week, when you think about it, you will say to yourself, "I'm all right, right now," and you will feel uplifted in knowing that this is so. But next week you will forget to do it. It makes you feel too complete, too secure. And being too secure is like being insecure, isn't that true? ¶I met a family from the South recently that was having quite a time trying to adjust to the security of success! The husband has been a salesman all of his life, only just meeting the more or less routine needs of his family, three girls and one boy. He and his wife had always nurtured a desire for a lot of money so that the family could live in complete security, and every month for years they had put away just a little savings, with an eye to making the type of investment, at the right time, which would satisfy their dream. ¶Not long ago they found themselves able to buy into land with "remote possibilities of oil." By spending the last of their savings to initiate drilling, by remote chance they did strike oil, bringing them almost immediate affluence through a chain of circumstances that has changed the entire pattern of their life. Now they feel more insecure than ever. When their money finally came in abundance, they found they really did not know what to do with it. They were worried because they had no experience in handling it. They felt totally transplanted, totally insecure in their apparent security. ¶After several conversations, they began to see that they had found their security in the desire for money; feeling that they did not have enough had become an integral part of the family's subconscious. Because they were not able to live in the eternal now, they could not catch up with their new condition of life. Many people who find security in material desires are not able to become accustomed to something they are not already acquainted with.

Saturday
LESSON 118
Be a Friend To Yourself

In the process of spiritual unfoldment, which brings you closer and closer to merging into the eternal now, you have to become accustomed to a new you. Become acquainted with yourself, become an old friend to yourself, and you will find living in the moment, in the inspiration of now, becoming second nature to the new you. Remember, it takes time to become an old friend to yourself, the same amount of time it would take to acquire a mature friendship with someone else. ¶In our beginning meditations on the Śaivite path of enlightenment, we must establish firmly in our intellect the basic truth of "the now." Now and its seeming counterparts, "then and when," are only ambiguous to us when the instinctive energies are scattered and unrelated and when there is absolutely no self-discipline of the vital forces which, when accomplished, harnesses man's individual awareness in such a way that he becomes, over long periods of time, actually aware that he is aware, as well as being aware that his awareness is entangled in the externalities of mind due to an eventful scattering of instinctive forces. Furthermore, his awareness persists in the intuitive know-how and ability to disentangle itself from that external state as it becomes yanked back, deep within its natural state, the eternity of the moment. This ability is acquired through regular and regulated practice of *yoga*, diaphragmatic breathing and simple, yet profound, inner, mental, intuitive practices performed daily at the same time. ¶Having preceded the practice of *yoga* by firmly establishing in the subconscious realm of the mind the inevitability of the permanency of the moment, called now, through all areas of thought, there is one dispelling power, and that is man's personal ability to withdraw his awareness from past and future and, from that static state, view out upon all areas of thought rather than wallow in them. We transgress our heritage on this planet through spending inordinate amounts of time in past and future and the mixture of the two. The penance is misery, confusion and sorrow, as we stumble over the furniture in a darkened room. Turn on the light, claim your heritage and live in the moment. Center awareness deep within the head. Sit in the center of the room. Enjoy the artifacts, rest in the center of the mind and view the panorama. Only by experiencing and acquiring the ability to reexperience, through the practice of *yoga,* the eternity of the moment can the aspirant allow deeper and deeper access to the fullness of his being.

Sunday
LESSON 119
Finding the Eternal Now

Before beginning a new project, meditate. Collect up the ramified forces flowing through and around your body and bring them all to one point by regulating the energies through the control of breath, *prāṇāyāma.* Thus, arriving at the now, if only for an instant, begins the auspiciousness of the moment, after which the project should be begun. By thus meditating and through this practice, inner results infiltrate worldly undertakings, and the opposing forces succumb to the clarity of your perceptions derived through initially being aware in the now, if only for a few seconds. ¶When you are experiencing the totality of the moment, you are not aware of the past, nor are you aware of the future or anything within the externalities of the mind. You are aware of the *ākāśa,* the primal substance of the superconsciousness of the mind. You are able to have a continuity of intuitive findings within it and gain much knowledge from within yourself. For the beginner on the path, the concept of the eternity of the moment is refreshing, and he does touch into it occasionally when he tries to meditate. This is encouraging to him, and he gains a new impetus to pursue his inner life more courageously than before. ¶It is impossible to intellectually try to experience the here-and-now state of consciousness, as it is impossible to describe the feeling one would have standing on the top of a tall mountain. Only through experience can these transcendental states be known. Therefore, become perfect in *yoga.* Your rewards will be great and your future sublime. ¶As the first attempt in finding the infinite reality of the eternity of the moment, sit quietly, draw all of your faculties into the center of your head and try to see the glowing white light there. When this light is seen, a high-pitched sound might also be heard, and you are then in the eternity of the moment. Bringing oneself to the repetition of this practice successfully and systematically, day after day, month after month, year after year is the *yoga* to be practiced to merge awareness deeper and deeper into superconsciousness. ¶Now, you can think and you can feel, and feeling is more convincing. When your mind is disturbed, your feeling is personality-centered. When your mind is quiet, your subtle feeling is superconscious, spiritually aware. Feel that you are the complete master of your body, of your mind and of your emotions. Can you really feel that? Feel the life within you. Feel your will dominating your mind. Your will is your soul in action. You may think about your will as being your soul in action, but you must feel the real you, the real "I am." Tell your subconscious mind twenty-four hours a day that this is true: that you are the master of body, mind, and emotions. For in one instant of realizing this, knowing this, feeling this to be true, you will find that you are all right, right now, in this instant, and you will find yourself entirely free from fear, worry, and doubt. Live completely, regardless of your circumstances—then the circumstances in which you divide yourself will adjust themselves to become as beautiful as the beauty of your soul.

Prema Vidhisāraḥ

प्रेम विधिसारः

Love Is the Sum of the Law

The ignorant prate that love and Śiva are two,
but none of them knows that love alone is Śiva.
When men know that love and Śiva are the same,
love as Śiva they ever remain.

TIRUMANTIRAM 270

Monday
LESSON 120
What Is Pure Love?

Love is the sum of all the spiritual laws. We may say that love is the heart of the mind. Anything that comes before you in life can be conquered through universal love, a force which is a demonstration of the soul. Universal love has nothing to do with emotional infatuation, attachment or lust. It flows freely through the person whose mind is unclouded by resentment, malice, greed and anger. But in persons whose minds are partially out of control and under the control of another, the force of the soul ends up as infatuation or attachment. ¶Pure love is a state of Being. Whereas everyone is running around trying to get love, it is found in giving. When a person begins to lose the idea of his own personality through concern for others, he will attract a like response to himself. The outgoing force of the soul in action brings freedom to the lower states of mind. The instinctive person is ordinarily so preoccupied with his own self, so wrapped up in his own shell, that he cannot give a thought to the welfare of another. He cannot give anything of himself. Such a person usually feels sorry for himself and finds other people unloving and unresponsive. He is still far from any realization of the Self within. ¶The unfortunate person who is burdened by resentment, for instance, feels that the world owes him more kindness than he is receiving. When he loses his resentment for the world simply by becoming interested in people, the world will once again reflect back the expression of this soul force, known as universal love. You may visualize this pure state of love as a force of light flooding out from the center of your Being. If you place sheets of paper too close to a light source, you temporarily block the light and scorch the paper. People are always scorching themselves by holding up against their own "inner-light paper" qualities such as resentment, malice and greed. Spontaneous acts of benevolence and selflessness, prompted by a will to perfection, lift the striving soul in feeling and begin slowly to remove the coverings from the light which is the soul. You can't expect immediate action, of course, because you may still carry the seeds of destructive qualities within you, and it is these seeds which continue to hold man in lower states of consciousness.

Tuesday
LESSON 121
Love Conquers Selfishness

The action and reaction of the self-centered state of mind creates tension and discord in mind and body. Often when the diaphragm is tight, the muscles are tense, breathing is difficult and your whole disposition is on edge. A person attains relaxation and peace through a benevolent act in which he loses himself in another's happiness. The cycles of tension and release, tension and release—which are constantly given birth to in the instinctive and intellectual state of mind—are only broken as the unfolding soul expresses itself in devotion, breaking up the crust of personal concern and hurt feelings. ¶Love may also be thought of as the full expression of the intuitive mind, a continuing flow from the source of Being. Most people would not be able to withstand the reaction to this force were it to be fully released within them. To suddenly relieve a person of all tension would be like making a poor man rich overnight. The instinctive mind feels lost and insecure under the impact of any sudden change in evolution. As the soul, the superconscious mind, or the light of God, begins to shine through the rest of the mind, the mind will either become reactionary or cooperative. Some people have a terrible fight within themselves as the soul begins to shine forth, and yet their only lasting satisfaction in life is in the outpouring of their individual soul qualities. ¶Sometimes students of Inner Being are able to control their actions or their speech when they become disturbed, but the thought force projected by their suppressed sulking is just as negatively effective. Seeking to understand the condition that has upset you will give control of the negative force and eventually lift you into the state of love which conquers all things. ¶Of course, the practice of understanding must begin at home. You must train yourself to know where you are in consciousness at all times. When you can become fully aware of the states of consciousness through which you pass, there will be no one whom you cannot understand, no one with whom you could not communicate through the medium of love. Until you learn the operation of this law as the sum of all laws, you will continue to harbor contention, to prefer argument and to walk the path of difference. Through *bhakti yoga*, the *yoga* of devotion, the combative mind becomes erased, absorbed into the consciousness of the One Self—the Being permeating all beings.

Wednesday
LESSON 122
Finding Your Security Within

With the help of devotion, you can soar within. You can not only pull away detachedly from unwholesome areas of the mind, but it is possible to keep yourself in an inward state of expanded consciousness. What is it all about when we are burdened? This is only the external odic force fields of magnetic energy in the area of the mind called the world and the subconscious. When we are totally aware in this limited state of consciousness, we have the feeling of being burdened. When we are aware in this state of mind, it is impossible to seek out an explanation or to accept an explanation from another. How many times during your life have you explained to your friends who were totally aware in the external area of the mind the reasons for their being there and the way to release themselves from these areas and soar within? You knew they knew what you were talking about, but they wouldn't accept what you had to say, possibly because they hadn't thought of if first. The magnetic areas of the odic force field of the external mind are that strong. They were burdened by the conscious and subconscious limited areas of the mind. Awareness had become submerged. ¶The only real security comes from within. Gain security, and if your security comes from within you, you become unburdened. However, if one gains his security from the external mind, then of course he will not accept help if help is given. What is help anyway, but man sharing with man? Who is the helper and who is the one who is helped? You have often heard teachers say, "Every time I give instruction, I learn more than my students." Is the teacher giving the opportunity to the students to learn, or are the students giving the opportunity to the teacher? Obviously, it is quite mutual. Who, then, is the great helper? The external ego does not give us help or assistance. It only ramifies awareness into even more externalized areas of the mind. The mind of light, your superconsciousness, is the only area of the mind where permanent bliss, security and steadfastness occur when awareness flows through it, even in the outer areas of your nature. The mind of light is the only thing that can uplift awareness, shuffling off the burdens of the external mind. It is the great teacher.

Thursday
LESSON 123
The Power Of Devotion

For eleven years I led a *bhakti* pilgrimage, a devotional pilgrimage, to the top of Mount Tamalpais in California, the first Sunday of every month. I never missed one. The devotees, in looking over three cities with me, could intuit that within each city there were problems. Each home in each city contained an area of the mind that was problem-ridden. ¶Those who had the devotion went to the top of the mountain. Hence, the opportunity to expand their awareness for an hour or so and look over the external states of the mind. There they set their pattern for meditation for the ensuing month. It takes great dedication, devotion and *bhakti* to disentangle awareness from that which it is aware of, to flow into and become aware of expanded areas of mind. The rewards are great. We are able to look over and through our expanded vision the totality of the exterior area of our mind and intuitively know the answer to the experiences that we are going through. ¶This may seem difficult to comprehend, but it is really very simple. When awareness is burdened in the exterior area of the mind, we simply release awareness from that area of the mind that it is aware of. Release the burden—but not by taking on more burdens or trying to find out the whys and wherefores of it all. In other words, we alleviate the pressures that awareness and our nerve system feel because of being involved in the exterior area of the mind and thus become devoted to our own superconsciousness. The power of devotion, love, *bhakti*, melts the odic-magnetic force fields, releasing awareness to soar into superconsciousness, the mind of light. And then we can focus, superconsciously, from our intuitive state of mind and look at the exterior world from a new perspective, from right within the very core of life itself. It does not take long. It does take one quality though—devotion—found in the *yoga* called *bhakti.* ¶What is devotion? Devotion involves going deep enough to understand the great principle of the fulfillment of one's duty. Who must be devoted to whom? Members of a family to their temple, a wife to her husband, a husband to his religion, children to their parents, the student to the teacher, the disciple to the *guru.* No matter what you are studying—mathematics, chemistry, philosophy, cybernetics, sociology, religion, a lifestyle—the professor should represent what you are going to be. That is why you are studying with him. Only through devotion will you be totally aware, open, free, inspired. Only through devotion will you become what you aspire to unfold within yourself.

Friday
LESSON 124
Bring Forth Good Qualities

Where do you get devotion? Not from the teacher. The teacher is only an awakener. He imparts knowledge to you, a vibration to you. He awakens you to the possibilities of the grandeur within yourself. Can a professor of geometry give you the total knowledge of that subject? No, he cannot. He can only show you the ways you can unfold the totality of the subject matter from within yourself. He gives you certain formulas and laws. You have to take them in and in and in where the solutions are. ¶How do we unburden awareness from the external areas of the mind through devotion? Our attitude has to be correct. Only in that way can we manifest the qualities that we want to manifest. Everyone has many different qualities and tendencies in his nature. Some are flowing freely. Others are suppressed. Others are repressed. Some are active and others temporarily inactive. Friends bring out the qualities and mirror the inner tendencies of each of us. When a person changes his life, he also changes his group of friends. It happens automatically. One group of qualities becomes inactive, and another group of tendencies begins to manifest itself in him. Our tendencies formulate our attitudes. Our attitudes, once consistently held, stabilize our perspective in looking at life. ¶The first step in unburdening awareness from the externalized odic-magnetic areas of the mind is to cause a *bhakti*, a love, a devotion, right within the nerve currents of your body. This is the first step. Get in love with the inner self. Begin to study the qualities of your nature, your tendencies. Write them all down on a piece of paper. Choose the ones that you wish to use and cross out the ones that you do not care for. Choose your qualities and tendencies as carefully as you choose your clothing. ¶Many people spend much time thinking about what they are going to wear. Hour after hour they are shopping in the stores. If you were to add up over a period of one year's time the number of hours they stood in front of the mirror dressing the physical form, it would be quite surprising. How about the inside? Do we dress up the inside, too? We can, you know. Choose the qualities and tendencies to wear this spring and in the summer and fall, too. Pick carefully the smile on your face. Let it come from deep within. We can dress up the face in all sorts of ways, but the qualities of our nature are those which really shine through. We can paint over greed and resentment, but the quality of *bhakti* devotion and love will shine through all paint. It is its own decoration. Dress up the inside. Make the qualities and tendencies of your nature match the outside. You will be surprised. You will be keeping awareness hovering, in inner space, like the hummingbird over the flower, looking out at the material world and seeing it as a flower. This is one of the great duties on the path. Bring forth the great qualities of devotion through the *yoga* called *bhakti.*

Saturday
LESSON 125
Live Your Inner Qualities

Devotion is the keynote to the fulfillment of duty. "What is duty?" "What are my duties?" Take a piece of paper. List all of your duties, all of the promises that you have made. A duty is very important. Devotion and duty lay the foundation for the spiritual unfoldment that everyone is talking about in this age. We do not find the path in books. We find the path in how we handle our individual lives. ¶Paint a mental picture of yourself as you want to be. Everyone has an ideal. You want to be kind; you want to be helpful at all times; you never want to miss an opportunity to serve or to help your fellow man. You want to be spontaneous, to be gracious, to be pure and direct in word, thought and deed. These are the qualities. The tendencies are there, for you are on the path. This is your new inner wardrobe. Wear it and wear it well. ¶How do you put on this wardrobe? Sit quietly and breathe deeply, eyes closed, and review the wardrobe, the qualities, the tendencies of the greatness within you. You will begin to feel that love, that softening, that bliss of inner peace which is there. ¶In the *yoga* called *bhakti*, you release an energy through the physical body, through the nerve system, from the central source of all energy. This energy is a constant flow, filling and thrilling every nerve current, muscle and sinew of your physical body. It will be a constant flow as you express the qualities that you have chosen. This constant flow of energy will permeate your physical body as a blessing to the world. This is the life of one who is in the fulfillment of the *yoga* called *bhakti*. ¶*Bhakti yoga* is the awakening of the love nature through the practice of devotion and giving. Giving begins new life. Giving is an essential for spiritual unfoldment, for until we give and give abundantly, we don't really realize that we are not the giver; we are just a channel for giving. Abundance, materially and spiritually, comes to you when you cease to be attached to it, when you can take as much joy over a little pebble as you could over a precious ruby. The power of giving is a very great power, a great power that comes to you through *yoga*. You hear about *yoga* powers—the power of levitation, the power of suspended animation—but the truly great powers are the power of giving, the power of concentration, the power of the subconscious control over your mind, body and emotions, the power of universal love—practical powers that can be used today.

Sunday
LESSON 126
Be a Master Of Giving

Why can't you spiritually unfold until you learn to give and give and give and give until it hurts? Because that hurt is your block. Many people give and they give generously, up to the point where they feel, "I have given a lot," or "I have given too much," or "I gave as much as I can give," or "I will give more when I can," or "I enjoy giving and I used to give a lot, but I can't give so much right now." These are the little blocks that come up within man's nature and undermine man's nature and bind him down to the depths of the negative areas of the subconscious mind. And then he can't progress. Why can't he progress? Because he can't have devotion unless giving unfolds as his light. Now, the man who has unfolded into giving doesn't qualify his giving, he doesn't even think about it. If he doesn't have a lot of material things to give, if he is going through circumstances which do not permit him, then what does he do? He gives what he can, in devotion, little things, to make people happy, little things to progress activity, little things to progress himself. He gives what he can, and he gives more than he can. And when something is given him, that gives him the power to give again. That is the great law. That is the great unfoldment. ¶When a seeker has unfolded to the power of giving, he doesn't think about himself so much, because he is spontaneous. He is always looking for an opportunity to do something good for someone else. When someone has not unfolded into giving, he thinks about himself a great deal, and he calculates his giving, because he has to give in proportion to something else. And by giving in proportion to something else, he is creating his future limitation. He is saying "I am just this big, and I will always be just this big because that is as far as my consciousness can go, just that much. So, I will hold my consciousness within this grave." But it doesn't work that way. The consciousness is not like that, because by limiting your giving, by limiting your consciousness, as time goes by it will shrink. And it will shrink until you don't know it. Your friends will notice, but you won't. It will shrink and shrink and shrink. And that is one of the things your friends won't tell you, that your consciousness has shrunk, and that you are not the same as you used to be. ¶This works in reverse, too. The person who has a heart full of joy, even if he doesn't have material possessions to speak of, always finds something to give; he gives what he has. He knows that he is not the gift, that he is not the giver at all, and when something comes his way, he gives of it freely. He is a vehicle for giving, and finally he is so full of abundance in consciousness that he knows he is not the giver, and he fulfills *bhakti yoga* in his life. If you give and give freely and spontaneously, you feel good about it, and if you do it again, you feel even better about it. But if you give and give selfishly, you feel bad about it, and if you continue to do so, you'll feel worse. If you give and give spontaneously, you will awaken your inner nature, and spiritual power will flow through you, and you will merge with God within you. But if you give, and give selfishly, by hanging onto your gift after you have given it, you close the door to spirituality. Giving is in many, many forms. The best way is to rely on the incomparable law of *karma.* Give freely, and your gift will come back to you often doubled soon after the gift is given. Then this opens the door for another gift to be given out. Your intuitive nature will tell you how you can give, when and where, and soon you will find yourself giving every minute of every day in the most spontaneous ways.

That which is neither conscious nor unconscious, which is invisible, impalpable, indefinable, unthinkable, unnameable, whose very essence consists of the experience of its own self, which absorbs all diversity, is tranquil and benign, without a second, which is what they call the fourth state—that is the *ātman*. This it is which should be known.

Atharva Veda, Muṇḍaka Upanishad 7. VE, 723

He who dwells in the light, yet is other than the light, whom the light does not know, whose body is the light, who controls the light from within—He is the *ātman* within you.

Śukla Yajur Veda, Bṛihadāraṇyaka Upanishad 3.7.14. VE, 708

The Self cannot be attained by the weak, nor by the careless, nor through aimless disciplines. But if one who knows strives by right means, his soul enters the abode of God.

Atharva Veda, Muṇḍaka Upanishad 3.2.4. BO UPM, 81

With his mind purified, with his consciousness purified, with patience, thinking "I am He," and with patience when he has attained the consciousness of "I am He," he is established by wisdom in the supreme *ātman* who is to be known in the heart.

Śukla Yajur Veda, Paiṅgala Upanishad 4.9. VE, 441

The ten abstinences are nonviolence, truth, nonstealing, chastity, kindness, rectitude, forgiveness, endurance, temperance in food and purity.

Śukla Yajur Veda, Tṛishikhi Brāhmaṇa 32-33. YM, 19

The cosmic soul is truly the whole universe, the immortal source of all creation, all action, all meditation. Whoever discovers Him, hidden deep within, cuts through the bonds of ignorance even during his life on Earth.

Atharva Veda, Muṇḍaka Upanishad 2.1.10. BASED ON PR, 682

As the sun, the eye of the whole world, is not sullied by the external faults of the eyes, so the one inner soul of all things is not sullied by the sorrow in the world, being external to it.

Kṛishṇa Yajur Veda, Kaṭha Upanishad 5.11. BO UPH, 357

Therefore, he who knows this, having become peaceful, controlled, detached, patient and concentrated, sees the *ātman* in himself and sees all in the *ātman*. Evil does not overcome him, but he overcomes all evil; evil does not consume him, but he consumes all evil. Free from evil, free from passion, free from doubt, he becomes a knower of Brahman.

Śukla Yajur Veda, Bṛihadāraṇyaka Upanishad 4.4.23. VE, 718

The Self resides within the lotus of the heart. Knowing this, consecrated to the Self, the sage enters daily that holy sanctuary. Absorbed in the Self, the sage is freed from identity with the body and lives in blissful consciousness.

Sāma Veda, Çhāndogya Upanishad 8.3.3-4. BE, 122

The Self is not grasped by eyes or words, nor perceived by the senses, nor revealed by rituals or penance. When the understanding becomes calm and refined, then in meditation, one realizes Him, the Absolute.

Atharva Veda, Muṇḍaka Upanishad 3.1.8. MC, 107

Vartamāne Jīvitam

वर्तमाने जीवितम्

Part Two

Living In the Now

Mahādevānāṁ Prema

महादेवानां प्रेम

Love of the Gods

My God is the melter of my heart of love. Let all adore my God, the Lord of primal love, first of beings, my Śiva, who again and again melts my heart. May He render me His love in foremost measure! Praise Him but once, the Pure and Holy One, and He will be your escort to heaven. He, Lord Śiva, decked in honeyed *konrai* blooms, sits enthroned in my love, steadfast and free.

TIRUMANTIRAM 274–275

Monday
LESSON 127
The Nature Of Devotion

Devotion in Hinduism is known as *bhakti.* It is an entire realm of knowledge and practice unto itself, ranging from the child-like wonder of the unknown and the mysterious to the deep reverence which comes with understanding of the esoteric interworkings of the three worlds. Hinduism views existence as composed of three worlds. The First World is the physical universe, the Second World is the subtle astral or mental plane of existence in which the *devas,* or angels, and spirits live, and the Third World is the spiritual sphere of the Mahādevas, the Deities and the Gods. Hinduism is the harmonious working together of these three worlds. Religion blossoms for the Hindu as he awakens to the existence of the Second and Third Worlds. These inner worlds naturally inspire in man responses of love and devotion and even awe. They are that wonderful. ¶Devotion in Hinduism occurs on many levels and at different cycles of time in the evolution of the soul. All forms of devotion are equally valid, and none claims itself as the only proper form of worship. There is devotion to the tribal Deities, to the scriptures, to the saints and to the *satguru.* But the most prevalent expression of worship for the Hindu comes as devotion to God and the Gods. In the Hindu pantheon there are said to be 330 million Gods. Even so, all Hindus believe in one Supreme Being who pervades the entire universe. ¶The many Gods are perceived as divine creations of that one Being. These Gods, or Mahādevas, are real beings, capable of thought and feeling beyond the limited thought and feeling of embodied man. So, Hinduism has one God, but it has many Gods. There are only a few of these

Gods for whom temples are built and *pūjās* conducted. Gaṇeśa, Śiva, Subramaṇiam, Vishṇu and Śakti are the most prominent Deities in contemporary Hinduism. Of course, there are many others for whom certain rites or *mantras* are done in daily ceremony, often in the home shrine. These include Brahmā, Sūrya, Sarasvatī, Lakshmī, Agni, Chandra, Ayyappan, Hanumān, Mariyamman and others. ¶The Hindu traditionally adopts an Ishṭa Devatā. This is a personal Deity chosen from the many Hindu Gods, often according to the devotee's family background or the feeling of closeness to one form of divine manifestation. It is the unique and all-encompassing nature of Hinduism that one devotee may be worshiping Gaṇeśa while his friend worships Subramaṇiam or Vishṇu, and yet both honor the other's choice and feel no sense of conflict. The profound understanding and universal acceptance that are unique in Hinduism are reflected in this faculty for accommodating different approaches to the Divine, allowing for different names and forms of God to be worshiped side by side within the temple walls. It may even happen that one may adopt a different personal Deity through the years according to one's spiritual unfoldment and inner needs.

Tuesday
LESSON 128
The Gods Are Living Realities

The Hindu religion brings to us the gift of tolerance that allows for different stages of worship, different and personal expressions of devotion and even different Gods to guide our life on this Earth. Yet, it is a one religion under a single divine hierarchy that sees to the harmonious working together of the three worlds. These intelligent beings have evolved through eons of time and are able to help mankind without themselves having to live in a physical body. These great Mahādevas, with their multitudes of angelic *devas,* live and work constantly and tirelessly for the people of our religion, protecting and guiding them, opening new doors and closing unused ones. The Gods worshiped by the Hindu abide in the Third World, aided by the *devas* that inhabit the Second World. ¶It is in the Hindu temple that the three worlds meet and devotees invoke the Gods of our religion. The temple is built as a palace in which the Gods reside. It is the visible home of the Gods, a sacred place unlike every other place on the Earth. The Hindu must associate himself with these Gods in a very sensitive way when he approaches the temple. ¶Though the devotee rarely has the psychic vision of the Deity, he is aware of the God's divine presence. He is aware through feeling, through sensing the divine presence within the temple. As he approaches the sanctum sanctorum, the Hindu is fully aware that an intelligent being, greater and more evolved than himself, is there. This God is intently aware of him, safeguarding him, fully knowing his inmost thought, fully capable of coping with any situation the devotee may mentally lay at His holy feet. It is important that we approach the Deity in this way—conscious and confident that our needs are known in the inner spiritual worlds. ¶The physical representation of the God, be it a stone or metal image, a *yantra* or other sacred form, simply marks the place that the God will manifest in or hover above in His etheric body. It can be conceived as an antenna to receive the divine rays of the God or as the material body in or through which the God manifests in this First World.

Man takes one body and then another in his progression through the cycles of birth and death and rebirth. Similarly, the Gods in their subtle bodies inhabit, for brief or protracted spans of time, these temple images. When we perform *pūjā,* a religious ritual, we are attracting the attention of the *devas* and Mahādevas in the inner worlds. That is the purpose of a *pūjā*; it is a form of communication. To enhance this communication we establish an altar in the temple and in the home. This becomes charged or magnetized through our devotional thoughts and feelings, which radiate out and affect the surrounding environment.

Wednesday
LESSON 129
Communing With the Gods

Chanting and *satsaṅga* and ceremonial rituals all contribute to this sanctifying process, creating an atmosphere to which the Gods are drawn and in which they can manifest. By the word *manifest,* I mean they actually come and dwell there, and can stay for periods of time, providing the vibration is kept pure and undisturbed. The altar takes on a certain power. In our religion there are altars in temples all over the world inhabited by the *devas* and the great Gods. When you enter these holy places, you can sense their sanctity. You can feel the presence of these divine beings, and this radiation from them is known as *darshan.* The reality of the Mahādevas and their *darshan* can be experienced by the devotee through his awakened *ājñā* vision, or more often as the physical sight of the image in the sanctum coupled with the inner knowing that He is there within the microcosm. This *darshan* can be felt by all devotees, becoming stronger and more defined as devotion is perfected. Through this *darshan,* messages can be channeled along the vibratory emanations that radiate out from the Mahādevas, as well as from their representatives, the Second World *devas* who carry out their work for them in shrines and altars. ¶To understand *darshan,* consider the everyday and yet subtle communication of language. You are hearing the tones of my voice through the sensitive organ, your ear. Meaning comes into your mind, for you have been trained to translate these vibrations into meaning through the knowing of the language that I am speaking. *Darshan* is a vibration, too. It is first experienced in the simple physical glimpse of the form of the Deity in the sanctum. Later, that physical sight gives way to a clairvoyant vision or to a refined cognition received through the sensitive ganglia within your nerve system, the *chakras.* Through these receptors, a subtle message is received, often not consciously. Perhaps not immediately, but the message that the *darshan* carries, direct from the Mahādeva—direct from Lord Gaṇeśa, direct from Lord Muruga, direct from Lord Śiva Himself—manifests in your life. This is the way the Gods converse. It is a communication more real than the communication of language that you experience each day. It is not necessary to understand the communication immediately. The devotee may go away from the temple outwardly feeling that there was no particular message, or not knowing in his intellectual mind exactly what the *darshan* meant. Even the words you are now reading may not be fully cognized for days, weeks or even months. The depth of meaning will unfold itself on reflection. ¶Visiting a Hindu temple, receiving *darshan* from the majestic Gods of our religion, can altogether change the life of a worshiper. It alters the flow of the *prāṇas,* or life currents, within his body. It draws his awareness into the deeper *chakras.* It adjusts his beliefs and the attitudes that are the natural consequence of those beliefs. But the change is slow. He lives with the experience for months and months after his visit to the temple. He comes to know and love the Deity. The Deity comes to know and love him, helping and guiding his entire evolutionary pattern. *Darshan* coming from the great temples of our Gods can change the patterns of *karma* dating back many past lives, clearing and clarifying conditions that were created hundreds of years ago and are but seeds now, waiting to manifest in the future. Through the grace of the Gods, those seeds can be removed if the manifestation in the future would not enhance the evolution of the soul.

Thursday
LESSON 130
The Meaning Of Icon Worship

Hindu temples are new to this side of the planet and the knowledge of the very special and entirely esoteric nature of the Hindu temple is unknown in the West. One of the first misunderstandings that arises in the West is the purpose and function of the "graven image." The Judaic-Christian tradition firmly admonishes against the worship of graven images–though, of course, in Catholicism saints and images, and in Eastern Orthodoxy their pictures, are reverently worshiped. The Hindu doesn't worship idols or graven images. He worships God and the great godlike Mahādevas. The image is only that, an icon or representation or channel of an inner-plane Deity that hovers above or dwells within the statue. The physical image is not required for this process to happen. The God would perform His work in the temple without such an image, and indeed there are Hindu temples which have in the sanctum sanctorum no image at all but a *yantra,* a symbolic or mystic diagram. There are other Hindu temples which have only a small stone or crystal, a mark to represent the God worshiped there. However, the sight of the image enhances the devotee's worship, allowing the mind to focus on the sacred bonds between the three worlds, allowing the nerve system to open itself to the *darshan.* ¶Sight is very powerful. Sight is the first connection made with the Deity. The sight of the icon in the sanctum stimulates and enhances the flow of uplifting energies, or *prāṇas,* within the mind and body. Each Deity performs certain functions, is in charge, so to speak, of certain realms of the inner and outer mind. Knowing which Deity is being worshiped, by seeing the image of the Deity there, unfolds in the mind's eye a like image and prepares the way for a deeper devotion. ¶In a Hindu temple there is often a multiplicity of simultaneous proceedings and ceremonies. In one corner an extended family, or clan, with its hundreds of tightly knit members, may be joyously celebrating a wedding. At another shrine a lady might be crying in front of the Deity, saddened by some misfortune and in need of solace. Elsewhere in the crowded precincts a baby is being blessed, and several groups of temple musicians are filling the chamber with the shrill sounds of the *nāgasvaram* and drum. After the *pūjā* reaches its zenith, *brāhmin* priests move in and out of the sanctum, passing camphor and sacred ash and holy water to hundreds of worshipers crowding eagerly to get a glimpse of the Deity. All of this is happening at once, unplanned and yet totally organized. It is a wonderful experience, and such a diverse array of devotional ceremonies and such an intensity of worship can only be seen in a Hindu temple. There is no place on Earth quite like a Hindu temple. ¶Esoterically, the Gods in the temple, who live in the microcosm, can work extraordinarily fast with everyone. There is so much going on that everyone has the sense of being alone. The weeping woman is allowed her moment of mourning. No one feels that she is upsetting the nearby wedding. No one even notices her. The temple is so active, so filled with people, that each one is left to worship as he needs that day—to cry or to laugh or to sing or to sit in silent contemplation in a far-off corner.

Friday
LESSON 131
The Centrality Of the Temple

Like the Hindu religion itself, the Hindu temple is able to absorb and encompass everyone. It never says you must worship in this way, or you must be silent because there is a ceremony in progress. It accepts all, rejects none. It encourages all to come to God and does not legislate a single form of devotion. Hindus always want to live near a temple, so they can frequent it regularly. People arbitrate their difficulties in the vicinity of the temple. The Hindu people treat the temple very seriously and also very casually. It's a formal-informal affair. Between *pūjās* some may sit and talk and chat while others are worshiping. You might even find two people having a dispute in the temple, and the Deity is the arbitrator of their quarrel, giving clarity of mind on both sides. ¶Each Hindu temple throughout the world has its own rules on how to proceed and what to do within it. In some temples, in fact most temples in South India, all the men are required to take off their shirts and enter bare-chested. However, if you are in a business suit in the South Indian temple in New York, that's all right. You are not required to take off your shirt. Every temple has its own rules, so you have to observe what everybody else is doing the first time you go. ¶Hinduism is the most dynamic religion on the planet, the most comprehensive and comprehending. The Hindu is completely filled with his religion all of the time. It is a religion of love. The common bonds uniting all Hindus into a singular spiritual body are the laws of *karma* and *dharma*, the belief in reincarnation, all-pervasive Divinity, the ageless traditions and our Gods. Our religion is a religion of closeness, one to another, because of the common bond of loving the same Gods. All Hindu people are a one family, for we cannot separate one God too far from another. Each in is heavenly realm is also of a one family, a divine hierarchy which governs and has governed the Hindu religion from time immemorial, and will govern Sanātana Dharma on into the infinite. ¶Hinduism was never created, never founded as a religion. Therefore, it can never end. Until the Persians attached the name *Hindu* to those people living east of the river Indus, and the name Hinduism later evolved to describe their religious practices, this ancient faith bore a different title—the Sanātana Dharma, the Eternal Truth. The understanding was that within every man the germ or cell of his total affinity with God exists as the perennial inspiration of his spiritual quest and wellspring of all revelation. This enduring sense of an ever-present Truth that is God within man is the essence of the Sanātana Dharma. Such an inherent reality wells up lifetime after lifetime after lifetime, unfolding the innate perfection of the soul as man comes more fully into the awakened state of seeing his total and complete oneness with God.

Saturday
LESSON 132
Standing in God's Presence

In the beginning stages of worship, a Hindu soul may have to wrestle with disbelief in the Gods. He may wonder whether they really exist, especially if his own intuition is obscured by assimilation of Western existentialist beliefs and attitudes. Yet, he senses their existence, and this sensing brings him back to the temple. He is looking for proof, immersed in the process of coming to know the Gods for himself. He is heartened and assured by hundreds of saints and *ṛishis* who have fathomed and found close and enduring relationships with the Gods, and who then extolled their greatness in pages of scripture and chronicle. ¶The devotee stands before the sanctum and telepathically tells the Gods a problem, and with hopeful faith leaves and waits. Days or weeks later, after he had forgotten about his prayer, he suddenly realizes the problem has disappeared. He attempts to trace the source of its solution and finds that a simple, favorable play of circumstance and events brought it about. Had the Gods answered his prayer, or would it have happened anyway? He brings another prayer to the Gods, and again in time an answer appears in the natural course of his life. It appears to him that the Gods are hearing and responding to his needs. Trust and love have taken root. He goes on year after year bringing the Gods into his secular affairs, while just as carefully the Gods are bringing him into their celestial spheres, enlivening his soul with energy, joy and intelligence. ¶The Hindu looks to the Gods for very practical assistance. He devoutly believes that the Gods from their dwelling in the Third World are capable of consciously working with the forces of evolution in the universe and they could then certainly manage a few simpler problems. He devoutly believes that the Gods are given to care for man on the planet and see him through his tenure on Earth, and that their decisions are vast in their implications. Their overview spans time itself, and yet their detailed focus upon the complicated fabric of human affairs is just as awesome. ¶When a devotee settles upon his Ishṭa Devatā, the one God to whom his endearment and devotion will be directed, that Deity assumes the position of his spiritual parent. Many of you are parents and know the inestimable value that correction and timely discipline serve in the raising of children into responsible, mature adults. The Gods are our spiritual parents. When a devotee is not living up to his best, betraying his own silent vows taken unto himself, his Ishṭa Devatā, or personal Deity, is present enough in his life, alive enough in his mind, to know this. The God has the ability to scan ahead in time and make a sharp and often painful adjustment or severe penalty in the life of the devotee to protect him from an even greater impending tragedy or mental abyss.

Sunday
LESSON 133
How the Gods Work with Man

The Gods do not treat everyone alike. The attitude that all souls are equal and subject to equal standards of right and wrong behavior is not an Eastern understanding. Nor is it the way the Gods view the souls of men. There are younger souls and older souls, just as there are children and adults. They live worlds apart in the same world. Souls living side by side may actually be hundreds of lives apart in their spiritual maturation, one just learning what the other learned many lives ago. The Gods discern the depth of the soul, and when they are approached they see the devotee not only as he is but as he was and will be. They help the devotee in understanding within the sphere of intelligence which they command. ¶Often one God will primarily direct one specialized mind stratum. He will come to know the problems and nuances indigenous to that mind region. Thus, the same misdeed performed by three souls of different ages under similar circumstances is viewed as three different misdeeds by the Gods. An older soul is more aware, more able to control himself and therefore more responsible for his actions. He should have known better and finds that his transgression brings painful retribution. Another less mature soul is still learning control of the emotions that provoked his misdeed, and he is sharply scolded. Still another soul, so young that awareness has not yet fathomed the laws of *karma*, of action and reaction, and who remains unawakened to the emotional mastery the situation demanded, is lightly reprimanded, if at all. The Gods in their superconscious judgment of human deeds and misdeeds are infinitely fair and discerning. ¶Their judgments are totally unlike the notion of a God in heaven who arbitrarily saves or condemns. In Hinduism all men are destined to attain liberation. Not a single soul will suffer for eternity. Therefore, the Gods in their deliberations are not making what we would consider personal judgments. Their decrees are merely carrying out the natural law of evolution. They are always directing the soul toward the Absolute, and even their apparent punishments are not punishments but correction and discipline that will bring the soul closer to its true nature. Now, of course human law is not like this, especially today, but in civilizations past and in the great religious Hindu empires of India, there were such equitable courts of law, with enlightened men of justice, that sentences and punishments were meted out upon careful scrutiny of the individual, his particular *dharma* and the duties and expectations it bound him to uphold. ¶It is through the sanction of the Gods that the Hindu undertakes the practice of *yoga*—that orthodox and strictly Hindu science of meditation that leads to merger of the many with the one. *Yoga* is the culmination of years of religious and devotional service and can only be successful with the support of the Gods who are the sentries guarding the gates of the various strata of consciousness. This sanction, once obtained, can and does allow the *kuṇḍalinī* force within the core of the spine to safely rise and merge with the Supreme that all Hindus know is the Absolute—timeless, causeless and spaceless. But first much work has to be done.

Upāsana Rahasyam

उपासनरहस्यम्

The Esoterics Of Worship

Offer oblations in love, light golden lamps. Spread incense of fragrant wood and lighted camphor in all directions. Forget your worldly worries and meditate. You shall attain true and rapturous *moksha.* Worshiping thus, there is nothing that you cannot attain. Worshiping thus, you shall inherit the wealth of Indra, heaven's king. Worshiping thus, you shall gain miraculous powers. Worshiping thus, you shall attain *moksha.*

TIRUMANTIRAM 1005–1006

MANIVEL...

Monday
LESSON 134
Lord Gaṇeśa, The Gatekeeper

Lord Gaṇeśa is the first God a Hindu comes to know. As the Lord of Categories, His first objective is to bring order into the devotee's life, to settle him into the correct and proper flow of his *dharma*—the pattern of duties, responsibilities and expectations suited to the maturity of his soul. As the Lord of Obstacles, He deftly wields His noose and mace, dislodging impediments and holding avenues open until the individual is set in a good pattern, one that will fulfill his spiritual needs rather than frustrate them. ¶Always remember that Gaṇeśa does not move swiftly. He is the elephant God, and His gait is slow and graceful. As the God of the instinctive-intellectual mind, His *darshans* are carried on the slower currents of mind, and so His response to our prayers is usually not overnight or sudden and electric, but more deliberate and gradual. Yet, our patience is rewarded, for His work is thorough and powerful, of matchless force persisting until our lives and minds adjust and our prayer has become reality. ¶Lord Gaṇeśa is also known as the Gatekeeper. Access to all the other Gods comes through Him. It is not that He would want to keep anyone from another God, but He prepares you to meet them and makes the meeting an auspicious one. This preparation can mean lifetimes. There is no hurry. It is not a race. Gaṇeśa will faithfully bar access to those who do not merit a divine audience and an ensuing relationship with the other Deities whose *darshans* are faster. Should a devotee gain unearned access and invoke the powers of other Deities before all preparations were concluded, *karma* would accelerate beyond the individual's control. Worship of

Lord Gaṇeśa, however, may begin at any time. ¶Gaṇeśa is the ubiquitous God. There are more shrines, altars and temples for Lord Gaṇeśa than for any other God. Gaṇeśa *bhakti* is the most spontaneous worship and the simplest to perform. It requires little ritual. Just the ringing of a small bell at the outset of a project before His picture or the burning of camphor or the offering of a flower is enough to invoke His presence and protection. Throughout India and Sri Lanka, there are small, unadorned shrines to Gaṇapati under shaded trees, along country roads, at bus terminals, along footpaths and in the city streets. His blessings are indeed everywhere. Helping Gaṇeśa, whose powers of mind outreach the most advanced computers we can conceive, are His *gaṇas,* or devonic helpers. These ministering spirits collect the prayers of those in need, ferret out and procure the necessary information and bring it before Lord Gaṇeśa's wisdom. ¶As we come closer to the wonderful Gods of Hinduism, we come to love them in a natural way, to be guided by them and to depend on them more than we depend on ourselves. The exuberant enthusiasm so prevalent in the West, of holding to an existential independence and expressing an autonomous will to wield the direction of our lives, loses its fascination as we mature within the steady radiance of these Gods and begin to realize the divine purpose of our Earthly sojourn. ¶One might ask how the Hindu can become so involved in the love of the Gods that he is beholden to their will? Similarly, one might ask how does anyone become so involved and in love with his mother and father, trusting their guidance and protection, that he is beholden to them? It works the same way. Where you find the Hindu family close to one another and happy, you find them close to the Gods. Where they are not close, and live in a fractured or broken home, the Gods will unfortunately have been exiled from their lives. They will not be invoked, and perhaps not even believed in.

Tuesday
LESSON 135
Your Will and The Gods' Will

Someone once asked, "They say true *bhakti* is giving your whole will, your whole being, to God. If you do that, aren't you making yourself completely passive?" Many think that the ultimate devotion, called *prapatti* in Sanskṛit, means giving up their willpower, their independence and their judgment for an attitude of "Now you direct me, for I no longer can direct myself, because I no longer have free will. I gave it all away." This is a good argument against *prapatti,* to be sure, but a gross misinterpetation of the word, which is the very bedrock of spirituality. This is not the meaning of *prapatti* at all. Not at all. I shall give an example. People who are employed work with full energy and vigor, utilizing all their skills on the job, day after day after day, year after year after year. They give of their talents and energies freely, but they do hold back some of the energies and fight within themselves. This is called resistance. That resistance is what they have to offer on the altar of purification. Getting rid of resistance, to be able to flow with the river of life, is what *prapatti* is all about. *Prapatti* is freedom. This truly is free will. Free will is not an obstinant will, an opposite force invoked for the preservation of the personal ego. This is willfulness, not free will. Free will is total, intelligent cooperation, total merging of the individual mind with that of another, or of a group.

Those who only in appearance are cooperative, good employees rarely show their resistance. They hold it within, and day after day, year after year, it begins tearing them apart. Stress builds up that no remedy can cure. In religious life, we must have *prapatti* twenty-four hours a day, which means getting rid of our resistance. ¶There are various forms of free will. There is free will of the ego, or the instinctive mind, there is free will of the intellect that has been educated in *dharma*, and there is free will of the intuition. For many, free will is an expression of the little ego, which often entangles them more in the world of *māyā*. For me, true free will means the *dharmic* will that is divine and guided by the superconscious. In reality, only this kind of will makes you free. ¶Hindus with Western education, or who were raised and taught in Christian schools, whether they have accepted the alien religion or not, find it very difficult to acknowledge within their own being the existence of the Gods, because the West primarily emphasizes the external, and the East emphasizes the internal. Thoroughly immersing oneself in the external world severs man's awareness from his psychic ability to perceive that which is beyond the sight of his two eyes. ¶You might ask how you can love something you cannot see. Yet, the Gods can be and are seen by mature souls through an inner perception they have awakened. This psychic awakening is the first initiation into religion. Every Hindu devotee can sense the Gods, even if he cannot yet inwardly see them. This is possible through the subtle feeling nature. He can feel the presence of the Gods within the temple, and he can indirectly see their influence in his life.

Wednesday
LESSON 136
Karma and Consciousness

The Hindu does not have to die to have a final judgment or to enter into heaven, for heaven is a state of mind and being fully existent in every human being this very moment. There are people walking on this Earth today who are living in heaven, and there are those who are living in hellish states as well. All that the Hindu has to do is go to the temple. As soon as he goes to the temple, to a *pūjā,* he is contacting the divine forces. During the *pūjā,* he is totally judged by the Deity. All of his *karma* is brought current, and he goes away feeling good. Or he might go away feeling guilty. That is good, too, because then he performs penance, *prāyaśchitta,* and resolves unseemly *karma* quickly. ¶It might be said that every day that you go to the temple is judgment day. Isn't it a wonderful thing that in our religion you can either go to heaven or hell on a daily basis, and the next day get out of hell through performing penance and ascend to heaven? The Hindu sees these as states existing in the here and now, not in some futuristic and static other-worldly existence. There are certainly inner, celestial realms, but like this physical universe, they are not the permanent abode of the soul, which is in transit, so to speak, on its way to merger with Śiva. ¶It is not necessary for the Hindu to wait until the end of life to become aware of the results of this particular life. Because he knows this and does not wait for death for the resolution of the results of his accumulated actions and reactions in life, his evolution is exceedingly fast. He lives perhaps several lives within the boundaries of a single lifetime, changing and then changing again. If he errs, he does not worry inordinately. He merely corrects himself and moves on in the progressive stream of human evolution. He is aware of the frailties of being human, but he is not burdened by his sins or condemning himself for actions long past. To him, all actions are the work of the Gods. His life is never static, never awaiting a judgment day; whereas the Western religionist who believes there is an ultimate reckoning after this one life is spent is piling up everything that he has done, good and bad, adding it to a medley in his mind and waiting for the Grim Reaper to come along and usher in the Day of Judgment. ¶Hinduism is such a joyous religion, freed of all the mental encumbrances that are prevalent in the various Western faiths. It is freed of the notion of a vengeful God. It is freed of the notion of eternal suffering. It is freed from the notion of original sin. It is freed from the notion of a single spiritual path, a One Way. It is freed from the notion of a Second Coming. Why, I think some of the *devas* in this temple are on their, let me see,... 8,450,000th coming now! They come every time you ring the bell. You don't have to wait 2,000 years for the Gods to come. Every time you ring the bell, the Gods and *devas* come, and you can be and are blessed by their *darshan.* They are omniscient and omnipresent, simultaneously there in every temple on the planet as the bell is rung. That is the mystery and the power of these great Gods who exist within the microcosm.

Thursday
LESSON 137
Oneness with Divine Law

Because it is relatively free from mistaken doctrines, the Hindu approach to life—and the Hindu approach to time and the Hindu approach to worry, and the Hindu approach to the subconscious mind—is very different from the Western approach. The Hindu knows that he is evolving through a succession of lives on the planet, and he is not in a hurry. The devout Hindu accumulates little *karma*, because his subconscious is constantly being brought current by the worship of the Gods. Thus, *karma* is controlled. The Hindu looks at religion as the most joyous expression life can offer. The Hindu considers all of mankind his brothers and sisters, all created by the same Creator, all destined to the same attainment. ¶When he visits the temple, he is seeking to understand the minds of the Gods, seeking their blessings and their guidance. He stands before the Deity in humble awe of the grandeur of a world he can only partially conceive. He inwardly tries to sense the Deity. If he is even slightly clairvoyant, he may see the Deity overshadow the image within the sanctum. At first he may see the image appear to move, thinking it his own imagination. He may observe the expression on the Deity change from day to day and from hour to hour. He may become aware of the Deity's influence in his life and awaken a love for the Gods whom he once only vaguely thought were plausible. ¶The Hindu is not an existentialist. He does not believe that God is unknowable. He does not believe in the dismal fate of mankind alone in the universe, with only himself to depend upon. The Hindu believes that he is born with his destiny and the patterns are set. He blends his will with the will of his religious community and with the will of the Gods in the temple, because he doesn't have the concept of a free will that is answerable to neither man nor God. ¶Belief is a pattern placed within the mind for a particular purpose, so that awareness will flow through that particular pattern for the rest of the person's life. Generally, the pattern is put into the mind of a child before he is thinking for himself, or your friends or family or teachers will put beliefs in your mind. You will say, "Yes, I believe that," without actually thinking it out for yourself. It is from our beliefs that our attitudes arise. Your individual awareness, your ability to be aware, has no way of functioning unless there are patterns within the mind for the *prāṇas* to flow through and around. You have to have a mind to work through. ¶First there are beliefs, and then attitudes. In the Hindu home and culture, beliefs and attitudes are taught very carefully and systematically with love and attention so that the individual becomes a productive member of the community even before leaving home. Those first mind impressions are important, and if they are correct and not fraught with misconceptions, they will properly guide the person through life with a minimum of mental and emotional problems. The person will correct himself or herself rather than having to be corrected by society.

Friday
LESSON 138
The Potency Of Tradition

This is one of the reasons that religious tradition is very, very important. Modern existential thought tells us that we can do anything we want to; we don't have to follow tradition. Out of such a belief comes a great sense of loneliness, a schism between the individual and all his ancestors, all the generations that preceded him on this planet. Out of such a belief comes the breaking up of culture, society, religion and families. ¶Tradition allows you to go through life's experiences in a controlled way, rather than just throwing yourself into life and upon life without forethought and preparation.

When you respect tradition, you call upon the collective wisdom of tens of thousands of years of experience. When you follow tradition, you share the solutions of untold problems, solved once perhaps before recorded history began in order that future generations might avoid them. Tradition is wisdom of the past inherited by the men and women in the present. ¶Our religion has a vast tradition, and not everyone can or does follow the entirety of it. There is the greatest freedom within Hinduism. You can choose to not follow tradition, but tradition is there to be followed when you choose to do so. Of course, we can take the path of trial and error, testing every single precept before adopting any. That is a tedious path which leads slowly to the eventual goal. By depending on our Gods, on our forefathers, on our religious ancestors, we move more swiftly along the spiritual path. In the early stages we tend toward untraditional ways. That is natural. Experience later shows us another way, and we begin to become traditionalists. This maturation comes to all souls over a series of births as they learn to perfect the intricate patterns of Hindu culture and religion. ¶There are certain traditions that can be broken up, that are lost and forgotten, covered over by the sands of time because they are traditions that men put in motion. Some traditions set in motion by people to solve certain problems at certain times have no relationship to our circumstances and in our times. ¶The Hindu tradition is initiated and administrated from the inner worlds, from the Devaloka. The Deities are the source of most tradition. They ordain the proper way to chant and the *mantras* to be used. They establish the language, the music, the dance, the systems of worship. Following the Hindu traditions better and better over the years attunes your mind to the great, positive mind flow of over one billion people on our planet. ¶Ours are the world's most ancient traditions. They are the most profound, based on an esoteric understanding of man and his purpose in life. Tradition guides experiences in life. It is a protective mind structure. Any experience that you have to go through is gently guided by this great mind structure. The old ways are world patterns that have come down through thousands upon thousands of years, which you have, in previous lives, lived through and known.

Saturday
LESSON 139
Microcosm, Macrocosm

The mind of man—and by that I mean his entire mental, emotional and spiritual structure—exists within the microcosm, which exists within the macrocosm that we can see and touch and that we call the physical universe. The Gods also live within the microcosm. The microcosm is within this macrocosm, and then again, within that microcosm is another dimension of space, another macrocosm. Similarly, you can look into a drop of water through the microscope and see a new dimension of space in which myriads of tiny creatures are experiencing a total existence. Those minute living things are in the microcosm; from where they stand they see it as a macrocosm. While you might say there is only one millionth of an inch between each of those little organisms swimming in the drop of water, to them it may seem like fifty yards. There are tens of thousands within that single drop, and yet they are not at all crowded, for it is a different dimension of space. This is how the microcosm can have an even bigger macrocosm than this one within it. ¶That bigger macrocosm is the Third World, the Śivaloka, where all the Gods and Mahādevas reside. It is within you, but it is ethereal, which means it is nonphysical. Your mind is in the microcosm. That is how it does all the things that it does. You can take your mind completely around the world in an instant, or across the galaxy. Right now we can take our minds to a star that is 680 million light years away from Earth. We can think about that star and see it in our mind. Time is not involved, nor is space. Thought is there instantly. The Gods are also in the microcosm, and in the macrocosm within the microcosm. From their view, all that they do for you, to help you work out a problem, even if they work on it for days of their time, happens faster than instantly. Since your mind, too, exists within the microcosm, the change takes place instantaneously. It then takes a day or two for the effects of that change to be felt in the macrocosm. Deep within your mind, in the microcosm, the problem vanished the instant you stood before the God in the temple. It takes you a few days, or at least a few hours, to catch up to the inner event and see the results in physical form.

Sunday
LESSON 140
Grace of The Gods

When you worship the God in the temple, through *pūjā* and ceremony, you are bringing that Divinity out of the microcosm and into this macrocosm. You supply the energy through your worship and your devotion, through your thought forms, and even your physical aura. The *pujārī* purifies and magnetizes the stone image for this to take place. The Gods and the *devas* are also magnetizing the stone image with their energy, and finally the moment is ready and they can come out of the microcosm into this macrocosm and bless the people. You observe that they stayed only for an instant, but to them it was a longer time. The time sense in the inner worlds is different. ¶If you want to get acquainted with the Gods, first get to know Lord Gaṇeśa. Take a picture and look at it. Put a picture of Lord Gaṇeśa in your car or in your kitchen. Get acquainted through sight. Then come to know Him through sound by chanting His names and hymns. This is how you get acquainted with your personal Deity. You will get to know Him just as you know your best friend, but in a more intimate way, for Gaṇeśa is within you and there ahead of you to guide your soul's evolution. As you get acquainted with Him, Gaṇeśa then knows that you're coming up on the spinal climb of the *kuṇḍalinī.* He will work with you and work out your *karma.* Your whole life will begin to smooth out. ¶Religion is the connection between the three worlds, and temple worship is how you can get your personal connection with the inner worlds. You never really lose connection with the inner worlds, but if you are not conscious of that connection, then it appears that you have. ¶The Gods of Hinduism create, preserve and protect mankind. It is through their sanction that all things continue, and through their will that they cease. It is through their grace that all good things happen, and all things that happen are for the good. Now, you may wonder why one would put himself under this divine authority so willingly, thus losing his semblance of freedom. But does one not willingly put himself in total harmony with those whom he loves? Of course he does. And loving these great souls comes so naturally. Their timeless wisdom, their vast intelligence, their thoroughly benign natures, their ceaseless concern for the problems and well-being of devotees, and their power and sheer Godly brilliance—all these inspire our love.

Prapattiḥ

प्रपत्तिः

Total Surrender

You may turn your bone to fuel, your flesh to meat, letting them roast and sizzle in the gold-red blaze of severe austerities. But unless your heart melts in love's sweet ecstasy, you never can possess my Lord Śiva, my treasure-trove.

TIRUMANTIRAM 272

Monday
LESSON 141
Softening of The Heart

The *yoga* of pure devotion is found at the beginning, the middle and the end of the path. Merging with Śiva is more and more a deeply felt experiential reality when the soul gives of itself to Śiva inwardly and outwardly in unabashed devotion. *Prapatti* truly is the key that unlocks the love needed as merger increases as the years pass by and, as Satguru Yogaswāmī said, "Love pours forth to melt the very stones." *Bhakti yoga* is not an intellectual study. It is a practice. It is also not an emotional experience. It is a devotional experience. There is a difference, which we will come to understand. *Bhakti yoga* is not a cure-all, nor a means to fast enlightenment. Rather, it is the foundation for enlightenment. It is not a technique. Nor is it a magic *mantra.* It is a way of life. The transformation that comes from living in the state of *bhakti yoga* is the softening of the heart. ¶External worship, *bhakti yoga,* is taught first on the spiritual path because it produces a softened, mellow heart. It is to waste the *guru's* time to give training in meditation and contemplation before the heart has been softened through *bhakti yoga.* The patient *guru* will wait until this has happened within the devotee. Otherwise, any accomplishment attained through intense *rāja yoga* practices will not be sustained. And the problems that arise within the devotee's subconscious mind—should he be taught *rāja yoga* before the proper preparation has been mastered—will go back on the *guru.* The *guru* will then have to act as the psychiatrist to solve the problems arising from the forced awakening. Whereas a mature *bhaktar* takes such problems, or negative *karmas,* which are sometimes aroused as a result of deep meditation, to the temple Deities, placing them at their feet to be dissolved. This will not happen for the devotee who has not experienced living in the state of *bhakti yoga*, because the relationship has not yet been established between himself and the Gods. Therefore, the wise *guru* starts his devotee at the beginning of the path, not in the middle. ¶The path begins with *charyā*, getting to know the Gods and developing a relationship with them through service. *Charyā* is *karma yoga*. Then *kriyā* is experienced. *Kriyā* is *bhakti yoga*. Once *bhakti yoga* has melted the heart, then the deep *yoga* concepts and meditation techniques of *rāja yoga* may be practiced. They are to be understood within the internal mind, not just memorized. The wise *guru* will never teach deep meditation techniques to angry, jealous, fearful devotees. Such devotees should first learn to serve selflessly, by performing *karma yoga* projects in the *ashram*, and then perform simple *bhakti yoga* until all anger has melted into love. ¶The inner knowing that "All is Śiva's will" is one of the first benefits of *bhakti yoga*. Only through true *bhakti* can the *yogī* achieve and maintain the inner state of Satchidānanda. It is only the true *bhaktar* who can sustain living with God and the Gods unreservedly and begin to internalize his devotion into deeper meditations. One cannot internalize devotion until it has been truly externalized. Here is an example to explain the process of the internalization of devotion. A devotee resents something said to him by another devotee and flares up in anger. The two devotees part, but the anger remains in the form of burning resentment. The emotion of anger has been internalized, but may later be unleashed on someone else.

Tuesday
LESSON 142
Foundations for Fruitful Yoga

Many Hindu teachers in the West teach purely *advaitic* meditation, with no theism or religious practice, but most who have come to the West from India were raised in Hindu homes. They have within them a firm religious, cultural foundation for *yoga.* Many do not pass the religious culture on to their Western devotees, however. In an orthodox Hindu community they would most likely teach in a more traditional way. *Advaita* philosophy is appealing to the Westerner. It does not require a change in lifestyle. ¶The nondual, *advaita*-based meditations do bring the devotees out of the conscious mind, but more often than not lead them into the subconscious. It is here, within the subconscious, that unresolved problems with family and one's own personal ego begin to appear. Without a proper religious-cultural background and traditional Hindu belief system, these problems are difficult to handle. This turmoil is certainly not the purpose of *advaitic* meditations, but it is a byproduct. The wise *guru* trains his devotees in traditional Hindu culture and values and teaches the beginning *yogas,* as well as temple protocol, music, the arts and dance. All these should be mastered to build a proper subconscious foundation within the mind. Karma *yoga* and *bhakti yoga* are the necessary prelude to the higher philosophies and practices. ¶Group meditation is all right, as the group can really help the individual, as does the individual help the group. Intense meditation awakens the *saṁskāras,* the impressions of the past, and intensifies the *prārabdha karmas,* bringing them into manifestation before their time. It has a greenhouse effect. ¶No one should perform intensive meditation alone until he or she can serve selflessly and accept praise and blame and criticism without complaint or resentment, but with a sweet smile. Only when a devotee has reached this stage is he or she firmly on the *kriyā mārga*, which will lead quite naturally to the *yoga mārga.* Then, finally, *rāja yoga* and other kinds of more refined, intensive *sādhana*s can safely be performed. These will clean up the *karmas* of the past without mental pain, once the proper foundation has been set within the mind and character of the devotee. ¶The progressive *sādhana*s of *karma yoga*, *bhakti yoga* and then *rāja yoga* are like clearing a path of its stones. First you remove the big stones. Then you walk back along the path. You still see big stones, but they are half the size as the first ones that were removed, and you remove these as well. Then you walk back along the path and remove more stones that stand out as large, and on and on until the path is clear. It is a refinement process. ¶The seeker on the path has to be soft, pliable, easy to get along with, as well as firm-minded. Therefore, *bhakti*, which is love in action, is a necessary prerequisite to success on the San Mārga, the straight path to God, toward merger with Śiva. All kinds of *yogic* techniques can be practiced, but they hold no fruitful rewards for those who are not firm-minded and not strong in the essential virtues. The prideful, antagonistic and difficult-to-get-along-with people must soften their hearts. This is done through *bhakti* and *karma yoga.* These practices alone will free the devotee from the *āṇava mārga*—the path of building up and keeping the personal ego strong. The *āṇava mārga* is a difficult path to leave for the San Mārga, but the results on the San Mārga are so much more rewarding in the long run. ¶It is often postulated by certain Indian schools of thought that once you reach a certain stage, *bhakti* should be set aside because it is dual by nature. But a devotee arriving into a high state of consciousness does not give up his love for God and the Gods. His devotion does not stop; rather it becomes more intense. He does not stop eating, relating to family, friends and other devotees. These are all dual things, too. Yes, it is true that some teachers preach this doctrine. But to avoid the *charyā mārga*, having perhaps never been on it, and say, "I am on a greater and much higher one; I don't have to do that" is another philosophy, not ours. ¶In Śaiva Siddhānta, the *mārgas* are progressive stages of character building. They are a foundation for good character, which is built on *bhakti.* Proper habit patterns created through the daily *sādhana*s of *karma yoga* and *bhakti yoga* lay this foundation within the mind, body and emotions. In case a devotee fails in pursuit of the higher *yogas*, he will always have his success on the *charyā mārga* to rely upon. For someone to say, "I now intellectually understand the *Vedas* and do not need to express love and devotion" is sad indeed. One who had really realized the truths of the *Vedas* would never say this.

Wednesday
LESSON 143
Bhakti Is the Foundation

Bhakti is a state of mind, an arrival at an inner state of consciousness. People who become angry, people who become jealous, people who are fearful, people who get confused are living in the *asura loka.* They are the ones who upset others and experience revenge. They have yet to come up even to the *āṇava mārga* and attain a little appreciation of themselves. They have yet to experience being secure in their own identity. ¶They have yet to "be their own person," "find their own space." They must first close the door on channeling *asuric* entities. Once firmly planted on the *āṇava mārga*, they begin feeling that they are God's gift to the world and may seek out a spiritual teacher. If the teacher does teach them *karma yoga* and *bhakti yoga*, they begin to realize that there are forces in the universe, souls in the universe, who are much greater than they are now or will ever be for a long time. Once this happens, the die is cast. They are on the spiritual path to their own eventual enlightenment. ¶Our scriptures, the Śaiva Siddhānta scriptures, are filled with stories of the greatest *jñānīs* who performed *karma yoga* and *bhakti yoga* and also spoke out the highest truths of *jñāna.* The tales explain that during auspicious days of the month they performed intense *rāja yoga tapas.* This is the *yoga*—the arms and the head and the torso of *yoga.* You do not perform only one *yoga* without all the others. It is an integral whole. ¶On occasion we observe devotees pilgrimaging to a temple, prostrating so devotedly. But after leaving the temple, they slap one of their children. We know that upon entering the house they argue with their spouse and complain about their in-laws. Where is the true *bhakti* here? This is what *bhakti* is not. Unfortunately, the children who observe this hypocrisy remember it for a long, long time. A child might think, "You love Lord Gaṇeśa, Mom, but you can't love me." When you love a baby, you will not hit it when it cries, even if the crying disturbs you. ¶Wise *gurus* will not initiate anyone into *rāja yoga* techniques who does not have a sweet nature and a natural outpouring of *bhakti.*

No one auditions for the symphony orchestra until he has mastered all that his first, second and third music teachers have taught him. ¶Suppose a devotee who is not virtuous is taught an intense *rāja yoga* meditation and practices it ardently over a long period of time until a burst of light is seen. Then the devotee, now feeling quite above others, argues with his parents, or flashes out in anger when talking to a friend. At that moment, all the good merit and benefits of the *rāja yoga* awakening are erased. This is because the *prāṇa* of higher consciousness has been dissipated by the angry words, which now burn deeper into the mind of others than they would have before. No, a kindly, gentle nature must precede *rāja yoga sādhanas*. That is for sure. ¶*Bhakti* is the base and the bedrock of spiritual unfoldment. A devotee who has an amiable nature, who is a good, considerate and giving person, is obviously a *bhaktar.* The disciplines of *bhakti yoga* make one a devotee, and a devotee is a very selfless type of person. These disciplines can take many forms, but the fruit of *bhakti yoga,* which is a loving disposition, must be attained before one can go further on the path with security. The proof is in the actions and attitudes of the individual. If he really sees Lord Śiva in and through all things, how can he not be a *bhaktar?* If he truly understands the law of *karma,* he cannot possibly resent any happening. He knows that the experiences of today were created in the past. He truly knows that today's actions mold the experiences of a future time. Yes, *bhakti yoga* is the bedrock of all minor and major enlightenments. Devotees who are very kind people, devotional, obedient, intelligent, will fulfill whatever assignments their *guru* gives—

be it a pure *advaitic* path, the *rāja yogas* or the path of *karma yoga.*

Thursday
LESSON 144
Lower States of Consciousness

When someone begins on the path from states of consciousness below the *mūlādhāra*, in the confused thinking areas of the mind, in the angry *chakras*, religion will be to him a superstitious, forboding, very unclear area. These *chakras* are also known as *talas,* or states of darkness, self-concealment and distortion. They are the "nether poles" of the higher *chakras* and of the seven corresponding *lokas.* Confused thinking we can define as "self-preservation thinking." When a person is within this *chakra*, the feelings of "me and mine" are strong. It is a state of outward passion and sense indulgence. This is the vibration of the *talātala chakra*, which could be translated as "under the bottom level," "place-non-place" *(tala-atala),* or "realm of nonbeing." In this fourth center below the *mūlādhāra*, the protection of one's small universe at all costs is the consciousness. ¶Should such a person ever become uplifted, since his consciousness is deep within the lower *chakras*, he would first come up in consciousness into jealousy, the *sutala chakra,* meaning "great lower region," a "good matter" state of spiritual darkness ruled by desire and passion. The feeling of jealousy is a higher consciousness than that of the *chakra* below, which confuses the thinking. The next upliftment, after jealousy and confused thinking, is the release into the *chakra* of anger, the second force center below the *mūlādhāra.* This is the *vitala chakra*, translated as "the region of the lost," "realm of division or confusion." The upliftment to follow anger is to enter the *chakra* of fear, a state of spiritual annihilation called the *atala chakra*, meaning "without bottom," or "no place." Fear is a higher consciousness than anger or jealousy. It is people who live in this *chakra* who make up the masses who fear God rather than love God. ¶The fifth *chakra* below the *mūlādhāra* is called *rasātala*, literally "state of sense enjoyment." This is the true home of the animal nature. Here personal selfishness predominates. Persons strongly in the consciousness of this force center care nothing for the problems and suffering of others. ¶Below this, dare we speak of it, is the *mahātala*, "the greatest lower region," where ego rules supreme. This is the realm of unconscionable acts, wherein perpetrators feel absolutely no remorse for the most heinous wrongdoings. The conscience is completely dormant for those locked in this realm. Negativity, depression and other dark states of mind are the order of the day for those in the *mahātala chakra*. Finally, at the bottom of consciousness is the *pātāla chakra*, "lower region of wickedness" or "fallen state," where dark ignorance rules. This is the realm of vicious destruction, of revenge, murder for the sake of murder. Basking in the twisted vibrations of this area of consciousness, depraved transgressors torture others without a thought, express malice without a twinge of conscience, harm others in innumerable ways for sheer enjoyment and take delight in the emotional, mental and physical suffering of fellow humans and all beings that cross their path. Hatred is the ruling force in the *pātāla chakra*; malice reigns supreme. Far from reason, and farther still from compassion and insight, are those who live in the darkness of this area of mind. ¶We can see that coming up through the lower *chakras* is quite an ordeal. But once the individual goes through the fear *chakra*, he comes to Lord Gaṇeśa's feet and enters the realms of memory and reason, clarity and understanding. It is at this point in the unfoldment through the *chakras*, which is a journey of consciousness, that he would begin thinking of others and seek to benefit them more than himself. From here on, the path of spiritual unfoldment is not as ominous as it was before. There are no threatening areas, except that it is possible to fall back into lower consciousness.

Friday
LESSON 145
Stewards of Vast Realms

The Gods are the controllers of these force centers within man. They live in the innermost areas of form. To enter the *mūlādhāra chakra*, the aspirant must go through Lord Gaṇeśa. And when the aspirant progresses to the *maṇipūra chakra*, Gaṇeśa will introduce him to Lord Muruga. Once this is accomplished, the devotee will worship Lord Muruga as the Be-All and End-of-All, just as Gaṇeśa was worshiped when consciousness was in His *chakras.* Lord Muruga is the controller of the *manipura chakra*, the *chakra* of willpower, and the two *chakras* above it, direct cognition and universal love. Now we can begin to see that the aspirant has to proceed in consciousness through the three *chakras* that Lord Muruga controls and meet all the tests before this God will introduce him to Lord Śiva. Lord Śiva's realm is *chakras* number six, seven and beyond. The aspirant still must go completely through the *chakras* of Lord Śiva's realm to become Śivaness—to experience His all-pervasiveness, and on into the essence of all essences, Paraśiva. ¶The aspirant who dearly loves Lord Śiva must finally go beyond Śiva's personal aspect to reach the impersonal side, and this is why, when he finally emerges from Paraśiva, he is really a true *bhaktar.* He is the true monistic theist. In the world of duality, theism is in itself a duality. Theism is very compatible with the mind of man, which is duality itself. Monism, on the other side, is beyond the mind itself. Monism is timeless, formless, and it is spaceless as well. True monism cannot be conceived by the mind. Yet, the mind does know of its existence. ¶When the devotee has proven himself, the Gods begin to take notice. We meet a God as we go up through the *chakras* above the *mūlādhāra.* We meet an *asura* as we go down through the *chakras* below the *mūlādhāra.* A God appears as each higher *chakra* breaks open. As the *mūlādhāra* opens and awareness comes through it, we encounter Gaṇeśa. When we experience fear and anger, we meet and are influenced by the *asuras* of fear and anger. In the *chakra* that governs confused and selfish thinking, we meet and are influenced by the *asura* who rules this realm. Descending to the still lower *chakras* of petty theft, fraud and stealing, grand larceny, murder and violence, we would meet professionals in these areas. ¶There are always inner Gods and outer Gods, for each *chakra* is a realm of consciousness with its own inner and outer hierarchy. A *chakra* is a world, a sphere of consciousness. There are astral helpers and physical-plane helpers connected to each *chakra.* These spheres of consciousness do interrelate. A mentally healthy individual is functional in about three *chakras,* or spheres of consciousness, at a time. A person with severe mental problems would be in a single sphere of consciousness and could not deal with things that happened to him outside that area of the mind, or *chakra.* ¶When you meet the God or *asura* of a particular realm, it would always be a conscious meeting, but you may not always see the God or the *asura.* His presence would certainly be felt. Some symbol would appear, such as an image of Lord Gaṇeśa, or of Lord Śiva. A lot of people are open to Śivaness now and see Him through His images. Terrorists are seeing their *asura* gods in their guns, explosives and other weapons. At this time in the Kali Yuga, all states of consciousness are out in the open. All of the fourteen *chakras* are manifest in one way or another on Earth. It is a very intense time on the planet, and likewise a ripe time for spiritual unfoldment.

Saturday
LESSON 146
How Bhakti Is Cultivated

Once a person rises in consciousness out of the *chakras* below the *mūlādhāra,* and the foundation of *bhakti* has been laid, then going into refined states of mind through meditation becomes easy. This is because devotion has removed the barriers. Those who love each other can communicate easily. The devotee who has reverence for a temple and devotion for the Gods within it can communicate easily with those Gods. *Bhakti yoga* is love on all levels of consciousness—physical, mental, emotional and spiritual. *Bhakti yoga* makes us feel good. When in a state of *bhakti yoga*—yoked with the Divine through love—meditation is natural, and one can "soar within" with ease. There are no barriers where love is concerned. ¶The greatest inhibiting factor in practicing *bhakti yoga* is the doubting, cynical, intellectual mind. Doubt and skepticism harden the heart and narrow the mind. People in this state cannot really become devotees until their heart softens and their tense intellect relaxes. They must fulfill the *sādhana* of reconciliation, which is to go before each person they know and worship that person as a God. This *sādhana* is done in meditation. The devotee has to meet each one by bringing up the person's face before him and sending kind thoughts and blessings of *prāṇa.* This must be done time and time again until love comes into the heart for each of them. Only after this *sādhana* has been accomplished will *bhakti* begin to bloom in the heart. The bloom of *bhakti* softens the heart and relaxes the intellect. ¶When you have the energy of *bhakti,* of love, flowing through your body, meditation is easy. You don't have to go through the preliminaries. You are already functioning in the higher *chakras.* The *bhakti* experience takes the *prāṇas* into the higher *chakras* from the lower *chakras.* But if you are living in the consciousness of personal, communal, national or international antagonism, entering meditation will be difficult. All the preliminaries will have to be carefully gone through—*prāṇāyāma,* deep concentration, the lifting of the *prāṇas* into the heart and throat *chakras,* etc. Then slowly the internal *bhakti* is complete, and the vibration of love begins to be felt. This is time-consuming. ¶The Śaiva Siddhāntin finds it much easier to do this preliminary work in the temple through the externalized *yoga* of *bhakti,* rather than trying to internalize the *bhakti* and lift the *prāṇas* while seated in lotus position, which is time-consuming and not as enjoyable. Whereas, to lift the energies from the lower *chakras* to the higher *chakras* through performing *bhakti yoga* in the temple during worship is easy, natural, and considered by the Siddhāntist as being a pure joy. ¶The best way to learn *bhakti yoga* is to choose the finest *bhaktar* among your religious group and emulate him. You can read about *bhakti yoga*, understand it intellectually and learn what it is supposed to do for you. That is fine. But to progress on the path up the spine, it is necessary to be a part of a religious group. The group helps the individual, and the individual helps the group. There are nearly always one or two real *bhaktars* within every religious group. Therefore, to learn *bhakti yoga*, emulate one of them. This, in itself, is forgetting yourself, as you copy another person's actions and attitudes. True, the person you choose may not measure up to your standards in other areas of life. But if in approaching the Deity, he shows true humility, patience and total surrender, be like him. If you join another Hindu group, visit another temple or *satsaṅga* group, pick out a true *bhaktar* there and emulate him or her as well. This is the way to learn *bhakti yoga*. Vegetarianism is an essential for the *bhakti yogī*, as is proper personal, cultural conduct in all matters of society. Śaivite culture and a consistent lifestyle keep the *bhakti yogī* always reminded of the Divine within the universe and within himself. Those who have no barriers to love find it is easy to see God in everyone.

Sunday
LESSON 147
Unconditional Surrender

What do we mean by internalizing worship? In external worship we are trying to see God and communicate with God with our two eyes and our physical nerve system. We enjoy His *darshan* and feel His *śakti*. In deep meditation, the external worship is deliberately internalized, and we are trying to see God with our third eye and feel God's all-pervasiveness through our psychic nerve system. Externalizing *bhakti* is really much easier than internalizing it. But once the externalized *bhakti* is perfected, it will be easy and natural to internalize *bhakti* right along. When this is accomplished, the most rigorous hurdles and time-consuming practices of *yoga*, which often lead the person onto *āṇava mārga*, will have been side-stepped. ¶To internalize worship, after the *pūjā* is over, sit before the Deity and draw into yourself all the *prāṇas* you feel around your body. Then draw those energies up the spine into the head. This is done with the mind and with the breath. It is very easy to do. It is especially easy when one is at the end of a major *karmic* cycle. The *bhakti* of uncompromising surrender, *prapatti*, to the God during a temple *pūjā* awakens the *amṛita*. The *amṛita* is the sweet essence from the *sahasrāra chakra*. It is the binding yoke to the Divine. Bind yourself in the lotus posture after temple worship and simply internalize all the feeling that you had for the God during the worship. That's all there is to it. The *yogī* yoked within enjoys the *amṛita* that flows from the cranium throughout his body. Devotees who want to awaken the higher *chakras* and sustain that awakening on the safe path will throw themselves into becoming uncompromising *bhaktars*. Then all the Gods of all three worlds will open their hearts and shower their blessings upon them. ¶What is my advice for those who find such uncompromising surrender hard to imagine but realize it is their next step on the path? Go on a pilgrimage once a year, read scriptures daily, perform *pūjā* daily, go to the temple at least once a week, if not more often—fulfill these disciplines, known as the *pañcha nitya karmas*. This is the basic Śaiva Siddhānta *sādhana*. ¶But on another level, one will not be able to fulfill the *pañcha nitya karmas* if he or she is not fulfilling the *yamas* and the *niyamas,* for these are the character-builders. We must possess a good character to be successful in *bhakti yoga.* Therefore, begin at the beginning. Right thought produces right speech, which produces right action. Right thought is produced through the knowledge of *dharma, karma, saṁsāra* and the all-pervasiveness of God. This knowledge correctly understood disallows the devotee from having wrong thoughts. He simply has right thought, and of course, right speech and action follow naturally. ¶Śaiva Siddhānta extols the *guru* and says that when the student is ready, one will appear. The *guru* will always restate the *dharma* to a devotee who is having problems with *bhakti yoga* practices. He will always direct the mind to the beginning teachings, for it would be obvious that the student does not understand one or more of them. If the devotee is not following the *pañcha nitya karmas* or the *yamas* and *niyamas,* it is obvious that purified knowledge of these four areas—*dharma, karma, saṁsāra* and Śivaness—needs to be strengthened. ¶Individual practices to advance spiritual unfoldment include prostrating before God, Gods and *guru,* full body, face down, arms and hands outstretched, and in that act, total giving up, giving up, giving up, giving up. In Sanskṛit it is called *prāṇipāta,* "falling down in obeisance." What are these devoted ones giving up? By this act they are giving the lower energies to the higher energies. It is a merger, a blending. When one is performing this traditional devotional act, awakening true *prapatti,* it is easy to see the lower energies from the base of the spine, the *mūlādhāra chakra,* rising, rising,

rising up the spine through all six *chakras* above it and out through the top of the head. It is transmuting, changing the form of, the base energies which breed conflict and resistance, "mine and yours" and "you and me," division, insecurity and separateness, into the spiritual energies of "us and we," amalgamation, security, togetherness. ¶Once the giving up of the lower is total—body and face on the ground, hands outstretched before the image of God, Gods or *guru*—those energies are surrendered into the higher *chakras* within the devotee, and it is a blissful moment, into the consciousness of "us and ours," "we and oneness," and inseparable love, thus claiming their individuality, not as a separate thing, but as a shared oneness with all. Thereafter, these devoted ones, having been transformed, are able to uplift others, to harmonize forces around them that they work with day after day after day, year after year after year. This total surrender, *prapatti,* is the meaning of Siddhānta. This is the true meaning of Vedānta. The combination of both, and the pure practice of *prapatti,* as just described, brings out from within the deeper meanings of Vedānta, the Vedic philosophy, without having to depend on the path of words, lectures and debates. My *satguru* was once heard saying, "It's not in books, you fool."

Āṇava Mārgaḥ

आणवमार्गः

The Path of Egoity

They are learned in Vedic lore. Knowing God is within them, they thought themselves to be God and plunged into distracting pleasures, forgetting all thought of God.

TIRUMANTIRAM 529

Monday
LESSON 148
What Is the Āṇava Mārga?

Much has been said of the path toward merger with Śiva, and much remains to be said. But the truth is this: most people on this Earth are following another path for the moment, the path of self-indulgence and self-interest and selfishness. No doubt, it is the most popular path, and it has its own *pandits* and masters, who teach how to perfect the path of the external ego, how to perfect worldliness, how to perfect the trinity of I, me and mine, how to perfect self-indulgence. But that is not the ultimate path, which is followed by the few, by mature souls. It is important for aspirants to know that the real path leading toward merger with Śiva has many detours, pitfalls and sidetracks that beckon unwary travelers. It is important for him or her to know about these side paths, to be warned, as I am doing now, to be wary of them, to be cautious, to be extremely careful. ¶One of these I call the *āṇava mārga,* or the path of egoism. True, it is not a traditional path, but it is a path well worn, well-known in all human traditions. In fact, you could say there are three such untraditional paths, three worldly *mārgas: āṇava, karma* and *māyā.* The last two bonds, *karma* and *māyā,* are the first to begin to diminish their hold on the soul as one proceeds on the path to enlightenment. And when these fetters begin to loosen, the *āṇava,* the personal ego identity, thoughts of "me," "my" and "mine," should also begin to go, but often don't. When *karma* and *māyā* begin to go, *āṇava* often becomes stronger and stronger and stronger. ¶The *karma mārga* is when the soul is totally enmeshed in the actions and reactions of the past and making new *karmas* so swiftly that little personal identity, or egoism, is experienced, like a small boat bouncing on a vast ocean of ignorance, the ignorance of the *māyā mārga.* This *mārga* is not spoken of at all in Hindu scripture, except indirectly, yet all the sages knew of its delightful distractions. It is truly there for the soul who is bound to ignorance of how to know *karma*, know *dharma*, or even know anything but the next and the next experience, as each is eagerly thrust upon him. Here the soul is bound by *karmas*, bound by *māyā*, giving the abilities to ignore. That is the path that has to be left once on it, the sidetrack to be ignored and passed by. A sharp turn, a firm decision, brings this unhappy soul onto the *āṇava mārga*, the path of extreme personal identity. Here the realization comes that "Yes! I am a person on this Earth with the rights of all. I am no longer bound and harassed by experience. I can adjust experience, create new experience for myself and for others. I can be the controller. I am I." ¶The I becomes the realization and sometimes the end of the path of the *karma* and *māyā mārga.* The I, that all-important personal identity, so strong, becomes the realization of the small and limited "self," which appears to be a big and real "self" to those who have found this path, which is not the spiritual path, but the path of grayness; while the *karma* and *māyā mārgas* are the paths of darkness. Yes, the *āṇava mārga* is a real *mārga*, a labyrinth. It truly is. ¶We are concerned to define *āṇava* because a word can be dispatched too quickly; a concept can be forgotten. *Āṇava,* the personal ego, finding oneself, with a small "*s*," the personal identity, gaining intellectual freedom are all modern clichés. Defining the *āṇava mārga* appeared in my mind as a necessary thing to do while I was helping devotees to understand the *charyā mārga*, the *kriyā mārga*, *bhakti yoga*, *karma yoga* and *rāja yoga*. To offset the negative with the positive better explains the positive. To understand the pure essence of ignorance, where it comes from, its values, beliefs and motivations, better defines the heights of wisdom out of which comes *dharma* and aspirations for *mukti*. Sometimes, in fact, we see *āṇava mārgīs* thinking they are *yoga mārgīs*. ¶We cannot advance on the path without a starting place. No race was ever won but that everyone began at the same place. To know where we are on the path of life progressing to *mukti*—which is one of the four tenets of life, *dharma*, *artha*, *kāma*, and *mukti*, merger with Śiva—we should not be deluded by the ignorance of what the *āṇava* actually is, and what *artha* and *kāma* are, the strength of their hold on the soul, preventing the *dharma* and the final attainment of *mukti*.

Tuesday
LESSON 149
Self-Concern, Self-Preservation

People who are living totally on the *āṇava mārga* are not religious, and if attending religious functions, they stand with folded arms, on the outside looking in. Their only emotions are for themselves, their immediate family and friends, but only if the latter prove useful to them. *Selfishness* and *avarice* are two descriptive words for their lifestyle. To their immediate family, they are protective, kind and resourceful, provided the spouse, sons and daughters are productive and equally as concerned for the family welfare. The animal instinct prevails of "Let's preserve the nest, the lair, at all costs." ¶The businessman on the *āṇava mārga* is generous by all appearances, gives enough to gain praise, adulation and to make friends. In proportion to his wealth, he gives a pittance. There is always some attachment to the gift, some favor to be eventually reaped. The gift is a purchase in disguise. The *āṇava mārgī* in giving charity would always want adulation, credit, name to be mentioned, and if it is a large amount, some control in the use of it. There are strings attached. He may even follow up years later and wreak criticism and havoc if the gift given in cash or kind is not maturing in value. ¶In contrast, the devotee of God on the *kriyā mārga* would know that he was only giving to himself through indirection, and place his gift freely in the hands of those he trusts. Trust is always preceded by love. There is no difference between the two, except the method of follow-up. The *āṇava mārgī* becomes the law. The *kriyā mārgī* knows that divine law will work for him if he follows the path of righteousness, while the *āṇava mārgī* is driven to manipulate the law in fulfillment of each of his concerns. ¶Emotional ups and downs are contingent to the *āṇava mārga.* Four steps forward, three steps backward, a step to the side, six steps forward, two steps backward, a step to the side, six steps backward, three steps forward, a step to the side—it is an amazing dance. It's a maze. They all think they are going someplace. This dance of ignorance is not one of Lord Śiva's favorite dances, though it is definitely one of His dances. He does it with a smile and a sneer, mirth and a tear on His face. He actually has most of the world doing this dance now. Ignorance is equally distributed throughout the planet. The intrinsic ability to ignore, consistently and persistently, the eternal truths of the Sanātana Dharma is one of the great qualifications of the *āṇava mārgī.* ¶Television is a window into the *āṇava mārga.*

We see extremely successful professional people who maybe have started on the *āṇava mārga* and have bypassed it to the artful acting portrayal of people on the *āṇava mārga.* We can see in their eyes, they have a life that is seeking and searching, understanding and knowing, and their magnetism keeps them before the public year after year after year. These are the professionals. Then we see on TV the *āṇava mārgīs* by the dozens. They come and go, are hired and not rehired. ¶Before the *āṇava mārga,* there is only confusion, unqualified thoughts, desires that are only motivative or directional, not crystallized into any kind of a concept that can be manifested toward a fulfillment. The confusion arises out of the drive for self preservation. All animal instincts are alive in such a human being. He does not hold to promises, does not seek to strive, is a proverbial burden on society. Society is made up of *āṇava mārgīs* and those who live in the other *mārgas.* Deception, theft, murder, anger, jealousy and fear are often the occupation and the emotions of those living without a personal identity, a well-defined ego. ¶A personal identity and well-defined ego is the *āṇava*, and the pursuit of the development of that is the *mārga.* Each *purusha,* human soul, must go through the *āṇava mārga*, a natural and required path whose bloom is the fulfillment of the senses, of the intellect and all the complexities of doing. It is prior to our entrance upon the *āṇava mārga* and while we are happily on the *āṇava mārga* that we create the *karmas* to be understood and overcome later, when we walk the *charyā* and *kriyā mārgas*. You have to understand before you can overcome. This is the time that we "do ourselves in" and later understand the all-pervasiveness of Śiva, the laws of *karma, dharma, saṁsāra.* Yes, of course, this is the time the mischief is done.

Wednesday
LESSON 150
Fear, Anger and Opportunism

Those who want to hold a position and those who don't want to hold a position combined, those who have no time to perform *sādhana,* who avoid their yearly pilgrimage, whose family cannot gather in the shrine room, who do not read scripture daily and attend a temple infrequently, if at all, they are doing extremely well on the *āṇava mārga,* in my estimation. Their *artha* and *kāma* are coming along just fine. Dharma is ignored, and *mukti* just may not happen. ¶Many people on the *āṇava mārga* perform *yoga, japa,* disciplines of this kind, and gain great adulation, as well as business contacts, through it. But nothing is gained other than a few minutes of quiet and aloneness. These are the opportunists, the people who make the world go 'round as we see it today. ¶*Swāmīs* are most precious to those on the *āṇava mārga,* giving blessings, amplifying their desires; adulation is sincere but not real. The *swāmī* is taken into their family as a personal figurehead of it, like a status symbol. They do not enter the *swāmī's ashram* to do *sādhana* and become a part of his life. And if the *swāmī* rebels, preaches *dharma* and holds back blessings, he is generally abused. "Love you, use you and abuse you" is the methodology of those on the *āṇava mārga.* All *swāmīs, gurus* and priests know this only too well. ¶The *āṇava mārgī* looks at God from a distance. He does not want to get too close and does not want to drift too far away, lives between lower consciousness and higher consciousness, between the *maṇipūra, svādhishṭhana* and *mūlādhāra* and the lower three, *atala, vitala* and *sutala,* which represent fear, anger and jealousy. He does not get into confused thinking. That is super lower consciousness, in the realm of the *talātala chakra.* He is guided by reason. That is why he can come into the other *mārgas.* ¶Therefore, God is at a distance. He sees himself pluralistically, separate from God, coexistent with God. Those who fear God anger easily. They fear their elders. They fear their government. They fear impending disaster, and they fear disease. God is just one item on the long list of things that they fear. They are not on the path of spiritual unfoldment. Their higher *chakras* are dreaming benignly, waiting for the consciousness to explore them. Only when someone begins to love God is he on the path of spiritual unfoldment. Only then is he a seeker. Only then does his budding love begin to focus on religious icons. Only then is he able to nurture his love into becoming a *bhaktar* and at the same time a religious person, a giving person. This is the *charyā* path. We come onto the *charyā mārga* from the *āṇava mārga.* We come to Lord Gaṇeśa's feet from the *āṇava mārga.* He is now the guide. The personal ego has lost its hold. ¶The *āṇava mārga,* and the glue that holds it together, is ignorance of the basic tenets of Hinduism. There is no way one can be on this *mārga* if he truly accepts the existence of God pervading all form, sustaining all form and rearranging all form. There is no way this *mārga* could be pursued by one understanding *karma,* seeing his manifest acts replayed back to him through the lives of others, his secret diabolical thoughts attacking him through the lips of others. The *āṇava mārga* does not include this knowledge. The *dharma* of a perfect universe and an orderly life, the consciousness of "the world is my family, all animals are my pets" is an abhorrent idea to someone on the *āṇava mārga*, especially if he is casted by birth in this life. The *āṇava mārgī* abhors the idea of reincarnation. To pay the bill of one's indiscretions in another life is not what *āṇava* is all about. There is a forgetfulness here. When you renounce your childhood, you forget that you ever were a child. You forget the moods, the emotions, the joys and the fears and all that was important at that time.

Thursday
LESSON 151
Surrender Is The Way Out

The *yoga mārga* must come naturally out of intense *bhakti* and internalized worship. The intensity of *bhakti* is developed on the *kriyā mārga*. The final remains of the ego are pulverized on the *charyā mārga*, where Śivathondu, selfless service, is performed unrelentingly with no thought of reward, but a hope that the *puṇya*, merit, will be beneficial in the long run. The *āṇava mārga* is easy to leave through total surrender to God, Gods and *guru*, along with *seva*, service to religious institutions. Surrender, *prapatti*, is the key. All the religions' teachings teach surrender to the divine forces. Great suffering, the psychic surgery kind of suffering, great repentance, is experienced in the overlapping of the *charyā mārga* with the *āṇava mārga*. The beginning knowledge of Hindu temple worship, scripture, being dragged into it by some aggressive teacher, later a desire for reconciliation—all this leads to penance, *prayaśchitta*, followed by serious *sādhana*. It is not without a great ordeal and effort, soul-searching and decision-making that one *mārga* bends into the other or bows before the other before it releases the consciousness to go on. One *mārga* must really bend before the other before one can be released. Before entering another *mārga*, it is a matter of giving up, which is painful, most especially for the *āṇava mārga* people, for whom suffering is no stranger. ¶How can someone on the *āṇava mārga* be convinced that there is a better way to live, think and act? The word here is *pursuit.* We are talking about pursuit. *Āṇava* people are always pursuing something, the fulfillment comes on the *āṇava mārga*, and there is fulfillment, but in a never-stopping pursuit of fulfillment. As soon as we stop the pursuit of fulfillment, we become unhappy, empty, feel unfulfilled and, I might even say, at times depressed. The *āṇava mārga* is the I-ness, me-ness, mine-ness; me, my, I. "I want, I give, I get, I collect." *I, me* and *mine* are the key words here. The true *āṇava mārgī* is the owner, the getter, the consumer, not always the producer, vulnerable to the emotions of fear, who uses jealousy as an asset to obtain. Anger is the motivating power to fulfill desire, by stimulating fear in others. He is a master of deceit. The true *āṇava mārgī*, perfected in the art, has at beck and call the eighty-four wiles of the lower emotions. ¶Why would someone begin to feel the need to change to a nicer way of life? The word *why* is the important word here. They are questioning, they are asking, they are intuiting another way of life. They have observed, obviously, others living a fuller life, fulfilled by the fulfillments of their pursuits, having left the *āṇava mārga. Āṇava mārgīs* have become aware of the existence of the *charyā mārgīs* and maybe a *kriyā mārgī* or two. It is the very force of the desire of pursuit that leads the *purusha,* the soul, to the *charyā mārga* into Śaiva Siddhānta. I see the whole thing like a tunnel—the *karma mārga*, the *māyā mārga*, the *āṇava mārga*, the *charyā mārga*, the *kriyā mārga*, *yoga mārga*—which the soul matures through as a child matures from a child to an adult. The problem is that it takes a little doing to define the pursuit. Therefore, the entrance of this tunnel, to be a good *āṇava mārgī*, is kind of crowded, and this is where the problem lies. To truly get on the *āṇava mārga*, to define the ego's identity, one must have the goal of pursuit. ¶There are two *mārga*s before the *āṇava mārga* begins, within the realm of deep ignorance. Here reside the masses who live in confusion, the professional consumers who know the generosity of society, who will never in this lifetime manifest a desire, a goal, a thought for the future worthy enough to be accepted on the *āṇava mārga*. They are the slaves of the *āṇava mārgīs*, those whom, as slaves, they manipulate without conscience.

Friday
LESSON 152
The Pernicious, Persistent Ego

Āṇava is one's personal ego, his identity and place in the world and position on the planet. If his motives are proper and the position is earned on account of good deeds, it is not *āṇava*. But if, when praised, he takes credit for himself, it is *āṇava*. *Āṇava* is the tricky substance of the mind. It is behind every door, it's peeking in every window. It is the first thing to come at birth and the last thing to go at death. To break the chain of *āṇava*, the yoking to the Infinite beyond comprehension in any state of mind must be complete and final. And yet, while a physical body is still maintained, the *āṇava* elf is still lurking in the shadows, saying "praise is better than blame, name must come into fame, and shame is to be avoided at all cost." This is the *āṇava* routine. It keeps people held down on the planet in the instinctive-intellectual mind of remorse and forgiveness and suffering the adjustments to circumstance that occur beyond their power of understanding. A big gun that shoots the bullet of the depth of knowledge of *karma,* the second bullet, of the deep understanding of the perfect universal energies, and the third bullet, of the *dharmic* way of a balanced life, kills the *āṇava* and brings that *purusha* onto the *charyā mārga,* onto the path of the Gods, the hospital of the soul at that point. The final conquering of the tenacious *āṇava* is the final *mahāsamādhi,* when all three worlds sing, "Mukti has been attained," the final goal of life that we on this planet know, merger with Śiva. ¶Because ignorance is all-pervasive, equally distributed throughout the world, one must leave the world and get a wise dome, wisdom, a wise head. He must transmute the energies from the solar plexus—nothing must affect him there—to his third eye, see into the past, see into the future, and with that seeing understand the present. ¶If we were to admit that there are really seven *mārga*s, we would find that *charyā, kriyā, yoga* and *jñāna* are progressive states of fullness, and the *āṇava mārga,* by comparison, is a static state of emptiness. This feeling of emptiness is a motivative, driving force of desire toward the attainment of the feeling of fullness. The feeling of fullness is the awakening of the higher *chakras,* of course. And the constant feeling of completeness is, of course, the permanent awakening of the *sahasrāra chakra.* The feeling of emptiness distinguishes the *āṇava mārga* from the other four *mārga*s, and this is why it is not included in Śaiva Siddhānta, but is not excluded either, because the *āṇava mala* is mentioned here and there and everywhere within the scriptures. For the sake of understanding individual ego in its struggles to be whole, we have delineated it as a path leading into *charyā*, *kriyā*, *yoga* and *jñāna*. ¶The path of the *āṇava* teaches us what to do and what not to do. It creates the *karmas* to be lived through and faced in many lives to come. And when *dharma* is finally accepted and understood and the religious patterns of life are encompassed in one's own personal daily experience, then and only then do we see the end of this path in view. So, the *āṇava mārga* is definitely not a never-ending maze or a no-man's land. Though a state of ignorance, it is still a state of experiential learning. All is leading, in evolution of the soul, to Sanātana Dharma. ¶Everything preceding *charyā* is *āṇava mārga*. People try to fill their emptiness with things. They work so hard for their money, thinking, "Oh, when I can buy this object for my home, I will feel fulfilled." They buy it with their hard-earned money. A day or two later, after ownership has taken effect, the initial fulfillment of ownership wanes, and unfulfillment, which has always been there, takes over, with the accompanying desire for the next fulfillment, object, or in the case of the intellectual, the next idea, group of ideas or new sphere of knowledge. There is no fulfillment in the instinctive-intellectual mind. This is the way it is. This is the way it has always been, and always will be, too.

Saturday
LESSON 153
Bound to The Path

A powerful businessman, a bum on the street, a highly educated scientist and the uneducated field worker could all be sharing the *āṇava mārga*. It is a path of gratification of the ego, or the gratification of other persons' egos. These days egos get gratified by going to heads of corporations, meeting important people and bowing before heads of state. It is on the *charyā mārga* that we learn that rich and poor, the powerful and lowly are all *purushas,* pure souls, *jīvas* encompassed in a physical body. And on this *mārga* we learn to bow before God and the Gods. We learn that their home, their officiating place, is the temple, the home shrine and under sacred trees. Being in their presence makes the *charyā mārgī* feel small. The first glimmer of the feeling of smallness is the first footstep on the *charyā mārga.* ¶Those who are not successful in life yet, and experience the repercussion of *karmas* of past lives denying them things, experiences, security and wealth, are the ruthless *āṇava mārgīs.* For those who have fulfilled their *dharmas,* and desire has waned for more—they don't need more money, they don't need more food, they don't need more houses, they don't need more respect—the *āṇava* wanes of its own accord, like an old leaf on a tree turns color and falls to the ground. They enter the *charyā mārga* and *kriyā mārga* with matured respect and humility. ¶The one who has little desires the most. He takes issues with the smallest things. The instinctive desire to save face is ever prevalent in his mind, for his face is all he's got. He doesn't have anything more. The rich and *āṇavically* powerful can buy new things, and when something goes wrong in life, change their image by retreating into their money, place, prestige and come out anew. Those full of *āṇava* who have satisfied, put to rest, the many desires of life, entering the *charyā, kriyā* and *yoga mārga*s gain a new spiritual face, a light in the eye and become looked up to even more than they were when they were sought out for donations for worthy causes. ¶Even the *jīvanmukta* doesn't like unjust criticisms, but he is bound by his wisdom to nondefensiveness, just, unjust, true or false. "Let them say what they have to say, and if it affects me, it is helping me on the way to my final *mukti.*" He would bless them for that. The *āṇava mārgī* is not like people on the other *mārgas,* who have mixed feelings about these issues. The *āṇava mārgī* is a prefect in retaliation. That comes as one of the powers or boons of living on this *mārga,* along with deception and the ability to lie one's way out of a situation. And to save face, place and position, no matter how lowly they might seem, is the goal of life for the *āṇava mārgī.* So, one should never drive the *yoga mārgīs, kriyā mārgīs* back to the *āṇava mārga,* because they would maintain their higher vision and be masters of the art and win at every turn. They should be left alone to pursue their goals. ¶In the Śaiva Siddhānta system of understanding, the progressive *mārgas* define the unfoldment of the individual soul, or the awakening of the *chakras.* When one comes to the temple because he wants to, has to and needs to live near one, he is on the *kriyā mārga.* This does not mean the *āṇava mārga* has not gone away or he has lost his personal identity. There is a little of the *āṇava* always with us right up to the moment of *mukti.* The *āṇava* presides through the fourteen *chakras,* but is most expressive before the awakening of the knowledge of the Gods and their abilities as helpmates to spiritual unfoldment. You don't get off the *āṇava mārga.* Individual ego slowly diminishes as the soul unfolds from *mārga* to *mārga.* Nandi the bull represents the ego, personal identity, and in a large traditional Hindu temple, we see many images of Nandi, getting progressively smaller as we approach the innermost sanctum. This indicates the soul's progression toward God or the diminishing ego.

Sunday
LESSON 154
Leaving the Āṇava Mārga

Āṇava still exists in the other *mārgas,* but it diminishes. It first starts out as the "I'll do it all myself. I need no one to help me." Fulfillment comes through fulfilling each individual desire. Self-preservation is a very important part of the personal ego. But then, later, as progressive steps are taken, spiritual identity fulfills the emptiness, as water fills up a container. Only at the moment that *mukti* occurs does the container vanish. Until then the *āṇava* is like smoldering coals in a burnt-out fire. New wood can be thrown upon them. They can be fanned up. Detractors to a spiritual movement will often try to reawaken the *āṇava* of its leader and kill out the rival movement by creating his downfall. ¶*Āṇava* comes strongly to the Hindu when not living up to Hindu Dharma, when not performing *sādhana,* when there is no desire for *mukti.* When he has a fatalistic view of *karma,* when his Sanātana Dharma does not include pilgrimage once a year, daily reading of scripture, home *pūjā,* temple worship, when he is overly involved in the acquisition of wealth, ignoring all the other goals of life—we have here the makings of a fine *āṇava mārgī.* Being overly involved with personal pleasures, *kāma,* neglecting *artha,* not understanding *karma,* we have the makings of a wonderful *āṇava mārgī.* Being overly involved in *dharma* or the desire for *mukti,* we have here the makings of a wonderful *karma yogī, bhakti yogī, rāja yogī, jñāna yogī.* The normal Hindu needs a normal balance of all the goals. It is no accident that the Hindu sages can understand the *āṇava* within man. Yes, of course, they passed through it themselves and are just tapping their own memory patterns, seeing the actions of others and knowing the outcome. ¶As the soul leaves the *āṇava mārga* and enters the *charyā* path, a budding love begins to unfold. He is now conscious in the *mūlādhāra chakra,* looking out through the window of memory and reason at the world around him. His personal ego, which had until recently been well placed on the *āṇava mārga,* is feeling bruised. It now has to deal with some very real challenges—loving one's country, loving the world, family, friends. The *charyā mārga* brings him into penance, which eventually brings him into *sādhana,* which is regulated penance. Without *sādhana,* penance tends to be spontaneous, erratic; whereas consistent *sādhana* is the regulation of penance. Now the soul begins dropping off the bonds of *karma, māyā* and *āṇava* as it unfolds into *bhakti,* love. This is true Śaiva Siddhānta. All this is not without being a painful process. Therefore, the protective mechanism of fear, which in itself is an avoidance process, is right there to help—in the *chakra* just below the *mūlādhāra.* The presence or absence of spiritual surrender and willingness to serve shows whether a person is on the *āṇava mārga* or on the *charyā mārga.* Devotees on the *charyā mārga* are striving to unfold spiritually and reach the *kriyā mārga.* People on the *āṇava mārga* are not striving at all. They are their own self-appointed teachers and proceed at their own pace. When we are on the *charyā mārga,* we have a lot of help from family, friends and our entire religious community. When we are on the *kriyā mārga,* the entire Hindu community, the elders and others all get behind us to help us along our way. Then when we are finally on the *yoga mārga,* we have all the *śaptha ṛishis* helping us. The *satgurus* are helping, too, and all three million *swāmīs* and *sādhus* in the world are helping us along the path at this stage. When we have entered the *jñāna mārga,* we are bringing forth new knowledge, giving forth blessings and meeting the *karmas* that unwind until *mukti.*

Japa Yogaḥ

जपयोगः

The Yoga of Incantation

The five-lettered Pañchākshara is the Lord's abode. Pañchākshara's manifest form is Namaḥ Śivāya. Its subtle form is Śivāya Namaḥ. Thus is He in that *mantra,* manifest and subtle.

TIRUMANTIRAM 919

ஓம் நமசிவாய

Monday
LESSON 155
The Magic Of Japa

Japa is the prelude to *rāja yoga. Japa* links Siddhānta with Vedānta through the repetition of the mantra *Aum Namaḥ Śivāya*—or *Aum Śaravaṇabhava* for the uninitiated. Those who are initiated into the sacred Pañchākshara, *Aum Namaḥ Śivāya,* have the advantage, because the repetition of this *mantra* will make them eventually see directly Śiva's perfect universe, and they in themselves will become a blend of Vedānta and Siddhānta. The unitiated are in preparation, using the mantra *Aum Śaravaṇabhava Aum,* thus quieting their minds, realizing the all-pervasiveness of Śiva and seeing that the natural state of the mind—when all *karmas* are temporarily suspended—is Satchidānanda, is peace, is bliss. Therefore, *japa yoga* is the prelude to *rāja yoga* and all other forms of *sādhana.* ¶ *Japa* is very widespread in Hinduism, more so than meditation. *Japa yoga* is easy to practice. The inexperienced can take it up immediately. It does produce certain results until they forget the *mantra,* which can happen! This may seem strange, but I have met devotees of *gurus* who had actually forgotten their *mantra,* even after paying a goodly sum to receive it. The innocent Americans and Europeans are the orphans and adopted children of Indian *gurus.* Some of these teachers, unaware of the critical differences of religion and culture of their new-found and eager devotees, respond by bringing them immediately into *japa* and *rāja yoga,* avoiding the known initiations and the basic philosophical and cultural foundations necessary for ultimate success. In the case of Indian devotees, these cultural and philosophical foundations would have been acquired within the family home. This foundation is necessary, as it directs the subconscious mind, which is the inner motor of a person, preventing him from opposing, inhibiting and invalidating the realizations that naturally occur when one practices *yoga*. So, first we learn the philosophy, then through *japa* and more advanced *yogas* we realize it. Whereas in performing *japa* and *rāja yoga* before you know the philosophy, what you previously learned may conflict with what you now realize. This can be very disconcerting. ¶When the philosophy is properly understood, we possess right thought, right speech and right action, which is proper behavior. This is culture. Hindu culture is very different from the European cultures, which are based largely on Abrahamic beliefs. Humility and obedience before elders and those who are wiser is a very big part of Hindu culture, as is the regard for knowledge and wisdom and the deeper philosophies. Therefore, a good character expressed day by day within the individual who is freed from anger and from contentious mental arguments is a central foundation for the practice of *yoga*. ¶One without such purity should not practice *japa yoga* lest he awaken the knowledge of his imperfections which are better to keep veiled. For knowing such could send him into states of remorse, early repentance—which means being penitent before one has the stability to take on the reaction of such a momentous discovery and undertaking. To meditate, one must be free from anger, jealousy and contention. *Karma yoga* should be practiced by the devotee prior to this to smooth out all character flaws. Śivathondu—which is another word for *karma yoga*—service to Śiva, is the platform for *japa yoga*. ¶Those who are victims to episodes of anger, to pangs of jealousy or to periods of fear should not meditate and should not perform *japa.* They should perform Śivathondu, attend group meditations and group *prāṇāyāma* sessions. This is because they must first be lifted up into the *mūlādhāra chakra* and above. They are living below it and must raise their consciousness in order to proceed deeply into themselves. It is the group itself in this case that will lift the individual who cannot easily lift himself. This process should be guided by a strong-minded, compassionate moderator.

Tuesday
LESSON 156
Japa Opens Inner Doors

One who performs *japa* properly will realize what he knows. You see, *japa* opens up the inner mind and focuses the energies of certain *chakras,* which are consciousness encased within the psychic nerve ganglia of the *nāḍī* network. Therefore, if he is a divine person, he will realize that Divinity. If he is an angry, selfish person, then he will realize that. We would want him to realize the former but not the latter. Through *karma yoga,* Śivathondu, the angry, hateful, contentious, competitive person will face himself through a series of small situations in which small realizations will occur. The instinctive nature and habits will be corrected until the individual is able to work smoothly over long periods of time. We would not want to open up his mind to the impurities, lest he become depressed or even morose and suicidal. Therefore, *japa yoga* obviously is an initiation that should come a little down the road, farther down the path. ¶Generally those who want to practice *japa yoga* and do have impurities working within them fall away from repetitive *mantras* very quickly, becoming a little afraid of what might happen if they are successful. Their own soul is watching after them in this early stage. Then there are those who are ardent, fanatical, you might say, who want to get results in a limited period of time and have no sense of the consequences. They work tirelessly to do this. The wise *guru* would discourage much practice of intense *mantras* or meditating alone, and would instead encourage *karma yoga*, giving to others, working for work's sake, serving for service's sake, not looking for rewards. Group meditations and group chanting are fine at this stage, as is temple worship until the purification process has had time to work its magic. ¶In short, there are two kinds of Hindus—a majority who worship in the temples without a philosophical background and those who do have such a background and take part in their religion, discussion of the higher knowledge and meditation upon it, feeling no need for the Gods or for temple worship. The Pañchākshara Mantra, *Aum Namaḥ Śivāya*, the center of the *Vedas*, is the link between the two, between Siddhānta and Vedānta, because it makes the mind realize what it knows. Every Siddhāntin knows a little about Vedānta and disregards it. And every Vedāntin knows a bit about Siddhānta and disregards it. Through chanting *Aum Namaḥ Śivāya*, finally you will realize what you know, including what you previously disregarded, and that blends the two—makes the whole person. The *purusha* becomes satisfied living in the physical body. The *jīva* becomes Śiva. ¶Initiation is essential for the ultimate results in chanting "Aum Namaḥ Śivāya," though, the uninitiated can and do say "Aum Namaḥ Śivāya." Within them it won't have much of an effect, but there will be an effect. This effect will be more potent and powerful once you have *dīkshā,* having studied and purified yourself through the purificatory process of *sādhana.* It would be so much better to chant "Aum Śaravaṇabhava" at this time, invoking Lord Muruga to bring the *guru* forth in your life who will initiate you. Muruga is the first *guru,* the first *swāmī* and renunciate. This is the preparatory stage.

Wednesday
LESSON 157
The Value Of Initiation

Oftentimes *japa* and chanting are the *ardha*-Hindu or non-Hindu's first introduction to Sanātana Dharma. An *ardha*-Hindu is often one who has been given a Hindu first name. It is our experience over the last fifty years that their *japa* has little effect unless they make the full commitment to becoming stalwart members of the Hindu religion and join a mature community. Those who are inside a department store handling and purchasing the merchandise and those outside looking through the window at the same merchandise are two different groups. *Ardha* means half, and *ardha*-Hindus are those who have come half way to making a full commitment and are still making up their mind. They are still on the outside looking in. Their *japa* doesn't have much power until they bring other aspects of their life into line with the Hindu Dharma. ¶For the non-Hindu who has not made a commitment, the universal *mantra Aum* is the most significant and precious of all *mantras.* This can be chanted by those of all religions, without restriction. The sounds of a city make "Aum." A child at birth says "Aum." A mother giving birth says "Aum." The last breath of a dying person is "Aum." Even the cows say "Aum." *Aum* is the *mantra* of Lord Gaṇeśa. All are striving for His holy feet. Those who are struggling with the lower nature, those who have not made a commitment to the Sanātana Dharma, a commitment which for the newcomers to the fold could be verified by their Hindu name on their passport, should all chant *Aum.* ¶To demonstrate the authority vested in the *mantra,* let me tell you a story. A minister in a court was summoned before the *mahārāja.* The minister also happened to be a *brahmin* priest, a *kulaguru* with the power to give initiation in the most sacred mantra, *Aum Namaḥ Śivāya.* The king asked him, "We would like you to initiate me into the sacred Pañchākshara Mantra." The *guru* said, "Yes, Majesty, I shall begin preparing you for your initiation." Then the king decreed: "No, we will take the initiation right now and never mind the preparations." The *kulaguru* objected, "This is quite impossible. My *guru* restricts me from giving initiation without due preparation." The king retorted, "So, we will do the *mantra* without you. Or else, explain to me how the *mantra* would work differently with the initiation than without." The *kulaguru* said, "Yes, Majesty, I shall give you an explanation." ¶In a loud voice the *guru* called to the five guards standing amidst the gathered audience, "Guards, come forward instantly and arrest this man, the *mahārāja,* he is into wrongdoings. He is demanding an initiation into the great Pañchākshara Mantra without the willingness to undergo the necessary preparations required by our noble *sampradāya.*" The guards stood silent, eyes wide, looking at the *mahārāja,* wondering what to do. The *mahārāja,* losing his composure upon hearing his minister's preposterous command, was struck with awe and thought, "What madness has overcome this holy man?" He then shouted to the guards, "Here, promptly: arrest this minister of mine, this *kulaguru* who is behaving in such an insolent manner against the throne. Tie him securely and take him away." The guards rushed forward without delay, grabbed the *guru* and held him tight. ¶The *guru* laughed and said, "Hold on a minute! I was just answering your question, Majesty. I spoke the *mantra* 'Arrest this man.' However, since I am not initiated into the court, not ordained to have that power, the guards stood idle and did not respond. You then gave the same *mantra*, 'Arrest this man.' Because you were carefully prepared and initiated as king, the guards responded." Upon hearing this, the *mahārāja* threw himself at the *kulaguru's* feet. The guards who had been hearing the entire conversation then released their captive, and themselves touched the holy man's feet and returned to their posts. In the months ahead the *mahārāja* meticulously prepared himself for and received his initiation. Now all three worlds cooperate with him. His kingdom flourishes, crops grow, the rains come when needed, the rivers run clear and the wells are always full, the cows are fat, the mangos fall sweetly from the trees, the Gods in the temples provide discipline for the king's subjects and Himalayan *ṛishis* regularly visit the kingdom, giving of their wisdom to one and all. Even though His Majesty chants, with the proper visualization, Aum Namaḥ Śivāya 108 times daily, one thing is missing: the king himself has not yet attained to full and complete God Realization. There is a story yet to be told.

Thursday
LESSON 158
Preparation And Propriety

The *mantra* is the name of the inner-plane being whom you are calling. If you say, "Aum Namaḥ Śivāya," are you ready to see what Śiva will show you, once He comes and lifts the veils? Maybe a little preparation—cleaning a few things, straightening up the house, the subconscious basement—is in order first. If you say, "Aum Śaravaṇabhava," is your mind really ready to become peaceful, or is it disturbed by fits of anger? But every soul is ready to say, "Aum," and come to the feet of the Lord of Categories, who will set everything in order from the many yesterdays. ¶If you are in the temple worshiping Lord Muruga, the mantra *Aum Śaravaṇabhava* obviously has a total overall effect. If you say "Aum, Aum, Aum" in front of Gaṇeśa, Gaṇeśa becomes conscious of your presence. The Deities are present in the temple. They may not be present in a person's home or under a tree. The main effect the *mantra* would have then would be to focus the concentration and quiet the mind. ¶If someone is already meditating and is self-instructed, not under a *guru,* and working for an eventual initiation to receive a *mantra* upon which to do *japa,* then whatever *japa* is performed should neither be too much nor too intense. We suggest for the non-Hindu *Aum,* and for the unitiated Śaivite *Aum Śaravaṇabhava,* 108 repetitions prior to meditation. This is totally on the safe side and will greatly enhance the meditation. ¶There is an idea that there is a special *mantra* for each person, and that a *mantra* should be secret. It has been my experience that *gurus* who are amassing wealth from unsuspecting Americans and Europeans will give all kinds of *mantras.* And they will be couched in a format that is sellable, like packaged merchandise. They will be made secret. But none of the traditional *mantras* that produce true realization and are lauded and acclaimed are secret. They are well-known by every Hindu in the world. Each Hindu throughout the world knows whether he has purified himself or not, and prepared himself or not, sufficiently to pronounce them—though he may pronounce them at any time he wishes, and an impact and a beneficial effect will follow in his life. But the spiritual impact of pronouncing a *mantra* after earning an initiation—this does not mean paying for it, but earning it through study and practice, character building, improving, proving oneself to one's *guru*—that effect is life-altering. It cleans the *karmas* of many past lives, perfects the lives of the future, and lays the foundation for *moksha* at the end of this or a future life. Let this not be misunderstood. ¶There are two classes of *mantras*, not powerful and powerful, meaning potentially dangerous. The only danger that a powerful *mantra* could have is opening a person to himself. The problem is not with the *mantra*, but with what is inside the individual when the *chakras* open and he can see his *karmas* of the past and his impending *karmas* of the future. That's why a *mantra* is carefully given, like a medical prescription. You don't give two aspirins to a baby. You give a half of one, or a quarter. And just as a child's physical body takes years to grow up, so do the mind and emotions. If the early adult years are put into training and purification through *karma yoga*, *bhakti yoga* and study of Vedānta, then there are no troubles on the path to enlightenment. To turn on a light in a dark room with a flick of a switch is quite a shock to the darkness of the room itself. Would we want this to happen within the individual on the path? No. We want to turn up the dimmer very slowly so he or she can gradually adjust to the brightness that was there all the time. ¶Many people want initiation because they want to get away from something. They want something to cure their ills. Others don't know what they want. They are disturbed, distraught with their *prārabdha karmas,* and they want relief. What they should be given is Śaiva Siddhānta—a comprehensive path of accomplishment. They should not be given a high-powered *mantra* that will, when it opens the mind, cause more frustration and disturbance from what the seeker sees. But once given such initiation—having no tools, mentally, emotionally or physically, to conquer the past *karmas* that the experiential emotions are intensifying (which should have been conquered through *karma yoga* and *bhakti yoga*)—the seeker falls into despair. It is the conscientious *guru's* responsibility to provide an on-going, progressive training prior to initiation and to continue it afterwards. Those who make their living by selling *mantras* would be considered fraudulent by traditional Hindu standards.

Friday
LESSON 159
The Esoterics Of Japa

Knowing the meaning of the *mantra* is very helpful when the devotee is visualizing it at the same time. Then he also knows when he reaches the goal which the *mantra* is supposed to produce within him. Since most *mantras* are in Sanskṛit, it is easy enough to find the meaning in the Sanskṛit dictionary. We must remember that the first *mantras* were given in the language spoken by the people. Sanskṛit *mantras* were given to people who spoke Sanskṛit. Yet, *mantras* could be phrased in other ancient sacred languages as well. It is just that the Sanskṛit language relates to the unfoldment of the inner being, which most other languages don't do as much. ¶*Japa* is a *sādhana*, and all *sādhana* is repetitive. *Japa* is taking a few words as a *mantra* and repeating it over and over again for mind control and personal enlightenment. This would attract good beings on the astral plane and strengthen the protective aura of the individual doing *japa*. There is no reason to think that performing *japa* would affect thc astral world in any way other than to bring forth goodness, compassion and admiration of the beings there toward the devotee performing this discipline. ¶*Namaḥ Śivāya Aum* and *Aum Śaravaṇabhava* have been revealed for spiritual unfoldment. They are not for magical purposes. Nor is *japa* intended for healing or other aims in the physical realm. ¶*Mantras* for *japa* are usually short, but not always. The Gāyatrī Mantra, consisting of thirteen words, is an example of a rather long *mantra*. True, Japanese Buddhists chant "Aum Namo Myoho Renge Kyo" for success, jobs and wealth, but this is not *japa* in the Hindu understanding. This is more along the lines of affirmation. *Japa* is very close to *rāja yoga*. *Japa* leads to spiritual renunciation, *rāja yoga* to enlightenment, stimulating the *chakras* of the head. *Japa* is never used in the Hindu tradition to pray for material things. Hindus do pray for material blessings, health and abundance but not through the use of *mantras* or *japa*. For these they turn to prayers, songs and ritual which stimulate the *chakras* of willpower, reason and cognition, giving the worshiper physical, emotional and mental vigor to bring the worldly goods into his hands. In summary, *japa* is religiously repeating just a few important, well-defined words, syllables or "seed sounds," called *bīja,* to awaken the higher nature. ¶Where did *mantras* come from? Mystical *ślokas* came from the *ṛishis* of ancient times who held conversations with the great *Mahādevas* and *devas* of the inner worlds. Out of this developed certain rituals that could, when performed properly, create certain causes in the physical world. In the English language we sometimes call these affirmations. An affirmation, as presented in our teachings, is generally for self-improvement. One is talking to his own subconscious mind. However, even in the English language, or any language, rituals are performed that do invoke the spirit forces of the religion. It just so happens that in Hinduism, Sanskṛit is the most accepted language of all, agreed upon by the Hindu hierarchy of all three worlds. ¶Because every sound has a color and creates a form on the astral plane when pronounced, the *mantra* must be pronounced properly, slowly, thoughtfully, with feeling, mentally seeing the color, mentally hearing the sound. The ideal way to perform *japa* 108 times is by also listening to the *nāda-nāḍī śakti,* the high "eee" sound one hears within the head when in a high state of consciousness. To perform *japa* quickly, as in a marathon, sometimes called "machine gun *japa*," brings little benefit. If you don't have time to do *japa*, don't do it at all. It should not be a meaningless ritual. It should be a very meaningful experience. ¶When we perform *japa* aloud, it is easier to concentrate the thought. The *mantra* is heard and therefore our mind does not wander. We must remember that the mind wandering into irrelevant thoughts mitigates the benefits of the *japa.* Therefore, we must remain concentrated. We perform *japa,* which is a *sādhana,* for pragmatic benefits. There is no other reason. Therefore, we should keep our mind on what we are doing. Visualize the proper colors that the *mantra* produces from one stage to the next. In *Śaravaṇabhava Aum* we visualize light blue fading into white and fading back into light blue, back and forth—"Śaravaṇabhava Aum, Śaravaṇabhava Aum, Śaravaṇabhava Aum." Blue is the color of the *ākāśa,* ether, and Śaravaṇabhava takes you there. Once the *japa* is perfected aloud, it may be done silently, simply by moving the lips but not making a sound, and then later making the sound internally without moving the lips. The ultimate accomplishment in the performance of *japa* is the *yoga* of going to sleep while verbally and mentally pronouncing the *mantra,* which continues during the sleeping hours. Upon awakening, the same *mantra* is still being repeated, mentally and then verbally, without a break in continuity. This is quite an accomplishment, but it has been done.

Saturday
LESSON 160
Getting the Most from Japa

There are some who in their spiritual exuberance follow the practice of doing 10,000 or 100,000 *mantras* a day in their *japa,* hundreds of thousands a month, millions a year. This is totally beneficial if under the direction of a *guru* who supervises the process. Most likely it would be given to an individual to conquer pride and arrogance. If a seeker is performing such intensive *japa* without the guidance of a *guru,* he then would be forcing a situation, using the *mantra* and the practice of *japa* like a drug, holding no concept in his mind of the results to be attained or even knowing if he has attained the results he should be attaining. It is the *guru* who always knows the results of the practice. But he never tells the results to the initiate. Attainment is never revealed intellectually until attainment has unfolded from within the individual, lest the intellectual knowledge of the attainment yet to be attained become a barrier to the attainment itself. ¶Each *guru* has his own methods of *mantra* initiation from his own *sampradāya.* It's a school of verbal teaching. Most importantly, preparation must be attained and maintained in order to convince an orthodox *guru* that the commitment is strong enough to make the initiation beneficial. Initiation from an orthodox *guru* begins a process of learning. It is not the end of a process of preparation after which the devotee is totally on his own once he pays his fee. There are many orthodox *gurus* in every country of the world. Choose your *guru* carefully by observing the devotees around him and what they have accomplished. If he has a preparation of training prior to initiation, qualifications to meet—such as vegetarianism, scriptural study, the performance of certain disciplines over a selective period of time—if he receives no fee for the initiation other than a gratuitous *dakshiṇā* afterwards—the amount left to the discrimination of the devotee, a love offering, or a contribution toward the payment of a *pūjā* in a temple to the priest—and if he provides ongoing, more intensive training and education, scripturally and culturally, after the initiation, preparing the devotee for the next stage of initiation, then you have a traditional *satguru.* ¶For the ultimate benefit in performing the *japa sādhana,* look on the Hindu Vedic calendar, *pañchāṅgam,* and choose the *amṛita yoga* days. These are the most auspicious. Next are the *siddha yoga* days. On any given day, the most auspicious time is during *gulika kāla.* These are the times when the forces of the universe—this means the entire universe, and most especially our galaxy—promote spiritual unfoldment. Of course, the daily experience of 108 repetitions should persist. Any intensification of this—1,008 times, for instance—would be best performed at a specially auspicious day and time. The most auspicious times of day are before sunrise and at sunset. The very best place and time to perform *japa* is in the temple after the *pūjā,* when all is quiet. This is the most ideal surrounding to repeat *japa* 108 times to gain maximum benefit. When performing *japa,* just breathe normally. *Japa* may be preceded by the *prāṇāyāma* practice that you have been taught by your *guru.* ¶*Japa* is a very good preparation for meditation. And you meditate on the *mantra* as you do the *mantra.* You can't meditate on the *mantra* without repeating the *mantra* inwardly. When the *mantra* is linked with meditation, it should be pronounced slowly so that you can meditate on each syllable of the *mantra* that is being repeated. You must remember that *japa* is the repetition of a few words or a few syllables. That is the *sādhana* of *japa.* Everything else is something else.

Sunday
LESSON 161
Pañchākshara Is Perfection

Aum Namaḥ Śivāya is such a precious *mantra* because it is the closest sound that one can make to emulate the sounds rushing out of the Self into the mind. Chanting it is profound because it is a sound channel which you can follow to get close to the Self of your self—sort of like following a river upstream to yourself.

Aum Namaḥ Śivāya can be equated with Śiva's drum of creation, called *damaru*. When "Aum Namaḥ Śivāya" is repeated, we go through the *chakras*, Na-Ma Śi-Vā-Ya Aum. The Aum is in the head *chakra*. Within *Namaḥ Śivāya* is each of the elements—earth, water, fire, air and ether—which in the mind are transmuted into all-pervasive consciousness, and that is also transmuted, into the great *chakra* way above the head at the end of the Aum. In just the breath, the space of time between the next repetition of "Aum Namaḥ Śivāya...Aum Namaḥ Śivāya...Aum Namaḥ Śivāya," the *prāṇas*, having reached Paraśiva, fall back into the spiritual, mental, astral and physical worlds, blessing them all with new energy, new life and new understanding. "Namaḥ Śivāya Aum, Namaḥ Śivāya Aum, Namaḥ Śivāya Aum, Namaḥ Śivāya Aum" is the constant process of life. It is the essence of life itself. We must realize that at any given moment we are a complete Paraśiva-Satchidānanda *jīva*, only working on the "Maheśvara part"—on the *jīva's* becoming Śiva. Paraśiva is there. Satchidānanda is there. The maturity of the *purusha*, of the *jīva*, the embodied soul, is not. Therefore, *Aum Namaḥ Śivāya* takes us into the reality above and beyond the relatively real. To know it is to experience it, and to experience it is to become initiated. ¶I have been performing *Aum Namaḥ Śivāya* for over fifty years. At first it had no meaning other than, "Wonderful, at last I got my *mantra*, and an assignment from my *guru* to perform *japa* regularly." As the *japa* progressed, all the inner worlds opened, all the doors of the mind. All the spiritual forces were unleashed, and the ability to control them came naturally. You see, *Namaḥ Śivāya Aum* brings the totality of the individual to the forefront and makes it manifest in daily life. This most pragmatic *mantra* is found at the center of the *Vedas,* in the hymn known as Śrī Rudram, and Śiva is at the center of *Namaḥ Śivāya Aum.* As the center of the *Vedas,* it blends Vedānta with Siddhānta, fusing them together with the fire of realization. So, I and all Śaiva Siddhāntists are a fusion of Vedānta and Siddhānta, with all doors open of understanding of the fourteen windows, the *chakras* of the mind, and even more than that. ¶My *satguru,* Śiva Yogaswāmī, placed great emphasis on *japa,* repeating the name of Śiva with concentration and feeling. This great Nātha *jñānī* explained, "May we not forget that *mantra* is life, that *mantra* is action, that *mantra* is love, and that the repetition of *mantra, japa,* bursts forth wisdom from within. *Japa yoga* is the first *yoga* to be performed toward the goal of *jñāna.* In the temple perform *japa.* Under the sacred tree, perform *japa.* I performed *japa* all of this life as a silent *sādhana,* and it is automatic now." Śiva Yogaswāmī enjoined his devotees: "Wear *rudrāksha* beads, repeat the Pañchākshara, let your heart grow soft and melt. Chant the letters five, and in love you will discover Śiva's will. Chant so that impurities, anxieties and doubts are destroyed. All hail *Namaḥ Śivāya.*"

Manoviśvam

मनोविश्वम्

The Universe Of the Mind

Bound by the primordial limitations, all living souls experience the five states: waking, dreaming, deep sleep, beyond deep sleep, the state beyond. Endless indeed are the bodies and organs that *māyā* endows. All souls alike, caught in birth and death, are struck by *karma*.

TIRUMANTIRAM 2160

Monday
LESSON 162
The Inner and Outer Being

Popular thought prevalent today is that we have an external mind to be shunned and an inner being to be reached. I look at the internal areas of the mind and the external areas of the mind as being one and the same, an integrated whole, one totality of mind. In my personal life I have proven this to myself time and time again for more than fifty-one years. ¶The inner universe of the mind is tremendous. It is much larger, more complex and better organized than any of the universes we can see with our physical eyes. The superconscious areas of mind deep within each of us are more advanced than the externalities of the material conscious world. ¶As an example, this planet, Earth, began in a very simple way. Man himself has made it extremely complex. Man has added to the planet all of the buildings, all of the systems, the laws, the cities, the countries, the states. Man has done this all himself. Quite often I humorously say, "The Gods created heaven and Earth and man decorated them." The inner mind is many times more complex than this. ¶Man is discovering new things within the sea and in outer space. All of these vast new discoveries are being registered within his subconscious mind. Only through his deep, intuitive, perceptive faculties, resident within the inner area of his mind, is he able to grasp these new findings, relate them to discoveries of the past and conditions of the present and hold a mountaintop overview of it all. But if he does not have this deep, intuitive, perceptive faculty awakened, man becomes confused by these new discoveries and fearful of his future. ¶Only the one who is inwardly awake, vibrant, alive and has the burning desire to know and be creative with that knowledge is content and at peace with himself and the world at large. For the more he knows about the external world, the more he discovers from deep within himself as he passes this knowledge on to the present generation, who will in turn pass it on to the succeeding generation, systematically and in an organized way. Many enlightened souls on the Earth today are handling the knowledge acquired from the exterior areas of the mind and the knowledge acquired from the depths of their own being in this way. To perform this mental activity, one does not have to be mystically inclined. A mystic is one who lives two-thirds within himself and one-third within the external areas of the mind. ¶A person who lives two-thirds within the external mind and only one-third within himself is not classified as a mystic. Let us look at the one-third of the inner area of mind in which he is living. It can be a delightful inner world or a very tragic area of the mind. This depends upon the character of the individual himself, the nature of his evolution and how he conducts himself in daily life. Although he is living only one-third within, intuitive flashes can penetrate the exterior walls of his consciousness strongly enough to change the history and course of humanity.

Tuesday
LESSON 163
The Mind's Three Phases

The totality of the mind is vast and complicated. However, it is helpful to look at the entirety of the mind in three basic phases: the instinctive, the intellectual and the intuitive. The instinctive mind is easy to become aware of and experience. It includes the impulses of our physical body, our cravings, our desires, our digestive system, and our emotional mechanism that works through the physical body. The systems of elimination and blood circulation and the regulation of the heartbeat are all within the instinctive mind. This phase of mind functions automatically, or instinctively. It is as much alive in the animal kingdom as among humans. ¶Man alone develops the intellectual mind and is responsible for its composition as he lives along through life. This phase is a mixture of man's instinctive desires and cravings coupled with the knowledge he has gained from others and from his own intuitive discoveries. Within man's intellect, he organizes a vast amount of knowledge that begins to accumulate from a very early age. Ninety percent of this knowledge deals with the externality of the world and mind itself. The intellect can consume most of man's time through an incarnation, and usually does, lifetime after lifetime. ¶The intuitive, or superconscious, phase is even more complex, more organized, more refined than the instinctive or intellectual phases. It is mystically known as the mind of light, for when one is in this state of mind, he may see light within his head, and sometimes throughout the entirety of his physical body, if his inner sight is developed enough. Otherwise, he just begins to feel good all over, as actinic energy permeates his nervous system. When intuitive flashes come, he knows the next thing to be done in a creative activity. This is the superconscious area of the mind. When man is extremely perceptive, tremendously creative and knowledge seems to come to him from the inside of himself spontaneously, he is a superconscious being. ¶*Instinctive* is a word that some may understand and others take offense at. Don't. It only means "natural or innate," naming the drives and impulses that order the animal world and the physical and lower astral aspects of humans. For example, self-preservation, procreation, hunger and thirst, as well as the emotions of greed, hatred, anger, fear, lust and jealousy, are all instinctive forces. They are very real in animals and humans alike. When the mind functions instinctively, it is controlled by the habit impressions made in the subconscious during its journey through the experiences of life. *Instinctive* also means that the driving force comes from the sexual nature. The nature is turned in that direction subconsciously, even though the conscious mind may not be cognizant of the fact. It also means that in the event of an emergency, the animal nature would take over completely, being jarred loose from lack of what I term "mind-control," or from what might be called self-control.

Wednesday
LESSON 164
Intellect and the Instinctive Mind

The first steps on the spiritual path consist in learning to harness these tendencies and impulses and transmute their energies into the higher nature. But we should not think of the instinctive mind as "bad," for it controls the basic faculties of perception and movement, digestion, elimination, ordinary thought and emotion and the many other vital functions of the physical being. Animals, birds, fish, reptiles and insects are the personification of the instinctive mind. Living mainly in the areas of fear, they react immediately to change. Their driving forces are sustenance, sex, shelter and security for their young and themselves. It is these instinctive drives that are the most difficult impulses for humans to deal with. They are, for people, the seeds of all the desires of all the entanglements within the four areas—sex, money, food and clothes—which we capture in one word, *desire*. Yes, it is desire that propels humanity onward. ¶The instinctive mind also has within it various forces: the force of fear, the force of anger, the force of jealousy and the dynamic force of self-preservation. It is what it is—instinctive. It impulsive and immediately reacts to all situations. Though it is a great force in developing the intellect, its greatest enemy is intuition, the mind of the soul, which guides humans out of the morass of the lower nature into sublimity. ¶Most of us find the intellect a saving grace when it comes from the transformation of the instinctive nature into something more substantial. Constantly we strive to broaden our intellect, increase our knowledge, govern the mind with organized thinking and control our emotions by repressing the instinctive nature. This is nature's way of increasing man's justification of that which has passed before the window of the mind and was not pleasing to his intellect, the justification being that enough knowledge has not been acquired by the intellect to sufficiently suppress the instinctive nature. ¶While the instinctive mind places great pulls on the individual, the intellectual mind often has a stranglehold. An intellectual person could run this explanation through his intellect and be able to explain it back better than we are unraveling it here, relating this point to that point exquisitely, yet deriving absolutely nothing from the conclusions to improve his own life. The next day his mental interest would be off on another subject.

Thursday
LESSON 165
Intellect And Intuition

Mystics never demean or belittle intellectual reasoning. The intellect is not bad. It is good and necessary when used correctly. But they also do not elevate it too highly, knowing it is not the whole mind, it is only one phase of the mind. Instinctive, intellectual and intuitive phases define the whole of the mind. We often use the terms "unfolding intuitive faculties" and "developing intuition" in an effort to encourage an individual on the path to work within himself in subduing his intellect so that he can actually observe the already functioning totality of his intuitive mind. ¶In order to subdue the intellect—that partial conglomerate of thought patterns and modes of procedure which accord with the culture of the day—it is first necessary to inwardly observe how one's acquired intellect actually functions. Observation is a faculty of the intuitive mind, and this particular aspect of observation only comes into usage after daily meditation has been maintained over a long period of time. Once an inkling of success in knowing intuition and how it differs from reasoning, emotional impulses and pre-programmed patterns within the subconscious awakens, the contest is won. Then and then only we can sustain this knowledge and dive deeper into the inevitable, all the time losing the future and the past, and loosening the reins of the intellect. ¶Some men say they are part of God, that the God Spirit is within them. The intuitive mind we consider to be that part of God's vast mind—our inspiration. If you have ever had a hunch and had it work out, that is the intuitive mind working within you. It has temporarily dominated your conscious mind and made it possible for you to look into the future and estimate its happenings. The intuitive mind is the essence of time, yet it understands time and timelessness, its essence. It is the essence of space, yet it comprehends space and spacelessness. It is real, yet it does not exist—real only when used, nonexistent to the lower realms of the mind. ¶Man's individual awareness is either captured by the nerve system of external consciousness of the animal bodies which his soul inhabits as vehicles to live in on Earth, or captured by his celestial nerve system. This, then, is the intuitive nature, the natural expression of the transcendental soul known as man.

Friday
LESSON 166
The Five States of Mind

Observing the great vastness of the mind, we can draw another conclusion and say that there are five states of mind: conscious, subconscious, subsubconscious, subsuperconscious and superconscious. The first state is the conscious mind, in which we perform our daily routines. When awareness is in the conscious mind, we are externalized. This means we take our direction mainly from memory of past experiences, from other people, from newspapers, magazines, radio, television or our emotions. The average man is aware in the conscious mind from the time he awakens in the morning until he falls asleep at night. That's what makes him average. Only when he becomes mystically inclined does he become consciously aware of some of the other four states. ¶The second state is the subconscious mind, the grand storehouse and computer of man. It faithfully registers all thoughts and feelings that pass through the conscious state, whether correct or incorrect, whether positive or negative. It registers them and acts or reacts accordingly. ¶The subsubconscious, the third state of mind, is a conglomeration of various actions and reactions that we have experienced in daily life. It is a subtle state composed of two or more vibrations of experience which mingle and form a third vibration. We have an experience. We react to it. Later we have a similar experience. We react to that. These two reactions merge in the subsubconscious, causing a hybrid reaction that lives with us many, many years. ¶The fourth state is the subsuperconscious mind. Deep, refined and powerful, it filters intuitive flashes from the superconscious mind through the subconscious gridwork. There are times when you want very much to find a clear answer from within yourself. However, being aware in the conscious mind predominantly, awareness is cut off from direct contact with the superconscious. So, you begin to ask questions of yourself. These questions are registered in the subconscious. The subconscious, like a well-programmed computer, begins to search for the right answer from the superconscious mind. Then, all of a sudden, you know the answer from the inside out. Finding solutions through insight or intuition is one of the functions of the subsuperconscious. It also is the source of all true creativity, inspiration, understanding and perfect timing in daily events. ¶The superconscious is the fifth state of the mind. Within it is one world within another world and yet another. All mystical phenomena and deep religious experiences come from the superconscious. It is the mind of light, beautiful and vast. When one is superconsciously alive, he feels joyously alive throughout the totality of his being—physically, emotionally and mentally—for new energies are working through his nerve system. This state of the mind is available to everyone to be aware in. The superconscious is the mind of bliss. It is vast, pure intelligence. The subsuperconscious mind is that aspect of the superconscious functioning through established subconscious patterns. ¶As we learn to identify these states, one from another, we also become more sensitive, like the artist who learns to observe depth, color and dimension within a beautiful painting. His sense of enjoyment is far superior to that of the average man who simply sees the painting as a nice picture, having no appreciation of the intricacies of color, depth, movement and technique.

Saturday
LESSON 167
Unfolding the Superconscious

The average man may have occasional subsuperconscious experiences and rare superconscious intuitive flashes. His awareness, however, is not attuned to know the intricacies of the working of his own mind. Therefore, he is not able to identify one from the other, making his sense of enjoyment less than that of the mature mystic. Because he is unaware of the higher states of mind, the average man may harbor his awareness deep in a subconscious state of suffering over the past for long periods of time, thereby completely ignoring his superconscious intuitive flashes when they come. As a result, his ability to bring awareness inward, out of the external, conscious and subconscious states of mind and into more blissful and refined areas, is lessened. Now *sādhana* is necessary for him to unfold his inner depth. Although he is unaware of these superconscious happenings within himself and unable to astutely pinpoint and dramatically distinguish them from his turbulent subconscious, his superconscious breakthroughs do have an effect upon the totality of his being. But when man lives externalized in the conscious and subconscious states, all the inner enjoyment and conscious abilities of exercising perceptive faculties are completely lost. The ritual of daily *sādhana* must be performed to quell the ordinary mind's tumultuous turbulence. ¶There are many mystics in the world today who have had no formal training and seem to unfold inwardly very rapidly simply by learning about the five states of mind, how to distinguish one from another, and how to move awareness within them consciously and systematically. They are participating in and enjoying some of the benefits of being able to experience step-by-step direct cognition of the five states of mind—conscious mind, subconscious mind, sub of the subconscious mind, subsuperconscious mind and superconscious mind. There is but one mind and, in its functioning, it works the same in everyone, as an autonomous, interrelated, self-perpetuating mechanism. Concentrate upon that mind. Find out what the mind is. Observe your thoughts, feelings and actions from within, and know that your mind is yours to use to the extent that you control the mind with the will. ¶Why must you study the mind? Because understanding alone is fifty percent of the control of the mind. This understanding is necessary to impress the subconscious deeply enough to secure awareness so that spiritual strength continues to come from within, from the superconscious through the subconscious. Before we can meditate, we have to know our way around within the mind. What part of you understands how the mind works? It is your superconscious. The subconscious can't understand how the mind works, because it's the repository. The subsubconscious can't understand. It's a collective repository. Your conscious mind can't understand either, for it is opinionated knowledge—looking at the world through the eyes of others. Only the superconscious and subsuperconscious can conceive how the mind works.

Sunday
LESSON 168
Understanding Is Control

When a situation comes up, I observe how the conscious mind looks at it. Then I ask how my subconscious would see it. Pondering further, I inquire how my subsuperconscious relates to it; then, how my superconscious views it. Through this process I get a clear picture of what happened, how it happened and if I should take it seriously. You might react strongly to a happening, but when you look closely you see it wasn't much to be concerned about. It is just the subconscious reacting, so you forget it. The subconscious was the problem. It is your subsuperconscious, intuitive understanding that makes such judgments. ¶Remember, these are not five separate departments. They all interrelate. The conscious and subconscious work together. The subsubconscious seems to work independently of both the conscious and the subconscious, but it is not really independent. It is just another aspect of the subconscious. The superconscious is our vast, pure intelligence. The subsuperconscious is one aspect of the superconscious, functioning through subconscious patterns. ¶As we begin working with ourselves, we remold the patterns that set the course of our life. We remold our subconscious mind. We begin to identify with infinite intelligence, not with the body or the emotions or the intellect. As we prepare for the realization of the Self in this life, we set new energies into action within our body. We begin to flow our awareness out of the past and into the present, right into the now. This steadies emotion. Then we cease to have concepts that the physical body or the emotional body is "I." We begin to claim spiritual independence and are able to watch the mind think. By remolding old habit patterns in the subconscious mind, we cultivate a contemplative nature and become nonviolent in thought and action, having that innate understanding of the *karmic* cycles of the working of the various states of mind. We are able to love our fellow man. It is easy to keep promises and confidences, for we have a certain restraint. We can begin to direct desires and acquire a certain inner poise which we did not have before, and we continually find new understanding through meditation. ¶In order to meditate, it is not enough to memorize the five states of mind—conscious mind, subconscious mind, sub of the subconscious mind, subsuperconscious mind and superconscious mind. It is not enough to memorize the processes of unwinding awareness and reprogramming the subconscious through affirmation, attention, concentration and observation. We must study out and apply these teachings to ourself. We must master them. This is the way we become a different person than we are today. When we simply memorize, we are only putting another intellectual covering over the beauty of our soul. ¶Surround yourself with superconscious people, people who are on the path. Being in their presence will help you, and their being in your presence will help them. The group helps the individual as the individual helps the group. This is provided the group is of one mind, both inner and outer. Place yourself in a good environment, a physically clean house, clean clothing, clean body, and among people who are shining forth from within. Do not surround yourself with people who are bound in the conscious mind, engrossed in jealousy, hate, fear and the other instinctive-intellectual qualities that cause contention in and among them. This will disturb you and hinder your progress on the spiritual path. If you are going to sit for meditation, you must follow these inner laws. ¶Do not argue with anyone anymore. A mystic never argues. Argument pulls awareness into the conscious mind and programs the subconscious in a strange way. It becomes mixed up. Then it has to be unscrambled. Also, never try to convince anyone of anything. If you are talking to a mystic, he will understand what you are going to say as you speak it. Usually before you have spoken he will have grasped the point of it. He is that sharp. He is that keen. If you are talking to someone who lives deep in the intellect of the conscious mind, he will want to discuss endlessly. He will want to argue subtle points, and the issue will never be fully settled, especially if you disagree with him. ¶The mystic sits in meditation and asks himself, "Who am I? Where did I come from? Where am I going?" He has the sensitivity to take a little flower and study it and conquer the functions of distraction as he works to hold his awareness at attention, like a well-disciplined soldier of the within, with a will supreme in governing that attention. This caliber of mystic will in this way learn to concentrate inwardly, as his supreme will dominates his powers of awareness, bringing forth the body of the soul into the physical elements so its keen inner observation is unfolded.

Jāgarachittam

जागरचित्तम्

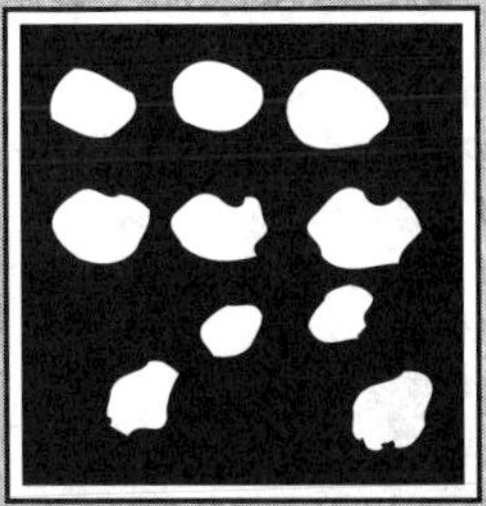

The Conscious Mind

In their bewildered thoughts are the three lions: lust, anger and ignorance. In their meandering thoughts are the four jackals: mind, intellect, will and egoity. In their sensory thoughts are the five elephants: taste, sight, touch, hearing and smell. These are the internal and external foes of the contending mind.

TIRUMANTIRAM 2214

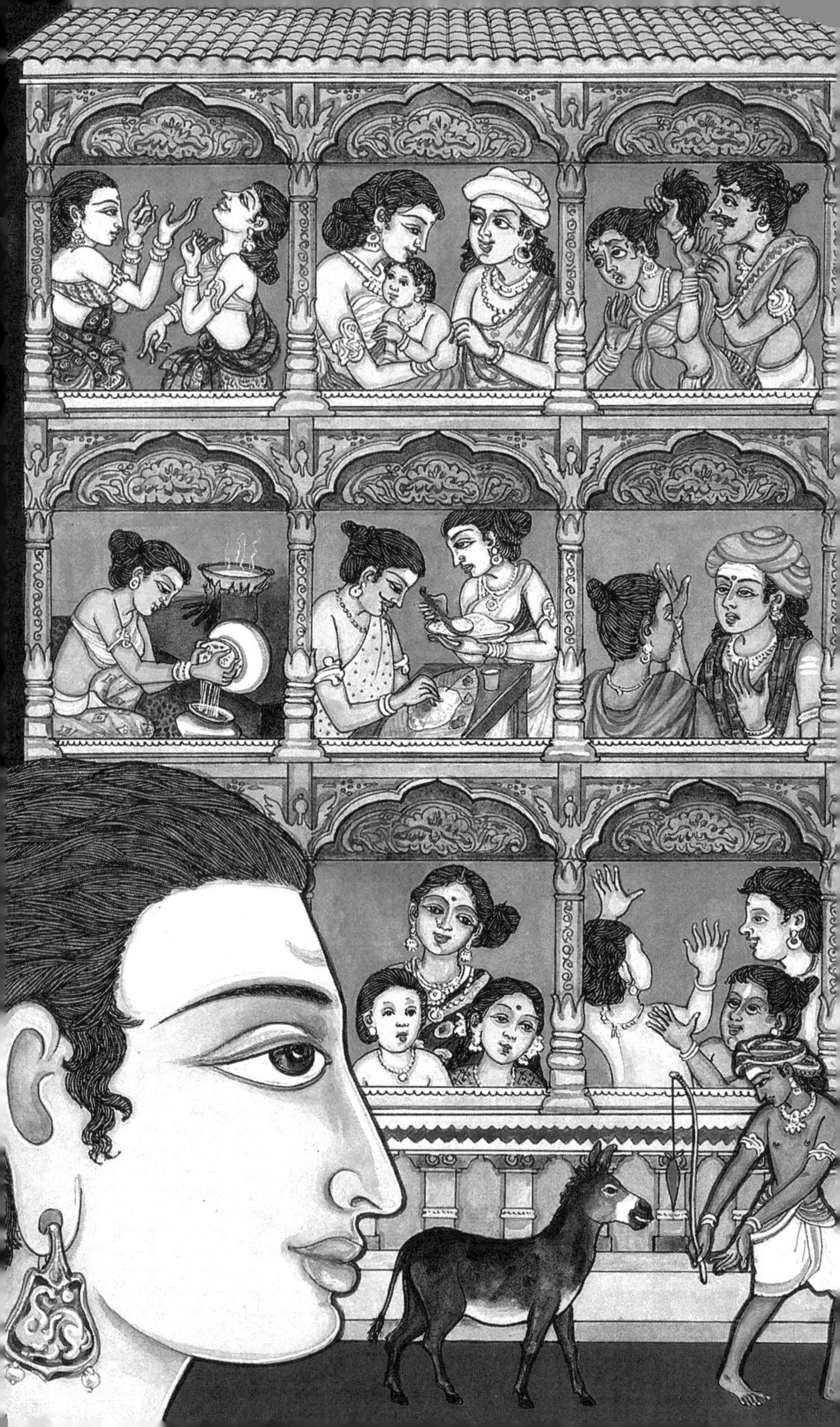

Monday
LESSON 169
Not Getting Bogged Down

When we live in the conscious mind, we are aware of other people's ideas. We listen with our ears, we see with our eyes, we feel with our fingers. We are involved in our physical senses, functioning instinctively as far as the physical body goes. We are functioning intellectually as far as our education goes, and we are dealing and working vibrantly and vitally in the world of external form. We can live in the conscious mind and be aware of that area of consciousness life after life after life after life, because the conscious mind is ever changing, perpetuated by its own novelty. One thing or idea leads us to another, and then on to another and another and another. We listen to people talk, and we want to know what they will say next. ¶The conscious mind is very curious. We taste something and we want to taste something else. We see something and we want to see something else. We feel something and we want to feel something else, and we go on and on, completely dominated by our five senses. This domination by the senses makes up the totality of the conscious mind. These five senses are constantly active, as energy continually flows out into the external world through them. The conscious mind makes up what is called the external world, and the external world is the conscious mind. We are all participating in making our own conscious mind as we go along through life. ¶Though the conscious mind is only seeming, it is very real while we are in it, as it glorifies in adding to itself. This process is called the intellect. As concepts and partial concepts are added one after another, the average person develops his or her intellect, and if it is not balanced by inner knowing, it holds the person firmly in the external realms of consciousness. Many people are trained to think, having had their conscious mind programmed in such a way, that the superconscious mind is nothing but a farce, that it doesn't exist at all, that the only reality is the external world, and pleasing the external senses is what life is all about. They are coached to believe that anything of an inner life or an inner nature is just pure fantasy, imagination, which only weak-minded people believe in. Many people live this way, with their awareness bogged down in the conscious mind—believing reality to be outside their physical body. The object of spiritual unfoldment is to transcend the conscious mind into superconsciousness and beyond.

Tuesday
LESSON 170
The Donkey And the Carrot

When we are in the conscious mind, we are like a donkey with a carrot in front of our nose. We are always walking to try to get that carrot. We are never satisfied, and we are never happy. The grass is always greener on the other side of the fence. No matter how much money we have, we want more. No matter how many clothes we have, we need more. No matter how many television programs we watch, there is always a better one coming up. No matter how many sights we have seen, the next one may surpass them all. No matter how much food we eat, there is always the next big wonderful meal to enjoy. No matter how many emotions we experience, the next set of those emotional experiences will be the high point of our entire life, and we are sure of it. That is the conscious mind. ¶When we live in the conscious mind, we only surmise. We make guesses. We are never quite sure if we are right. Therefore, we are insecure, because the conscious mind only knows what has gone before it. It is certain only about the past. If it has been provided with a good memory, then it knows the past very well. But without a good memory, the conscious mind doesn't know the past well at all. So, when we are in the conscious mind, we have one predominant and solid quality that we really can be sure of, and that is fear. We are afraid! We're afraid of the future. And many of the things in the past petrify us, for we don't want them to happen to us again. We don't know quite how to avoid them, because with awareness caught in conscious-mind concerns, our superconscious faculties are temporarily cut off. The superconscious mind is seen as a figment of imagination, a product of superstition. ¶The conscious mind is the real enemy, the real barrier, the real distractor to someone on the path of enlightenment. It is intriguing. It is the temptress. It leads us on and on and on, life after life after life after life after life after life after life. It is a wonderful state of mind, however, as long as our superconscious faculties are also available for awareness to flow into once in a while to become refreshed and renewed by a change of perspective and influx of energy. Otherwise, the conscious mind is a difficult and onerous state of mind in which to live, day after day after day. The spiritual path leads us out of the morass of the darkness of the conscious mind into the mind of light, which we call superconsciousness.

Wednesday
LESSON 171
Reason Reigns Supreme

It really hardens a person to live in the conscious mind all the time, because he has to build an ego shell around himself for protection, and that makes him insensitive and rough. One of the biggest protective influences of the conscious mind is anger. Anger makes a person cunning in his thinking, and of course the predominant underlying quality of anger is fear. He is always afraid of something. It is generally something that may happen or is going to happen. He is always in conflict with someone. These are the motivating forces of the conscious mind: anger and fear. Most people live in the conscious mind unconsciously. ¶The conscious mind is the area of the mind where memory and time are Gods, and reason is the Supreme Ruler. "If it is not reasonable, it is not acceptable," declares the conscious mind, and "If we can't measure it, it does not exist." That is the conscious mind. It is active. It is alive. The conscious mind perpetuates itself, and we all help it to do that. It is carried on in ramification by its own novelty. We can always find in the conscious mind some distraction to please us, to intrigue us, to dominate our awareness of other states of consciousness. And we don't have to look very hard to find it. ¶The mystic's goal is to control awareness while he is in the conscious mind—to know where he is in consciousness. When he finds he is aware in the conscious mind, and the five senses have become his ruler, he then controls his awareness within the conscious mind itself. He does this in a number of ways. One way is through the control of breath. Breath is life, and life is breath. Breath is the controlling factor of awareness. Awareness rides on breath. Breath is also a controlling factor of our willpower. A seeker must develop a dynamic will to walk the path of enlightenment, so that he does not stumble or falter, but continues onward no matter how difficult the path seems to be for him. ¶The mystic loves the conscious mind, for he sees it like an adult sees the toys of children. An adult does not take children's toys too seriously, but the child does. Meditate on that comparison. Meditate also upon the conscious mind while you are aware in it. Write down on a piece of paper the various areas of daily experience over a period of three days to which you are most attached. Then meditate on those time periods until you are able to see the chemistry that makes the conscious mind appear to be what it is. When you live two-thirds within yourself, even physical things begin to look transparent to you.

Thursday
LESSON 172
Like Writing On Water

Spiritual unfoldment leads us along the path into the illumined knowing of where we are in consciousness at any point in time. There are many methods through which this may be accomplished. ¶Carefully choose one path and then stay with it with extreme loyalty. For this, a preceptor is needed, a spiritual guide, to answer questions, to raise questions for you to find answers to within your meditations. It is an arduous journey. The rewards come only near its end. ¶To live positively in the conscious mind each day, exercise at least a half hour. Keep the vital energies of the body high and healthy. Eat simply and follow a vegetarian diet, feeding the stomach rather than the mouth. Be considerate of others always and live inconspicuously, almost transparently, by not ruffling your surroundings, by keeping the home neat and clean, by passing through a room or place and leaving it in a nicer condition than before you arrived. Seek fresh air and learn to breathe deeply. Get out in the sun. Move the physical body, walk briskly, dance, keep the energies vibrant and buoyant. Be close to nature. Grow food. Develop an art or craft so the hands are active, creative. Of course, being neat and attractive in personal appearance keeps the thoughts of others toward you positive. This is the way to live in the conscious mind. Try to live life as though you are walking in the rain without getting wet, or carefully writing on water. No ripples, no disturbance, no reactionary residue that has to be faced at some future date. ¶When we live unconsciously in the conscious mind, we most often look at the physical body as who we are. We say, "I am hungry," "I am happy," "I am not feeling well," "I want to go to America" or "I have just come to Bangalore." Instead of "I am not feeling well," we mean our physical body is not feeling well. Instead of "I want to go to America," we mean we want to take our physical body to America. Our language is a conscious-mind language. The perspective of our language is constructed to make the conscious mind the real thing, the entire reality of the world. From little children we have been taught that the conscious mind is real and that anything other than this real, solid, conscious mind is to be doubted. ¶The mystic walks in the opposite direction. He goes against the crowd. He learns to swim upstream. It is a little more difficult for him, but oh so worth it. The seeker has to learn that the conscious mind is only a vast dream created by many, many people who are dreaming openly. They are dreaming, and every mystic knows it. They are forming the dream by what they say, by their emotions, by what they think and by that in which they involve themselves. The mystic knows there is no enduring reality to the vast dream made up by people themselves, by their desires, their relationships, their cravings and their insecurities.

Friday
LESSON 173
Shrouding the Soul Body

If we were alone in a desert, there would not be much of the conscious mind present. Our emotions would subside. Our perceptions would be keen and uncluttered. Our senses would awaken. Our reality would be mostly an inner reality. We would have to call upon our inner resources to subsist. But as soon as a city grew up around us with hundreds of people in it, we would experience the development of a vast conscious mind, for everyone would contribute just a little bit to it. Problems, projects, confusions and involvements of every kind would assert themselves, absorbing our awareness. ¶Most of the inner resources we relied upon formerly would be forgotten as we ceased to depend upon our own strength and innate intelligence. We would begin depending upon a rule book. We would rely on what someone else thought, on what was taught in the universities, stored in the libraries, legislated by politicians and promulgated by the news media. We would follow opinion religiously and develop an intellect. And one by one, all of these layers of the conscious mind would cover the soul, making the outer more evident than the inner. ¶The beautiful, radiant body of the soul would be covered in the very same way that we would take a gorgeous lamp glowing with light and put pieces of fabric over it. First we would put a yellow piece of fabric over it, an intellectual coating. Then we might argue about some intellectual concept. Others would say, "I don't believe you." And you say, "I know I'm right." Then we would put a pink piece of fabric over the lamp. Pink is the color of emotion and self-aggrandizement. Perhaps we would continue trying to help our friend, and he would say, "I don't want any help. Get out of here!" We might become angry with him and put a red piece of fabric over the lamp. And when we are depressed amid all these mixed emotions, we cover the light with a black piece of fabric. When jealous of our fellow man, we drape a dark green piece of fabric over it. Where is the light of the body of the soul, that crystal-clear light? It's there, temporarily covered. ¶The body of the soul actually looks like a plastic body filled with light. You have seen mannequins with arms, legs, torso and head made completely out of transparent, neon-like plastic. If you were to put a light in such a mannequin, it would glow. This is what your soul body, your psyche, looks like. The conscious mind has truly become a reality for those who have layer upon layer covering this body of the soul. They are living with all of those emotions vibrating in them. Greed, hate, resentment, jealousy and anger are all totally alive on the inside. Yet, plastered on the outside of it all are beautiful, superficial emotions.

Saturday
LESSON 174
Conscious and Subconscious

Remember, the sum total of the conscious mind only knows what has preceded it, what has gone before it—the past, what it can remember. It will only accept that which seems to be reasonable. So when the process of going inward persists, the sheaths have to be removed, one after another. The senses have to be quieted, the subconscious mind reeducated. This is how the conscious mind and the subconscious mind work hand in hand. ¶The subconscious mind is like a great computer. It responds to the programming that has been set in motion through all the previous lives. Our reaction and habit patterns of this life form our tendencies of the next life, and the tendencies of our last life make our reactions and habit patterns of this life. Life after life after life, we have been programming the subconscious mind. It has been mainly programmed by awareness caught in the instinctive emotions of the senses of the conscious mind itself. ¶The conscious mind can become just as vast and wonderful, or as terrible, as we want to make it. It is not to be feared. It is not to be ignored, either. It is to be understood. The conscious mind is a state of mind just like all the others, for there is only one mind. Our individual awareness flows through the various phases of that one mind. ¶The conscious mind is primarily an odic force structure. Odic force is the emanation of actinic force through the physical body. Hidden tendencies, repressions, suppressions and reactionary habit patterns accumulate in the subconscious mind and give enough ballast of odic force for awareness to be neatly attached to everything of which it is aware. We are then in the conscious mind most of the time, and not inwardly oriented. ¶When people are caught in the conscious mind and believe it to be absolute, they believe in finite terms such as: "When you're dead, you're dead. So live your life and really get as much as you can out of it, because when you're dead, you're dead, and that's the end of it." They believe that the external world is absolutely real, and that anything of an inner life is simply imagination. They live a rather shallow life, perpetuated by their emotional habit patterns and reactions. They anger quickly. They are quick to become jealous. They are suspicious, and they become emotionally attached to other people, with whom they later argue or fight. They love to be entertained. They seek entertainment, trying to get more of everything that is possible to get. Their desire nature is never satisfied in their conscious-mind experience. Awareness has been enmeshed in these conscious-mind desire cycles for such a long period of time that to release it and dive deep within, we must first gain mastery of awareness through attention and concentration. ¶After awareness is wise to the conscious mind and the subconscious has been positively reprogrammed, attention and concentration bring us into subsuperconscious states. We begin to breathe regularly and diaphragmatically. We become aware of only one thing at a time in the physical world, allowing one thing to attract our attention, rather than continuing to ramify. This practice begins to weave awareness into subsuperconscious, perceptive states.

Sunday
LESSON 175
The Meaning Of Detachment

You have heard the statement "Being in the world, but not of it." This is done through detachment. It is an attitude. It is a perspective. It is how we hold ourselves within that really matters. Basically, that is the only difference in the beginning stages between one who is on the spiritual path and one who is not on the path—it is how awareness is held within, the perspective from which the conscious mind is viewed and responded to. ¶The conscious mind is created and ramified by man himself. It is carried on by its own novelty. It goes on and on and on, and awareness can go on and on and on and on in it. Only in those quiet moments of retrospection does someone who lives in the conscious mind relax, turn inward and understand a little philosophy. This pondering gives release, a new influx of energy. The object in being on the spiritual path is not to have just a little influx of energy, but to be the energy itself—consciously. The object is to have awareness basically attached to the primal life force, and to see that and experience that as the real thing, rather than be attached to a collection of possessions and memories in the material world. ¶Anyone who is strongly in the conscious mind has a feeling of possession and a feeling of fear. We're afraid of losing possessions. We own something. We love it! We break it! We cry! Our nerve system hurts when the odic force detaches. It was attached to that which we owned. Emotional involvement is a function of odic force. Holding awareness within the higher states of mind does not mean we cannot own anything. It means we will love it more when we do, but we will not be attached to it to the point that we become emotionally torn when it goes away. ¶Understanding of the forces comes as we unfold on the path. Someone who is not involved deeply in the conscious mind is not subject to as many instinctive emotions. He is more of a real person, more himself. Most people think of the conscious mind as the entirety of the mind. But actually it is only one-tenth of the mind's entirety and, therefore, should not frighten us in any way. Nor should we wish to retreat from the conscious mind. The only retreat is simply to detach awareness from that which it is aware of and allow it to go soaring within to that indefinable source from which all energies spring. Dive into the source and lose awareness within it and attain your ultimate goal.

Saṁskārachittam

संस्कारचित्तम्

The Subconscious Mind

Light the lamp of mind and dispel the darkness of egoity. Extinguish the fire of wrath and brighten all lamps within. Thenceforth alike, the mind's light is an undying lamp indeed.

TIRUMANTIRAM 602

Monday
LESSON 176
The Form of the Subconscious

What is your subconscious mind? Think about this for a minute. Realize that everything that has once passed through your conscious mind in the form of experience is resident right now within your subconscious. Not only that, but imbedded within the cellular structure of your body, in the DNA code—one of the most formidable discoveries of modern science—lie all the experiences of your genetic history. The life, the biological evolution of your forefathers, is all registered in the molecular strands of your subconscious, capable of being recalled into memory. ¶In our study together we will be concerned with much more than the negative areas of the subconscious. We will discover that the subconscious can be a great help in our daily life—once we learn to impress it properly, and consciously utilize the latent powers within it. Then it ceases to be a deterrent to well-being, and becomes a valuable tool, available at all times and under all circumstances as we progress through the experiences of life. ¶The subconscious mind, like the conscious mind, has a form of its own. It is given form, shape and momentum by the nature of your experiences in life and the way you react to them. Most people are not happy with the form of their subconscious mind. They are still reacting to early experiences, early environments. Some people go to great expense in trying to change the form of their subconscious, through therapy or travel, but because there is no absolution in either, in time they generally manage to recreate their subconscious in the same old form. Childhood experiences do have a profound influence on one's make-up in this life, but these influences are by no means binding. Any attitude, any personality conflict or block in the subconscious can be demagnetized and resolved. ¶How do we change the form of the subconscious? We purify it by resolving in understanding those experiences which have created it. How do we resolve those experiences through understanding? We bring them up into the light and face them without reaction. By resolving our reactive experiences in understanding, the subconscious becomes more and more transparent to our own view and, therefore, necessarily undergoes positive change. To be able to objectively observe one's own experiences without reaction is one of the powers acquired through the performance of *sādhana.*

Tuesday
LESSON 177
Resolving Past Experiences

Suppose when you were young you stole some money from your mother's purse. "She promised me this once and broke her promise," you rationalize. "Besides, I really need it," you add. Then, because you are not particularly pleased with yourself, you pack this experience away in a corner of the subconscious where you will not need to think about it. You suppress it. But the next day, your mother casually mentions the subject of money to you, and you react or emotionally re-enact the experience. You feel guilty. Not wanting to think about it, you suppress it again, deeper in the subconscious. Suppose then later in life your mother has become seriously ill, and in a reflective mood you realize that you have not been close to her for many years. Mixed in with a rush of buried memories you come across the incident of the stolen money. ¶For the first time you appreciate and realize the sense of guilt that had lingered, influencing your life since that time in a hundred subtle ways. In the light of understanding, the experience suddenly becomes clear to you, and you objectively and unemotionally see yourself as you were at that time. You feel relieved and strangely lifted, not because you were able to analyze why you stole the money, but because in totally facing and accepting yourself in that circumstance you realize that you have expanded beyond it into a new realm. ¶Intuition travels through a purified subconscious. Before we can utilize the superconscious or intuitive realms of the mind, we must be able to resolve those past experiences which may still vibrate in our subconscious. Realize, however, that you need not seek out mental repressions. Simply face each one honestly as it naturally arises in life. Imagine that you are trying to arrive at an important business or family decision. All the facts you need to know have already been outlined, yet you find yourself frustrated in not being able to arrive at a clear decision. The more you concentrate upon the problem, the more obscure does the answer seem. What your conscious mind isn't aware of is that the personality problems you are having with your superior at the office, or with your spouse at home, are clouding the issue. Soon after, while relaxing on a family outing, thinking about nothing in particular, a great feeling of compassion, forgiveness and understanding wells up within you, and all at once that "bright idea" needed to solve the problem comes to you unbidden.

Wednesday
LESSON 178
A Channel To Intuition

Why does intuition come at this time? Your mind being at rest and no longer disturbed, intuition can flow through it unhampered. Then, too, the elements of a problem have a way of piecing themselves together in the subconscious when it is allowed to relax. Your best answers often come after you have removed the searchlight of your conscious mind's focus for a time. This is the superconscious working through the subconscious, making it subsuperconscious. ¶You have now unfolded the key to living an intuitive and productive life. People who live positive lives have clear goals well impressed in the subconscious mind. They often draw upon their subsuperconscious mind, though they may call it by another name—perception, insight, intuition, instinct or sixth sense. ¶The subconscious mind may appear to be a very complex state of mind, as anything is when we do not understand it. Through daily *sādhana* you will learn how to clear the subconscious of its unnatural states of confusion and how to keep it clear, transparent. Through *sādhana* you will understand the relationship of the subconscious to the instinctive mind. ¶The subconscious mind performs many, many functions for us. In fact, it would be impossible to do without it. But think of some of the uses of the subconscious—the skills which your memory bank acquires, such as typing, driving, playing musical instruments or speaking language. As soon as any learning process becomes subconscious, the conscious mind is free to direct its attention to new areas of learning. Even all the processes of the physical body are governed by the subconscious mind. Can you imagine having to think through and control your heartbeat, or your digestion every time you enjoyed a meal, or the intricacies of muscular coordination? It is only when we interfere with the natural processes of the subconscious—which are very intelligent if left alone—that we become aware of our dependence upon this positive state of mind. ¶Here is an exercise in using the subconscious constructively. Before going to sleep at night, decide what time you want to awaken yourself in the morning. Visualize the hands of a clock at that time and impress yourself with the feeling of waking up at the particular hour which you set for yourself. Then, just before you go to sleep, forcefully impress your subconscious with the command to awaken yourself at whatever hour you have chosen. Confidently anticipate that your subconscious will do this. Don't worry, don't doubt, don't question—just observe the way in which your subconscious works for you if you but let it. ¶The subconscious mind is a storehouse, a reflection of all previous conscious mind experiences. The power of our decisions creates our reactions of tomorrow. When tomorrow's reactions happen, they program the subconscious. We have to be careful that our programming is just right, so that the channels to superconsciousness begin to open through the subconscious.

Thursday
LESSON 179
Confronting Memories

When man finally turns inward, sits down and asks "Who am I? Where did I come from? Where am I going?" what is the first thing he discovers? The subconscious mind, of course. ¶Do not be afraid of the subconscious. It is useless to be afraid of the past. If memories come up from the subconscious as if they happened yesterday, and you begin reacting emotionally and even physically all over again, say to yourself, "Welcome, welcome, welcome, memory from the past. My goodness, you're shaking my emotional body. I remember going through these emotional states years ago, and here we are reliving this film over again. But now I am on the spiritual path to enlightenment. I am the Self. One day I'm going to realize it fully. I only live in this physical body. I use these emotions, but I won't be used by them. They are my tools. So here you are, my memory pattern, trying to make me feel like I did five years ago before I reprogrammed my subconscious and awakened spiritually. Oh, memory from the past, you have tested me well. Thank you." Then, like a good secretary, write down on a piece of paper everything you can remember about these experiences that have come before your vision, and burn the paper when you have finished. Write down the entire experience that you are reacting to emotionally. ¶This paper-burning serves three purposes. First, it is symbolic to the subconscious that you are not going to react anymore to that particular problem. You have, through the act of writing it down, taken it out of the subconscious. Second, burning the paper means that no one else will read it, which might cause other problems. It also means that through the act of burning subconscious memories, you have released them forever. ¶When you begin to meditate, you become keen and perceptive enough to begin to see within yourself. Occasionally, you will see into the subconscious area and begin emotionally to relive the past. This means that many of the predominantly strong memory and reactionary patterns of the past loom up before you, one after another, and you may begin to react to them all over again, emotionally and even physically. These are not real experiences. It is only a layer of the subconscious exposing itself to your inner vision, indicating that reprogramming is needed. Handle each layer dynamically. Welcome the thoughts and accompanying feelings in a hospitable way. Do not fear them or regret them, and certainly do not criticize yourself for having them. Simply remove them from the subconscious by writing them down and burning the paper. The reaction will subside, but the memory will linger as an education upon which you can formulate decisions for the future, thus avoiding the same problem.

Friday
LESSON 180
Never Fear The Past

Generally people start meditating and do fairly well in the beginning, for their great desire to unfold spiritually propels them within themselves. But when the subconscious mind begins to upheave its layers—as it naturally must for the unfoldment process to continue beyond an elementary stage—meditators become afraid to look at the subconscious patterns of their seemingly not-so-perfect past. To avoid facing themselves, they stop meditating, and the subconscious subsides. The once-meditating seeker returns more fully to the conscious mind and becomes distracted again in order to forget "all those terrible things." At the time, the remembered past seemed to be terrible because the impressions were strong, magnified by sensitivities awakened through meditation. ¶For many years thereafter the one-time meditator can be heard to say, "I'd like to meditate, and I do sometimes, but I don't have time, really, to meditate. What he is actually saying is, "Most of my time is use up distracting myself so that I won't have to meditate anymore and won't have to face my bothersome subconscious." ¶On the path to enlightenment, you have to face everything that has gone into the subconscious, not only in this life, but what has been registered in past lives. Until you do, you will never attain Self Realization. Your final obstacle will be that last subconscious area that you were afraid to face, looming up before you in the form of worries, fears and repressions that you will wish to push away, hide from, so that neither you nor anyone else can see them. ¶To hear of the Self is a great blessing, indeed, but to desire to realize the Self means that in this and your past lives you have gone through all of the experiences that this Earth consciousness has to offer. You have died all of the deaths and had all of the emotional experiences. You have had the good of the world and the bad of the world, and the mixed good and bad of the world through all of your many lives before you come to the life where you say, "I want to realize the Self in this life." Now you begin to tie up all the loose ends of past experiences that have not been fulfilled or resolved, because those loose ends are what bring you back to birth.

Saturday
LESSON 181
Meditation's Great Obstacle

Things that you cannot face in yourself you will hate when you see them in someone else. To counteract this, your universal love, the platform for Self Realization, must be awakened into the emotions of the instinctive mind and filter out into the conscious mind. So, as you are meditating and the various aspects of your subconscious come up, face them positively, reprogram them beautifully, and they will settle back into simply a memory pattern, resolved and incapable of disturbing you again. ¶If you see something in someone else you do not like and it is affecting you emotionally, sit down and face it within your own subconscious mind. The sore spot is located there. If you feel someone is doing something that you do not think he should be doing, and this really gets on your nerves, just know that under the right circumstances you may do the same thing because the tendency to react to it is there in your subconscious. Get into yourself and reprogram that area of your subconscious with good, positive affirmations. Firm up your lifestyle, be more strict with yourself, use your willpower and think positively. Do not allow a weak link in a chain of habit patterns to bar your spiritual unfoldment even for a moment. Sometimes we detect the weak link in our own chain by looking into the lives of other people. ¶If your parents are living the type of life that grates on your nerves, begin to realize now that perhaps when you become their age you may live a similar life. The grating effect that you feel indicates that the seeds of that kind of life are just coming up, and you are trying to suppress them by criticizing your parents, whereas what you should be doing is strengthening yourself through having compassion toward them. ¶One of the biggest barriers on the spiritual path is to dislike our own subconscious as we become familiar with it. We must watch this pitfall very closely. The subconscious mind is not an enemy. It is just a well-used piece of equipment that we are renewing. If we make an enemy out of the subconscious mind and walk around hanging our head, wondering why this happened and why that happened, and "If it were not for the subconscious I would be farther along the path," we are simply programming the subconscious to become an even more formidable barrier. Instead, we have to bless the subconscious mind and look at it as a vital tool to help us in our spiritual evolution. ¶Take a mountain-top attitude. If you are having a difficult day, tell yourself, "I'm working with my subconscious mind. Admittedly, things are not working out very well for me today, but I think I will have it all adjusted by evening." Run to the store, buy a lot of paper, do a lot of writing and burning and clear up various subconscious areas and release awareness to soar within again. This is called the *vāsanā daha tantra.* ¶The point I want to make is: do not fear the subconscious mind. Realize that it has not been programmed as it should be. Therefore, the program has to be changed. Realize that your superconsciousness is the master programmer. Get busy and reprogram your subconscious through the power of affirmation. You can do it through the powers of meditation. ¶Of course, there is a portion of the subconscious mind that remains more or less the same, handling the instinctive, involuntary processes of the physical body. But by following a *sattvic* diet, which is conducive to meditation, this area of the subconscious also begins to improve. As we improve food intake and elimination processes, we stop storing up poisons in our cells. As stored poisons are released within the body, they are eliminated regularly. This more physical area of the subconscious mind is also improved through proper breathing, proper posture, *haṭha yoga,* getting plenty of sun, exercise, walking and all of the many wonderful things that benefit the physical body. ¶Add to your contemplative lifestyle a craft. Working with your hands in doing a craft as a hobby, taking physical substance and turning it into something different, new and beautiful—this kind of creativity is important in remolding the subconscious mind. It is also symbolic. You are actually remolding something on the physical plane and, by doing so, educating yourself in the process of changing the appearance of a physical structure, thus making it easier to change the more subtle mental and emotional structures within your own subconscious mind.

Sunday
LESSON 182
Seeing Oneself In Others

It is a principle on the path that until we are rather advanced, we do not really know whether we have reprogrammed the subconscious mind or not, or if the reprogramming has been done correctly. However, we do know when we create something with our hands whether it is done correctly and carefully. We also know when it is finished, for we can see it on the physical plane. Taking a physical substance into our hands, using it carefully and systematically, and disciplining ourselves to finish that which we have begun is a powerful process. By doing this, we overcome habit patterns of carelessness and of not being able to pay attention to details. We also overcome the habit of becoming distracted. So, choose a hobby or a craft. It should be something that you do with your hands that changes the form of physical objects, such as taking clay and out of it making a beautiful vase or using yarn to weave a lovely tapestry. ¶As soon as the subconscious mind has been positively reprogrammed, even just a little, the channels of intuition begin to open, and you feel peaceful. Disturbances within your mind subside. At this stage on the path you often wonder if you are making progress anymore. You hold a consciousness like being in an airplane going at a thousand miles an hour while holding the feeling of not moving. When you feel as if nothing is happening to you inside anymore, you are living in an intuitive state, the eternity of the moment. Your intuition is now penetrating your external mind all of the time. ¶When your subconscious has been cleared of past reactionary patterns and reprogrammed thoroughly, you do not take exception to things that happen in the world. In understanding, you love everyone and embrace every event. You intuitively sense just what they are all going through, because you have, in your memory banks, knowledge of each happening acquired during all the lives you have ever lived. This becomes available to you subsuperconsciously. You begin remembering when you went through the very same thing your friend is going through. It may have been a life or two ago, but you went through it all the same. Therefore you know his next step, because you know how you got out of the same experiential pattern yourself. Then you begin to know that your soul body and your physical body are becoming one. You are slowly beginning to realize that you truly are an effulgent, spiritual being living on the Earth. ¶The only thing that is not spiritual, seemingly, is the subconscious mind, but that is an illusion because it has been programmed in a haphazard way. You have gone along through your many, many lives, having many, many, many experiences. It has collected up diverse habit patterns and erratic programming. When you attack this programming positively and work with it, the subconscious becomes a tremendous tool and is no longer the unfriendly obstacle that it was. It becomes subsuperconscious and new energies start flowing into the physical body. New understanding begins to come from within. Your perspective in looking at life is steady now. ¶Man has not always realized that a subconscious area of mind exists. For hundreds of years, humanity in the West believed that the conscious state was the only reality. Humanity has had religious inclinations also, and believed in superconsciousness, but felt that superconsciousness was totally outside and away from the individual self. That is why God is talked of as being way up in the heaven, and the angels high in the sky. These beliefs caused the superstition, religious misunderstandings and contradictions that have come down to us through the ages. ¶Why was God supposed to be outside the being of man, way up in the sky? It was because the subconscious area of mind was in-between. From this limited perspective, man saw himself as a little, insignificant nothing that has come from someplace, not knowing for sure when or how he got here in this conscious state. He knew he was a kind and hateful, generous and greedy, jealous, intellectual, instinctive being. He knew that. He knows it today. That is how one gets along through life. You have to fight for what you want. You have to argue. You have to be jealous, or else how are you going to get anyplace? You have to be quick-tempered to dominate others. You have to scare people, get your own way and elbow your way through life. That is the way to live when totally in the conscious mind.

Vāsanāchittam

वासनाचित्तम्

The Sub of the Subconscious Mind

Light and darkness live together in the mind, and thus the soul seeks grace and ignorance at once. The *jīva's* inner knowing is bereft of light. Apart from those who have attained wisdom, the rest despair of ever dispelling their mind's darkness.

TIRUMANTIRAM 1010

Monday
LESSON 183
Where One Plus One Equals Three

There is one area of the subconscious mind that seems rather devious and extremely hard to program. It is called the sub of the subconscious mind. It often could seem like faulty software in the computer. But when finally programmed correctly, it can become the greatest asset. It brings us good luck and assists with perfect timing through life. At times we feel as if nothing is happening to us anymore. Everything is going along smoothly. We walk up to a closed door and the door opens for us. We walk up to a telephone and it begins to ring. These signs show us that the subsubconscious is going along very nicely. As soon as we do not enjoy this fine timing, it is generally because of the sub of the subconscious area. For when two programs of a similar nature go into the subconscious computer at different times, they mix and mingle and form a third program within the subconscious that is difficult to fathom intellectually. This is recorded in the sub of the subconscious. For this reason, the sub of the subconscious mind seems awesome and foreboding. If both of the programs are good, beneficial, positive and spiritually vibrant, things go smoothly for us. But if they are not, this area of the subconscious can be very disturbing. Remedies are deep introspection and emotional-intellectual honesty. The subsubconscious can become very powerful, creating healthy new tendencies in this life and molding a dynamic personality. ¶Two thoughts, at different times, sent into the subconscious mind, form in what is called the sub of the subconscious a totally different rate of vibration when intermingled—that is, if the psychological arrangement of the mind was the same at the time each thought entered it. This subconscious formation of thought turns into feelings of the lower, instinctive nature and causes the external mind to react to situations in a way that it normally would not have done. ¶The subsubconscious mind not only attracts situations that express its contents, but creates situations by playing upon the subconscious itself. The sub of the subconscious mind, therefore, is the part of the subconscious that stores and manages the unfathomable result of the combinations of intense, emotionally-charged experiences, either positive or negative. These combinations create a third, hybrid reactionary condition quite unlike either experience alone could have caused. ¶Color shall be our example. Blue stands alone as a color, and so does yellow. When they merge, they make a third color, green, which creates a mood when you look upon it, different than the mood that arises from looking upon blue or yellow alone. Only in understanding that green is a composite of yellow and blue is the mystery dispelled. Add white to red and you get pink. Add water to soil and you get mud. This is easy to understand and shows the nature of impressions coming together in the subconscious. Add oxygen to hydrogen and you get water. That is a mystery which parallels the nature of the subsubconscious mind, a realm where one plus one equals three, while in the subconscious the sum is two.

Tuesday
LESSON 184
Fathoming the Unfathomable

Yes, two different reactionary thoughts of a similar vibration sent into the subconscious at different times under similar psychological conditions create a third, different subconscious happening. This happening registers in the subsubconscious and continues to vibrate there until it is dissolved and reabsorbed within the subconscious itself. If psychological structures build up as problems in the subsubconscious and are not resolved, they can inhibit or hold back the superconscious. One then easily feels depressed and subject to many lower emotions. Then the concept that one is a self-effulgent being seems quite distant, indeed. When the subsubconscious build-up is problem free, superconsciousness is there, bringing success and well-being. ¶The subsubconscious concerns us primarily as the state of mind which relates to congested subconscious force fields, or *vāsanās,* caused by two similar intense emotional reactions at psychological moments. The resultant deeply suppressed emotions are puzzling to the seeker because, unless he is able to resolve through periodic review his subsubconscious, he may find them welling up from within him unbidden, and he knows not why. The subsubconscious influences us when we are encountering an experience similar to one that caused one of the two component reactions. This releases highly unexpected emotional responses, inobvious reactions and new behavioral patterns, some positive, some negative. The hybrid formation continues to react within the subsubconscious mind until resolved. Once understood, the mystery is gone. The *vāsanā* loses its emotional power. To a very great extent, it is the subsubconscious that harbors our subliminal aspirations, self-esteem, impulses toward success, neuroses and overall psychological behavior. ¶An example of this state of mind is as follows. A young man goes to an office party and accidentally spills coffee on his suit. Being a gentle, shy man, he becomes embarrassed and emotionally upset when everyone turns to look at him. Many months later, he attends his sister's wedding. In her excitement at the reception, she accidentally spills tea on her beautiful new *sārī.* She is naturally embarrassed. But it is a psychological moment for him, intensified by his attachment to his sister, and he becomes more embarrassed for her than she is for herself. ¶A year later he discovers that each time he attends a social gathering, his solar plexus becomes upset, his digestion is affected, he gets a headache and has to leave. The fear mechanism, stimulated by the subsubconscious mind, is protecting him from another upsetting condition among a group of people. This continues for a number of years until the subsubconscious, in a semi-dream state, reveals itself to him and he sees clearly how the two reactionary thought patterns, caused by the dual experiences, met and merged and gave rise to a different conscious experience—the indigestion, the headaches and the dread of being among people. Once the obstacle was resolved in the light of understanding, he would be able to be among people in gatherings without these ill effects.

Wednesday
LESSON 185
The Mind's Potent Alchemy

It is only when the emotionally charged experiences that go into the subconscious are of a strictly instinctive nature that the subsubconscious is uncomely or not beneficial and becomes a strong hindrance to well-being. On the other hand, experiences of a positive, intellectual or spiritual nature merging in the subconscious can create a subsubconscious that is quite dynamic and helpful, giving courage and competence in worldly affairs. Feelings of security, love and compassion can come up from the subsubconscious during psychological moments in one's life to counteract and eliminate or subdue feelings of jealousy, hatred and anger, which are natural to the instinctive mind. ¶For example, a man's business flourishes during the summer. The next winter he experiences great exhilaration and satisfaction at winning a skiing competition. The summer success and the winter accomplishment merging in the subconscious create a third, different impression which builds an abiding confidence and impulsion toward future victory. The next year, he goes into a second business and again prospers. His competitors wonder how he has avoided the seasonal ebbs and flows of this particular business. "How has he been so lucky?" they wonder. The strong impression of being successful planted in the subsubconscious has created a positive habit pattern for the forces of the subsuperconscious to flow through. ¶The subsubconscious can also be formed by the blending of strong, intuitive, religious or mystical impressions. For instance, a devotee has an elevating vision of a Deity in an early morning dream or a conscious vision during meditation. A year later, while meditating, he has the experience of flying through the *ākāśa* in his astral body. These two impressions merge in the subconscious and create an deep-seated faith and unwavering certainty in the inner realities. Such *vāsanās* bring up courage and eliminate the fear of death, replacing it with the assurance that life is eternal, the soul is real and the physical body is but a shell in which we live. Now we have seen that the subsubconscious state of mind can be beneficial, or it can hold impressions that are actual obstacles in our path that must eventually be dealt with and overcome. Both positive and negative impressions can lie vibrating within it at the same time without interfering one with another.

Thursday
LESSON 186
Resolution Through Dreams

Through the powers of meditation, one can straighten out a few of the subsubconscious mind's predominant misprogrammings that cause tendencies that make us act in certain ways. The subsubconscious mind can be understood consciously when the thoughts which created this "sub" are traced. These will usually be found when the conscious mind is at its lowest ebb. When resting it is possible to study the sub of the subconscious mind with ease. The body is relaxed and the conscious mind has loosened its hold on external objects. When study has commenced, trace through the thought pictures consciously, without disturbing the over-all picture. Take into consideration the fact that all thought stems from a series of influences within the ego. These influences take form and shape in thought. When you manifest pictures before you, trace them to their conception by holding the consciousness lightly over the mind, blotting out all distractions that may creep into the mind in an effort to disturb your consciousness. Take your findings, whatever they may be, and consciously think them through until all doubts have been dispelled. You will then find that through your conscious effort the sub of the subconscious mind has been understood consciously as well as subconsciously. ¶Generally this process occurs automatically. We resolve the obstacle in the dream state. When we meditate deeply before sleep, we pass through the dream world and enter superconsciousness. From here, the work is done on the subsubconscious mind. Should we try to remember these dreams or analyze them, and meditate at the same time, we would reimpress them again in the subconscious and strengthen these same patterns and tendencies. When we have had a long series of peculiar dreams, often this is the subsubconscious mind working out these habit patterns and tendencies and throwing them back into the subconscious to be programmed beautifully and correctly. To clear the subsubconscious of uncomfortable happenings, especially if you are living a good, religious life and performing regular *sādhana*, you can simply command it to clear itself. It will do so during the in-between dream state that you have experienced just before awakening. Therefore, the advice is, when you are going through your first stages of unfoldment, clarifying and reprogramming the sub of the subconscious mind, do not analyze your dreams.

Friday
LESSON 187
Not Analyzing Your Dreams

When the ego functions in subconscious or subsubconscious dream states, situations are created. These situations, remembered while in a conscious state termed "awake," will create on the conscious plane similar happenings. Here again we have a manifestation of the subsubconscious mind in the dream. It is apparent that we dream things that we could not have possibly thought up. Such dreams are a conglomeration of seemingly unrelated happenings that pass through the mind. The unrelated happenings do, however, reimpress the subconscious and conscious mind if remembered, and in turn impress the subconscious again, and similar happenings are created in our everyday life. This, perhaps, is hard to believe, but as each of us thinks back over our life, we can pick instances where this rings true. ¶To change this picture, use the power of the subconscious mind to clear its sub and release within you the full abundance you were born to live. When using the subconscious mind in manifesting control over this situation, take into consideration that it is not able to eradicate the vibration. But during sleep your subconscious will make it possible for you to continue working out the rate of vibration created while in the dream state and remembered while awake. Simply tell your subconscious mind, when you are in the process of remembering a dream, to work out the remaining particles of that experience during sleep rather than recreating it on the physical plane. ¶When awakening after having had some bad dreams, say to yourself, "Great! I must have really started reprogramming the sub of the subconscious mind last night. I certainly should be feeling more positive with a stronger will in a day or two." The key is to forget about your dreams as soon as you awaken if you are practicing attention, concentration and meditation. ¶When the ego wakes up from sleep, the physical body should immediately be put into action. To go back into the state of sleep immediately after naturally becoming conscious causes the five positive currents to be unconventionally depolarized; the ego passes into the subsubconscious regions.

Saturday
LESSON 188
Helpmate or Hindrance?

The sub of the subconscious mind can and does create situations of an uncomely nature. The subsubconscious mind, through its natural magnetism, attracts so-called temptations and unhappy conditions. The conscious mind, weakened by harmful practices, falls into this self-created trap. There the ego seemingly suffers between the subconscious thoughts that created the "sub," the ego's conscious expressions, and its subsuperconscious knowing. Guilt is one of the results of this state, also pride and anguish. These are a few of the qualities resulting from the subsubconscious state of mind. When the "sub" is controlled through a deep understanding of its inner workings, the ego, or consciousness, is free from being bound in identifying itself with the mind, body and emotions. The ego, or consciousness, can then progress towards the dynamic realization of your real Self—beyond the mind, the mind that is under your control. Otherwise, the ego is caught in the cross-section between the conscious mind and its subsuperconscious knowing, resulting in superstition, ideology, fanaticism and an argumentative nature. ¶The subsubconscious mind is very simple. We can compare it to *kumkum,* the red powder worn as a dot on the third eye, which is a combination of yellow turmeric and pale-green lime juice. We can also liken it to ice, formed when water meets with freezing temperature. Cooking is perhaps the best common example. We place vegetables in a pot on a stove or fire, and we add the delicious curries. With the heat coming up from beneath the pot, the ingredients merge together as one. The vegetables no longer taste like they formerly did and neither do the spices. It is not possible to separate the vegetables from the spices once the cooking has begun. ¶A traumatic emotional experience occurs and is recorded in the subconscious. This we liken to placing the vegetables into the pot. Eight months later, a similar experience happens and is reacted to with equal emotion. It happens, it is reacted to, it goes into the same pot. The vegetables have joined the spices. A subconscious remembrance of the previous experience comes up and is accompanied by a heat of emotion. This is the heat that welds the two impressions together, just as fire cooks the curried vegetables. The two experiences have now become one, inseparably blended together in the subconscious, making a third impression, or *vāsanā,* totally different from the two impressions that manufactured it. It is unique and complete within itself, driven forward by an emotional force even greater than its two component experiences. ¶It is this subliminal power that makes the subsubconscious mind an overwhelming hindrance or a tremendous helpmate when used properly. When existing in negative ignorance, it is a deterrent on the path to enlightenment. The solution to eliminating the power of emotion that compels these blended *karmas* forward is simple. We only have to understand the ingredients—the vegetables and the spices—and resolve each one separately. Once cognized, even the most complex patterns can be resolved or unraveled through writing down one's inmost feelings and burning the paper in an ordinary fire. This is called the *vāsanā daha tantra.* Remember, however, that it is not necessary to remove each and every negative impression, one by one. Rather, we seek to strengthen the positive impressions. This in itself is sufficient and will allow unseemly impressions to be naturally resolved.

Sunday
LESSON 189
Uncovering the Light of the Soul

As we study the mystical teachings of our religion, we begin to reprogram the subconscious mind and mold it like we mold clay. We become more conscious of our fears. We tell ourselves, "There is nothing to be afraid of. There is not one thing to be afraid of." We are able to talk to the subconscious mind in this way. It is called affirmation. "I am a fearless being. I am a fearless being," we keep saying to ourselves time and time and time again. In affirming this truth we begin reeducating or reprogramming the subconscious mind. Finally, we begin to remove the layers upon layers covering the soul. ¶In India there is a traditional analogy of a lamp whose light is concealed by a screen of colored pieces of cloth. It is said we can uncover the lamp, representing the light of the soul, by reprogramming the subconscious. First we take off the black piece of cloth. The dark green one is still there, so little light comes through as yet, and we are faced with the instinctive emotion—our great protective power of being jealous. Both fear and jealousy are protective mechanisms of the mind. We work with our jealous nature as we make other affirmations. "I have all that everyone else has. The same power that is within everyone is within me." In this way we begin reprogramming the subconscious and gain more and more confidence in ourselves. Jealousy is inferiority. We feel we lack that which someone else has, so we try to cut them down a little bit to our size. Jealousy makes people mean. Finally, we work our awareness through this dark green sheath of jealousy, and we remove that sheath from the lamp of the soul. A little more light now shines through, and we begin to feel good about ourself—"I'm not so bad after all. In fact, I'm pretty good." We become more confident and penetrate even deeper while working on the next instinctive quality, and the next and the next and the next. Finally, as we take off the last sheath, we find that we are That which we were all the time. We are inwardly free. We have removed awareness from the conscious mind and brought it through the subconscious state into pure superconsciousness. Now the physical body seems to us but a shell, a place in which we live in order to express ourselves on the surface of the Earth. The spiritual body seems to us to be our real body, and we wonder why we didn't realize that before.

Karaṇa Chittam

करणचित्तम्

The Superconscious Mind

You need no shouting when you withdraw into understanding. You need no speaking when you are seated in superconsciousness. You need no holy rites when you are inwardly detached. You need no meditation when you have reached the actionless state.

TIRUMANTIRAM 1634

Monday
LESSON 190
Consciously Superconscious

We have to adjust our subconscious to the idea that we are a superconscious being, rather than an instinctive being or an intellectual being driven by the impulses of the five senses. Awareness is the core of us. If we dropped off this physical body today, we would be a superconscious being without a physical body. If we stepped into another physical body tomorrow, we would still be a superconscious being, but with another physical body, different than the one we had yesterday, with an entirely new subconscious and new external environment. ¶I would like you to visualize dropping off your physical body and going over to, say, Sri Lanka or Bosnia to pick up a brand new body. See yourself stepping into it, adjusting your nerve currents within it, getting up from the battlefield, putting it into the hospital and healing it up and going home to its parents with a medal of valor. ¶You would have a new physical body, a new subconscious mind and a new external environment to adjust to. In this new body you would soon forget that you are a superconscious being. You would be so involved in being Ānanda from Toronto who recently arrived there as a refugee from the war. But the superconscious being of you would know that it was a superconscious being, and finally Ānanda would begin to know it, too. New rays of light would be coming through Ānanda's aura. The subconscious would be reprogrammed quickly, and pretty soon Ānanda would become a man who meditated, in the very same way you meditated before you dropped off your old body and picked up Ānanda's body on the battlefield. There would not be much of a break in continuity. This gives you a brief look at reincarnation. Your subconscious can readily adjust to this simple concept. ¶There is one theory of reincarnation that holds we do not have to incarnate as little babies, but that we can incarnate as full-grown people when we know how it is done. More evolved souls can do this because they know the inner laws. Less evolved souls must incarnate through the womb, because this is the process that is most instinctively natural. This is one of the fringe benefits of becoming conscious in the superconscious body. Become consciously superconscious. That is the goal.

Tuesday
LESSON 191
When Are You Superconscious?

It is easier to know when you are not superconscious than when you are superconscious, because your superconsciousness is such a natural state. It is such a beautiful state. It is such a full, wholesome state to be in, that you are not aware generally that you are superconscious. ¶When you are not feeling too well within yourself, you are not superconscious. When you are feeling really good and satisfied within yourself, you *are* superconscious. When your timing is right, when everything is happening just right during the day, you are superconscious. When nothing seems to be happening right, then your awareness is flowing through one of the congested areas of the thought realm. When everything seems to be going wrong, you are flowing through an instinctive area or a congested intellectual area. ¶When you are arguing with yourself, you are not superconscious. You are flowing through an area of the intellectual mind, taking two points of view and flowing from one to another. When discussing something with someone, you are not superconscious, for superconsciousness is a one-way street. You speak right from the core of existence without really thinking about what you are going to say. You just speak out and hear what you said afterwards. ¶When you are arguing with someone, you are not superconscious. You have moved into a congested area of the thought strata of the mind and you are verbalizing it, and are congesting the aura, too. Then awareness has to be unwound from that area of the mind and directed back again to superconsciousness. When you are disturbed about yesterday, or even have a consciousness that there was a yesterday, you are not in a superconscious state. When you are afraid, you are not in a superconscious state. When you are peaceful, when you are calm, when you are in the eternity of the moment, when you feel secure on the inside of you, you are in a superconscious state. Superconsciousness is not something you will get, because you have never been without it. You are superconscious this very minute, and functioning in all five states of the mind.

Wednesday
LESSON 192
Becoming Aware of Energy

Become aware of the totality of Being. This does not take a lot of time. The easiest way, the simplest way, is to be aware of the spine and the energies within the head. Locate the consciousness of energy. Be aware of energy. When you are aware of energy, you automatically forget what you were previously aware of and it fades away. You leave the consciousness of the instinctive-intellectual area of the mind and move into superconsciousness. If you can remain totally centered in awareness of the energy within your spine and the energy within the head, you become aware of the same energy within everybody and everything you see. You are immediately in a superconscious state when this happens. ¶Therefore, the simple goal is, stay in this consciousness of energy for the rest of your life. It is just that easy, but it is not quite that simple to accomplish, because you have already trained your awareness to move into other channels of the mind, and it will do that automatically as soon as you cease to be aware of the energy within the spine. Then you forget that you are a superconscious, immortal being and begin to think you are only temporal. You may begin to think that there is a past, or that there is a future, and begin to feel that the eternal now is an insecure time. You may find yourself beginning to lean on other people rather than on your own spine. ¶When you discover this happening, then begin to meditate. Go deep within yourself again and find superconsciousness. Seek the company of people who center their awareness within. This will make it easier for you to do so. Being around people who center awareness in the external areas of the mind is difficult because they draw your awareness into the external areas of the thought strata. ¶People who really value awareness being "hooked," shall we say, into the inner areas of energy, and have studied that function of energy, draw your awareness into it. When this happens, you begin to see from inside out. You actually see from the inside of everything that you look at to the exterior of it. You look at a tree. You first see the energy within the tree. The bark is the last thing you see. When you are in an outer consciousness, first you see the bark of the tree and then you intellectually surmise that there must be energies within it because you happen to notice that a leaf is growing and assume that it must be alive.

How awkward awareness is when it is stumbling around in the external area of the mind. And how smooth awareness flows freely when it is dynamically cruising into inner layers of inner space. ¶We shall now compare the superconscious mind to an onion of seven layers, each interior layer more subtle than the outer ones. 1) Experiencing the consciousness of the eternity of the moment, as if the world was revolving around you; 2) Experiencing a cosmic energy, a divine force, flowing through your external mind which is more real to you than the external mind itself; 3) Experiencing hearing voices singing, music playing—the divine sounds of the flute, *mṛidaṅga, vīṇā* and *tambūra*—while in meditation or early in the morning just before awakening; 4) Experiencing seeing the faces of Gods or *devas,* or a *ṛishi's* face, looking into yours while in meditation or early in the morning just before awakening; 5) Experiencing the peace and inner poise of the all-pervasive Satchidānanda; 6) Experiencing the *ānandamaya kośa,* the body of the soul, as it comes into conscious union with the physical body; 7) Experiencing being on the brink of the Absolute, Paraśiva, the void, having lost consciousness of the physical body and of being any of the five states of mind. These seven states of superconsciousness are only a few, to be sure, of this vast area of mind.

Thursday
LESSON 193
Learn to Move Awareness

You must not think the superconscious mind is way out of your reach simply because of the word *super,* because it is quite the contrary. It is within you. It has always been within you. All you have to do is to reprogram the subconscious a little and move awareness out of the conscious mind, and your journey is within.

You are superconscious now. You have to accept that. You do not have to "get to be" superconscious. This is not something that is going to happen to you all of a sudden and then cause you to be different. The thing that is going to happen to you is that you will release your individual awareness from the so-called bondages of the habit patterns of the external mind that it had been accustomed to flowing through. Once it is released, you will automatically flow into other inner areas of the mind because you have been studying about them and now have the map clearly outlined for you. ¶You might be wondering why, if you are supposed to be superconscious right now, you have not had the wonderful experiences that I have told you about. This is easy to answer. You may be superconscious now but not consciously superconscious all of the time, or even for long enough periods to have these beautiful experiences. So when I say you are superconscious right now, that is true, or you would not even be hearing about it. ¶It is no accident our meeting in this way to share some of my inner life and this particularly deep subject matter. It is providential, I would say, and has occurred at the proper time of your unfoldment on the path. Though you are superconscious right now, awareness is still externalized enough that you touch into it only a little bit and then are pulled back to the subconscious or to the conscious mind. ¶Through regular practice of meditation, one learns to move awareness through the superconscious areas like a dancer learns to move across the stage according to the rhythm of the music. It takes much practice for the dancer to acquire the technique in the preparation of himself to fulfill his calling. He has to live a disciplined lifestyle. It is the same for the contemplative. He has to work with and exercise the currents of awareness so dynamically that he can flow into a superconscious area and remain there long enough to look around a little bit and enjoy it.

Friday
LESSON 194
The Use Of Intuition

Intuition is the natural way in which man expresses himself on Earth or any other planet on which he might find expression of his being. This natural flow of *mana,* the Polynesian word for *prāṇic śakti,* from and through him only becomes inhibited when he disconnects from the nerve system of the celestial into the nerve system of the animal. When this occurs, there, therefore, is a disconnect between superconsciousness and external consciousness. Man's individual awareness is either captured by the nerve system of external consciousness, of the successive animal bodies which his soul inhabits as a vehicle to live on Earth in, or man's individual awareness is capture by his celestial nerve system, matured on aged planets in the galaxy prior to arrival here on Earth. This, then, is superconsciousness—the natural expression of the transcendental soul known as man. ¶Intuition day by day occurs spasmodically, but it does occur. And systematically one can gear his observation of his own intuitional faculties and find out exactly when these intuitive functions occur within him. It is a well-defined fact that we have the faculty of precognition of coming events. It is also concurrently known that feelings of fear may precede impending danger. It is for the individual to disentangle and sort out within his own daily experiential pattern which is which. In this way he becomes knowledgeable in the great university of his own mind as to what is a daily intuitive occurence and what is not. ¶How does one distinguish between intuition and usual thought-feeling processes? Desires come through feeling, warmth of emotion, as do thoughts, schemes, ways of manipulating the media forces for one's own personal benefit or that of a loved one. This is contrary to the power of intuition, which runs cold and is direct, like a bolt of lightning in the inner sky or the subtle rainbow of an etheric aura which bypasses the processes of current thinking, giving answers before the question and solving problems before they have accrued. ¶It is only through *sādhana* and divesting oneself—in order to perform *sādhana*—from the social structure of the conglomerate of mortals that surround you that you will actually be able to prudently delineate between true intuition and the imposing factors of need and greed that often seem paramount when living up to the externalities of the instinctive nerve system.

Saturday
LESSON 195
Subduing The Intellect

Here's a fine example of the use of intuition. You have often been in a situation in your own mind where you felt a subtle, direct impulse from deep within you as to how you should proceed. Most probably you denied it as fantasy and commenced in a logical way to fulfill your impulses and desires from previous patterns of experience only to find that you would have traversed agonies and confusions had you followed the subtle impulse of direction which was rejected to enhance established patterns of procedure. But I might add that that first impulse must have registered itself as cold and clear, direct and profound. Only if it did would it have indelibly imprinted itself within your memory patterns, clear and sharp, thus distinguishing itself clearly from all warm, emotional feelings that appear to be reasonable and totally in line with the current pictures of the day. ¶In current events, most people guide their lives on prior reasonable patterns. This knowledge is only prophetic. It has absolutely no relation to the other courses of action entered into by intuitive decision, which in turn would encase man's individual awareness into the strong, dynamic superconscious being that he ever was, is now and always will be. ¶Though we often use the terms "unfolding intuitive faculties" and "developing intuition," they are only used in an effort to encourage the aspirant on the path to work within himself in subduing his intellect so that he can actually observe the already functioning totality of the intuitive area of the mind. ¶In order to subdue the intellect, that conglomerate of thought patterns and established modes of procedure according to the culture of the day, it is first quite necessary to inwardly observe how one's acquired intellect actually functions. Observation is a faculty of the intuitive area of the mind, and this particular aspect of observation that I have just described comes into usage only after regular periods of meditation have been maintained over a long period of time. True, our intuitive faculties do constantly mingle through thought sequences each day, but our ability to distinguish one from another is accrued only through regulated discipline of our individual power of awareness. Once an inkling of success comes in knowing intuition and how it differs from reasoning, emotional impulses and preprogrammed patterns within the subconscious, the contest is won. Then and then only we must persist to sustain this knowledge and dive deeper into the inevitable, all the time losing the future and the past, and loosening the reins of the intellect.

Sunday
LESSON 196
The Self Never Changes

When you begin to sense this changeless existence within, your intuition begins to awaken, and if you function through the use of your intuition you are able to clear many misunderstandings about the experiences of life. In this clarity, intuition is born. Right now you perhaps think you are the mind; you may feel remote from your Inner Being, but ask yourself each time you think you have found yourself, will this change? You will find that every image you hold of yourself is subject to change—even your soul, or your superconscious mind, is subject to change through evolution and, therefore, is impermanent. Only the Self, the very core, is eternally the same, eternally Real. Find your Inner Being through feeling; realize it is closer to you than your hands or feet, closer to you even than your breath. Your mind will want to leave this consciousness as soon as you attain it, but gently guide your mind back through the channel of concentration until once again you become rejuvenated, uplifted in the awareness of That which has never changed. That is your very Self, and That is God. ¶Jñānaguru Yogaswāmī said, "Search without searching." By this he meant that as long as we are searching for God in meditation, there are two—God and the seeker. He did not mean that we should stop looking for God, stop meditating or stop striving and live an ordinary life or give up *sādhana*. He was saying that to deepen your meditation, while seated in the lotus position, doing *prāṇāyāma,* to deepen this state, stop looking and begin to realize that you are That which you are looking for. As long as there is searching, Paraśiva has not been found, for searching is two, and It is one. But you must keep searching until It is found. How to attain That? Satguru Yogaswāmī said, "Stop looking, and just be." Give up consciousness which is seeing and registering that which has been seen. Become the sound, *nāda,* just be and merge into the Ultimate Quiet. When the disciple is on the brink of the Absolute, the timeless Paraśiva, twoness disappears in the overpowering presence of Śiva, and consciousness is absorbed and annihilated in His transcendental Being, which is nondifferent from the disciple's. However, if the disciple continues looking for this experience and thus, in the act of his search, solidifies himself and the sought-after experience as two different things, he becomes the obstacle and the problem to be eliminated. In the end, the Great Mystery is known as one, as two, as neither one nor two.

Anukaraṇa Chittam

अनुकरणचित्तम्

The Subsuperconscious Mind

In the hint of His grace, the whole universe shall be revealed to you. When the darkness of ignorance lifts, the Great One stands revealed. When you seek Him, your swarming thoughts centered on Him, you shall see the light of *jñāna*, and thus become immortal.

TIRUMANTIRAM 1794

Monday
LESSON 197
The State of Perfect Timing

After the subconscious mind has been very, very carefully reprogrammed into the contemplative lifestyle, there is little difference to us between the subconscious and the superconscious states. Therefore, basically, we have moved our awareness into an entirely new mind structure, or at least it seems new to us. This is called the subsuperconscious mind, or the area of the superconscious that has a subconscious which is connected with the physical-body functions and everyday life affairs. ¶The subsuperconscious state is the total man, functioning at a higher vibratory rate than he did when in the instinctive-intellectual area. What is the subsuperconscious mind? It is the superconscious of the devotee, well-programmed in the contemplative life. This devotee can work with himself and move awareness freely through any area of the mind that he wants to, consciously, without being hindered by habit patterns and reactionary conditions of the past which were programmed in the subconscious for him by parents, schoolteachers, friends and the public in general as he came along through life from birth. ¶When your timing is perfect and everything works correctly around you, things happen as you expect them to happen, or even better, you are in the subsuperconscious area of the mind. Certainly you are not in the subconscious area or in the external conscious mind. You are subsuperconscious. You are aware within the inner realms and the external realms at the same time. When you feel stationary, stable, as if the whole world stopped and there is only you in the center, and yet you are able to converse with your friends—this is a subsuperconscious state. Subsuperconsciousness is really awareness traveling, propelled by energy and willpower. ¶The devotee who has developed the subsuperconscious area of the mind can sit quietly as a being of pure cosmic energy and observe the many thoughts of the mind without being affected by them. The intuitive knowing that we are pure awareness, the soul, and not the thoughts that we think gives the security to move from concentration into deeper meditation. The subsuperconscious state gives that inherent feeling of inner stability, the feeling of being stationary or centered within the realms of the thinking mind. ¶Let us look at a mystic walking down the street who is conscious of his energy, only doing one thing—walking, moving the physical body. He is aware of pure energy moving that physical body and walking, and yet many different things are passing by him, or he is passing by them. He sees store windows, automobiles, people, things. Many, many things are happening around him as he is walking down the street conscious of being pure energy. ¶Man in the subsuperconscious area of the mind in meditation is sitting as a being of pure energy. Even if many thoughts go past his vision, he knows he is flowing through the world of thought as a subsuperconscious state of awareness. Awareness is in a stationary state within the realms of the thinking mind. When we are out of the thinking mind, we are in the conceptual, subsuperconscious areas.

Tuesday
LESSON 198
Reprogramming The Subconscious

Superconsciousness functions through the conscious mind as well as the subconscious. Basically, we have no need for those two particular categories of mind unless we slip out of superconsciousness and start to rebuild a subconscious by spending too much time with awareness flowing through the conscious area of the mind, or the world of the senses, which is separate, in a way, from superconsciousness. In short, this is called worldliness. When we neglect our religious life and spend too much time only being aware in the environment of the external world, a subconscious begins to build, clouding the inner sky and separating us from the sun, God Śiva. Is worldliness having two Mercedes, a large house, lots of money, and everything that you want in life? No, those are the tools that you must have to fulfill your *dharma*. Worldliness is the animal nature, the nature that gets angry, jealous, hateful. That's worldliness. So, when the subconscious mind becomes too full, then we are totally in the conscious mind and don't want to have any desire to look inside ourselves, because we are afraid of what we might see, and then we are worldly. ¶The subconscious mind is divided into two sections. One regulates the involuntary processes of the body and the other the involuntary processes of the emotions, the instinctive habit patterns, our action and reaction process and all the things we experience in everyday living. Most people on the path have experimented with proper nutrition, have closely watched their diet, and have seen that it has had an immediate effect upon the physical body. The body began to change, to look different and feel better to live in. It became more vibrant and slender as the food intake had its chemical reactions upon the cells. Generally, unless they had acquired a deep understanding of nutrition, or it became a part of their lifestyle, they drifted back to their old patterns of eating. They found that the body quickly changed into the way it used to behave, look and feel, because of the improper chemical balance from the food intake. This is what can happen in the part of the subconscious mind which handles the involuntary processes of the body. ¶The very same thing happens in the part of the subconscious mind that handles the processes of the emotional body. The aspirant on the spiritual path can work diligently with himself and put a fine program into his subconscious, but if he does not use that program and keep up the intensity by traveling on the path—if he sits down on the path where he is and stops striving, if he allows previous habit patterns, action and reaction processes, to remold his subconscious again from the instinctive areas of the mind—the subconscious will rebuild itself or reprogram itself, all by itself, into the same conditions it had before he started working with it. ¶Be alerted to this. Be careful with the subconscious mind. If you are on the path, keep moving along. Stay in a good environment. Keep up the intensity and associate with those who are on the path, those who are working with themselves, those who are inwardly striving, and by their example and the vibration of their being, they will inspire and help you work with yourself and inwardly strive. ¶When old habit patterns start to reprogram the subconscious mind almost without your knowing it, the vibration of those that are striving on the path around you will check those qualities from gaining too much power. We are influenced by our environment. We are influenced by the people around us. Therefore, be with the people that can influence you the best until you are reprogrammed powerfully enough to influence those around you.

Wednesday
LESSON 199
Defining the Sub-Superconscious

The subsuperconscious mind is a quiet subconscious. That is actually what it is. It is the subconscious that has been made to be peaceful by putting into it a contemplative lifestyle. It is a receptacle for the superconscious areas of mind to permeate the physical body from the psyche, so that the body of the soul can look out through the eyes of the physical body, radiate through the cells of the physical body and allow superconscious rays to radiate out through the aura. ¶Would you like to try to locate the subsuperconscious state of mind? Look at the room around you. That is the conscious mind you are aware in. Next, focus on your feelings and be aware of what you are thinking. You are now aware in the subconscious mind. Next, feel your spiritual identity, feel the power in your spine. Sit up straight. Feel powerful energy on the inside of your spinal cord. At the same time you are identified with being the energy in the spine, and separating the feeling of energy from the physical spine, look at the room around you and become conscious of your personal thoughts and feelings. Doing this brings you into a subsuperconscious state, because you are conscious of your superconsciousness, the power and energy and life and spiritual forces resident right within the body. Simultaneously, you are conscious of your thinking faculty, the room around you and yourself as being pure energy. It is that easy to be in a subsuperconscious state, more difficult to remain in it for long periods of time. ¶The feeling of the eternity of the moment is experienced upon the first arrival into the subsuperconscious state of mind. This occurs when the subconscious state of mind is in a quiescent state, a state of full receptivity to superconsciousness. It has not been destroyed, but has been purified of all barriers, such as negative attachments. When this occurs, the devotee has the feeling that there is no future, there is no past and the only reality is the eternity of the moment. ¶The subconscious mind, thus opened to the influx of actinic power, creates a force field called an *actinodic* force field. That is, the odic forces of the subconscious, having been permeated with enough actinic energy so that the odic forces are quieted, organized and controlled through actinic power, form a new state of mind called the subsuperconscious state of mind. ¶Great vistas of creativity are opened to those who learn to keep open and receptive to the subsuperconscious mind. Music, art, drama and dance flow most spontaneously, and answers to questions in the subconscious, previously unanswered, come forth in intuitive flashes, without the use of reason, while not conflicting with reason. A feeling of contentment and confidence resides within an individual who has learned to consciously identify and use the subsuperconscious mind.

Thursday
LESSON 200
Security in Superconscious

When the superconscious forces diminish, the subsuperconscious mind, in effect, recedes from the actual consciousness of the devotee, and he becomes simply conscious of his subconscious mind. In the very same way, from time to time, the conscious mind overshadows the subconscious mind, and the devotee becomes conscious fully in the external world, the subconscious mind receding from his conscious awareness of it. Therefore, the object of the devotee is to control the materialistic forces and the impressions that they create in his mind, so that he can become consciously conscious in the state of mind he chooses.¶The greatest sense of security is the feeling: "I am all right, right now." Simply believing this temporarily quiets not only the conscious but also the subconscious instinctive fears and brings forth an immediate influx of intuitive, superconscious awareness through the subconscious, giving security and solidarity to the entirety of the mind by expanding consciousness through actinic energy. As we expand our consciousness through the conscious control of actinic energy, we become aware of new attributes and possibilities within our nature. Also, we become aware of the realms of knowledge within us that can be tapped through our continued *sādhana.* ¶Meditation is conscious use of the subsuperconscious mind to solve problems that confront us in our daily activity and derive creative solutions from the inner recesses of our own mind. Another way of using the superconscious forces is through affirmation. When you say to yourself, "I'm all right, right now," you immediately bring the forces of the mind together. All fears, worries and doubts cease. An influx of actinic energy fills the subconscious, and a sense of dynamic security permeates your being. ¶To consciously use the subsuperconscious mind, before you go to sleep at night repeat this affirmation to yourself, over and over again: "Tomorrow, I shall awaken filled and thrilled with cosmic energy of God Śiva, creatively alive and in tune with the universe." Say this several times unto yourself and feel the actinic force begin to move, the life force begin to move within your body. You will awaken in the morning filled and thrilled with creative energy and with a desire to be productive, to create. Answers to problems will be immediately unfolded from within yourself. You will experience the mechanism of playback, of finding solutions to questions that have been unanswered within your subconscious mind perhaps for years. All this and more will come to you through the grace of God Śiva and our many Gods if you diligently and regularly fulfill your *sādhana.*

Friday
LESSON 201
Subsuperconscious Breakthroughs

A devotee who can command his mind to be instantly creative, and be consistently successful, has acquired a conscious control of the use of the subsuperconscious state of mind. This is because the subconscious mind—made of odic force, a sticky-like substance that absorbs impressions, holds impressions and files them (not always, however, in an organized way)—has been understood, dissolved and brought in line with the cosmic forces through living a religious life. In this pure condition, the devotee's attempts to direct his own mental forces are quite naturally successful. Unobstructed, the superconscious forces flow into the life of the devotee, and creativity is in abundance. Once the first breakthrough has been made, we find that these brilliant rays from the cosmic mind—which we also call Satchidānanda, the mind of God Śiva, the Gods and your immortal soul—penetrate the sticky-like substance of the subconscious, reorganizing and purifying it. ¶The next time you feel physically, mentally or emotionally fatigued, use your willpower to command access to the cosmic energies that exist deep inside of you. Do not allow the body or mind to fall into lethargic, depressed states. Feel the life forces stirring, flowing out to invigorate every cell of your being. ¶When you can see a white light aglow in your head in a darkened room, or even see a flash of it, or hear the inner, high-pitched sound, "eee," humming in your inner ear, then you know that you are consciously functioning in the subsuperconscious state of mind. Devotees who have had their first flash of white light in their head or heard the constant high-pitched "eee" in their inner ear have awakened the process of the subsuperconscious state of mind, and it works quite automatically after that. All they have to do is to learn how to consciously use their subsuperconscious transcendental powers. All this will naturally occur through their continued *sādhana.* ¶The first breakthrough of the clear white light is subsuperconsciousness. The odic force fields of darkness which are seen within oneself are created by beliefs that conflict with the Sanātana Dharma, resentment and past conflicting *karma.* These are built up through the centuries of man's intermingling within his own species. This inner darkness or odic force has created man's subconscious mind, and conscious mind, the way he knows it today. Every devotee is inwardly desirous of breaking through the barriers of this inner darkness, realizing the discontent caused by the influx and outflow of connecting odic forces, not only between himself and family, friends and relations, but also in his association with the world at large.

Saturday
LESSON 202
Bursts of Light And Intuition

Intense desire for spiritual unfoldment eventually manifests itself in a breakthrough of actinic will, which permeates the subconscious mind of the devotee until he completely identifies himself as an actinic being. This happens from within the deeper realms of man's mind and eventually manifests itself into consciousness, then into thought patterns and then finally into speech and action. Actinic will also appears from the transference of desire from material objects and activity into finding some real solution within oneself for the eventual quest of all men, peace of mind. This actinic force becomes so strong, finally there is a breakthrough or burst of light. This happens quite naturally within many people who have not even availed themselves of classical *yoga* teachings. This first breakthrough throws into orbit, so to speak, the subsubconscious state of mind, for an infinitesimal flow of actinic force thereafter begins to permeate the subconscious mind, easing darkness or confusion or pressures of the conglomerated, accumulated force fields. After this first breakthrough, the devotee becomes more creative, kinder, a little happier and more metaphysically inclined, for the subsuperconscious mind becomes another building force field. ¶Occasionally devotees have flashes of intuition, bursts of prophetic knowing. Some devotees also occasionally enter trance states, when messages may come through their voice from the superconscious mind without their conscious-mind knowledge. When the trance subsides there is usually no memory of what they said or did. Such subsuperconscious states are often brought forth by intense religious emotion, which occasionally becomes so overwhelming that it pierces the worldly subconscious and conscious mind. ¶Your belief in your subsuperconscious power will also unfold your destiny in this life. "I will be what I will to be." "I will do what I will to do." You can repeat these two affirmations over and over, time and time again and rearrange, restructure, the forces of your subconscious mind and create a great inner peace within yourself. Turn on to actinic force and bring the forces of superconsciousness through your subconscious. This creates feeling, a feeling that you are what you say you are—positive, direct, full of life and energy and creative power. Your subsuperconscious mind proves this through your conscious mind, not only through feeling, but you will find yourself acting out the part in all kindness and security, but exercising the positive will of "I will be what I will to be" and "I will do what I will to do."

Sunday
LESSON 203
Proceed with Confidence

There are those who simply follow the pattern of odic force fields of others and never realize their actinic destiny, because they have never had the ability to break through the odic force barriers with their actinic power. Actinic destiny is found by those who stand out from the masses and actually do something, who live a creative life for the benefit of others. Actinic power creates through the subconscious, but it is a flowing-through or flowing-out power. Odic power is a holding onto, a sort of sticky type of power. ¶Move through odic force fields unnoticed. Those who have awakened their subsuperconscious powers often become exuberant and, more than often, a wee bit egotistical. And yet, a deeper subsuperconscious attribute is that of humility. Humility, within itself, is a power, a power of the fullness of the subsuperconscious mind, giving you the ability to move through the odic force fields unnoticed. ¶Because of the nature of odic forces—which constitute people in their conscious and subconscious mind, cities, nations and events—the flow of actinic force can or could be disturbing to certain force fields. The consequences have, through history, been disastrous from time to time. Therefore, keep your subsuperconscious knowledge and powers where they are, as an inner mechanism of you, available to your conscious use. Do not advertise your subsuperconscious power, because odic force fields of jealousy or fear could be stimulated against you. Therefore, learn to move inconspicuously in the odic-force world, while contributing to the beauty of the world through your conscious use of your subsuperconscious mind. ¶All that is beautiful has come from the subsuperconscious powers awakened within man. So, let your life shine by your actions rather than by your advertising subsuperconscious powers. There is no pride so great or hard to be rid of than spiritual pride. Having the availability of actinic force working through the subconscious mind can very easily become distorted into building up even a greater odic subconscious mind. ¶And now, on the lighter side of thinking, here is another way to use your subsuperconscious powers consciously. When you know the next thing to do, or the right thing to say, this is your subsuperconscious mind. Practice feeling confident, secure in the consciousness of the eternal now. Absorb the feedback from groups of people, or people you are talking with, and when your subconscious mind has collected the feedback, feel dynamically the eternity of the moment, and you will know just the right thing to say, or the next thing to do. This is using your subsuperconscious powers consciously. ¶The greatest thing that a devotee must learn is that all knowing is within oneself. Therefore, go to your innerversity, your great subsuperconscious school, and bring forth knowledge. In order to do this, be confident within yourself. In order to be confident within yourself, have no fear. In order to have no fear, say to yourself, "I am all right, right now." This will quickly bring you into the consciousness of the eternity of the moment. You will feel actinic force permeating, or more life permeating, your body, which is subconscious, and your subsuperconscious state of mind will be active. That is, go ahead in full confidence that you are the knower of all that is known.

Chintana Bhāvaḥ

चिन्तनभावः

The Nature of Thought

When the *prāṇa* of the breath is contained within and not exhaled, the thoughts, too, are contained there, and the Lord shall leave you not.

TIRUMANTIRAM 586

Monday
LESSON 204
Thought and Awareness

The mystic, while in the beginning stages, tries diligently through his *sādhana* to extract his awareness from the thinking area of the mind, while simultaneously trying to perceive without thinking about what he has perceived. It is the overview of what has been perceived that the mystic endeavors to superconsciously grasp in a series of flashes. He well knows that thinking is the more externalized strata. The mystic constantly, through every waking moment and even during sleep, endeavors to strengthen his acute observation through perceiving the overview of thought strata rather than thinking through them. My *guru* often said, "There is a chair at the top. Sit in it and look at the world from that perspective." The mystic constantly sits in this chair, looking at mind from the threshold of the Absolute. ¶It is the baser emotions, when stimulated, that bring awareness from inner depths into the thought strata of the mind, thus strengthening human emotions and feelings with powers of reason and memory. Therefore, for those not too deeply engaged in the external emotional traps, certain *sādhanas* can be performed to regulate and control these instinctive drives. When they are less impulsive and forceful, one has a sense of being able to control one's thoughts. Later on, if the *sādhana* persists, the sense that awareness travels in and among these thoughts is felt, and still later the perceptions occur of hovering above thought, looking out upon the thought strata of the mind or a portion of it. ¶To give an example of the thought state, and a deeper state of not thinking but perceiving thoughts, imagine sitting before a television set. The set has not been turned on, and you are thinking about various things that involve you personally and wish to distract awareness from them by watching a television program. When you turn to the program, sitting across the room from the set, you have the sense of perceiving the thoughts, moods and emotions of the program, without necessarily thinking yourself. You perceive. Similarly, the mystic can be called the watcher of the play of life, for he is totally identified with his inner depths, rather than the thought strata and structures he perceives. ¶The mystic lives in a state similar to that of a child, for a child does not think, but perceives. He, of course, reacts emotionally to some of his perceptions, but it is only when he reaches twelve or fourteen, sometimes younger, that he begins to enter the thought strata of mind. The mystic has deliberately arrived at this state of the child through *sādhana* and, of course, has awakened the facilities in himself to go into the next succeeding, even more refined, areas of consciousness. ¶The entire concept of creating a thought, or thoughts of the mind already being in existence, or thoughts and concepts disintegrating or being destroyed because they are no longer used, is totally dependent upon the nature of the *sādhana* of the mystic. There are four different perspectives in looking at the mind from within oneself. In Shum, these four perspectives are called *shumef, moolef, simnef* and *defee.* And of course, many more combinations of these perspectives can be utilized and have been, thus creating the various philosophical and metaphysical outlooks that we know today. How thought is seen within one's mind totally depends on the positioning of one's individual state of awareness. This, in turn, depends upon prior *sādhana* he has performed.

Tuesday
LESSON 205
Thought and Manifestation

Thought and matter are synonymous. They have only to be seen in this way to be understood as such. From the external area of the mind, matter seems to be separate from thought. However, from the central, internal perspective of the mystic, thought, energy and matter are one. Things and forms are and have been manifestations of thought conglomerates though the ages. And, of course, as you look upon animate and inanimate matter with your own faculties, they are immediately reduced to thought. This is the way it is seen by the mystic who has attained Self Realization. He also knows thought to be of an apparent, more permanent nature than animate and inanimate objects, which appear to change rather rapidly. ¶Therefore, we now have the hypothesis that thought, energy and manifested form are one and the same, only seen as different by the unenlightened. Therefore, we must concur that instantaneously upon thinking about any segment of manifested form, we are simply moving individual awareness into the subtle ether of the mind where the form exists in unmanifest state. By "unmanifest," I mean not having physical size, shape and density. Therefore, if matter were not thought, how could it be reduced to thought? This then leads us to another view of form, thought and energy, and that is of the all-pervading energy, the base of all form and thought, the primal substance of the mind—internal and external manifestations of form. Were this to be removed, there would be no form, no thought—either interior or exterior. Man's individual awareness is of the nature of this all-pervading actinic energy of the universe. I say "of the nature of" because it has several other qualities as well, being a bridge between the viewing of form and formlessness. ¶There are various strata of thought, and of these the most obvious, of course, is what normally is termed thinking. The motivation thought stratum of the astral plane, because of its being more refined in nature, therefore more permanent, precedes all externalized thinking. We are not aware of this until we begin to meditate often, having perfected concentration and meditation. However, there is yet another area of thought, which can be viewed from the fifth dimension of the mind, and here we see form in all phases of manifestation from one point in inner space and time. We can look to the future and to the past, viewing one singular object, and see a change in manifestation as new, individual frames on a motion picture film, each one being slightly different from the other. This really has to be experienced to be believed—that all phases of manifestation and all of the various and varied forms of the universe exist in the great circle of life. Therefore, we can conclude that it is the point in time and space where our awareness resides that keys us in to seeing only one frame at a time on this circle of creation, preservation and dissolution of form, which leads into the creation of the same form again. ¶The mystic, once recognizing his particular point in time and space, can travel around this circle of life at will, his control being prior *sādhana* performed well during early years of unfoldment.

Wednesday
LESSON 206
Awareness Externalized

In concentrating on a flower, one of the *sādhanas* that you have been given, when awareness is held steady and only the flower exists within the mind, as well as outside your body, close observation and scrutiny of the flower can then begin. An intuitive flash will bring knowledge of the complete cycle of that particular form in all phases of its manifestation. This intuitive flash comes to those just beginning the processes of meditation. Later on, the process can be slowed down and sustained. We cannot be imaginative here or fantasize, for only through actually keying into the particular area in time and space does one begin to contemplate future and past in relationship to it. ¶Living in the external area of the mind, it appears that thoughts are always changing. New concepts come and old ones go, as do customs and systems of living. From an inner perspective, it is similar to riding on a train, seeing the countryside, animals, people and buildings quickly pass by. Everything seems to be changing, but it is only you who is traveling through space. So it is within the mind. You travel through inner space rapidly or slowly, depending upon the nature of your *sādhana* or your natural emotional velocity. It is through holding fast to this perspective that a swift inroad to further enlightenment can be attained. If you hold to the perspective that ual awareness automatically traps itself into the pygmy consciousness as a victim in a vast, ever-changing conglomerate of *prāṇic* mind substances. You have experienced this, no doubt, as it is the experience of those who have not awakened to the inner path. ¶What we must seek to see is the all-pervading energy which permeates all form. It is not necessary to centralize on one thought or sequence of pictures as opposed to another to gain this new perspective, for we cannot, in a sense, climb up to it. We have to drop down into it by going deep within the essence of the mind and intuiting the all-pervading force. We come out of that state as a pure, unhindered awareness, able to flow and focus detachedly in the accustomed areas of mind that make up what we term "our life," and as new cavities of mind awaken before our vision, we flow in and out of them unhampered or hindered by what is seen.

Thursday
LESSON 207
The Sources Of Thoughts

Sometimes the thoughts you think are not your own. Your individual awareness may have inadvertently been pulled into an area of the mind that someone else is aware in. So, unintentionally you may be reading someone else's thoughts as your own, and if they are of a nature that you do not approve, it is possible that you may be disappointed in yourself. Keen discernment must always be employed by the aspirant on the path in order to decipher which is which. This is difficult, but you should always question thoughts that just pop into your head to find out whether they are, in fact, your own or those of another. ¶A general outline that you can follow in deciphering your personal thoughts from those of another is this. As soon as you begin to question your thinking with this in mind, if the thoughts are yours, you will continue thinking in the same way after the questioning has subsided. However, if they are those of another, through the simple act of questioning whether they are or not, you have removed awareness from the area of mind they are vibrating in. Then when the questioning has subsided, you will forget that trend of thought and go on with one of your own. Their thoughts will fade from your memory in a similar way dreams do when you awaken in the morning. ¶This is by no means an inference that you should every minute of the day question your thinking as I have just described. For, more than often, with people whom we love as well as with other friends and acquaintances, you would want to be always drifting into the areas of mind they are in, and they with you. It is only on rare occasions that thoughts of an uncomely nature, of an instinctive nature, especially sexual, may militate against your *sādhana.* My advice is rather than blame yourself, first question to see if such fantasies are actually your own. Mass hysteria and fear of a national or global disaster can also be picked up by the sensitive individual, sometimes unknowingly. Along the same lines, we should be alert to this. ¶There is a Śaivite hermit, the venerable Markanduswāmī, living in a humble mud hut in Sri Lanka. He is very old, and was for many years a disciple of Jñānaguru Yogaswāmī. In fact, his every utterance is a quote from his *guru.* One afternoon at his hut he described Yogaswāmī's approach to dealing with thought during meditation. He said, "Yogaswāmī said, 'Realize Self by self. You want to read this book, that book and all these books. The Book of Infinite Knowledge is here (pointing to his chest). You'd better open your own book.' The prescription he gave me to open that book is this: 'When you are in meditation, you watch the mind. Here and there the mind is hopping. One, two, three,...a hundred. In a few seconds the mind goes to a hundred places. Let him be. You also watch very carefully. Here and there this mind is running. Don't forget Self for a second. Let him go anywhere, but if he goes to a hundred places, you must follow him to a hundred places. You must not miss even a single one. Follow him and note, *He is going here. Now he is going there.'* You must not miss even a single one. That is the prescription Satguru Yogaswāmī gave me to open this inner book. He said, 'Watch very attentively and learn to pick up things coming from within. Those messages are very valuable. You can't value them. Realize Self by self and open this inner book. Why don't you open your own book? Why don't you make use of it? Why don't you open your own book? What an easy path I am prescribing for you!' "

Friday
LESSON 208
Being the Watcher

We can see that from the mystic's point of view, he is the watcher. And as the mirror is in no way discolored by what it reflects, so is the mystic in his perfected state. Your perfected state, too, as the watcher is right there, deep within you. The next time you sit for meditation, follow my *guru's* advice to us all and witness your thoughts. Be that stationary awareness, holding form in its own perfection. All you have to do is to watch your mind think. Then and only then are you experiencing your perfect state of inner being. The only difference between the *jñānī* and the novice is that the *jñānī* stays in there longer as the watcher, whereas the novice experiences this only momentarily from time to time. ¶This is the result of a great abundance of your *sādhana,* and as the watcher, once stabilized within a new platform, a new beginning is commenced. There is much preparation that you can perform to attain this prolonged state more rapidly. There are some do's and don'ts to be heeded and explicitly obeyed. Do regulate your in-breath to equal the same number of counts as your out-breath, and feel the bliss of your body as it becomes relaxed and harmonized. Don't allow indulgence in sexual fantasy for even one moment. Do correct your diet to that of *sattvic* foods that grow above the ground. Don't indulge in mental argument with yourself or anyone else. ¶These four suggestions are the basic formula for cleansing the dross from the mind as well as from the subconscious by not putting more into it. Assuredly, results are dimmed if an aspirant meditates in the morning, engages in mental argument in the afternoon and sexual fantasies before sleep, or at any other time. His *yogic* discipline then would simply strengthen his fantasies and their repercussions, as well as the excitement of mental argument. Therefore, having these two greatest barriers out of the way, the path is clear, the *sādhana* easier to handle and the results cumulative. ¶At the beginning of your practice of trying to decipher the nature of awareness as opposed to the nature of thought—which must be satisfactorily done before awareness can truly be detached—refrain from criticizing yourself or others as you begin to observe the many things you have been thinking about all these many years. For, it is a fact that once you are able to observe your own thoughts even a little—though you may be unhappy with many of those thoughts, as they do not ascribe to the new philosophy and outlook which you have become interested in and appreciate and even though you may abhor some thoughts and attitudes—you are already detached from them somewhat. So, don't make matters worse by criticizing yourself for the thinking and mental habit patterns you are observing. This can cause tension in the nerve system and work directly against the *prāṇāyāma* that you may be practicing, and nullify the results. Rather, claim yourself to be the watcher at this early stage, and obey the two don'ts that I have just mentioned. Beautiful philosophical thoughts and refined feelings will fill in and take the place of minutes or hours previously used in mental argument and instinctive fantasy.

Saturday
LESSON 209
Seeking a New Perspective

In the philosophical-theological perspective of the mind which I call *moolef,* we see thoughts as traveling from one to another. This is what they seem to do, from one point of view. They not only travel from one person to another, but are seen to pass rapidly before our vision, ever demanding and commanding our awareness to travel with them. We are then faced with the tedious task of quieting the mind by endeavoring to control these thoughts. Through breath control and various forms of prior understandings, which are cumulative as we persist in the performance of our *sādhana,* the deep, mystical perspective which I call *shumef* soon situates individual awareness deep enough within ourselves, undisturbed by physical or emotional upheavals and intellectual tangents, that the world of thought may be viewed as stationary, and it is awareness that moves from thought to thought, scanning and registering what it sees. This, as I have mentioned before, is the perspective to be sought and attained through the performance of *sādhana.* ¶Remaining in one place in the inner depths of the mind, totally aware of being in that one place, as well as aware of that which is happening about you, is the state to be attained and maintained throughout your life. By being the watcher, ignorance is dispelled, emotion is quelled, and the foreboding stampede of excitement is subdued. By being the watcher, the overview of life is precise, and an equal balance between the inner and the outer is maintained. ¶During the course of this practice, you may feel totally apart from what you had come to believe were the realities of life. It must always be remembered that an initial dissatisfaction had occurred, compelling the search within to begin. It was this dissatisfaction that first consciously established the deep, inner state of being able to watch your mind think and experiences occur. But this state, once attained, is not easy to maintain. Practice is needed to give confidence and accept new habit patterns in the outer realms of daily expression. The practice is the constant pulling of awareness within and from there, that one central point, looking out upon the mind. Only in performing this act time and time again does success come and stay. ¶If you have never experienced watching your mind think, observing your emotions play, watching your body move while living within it, then you may find it difficult to conceive of this state of perpetual permanence within one central point deep within. ¶As we have to start somewhere, let's begin with the body. The eyes watch the hands at work, and while doing this, we can think about the hands. Also, one step deeper, it is possible to think about the eyes and inwardly observe the mechanism of sight. There is a "you" in there that is observing this mechanism of sight, the eyes, the eyes seeing the hands, the thoughts about the hands, eyes and sight. This "you" is the watcher, the witness—the state that the mystic is consciously conscious in. Becoming conscious in this state through this one simple practice is possible for short periods of time, and once you have understood the principle involved, success is assured.

Sunday
LESSON 210
Become The Watcher

We must be aware that it is only reawakening consciousness into a natural state, and that there is nothing mystical, difficult or inward that has to occur to hold an awareness of the inner and outer simultaneously from one central point in the mind. It is only because one is not accustomed to thinking in this way that it may seem difficult. But little children are in this state much of the time, and it is natural to them. ¶The beginning stages of watching the mind think I shall describe as similar to sitting quietly with your eyes open and while not thinking about anything in particular, simply looking at what is around you—all of the time feeling somewhat empty on the inside, but seeing what is in front of you, to the left side of you, to the right side of you, above you, below you, and knowing what each object is, but not thinking about any object or collection of objects. Your eyes are watching; who lives behind them is the watcher. The objects that the mind perceives are similar to thoughts. ¶When you close your eyes and begin thinking about the objects you have been looking at, duplicating your surroundings in your mind by creating thought pictures of those objects, there is a deeper you who is the watcher of those thoughts. This you can practice all through the day almost anywhere you are. It takes no particular skill or practice. It can be done at any time. You are simply becoming conscious of the natural processes of awareness, consciousness and thought which have been going on day after day all through your life up to this point. ¶Each time you practice being the watcher, using the method just outlined, as soon as you begin to succeed, you will immediately receive the impact of realization of the extent of involvement in the external mind that had occurred between these periods of practice. You will find that the more you practice regularly, increasingly, more frequently, you will remember to continue "the witness" in the midst of daily life—while riding in conveyances, talking with people, shopping in crowded stores, even in the midst of a disagreement or at the pinnacle of a creative flow. "You," the watcher, will preside, and in presiding will carry that inner presence so necessary for a full and fruitful life. ¶With this in mind, be encouraged, for we must remember that total involvement in the externalities of the mind seems to be the cultural trait of this century. Therefore, it may take a few years to change the pattern. To send awareness soaring within to home base is not easy when the rest of the world is plunging in the opposite direction. If at first you only succeed a few minutes a day being able to watch the mind think or watch the eyes see, that is sufficient, as long as the practice is regular and consistent, day after day. ¶Other kinds of practice previously outlined in the *sādhana* of this book will strengthen this ability and increase your capacity to maintain that equal balance between the inner and the outer, if performed with regularity. This intricate study of awareness steadied versus fluctuating thought can only be pursued by taking the slow and sometimes arduous approach, not being overly enthused by success or discouraged by failure.

Sthūlaśarīraṁ Prāṇamayakośaścha

स्थूलशरीरं प्राणमयकोशश्च

13

The Physical and Prāṇic Bodies

The gross body with prominent presence, the subtle body that takes invisible shape, and the causal body that is known by inference—all these bodies ultimately merge in the Lord's feet.

TIRUMANTIRAM 2130

MANIVEL

Monday
LESSON 211
Meet Your Physical Body

Introduce yourself to your physical body by looking into a mirror today, a full-length one if possible. Say to yourself aloud, "I am not my physical body. I am much greater than my physical body." You will immediately see this to be true if you approach the mirror and stand before it with these two thoughts in mind. Then listen to yourself saying, "I am not my physical body. I am much greater than my physical body." The physical body is only one of the vehicles through which your highest being functions. To gain a concept of how much greater you really are, you must first begin bringing those several vehicles under your conscious control. This is done first by using the power of understanding, which is about fifty percent of the application of control when it comes to the world of the mind. ¶Quite often new aspirants coming to me to enter the classical *yoga* path will say, "I am sick of this body and its desires. I want to renounce it and live entirely spiritually." There is nothing wrong with such a resolve, except that usually the aspirant really means, "I have no control over my body. I don't understand it, nor any of my emotional drives. They control me, and somehow I can't get away from the consciousness of them." ¶As long as you react to your physical body, despising or cherishing it too much, you cannot progress well in *sādhana* or religious life. However, through the practice of concentration of the flow of thought forces, and through the deliberate use of your willpower, the power of cognition, deep understanding will unfold within you, acting as a controlling agent of the odic forces that sometimes can be so turbulent. ¶As an exercise in concentration, locate the different parts of your physical body through feeling while sitting still. Feel all of your muscles. Feel each bone. Locate them with your mind's eye. Feel every organ, your heart, your liver, etc. Feel your circulatory system, the warmth, the flow. You are using the feeling faculties of the subconscious mind, the part of the subconscious that governs the involuntary processes of the body. The other part governs the involuntary processes of the mind, such as habits. In feeling the various parts of the body you are actually becoming consciously conscious of odic force, using the aggressive vibration of this force to become conscious of the physical body.

Tuesday
LESSON 212
Expressions of Actinic Force

Did you know that the physical body reflects the higher states of your consciousness and actually registers the flow of actinic force? There are advanced *yogīs* who can look at the physical body of a beginning seeker and observe how evolved he may be on the spiritual path. He would also be able to intuit from his observation the remaining subconscious seed experiences that yet must be worked out either physically or mentally. ¶Your physical body will express the highest that is within you when the actinic forces are flowing freely through it. Often the physical body reflects the lower nature when the odic forces are turbulent and in or out of control. The best way to keep the actinic force flowing through the physical body is practicing the art of giving, doing little things for others that you have not been asked to do. This keeps you creative, and being creative is actinic, superconscious and religious. Giving, doing without thought of return, affectionate detachment, creates an odic vacuum which your actinic, spiritual forces flow into and fill. As you practice this *bhakti* and *karma yoga* art, your relatives and friends, even strangers, will recognize your unfoldment, for the actinic forces, the real you, will permeate your physical body, making each of your features alive. ¶You can only detach yourself from your odic physical body when you know that a higher you exists, when you have gained stability by identifying yourself as actinic force. Don't mistake your personality or ego for your actinic individuality. ¶Often the two terms *individuality* and *personality* are taken to be synonymous, but this is far from true. In classical *yoga* teachings we look at individuality as being the actinic energy, or the clear white light, the pure energy substance of the mind, which is constant, ever unfolding itself, peaceful and controlled. The personality we consider as the various masks or personae which cover the individuality. The personae which are heavy, dark and glued on to one's face, so to speak, are those of an intense ego, congested odic force. They are most difficult and rather painful to drop off, or even to pull off. The personae which are transparent allow the clear white light from the actinic being to shine through. One can have many of these personalities and have fun using them constructively in the world, doing things of the world, always recognizing that the clearness of actinic vision shines through the mind-constructed personality of the individual's race, occupation, social background and various accomplishments.

Wednesday
LESSON 213
Personality and Individuality

Many people become attached to their personality and suffer when it changes. One cannot, however, be attached to his individuality. In identifying the difference between personality and individuality, we can say that man's individuality is the actinic, superconscious mind, which is constant, permanent, ever-unfolding and secure, and deep within, at a more intense rate of vibration than his odic conscious and subconscious mind, which make up the ever-changing personality. It is conceivable that man can have many different personalities, but he can have only one constantly unfolding individuality. And so it is the ego or personality masks we must identify as being the unreal and impermanent, and the actinic individuality as being the permanent, secure, ever unfolding and refined actinic phase of the mind. This week do an internal concentration on the words *personality* and *individuality.* Try to locate your individuality by identifying your several masks or personalities that you have created in this life and write your findings on why you can get attached to personality but cannot get attached to individuality. ¶You perhaps have had a series of good, positive and constructive experiences. They have gone deep into your subconscious mind. The subconscious mind has reorganized itself, giving you a more positive, constructive, fruitful outlook on life. As a result, several weeks later your friends say to you, "You look different. Your face has a glow. You appear eight years younger." These compliments also go into your subconscious mind, and you begin to feel good about your physical body. These good feelings, constructive, healthy feelings, again go into the subconscious mind and build from within itself a new atomic structure for the physical body. You take a new lease on life. Your body grows younger because your mind has had good impressions placed within it.

¶Think on this. Be renewed by a change of your mind, and seek for the constructive experiences with a positive reaction. Allow the reaction to bear fruit within the subconscious mind. Concentrate and feel the good feelings permeating the nerve currents running through the physical body, thus being renewed actinically from within. Good feelings are like food to the physical body. Food from deep within the nervous system, fed out through the circulatory system, right out to the skin, makes for an inner glow which can be seen on your face and through the rest of the body. This constitutes happy organs. In other words, all of the organs of the body are working in perfect timing, one with another, being proportionately fed by actinic energy and the vital odic forces. A good, well-balanced "force diet" makes for healthy organs and controlled, calm, central and sympathetic nerve systems.

Thursday
LESSON 214
Tuning Up With Haṭha Yoga

When we live in our personality, we are limited, but our individuality reigns supreme. A balance of actinic and odic forces running through the physical body bursts forth into individuality within the aspirant on the spiritual path. This cherished individuality, the feeling that you are the center of the universe, and your created world revolves around you, does not make one egotistical, but rather forms within the consciousness a deep humility, or a deep feeling of the realities of life, thus laying a solid foundation for meditation. ¶*Haṭha yoga* is a science of perfecting the physical body through the use of certain postures, or *āsanas.* In a deeper sense, it is a system of handling the physical body so that you are able to gain a conscious, actinic control of the odic forces of your subconscious mind. When the body is tuned up to a rhythmic pitch, you can single out the seeds of basic odic desires and destroy them. ¶The practice of *haṭha yoga* places the physical body in different *āsanas* in a regular, routine arrangement, so that the nerve currents in the body area are tuned up to a perfect pitch. No stretching, no straining, no pulling, no stresses. Once you have memorized the correct postures of *haṭha yoga* in their progressive order, you will find that after practicing them for only a few minutes, your mind will be able to concentrate itself without any effort whatsoever. You will be in an automatic state of subconscious concentration because you will have no nerve strain to distract your mind or bottle up the odic force. You will find yourself more alive consciously, and much more alive subconsciously, than you have ever been before. A child can do most of the *haṭha yoga* postures quite naturally. When you can, too, you will have that youthful freedom of mind flow again. ¶*Haṭha yoga*, practiced correctly over a period of time, makes the mind so acute that you become able to "single out the seed of desire by disregarding all other corresponding erroneous thoughts." In other words, in the practice of this science alone, the *yoga* student begins to burn out congested seeds of desire from within without even thinking about them. As you become more and more perfected in *haṭha yoga*, the odic forces, both passive and aggressive, become adjusted, balanced and controlled. ¶Through the practice of *haṭha yoga*, the physical body becomes a perfect vehicle for the mind to live in. The tensions which have been built up through the years become fleeting, and the mind becomes actinically alive. This enables the *yoga* student, as he presents himself to the *yoga* master for personal training, to single out the seed of desire and, in the light of understanding, destroy it. This retroactively brings forth a great wisdom through the conscious use of the subsuperconscious mind. When this happens, you don't have to think to know. You know, and thinking is the result. Affectionate detachment from friends and relations is automatically accomplished, and a greater love for them flows in through actinic understanding.

Friday
LESSON 215
The Sheath Of Vitality

In the West we have only a few close equivalents for the Sanskṛit word *prāṇa,* and they are *odic force, actinic force* and *energy.* But *prāṇa* is not really a form of energy or a force; it is the sum total of all energy, all force, in its various manifestations. Science has proven that all matter is in vibration, that the difference in these vibrations are what gives matter its form. At one time scientists believed the atom to be the smallest unit within matter, but progressively smaller units have been discovered. When the smallest subdivision of matter is reached, *prāṇa,* or pure energy, remains. *Prāṇa* is the sum total of energy, because the whole material universe is, in a sense, manifested from it. ¶The odic *prāṇic* sheath is the health body, *prāṇamaya kośa,* hovering just within and through the physical body, extending out from the physical body about two to five inches. Odic *prāṇa* is physical vitality. Actinic *prāṇa* and willpower are one and the same. ¶You have probably read of cases of suspended animation, men buried alive for hours or days without air or food. When this actually occurs and it is not faked, it is usually due to the control of *prāṇa.* After extensive training, odic force can be stored in a static state in the body and then used in the absence of air or food, for it is the essence of air or food. Some animals that hibernate do this as well. Frogs have been found buried in earthen mounds in the United States and are said to have been hibernating there hundreds of years without food, water, or air, yet once liberated they showed every sign of life. And man can do it, too, with proper training over a long period of time. This, of course, is not a complete unfoldment of the meaning of life. It is only the conquest of the second aspect of man, odic *prāṇa.* ¶Breathe deeply in and out, in and out, in and out. As you breathe in, feel as though you are pulling odic *prāṇa* into you as well as air. As you breathe out, feel as though you are sending out the air, but keeping the odic *prāṇa* in the body, all the time storing it in the solar plexus. Soon you should begin to feel full of energy, solid and stable. ¶Here is another exercise. Select a dimly lit place that you can use as a background against which to view your hand, such as a closet. Open your right hand, in which you have been storing odic *prāṇa*, and hold it against the dark background. With your eyes half open, gaze at your hand relaxed. Don't try too hard. You should be able to see the odic *prāṇa* around each of your fingers. It will be seen as a cloudy, vaporous substance. If you are in perfect health, the odic *prāṇa* will be clearer and more readily apparent. Some sensitive *yoga* students can see the odic *prāṇa* around the physical body of people.

Saturday
LESSON 216
Experience Odic Prāṇa

Fill six glasses with water. Place them on a table before you. Take one of these glasses of water and hold it in one hand while with the other hand you shake the fingertips into the glass but without touching the water. Feel the odic *prāṇa* falling from the hand and fingers into the water, being absorbed into the water and held there. Thus we have mixed two forms of odic power, that of the physical-health odic *prāṇa* and the odic manifestation of water. This creates magnetism when these two forces come together in the external, odic water. Mark the glass of water that you have magnetized so that only you will later be able to identify it, then place it with the other five glasses. Switch the glasses around so that it is not apparent which glass was magnetized. If you are doing this exercise by yourself, you may close your eyes when you switch the glasses so that you do not identify the glass that has been magnetized. Now, the test. Close your eyes and drink from each glass. You close your eyes so that your taste will be most keen, and you will not be distracted by anything you see, having your entire mind on your taste buds. As you taste each glass of water, you will notice a distinct difference in the taste of the water in the glass you magnetized with odic *prāṇa*. ¶You will achieve a great control over your *prāṇic* sheath by learning to breathe diaphragmatically. The following experiments, coupled with diaphragmatic breathing, will help you awaken your own knowledge of the controls over odic *prāṇa* and your own odic *prāṇic* sheath. Take a deep breath through the nostrils, at the same time holding a mental picture of taking odic *prāṇa* into the body from within the air. You may visualize it in the form of a vapor, like the odic *prāṇa* you perhaps saw around your hand. Visualize the odic *prāṇa* going all the way down to your solar plexus, while the air is only held in your lungs. The odic *prāṇa* stays in your solar plexus while you exhale air from the lungs. From the solar plexus area, the odic *prāṇa* will automatically flow through the muscle tissue to the blood and begin to store up in various nerve centers in reserve for future use. In mastering this exercise, you will build up the vital body energies and calm the nerves. It is not necessary to do this often, only when you feel the need of storing up odic *prāṇa.* ¶Odic *prāṇa* is often used unknowingly for healing various physical distresses, emotional upsets and mental strains. A child runs to his mother; the odic *prāṇa* coming from the mother, freely flowing toward the child, comforts any distress the child may be going through. The child runs off vigorously, taking a good supply of odic *prāṇa* from his mother through absorption. You can supply odic *prāṇa* to any part of your body that may be ailing, and gain some relief. For emotional distress, store odic *prāṇa* in the solar plexus, and to relieve mental strain store it in the upper back and chest area. ¶As you inhale odic *prāṇa,* draw a mental picture of the process. When you make a mental picture, you are also employing odic force to form the picture, for all mental pictures are made out of odic force. After the mental picture of the physical area in your body that is in distress is well formed, visualize the odic *prāṇa* being sent to that particular organ or part of the body. Inhale, then hold your breath a few seconds as you visualize the odic *prāṇa* flowing from the solar plexus to that area of your physical body.

When you manage to flow enough odic *prāṇa* into the distressed area of your physical body and the health body becomes more vibrant, you will notice the distress ease. Do this for short periods of time. Remember, inhale, hold a few seconds while sending the energy to the distressed area, then exhale the air, holding the odic *prāṇa* in the part of the body that needs extra energy most. "Where awareness goes energy flows." All breathing should be through the nostrils, not the mouth, deep and slow, natural and rhythmic.

Sunday
LESSON 217
Trace the Source of Prāṇa

Prāṇa is not air, of course, yet it is contained in the air in a certain manifestation. Much *prāṇa* is found in the air among the trees or near the ocean. All of nature and the forces of nature are various manifestations of odic *prāṇa* that have taken visual shape. Plants feed on the odic *prāṇa* in the air. You can absorb *prāṇa* simply by walking through a grove of trees. The air is filled with it. Take a walk today, out into the odic force field of nature and absorb the *prāṇa* in the air through your breath and through the pores of your skin. You will feel the *prāṇa* entering into your *prāṇic* sheath, or vital health body, and remaining there while you exhale. ¶Sit quietly and use the internal method of concentration when you think on this. Each time your mind wanders, pull it firmly back to the subject of concentration. Remember, in concentration, that the process of making the mind return to the object or subject of concentration forces a flow of odic as well as actinic *prāṇa* through the most subtle nerve currents, causing them to grow strong, so that soon your concentration will be effortless as your subconscious responds to your conscious-mind concentration efforts, causing a new process called meditation to occur in the wonderful world of the mind. ¶Concentrate on the *prāṇic* health body flowing through and just within your physical body. Mentally go over the exercises we have done this week in proving the flow and existence of odic *prāṇa* to the subconscious habit mind, so that by establishing a new habit pattern, the subconscious will aid instead of barricade your natural unfoldment on the path to enlightenment. Your subconscious needs certain proofs of these inner laws to solicit full cooperation. ¶Mentally trace odic *prāṇa* to its source and cause. Does it come to an end? If so, where? Where does actinic *prāṇa* begin? You will soon find that odic *prāṇa* does come to an end, for it merges in the subconscious area of the mind into the subsuperconscious. You will find that odic *prāṇa* depends on the existence of actinic *prāṇa* for its existence. As you concentrate on the interrelated flow of odic *prāṇa* and ascertain the area of the inner mind where actinic *prāṇa* begins, you should conceptually see how you have been controlling odic *prāṇa* during this entire week through the use of your subsuperconscious state of mind. ¶You are maturing through the knowledge of the within of your Being, which you have been studying these last few months. Remember, in the wonderful world of the mind, understanding, gaining mental perspectives, finding proof, no matter how small, within ourselves—these form important controls over the mind. The art of concentration, though the basic and most fundamental control of all, is not the only control over the mind on the classical *yoga* path to enlightenment. Harmony is control of even deeper aspects of the mind, as are understanding and actinic love. As we expand our consciousness on the *yoga* path to enlightenment, we hear more, see more, feel more, know more within ourselves. This is intense. We must not fear intensity, for intensity is actinic. Your actinic Being is intensity itself, actively alive and always shining out. Man can be thought of as seven aspects of form, but the Self is beyond the mind or beyond form, for mind is form. Mind is consciousness; consciousness is form. The Self is formless. Therefore, you can contemplatively say, "I am That, I am."

Sūkshma Śarīram

सूक्ष्मशरीरम्

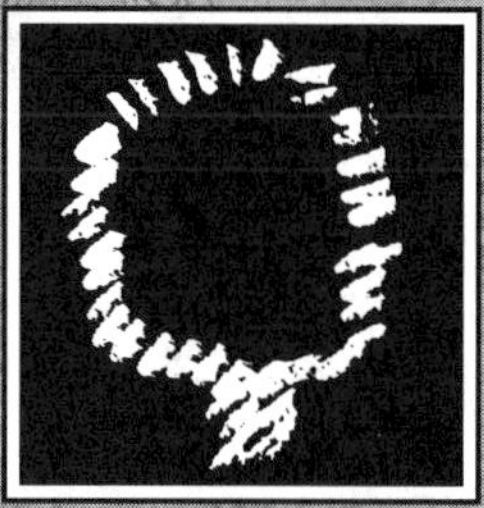

The Astral Body

Into the union, the Holy One entered. Gathering *tattvas* five and twenty, Śiva fashioned the five-sheathed body. Munificent indeed was His gift! A veritable bundle of desire He made.

TIRUMANTIRAM 465

Monday
LESSON 218
Your Astral Counterpart

You will recall from last week the first aspect of man, the physical body, and the second aspect, the vital health body. The third aspect is the astral body. ¶The astral body is almost an exact duplicate of the physical body. However, changes that appear upon the physical body, such as aging, first occur within the structure of the astral body. The astral body is of the subconscious mind, at the level of the memory and reason *chakras.* It can be easily disturbed and is sometimes called the emotional body. It is made of odic *prāṇa* and kept intact by the general life flow of actinic *prāṇa* bursting constantly forth from its atomic structure. Being the exact counterpart of the physical body, the astral body appears like the physical body in size, shape, in every sense except weight. It differs in weight because it is composed of astral odic matter. This matter vibrates at a higher rate of vibration than what we might call physical matter. ¶Try to picture for yourself the fact that the physical body and astral body are of different vibrations and fit one inside the other, connected by the energy factor, which is the odic *prāṇic* energy of the vital health body. The astral world vibrates just inside the physical world that we see through our physical eyes and feel with our physical hands. Therefore, it is an exact duplication of everything that exists materially to our physical senses. This is logical to us, knowing and having identified the states of mind, for each state of mind is a form of vibration working together with all the others. The "one mind" is in different forms of vibration, all working together, one aspect within the other. ¶As we can walk and talk using our conscious mind and our physical body as a vehicle during our waking hours, so can we walk and talk using the duplicate of the physical body, our astral body of the subconscious mind, during the hours we are asleep. When we are in the astral body in the subconscious world, other people are also in that world, and forms of communication take place, as in the physical world. ¶There is a cord of odic and actinic force which connects the two bodies. It is called the silver cord. Should someone travel too far from his physical body astrally, or have an intense astral experience, an extra supply of energy would be drawn from the vital health body and the physical body, and he would be tired on awakening. ¶The inner study of you can be complicated, for you are a most complex being of many dimensions. As we embark on this week's study of the inner you, it may be helpful to have a list which you can refer to now and then to put together the pieces in the right order. The age-old teachings which are captured in this book boldly claim "man" to be more than is usually understood, that being a mortal body with an intellect, small or large. Man, as the mystics understand him, is the immortal soul surrounded by seven aspects. Here follows a summary of the "seven aspects of man" established around the actinic causal body of the soul, *ānandamaya kośa,* "sheath of bliss:" 1) thc physical body, *annamaya kośa,* "food made sheath;" 2) the vital health body, *prānic* sheath, *prāṇamaya kośa;* 3) the astral body, instinctive aspect of *manomaya kośa;* 4) the human aura and instinctive mind, *prabhāmaṇḍala* and *manas chitta;* 5) the intellect, odic causal sheath, *buddhi chitta;* 6) the subtle nerve system, *nāḍīs* and *chakras;* 7) the intuitive mind, actinodic causal sheath, *vijñānamaya kośa,* "sheath of cognition." ¶Just as we have school, entertainment, discussions and meetings with friends in the conscious mind on the physical plane, so do we go to school, enjoy entertainment, discuss problems and meet and talk with friends on the astral plane. And as the subconscious mind receives impressions from the conscious mind during our waking hours, so does the conscious mind receive impressions from the subconscious mind as we go through experience during our sleeping hours. ¶In the same way, people have seen with the eyes of their astral body, while simultaneously conscious through their physical eyes, people on the astral plane. Similarly, those who are traveling on the astral plane can see people on the physical plane, as they look out through the odic astral force field into the gross conscious-mind world. Travel is much faster on the astral plane, as it is done through desire, and the astral body is a much more refined rate of vibration than is the physical body, which functions close to the time sequence as we know it.

Tuesday
LESSON 219
Life on the Astral Plane

Each night when you read your lesson in this book, realize that therein is your key to entry into the astral school of Himālayan Academy. Going to sleep thinking about the lesson you have been reading, try to wake up slowly in the morning and, with effort, recall what you have been doing during the night on the astral plane. ¶The astral world is a plane in space, just as the physical world, as we know it in the conscious mind, is a space plane. It is the particular rate of vibration which each of these worlds generates that determines the space plane it occupies. Looking out through the conscious mind, we perceive outer space. Looking into the subconscious mind, we perceive inner space. As the habit patterns of the subconscious mind control many of our conscious-mind happenings on the physical plane, so does the superconscious mind control many of the occurrences of the astral plane through the subconscious astral body. This has to do with the awakening of the subsuperconscious mind. The subsuperconscious mind becomes stronger and stronger, providing we exercise our intuition on the conscious-mind level. ¶Just as you choose your friends on the physical, conscious plane, so do you attract kindred beings to you in the astral world. By keeping our homes clean and peaceful, by keeping our bodies and clothing fresh and clean, the odic force becomes quite pure and enables us to be more actinically alive. This condition also keeps lower astral people away from us, so long as we do not ourselves enter into an instinctive, astrally odic vibration. The spiritual, actinic vibration keeps all lower astral influences away, just as doors, locks, windows and walls discourage unwanted entrance into buildings. ¶It is not advisable to admit lower astral entities if you are sensitive to this possibility, for doing so creates a double influx of odic force, whereas the striving of a *yoga* student is to become actinically superconscious and not to intensify the odic subconscious. Astral entities live in their own world on the astral plane. Possibly you enter this plane at night, too, but during the day we must attend to our conscious-mind activities and take care of our immediate programs, keeping the two worlds apart as distinctly as our sleeping state is separated from the state of being awake. ¶When the physical body dies, this automatically severs the actinodic silver cord that connects the astral and physical bodies. Then the process of reincarnation and rebirth eventually begins. The physical body remains on the physical plane as a conglomeration of magnetic forces and begins to dissolve into the forces of surrounding nature. The actinic life of the physical body and the vital health body travels up the silver cord as it dissolves and lends a tremendous charge to the astral body. This movement registers on the subconscious astral body all conscious-mind memory patterns of the life just lived, and the person becomes fully conscious on the astral plane. ¶This tremendous charge of odic and actinic force registering upon the astral body at the time of transition, or death, is what stimulates and gives the initial impulse to the process of reincarnation. This process is largely controlled by the activity of subconscious habit forces. ¶Before the reincarnation cycle fully takes hold, however, the person just departed often quickly recreates the same states of consciousness, the same interests he was accustomed to on the physical plane, and he may go on as usual, meeting his family who visit him during their sleeping hours in their astral bodies. Although the astral body is still bound by the habit patterns of its physical life, it continues to wear away from the moment of transition, and odic force is continuously fed back to the physical plane in an effort to make contact again with family, friends or loved ones through the medium of memory and desire. Another physical body is created, and a reentry into the conscious world is made. The old astral body is dropped off, and the newly generated actinic forces give life to a new physical body and a new health body, along with a new astral body. The new astral body is the sum total of all preceding subconscious experience, and it may be quite mature during the time the physical body is only a child. The odic astral form that was left behind is called an astral shell and eventually corresponds to the corpse of the dead physical body.

Wednesday
LESSON 220
The Aura and Instinctive Mind

As we begin the study of the fourth aspect of man, let us hold in mind the first three: the physical body as the first aspect, the vital health body as the second aspect and the astral body as the third aspect. The fourth aspect is the instinctive mind and the human aura, the colorful spectrum that registers whatever state of mind the person passes through. The human aura is the reflection of specific evolution. But it registers most clearly the basic reactionary patterns of the instinctive mind. ¶Within the instinctive mind there are both aggressive and passive odic forces. Some of these are fear, anger, jealousy, deceit, pride, greed—and then there is that form of attachment sometimes called odic or magnetic love, as well as happiness and affection. These emotions are either aggressive or passive, depending upon the motivating factors involved. The motivating factors are desire, a lack of control of odic force, or a type of actinic, superconscious flow which motivates from within to the externals of human consciousness. When this actinic flow is in action, the more refined emotions of compassion, benevolence and joy are experienced. Basically, all of these qualities may be defined as being either odic or actinic. The actinic forces flow from the core of the soul out through the odic force field, and when the actinic forces become diminished, odic forces congeal and rush in to fill the gap. ¶Fear is passive odic force. Anger is aggressive odic force. The two basic colors of the odic aura are gray and red. Gray is the color of fear, which when it leads to depression or intense fear, becomes black. Red is the aura's registration of anger. In a suppressed state of the instinctive mind, when desire has not been met, the aura registers a reddish black to portray the emotion of lust. ¶Fear dominates the lives of many people, even when they have no reason for being afraid. It is a protective mechanism of the lower, instinctive nature inherent in every human being; animals, too. The fear of the darkness, for instance, was born in primitive man's lack of a shelter. Long before he discovered the use of fire or even learned to live in caves, he trembled in the darkness when the sun went down each day, for he knew he was at the mercy of wild animals and other dangers of the night. Even today, the ability of men to fear endows them with a natural caution in the face of the unknown. The gray cast permeates the aura during protective investigation until it is proven that a condition of safety exists. ¶Today man still retains fear of the darkness. But now he surrounds himself with electric light, symbolizing the new golden age in which his actinic force has begun to penetrate through the instinctive mind, refining this mind just as the glow of electricity refines the vibration of the Earth at night. Among other forms of fear are fear of death, fear of poverty, fear of water and fear of high places. ¶Anger is also, like fear, an instinctive control, and at one time served its purpose. The onrush of anger served to protect man's private interests in critical situations by injecting adrenaline into his blood and thus preparing him for defense. But as man evolves closer to his real, actinic being, he discovers that actinic love, understanding, compassion and wisdom are higher qualities than anger. Two more instinctive emotions that motivate the passive and aggressive odic forces into action are jealousy and deceit. ¶The actinic age is bursting forth upon this planet. Its signposts heralding the spiritual mind of man are portrayed in symbolic happenings upon the Earth, such as the electric light, atomic energy, probes into space, probes into the subconscious, probes into prior lives and dangerously expanding states of awareness stimulated by chemicals. All this and more show us that man has outgrown the lower, instinctive emotions such as jealousy, portrayed in the odic aura around and through the body in the color of dark green, and deceit, portrayed as green-gray.

Thursday
LESSON 221
Harnessing Instinctiveness

Yes, man has outgrown jealousy and deceit, but how often does he realize this? The newspapers are filled with examples of people who let themselves be controlled by these emotions. When jealousy is felt, one feels that the person they admire has more control over the odic and actinic forces than they do, and in a frantic effort to balance the forces, they devise plans to tear down the odic forces or cease the flow of actinic forces of their prey. Jealousy is treacherous when it turns active and aggressive and makes a person deceitful. ¶Many people do not feel deceit to be an emotion after it has been existent in their nature long enough to become a habit. Instinctive emotions often become habits when allowed to be indulged in too much, especially these basic and baser ones—fear, anger, jealousy and deceit—

all of which are resident in the lower *chakras,* below the *mūlādhāra chakra.* ¶Fear, anger, jealousy and deceit produce an odic aura web of green, gray, black and red, running through and through the organs of the astral body, affecting the organs of the physical body, as well as draining the vital health body of needed odic power. This cuts the actinic flow to a minimum, so that the only life in the body exists in a dull, crafty sparkle in the eyes. ¶These basic, instinctive emotions of the subconscious mind are the substance through which we evolve. As more control of the forces is effected, the colors of the aura lighten and the nature is refined. This refining process is done quickly through discipline on the *rāja yoga* path to enlightenment. Every effort that you make to curb and control your base, instinctive nature brings you that much closer to your spiritual goal. There is a very true saying, "You are only as actinic as your lowest active odic force." Those things to which you still react represent your low points and must be turned into actinic understanding before you can dissolve the odic force field that contains them. ¶Another dimension of the instinctive mind is the habit mind. Habits are built into us from childhood. Some remain conscious and others enter the subconscious. The most difficult to overcome are our habitual identifications with the force fields of our city or state, our country, our race, and even the world itself. The many ramifications of human behavior which pertain to a study of the habit mind could fill many books. Prejudice is one of the negative emotions contained in the habit mind. We may not think of prejudice as being a habit, but it is. Many adults retain very strong habitual prejudices. They do not care for people who do not belong to their particular race, caste or social class. ¶When there is any sudden shift or disturbance in the race's instinctive mind, its forces may very suddenly and quickly become aggressive, arousing the lower instinctive emotions. When, however, the race mind is allowed either to run its natural evolutionary course, or it is kept under control and its own sense transcended, then man realizes that he cannot judge himself or another on the basis of race, color, caste, creed or nationality, but rather on the basis of spiritual individuality. ¶Make a list of all the negative emotions which still reside in your instinctive force field. Should you find that you are dominated by one or more of these emotions, admit it to yourself honestly. This admission, this facing yourself, loosens the hold of the odic force and allows some actinic force to penetrate and dissolve the lower force field of the instinctive emotion you are examining. First step—admission; second step—observation. When, for instance, you become angry, fearful or jealous, observe yourself in this action. Immediately become aware of actinic force. Become an empty being of colorless energy; see the dark auric colors dissolve into a radiance of blue, yellow, lavender and white. You can do this with your present understanding that the actinic force is much higher than the instinctive mind, much greater than the astral or the physical or health bodies.

Friday
LESSON 222
The Intellect, Or Outer Ego

The fifth aspect of the soul is the odic causal sheath, or intellectual mind, known in Sanskṛit as *buddhi chitta.* It functions on the odic causal plane within the Second World of existence, Antarloka, the creative realm of the intellect. Here the individual organizes information, gains new ideas or new ways of looking at old projects, and uses this knowledge to move vast magnetic force fields around on the Earth's surface. This plane is primarily subconscious, with occasional influences from the superconscious. It is basically a mental plane where odic forces are manipulated. The intellect is the aspect of the soul you use when you sit and think, memorize or reason. The intellect can also be projected to distant places without leaving the physical body. Through this aspect, the adept can perceive what is there and accumulate knowledge or information. ¶The first shining forth of man's individuality comes when he has the conscious control of the intellectual mind. After the practice of internal and external concentration has been perfected and the subconscious processes of meditation have taken hold, the thought forms of the *yoga* student become distinct and clear. A thought form is made of astral matter. It is odic force and has a color and is created within the consciousness of man. The intellectual mind works through the mechanism of creating, preserving and destroying thought forms. The intellect is the manifestation of a series of well-constructed thought forms. Therefore, the better a person is educated, the more distinctly and clearly does the intellect function. ¶There are people all over the world today who have only unfolded to the fourth and fifth aspect of man and are guided simply by the habit patterns of the instinctive-intellectual mind. But the governing of the odic force fields in the world as it is today is done through the conscious control of the intellect or the odic causal sheath. ¶Diplomacy, a kind of love—one not wanting to hurt one's fellow man, suppression of the emotions of hate and anger—brings about a kind of harmony. These are products of the intellect which when developed into a strong intellectual sheath is able to control the baser emotions through controlled memory, controlled reason and controlled willpower, the three faculties of our ability to govern forces of nature. ¶Neither overrate nor underrate the intellect, for it fills several important functions in life, the great experience. But remember, the intellect is not the totality of man, it is only, figuratively speaking, the fifth aspect. The intellect is not the full mind, it is only one part, about one-tenth of the mind. The subconscious and the superconscious make up the other nine-tenths. ¶Opinionated knowledge is a faculty of memory. We study, we listen, we hear and we quote the opinions of others. Opinionated knowledge is stored up in the memory gridwork of the subconscious mind. This provides security, or a platform, for the intellect, making it strong, developing an ego. Therefore, intellect is our ego. The ego separates people from people, nations from nations and the soul from realization of the Self. ¶"Your real education is the innerversity." Perhaps you have been thinking that this statement is anti-intellectual, against education. Let's examine the real meaning, function and purpose of education. Education is not worn. It does not stick to you. It is not your collection of someone else's opinions. Through education, you stimulate your intellect. Education is that which you bring out from within yourself as a result of your personal interest in the fulfillment of your birth *karmas,* or *prārabdha karmas.* Education means exposure to new ideas and old opinions, giving you the tools to explore your own opinions freely, make decisions, research and review them and advance your understanding of God, soul and world. This is education. It is not static. It is as fluid as a river. Or it should be. You have the choice, the ability, to remold your intellect any way you want. The great truths of life are a part of your being. They are within you. They unfold to you slowly as you evolve your comprehension of them. Yet, they are always there within you, waiting to be realized. ¶The only real, permanent education is your unfoldment into the building of the intuitive mind through the control of the intellect. ¶Since the intellect is made fundamentally of thoughts which are ever creating, preserving and destroying themselves, the control of thoughts builds the seventh aspect of man, the intuitive mind, or *actinodic* causal sheath, known in Sanskṛit as *vijñānamaya kośa.* Intuition, knowing, awareness and understanding—these are products not of the intellect, but of the intuitive mind. The dedicated student who has applied himself seriously leaves college not with a "know it all" feeling but with an awareness of the limits of the intellect, and profound respect for the vast amount of knowledge that he has yet to discover or unfold. Conceit is a sure sign of insecurity; humility denotes awareness.

Saturday
LESSON 223
The Intuitive Nature

Observe the intellect as it is manifested in the world around you. You can see its limits. You can also see when it becomes a tool for the intuitive mind. When you discover great truths in the books you read, when creative ideas come to you, observe, with affectionate detachment, the people around you, the situations in life through which you pass. As you have learned, observations give birth to understanding, and understanding comes from your superconscious mind. Thus, the intellect must be developed to a certain extent and then controlled, through the control of thought. ¶Thought forms are manifestations of astral matter, or odic force, and travel through astral space, or odic force fields, from one destination to another. They can build, preserve and destroy. Thought forms can also protect, and they can create. Thought forms can also be seen, just as auras can be seen. ¶The intellect is the external ego, but it is only the external ego when it is in control and has cut itself off sufficiently from superconsciousness by becoming opinionated. When the intellect represents the ego, we say a person is unable to change his mind, no matter how much you try to convince or talk with him. He is stubborn, unyielding, even unfriendly if he becomes agitated or disturbed in his effort to hold the intellect together. ¶Should the intellectual nature become disturbed, the astral body then takes over and the instinctive mind or the instinctive qualities are prevalent at that time. This is quite apparent in undisciplined people, because the intellectual nature is undisciplined. When the astral body and the intellect work hand in hand, they create an instinctive-intellectual individual filled with opinionated knowledge, undisciplined instinctive drives, and emotions of hate and fear that have not been transmuted into the realms of reason and controlled through allowing a gridwork of positive memory patterns to build. ¶Within man, and functioning at a different rate of vibration than the intellect is found the power or the motivating force of the mind, the *chakras,* or force centers. There are seven of these basic force centers, which are stimulated into action and unfoldment by the *iḍā, piṅgalā* and *sushumṇā* currents. The *iḍā* and *piṅgalā* are odic psychic currents (the Chinese *yin* and *yang*) interwoven around the spinal cord. Directly through the spinal cord runs the *sushumṇā* current, which is actinodic. The *iḍā* current is passive odic force; the *piṅgalā* current is aggressive odic force. The *sushumṇā* is an actinodic current. These currents govern the sixth aspect of man, the *chakras.* These currents are like the reins which will guide a horse as we ride in one direction or another. ¶The intuitive nature, man's seventh aspect, is composed of a greater amount of actinic energy than odic. It is formed by the *sushumṇā* current that runs between the *iḍā* and *piṅgalā* currents up through the spinal cord. However, it is the state of mind that a *yoga* student must learn to identify as his own, so to speak. Until this time, he usually identifies with the intuitive mind of his *guru.* This identification serves as a constant reminder of the existence of his own intuitive nature. Many students seem to know when the *guru* is in a higher state of intuitive awareness, but they may fail to realize that the knowing or recognition of that state is their own higher state of intuitive awareness, occurring simultaneously with that of the *guru.* This is one of the great benefits awarded a *yoga* student working in the *guru* system: his opportunity to identify with the intuitive mind of the *guru.* ¶When the *yoga* student learns to control his own odic force field to the point where he no longer identifies with his physical body, his astral body or his intellect, he can then identify his external ego with his intuitive nature, or subsuperconscious mind. This new and humble identity is a sporadic sense in the initial stages on the *yoga* path, for only when the student is really actinic does he utilize the intuitive mind consciously, perceiving it through the faculties of cognizantability. One does not entertain thoughts when in this state of full awareness. In this consciousness, one views and perceives through the *anāhata chakra* of direct cognition. The intuitive nature is the most refined aspect of the astral body. Although the intuitive aspect is made primarily of actinic force, there is enough odic force within it to enable man to enter into the realm of creation in the material world. This seventh aspect of man is a plateau, a leveling off of one cycle of evolution and the beginning, at the same time, of another.

Sunday
LESSON 224
Soul Body, The Real You

Within all seven aspects of man lies the body of the soul, the actinic causal body, *ānandamaya kośa,* the real you. The soul body has a form just as the astral body has a form, but it is more refined and is of a more permanent nature. It is this body which reincarnates, creating around itself new physical and astral bodies, life after life after life. This process matures and develops the body of the soul. Hence we have old souls and young souls, depending on the maturity and unfoldment of the soul body, or depending upon the number of lives or the intensity of maturing experience which the individual has passed through. ¶The body of the soul is pure light, made of quantums. It is indestructable. It cannot be hurt or damaged in any way. It is a pure being, created by Lord Śiva, maturing its way to Him in final merger. The body of the soul is constant radiance.

Its mind is superconsciousness, containing all intelligence, and is constantly aware, does not sleep and is expanding awareness as the soul body matures. For the soul-realized person, awareness travels through the mind as a traveler travels from city to city, country to country, never caught in any one area for longer than necessary, always consciously conscious of awareness in consciousness at every moment. The body of the soul lives in the eternity of the moment, simultaneously conscious of past and future as a one cycle. The true nature, everlasting secure personal identity, is realizing oneself as the soul body. This is truly finding our roots, our source, our indestructable, ever-maturing soul. ¶In the years that follow complete illumination, or realization of the Self, in obtaining a stabilized *nirvikalpa samādhi*, a body of pure actinic golden energy, the *svarṇaśarīra*, begins to form. I experienced this beginning to happen in me in 1955. At that time there was only enough odic force to hold the physical body together in material activity. This new actinic body is built through the consecutive practice of *nirvikalpa samādhi* on a daily basis, which forms one of the highest disciplines of *siddha yoga*. ¶However, it should be mentioned that the first great attainment to be striven for by the aspirant is the experiencing of inner light, which is taught to family people and renunciates alike, implying that he has enough inner dominion and control over the intellect that the radiance within the head or body is actually seen. This implies also a working control of the *maṇipūra chakra* and a conscious awareness of the working of the *anāhata chakra* of cognition, allowing a burst of actinic energy to the *viśuddha chakra* of love. ¶The next step for aspirants is what is known as "touching into the Self." When this occurs, the soul body is released, made completely autonomous, so that they can then be trained in its conscious use and control. It is in this body that they attend higher plane schools and communicate through vibration with others in the soul body. From then on, it is for them to train with the *guru* personally so that they learn to use and control the body of the soul. With this control and altered consciousness, they eventually come into a sustained realization of the Self, *nirvikalpa samādhi,* in this or a future life, for the next phase on the path to merger is to make ready and then sustain renunciate life in the truest sense by becoming a Nātha *sannyāsin.* ¶It must be said that many frustrate themselves by seeking realizations beyond their abilities, while not accomplishing the realizations that are within their abilities. We must remember that *savikalpa samādhi* relates to the *anāhata* and *viśuddha chakras,* sustained by a purified intellect and a dynamic will. Whereas *nirvikalpa samādhi* is of the *ājñā* and *sahasrāra chakras* and those above and is sustained by complete renunciation of the world to the point where the world renounces the renunciate. These are the venerable *sannyāsins.* ¶Control of the mind builds the intuitive nature. By directing the flow of thought, perceptively discriminating between actions, aware of attending reactions, the *yoga* student soon learns the use of his actinic power. In order to hold an expanded consciousness, this power must be brought into use, and when it flows through the intellect, it automatically changes the chemistry of the intellect while it begins to build the intuitive nature. ¶Reverse your thinking about yourself. Feel that you come out of timelessness, causelessness, spacelessness. Visualize the pure radiant body of light, the being of the soul, the "I Am," the "Watcher." Then around that is formed the intuitive mind, and around that is formed the intellect. Then the *chakras* come into view, governing the highest to the lowest states of mind, and the *iḍā, piṅgalā* and *sushumnā* currents. The instinctive nature is formed around this, then the human aura, through which thought forms are created, then the vital health body, and then the physical body.

Mānava Prabhāmaṇḍalam

मानवप्रभामण्डलम्

The Human Aura

That light within is as pure as the lightening's light. It is light that is great and red. It is the light of Śiva that beams *jñāna*. It is the light of *chakras* above. It is the light born of constant awareness of the pure sound, Aum. It is the light that is blended from all these lights.

TIRUMANTIRAM 2686

MANIVEL...

Monday
LESSON 225
The Remarkable Human Aura

The human aura extends out around the body from three to four feet, even from five to six feet in the case of more evolved souls. It is made up of a variety of vibratory rates or colors. Each area of the mind that awareness flows through reflects a change in these vibratory rates of colors in the human aura. When you have developed a certain psychic sight, by seeing through the eyes of the soul, you will be able to look at a person, see the aura around him and know immediately the area of the instinctive, intellectual or superconscious mind he is aware in at that particular time. ¶For instance, if someone's awareness was flowing through the realms of depression, that is, the area within the vast mind substance that contains the vibratory rate of depression, his aura would look rather gray, dim and dismal. If he was aware in the feeling of a genuine love for all humanity, his aura would look light blue, fringed and tinged with yellow. However, if his love for humanity was of a superficial, emotional nature, being more idle talk and emotion than sub-superconscious compassion, his aura would be pink or reddish, telling you there was still a lot of instinctive fire, and should an upsetting circumstance occur, he could easily forget about universal love and become quite angry. Then the pink would turn to flaming red streaked with black. After this, if he were to feel remorseful about the emotional upheaval, the aura would turn to dark blue, and you could hardly see his face for the deep blue mist that would form around his body. If awareness was flowing through the area of the mind of inferiority and jealousy, the aura would be dark grayish-green in color. Someone with healing inclinations would have a pale green aura. A student increasing his intellectual knowledge would have an aura of brilliant yellow. The combinations are almost endless. ¶Several colors often appear in the aura at the same time. For example, the red of suppressed desire and seething anger might appear along with the yellow of intellectual involvement. This person's head would be surrounded in yellow, and the lower part of his body streaked in red. Even a touch of very dark green might appear, showing that jealousy caused his anger. It becomes easy to diagnose emotional problems simply by looking at the vibratory rate of the aura's colors and judging the area of the mind awareness is flowing through.

Tuesday
LESSON 226
Color's Ceaseless Ebb and Flow

The vast plasma of the mind is complete and finished in all of its various states, departments, areas and moods. It only seems as though it is being created as we move our awareness through it. Each area of the boundless universe of the mind has its own colors and sounds. We interpret them through our nerves and register them as feelings. When we separate awareness from that which it is aware of, it is possible to separate feeling from that which we feel. Then we can become aware of the sound of feeling and the color of feeling, as well as the color of sound, the sound of color and the feeling of sound. It will require some good meditation on your part to fully grasp this concept. But in time you will come to understand the complete gamut of emotion and its vibratory rates as you begin to become aware of the aura around the physical body. ¶When someone is flowing his awareness through subsuperconscious areas of the mind and programming his subconscious anew, his aura rapidly changes. You know he is progressing on the path, for his aura goes through various changes of color patterns week after week as he works inwardly with his awareness. A devotee sitting in meditation, diligently working within himself, will in the course of half an hour change the colors of his aura from three to four to five times, as he moves his awareness from the instinctive-intellectual areas into the brilliancy of subsuperconscious realms. His aura will take on shades of light blue and light yellow interlaced with white. Then as he moves into superconsciousness, rays of light from the central source of energy will begin to emerge from the core of his spine and flood out through his aura and penetrate the atmosphere of the room. You feel his presence as a *darshan.* ¶The sub of the subconscious mind has an aura of its own deep within the outer aura that we have been describing. It is seen "within" the physical body itself and is different from the daily emotional-intellectual aura which appears around the physical body as a result of awareness being in one area of the mind or another. All the reactionary conditions of our past which are currently reacting in our subconscious mind are reflected in the colors of this inner subconscious aura. Oddly enough, the inner aura looks much like a modern art painting. This part of the aura does not flood out around the body, but hovers deep within the body in the area of the chest and torso. Peering deep into the torso, one can see its various colors. They do not move. Modern art painters may without knowing it be depicting the subsubconscious aura of themselves, their family and their friends, for that is exactly what some paintings look like. ¶The inner aura might look like this: on the left side of the chest, a large area of green; down in the lower abdomen, a patch of red; near the throat, yellow; and across the heart area are streaks of orange or purple. These colors do not move. They just remain there vibrating, and the rest of the aura moves around and through them.

Wednesday
LESSON 227
Working With The Inner Aura

As soon as one begins to meditate, to gain enough control of awareness, the colors begin to move a little. When the meditator breaks out of his ordinary daily life habit patterns by beginning to reprogram his subconscious mind, his inner aura begins to change. When after a good meditation a predominant subconscious reactionary pattern comes before his vision as if it happened yesterday, and he begins to react to it all over again, one of these color patterns may move up to the throat area. He will have to swallow. At that point, if you ask the question, "What's on your mind?" he would speak out this reaction. I always recommend it be written down and burned instead of spoken. Then that color leaves, never to reappear, and another one rises from underneath. A green color might leave and a brown one come up in its place. These repressed areas eventually will dissipate, and awareness, once divided in many different ways, will pull in its tentacles from externalized areas of the mind until it can move freely through all areas of the mind. ¶Each time one of these deep-rooted subconscious reactionary conditions leaves, the inner aura becomes more fluid, brighter and less rigid. The devotee becomes more wholesome. After an entire subconscious cleansing, due to maybe a year of someone working with himself and developing and reprogramming his subconscious mind positively, the chest would turn into a pure sheet of very beautiful yellow, and rays of white light could be seen coming out from within it. This would continue until the devotee stopped working with himself. And if he began dwelling more in subconscious areas or encounters a condition in life which he is not able to face within himself and regresses into resentment, selfishness, self-pity and spite, the chest would cloud again and look exactly like a modern art painting. ¶The mind is like a vast universe. Man's individual awareness travels through the mind from one planet to another, one area to another. Or, if we compare the mind to the world, man's individual awareness travels through the mind from hate to love, to joy, to sorrow, to all the various ideas and concepts within the mind as he would travel from country to country, city to city. Therefore, the human aura is very consistent. Each time man's individual awareness flows through love, the human aura reflects the pastel colors of love, as it would reflect the colors of hate, fear, jealousy, exuberance, compassion and the various areas of the intellect. One can learn to read the colors of the human aura and know in what area of the mind the awareness of the person is flowing.

Thursday
LESSON 228
The Art of Seeing Auras

The big question always arises, "How do we know whether or not we are seeing an aura, or if it is just our imagination?" Actually, there is no such thing as imagination, according to the general use of the word. When we go within ourselves, we find that each thing that is so-called imagination, or "in the world of image," actually exists within the refined substance of the mind, and we are just becoming aware of it where it is imprinted in the vast internal substance of the mind. Only when we become aware of something that we imagine for a long enough period do we bring it out of the subtle areas of the mind and impress it upon the memory patterns of the physical brain. At that point we do not call it imagination. We begin to call it real. Finally, if we can bring it into physical manifestation, then we really begin to call it real. I suppose that this is the way man's individual awareness has become externalized, so that he looks at the external world as real and the internal, refined areas of the mind as being unreal or elusive. It was not always so, however, because with the absence of the things to externalize man's individual awareness, man is naturally within himself. ¶When awareness is within the very depths of the mind, so that color and light and sound are one and the same to him, he then looks at his fellow man from the inside out. He would first see the spine of someone he was looking at, and the lights within the spine, and then he would see the inner aura, then the outer aura of the individual, and last he would see the physical body. When awareness is externalized to the point where we see physical things as reality, then we see the physical body first, and have to strain to see the aura and the internal layers of consciousness. ¶Go within yourself and all things will be unfolded to you on the inner planes of consciousness, as well as in the external states of mind. You will begin to see through them all. Seeing an aura is like seeing through someone. Their physical body begins to fade just a little bit, and we see where their awareness is flowing in the wonderful world of the mind. ¶The colors around the person are first seen within your own mind. You would not clearly see them around their physical body. Later, after becoming adjusted to this new form of sight, you may see colors around an individual's physical body. ¶Where do these colors come from? All things in the mind are sound and color. Look around you and observe each vibratory rate of every physical object as having a sound as well as a color. Everything is sound. Everything is color. Everything is shape. Therefore, in the refined areas of the mind, all things are color and all things are sound, recognizable through the sixth sense of the all-seeing eye. This faculty is always awake. You only have to learn how to be aware of and use it, in a similar way an artist must learn to distinguish with his physical eyes between one shade of color and another and between the dimensions in a painting.

Friday
LESSON 229
Psychic Sight's Use and Misuse

The mystic learns how to use his already developed sixth sense, his third eye. It is used all the time, constantly, day in and day out, though not consciously. For example, someone may walk into your home. You look at him and say, "You are not feeling very well today. You seem disturbed." How do you know? Inside yourself you are seeing his aura. If he enters looking bright and shiny, you know how he feels inside because you see his aura. ¶The spiritual path to realization of the Self, however, is not to see and analyze auras. The quest is to flow awareness through even the core of energy itself, into the vastness of the Self God, where awareness completely aware of itself, dissolves in its own essence, and merges into timelessness, into causelessness, into spacelessness, into Śiva, beyond that still, still area of the mind. Yes, learning to read auras can be a hindrance on the path to enlightenment because one can become the center of attraction, for everybody wants to know what his aura looks like. The aura is constantly changing. To give a reading of a friend's aura would be like telling him what kind of clothes he is wearing. The next day, he may be wearing something different. Also, when you can see someone's aura, quite often you do not notice it. Generally if you do have this awakened inner perception of auras, you would only notice someone's aura if it were peculiarly dull or strongly radiant. A mystic who has control of this faculty does not generally see auras all of the time, but just when he wants to. But if a person's aura were outstanding in a certain way, naturally it would stand out clearly and be seen easily. And so, when we look into such an aura, we are actually looking into the area of the mind in which his individual awareness is traveling, for the mind is always totally in a state of creation with awareness flowing through the mind just as the traveler roams the world. ¶The mystic has to caution himself not to become overly involved in the emotions of others. He must protect his inner life by living two-thirds within and only one-third in the external realms of consciousness. And he must be wise enough to know that each one has to walk either over or around all the boulders in his path. In other words, if you are around people who are not good, who have dark auras, who have deep-rooted subconscious areas that represent a lot of black, gray, red, green blobs hidden in the psychic nerve currents of their chest, and you are not quite out of that area yourself, the vibratory rate of those people will draw you back into those areas of the mind. That is why those who live the contemplative life like to be among themselves. They like to be with people of the same lifestyle. It is necessary. It is extremely necessary to surround yourself with a good environment to make progress on the spiritual path past a certain point. You can meditate a little bit to move awareness into a peaceful area of the mind or get a little burst of inner light, or practice breathing and have a healthier body and a sound nerve system. But if you really want to go deep within toward your goal, you have to move awareness, physical body, emotional body, mental body, in with a group of people that are thinking along the same lines and living the same lifestyle. The group helps the individual and the individual helps the group. ¶The gift of psychic vision should be developed very gradually through the stages of *sādhana.* The veiling grace of Lord Śiva is for very good reason. Some people are born with psychic sight and maintain it throughout their lifetime. As this faculty was developed in a prior birth, the wisdom and understanding of its proper use comes naturally to them. But more commonly, psychic sight develops slowly, almost imperceptively, through an unbroken continuity of *sādhana.* Through the unveiling grace of Lord Śiva we are allowed to see what needs to be seen at the proper time in our life when we can sustain the resultant reactions. ¶We often observe the facial expressions and body language of friends and strangers and thus learn the contents of their conscious and subconscious mind, and from this deduce how they are thinking and feeling. But much can be concealed if we see no deeper. For example, someone may be smiling when he is really feeling depressed. However, when we see with our astral vision, there is no mystery. When we peer into their subconscious mind, we see the colors of their moods and emotions that perhaps are not reflected in their faces. Yes, colors and auras do relate to the five states of mind, conscious, subconscious, sub of the subconscious, subsuperconscious and superconscious.

Saturday
LESSON 230
Chakras And Nāḍīs

There are seven great force centers of psychic nerve ganglia, called *chakras,* within in the physical body, the astral body and the body of the soul. Each *chakra* is a spinning vortex of mind power, a vast collective area of many, many different thought strata of odic and actinic energy. When awareness flows through any one or more of these areas, certain functions happen, such as the function of memory, the function of reason and the function of willpower. As the *chakras* spin, releasing energies into the body, these energies permeate the physical cells with life and vitality and radiate out through the force fields that surround the body. The forces are cloud-like or fog-like in consistency and reflect these energies in much the same way as a cloud reflects the rays of the sun. You have watched clouds in the sky at sunset. They appear to change color from white to pink to orange and then to darker shades. Of course, the clouds do not change. The light waves change. The clouds faithfully reflect the color of the light. In a similar way, the human aura is a reflection of the wave length of energies generated in our mind by our emotions and from our body. The basic odic and actinic energy of the aura itself does not change. It is the energies emanating from the *chakras* that change. The aura simply mirrors those energies as color vibration. ¶Within the aura are psychic nerve currents called *nāḍīs.* It is through these *nāḍīs* that you feel someone standing next to you without turning your head to look at him. Also, by standing next to a person, two or three feet away, you can feel how he is feeling. Feelings are transferable, for feelings are vibrations which can be felt through the subtle nerve system. You feel them with these astral *nāḍīs* that extend out from the body into and through the aura. Oftentimes you may identify with the feelings that you pick up from others and begin to feel that way yourself, while actually you are just picking up the vibration from someone near you. As we have learned, through the clairvoyant vision these feelings can be seen as colors in the astral atmosphere surrounding your acquaintance. As feelings are transferable, the colors within our aura are transferable, too. We now know that our aura, and the thoughts and feelings which give rise to it, affects and influences those around us. In a sense, we "rub off on one another." A positive example is the way in which the pure and healthy aura of the faithful and devoted Hindu wife enhances the aura of her husband. His mental state is generally more positive as a result, and his business prospers.

Sunday
LESSON 231
Improving Your Aura

With the knowledge of the affect that we have on others through our mental and emotional astral atmosphere, we gain a wonderful *siddhi:* the ability to develop and improve our own aura and thus our daily mental and emotional state, and at the same time the power to improve the aura and mood of those around us. Your *sādhana* now is to take pains to develop your aura in the direction of more desirable colors and to gradually eliminate undesirable ones. ¶Now we shall begin to understand how to perform this new *sādhana.* It works in two ways: 1) by visualizing one or more bright, positive colors flooding your aura, immediately your awareness leaves the undesirable area of the mind (such as depression, anger or jealousy), and you experience more positive feelings; 2) by consciously moving your awareness into more positive areas through the repetition of positive affirmations or *mantras*, while at the same time working to bring through the corresponding feelings, such as joy, happiness or contentment. In this way the aura is infused with bright, positive colors. Consciously working to improve one's own aura becomes doubly important when we remember that its colors, being magnetic, react back on our mind and emotions, thus intensifying and neutralizing the original mental states which called them forth. We have all found this to be true through the lesson that any negative mood or mental state seems to hold one in its clutches of its own accord, and it takes willpower to pull oneself into a more positive frame of mind. But, as you may have found in your previous experience with *sādhana*, consistent effort does yield results. You can steady and strengthen your mental and emotional faculty just as you can strengthen your physical muscles and steady your nerves through exercise and practice. ¶By consistently visualizing desirable colors in your aura, especially during moments of trial and emotional turmoil, you can become quite facile and skillful in controlling your individual awareness. Brightening up your aura in this way neutralizes the remnants of negative emotion and charges the aura with actinic energy. Automatically, feelings of depression and despair give way to courage and confidence. Feelings of jealousy and resentment give way to confidence and compassion. ¶As you continue with this *sādhana,* you will see how well it can work for you. This practice will also help you to further build and mold your character in accordance with the *yamas* and *niyamas* by keeping your awareness out of the darker or more dense states of the mind. You will soon develop a strong and more attractive personality which will naturally uplift others. ¶You have discovered the five states of mind: conscious, subconscious, sub of the subconscious, subsuperconscious and superconscious. You also understand the three phases of the mind: instinctive, intellectual and superconscious. Now we are learning about our individual awareness, what it is and how it travels through the vast universe of the mind just as a traveler moves from place to place on the Earth. In each place that the traveler visits, he is affected by the vibrations around him. He absorbs the thoughts of others and their moods. He is influenced by the events he participates in. Similarly, when your individual awareness travels through the mind, it is influenced or colored by the vibrations within each area of the mind it becomes aware in. This influences your nerve system and lays the foundation for your thoughts and feelings, thus giving rise to the colors in your aura. These colors are ever changing because your own awareness is constantly moving through the vast universe of mind substance.

Varṇa Chamatkāraḥ

वर्णचमत्कारः

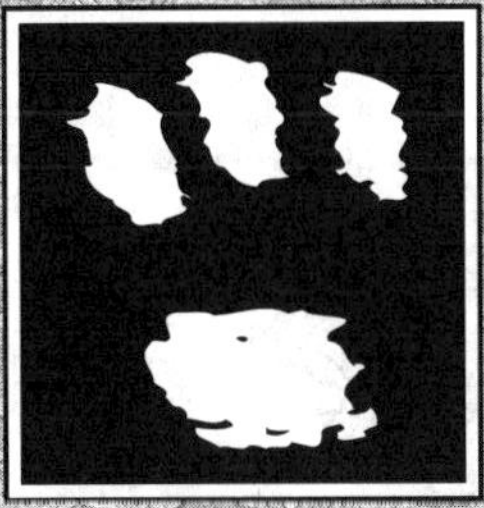

Color's Magic

Earth shines as golden in the body; water appears white; fire, red; air, dark; ether, smoky. Thus do the five elements appear within, concealed.

TIRUMANTIRAM 2145

Monday
LESSON 232
Color-Flooding Your Aura

You as a devotee have often gone to the temple with your problems and placed them at the feet of the Deity. In the unseen world of the Devaloka what actually happens is that the Deity and His many *devas* work with your problems by working with your aura, most especially the inner aura, by disintegrating or clearing up any congestion they find. They lighten the darker colors that were created by traveling through troubled states of mind, infusing them with rays of white and violet light from the inner sanctum. We rarely see this happening, but we can certainly feel it, and we depart the temple feeling relieved and freed from congestion and worry. Often we can hardly remember what we were upset about. ¶You can also flood your aura with rays of white and violet light, just like the Deities and *devas* do. If you are in a bad mood because of having just become angry with someone because you were jealous of him, there is a remedy that you can perform for yourself. Your aura is now brownish with murky dirty green, possibly accented with black and red sparks. To counteract this heaviness, just add white. Visualize white light flooding out from the center of your spine into and through your aura. Visualize violet rays flooding into your new white aura, invigorating and cutting through the darkness. ¶When you go as pure awareness, right into the center of your spine and flood white mind substance out into your aura, the white mixes with the black, and gray appears in your aura. Immediately you experience fear, but this emotion soon passes as more white enters the aura. The gray soon disappears. As still more white enters the aura, the flaming red of anger turns to the pink shades of tolerance and compassion. The dark browns and the murky dark green of jealousy turn to the emerald green of confidence and humility. A feeling of peace and contentment comes as the new colors react back on the emotions. All this and more happens to you from within you because you deliberately moved your individual awareness deep into the center of your spine and flooded white rays of light out through your aura. It takes but a little effort on your part, a little concentration, persistence and faith in your ability to change your own mood by a positive effort of will. You, too, can do as the *devas* do. Try it today. ¶You have no doubt experienced difficulty in getting up in the morning. What is the remedy for this? What color would you flood your aura with to invigorate your physical body in the early morning? Flood your aura with red, of course, a nice bright red. It doesn't take much effort to visualize the color red. You will know that you have succeeded when all of a sudden your physical vitality awakens and you feel invigorated and ready to jump up for a wonderful day. ¶All of us at one time or another experience mental laziness. What is the remedy? Simply flood your aura with yellow by visualizing yellow light all around you, and soon you will be drawn into the thinking area of the mind and be able to progressively pursue your studies. Visualizing orange strengthens your intellectual aggressiveness because red is added to the yellow. So if you want to become intellectually aggressive, a quality needed to succeed in the business world, after you have succeeded in flooding your aura with yellow light, then flood your aura with orange light and experience the change for yourself.

Tuesday
LESSON 233
Blessings and Their Opposite

If resentment and anger are not conquered in this life, all the *karmas* of the creation of these upsets through life condense and go to seed. In the next life, in condensed form, the colors of the inner aura of the sub of the subconscious mind remain in the mind substance of the baby, waiting for similar situations to occur, to burst out in a full array of color and take over the outer aura emotions and the conscious and subconscious mind. As the baby grows physically, the inner aura grows, too. That's why parents often sing religious songs and bless the baby with white light, to help in harmonizing the seed *karmas* so they don't awaken in all their negative power. They work to lighten the colors with white light, and the *karmas* are lightened. Thus, the wise Hindu parent attempts to subdue the sub of the subconscious mind reflected in the permanent aura of the child even at an early time in life. Each area of this *prāṇic* montage of color represents a whole conglomerate of experiences the child had in past lives but did not resolve and therefore must go through again in this life. ¶Yes! You can bless yourself as well. With little effort at all, go within yourself and become aware of the center of your spine where the white light is and let the light shine out, flooding your entire aura. As it does so, it also will neutralize the more permanent inner aura, lightening the heavier colors, if any, into shades and hues that will inspire and invigorate your future life. When the darker colors are finally gone, they are gone forever. This is indeed a blessing you can give yourself, or which the Deity can give you in the temple with the instant power of His rays. ¶You might be wondering at this time, what exactly, then, is a curse? A curse is just the opposite of a blessing. When someone becomes angry at you, or you become angry with someone, they are actually cursing you, or you them. This is because powerful vibrations of red and black, grays and muddy, brownish greens are being sent from one person to another. Truly, this hurts, and bad *karma* is made. ¶Our holy scriptures tell us that we must purify our intellects. What does this actually mean? It means that we must lighten up the colors that are within our subconscious and sub of the subconscious mind. When the intellect is finally purified, the outer aura shows many pastel colors in and through it. The permanent inner aura will be filled with beautiful patterns of golden yellow, blue and lavender. But, once the intellect is purified, good mental maintenance must occur daily so that congested areas are not recreated out of habit. This is the great value of a regulated religious life and daily *sādhana.* ¶To keep the colors of our subconscious and subsubconscious refined, our religion tells us to go on a long pilgrimage once a year. This means we take our inner aura that has been building up through the year and place it at the feet of the Deity at some far-off temple. While on the pilgrimage, we are able to collect all its colors, emotions and deep feelings and leave them, along with our offering of fruit and flowers, at the God's holy feet to be disintegrated by Him. So great are the Gods of our religion. ¶To keep the colors of our subconscious and subsubconscious refined, our religion tells us to read scripture daily because their high-minded thoughts and concepts bring purple, lavender, pink and yellow into our aura. To keep the colors of our subconscious and subsubconscious refined, our religion tells us to perform *pūjā* daily to personally invoke the higher beings in the Devaloka at our own home shrine and obtain their blessings. It may interest you to know that such blessings lighten not only the aura of each one in the household but also the physical building itself. ¶To keep the colors of our subconscious and subsubconscious refined, our religion tells us to provide the essential sacraments in life for the children, so that the permanent impressions of these special combinations of color and sound are placed into the inner aura of the subsubconscious mind and added to the ones that are already there from previous *saṁskāras.*

Wednesday
LESSON 234
Exploring the World of Colors

Sometimes you may experience stressful moments during your daily *sādhana.* They will soon pass, never to reappear, so do not be worried. What is actually happening is that the white light coming out from within you penetrates various pockets of the inner aura, and one by one they are being lightened up. However, each time the inner light penetrates one or another of these congested subsubconscious pockets of color, the memories of what created them are stirred. This brings up, to be reexperienced, the corresponding thoughts, feelings and emotions. Because they are unbidden, the stress of this intrusion is felt in the external nerve system. Be assured, it will pass. Breathe deeply and, be assured, it will pass. Breathe deeply and diaphragmatically and all will be well. This is a form of mild, self-imposed psychic surgery, as the colors adjust to the rays of white light from deep within your spine through the grace of Lord Śiva. ¶If your child is crying uncontrollably and you can't get to sleep, what color would you bless him with? Would you get angry and yell, "Why don't you go to sleep! I told you, you're disturbing your father!" Flashes of red? The child would be terrified. No, you would harmonize the child's emotions with shades of blue and pale green. An important part of your *sādhana* is to familiarize yourself with the mental-emotional counterpart of each of the colors. You can familiarize yourself with the individual physical, mental and spiritual effect of each color simply by looking at one color after another and experiencing the results. Each color and the emotions it reflects are like two sides of the same coin. Learn them so well that the thought of one immediately brings the idea of the other. This knowledge is the foundation of your color *sādhana*. Enter into this wonderful world of color with interest and earnestness. ¶You can perform color *sādhana* in a number of ways. For example, study the way various colors in your immediate environment make you feel. How do you feel when you enter a room that is painted blue? White? Yellow? Another way to study color is to visualize each of the colors within your conscious mind. Place before you a piece of paper of the color you wish to visualize. Look at the paper and then close your eyes and try to see the exact same color in your mind. Then open your eyes and look at the paper again and with eyes still open turn your head away from the paper and try to see the color in your conscious mind. Literally fill your mind with the color of the paper. After you have accomplished this exercise with one color, repeat it with another, then another and then another. By using your great soul faculty of observation and through the grace of Lord Gaṇeśa, you will perceive many proofs of the significance of color. You will soon amass a stock of experiences within your subconscious mind of each color and its corresponding mental-emotional state.

Thursday
LESSON 235
Methods for Self-Improvement

The next phase of your *sādhana* can begin when you have memorized the colors and their corresponding mental and emotional states and this knowledge is clearly defined in your conscious and subconscious mind. Start by giving yourself a thorough, honest, emotional and mental-maintenance examination. Begin by analyzing your fine, noble qualities and writing them on a piece of paper. Then, on the same piece of paper, note your weak, instinctive frailties. These are qualities you would like to get rid of or change to bring your nature into a more refined level of consciousness. Now, perhaps for the first time, you will be looking at yourself as a total physical, emotional, mental and spiritual being. ¶Next, decide which weakness needs attention first and begin applying what you have learned about flooding your aura with the color that will effect the changes you desire. If you are persistent in your efforts, you will be pleased with the results. Choose a failing in your character, such as jealousy. Once you've made up your mind to deal with jealousy and lighten the ugly, dark-brownish-green in your inner and/or outer aura, make a clear mental picture of light green and yellow and flood those colors into your aura by just a slight effort of your will. You do not have to exert much effort to do this. You need only relax and hold a clear mental picture of the desired colors. Visualize the two colors and project them out from the center of your spine into your inner and outer aura. That is all you have to do. As soon as the light green and yellow flood your aura, you will feel an immediate change in your mental and emotional state. The antagonistic feelings of jealousy will begin to fade. The opposite mental quality of understanding and the emotional quality of self-assurance will automatically be strengthened as a result. ¶Once you perfect this technique on one or two difficult traits, such as jealously, anger or resentment, you can begin to transform other weak areas of your nature, such as shyness, lack of self-confidence or being overly critical of others. The procedure is the same. And the best time to work on the area is when you have been propelled into it by something that happens to you. Each time you feel yourself entering one of these areas of the mind, and your awareness is consumed by one of these feelings—in which case your aura has taken on its corresponding colors—simply visualize the counterbalancing color and flood it into your aura. ¶If you are overtaken by anger and resentment—blackish red with streaks of yellow—visualize light blue entering your aura and surrounding your body. The light blue will neutralize the fiery reds, and before you know it the anger, and resentment are gone. Visualizing the light blue color actually drew your awareness out of certain areas of the instinctive mind into intuitive states. Instead of anger, you experience compassion and understanding. By making this part of your *sādhana*, you have acquired a fine new tool to cope with your instinctive-intellectual emotions and mental states. ¶There will be times, of course, when the pull of the instinctive-intellectual areas will be so strong that it will be difficult for you to visualize a counterbalancing color. So strong are the pulls of the lower nature that it may even be distasteful to think of the intellectual and superconscious colors. However, through performing this *sādhana* regularly, there will come a time when each time your awareness is pulled into an undesirable instinctive area, you will be able to exercise the inner nerve system of your soul body and bring the instinctive, intellectual elements of your nature under your control.

Friday
LESSON 236
Charging Your Aura with Prāṇa

I want to encourage you and to give you confidence to flood your aura with colors. It takes but a little of your willpower to do this. The intent itself is the thrust of awareness required. Willing consists of a mental command, leaving the rest to the natural mechanism of the mind. Therefore, let us pray to our dear Lord Gaṇeśa to help us remove the obstacles of doubt and fear. ¶If you are working through the day to bring a certain color into your aura, carry something with you or wear something of that color. The more you are aware of the color you are working with through the day, the better the results. This is because your attention will automatically take up the impression of it, and the corresponding quality will be enhanced in your character. A little practice during your half-hour *sādhana* period and through the day, and some positive experiences with color will soon give you the confidence you need. Patience, perseverance and earnest interest will be the keys to your success. ¶As you know, it is not uncommon for the emotions of one person to affect those around him. It is therefore important that you learn how to "charge" your aura with *prāṇic* energy so that the darker colors from the auras of others do not penetrate your own. If and when they do, you will experience their moods and emotions and may interpret them as your own. But actually you have simply accepted into your aura the dark reds, muddy browns and greens from their aura. You simply did not have enough *prāṇa* in your aura to ward off the intrusion. Such mental thought forms and undesirable colors from others' auras are often called psychic influences. ¶To protect yourself from psychic influences, you can charge your aura with the vital *prāṇa* from your own *prāṇic* body. To do so, sit quietly, breathe deeply and mentally get in touch with your *prāṇic* body, first by visualizing it and secondly by feeling it. The *prāṇic* body of most people extends out from the physical body about one or two inches, depending on the level of vitality. Of course, the *prāṇic* body also completely permeates the entire physical body. As you sit quietly, breathing deeply and slowly, become intimately aware of the vitality, the *prāṇa,* running throughout the physical body. As you breathe in, feel the vitality of your body. Feel the magnetic energy within it. Feel its life. Then, as you breathe out, mentally and through feeling release some of this vitality, this *prāṇa*, this life-force, and send it out into your aura. Keep sending it out on the out-breath to the aura's outer edges all around your body, from your head to your feet. The outer edge of the human aura is about three or four feet away from the physical body. After you have charged your aura with vital *prāṇa* in this way about nine times, you should begin to feel a magnetic shell being built around the outer edge of your aura. ¶You will feel very secure and content as you sit within your own aura, which is charged with *prāṇa* from your own *prāṇic* body. You are protected from all kinds of psychic influences, seen and unseen. But the *prāṇa* within your aura will eventually wear away, and you will have to recharge it when it does. For the beginner, it only lasts an hour or two before it has to be rebuilt. When you become more advanced in this practice, it will happen almost subconsciously, or automatically, when you sense the need. Once you master this simple method of charging your aura with *prāṇa*, you will soon develop an immunity to undesirable thought forms and emotional colors of those around you. This is a great aid to prevent taking on the negative influences of the place we are about to visit, the person we are about to meet or the gathering we are about to enter.

Saturday
LESSON 237
Protective Emanations

After you have quickly increased the *prāṇic* strength of your aura, you can easily flood it with any color you wish. Each color has its own special protective qualities, which can be chosen to counteract or balance out the particular vibrations you are or will be experiencing. Let's take the example of protecting yourself from the auric emanations of persons who are ill, a condition you will encounter if you visit a hospital. You can easily counteract this influence by flooding your aura with colors of health and physical strength. This will not only protect you, but it will also improve the condition of those around you. How do you do this? Become aware of your spine and visualize a stream of white light in its center from the base to the top of your head. Then mentally draw from this pure white light warm red and vibrant pink. As a healing power, visualize pale green surrounding the patient, a color many modern hospitals have adopted to invoke healing. To increase your vitality even more, visualize yourself effortlessly performing some strenuous physical or athletic feat. For example, mentally go through all the motions of lifting something heavy with ease and you will soon feel the energy rising within you. ¶The aura of the successful doctor or nurse invariably shows the presence of bright reds and vivid pinks. Most successful doctors and nurses who are in contact with their patients possess the mental and emotional vibrations of strength, power and confidence. They remain cheerful and bright despite the negativity of the many around them suffering from disease and despair. The doctor's strong aura, well protected, does not absorb the gray shades of his patients. Gray in the aura, which indicates fear, opens the individual to all kinds of negative influences. ¶If you are going to have an important intellectual discussion with someone and want to be sure to remain poised and centered, what colors should you flood your aura with? The answer: bright oranges and yellows. This will bring a new energy to enhance your intellect and protect you from being overpowered by the intellectual force of someone else. You have probably experienced times when you were overwhelmed in this way and came away from a discussion regretting having been swayed from your original perspective. This technique can help prevent this by making you mentally stronger and more agile. This is also a way to help overcome shyness. Surrounded by a vibrant aura charged with bright orange and yellow, you are a secure and confident individual, able to enter into discussion with new self-assurance. The vibrations of others tend to rebound from your aura. You are relaxed and friendly, and intelligence pours forth uninhibitedly from you. One more thought on this subject: it is also wise to hold a mental image of your head being surrounded by a golden aura of yellow light. This will create the vibration in which thoughts flow freely without interruption and perception is quickened as you speak.

Sunday
LESSON 238
Shielding Your Emotional Nature

Now, perhaps most importantly, you must learn how to protect your emotional nature. The emotional nature is often the most vulnerable and easily influenced of all. You will have to admit that far too often you have been moved into action by your emotions rather than your intellect. To guard your emotions is to keep the instinctive nature harnessed under the firm reins of your intellect. The colors used to harmonize and protect the emotional nature are light blue and violet. By flooding your aura with beautiful sky blue and vivid violet, you quiet your own lower emotions and feelings and become impervious to the negative feelings and moods of those around you. With the advent of these colors, your individual awareness is transported into the more refined, uplifting realms of the subsuperconscious mind. Always remember that by flooding your aura with bright sky-blue and lavender you are automatically building an armor to protect yourself from others' lower feelings and passions, such as anger, jealousy, hatred and lust. So, make a study of bright, clear blues and violets and select the ones that appeal to you the most. Intuitively you will know which hues are best for you. Beautiful hues of blue and violet will always be found in the auras of successful teachers, missionaries, social workers and those who work among those of lesser emotional and mental refinement than their own. ¶There is one last part of this *sādhana* that you should learn to make your understanding of the human aura complete, and that is the knowledge of the auric circle. The auric circle is an energy shell around the aura itself. It acts as a shelter or shield against all forms of psychic influences directed consciously or unconsciously against the individual. Unlike charging the aura with *prāṇic* energy through breathing, the auric circle is quickly and easily formed by making a mental image of an egg completely surrounding your aura. The shell should be visualized as a great oval of translucent white light with an opening at the top the size of your head. It is egg-shaped or oval because it fringes the aura as the shell encases an egg. It should be visualized about three to four feet in depth at the widest point, tapering to about two feet at the head and feet. ¶It takes but a little effort of the will to visualize and project this protective, translucent shell around your aura on the *astral* plane. Though you may not see it, you will feel its protective presence. Once you have built up the protective shell around your aura, then it needs only to be renewed from time to time. You can easily do so by extending both arms out in front of you waist high. Then press the palms of your hands together and visualize energy flowing from your solar plexus into your hands. Once the flow of *prāṇa* is established, slowly part your hands while feeling the *prāṇa* emanating from your finger tips. This *prāṇa* remains in the outer shell of your aura. Move your arms out to the side and then completely around to the back of your body until the fingers and palms touch again. All the time you are doing this, keep sending the *prāṇa* out into the shell of your aura from your fingertips. Strengthening the protective circle around your aura in this way from time to time will be quite helpful to you in manifesting a fuller and more joyous life, because it will definitely ward off all forms of psychic attack or evil influence, no matter what the source. The auric circle surrounding a vibrant aura charged with the proper colors, fortified by sending the vital *prāṇas* from the *prāṇic* body, affords protection against the draining of physical strength by *astral* entities in extreme cases of *astral* attacks. In short, this protective, translucent, white shell is a spiritual shield which filters out those influences which would be harmful or upsetting to you. Before beginning your prayers or meditations, you should always strengthen this protective shield.

Nidrā Svapnāni cha

निद्रा स्वप्नानि च

Sleep and Dreams

The gross body of the waking state, the subtle body of the dream state, both made of twenty-five *tattvas*, are verily of *bindu's* power. That power, permeating the soul, penetrates the states of waking and dreaming.

TIRUMANTIRAM 2187

Monday
LESSON 239
The World Of Dreams

Dreams have been a mystery and a puzzle to people of all ages throughout time. The wonderment of dreams has been apparent in history, philosophy and now even in science. This leads us to assume that the dream state is not unlike the waking state, for especially in this technological age of communication, we live more in our mind than in our physical body. Millions are computer-literate and deal in concepts far beyond the normal state anyone would have found himself in one hundred years ago. The mind never sleeps—only the physical body experiences this indulgence—and the physical brain perceives and records what passes through the mind, but the astral brain perceives and records... oh-so-much more! Therefore, keeping this in mind, there is a continuity of consciousness twenty-four hours a day, but not all of it is perceived or recorded by the physical brain, either through the day or through the night. This is why it is difficult to remember all the details of one's life and experience, even as short a time as forty-eight hours ago. It is only the important things, those which make the strongest impression within the physical brain's memory patterns, that are remembered. ¶In the inner worlds, inner universe, there is a life not unlike this one that we experience as a *jīva*, but far more complete, intricate, logical and much more advanced. Within this world, the Antarloka, there are great schools where students gather to learn of a more productive future that they can participate in creating when they incarnate. Here, they mix and mingle with other souls whose physical bodies are sleeping and whom they will work and cooperate with during their next cycle of birth. It is a well-planned-out universe, both the outer universe and the inner universe. The value of sleep for the person on the path is to gain the ability to bypass the lower dream state and soar deeper within to these inner-plane schools. This is done by the repetition of *mantras, japa yoga,* just before sleep, after relaxing the body through *haṭha yoga* and diaphragmatic breathing. ¶It is almost traditional in many cultures to try to remember one's dreams, and dreamologists will even interpret them for you. This all borders close to the realm of superstition and is far less desirable for spiritual growth than other more pragmatic types of practices. A beginner on the path, or even one in the intermediate phase, should endeavor to forget dreams and strengthen the fibers of the mind and psyche through daily *sādhana.* There is actually a time, on the *yoga mārga,* after the *charyā* and *kriyā mārgas* have been well mastered and passed through, that the remembrance of one's dreams is beneficial and fruitful, but this would only be between the *guru* and the *śishya.* ¶When *japa* is well performed and the sincere desire is maintained to transcend the forces of the physical body and enter into the astral schools of learning, the aspirant would have dreamless nights. A deep sleep would prevail. There may be a few seconds of dreaming just before awakening, to which one should not pay any attention, as the astral body quickly reenters the physical. But a deep, dreamless sleep is in itself an indicator that the *purusha* is totally detached from the physical forces and totally intact and functioning in the Devaloka. Himālayan Academy is an academy in the Devaloka in which *ṛishis* of the Nandinātha Sampradāya teach, help and guide tens of thousands of devotees of God Śiva who have been influenced by the words and teachings of our *sampradāya.* ¶We want to forget bad dreams as quickly as possible, lest by remembering them through the conscious mind we impress them in the immediate subconscious and make them manifest in daily life. Thinking about a bad dream is to create. Forgetting it is to avoid creating. Therefore, if you have the slightest worry about dreams and are not directly under a *guru's* guidance on a daily basis, it is best to let them slide by and consider them unimportant and not a part of you, as you would consider a television program to be. ¶Really bad nightmare kinds of dreams are not natural to the sleeper's mind. Therefore, we must assume that they are produced by outside influences, such as what the neighbors are going through in the next apartment, the apartment above or the apartment below, or what a dear friend or relative may be experiencing in daily life. Subjective as they are, the frustrated, confused, even threatening, dreams of this nature are taken to be one's creation or one's own problem. However, this is more than often not true. A child may be tormented by nightmares and wake up screaming, and the solution would be to have it sleep in another room, away from the next-door apartment where the husband and wife are battling, entertaining hateful thoughts. These kinds of quarrels permeate the inner atmosphere one hundred yards around, as far as the loudest voice could be heard if there were no walls. This is why those on the path seek the quiet of a forest, a life away from the city, in order to perform *sādhana* in their spiritual pursuit. Dreams of capture and chase are not products of one's own mind. They are definitely outside influences.

Tuesday
LESSON 240
Experiences on The Astral Plane

When we are in a dream, it seems so real to us. When we wake up, we reflect on it as a dream, which is usually thought of as unreal. Similarly, Indian philosophers enjoy saying that we are in this life and it seems real until we wake up, through spiritual enlightenment, to a greater reality. If we postulate that dreams are real, we must then acknowledge that what we remember of them is our uninhibited states of consciousness, experience, unencumbered by society, local and national customs or inhibitions planted into the mind by parents at a young age. Knowing this will let us know who we really are, underneath the facade, encumbered by society, suppressed by beliefs and attitudes of the waking state. We are free in our dreams. No one is looking at us. Society, family and friends are not judging us. ¶*Āyurveda* physicians state that those of the *kapha dosha,* which is water and earth, often dream of water. One who is of the *pitta dosha,* fire nature, dreams of fire. A *vata,* or air nature, dreams of air. But they also say that it may be best to forget your dreams because they might be produced by indigestion or constipation. And these may be dreams you would not want to remember. Nevertheless, if dreams depict who we really are, it may be beneficial for those under the guidance of a *satguru* to write them down each morning upon arising and put them at his holy feet at the end of each month. This would be strictly a *guru-śishya* training relationship and for a specified period of time, not more than four months. It might be scary, even disheartening, for you to do this for yourself. And *satgurus* would recommend that you forget your dreams upon awakening, for if remembered they may bring that reality into the awakened reality and produce experiences you would not want to experience. ¶One more thing comes to mind—this is that occasionally I have experienced being absolutely aware, fully conscious of the physical body, eyes closed, while simultaneously seeing through the eyes of the inner body and communicating through thought with astral people in my room. Sometimes when the *maṭhavāsis* have been late to feed me because I was napping but fully conscious, the guardian *devas* would come before me with delicious food, nicely prepared, and with their astral hands spoon it into my mouth, and I actually smell and taste it. When the astral meal is over, I am not physically hungry anymore. During the height of the Sri Lanka civil war crisis, when thousands of my devotees there were being killed day after day, several times during the day I deliberately took naps off and on. Just before these sleeps and just before awakening in the morning, I would meet with those who had been killed and bless them one at a time as they came before me. I was totally conscious as my astral hand would put the blessing, the mark of *vibhūti,* Śiva's sacred ash, upon their forehead. Then they would go on into the Śivaloka. This type of physical-astral experience is definitely not a dream, nor is it a superconscious vision. It is an actual, intense human happening involving this world and its astral double, coexisting in communicative activity. Unlike dreams, which are quickly forgotten, these physical-astral experiences, not unlike superconscious visions, leave an indelible mark in the physical brain and are more vivid months and even years later than when they were experienced. ¶For three or four years in the late fifties, I researched the death experience and its astral interface with this apparent reality. The dream world was explored, and the astral interface with waking consciousness within it. We discovered that there are many thousands of astral lovers who regularly visit women to satisfy their sexual desires. These women are single, either not married yet, or divorced, or married, but their husbands were not able to satisfy them. It was also discovered that because of this psychic phenomenon, women who have had unhappy marriages are more attracted than men to spiritualism, as it was called in those days. Such astral male lovers are called *gandharvas* in the *Vedas,* and their female counterparts are the *apsarās.* These are definitely experiences, astral-physical-plane interface experiences, as real as happenings during the waking day.

Wednesday
LESSON 241
Interpreting Our Dreams

In the early 1980s, just before Sri Lanka's civil war, I was invited by the government to travel through the country and visit all who were attached to our Śiva Yogaswāmī *paramparā* during the past century. There were massive parades for miles and miles in villages we passed through, grand receptions, rides on great chariots and hundreds of garlands from those that came alive for the event. All during these times, knowing that war was eminent, I preached that Śiva's devotees do not fear death, it is only a passing into another life. Later, at the height of the civil war, when my devotees were experiencing the transition and the killing and torture, it was perplexing to me to understand how people that were so high in consciousness and culture could go so low. In many, many astral, conscious states, I visited the lowest *chakras*, protected by *devonic* helpers and unseen by those within them, and discovered for myself these regions before ever reading about them. Having never read a book from cover to cover in my life and having been trained from very early years, sixteen or seventeen, to have the experience first and then somehow or other it would be verified by scripture later on, this was my path. I was told that to know what was coming up in the experiential pattern of spiritual unfoldment could be to put into thc subconscious mind the experience and memories of it, which would not be the experience at all. This, I was taught, would build a spiritual pride that would detour one from the path to Self Realization. Very carefully I observed this, fully understanding the wisdom of the advice. It was amazing to me to have verified in obscure scriptures that the *chakras,* or *talas,* below the *mūlādhāra* were exactly as when I visited each of them, guided by mighty *devas* who had the power to go anywhere within the mind. Life has taught me that knowledge is best when it is experiential, not intellectually learned and then remembered. This I have endeavored to impress upon my devotees over the past five decades. ¶Hindus say there are kinds of dreams conjured from the needs of the individual, and then there is another kind that is sent by the Gods. I myself have appeared in dreams to people that have never seen me, seen my picture or even knew of my physical existence. Gods communicate by pictures. Therefore, certain kinds of dreams have meaning if they are sent by the Gods. Signs, symbols and body language to the Asian people have great meaning. For instance, folding your arms across the chest in the West is resting them; in the East it is a sign of disdain. Dreams from the Gods come to very religious people who live a disciplined life of *sādhana,* rising at four in the morning, and living Hindu Dharma to the best of their ability to understand it. They have attracted the attention of the Gods because they have penetrated the realms of the Gods. If they let down, then they would not have those kinds of visitations any longer. ¶The average lifetime is about eighty years in the United States. The average time someone sleeps is about one third of their life. Therefore, we are dreaming about twenty-seven years of our life. We assume that dreams only occur when the physical body is asleep. But what about the unproductive thoughts, the daydreams, thinking about unfounded fears, the uncontrolled states of waking mind, mental arguments, mental fears, the uncontrolled combative thoughts, fantasies—sexual, violent, tender, loving, worrisome, fretful, indecisiveness or gruesome? ¶If someone confesses his dreams he has at night, he should also confess his dreams during the day. The ancient scriptures say that dreams are like our waking thoughts in this way: if we dream and forget the dream, it is as though the dream had never happened. If you think a thought during the day and forget the thought, it's as though the thought had never happened. It's when we remember and speak out a dream or remember and speak out a thought that it has reality on this plane.

Thursday
LESSON 242
Shielding Your Emotional Nature

Some dreams come from the person's nature, *vata, pitta, kapha,* and others from the emotional nature, some from subconscious fears, and some from just playing back experiences in daily life. But certain dreams are brought by the Gods. We might not call these dreams, by our way of defining them. And there are prophetic dreams. Prophetic dreams come from the superconscious mind, beyond the subconscious. It is a state of mind that sees into the future and into the past simultaneously, is able to read the *ākāśic* records. During intense periods of one's life that will manifest in the future, be they good, bad or mixed, it is this state of mind within every human soul that is tapped, or that of its own volition infiltrates its wisdom in coming events upon the physical brain through what is called a prophetic dream. There is no mystery here. Sincere souls should be warned of impending dangers or good fortune that might disrupt their current mundane lifestyle. To be forewarned is to be forearmed. Like visions of the Gods and astral-physical interfaces, prophetic dreams, which are more like visions, are also remembered and cannot be forgotten. They are remembered day after day even more vividly than when they occurred. Let's not be unaware that our own superconsciousness, our third eye, our *dūrdarśana,* our far-seeingness, can warn us of events. ¶If you dream that you are dying, in Hindu thought it means you are going to live. But if you dream your teeth are falling out, you are going to die. And we must know that this has been tried and tested and proved worthy over thousands of years of experience. I myself, being of a *kapha dosha,* dream of water. When the water is calm, I know that there will be no mental disturbances in the foreseeable future. But when there are dashing ocean waves, I know that within 72 hours, three days, there will be a mental disturbance with an aggression of mental force. This has been proven to my external, conscious mind time and time again. The ancient texts speak of giant floods that consume the world, as in typical dreams. The single most talked about dream in Indian lore is of flying. ¶If you remember a dream a month later, it is not an ordinary dream. It has meaning. Therefore, if you are prone to go to a dream analyst, and you want to get the right knowledge from his perception, present to him an astral-physical interface, a dream or a vision, at least thirty-one days after it has happened and which is still important to you and a part of your life. This is the best advice we can give for an honest appraisal. This is very good *satguru* advice. ¶The most prophetic dreams come in the early hours just before sunrise. The more subconscious-cleansing type dreams come before that time. But in my own experience, the really impressive dreams come just before waking up at three or four o'clock in the morning. It's always a couple of hours before sunrise. Eleven or twelve o'clock? No! These are kind of witchy times, subconscious times, and dreams experienced then just fade away. ¶When you wake up during the night, discipline should be applied lest you just roll over in a semi-conscious state and return to the dream world, going back into a subconscious or lower astral area—which might be negative, might be positive, you don't know. To avoid this, you should become fully awake. The ideal practice for seekers is to sit up when you wake up during the night. Sit and listen for a minute or two to the *nāda-nāḍī śakti* or go into the light within your head if you are able. Then, if you wish, consciously lay down and go back to sleep, just like you did when you went to bed in the first place. ¶If you then have difficulty returning to sleep, you can assume you have had sufficient rest for your physical body. In such a case, don't force yourself to return to sleep, waiting for the alarm to ring, which is a kind of indulgence. Instead, get up. That means fully get out of bed, get dressed and do something useful. If you just roll over and go into the semi-conscious dream world, you can go into subconscious areas, into the Pretaloka, and even have astral attacks from astral entities, and even into the *talas* below the *mūlādhāra.* This drains the physical and astral energies of their life and vigor. In my early training, both ways were tested, so the knowledge from actual experience is evident. Follow the formula: "Wake up, get up." One of my *sādhanas* practiced in Sri Lanka in the late '40s was to sleep for only two hours, wake up with the help of a small alarm clock, sit in the lotus posture and meditate as long as possible, reset the alarm for another two hours, and repeat until just before sunrise. ¶When people begin to meditate and are on the spiritual path, working with themselves—and this means that they do accomplish making a difference in their behavior, their beliefs, attitudes and daily actions—their dream life will reflect these results as well. For them, the dream *karmas* can be worked out. *Karma* is often qualified as a force that is sent out from us and returns to us, generally through other people. Nearly always, *karma* is related to the waking state. However, we do experience emotions in dreams. The world within is as solid as is the body in which we find ourself in the awakened state. We do experience in the inner worlds, while the physical body is asleep, forces going out from our thoughts, feelings and what we say and think, and these obviously are dream *karmas*, real *karmas* that will eventually manifest on the physical plane unless reexperienced and dissolved within the dream world itself. The reason why dream *karmas* can only be worked out by those who are performing *sādhana* and making actual changes in their lives is because they have effected a certain soul control over their mind, physical body and emotions, and this naturally carries over into the dream reality.

Friday
LESSON 243
Working with The Dream State

We really should have another word for this dream reality, as the word *dream* has taken on connotations of something that only exists in one's imagination. These kinds of dreams—when a person is in his astral body and can feel what he touches, emote to his experiences, think and talk—are not what is known as the dream state. This is an astral experience, similar to the death experience, but the astral body is still connected to the physical body. Dreams and death are brothers, with the exception that the silver cord is not broken, which is the psychic cord of actinodic energy, or the umbilical cord between the astral body and its physical duplicate, or of the physical body and its astral duplicate. Therefore, when one begins the regular practice of *sādhana,* meditation, *mantras*, correcting behavioral patterns in daily life, the astral body is able to disconnect from the physical body and an astral reality is experienced, which is not a dream when remembered, in the sense that dreams are usually denoted to be. ¶The English-language concepts of dreams—such as "when I wake up," "when I was dreaming" or "I tried to remember my dream"—set the pattern for the psychology behind dreams in the Western context. We could say, "I realized I was consciously active as I reentered my physical body and tried to impress in my physical brain the creative work, activity, thoughts, feelings and experiences that happened throughout the night." This would be affirming twenty-four-hour consciousness, of which the physical body plays a very small part in its apparent reality. ¶Because they are experienced, because they affect our waking life and because many of them are portents of the future: these are reasons Ādi Śaṅkara gave in saying that dreams are real in many respects. In the West, dreams are thought of as more or less unreal. In the East they are thought of as both real and unreal. The Sanskṛit word for dream, *svapna,* is etymologically related to the Greek word *hypnos* and includes the content of dream and the form or process of dreaming. It is one of four *avasthās,* or states of consciousness, given in the *Upanishads: jagrat,* the waking state; *svapna,* the sleeping or dreaming state; *sushupti,* deep sleep; and *turīya,* the fourth state, also called *samādhi.* ¶We have spoken earlier about the twenty-four-hour consciousness of the mind and how even in the waking state an uncontrolled mind is dreaming and fantasizing, and we made the point that it is only the physical body that experiences the phenomenon of sleep. The astral body does not have to. It can remain awake and active twenty-four hours a day, because it is always functioning within the physical body during the physical body's waking hours as well. We actually live in our astral body twenty-four hours a day. That is the true home of the soul, mind, emotions, seed *karmas.* The astral body, when fortunate enough to have a physical body, uses it at least half a day every day, when that body is not sleeping. ¶More and more subtle dimensions of consciousness are dealt with in *sādhana.* Ultimately, perhaps, one even begins to work with dreams in subtle ways. The Hindu idea that one would not steal or injure even in a dream seems to reinforce this subtlety. A dream that might not mean anything to an ordinary person, say an incident of stealing, might be thought important to an adept. Often religious people suppress their natural feelings in order to live up to religious concepts of virtue and ethics that they have not naturally worked into and earned by clearing up their past behavioral patterns through daily *sādhana,* self-inquiry and change in belief through belief therapy. This means totally eradicating one belief and replacing it with a new one that is more in line with the religious principles they have decided to mold into their life than were the older ones. Because of this suppression, the expression of the desires is released and experienced during dreams. Many people who have accomplished these repressions exceedingly well have repetitive dreams. Here the *guru* would take note of the dreams that were occurring to see if they were actually suppressed desires, feelings and emotions that had to be talked about in the light of day and changed, especially if they are recurring. The recurrence of the same or similar dream experience indicates that work needs to be done within the seeker, who has set for himself too high a standard during the waking state and is not performing enough *sādhana* and *tapas* to maintain that standard. Therefore, the letdown comes when no one is watching. During dreams he can do what he really wants to do. ¶The key here for the seeker is not to carry the dream into daily life and then start to do what he did in the dream in the physical world. This would only make more *karmas* and compound the situation, stop the *sādhanas* and open a door for perhaps endless other *karmas* or a complete life change, change of personality. The remedy is, if possible under the guidance of a *guru*, to perform certain *sādhanas, tapas,* penance, self-inquiry, even a penance for having the dream, while remembering the high standards of virtue and good conduct that should have been maintained during that sleep cycle. This explains the Hindu point of view that one should not steal even during dreams, commit adultery, harm anyone or act against *dharma*, the *yamas* and *niyamas,* in any way.

Saturday
LESSON 244
The Continuity Of Consciousness

In India there is the concept that dreams affect not only the dreamer himself but those around him as well. Partially this is because the concept of self is intertwined with everything else: family, community, village, cosmos. Thus, a dream by the *guru* would affect all of his monks. The dreams that a *guru* would dream would become the teachings of the *guru* to all *śishyas.* But because the *śishyas* were in tune with his inner mind, the knowledge would be imparted to them at the same time that the dreams were occurring. Therefore, they would very rapidly pick up on the teachings that developed out of the dreams. ¶Similarly, families, friends, loved ones and relations are all connected. To be connected to a *guru* would not disconnect you from your family, but only from the members of the family that were not connected to the same *guru.* They would, all of a sudden, be on the outside of the family looking in, because they would not be in the inner, dream, astral, inner-plane school phenomenon that being connected to a *guru* provides. When entire families are of the same *sampradāya* and hold allegiance to the same *paramparā,* all goes well in the continuity of consciousness through the entire life cycle. ¶There is no reason to think that dreams are individually secret in the vibrations they create and that they do not affect the inner minds of those the person is connected to. But then again, this applies to people who are doing regular spiritual disciplines and are tapping inner resources and through these inner resources are tapping the higher dimensions of the mind and striving for higher consciousness. ¶The first thing a *guru* would do, or which you can do, if somebody tells about their dream, is to discern if he is an undisciplined person. If so, the dream obviously reflects his undisciplined nature. If he has been disciplined in the past and is now resting on his accomplishments and has let down on his disciplines, or if he is currently doing *yoga* at a certain time each day, this knowledge itself will show in the dream's quality. ¶In India, dreams are also understood to be good and bad omens. The *Atharva Veda's* appendix sixty-eight is all about the symbolism of dreams. Traditional good omens are dreaming that you have been killed, that your house has burned down. Indian dream analyzers actually interpret those dreams as positive. Dreaming that your teeth are falling out is bad. Being covered with oil is bad. Dreaming of a woman in a green or red *sārī* is bad, though dreaming of a woman in general is considered auspicious. If you dream that someone gave you an umbrella or that you are riding on a camel, that is good. It is only ignorance—which is the ability to ignore—to pass over an entire subject area of knowledge with a superficial reason or comment. These age-old traditions which have stood the test of time are obviously a systematic investigation by many learned people of what tens of thousands of men and women have experienced after having had dreams of these kinds and thus formulated these postulations. The Western rationalist would write them off simply as superstition. ¶The word *superstition* comes from the Latin *superstitio,* originally meaning "a standing still over." *Webster's Dictionary* defines *superstition* as "any belief or attitudc based on fear or ignorance that is inconsistent with the known laws of science or with what is generally considered in the particular society as true and rational, especially such a belief in charms, omens, the supernatural, etc." These simple words are very important because they have the power to block out from human consciousness vast amounts of mystical knowledge. The Hindu looks at time not in a twenty-four-hour day, but a cycle of lifetimes, of many lives, and from creation of the soul to its eventual fulfillment of merger in Śiva. The Westerner looks at time as a straight line. It has a beginning; it has an end. The line begins at birth and ends at death. Therefore, such a short line of consciousness cannot waste time in superstition, imagination. Whereas the Hindu believes that the knowledge acquired in one life should be carried over to the next life, the next and the next. It is an ever-building, ever-growing maturation of not only the soul but the many bodies it inhabits. ¶The theme that we are working with is the continuity of consciousness from birth to death, but even more, from the creation of the soul to its final merger into its creator, having fully matured into the image and likeness of the creator and the experiential consciousness, twenty-four hours a day, as creating *karmas.*

Sunday
LESSON 245
Shared Dreams; Inner Darkness

It is the one-life belief that creates the big distinction between waking and sleeping. It is the super misconception that the objective reality is real and the subjective reality is fantasy, unreal. Quite the contrary, the subjective reality is real and the objective reality is less real, from the Hindu point of view. Both the subjective and objective realms are given reality by the previous *saṁskāras* impressed within the soul, and when done with and healed, those subjective and objective realities fade away. It is because of these *saṁskāras* that people do not merge with Śiva as Śiva, why the *jīva* does not become Śiva immediately. Experiences had and *karmas* made in a physical birth will require a physical birth to heal them. Experiences and *karmas* made in the dream world will require sleep experience to heal them. ¶One of the strong themes in Hindu dream thought is that of shared dreams. This means two people having the same dream and confirming it later by talking about it, two people communicating in a dream which reflects later in reality, or two people entering a dream together. Tibet's *gurus* and disciples would dream the same dream consciously, being of such one-mindedness, with the purpose of creating something on the physical plane, and if they pooled their minds like that, they would be able, according to our tradition, to create something that never existed before. ¶Two people sharing the same dream and communicating within that dream is a definite astral plane experience. People endeavoring to have the same dream is a systematic teaching of the Nandinātha Sampradāya, such as entering inner-plane schools where everyone is learning from great Nātha adepts. People having the same dream and then talking about it and saying "Yes, I had a dream like that at the same time" may be a prophetic message from the Gods and *devas,* a form of channeling. The intelligent souls living in the inner world want to communicate something to those in the outer world and can't communicate it directly through a psychic, so they try to communicate it through dreams through numerous people. These are usually very prophetic dreams. Dreams of this kind should not be taken overly seriously if only two people have them, because one might be just agreeing with the other that he had also had it, compromising or looking for favors. If two people have had the same dream, they should look for a third person who has also had the same dream. This is the protective step to take. The inner-plane beings will project the same image and knowledge through five, ten, fifteen individuals, so there will always be a third person, or a fourth or a fifth. Then these prophetic kinds of dreams can really be taken seriously. With these kinds of projected dreams, there is no need to panic, because they are projected by the great overseers of this planet, long before anything forboding would happen, to give inhabitants a chance to understand and adjust the situation. They are not given in the framework of something happening in two or three days or a week or two. ¶Enlightenment gives experiential understanding of all states of mind, from the nothing which is the fullness of everything and the fullness which is the emptiness of nothing, into sound, color, combinations of colors and sounds, which is form. The forms that interrelate with forms make *saṁskāras*. The forms of the *saṁskāras* remembered separate and categorize the forms, and *voilà,* human life is created. Enlightenment means seeing the entire picture simultaneously, because when the light is turned on, everything in the room is seen. When the light is turned on in the mind, everything in the mind is seen. There are no mysteries, no dark areas, no gray areas. Unlike turning on the light in the room, which immediately produces shadows, enlightenment illumines everything in the mind from the inside out. There are no shadows, no mysteries. Yes, dreams are no mystery to the enlightened, but are seen no differently than the waking state. There is only one reality in form, which is the pure consciousness which is conscious of form, and this reality is what realizes itself as formless, timeless, spaceless. ¶An enlightened man does not dream or live differently, but simply sees his dreams and waking life differently. The unenlightened person has definitely a darkness, many gray areas in the struggle for enlightenment. Or, if he is not struggling for enlightenment, the blackness within is his reality. An occasional flash of light, which might come with a bright, unexpected idea, is like a word from the Divine, considered a word from the Divine. The unenlightened are blinded by their own good deeds, mixed deeds and bad deeds of the past, couped up in darkness and held there by their lethargy and inability to attempt a *yoga,* a union, with the Divine. As a single leaf from a tree can guard your eyes from the bright impact of sunlight when held between you and the sun, so can one single belief—and the religious ones are clung to most religiously—hold a believer in dark areas of the mind.

There is nothing higher than dharma.
Verily, that which is *dharma* is truth.

Śukla Yajur Veda, Bṛihadāraṇyaka Upanishad 1.4.14. BO UPH, 84

The mind operating at the sensory level is the root cause of all worldly knowledge. If the mind is dissolved, there will be no worldly knowledge. Therefore, keep the consciousness fixed on the Supreme Being in deepest concentration. *Adhyātma Upanishad* 26

Borne along and defiled by the stream of qualities, unsteady, wavering, bewildered, full of desire, distracted, one goes on into the state of self-conceit. In thinking "This is I" and "That is mine" one binds himself with himself, as does a bird with a snare.

Kṛishṇa Yajur Veda, Maitrī Upanishad 3.2. UPH, 418

By means of the hymns one attains this world, by the sacrificial formulas the space in-between, by holy chant the world revealed by the sages. With the syllable Aum as his sole support, the wise man attains that which is peaceful, unageing, deathless, fearless—the Supreme.

Atharva Veda, Praśna Upanishad 5.7. VE, 775

The resplendent Self, through the ecstacy of spiritual joy, inspires all virtuous thoughts among men of divine nature. *Ṛig Veda* 8.32.28. RS VOL. 9, PG. 3,025

Vāsanā is divided into two, the pure and the impure. If thou art led by the pure *vāsanās,* thou shalt thereby soon reach by degrees My Seat. But should the old, impure *vāsanās* land thee in danger, they should be overcome through efforts.

Śukla Yajur Veda, Mukti Upanishad 2. TH, 7

When cease the five [sense] knowledges, together with the mind, and the intellect stirs not—that, they say, is the highest course.

Kṛishṇa Yajur Veda, Maitrī Upanishad 6.30. TP, 443

The spirit of man has two dwellings: this world and the world beyond. There is also a third dwelling place: the land of sleep and dreams. Resting in this borderland, the Spirit of man can behold his dwelling in this world and in the other world afar, and wandering in this borderland he beholds behind him the sorrows of this world and in front of him he sees the joys of the beyond.

Śukla Yajur Veda, Bṛihadāraṇyaka Upanishad 4.3.9. TU, 134

The mind is said to be twofold: the pure and also the impure; impure by union with desire—pure when from desire completely free!

Kṛishṇa Yajur Veda, Maitrī Upanishad 6.34. UPH, 447

Japa is the happy giver of enjoyment, salvation, self-fulfilling wish. Therefore, practice the *yoga* of *japa* and *dhyāna.* All blemishes due to transgressions of rule, from the *jīva* up to the Brahman, done knowingly or unknowingly, are wiped away by *japa.*

Kulārṇava Tantra 11.1. KT, 111

Only by a tranquil mind does one destroy all action, good or bad. Once the self is pacified, one abides in the Self and attains everlasting bliss. If the mind becomes as firmly established in Brahman as it is usually attached to the sense objects, who, then, will not be released from bondage?

Kṛishṇa Yajur Veda, Maitrī Upanishad 6.34. VE, 422

Samagre Vilayam

समग्रे विलयम्

Part Three

Merging In the All

Karma Prākṛitika Vidhiḥ

कर्म प्राकृतिकविधिः

८८

Karma, the Natural Law

Unaware of the evil fruits that *karma* brings, they choose not to attain the *jñāna* which grants liberation from *karma.* "Renounce *karma* and be liberated"— this Vedic teaching is unknown to them who, wallowing in *karma,* will never reap the rich harvest.

TIRUMANTIRAM 2557

Monday
LESSON 246
The Law of Cause and Effect

Memory patterns are extremely magnetic. They cause us to have experiences of the type that make us wonder, "Why should that have ever happened to me? What did I do to attract this? What did I do to cause that? I don't deserve this happening to me." The vibrations that cause these experiences were put into effect in this or a past life. *Prāṇic* forces deep within imprint memory patterns of these actions we put into motion, causing us to face the reactions of them in this life. We face those reactions collectively through other people and through our own action. We are impelled to do certain things. Why? We call it *karma. Karma* means cause and effect. We throw a boomerang. It travels out into the air, turns around and comes back to us with equal force. In a similar way, our actions and even our thoughts set up patterns of reaction that return to us with equal force. This is the natural law of *karma.* Every action, every effect, in the universe has been preceded by a specific cause or set of causes. That cause is in itself an effect of prior causes. The law of *karma* is the law of cause and effect, or action and reaction. ¶When we cause a traumatic disruption within ourselves or within others, the action is imprinted in the memory patterns of the *mūlādhāra chakra.* The seed has been planted and will remain vibrating in the depths of the mind even though consciously forgotten. We carry it over from life to life, from birth to birth until one day it blossoms into the fruit of our action—reaction. ¶The reason patterns of the *svādhishṭhāna chakra,* just above memory, do not understand these experiences at all, because that *chakra* functions at a different rate of vibration. So, only after the event has occurred, or the impulses have come, can we reason them out rationally. Since we have forgotten our past life and are only left with the *prāṇic* reverberations deep in the memory cells, we don't know the causes. In fact, there seems to be no cause for many of the things that happen to us in life, no reason or justification. This can be frustrating. However, that is *karma*, and it is generally written off by saying, "That's *karma*." It is an effect to a previous cause. ¶The best attitude to hold when you first recognize the existence of *karma* is to realize that, true, it is a joy or a burden, and to stand straight, carrying that joy or that burden well balanced, seeking at all times not to add to it. Carry your *karma* cheerfully. Then begin the tedious task of unwinding these multitudinous patterns through performing daily *sādhana*. Each next step will become quite obvious to you as you begin to find that you are the writer of your own destiny, the master of your ship through life, and the freedom of your soul is but yours to claim through your accomplishments of your *yoga*.

Tuesday
LESSON 247
How We Face Our Karma

How can we work out *karma*? There are thousands of things vibrating in the *mūlādhāra chakra*, and from those memory patterns they are going to bounce up into view one after another, especially if we gain more *prāṇa* by breathing and eating correctly. When meditation begins, more *karma* is released from the first *chakra*. Our individual *karma* is intensified as the ingrained memory patterns that were established long ago accumulate and are faced, one after another, after another, after another. ¶In our first four or five years of striving on the path we face the *karmic* patterns that we would never have faced in this life had we not consciously sought enlightenment. Experiences come faster, closer together. So much happens in the short span of a few months or even a few days, catalyzed by the new energies released in meditation and by our efforts to purify mind and body, it might have taken us two or three lifetimes to face them all. They would not have come up before then, because nothing would have stimulated them. ¶First, we must know fully that we ourselves are the cause of all that happens. As long as we externalize the source of our successes and failures, we perpetuate the cycles of *karma*, good or bad. As long as we blame others for our problems or curse the seeming injustices of life, we will not find within ourselves the understanding of *karmic* laws that will transmute our unresolved patterns. We must realize that every moment in our life, every joy and every sorrow, can be traced to some source within us. There is no one "out there" making it all happen. We make it happen or not happen according to the actions we perform, the attitudes we hold and the thoughts we think. Therefore, by gaining conscious control of our thoughts and attitudes by right action, we can control the flow of *karma*. *Karma,* then, is our best spiritual teacher. We spiritually learn and grow as our actions return to us to be resolved and dissolved. ¶The second way to face *karma* is in deep sleep and meditation. Seeds of *karma* that have not even expressed themselves can be traced in deep meditation by one who has many years of experience in the within. Having pinpointed the unmanifested *karmic* seed, the *jñānī* can either dissolve it in intense light or inwardly live through the reaction of his past action. If his meditation is successful, he will be able to throw out the vibrating experiences or desires which are consuming the mind. In doing this, in traveling past the world of desire, he breaks the wheel of *karma* which binds him to the specific reaction which must follow every action. That experience will never have to happen on the physical plane, for its vibrating power has already been absorbed in his nerve system.

Wednesday
LESSON 248
Working It Out On the Inside

A third way that past actions are re-enacted is through the actual intense reactionary experience and working with yourself, conquering inner desires and emotions. When something happens to you that you put into motion in a past life or earlier in this life, sit down and think it over. Do not strike out. Do not react. Work it out inside yourself. Take the experience within, into the pure energies of the spine and transmute that energy back into its primal source. In doing so, what happens? You change its consistency. It no longer has magnetic power, and awareness flows away from that memory pattern forever. You could remember the experience, but your perspective would be totally detached and objective. This is the most common way *karma* is resolved, in day-to-day experiences. By living an inner life, you stop creating uncomplimentary *karma* and can therefore consciously face the reactions of the past without the confusion of additional day-to-day reactions. ¶Everyone lives an inner life. When you are thinking over that film that you saw last week, that is inner life. When you are deeply involved in a reactionary area because of something that has happened or is happening to someone else, you are living inwardly the same experience that you think they are going through.

¶In your life, someone you love has gone through an experience, and you have shared it with him. You felt his suffering and began to live it through dramatically. Actually, that same experience under a different set of conditions would have been happening to you, but it was happening to you in an indirect way through observation. You were able to vicariously work through this *karma.* ¶Perhaps your friend is destined to lose his leg in this life because he caused someone else to lose a leg in a past life. If he is living as an instinctive being, with all the energies flowing through the first two *chakras,* memory and reason, and through the passive physical forces, that experience will come to him in full force. However, perhaps he has his energies flowing through aggressive intellectual forces. Even if he is not consciously on the path of enlightenment, but is kindly and subdues his instinctive reactions by his intellect, that *karma* would still come back to him, but he would experience it in a different way. ¶One morning he may pick up the newspaper and read about an automobile accident in which someone has lost a leg. This news jars him. His solar plexus tightens. His reaction is so severe that he cannot eat his breakfast that morning. He does not know why, but all day he lives and relives every experience the article describes. He wonders, "What if this had happened to me? What would I do? How would I face it? How would I adjust my consciousness to it?" At work he imagines himself going through life with one leg—the therapy, the family concern, the emotional adjustment. It may take him three or four days to work his awareness out of that reaction. He does not know why that particular article in the newspaper impressed him so much. It seems foolish to him to think so much about the event and he tries to forget it. Soon thereafter, while hiking in the mountains, he stumbles and falls, cutting his thigh on the jagged rocks, tearing a few ligaments. The full force of the *karmic* experience comes, but because of his present goodness and previous blessings earned through control of his intellect, he receives the experience as a minor wound and an emotional reaction to another's losing his leg. This seed *karma* is worked through within himself in this way. He does not have to lose a leg, as he would if he were living in the instinctive mind of fear, anger and jealousy.

Thursday
LESSON 249
The Effect of Self Realization

"I am the master of my fate." This is how you become the master of your fate and the ruler of your own destiny. Through meditation you can bring everything to the now. "What happens when all the *karma* of all my past lives is worked out and I finally bring myself up to the now? Then what happens?" you might ask. You would truly be an artisan, an absolute expert, at working out *karma* in the mental and spiritual spheres, and could begin to help working out *karma* for other people. *Karma* is transferable. One can take on some of the *karma* of other people, work it out for them and make their burden a little easier for them. ¶After the realization of the Self, Paraśiva, the forces of *dharma* and previous *karma* still exist, but through the force of the realization of God, much of the impending impact of *karma* has dwindled, and it is faced differently, treated differently. Prior to the experience of realization, *karmas* were dealt with in individual increments. After realization, the sum total is seen. The spiritual destiny is realized. The *karma* and *dharma* and the future manufacturing of *karma* is viewed from within out, as a totality. ¶One does not have the experience of realizing the Self until all of his *karma* is in a state of resolve. This means that the action-and-reaction patterns were balanced out, one against the other, through his ability to be steadfast in his *yoga, brahmacharya* and previous superconscious insights which have revealed the true nature of himself. When this begins to occur in him, he actually sees that man is not man, man is the Self, God, for his *karma* and the forces of his *dharma* have begun to become transparent to him. ¶Through the power of his realization, the *karma* is created and simultaneously dissolved. This occurs for the one who lives in the timeless state of consciousness. If one were to realize the Self each day, he would live his life like writing his *karma* on the surface of water. The intensity of the Self is so strong that action and reaction dissolve, just as the water's surface clears immediately when you remove your finger from having written or made designs upon it.

Friday
LESSON 250
The State Of Resolve

When you hear the high-pitched sound "eee" in your head, your *karma* and your *dharma* are at that moment well balanced in this life. This is reassuring to know, as is the fact that if you persist in this state for an exceedingly long period of time, you would come into the realization of the experience of God. However, as you doubtless have already experienced, distractions you have set into motion teasingly bring awareness into another area, and almost without your knowing it, the high-pitched "eee" sound has faded and a thought has taken its place. ¶When you are in a state of resolve—

and *resolve* is the key word here; this means you have resolved the major *karmas* of conflict—good fortune and all the emotions arise, both generated through understanding the awakened philosophies by the practice of *yoga* and the results obtained. Then the *karmas* of the head *chakras* begin to unfold, resulting in these sublime feelings. These *karmas* are only experienced after many Paraśiva experiences, but they are felt before as a blissful impending future. It is from these *karmas* the word *bliss* derives. Only beyond the beyond the beyond—within the vastness within the heart and core of the universes, when space turns to spacelessness, time stops and *māyā's* endless cycles are no more—are there no more *karmas*. *Māyā's* endless cycle of creation, preservation and dissolution are *karmas* in the manifold creations of this process.

Saturday
LESSON 251
The Role of The Satguru

Responsibly resolving *karma* is among the most important reasons that a *satguru* is necessary in a sincere seeker's life. The *guru* helps the devotee to hold his mind in focus, to become pointedly conscious of thought, word and deed, and to cognize the lessons of each experience. Without the guidance and grace of the *guru*, the devotee's mind will be divided between instinctive and intellectual forces, making it very difficult to resolve *karma*. And only when *karma* is wisely harnessed can the mind become still enough to experience its own superconscious depths. ¶The *guru* guides and also shares a bit of the heavier burdens, if one is fortunate enough to be dedicated enough to have a *guru* who will lend his powers in this way. But each aspect of the *karma*, the outgrowth of the *dharma*, must be passed through by the disciple, creating as little as possible of a similar *karma* on this tenuous path of the repetition of the cycles of life. ¶The *guru* is able, because of his enlightenment or *tapas*, or as his *tapas*, to take upon himself the *karma* of another. Just what exactly does this mean? You have already found such persons at the moment of your birth—your mother and your father, who perhaps unknowingly, took the full impact of your *dharma*, and continue to take the impact of the *karma* you create, deeply within their nerve systems. If your *karma* is of a heavy nature, it could disrupt the entire home, and they could suffer because of it. On the other hand, if your *dharma* is *devonic*, full of merit accrued by generosity, good deeds and graciousness in your former life, your presence in their home is a blessing, and the force of your arrival may mitigate influences in their minds of an uncomely nature, bringing peace, harmony and forbearance into the home. The *guru* may take unto himself, into his nerve system, some of the heavier areas of your *karma* in the same way your parents performed this function for you perhaps unknowingly. ¶Planetary changes activate new *karmas* and close off some of the *karmas* previously activated. These *karmas* then wait in abeyance, accumulating new energy from current actions, to be reactivated at some later time. These *karmic* packets become more refined, life after life, through *sādhana.* All of this is summed up by one word, *evolution.* ¶The planets do not cause the events or the vibrations that individuals react to either positively or negatively. The magnetic pulls of light or the absence of light release that which is already there within the individual. If not much is there, not much can be released. The magnetic pulls and the lack of magnetism are what *jyotisha* (Vedic astrology) is telling us is happening at every point in time. Two things—magnetism and its opposite. On and off. Light and dark. With and without. Action and no action. Therefore, these keys release within the individual what was created when other keys were releasing other *karmas.* It is our reaction to *karmas* through lack of understanding that creates most *karmas* we shall experience at a future time. The sum total of all *karmas,* including the journey through consciousness required to resolve them, is called *saṁsāra.*

Sunday
LESSON 252
The Varieties Of Karma

What do we mean, exactly, by the terms good *karma* and bad *karma*? There is good *karma* as well as bad, though we say there is no good nor bad—only experience. Still, some *karmas* are more difficult to bear, experience and reexperience than others. This is where it is extremely important to inhibit the tendencies to let loose the forces that externalize awareness, while at the same time performing the *sādhana* of realizing the Source through internalizing awareness. It is this constant pull between the inner and the outer, or individual awareness soaring back and forth between the externalities and internalities, that keeps churning the fiery forces of *karma* into the smoldering coals of *dharma.* Good *karma* is denoted by good merit, since every cause has its due effect. Therefore, so-called bad *karma* brings injury, pain, misunderstanding and anguish, which when suffered through completes the cycle. ¶Ancient *yogīs,* in psychically studying the timeline of cause and effect, assigned three categories to *karma.* The first is *sañchita,* the sum total of past *karma* yet to be resolved.

The second category is *prārabdha,* that portion of *sañchita karma* being experienced in the present life. *Kriyamāna,* the third type, is *karma* you are presently creating. However, it must be understood that your past negative *karma* can be altered into a smoother, easier state through the loving, heart-*chakra* nature, through *dharma* and *sādhana.* That is the key of *karmic* wisdom. Live religiously well and you will create positive *karma* for the future and soften negative *karma* of the past. ¶Right knowledge, right decision and right action imperceptively straighten out, unkink and unwind ignorantly devised or contrived past actions. The key word is *reform.* Re-form, re-make, re-cast. To put into a molten state and be reformed is what happens to our *karma* when we enter *dharma. Adharma* is creating *karma,* good, not so good, terrible, mixed and confused. *Dharma* reforms all of this—reshapes and molds, allowing the devotee to do good and think good, to be clearly perceptive. Putting all the *karma* in a molten state is *bhakti.* Happy *karma,* sad *karma,* bad *karma,* when consciously or unconsciously wanted to be held onto, inhibits *bhakti. Bhakti* brings grace, and the sustaining grace melts and blends the *karmas* in the heart. In the heart *chakra* the *karmas* are in a molten state. The throat *chakra* molds the *karmas* through *sādhana,* regular religious practices. The third-eye *chakra* sees the *karmas,* past, present and future as a singular oneness. And the crown *chakra* absorbs, burns clean, enough of the *karmas* to open the gate, the Door of Brahman, revealing the straight path to merging with Śiva.

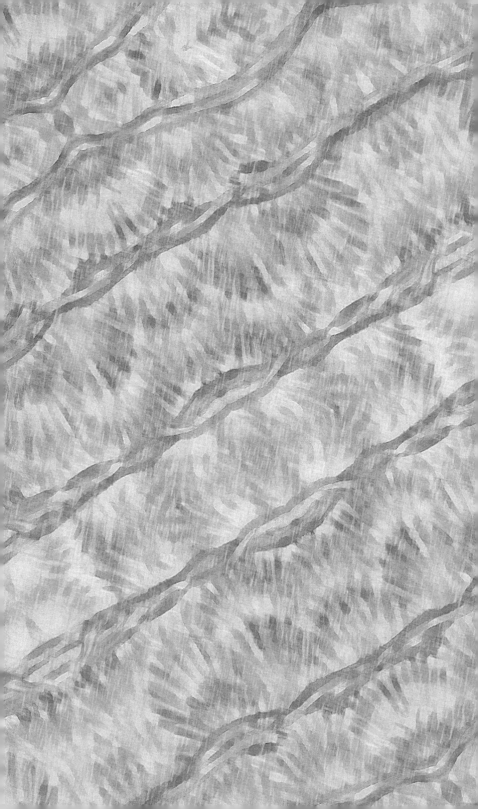

Dhyāna Kalā

ध्यानकला

The Fine Art Of Meditation

Closing the gateway below the *mūlādhāra,* center your thought on the door of Brahman above the *sahasrāra* and meditate on that into oneness. Fix your lance-like vision on that vast inner space. Thus practicing *kuṇḍalinī yoga,* you shall vanquish time.

TIRUMANTIRAM 583

Monday
LESSON 253
What Is Meditation?

Many seekers work or even struggle regularly with their meditations, especially those who are just beginning, "How does one know if he is really meditating or not?" That's a question that a lot of people who meditate ask themselves. When you begin to *know*, having left the process of thinking, you are meditating at that point. When you sit down and think, you are beginning the process of meditation. For instance, if you read a metaphysical book, a deep book, and then sit quietly, breathe and start pondering what you have been reading, well, you're not quite meditating. You're in a state called "concentration." You're organizing the subject matter. When you begin to realize the interrelated aspects of what you have read, when you say to yourself, "That's right. That's right," when you get these inner flashes, the process of meditation has just begun. If you sustain this intensity, insights and knowledge will come from the inside of you. You begin to connect all of the inner flashes together like a string of beads. You become just one big inner flash. You know all of these new inner things, and one insight develops into another, into another, into another. Then you move into a deeper state, called contemplation, where you feel these beautiful, blissful energies flow through the body as a result of your meditation. With disciplined control of awareness, you can go deeper and deeper into that. So, basically, meditation begins when you move out of the process of thinking. ¶I look at the mind as a traveler looks at the world. Himālayan Academy students have traveled with me all over the world, in hundreds of cities, in dozens of countries, as we've set up *ashrams* here and there on our

Innersearch Travel/Study programs. Together we have gone in and in and in and in amid different types of environments, but the inside is always the same wherever we are. So, look at the mind as the traveler looks at the world. ¶Just as you travel around the world, when you're in meditation you travel in the mind. We have the big city called thought. We have another big city called emotion. There's yet another big city called fear, and another one nearby called worry. But we are not those cities. We are just the traveler. When we're in San Francisco, we are not San Francisco. When we're aware of worry, we are not worry. We are just the inner traveler who has become aware of the different areas of the mind. ¶Of course, when we are aware in the thought area, we are not meditating. We're in the intellectual area of the mind. We have to breathe more deeply, control the breath more and move awareness out of the thought area of the mind, into that next inner area, where we begin to know. Such an experience supersedes thinking, and that is when meditation starts. I'm sure that you have experienced that many, many times. ¶Many people use meditation to become quieter, relaxed, or more concentrated. For them, that is the goal, and if that is the goal, that is what is attained, and it's attained quite easily. However, for the deeper philosophical student the goal is different. It's the realization of the Self in this life. Meditation is the conveyance of man's individual awareness toward that realization. Each one, according to his evolution, has his own particular goal. If he works at it, he fulfills that goal. For example, a musician playing the piano might be satisfied with being able to play simple, easy tunes to entertain himself and his friends. Yet, another musician more ambitious in the fine arts might want to play Bach and Beethoven. He would really have to work hard at it. He would have to be that much more dedicated, give up that much of his emotional life, intellectual life and put that much more time into it. So it is in meditation.

Tuesday
LESSON 254
Meditation Is a Fine Art

Meditation is a fine art and should be approached in the same way the fine arts are approached. That's the way we teach meditation at Himālayan Academy, as a fine art. The artist-teachers are not running after the students. You don't learn a fine art that way. You go to your teacher because you want to learn. You might go a long distance. You want to learn, and so you study. He gives you something to work on. You go away and you work on it, and you come back having perfected it. That's how we expect Academy students to progress along the path. Something has to happen on the inside, and it usually does. ¶Controlling the breath is the same as controlling awareness. They go hand in hand. During meditation, the breath, the heartbeat, metabolism—it all slows down, just like in sleep. You know, deep meditation and deep sleep are extremely similar. Therefore, the practice of *prāṇāyāma* and regulation of the breath, the *prāṇas,* the currents of the body, should really be mastered first. In the very same way, the dancer doesn't just start out dancing. He starts out exercising first. He may exercise strenuously for a year before he begins to really dance. The pianist doesn't sit down at the piano and start with a concert. He starts with the scales and with the chords. He starts by limbering his fingers, by perfecting his rhythm and posture. Meditation has to be taught like one of the fine arts. It's only the finely refined person who can really learn to meditate. Not everyone who wants to meditate can learn to meditate. Not everyone who wants to learn to dance or to play the piano can learn how to really, really do it. We need this preparation of the physical body so that the physical and emotional bodies behave themselves while you are in a deep state of meditation. ¶Your breath will slow down until you almost seem to stop breathing. Sometimes you do, and you're breathing with an inner breath. You have to educate yourself to that so it doesn't make you fearful and bring you out of meditation with a jerk and a gasp, which can then inhibit you. You can get fearful in meditation. So, good basics must be learned for one to become a deep meditator. You can spend hours or years working with the breath. Find a good teacher first, one who keeps it simple and gentle. You don't need to strain. Start simply by slowing the breath down. Breathe by moving the diaphragm instead of the chest. This is how children breathe, you know. So, be a child. If you learn to control the breath, you can be master of your awareness. ¶The sense of *bhakti yoga*, a sense of devotion, is extremely important on the path. Unless we have a great *bhakti*, a great devotion, we can easily be shaken from the spiritual path. It's the fuel that keeps us motivated. If we prepare our room before meditation by lighting an oil lamp or candle, a stick of incense, or only setting out a few fresh flowers, it puts us in a state of readiness; and for any serious thing that we do, we must prepare. If you're going to cook a fine meal for a special guest, you take a bath first. You prepare yourself; you get ready. You get mentally, emotionally and physically ready. Meditation is the same thing. Physical preparations have their effect on the mind and emotions, too, turning awareness within and creating a mood and environment where there are fewer distractions. If you would prepare for meditation as exactly and precisely as you prepare yourself in the external world to go to work every day, your meditations would be much improved.

Wednesday
LESSON 255
Thought, Diet And Desire

Devotees occasionally ask, "When you experience a thought you don't like, should you go around the thought, or go to the center of the thought and find out why you don't like it?" Look at thoughts as people. I see thoughts when I'm in the world of thought like a school of fish. I'm there in the ocean, sitting and looking, and a school of fish goes by, right in front of me. Well, look at thoughts as people. You are aware of other people, but you are not other people. You are just aware of other people. So, when you see someone you do not like, you don't have to do anything about it. Let him be. It's the same with thoughts. When a thought comes passing by that you don't like, let it go. You don't have to glue yourself onto it and psychoanalyze it; it doesn't do the thought any good to be psychoanalyzed by you! ¶A vegetarian diet is a big help on the spiritual path. Of course, it's only one of the helpers on the path. I've worked out a very simple look at food. I look at food in four ways. You have four types of food: fresh food, dead food, clean food and dirty food. Not necessarily all fresh food is clean food. Much fresh food that we get nowadays is dirty food, because food is like a sponge. It will sponge up into itself chemicals, smog and inorganic substances. These are harmful to the physical body, because the physical body is organic. So, the object of nutrition for meditation is to eat clean, fresh, organically grown food and to avoid eating dead, chemically grown, dirty food. Every time you have a delicious dinner in front of you, ask yourself the question, "Is this clean fresh food or dead dirty food? Or, is this clean dead food or is it fresh dirty food?" After that, have a wonderful dinner, if you can! Basically, we eat one-third fruits, nuts and seeds and two-thirds fresh vegetables, salads, grains and dairy products. Such a diet keeps the physical and emotional forces subtle and refined, which therefore makes meditation subtle and refined, too. The within is very refined. We always try to the best of our ability, and we're not finicky at all about watching the combination of foods. ¶We have talked before about desire and transmutation. The idea of transmuting one's desires really means becoming aware of something inside that you want even more than the external desires. Ultimately, man's greatest desire and urgency is for the realization of the Self in this life—the core of his Being. Realize that and live with it and enjoy it while on this planet. Once we intensify that desire, other desires become less intense, only because we are less aware of them. They are still intense for the people who are aware of them, because they still exist, right in the mind substance. ¶Here's a wonderful meditation that I think you will enjoy. It shows you how simple the mind can be. How many hairs are there on your head? Thousands, but there's only one hair in the total mind structure. People have thousands, and animals even have more, but basically there is only one hair. Think about that. There is only one eye. People have two, and so do animals. But study one eye and you know them all. There's only one tooth. People have a lot of them, and so do animals, but there is basically only one in the universe of the mind. Meditate on that and bring everything to the one. Then, when you get it all worked out—that there's only one hair, there's only one eye, there's only one tooth, there's only one fingernail, and there's only one of everything—start throwing those few things away. Throw away the tooth and make it disappear. Throw away the hair and make it disappear. This will take you right to the essence, the total essence of your being. Of course, probably your awareness will wander in the meantime, and you won't get through this meditation. But keep working at it and working at it and really make everything extremely simple. We look at the world with our two physical eyes and we see such a complexity that it's almost mind-boggling to encompass the entirety of it all. It's much simpler than that on the inside.

Thursday
LESSON 256
Energy and Meditation

Highly emotional states should be avoided by one who meditates. The reaction to the emotional experience is too strenuous for him to live with. It takes quite a while for that reaction to re-enact back through his nerve system. When one goes through an emotional state, it takes seventy-two hours for the basic emotional system to quiet and about one month for him to unwind out of the reaction to the action. So, he must really watch the emotions and keep that power very much under control. Therefore, one who meditates should not argue. One who meditates should not allow himself to become emotional. Then should he suppress his emotion? Well, if he is so emotional that he has to suppress his emotions, then he is not going to be meditating anyway, so we don't have to bother about it. ¶Let's intensify a few ideas about meditation. Put power into your meditation. Put power into your meditation so that whether you sit for five, ten or fifteen minutes a day, you go into meditation with full force and vigor. In this way, you come out of your meditation with something more profound than the thought or feeling you took within. You then begin to build up a tremendous, dynamic force, a reservoir within yourself which acts as a catalyst to push you on to contemplative states. A contemplative state of consciousness is by no means a passive state of consciousness. It is a very dynamic state of consciousness, so dynamic that the best you can do is to sit still without moving physically as you begin to enjoy it. Meditation, as you may know, is a very active state, where every thought and every feeling is directly under the flow of your will and cognition. Of course, we must remain relaxed also, being certain not to externalize our efforts, to become outwardly fanatical or pushy. There is an inner will and an outer will. We must use the inner will in our daily efforts to meditate. ¶Meditation does not have to be prolonged to accomplish what you want to gain in unfoldment through your perceptive insights. Ten to thirty minutes is enough in the beginning. However, after you have finished with a dynamic meditation, you might sit for a longer time in the bliss of your being and really enjoy yourself as the pure life energy radiates through your nervous system. Meditation is essentially work, good hard work, and you should be willing to work and expend energy so that you can meditate. *Karma yoga* activity, the ability to serve in the temple selflessly, whole-heartedly and accurately, is a must if you want seriously to amalgamate the instinctive forces that demand reward for work and be able to meditate with full force, vim and vigor. ¶There are many ways to prepare yourself for meditation. First, generate energy. Jump up and down, exercise, do knee bends, do push-ups and get your mind active and interested in something. It is impossible to meditate unless you are interested in what you are meditating on. Perhaps you have found this out. Then sit down dynamically. Close your eyes. Breathe, keeping your spine straight and head balanced at the top of the spine. The spine is the powerhouse of the body. Feel the power of it. Now go full force into the challenge you have chosen to take into meditation. Observe, investigate, elucidate and stay within. Keep your body motionless until you bring out something more than you intellectually knew before, a new observation or a new thought sequence. Your meditations cannot be a milk-toast state of consciousness, a passive-magnetic state of mind.

Friday
LESSON 257
Overcoming Karma

Seekers ask, "How can I stay awake when I meditate? I fall asleep almost every time. This happens even during the day. It's terrible." The answer is, it is absolutely impossible to go to sleep while in meditation and still call it meditation. It is possible to put the body to sleep deliberately and then go into meditation. If you catch yourself dropping off to sleep while sitting for meditation, you know that your meditation period is over. The best thing to do is to deliberately go to sleep, because the spiritual power is gone and has to be invoked or opened up again. After getting ready for bed, sit in a meditative position and have a dynamic meditation for as long as you can. When you become sleepy, you may put yourself to sleep by deliberately relaxing the body and causing the *prāṇas* to flow. Mentally say: "*Prāṇa* in the left leg, flow, go to sleep; *prāṇa* in the right leg, flow, go to sleep; *prāṇa* in the right arm, flow, go to sleep; *prāṇa* in the left arm, flow, go to sleep; torso actinodic *prāṇa,* flow, go to sleep; head with inner light, go to sleep." Then the first thing you know, it is morning. ¶How does meditation affect one's *karmas*? *Karma* is congested magnetic forces, and meditating is rising above *karmic* binding influences. You can control the congestion of *karma* or avoid the congestion and thus control your *karma.* This proves to yourself that you are the creator, the one who preserves and the destroyer simultaneously on the higher levels of consciousness. Yet, you have to come back occasionally to the "little old you" on this level and do the things that you have been accustomed to doing as a human, until you fully have the complete realization of the Self God—the *emkaef* experience. Then you penetrate the doors of the Absolute into the core of existence itself, and you become the Self that everyone is searching for. But to overcome *karmic* patterns, the will must be tremendously strong and stable, and that means we must demand perfection in our life. ¶Why would you ever want to place demands of perfection upon yourself? You now walk the path of perfection, and you must be so to walk that path. What is this perfection? First, it is a clarity of cognition. Second, it is a bursting of actinic love for your fellow man. Third, it is an openness and willingness to serve and fit in, in any capacity. Fourth, it is living a contemplative lifestyle better every day. Fifth, it is mastering all of your *yoga* disciplines given to you by your *guru*. Sixth, it is the ability to hold responsibility, maintain a continuity of your own *karma yoga*, yet have the mobile quality to be ever ready to do something different without losing continuity of what you have been doing in holding your responsibility. ¶If you can gear yourself to accomplish all this, you are on the path of enlightenment and you will surely prove to yourself, when you have your realization, that you are a free man in a free world, subject to nobody, to no power, even the power of *karma*. How could That which is formless and causeless be subject to anything?

Saturday
LESSON 258
Finding Your Guru

I am often asked, "When one feels it's time to travel the spiritual path, do you recommend he aggressively seek a *guru* or passively wait and see what happens?" When one is ready to swim, should he walk around the swimming pool, or should he dive in and get on with it? Naturally, he should dive in and take each thing that comes along in a very positive way. That is the thing to do. Otherwise, in waiting and putting it into the intellectual mind, all the different doubts come up and make a big fog which again he has to live through. He missed his timing. ¶The *guru*-disciple relationship is so central in Hinduism. A *guru* is a helper on the inner path. Visualize a rocky stream path leading up a high mountain. The *guru* is there to help you over some big boulders and through the swamps and to send out a scout to help you back on the inner path if you become externalized. You don't need a *satguru* all the time. Most of it you have to do yourself, after you have his grace and learn the rules. But, he is there when you need him inwardly; he is just there, and that is reassuring. Do everything that you possibly can for your *guru.* The *guru* is like the wind. You may not always have him as close to you, so throw yourself into his work selflessly. He has a mission that came to him from his *guru* and his *guru's guru.* It is your mission in this life, too, realization of the Self God within and helping others do the same. ¶I have been asked many times, "How does one choose a *guru*?" Well, if you are in a crowd of people and you hadn't seen your mother and father for five or ten years, you would immediately know them. You could pick them out of a large crowd. You'd immediately know. Not necessarily by how they looked, but by the vibration. You'd immediately know. And so it is with the *guru.* There are, shall we say, commercial *gurus.* Pick a *guru.* Here a *guru*, there a *guru.* A *guru*, in the classical sense of the word, doesn't have a great many devotees. He might have a lot of people who think he's really great, especially if he chants well or does something that is outstanding. It's easy to get a lot of followers. Traditionally, a *guru* can only take a few close disciples, and he generally does. ¶If you're looking for a *guru*, try to feel his vibration. Better still, talk to his students to see if they have any substance. Ask them, "Have you had any inner experience?" If they start talking about everything, telling you all about it or try to convert you, be cautious. On the other hand, if they look content within themselves and test you out a little to see if you're sincere, you know that they're taught to be wise. Look at the students. See how they interact among themselves. Observe closely what they do. Note how well disciplined they are. In this way, you get to know the caliber of the man who is their *satguru.* Find out who his *guru* is and where the line of *darshan* power comes from. Then you get to know, to really know. Don't be too hasty in picking your *guru.* That is the best advice. Maybe it's not for you in this life to have a *guru.* Maybe next life or the life after that. There's no hurry, and yet there is a great sense of urgency on the spiritual path, a great sense of urgency. Don't go hunting for a *guru.* Just be alert enough to know when you encounter him. ¶How does one know whether an inner experience is real or imaginary? Well, we don't have to go very far in answering that question because everyone has inner experiences. Two people are in love. They fight. They separate. That's an inner experience. And it's real, isn't it? That emotion, that tearing apart, those wonderful mental arguments where nobody quite wins—they're all real. Even such an argument is an inner experience, but of a more externalized, instinctive-intellectual or gross nature. Yet, it's very real. It shakes the muscles. It can even make us perspire. It lives within us. It could keep us awake at night or give us disturbing dreams. It's a real and a vital experience. We have to go through these grosser inner experiences first before our inner life becomes more refined. They are just as real—seeing light within the body, light within the head and hearing the inner sounds. All of the things you have read about come to you after you have gone through the inner experiences of the instinctive and intellectual mind. First we go through our inner instinctive experiences, then our intellectual experiences, then our intuitive or creative experiences. Finally, we come to the Self, which we realize is the totality of all inner experiences, being beyond experience itself.

Sunday
LESSON 259
Going Into Meditation

The refined, inner energy that you experience in your deepest meditations is always there, was always there and shall always be there. It's just there. You don't have to call upon it. It's just there. Just be aware that you are it, and not that you are any other of the many other types of things that you can be. Just be that intangible, tangible energy and don't be the emotions that you feel. Don't be thoughts that you think. Don't be the stomach that's hungry. Don't be the body that's moving. Don't be the place that you're going to. Just be that energy. Then you can do anything in the external world and really enjoy life. ¶Here are some basic signposts for successful meditation. Remember them and do them slowly on your own. First, sit up nice and straight with the spine erect and the head balanced at the top of the spine. Proper posture is necessary because the very simple act of equalizing the weight and having it held up by the spine causes you to lose body consciousness. Just the equalizing of your weight can do that. Breathe deeply and rhythmically. Feel the energies of the body begin to flow harmoniously through the body. Now, try to feel the warmth of the body. Simply feel the warmth of the body. Once you can sense physical warmth, try to feel the totality of the nerve system at one time—all of the five or six thousand miles of nerve currents. It's simple. Feel it all at one time and grasp that intuitively. Now, this nerve current is being energized from one central source, and we're going to find that source. It's in the central core of the spine. Feel that energy flow through the spine and out through this nerve system, which finally causes warmth in the physical body, which you've already felt. But now don't feel the warmth of the body. Don't feel the nerve system. Feel only the power of the spine. Once you have done this, you are ready to meditate. You're alive in your body. You look alive. You look vital. Your face is beginning to glow. Next, simply sit in a state of pure consciousness. Be aware of being aware. Don't be aware of a second thing. Simply be aware that you are aware—a totality of dynamic, scintillating awareness, vibrant right in the central source of energy. It's closer to what you really are than your name, than your intellectual education, than your emotional behavior or the physical body itself, which you only inhabit. From this point in your own personal meditation, you can take off and travel in many different directions. If your *guru* has given you a *mantra*, for instance, contemplate on the inner vibrations of the *mantra*. Chant it to yourself, or follow whatever inner instructions he has given you. ¶Coming out of meditation, we perform this process in reverse. Again feel the power of the spine and let that power flow right out through the nerve system, energizing the miles and miles of nerve currents. Feel your nerve system coming to life. Feel the warmth of the body as we come back into physical consciousness. Finally, open your eyes and view the external world around you and compare it to the internal world that you very rapidly just touched into in your meditation. It's easy to remember this entrance and exit to meditation. Do it often. Get to know the energy flows of the body. Live in the pure energy of the spine. Lean on no one. If you must lean on something, make it your own spine.

Merudaṇḍa Śaktayaḥ

मेरुदण्डशक्तयः

Powers of the Spine

When the breaths of *iḍā*-moon and *piṅgalā*-sun course their way unhindered through the spinal channel, your body will be imperishable, and abiding joys shall arise even here in this world below. This is the true way of Śiva *yoga.*

TIRUMANTIRAM 883

Monday
LESSON 260
The Iḍā and Piṅgalā Currents

In the esoterics of unfoldment on the path of enlightenment, there are some mechanics about what happens inside of the human body, its nerve system, that you should know about. There are two basic forces working within the body, as I have explained, the instinctive area of the mind and the intellectual area of the mind. Within these are two forces working that flow out from the central source of energy through their respective currents. They are called the *iḍā* and the *piṅgalā* forces. ¶The *iḍā* current is pink in color. It is the vibration of the physical body. It is the Earth current. When the energy is flowing through that current, or *nāḍī*, we are more conscious of the physical body, or more in physical consciousness. We are not in the world of thought but in the world of feeling. We feel very strongly and experience very strong emotions when the energy is flowing through the *iḍā* current. ¶In some people the energy flows through the *iḍā* current constantly. They have very strong emotions and deep sentiments. They live in their emotion most of the time, emoting over one thing or another. They emotionally and deeply feel through this *iḍā* current how other people feel. They take other people's feeling onto themselves and have a preoccupation with their physical bodies. This is the current that can produce another human being in a woman, or develop athletic abilities in a man. ¶When the vibratory force of energy flows through the *iḍā* current, the entire physical body responds. It is physically active. We like to work. We like to move. We like to exercise. We like to do things. We enjoy equally the base emotions and the movements of the physical body. ¶When the energy flows through *iḍā* in some people, they actually enjoy suffering. There are people deep in this current who if they did not have something to suffer over would not feel whole. They would feel they were not living fully enough on this planet. They would not feel human, for the *iḍā* current is the current of being human. It is very base. It is very earthy. Still, those living in this current are intuitive. They do have intuition, but their intuition conflicts with their heavy emotion, so intuition comes through periodically, in intuitive flashes. They may even become superstitious because of this. The *iḍā* current flows most strongly through the left side of the physical body. ¶The *piṅgalā* current is quite different. Blue in color, it is the current of the intellect, flowing mostly through the right side of the body. When the pure life energy is flowing through the *piṅgalā* current, we are not as conscious that we have a physical body. We are aware in the mind. We are inquisitive. We like to talk a lot. We like to argue. We like to reason. We enjoy discussion. It is the intellectual current. We like to read. We like to memorize the opinions of other people. We like to memorize our own opinions and tell them to other people. We like to do business. When the energy is flowing through the *piṅgalā,* we do not emote much. We think over our emotions. We analyze our feelings and thoughts. This is the aggressive human current. ¶People living in this current do not pay much attention to the physical body. They let it take care of itself. They also are inclined to let other people do the emoting. They become powerfully strong in that aggressive type of intellectual force. When we are in the *piṅgalā* current, we are headstrong, somewhat pushy, pushing ideas across to other people, and inclined to be argumentative. We have a strong facility of reasoning. It is a very positive and powerful current.

Tuesday
LESSON 261
The Spine's Central Energy

Once in either current for a long time, it is difficult to flow awareness out of it. There are some people who are predominantly *piṅgalā,* aggressive in nature and strong in their human elements in that area. There are some people who are predominantly *iḍā,* human, physical and earthy, and full of feeling. And there are some who switch from one to the other. These are the more rounded and well-adjusted type of people, who can move awareness through the *piṅgalā* current and through the *iḍā* current and adjust the energies almost at will. ¶We have still another basic strong current that you should know about. It is called *sushumṇā.* Within this massive current are fourteen other smaller currents which govern the instinctive, intellectual, conscious, subconscious, sub of the subconscious, subsuperconscious and superconscious areas of the mind. The *iḍā* and the *piṅgalā* are two of these fourteen, so this leaves twelve more within the *sushumṇā.* ¶When we begin a religious pilgrimage or retreat into *sādhana* and we want awareness to dive deep within, we have to withdraw the energy of the vibrating *iḍā* and the vibrating *piṅgalā* current into *sushumṇā.* This is quite a chore, because these currents have had energy flowing in them for a number of years. So, to rechannel that energy is to rechannel the entire circumference of awareness into the *sushumṇā* current. This takes a lot of practice. ¶Breathing, of course, is a major function of control here. *Haṭha yoga* is a major function, too. Sitting in the lotus position conquers a great deal of the *iḍā* current. The practices of concentration and observation conquer a great deal of the *piṅgalā* current. Some good, solid study that disciplines awareness, such as the study of math, music or a skill, moves awareness into the *piṅgalā* and helps balance these two currents. ¶Then the next step is to bring awareness into *sushumṇā.* This is the path. However, if awareness is flowing through the *piṅgalā* current already and is extremely aggressive, that means the entire nature of the individual is extremely aggressive, intellectual, and it is extremely difficult for him to withdraw those energies into the *sushumṇā* current. Why? Because he will argue within himself mentally and reason himself out of it. He will simply go to another book, or have a different intellectual look at it, or go to another teacher, or watch television instead, or go to another lecture. He will never quite get around to bringing in this aggressive *piṅgalā* energy from the intellect back to its source, *sushumṇā,* so that he can go within and experience superconscious realms of the inner mind consciously. ¶These two forces, the *iḍā* and the *piṅgalā,* are the big challenges. They are what makes a person "human" in the popular sense of the word. It is the degree of energy that flows through the areas of the *iḍā* and *piṅgalā* that forms one's nature, his actions, reactions and responses. The areas of his external personality are governed by these two currents.

Wednesday
LESSON 262
Withdrawing Into Sushumṇā

How do you bring about a balance? It is done by regular practice of the five steps. Choose a time to withdraw deliberately the energies from both the *iḍā* and *piṅgalā* currents and to move awareness into *su-*

shumṇā in a very positive way. In the morning when you awaken and at night before you sleep are the best times. Breathe regularly, the same number of counts in and out. Sit in the lotus posture. When you sit in the lotus posture, you are actually short-circuiting the *iḍā* current to a certain extent. When you are breathing regularly, through the control of the breath, you are short-circuiting the *piṅgalā* current to a certain extent. Then, when awareness flows into the core of energy within the spine, you soon become consciously conscious of the *sushumṇā* current. At that point, awareness is within and begins immediately to draw upon all the externalized energies of the body, and these two psychic currents are drawn within to their source. ¶When we chant the mantra *Aum,* and do it correctly, we pronounce the AA so that it vibrates the physical body. The OO has to vibrate through the throat area, and the MM, the head. In doing this, we are deliberately moving awareness out of the *mūlādhāra* and *svādhishṭhāna chakras,* deliberately harmonizing all the forces of the instinct and physical body, and of the *iḍā* and the *piṅgalā* currents. Chanting the AA and the OO and the MM brings the *sushumṇā* into power. We are transmuting and changing the flows of all the energies through the physical and astral body and blending them as much as possible into the body of the soul. ¶The mantra *Aum* can be chanted at any time. It can be chanted silently and cause the same vibration through the body. When you chant Aum, the *iḍā* and the *piṅgalā* blend back into the *sushumṇā.* ¶You will actually see this happening. You will see the pink *iḍā* current begin to blend back into the golden center of the spine. At other times it is seen winding through the body. The same happens with the *piṅgalā* force. It, too, moves back into the spine, until you are all spine when you are centered in the *sushumṇā.* This is how it feels, like being all spine. This beautiful, pure energy flows out through the *sushumṇā* and the *iḍā* and the *piṅgalā* and then on out through the body. This energy becomes changed as it flows through the first three or four *chakras.* It makes what is called *prāṇa.* This energy runs in and through the body. It is a great mind energy which is in the world of thought. All the stratas of thought are *prāṇa.* The human aura is *prāṇa.* ¶*Prāṇa,* or odic force, is transferred from one person to another through touch, as in a handshake, or through a look. It is the basic force of the universe, and the most predominate force found within the body. You have to really study *prāṇa* to get a good understanding of what it is. It runs in and through the skin, through the bone structure, through the physical body and around the body. ¶Breath controls *prāṇa.* This practice is called *prāṇāyāma.* It is the control of *prāṇa,* the regulation of *prāṇa,* or the withdrawal of *prāṇa* from the external world back to its primal source. That is why *prāṇāyāma* is so important to practice systematically, regularly, day after day, so we get all the *prāṇa* into a rhythm. In this way we get a rhythm of the pure life force flowing through *iḍā, piṅgalā* and *sushumṇā* and out through the aura. We gain a rhythm of awareness soaring inward, into refined states of the *ājñā chakra* and *sahasrāra chakra,* the perspective areas from which we are looking out at life as if we were the center of the universe. This is how we feel when we are in these *chakras.*

Thursday
LESSON 263
An Exercise in Energy Balance

Control of the *prāṇa* is also guided through nutrition. Food and air contain a great deal of *prāṇa. Prāṇa* is transferred from one person to another, from a person to a plant, from a plant to a person. It is the life of the world of form. We should eat types of food that contain a great deal of *prāṇa* so that we are making *prāṇa* ourselves. Consider the physical body as a temple, with plumbing and electricity. To maintain this temple, watch what you eat and be conscious of the areas where you flow awareness in the world of thought. The vibration of certain thoughts upsets the nerve system of this physical-body temple. Also, be careful of the people that you mix with, so that their awareness and vibrations do not pull your awareness into unwholesome areas and the vibrations of their aura do not affect your temple. This is extremely important to observe, especially during the first few years of unfoldment. ¶When we are in ideal surroundings, in the shrine room of our own home, we can balance the passive and active currents of the body—the *iḍā* and *piṅgalā* forces. First, do this simple *prāṇāyāma.* Breathe easily, in and out, in an even rhythm, say, four heartbeats to the inhalation and four heartbeats to the exhalation. This steady rhythm will soon begin to balance the *iḍā* and *piṅgalā.* ¶As the *piṅgalā* force becomes quieted and regulated, you will hear a ringing about an inch above the right ear. This is the sound of the nerve current of the *piṅgalā nāḍī.* And as the *iḍā* force becomes quieted and regulated, you will hear a ringing about an inch above the left ear. This is the nerve sound of the *iḍā nāḍī,* slightly different from the tone of the *piṅgalā nāḍī.* The direction of energy flow in the *piṅgalā nāḍī* is up, whereas the *iḍā nāḍī* flows downward. When the energy in the two *nāḍīs* is balanced, a circle is formed, creating a force field in which the *sushumṇā nāḍī* is regulated. ¶Now, to bring the *sushumṇā* force into power, listen to both tones simultaneously. It may take you about five minutes to hear both tones at the same time. Next, follow both tonal vibrations from the ears into the center of the cranium, where they will meet and blend into a slightly different sound, as two notes, say, a "C" and an "E," blend into a chord. The energy of the *nāḍīs* is then flowing in a circle, and you will enter the golden yellow light of the *sushumṇā* current. Play with this light and bask in its radiance, for in it is your bloom. The unfoldment progresses from a golden yellow to a clear white light. Should you see a blue light, know that you are in the *piṅgalā* current. If you see a pink light, that is the color of the *iḍā*. Just disregard them and seek for the white light in the tone of the combined currents until finally you do not hear the tone anymore and you burst into the clear white light. Thus you enter *savikalpa samādhi—samādhi* with seed, or consciousness, which is the culmination of this particular practice of contemplation. ¶After doing this for a period of time, you will find that you lose interest in the exterior world. It will seem transparent and unreal to you. When this happens, you have to learn to bring your consciousness back through meditation, deliberately into the processes of inner knowing and thought, and back into the exterior world through concentration. It requires a deliberate concentration then to make the exterior world seem real again to you. ¶Now is the time for devotees who have worked diligently in concentration and meditation and in clearing up personal problems to enjoy their *yoga* and be happy in their attainments, to enjoy the bliss that is their heritage on Earth.

Friday
LESSON 264
The High "eee" Sound

Within the quantum level of consciousness there originates a vibration, a steady vibration, that can be heard with the inner ear as a high-pitched "eeeee," as if a thousand *vīṇās* were playing, as if all the nerve currents in the astral body, physical body and the body of the soul were singing in harmony. It is a divine combination of the *iḍā* and *piṅgalā* tones blended together in the *sushumṇā.* Each lineage of *gurus* has embedded within the psyche of tradition a certain combination of sounds, and that listening to this mystic sound holds all devotees close to their *satguru* and all those who preceded him. It is also said that when one is in another birth, the sound is the same, and this will eventually lead the aspirant back to his spiritual lineage. Listening to the *nāda,* as it is called in Sanskṛit, or *nāda-nāḍī śakti,* brings the threshold of bliss and shows that the balance of all *karmas* has been attained. Listening to the *nāda* and tracing it into its source carries the seeker's awareness to the brink of the Absolute. There are today mystical orders that do nothing but listen to the *nāda* while looking at and enjoying the *darshan* of their *guru's* picture. ¶Many sincere seekers wonder why they cannot hear "eeeeee," the *nāda,* during their meditation, whereas others not only hear it during meditation but during the day when talking, shopping or just meandering through the garden. This is to say, it is there when awareness enters that area of the mind. The mind has to be made empty. That means resolving all unresolved conflicts within the subconscious. The striving to hear the *nāda* will bring up unresolved issues. They may plague the conscious mind until resolved. At first you might disregard them and feel they will go away as abruptly as they came. But later, when they persist, and the major one is deception—yes, we can even deceive ourselves—we are inwardly forced to face up to, admit our secrets and make amends. When deception goes, the *nāda* comes. When the subconscious is heavy, the *nāda* and the brilliant colors it radiates fade. Failure on the path puts the *nāda* out of range of the inner ear of the soul. ¶The mystical *nāda,* it's a medley of sounds, and each sound which is there has a color, but may be covered, as is the light of the mind of the soul, the clear white light. It is covered, but not permanently. Admittance of the mistakes, the experience of repentance and the performance of penance, called *prāyaśchitta,* lay the foundation for a reconciliation that will release the force of lower nature into the higher and uncloud the veil that hid the inner light, that hid the *nāda*—that incomprehensible high-pitched "eee," sounding within the head, that incomparable source of inner security, contentment and outpouring of love. When you hear the *nāda,* endeavor to project it in love's outpouring to all those who are in your orbit of communication. They will feel the blessings when your divine love is projected through your *nāda* into their *nāda.* This is the height of selfless consciousness, universal love, a constant mystically outpouring and experience of oneness. The *sushumṇā* is *nāda* and more. *Nāda śakti* is. It just is.

Saturday
LESSON 265
Kuṇḍalinī, the Spiritual Force

Haṭha yoga (ha-piṅgalā and *ṭha-iḍā)* balances the two forces, the *iḍā* and the *piṅgalā.* The straight, erect spine releases the *actinodic* flow of the *sushumṇā* current. The mind centered in the contemplative atmosphere, cognizing timelessness, causelessness, spacelessness while sitting in the lotus position, awakens the pineal and pituitary centers, and the door of Brahman at the top of the head. ¶The force of the *actinodic* causal body, the sheath of cognition, *vijñānamaya kośa,* a pure actinic force running through the *sushumṇā* current, is called the *kuṇḍalinī.* As this *kuṇḍalinī* force becomes activated, the *sushumṇā* power begins to grow, or the *actinodic* causal body begins to grow, and the higher *chakras* of cognition and universal love begin to spin faster. Once *kuṇḍalinī* power has been activated, its force expands or contracts consciousness. As man's consciousness expands into actinic spheres, more *kuṇḍalinī* power is used. This power is lessened as his consciousness emerges into the limited fields of the odic world. ¶Often known as the serpent power, the *kuṇḍalinī* is coiled at the base of the spine in the instinctive man who resides mostly in the force fields of memory and fear. When this power becomes uncoiled, the serpent, or *kuṇḍalinī,* luminously raises its head, and finally, after *nirvikalpa samādhi,* it lifts its power to the top of the head. ¶When *nirvikalpa samādhi* has been practiced daily for many, many years—according to the classical *yoga* teachings, for twelve years—and the golden body has been built, the *kuṇḍalinī* force coils itself in the *sahasrāra chakra* of the *yogī,* at the top of the head. This is known as the *manas chakra,* located about where the hairline begins at the forehead. This *chakra* eventually becomes the *mūlādhāra chakra*, or the memory-pattern *chakra*, of the golden body. The *manas chakra* is fully activated when the golden body is fully unfolded. This is known in Hindu and Egyptian mystic schools as the golden body of light, for it registers in the minds of those who look upon it, to their soul body, as a golden ball of light or a golden body.¶When the *kuṇḍalinī* rises into the realms of pure actinicity, the pineal gland and pituitary center are activated. When these two centers are activated simultaneously, the forces of both of them merge, bringing man into *nirvikalpa samādhi.* Therefore, the aggressive odic force merges with the passive odic force, in perfect balance, and the *actinodic* power of the *sushumṇā* current comes into perfect balance, poised with the *kuṇḍalinī* force. The *yoga* adept finds himself on the brink of the Absolute, cognizing That which he cannot explain, knowing there is something beyond which the mind does not know, conceiving That which cannot be conceived, because form, which is mind, cannot conceive formlessness. Then the *yogī* touches into the Self and becomes a knower of the Self, merges with Śiva. ¶When the *iḍā, piṅgalā* and *sushumṇā* forces merge and reside in perfect balance, the third eye awakens. When the pituitary, pineal glands and the *sushumṇā* source are in perfect balance, man is able to perceive consciously into other worlds of the mind. The golden body, as it begins to grow after the renunciate, or *sannyāsin,* attains *nirvikalpa samādhi,* is built by man's service to his fellow man.

Sunday
LESSON 266
The Way After Realization

When a *yoga guru* brings others from darkness into light and from light into Self Realization, he is also strengthening his own golden body. When a *satguru* makes it easy for his *sannyāsins* to remain in the practice of Self Realization, encouraging them and demanding of them the practice of *nirvikalpa samādhi,* he helps them hold their forces in check through the power of his golden body. ¶After *nirvikalpa samādhi,* the *sannyāsin* has a choice to serve mankind or to wait for mankind to unfold into the consciousness that he has attained. This is called being a *bodhisattva* or *upadeśī,* one who serves, or an *arahat* or *nirvāṇi,* one who waits. The golden body begins to grow through service and by bringing others into enlightenment as a *bodhisattva,* or through the constant practice of *nirvikalpa samādhi* while living a strictly secluded life as an *arahat,* only mixing with those of his own level of realization. ¶The *sahasrāra chakra* at the top of the head and the *ājñā chakra* at the brow, or the third eye, are the two controlling force centers of the soul body. These force centers become the two lowest *chakras* of the *yoga* master's new golden body, *svarṇaśarīra,* as this body begins to build after his first *nirvikalpa samādhi.* ¶The usual experience before *nirvikalpa samādhi* is for the aspirant to become a knower of the Self. This could occur at any time during his training. In order to attain this experience of "touching into the Self," he must have a complete balance of all odic and actinic forces within him. A noted change in his life pattern often occurs after he becomes a knower of the Self, for the soul body has become released into orbit, and he has then a subsuperconscious control of this body. In other words, the odic-force tie has been released. This body has quickly matured. Then, if practicing contemplation as prescribed by his *satguru* and finally working out the various *karmic* binds or holds in the lower odic force field with the help of the *guru,* he attains complete Self Realization, or *nirvikalpa samādhi.* Then the golden body, *svarṇaśarīra,* is born through the merging of the forces of the pituitary and the pineal gland, setting the *sahasrāra* into a constant spinning motion. This constant spinning motion generates the force which propels the *yoga* adept back into *nirvikalpa samādhi.* Each time he goes into *nirvikalpa samādhi* he intensifies a little the spinning movement of this *chakra,* unfolding it a little more, and as this occurs, the golden body begins to build. ¶When the *yoga* adept touches into the Self and becomes a knower of the Self, attains *nirvikalpa samādhi,* becomes Self Realized, *yoga* powers come to him. These *yoga* powers are often renounced, depending upon the rule of the order to which he belongs, whether it be a teaching order or an order of hermits. According to the need, a power is developed. The powers that a *yogī* can use are as many as the petals within the *sahasrāra chakra.* They are 1,008. These powers are conceived through the *nāḍīs*—small, elastic-like psychic nerve currents extending out into and through the aura of the body. The *nāḍīs* work in conjunction with the *chakras,* and with the major currents of the body, *iḍā, piṅgalā* and *sushumṇā.* ¶Remember, when the *kuṇḍalinī* force becomes strong within you during a meditation, just sit and be aware that you are aware, a blissful state called *kaef* in Shum, the language of meditation. You will feel very positive and experience yourself as a great, big ball of energy. When the energy begins to wane, try to absorb it into every cell of your external body, then continue your meditation exactly where you left off. In this way you will build a strong, disciplined nerve system and subconscious mind. This will lead you naturally onto the next inner plateau, then to the next and the next. ¶Never allow yourself to be complacent in your spiritual attainments. Always continue to strive. Even *ṛishis, swāmīs* and *yogīs* who have totally realized Paraśiva continue to work on themselves from within themselves. They don't let down, because if they did it would be many years before they had the next experience of the timelessness, formlessness, spacelessness of the unspeakable Paraśiva experience. The message, therefore, is, at the beginning of meditation and at the end, keep striving. Don't turn back, but proceed with confidence.

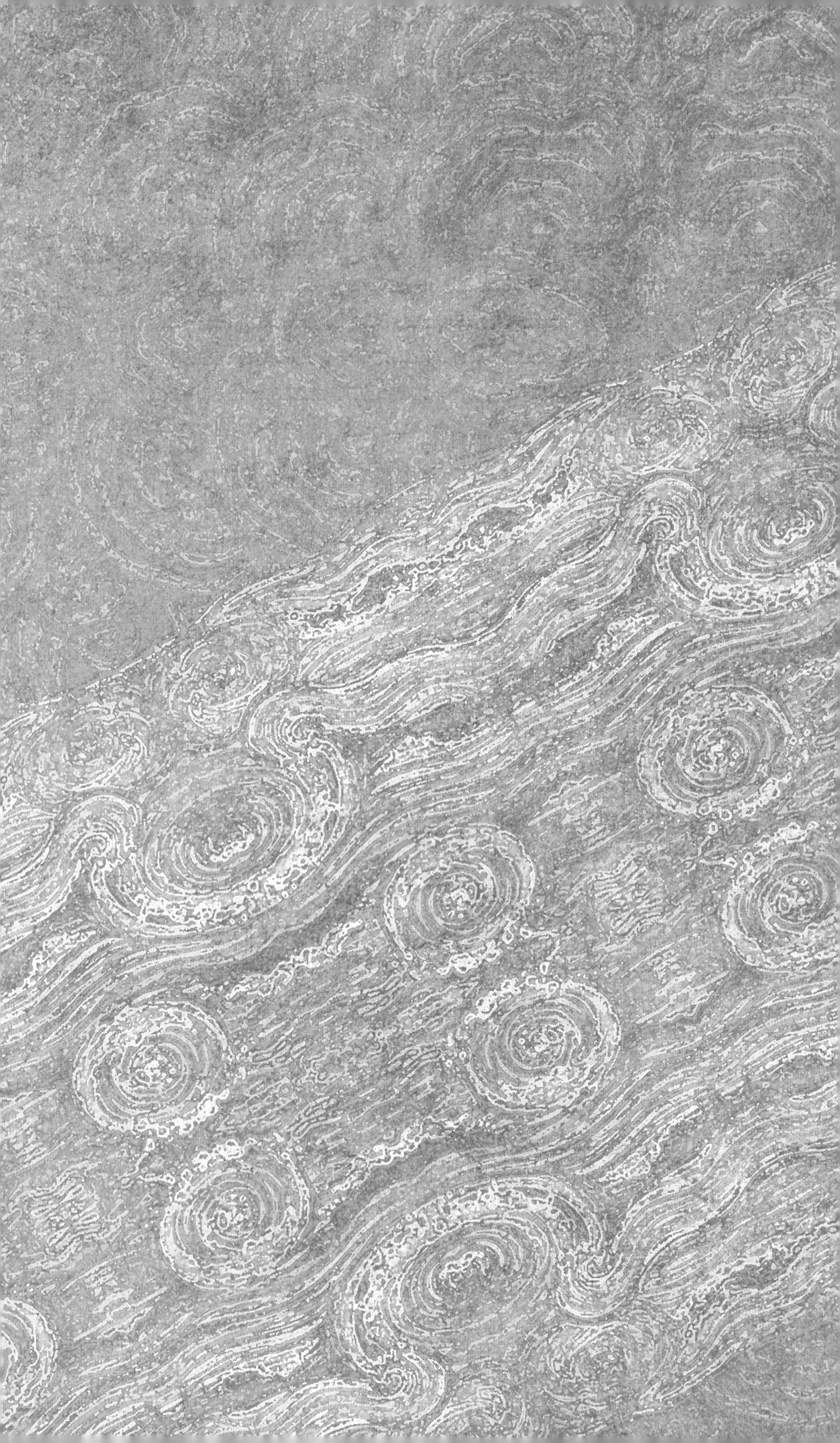

Tyāgajīvanam Paddhatidvayaṁ cha

त्यागजीवनं पद्धतिद्वयं च

Renunciate Life And the Two Paths

He is *dharma.* He is birthless and kinless. He abides in the wilds, living by alms. He has renounced all, and to all those who renounce, He destroys their bonds of birth. You unknowing ones, know this.

TIRUMANTIRAM 1616

Monday
LESSON 267
Distinguishing The Two Paths

There are two traditional paths for the devout Hindu of nearly every lineage. The first is the path of the renunciate. The second is the path of the householder, who guides human society and produces the next generation. The ancient *ṛishis* evolved well-defined principles for both, knowing that unmarried aspirants would most easily unfold by adhering to principles of nonownership, noninvolvement in the world and *brahmacharya,* while married men and women would uphold the more complex and material family *dharma.* Though the principles or guidelines for these two paths are different, the goal is the same—to establish a life dedicated to spiritual unfoldment, hastening the evolution of the soul through knowledge of the forces at work within us, and wise, consistent application of that knowledge. ¶In our *Holy Orders of Sannyāsa,* the two lifestyles of Hindu renunciates are described as follows. "Some among them are *sādhus,* anchorites living in the seclusion of distant caves and remote forests or wandering as homeless mendicants, itinerant pilgrims to the holy sanctuaries of Śaivism. Others dwell as cenobites, assembled with their brothers, often in the *ashram, aadheenam* or *maṭha* of their *satguru,* but always under the *guru's* aegis, serving together in fulfillment of a common mission. These devotees, when initiated into the order of *sannyāsa,* don the saffron robes and thereby bind themselves to a universal body of Hindu renunciates, numbering today three million, whose existence has never ceased, an assembly of men inwardly linked in Śivasambandha, their mutual dedication to Śiva, though not necessarily outwardly associated." ¶We can thus see that in the strictest traditions, the renunciate path includes only those who have received initiation, *sannyāsa dīkshā,* from a qualified preceptor, for only they have fully and irrevocably renounced the world and closed off all other options for their future. However, depending on the tradition, the renunciate path broadly includes the wandering *sādhu,* or homeless mendicant, and the *sādhaka* under vows preparing for *sannyāsa* at some future time. ¶We have studied the three primary currents in the human nerve system. The aggressive-intellectual current is masculine, mental in nature and psychically seen as blue in color. This current is termed in Sanskṛit *piṅgalā.* The passive-physical current is feminine, material in nature. This current, which is pink or red, is known as *iḍā.* The third current is spiritual in nature and flows directly through the spine and into the head. Being yellowish-white, the *sushumṇā,* as it is called, is the channel for pure spiritual energies that flood into the body through the spine and out into the 6,000 miles of nerve currents. Depending on the nature and *dharma,* each individual's energy expresses itself as predominantly physical or intellectual—passive or aggressive—or spiritual. However, in the *sannyāsin* the two forces are so precisely balanced that neither is dominant, and he therefore lives almost totally in *sushumṇā.* The monastic, whether a monk or a nun, is in a sense neither male nor female, but a being capable of all modes of expression. ¶At times, the renunciate's *sādhana* is austere, as he burns layer after layer of dross through severe *tapas.* He wears the saffron robe, studies the ancient ways and scriptures. He chants the sacred *mantras.* He reflects constantly on the Absolute.

He lives from moment to moment, day to day. He is always available, present, open. He has neither likes nor dislikes, but clear perceptions.

Tuesday
LESSON 268
The Meaning Of Renunciation

Having stepped out of his ego shell, the *sannyāsin* is a free soul. Nothing binds him. Nothing claims him. Nothing involves him. Without exclusive territory, without limiting relationships, he is free to be himself totally. If he has problems within himself, he keeps them silently within and works them out there. If he speaks, it is only to say what is true, kind, helpful or necessary. He never argues, debates, complains. His words and his life always affirm, never negate. He finds points of agreement, forsaking contention and difference. No man is his enemy. No man is his friend. All men are his teachers. Some teach him what to do; others teach him what not to do. He has no one to rely upon except God, Gods, *guru* and the power within his own spine. He is strong, yet gentle. He is aloof, yet present. He is enlightened, yet ordinary. He teaches the basic philosophy of monistic theism, or nondual Reality. He speaks wisely of the Vedic scriptures and ancient *śāstras* and lives them in his own example. Yet, he consciously remains inconspicuous, transparent. ¶He is a man on the path of enlightenment who has arrived at a certain subsuperconscious state and wishes to stay there. Therefore, he automatically has released various interactions with the world, physically and emotionally, and remains poised in a contemplative, monastic lifestyle. The basic thought behind the philosophy of being a *sannyāsin* is to put oneself in a hot-house condition of self-imposed discipline, where unfoldment of the spirit can be catalyzed at a greater intensity than in family life, where the exterior concerns and overt responsibilities of the world predominate. ¶The *sannyāsin* is the homeless one who remains detached from all forms of involvement—friends, family, personal ambition—finding security in his own being rather than attaching himself to outward manifestations of security, warmth and companionship. He is alone, but never lonely. He lives as though on the eve of his departure, often abiding no more than three nights in the same place. He may be a pilgrim, a wandering *sādhu.* He may be a monastic contemplative living in a cloistered monastery or semi-cloistered *ashram.* In preparation for *sannyāsa,* the aspirant leaves behind family, former friends and old acquaintances and steps out into a new pattern of subsuperconscious living. He strives to be all spine-power, all light. When we see him trying, although he may not be too successful at it if he is going through some inner turmoil or challenge, we know he is striving, and that is an inspiration to us. His very existence is his mission in life. He has dedicated himself to live a life of total commitment to the path of *yoga,* and by doing so he sustains the spiritual vibration for the householders. It is the renunciate who keeps the Vedic religions alive on the Earth. He keeps the philosophy vibrant and lucid, presenting it dynamically to the householders.

Wednesday
LESSON 269
The Stage of Path-Choosing

The two paths—householder and renunciate—every young man has to choose between them. In Hindu tradition the choice is made before the marriage ceremony, and, if not, during the ceremony itself. The choice must be his and his alone. Though guided by the advice of parents, elder family members and religious leaders, the choice is his and his alone as to how his soul is to live through the birth *karmas* of this incarnation. Both paths take courage, great courage, to step forward and embrace the responsibilities of adult life. ¶In making this decision in our tradition we have found it valuable for the young man to spend time in a Hindu monastery where he can live the monk's life for a period of six months or more and receive spiritual and religious training that will enhance his character for a positive future, no matter which path he chooses. Only by living for a time as a monk will he come to truly understand the monastic path and be empowered to make a knowledgeable choice between that path and the traditional *dharma* of the householder, raising a family and serving the community. One of the best times for this sojourn apart from the world, setting aside life's usual concerns, is just after high school or during an interim break. Then, after the time in the monastery, a firm and positive consideration should be made, in consultation with family and elders, as to which of the two paths he wishes to pursue. Once this decision is made and blessings given by the family preceptor, a path-choosing ceremony, Ishṭa Mārga Saṁskāra, should be held in the presence of the religious community to which he belongs, thus making the decision known publicly to one and all. ¶Path-choosing is a beginning, pointing a direction, declaring an intention. Marriage becomes a lifetime commitment only when the final marriage vows are spoken. This is preceded by months or even years of choosing a spouse, a process that calls forth the wisdom of the two families, community elders, religious leaders and those who are trained to judge astrological compatibilities. Renunciate life in our Nātha tradition and many others becomes a lifetime commitment only when final, lifetime vows of renunciation of the world are voiced. This is preceded by ten or more years of training during which the postulant monastic renews temporary vows periodically, at two-year intervals. During this lengthy time of training, the *sādhaka* is free to choose not to renew his vows at any juncture and opt instead for the path of the householder and be welcomed back into the family community. In some lineages, no formal vows are even taken, but there are traditionally understood norms of conduct, proprieties and protocol to be adhered to. For choosing the renunciate path is indeed not just like taking a position in a corporation. It is embracing a way of life, an attitude of being. ¶We might say that one does not choose renunciation, but rather is chosen by it, when the soul is matured to the point when the world no longer holds a binding fascination. While considerations of the order that one will join are practical realities, it is vital that the young man choosing renunciate life do so not seeking place or position in a particular order, but sets out as a free spirit, unencumbered, under the guidance of his *satguru,* willing to serve everywhere and anywhere he is sent, be it in his *guru's* central *ashram,* a distant center, a monastery of another *guru* or alone on an independent *sādhana.* The clear path is to define the path itself. Then, proceed with confidence.

Thursday
LESSON 270
The Way of The Bachelor

Of course, not all are necessarily able to set forth with perfect clarity in life. Thus, both the renunciate and householder communities accept singles who are not selfish and self-indulgent, who gather together into their respective home-like environments, sharing finance, food and worship. It is in Hindu culture the way of the unmarried devotees, who, whether woman or man, wears white and abjures the family *dharma* while not necessarily joining an *ashram,* wandering as a *sādhu* or following any monastic regimen. This is not a formal path, but it is a spiritual lifestyle which if successfully fulfilled is an alternative for those who cannot follow one of the two traditional paths. Singles who succeed in living harmoniously with one or more like-minded individuals may be considered worthy to enter *ashrams* in association with a *guru* and under the authority of a rigorous discipline greater than they could provide for themselves. ¶This might be called the way of the spiritual bachelor or spinster—the *brahmachārī* or *brahmachāriṇī.* These are humble men and women, often under simple vows, who are not following the traditional renunciate path, but don't intend to marry and so remain celibate and dedicate themselves to serving God, Gods, *guru* and humanity. Among them are those who are still deciding between the two paths, even at a later age. It usually does not include those whose spouse has passed on or who have suffered a divorce, as they are considered still a spouse, nor others whose heavy *karmas* would disallow them from entering a traditional order for one or more reasons. This life of bachelor or spinster can, when strictly and sincerely followed, be a joyous and useful life in service to *dharma* and fulfillment of spiritual goals. This is provided that devotees do not isolate themselves but eagerly and persistently serve the family community and the renunciate community with dedicated, cooperative effort, and get along one with another in harmony, love and trust, in the spirit of true Sivathondu, service to Śiva, never alienating themselves from others, but stepping forward as best they can to serve selflessly and wholeheartedly. The positive cooperation of their untiring energies is truly recognized in all three worlds. ¶There is another group that has no path, who neither marry nor follow the path of discipline and who are self-indulgent, unwilling to live with others and benefit from hastening their *karmas* through interaction, so that this puts many of their *karmas* on hold for another life. These souls think they are making spiritual progress, but they are, in fact, making new unwholesome *karmas* through a selfish lifestyle of noncommitment and unexamined egocentricities. They fail to realize or accept that interaction with others, whether householders or monastics, is needed to bring up quickly the *karmas* to be resolved in this birth and perhaps the next, and that avoidance of others offers no stimulus for progress. ¶Such single men and women may delude themselves into thinking they are *sādhus,* mendicants, *yogīs* or mystics, but in actuality they have invented their own routines which are not in harmony with the *sādhu* path of strictness and tradition. Following a self-chosen, self-defined path, they answer up to no one and, therefore, deal with the clever avoidance syndrome. ¶They are considered to be like children by both the renunciate and the householder.

Both groups constantly work to set aright these obstinate, unruly seekers, to bring them into a lifestyle of unselfish behavior, of interaction with others, encouraging them to replace egocentric patterns and preferences with the higher qualities of selfless service, group involvement and, above all, *prapatti*, humility, total surrender to the Divine within the temple and themselves. They are encouraged to overcome anger, back-biting, fear, jealousy, overt intellectual knowing, and talkativeness with the *sādhana* of silence, *mauna*, to bring forth the humility needed to make spiritual progress in this life. Many, however, are sincerely committed to noncommitment. Strange as it may seem, these unguided souls use up their allotted time for guidance and then beg for more. Those who walk on neither of the two paths are a daily burden to both the householder and the *sannyāsin.*

Friday
LESSON 271
Those Following Neither Path

It is necessary for spiritual unfoldment on the path to enlightenment to live among others, be loyal, faithful, not promiscuous, to settle down and establish a cooperative routine of community life. Living among others—even having roommates who think, believe and have adopted the same spiritual, religious disciplines—grants the burden of good conduct, prompt resolution of problems and an abidance of sharing, giving and caring during the trials and happinesses that naturally arise in living with others. ¶Those who are self-indulgent have no inclination to share companionship in a family, an *ashram* or spiritual community, as getting along with others is burdensome, bothersome, impossible to even imagine. Their subconscious is so full of dross that their aloneness relieves it somehow—through self-indulgence on the Internet, sweets, preferential foods and avoidance of confrontations of any kind which might or would conjure up anger, distance and dispel the little I-ness into I-dentity within a group where *kukarmas* and *sukarmas* are shared as their life on the spiritual path moves upward and upward and upward. ¶All *gurus* should disallow and throw such seekers out of their *ashrams*, lest they become accomplished detractors and herald an Internet site against them. Their only purpose is to infiltrate, dilute and destroy—not always consciously, perhaps, but subconsciously—and to bring everything down to their own level. The borderline conflicts that they create, where no one is exactly right and no one is exactly wrong, hold back the spiritual work, the mission of the lineage, temporarily, perhaps only for a moment, an hour or a day. Their mission of preaching indecision to those who have decided is fulfilled. When they tire of their new surroundings and are ready to move on, they infiltrate another group, endeavoring to take along with them those they have converted to their ways. All *satgurus, gurus, swāmīs,* heads of Hindu orders and those of other faiths, too, have recognized this problem and are alerted to potential infiltration, dilution and disruption of their group by those who do not belong because they will not follow the accepted patterns and instead endeavor to adjust them, dilute them into the nothingness which they would find inside themselves if they were even to spend a moment or two alone. ¶Other faiths are a little better disciplined in demanding followers to be totally converted to their particular denomination and not admitting into their sanctuaries, monasteries and administrative bodies those who have not taken up a strong commitment. It is here the trouble lies for Hindu-based organizations, bringing in members of Abrahamic religions, faiths which are, by their own proclamations, dedicated to the destruction of Hinduism. Truly devout born members of Hinduism would never turn against the cause they support, nor would those who join the faith by valid adoption or conversion—for to make their unwavering commitment, they made sacrifices, be it a family inheritance or alienation from their community, such as Jews, Christians and Muslims have faced who left their fold and converted to the Sanātana Dharma. The voice here is commitment to an established religion and fully converting to it by severing from any and all prior affiliations. Also, there should be zero tolerance for inharmonous conditions. So many *gurus* live surrounded by conflicts amongst followers as a way of life. No wonder they pass on before their time. ¶It has always been my advice to *gurus* and *swāmīs* to impose aloneness as a *prāyaśchitta*, penance, on dissidents who have infiltrated their core. In their aloneness, they would experience the torment of their own misdeeds, and their departure would be imminent, or in their aloneness their soul might shine forth and deliver a message to their errant mind—perhaps preprogrammed by others who sent them to break up the group—and emancipate them from the destructive and disruptive path they are on. Those within the *ashram* pursuing a higher path, training for true renunciation, are then freed from the detractors. The detractors are also freed to find good spouses and raise good families within the confines of their faith. Every group has such misfits within it from time to time. Wise *gurus* and *swāmīs* will ferret them out and send them on their way before they make too many bad *karmas* that will sorely impact their next birth. ¶Many devotees ask about realization amidst family life, not renouncing the world, but just changing your attitude about life. "I mentally renounce the world and therefore I am a *sannyāsin.*" Realization in family life is in the *anāhata* and *viśuddha chakras,* which then stimulates the *chakras* above into psychic abilities of various kinds: astral projection, foreseeing the future, reincarnation-readings of past lives and more. These realizations are stabilizing to the families, especially to the elders of the extended family when three generations live in one house. However, the family man would not want to seek for timeless, formless, causeless Paraśiva, because this would be a foundation, a starting point, for detaching from the family, and he would never look back. To renounce the world may not be possible, but if he were to continue seeking for total transformation, the world would renounce him. The family would find their newly acquired mendicant incompatible with their desires and goals. The wife would find her spouse more interested in himself than her, with difficulties in maintaining income, continuity of family duties, distaste for work in the world, and the desire to retire into mountain caves, or at least a peaceful forest. All these thoughts, desires and feelings manifest in deserting family duties, or *gṛihastha dharma,* and its penalty is bad merit and breaking the vows that fulfill that dharma. So, you can see the dilemma that entangles stepping over the fiery line without the proper preparation, qualifications and initiations. It is the *sannyāsa* initiation that gives permission, the starting point for the experience of Paraśiva and the aftermath of transformation. This is what the orange robes signify in orders that set for themselves this ideal as their true goal.

Saturday
LESSON 272
A Message To Sannyāsins

To further delineate the nature of renunciate life, I would like to share with you a letter I wrote to the *sannyāsins* of my Śaiva Siddhānta Yoga Order. It constitutes the introduction to *Holy Orders of Sannyāsa,* the vows and ideals they live by. ¶"The first part of your life was lived for yourself; the second part will be lived in the service of others, for the benefit of your religion. You have been tried and tested through years of training and challenges and proved yourself worthy to wear the *kavi,* the orange robes, and to fulfill the illustrious Śaiva *sannyāsin dharma.* ¶"The *sannyāsin* harkens close to Śiva and releases the past to an outer death. Remembering the past and living in memories brings it into the present. Even the distant past, once remembered and passed through in the mind, becomes the nearest past to the present. *Sannyāsins* never recall the past. They never indulge in recollections of the forgotten person they have released. The present and the future—there is no security for the *sannyāsin* in either. The future beckons; the present impels. Like writing upon the waters, the experiences of the *sannyāsin* leave no mark, no *saṁskāra* to generate new *karmas* for an unsought-for future. He walks into the future, on into the varied *vṛittis* of the mind, letting go of the past, letting what is be and being himself in its midst, moving on into an ever more dynamic service, an ever more profound knowing. Be thou bold, *sannyāsin* young. Be thou bold, *sannyāsin* old. Let the past melt and merge its images into the sacred river within. Let the present be like the images written upon the water's calm surface. The future holds no glamour. The past holds no attachment, no return to unfinished experience. Even upon the dawn of the day, walk into your destiny with the courage born of knowing that the ancient Śaivite scriptures proclaim your *sannyāsin's* life great above all other greatness. Let your life as a *sannyāsin* be a joyful one, strict but not restrictive, for this is not the path of martyrdom or mortification. It is the fulfillment of all prior experiential patterns, the most natural path—the straight path to God, the San Mārga—for those content and ripened souls. Leave all regret behind, all guilt and guile, others will preserve all that you proudly renounce. Let even the hardships ahead be faced cheerfully. ¶"Never fail to take refuge in your God, your *guru* and your Great Oath. This is the highest path you have chosen. It is the culmination of numberless lives, and perhaps the last in the ocean of *saṁsāra.* Be the noble soul you came to this Earth to be, and lift humanity by your example. Know it with a certainty beyond question that this is life's most grand and glorious path, and the singular path for those seeking God Realization, that mystic treasure reserved for the renunciate. Know, too, that renunciation is not merely an attitude, a mental posture which can be equally assumed by the householder and the renunciate. Our scriptures proclaim that a false concept. True renunciation must be complete renunciation; it must be unconditional. There is no room on the upper reaches of San Mārga for mental manipulations, for play-pretend renunciation or half-measure *sādhana.* Let your renunciation be complete. Resolve that it will be a perfect giving-up, a thorough letting-go. Let go of the rope. Be the unencumbered soul that you are. Be the free spirit, unfettered and fearless, soaring above the clamor of dissension and difference, yet wholeheartedly and boldly supporting our Śaivite principles against those who would infiltrate, dilute and destroy. All that you need will be provided. If there is any residue of attachment, sever it without mercy. Cast it off altogether. Let this be no partial renunciation, subject to future wants, to future patterns of worldliness. Give all to God Śiva, and never take it back. To make this supreme renunciation requires the utmost maturity coupled with a dauntless courage. It requires, too, that the wheel of *saṁsāra* has been lived through, that life hold no further fascination or charm.

Sunday
LESSON 273
A New Spiritual Birth

"Through experience the soul learns of the nature of joy and sorrow, learns well to handle the magnetic forces of the world. Only when that learning is complete is true *sannyāsa* possible. Otherwise, the soul, still immature, will be drawn back into the swirl of experience, no matter what vows have been uttered. True renunciation comes when the world withdraws from the devotee. *Sannyāsa* is for the accomplished ones, the great souls, the evolved souls. *Sannyāsa* is not to be misinterpreted as a means of getting something—getting enlightenment, getting *puṇya,* or merit. *Sannyāsa* comes when all getting is finished. It is not to get something, but because you are something, because you are ready to give your life and your knowledge and your service to

Śaivism, that you enter the life of the *sannyāsin.* The *kavi,* or saffron robes, are the royal insignia of the *sannyāsin.* Those in *kavi* the world over are your brethren, and you should feel one with each of these hundreds of thousands of soldiers within. ¶"The ideals of renunciation as practiced in the Sanātana Dharma are outlined fully in these *Holy Orders of Sannyāsa.* Live up to them as best you can. You need not be a saint or *jīvanmukta* to enter into the ancient world order of *sannyāsa.* Renunciation in its inmost sense is a gradual process. It does not happen instantly when a vow is spoken. Do not mistake *sannyāsa dīkshā* as the end of effort, but look upon it as a new spiritual birth, the beginning of renewed striving and even more difficult challenges. There will remain *karmas* to be lived through as the soul continues to resolve the subtle attachments, or *vāsanās,* of this and past lives. It is enough that you have reached a knowing of the necessity of *tyāga.* It is enough that you renounce in the right spirit and pledge yourself to meet each challenge as befits this tradition, bringing honor to yourself and your religion. ¶"Finally, you are charged with preserving and defending the teachings of the Śiva Yogaswāmī Guru Paramparā and the Śaiva Dharma as brought forth in *Dancing with Śiva—Hinduism's Contemporary Catechism* and *The Holy Bible of the Śaivite Hindu Religion.* You are cautioned against being influenced by alien faiths or beliefs. You are the vault, the repository, wherein are kept the priceless treasures of Śaivism, secure and available for future generations. All who accept these Holy Orders accept a selfless life in which all monastics work their minds together, thus keeping the *saṅgam* strong and effective. You must not veer from the San Mārga, nor follow an individual path, nor remain remote or aloof from your brother monastics. It is a serious life which you now enter, one which only a *sannyāsin* can fully undertake. Remember and teach that God is, and is in all things. Spread the light of the One Great God, Śiva—Creator, Preserver and Destroyer, immanent and transcendent, the Compassionate One, the Gracious One, the One without a second, the Lord of Lords, the Beginning and End of all that is. Anbe Śivamayam Satyame Paraśivam."

Narā Nāryaścha Naikāḥ

नरा नार्यश्च नैकाः

Men and Women Are Not the Same

Course the breath in appropriate ways through the feminine *iḍā* and masculine *piṅgalā nāḍīs.* Seat yourself in agreeable *āsanas* and, directing the breath within, ascend upward through the triangle-shaped *mūlādhāra.* Truly, you may see the feet of the Lord who is timeless eternity.

TIRUMANTIRAM 2173

Monday
LESSON 274
The Ideals of Family Life

If both husband and wife are on the spiritual path, the householder family will progress beautifully and deeply. Their love for one another and their offspring maintains family harmony. However, the nature of their *sādhana* and unfoldment of the spirit is different from that of the *sannyāsin.* The family unit itself is an odic-force structure. It is a magnetic-force structure, a material structure, for they are involved in the objects and relationships of the world. It is the family's effort to be "in the world but not of it" that gives the impetus for insight and the awakening of the soul. The struggle to maintain the responsibilities of the home and children while simultaneously observing the contemplative way, in itself, provides strength and balance, and slowly matures innate wisdom through the years. ¶The successful Hindu householder family is stable, an asset to the larger community in which it lives, an example of joyous, contented relationships. Members of the family are more interested in serving than being served. They accept responsibility for one another. They are pliable, flexible, able to flow freely like water. They worship and meditate daily without fail and strictly observe their individual *sādhanas.* Their insight is respected and their advice sought. Yet, they do not bring the world into the home, but guard and protect the home vibration as the spiritual center of their life. Their commitments are always first to the family, then to the community. Their home remains sacrosanct, apart from the world, a place of reflection, growing and peace. They intuitively know the complex workings of the world, the forces and motivations of people, and often guide others to perceptive action. Yet, they do not display exclusive spiritual knowledge or put themselves above their fellow man. ¶Problems for them are merely challenges, opportunities for growth. Forgetting themselves in their service to the family and their fellow man, they become the pure channel for love and light. Intuition unfolds naturally. What is unspoken is more tangible than what is said. Their timing is good, and abundance comes. They live simply, guided by real need and not novel desire. They are creative, acquiring and using skills such as making their own clothing, growing food, building their own house and furniture. The inner knowing awakened by their meditations is brought directly into the busy details of everyday life. They use the forces of procreation wisely to produce the next generation and not as instinctive indulgence. They worship profoundly and seek and find spiritual revelation in the midst of life. ¶Within each family, the man is predominantly in the *piṅgalā* force. The woman is predominantly in the *iḍā* force. When the energies are the other way around, disharmony is the result. When they live together in harmony and have awakened enough innate knowledge of the relation of their forces to balance them, then both are in the *sushumṇā* force and can soar into the Divinity within. Children born to such harmonious people come through from the deeper *chakras* and tend to be highly evolved and well balanced.

Tuesday
LESSON 275
Maintaining The Balance

Should the woman become aggressively intellectual and the man become passively physical, then forces in the home are disturbed. The two bicker and argue. Consequently, the children are upset, because they only reflect the vibration of the parents and are guided by their example. Sometimes the parents separate, going their own ways until the conflicting forces quiet down. But when they come back together, if the wife still remains in the *piṅgalā* channel, and the husband in the *iḍā* channel, they will generate the same inharmonious conditions. It is always a question of who is the head of the house, he or she? The head is always the one who holds the *prāṇas* within the *piṅgalā*. Two *piṅgalā* spouses in one house, husband and wife, spells conflict.

¶The balancing of the *iḍā* and *piṅgalā* into *sushumṇā* is, in fact, the pre-ordained spiritual *sādhana*, a built in *sādhana*, or birth *sādhana*, of all family persons. To be on the spiritual path, to stay on the spiritual path, to get back on the spiritual path, to keep the children on the spiritual path, to bring them back to the spiritual path, too—as a family, father, mother, sons and daughters living together as humans were ordained to do without the intrusions of uncontrolled instinctive areas of the mind and emotions—it is imperative, it is a virtual command of the soul of each member of the family, that these two forces, the *iḍā* and *piṅgalā*, become and remain balanced, first through understanding and then through the actual accomplishment of this *sādhana*. There can be no better world, no new age, no golden future, no peace, no harmony, no spiritual progress until this happens and is perpetuated far into the future. This is the *sādhana* of the father. This is the *sādhana* of the mother. And together they are compelled by divine law to teach this *sādhana* to their offspring, first by example, then through explanation of their example, as youths mature into adulthood. Those unfortunate couples who neglect or refuse to perform this *sādhana*—of balancing the *iḍā* and *piṅgalā,* and from time to time bringing both into the *sushumṇā*—are indeed distressed by their own neglect. At the time of death, as their life ebbs into the great unknown, they will, in looking back, see nothing but turmoil, misunderstanding, hurts—physical hurts, emotional hurts, mental hurts. Their subconscious will still be hurting, and they will know the hurt they gave to others will follow them into the next world, then into the next, to be reexperienced. Their pain knows no cure during their last few hours before transition from the physical body into one of the *astral* worlds they earned access to, as their good deeds, misdeeds and wrongful deeds are gathered together and totalled. Therefore, it is for the wise, the understanding, the hopeful parents to follow the *iḍā-piṅgalā-sushumṇā sādhana* daily, weekly, monthly, yearly. This is the path for the family persons toward merger with Śiva. It truly is.

Wednesday
LESSON 276
Spiritual Leadership

Who is the spiritual leader of the house? The man or the woman? *Dancing with Śiva* states: "The husband is, first, an equal participant in the procreation and upbringing of the future generation. Second, he is the generator of economic resources necessary for society and the immediate family. The husband must be caring, understanding, masculine, loving, affectionate, and an unselfish provider, to the best of his ability and through honest means. He is well equipped physically and mentally for the stress and demands placed upon him. When he performs his *dharma* well, the family is materially and emotionally secure. Still, he is not restricted from participation in household chores, remembering that the home is the wife's domain and she is its mistress." ¶If this happens, everything works out naturally in the home in a very harmonious way. If this does not occur, then the *prāṇic* forces do not flow as well for the family. Why? Because the stabilizing influence of the *prāṇas,* under control and well balanced, has not come to pass. As a result, there can be no effective invoking of God, Gods and *guru.* Arguments, rude and harsh words fly back and forth, children are maltreated, and backbiting of the husband, relatives, friends and neighbors is not uncommon. Adultery with prostitutes or casual pickups tempt, distract and burden the husband with guilt, especially during his wife's monthly retreat and during pregnancy. The life of a family going through such *karmas* is chaos. The children, who modern psychiatrists and ancient seers say are guided by the example of their parents, are thrown overboard, as from a ship they safely boarded with full confidence. Reality points out that there are no, never have been, nor ever will be, delinquent children. Delinquent parents are the culprits—"the parents are what is wrong with society; children are only guilty of being guided by their example." ¶The wise men of ancient times understood how the *prāṇic* life forces flow within man and woman. They knew that the family man's being in the *sushumṇā* current stabilizes the forces of the home. If he is meditating and going within himself, his wife will not have to meditate as much. She and the children will go within to their Divinity automatically on the power of his meditation. If he radiates peace, Divinity and confidence, they will too, without trying, without even being conscious of it.

¶One thing to remember: the family man is the *guru* of his household. If he wants to find out how to be a good *guru,* he just has to observe his own *satguru,* that is all he has to do. He will learn through observation. Often this is best accomplished by living in the *guru's ashram* periodically to perform *sādhana* and service. Being head of his home does not mean he is a dominant authority figure, arrogantly commanding unconditional obedience, such as Bollywood and Hollywood portrays. No. He must assume full responsibility for his family and guide subtly and wisely, with love always flowing. This means that he must accept the responsibility for the conditions in the home and for the spiritual training and unfoldment of his wife and children. This is his *purusha dharma.* To not recognize and follow it is to create much *kukarma,* bad actions bringing back hurtful results to him in this or another life.

Thursday
LESSON 277
The Role of Wife and Mother

When the wife has problems in fulfilling her womanly duties, *strī dharma,* it is often because the husband has not upheld his duty nor allowed her to fulfill hers. When he does not allow her to, or fails to insist that she perform her *strī dharma* and give her the space and time to do so, she creates *kukarmas* which are equally shared by him. This is because the *purusha karmic* duty and obligation of running a proper home naturally falls upon him, as well as upon her. So, there are great penalties to be paid by the man, husband and father for failure to uphold his *purusha dharma.* ¶Of course, when the children "go wrong" and are corrected by the society at large, both husband and wife suffer and equally share in the *kukarmas* created by their offspring.

In summary, the husband took the wife into his home and is therefore responsible for her well-being. Together they bring the children into their home and are responsible for them spiritually, socially, culturally, economically, as well as for their education. ¶What does it mean to be the spiritual head of the house? He is responsible for stabilizing the *prāṇic* forces, both positive, negative and mixed. When the magnetic, materialistic forces become too strong in the home, or out of proper balance with the others, he has to work within himself in early morning *sādhana* and deep meditation to bring through the spiritual forces of happiness, contentment, love and trust. By going deep within himself, into his soul nature, by living with Śiva, he uplifts the spiritual awareness of the entire family into one of the higher *chakras*. How does he accomplish this? Simply by moving his own awareness into a *chakra* higher than theirs. The awareness of his family follows his living example. ¶The family woman has to be a good mother. To achieve this, she has to learn to flow her awareness with the awareness of the children. She has been through the same series of experiences the children are going through. She intuits what to do next. As a mother, she fails only if she neglects the children, takes her awareness completely away, leaving the children to flounder. But if she stays close, attends to each child's needs, is there when he or she cries or comes home from school, everything is fine. The child is raised perfectly. This occurs if the wife stays in the home, stabilizing the domestic force field, where she is needed most, allowing the husband to be the breadwinner and stabilizer of the external force field, which is his natural domain.

Friday
LESSON 278
How Forces Can Go Awry

Odic force is magnetic force. Actinic force comes from the central source of life itself, from Lord Śiva. It is spiritual force, the spirit, pure life. The blend of these two forces, the *actinodic,* is the magnetic force that holds a home together and keeps everything going along smoothly. If a family man and woman are both flowing through the aggressive-intellectual current, the magnetic-odic forces become strong and congested in the atmosphere of the home, and inharmonious conditions result. They argue. The arguments are never resolved, but it is a way of dissipating the odic forces. If the man and the woman are flowing through the passive-physical current, the magnetic odic forces are not balanced. They become physically too attracted to one another. They become unreasonable with each other, full of fear, anger, jealousy, resentment, and they fight or, worse, take their frustrations out by beating, calling names and hurting, in many other ways, each other and their own children who came trustingly into their family. True, it is within the child's *prārabdha karmas* to experience this torment, but it is the duty of the parents to protect them from it, creating an environment in which unseemly seeds will not germinate. True, it may be the child's *karma* to experience torment, yet the parents do not have to deliver it. Wise parents find loving means of discipline and protect themselves from earning and reaping the unseemly *karmas* through improper *hiṁsā* methods of punishment. ¶However, if each understands—or at least the family man understands, for it is his home—how the forces have to be worked within it, and realizes that he as a man flows through a different area of the mind than does his wife in fulfilling their respective, but very different, birth *karmas*, then everything remains harmonious. He thinks; she feels. He reasons and intellectualizes, while she reasons and emotionalizes. He is in his realm. She is in her realm. He is not trying to make her adjust to the same area of the mind that he is flowing through. And, of course, if she is in her realm, she will not expect him to flow through her area of the mind, because women just do not do this. ¶Usually it is the man who does not want to, or understand how to, become the spiritual head of his house. Often he wants the woman to flow through his area of the mind, to be something of a brother and pal or partner to him. Therefore, he experiences everything that goes along with brothers and pals and partners: arguments, fights, scraps and good times. In an equal relationship of this kind, the forces of the home are not building or becoming strong, for such a home is not a sanctified place in which they can bring inner-plane beings into reincarnation from the higher celestial realms. If they do have children under these conditions, they simply take "potluck" off the lower astral plane, or Pretaloka. ¶A man goes through his intellectual cycles in facing the problems of the external world. A woman has to be strong enough, understanding enough, to allow him to go through those cycles. A woman goes through emotional cycles and feeling cycles as she lives within the home, raises the family and takes care of her husband. He has to be confident enough to understand and allow her to go through those cycles. ¶The *piṅgalā* force takes man through the creative, intellectual cycles. Man brings through creativity from inner planes. He invents, discovers, foresees. We normally consider it as all having been created within his external mind, but it is done through his *piṅgalā* force operating on inner planes of consciousness. He is not going to be smooth always and living in superconscious states, for he has to go through experiential cycles. He must be inspired one day and empty the next. He must succeed and fail. He is living his destiny and working out *karmas.*

Saturday
LESSON 279
Nurturing Harmony

A woman living in the *iḍā* current goes through her emotional cycles, too. Her moods change regularly. She laughs, cries, sulks, enjoys. He has to be wise enough to allow her to have these ups and downs and neither criticize nor correct her when she does. If conditions become strained within the home, the man of the house becomes the example by feeling the power of his spine and the spiritual force of Śiva within it. He finds that he remains calm and can enjoy the bliss of his own energy. He finds ways and means to create joy and happiness and make odic forces that may have gone into a heavy condition beautiful, buoyant and lovely again. ¶Rather than arguing or talking about their cycles, the man who is spiritual head of his house meditates to stabilize the forces within himself. He withdraws the physical energies from the *piṅgalā* and the *iḍā* currents into *sushumṇā* in his spine and head. He breathes regularly, sitting motionless until the forces adjust to his inner command. When he comes out of his meditation, if it really was a meditation, she sees him as a different being, and a new atmosphere and relationship are created in the home immediately. ¶The children grow up as young disciples of the mother and the father. As they mature, they learn of inner things. It is the duty of the mother and the father to give to the child at a very early age his first religious training and his education in attention, concentration, observation and meditation. ¶The parents must be fully knowledgeable of what their child is experiencing. During the first seven years, the child will go through the *chakra* of memory. He will be learning, absorbing, observing. The second seven years will be dedicated to the development of reason, as the second *chakra* unfolds. If theirs is a boy child, he is going through the *piṅgalā*. If a girl child, she is going through the *iḍā* current and will go through emotional cycles. By both spouses' respecting the differences between them and understanding where each one is flowing in consciousness, there is a give and take in the family, a beautiful flow of the forces. ¶The *āchāryas* and *swāmīs* work with the family man and woman to bring them into inner states of being so that they can bring through to the Earth a generation of great inner souls. It is a well-ordered cycle. Each one plays a part in the cycle, and if it is done through wisdom and understanding, a family home is created that has the same vibration as the temple or a contemplative monastery. ¶In summary, woman is in the *iḍā* current predominantly and does not think or flow through the same areas of thought strata as the man does. If he expects her to think the same way that he is thinking, he is mistaken. Once they have a balance of the forces in the home, she is not going to be analytical. She will be in thought, of course, but she will not indulge in his ramified thinking. She is naturally too wise for this. If he wants to have discussions with her or use her as a sounding board, he is inadvisedly guiding her into the *piṅgalā* current. And if she is going through one of her emotional cycles at the time, she will become upset with him for apparently no reason at all. He has to realize that her intuition is keen, and that she will have from time to time profound intuitive flashes. She might explain to him spontaneously the answer to something he has been thinking about for days, without his having verbally expressed to her what was on his mind. This happens quite often in the positive, harmonious home.

Sunday
LESSON 280
Mutual Appreciation

Tremendous confusion can exist within the family if the man and the woman think that they are the same and are flowing through the same areas of the external mind. The only area that they should flow through together is the *sushumṇā*, the spiritual. And when they are both intently in the intuitive mind, they will unravel deep and profound things together. She is in the home, making things nice for him. When he returns from his mental involvements in the world, it is up to him to get out of the intellectual mind and into the spiritual currents of his superconsciousness in order to communicate with her at all, other than on a subconscious, physical or materialistic level. ¶For harmony to prevail between a man and a woman, he has to live fully within his own nature, and she has to live fully within her own nature. Each is king and queen of their respective realms. If each respects the uniqueness of the other, then a harmonious condition in the home exists. ¶A good rule to remember: the man does not discuss his intellectual business problems with his wife, and she does not work outside the home. He solves his problems within himself or discusses them with other men. When he has a problem, he should go to an expert to solve it, not bring it home to talk over. If he does, the forces in the home become congested. The children yell and scream and cry. A contemplative home where the family can meditate has to have that uplifting, temple-like vibration. In just approaching it, the *sushumṇā* current of the man should withdraw awareness from the *piṅgalā* current deep within. That is what the man can do when he is the spiritual head of the home. ¶A woman depends on a man for physical and emotional security. She depends on herself for her inner security. He is the guide and the example. A man creates this security by setting a positive spiritual example. When she sees him in meditation, and sees light around his head and light within his spine, she feels secure. She knows that his intuition is going to direct his intellect. She knows he will be decisive, fair, clear-minded in the external world. She knows that when he is at home, he turns to inner and more spiritual things. He controls his emotional nature and he does not scold her if she has a hard time controlling her emotional nature, because he realizes that she lives more in the *iḍā* force and goes through emotional cycles. In the same way, she does not scold him if he is having a terrible time intellectually solving several business problems, because she knows he is in the intellectual force, and that is what happens in that realm of the mind. She devotes her thought and energies to making the home comfortable and pleasant for him and for the children. He devotes his thought and energies to providing sustenance and security for that home. ¶The man seeks understanding through observation. The woman seeks harmony through devotion. He must observe what is going on within the home, not talk too much about it, other than to make small suggestions, with much praise and virtually no criticism. He must remember that his wife is making a home for him, and he should appreciate the vibration she creates. If he is doing well in his inner life, is steady and strong, and she is devoted, she will flow along in inner life happily also. She must strive to be one with him, to back him up in his desires and his ambitions and what he wants to accomplish in the outside world. This makes him feel strong and stand straight with head up. She can create a successful man of her husband very easily by using her wonderful intuitive powers. Together they make a contemplative life by building the home into a temple-like vibration, so blissful, so uplifting.

Chiti Chakrāṇi

चित्तचक्राणि

Spinning Wheels Of Consciousness

Piercing the *chakras* that are multi-petalled—four, six, ten, twelve and sixteen—behold then the twin petalled *ajñā* center. You have indeed arrived at the holy feet of the timeless, causeless One.

TIRUMANTIRAM 1704

Monday
LESSON 281
14 Regions of Consciousness

Hindus scriptures speak of three worlds, fourteen worlds and countless worlds. These are different ways to describe Śiva's infinite creation. Of the fourteen worlds, seven are counted as rising above the earth and seven as descending below it. Correspondingly, there are fourteen great nerve centers in the physical body, in the astral body and in the body of the soul. These centers are called *chakras* in Sanskṛit, which means "wheels." These spinning vortices of energy are actually regions of mind power, each one governing certain aspects of the inner man, and together they are the subtle components of people. When inwardly perceived, they are vividly colorful and can be heard. In fact, they are quite noisy, since color, sound and energy are all the same thing in the inner realms. ¶When awareness flows through any one or more of these regions, the various functions of consciousness operate, such as the functions of memory, reason and willpower. There are six *chakras* above the *mūlādhāra chakra*, which is located at the base of the spine. When awareness is flowing through these *chakras*, consciousness is in the higher nature. There are seven *chakras* below the *mūlādhāra chakra*, and when awareness is flowing through them, consciousness is in the lower nature. In this Kali Yuga most people live in the consciousness of the seven force centers below the *mūlādhāra chakra.* Their beliefs and attitudes strongly reflect the animal nature, the instinctive mind. We want to lift our own consciousness and that of others into the *chakras* above the *mūlādhāra.* This brings the mind out of the lower nature into the higher nature. We do this through personal *sādhana*, prayer, meditation, right thought, speech and action and love for Lord Śiva, who is All in all. ¶The *mūlādhāra chakra*, the divine seat of Lord Gaṇeśa, is the dividing point between the lower nature and the higher nature. It is the beginning of religion for everyone, entered when consciousness arrives out of the realms below Lord Gaṇeśa's holy feet. ¶The physical body has a connection to each of the seven higher *chakras* through plexes of nerves along the spinal cord and in the cranium. As the *kuṇḍalinī* force of awareness travels along the spine, it enters each of these *chakras*, energizing them and awakening in turn each function. In any one lifetime man may be predominantly aware in two or three centers, thus setting the pattern for the way he thinks and lives. He develops a comprehension of these seven regions in a natural sequence, the perfection of one leading logically to the next. Thus, though he may not be psychically seeing spinning forces within himself, man nevertheless matures through memory, reason, willpower, cognition, universal love, divine sight and spiritual illumination. ¶It may help, as we examine each of these centers individually, to visualize man as a seven-storied building, with each story being one of the *chakras*. Awareness travels up and down in the elevator, and as it goes higher and higher, it gains a progressively broader, more comprehensive and beautiful vista. Reaching the top floor, it views the panorama below with total understanding, not only of the landscape below, but also of the relation of the building to other buildings and of each floor to the next. ¶In Sanātana Dharama, another analogy is used to portray the *chakras*—that of a lotus flower. This flower grows in lakes and pools, taking root in the slimy mud below the surface where no light penetrates. Its stem grows upward toward the light until it breaks the surface into fresh air and sunshine. The energy of the sun then feeds the bud and leaves until the delicate lotus blossom opens. The first *chakra*, is called the root *chakra*, *mūlādhāra.* Awareness takes root in the baser instincts of human experience and then travels through the waters of the intellect, becoming more and more refined as it evolves, until finally it bursts into the light of the superconscious mind, where it spiritually flowers into the 1,008-petaled lotus *chakra* at the top of the head. By examining the functions of these seven great force centers, we can clearly cognize our own position on the spiritual path and better understand our fellow man.

Tuesday
LESSON 282
Mūlādhāra, the Realm of Memory

The *chakras* do not awaken. They are already awakened in everyone. It only seems as if they awaken as we become aware of flowing our energy through them, because energy, willpower and awareness are one and the same thing. To become conscious of the core of energy itself, all we have to do is detach awareness from the realms of reason, memory and aggressive, intellectual will; then turning inward, we move from one *chakra* to another. The physical body changes as these more refined energies flow through it and the inner nerve system, called *nāḍīs,* inwardly becomes stronger and stronger. The *mūlādhāra chakra* is the memory center, located at the base of the spine, and is physically associated with the sacral or pelvic nerve plexus. *Mūla* means "root" and *adhāra* means "support," so this is called the root *chakra.* Its color is red. It governs the realms of time and memory, creating a consciousness of time through the powers of memory. Whenever we go back in our memory patterns, we are using the forces of the *mūlādhāra.* ¶This *chakra* is associated also with human qualities of individuality, egoism, materialism and dominance. Man lives mostly in this *chakra* during the first seven years of life. This center has four "petals" or aspects, one of which governs memories of past lives. The other three contain the compiled memory patterns and interrelated *karmas* of this life. When this *chakra* is developed, people are able to travel on the astral plane. It is complete within itself, but when the first two *chakras* are charged with gross, instinctive impulses and developed through Western education, with its values and foibles which contradict Hindu *dharma,* they can create together a very strong odic force which, when propelled by the worldly will of the third *chakra* toward outer success and power, can dominate the mind and make it nearly impossible for awareness to function in the higher force centers, so great is the material magnetism. Men living fully in these lower three *chakras* therefore say that God is above them, not knowing that "above" is their own head and they are living "below," near the base of the spine. ¶You have seen many people living totally in the past—it's their only reality. They are always reminiscing: "When I was a boy, we used to… Why, I remember when… It wasn't like this a few years ago…" On and on they go, living a recollected personal history and usually unaware that they have a present to be enjoyed and a future to be created. On and on they go, giving their life force energies to the task of perpetuating the past. The *mūlādhāra* forces are not negative forces. Used and governed positively by the higher centers, the powers of time, memory and sex are transmuted into the very fuel that propels awareness along the spinal climb and into the head. Similarly, the mature lotus blossom cannot in wisdom criticize the muddy roots far below which, after all, sustain its very life. ¶The center of man's reasoning faculties lies in the second, or hypogastric, plexus below the navel. It is termed *svādhishṭhāna*, which in Sanskṛit means "one's own place." Its color is reddish orange. Once the ability to remember has been established, the natural consequence is reason, and from reason evolves the intellect. Reason and intellect work through this *chakra*. We open naturally into this *chakra* between the ages of seven and thirteen, when we want to know why the sky is blue and the "whys" of everything. If very little memory exists, very little intellect is present. In other words, reason is the manipulation of memorized information. We categorize it, edit it, rearrange it and store the results. That is the essence of the limited capacity of reason. Therefore, this center controls the *mūlādhāra*, and in fact, each progressively "higher" center controls all preceding centers. That is the law. In thinking, solving problems, analyzing people or situations, we are functioning in the domain of *svādhishṭhāna*. ¶This center has six "petals" or aspects and can therefore express itself in six distinct ways: diplomacy, sensitivity, cleverness, doubt, anxiety and procrastination. These aspects or personae would seem very real to people living predominantly in this *chakra*. They would research, explore and wonder, "Why? Why? Why?" They would propose theories and then formulate reasonable explanations. They would form a rigid intellectual mind based on opinionated knowledge and accumulated memory, reinforced by habit patterns of the instinctive mind.

Wednesday
LESSON 283
The Centers of Reason and Will

It is in the *svādhishṭhāna chakra* that the majority of people live, think, worry and travel on the astral plane. If they are functioning solely in the reasoning capacity of the mind, devoting their life's energies to its perpetuation in the libraries of the world, then they would take the intellect very seriously, for they naturally see the material world as extremely real, extremely permanent. With their security and self-esteem founded in reason, they study, read, discuss, accumulate vast storehouses of fact and rearrange the opinions and conclusions of others. When guided by the higher *chakras* and not totally entangled in ramifications of intellect, the powers of *svādhishṭhāna* are a potent tool in bringing intuitive knowledge into practical manifestation. Reason does not conflict with intuition. It simply comes more slowly, more cumbersomely, to the same conclusions. Nevertheless, the intellect, in its refined evolution, can harness and direct the base instincts in man. ¶Within the third center, called the *maṇipūra chakra*, are the forces of willpower. *Maṇi* means "gem," and *pūra* means "city," so *maṇipūra* signifies the "jewelled city." Its color is yellow. It is represented in the central nervous system by the solar plexus, where all nerves in the body merge to form what has been termed man's "second brain." This is significant, for depending on how the energy is flowing, the forces of will from this *chakra* add power either to worldly consciousness through the first two centers or to spiritual consciousness through the fourth and fifth centers. In Hindu mysticism, this dual function of willpower is conveyed in its ten "petals" or aspects, five which control and stabilize the odic or material forces of memory and reason, and five which control the actinic or spiritual forces of understanding and love. Therefore, the *maṇipūra* energies are actinodic in composition, while *mūlādhāra* and *svādhishṭhāna* are purely odic force structures. When awareness functions within the realms of memory, reason and aggressive willpower, men and women are basically instinctive in nature. They are quick to react and retaliate, quick to have their feelings hurt and quick to pursue the conquest of others, while fearing their own defeat. Success and failure are the motivating desires behind their need to express power and possess influence. Consequently, their life is seeded with suffering, with ups and downs. They look for a way out of suffering and yet enjoy suffering when it comes. They are physically very hard working and generally not interested in developing the intellect unless it can help them achieve some material gain. In these states of consciousness, the ego rises to its greatest prominence, and emotional experiences are extremely intense. If, on the other hand, the willpower has been directed toward higher awakening, awareness is propelled into deeper dimensions. Gains and losses of material possessions and power no longer magnetize their awareness, and they are freed to explore higher centers of their being. Inwardly directed, the willpower gives resolute strength to these aspirants, strength to discipline the outer nature and to practice *sādhana.*

Thursday
LESSON 284
Cognition and Divine Love

¶With the spiritual will aroused, awareness flows quite naturally into the *anāhata chakra*, the heart center, governing the faculties of direct cognition or comprehension. Connected to the cardiac plexus, this *chakra* is often referred to as "the lotus of the heart." Its twelve "petals" imply that the faculty of cognition can be expressed in twelve distinct ways or through as many masks or personae. Its color is a smoky green. Man usually awakens into this region of cognition around age twenty-one to twenty-six. Life for seekers in this *chakra* is different than for others. It is in *anāhata*, literally "unstruck sound," that the aspirant attains his mountaintop consciousness. Instead of viewing life in its partial segments, like seeing just the side of the mountain, he raises his consciousness to a pinnacle from which an objective and comprehensive cognition of the entirety is the natural conclusion. Uninvolved in the seemingly fractured parts, he is able to look through it all and understand—as though he were looking into a box and seeing the inside, the outside, the top and the bottom all at the same time. It looks transparent to him and he is able to encompass the totality in one instantaneous flash of direct cognition. He knows in that split second all there is to know about a subject and yet would find it difficult to verbalize that vast knowing. Various highly endowed psychics are prone to utilize this force center, for such spiritual powers as healing are manifested here. ¶People with the *anāhata chakra* awakened are generally well-balanced, content and self-contained. More often than not, their intellect is highly developed and their reasoning keen. The subtle refinement of their nature makes them extremely intuitive, and what is left of the base instincts and emotions is easily resolved though their powers of intellect. It is important that the serious aspirant gain enough control of his forces and *karmas* to remain stabilized at the heart center. This should be home base to him, and he should rarely or never fall below *anāhata* in consciousness. Only after years of *sādhana* and transmutation of the sexual fluids can this be attained, but it must be attained and awareness must settle here firmly before further unfoldment is sought. ¶Universal or divine love is the faculty expressed by the next center, called the *viśuddha chakra.* This center is associated with the pharyngeal plexus in the throat and possesses sixteen "petals" or attributes. Whereas the first two centers are predominantly odic force in nature and the third and fourth are mixtures of odic force and a little actinic force, *viśuddha* is almost a purely actinic force structure. On a percentage scale, we could say that the energies here are eighty percent actinic and only twenty percent odic. Whenever people feel filled with inexpressible love and devotion to all mankind, all creatures large and small, they are vibrating within *viśuddha.* In this state there is no consciousness of a physical body, no consciousness of being a person with emotions, no consciousness of thoughts. They are just being the light or being fully aware of themselves as actinic force flowing through all form. They see light throughout the entirety of their body, even if standing in a darkened room. This light is produced in the *ājñā chakra* above through the friction occurring between the odic and actinic forces and perceived through the divine sight of the third eye. The sense of "I," of ego, is dissolved in the intensity of this inner light, and a great bliss permeates the nerve system as the truth of the oneness of the universe is fully and powerfully realized. *Viśuddha* means "sheer purity." This center is associated with blue, the color of divine love. ¶The *jñānī* who has awakened this center is able for the first time to withdraw awareness totally into the spine, into the *sushumṇā* current. Now he begins experiencing the real spiritual being. Even at this point he may hold a concept of himself as an outer being, as distinct from the inner being he seeks. But as he becomes stronger and stronger in his new-found love, he realizes that the inner being is nothing but the reality of himself. And as he watches as the outer being fades, he realizes that it was born in time and memory patterns, put together through the forces of reason and sustained for a limited period through the forces of will. The outer shell dissolves and he lives in the blissful inner consciousness that knows only light, love and immortality.

Friday
LESSON 285
Divine Sight And Illumination

The sixth force center is *ājñā*, or the third eye. *Ājñā chakra* means "command center" and grants direct experience of the Divine, not through any knowledge passed on by others, which would be like the knowledge found in books. Magnetized to the cavernous plexus and to the pineal gland and located between the brows, the *ājñā chakra* governs the superconscious faculties of divine sight within man. Its color is lavender. Of its two "petals" or facets one is the ability to look down, all the way down, to the seven *talas,* or states of mind, below the *mūlādhāra* and the other is the ability to perceive the higher, spiritual states of consciousness, all the way up to the seven *chakras* above the *sahasrāra.* Thus, *ājñā* looks into both worlds: the odic astral world, or Antarloka, and the actinic spiritual world, or Śivaloka. It, therefore, is the connecting link, allowing the *jñānī* to relate the highest consciousness to the lowest in a unified vision. This center opens fully to the conscious use of man after many experiences of *nirvikalpa samādhi,* Self Realization, resulting in total transformation, have been attained, although visionary insights and, particularly, inner light experiences are possible earlier. ¶The composition of this *chakra* is so refined, being primarily of actinic force, that a conscious knowledge of the soul as a scintillating body of pure energy or white light is its constant manifestation. From here man peers deeply into the mind substance, seeing simultaneously into the past, the present and the future—deeper into evolutionary phases of creation, preservation and destruction. He is able to travel consciously in his inner body, to enter any region of the mind without barrier and to reduce through his *samyama,* contemplation, all form to its constituent parts. ¶It is not recommended on the classical Hindu *yoga* path for one to sit and concentrate on this force center, as the psychic abilities of the pineal gland can be prematurely awakened over which control is not possible, creating an unnecessary *karmic* sidetrack for the aspirant. Visions are not to be sought. They themselves are merely illusions of a higher nature around which a spiritual ego can grow which only serves to inhibit the final step on the path, that of the Truth beyond all form, beyond the mind itself. Therefore, the pituitary gland, which controls the next and final center, should be awakened first. This master gland is located about an inch forward and upward of the left ear, near the center of the cranium. At that point one can inwardly focus awareness and see a clear white light. This light is the best point of concentration, for it will lead awareness within itself and to the ultimate goal without undue ramification. ¶The *sahasrāra,* or crown *chakra,* is the "thousand spoked" wheel, also known as *sahasradala padma,* "thousand-petaled lotus." Actually, according to the ancient mystics, it has 1,008 aspects or attributes of the soul body. However, these personae are transparent—a crystal clear white light, ever present, shining through the circumference of the golden body which is polarized here and which seems to build and grow after many experiences of sustained *nirvikalpa samādhi,* manifesting a total inner and outer transformation. ¶The crown center is the accumulation of all other force centers in the body, as well as the controlling or balancing aspect of all other sheaths or aspects of man. It is a world within a world within itself. When the *yogī* travels in high states of contemplation, when he is propelled into vast inner space, he is simply aware of this center in himself. In such deep states, even the experience of light would not necessarily be seen, since light is only present when a residue of darkness is kept, or since light is the friction of pure actinic force meeting and penetrating the magnetic forces. In the *sahasrāra,* the *jñānī* dissolves even blissful visions of light and is immersed in pure space, pure awareness, pure being. ¶Once this pure state is stabilized, awareness itself dissolves and only the Self remains. This experience is described in many ways: as the death of the ego; as the awareness leaving the mind form through the "door of

Brahman," the *brahmarandhra,* at the top of the head; and as the inexplicable merger of the *ātman,* or soul, with Śiva, or God. From another perspective, it is the merger of the forces of the pituitary with the forces of the pineal. Great inner striving, great *sādhana* and *tapas,* first activate the pituitary gland—a small, master gland found near the hypothalamus which regulates many human functions, including growth, sexuality and endocrine secretions. It is inwardly seen as a small white light and referred to as "the pearl of great price." When the pituitary is fully activated, it begins to stimulate the pineal gland, situated at the roof of the thalamic region of the brain and influencing maturation of consciousness expansion. The pineal is inwardly viewed as a beautiful blue sapphire. For man to attain his final, final, final realization, the forces of these two glands have to merge. Symbolically, this is the completion of the circle, the serpent devouring its own tail. For those who have attained this process, it can be observed quite closely through the faculty of divine sight.

Saturday
LESSON 286
The Unfoldment Of Humanity

This is the story of man's evolution through the mind, from the gross to the refined, from darkness into light, from a consciousness of death to immortality. He follows a natural pattern that is built right in the nerve system itself: memory, reason, will, direct cognition, inner light perceptions of the soul, which awaken a universal love of all mankind; psychic perceptions through divine sight; and the heavenly refinement of being in the thousand-petaled lotus. ¶During each age throughout history, one or another of the planets or *chakras* has come into power. Remember when the

Greek God Cronus was in supreme power? He is the God of time. Mass consciousness came into memory, or the *mūlādhāra chakra,* with its new-found concern for time, for a past and a future, dates and records. Next the mass consciousness came into the *svādhishṭhāna* and its powers of reason. Reason was a God in the Golden Age of Greece. Discourse, debate and logic all became instruments of power and influence. If it wasn't reasonable, it wasn't true. Next the *chakra* of will came into power. Man conquered nations, waged wars, developed efficient weapons. Crusades were fought and kingdoms established during the period. Our world was experiencing force over force. Direct cognition, the *anāhata chakra,* came into power when man opened the doors of science within his own mind. He cognized the laws of the physical universe: mathematics, physics, chemistry, astronomy and biology. Then he unfolded the mind sciences by penetrating into his subconscious mind, into the *chakras* where he had previously been. With man's looking into his own mind, psychology, metaphysics and the mind religions were born. ¶Now, in our present time, the mass consciousness is coming into *viśuddha*—the forces of universal love. The forerunners of this emerging Sat Yuga, popularly called the New Age, are not worshiping reason as the great thing of the mind or trying to take over another's possessions through the use of force. They are not worshiping science or psychology or the mind religions as the great panacea. They are looking inward and worshiping the light, the Divinity, within their own body, within their own spine, within their own head, and they are going in and in and in and in, into a deep spiritual quest which is based on direct experience, on compassion for all things in creation. ¶As the forces of the *viśuddha chakra* come into prominence in the New Age, it does not mean that the other centers of consciousness have stopped working. But it does mean that this new one coming into prominence is claiming the energy within the mass consciousness. When this center of divine love gains a little more power, everything will come into a exquisite balance. There will be a natural hierarchy of people based on the awakening of their soul, just as previous ages established hierarchies founded on power or intellectual acumen. With that one needed balance, everything on the Earth will quiet down, because the *viśuddha chakra* is of the new age of universal love, in which everyone sees eye to eye, and if they do not, there will always be someone there to be the peacemaker. Look back through history and you will see how these planetary influences, these great mind strata of thought, have molded the development of human society.

Sunday
LESSON 287
Chakra Cycles In Each Lifetime

The same cyclical pattern of development in human history is evident even more clearly in the growth of the individual. In the seven cycles of a man's life, beginning at the time of his birth, his awareness automatically flows through one of these *chakras* and then the next one, then the next and then the next, provided he lives a pure life, following Sanātana Dharma under the guidance of a *satguru*. ¶In reality, most people never make it into the higher four *chakras*, but instead regress back time and again into the *chakras* of reason, instinctive will, memory, anger, fear and jealousy. Nevertheless, the natural, ideal pattern is as follows. From one to seven years of age man is in the *mūlādhāra chakra.* He is learning the basics of movement, language and society—absorbing it all into an active memory. The patterns of his subconscious are established primarily in these early years. From seven to fourteen he is in the *svādhishṭhāna chakra.* He reasons, questions and asks, "Why? Why? Why?" He wants to know how things work. He refines his ability to think for himself. Between fourteen and twenty-one he comes into his willpower. He does not want to be told what to do by anyone. His personality gets strong, his likes and dislikes solidify. He is on his way now, an individual answerable to no one. Generally, about this time he wants to run away from home and express himself. From twenty-one to twenty-eight he begins assuming responsibilities and gaining a new perspective of himself and the world. Theoretically, he should be in *anāhata,* the *chakra* of cognition, but a lot of people never make it. They are still in the bull-in-the-china-shop consciousness, crashing their way through the world in the expression of will, asking why, reasoning things out and recording it in memory patterns which they go over year after year after year. ¶But if awareness is mature and full, having incarnated many, many times, he goes on at twenty-one to twenty-eight into the *anāhata chakra.* Here he begins to understand what it's all about. He comprehends his fellow men, their relationships, the world about him. He seeks inwardly for more profound insight. The *chakra* is stabilized and smoothly spinning once he has raised his family and performed his social duty and, though he may yet continue in business, he would find the energies withdrawing naturally into his chest. It is only the renunciate, the *maṭhavāsi,* the *sannyāsin,* who from twenty-eight to thirty-five, or before, depending on the strictness of his *satguru,* comes into the *viśuddha chakra,* into inner light experiences, assuming a spiritual responsibility for himself and for others. This awakening soul appreciates people, loves them. His heart and mind broadly encompass all of humanity. He is less interested in what people do and more in what they are. It is here that, having withdrawn from the world, the world begins to renounce him. Then, from thirty-five to forty-two, or before, he perfects his *sādhanas* and lives in the *ājñā chakra,* experiencing the body of the soul, that body of light, awareness traveling within naturally at that time, withdrawing from mundane affairs of the conscious mind. From forty-two through forty-nine he is getting established in the *sahasrāra chakra* in a very natural way, having met all of the responsibilities through life. ¶This is the exacting path a devotee would follow under the training of a *satguru.* Ideally, and traditionally, the young man should come under the training of a *guru* at about fourteen years of age, when he is just coming into the *maṇipūra* area of will. At this point, the will is malleable and can be directed into the channels of the inner climb, rather than directed toward the outer world, though he may work or study in the outer world, too. But his motivation is inner. Carefully guided, awareness flows through each of these force centers, and at fifty years of age, he is fully trained and mentally prepared to take on intense spiritual responsibilities of his *sampradāya* and soar even more deeply inward in a very, very natural way.

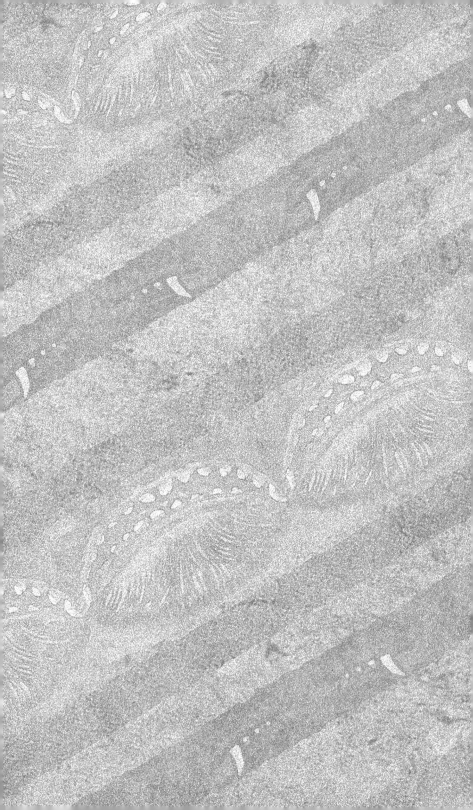

Chiti Kramika Vikāsaḥ

चित्तक्रमिकविकासः

The Evolution Of Consciousness

Guiding the *kuṇḍalinī* through the six *chakras*, with single-minded purpose they direct the mind, sitting immobile, like a wooden stake, impervious to touch or sound. To the wise *yogīs* who thus set their aim high, the Lord grants His grace.

TIRUMANTIRAM 1457

MANIVEL

Monday
LESSON 288
Iḍā, Piṅgalā And Sushumṇā

In mystic cosmology, the seven *lokas,* or upper worlds, correspond to the seven higher *chakras.* The seven *talas,* or lower worlds, correspond to the *chakras* below the base of the spine. Man is thus a microcosm of the universe, or macrocosm. The spine is the axis of his being, as Mount Meru is the axis of the world, and the fourteen *chakras* are portals into the fourteen worlds, or regions of consciousness. The actinodic life force within the *sushumṇā* current runs up and down the spine and becomes very powerful when the *iḍa* and *piṅgalā,* or the odic forces, are balanced. Then man becomes completely actinodic. He doesn't feel, in a sense, that he has a body at that particular time. He feels he is just a being suspended in space, and during those times his *anāhata* and *viśuddha chakras* are spinning and vibrating. When, through the practice of very intense, sustained states of contemplation, he merges into pure states of superconsciousness, the *iḍā* and the *piṅgalā* form a circle. They meet, and the pituitary and the pineal glands at the top of the head also merge their energies. This produces deep *samādhi.* The pituitary gland awakens first and through its action stimulates the pineal. The pineal shoots a spark into the pituitary, and the door of Brahman, the Bramarandhra, is opened, never to close. I once saw the *sahasrāra* on a long stem above my head when I was in New York in 1953 or '54. ¶The *sushumṇā* force also merges, and the *kuṇḍalinī,* which is at this time playing up and down the spine like a thermometer, as the fire-heat body of man, rises to the top of the head, and man then goes beyond consciousness and becomes the Self and has his total Self Realization, *nirvikalpa samādhi.* ¶The *iḍā nāḍī* is pink in color. It flows down, is predominantly on the left side of the body and is feminine-passive in nature. The *piṅgalā nāḍī* is blue in color. It flows up, is predominantly on the right side of the body and is masculine-aggressive in nature. These nerve currents are psychic tubes, shall we say, through which *prāṇa* flows from the central source, Śiva. The *prāṇa* is flowing down through the *iḍā* and up through the *piṅgalā*, but in a figure eight. The *sushumṇā nāḍī* is in a straight line from the base of the spine to the top of the head. The *iḍā* and *piṅgalā* spiral around the *sushumṇā* and cross at the third *chakra*, the *maṇipūra,* and at the fifth *chakra*, the *viśuddha,* and meet at the *sahasrāra.* This means that there is a greater balance of the *iḍā* and the *piṅgalā* in man's will center, or *maṇipūra chakra*, and in his universal love center, or *viśuddha chakra*, and of course at the great *saṅga* center, the meeting place of the three rivers, the *sahasrāra chakra.* ¶The *sushumṇā nāḍī,* flowing upward, is the channel for the *kuṇḍalinī śakti,* which is white. It is the cool energy, as white contains all colors. When this happens, and it happens almost imperceptibly under the *guru's* watchful eye, consciousness slowly expands. The novice only knows of the subtle yet powerful spiritual unfoldment when looking back from the time the practices were begun. Now he sees how life was then and how now his soul's humility has overtaken the external ego. ¶Through breathing exercises, meditation and the practice of *haṭha yoga*, the *iḍā* and the *piṅgalā,* or the aggressive and passive odic forces, are balanced. When they are balanced, the *chakras* spin all at the same velocity. When the *chakras* spin at the same velocity, they no longer bind awareness to the odic world; man's awareness then is automatically released, and he becomes conscious of the actinodic and actinic worlds. ¶Those *chakras* at the crossing of the *iḍā* and *piṅgalā* are the more physical of the *chakras*, whereas those it skips are energized by the *sushumṇā* itself. When the *yogī* is really centered within, the *iḍā* and *piṅgalā* then blend together in a straight line and merge into the *sushumṇā*, energizing all seven *chakras*, and in the older soul, slowly, very slowly, slowly, begin to energize the seven *chakras* above the *sahasrāra*. When this happens, he no longer thinks but sees and observes from the *ājñā chakra* between the eyes. He is totally consciously alive, or superconscious. It is only when his *iḍā* and *piṅgalā* begin functioning normally again that he then begins to think about what he saw.

Tuesday
LESSON 289
Kuṇḍalinī Out of Control

There are three channels through which the spiritual energies of the *kuṇḍalinī* can rise. The one recommended is the *sushumṇā*. The other two are to be avoided. When the *kuṇḍalinī śakti* flows outside of the *sushumṇā nāḍī* into and through the *iḍā nāḍī* on the left side of the spine, which corresponds to the left sympathetic nerve system, it is fragmented into other smaller and more sensitive nerve currents connected to the organs of the physical body. It produces heat within this formerly cool *nāḍī* network. The person becomes overly emotional, feminine in nature, talks a lot, often has hurt feelings, cries at the least provocation and engages in other emotional behavior patterns that center around the personal I-ness. Such persons always want to help others, but rarely actually do. This heat, though astral, is felt in the physical body in the solar plexus. When provoked, it angers, and is always quick to defend the personal ego in saving face. Similarly, when the serpent power flows up through the *piṅgalā nāḍī* and into the sympathetic nerve network on the right side of the body, the person becomes overly intellectual, very masculine in nature, talks little, has steel nerves and patterns centering around the conquest of others through intellectual debate. He is prone to long silences, holding in emotions, and to secret patterns of behavior to stimulate or satisfy base desires. In other words, he is not open, smiling, friendly, companionable. In either case, the *kuṇḍalinī śakti* rising through the *iḍā* or *piṅgalā* can move upward only to the *viśuddha chakra* and no farther. This is the impasse. ¶The misdirection of the *kuṇḍalinī* happens most often to the less disciplined, those more eager for attainments on the fast track, those not under the watchful eye of the *satguru*. Nevertheless, the novice feels a dynamic awakening of power. This heat, produced by the *kuṇḍalinī śakti* flowing through either of these two *nāḍīs* of the sympathetic nerve system, can and often does produce jerks in the body, spine and neck. ¶More often than not, the jerking body, twisting neck and the "I now know it all" attitude are taken for a highly spiritual experience and even validated as such by certain teachers. But it is as if we were driving on a rocky road, thinking it to be a smooth highway. It is an unusual experience, to be sure, building the personal ego into something it was never intended to be. When this happens to a devotee, the wise *guru* or *swāmī* recommends that all spiritual practices be immediately stopped. *Japa* should be stopped. All *prāṇāyāma* except the simplest regulation of the breath should be stopped. Reading scripture should be stopped, worship of all kinds should be stopped. Anything other than wholesome, humbling *karma yoga*, such as cleaning bathrooms, should be stopped. Growing food should be encouraged. Bare feet on the ground and at the same time hands in the dirt is the best way to bring the rampant *kuṇḍalinī* down to the *mūlādhāra chakra.* Once it is down, it can be directed up through the right current, but only when the devotee does not have conflicting patterns in his life. ¶Unlike the subtle movement of the divine serpent power through its proper channel, the *sushumṇā nāḍī* within the spine, its misdirection may reflect a dramatic change in the nature, turning the once humble student into an ego giant, either overly emotional and self-centered or intellectually argumentative; both types are not self-reflective in any way. From a perhaps once shy person, we now have a "Come to me, I will fix you, repair you, inspire you, for I am aware," or worse, "I am enlightened." Once the spiritual ego has taken over, some even claim to have attained more than their teacher. They don't need a teacher anymore. For them, the *guru* is on the inside, and their heated discussions, emotional outbursts and challenging positions, eventually take their toll on their own being.

Wednesday
LESSON 290
Quelling the Kuṇḍalinī

As it is said, "What goes up must come down." This is especially true with the *kuṇḍalinī śakti* moving through either of the other of the two wrong channels, where it can produce "dis-ease"— discomfort, physically, emotionally, intellectually and astrally—that no doctor's effort can fathom the cause of or effect a cure.

At various junctures, as it rises, the *kuṇḍalinī śakti,* or serpent power, attacks the organs in the vicinity of the *chakra* it is passing through, biting and poisoning them on the astral level. As it climbs, each one of the astral organs is hurt and felt as a physical ailment. This often reflects as a symptomatic problem in the kidneys, then stomach problems and later heart problems and thyroid difficulties. At each juncture, the doctor would be perplexed by the ailment, unable to find a medical cause, then doubly perplexed when that problem leaves and the next one arises. Though treatments and multiple tests are more than often given, the source of the problems is usually undetected. ¶A devotee going through this experience often challenges the will of his *satguru,* whereupon he is left to his own devices, as it lies beyond even the *guru's* ability to help or guide him further. For the rule is: the *guru* takes nine steps toward the seeker for each humble, cooperative, eager step the devotee takes toward him. When the devotee balks, begins to argue and challenge the *guru's* will, this is the *guru's* signal to withdraw, a mystical sign that his ninth step had been taken. Should he take the tenth, he enters without a welcome and tangles when step eleven and twelve are taken. To withdraw then would cause an unwanted *karma* of hurt, pain and anguish. So, the wisdom of the ancients is "For every one step taken toward the *guru,* the *guru* takes nine toward the devotee." ¶Then Śrī Śrī Śrī Viśvaguru Mahā-Mahārāj-ji steps in and takes over, and the failed aspirant either is corrected by the forces of circumstance to give up spiritual pursuits for financial or other reasons, or he spins off the spiritual path into Viśvaguru's *ashram,* called Bhogabhūmi, place of pleasure (another name for Earth). It is the biggest *ashram* of all. Here followers learn by their own mistakes and make fresh new *karmas* to be experienced in yet another life. ¶To avoid these problems, and worse, the *kuṇḍalinī śakti* has to be brought down all the way—slowly, not abruptly, lest the person become suicidal—all the way to the base, to the *mūlādhāra chakra*, and then redirected up the proper channel. As pride comes before a fall, the fall of the spiritual pride is again another hurt, a final bite from the serpent, and as the poison flows through all organs, and temporary physical, mental and emotional suffering is the consequence.

Thursday
LESSON 291
Striving and One's Dharma

Many seekers want a future of wealth, family and friends and they want the very highest spiritual illumination, too. This is their spiritual pride setting an unrealistic pattern. We must remember that after one renounces the world, with his entering the higher *chakras—viśuddha, ājñā* and *sahasrāra*—the world renounces the individual. If married, he no longer can fulfill his *purusha dharma*, his family duties. He can no longer hold employment that offers benefits for longevity. His perspective of the world and advancement in it has been changed forever. As a ship floats aimlessly on the ocean without a rudder, so does the unprepared soul meander who has forced his way, uninvited through initiation, into the realm of the saints and sages of Sanātana Dharma. This is why householders and all who have not properly prepared themselves, been well schooled and tested by a competent preceptor, should not go too deeply into *rāja* or *kuṇḍalinī yoga* practices. ¶If they are prone to anger, jealousy, contempt and retaliation, they should abstain from any of the *yogas* of *japa* or exploratory meditation. These will only intensify and *prāṇanize* the lower *chakras* that give rise to demonic forces. Rather, they should perform the always healing *vāsanā daha tantra* and confine themselves to *karma yoga*, such as cleaning in and around the temple and picking flowers for the *pūjās*. These simple acts of *charyā* are recommended, but should be not extended to intense worship. ¶Then, and only then, their life will be in perspective with the philosophy of Sanātana Dharma and begin to become one with Śiva's perfect universe. *Brahmadvara*, the door to the seven *chakras* below the *mūlādhāra*, will then be sealed off as their experiential patterns settle into the traditional perspective of how life should be and each individual should behave within it. ¶The use of drugs is another foreboding danger, for certain stimulants set in motion the *kuṇḍalinī* simultaneously into higher and lower regions. For instance, when the user of drugs, like an intruder, forces his way into the experience of the oneness of the universe, the totality of now-ness and all-being, by touching into the fourth *chakra, anāhata*, simultaneously every other center below the *anāhata* is stimulated, meaning *svādhishṭhāna* and the first, third, fifth and seventh below the base of the spine—the centers of reason, fear, jealousy, selfishness and malice. Noticeable mood swings of those who rely on drugs hamper the person throughout life. Only severe *prāyaśchitta*, penance, can set the course toward spiritual healing.

Friday
LESSON 292
Seven Centers of Instinctiveness

The seven *chakras*, or *talas*, below the spine down to the feet are all seats of instinctive consciousness, the origin of fear, anger, jealousy, confusion, selfishness, absence of conscience and malice. ¶The first *chakra* below the *mūlādhāra*, called *atala* and located in the hips, governs the state of mind called fear. When someone is in this consciousness, he fears God as well as other people—even himself at times. In the *chakra* below that, called *vitala* and located in the thighs, anger predominates. Anger comes from despair or the threatening of oneself-will. When people are in the consciousness of this *chakra,* they are even angry at God. With their wrath, they often strike out at those around them, leaving a trail of hurt feelings behind them. From sustained anger arises a persistent, even burning, sense of resentment. ¶The third *chakra* below the *mūlādhāra,* called *sutala* and located in the knees, governs jealousy. Jealousy is actually a feeling of inadequacy, inferiority and helplessness. When mixed with anger it causes terrible reactions within the nerve system of the astral body. When people are in the consciousness of this *chakra,* they often deny the existence of God and are contentiously combative with one another. ¶The fourth *chakra* below the *mūlādhāra,* called *talātala* and located in the calves, governs instinctive willfulness, the desire to get rather than give, to push others no matter what the reactions may be, all to benefit oneself. When people are in the consciousness of this *chakra* they proclaim the existence of materialistic advancement over everything else. Greed, deceit, coercion, bribery and lust prevail. This is truly a "dog-eat-dog" state of mind.

¶The fifth *chakra* below the *mūlādhāra,* called *rasātala* and located in the ankles, is the true home of the instinctive mind. When people are in the consciousness of this *chakra* they see to the well-being of "number one" first, "me, myself and I." Memory, reason, willfulness; thoughts, feelings and actions without conscience are all motivating factors here, governed by anger and fear. To this state of mind, jealousy, anger and fear are experienced as intense, even high, states of consciousness. There are even philosophies that have been conceived based on the states of consciousness experienced in these five *chakras* below the *mūlādhāra.* One of these is existentialism. Many true atheists reside in the fifth chakra below the *mūlādhāra,* and it is in this *chakra* that a great part of the mass consciousness resides at this time in the Kali Yuga. ¶There are still two more *chakras* below this one. The sixth *chakra* below the *mūlādhāra,* called *mahātala* and located in the feet, is "theft without conscience." Persons living here feel that "the world owes them a living." They simply take what they justify to be theirs anyway. The seventh *chakra* below the *mūlādhāra,* called *pātāla* and located in the soles of the feet, governs revenge, murder for the sake of murder, malice expressed through the destruction of others' goods, properties, minds, emotions and physical bodies. Hatred abides here. Malice reigns supreme. This is the consciousness of terrorists and those who support terrorists with vigor and enjoy from afar their every killing, rape and torturous act. Reason seldom influences those who live in this state of mind. ¶From here, at the bottom, there is no other way to go. The only way is up. Evolution takes its toll in bringing the consciousness of these wanton souls up and up into personal ego and some semblance of self-esteem, and then up into the ability of being jealous, then up into conquest of their fears and memory of their past actions, fearful that these horrific events might be repeated, then finally ascending into memory and reason, then into willpower in the *maṇipūra chakra.* Here they may become religious, repentant, resistant to ever, ever wanting again to face the experiences they look back at constantly and cry about in their remorse. Yes, there is only one path. It goes up or it goes down. ¶Here, in the *maṇipūra chakra,* which coordinates with the *chakra* of memory, they are ready to practice *prāyaśchitta,* penance, whatever it takes to extract the emotion from the memories which are tangled together deep in the subconscious. This is a painful process. But evolution makes it necessary to be lived through. Once accomplished—and practically speaking it is not easily or always accomplished—this changes for the better the course of the *prāṇas* that flow through the subconscious, the sub of the subconscious and subsuperconscious mind for themselves, their family, ancestors and progeny several generations back and many generations into the future. ¶To further explain, those who are well settled in consciousness within these seven *chakras* below the *mūlādhāra* are not interested in religion. They are irreverent and deny the existence of God. It is here that superstitious fears often prevail. There are no rules. There is no conscience. The various interrelated states of consciousness found within these seven *chakras* foster chaos, confusion, feelings of hopelessness, despair—all *adharmic* states of mind. These are the rates of vibration of the instinctive mind below the *mūlādhāra*, where Lord Gaṇeśa sits in all His majesty.

Saturday
LESSON 293
Consciousness And the Chakras

Gaining stability in any of the *chakras* above the *mūlādhāra* avails a certain control over the related *chakras* below the *mūlādhāra*. For example, the *mūlādhāra* has power over the second, fourth and six *chakras* below the base of the spine, the centers of anger, confusion and absence of conscience. *Maṇipūra*, the third *chakra*, has power over the *mūlādhāra* and the same Narakaloka centers in an even more expansive way. The reason center, *svādhishṭhāna*, *chakra* two, controls the centers of fear, jealousy and so on. The cognition, seeing-through-worldliness *chakra—anāhata—*the fourth center above the *mūlādhāra*, controls the reason *chakra*, and the centers of fear, jealousy, egotistic self-preservation and so on. ¶All the *chakras*, indeed, are functioning in everyone, as everyone has willpower, memory, reason and so on. But each soul has a home base. The *ahiṁsā* person whose home base is *anāhata chakra* would not harm others because he perceives the unity of all. The person living in the *ājñā chakra* above could never harm others because he is immersed in divine love. The home base of the terrorist who takes pleasure, joy and pride, and receives medals of honor for his disdain of human rights, is the *pātāla chakra*, at the bottom. The average person, and this is what makes him average, functions predominantly in about six *chakras*. These would be six below the *mūlādhāra* for someone for whom fear is the high point. Three within that six are the sustaining elements. ¶The upper seven *chakras* spin clockwise, and this spinning creates the *śānti*, or ever-growing peace, within an individual dominated by them. The lower seven spin counterclockwise, and this produces an ever-growing turmoil within one so affected. The vulnerable part of spiritual unfoldment is when someone is in the higher *chakras*—for example will and reason—and has one or more lower *chakras* open as well. This means one set of *chakras* is spinning clockwise and the other set is spinning counterclockwise, which accounts for great mood swings, elation, depression, self adulation, self condemnation. So, *brahmadvara,* the doorway to the Narakaloka just below the *mūlādhāra,* has to be sealed off so that it becomes impossible for fears, hatreds, angers and jealousies to arise. Once this begins to happen, the *mūlādhāra chakra* is stabilized and the renegade becomes a devotee of Lord Gaṇeśa. You cannot come to Gaṇeśa in love and respect if you are an angry or jealous person. That is our religion. ¶As awareness flows through the first three higher *chakras,* we are in memory and reason patterns. We see the past and the future vividly and reside strongly in the conscious and subconscious areas of the mind. When awareness flows through the *anāhata* and *viśuddha chakras,* our point of view changes. We begin to see ourselves as the center of the universe, for now we are looking out and seeing through the external world from within ourselves. We look into the primal force within ourselves and see that this same energy is in and through everything. ¶The *chakras* also relate to our immediate universe. Put the sun in the center, representing the golden light of *sushumṇā.* The Earth is the conscious mind; the moon is the subconscious mind. The vibratory rates of the planets are then related to the seven *chakras;* the first *chakra, mūlādhāra,* to Mercury; the second *chakra, svādhishṭhāna*, to Venus; the third *chakra*, *maṇipūra*, to Mars; and so forth. In this way, if you know something of Vedic astrology, you can understand the relationship of the influence of the planets as to the formation of the individual nature, and how these various *chakras* come into power, some stronger than others, depending upon the astrological signs, for they have the same rate of vibration as the planets. Now you can see how it all ties together. ¶Through the knowledge of the *chakras*, you can watch people and see what state of consciousness they are functioning in. It is helpful to know that all souls are inwardly perfect, but they are functioning through one force center or another most of the time, and these force centers determine their attitudes, their experiences, how they react to them and more.

Sunday
LESSON 294
Closing the Door To Lower Realms

When at the moment of death you enter the astral plane, you only are in the consciousness of the *chakras* that were most active within you during the later part of your lifetime and, accordingly, you function in one of the astral *lokas* until the impetus of these *chakras* is expended. It is the *chakras* that manufacture the bodies. It is not the body that manufactures the *chakras*. Since you have fourteen *chakras*, at least three are the most powerful in any one individual—for example, memory, will and cognition. Each *chakra* is a vast area of the mind, or a vast collective area of many, many different thought strata. Generally, most people who gather together socially, intellectually or spiritually are flowing through the same predominant *chakra*, or several of them collectively. Therefore, they are thinking alike and share the same perspective in looking at life. ¶The *chakras* exist as nerve ganglia that have a direct impact on organs in the physical body, as psychic nerve ganglia in the astral body and as spinning disks of consciousness in the body of the soul, *ānandamaya kośa.* The power to close off the lower *chakras*—to seal off the doorway at the lower end of the *sushumṇā*—exists only when the soul is presently incarnated in a physical body. All fourteen *chakras,* plus seven more above and within the *sahasrāra,* are always there. It is up to the individual to lift consciousness from one to another through right thought, right speech, right action, showing remorse for errors committed, performing regular *sādhana,* worship, pilgrimage and heeding other personal instructions the *satguru* or *swāmī* might guide the person through. All this and more teaches the *prāṇas* of consciousness, and most importantly, individual awareness, the art of flowing up through the higher centers through the process of closing off the lower ones. ¶Spiritual unfoldment is not a process of awakening the higher *chakras,* but of closing the *chakras* below the *mūlādhāra.* Once this happens, the aspirant's consciousness slowly expands into the higher *chakras,* which are always there. The only thing that keeps the lower *chakras* closed is regular *sādhana, japa,* worship and working within oneself. This is demonstrated by the fact that even great *yogīs* and *ṛishis* who have awakened into the higher *chakras* continue to do more and more *sādhana.* They are constantly working to keep the forces flowing through the higher centers so that the lower ones do not claim their awareness. ¶Now, all of this, perhaps, seems very complex and esoteric. But these are aspects of our nature that we use every day. We use our arms and hands every day without thinking. If we study the physiology of the hands, we encounter layer after layer of intricate interrelationships of tissues, cells, plasma. We examine the engineering of the structural system of bones and joints, the energy transmission of the muscular system, the biochemistry of growth and healing, the biophysics of nerve action and reaction. Suddenly a simple and natural part of human life, the function of the hands, seems complex. Similarly, we use the various functions of consciousness, the *chakras*, every day without even thinking about them. But now we are studying them in their depths to gain a more mature understanding of their nature. ¶Actually, there are more *chakras* above and within the *sahasrāra*. Buddhist literature cites thirty-two *chakras* above. Āgamic Hindu tradition cites seven levels of the rarefied dimensions of *paranāda,* the first *tattva,* as chanted daily by hundreds of thousands of priests during *pūjā* in temples all over the world. Their names are: *vyāpinī, vyomāṅga, anantā, anāthā, anāśṛitā, samanā* and *unmanā.* I have experienced these higher *chakras* or *nāḍīs* as they are, in this subtle region, as conglomerates of *nāḍīs.* These force centers are not exactly *chakras,* as they are not connected to any organ or part of the physical body. They are *chakras* or *nāḍīs* of the body of the soul, which when developed as a result of many, many, many Paraśiva experiences, slowly descend into the mental and astral bodies. The mental body becomes permanently different in its philosophical outlook, and the astral body begins to absorb and be transformed by the golden body, or *svarṇaśarīra.*

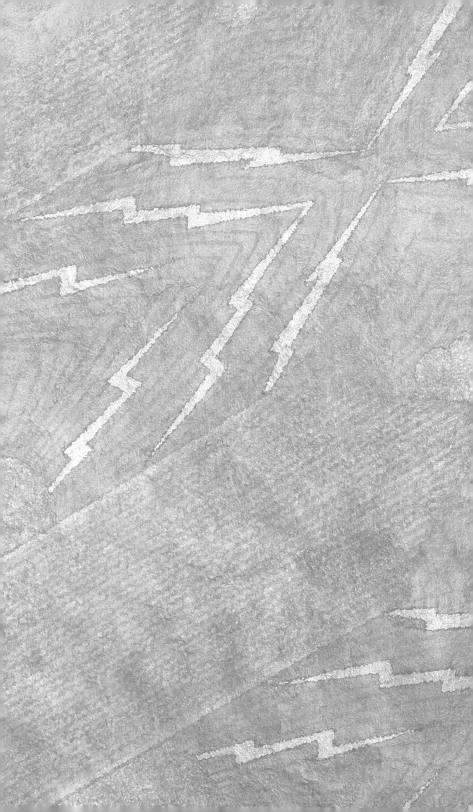

Śaktikshetrāṇi Ātmikarakshā cha

शक्तिक्षेत्राणि आत्मिकरक्षा च

Force Fields and Psychic Protection

Countless *devas* glorified my Lord. "O! Southern breeze, fragrantly cool," they praised, "O! Bounteous One," they adored. Yet this they do not know: from beyond the vast spaces He grants His divine protection.

TIRUMANTIRAM 1715

Monday
LESSON 295
Nature's Two Basic Forces

There are two basic forces in the universe, which you can look up in the dictionary. One is called odic force. The other is actinic force. Odic force is magnetic force. Odic force is the force of collective energies that make things—trees, chairs, tables, houses, the physical body. Odic force is of the material world—dense and heavy. The aura around the physical body and the forces of nature which govern much of man's life on Earth are odic force. ¶Actinic force is your pure life force coming from the central source deep within out through the nerve system. But as soon as this pure life force begins to mingle with the astral atoms and the physical body atoms, it turns to odic force. The study of these two forces can give you a great awakening—two primal forces. ¶The *sahasrāra chakra*, the *ājñā chakra,* the *viśuddha chakra*—the top three, in the head and throat centers—are primarily actinic force centers of rarefied inner consciousness within the superconscious itself. The *anāhata chakra,* the one at the heart center, which allows us to look out into the external world and within to the internal areas, is primarily a mixture of actinic force and odic force. It's called actinodic. It's a mixture of these two forces. However, the lower three *chakras—maṇipūra, svādhishṭhāna* and *mūlādhāra*—are primarily odic force *chakras.* They are the forces that make up what we call the world. ¶The *iḍā* and *piṅgalā* forces are basically odic forces. So, therefore, when the odic force is withdrawn back into the *sushumṇā,* back into its actinic substance, we lose complete awareness of the external world. That is how we enter meditation, by withdrawing the odic forces. The *prāṇa* is the in-between. It is the actinodic force that flows in and through odic and actinic forces. It is the binder of these two forces. ¶But it's easier to relate to the word *odic* and the word *actinic* and compare these two forces, because you can feel them through your physical body. Lift your arm. The movement of the spirit within is actinic force, and all the rest that happens is odic force, including the arm itself, the vibrations around the arm. They're all odic force. The mixture of what is going on is actinodic force, which is the closest, in looking at it in this way, that we come to *prāṇa.* ¶When we are in actinic force and we are aware of it, we have harmony, we have peace in all of our external life. Everything goes right and everyone sees eye to eye and finds points of agreement, one with another. There's no argument, and there's no confusion. However, when we become conscious in and awareness is flowing through the odic force realms, awareness actually thinks it is odic force. Then we have inharmonious conditions to live in. No one sees eye to eye, one with another. There's argument, and there is contention. ¶Look at these *chakras* as vast fields of collective related and interrelated thought realms, like vast cities, and look at awareness as the traveler through these *chakras.* When you are flowing awareness through one of these vast energy fields of actinodic force or actinic force with these thought or perceptive layers within it, you think a certain way as you hit each of these strata of thought. Think of it in that way. As you travel through, the nerve ganglia within the spinal cord are registering all this and bringing what you are experiencing into your immediate consciousness. You become aware of it through the nerve ganglia within the spine.

¶Through a mixture of actinic and odic force, willpower and awareness motivate the travels through these layers of the mind. When the nerve force does begin to register, when you're in a certain *chakra,* it begins to vibrate, and it throws off color and it throws off sound, and then, within you, you do see these disc-like wheels spinning. I have experienced that. I have seen them, and they're just like they are represented in the picture books, but much more vivid. They have sounds—in fact, they're quite noisy—because color and sound and energy are all the same thing in the inner realms, and that is how they have produced these images that you see in books on mysticism and occultism. However, they're greater than that. They are great energy fields in the inner man, and they flow. They are what make up people. The physical body has a connection to each one of these seven *chakras,* though you may not be aware of all of them, you may only be aware in one of them or two of them, and that is the way you think.

Tuesday
LESSON 296
Controlling Odic Force Fields

Occasionally, a devotee will come along in meditation and have sublime inner experiences. He's experiencing the *viśuddha chakra,* and he has inner light experiences. He's just on top of the world. A month later, he meets some *karmic* boomerang. He doesn't have the stamina or the discipline to hold awareness within, and he starts flowing through the second *chakra,* and he's saying, "I've never had any experiences at all. I wonder why? (the second *chakra* is reason) I wonder why I don't have some inward experiences," and why this and why that and why something else. "I wonder why I'm even doing meditation." He's wondering why all the way along, and he's quite argumentative. ¶I say, "Don't you remember the beautiful experience that you told me about? You came all wide open." "Oh, no, no, no." He doesn't remember that at all. "What experience?" he asks. "Don't you remember? You were right here in the temple," I say, trying to lead him gently back to his experience, "and your head turned into a sea of light. You sat there for an hour and then came and told me all about it." Then we pretend it only happened a moment ago, and he is back within again. This happens quite regularly. Therefore, to stabilize awareness, so it does not flow through the first *chakra*, the fifth *chakra*, the third *chakra*, the second *chakra*, to stabilize awareness, what do we do? Attention, concentration, meditation. Attention, concentration, meditation. Work daily within ourselves so we stabilize, and so that willpower and awareness become one and the same great motivating force, so we travel through the areas of the mind that we want to, not propelled by the forces of *karma* as they boomerang back, not propelled by those forces. We have to work within daily to stabilize the breath and the body so that will and awareness become one and the same great motivating force. Then, when the patterns and stumbling blocks of the past loom before us, we have the strength to stay within and maintain the continuity of one inner unfoldment after another. ¶These magnetic forces are either passive or aggressive in their manifestation. Business advertising is one example of aggressive odic force in use. Sexual magnetism is one example of passive odic force. Our physical body is composed of a subtle balance between active and passive magnetic forces. When the aggressive odic force becomes too active, the passive forces become disturbed and illness results, generally of a mental or emotional nature. When the passive odic forces become overstimulated, physical ailments of a purely physical nature result. ¶Odic forces are colorful and are of the conscious and subconscious world. Actinic force is colorless and very refined in color and is the vibration of deeper consciousness. When the mind is in a disturbed state, the odic forces are out of balance with each other. The trained *yoga* adept knows how to open himself to the inflow of actinic force, which then quiets or appeases the odic discharge. The evolution of the adept through meditation depends on the measure of his control and use of the odic forces as he enters into the consciousness of the actinic world. Many people start on the path of Self Realization in an almost involuntary way, simply by asking the fundamental question, "Who, or what, am I?" In so doing, they turn the mind fiber in upon itself and become tuned into the substance of actinic force. ¶Everyone has his own actinic wave length or actinic ray upon which, or within which, his awareness glides in the realms of expanded consciousness. A *satguru's* actinic ray is actually heard as *nāda,* the "eeee" sound. This mystic sound the *guru* hears as he tunes into his *guru.* His *guru* listens to the same sound to be one with his *satguru,* and on and on, back in time, which is within the "now." To become one with, or of a similar vibration with, the actinic vibration of the *satguru* is synonymous to listening to the sound of the *guru*'s lineage. This is called the *nāda-nāḍī śakti.* The devotee endeavors in this meditation to listen to his *guru*'s *nāda,* not his own, but that of his *guru,* his *guru*'s *guru* and all the others back in time. This is oneness, the oneness of a devotee merging into the *satguru's* lineage.

Wednesday
LESSON 297
Creating the Golden Yoke

Each lineage has within it a *nāda* of a different velocity of sound, varied in pitch and depth. This is Hindu mysticism. This is the magic of Hindu oneness. This is *sampradāya.* This is *paramparā.* This is what I want you to do: in the beginning, don't try to hear your *nāda.* Try instead to hear mine. You will know you are hearing my *nāda* and not your own when it is slightly louder. This is *nāda-nāḍī śakti.* This is your first *siddhi.* It will bring many good benefits into your life, smooth out the *karmas,* bringing you from future to future, keep you inspired and on the subtle path, strengthening your psychic protection, strengthening your personal force field and that of all the loved ones connected to you, whether they themselves hear *nāda* or not. ¶There is a large religious movement in India whose one and only practice is to gaze at the founder's picture and to listen to the inner sound, which is the followers' connection to him and thus to the Divine in all. I'm hearing the *nāda* now, as I speak, that of my *satguru,* Yogaswāmī; his *satguru,* Chellappaswāmī; and his *satguru,* Kadaitswāmī, and that of innumerable *ṛishis,* back to Tirumular and his *satguru,* Nandinātha, and those beyond and beyond and beyond, to the beginning of time, for there has never been a time on this planet or any of the earths the same distance from other suns in our galaxy or any of the others when our Nandinātha Sampradāya has not existed. *Nāda* is always present and within divine lineages of Sanātana Dharma, the eternal path, the eternal religion, the eternal truth, more advanced than modern science, but not conflicting in any way with the discoveries of science, as these good souls penetrate into Sanātana Dharma and unravel its mysteries. ¶There are advanced forms of communication and training that utilize these energy rays. Two people may be a continent apart, entirely separated from each other's odic, conscious and subconscious force fields, and still be subject to actinic mind communication. This has been called soul communication. It is possible because in the superconscious mind, where actinic rays exist, time and space are conceptually different. ¶In the evolutionary cycle, man eventually becomes conscious of the actinic force as it flows through the odic areas of the mind. On these rays, education comes from the inside of himself out to the conscious mind. A person going through such an experience feels he has tapped a higher, intuitive resource. Psychically seen, an intellect developed in this manner, rather than through mere sensory observation, has a golden appearance. The education of the mind's odic force field from its actinic source creates what I call the "golden yoke." It is the yoke of liberation, because in its exercise one penetrates to the very depths of the inner being. In so doing, the inner awakening and knowledge brought forth from this superconscious realm registers on the odic force field of the conscious mind's intellect. It is known that sages have learned languages, mathematics and all flows of knowledge in meditation. Uneducated men have become scholars by opening what Jñānaguru Yogaswāmī called "your own book." ¶Now, we can lose this expanded consciousness, once it has been gained, by allowing ourselves to become identified again with the odic world. As soon as we stop making the effort to penetrate the actinic realms, the ordinary forces of attachment, fear and desire force in upon us. It then requires extra effort to balance the forces and penetrate the life-giving, light-giving regions in meditation. When this happens again, one has the experience of seeing light within the cranium, the friction of the actinic force permeating and lighting up the odic force field. ¶A *guru*-disciple relationship may be established on the actinic plane for years before a physical meeting and training takes place. The study and unfoldment begins when one turns within himself, creating the irrevocable "golden yoke" and attuning himself to the same actinic ray of consciousness in which the *guru* functions. Teachings can then be conveyed on these rays, as long as *guru* and disciple are in harmony. By working with this golden yoke, one's *karmic* experiences are hastened, but at the same time they are encountered in a more orderly fashion.

Thursday
LESSON 298
The State of Contemplation

The force field of actinic consciousness is one which a *guru* has worked perhaps for many years to enter. His awareness of it is his control of it. This mechanism works in the same way a corporate executive guides the forces of his business, through knowledge of the field and experience. A *guru* learns control of actinic force fields just as a businessman learns to control his odic force fields. ¶The odic force and the actinic force make up this planet. The action and interaction of these two forces working together cause the life that we see on Earth. Quite often in meditation I see the planet as completely transparent, just like a tremendous, transparent, translucent sphere. It looks light, and it is floating in a clear space, a blue space. This space is called *ākāśa.* I am seeing the planet in the *ākāśa,* vibrantly seeing the collective odic and actinic forces working within and through it. ¶Coming out of this state, one can see easily the way in which human beings are created. The woman holds the power of the odic force field. The man holds the power of the actinic force field. Between them they cause a chemicalization that brings through the soul and the physical and emotional body of a newborn child. ¶Depending upon this chemical balance, they give birth to an old soul or a young soul. That is why it is so important for families to have a deeply religious life. What is a religious life? It is the balance of these two forces, the odic force and the actinic force. It is so important that there is an absolute harmony between the man and the woman. This guides and governs the inner currents of the children until the age of twenty-one. At that time, the inner forces dissolve from the family and are governed by their own superconscious mind. ¶I have seen this all happen from the inside. It is a vast and beautiful picture. Of course, with vast populations now covering the planet, it is happening more than ever—more births, more deaths, more forces to contend with. At this time in the evolution of this planet, the actinic forces are breaking through the odic force fields due to the planetary configurations, making this an actinic age, an age of light and great illumination, an age of contemplation. ¶The state of contemplation is not just peacefully sitting and getting all jazzed up on the inside. It is as refined an activity as penetrating subtle thoughts and feelings on the superconscious plane until all intellectual structure dissolves in the atom's essence within superconsciousness. If you have ever had the experience of tracing a vibration of consciousness to the point where consciousness is no more, you will know how subtle is the fiber of an actinic ray. The explosion of light so commonly associated with the contemplative state is only the first breakthrough. After this, an aspirant is ready to begin the study which will give him the mastery of these subtle forces. ¶Striving in meditation for a continuing contemplative awareness, a strong actinic vehicle is built. The aura of a person who has created access to this inner world gives evidence of a higher energy source. This is what is behind the ancient myths wherein the Gods rode through the skies in golden chariots. The golden chariot is the actinic vehicle of the superconscious. A *satguru* must be able to control his travel on more than one actinic ray. In doing so, he is able to establish a continuity of contact in the deeper consciousness within his various disciples. It is on an actinic ray that intuitive knowledge is gained and passed along. ¶At first the odic forces seem warm and friendly, and the actinic force registers more as an emptiness or nothingness existing inside of you. But if you can find out what and where this nothingness is, you will not have to think anymore about purging the subconscious, because the actinic flow will take over the outer mind and you will find yourself lifted in love, light and perception.

Friday
LESSON 299
Heightened Sensitivity

People are worried about the world's coming to an end. Every now and then a religious sect proclaims the new coming of the end of the world. But although the Earth as we know it continues its steady progress around the Sun, the conscious mind for thousands of people has come to an end, for the simple reason that they are no longer interested in it. For them, the world of inner sounds and colors has opened its far more attractive fare. But the job of sustaining and maintaining expanded awareness is not accomplished by losing the controls over one's powers of awareness. The actinic world is only attained and sustained by initiating definite controls over the odic world. One state of consciousness is controlled in the process of awareness moving and expanding into another state. ¶As we progress along the path, we become more and more and more sensitive. This sensitivity is a wonderful thing. It's like graduating from being an old battery-set radio of the 1920s and '30s to a sophisticated, solid-state television. This sensitivity that you will begin to recognize is so refined and yet so strong. You communicate with yourself through the nerve currents which extend out, around and through the physical body-physical nerve currents as well as psychic nerve currents. Before we get deeply within on the path, we're not too sensitive. But as this sensitivity develops, we begin to see through our hands. We begin to hear feeling. We begin to see sound, and all sorts of new faculties manifest. ¶Now, this can be very distressing, because we see things that we ordinarily would not be able to see. We hear meaning in what people say that ordinarily we would be unaware of, and we can become very disappointed in life, in people or in ourselves. This may seem like falling into a bog on the path, and we don't want to do this. We want to be sensitive, and yet we want protection, psychic protection. Our dreams become more well defined, but we don't want to be vulnerable to negative areas of the mind, disruptive areas, experiential areas of the astral plane while we are sleeping. Neither do we wish to be attacked on the astral plane by the mischievous beings, entities that are on that particular side of life. ¶We need this astral protection. We need this psychic protection. The group helps the individual and the individual helps the group. The force field of a group of people on the path goes along at a certain rate of intensity which is not broken, and this gives us tremendous psychic protection. In the very same way, a positive group of people only admit into their midst other positive people. A group of businessmen have a well-managed force field, and generally only a businessman of their same caliber can come and mix with them. A group of artists has a force field, and only artists of the same caliber can get into it. Why? If they let everybody in, they wouldn't have a force field. The business would fail. The art would go into chaos. Friendships would be destroyed because of other influences coming in and amongst the people. ¶Force fields protect and sustain not only our outer forms of expression, but deep spiritual layers as well. When we go "out" into superconsciousness, if we are sensitive and unable to protect our subconscious mind, all sorts of other types of influences can enter. We don't want this to happen, and it's not necessary. It is a deterrent on the path, for we then are exposed to unseemly astral influences that detract us from our quest. ¶Make friends with those who are on the path. Be with fine, positive people. Don't be with negative, complaining people who have no relationship to what you are doing on the inside or who are criticizing you for what you are doing. There's the old statement, "One bad apple can turn the whole bushel rotten." Maybe that will be reversed in the New Age; a lot of things are changing in the New Age. Maybe at some time a whole bag of good apples will make a bad apple good, but so far it hasn't occurred. Until such a time, we have to be wary of a natural law of nature and live among others of virtuous character and conduct, others who share spiritual insights and seeking.

Saturday
LESSON 300
Undesirable Influences

Being on the path is a marvelous thing, but it is a path. There are jungles on either side, and if we wander off into the jungle, taking too many liberties, continuity of the vibration of our unfoldment will begin to wane. Suppose you are meditating regularly in the morning and at night, day after day. Perhaps they're not long meditations, but they are regular. You are generating a certain vibration out of it. If you then stop that routine and take your awareness into feeling sorry for yourself or mentally arguing with a friend, you lose the subtle thread of superconsciousness. You're going through an old, old pattern and it will be difficult to get back into the vibration of meditation. Your dreams at night may become nightmares. Your circle of friends may change. This is called, in a sense, spinning out into a different area of the mind. If you have not yet experienced this yet, it's not a recommended experience on the path. And if you have experienced it, you know what I am talking about, and you know the importance of protecting yourself and your meditations. Psychic protection, to sensitive people, is extremely important. It involves every detail of life—your home, friends, clothes, diet, even your dreams. You should live in places that are clean, very clean. Paint your place. Assure yourself that the inner atmosphere is clean and unpolluted. ¶We have an outer atmosphere and we have and inner atmosphere. The inner atmosphere can become polluted, too, just like the outer atmosphere can. All sorts of influences from the *astral* plane can come in on the inner atmosphere, and this we don't want. We want the inner flow of the inner atmosphere, which is within this atmosphere of air and ether, to be absolutely peaceful and sublime. How is this done? By keeping your house, your meditation room, as clean as possible. By entertaining few guests and then only people of the same caliber and nature. Guests should not stay more than three nights. Why? Because otherwise they bring too much distraction, too many other influences into the home. Finally, the whole atmosphere may be disrupted. Many families have broken up and lost their home, and children have gone homeless, simply because guests have stayed too long and worked into the inner atmosphere and brought in too many influences of a distracting and disturbing nature. This is an old, old traditional custom of hospitality that dates back many thousands of years, and these old customs are based on sound judgment. If they are understood and followed, they assure and protect our contemplative life. ¶Keep your environment positive, so that the inner feeling is always content. Keep your home shrine or meditation space radiant, so that the inner feeling there is always uplifting. As you advance along the path, the radio mechanism will become highly tuned, very positive. Being positive, it will register all types of influences. Influences that are distasteful to you will come through as strongly as influences that are really magnificent. You have to learn to shield out the static by finely tuning this mechanism. That is why you strive for mastery of *sādhana,* mastery of concentration, your ability to hold awareness where you want it, when you want it for as long as you want it, and mastery of your ability to experience *kaef,* pure awareness aware only of itself, by taking awareness out of the entire context into just being aware. This practice of *kaef* is one of the fundamental protectors from psychic or *astral* invasion, for when you are in that state, great clarity and willpower persist and the lower states are transcended. ¶To attain and sustain *kaef* is a simple practice. You pull awareness out of the thought processes. You pull awareness out of the emotion processes. You pull awareness out of the bodily processes, and you're just completely on that pinnacle of being aware of being aware. That's so necessary to practice every day, even if you do it for a split second. ¶The experience of *kaef* can be attained by anyone on the face of the Earth, at least for a split second, because it's so easy to be aware of being aware. To hold that experience and to stabilize the physical and emotional elements long enough to hold that intensity for even a minute takes more practice—not too much, but consistent practice. To maintain *kaef* for two minutes requires more effort, more will, more dedication to the life of *sādhana.* Five minutes requires more. That's the test.

Sunday
LESSON 301
Sensitivity and The Third Eye

When you meditate, you become inwardly strong. You become extremely sensitive, and sensitivity is strength. But if you are not psychologically adjusted to the things you may be hearing and seeing and the depth to which you might see, you might see things that will be disturbing to you, that will upset your nerve system. Now, it is true that if you are centered in yourself completely enough to be all spine and just a being of energy, you can go anyplace in any type of environment, inside or outside, and the environment would be better for your having been there. You would not absorb any of the distracting or negative vibrations. But until that day comes, it is better to be wise and live in a positive vibration and among people who can help stabilize the force field around you, so that your inner life goes on without interruptions—of spinning out, having to crawl back, and spinning out and then having to crawl back. Why go through all those frustrating experiences which are inconvenient, time consuming and totally unnecessary?

¶Part of the psychic pitfall is the belief that in order to be spiritually awakened, one must also be psychically awakened, seeing auras, visions, hearing celestial music and such. We do not have to awaken the third eye. To me, that is a translation error made in the old scriptures. This third eye has never been asleep. It's always awake. We are not aware, however, of the visual mechanism of the third eye. The artist doesn't have to learn to see to distinguish hundreds of shades of color in a painting. He has only to learn how to be aware of his ability to see hundreds of different shades within a painting. The untrained eye cannot see such subtle variation of tones and hues, but just looks at the painting.

¶It is the same with the third eye. It doesn't have to be awakened. It's always awake. As we become more and more sensitive, the third eye becomes more and more apparent to us, because we keenly observe through that faculty more than we did before. ¶If you are standing on a crowded bus and another passenger is just about to crash down on your foot with his foot, you will intuitively move it out of the way. You have often noticed that you moved your foot or some other part of your body out of the way of danger just in time. Well, your third eye wasn't asleep then, and you didn't see that foot coming down on you with your physical eyes. You saw it with your third eye. ¶We use this third eye all the time. When someone greets you who is apparently looking fine and you sense otherwise, thinking, "I feel he's disturbed. I wonder what's wrong," you're seeing his inner condition with your third eye. When you walk up to someone's house and you have the feeling that nobody is home because you don't feel vibrations coming from the house, you're seeing this with your third eye. We see and respond to things seen with the third eye every day, whether we are fully conscious of it or not. ¶The third eye does not have to be awakened. In fact, it is harmful to consciously make efforts to see things psychically—a big sidetrack on the eternal path. We become sensitive to the use of it by using it, going along with our natural meditational practices in a regular way, morning and night, morning and night, when you awaken in the morning and just before you go to sleep at night. All sorts of wonderful things come to you. Protect yourself as you protect a precious jewel. Guard your awareness from coarse influences and you will enjoy the bliss of the natural state of the mind—pure, clear and undisturbed.

Darśanam, Guru Kṛipā

दर्शनं गुरुकृपा

Darshan, Grace Of the Guru

He taught me humility, infused in me the light of devotion, granted me the grace of His feet. After holy interrogation, testing me entirely, He revealed to me the Real, the unreal and real-unreal. Undoubtedly, the Śiva-Guru is Iraivan, the worshipful Lord Himself.

TIRUMANTIRAM 1573

Monday
LESSON 302
Training from A Satguru

Several thousand years ago, a *yoga* master was born from his own realization of the Self. He was born from his search within, where he found Absolute Existence deep inside the atomic structure of his being. This master's realization came as he controlled the mind and penetrated through it to the very core of its substance. After Self Realization, his mind opened into its fullness of knowing. This knowledge he then imparted, as needed, to the students who came to him curious or eager to solve the philosophical and metaphysical puzzles of life. The first esoteric universities formed around the master in this way. Other masters have since come and gone. Each in turn battled and conquered the fluctuating mind and penetrated into the depth of being. Students gathered around them in a most natural sequence of events. Each master brought forth from his intuition the related laws and disciplines needed so that they, too, might attain Self Realization, *emkaef,* as it is called in Shum, the language of meditation. ¶This is known as the *guru* system of training. It is personal and direct. An advanced devotee is one whose intuition is in absolute harmony with that of his master. This is the way I teach, not in the beginning stages when my devotees are probing the subject matter for answers, but after they have conquered the fluctuation of the patterns of the thinking mind. When they reach an advanced level of control and rapport with me, they have become *śishya,* dedicated their lives to serving mankind by imparting the teachings of Advaita Īśvaravāda—the nondualistic philosophy of the *Vedas,* the basic tenet of which is that man merges into God. ¶Advice can be given freely, but unless the seeker is dedicated to the path of Eternal Truth, it is taken only on the intellectual plane and quoted but rarely used. Therefore, the wise *guru* gives challenges—spiritual assignments known as *sādhana*—advice, spiritual direction and guidance merge with the aspirant's own individual will. This causes daily, recognizable results from actions taken to produce accomplishment physically, emotionally, intellectually and spiritually. Each seeker sets his own pace according to his character, his ability to act with care, forethought, consistency and persistence in the *sādhana* given to him by his *guru*. ¶There are five states of mind. Each one interacts somewhat with the other. The conscious mind and the subconscious mind work closely together, as does the sub of the subconscious with the subconscious, and the subconscious with the subsuperconscious. The superconscious is the most independent of them all. Being the mind of light, when one is in a superconscious state, seeing inner light is a constant experience of daily life. To attain states of this depth and still function creatively in the world, a solid training under a *guru* is requisite. ¶The power to meditate comes from the grace of the *guru*. The *guru* consciously introduces his student into meditation by stimulating certain superconscious currents within him. The grace of the *guru* is sought for by the *yogīs* and is well understood by them.

Tuesday
LESSON 303
Darshan's Mystic Power

Little is known of the *guru's* grace or the power of *darśana* in Western culture. *Darśana* (more popularly *darshan)* is a Sanskṛit word meaning "vision, seeing or perception." But in its mystical usage, it is more than that. *Darshan* is also the feeling of the emotions of a holy person, the intellect, the spiritual qualities that he has attained and, most importantly, the *śakti,* the power, that has changed him and is there constantly to change others. *Darshan* encompasses the entirety of the being of a person of spiritual attainment. In India, everyone is involved in *darshan.* Some at a temple have *darshan* of the Deity. Others at an *ashram* have *darshan* of their *swāmī* or on the street enjoy *darshan* of a *sādhu.* And most everyone experiences *dūrdarshan.* That's the word for television in India, meaning "seeing from afar." Even this seeing, through movies, news and various programs of mystery, tragedy, humor, the fine arts and culture, can affect our emotions, intellect, pulling us down or lifting us up in consciousness. Seeing is such a powerful dimension of life, and it affects us in so many ways, inside and out. *Darshan,* in the true meaning of this mystical, complex and most esoteric word, conveys all of this. ¶The concept of *darshan* goes beyond the devotee's seeing of the *guru.* It also embraces the *guru's* seeing of the devotee. Hindus consider that when you are in the presence of the *guru* that his seeing of you, and therefore knowing you and your *karmas,* is another grace. So, *darshan* is a two-edged sword, a two-way street. It is a process of seeing and being seen. The devotee is seeing and in that instant drawing forth the blessings of the *satguru,* the *swāmī* or the *sādhu.* In turn, he is seeing the devotee and his divine place in the universe. Both happen within the moment, and that moment, like a vision, grows stronger as the years go by, not like imagination, which fades away. It is an evergrowing spiritual experience. The sense of separation is transcended, so there is a oneness between seer and seen. This is monistic theism, this is *Advaita Īśvaravāda.* Each is seeing the other and momentarily being the other. ¶*Darshan* embodies *śakti. Darshan* embodies *śānti. Darshan* embodies *vidyā,* perceiving on all levels of consciousness for all inhabitants of the world. It is physical, mental, emotional, spiritual perception. Hindus believe that the *darshan* from a *guru* who has realized the Self can clear the subconscious mind of a devotee in minutes, alleviating all reaction to past actions and alter his perspective from an outer to an inner one. *Darshan* is the emanating rays from the depth of an enlightened soul's being. These rays pervade the room in which he is, penetrating the aura of the devotees and enlivening the *kuṇḍalinī,* the white, fiery, vapor-like substance that is actually the heat of the physical body in its natural state. ¶In the Orient, whenever the cloud of despair covers the soul of a devotee, the *darshan* of a *guru* is sought. Whenever it becomes difficult to meditate, his grace is hoped for to lift the veil of delusion and release awareness from the darker areas of mind to soar within. Consciously merge into the inner being of yourself, and you will know your *guru* when you find him.

Wednesday
LESSON 304
The Scent Of a Rose

If you were to travel through India on a spiritual pilgrimage, you would undoubtedly hear much about the Sanskṛit word *darshan.* The religious leaders of the Orient are categorized according to the *darshan* they give, for there are various kinds of *darshan. Darshan* is the vibration that emanates from the illumined soul as a result of his inner attainment, be he a *yogī, pandit, swāmī, guru* or a *ṛishi.* Usually the *yogī, swāmī,* saint or sage attracts his following not so much by what he says as by the *darshan* he radiates. Hindus travel for miles to receive the *darshan* of an illumined soul established in his enlightenment. Perhaps he doesn't even speak to them. Perhaps he scolds some of them. Perhaps he gives the most inspired of talks to them. In any case, they feel the *darshan* flooding out from him. ¶A great soul is always giving *darshan.* The Hindus believe that the *darshan* coming from a great soul helps them in their evolution, changes patterns in their life by cleaning up areas of their subconscious mind that they could not possibly have done for themselves. They further believe that if his *darshan* is strong enough, if they are in tune with him enough, by its power the *kuṇḍalinī* force can be stimulated enough that they can really begin to meditate. This is called the grace of the *guru.* The ability for one to meditate comes from this grace. You must have it before you can begin to meditate, or you must do severe austerities by yourself instead. *Darshan* is not well understood in the West, because the West is outwardly refined but not necessarily inwardly refined. The peoples of the Orient, by their heritage, are inwardly sensitive enough to understand and appreciate *darshan.* ¶*Darshan* and the unfolding soul on the path are like the rose. When the rose is a bud, it does not give forth a perfume. Unfoldment is just beginning. We admire the beauty of the bud, the stem and the thorns. We are aware that it has the potential of a magnificent flower. In the same way, we appreciate a beautiful soul who comes along, seeing in him the potential of a spiritual mission in this life. ¶In the life of a bud, nothing happens until unfoldment begins. The same is true for the fine soul. It happens occasionally that someone comes along and picks the bud. This means the fine soul is in the wrong company. Now neither the bud nor the soul can unfold. But when they are well protected in a garden or *ashram* by a careful gardener, or *guru*, the bud and the soul unfold beautifully. ¶With just their first little opening to the world, they begin to see the light of the outer and inner sun shining down into the core of their being. It is still too early, of course, for the rose to have a noticeable fragrance, or the soul a *darshan*. We might appreciate them closely, but we would detect little in this early and delicate stage of unfolding. At this time, the unfolding soul might say, "I can see the light in my head and in my body." And the sun's rays keep pouring into the rose, penetrating into the stem and as deep as the roots. It is feeling stronger and unfolding more and more. If no one picks it because of its unfolding beauty, the rose continues to unfold until it opens into all its glory. Then a wonderful thing happens. The delicate perfume of the rose fills the air day and night. It is the *darshan* of the rose. ¶To some people, the bouquet of the rose is very strong; to others, it is rather weak. Is the emanation of the rose stronger at one time than another? No. It is always the same. It goes on and on and on, maturing all the while into a deeper, richer, more potent scent. Soon it is filling the entire garden. But to the one who comes into the garden with a stuffy nose, there is only the beauty of the flower to experience. ¶In the same way, one who is closed on the inside of himself misses the *darshan* of the awakened soul. He sees in the greater soul just another ordinary person like himself. The *darshan* is there, but he is too negative to feel it. But the *darshan* permeates him just the same. He goes away from the garden not having smelled a rose, but carrying the perfume of the rose himself. If you stand away from the rose, you smell less of its fragrance. Bring yourself really close, and more of its strong and sweet scent will penetrate your body.

Thursday
LESSON 305
Sensitivity To Darshan

Darshan from a great soul, like the pollen of the flowers, can stimulate healthy sneezing and cleansing if one's subconscious happens to be congested. Call it, if you like, an allergy to flowers. Some people have allergies to *gurus*, too. The *guru's darshan* lifts repressed subconscious patterns that have been out of the flow of the cosmic pattern of regenerative life, bringing them up before one's conscious attention. Instead of feeling wonderful, the visitor to the garden feels miserable, as the fire is brought up from within, releasing his awareness to view the polluted state of the subconscious mind. ¶Some people are more sensitive to fragrance than others. Others are so selfless and sensitive, they can become the fragrance itself for a time. In such a person, the rose smells sweet through every pore of his body. He is not in the least aware of any subconscious congested area of the mind. He sits in the garden and goes deep into meditation on the subtle fragrance of the flowers. The same principle relates to the unfolded soul. *Darshan* pours forth from within the unfolded soul just as fragrance flows from the rose—stronger at some times than at others because some devotees are more in tune than others. For them, the room begins to ring and vibrate. Some people are so sensitive that when a great soul comes to the same town, they feel his presence. This shows their inner attunement to the constant flowing power of the *darshan.* ¶Everyone has some feelings radiating from within, but they are emanations that fluctuate. Because you feel these vibrations coming from them, you can intuit how they are feeling. They do not emanate a constant or a building flow. It is a fluctuating flow of emotional, or astral, energy. The *darshan* I am explaining is really the energies flowing from the deeper *chakras, sahasrāra* and *ājñā,* the seventh and sixth *chakras,* or psychic force centers, in the head, through the *kuṇḍalinī* force within the spine. These energy flows do not fluctuate as the emotional odic-force energies do. They go on day and night and night and day through the illumined soul. Those devotees who are in tune with the *guru* can feel his physical presence when he enters their town because the *darshan* gets stronger. And it feels to them more ethereal when he is farther away. ¶These energy flows are very important to study, because it is possible to draw and enjoy a great *darshan* from an illumined soul if you approach him in just the right way. If you can become as a sponge when you approach him, you will draw out inspiring talks and gracious blessings from him. The Hindu is conscious that he is drawing *darshan* from his *ṛishi* or his *satguru,* just as you are conscious of drawing the perfume of the rose into your body. When approaching a soul who is known to give *darshan,* be in the same area of the superconscious mind that you feel he must be in. The *guru* does not have to be necessarily functioning in that same area. He could be externalized in consciousness at the time. This is not important. It does not stop his *darshan* at all. The *guru,* feeling you draw the *darshan,* would immediately go within and enjoy it himself. Once *darshan* is there in him, it is always there.

Friday
LESSON 306
Protection and Stabilization

Hindu devotees are very careful not to upset their *guru,* for they do not want his forces strongly directed at them. It is the same *darshan,* however. At a time such as this, it is like a distilled perfume from the rose. It becomes too potent. Therefore, the devotee tries to maintain a good atmosphere around the *guru* so that his *darshan* is pleasant and natural. The *darshan* of a *guru* is the power that stabilizes the devotee on the path. The philosophies, teachings and practices that he is given to do are important, but it is the power of *darshan* that is his stabilizing influence, enabling him to unfold easily on the path of enlightenment. ¶*Darshan* is a mystical power emanating from the adept who has gone deep enough within to awaken this power. By stabilizing that power, he gives psychic protection to his disciples and devotees, even during their sleep at night. The same power grants them the ability to meditate without the prior necessity of extensive *tapas. Satguru darshan* releases the awareness of the devotee out of the area of the mind which is constantly thinking into sublimity. ¶A beginning meditator is usually aware most of the time in the area of consciousness where thoughts run constantly before his vision. He finds it difficult to go deeper. All efforts fall short of the divine life he inwardly knows he can live, as he is bound by the cycles of his own *karma.* The *satguru's* power of *darshan* releases the meditator's individual awareness from the thinking area of mind and stabilizes him in the heart *chakra,* and he begins to awaken and unfold his Divinity. ¶Devout Hindus sit before a *satguru* and in seeing him, draw the *darshan* vibration from him, absorbing it into themselves. They are sensitive enough to distinguish the vibration of *darshan* from the other vibrations around the *guru.* They also believe that any physical thing the *satguru* touches begins to carry some of his *darshan* or personal vibration, and that when away from him they can just hold the article to receive the full impact of his *darshan,* for the physical object is a direct link to the *satguru* himself. It is *darshan* vibration that makes a human being a holy person. When we say someone is holy or saintly we are feeling the radiations of that divine energy flooding through him and out into the world. ¶The inner life of a devotee has to be stabilized, cherished and well protected by the *guru.* The *guru* is able to do this through his well-developed facilities of *darshan,* even if his devotee lives at great distances from him. Unless the inner vibratory rate of the devotee is held stable, he will not come into his fullness in this life. If a plant is transplanted too often, it won't come into its full growth. If the bud is picked before it blooms, it will not flower or give forth its redolent fragrance. Yes, the grace of the *satguru* fires the ability to meditate in the seeker, the erudite Hindu believes.

Saturday
LESSON 307
Relationship With a Guru

A child living with his family who does right by his family in honoring his mother and his father reaps a reward—for that mother and father are going to gladly see to all his needs in the emotional, intellectual and material world. But if the child negligently begins to play with the emotions and intellect of his mother and father by not living up to their expectations, they will be relieved when he is old enough to leave home and be on his own. During the time he is still at home, they will, of course, talk with him and work the best they can with the negative vibrations he generates, as their natural love for him is a protective force. ¶As it is with the parents, it is much the same with the *guru.* A devotee coming to his *guru* who is evolved, honest and able is first asked to do simple, mundane tasks. If they are done with willingness, the *guru* will take him consciously under his wing for a deeper, inner, direct training, as he fires him to attain greater heights through *sādhana* and *tapas.* This *darshan* power of the *guru* will then be constantly felt by the disciple. But if the disciple were to turn away from the small tasks given by his *guru,* he would not connect into the deeper *darshan* power of the *satguru* that allows him to ride into his meditations deeply with ease. If the devotee breaks his flow with the *guru* by putting newly awakened power into intellectual "ifs" or "buts" or—"Well, now I know how to meditate; I don't need you anymore. Thank you for all you've done. I've learned all you have to offer me and must be on my way"—or if he merely starts being delinquent in his efforts, then the *guru*-disciple relationship is shattered. ¶Still a certain *darshan* power goes out to him, but the *guru* no longer consciously inwardly works with him as an individual. He knows it is too dangerous to work with this fluctuating aspirant, for there is no telling how he might take and use the accumulating power that would later be awakened within him. The *satguru* makes such a one prove himself to himself time and time again and to the *guru,* too, through *sādhana* and *tapas. Sādhana* tests his loyalty, consistency and resolution. *Tapas* tests his loyalty as well as his personal will, for he does *tapas* alone, gaining help only from inside himself, and he has to be aware on the inside to receive it. A wise *guru* never hesitates to put him "through it," so to speak. ¶A *guru* of India may give *tapas* to a self-willed disciple who insisted on living his personal life in the *ashram,* not heeding the rules of his *sādhana.* He may say, "Walk through all of India. Stay out of my *ashram* for one year. Walk through the Himālayas. Take nothing but your good looks, your orange robe and a bowl for begging at the temples." From then on, the *guru* works it all out with him on the inside for as long as the disciple remains "on *tapas.*" Maybe the *guru* will be with him again, yet maybe not; it depends entirely on the personal performance of the *tapas.* ¶This, then, is one of the reasons that it is very, very important for anyone striving on the path to first have a good relationship with his family—for the *guru* can expect nothing more than the same type of relationship eventually to arise with himself or between the aspirant and some other disciple. As he gets more into the vibration of the *guru,* he is going to relax into the same behavioral patterns he generated with his parents, for in the *ashram,* many of the same vibrations, forces and attitudes are involved.

Sunday
LESSON 308
The Devotee's Responsibilities

The aspirant may go to his *guru* and be one with him by preparing himself to receive his grace. As a result he may be able to meditate, to keep his personal *karma* subdued sufficiently to quiet the inner forces. Once a *guru* has been chosen, the aspirant must be loyal to him and stay with that one *guru* only. He should not go from one to another, because of these subtle, powerful inner, connecting vibrations of *darshan* and the training received through the power of a *satguru's* use of *darshan.* These inner, mystical laws protect the *guru* himself against people who wander from one *guru* to another, as well as warn the seeker against the fluctuating forces of his own mind as he creates and breaks the subtle yet powerful relationship with a holy person. ¶*Satguru darshan* opens psychic seals in the devotee by moving his awareness out of an area that he does not want to be in. Similarly, a blowtorch changes the consistency of metal. The *satguru* is like the sun. He is just there, radiating this very pure energy like the sun evaporates water. The *satguru* hardly does anything at all. It is the seeker who opens himself to the great accumulated power of *darshan* which the *guru* inherited from his *guru* and his *guru's guru,* as well as the natural *darshan* he unfolded from within himself through his evolution and practices of *sādhana* and *tapas.* It's all up to the aspirant at first. ¶A *satguru* doesn't do a thing. The *guru* can amuse himself externally with anything. It does not make any difference in his *darshan* when he is at a certain point in his unfoldment. If you are around him long enough, and if you are honest with yourself and persistent in the tasks he asks you to perform and directions he gives you, psychic seals lift after awhile. But you have to do your part. He does his in an inner way, and as he does, you will feel the psychic seals melt away under his fiery *darshan,* just like a blowtorch penetrates and transforms the metal it touches.

Ādhyātmika Praśikshaṇam

आध्यात्मिकप्रशिक्षणम्

Spiritual Training

Gathering the strands of my fetters, he knotted them together and then wrenched them off. Thus freeing me from my fond body, straight to *mukti* he led me. Behold, of such holy potency is the presence of my *guru* divine!

TIRUMANTIRAM 1574

Monday
LESSON 309
The Meeting of Two Darshans

Once someone said of my *guru*, Yogaswāmī, "You have to make yourself like a fool to go in front of that man. He will speak as a madman of God to you. But if you go to him in an ordinary state of consciousness, he will say, 'I'm just like you. Go away. I have nothing to say. Nothing comes from the inside. Go away!'" You have to be an intellectual fool to be in front of the *satguru*. If you hear ordinary things from the *guru*, look closely at yourself. He is your closest mirror. He is only biding his time with you until the extraordinary ones come along to utilize his depths. Most *gurus* enjoy an exquisite inner life that is so refined and interesting, it keeps them very well occupied. The *darshan* of a *satguru* in Sri Lanka and India is judged by how one feels on the inside after leaving his presence—not necessarily by the feelings that persist while in his presence—because the *guru* could be emotionally upset in the presence of a clever visitor. So, it is only after one leaves, while experiencing his reaction to having been with the *guru*, that the depth of the *guru's darshan* is judged. The *darshan* of a *satguru* siphons your own bliss in a similar way that liquid is siphoned. A *guru* works with *darshan* in two ways. One way is through giving it deliberately; that is the "flow-out" of *darshan*. Another way is to pull the flow within of external forces; that is the "flow-in" of *darshan*. He is siphoning it from his devotees. At the same time, he is giving, too, of his natural *darshan*. ¶Each *guru* has a natural *darshan*, according to his unfoldment and training. When they are personally going through something, their vibratory rates change from time to time. Basically, there is only one *darshan*, which is right from his soul, but going through various unfolded channels, like a prism, it can come to many powers. From some *gurus* the *darshan* is deeply loving, warm and gentle. From others it is fiery, sharp and profoundly detached. Many have a *darshan* so deep it cannot be readily felt, so withdrawn is their consciousness from this plane. ¶The vibration of the soul of an aspirant on the path when he is meditating is realized by the *satguru*, and this is the time he helps the most. The bliss of the aspirant is the ultimate of what he wants to bring forth first. The *darshan* of the *satguru* will syphon that from him if the intellect or emotion of the aspirant does not get in the way and obstruct and interrupt the process. If you are a meditator who has had inner experiences of light and are living a strict, disciplined life, you will reach a point in your unfoldment of sensitivity enough to feel and distinguish the *darshan* of a *satguru*. Soon the feeling will switch, and you will begin enjoying your own bliss of superconscious *darshan*. These two *darshans*—yours and that of the *satguru*—then meet, causing a spiritual dynamic strong enough that another meditator entering the area would automatically be inclined to go into deep meditation even if he were a beginner. ¶Devotees may say, "I have realized the Self." How does one know if this is true or not? One does not ascertain this by philosophically questioning, because they know all the right answers. They have memorized them. Look at the aura! Yes! That is telling. And then encourage them to do it again. He did it once. Do it again. The channel is open. The wise *satguru* will simply watch and feel the devotee's *darshan*. If the devotee truly has had the realization of the Self, how wonderful. The *dar-*

shan will grow stronger. It does not get weaker. It becomes better and better as the months and years go by. But if the feeling that comes forth from within him begins to feel terrible a few weeks after the illumination, it becomes apparent that he undoubtedly had a fine inner experience, but did not go all the way to the source of it all. ¶The *darshan* of an adept sitting in Satchidānanda is quite different than the ordinary daily *darshan.* It is extremely intense, and it causes that ringing sound to vibrate the inner atmosphere in the minds of everyone. No one feels like moving during this holy time, so intensely alive are they. The high-pitched *darshan* of Satchidānanda is so intense that the physical body does not move, hardly breathes. This you experience when you are in the presence of someone who is going in and out of Satchidānanda and Paraśiva. It is a different kind of *darshan*—awe inspiring. ¶The vibration of *darshan* knows no time or space. You see *darshan* when the *satguru* is around, and you can feel his *darshan* when he is miles away, even at times stronger. Look at *darshan* as great wires of communication, much like an open telephone line, enabling you to pick up the receiver and always find someone at the other end of the line. Subconscious problems only arise when the devotee does not feel the *guru's darshan.* During these times, his personal ego takes over and he becomes confused and ashamed.

Tuesday
LESSON 310
Loyalty to One's Satguru

A devotee on the path who has a *satguru* should not seek *darshan* from another *guru* unless he has permission from his own *guru* to do so. Why? Because he should not become psychically connected with the other *guru.* The *darshan* develops inner psychic bonds.

Another *guru* does not want to influence the unfoldment of the aspirant either. However, if he has permission to absorb *darshan* from someone else, then of course, there has been an inner agreement between the two *gurus* that no connection will result, and the disciple will not be distracted from his *sādhana* by conflicting new methods. ¶It is not good for a student on the path to run around to various teachers and lecturers and gain reams of miscellaneous knowledge about the path and related occultism. He becomes magnetically attached to the students of the various teachers and sometimes to the teachers themselves. The teachers do not like this "browsing" on the part of the *guru*-hopper, either, for it impairs the unfoldment of their own students, as it goes against the natural flow of unfoldment on the path. It is also energy draining and time-consuming for the *guru* or *swāmī*. ¶One must look at spiritual unfoldment in the same way one approaches the study of a fine art. If you were studying the *vīṇā* with a very accomplished teacher, he would not appreciate it at all if you went to three or four other teachers at the same time for study behind his back. He demands that you come and go from your lesson and practice diligently in between. By this faithful and loyal obedience, you would become so satisfied with the results of your unfolding talents that you would not want to run here and there to check out what other maestros were teaching and become acquainted with their students. Students only run from teacher to teacher only when they do not obey the teacher they have. ¶The wise *guru* or *swāmī* who takes his mission seriously and knows human nature to its core makes it very difficult for a devotee who departed his fellowship to later return. First he requires a detailed written explanation of the reasons for leaving, and a full written confession as to what occurred during the time away. This is all verified through background checks and in-depth personal interviews. Then to test the sincerity, penance, *prayaśchitta,* is given and performed before readmitance can even be considered. Upon hearing of these soul-searching procedures (known as *vrātyastoma*), most will bow out without a word and seek less demanding groups, thus proving their insincerity. These time-proven methods prevent detractors from returning to further disrupt the group from the inside more effectively than they could from the outside. If the seeker is qualified to be re-admitted after completing his *prayaśchitta,* he must begin at the beginning study level and be given no special privileges, positions or recognition in respect of his prior association. The protection of the fellowship is of utmost importance for the benefit of each devotee, and for the continuing spiritual unfoldment of the *guru* or *swāmī* himself. One should not be so naive to think that disgruntled former devotees would not seek reentrance for the purpose of disrupting the organization, or be sent on a mission from an adversarial group to rejoin in order to disrupt. All this and more has happened to *gurus* and *swāmīs* since the turn of the century. ¶There are three kinds of *gurus* that are traditionally available to guide the soul. The first, of course, are the parents. Next is the family *guru,* or a *guru* chosen by the children. The third *guru,* often the most suave, the most attractive, but in reality always the most demanding, is Viśvaguruji Mahā-Mahārāj. He does live up to his name in all ways, for *viśva* means "everything and everyone in the world," and *guru,* of course, means "teacher." Mahārāj is "great ruler." Viśvaguruji, as I call him, seemingly teaches so patiently, yet accepts no excuses and remains unforgivingly exacting in his lessons. Everyone living on this planet has a *guru,* whether they know it or not. ¶When the world becomes the teacher, the lessons can be rough or enticing, unloving or endearing, unpleasant or full of temptuous, temporary happiness. The world is relentless in its challenges, in the rewards it offers, the scars it leaves and the healing it neglects. The unrelenting Viśvaguruji works surreptitiously through the people you meet, as past-life *karmas* unfold into this life. He never gives direct advice or guidance, but leaves the lessons from each experience to be discovered or never discovered. His *sūtra* is "Learn by your own mistakes." His way of teaching is through unexpected happenings and untimely events, which are timely from his point of view. Unnecessary *karmas* are created while the old ones that were supposed to be eliminated smolder, waiting patiently for still another birth. Pleasure and pain are among his effective methods of instruction. Viśvagurujī is the teacher of all who turn their backs on parents, elders, teachers, *gurus* or *swāmīs,* laws and traditions of all kinds. It is not a lingering wonder why someone who once abandoned a loving *guru* or *swāmī* would want to return from the world and go through the *vrātyastoma* reentrance procedures, no matter what it takes.

Wednesday
LESSON 311
The World As Your Guru

Those on the *āṇava mārga,* the path of the external ego, often claim to be their own *guru.* Some untraditional teachers even encourage this attitude. However, being one's own *guru* is a false concept. Traditionally, one would be his "own *guru*" only if he were initiated as such, and his *guru* left the physical body. Even then he would be bound by the lineage within the sect of Sanātana Dharma he dedicated his life to, and would still maintain contact with his *guruji* within the inner world. Therefore, he would not really ever be his own *guru* at all. Being one's own *guru* is a definite part of the *āṇava mārga*, a very important part. It is raw, eccentric egoism. A teenager doesn't become his own teacher in school. A medical doctor doesn't become his own professor and then get a license to practice, signed by himself. Nor does a lawyer, an engineer or even an airline stewardess. So, logic would tell us that those pursuing something as sensitive, as personal and final as the path to perfection cannot on their own gain the necessary skills and knowledge to be successful in this endeavor. ¶Well, we are having fun here, aren't we? But it is also a serious subject. Think about it. In the realm of training and responsiveness, we can say that there are two basic *mārgas*, or stages: the *āṇava mārga* and the *jñāna mārga*. Those on the *jñāna mārga* know they need someone in their life who has already attained what they are seeking to attain, who can see ahead of their seeing and consciously guide them. This is the traditional path of Hindu Dharma leading to Self Realization. ¶Those on the way of external ego have met many teachers, tested them very carefully, and have found them all not meeting up to their standards. They are the devotees of Śrī Śrī Śrī Viśvaguru Mahā-Mahārāj-ji, members of his Bhogabhūmi Āshram, place of pleasure. The regular daily *sādhana* is stimulating the desire for sex, for money, for food, for clothing. ¶Unlike other *ashrams*, here there are no apparent boundaries or clear-cut guidelines. Followers are free to do as they please. All classes are open to everyone, from the most refined studies to the most devious and low-minded. Advanced low-level classes feature how to "do in" your enemies and remain undetected; how to access pornography on the Internet, one of the great tools of the *ashram*, and then participate in the pleasures it recommends. There are courses on effective ways to beat the children, abuse the wife or husband, to maximize domestic chaos. Executive education includes how to climb a corporate ladder, the pros and cons of saving face when rightly accused, and downing your accuser as misinformed or as a perpetual liar. One whole department is dedicated to self-indulgence. Advancements in technology provide never-ending novelty. There's experiential training in crime and punishment, in terrorism and being terrorized, revenge, retribution and the quest for forgiveness. Viśvagurujī has licenced assistant teachers all over the globe, in every city and small community in every country. In fact, every facet of our lovely planet participates in his training programs at every moment in time. ¶Mid-range subjects include politics, how to lose and still gain in the process. Love and relationships is very popular, with intensives in promiscuity, marriage, infidelity and divorce. How to find your little self and make it big—name and fame—is among the top ten pursuits. There are numerous variations on the acquisition and loss of property. Suicide and threatening suicide to get your own way have many students. Certain subjects are compulsory, including the quest for health and longevity, and the reality of decline, death and dying. The emotional wing is always full, especially the sessions on joy and sorrow. Anger is overcrowded, and jealousy, too. The list goes on and on. How to be totally committed to being noncommitted keeps many from advancing into higher grades. Keeping your children from becoming interested in religion, lest it hamper their education and job possibilities, has lots of apparently intelligent advocates. Making a living is one of the largest branches, with a recent addition of remaining sane while holding three jobs. Understanding your rebellious teenager and other parenting challenges are very big. How to have a family and neglect it at the same time (subtitled "latch-key kids") is the latest rage. ¶Most *ashramites*, or *bhogīs*, are swamped with so many subjects, they struggle twenty-four hours a day and still never catch up. This is a very tough school, and the odd thing is, enrollment is automatic; even without applying for a course, you wind up studying it. It's the default when the guidance of other *gurus* is rejected. Viśvaguruji has many doors for entering his *ashram* and only one for exiting. Gradually, eventually, and it may take many lifetimes, everyone comes to see that he is leading them to an understanding that every freedom has its price, every action its reaction, that the path to perfection is up and up and up. ¶So, you can tell your friends, "I have a *guru* and you have one, too. Everyone has a *guru*, whether they know it or not." All three *gurus*—parents, family *guru* and Viśvaguruji—unanimously say, "It's a dirty job, but somebody has to do it." Viśvaguru's school of hard knocks eventually delivers all errant seekers back to a *satguru*, shaman, rabbi, priest or minister. In order not to repeat his training, you either learn through the tough reactions of his courses or gentler lessons under the guidance of the two other traditional *gurus.* All *gurus* are conspirators in the evolution of the soul, and Śrī Śrī Śrī Viśvaguru Mahā-Mahārāj-ji is no exception.

Thursday
LESSON 312
Temple and Home Shrine

Through *darshan* power, the *guru* is able to communicate with his disciples. Information is passed on these rays of *darshan.* Unfoldment is guided on these rays of *darshan.* A beginning student cannot feel the *darshan.* That means he is not inwardly connected or "hooked in." He does not have that open line. That is why the *satguru* often puts out some sort of intellectual book or pamphlets, to hold the intellect in check until the student goes deeper within. After deep study of the *guru's* works, they then begin to feel his *darshan* occasionally from a distance, but not all the time. ¶A devotee does not have to be with his *guru* physically all of the time to unfold as a beautiful flower on the path. But he does have to be with the *satguru's darshan* all the time, for that waters, protects, guides the unfoldment superconsciously. The *guru* is within him—not the physical presence of his teacher, however holy, but the divine spheres of his *guru's* superconscious being. The law is, though, that only his *guru* can bring him into this realization fully and permanently. ¶A temple can be prepared to emanate a certain kind of *darshan* as strong as, if not stronger than, a *guru's.* When a Hindu temple is established, a *satguru* who has a strong *darshan* is invited to come and help the priests prepare the main altar in the temple, which initiates the flow of *darshan* and *śakti.* This is done through the use of *actinodic* force.

Certain physical elements are magnetized with *actinodic* power within the shrine through the chanting of *mantras* and by various other means. This brings the vibratory state of the physical element that holds this new vibration to a high pitch. The *darshan* vibration penetrates the ethers. ¶In a similar way, you have magnetized your clothing without realizing it with your personal vibration. A very sensitive "medium" could be blindfolded and by holding in his hand a piece of your clothing identify it as yours and tell something about you. That is why a temple has to be visited with the proper attitude, for a minute part of your *actinodic* force is left in the temple as you stand in front of the altar feeling the *darshan* radiating from it. The altar *darshan* builds up over many, many years as devotees come and go and priests chant the sacred *mantras*, permeating the temple with this *darshan* force, storing it in a great battery which takes in and emanates out. ¶*Darshan* is extremely important in spiritual unfoldment, because it catalyzes the crown *chakra.* It catalyzes the refined, superconscious being of man, energizing and strengthening it, in the very same way a violent or sensuous movie and the vibrations of the people sitting within the theater catalyze the lower *chakras. Darshan* catalyzes the crown *chakra,* the all-seeing-eye *chakra,* the universal-love *chakra* and the *chakra* of direct cognition in a similar way. That is why once a temple has been established, it should be approached and treated in a certain sensitive way to keep its *darshan* flowing strongly and profoundly. It builds in power through the years and stabilizes the spiritual unfoldment of all pilgrims who know of its existence, especially those who pilgrimage to the temple to be blessed by it. ¶If you get a little cloudy, a little foggy, and *karma* becomes heavy to the point you feel you cannot handle it yourself, then you can tune into the temple *darshan* if you do not have a *satguru*, for it works much the same way. Each devotee should establish a shrine in his own home which is connected in vibration with the *darshan* of the temple, which is again connected with the *guru* who helped the priests begin the flow for the temple. ¶The home shrine can bring through some of the vibration by your simply using the five elements: earth, air, fire, water and ether. This would be taught by the wise elders. This, then, is the cycle of *darshan:* from the *satguru*, the temple, the home shrine and back to you. If you want to begin a little shrine yourself, you need a stone blessed at the temple, which holds the vibration of the *darshan* there, nice, fresh air; and you have to reserve a space, preferably a private room. It must be neatly arranged and be clean and clear of worldly vibrations, a room set apart from all others. In it you must have the five vibrations occurring: earth, air, fire, water and ether, and it must be connected into the *darshan* of the temple.

Friday
LESSON 313
"Catching" The Darshan

The advanced *yoga* adept can go inside himself through the practice of *mahāyoga* and awaken the flame at the top of his head and experience the five vibrations inside himself, deep within the psychic centers of the head, which is the inner temple. For the beginning meditator who has not done *sādhana*, this is difficult, and the outer temple and its *darshan* is a great aid. There are many catalysts on the path that aid in making you strong, so that you can lean on your own spine and bring through your own bliss. We must remember that the *satguru* is a helper on the path. His renunciate *sannyāsins* are also sometimes helpers, too. The meditator should not lean on his *guru* or the other disciples, who may be stronger and more advanced in their *sādhana*. He must rely only on himself, lean on his own spine and unfold spiritually. ¶In the *ākaśa*, all form exists in all phases of its manifestation. A mystic sculptor can take clay or stone and bring forth an image of the *satguru*. As soon as he feels the *darshan* coming through the form, he knows he is nearly finished. Everything is in one place. It's only the physical two eyes doing such wonderful things as to make us think things are in different places in the conscious mind of time and distance. But everything in the *ākāśic* plane of consciousness is in one place. So, all the mystic sculptor has to do to get the *satguru darshan* is to make the form of the *guru* in the exact same way it already exists in the *ākāśa* when the *darshan* was the strongest at the highest point in his life on Earth. ¶In a similar way, one can receive *darshan* through a picture of the *satguru*. The *darshan* does not really come from the picture, but from the *ākāśa* where the inner *guru* exists. The picture only acts as a point of concentration, but enough of a focal point to tune the devotee into the *ākāśa* at the exact moment, which is "now," when that picture was taken or painted and the exact feeling of the *darshan* at that particular time and its accumulated effect up to the present moment. Then the totality of the *satguru's darshan* is felt. ¶In intellectually knowing how the system of *darshan* works in many of its various phases, it is easy then to participate in it, and by meditating on some of these principles that

I have outlined, you can catch the knack of it.

Saturday
LESSON 314
The Power of Prostration

Prostration at the holy feet of the *satguru* has been performed in Hindu India and Sri Lanka for thousands of years. It's an ancient custom and a very valuable one, because it separates the people who can prostrate from those who cannot. It separates the deeper souls from those still going through the intellectual and instinctive areas of the mind. It allows the aspirant himself to know where he is on the path, and it allows the *satguru* to know at a glance, without thought, where the seeker is on the spiritual path by the emanations out of the spine as he prostrates himself face down before him. ¶Prostration issues forth definite energies when done before the *guru* or the temple Deity. The ego is naturally subdued, humility strengthened, and the soul of *guru* and disciple enjoy deep rapport in that moment. ¶Śaiva Siddhāntins have always had blind *bhakti* for God, Gods and *guru*. Their mothers and fathers are often included and showered with the same feelings of love. They are by nature very sweet people. Jñānaguru Yogaswāmī had this to say about *guru bhakti*: "*Guru bhakti* is the greatest blessing. Cherish it and relish it and be refreshed! Advance on the path of *dharma*. Call on the name of 'Śaṅkara Śiva.' Know that there is not one wrong thing. And proclaim that all is truth. Seek for the grace of God. Repeat 'Śivāya Namaḥ.' You must realize Self by self. In you will peace and patience shine, and you will be your own support. Let 'like' and 'dislike' be snuffed out. Ponder not upon past *karma*. Resolve to kill the 'three desires.' " ¶Devotees often transfer to their *guru* whatever feelings they have for their mothers and fathers. This does not mean that they cease to love their mother and father when they accept a *guru.* It means that if they have problems at home, they will have similar problems with their *guru.* If they love and honor their parents, they will love and honor their *guru.* Devotees who have true *bhakti* are filled with love for all beings. Their children will never upset them. They care for their pets and love their mother and father. They do not go to a *guru* to escape unhappiness at home. They go to a *guru* because their mother and father have taught them all they know, and now they must move onward. Even in this move, the parents' blessings are sought to either follow the family *guru* or another. This is the traditional way. This is Śaiva Siddhānta. ¶There are emanations that come out of the spine wherever the individual is functioning, different types of instinctive, intellectual feelings or those of superconsciousness. The meditator works with those forces. He transmutes his energies to the crown *chakra.* You must work diligently to get there, and then you have it for eternity. This is the great heritage that is your right to receive by living on this planet. ¶Transcendental beings, who have nerve systems so highly developed that they do not need a physical body in which to function and help those on Earth, can give a vital and a vibrant *darshan* which will help and stabilize you on the path. Delicate, subtle actinic beings that have once lived on the Earth and, just like you, have meditated, worked with their forces, attained Self Realization, brought forth *darshan* and finally dropped off the physical body, vowing to serve the people of the Earth. Hindus call them *devas,* Gods or Deities. All of them are right here, because everything is in one place.

Everything of a same or similar vibration is in one place in the *ākāśa.* The great actinic bodies of all these evolved beings are right here. You can invoke the *darshan* of the Gods, too, if things really get rough for you on the path up the spine. These *devas* or Gods visit various temples at auspicious times, traveling in the *ākāśa loka,* which is close to time-space consciousness.

Sunday
LESSON 315
Yoking with the Inner Worlds

An advanced adept can, in meditation, travel in the *ākāśa,* too. He can go to India, Sri Lanka, America in three different ways: by projecting himself mentally "out there" in the *ākāśa,* by sitting and bringing Sri Lanka here, or by traveling in his *astral* body and actually being there. People would see him there if they were inwardly awakened. The great *devas* or Gods visit temples and participate in keeping the *darshan* vibration going strong. They help the *satgurus,* too. They help the disciples of the *satgurus* by giving a wonderful psychic protection. They can usually be contacted by ringing a bell. ¶The bell is one of the things that penetrates in vibration into the *ākāśa.* If you trace the evanescent tones of a bell in and in and in, right into the light, it will be the last sound you will hear before soundlessness occurs. All other sounds will fade away, and you will only hear the bell as the last overtone of sound. On the tone of a bell you can bring a *yogī* safely out of deep meditation. He will begin to hear that sound, and will come out into normal consciousness after a while. Otherwise you might talk to him, and he might not even hear you. You can awaken a sleeper out of deep sleep by ringing a bell softly. The soft tones of the bell will penetrate into the depths of his sleep or meditation and bring him out in a very nice way into physical consciousness. As a bell is the first, so the flame is the second thing that penetrates that deeply into consciousness. ¶The inner-plane being, once contacted, would then use the water on your home altar to put in all of the accumulated unwholesome vibrations found in the room. He would then charge the stone on the altar with his *darshan.* The inner-plane being or *deva* would come to the *pūjā,* summoned by the bell. The power of the flame would give him the ability to work within the room, and he would go around collecting all the negative vibrations from everybody, old *karma* and magnetic collections of thought and emotion, and put it all in the water. After the *pūjā,* the water should be thrown out. It may start to get cloudy. In the meditation room, the water should always be kept fresh, because it even collects odic force on its own. ¶The odic force is what causes all the problems on Earth. Water itself is odic force, so it collects the conflicting vibrations in its elements. The actinic forces do motivate odic forces, as well as create odic force. So, when in the large temples of India the ceremony is at a certain pitch and height, the *darshan* of the Deity that the temple is built for is felt because He visits the temple in his spiritual body. He might just come for a short period of time, but the vibration of the *darshan* is felt in a very dynamically uplifting way, a vibration similar to that of a *satguru,* but different because it comes from an inner plane. It protects one from old experiences coming up from the subconscious to repeat themselves, *karmas* that perhaps might take years to live through again. This inner protection is one of the many wonderful ways that *darshan* works for the good of people on the path.

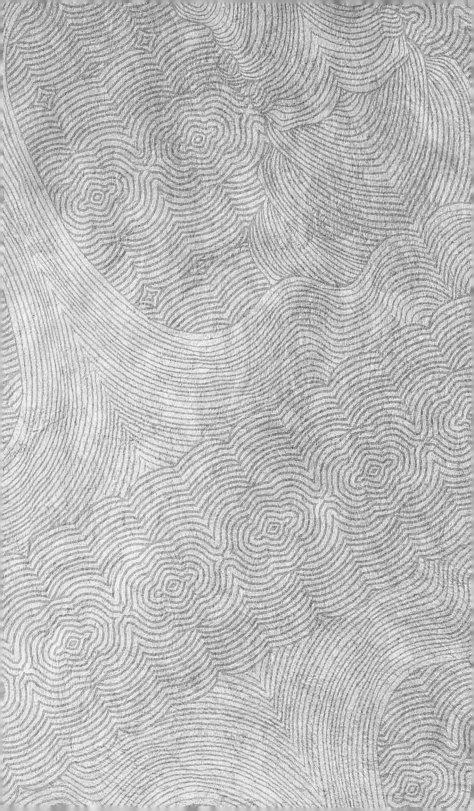

Jñāninaḥ Tad Darśita Mārgaścha

ज्ञानिनः तद्दर्शितमार्गश्च

Jñānīs and the Path They Teach

The great knowers seek the Lord of the heavens. Those who seek the company of these great ones will attain Śivaness. They become the path of virtue and are truly blessed. To consort with the great knowers is indeed bliss supreme.

TIRUMANTIRAM 545

Monday
LESSON 316
The Holy Path To Śiva's Feet

So many in the world are unaware of the great joys that are the reward of a religious life lived well. They seek their fulfillment outside of themselves and fall short time and time again. One day they will conclude, as you all have, that it is the inner life, the spiritual life that alone brings eternal, unchanging happiness. This outer world and consciousness can never bring the soul real contentment, real fulfillment. Oh, you can find a temporary happiness, but it will be followed by its opposite in due course. The outer consciousness of the material world is by its very nature a bondage. It binds one through *karma.* It binds one through *māyā.* It binds one through *āṇava,* or ego identity and ignorance. That is the nature of the world, to bind us. ¶When the soul has had enough experience, it naturally seeks to be liberated, to unravel the bonds. That begins the most wonderful process in the world as the seeker steps for the first time onto the spiritual path. Of course, the whole time, through all those births and lives and deaths, the soul was undergoing a spiritual evolution, but unconsciously. Now it seeks to know God consciously. That is the difference. It's a big difference. By this conscious process of purification, of inner striving, of refining and maturing, the *karmas* come more swiftly, evolution speeds up and things can and usually do get more intense. Don't worry, though. That is natural and necessary. That intensity is the way the mind experiences the added cosmic energies that begin to flow through the nervous system. ¶So, here is the soul, seeking intentionally to know, "Who am I? Where did I come from? Where am I going?" A path must be found, a path that others have successfully followed, a path that has answers equally as profound as the seeker's questions. In Śaivite Hinduism, we have such a path. It is called the Śaiva Neri, the Path of Śiva. It is a wide and unobstructed path that leads man to himself, to his true Self that lies within and beyond his personality, lies at the very core of his being. ¶I want to speak a little about this inner path today. You all know that it is a mystical path, full of mystery. You cannot learn much of it from books. Then where to look? Look to the holy scriptures, where the straight path to God is described by our saints. Look to the great masters, the *siddhas,* or perfected ones. Look to the *satgurus,* who have themselves met and overcome the challenges that still lie ahead for you. Look to them and ask them to help you to look within yourself. Much of the mysticism which is the greatest wealth of Hinduism is locked within these masters, who in our tradition are known as the *satgurus,* the sages and the *siddhas.* There is much to say on this. As Yogaswāmī told us, "The subject is vast and the time is short!"

Tuesday
LESSON 317
Four Stages Of Evolution

Let me begin with something that may at first come as a surprise to you. All men and women on the Earth are doing exactly as they should and must do. People complain, "I wish I were rich. I wish I lived somewhere else. I really should be a doctor. If only things were different." But in the final analysis, we are all doing exactly as we want, as we must, doing what is next on our personal path of evolution. Nothing is wrong. Nothing should be that is not. Even the drunk, even the thief, is part of the cosmic dance of God Śiva. Not that you should ever think of being a thief, for there is much difficult *karma* there. Just realize that he, too, is evolving. He, too, is Śiva's creation, and what he does is, for him, somehow necessary. ¶Just look at the world. Warriors have to fight their battles. Priests have to take care of their temples. Businessmen must sell their goods. Farmers must grow their crops and tend their flocks. Teachers must pass on knowledge. Each one has to do what he has to do in the great cosmic dance of Śiva. Each one follows the path of service leading to devotion, which leads to spiritual disciplines of *yoga.* Finally, that *yoga* culminates in the attainment of Truth, or God Realization. These are the four *mārgas* leading the soul to its very Self. ¶For Hindus, the path is seen as divided into four stages or phases of inner development. Some say *karma yoga, bhakti yoga, rāja yoga* and *jñāna;* others say *charyā, kriyā, yoga* and *jñāna.* Either way, it is basically the same—progressive stages followed by the soul in its quest for God. We are speaking here of the way the ancients attained their realizations, how they lived their lives, suffered, went through mental pain in their *tapas,* walked the San Mārga path through life—*charyā, kriyā, yoga* and *jñāna*—and in that process unwound the *karmas* of the past, learned to live fully in the present, abashed the person of themselves to be the soul of themselves. They practiced true *yoga* to obtain release from rebirth, *moksha,* which only the realization of the Absolute Truth can give. There is, of course, no action too great to render to persist on the path of enlightenment, once the path has clearly been defined. ¶*Jñāna* is the last stage. Most people don't understand *jñāna.* They think it is little more than intellectual study of the path, a simple kind of wisdom. But *jñāna* does not mean simplistic reading of scriptures or understanding of philosophical books and knowing pat answers to stereotyped questions. *Jñāna* is the blossoming of wisdom, of enlightened consciousness, of true being. *Jñāna* is the state of the realized soul who knows Absolute Reality through personal experience, who has reached the end of the spiritual path after many, many lifetimes. ¶ *Yoga* is the path of *sādhana,* or discipline, leading the advanced soul toward *jñāna. Yoga* is divided into eight parts, ranging from the simple physical disciplines and diet, up to the deepest contemplation gained through perfect control of mind. *Yoga* does not mean just sitting in lotus for half an hour each day in a penthouse or doing *haṭha yoga āsanas* for health and beauty. It means *yoga* as performed by the *yogīs* of yore, the renegades from society, *tapasvins* ready to face the fire of *sādhana,* brave souls who have given up all else in their search for Truth, persevering with an iron will until they accomplish what they seek. ¶ *Kriyā* is basically worship and devotion, or the expression of our love of the Divine through various ceremonies and rituals. *Kriyā* does not mean mindlessly or superstitiously attending temple services, to look good in the community, to be with friends, to gossip or talk of politics and other human affairs. It is a genuine communion with the inner worlds, a profound stage in which the heart swells and eyes overflow with internalized worship, love and surrender. ¶ *Charyā* is service, but it does not mean empty service, unthinking performance of traditional rites or just marrying off daughters, thus forestalling premarital affairs. It is service done selflessly, it is *dharma* performed consciously, it is worship offered wholly and it is goodness in thought, word and deed.

Wednesday
LESSON 318
Devotion and Guru Guidance

Of course, our most cherished theology is monistic Śaiva Siddhānta, the *advaitic* teachings inherited from our *guru paramparā* who outlined the course we are on. This teaches us that God and man are ultimately one. This teaches us that our Supreme God, Śiva, is the creator of the universe, and He is also the creation. He is not different from it. ¶We must go to the temple and worship, with all our heart, God in form before our *karmas* are cleared, our responsibilities paid, and we realize the formless perfection of God Śiva. The *guhā,* the cave of consciousness, opens its doors for us to sit comfortably, mentally undistracted, within the cavity within the head, there to begin the *yoga* of union for personal, spiritual, everlasting attainment. Śaiva Siddhānta outlines the path that we are on. It tells us how to attain these goals. ¶The saints who sang the hymns of *Tirumurai* inspire us onward and inward. The illustrious, venerable Ṛishi Tirumular captured the essence of the *Vedas* and the *Āgamas* in his epistles, promulgating the rules and regulations that we must follow, setting forth the attainments that we may expect to reach. Over two thousand years ago the great *siddha,* Saint Tirumular, taught, "Offer oblations in love. Light the golden lamps. Spread incense of fragrant wood and lighted camphor in all directions. Forget your worldly worries and meditate. Truly, you shall attain rapturous liberation." ¶It is said in our Hindu scriptures that it is necessary to have a *satguru.* However, it is also possible for an individual to accomplish all of this by himself without a *guru.* Possible, but most difficult and exceedingly rare. There may be four or five in a hundred years, or less. Scriptures explain that perhaps in past lives such a soul would have been well disciplined by some *guru* and is helped inwardly by God in this life. With rare exceptions, a *guru* is necessary to guide the aspirant on the path as far as he is willing and able to go in his current incarnation. Few will reach the Ultimate. The *satguru* is needed because the mind is cunning and the ego is a self-perpetuating mechanism. It is unable and unwilling to transcend itself by itself. Therefore, one needs the guidance of another who has gone through the same process, who has faithfully followed the path to its natural end and therefore can gently lead us to God within ourselves. Remember, the *satguru* will keep you on the path, but you have to walk the path yourself. ¶All *gurus* differ one from another depending on their *paramparā*, their lineage, as well as on their individual nature, awakening and attainments. Basically, the only thing that a *guru* can give you is yourself to yourself. That is all, and this is done in many ways. The *guru* would only be limited by his philosophy, which outlines the ultimate attainment, and by his own experience. He cannot take you where he himself has not been. It is the *guru's* job to inspire, to assist, to guide and sometimes even impel the disciple to move a little farther toward the Self of himself than he has been able to go by himself.

Thursday
LESSON 319
Duties of The Disciple

It is the disciple's duty to understand the sometimes subtle guidance offered by the *guru*, to take the suggestions and make the best use of them in fulfilling the *sādhanas* given. Being with a *satguru* is an intensification on the path of enlightenment—always challenging, for growth is a challenge to the instinctive mind. If a *guru* does not provide this intensification, we could consider him to be more a philosophical teacher. Not all *gurus* are *satgurus.* Not all *gurus* have realized God themselves. The idea is to change the patterns of life, not to perpetuate them. That would be the only reason one would want to find a *satguru.* ¶Some teachers will teach ethics. Others will teach philosophy, language, worship and scriptures. Some will teach by example, by an inner guidance. Others will teach from books. Some will be silent, while others will lecture and have classes. Some will be orthodox, while others may not. The form of the teaching is not the most essential matter. What matters is that there be a true and fully realized *satguru,* that there be a true and fully dedicated disciple. Under such conditions, spiritual progress will be swift and certain, though not necessarily easy. Of course, in our tradition the *siddhas* have always taught of Śiva and only Śiva. They have taught the Śaiva Dharma which seeks to serve and know Śiva in three ways: as Personal Lord and creator of all that exists; as existence, knowledge and bliss—the love that flows through all form—and finally as the timeless, formless, causeless Self of all. ¶When we go to school, we are expected to learn our lessons and then to graduate. Having graduated, we are expected to enter society, take a position comparable to our level of education. We are expected to know more when we leave than when we entered, and we naturally do. When we perform *sādhana,* we are expected to mature inwardly, to grow and to discipline ourselves. And, in fact, we do become a better, more productive, more compassionate, more refined person. ¶But when we perform *yoga,* we are expected to go within, in and in, deep within ourselves, deep within the mind. If *yoga* is truly performed, we graduate with knowledge based on personal experience, not on what someone else has said. We then take our place among the *jñānīs*—the wise ones who know, and who know what they know—to uplift others with understanding in *sādhana* and in *yoga*.

Friday
LESSON 320
Attaining The Ultimate

In other words, the practice of *yoga* well performed produces the *jñānī*. The *yogī* has the same experiences, if he is successful, and comes out with the same independent knowledge which, when reviewed, corresponds perfectly with what other *jñānīs* discovered and taught as the outcome of their *yogic* practices. This kind of knowledge surpasses all other knowing and is the basis of all Hindu scriptures. The *jñānī* is a rare soul, a highly evolved soul. He speaks of Truth from his experience of it and gives it a personal touch. As Śrī Rāmakṛishṇa said, you go into yourself a fool, but through the practices of *yoga* you come out a wise man. That is the *jñānī*—the knower of the Unknowable. ¶The *yogī* who is in the process of *yoga*, who has not graduated to God Realization, is not yet a *jñānī*, though he has all kinds of realizations along the way, some sustained, others yet to be sustained. The *yogī* is seeking, striving, changing, unfolding, trying with all his heart to become, to know his ultimate goal. When the merger has become complete, when two have become one, he is no longer a *yogī*, he is a *jñānī*. When the student graduates from college, he is no longer a student, he is a graduate. The merger of which I speak is Paraśiva, to be experienced by the *sannyāsin* who has turned from the world and into himself. ¶There is yet another realization which can be described as experiencing God Śiva as Satchidānanda, as light and love and consciousness. This also may be achieved through *yoga.* When one experiences this expanded state of being, this cosmic consciousness, he comes back knowing he has had a fantastic experience, but no *jñāna* persists, for he has yet to attain the Ultimate. Family people can attain this second state through diligent effort, and even attain to Paraśiva at the point of death, or before if the path of renunciation is entered upon fully after life's obligations have been fulfilled. But there are few, very few, who have attained the highest of the high, Paraśiva, after having been householders, having fulfilled their family *dharma,* freed from any and all worldly endeavors, plunged into total, total, abandonment of spouse, family, friends, associates of all kind, taking no disciples, shunning devotees and forever living alone on alms, to seek the highest of the high. As said, even following such a strict path, there are few, very few, who attain to Absolute Reality. But all who strive have done powerful preparation for their next life. ¶My *satguru,* Śiva Yogaswāmī, often said, "Lord Śiva is within you. You are within Lord Śiva. Lord Śiva, with all of His powers, cannot separate Himself from you." Śiva Yogaswāmī told us to go to the temple, to worship at the temple. He also told us to go within ourselves, into Śivajñāna. He did not tell us *not* to go to the temple. He did not try to break our faith. He tried to build our faith and make us strong. He guided us on the straight path, the path of the Śaivite saints, leading us to the feet of Śiva. ¶Śiva Yogaswāmī himself, though completely Self realized, went regularly to the temple, worshiped Śiva there, then plunged within himself in the aftermath of holy *pūjā,* drawing near to Śiva through meditation. He never advocated, nor has any Śaivite *satguru* advocated, that advanced devotees give up *bhakti,* give up the temple. No! Never! They taught that Śiva is within and cannot be separated from you, but they also wisely directed us to seek Him and worship Him in the temple.

Saturday
LESSON 321
The Nature Of God Śiva

Śiva has a form. He is also formless. But He does have a form, and He exists in the realm of highest consciousness called the Śivaloka. Śiva has a mind, a superconscious mind that permeates like a plasma all the forms that He creates, all the forms that He preserves and all the forms that He absorbs back into Himself. Śiva is very close to each and every one of us. Śiva's mind permeates all of us. But when we want to see Śiva's form and receive His *darshan,* we go to the Śiva temple, and when the holy priest invokes God Śiva, God Śiva hovers in His body of golden light over the Śivaliṅga. In deep meditation, Śivajñāna, we can, within the temple of our own heart, see God Śiva's Holy Form. ¶God Śiva creates. God Śiva preserves all His creations and, when the creation is no longer needed, absorbs it back into Himself, to create again. Śaivites all over the world love God Śiva. God Śiva loves His devotees. For each step the devotee takes toward Śiva, Śiva takes nine steps toward the devotee. Such are the final conclusions of Śaiva Siddhānta. ¶There is no reason to ever become confused about the many Deities in our wonderful Hindu faith. Is Lord Gaṇeśa our Supreme God? No. Is Lord Muruga our Supreme God? No. They are Gods, two of the many Gods that God Śiva has created. But God Śiva is Supreme God, timeless, formless, spaceless, permeating all form, and yet having a form. He is the fullness of everything that fills people from within out. ¶In Śaivism we become strong, we become fearless, through our worship of Śiva. Members of the Śaiva Samayam, the Śaivite religion, do not fear death, for they know about rebirth. Members of the Śaiva Samayam do not fear an eternal hell; there is no eternal hell. Members of the Śaiva Samayam do not fear their ministers, their priests, *swāmīs* or *gurus*. Members of the Śaiva Samayam do not fear God. The lack of fear, therefore, makes you strong. Our saints tell us in the sacred hymns of the *Tirumurai* that the worship of Śiva makes you strong. The worship of God Śiva brings you intelligence. The worship of God Śiva will bring you knowledge of your divine, inner Self. Remember this as you go forth in life: we do not use weapons in our religion. We follow the path of nonviolence, noninjury to other beings. Our only weapon is our mind, our intelligence. ¶Unfortunately, in some, though not all, of the Judaic/Christian sects, the fear of God is prevalent. The distinction between good and bad, heaven and hell, is predominant, causing fears, apprehension and deep mental conflict. Hence, this psychological set-up is not conducive to the practice of *yoga*, for it arbitrates against the very idea of oneness of man and God which the *yogī* seeks. Those who have been so indoctrinated often try to meditate, but necessarily do not succeed in its deepest attainments, because of subconscious barriers placed there by a dualistic philosophy.

Sunday
LESSON 322
When the Quiet Comes

In order to really meditate to the depth of contemplation, and not merely to quiet mind and emotion and feel a little serenity, you have to be a member of a religion that gives the hope of nondual union with God, that teaches that God is within man, only to be realized. Meditation, if it is to lead to *jñāna,* must begin with a belief that there is no intrinsic evil and encompass the truth of *karma,* that we are responsible for our own actions. Such meditation must be undertaken by a member of a religion that gives a hope of a future life and does not threaten failure with eternal suffering, should failure be the result. Such meditation is possible, in fact required, of those who follow the Hindu Dharma. Hence, the practice of *yoga* is the highest pinnacle within our most ancient faith. ¶If you go through the entire holy scriptures of Śaivism, you will not find our saints singing hymns to Adonai, Yahweh, Buddha or Jesus. Our saints told us to worship God Śiva, the Supreme God, to worship Gaṇeśa first before worshiping Śiva, to worship Lord Muruga. In the old days, there were millions of Śiva temples, from the Himālayan peaks of Nepal, through North and South India, Sri Lanka and what is now Malaysia and Indonesia. Everyone was of one mind, worshiping Śiva together, singing His praises with a one voice. As a result, India was spiritually unified. It was then the wealthiest country in the world. The worship of Śiva will give you wealth. The worship of Śiva will give you health. The worship of Śiva will give you knowledge. The worship of Śiva will fill your heart with love and compassion. ¶The Śaiva Samayam is the greatest religion in the world. The Śaiva Samayam is the oldest religion in the world. The Śaiva Samayam has *yoga.* It has great temples, great *pandits, ṛishis* and scriptures. All the saints who sang the songs of Śiva told us how to worship Śiva and how we should live our Śaivite lives. We must all follow those instructions. In singing those songs to Śiva, Śiva will give you everything that you ask for. He will give you everything that you ask for, because Śiva is the God of Love. Our saints have sung that Śiva is within us, and we are within Śiva. Knowing that, fear and worry and doubt are forever gone from our mind. ¶When the mind has resolved all of its differences through worship, penance, *dhāraṇā, dhyāna,* then the inner which is stillness itself is known. Then the inner is stronger than the outer. It is then easy to see every other person going through what has to be gone through during his or her particular stage on the path. Opposites are there, but no opposites are seen. This is why it is easy for the wise—made wise through spiritual unfoldment—to say, "There is no injustice in the world. There is no evil, no sin." ¶We only see opposites when our vision is limited, when we have not experienced totally. There is a point of view which resolves all contradictions and answers all questions. Yet to be experienced is yet to be understood. Once experienced and understood, the Quiet comes. The *karmas* are quiet. This is the arduous path of *charyā, kriyā* and *yoga* resulting in *jñāna.* This is the path of not only endeavoring to unfold the higher nature but, at the same time and toward the same end, dealing positively and consciously with the remnants of the lower nature. Following this spiritual path, we find ourselves effortlessly replacing charity for greed and dealing with, rather than merely suppressing, the instinctive feelings of jealousy, hatred, desire and anger.

Svātmanaḥ Pūrṇatādvayam

स्वात्मनः पूर्णताद्वयम्

8

The Two Perfections Of Our Soul

The Primal One, the indivisible great, Himself into several divided. As form, formless and form-formless, as *guru* and Śakti-Lord in numerous forms, He became immanent in *jīvas* and transcendent, too.

TIRUMANTIRAM 2481

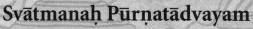

Monday
LESSON 323
Śiva's Three Perfections

We shall now discuss the three perfections of our Supreme God Śiva: Paraśiva, Satchidānanda and Maheśvara. Isn't it wonderful to know that two of God's three perfections are inherent in the soul of man? What are those three perfections? The great God Śiva has form and is formless. He is the immanent Pure Consciousness or pure form; He is the Personal Lord manifesting Himself as innumerable forms; and He is the impersonal, transcendent Absolute beyond all form. We know Śiva in His three perfections, two of form and one formless. First, we worship His manifest form as Pure Love and Consciousness, called Satchidānanda in Sanskṛit. Second, we worship Him as our Personal Lord, Maheśvara, the Primal Soul who tenderly loves and cares for His devotees—a Being whose resplendent body may be seen in mystic vision. In our daily lives we love, honor, worship and serve God in these manifest perfections. Ultimately, in perfectly simple, yet awesomely austere *nirvikalpa samādhi,* we realize Him as the formless Paraśiva, sought for and known only by *yogīs* and *jñānīs.* We cannot speak of His Absolute Reality which is beyond qualities and description, yet knowable to the fully matured soul who seeks God within through *yoga* under the guidance of a *satguru.* ¶For the sake of understanding the mysteries of the soul, we distinguish between the soul body and its essence. As a soul body, we are individual and unique, different from all others. Our soul is a self-effulgent body of light which evolves and matures through an evolutionary process. This soul body is of the nature of God Śiva, but is different from Him in that it is less resplendent than the Primal Soul and still evolving, while He is unevolutionary Perfection. We may liken the soul body to an acorn, which contains the mighty oak but is a small seed yet to develop. Even when God Realization is attained, the soul body continues to evolve in this and other worlds until it merges with the Primal Soul, as a drop of water merges with its source, the ocean. This is the destiny of all souls without exception. ¶At the core of the subtle soul body is Satchidānanda, or immanent Love, and at the core of that is Paraśiva, or transcendent Reality. At this depth of our being there exists no separate identity or difference—all are one. Thus, deep within our soul we are identical with God this very moment, for within us are the unmanifest Paraśiva and the manifest Satchidānanda. These are not aspects of the evolving soul, but the nucleus of the soul, which does not change or evolve. They are eternally perfect and one with God Śiva. From an absolute perspective, our soul is already in nondual union with God in His two perfections of Satchidānanda and Paraśiva, but to be realized to be known. Satchidānanda is the superconscious mind of the soul—the mind of God Śiva. Paraśiva is the inmost core of the soul. We *are* That. We do not *become* That. There exists no relation between Satchidānanda, which is pure form and consciousness, and Paraśiva, which is without form. Paramaguru Śiva Yogaswāmī taught us, "You are Śiva. I am Śiva. All are Śiva. Even as Śiva is immortal, so too are we."

Tuesday
LESSON 324
Form and Formlessness

We must caution each and all not to think of the external mind as God, which would be a self-deception. Man's personality or individuality is not God—neither is the ego, the intellect, or the emotions. Though the unenlightened sometimes make this mistake, I believe you will readily ferret out the difference. Paraśiva, the Self God, lies resident at the core of man's existence, far beyond the reach of the external phases of consciousness; yet these exist only because That exists, the timeless, causeless, spaceless God Śiva beyond the mind. ¶The other perfection inherent in the soul of man is Satchidānanda—Being, Consciousness and Bliss. When mind force, thought force and the *vṛittis,* or waves of the mind, are quiescent, the outer mind subsides and the mind of the soul shines forth. We share the mind of God Śiva at this superconscious depth of our being. In entering this quiescence, one first encounters a clear white light within the body, but only after sufficient mastery of the mind has been attained through the disciplined and protracted practices of *yoga.* ¶Hearing the *vīṇā,* the *mṛidaṅgam,* the *tambūra* and all the psychic sounds is the awakening of the inner body, which, if *sādhana* is pursued, will finally grow and stabilize, opening the mind to the constant state of Satchidānanda, where the holy inner mind of God Śiva and our soul are one. I hold that Satchidānanda—the light and consciousness ever permeating form, God in all things and everywhere—is form, though refined form, to be sure. Satchidānanda is pure form, pure consciousness, pure blessedness or bliss, our soul's perfection in form. Paraśiva is formless, timeless, causeless, spaceless, as the perfection of our soul beyond form. ¶Though it is supreme consciousness, Satchidānanda is not the ultimate realization, which lies beyond consciousness or mind. This differs from popular interpretations of present-day

Vedānta, which makes these two perfections virtually synonymous. Modern Vedānta scholars occasionally describe Satchidānanda almost as a state of the intellect, as though the perfected intellect, through knowledge, could attain such depths, as though these depths were but a philosophical premise or collection of beliefs and insights. This is what I call "simplistic Vedānta." ¶To understand how these two perfections differ, visualize a vast sheath of light which permeates the walls of this monastery and the countryside around us, seeping in and through all particles of matter. The light could well be called formless, penetrating, as it does, all conceivable forms, never static, always changing. Actually, it is amorphous, not formless. Taking this one step farther, suppose there were a "something" so great, so intense in vibration that it could swallow up light as well as the forms it permeates. This cannot be described, but can be called Paraśiva—the greatest of all of God Śiva's Perfections to be realized. This, too, can be experienced by the *yogī,* in *nirvikalpa samādhi.* Thus, we understand Paraśiva as the perfection known in *nirvikalpa samādhi,* and Satchidānanda as the perfection experienced in *savikalpa samādhi.* By the word *formless* I do not describe that which can take any form or that which is of no definite shape and size. I mean without form altogether, beyond form, beyond the mind which conceives of form and space, for mind and consciousness, too, are form.

Wednesday
LESSON 325
Being and Becoming

Out of the microcosm ever comes the macrocosm. Out of Paraśiva—which is timeless, causeless and formless—ever comes all form. This is the great mystery without a reason why. Out of pure consciousness ever comes the light which binds all form together in specific bondage, individualizing forms, souls, one from another. This is ever happening, as simultaneously struggling souls remove their bondage through the grace of God Śiva to come into Satchidānanda, later to be absorbed into Paraśiva. This, too, is a great mystery without a reason why. ¶The existence called Paraśiva pervades the infinite Satchidānanda, sustaining it just as the Divine Light of God Śiva's mind pervades and sustains the gross forms of this world. Paraśiva does not create Satchidānanda, yet Satchidānanda is sustained because of the existence of nonexistence. Now, you might ask, "Why?" The answer is that this is the will of our great God Śiva. ¶Therefore, first we seek to gain an intellectual clarity as to the path we are on. This purified intellect gives a philosophical clarity and should not in any way be mistaken for attainment. In the technological age there are thousands who are intellectually clear as to the task at hand, how to obtain the objective, and they have the necessary skills to begin. They do not delude themselves that they have already begun or attained anything until failure has been many times encountered, that failure conquered and success achieved in its place. Thus, we draw a distinction between the seasoned *yogī* whose knowledge has its source in superconsciousness and the armchair Vedantist who often thinks his intellectual comprehension is some kind of advanced attainment. It is not. Peoples of the West have come too far in technology, too far in the understanding and use of the mind, too far in personal study of Vedānta to be impressed by this anymore. ¶The two perfections explain well the deep questions man asks himself, questions which bring forth far too few answers. Through meditation upon the two perfections inherent in the soul, we can penetrate the mystery of the oneness of man and God. Man and God are one, yet God Śiva has yet a third perfection, Maheśvara, the Primal Soul, already perfect and complete, whereas man's soul body is still maturing, still evolving. One day, the soul body of man will merge with God Śiva in this third perfection. So, we see that man is both being and becoming. He is already perfect, for the essence of his soul, Paraśiva and Satchidānanda, exists eternally within him as him, having never been created. Yet, man is evolving, becoming, for his individual soul body, created by God Śiva, is not yet perfect, is still evolving through time, eventually to mature into the image and likeness of the Primal Soul and Creator, Maheśvara. ¶I might surprise you when I say that man's soul is created and not created. True, the soul body of light was created by God Śiva Himself. Within this body of light and consciousness exist, without beginning or end, the two perfections of Paraśiva and Satchidānanda. We find the paradoxes of oneness and twoness, of being and becoming, of created and uncreated existence subtly delineated through an understanding of the three perfections of our great God Śiva.

Thursday
LESSON 326
The Point Of Conception

The point of conception is the apex of creation. At what point do we conceive, and how do we create? Let's expand our consciousness, really expand our consciousness, and begin to know that creation is merely recognizing what is already there—that there is nothing new; everything is within you and it is portrayed on the outside as you become aware that it is already created, finished, within you. ¶What makes the point of conception the apex of creation? It is the story of you. Expand your consciousness to take in the sun, the moon, the planets, the Earth, everyone. And when your limited consciousness focuses upon one thing, you say, "There is the sun, and in a few hours I will see the moon." And in a few hours you do see the moon. You are the creator, but you only create to the lower realms of the mind. Everything is within you: the sun, the moon, the planets, all of the people functioning through all their different states of consciousness, all of the various manifestations of form. They are all within you. ¶As you become aware of one thing at a time, you are really creating it into the lower realms of your mind. You are translating it into the lower realms of your mind. Your recognition of what is is the way you create it to yourself. This is deep. This is in the realm of contemplation. And only in the realm of contemplation will you begin to conceive of it. ¶Those of you who have had the power enough to concentrate enough of the mind in order to contemplate should begin to be very godlike in your everyday life. You should work very, very hard to do each thing perfectly that you do in your conscious mind, to finish each job, and to have consideration for others at all times. That will take you into the next stages of contemplation. ¶When we become careless in our lower realms of the mind after having reached contemplation, we use that great God-power in a negative way and build great barriers within ourselves that hold us in the lower realms of the mind. But when we strive diligently to perfect devotion, which is *bhakti*, to perfect service, which is *karma yoga*, at all times—twenty-four hours a day, the vigil is—then we release barriers, barriers that we are going to meet perhaps next year or the year after. We burn up and clean up *karma* that will come even in your next life. And you go from one stage of contemplation and become stable in the next stage of contemplation, until you begin to live on the very brink of the Absolute. And it's on the brink of the Absolute that you can begin to realize that the point of conception is the very apex of creation. You realize all form, and then you realize formlessness. ¶The struggle with the mind is an easy struggle if you are constantly vigilant, all of the time, doing always what you know you should do, not allowing the mind to become instinctive, not excusing the mind when it does become instinctive, not allowing the mind to justify, rationalize, excuse, become combative, but making the mind always remain poised, like a hummingbird over a flower, so that you begin to live in the eternal now, constantly, permanently. And then the within becomes natural to you, not something you hear about, study about, talk about, sing about, for you become open, awakened, within.

Friday
LESSON 327
Expanded Consciousness

Contemplation is man's power over his mind as he begins to go within himself. Concentration is man's power over his mind as he goes through life working out life's problems. And meditation is man's wisdom. ¶Let's expand our consciousness once again, and see if we can become conscious of the entire universe all in one instant. Where is that universe? It is very real to you in that instant, but where is it? You might look above and say, "It's out there," but where is "out there?" Where do you conceive "above?" You might say the sun is way up in the sky. So is the moon. But where is the focal point of your conception? How do you create the sun, and how do you create the moon? You might say the sound of a waterfall is twenty feet away from you. Where is that sound created? Where do you conceive it? Only to the lower realms of the mind is the sun so many million miles away, or the waterfall so many feet from where you are sitting right now. Expand your consciousness, and you begin to know this truth. Do all the petty little things that you can do if you give way to the negative states of mind, and you bind yourself to the lie and live in the lie, like an animal would live in a cage. "Know the truth, and the truth will make you free." ¶Therefore, freedom does not come through what you have remembered, how well you can rationalize, how well you can talk yourself into and out of situations, how well you can excuse negative happenings. The knowing state of consciousness in which you can know the truth only comes when you can control the lower state of mind and live a godlike life each day, and then your consciousness does expand automatically. Your daily life becomes a life of inspiration, and in your expanded consciousness you begin to know the truth, and that knowing of the truth sets you free from the lower state of mind which you then realize is the lie, the eternal lie. The point of conception is the apex of creation.

Saturday
LESSON 328
Clinging to the Light Within

Many years ago, during the spring at our Mountain Desert Monastery, a young man wrote to me saying that he intended to give up the world and become a Hindu monk. Here is a letter that I wrote in response and an inspired talk I sent to him to ponder, entitled "On the Brink of the Absolute." ¶"Namaste! Your lovely letter arrived just as I returned to the monastery today from our India Odyssey pilgrimage to my *ashram* in Alaveddy, Sri Lanka, and eight other countries. That good timing indicates that you are on an inner beam, no doubt from the efforts already expended in your spiritual quest. From your letter, it is certain that you have exhausted the many dead-end trails on the path. Your decision to be a renunciate monastic is a good one. It is a big step and I know you have thought it over well. Times are changing. Dedicated souls like yourself are needed as helpers on the path in our monastic orders to stabilize and teach those who are seeking. It is time now for the Western mind to rediscover the vast teachings of Śaiva Siddhānta Hinduism. ¶"I am going to give you the first of many challenges we may share together in this life. It is to meditate deeply every day for one full month on a talk I once gave to a small gathering of *maṭhavāsis,* monks, at the San Francisco Temple. In fact, it was August 28, 1960. Like you, they were beginning to experience the blissful and peaceful areas of their inner being, and we spoke of enlightened insights one has on the very brink of the Absolute. You will be challenged by this assignment. Remember, the rewards are more than worth the effort required. ¶"It is my duty as your spiritual teacher to assure you that there will be trials. The *sannyāsin's* life is not easy. It will demand of you more than you ever thought possible. You will surely be asked to serve when tired, to inspire when you feel a little irritated, to give when it seems there is nothing left to offer. To drop out of this great ministry would not be good for you or for those who will learn to depend on you. A Hindu monastic order is not a place to get away from the world. You must teach us and yourself to depend on you, so that twenty or thirty years from now others will find strength in you as you fulfill your *karmic* destiny as a spiritual leader in this life. ¶"Therefore, read carefully these words. Weigh your life and consider well where you wish to devote your energies. The goal, of course, is Self Realization. That will come naturally. A foundation is needed first, a foundation nurtured through slow and arduous study, through *sādhana* performed and the demands placed by the *guru* upon the aspirant. "This is a wonderful crossroad in your life. Do not hurry into it. Do this assignment and should you wish a more disciplined and intense training, do *sādhana.* Settle your affairs of the world. Then we can sit together...." ¶The higher states of consciousness very few people are familiar with, having never experienced them. They are very pleasant to learn of, and yet out of our grasp until we have that direct experience of a higher state of expanded consciousness. The mind, in its density, keeps us from the knowledge of the Self. And then we attain a little knowledge of the existence of the Self as a result of the mind freeing itself from desires and cravings, hates and fears and the various and varied things of the mind. I say "things" because if you could see hate, you would see it as a thing that lives with one as a companion. If you could see fear, you'd see it as a thing, and as understanding comes, that thing called fear walks away down the road, never to return. ¶As you unfold spiritually, it is difficult to explain what you find that you know. At first you feel light shining within, and that light you think you have created with your mind, and yet you will find that, as you quiet your mind, you can see that light again and again, and it becomes brighter and brighter, and then you begin to wonder what is in the center of that light. "If it is the light of my True Being, why does it not quiet the mind?" ¶Then, as you live the so-called "good life," a life that treats your conscience right, that light does get brighter and brighter, and as you contemplate it, you pierce through into the center of that light, and you begin to see the various beautiful forms, forms more beautiful than the physical world has to offer, beautiful colors, in that fourth-dimensional realm, more beautiful than this material world has to offer. And then you say to yourself, "Why forms? Why color, when the scriptures tell me that I am timeless, causeless and formless?" And you seek only for the colorless color and the formless form. But the mind in its various and varied happenings, like a perpetual cinema play, pulls you down and keeps you hidden within its ramifications.

Sunday
LESSON 329
To the Depths Of Your Being

In your constant striving to control that mind, your soul comes into action as a manifestation of will, and you quiet more and more of that mind and enter into a deeper state of contemplation where you see a scintillating light more radiant than the sun, and as it bursts within you, you begin to know that you are the cause of that light which you apparently see. And in that knowing, you cling to it as a drowning man clings to a stick of wood floating upon the ocean. You cling to it and the will grows stronger; the mind becomes calm through your understanding of experience and how experience has become created. As your mind releases its hold on you of its desires and cravings, you dive deeper, fearlessly, into the center of this blazing avalanche of light, losing your consciousness in That which is beyond consciousness. ¶And as you come back into the mind, you not only see the mind for what it is; you see the mind for what it isn't. You are free, and you find men and women bound, and what you find you are not attached to, because binder and the bound are one. You become the path. You become the way. You are the light. And as you watch souls unfold, some choose the path of the Spirit; some choose the path of the mind. As you watch and wonder, your wondering is in itself a contemplation of the universe, and on the brink of the Absolute you look into the mind, and one tiny atom magnifies itself greater than the entire universe, and you see, at a glance, evolution from beginning to end, inside and outside, in that one small atom. ¶Again, as you leave external form and dive into that light which you become, you realize beyond realization a knowing deeper than thinking, a knowing deeper than understanding, a knowing which is the very, very depth of your being. You realize immortality, that you are immortal—this body but a shell, when it fades; this mind but an encasement, when it fades. Even in their fading there is no reality. ¶And as you come out of that *samādhi,* you realize you are the spirit, you become that spirit, you actually are that spirit, consciously, if you could say spirit has a consciousness. You are that spirit in every living soul. You realize you are That which everyone, in their intelligent state or their ignorant state, everyone, is striving for—a realization of that spirit that you are.

¶And then again for brief interludes you might come into the conscious mind and relate life to a past and a future and tarry there but for a while. But in a moment of concentration, your eye resting on a single line of a scripture or anything that holds the interest of the mind, the illusion of past and future fades, and again you become that light, that life deep within every living form—timeless, causeless, spaceless. ¶Then we say, "Why, why, after having realized the Self do you hold a form, do you hold a consciousness of mind? Why?" The answer is but simple and complete: you do not; of yourself you do not. But every promise made must have its fulfillment, and promises to close devotees and the desire that they hold for realization of their true being hold this form, this mind, in a lower conscious state. Were the devotees and disciples to release their desires for realization but for one minute, their *satguru* would be no more. Once having realized the Self, you are free of time, cause and change.

Ātmā Paraśivaḥ Samādhiścha

आत्मा परशिवः समाधिश्च

Soul, Self and Samādhi

Meditating in oneness, I visioned Paraparam. Meditating in oneness, I realized the Śiva-state. Meditating in oneness, I experienced transcendental awareness. Meditating in oneness, I witnessed aeons upon aeons.

TIRUMANTIRAM 2953

Monday
LESSON 330
More Solid than A Neutron Star

The Self is like a neutron star, one millions times harder than a diamond, not light, not dark, not within, not without, all things and nothing. You can't smell it, yet you sense its smell. You can't hear it, yet you feel its noise. You can't see it, yet you are blinded by the thought of its light. You can't know it, yet you know it; and knowing it is irresistible. The compact neutron star is heavier than heaviness itself, lighter than a balloon within air, space, nonspace, matter, nonmatter, air, the absence of air, light, the absence of light. How can we compare the neutron star to the Self, which is a trillion times greater, infinitely greater? There is no comparison, only an analogy of its greatness, of the stability-of-hardness, ever-present Self within each and every one of you. Quell the wanderings of the external mind. Bring it in through breathing, regulated breath. Quell the waves of the subconscious mind by bringing it into right belief, right words, right action—*dharma*—thus acknowledging all wrong actions, wrong words, wrong belief with penance, perseverance and final dissolution. Then there is nothing left but *dharma*—right action, right thought, right speech—within every experience of life. *Dharma* is sustained. ¶The neutron star: a trillion times more solid is the Self, which is you this very moment. Feel strong, feel secure, feel invincible, untouchable and yet able to be touched. Claim your heritage. Learn to work with yourself within yourself to accept your inherent identity. Don't waste your time looking for your religious roots, racial roots, from the past. Once found, they will only give you momentary fulfillment. Accept and learn to deal with the realization of your acceptance of the undisputed fact of the strength of the Source. You are always your Source, emanating, ever emanating, creation, preservation and dissolution, but to create again to preserve the whims and fancies of the emanations of the neutron star. The emanations of the star, of which the Self, Paraśiva, you, is a billion times more compact, is this *māyā* of a constant, intricately complex series of performing, sustaining and cancelling out to perform again. Let's all dance with Śiva and unfold within ourselves Śiva consciousness—the all-rightness of whatever happens, of all the happenings in the perfect universe called Śivaness.

Tuesday
LESSON 331
How the One Becomes Many

The Self is timeless, causeless and formless. Therefore, being That, it has no relation whatsoever to time, space and form. Form is in a constant state of creation, preservation and destruction within space, thus creating consciousness called time, and has no relationship to timelessness, causelessness or formlessness. The individual soul, when mature, can make the leap from the consciousness of space-time-causation into the timeless, causeless, formless Self. This is the ultimate maturing of the soul on this planet. ¶Form in its cycle of creation, preservation and destruction is always in one form or another, a manifest state or a gaseous state, but is only seeming to one who has realized the Self. Śiva in His manifest state is all form, in all form and permeating through all form, and hence all creation, preservation and destruction of form is Śiva. This is the dance, the movement of form. No form is permanent. Śiva in His unmanifest form is timeless, causeless, spaceless—hence called the Self God. Hence, Śiva has always existed, was never created, as both His manifest and unmanifest states have always existed. This is the divine dance and the mystery revealed to those who have realized the Self. ¶The soul merged out of Śiva as the Self in His timeless, causeless, spaceless, unmanifest state and from Śiva as the Creator, Preserver and Destroyer in His manifest state of all form. The core of the merger between these two states, or the apex, causes a cell which breaks loose another cell, thus spawning souls. Each time the Being of Śiva goes from His manifest to His unmanifest state, it spawns a soul. ¶Where the Śakti unites with the unmanifest and Śiva unites with the manifest, this natural process, which continues even into the *sahasrāra* of man, is the core from whence creation comes. ¶Each God has a vehicle through which he is represented—Gaṇeśa the mouse, Muruga the peacock, and Śiva rides in man. The origin of man—being spawned from Śiva, the birthless, deathless God—therefore, is as a pure, taintless soul. After thus being spawned, the soul goes through a maturing process. This slow growth is in three basic categories: *karma* exercises, *āṇava* clouds, *māyā* distorts. This classroom of these experiences finally matures an intelligence free enough from the bondage of the classroom of *āṇava, karma* and *māyā* to realize its own Divinity and at-one-ment with Śiva as a taintless, pure soul. This, then, is the foundation, after once attained, for final liberation, Self Realization, to be sought for.

Wednesday
LESSON 332
Realization And Evolution

When the soul is spawned, it is a release of energy. This energy, once released, accumulates more energy around it from the manifest world, which is also Śiva.

The impact of the spawning is so strong that finally a body is created around this tiny cell, which looks exactly like the Primal Soul body of the God that spawned the soul into being. The word *soul* in itself, meaning core, refers to this cell. The body of the soul, the actinic causal body, as it becomes denser, moves into another plane of manifest being and begins on its own to create, preserve and destroy, for it now is form, taking on the same nature, which is its nature, of Śiva in manifest form. The only difference now between this soul and Śiva is that Śiva can be in unmanifest state, but the soul is caught in the activity, the so-called bondage, of the manifest state. It has not yet completed the cycle. Once this soul has completed the cycle of the manifest state, then quite naturally it merges back into itself and realizes, or is, the unmanifest state. ¶After realization of the Self, to attain actual liberation from rebirth requires the willful and deliberate act of the adept at the point of death to direct the course. If he feels and knows that he has yet to perform actions of service on this planet, once the physical body has been parted from, he will find himself on an inner plane in which he can prepare to return at the proper place and proper time to fulfill his desire. However, should he have felt well satisfied with his many lives, as they play before his vision during his transition from his physical body, now ready to go on in this liberated state, he would find himself on an inner plane whence it would be impossible to reenter flesh. Thus, *moksha, kaivalya,* liberation from earthly birth, has been attained, and the way is open to further evolution on the subtle planes. ¶Embodied souls have attributes that are constantly refining themselves as they traverse the instinctive nature toward the Divine. These qualities are becoming more and more like Lord Śiva's. His personality, attributes and qualities are described by the 1,008 names given to Him, for no single name is adequate to depict His attributes. Similarly, a person could not be adequately explained by one word. Now you can see the similarity between Lord Śiva and His offspring.

Thursday
LESSON 333
Maturation Of the Soul

There is nothing separate from Lord Śiva, who pervades all. The seeming separateness is the forgetting, lack of awareness or inability to be aware at all. Thus, all souls—Gods and men—are inseparable, tied into, a direct extension of Śiva, immanently close. The fearful distance is the state of the soul in the *kevala* or *sakala avasthais,* not in the *śuddha avasthai,* in which the enjoyment of the bliss of the oneness is felt. But the oneness is no less there in the *kevala* state. Souls, young and old, are directly connected to Lord Śiva—closer than breathing, nearer than hands or feet. He is the eye within the eyes of the beholder of His form, in souls young and old. Therefore, sight is the first experience of *darshan.* ¶You become everything when you merge in Śiva, but you are no longer you. Before that, you evolve to a perfect likeness of the Primal Soul. The final destiny of the soul is to fully mature its soul body, at which time it would be identical to Śiva. Therefore, this process leads the soul through three states or *avasthais*: *kevala, sakala* and *śuddha.* Once having been spawned, the soul exists in a quiescent condition, not being aware of itself. This is the *kevala* state—soul not being aware of itself. Eventually it hits matter, magnetizes matter around it—its first etheric body. This etheric body slowly develops into a mental, then emotional and astral body, and finally a physical body. This begins the *sakala* state—soul being aware of the mental plane, astral plane and finally the physical world. It is in the latter stages of the *sakala* state that religion begins, when the soul has completed enough of this process to realize its individual identity, apart from the mental matter, the emotional or astral matter and the physical matter. All through this process, the all-pervading Śiva nurtures the soul into its maturity on the onward march of its evolution. Lord Śiva does not create a soul, then, unattached from it, wait for it to return on its own volition. Rather, He creates the soul and energizes it through its entire evolution until, at the end of the *śuddha avasthai,* the final merger occurs, *viśvagrāsa,* absorption, by His grace. ¶All souls, Mahādevas, *devas,* people *devas*—and in all states, *śuddha, sakala, kevala*—have exactly the same relationship with Śiva. None is more favored, more dear or cared for than another. In the *śuddha avasthai,* the mental body is purified in the soul maturity and thus reflects its nature, Śiva's nature, more than in the *kevala* or *sakala* state. Therefore, those older souls are doing the same work as the Lord naturally does. This is the loving caring for other souls. This is the innate nature of the soul and the absolute nature of Śiva. As the light cannot detach itself from its rays, Lord Śiva cannot withdraw Himself from His creations.

Friday
LESSON 334
The Body Of the Soul

All concepts of time, space, mind, universe, microcosm and macrocosm are what occur when inhabiting a physical body. But they are only concepts, not relating to what actually occurs. The seven *chakras* of the physical body produce their frameworks, relationships. The Self, the realization of God, Paraśiva, is immanent now within everyone, only realizable according to the soul's evolution, which can be hastened through the practice of *yoga.* Therefore, to look for realizations through correlations or to seek correlations as destinations is futile. This is because what you seek after already exists in its fullness within each soul. ¶Those in the *kevala avasthai,* are creating forms around the soul and are not inwardly directed. Those in the *sakala avastai* are deciphering their creations and not interested. Those in the *śuddha avasthai* perceive, little by little, a fullness—that within which has never changed since the first cell broke away containing within it the fullness of Śiva, His *samādhi,* as well as form. ¶Our soul is an immortal, effulgent being of light created by God Śiva in His image and evolving to union with Him. Its uncreated divine essence is Pure Consciousness and Absolute Reality, eternally one with Śiva. The unfoldment of the soul through the *avasthais* of existence can be understood in the analogy of the fragrant lotus rising above the water, drawn up by the sun, having come from the mud below. The mud is *kevala,* the lotus and its blossoming is *sakala,* and the sun is *śuddha.* ¶One day you will see the being of you, your divine soul body. You will see it inside the physical body. It looks like clean, clear plastic. Around it is a blue light, and the outline of it is whitish yellow. Inside of it is blue-yellowish light, and there are trillions of little nerve currents, or quantums, and light scintillating all through that. This body stands on a lotus flower. Inwardly looking down through your feet, you see you are standing on a big, beautiful lotus flower. This body has a head, it has eyes, and it has infinite intelligence. It is tuned into and feeds from the source of all energy. ¶The soul form, which is another way of naming the "soul body," evolves as its consciousness evolves, becoming more and more refined until finally it is at the same intensity or refinement as the Primal Soul. The experiences of life, in all the various planes of consciousness, are "food for the soul," reaping lessons that actually raise the level of intelligence and love. Thus, very refined souls are walking intelligences, beaming with love. The "soul body" is not like any other body, because it is the Being itself, not an encasement for the being. ¶I chose the term *soul body* many years ago to convey the very real fact that souls do have a human-like form that can be seen in mystic, superconscious vision. It was a way of describing the actual nature of the soul, which is not simply a ball of intelligence, or a point of awareness. But the body of the soul cannot be separated from the soul. They are one and the same. If you take away the form of the soul, all bonds are broken and *jīva* becomes Śiva.

Saturday
LESSON 335
The Death of The Small Self

When the emotions begin to react in a systematic way, and hate and fear and jealousy and love and passion and all of those emotions begin to function properly, and awareness flows out into the conscious mind, the physical body begins to assume a mature, intelligent appearance. You can look at the person and judge, "By looking at his body, I see that he is an intelligent man." That means all of his instinctive and intellectual faculties are developed and working simultaneously together. However, he may be yet to turn inward. Perhaps you can ascertain this by looking into his eyes. Perhaps in this life he will turn inward, when he has satisfied some of his desires he is setting into motion. As soon as he begins to turn inward, he begins to nourish his spiritual body. It starts to grow within the emotional body. It grows like a child, fed by all of his good deeds. All of his selflessness and selfless actions toward others feed that body. All of his working with himself, conquering instinctive emotions within himself, is food for that body, as it draws from the central source of energy. All of his selfishness and greed and giving power to thc instinctive elements starve this spiritual body. You have heard about the suffering of the soul. As it unfolds, it cries out and wants more attention. This is man's struggle within himself. ¶Finally, the spiritual body grows up into a mature body and unfolds the subsuperconscious mind, grows up more and becomes aware in the superconscious mind, taking on more spiritual force from the Infinite. Ultimately, it takes over the astral emotional-intellectual body. ¶That is the whole story of the inner awakening that is occurring within each of us. The mere fact that it makes sense to you as you read about it means you are in the process of this experience of superconsciousness moving out into the conscious plane. ¶Ultimately, you begin to go through the harrowing experiences of past *karma* with your eyes firmly set upon your ultimate goal: Self Realization. As you live your life in service to mankind, reprogramming your subconscious and facing all of the things that you didn't face fully through your many past lives while working with your emotions and intellect, finally you come to the crucifixion of the ego. This happens when your last experiences have begun to fade and you no longer see yourself as a "Mr. Somebody" who came from some community somewhere, who is of a certain nationality and who, incidentally, distinguishes himself from all other people because he is on the path to enlightenment and he knows a lot of people that are not. ¶This great spiritual pride of the personal ego finally is crucified. It is put on the cross of man's own spiritual discernment. The death of the ego is a tremendous experience. You go through the dark night of the soul and feel that your family, friends and even the Gods have deserted you. During this time, you do not see light anymore. You see blackness all through the body, as all of the accumulated experiences of the many, many lives come in on you and you are not even aware where your awareness is in the mind. You can't figure it all out. It happens too rapidly. Then finally: "I am That. I am." You burst into the Self God.

Sunday
LESSON 336
Birth of the Golden Body

The golden body, *svarṇaśarīra,* is a body made of golden light. After many experiences of Paraśiva, it gradually descends from the seven *chakras* above the *sahasrāra* into the *ājñā chakra,* which then becomes the soul's *mūlādhāra,* then down into the *viśuddha chakra,* which then becomes its *mūlādhāra,* and then down into the *anāhata,* which then becomes its *mūlādhāra.* ¶All seven *chakras* above the *sahasrāra* slowly come down and down and down until the entire astral body is psychically seen, by mystics who have this sight, as a golden body. The astral body slowly, slowly, slowly dissolves into the golden body. That is what I have seen happen. That is what our *paramparā* and our *sampradāya* know from experience. Experience is the only true knowing—a knowing that can be verified in books, through others who have the same knowing, but a knowing that no others know who have not had the same experience. To them it is only a concept, a nice one maybe, but just a concept or written off as an opinion. ¶When the golden body fully enters the physical, having taken over the astral, the knowing that is known comes unbidden. It is beyond reason but does not conflict with it. It is a living scripture but does not conflict with those written by seers of the past who have seen and their records have become scripture. So great is the Sanātana Dharma that it defies all who doubt it, all who disdain it, all who disregard it, all who degrade it, with personal realization of its Truth. ¶This golden body, which begins to build into a golden body after the experience of *nirvikalpa samādhi,* is connected to the *sahasrāra chakra.* In other words, the *sahasrāra chakra* is the home base in the physical body for the golden body. There are twelve basic unfoldments to this *chakra* as the golden body grows. When the realized *sannyāsin* travels in high states of contemplation, he moves freely in his golden body and can help and serve mankind. Over time, he gains a conscious control of the *sahasrāra chakra* as a force center which propels him into inner space. ¶It is this golden body, as it refines and refines and refines itself within the Śivaloka after *moksha,* that finally merges with Śiva like a cup of water being poured into the ocean. That same water can never be found and put back into the cup. This truly is *svarṇaśarīra viśvagrāsa,* the final, final, final merging with Śiva.

Paraśiva Darśana Dāyitvam

परशिवदर्शनदायित्वम्

The Responsibility Of Enlightenment

Their thoughts are filled with Śiva, having destroyed the soul's triple bondages. Pure Śaivas they have become, and they shall not return to worldly bondage. Shouts, confusion and fights in this world they do not indulge in. They remain immersed in constant inner sound and endless inner space. ¶The wise impart divine knowledge only to those fully ripened to receive it. With you facing east or south, your disciple facing west or north, take him gently to the limits of the vast infinite. In this way instruct him, with the *śakti* of the Lord centered in your mind.

TIRUMANTIRAM 2970 & 1701

Monday
LESSON 337
After the First Great Samādhi

Rare are the diligent *sannyāsins* who, after working for many years within themselves, each in his own time, burst through superconsciousness into *nirvikalpa samādhi,* the realization of the timeless, causeless, spaceless Self. Many strive to attain Self Realization during many lifetimes and then for many years in their present birth. The many lives have brought certain accomplishment which leads to their first breakthrough into *nirvikalpa samādhi.* The first breakthrough into *samādhi* happens quickly, so that the subtle parts of the mind, shall we say, are not consciously aware of what is actually taking place and what has actually happened, because they are not used to being consciously aware in the higher states of consciousness. However, when the renunciate has broken through to the Self, Paraśiva, he has the possibility of the full use of his mind, the higher states of consciousness as well as the full understanding of lower states of consciousness and how his individual awareness travels from one state to another. The mere fact he has broken through to *samādhi* means that he was able to justify experience enough in his subconscious mind so that his subconscious mind could fall into line, into the habit pattern of pure concentration. When the conscious mind is in concentration upon one single thing, the subconscious mind is in concentration also, following the pattern of the conscious mind, on one particular thing. Then that expands consciousness automatically into the superconscious state of mind. With the understanding of the functioning of the superconscious mind, and not being deluded by any of the ramifications of the superconscious mind, often a renunciate has managed to go right into the very core and actually break through to the Self. This is what has happened to him. ¶Each soul comes into Self Realization differently, because each has a different mind, a different subconscious mind and a different conscious mind, with a different nature, so naturally his reaction through experience before the experience of Self Realization and his reaction afterwards, being of the conscious and subconscious mind, is going to be different, depending upon his background and understanding and his nationality, etc. ¶The teachings of *yoga* are so basically simple and so basically concrete. And the most beautiful thing in the world, on contemplation, is the simplest thing in the world. The most beautiful design is the simplest design. So, simply since one has realized the Self and gone into *nirvikalpa samādhi* once, then obviously the simplest thing to do is to do it again. This is the practice of *samādhi.* When one has accomplished this a second time, do it again. Realize the Self again and again and again. Each time the renunciate comes out of *samādhi,* he will rebound, and it is like popping back into a different aspect of the mind. Or he will actually have more conscious awareness of the mind and totality of the mind. In other words, he will have a greater capacity of expanded consciousness. Or, in still other words, he will become consciously more superconscious for longer periods of time each time he experiences *nirvikalpa samādhi.* ¶When a beginning devotee is going up the path, he is spontaneously superconscious now and again. After his first *samādhi,* he has realized that he has had longer periods of superconsciousness. After his second *samādhi,* he will be more and more aware of the superconscious mind, and after the next *samādhi*, he will be even more and more aware of the superconscious mind. However, each will unfold the superconscious mind and superconscious possibilities, powers, etc., differently than another, due to the fact that all have different backgrounds, personalities and such; for though he realizes the Self, the entirety of the basic nature does not change. However, his understanding of his own control of his tendencies, the overall control that he has, and his ability to mold his own life—that starts a process which transforms him gradually and increasingly as he becomes more and more familiar with the laws of going into and out of *nirvikalpa samādhi.*

Tuesday
LESSON 338
Bringing Others Into Realization

The lesson I want to point out is that once the soul has realized the Self, it is now on the road to realizing it again, and realizing it again and again. It is just as simple as that, and the warning that I would give is: do not become fascinated in the aftermath of any experience of the Self—so that the inner mind is always reaching for the highest *samādhi*, not being intrigued with the superconscious that is after *samādhi.* When one is intrigued with the superconsciousness after *samādhi*, this builds up the forces, not only of the mind but all the psychic forces, and brings the *maṭhavāsi* into a realm of occultism. This is something to guard against, because when he is intrigued with the aftermath, with the possibilities and the ramifications of the mind, this will eventually lead him around and around in circles, because the mind can offer nothing other than ramifications. In the beginning teachings, all devotees learn that the mind created itself, created itself and created itself. Well, even the superconscious mind does this. ¶What must be really sought after, in order for one as a Self-Realized person to fulfill his destiny of bringing others into Self Realization, is a pure *samādhi* which will keep the pure teachings of *advaita yoga* alive on the Earth through the *sannyāsins.* Everything on Earth comes through people. Everything of advanced knowledge has come through people. Self Realization is the pure teachings of *yoga,* attained on the Earth through people who talk, breathe, live just like the Self-Realized soul does. ¶If he goes into *nirvikalpa samādhi* and becomes ramified in the psychic powers that come after *samādhi,* after his first *samādhi,* his second *samādhi,* his third *samādhi,* he will become more intense and will realize new possibilities within himself. If he remains on those planes of the phenomena of the occultism of the mind, then he gains new and fascinating powers of the mechanism of the mind, but he loses the power to bring others along the path into *samādhi.* If the renunciate maintains a clean *samādhi* and comes back into the mind, he realizes he has had some extrasensory perceptions, and he does not use them. He does not use them at all unless, of course, he uses them quite naturally, just as naturally as he would enjoy a meal, but he does not dwell on supernatural powers as anything special. He is at every point in time just who he is. ¶What the renunciate is taught to dwell on would be the next time and the next time he would be going into *samādhi.* Then he awakens a strong current within himself that can bring others into *samādhi.* By dropping off unessential powers, he gains one great power. That is the one great power that those who have realized the Self want, the power to bring others into Self Realization. You can only do that by having first attained a pure Self Realization yourself and going into *samādhi* again and again and again. Remember, the *sannyāsin*'s destiny is this: having realized the Self, bring others into the pure realization of the Self, and teach other *sannyāsins* to go into *samādhi* and come out with a well-balanced mind, without deviating one way or another on the psychic planes.

Wednesday
LESSON 339
Finding the Light's Center

After his first *nirvikalpa samādhi,* the renunciate's concentration and his practice of concentration should be easier. His first step in practicing *samādhi* would be to concentrate upon one physical object, that is if he cannot see his inner light. And if his mind is confused, he won't be able to see the inner light, like before he went into his first *samādhi.* Only after he has gone into *samādhi* many, many, many times, where his whole body becomes filled with light, will he then see his inner light all the time, twenty-four hours a day. But at first he won't. He will have his first breakthrough, but he won't see the light all the time. ¶If he doesn't see the inner light, he must concentrate, get his mind quiet, write down his confessions and understand the different experiences he has gone through, in the very same way he has been taught in his beginning study. Then, finally, when his inner light—which he will soon begin to find right at the top of the head—comes into prominence, he must turn his concentration onto that. And, with enough mind power, he should be able to hold that inner light, a very bright white light looking just like a star, right at the top of the head. This will give him figures and conscious-mind forms, about three inches in diameter, and then he would concentrate the light into a three-inch diameter. He may not always know where the center is, especially if he has been involved in his Śaiva *seva.* If that is so, he should press the top of his head with his finger, and that will indicate to him where the center of that light should be. This will immediately center his awareness in the center of the light. Then he tries to part it, tries to open it up like a camera lens, and comes into brilliant, very brilliant, light. It will just be scintillating, much brighter than a star. It will be like a carbon-arc light. This is very brilliant and very powerful. The renunciate is then schooled in how to hold that to a three-inch diameter, because the tendency will be for that light to fill up his whole head. He will feel very blissful. We don't want that to happen. We don't want the emotions or the lower mind to get out of control simply because he found a bright light in his head. ¶He has seen other seekers, as they were just awakening in the inner light, get so carried away about the inner light, that it throws them into an emotional state and they can get fanatical about it. It doesn't give them any inner wisdom or anything like that. So, remembering this, the wise *sannyāsin* will not allow himself to get emotional about the inner light, because seeing this light indicates that he is only beginning to come into his superconscious. The light, really, is the friction of the superconscious mind against the conscious and subconscious mind. In my way of looking at it, it is an electrical friction. The odic forces and the actinic forces merging causes light and sound. ¶So, when he sees this brilliant light right in his head, more brilliant than he has ever seen, intensified brilliance—he tries to find the center of it. When he finds the center of it, again trying to open up that light like a camera lens, he will then come into a state of consciousness called Satchidānanda, a state of pure consciousness, a state of pure bliss, *savikalpa samādhi.* Here he won't be in a brilliant light anymore. Above him it will look like he is looking way up in the sky, into outer space, and the color of it will be a whitish blue. That will be the *ākāśa* he will be in.

Thursday
LESSON 340
Distractions And Sidepaths

In the *ākāśa,* he would be able to go into all sorts of psychic phenomena. We don't want that. We don't want to utilize the *ākāśa* in that way, because then we cause the growth of gross matter in the subconscious mind, which is capable of imprinting into the *ākāśa* things that we want to happen. Then we could go in the *ākāśa* and see them. We will see those forms change shape from what we have, from our own subconscious, imprinted in the subconscious. Then, through the power of the light, it takes form in the *ākāśa,* and we can have a little world of our own going around on the inside, and that is called psychism or occultism. We don't want that. Nor do we want to tune in with anybody else who is also in the *ākāśa,* because that leads us away from the purity of *yoga.* ¶Now, for instance, if I were in the *ākāśa* and two other adepts were in the *ākāśa,* then we could tune in with one another, and I might even see their faces in the *ākāśa.* We would guard against this, because that would be allowing the superconscious mind to take form. When the superconscious mind takes form, then that means the consciousness is lowered and we are being led away from our goal, and the next thing we knew we would come through the subconscious back to the conscious mind. We want to avoid this. We don't want to come through the subconscious to the conscious mind. From *samādhi,* we want to come directly from the superconscious into the conscious. So, we avoid all form and colors that we might see in the *ākāśa.* ¶When the *sannyāsin* arrives at that state, the next lesson will occur. He will be in a pure state of consciousness, pure bliss. It will appear to him as spaceless. He will be having a feeling of timelessness, a feeling of formlessness, but it is not the Self. It is taken as the Self, but it is not the Self, for it still has consciousness. In summary, we have discovered how to come out of darkness into light in the practice of *samādhi,* and how to go through two different stages of light into a realm of pure consciousness which we call the *ākāśa.* ¶As we have previously studied, there are seven different states in the superconscious mind, seven different states and usages. The very first is the light. And the pure consciousness state that we just discussed is the seventh state. All the others we want to avoid. It is not that it wouldn't be possible to get into them and develop them, but we want to definitely avoid them, because they are, shall we say, deterrents to the purities in the Self. So, we shall avoid them by going from basic inner light to a more intense light and popping out into a pure state of consciousness. The *sannyāsin* will still have an overall consciousness of the physical body. As a matter of fact, when he is looking down at the physical body, it might just appear like a shadow to him. It is not advisable for him to look down at the physical body in consciousness, for that will lead him down into the sixth or fifth plane of consciousness, and we don't want to be there in the superconscious. Then other things will intervene, and he won't achieve the *samādhi.* He will have to come out and start over again. So, these investigations we want to avoid, because they are not necessary, ever, though they are not impossible. When he is in his pure state of consciousness, then he has to look for the continuation of the *kuṇḍalinī* force or, shall we say, the continuation of the nerve currents that house the *kuṇḍalinī* force. In conscious-mind terms, that will look like a tube or a nerve current which would be issued right from the top of the head. ¶In this state of pure consciousness, like in outer space, he tries to find just one nerve current right at the top of the head. When he finds this nerve current at the top of the head, he is taught to concentrate on it from where it begins at the top of the head right up to the end of it, and soon he finds the end of it. The experience of experiences. Of course if he has a mishmash in his subconscious mind, he won't be able to hold this pure state of consciousness. The subconscious mind in its power and intensity of this contemplation will begin picking up, and he will be coming right back in the outer consciousness. If his subconscious is fairly clean and under control, then he will be able to hold it, and he will hold it quite naturally. It will be a natural state to him after Self Realization. ¶So, then, the next thing to do is to find this nerve current. In conscious mind terms, it may issue out about one-half inch in diameter. In superconscious-mind terms, it may be eleven feet in diameter, because the superconscious mind can magnify or it can diminish. It has that power almost at will. He must try to find the center of this nerve current, and then he comes into the core of this *ākāśa,* the very atomic structure that makes it up.

Friday
LESSON 341
Dharma after Self Realization

What is life like after realization? One difference is the relationship to possessions. Everything is yours, even if you don't own it. This is because you are secure in the Self as the only reality, the only permanence, and the security that depends on having possessions is gone. After Self Realization, we no longer have to go into ourself. Rather, we go out of ourself to see the world. We are always coming out rather than trying to go in. There is always a center, and we are the center, no matter where we are. No matter where we are, no matter how crude or rotten, the vibrations around us will not affect us. Curiosity is the final thing to leave the mind, which it does after Self Realization. The curiosity of things goes away—of *siddhis,* for example. We no longer want power, because we are power, nonpower, unusable. And we don't have the yearning for Paraśiva anymore; we don't have the yearning for the Self. And Satchidānanda is now to us similar to what the intellect used to be. If we want to go to a far-off place, we go into Satchidānanda and see it. It is that easy. *Samyama,* contemplation, is effortless, to you now, like the intellect used to be, whereas before, *samyama* was a very big job which took a lot of energy and concentration. Therefore, before Paraśiva, we should not seek the *siddhis.* After Paraśiva, through *samyama,* we keep the *siddhis* we need for our work. ¶But Paraśiva has to be experienced time after time for it to impregnate all parts of the body. Our big toe has to experience it, because we are still human. From a rotten state of consciousness, feeling totally neglected, that nobody loves us, we have to realize Paraśiva. When ill and feeling we may die, we have to realize Paraśiva. When concentrating on our knees, we have to bring Paraśiva into them. The knees are the center of pride, and this helps in attaining ultimate humility. So it is with every part of our body, not only the pituitary center, the physical corollary of the door of Brahman—that is the first place—but with every part of the body. The pituitary gland has to be stimulated sufficiently to open the door of Brahman. But only the strictest *sannyāsin* disciplines would induce this result. Ears, eyes, nose, throat, all parts of the body have to realize Paraśiva, and the *siddha* has to do this consciously. The calves have to realize Paraśiva. All the parts of the lower body have to realize Paraśiva, because all of those *tala chakras* have to come into that realization. ¶Then, finally, we are standing on the *mūlādhāra chakra* rather than on the *talatala chakra.* Then, finally, our feet are standing on the *svādhishṭhana chakra,* and so on. And this is the true meaning of the holy feet. Finally, we are standing in the lotus of the *maṇipūra chakra.* And doubly finally, the *kuṇḍalinī* coils up in the head and lives there rather than at the bottom of the spine. ¶For ultimate freedom, everything has to go away, all human things, possessions, love, hate, family, friends, the desire for attention and community acceptance. The *sannyāsin* renounces the world, and then, if his giving up is uncompromisingly complete, the world renounces the *sannyāsin.* This means the world itself won't accept him as it once did as a participant in its mundane transactions of a job, social life, home and family. Earlier friends and associates sense his different view of their existence and now feel uncomfortable with him. Slowly he joins the band of hundreds of thousands of *sannyāsins* throughout the world, where he is joyously accepted. All must go, the past and the future, and will naturally depart as the great realization deepens, as it penetrates through all parts of the body and all states of the mind. This alone is one good reason that family people and noncommitted singles are never encouraged to strive for realizations higher than Satchidānanda, and then only for brief periods now and again at auspicious times. For family people, *gṛihasthas,* to go further into themselves would be to earn the bad *karmas, kukarmas,* of subsequent neglect of family *dharma,* and to lose everything that the world values. ¶When the renunciate finally attains Paraśiva, everything else will fall away. It all has to fall away to attain Paraśiva. But it doesn't totally fall away when he attains Paraśiva, because he arrives into Paraśiva only with a tremendous amount of built-up effort. All the Gods have given permission. Lord Śiva has given permission, and He now says, "Enter Me." That is grace, His grace.

Saturday
LESSON 342
Enlightened? Stay Enlightened.

A *sannyāsin* of attainment has had many, many lifetimes of accumulating this power of *kuṇḍalinī* to break that seal at the door of Brahman. Here is a key factor. Once it is broken, it never mends. Once it is gone, it's gone. Then the *kuṇḍalinī* will come back—and this gives you a choice between *upadeśī* and *nirvāṇī*—and coil in the *svādhishṭhāna, maṇipūra, anāhata,* wherever it finds a receptive *chakra,* where consciousness has been developed, wherever it is warm. A great intellect or a *siddha* who finds the Self might return to the center of cognition; another might return to the *maṇipūra chakra.* The ultimate is to have the *kuṇḍalinī* coiled in the *sahasrāra.* ¶I personally didn't manage that until 1968 or '69 when I had a series of powerful experiences of *kuṇḍalinī* in the *sahasrāra.* It took twenty years of constant daily practice of tough *sādhanas* and *tapas.* I was told early on that much of the beginning training was had in a previous life and that is why, with the realization in this life, I would be able to sustain all that has manifested around me and within me as the years passed by. Results of *sādhanas* came to me with a lot of concentrated effort, to be sure, but it was not difficult, and that is what makes me think that previous results were being rekindled. ¶The renunciate's path is to seek enlightenment through *sādhana,* discipline, deep meditation and *yogic* practices. That is the goal, but only the first goal for the *sannyāsin.* To stay enlightened is even a greater challenge for him. This requires a restrictive discipline—not unlike a military, at-base, on-call life, twenty-four hours a day—even in his dreams. ¶Many people have flashes of light in their head and think they are totally enlightened beings, then let down in their *sādhana* and daily worship to later suffer the consequences. Enlightenment brings certain traditionally unwanted rewards: attention, adulation; one becomes the center of attraction, knows more than others and can exist on words, sentences, paragraphs, chapters, for a long time, even after the light fades and human emotions well up and new mixed *karmas* build. He then may become known as having attained the erratic human behavior of the "enlightened" person. This is totally unacceptable on the spiritual path. Once enlightened, or "in-light," even to a small degree because of daily *sādhana,* stay enlightened because of daily *sādhana.* Once having intellectually realized Vedic truths and become able to explain them because of study and daily *sādhana,* then realize these truths by intensifying the daily *sādhanas,* lest the remaining *prārabdha karmas* germinate and create new unwanted *karmas* to be lived through at a later time. ¶The advice is, having once attained a breakthrough of light within the head, wisdom tells us, remain wise and do not allow these experiences to strengthen the external ego. Become more humble. Become more self-effacing. Become more loving and understanding. Don't play the fool by giving yourself reprieve from *prāṇāyāma, padmāsana,* deep meditation, self-inquiry and exquisite personal behavior. Having once attained even a small semblance of *samādhi,* do not let that attainment fade into memories of the past. The admonition is: once enlightened, stay enlightened. ¶Enlightenment has its responsibilities. One such responsibility is to have respect for and pay homage to the *satguru* and the *satgurus* of his lineage. These are the ones who, in seen and unseen ways, have helped you on your path. Another is to keep up the momentum. The wise know full well that the higher *chakras,* once stimulated, stimulate their lower counterparts as well, unless the sealing of the passage just below the *mūlādhāra* has been accomplished. Diligence is needed, lest higher consciousness fall unknowingly on the slippery slide of ignorance into the realms of lower consciousness, of fear, anger, resentment, jealousy, loneliness, malice and distrust. The faint memories of the beginning enlightenment experiences still hover, and while now in lower consciousness but still emulating the higher qualities in personal behavior, the now unenlightened claims full benefit for the previous enlightenment. Shame! This is because he did not maintain his disciplines after enlightenment. He let down and became an egocentric person.

Sunday
LESSON 343
Insisting On Sādhana

Many *gurus* and *swāmīs* don't insist on continued disciplines and *sādhanas* after a few inner accomplishments have been made. The beginning is the end of the course to them. These *gurus* and *swāmīs* are modern, and often take an easy approach of not putting excessive demands upon themselves or their devotees. Traditional Sanātana Dharma, however, insists on daily *sādhana* for the enlightened one who desires a greater on-going transformation and for the unenlightened who has little or no anticipation of becoming enlightened. ¶*Pūjā* bells are heard ringing before sunrise throughout the homes of India in every city. In these early morning hours, men and women are priests and priestesses in their own home. Children learn *ślokas; haṭha yoga* is a daily exercise; *prāṇāyāma* is done for maintaining a healthy mind and body. Discipline is the criterion of being a good citizen. In Hinduism it happens to be a religious discipline. The effects of abandoning the earlier *yogas* upon reaching a certain stage of spiritual unfoldment for *gurus* and *swāmīs* is reflected in the lives of their students. When they began to teach, they would not be inclined to take their devotees through the beginning stages; they would not impart the practices of the first two *mārgas—charyā* and *kriyā.* They would be more inclined to start the beginners out at the upper stages, where they themselves are now, and abandon the beginning stages. This would be, and is, a mistake, one which many *gurus* and *swāmīs* have lived to regret when their own disciples began to compete with them or turned sour when unable to attain the expected results. Traditionally, the character has to be built within the devotee as a first and foremost platform before even the hint of an initiation into inner teaching is given. This purifying preparation involves repentance, confession and reconcilation through traditional *prayaśchitta,* penance, to mitigate *kukarmas.* This crucial work often takes years to accomplish. ¶Once some level of enlightenment has been attained, this is the time to intensify the *sādhana,* not to let up. When we let up on ourselves, the instinctive mind takes over. We are still living in a physical body. Therefore, one foot must always be kept firmly on the head of the snake of the instinctive-intellectual nature. The higher we go, the lower we can fall if precaution is not taken. Therefore, we must prepare devotees for a sudden or slow fall, as well. They should land on the soft pillows of consistent daily *sādhana,* worship of God, Gods and *guru,* and the basic religious practices of *karma yoga* and *bhakti yoga.* Without these as a platform, they may slide down in consciousness, below the *mūlādhāra,* into the *chakras* of fear, anger, doubt and depression. ¶The scriptures are filled with stories of certain *ṛishis* who reached high levels, but had given up all their *bhakti* and *japa.* When difficult personal *karma* came, each fell deep into the lower nature, way below the *mūlādhāra,* to become demon-like to society rather than a holy seer and a guiding force. ¶The whole idea that *bhakti* is for beginners is a modern expedient. It was created by modern people who do not want to do the daily *sādhanas,* who do not believe the Gods really exist and who are so bound in their individual personality that they do not accept the reality that God is in and within everything. This non-belief, lack of faith, changes their values very slowly at first, but changes them nonetheless into those that cry, "Personal freedom is what is sought, making the little ego big, and then bigger." Traditional disciplines and the spiritual teachers who know them so well nowadays come under the purview of these "free thinkers," later to regret it. This is similar to children being the head of the house, telling their parents what they will do, and what they will not do. ¶Only the strongest and bravest souls can succeed in enlightenment and maintain and develop it until true wisdom comes as a boon. Therefore, we reaffirm, having attained a small degree of enlightenment, or a fuller enlightenment, stay enlightened, because *mukti,* the transference from the physical body through the top of the head at the point of death, has not yet occurred. And only after that happens are we enlightened forever. This is the beginning of the ultimate merging with Śiva in a physical body! Thereafter follows *viśvagrāsa,* the final, final, final merger whence there is no return, where *jīva* has in reality become Śiva, as a bowl of water poured into the ocean becomes the ocean. There is no difference and no return.

Punarjanma

पुनर्जन्म

Reincarnation

Like the prancing steed that leaps forward, the *jīva* also traverses near and far. Like those who doff and don one garment and another, the *jīva,* too, moves from one body to another.

TIRUMANTIRAM 2131

Monday
LESSON 344
The Transition Called Death

Death—what is it? The dropping off of the physical body is the time when all of the *karma*-making actions go back to seed in the *mūlādhāra chakra,* into the memory patterns. All of our actions, reactions and the things we have set in motion in the *prāṇic* patterns in this life form the tendencies of our nature in our next incarnation. The tendencies of our nature in the present incarnation are the ways in which awareness flows through the *iḍā, piṅgalā* and *sushumṇā* currents. ¶These tendencies of man's nature also are recorded under the astrological signs in which he is born. Man comes through an astrological conglomeration of signs, or an astrological chart, according to his actions and reactions and what he set in motion in the seed-*karma* patterns of his past life. So, we are always the sum total, a collection, of all the *karmic* experiences, a totality of all the seed patterns that have happened to us, or that we have caused to happen, through the many, many lives. We are now a sum total, and we are always a continuing sum total. ¶A past life is not really so many years ago. That is not the way to look at it. It is now. Each life is within or inside the other. They exist as *karmic* seeds that appear in the *prāṇic* force fields in our life now and, like seeds, when watered they grow into plants. These seeds are nourished by *prāṇa.* When we die, or when we discard the physical body, that is the end of a chapter of experience. Then we pick up a new physical body. This begins a new chapter that is always referring back to the last chapter for direction. These are tendencies. ¶This is the entire story of what happens after we die. We simply step out of the physical body and are in our astral body, going on in the mind as usual. The awareness does not stop simply because the physical body falls away. The *iḍā* force becomes more refined, the *piṅgalā* force becomes more refined, the *sushumṇā* force is there like it always was, but all are in another body that was inside the physical body during life on Earth. ¶One great peculiarity about man is that he individually feels that he is never going to die and goes on through life planning and building as though he were going to live forever and ever. The fear of death is a natural instinctive reflex. We encounter it sometimes daily, once a month, or at least once a year when we come face to face with the possibility of obliteration of our personality and of leaving the conscious mind. The fear of change or fear of the unknown is an ominous element in the destiny of a human being. The study and comprehension of the laws of reincarnation can alleviate this fear and bring an enlightened vision of the cosmic rhythms of life and death. It is a simple process, no more fantastic, shall we say, than other growth problems we experience daily. A flower grows, blossoms and withers. The seed falls to the ground, is buried in the earth, sprouts and grows into a plant and a flower.

Tuesday
LESSON 345
Desire, Death And Rebirth

Where are we born after we die? How do we become born again? You are born again in the same way you died. After some time, the astral body cannot stay on the astral plane anymore, because the seeds of *prāṇic* motion have to be expressed on the physical plane again due to one's activity on the astral plane. A new physical birth is entered. Generally, this happens through a newborn child's body, but a more advanced soul who has his spiritual body well developed can pick up a body which is fifteen, sixteen, seventeen, eighteen, nineteen, twenty years old and go right along in life from that point. ¶In what country do you become born? It all depends upon what country you were thinking about before and when you died. If you had a desire to go to Canada, most likely you will be born in Canada next time around. If you had been thinking about going to South America a year or two before you passed away, you would be reincarnated in South America, because that was your destination. If you were very much attached to your own particular family and you did not want to leave them, you would be born back in that immediate family again, because your desire is there. The astral body is the body of desire. ¶Students probing the mysteries of reincarnation often ask, "If reincarnation is true, why can't I remember my past lives?" They might just as well ask another question: "Why do we not remember everything in detail in *this* life?" The memory capabilities, unless highly trained, are not that strong, especially after having endured the process of creating a new body through another family and establishing new memory patterns. However, there are people who do recall their past lives, in the very same way that they remember what they did yesterday. Former-life memory is that clear and vivid to them. ¶However, it is neither necessary nor advisable to pursue events, identities or relationships that may have existed in previous lives. After all, it is all now. We don't think it important to remember details of our childhood years, to wallow in happy or unhappy nostalgia. Why pursue the remembered residue of what has already come and gone? Now is the only time, and for the spiritual seeker, past life analysis or conjecture is an unnecessary waste of useful time and energy. The present now is the sum of all prior thens. Be now. Be the being of yourself this very moment, and that will be the truest fulfillment of all past actions. ¶The validity of reincarnation and its attendant philosophy are difficult to prove, and yet science is on the threshold of discovering this universal mechanism. Science cannot ignore the overwhelming evidence, the testimony of thousands of level-headed people who claim to remember other lives or who have actually died and then returned to life, and the impressive literature spanning Hindu, Tibetan, Buddhist and Egyptian civilizations. Thus, the pursuit of various theories continues in an effort to bring theory into established law according to the reason and intellectual facilities of man. Those living in the heart *chakra, anāhata,* are able to cognize and know deeply the governing mechanism of rebirth from their own awakening. ¶There are at least three basic theories or schools of thought related to reincarnation. At first they may seem to conflict or contradict one another, but further elucidation indicates that they are all correct. They are just different aspects of a complex mechanism.

Wednesday
LESSON 346
Theories of Reincarnation

According to one theory of reincarnation, life begins with sound and color. Sound and color produce the first forms of life in the atomic structure of our being through binding the seed atoms together. At this point, life as we know it begins. It remains in a seed state or state of conception until the instinctive and intellectual cycles evolve into maturity through the process of absorption of more atoms into the astral body. This process continues until a physical body is formed around the astral body. But that is not the culmination of this theory. The cells and atoms of these bodies themselves evolve, becoming more and more refined as cycles of experience pass until complete maturity is reached in a physical body which is refined enough to attain *nirvikalpa samādhi* and begin the next process of building a golden body of light. According to this theory, the soul takes on progressively more advanced bodies, evolving through the mineral, vegetable and animal kingdoms, slowly acquiring knowledge through experience. There may even be a life that seems to regress, such as a man incarnating as a cow to gain needed lessons of existence. ¶A second concept in this theory explains the lower evolutionary rate of animals, insects, plants and minerals. According to this principle, animals and lower forms of life function under what is called a "group soul." They do not have an individual astral identity, but share a group astral atomic structure. That is one reason for the lack of so-called individuality among these groups and why animals move about in herds and birds live together in flocks—indicating the movement of the one group soul, so the theory goes. ¶In another theory, when man dies, he goes on to the astral plane after breaking the silver cord which binds him to the physical body. During out-of-the-body experiences, this silver cord is often seen as a cord of light connecting the physical, astral and spiritual bodies. When awareness leaves the physical body, it passes through one of the *chakras*. If our life has been one of baser emotion and reason, we would exit through one of the *chakras* near the base of the spine, either the *mūlādhāra* or *svādhishṭhana,* and begin a conscious existence on a lower astral plane. From there we would work out various experiences or reactionary conditions caused by congested mental and emotional forces which impressed our subconscious mind during the course of our lifetime. On the astral plane, we relive many experiences by reactivating them, creating for ourselves heavens or hells. When the lessons of that life had been learned and the reactions resolved, we would be drawn back into a family, into a new physical body, in order to gain more experience in the light of the new knowledge acquired while on the astral plane. ¶If we have evolved to the point that our life was one of service, understanding and love, then we would exit through the next higher *chakras,* for that is where awareness has been polarized, and our astral existence would be of a deeper, more refined nature. However, if we had discovered and practiced a dedicated spiritual life, then our exit would be through the top two *chakras,* which do not lead awareness onto the astral plane but take it into the Third World of divine existence, never to reincarnate again into the physical world. After *nirvikalpa samādhi* is attained and perfected so that the *mahāyogī* can go into it at will, he leaves the body consciously through the door of Brahman, the center of the *sahasrāra chakra* above the pituitary gland at the top of the head. This depends on whether or not the golden actinic causal body, which has been developed after Self Realization, is mature enough to travel in actinic force fields on its own.

Thursday
LESSON 347
Earth Peoples' Shared Wisdom

Therefore, reincarnation is a refining process, attributing to the evolution of consciousness. To the watchful observer, the evolution of man's inner bodies can be seen reflected in the tone and form of his physical vehicle. Being a reflection of the inner bodies, the physical shell can and does pass through radical transformation as the spiritual path is followed. Some people seem to reincarnate within this very life, changing themselves so deeply through *tapas* and *sādhana* that they are totally renewed or reborn on the physical plane. Their new light and energy pass through the very cells of the body, invigorating and strengthening it. Still, the inner bodies are more malleable than the physical forces and generally evolve more quickly, becoming quite different and more refined in this life than the physical shell. In the next life, the physical structure will be entirely different, as the spiritual body manifests a new physical body more like unto itself. ¶Other theories propose that the soul remains on the astral plane after death. After reviewing all of our Earthly experiences on the playback, we release the astral body and enter the heavenly realms of consciousness, never coming back to the physical plane, or at least not for a long time. Many cultures, such as the Native American Indian culture, recognize this basic law of reincarnation in their "Happy Hunting Ground" concepts. Also related to this theory is the belief that when something is destroyed through fire on the physical plane, whether animate or inanimate, it will be found again on the astral plane. For example, when an Indian brave died, his saddle, clothing and valuables were buried and sometimes burned along with his body so that he might continue using these possessions to live well on the inner, astral, plane. These theories of reincarnation assure us that we will meet our loved ones and friends on the inner planes after death. Similar traditions exist among the Hindus in Bali and the Shintoists in Japan. ¶By exploring the theories of various civilizations we discover that man can either incarnate soon after his death, with little or no interlude, or he may remain for thousands of years on the astral plane, evolving in those force fields, just as on Earth he evolved from experience to experience. How long he will spend on the astral plane depends on how he has created or chosen what he wants to do while on Earth. If he left things undone and felt compelled to accomplish more, to see more, then he would return quickly to another body in fulfillment of the desire for Earthly experience. However, were he satisfied that life had taught him all of its lessons and wished to exist away from the physical plane in mental and spiritual spheres, he might never return to inherit another body. ¶If we study the Pyramids and explore the intricate ceremonies which the Egyptians provided for their death, we find that they kept the body preserved with elaborate chemical and environmental treatment. When the elements of the physical body are kept intact and not allowed to decompose, the departed may remain consciously on the astral, mental or spiritual plane for as long as he wants. A contact can even be maintained on the physical plane through these laws. However, as soon as the physical body begins to disintegrate, awareness is polarized once again and pulled back to the lower *chakras* and the physical plane. Actually, as the elements of the previous body disintegrate, all of the instinctive-mind atoms form a force field around that body. This generates a power center. When the body is completely disintegrated, the force field is dissolved, and the soul reincarnates at that time. The Egyptians believed that if a body could be durably mummified, the deceased could enjoy a fine life on the inner planes for thousands of years. Modern science can freeze bodies and thus preserve them perfectly, thus opening up possible research into these principles one day.

Friday
LESSON 348
Yoga Adept's Special Pattern

These first laws of reincarnation dealing with the astral plane governed by the powers of the first three *chakras* seem to be quite valid when man is living in his instinctive mind. However, when he passes from the physical body through the will, cognition, or universal love *chakras,* he comes into a different reincarnation law. He then is living on two planes at the same time and, according to this theory, would have representative bodies on both planes. His evolution on the physical plane would be quick, since his only physical, conscious expression would be a small animal, perhaps a little bird or cat or some extremely sensitive animal. This creature would represent and polarize the advanced soul's instinctive mind on the physical plane while he evolved at an accelerated pace on vast inner planes. This dual existence would continue until such time as the process of reincarnation was intensified and the vibration of the Earth was strong enough in his mind to pull awareness back dynamically to another human life. This might take years, and it might take centuries. ¶In a sense, this mystic would be held through the power of the higher *chakras* in a very subtle force field and only touch into physical consciousness sporadically by using different bodies of animals and people for a few minutes or hours to contact the Earth. He would not necessarily be conscious of doing this. His awareness would exist predominantly on the inner planes. ¶This is one reason we find some of the Indian religions forbidding the killing of animals of any kind. They believe an animal may be a great saint or *jñānī* who has passed on. Nonkilling of animals, especially cows, is widely observed in India even today. Of course, many consider such a theory senseless, ridiculous, fraught with superstition. However, we could look at everything which we don't yet understand as superstitious until we comprehend the intricate mechanism of the laws of the governing force fields. ¶Another postulate of this theory is that an advanced being living in his inner bodies, having left consciousness through one of the higher *chakras,* would be working out a certain amount of *karma* by helping others who are still in physical bodies to work out their *karma.* For various reasons, this being would not be able to return to Earth consciously. What, then, would cause him to reincarnate? It would be the intellectual clarity and spiritual intensity of the mother and father in the process of conception or planned conception. They would have to reach very deeply into the inner planes in order to provide the channel for a high reincarnation, whereas couples cohabiting in lust or free-for-all sex more or less take potluck off the astral plane. This indicates briefly an ancient but neglected law: that the parents—through their love for one another, through their devotion and through their states of consciousness during the days of conception—attract to themselves either old souls or young souls. ¶Generally, the soul, at the time of conception, chooses the body he will inhabit but does not actually enter the womb until the infant body takes life and begins to move and kick. Similarly, on the physical plane we may buy an acre of land and plan the house we wish to live in, but not actually move in until months later when the house is completed.

Saturday
LESSON 349
Reincarnating Prior to Death

The next theory of reincarnation, governed by the throat, brow and crown *chakras*, states that when an advanced soul leaves the body through the brow *chakra*, or third eye, he enters a highly refined force field world from which he is able to pick and choose exactly when and where he will return. At this point he does not have to reincarnate as an infant, but could take an already well-matured physical body. In such a case, the soul inhabiting the body would have *karmically* ended this life and be involved in the reincarnation process, either dead or preparing to die. The advanced *yogī* would flow his awareness into the nerve system of the body, revitalizing it with the spark of his will and consciously bring it back to life. ¶He would face the problem of amalgamating himself with the memory cell patterns still resident within the mature brain. Affectionate detachment would have to be practiced as he adjusted to his new family and friends who wouldn't feel as close to him anymore. They would sense that he had changed, that he was somehow different, but would not understand why. Once his mission in that body had been completed, he could leave that body consciously, provided he had not created too much *karma* for its subconscious while inhabiting it. All such *karma* would then have to be dissolved before dropping off the body. This practice is exercised only by souls who have sufficient mastery of the inner forces to leave consciously through the *ājñā chakra* at death. Those who leave through that force center unconsciously would then reincarnate as an infant. ¶A related law, for those far advanced inwardly, states that the reincarnation process can begin before actual death takes place. While still maintaining a body on this planet and knowing that death is imminent, the inner bodies begin their transition into a new body at the time of conception. After a three-month period, the first signs of life appear and the advanced being enters the newly forming physical body. During the nine-month gestation cycle, the waning physical body is in the slow process of death, and exactly at the time of birth the death finally comes. ¶If evolution continues on the astral and other inner planes, and is in some ways more advanced in these realms, then do we need a physical body at all to unfold spiritually? Is it perhaps an unnecessary burden of flesh? According to classical *yoga* precepts, you must have a physical body in order to attain *nirvikalpa samādhi*—the highest realization of God, the Absolute. This is due to the fact that on the refined inner planes only three or four of the higher *chakras* are activated; the others are dormant. For *nirvikalpa samadhi,* all seven *chakras,* as well as the three major energy currents, have to be functioning to sustain enough *kuṇḍalinī* force to burst through to the Self. The very same instinctive forces and fluids which generate material involvement, uncomplimentary *karma* and the body itself, when transmuted, are the impetus that propels awareness beyond the ramification of mind into the timeless, spaceless, formless Truth—Śiva.

Sunday
LESSON 350
To Die a Conscious Death

If you were to die at this very moment, where would what you call *you* go? Where would your awareness be drawn? The laws of death and reincarnation tell us that your awareness would go into various refined force fields of the mind, similar to some states of sleep, according to where you are in the mind at the time of death. By a similar law on this plane, when a wealthy executive and a mendicant enter an unfamiliar town, one finds himself lodged at the finest hotel among other businessmen of his caliber, and the other is drawn of necessity to the slums. The entire process of reincarnation is the inner play of magnetic force fields. ¶Should you reincarnate now, you would undoubtedly enter a force field which would approximate where you are inside yourself, unless, of course, you had broken through barriers into a force field different from the one in which you are now living. In other words, to use an analogy that can also be applied to states of instinctive, intellectual and superconscious awareness, if you were living in America, but had your mind centered in the force field called France, owned things imported from France and spoke fluent French, you would undoubtedly reincarnate in France and act out that drama to its conclusion. ¶Reincarnation and *karma* in its cause-and-effect form are practically one and the same thing, for they both have to do with the *prāṇic* forces and these bodies of the external mind. The *sannyāsin's* quest is Self Realization. To make that realization a reality, he always has to be conscious consciously of working out these other areas. Why? Because the ignorance of these areas holds and confuses awareness, preventing him from being in inner states long enough to attain the ultimate goal of *nirvikalpa samādhi.* ¶Little by little, as he goes on in his esoteric understanding of these mechanics, he unwinds and reeducates his subconscious. He conquers the various planes by cognizing their function and understanding their relation one to another. This knowledge allows him to become consciously superconscious all the time. He has sufficient power to move the energies and awareness out of the physical, intellectual and astral bodies into *sushumṇā.* Then the *kuṇḍalinī* force, that vapor-like life force, merges into its own essence. ¶It is therefore the great aim of the aspirant on the path of enlightenment to live a well-ordered life and control the forces of the mind that propel him into cycles of life and death. He must strive to gain a fundamental knowing of the life-death-reincarnation processes, and to be able at the point of death to leave the body consciously, as a matter of choice, depending upon the consciousness leading to the moment of transition. He must throw off the false identification with this body or that personality and see himself as the ageless soul that has taken many, many births, of which this is only one, see deeper still into the total unreality of life and death, which only exist in their seeming in the outer layers of consciousness, for he is the immortal one who is never born and can never die.

Mṛityur Maraṇaṁ cha

मृत्युर्मरणं च

Death and Dying

Blessed indeed are those who die. If in death they unite as one with Śiva, then, even dead, they are alive. They who are dead to the bonds of *karma, māyā* and *āṇava* are the true *siddhas,* who merge into Śiva.

TIRUMANTIRAM 1907

Monday
LESSON 351
Preparations For Transition

People ask, "What should a person do to prepare to die?" Everyone is prepared to die, and whether it happens suddenly or slowly, intuitively each individual knows exactly what he is experiencing and about to experience. Death, like birth, has been repeated so many times that it is no mystery to the soul. The only problem comes with conflicting beliefs, which produce fear and anxiety about death. This temporary ignorance soon subsides when the failing forces of the physical body reach a certain level. At this point, the superconscious intelligence, the soul itself, is there. We can compare this to restless sleep and deep sleep. ¶When one knows he is going to depart the physical body, he should first let everybody know that he knows and give relatives security by explaining to them that soon they won't be seeing him in a physical body anymore. He should consciously go over his wealth, his properties, be the executor of his own will. From the Hindu point of view, the knowledge of one's immanent departure begins the *sannyāsa ashram* for the individual. In this *ashram,* the devotee traditionally divests himself of all material belongings, effecting a conscious death before the actual death. He is the executor of his own will, taking care of everybody and not leaving these things to others to deal with after his passing. ¶After everything is settled, all personal possessions disposed of, then he begins meditation and awaits the fruitful hour, trying to exit through the highest *chakra* of the attainment of this life. Each *chakra* is a door through which we can depart. The dying should always remember that the place where one will reincarnate is the place that he is thinking about prior to death. So, choose your desires wisely. The last thoughts just before death are the most powerful thoughts in creating the next life. One must also realize that if he and others are aware that he will soon depart, others in the inner worlds also realize he will soon be making his transition and are busy making adjustments and preparations for his arrival. ¶With a sudden death—uncalled for, unbidden and unexpected—a totally different sequence of events occurs. There is no settlement of affairs, and the chaotic situation, emotional and otherwise, persists in the inner worlds and even into the next life. Property is not distributed, and nothing is settled. Negative *karmas* and positive *karmas* are all cut short. The situation can be summed up in one word, *unfulfillment.* Once in the inner world, the deceased feels this unfulfillment and is restless and anxious to get back. He is in a place he did not intend to be, and does not want to stay. So, in the inner world he is with a whole group of those who almost immediately reenter the flesh, for he is too agitated to stay very long on the inner planes. It's like an emergency ward or intensive care unit. ¶Chances are it would be difficult for such a soul to get a birth. Perhaps there would be an abortion or miscarriage a couple of times before there was a successful birth. These are the disturbed children we see, emotionally distraught, needing special care. They cry a lot. Some of the damage that occurred in the previous birth, some dramatic event experienced in the past life, perhaps the cause of death itself, may even show up in this life as a birthmark. ¶In preparation for death, one can soften the *karmas* of future births by making amends with others, settling scores, doing everything to tie up loose ends, seeking the forgiveness of those harmed, to get the mental-emotional matters of this life all worked out. ¶In some cases, this process may in itself prolong life, for with the release of old tensions and conflicts there comes a new freedom which may reflect even in the health of the body. But it is traditional for the householder to fulfill the natural term, then, as a renunciate, distribute to loved ones all worldly possessions and leave the community, go off to Varanasi or some other holy place and await the fruitful moment. It would be creating an unnecessary *karma* to return, taking everything back that one gave away and then continue on as before. If people he knew visit him at this time, he should not know them. He is like a *sannyāsin,* free to give of his wisdom. His eyes see them; his mind does not. This traditional practice is for the attainment of *moksha,* or an exceptional birth of one's own choosing as a herald of *dharma.*

Tuesday
LESSON 352
Sudden Death, Boon or Bane?

As the physical forces wane, whether at sudden death or a lingering death, the process is the same. All the gross and subtle energy goes into the mental and emotional astral body. In the case of a sudden death, the emotions involved are horrendous. In the case of a lingering death, the increasing mental abilities and strength of thought is equally so. As we know, intense emotion manifests intense emotion, and intense thoughts manifest intense thoughts. These intensities would not remanifest until entering a flesh body again. This is why it was previously explained that sudden death—with its intense emotion, the intellect not having been prepared for it—would produce difficulties in getting born and in the first few years of getting raised, leading to miscarriage and abortion and later child abuse. All these experiences are a continuation of the emotional upheaval that happened at the sudden departure. The emotional upheaval of the person is compounded by the emotional upheaval of the friends, family and business associates when they finally hear of the sudden departure. Similarly, when that person reincarnates, the family and friends and business associates are aware of the special needs of the child, anticipating the crying and emotional distress, which eventually subsides. ¶However, if the person was prepared for death, no matter when it might arrive, sudden or otherwise, his mental and emotional astral body would have already been well schooled in readiness. Sudden death to such a soul is a boon and a blessing. The next birth would be welcoming and easy, one wherein he would be well cared for and educated by loving parents. ¶Nevertheless, the thought force of the departing person is very strong, as his energy transmutes into the mental body. That's why nobody wants the departing person to hate them or curse them, because the thought force is so strong. Even after he has departed, that same thought force will radiate many blessings or their opposite on the family or individuals. In the case of blessings, this is the basis of ancestor worship. Ancestors are even more immediate than the Gods, so to speak. They will help you hurt somebody, or to help somebody, depending on who they are. Ancestors are even more accessible than the Gods, because you don't have to be religious to contact them. ¶People wonder whether death is a painful process, such as in the case of cancer victims. Cancer, which produces a lot of pain, is a process of life which results in death, but death itself is not painful. Death itself is blissful. You don't need any counseling. You intuitively know what's going to happen. Death is like a meditation, a *samādhi.* That's why it is called *mahā* (great) *samādhi.* A Hindu is prepared from childhood for that *mahāsamādhi.* Remember, pain is not part of the process of death. That is the process of life, which results in death. ¶When somebody is about to have a tremendous accident and, for example, sees his car is going to run into a truck or his plane is going to crash, he experiences no pain whatsoever, as he dies before he dies.

Wednesday
LESSON 353
Interfering with Death's Timing

People always lament when someone dies quickly, saying, "His life was cut short so suddenly." But with such a death there is no pain, as the soul knows it's coming. It's really so much better than a slow, lingering death. The problem comes when doctors bring the dying back. Then a lot of pain is experienced. The doctors should let them die. ¶To make heroic medical attempts that interfere with the process of the patient's departure is a grave responsibility, similar to not letting a traveler board a plane flight he has a reservation for, to keep him stranded in the airport with a profusion of tears and useless conversation. Prolonging the life of the individual body must be done by the individual himself. He needs no helping hands. Medical assistance, yes, is needed to cauterize wounds, give an injection of penicillin and provide the numerous helpful things that are available. But to prolong life in the debilitated physical body past the point that the natural will of the person has sustained is to incarcerate, to jail, to place that person in prison. The prison is the hospital. Prison is the sanitarium. The guards are the life-support machines and the tranquilizing drugs. Cellmates are others who have been imprisoned by well-meaning professionals who make their living from prolonging the flickering life in the physical body. The misery of the friends, relatives, business associates and the soul itself accumulates and is shared by all connected to this bitter experience to be reexperienced in another time, perhaps another lifetime, by those who have taken on the grave responsibility of delaying a person's natural time of departure. ¶*Āyurvedic* medicine seeks to keep a person healthy and strong, but not to interfere with the process of death. Kandiah Chettiar, one of the foremost devotees of Satguru Yogaswāmī, explained to me fifty years ago that even to take the pulse of a dying person is considered a sin, to inhibit the dying process. In summary, we can see that the experience of dying and death is as natural as birth and life. There is little mystery there to be understood. ¶To perpetuate life, you perpetuate will, desire and the fruition of desire. The constant performing of this function brings the actinic energies of the soul body into physical bodies. To give up one's own personal desires is the first desire to perpetuate. Then to help others to fulfill their highest aspirations is the next challenge. Then to seek for ultimate attainment and fulfill that lingering desire takes a tremendous will. Then to lay a foundation for the betterment of peoples everywhere, in spreading the Sanātana Dharma to those open and ready to receive it and make it available to those who are not, is the ultimate challenge. This perpetuates life within the physical body, which of itself renews itself every seven years.

Thursday
LESSON 354
Leaving via the Highest Chakra

Many have asked what is meant by leaving through a certain *chakra* at the point of death? Let's take an example of a person of whom people say, "His mind is in his butt." They mean his awareness is down at the bottom, so to speak. He is ogling pornography. He's swearing, angry, self-indulgent all the time. That is the world he would go into if he died in this state of mind, the lower world of selfish self-gratification, where lust is not lust, but a way of life, for nothing else is happening but that—just lust, twenty-four hours a day. Or it is sometimes said, "She is such a motherly woman. She is all heart, really a perceptive lady." That is where she would go at the moment of death—out through the throat *chakra,* the universal love *chakra,* and experience a heaven world beyond expectations, beyond descriptions of any kind. Just as a traveling businessman would go to a hotel where others have come for similar purposes, she would go to a world where everybody is a heart person. That is why you cannot spiritually unfold so much in the inner world, because everybody is the same in each stratum of consciousness. You would have to study and do disciplines to get into the next *chakras,* but you would never have the lower ones to contend with if you had not been in the lower ones during your physical life. ¶If somebody dies in the states of anger and fear, he goes into the lower worlds of those states of consciousness. And in that realm there would be hundreds of thousands of people in that same state of consciousness. Whatever is in the mind at that moment—a country, a family, community—will have a strong impact on where he goes in the inner world, and on the nature of future *saṁskāras.* The thoughts at death are the next *saṁskāras* of the astral body. Even if you have the thought, "When you're dead you're dead," your astral body might just float over your physical body and be "dead." Someone would have to revive you and explain to you that you are in your astral body and are as alive as you ever were, but not physically. ¶At death you leave through a nerve ganglia of consciousness, a *chakra.* Most people live in about three *chakras,* and they see-saw back and forth among those states of mind. Each one is a window, and at death it becomes a portal, a doorway. So, it is the state of mind at death that gets you into one *loka* or another within the Śivaloka, Devaloka, Pretaloka or Narakaloka. ¶The ideal is to leave through the top of the head, through the door of Brahman, to get into the Brahmaloka and not have to come back. The dying person should, at the time of transition, concentrate awareness at the top of his head and willfully draw up into it all the energies from the left and right legs and arms, one after another, then the energy within the entire torso, and all the energies within the spine, from the *mūlādhāra chakra,* up into the *ājñā* and *sahasrāra.* With all the energies gathered at the top of his head, he will leave through the highest *chakra* he experienced this lifetime. This would put him in a great place in the inner world. ¶Maybe at age eighteen he reached the *viśuddha chakra* for a very short time. He will revive that experience just before death as he is going through the playback of his life, and he will go out through that *chakra.* But if he is thinking about lower things, he will go out through the lower *chakras.* If he goes out through a lower *chakra,* or portal, he can in the inner world eventually work his way back to the *viśuddha chakra,* with a lot of help from the *devonic* guides and their advisors, but he cannot go beyond it until he gets a new physical body. ¶The portal is where the physical eyes hook into or go into. Through that portal you go into that world. This is why a departing person, in the spirit of *kaivalya,* perfect detachment or aloneness, gazes at pictures of God, Gods and *guru,* and sings or listens to hymns sung by loved ones, so that the experience of death truly does take him to the highest plane he experienced in this birth, or even higher if he experienced a higher state in a previous birth. ¶The astral body carries the *chakras.* The *chakras* are in the astral body. The astral body lives in the physical body, and when death comes, it is going to live without the physical body. The same *chakras* are within it. At the moment of death, you have the opportunity to stabilize yourself in the highest *chakra* you have experienced in this life.

Friday
LESSON 355
An Event Worth Celebrating

The tunnel of light that is experienced by so many people at the point of death is the portal they are going through, the window, the *chakra.* It is a tunnel, and it has distance, because it takes time, consciousness, to go from one end to the other. Passing through the tunnel is leaving this world and going into another. You do that in meditation, too. You leave the light of the physical plane and go into the light in the inner world. Death takes place in a short period, but is a foreboding affair to those who have never meditated. But dying is not such a dramatic experience really. Every night you "die" and leave your physical body. It is very similar. Every night mystics leave their physical body, go and meet and converse with other mystics on the inner planes. That's why they know each other when they meet on the physical plane. *Samādhi,* the exalted meditative state, which literally means "holding together completely," is also a word used to describe dying. Why is that? Because deep contemplation is similar to a death experience; only the silver cord is not separated. This cord is an astral-*prānic* thread that connects the astral body through the navel to the physical body. It is a little like an umbilical cord. The only full separation comes when the cord is cut at *mahāsamādhi,* the true death of the physical body. People die all the time, but if the cord is not broken, they come back. You die all the time. The cord being broken makes for a twenty-four-hour consciousness in the inner world, as compared to a sixteen-hour consciousness in the physical world. ¶Many people wish that they were dead and give up on life, look at death as an escape rather than a fulfillment. These cumulative thoughts and desires can create the near-death experience. The welcoming *devonic* helpers of Lord Yama, the benevolent God of the death experience, don't pay any attention, because they know the person is not going to die. The person thinks he is going to die, but they know he is not. He has just conjured it up. Just like a conjured illness. ¶If a person knows he is terminally ill, that knowledge is a blessing, for he can prepare. He should not hesitate to tell his relatives he is going to die, and that is a wonderful blessing for them, as they can prepare for his great departure. Now all know he has finally arrived at the end of his *prārabdha karmas* and is going to fly. In turn, family and friends should release him, be happy.

He is going to be happy with no physical body. For they know they will be as close to him in his astral and soul body as they were in his physical body. They will visit him every night when they sleep, in the inner worlds, and learn many things from these loved ones as to how to prepare for their own great departure, be it sudden or prolonged. Don't cry; you will make him unhappy. You should be happy for him, because he is going to be happy. It is not a sad occasion. For Hindus, death is a most exalted state, an incredible moment that you spend your whole life preparing for. Birth is the unhappy occasion. Death should be a big party. He has just gone through his day of Brahma. ¶The sadness at death comes from Western attitudes. Western thought has to be reversed. Here a child comes into birth. It is sad, because he was all right before he was born. Now his *prārabdha karmas* are going to start to explode. He has to deal with his past, which he did not have to deal with in the Devaloka. He has a chance to make new *karmas.* The time of birth is the grave time. When he dies, that means that section of the *jyotisha* is finished and he can go and have a great rest and be with intelligent people. It is great inside there and difficult out here. ¶When someone tells me they or a loved one have cancer, AIDS or some other incurable disease, my counsel is this. Everyone dies, but it is a blessing to know when you are going to die, because then you can prepare for it, make a decision whether you are going to be reborn, do intense *sādhanas,* make preparations. Eastern men don't fight terminal cancer or AIDS. They go to an astrologer or palmist, ascertain their time of death, then prepare themselves. It's really a blessing. It's best not to fight it or "cure it," since you are interrupting your timing. Just let it happen. Heed the wisdom of the *Vedas,* "When a person comes to weakness, be it through old age or disease, he frees himself from these limbs just as a mango, a fig or a berry releases itself from its stalk." ¶Hindus go to special sacred places to die, because that's where holy people live, in that part of the astral plane. That place has access to other planets, or to the moon. A lot of people go to the moon when they die and live there. Jews who die go to Israel. That's their holy land. You can get caught in the astral plane or some *bardo* mind-flow that would contain you for a long time, and then get a bad birth if you do not go to a special place to die. So, you want at least to die near a temple. A temple is connected to the three worlds. We brought India to the West with our temples and by encouraging more to be built. The Indian people don't mind dying in the West since all the temples are here. They love all the temples they have built, especially our Kadavul Temple, for it feels so sacred to them. All of the temples in the West are connected to other temples in Sri Lanka and India.

Saturday
LESSON 356
Death Rites And Rituals

A lot of people who are about to die do not believe in life after death, so they remain hovering over their physical body when it is lifeless. Astral-plane helpers have to come and "wake them up" and tell them that their physical body is dead and explain that they are all right and are alive in their astral body. It is often not an easy process getting them readjusted. ¶Is there really a Lord Yama, a Lord of Death, devotees often wonder? The answer is yes, not only He, but there are a lot of Lord Yamas, a wide group of well-trained helpers. These tireless inner-plane attendants work, as part of the Yama group, with the doctors and nurses who are involved with terminal cases, those who assist in the transition process, those who take care of disposing of bodies. These are the Yama helpers in the physical world. Executioners, murderers and terrorists are a less noble part of the Yama group. Anyone, other than family and close friends and religious helpers, who is involved in the transitional process two weeks before and after death is part of the Yama group, including ambulance drivers, hospice staff, nurses, morticians, medics, autopsy staff, insurance agents, grave diggers, wood cutters who prepare fuel for funeral pyres, body baggers and coffin makers. Medical doctors and nurses who secretly err in their practice, after dying, join Lord Yama's recruits, in the inner world as *prāyaschitta* to mitigate the *karma* they created. ¶I am speaking especially about modern doctors who operate too freely, even when sometimes it may not be necessary. It is not uncommon that the patient dies on the operating table due to a known mistake on the surgeon's part. Yet, somehow or other, physicians are regarded by the public as monarchs, Gods, above the law. But the *karma* relating to manslaughter nevertheless is constant and unfailingly takes effect in this life or another. A common civilian, or the same doctor, running down a pedestrian would naturally be prosecuted to the full extent of the law, fined and maybe jailed. But the secret manslaughters are never admitted, never accounted for; no one is held accountable—except that the unrelenting law of *karma* reigns as supreme judge and jury. ¶There is an entire industry that lives on the fact of death. If a doctor says,

"Two weeks to live," then the inner-plane Yamas are alerted and step in. Lord Yama is Lord Restraint, restraining life and getting it started again on the other side. Then the Yama workers, who are like nurses, say, "You are Catholic; you go to Rome. You are Jewish; you go to Jerusalem. You are Muslim; you go to Mecca. You are Hindu; you go to Varanasi," and so forth. In the lower astral, it's all segregated. In the higher worlds it is all oneness. ¶In preparing the body for cremation, embalming should not be done. It is painful to the astral body to have the physical body cut or disturbed seriously within seventy-two hours after death. The soul can see and feel this, and it detains him from going on. As soon as you tamper with his physical body, he gets attached, becomes aware that he has two bodies, and this becomes a problem. Ideally when you die, your physical body goes up in flames, and immediately you know it's gone. You now know that the astral body is your body, and you can effortlessly release the physical body. But if you keep the old body around, then you keep the person around, and he is aware that he has two bodies. He becomes earthbound, tied into the Pretaloka, and confused. ¶Embalming preserves the physical vehicle. For a *jīvanmukta,* he might want to leave, but some people might want to keep him around for a while for their own benefit. The best way for him is to go off into the hills, to die in the forests where no one knows and none of these questions arise. More than many great *sādhus* have done this and do this to this day. For my *satguru,* Śiva Yogaswāmī, they did the right thing by cremating him; they released him and did not try to tie him to the Earth. To come and go from the

Śivaloka to the Pretaloka is his choice and his alone. To me, embalming or entombing is a divisive way to hold on to the holy man, and I feel it will draw him back into birth. True, in our scriptures it is recommended that the body of a perfectly liberated saint not be cremated but interred instead in a salt-filled crypt. This may be done so that devotees can continue to be served, but in our lineage it is not the way. In our tradition, the body of the departed is cremated within twenty-four hours. This purifies the physical elements and releases the deceased to the inner worlds. In contrast, the Egyptians wanted their pharaoh to be born again as a king. They didn't want a young soul to be their king. So all their preparations helped him to be born into the royal family. The Hawaiians did the same thing, royalty perpetuating royalty.

Sunday
LESSON 357
Beyond Liberation

In the later stages of evolution, physical life can be so joyous that one might ask, "Why wish for liberation?" But not wanting to be reborn is not the goal. Obtaining the stability of mind and spirit so that you can function even on the physical plane better, without the necessity of having to do so, is a better goal. After *mukti*, liberation, one still has responsibilities to complete certain *karmic* patterns. Even the *sapta ṛishis,* seven sages, have their offices to perform in guiding the Sanātana Dharma, though they do not have to be reborn in a physical body to do their job. *Mukti* does not call an end to intelligence, does not call an end to duty. *Mukti* calls an end to the necessity for a physical birth. It's like death—you don't want to die, but you do anyway. When on the inner plane, you don't want to be reborn, but you are anyway. You have to do these things. The ideal is to live out one's Earthly life to its full extent, not to shorten it in any way, for during the elderly years, after ninety and the twenty or thirty years thereafter, the *sañchita karmas* in the great vault which are waiting to come up in another life begin to unfold to be lived through and resolved in this one. By no means should suicide ever be considered, for it cuts short all *karmic* developments of the current life and may require additional births to work through the lowest possible experiences still held in the great *sañchita* vault. Many incarnations may elapse after an untimely self-inflicted death before the soul returns back to the same evolutionary point at which the suicide was committed. Suicide is no escape. It only prolongs the journey. ¶The goal is realization of Paraśiva as the ultimate personal attainment. This is *nirvikalpa samādhi. Savikalpa* is the by-product of this. Even having had this experience, if the *sādhana* and *tapas* and discipline are not maintained, *mukti,* liberation, will not be the product of effort. The knowledge of Paraśiva, in its total impact, must impact every area of mind, every nook and cranny of the mind. Therefore, the goal is realization; and liberation from rebirth is the by-product of that essential goal. If a soul becomes realized but still has the desire to come back to finish something, he will come back partially enlightened. Hinduism will be an open book to him, and he will understand all of the basic truths and be able to explain it all naturally. He will find his enlightenment later in life and go on, having experienced what he had to. ¶There is a choice one makes upon becoming illumined and understanding the whole process—whether to be a *bodhisattva* or an *arahat,* an *upadeśī* or a *nirvāṇī.* This is based on a belief and an attitude in the heart and soul. A *nirvāṇī* says, "I'll move on and wait for everyone to catch up with me." An *upadeśī* says, "I'll help everyone on the path." Occasionally an *upadeśī* has tasks to fulfill, but they are self-assigned, for this is a personal choice. Likewise, a *nirvāṇī* will work and make a great attainment. Then he will spin out his own *karmas* and make his transition. The *upadeśī* will make his attainment and then work with his own *karmas* slowly while helping others along the path. Who is to say which is the best choice? It's a totally individual matter. I personally am an *upadeśī.* No detail is too small for me to handle. A *nirvāṇī* would not take that attitude. ¶In the inner worlds, one who has transcended the need for a physical birth is there like he is here. He has a twenty-four-hour consciousness. He does not have to eat unless he wants to, and he doesn't have to sleep, so he has a total continuity of consciousness. He has Paraśiva at will and is all-pervasive all of the time. He does have duties. He does relate to brother souls in the same stratum, and he does evolve, continuing in evolution from *chakra* to *chakra* to *chakra,* for there are *chakras,* or *nāḍīs,* above the *sahasrāra* for which he does not need a physical body. This, again, is for the *upadeśī.* The *nirvāṇī* would not turn back, but proceed onward. The first realization of Paraśiva, the impact of the aftermath, allows you the decision to choose between the dispassion of the *nirvāṇī* and the compassion of the *upadeśī.* ¶The Śaiva Siddhānta perspective is that Śiva's wonderful universe of form is perfect at every point of time, complete and totally just, and every soul in all stages of evolution, is an intrinsic part of it, even Śiva Himself. The true *mukti* of everyone and of the universe itself would be at *mahāpralaya;* but meanwhile, *mukti* is defined in our vocabulary as freedom from rebirth in a physical body. But many other bodies drop off, too. There are more intelligences to come into, great creations of form. Upon death, even a Self-Realized soul does not necessarily "disappear" into nothingness or Allness. The absolute goal, Paraśiva—timeless, formless and causeless—is a release, but not an end. There is, of course, an end, which we call *viśvagrāsa.* This is total merger, a union with That from which the soul never returns—*jīva* became Śiva. So, whatever inner body the *jīvanmukta* is functioning in, in the thereafter, he has no need for Self Realization, the seal has already been broken and never heals. So, claiming "I am That, I am"—That being the Absolute, Paraśiva—is the total stabilizing one-ment of all the *māyās* of creation, preservation and destruction of the individual mind, as well as the mind of reality it goes through.

Mānava Mātrakṛite Antima Siddhāntāḥ

मानवमात्रकृते अन्तिमसिद्धान्ताः

The Final Conclusions For All Mankind

I freed myself from the fetters the Creator bound me with. I learned the way of reaching Śiva. I destroyed my *karmas* with the sharp sword of realization and stood ego-lost. And now I hasten toward the city of God.

TIRUMANTIRAM 2962

Monday
LESSON 358
Wisdom of The Ages

Religion as it is known today is an offshoot of various ethnic groups that gathered together in the twilight of human history and forged systems of law, worship, culture and belief. The unique circumstances of geography, language, communications and race isolated one group from another and differences were born and preserved: differences of belief and custom. As these small communities varied, so did the systems which satisfied each one. From their inception they absorbed the singular thought patterns postulated by their culture and their leaders, and these distinctions were perpetuated from father to son, from *guru* to disciple, from one generation to the next. The leader was the shaman, the priest, the *āchārya,* the philosopher-king. He was well versed in religious matters among them and naturally became the authority, the tribal priest. Religion in the early days was tribal, for man's early experience was tribal. Being tribal, religion was political. The political character has been preserved, as we find it today, in the world's many religions, which are, for the most part, the common beliefs of the various races and/or nations on the Earth. ¶Five, ten thousand years ago in the Himālayas and across to the Indus Valley, ancient *ṛishis* and sages studied and meditated upon the eternal truths passed down to them and in conclaves jointly concurred as to the results of their personal findings on the inward path. Following an already ancient tradition, they were sent on missions—to Kashmir, China, Greece, Egypt, Arabia, Mesopotamia, South India, Southeast Asia and to every traversable part of the world—with the same message, digested and concise, given out with the power and force of their personal realizations of the final conclusions. ¶Today I am going to speak about Hinduism and the conclusions drawn by its early sages and saints as to the orderly evolution of man's soul and the ultimate spiritual goal of that evolution, the culmination of the countless accumulated passages of the soul on its journey to Truth. The ancient ones, the *ṛishis* and sages who formulated these final conclusions, recorded them as scriptures which still exist today. They were not interested in preserving a sectarian view of religion. Rather, they laid down their conclusions for all mankind. They had realized God within themselves, and from that inner realization they spoke out with boundless humility and undeniable authority. These teachings were recorded in the early *Vedas*. They blossomed in the *Upanishads*. They were detailed in the *Āgamas*. They came to be known as the Sanātana Dharma, the Eternal Path. ¶According to ancient Hinduism, all is Śiva, all is God. God is both immanent and transcendent, both *saguṇa* and *nirguṇa*, with and without form. There is but one God. He manifests variously as the formless and Absolute Reality, as the rarefied form of Pure Consciousness, Satchidānanda, Pure Energy or Light flowing through all existence, and as the personal Lord and Creator, the Primal Soul. As the Immanent Lord, Śiva created the soul, and the world of form and experience, that it might evolve toward and merge with the Absolute. ¶The *Śvetāśvatara Upanishad* (3.1-2 UPP) speaks of God as both immanent and transcendent, and I would like to quote for you from it. "He is the one God, the Creator. He enters into all wombs. The One Absolute, impersonal Existence, together with His inscrutable *māyā,* appears as the Divine Lord, endowed with manifold glories. With His Divine power He holds dominion over all the worlds. At the periods of Creation and Dissolution of the universe He alone exists. Those who realize Him become immortal. The Lord is One without a second. Within man He dwells, and within all other beings. He projects the universe, maintains it, and withdraws it into Himself." Elsewhere, the *Śvetāśvatara Upanishad* (3.8-9 VE) speaks of God as the Primal Soul, "I have come to know that mighty Person, golden like the sun, beyond all darkness. By knowing Him, a man transcends death; there is no other path for reaching that goal. Higher than Him is nothing whatever; than Him nothing smaller, than Him nothing greater. He stands like a tree rooted in heaven, the One, the Person, filling this whole world." And the *Muṇḍaka Upanishad* (2.1.2 MC) speaks of God as the unmanifest, *Nirguṇa Brahman:* "Self-resplendent, formless, unoriginated and pure, that all-pervading Being is both within and without, anterior both to life and mind. He transcends even the transcendent, unmanifest, causal state of the universe."

Tuesday
LESSON 359
Impetuous, Impatient

The final goal of human life is realization and liberation—realization of the Absolute, Unmanifest, Paraśiva, Nirguṇa Brahman, and liberation from birth. This realization cannot be brought about solely by an effort of the mind, by any discipline or method. *Sādhana* and *tapas* and *bhakti* are necessary for purifying the mind and body in preparation for God Realization, but it is by the grace of the *satguru* that it is attained. ¶The North American Hindu—and in these words we include the Indian Hindu who lives in America whether in the first generation, the second, the third or the fourth—often wants to begin at the end of the path rather than at the beginning. There is a distinct lack of patience on this side of the planet. Our desire, our lack of knowledge which breeds undue desire, impels us beyond our abilities and before our time. We want everything right now. We are impatient and perhaps unwilling to wait for the natural fulfillment of desire, for the natural unfoldment of the soul. We seek to force it, to strive for greater attainments than we are prepared to sustain. We want illumination, and we want it now. But results cannot be obtained unless we have the patience to begin at the beginning and to follow through systematically. We must take one step and then another. There are no shortcuts to enlightenment, but there are detours. Impatience with the natural process is one of them. ¶If you find a green melon in an open field, will it help to expose it to more sun? To more heat? Will it ripen faster and taste sweeter? No, it will not. It ripens from the inside out. The process cannot be forced. The melon will grow ripe without intervention. Similarly, the soul will mature in its time. I am not saying that you should not strive, should not make even great inner efforts. I am saying that impatient striving, the kind of striving that puts aside all common sense and says "I am going to get realization no matter what" is itself an obstacle to that realization which is not a something to get. Hindus in the West have much to learn from Hindus in the East when it comes to contentment with their *karma* and *dharma*. We must work to perfect an inner serenity that can accept spending a lifetime or several lifetimes in search of Truth, that can accept that some of us are by our nature and unfoldment better suited to service and devotion, and others to *yoga* and the various *sādhanas.* This is a far more enlightened perspective than the Western notion which subtly maintains that there is but a single life in which all the final goals must be reached. ¶The eternal path, the Sanātana Dharma, has been well charted by the great illumined minds, developed minds, spiritually unfolded minds, realized minds on this planet. No one can skip, avoid, evade or abstain from any part of that path. As Euclid could find for his impatient crowned pupil no special "royal road" to geometry or philosophy, so there is no privileged "royal road" to spiritual illumination. Similarly, a marathon runner cannot begin the race twenty miles from the starting point. A mountain climber cannot refuse to climb the lower, perhaps less challenging, cliffs. The natural laws known to all men do not allow it. The natural law known to himself, his own conscience, does not allow it. It is the same on the spiritual path. ¶The eternal spiritual path, the way of God, is broad. It accepts all and rejects none. No matter where a seeker is in his inner development, the eternal path embraces and encourages him. If he is a simple man, the path for him is simple, unsophisticated, answering the needs of his everyday life, yet opening him to more and more subtle ways of worship and living. If he is an advanced soul, a mature soul, he will find within Hinduism the San Mārga, the pure path to the Absolute.

Wednesday
LESSON 360
The Process Of Evolution

When a beginning devotee comes to the temple to worship Śiva, he sees Śiva as a man, a person not unlike himself, yet more than a man, for He is a God, the God of Gods, so powerful, so aware and complete within Himself that He is the center of endless universes. In coming to worship Śiva, this devotee prostrates himself before the Deity just as if he were in the presence of the grandest potentate or majesty imaginable. Śiva is that to him. We know how wonderful it can be to approach a distinguished and honored personage. It makes us feel special. It brings out the best within us. The same thing happens to this man. He feels himself in the presence of the Supreme Lord, and he brings the best of himself to the temple. ¶If he has a problem, if something is not going well in his family or in his business, he will come to the temple with special offerings. The priest takes that offering into the inner sanctum for the *pūjā*. During the *pūjā* it is blessed and then some of it is returned to the worshiper to take back to his home, carrying the vibration of the temple into his everyday life. During *pūjā* he will concentrate his efforts on opening himself to the divine influence of Lord Śiva. And as he leaves the temple, he will look for a break in the problem, for a new perspective to arise as a result of his worship in the temple. He will look for some telling signs from his environment—the way the lizard chirps, how many crows come down, and even what kind of people walk by his house. Perhaps the solution to his problem is simply a new way of seeing it, a different perspective that gives him the insight to handle the matter, or there may be a change in his external circumstances. ¶As this man worships, he grows more and more devoted, becomes capable of a profound understanding of the rituals and practices of his early *saṁskāras.* From the practice of putting holy ash on his forehead and the feeling that goes through his nervous system whenever he does that, he begins to discover sound reasons for doing it, reasons he can confidently tell his children. His worship leads him little by little into new realms of consciousness. ¶Another man, more refined and awakened, may have worshiped during the exact same *pūjā.* This devotee came to worship the same Deity, but to him it was not only an ethereal being external to himself. He perceived it also as an essence pervading the universe, a oneness of pure consciousness flowing through all form, and he worshiped that Satchidānanda in the sanctum and equally within himself. As the energies of the *pūjā* reached their crescendo, he could feel that pure essence of consciousness as himself. After the *pūjā,* he went to a secluded corner of the temple, there to meditate, to bask in the *kuṇḍalinī* energy awakened in him through his temple worship until he knew himself as one with that vast sea of pure life energy and light. He went home feeling peaceful and calm and just at one with everyone and everything that came along in his life. He has no awareness of time and just lives fully in the intensity of the moment. When he applies holy ash at the temple or in his shrine room at home before he sits down to meditate, he sees it as the ash of those forces which hold him in individual consciousness—the forces of *karma* and ego and desire. He applies the ash so that it makes three distinct lines across his forehead. They are lines to impress him with the need to keep these three forces subdued in his life. ¶This man lives in tune with the worship of Lord Śiva and the *darshan* he receives, and opens up within himself from that worship. Everything in his life flows smoothly and harmoniously. He is in touch with a divine voice within himself and he follows it as his own will. His life is simple. And he feels himself complete. Neither fretting over the past nor worrying about the future, he lives totally in the present. His evolution is steady and graceful. He grows greater in his capacity to hold those moments of *darshan* he feels until he carries that *darshan* steadily through every aspect of his life. That is his only experience. He is a witness to what goes on around him—doing it perfectly but detached from the doing. He sees light within his head when he meditates. And that grows until he knows that the light is more real than anything he considers himself. That way his unfoldment continues. He comes to be purer and purer, more and more aware of the real. ¶A third man, living under strict vows and the guidance of his *satguru,* having long ago perfected the harmony and discipline that allowed him to see himself as the Pure Consciousness within all beings, is immersed within states of contemplation, whether in a mountain cave or before a temple sanctum. His goal is to find the source of that energy, and the source of that source, and the source of that, until he realizes That, Paraśiva, the Absolute beyond all form. He experiences himself and Śiva as one.

Thursday
LESSON 361
From Caterpillar To Butterfly

To all these devotees, in their different stages of spiritual evolution, Lord Śiva is the Supreme God. To the first, He is the Primal Soul, the Creator, Preserver and

Destroyer of existence. To the second He is the Primal Soul as well as Pure Consciousness, the substratum of existence, the divine energy coursing through and animating every atom within the microcosm and the macrocosm. To the third He is the manifest Primal Soul and Pure Consciousness and the unmanifest Absolute, Paraśiva, that transcends form itself. These three perspectives are not exclusive of one another, but encompass one another as the lotus of the mind opens to an ever widening understanding of God. Each is true according to where the devotee is on the path. ¶This Eternal Path is divided naturally into four separate categories. The *Bhagavad Gītā*—the popular book which you all know from your studies in Vedānta and which has made Hindu philosophy well known in America—defines these as four separate nonprogressive paths, called *karma yoga, bhakti yoga, rāja yoga* and *jñāna yoga.* In Āgamic scripture these are defined a little differently and are considered to be four stages of a progressive path, termed *charyā, kriyā, yoga* and *jñāna.* These are all Sanskṛit terms. According to the Āgamic tradition, these four categories are the natural sequence of the soul's evolutionary process, much like the development of a butterfly from egg to larva, from larva to catapillar, from caterpillar to pupa, and then the final metamorphosis from pupa to butterfly. Every butterfly, without exception, will follow this pattern of development, and every soul will mature through *charyā* to *kriyā,* through *kriyā* to *yoga* and into *jñāna. Charyā,* or *karma yoga,* may be simply defined as service. *Kriyā,* or *bhakti yoga,* is devotion. *Yoga,* or *rāja yoga,* is meditation, and *jñāna* is the state of wisdom reached toward the end of the path as the result of God Realization and the subsequent enlivened *kuṇḍalinī* and unfoldment of the *chakras* through the practices of *yoga.* The soul does not move quickly from one stage to another. It is a deliberate process, and within each stage there exist vast libraries of knowledge containing the sum of thousands of years of teachings unraveling that particular experiential vista. ¶The evolution of the soul through the stage of *charyā* or service may itself take many, many lives. We see people every day who are working to be of service, to be more efficient, to be more useful to others. They are not necessarily inclined toward devotion, yet they may be deeply concerned with humanitarian programs, with selflessly helping their fellow man. An entire life may be spent in *charyā,* and the next life and the next. It is a slow process, with its own timing. Not every stage of experience can be accepted at once. ¶The path of *charyā* begins with the avoidance of wrongful action, and can be likened to the early training of a child in which he is told, "Don't do this. Do this instead. Don't behave in that way. This is the proper behavior." In early life a child learns what is right by being told what not to do. In spiritual life, too, we have these avoidances, these restraints. The seeker is advised to avoid over-eating, criticism of others, anger, hatred, envy and deceit. This gives him guidelines that stabilize him in the beginning, controlling the instinctive mind. These inner reins help him to know what is right, help him to control his *karma* and educate his intellect by laying a foundation of quiet within the instinctive mind, a foundation upon which the intellect may build a knowledgeable structure. ¶*Charyā* is the state of overcoming basic instinctive patterns and learning to work for the sake of work rather than the fruits of our labor. It is the simple fulfillment of right action and the first step on the spiritual path in our religion. Our duty to our parents, to our community, to the wife and children, to the temple in the town or village—all this must be fulfilled for *charyā* to be perfected. One goes to the temple at this stage of unfoldment because it is expected of him. He goes there not to practice *yoga*, not to evolve a personal relationship with the Deity, but because he must. It is his duty. His instinctive mind at this stage of his evolution is so strong that it must be governed firmly by external laws, external forces. He either obeys or suffers the consequences of disobedience. It is his fear of the consequences that motivates him more than anything else. Certainly he may feel guilty or fearful when he approaches the temple, for he is aware of his own transgressions and omissions. But little by little he gains confidence and understanding. His conscience begins to take the place of outer sanctions and gradually becomes his guideline. Whereas before he never felt guilty even for his worst transgressions, now he begins to feel remorse for misdeeds. Tendencies toward selfishness lose their hold on the devotee as he strives to become the perfect servant to God and mankind.

Friday
LESSON 362
Service, Worship Understanding

The sequential pattern of evolution is experienced by each individual in a microcosmic sense in each lifetime. Even if they have been experienced in a previous life, the lessons contained in each stage are, in a sense, relearned in childhood. If we have previously learned them, then they will be quickly mastered. But if we have not learned these lessons in another life, we draw to ourselves in this life the experiences that we need to do so. This knowledge is an inheritance that comes along with the physical body. In other words, experiences from other lives affect the patterns of experience in this life. With basic inherited knowledge, the soul develops an intellectual mind through the good graces of its own personal *karma* and destiny, provided his intellectual mind is in accordance and in harmony with the precepts of his religion. ¶If not, he has problems. Those problems can be overcome, but they are problems while they are being overcome. If his beliefs are not in harmony with his religion, that conflict can stagnate and congest his natural advancement and must be resolved before he can move on to the second stage. ¶In the stage of *charyā*, similar to *karma yoga*, the devotee naturally awakens a desire to work for the sake of work, to serve for the sake of service. He does this in his daily life and through helping in the temple in practical ways—through sweeping the marble floors, polishing the brass oil lamps, weaving fragrant garlands for the *pūjās*, helping other devotees in their lives, and in general through a humble and unseen kind of service. This humble service is itself a means to break the stagnant congestion of erroneous beliefs. Worship during the *charyā* stage is entirely external, yet it is entirely meaningful to the devotee. In *charyā* the devotee looks upon the stone image in the temple sanctum with his physical eyes, and to him *darshan* of the Deity is the physical sight of the stone image of God. ¶As the devotee unfolds into the next stage, of *kriyā* or *bhakti yoga*, he will want to worship and serve in the temple in more internalized ways. He will seek to understand why a stone image is a stone image, why stone images are needed at all. He will begin to think about the purpose of worship, the meaning of worship, the experience of worship. He will wonder to himself about the ancient customs and protocol and why these customs are followed in his community. He will delve into the scriptures, learning and studying about his religion. Singing the sacred hymns, chanting the names of the Lord and performing *japa* will become an important part of his devotion, which is partly internal and partly external. Devotion will well up from the recesses of his soul as he purifies himself. His heart begins to open as he evolves out of the instinctive mind into a spiritualized intellect, an intellect that is developed from within himself. His instinctive nature is subsiding, and his intellectual nature is emerging as he comes into a full understanding of the laws of *karma*. As his intellect controls the instinctive mind, he understands for the first time the cause and effect, the action and reaction of his physical and mental activities. ¶*Kriyā* blossoms into its fullness when there arises in his heart a desire, a strong desire, to know and experience God, to penetrate into the realms of consciousness and reality beyond the physical plane revealed by his grosser senses. He expresses this desire through continued worship in the very special environment of the Hindu temple or his home shrine. He worships the personal aspect of God, and his attitude is no longer one of fear, of a servant to a master, as it was in *charyā*. In *kriyā* he looks upon God as a dutiful son to his father. He perceives that God is his personal Lord, concerned for the welfare of mankind, and he approaches God in a human, personal way. He wants to serve God not because he fears the consequences of being an infidel, but because he wants to be in harmony with a higher reality which he reveres, to be attuned to the *darshan* of the Deity.

Saturday
LESSON 363
The Blossoming Of Devotion

For those in *kriyā*, *darshan* is not only the physical sight of the stone image in the temple. It is also an inner communion, a receiving of the blessings and the messages and the rays of Second and Third World beings, who are actual conscious entities and whose consciousness is canalized through the sacred image by esoteric temple practices. This is a deeper perception of the *darshan* of the Deity. Other forms of religious expression naturally come forth for the devotee in this stage of unfoldment, such as attending *pūjās* regularly, chanting, undertaking pilgrimages to temples and holy places and studying the scriptures. ¶Midpoint in this stage of development of the soul, the devotee may psychically experience an aspect of God that he has been worshiping in the temple. He may see the Deity in a dream or have a vision of Him during a quiet period when he is sitting with his eyes closed after a *pūjā*. After this experience, he centers his life fully around God and learns to psychically attune himself to His *darshan,* His will. Once he fully understands his religion, if he has sufficient means he may express his eagerness to serve through building a temple, or participation in such a project. Indeed, this is the great culmination of *kriyā*. It is through the devotees in the *kriyā,* or *bhakti yoga,* stage of the unfoldment of the soul that we have all over the world today magnificent Hindu temples, built by people who have performed well, who have controlled their thoughts and actions, who have understood the laws of *karma* and the penalties of wrong action. They have avoided wrong action not out of fear, but because they have evolved into performing right action. Having released themselves from the dense fog of the instinctive mind, they can now build temples of great beauty which reflect the beauties they have discovered within themselves in their personal communion with God, who to them is not an awesome master who might punish and discipline, but a loving father. ¶As he matures in *kriyā*, the devotee unfolds a more and more intense love of God, to the point that he may well shed joyful tears during intense moments of worship. When that love is constant from day to day, when it is strong enough that he is capable of surrendering his individual will to God's Cosmic Will, then *kriyā* or *bhakti yoga* has reached its zenith. This giving up of his own will is a slow process as he unwinds the last remaining strands of his external will from the instinctive mind. His will was born of intellectual concepts, and these concepts, too, he releases unto God, feeling within his inmost being that he knows little of the grand mysteries of existence, an admission he could not make earlier. He realizes that he receives his inspiration, his energy, his very life, from God. ¶At this stage of *kriyā* the devotee learns patience. He learns to wait for the proper timing of things in his life. He is in no hurry. He is willing to wait for another life, or for many more lives. There is no urgency. He trusts God and trusts the path he is on. He settles down, and his life comes into a balance. He observes that he is in an evolutionary process along with thousands and millions of others. He embraces other devotees with renewed love and appreciation. He patterns his life in such a way that the temple is the hub of his culture, his religious activity and observance, his very thinking. From the temple or his home shrine, he goes forth to spend his days in the world, and to the temple or shrine he returns from the world. His life comes and goes from that sacred place. ¶In the stages of *charyā* and *kriyā,* the deep-seated impurities of the mind are cleansed as past *karmas* are resolved and a foundation laid for the third stage on the divine path, that of *yoga. Yoga* is a very advanced science. It cannot be sustained except by the soul that has unfolded into the fullness of *charyā* and *kriyā* and maintains the qualities of service and devotion as meditation is pursued. The devotee who has served God well now embarks upon finding union with God in his sanctum within. He remains enveloped in the *darshan* of the personal Lord he carefully cultivated during *charyā* and *kriyā,* and on the power of that *darshan,* he is drawn within by the Primal Soul Himself to rarefied states of consciousness and the stillness of meditation.

Sunday
LESSON 364
The Journey Called Yoga

To the meditating *yogī, darshan* is more than a communication radiating out to him from an external God or Mahādeva. It is a radiant light shining from the sanctum sanctorum of his own *sahasrāra chakra.* Worship for him becomes completely internal as he follows that light, that *darshan,* seeking to know its source. In *yoga,* the devotee worships the transcendent aspect of God. He strengthens his body and nerve system. He disciplines the energies of mind and body. He learns to regulate his breath and to control the *prāṇas* that flow as life's force through his nerve system. In this process the *kuṇḍalinī śakti* is lifted and the multi-petaled *chakras* unfold in all their splendor. The subtle realms within the devotee are revealed layer by layer as he methodically perfects attention, concentration, meditation and contemplation. ¶Lord Śiva now brings the earnest devotee to meet his *satguru,* who will guide him through the traditional disciplines of *yoga* on his inward journey. It is his spiritual preceptor, his *guru,* who takes care that he avoids the abysses and psychic pitfalls along the path. ¶In this stage of *yoga,* the devotee looks upon God as a friend, a companion. He strives with a diligence and energy he never knew he possessed, with a dedication he once thought impossible, and as he strives his willpower is awakened. Finally, one day, in his first *samādhi,* he penetrates to the essence of being. In this ultimate experience, which remains forever beyond description, he has reached the union which is *yoga.* ¶Returning from this state of ineffable fulfillment, the devotee brings back into his life a new understanding, a new perspective. He is never the same after that experience. He can never again look at life in the same way. Each time he enters into that God Realization, that *samādhi,* he returns to consciousness more and more the knower. His knowing matures through the years as his *yoga sādhana* is regulated, and as it matures he enters ever so imperceptibly into the fourth and final stage of unfoldment, into *jñāna.* ¶One does not become a *jñānī* simply by reading philosophy. That is a great misconception. Many people believe that you can spiritually unfold or evolve into a *jñānī* through reading books, through understanding another's unfoldment or performing meditations that he once performed. Understanding another person's wisdom does not make us wise. Each has to experience the fullness of the path to enlightenment himself. ¶The *jñānī* becomes one who postulates that what he has himself realized are the final conclusions for all mankind. His postulations are filled with assuredness, for he has experienced what the *Vedas*, the *Āgamas* and the *Upanishads* speak of. He has awakened the power and force of his own realization. He knows. He becomes the embodiment of that knowing, of the Truth he once sought as something other than himself. He finds within the scriptures confirmation of his realization echoed in the verses of *ṛishis* written at the dawn of human history. This matured soul sees reflected in their writings that same state of complete merging with the Divine that he himself has come to know as the timeless, formless, spaceless Absolute which he once worshiped symbolically as a stone image in previous life wanderings within the instinctive mind, or avoided and resented because the temple to him represented an awesome and fearful threat to his impurities. ¶He has removed the veils of ignorance, removed the obstacles to understanding. He has come into his true being, union with God, union with Śiva, and in this serene state he sees God as his beloved, as that which is dearer to him than life itself, as he is consumed by that all-encompassing love. There is for him no more an inner and an outer life and consciousness, for they have melted and merged into a single continuum. He is That, and for him it is clear that all are That. Unknown to himself, he has become the temple of his religion, capable of imparting knowledge merely by the power of his silent presence. He has become the source of light and *darshan* which radiate out through the *nāḍīs* and *prāṇas* of his being. This great soul is found in his reveries sweeping the temple floor, polishing brass lamps, weaving fragrant garlands, expounding *smṛiti* and being the humble Śivanadiyar, slave to the servants of the Lord, as he lives out the final strands of *karma* of this last birth. ¶The final conclusions of the world's most ancient religious tradition, the Sanātana Dharma, are that mankind is on a spiritual path as old as time itself, that this journey progresses from birth to birth as the soul evolves through the perfection of *charyā* into the perfection of *kriyā*, and from there into the perfection of *yoga*, emerging as a *jñānī*. This is the path followed by all souls. Whatever religion they espouse, whatsoever they may believe or deny, all of mankind is on the one path to Truth. It begins with the *dvaita* of *charyā* and ends in the *advaita* of *jñāna*—the *advaita* postulated in Vedānta and in the Śuddha Siddhānta of Śaiva Siddhānta.

Monday
LESSON 365
Eternal Questions

Many people think of the realization of timeless, formless, spaceless Paraśiva, *nirvikalpa samādhi*, as the most blissful of all blissful states, the opening of the heavens, the descent of the Gods, as a moment of supreme, sublime joyousness. Whereas I have found it to be more like cut glass, diamond-dust *darshan*, a psychic surgery, not a blissful experience at all, but really a kind of near-death experience resulting in total transformation. The bliss that is often taught as a final attainment is actually another attainment, Satchidānanda, an aftermath of *nirvikalpa samādhi,* and a "before-math." This means that Satchidānanda, *savikalpa samādhi,* may be attained early on by souls pure in heart. It also means that one need not gauge the highest attainment on the basis of bliss, which it transcends. ¶In my experience, the *anāhata chakra* is the resting place of dynamic complacency, of thoughtful perception and quietude. Those of a lower nature arriving in the bloom of this *chakra* are released from turbulent emotions, conflicting thoughts and disturbances. This to many is the end of the path, attaining peace or *śānti.* Once one attains *śānti* as just described, in my experience, this marks the beginning of the path, or part two, the second level. It is from here that the practices of *rāja yoga* take hold, once *śānti* is attained. In the *anāhata chakra* and *viśuddha chakra,* Satchidānanda, the all-pervasive being of oneness, of the underlying being of the universe, is attained, experienced. ¶But unless *brahmacharya,* chastity, is absolutely adhered to, the experience is not maintained. It is here that relations between men and women play an important part, as in their union temporary oneness occurs, followed by a more permanent two-ness and ever-accumulating distractions, sometimes along with insolvable difficulties. Those who practice sexual *tantras,* seeking Self Realization through this path, will agree with this wisdom. ¶Does Self Realization bring bliss to the realized one? Self Realization is in several stages. Realizing oneself as a soul—rather than a mind, an intellectual and emotional type or a worthless person—gives satisfaction, security, and this is a starting point. Realization of the Self as Satchidānanda gives contentment, a release from all emotions and thoughts of the external world, and the nerve system responds to the energies flowing through the *viśuddha* and *anāhata chakras.* Realizing the Self that transcends time, form and space, Paraśiva, is a razor-edged experience, cutting all bonds, reversing individual awareness, such as looking out from the Self rather than looking into the Self. ¶There are many boons after this transforming experience, if repeated many times. One or two occurrences does make a renunciate out of the person and does make the world renounce the renunciate, but then without persistent effort, former patterns of emotion, intellect, lack of discipline, which would inhibit the repeated experience of Paraśiva, would produce a disoriented nomad, so to speak. Therefore, repeated experiences of the ego-destructive Paraśiva, from all states of consciousness, intellectual, instinctive, even in dreams, permeates the transformation through atoms and molecules even in the physical body. It is then that the bliss can be enjoyed of Satchidānanda—and simultaneously, I would say, Satchidānanda and the rough, unrelenting, timeless, formless, spaceless Paraśiva merge in a not-merging way, such as light and darkness in the same room. This is different than the concept of *sayujya samādhi,* which is maintaining the perpetual bliss within the fourth and fifth *chakra* and stimulating the sixth and seventh. For this to be maintained, a certain isolation from worldly affairs and distracting influences is required to prevent the reawakening of previously unsatisfied desires, repressed tendencies or unresolved subconscious conflicts. ¶Someone asked, "If realization in and of itself is not blissful, then what impels a soul that has arrived at bliss to strive for further realizations?"

We are all moving forward to our ultimate goal of merging with Śiva. Bliss quiets the senses. It is the natural state of the mind when unperturbed by previous desires unfulfilled, desires yet to be fulfilled and the desires known to not be fulfillable. As long as the *anāhata* and *viśuddha chakras* spin at top velocity, the senses will be quieted, few thoughts will pass through the mind unbidden, and the understanding of the *Vedas* and all aspects of esoteric knowledge will be able to be explained by the preceptor. Many choose to remain here, as the explainers of the inexplainable, and not go on. Deep into the sixth, seventh, eighth, ninth, tenth, eleventh *chakras,* into the beyond of the beyond, the quantum level, the core of the universe itself, there comes a point when the powers of evolution move one forward, and even these desireless ones desire the greatest unfoldment, once they have found out that it is there to be desired. ¶Realizing Paraśiva is merging with Śiva, but it is not the end of merging. At that pinpoint of time, there are still the trappings of body, mind and emotions that claim awareness into their consciousness. Ultimately, when all bodies—physical, astral, mental, even the soul body—wear out their time, as all forms wear out in time, bound by time, existing in time, as relative realities, then *viśvagrāsa,* the final merger with Śiva, occurs, as the physical body drops away, the astral body drops away, the mental body drops away, and the soul—a shining, scintillating being of light quantums—merges into its source. As when a drop of water merges into the ocean, it can never be retrieved, only Śiva remains. Aum Namaḥ Śivāya.

Behold the universe in the glory of God, and all that lives and moves on Earth. Leaving the transient, find joy in the Eternal. Set not your heart on another's possession.

Śukla Yajur Veda, Īśa Upanishad 1. UPM, 49

According as one acts, so does he become. One becomes virtuous by virtuous action, bad by bad action.

Śukla Yajur Veda, Bṛihadāraṇyaka Upanishad 4.4.5. UPH, 140

Iḍā is the Gaṅgā of the lower world, *piṅgalā* the river Yamunā, and between *iḍā* and *piṅgalā* is *sushumṇā*, the subtle river Sarasvatī. It is said that to bathe in the confluence of the three rivers leads to the Great Result.

Śukla Yajur Veda, Tṛishikhi Brāhmaṇa 316-317

With earnest effort hold the senses in check. Controlling the breath, regulate the vital activities. As a charioteer holds back his restive horses, so does a persevering aspirant restrain his mind.

Kṛishṇa Yajur Veda, Śvetāśvatara Upanishad 2.9. P, 192

O self-luminous Divine, remove the veil of ignorance from before me, that I may behold your light. Reveal to me the spirit of the scriptures. May the truth of the scriptures be ever present to me. May I seek day and night to realize what I learn from the sages.

Ṛig Veda, Aitareya Upanishad, Invocation. UPH, 95

One alone is God; there cannot be a second. It is He alone who governs these worlds with His powers. He stands facing beings. He, the herdsman of all worlds, after bringing them forth, reabsorbs them at the end of time.

Kṛishṇa Yajur Veda, Śvetāśvatara Upanishad 4.1.11. VE, 621

Lead me from unreality to reality. Lead me from darkness to light. Lead me from death to immortality.

Śukla Yajur Veda, Bṛihadāraṇyaka Upanishad, 1.3.28. HH, 202

The desire for true knowledge arises in a person who is free from attachment and possessed of discriminative faculty. With a view to uplift that conscious soul from the ocean of mundane life, Lord Śiva unites him (with a sense of longing). The person thus united is directed to an *āchārya* by God.

Mātaṅga Parameśvara Āgama 50-51

When nourishment is pure, nature is pure. When nature is pure, memory becomes firm. When memory remains firm, there is release from all knots of the heart.

Sāma Veda, Çhāndogya Upanishad 7.26.2. PU, 489

As one not knowing that a golden treasure lies buried beneath his feet may walk over it again and again yet never find it—so all beings live every moment in the city of Brahman yet never find Him, because of the veil of illusion by which He is concealed.

Sāma Veda, Çhāndogya Upanishad 8.3.2. UPP, 121

The Self is not realized through instruction, nor by intellectual power, nor by much hearing. It can be reached only by the one whom the Self chooses. To him the *ātman* reveals its form. He who has not renounced evil ways, who is not at peace, who cannot concentrate, whose mind is not composed cannot reach the Self, even by right knowledge.

Kṛishṇa Yajur Veda, Kaṭha Upanishad 1.2.24-25

The sub-su
works upon t
of the consc
full physic
will not be
the "sub" of
will lock t

Jñātṛisāmarthyatvam Manojayaḥ

ज्ञातृसामर्थ्यत्वं मनोजयः

Cognizantability

The Conquest of the Mind

THE TRUTH

What you are to the mind
You are not in Truth.
What seems—isn't.
What could be—can't.
What appears to be is not enough
Even to be apparent,
For the seer is what he sees,
—And isn't in Truth.

August, 4, 1959

Manasaḥ Sthitipañchakam

मनसः स्थितिपञ्चकम्

Section One

The Five States of Mind

Conscious

Subconscious

Subsubconscious

Subsuperconscious

Superconscious

HAVE YOU EVER SEEN THE MIND? NO, YOU HAVE NOT! YOU HAVE SEEN THE EFFECTS OF THE MIND THROUGH ITS MANY PHASES AND ITS many ramifications. Also, you have felt the results of the mind in your own life and in the lives of others. Come on a tour of the mind with me, into its depths, and find out how simple, or how complex, it can be. See for yourself how easy it is for you to control your mind and fathom your problems from the innermost recesses of your being. All that and more "Cognizantability" will awaken in you.

You may not understand everything that you read, but you will acknowledge much more than you anticipate. You will become aware of your mind as it is, because the mind, as you will find out, is the essence of time and space. You only create time and hold a consciousness of space in the lower realms of your mind.

Through the study of "Cognizantability" you can learn to awaken and use the mind in its entirety to solve problems of any nature for the attainment of true and deeply satisfying happiness. You do not have to work too hard at this study. You must only have the concentration to read all of the aphorisms and their commentaries several times, and then, strange as it may seem, your own subconscious mind will take over the study for you, completing your task. When you finish reading "Cognizantability" the first time, go over it again and study it thoroughly. At this time you will begin to understand what was confusing to you the first time you read it. Now you are going to get the treat of your life. Take "Cognizantability" apart and try to disprove to yourself everything you have read. Do this, and you will do much for yourself.

"Cognizantability" is comprised of aphorisms and their explanation of the interrelated five states of mind. An aphorism, as you know, is a short, easy-to-remember statement. I have given a brief explanation of each aphorism, with some practical examples of how the study of the five states of mind can help you gain a greater control of the mind. The mere reading of the precepts will do no great good, other than perhaps stimulate some intellectual thought along psychological and philosophical lines. The practical, consistent practice of certain keys to be found by you in the precepts will, however, produce results. As the time element is involved in our daily lives, so much so that very often we do not have time to do the things we feel we should do, let alone those we would like to do, I have often told my students that the consistent practice for even five minutes a day after many days will definitely produce remarkable results—like the man who decided to construct a fence around his house, but being pressed for lack of time he could only manage to put one stake in the ground every day. There wasn't much to be seen after two weeks of his labor, and of course, this afforded much backyard gossip for the neighbors. All gossip stopped, however, when in only two months time of his consistent labor of placing one fence stake in the ground every day the fence stood complete to be enjoyed by owner and neighbors alike.

You will find as you turn the pages at random that each precept is separate and complete in itself, yet they are all interrelated and should be read in a broad sense as well as be studied individually. It is suggested that "Cognizantability" be read in its entirety first, then each chapter should be studied as a unit. Following this, each precept may be taken separately and digested through the subconscious mind. "Cognizantability," intuitively read, will feed the intellect into a healthy cognition of its contents.

When "Cognizantability" has been read by you, it must be digested. I suggest that you do not try to digest it consciously, but take one aphorism a day. Think it over carefully. It will unfold itself in your mind. Be careful to remember it correctly, or jot it down on a piece of paper and carry it with you. All is now ready for you to really unfold your inmost nature. Just open up and allow the subsuperconscious mind to take over.

Many books are written on psychology, philosophy and metaphysics. But this treatise incorporates the essence of all three. All you need to know about the mind is within these pages. Endless ramifications and systems of thought can be, and have been, constructed, but here is a lasting and correct way to produce results in your everyday life.

Concentration is a thing hoped for, but seldom attained. Meditation is the outcome of a concentrated mind. Not only must the conscious mind be concentrated, but the subconscious mind as well, for meditation to begin. Once the mind becomes pointedly concentrated, even for an instant, something remarkable begins to happen. Concentration releases into the field of consciousness the resources and actions of other parts of the mind which were hitherto seemingly and unadvisably shut off. The result is concentration not only of the conscious mind, but also, toward the same goal, the forces of the subconscious mind as well. When this happens, there takes place what is known in *yoga* and Buddhist literature as meditation. Meditation is an integrated state of mind quite different from the ordinary processes of sequential thought.

The deeper one goes into this state, that is, the more one succeeds by concentration in releasing blockages, the more the various rivers of the mind flow in, and a progressively wider and deeper cognition and understanding unfolds. This, of course, must be experienced, but the experience does come as we make progress in our attempt to hold the mind consciously and subconsciously one-pointed in concentration. The next step is called contemplation and comes as a steady growth out of meditation. One unfolds into the other. Contemplation is a state rarely, if ever, attained by the average man; it need not concern us too much here, as it flows quite naturally out of successfully sustained meditation. There is nothing fearsome or dangerous about it, but it is an experience quite different from either our ordinary sense perceptions or reasoning processes. It is in the nature of direct cognition of something through identity or oneness with it. The aim, of course, is the realization of the Self.

It is through this process that George Washington Carver achieved his tremendous knowledge of the peanut, leading to many inventions and uses for it. It is by this process, or an approximation of it, that some of our great scientists have come to some of their profound insights into the workings of the universe. It is by contemplation and its final succeeding state, *samādhi,* or *nirvāṇa,* that the *ṛishis* of old, the great saints of all religions, achieved their revelations. We are not trying to attain everything at once here, but you can see the road we are on. Each way station produces bountiful rewards in greater understanding of ourselves and the world about us, greater control and richness in our lives.

We do not have to worry now about the last stages of the journey, but can well keep in mind the principal geography—the five steps of attention, concentration, meditation, contemplation and *samādhi.* It is immaterial whether we now consciously seek the ultimate goal, *samādhi,* which is "Union with God," the realization of the Self or Truth, but whatever our needs are now, the way to their solution lies along the path indicated. As you progress in the earlier stages of concentration and meditation, solutions to your immediate apparent problems will unfold, and your life will gradually change course toward greater fulfillment and satisfaction of your real needs.

These aphorisms should not be confused with the popular concept of affirmations! Some people direct their energies, through concentration, on the repetition of affirmations, ignorant of how and why they do or should. Sometimes they come to a conclusion that it must be beneficial, by the eventual outcome. When one begins to affirm a positive statement, a well-qualified foundation of what is desired and the responsibilities entailed, as well as the vibratory rate of the words themselves, must be taken into careful consideration before repetition to impress the subconscious state of mind. An aphorism is different. It is a well-qualified, easy-to-remember statement to be thought over and placed in the subconscious mind, where the deeper understanding of such a statement will gradually be unfolded from within yourself.

In reading "Cognizantability" you will learn much about aphorisms. Should you be one who uses affirmations, you will be happy to learn that when you open the door to the superconscious mind, you will need no helpers or crutches. You need nothing but the willpower within you to help, protect and provide for you and give you self-respect. Yes, I said respect, for that is the last thing we acquire. Respect is too often reversed into pride, inferiority, and lack of understanding by imposing superiority on oneself. Yes, respect for oneself is the last acquired possession on the journey through the mind. For Self is not known until mind is put in order and mind cognizes itself, dissolving itself into its own bed of peace.

Before you turn the page and begin the study of "Cognizantability," I am going to impart to you two statements to exercise your mind. Number One: How can we forget what is forgotten? Number Two: How can we remember what is remembered?

These are two statements that can be discussed, talked about and dismissed, without ever coming up with concrete conclusions. Now, let us take into consideration the following: How can we remember what has been forgotten? That is the way you would write it, but I said, "How can we remember what is remembered?" And this is what it means: that nothing is forgotten. It is all locked up in the mind and can be brought out by the proper handling of the mind.

The next statement: How can we forget what is forgotten? Now that is even more ambiguous than the one I just explained. However, it is easy when you look at it in the right light—in the light of desire. For desire is the force that drives humanity onward and through all phases of the mind. Desire is the only thing that holds this world together. So, how can we really forget what is forgotten? Have not all things been forgotten when the focus of desire has been transmuted into the realm of desirelessness? So, truly, how can we forget what is forgotten when through changing our desire we change our life? By changing our life we change those around us and so the world. What was forgotten is that the desire changed. However, it still exists in the halls of memory, in the essence of time, cause and space, the superconscious mind, of which you will learn more later. So, on with the study, and may it lead you into that for which you were destined—peace, power and a positive, unfolded life.

Vedic Dharma, man's spiritual, philosophical and devotional laws and guidelines, leads him through practice to the Ultimate within himself. For many thousands of years each preceptor has elucidated portions or all of these systematic teachings to his closest disciples, thus adding to the ever growing wealth of Hinduism.

It was when we were finishing the lexicon of *Dancing with Śiva* in 1993, forty-four years after the aphorisms of "Cognizantability" were unfolded, that—surprisingly—we found that the five states of mind, that were so unexpectedly unfolded in 1950, have names in the Sanskṛit language, which I had no knowledge of then. The various definitions of mind and consciousness, which form the essence of the aphorisms, were, in a way, retrofitted with the assistance of eminent contemporary Indian scholars who knew the Sanskṛit nomenclature and made connections between the traditional terms and the subsuperconscious messages of so many decades ago. They are as follows: conscious mind, *jagrat chitta* ("wakeful consciousness"); subconscious mind, *saṁskāra chitta* ("impression mind"); subsubconscious mind, *vāsanā chitta* ("mind of subliminal traits"); superconscious mind, *karaṇa chitta* ("causal mind"); and subsuperconscious mind, *anukaraṇa chitta* ("sub-causal mind"). My *satguru* was truly right when he so often said, "There is nothing new. It was all finished long ago."

The five states of mind and the basic laws of transmutation here again outline for the seeker needed knowledge and tools to unleash the force of awareness from the seeming bondages of mind to realize the Self God beyond all aspects of mind, time, space and causation. Learn to distinguish the vibratory rate of each state, using them as a road map of the within to know where you are in consciousness at all times. In doing so, the vibration of your individual awareness when opposed to the state of mind will become apparent. Thus, in thoroughly understanding the vibratory rate of duality, awareness versus a state of mind, it is possible to retroactively realize the pure, nondual state.

The precepts represent milestones or landmarks along the road to the superconscious. Using these as points of departure, we can survey what has passed, be aware of our progress and view our approaching destination.

In this treatise you will find the door to be
unlocked to realize your own Self.
The knowledge contained herein has
assimilated the wisdom of the psychology
and metaphysics of the West, the ancient
yoga philosophy of the East, and is presented
in a way easy to understand and simple to master.
When you read and reread it, you will be happily
rewarded with what is unfolded to you.

CANTO ONE

The Conscious and Subconscious Mind

THE FIRST APHORISM

There is but one mind. It functions in various phases, namely: instinctive, intellectual and superconscious. These phases are manifested consciously as well as subconsciously.

The mind is open to various actions found in the sympathetic nervous system. It is smoothly transformed into all kinds of intellectual and instinctive thoughts and feelings. I liken it to the sympathetic nervous system. That is to say that the conscious mind acts in sympathy with the subconscious. ¶All act as one unit, but for better understanding and appreciation, we have found it necessary to break it down into several parts. All these function together consciously as well as subconsciously, instinctively as well as intellectually. ¶We do not prove anything in this guide. We only make it possible for you to prove it for yourself, consciously, from the results of what you comprehend subconsciously. These aphorisms are explained in simple language so they may be understood in their entirety by everyone, for there is but one mind, and in its functioning it works on itself, the same in everyone, only varying its actions between the instinctive, the intellectual and the superconscious or intuitive spheres. ¶In the study of this aphorism, call it a simple one if you will, but take into consideration the meaning of each word involved. *Instinctive,* for instance, is a word that some may understand and others may take offense at. It means, in this case, that when the mind functions instinctively it is controlled by the habit impressions made in the subconscious during its trip through the experiences of life. Instinctive also means that the driving force of awareness comes from the sexual nature; the nature is turned in that direction subconsciously, even though the conscious mind may not be cognizant of the fact. It also means that in the event of an emergency, the animal nature would take over completely, being jarred loose automatically from lack of what I term mind control, or you might call it self control. ¶Most of us find the intellect a saving grace when it comes from the transformation of the instinctive nature into something more substantial. Constantly we strive to broaden our intellect, increase our knowledge, govern the mind with organized thinking, and control our emotions by repressing the instinctive nature. This is called, in terms easy to understand, nature's way of increasing man's justification of what has passed before the windows of the mind that was not pleasing to the intellect—the justification being that enough knowledge had not been acquired by the intellect to sufficiently suppress the instinctive nature. Hence, man studies himself, promoted by the forces set up in his mind from previous happenings. He sells himself on the idea that he can do nothing of himself, that a power greater than himself governs all, and he calls that power by various names: God, Christ, Jehovah, etc. This God he bows to; it is somewhere, it is all powerful, it is supreme. ¶Some men say they are a part of this God, that the God Spirit is in them. Let them tell us what part of this God Spirit they are and where is the God Spirit. In which part of them can it be found? Ask that question and you will get yourself into a lengthy discussion. The superconscious mind we consider to be that so-called part of God, our inspiration. If you have ever had a hunch and had it work out, that is the superconscious mind working within you. It has dominated your conscious mind and has made it possible for you to look into the future and estimate its happenings. The superconscious mind is the essence of time, yet it understands time, and timelessness is its essence. It is the essence of space, yet it comprehends space and spacelessness. It is real, yet does not exist—real only when used, nonexistent to the lower realms of the mind only when in its natural state. You will learn how to tap the superconscious power consciously later on in this study. I am now only introducing it to you. ¶You are beyond that state of mind, however. The real you, the Self, is beyond the mind. Your road leads through the conscious and subconscious control of the mind. Then the doors are found to the superconscious and opened consciously, leading you to the realization of your true Self, the you beyond a stilled mind.

THE SECOND APHORISM

The conscious mind, within itself, is insanity in its natural state; its only balance comes from a subconscious consciousness of the superconscious. When the consciousness sinks into perverted, instinctive phases of thought and feeling, resulting in physical action, thus eventually cutting itself off from the superconscious and intellectual spheres through untimely and immoral practices, it (the conscious mind) falls into its natural state, termed insanity.

The conscious mind is not the only state of mind that is insane, as we call it. The subconscious is as well. The only balance we have comes from a subconscious understanding of the superconscious, or God-consciousness. If this were not true, the instinctive nature would take over the entire mind and bring total insanity. The mind would magnify all it did not comprehend, and a complete loss of mental and physical coordination would result. ¶The super, all-knowing consciousness, however, steps in through the subconscious (this is reflected outside by churches, ministers and priests), keeping the consciousness deep enough to hold the balance between the conscious and subconscious mind, for the subconscious is but a reflection, a storehouse, of all conscious mind happenings. It holds its balance only through the use of the will—the instinctive desire to create. ¶When the creative forces are dissipated through sex and the lower emotional forms of enjoyment, the subconscious loses the guide-power of the will. The will loses its strength, for the vital forces in the body have been thrown away or used up faster than they can be replaced. In turn, the conscious mind reacts, thinking assumes distorted or irregular proportions and a mental unbalance occurs. ¶The creative forces must be transmuted to be of use in holding the conscious and subconscious mind concentrated to the point where the superconscious mind can be tapped consciously; otherwise, the conscious mind will tend to fall into its natural state of insanity, neurosis, nervousness, depression and despair.

THE THIRD APHORISM

The conscious mind is only one-tenth of the mind. The subconscious of the conscious mind, the subconscious, the superconscious and the subconscious of the superconscious mind are the other nine-tenths.

We can all plainly see why the conscious mind is only one-tenth of the entire mind. Yet it is in the conscious mind that we live most of our waking hours. The subconscious mind, the sub of the subconscious, the superconscious and the subconscious of the superconscious are the other nine-tenths. They are what we will learn to control and use—control the former and use the latter. Call on the subconscious of the superconscious, and you will get results if you call correctly. To make this contact, we have to understand repression. Repression is a series of hopes, doubts, fears and impulses that have never reached the surface of the mind. Yet, the conscious mind knows of them to an extent, but because they have sent their messages in cleverly disguised, the conscious mind, just as cleverly, has pushed them down in an effort not to be disturbed. ¶Get your freedom from within, we say, but how is another story, a different story and a long story. It means that work must be done, and done well. All repressions must be realized and consciously understood. Then, and only then, will the subconscious of the superconscious mind flow freely out through the conscious mind, and the book of knowledge so often talked about in all of the philosophies and religions will open its pages to you, chapter by chapter, will unfold into a conscious realization of your true Self.

THE FOURTH APHORISM

The intellect strengthened with opinionated knowledge is the only barrier to the superconscious.

Opinionated knowledge can be harmful, for it is strictly of the subconscious realm of the mind. It is stored away in an effort to set up some security for the conscious and subconscious states of mind, something for them to cling to and lean upon—that is, the opinions of others, intellectual assertions made on happenings of the past based upon only what the eye and ear have received. This well-formed barrier makes it possible for the mind to convince itself of anything outside of reason or within the realm of reason. It manufactures a large percentage of the world's so-called thinkers. When, however, you ask them their own opinions, they only formulate opinions of others and culminate them into one of their own. This makes one think that by this rearrangement of knowledge the thinking process has been stimulated. However, it has not. It has only run its natural course and is conditioned only by the faculty of memory. Memory, too, plays a part in the intellect, as you well know, for if very little memory exists, very little intellect would be present. ¶When the superconscious mind is tapped, the essence of memory has been reached. All knowledge is awakened from within to the extent of the intellect. Your intellect at this very moment may be searching for a way out of accepting this treatise. That is why I say try to intellectually disprove all you read here after you have read and re-read it. Give your mind a break and let it make you think by turning itself back on itself. You'll be pleased with the outcome.

THE FIFTH APHORISM

There is but one mind. The consciousness, or Ego, functions within the mind's various phases. The one-tenth of the mind, of the conscious plane, in ramification, is carried on by its own novelty. The object is to control the conscious mind and become consciously conscious.

This, then, is the essence of what we are first working for: to become consciously conscious. It is bringing the mind to a state of constant concentration so that it can look in on itself and cognize its own nature. This is easy, for all you have to do is to watch your mind think, and to begin this interesting activity, just tell yourself one little truth. Tell yourself that you are not your mind, because you can control your mind with your will. You can if you really try. Tell yourself that, and you'll see how fast the mind objectifies itself long enough for you to study it. ¶Oh, yes, we have to observe the conscious mind in all its activities. You will see how it ramifies and is carried on from one thing to another by the simple novelty of thinking. It has not the concept of conclusion in some things. It has not the desire of understanding in others. ¶You will thank me for suggesting this tour to you, and you will bless yourself with your results gotten from within. The great creative forces used by all who create the artistic, the different and the new will begin working within and for you when you step out and watch the mind. The Ego that I mention here has nothing to do with being egotistical. It is the life essence, the link to the real Self of you that passes through all states of mind, like you pass through the experiences of life. This Ego you will realize when watching your mind at work.

THE SIXTH APHORISM

The subconscious of the conscious mind is but a reflection of the subconscious of the superconscious mind.

We have studied the conscious mind and its relation to the other states of mind and have found that it is only one-tenth of the mind. It has not the power to act on its own for any length of time without being carried on by its own novelty through ramification. The subconscious of the conscious mind is the storehouse for the conscious mind. All the happenings of each day and all reactions are stored up there. It is only a reflection of the subsuperconscious, for when all the repressions are released, the subsuperconscious takes over the subconscious mind. For, through the power of understanding generated by the superconscious through the subconscious, the subconscious is dissolved, and the true, intuitive, all-knowing, superconscious self returns to its rightful position in the picture of the mind. All the confusion of the subconscious clears, and the Ego looks as naturally within as without, simultaneously.

THE SEVENTH APHORISM

There are two sections to the subconscious of the conscious mind and the subsuperconscious mind. One section controls the physical, and the other controls the mental.

The first section of the subconscious controls the involuntary processes of the body. The next controls the involuntary processes of the mind. When the subconscious is in control, the control is at one rate of vibration. When the subsuperconscious is in control, after the subconscious has become understood, concentrated and cleared of all confusion, the vibratory rate is higher. ¶The vibratory rate we speak of here is likened to class distinction: breeding, culture, the world today. The difference between the working man and a businessman is the feeling of security. Every organ of the body takes on a new tone; the mind reacts more smoothly to life; the emotions contrast evenly between cause and effect; the sexual forces assume their natural function, and the transmutation of the creative fluids begins.

THE EIGHTH APHORISM

An uncultured nature is the result of repressed tendencies. Such a nature must be analyzed subconsciously through the conscious and subsuperconscious mind. The conscious unraveling of the repressions will then commence. This is the key to awakening the superconscious regions.

The subconscious mind analyzes a problem two ways: first from the plane of reason; second from the plane of intuition. Intuition works through but it does not use the process of reason. Intuition is more direct than reason and far more accurate. ¶The conscious mind builds us into a personality, desirable or undesirable. We can readily change this personality by releasing hidden repressions. Repressions are unfulfilled suppressed desires, like those that lurk in the corners of the mind and pop out at psychological moments until they are suppressed again by the conscious mind. This is the problem we face before we can unlock the superconscious realm of the mind. This problem can be totally impossible, or it can be made easy, depending upon the approach. ¶It is a well-known fact that when the mind releases tendencies that have long been suppressed, reaction occurs. This reaction is what we must anticipate and take into consideration at all times. It is the cause of new repressions if allowed to dominate the consciousness. ¶Following through on this line of thought, I shall take you into a typical familiar case that will cause your subconscious mind to recognize the way to dig out repressions. This case is that of a person who always wanted to drink but never had the nerve to do so because of public opinion and family ties. Subconsciously this person had always wanted to get drunk and experience that expression of release. It was a repressed desire that was not realized, and it showed itself in the form of condemnation of all who do drink. It was impossible for anyone to mention liquor without being obliged to listen to a lengthy discourse on the evils of drinking. This person knew subconsciously he would like to have this experience, but consciously fought it desperately until one day a friend offered him a drink at a social business affair. It was rather rude and almost impossible to refuse. Instead of letting the drink idle away on the table during the ensuing conversation, old man subconscious took over and the drink disappeared, and another took its place. This went on until three drinks, unnoticed by the conscious mind of the person, disappeared. When his conscious mind realized what had happened, a strong reaction followed, the effects of which lasted many weeks. The entire system was upset, physically, mentally and emotionally. But the secret was out. "Like attracts like," and desire will have its fulfillment. The conscious mind began to realize its deep-seated subconscious repression, painfully at first. Then the problem came up of how to remove this repression without suffering the reaction, and the answer followed: overcome all reactions to persons who drink, learn to accept it as one of the experiences in life, make the most of it, bend a little, be strengthened by understanding and tempered with compassionate love. Try to understand the cause and not react to the effect. ¶This was done, and the repression was loosened. Then one day some friends threw a party and all got drunk including our friend, and Mr. Repression was out in the open to be viewed consciously, and as repressions cannot stand the light of understanding, it vanished. The reaction was also supported with the understanding that every cause has its reaction, and the realization that the reaction to a reaction must be understood, not repressed. This keeps the body, mind and emotions from losing their subconscious control. ¶The matter was ended. No more does this person enjoy talking against drink, but rather talks intelligently of its harmful effects on the body, mind and emotions based on experience. When offered a drink, a polite "No, thank you. I drank once and had enough" is the reply. No longer is the repression lurking in the subconscious. No longer is the desire suppressed as it creeps into the conscious mind. The operation has been successful, and nature has healed the wound; the nature of perfect love, through a conscious understanding of a subconscious desire, dissolved the repression. ¶This, then, is the problem we face in unlocking the door to the superconscious mind: to school the subconscious mind in the arts of concentration and meditation. Some say they meditate while working or riding on the bus. This is a wrong concept of the word, a sign of emotional desire for attention, for meditation only comes when the subconscious mind has been released of all repressions. A repression is a desire that is only found when an emotional reaction takes place in the conscious and subconscious mind, such as dislikes, hates or fears. For we only react to that in others of what is locked in a corner of our own subconscious mind in the form of an experience we have yet to go through, either physically or mentally.

8/4/59.

The Truth

What you are to the mind
you are not in Truth.

What seems isn't.
What could be, can't
What appears to be is not enough
even to be apparent
For the seer is what he sees
and isn't in Truth.

CANTO TWO

The Subsuperconscious and Subsubconscious Mind

THE NINTH APHORISM

The superconscious mind working through the subconscious of the conscious mind is the essence of reason. It is known as the subconscious of the superconscious or the subsuperconscious mind. The superconscious mind functions beyond reason yet does not conflict with reason.

This in itself is easy to comprehend. The explanation is clear and concise. To elaborate on the last statement, I will say that to follow a line of thought, then into its depths, through the use of reason takes time. When the depths are reached instantaneously through contacting the superconscious, all the essence is unfolded without the use of reason, space or time. Yet it does not conflict with reason, because the end result is the same in any case. All the time spent in reason requires the mind to open its superconscious resources through the subconscious for the final answer. Hence, training the mind in the arts of concentration and meditation is of great value in this instance.

THE TENTH APHORISM

Two thoughts sent into the subconscious mind at different times, with the same rate of intensity, are different from their separate conscious expressions. This self-created state manifests itself at a much later time on the conscious plane, creating disturbance to the mind.

Two thoughts, at different times, sent into the subconscious mind form in what is called the sub of the subconscious a totally different vibration when intermingled—that is, if the psychological arrangement of the mind was the same at the time each thought entered it. This subconscious formation of thought turns into feelings of the lower instinctive nature and causes the external mind to react to situations in a way that it normally would not have done. ¶This thought formation is taken apart in only one way. It is dissected only through the transmutation of the regenerative forces. It is well and good to believe that sex is a necessary part of life, but the dissipation of the creative energies is not. These forces must be sent back into the body to give strength of character and power over the subconscious mind and its sub; this awakens the subsuperconscious mind in all its peace and glory. ¶When the sex energies are transmuted, they lead the mind calmly into itself, in a way that is not only constructive, but totally satisfactory in all lines of endeavor, be it extroversion or introversion. All one needs to do is release into understanding all fears, worries and doubts about sexual expression. And the consciousness of comprehension will awaken the mind, and all attempts to bring forth knowledge and freedom from within will be fulfilled.

THE ELEVENTH APHORISM

The sub of the subconscious mind can only be created through the conscious mind or the subconscious of the conscious mind.

This sub of the subconscious mind is to be studied objectively before we go into it deeply. It has a great many uses. In our understanding that part of the mind as an object, we must first break it down into its patterns as related to us at the present time. Then have all of the qualified thoughts sorted out and blended into a picture of what has been created. This is easy when concentration upon the mind as an object has been perfected.

THE TWELFTH APHORISM

The sub of the subconscious mind can be understood consciously when the thoughts which created this sub are traced. These will usually be found when the conscious mind is at its lowest ebb.

When resting it is possible to study the sub of the subconscious mind with ease. The body is relaxed, and the conscious mind has loosened its hold on external objects. When study has commenced, trace through the thought pictures consciously without disturbing the overall picture. Take into consideration the fact that all thought stems from a series of influences within the Ego. These influences take form and shape in thought. When you manifest pictures before you, trace them to their conception by holding the consciousness lightly over the mind, blotting out all distractions that may creep into the mind in an effort to disturb your consciousness. Remember to take your findings, whatever they may be, and consciously think them through until all doubts have been dispelled. You will then find that through your conscious effort the sub of the subconscious has been understood consciously as well as subconsciously. The principle is to keep your mind quiet while you are studying a problem and do not react subconsciously to the study of the problem. Sit back and quietly allow the problem to unfold before your vision.

THE THIRTEENTH APHORISM

Should superconscious expressions be dropped into the subsubconscious, they must first pass through the conscious plane, or be given to the subconscious of the conscious mind by the subsuperconscious mind and from there dropped into the sub of the subconscious mind.

This aphorism is very clear and you will have no trouble separating the superconscious and the subconscious thoughts that have blended in the subsubconscious mind once you have perfected the objective study of the mind. Since we are all victims of the subconscious state of mind, we must keep it in a state of transparency by paying constant attention to this state of mind in our daily meditations.

THE FOURTEENTH APHORISM

The sub of the subconscious mind can, and does, create situations of an uncomely nature.

It is well known that repressions are formed by a series of suppressed desires. When these repressions are released, the emotional unit undergoes a change. It is also well known that all the thoughts placed into the subconscious remain there until they materialize into something definite. Then they will reappear. ¶It is a little bit different with the subsubconscious state of mind, for it not only attracts situations that will bring these thoughts out, but it creates situations by playing upon the subconscious mind itself.

THE FIFTEENTH APHORISM

The subsubconscious mind, through its natural magnetism, attracts so-called temptations and unhappy conditions. The conscious mind, weakened by harmful practices, falls into this self-created trap. There the Ego seemingly suffers between the subconscious thoughts that created the "sub," the Ego's conscious expression, and its subsuperconscious knowing.

Guilt is one of the results of this state, also pride and anguish. These are a few of the qualities resulting from the subsubconscious mind. When the sub is controlled through a deep understanding of its inner workings, the Ego, or consciousness, is free from being bound in identifying itself with the mind, body and emotions. The Ego, or consciousness, can then progress toward the dynamic realization of your real Self—beyond the mind, the mind that is under your control. Otherwise, the Ego is caught in the cross-section between the conscious mind and its subsuperconscious knowing, which results in superstition, ideology, fanaticism and an argumentative nature.

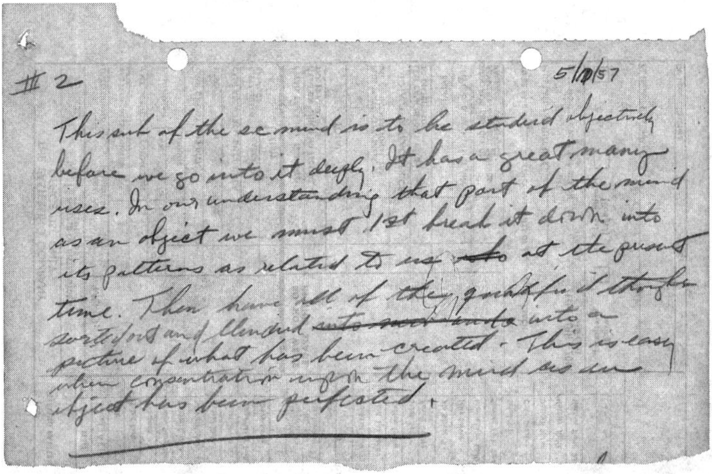
II 2 5/[illegible]/57

This sub of the sc mind is to be studied objectively before we go into it deeply. It has a great many uses. In our understanding that part of the mind as an object we must 1st break it down into its patterns as related to us ~~to~~ at the present time. Then have all of the qualities [illegible] through sorted out and blended ~~into [illegible]~~ into a picture of what has been created. This is easy when concentration upon the mind as an object has been perfected.

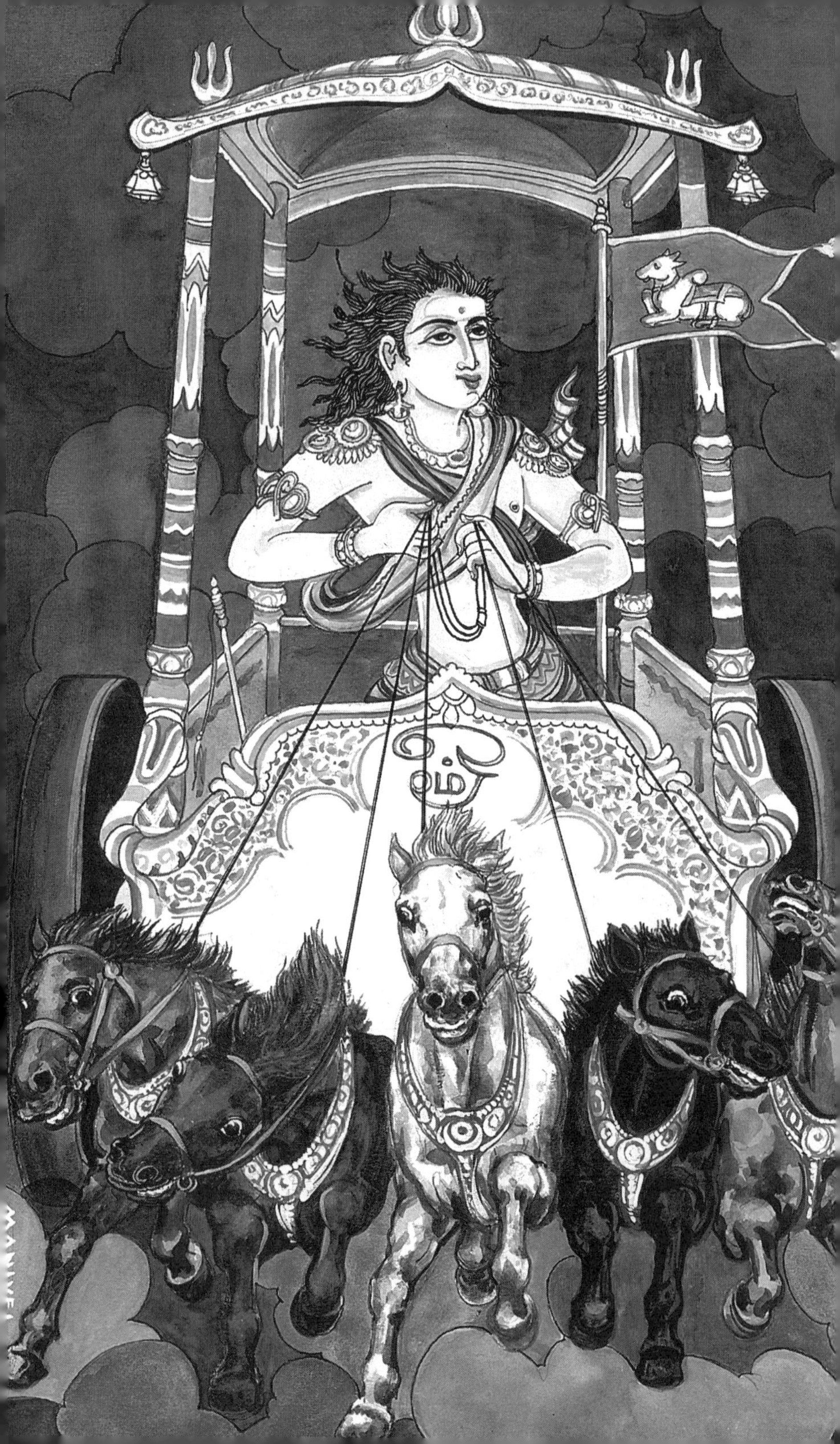

CANTO THREE

Control of Consciousness

THE SIXTEENTH APHORISM

Some reactions are healthy; others are unhealthy. The reaction to a reaction is destructive, whereas the reaction itself, when viewed with a balanced mind, eventually becomes an asset.

Reaction is what makes the world go round. It is the driving force which makes it possible for us to continue living and creating in our subconscious search for the inner being, our craving to bring forth our latent forces to the conscious plane. ¶Reactions are twofold: a reaction to a reaction; or just a normal reaction to something we do, or do not, understand. This is why a strong foundation must be established in organized thought before we dive deeper into the mind to conquer reaction. This takes only a little study to accomplish. ¶When you react to a situation, don't re-enact it or go over it in your mind again after it has happened. Wait until the emotional nature has completely composed itself. Then take apart the reaction, little by little—being sure you do not upset yourself again—and find out its basic cause. Only then can you come to terms with yourself and arrange a working agreement with your own mind. ¶Handling your mind in this way takes discipline; it is one of the first steps in concentration. If you cannot think the reaction through and arrive at the cause, make a problem of it on paper. Write down everything that comes into your mind about the reaction until it has been assimilated. In this way you turn every reaction into an asset. Doing that will add wisdom, color and vitality to your life.

THE SEVENTEENTH APHORISM

The conscious mind creates the future by what has gone before, through its subconscious. Should memory be weakened, due to abusive practices, its creations are distorted.

This creation is sometimes distorted when the faculty of memory has been weakened due to improper diet or lack of sexual controls. The inability to come to terms with oneself often makes one dull and somewhat blank. Then the subconscious mind receives a distorted, unqualified impression. When the impression is ready to be qualified, it comes out in the outside world as an experience uncomprehendible to the conscious mind. ¶It is of the utmost importance that the body be kept strong and healthy, that the vital fluids be conserved, that the memory gain conscious and subconscious control over every situation, and that the subconscious receive impressions fully qualified and well organized. ¶The future is created by the impressions we have put into the subconscious in the past and those impressions we are placing there continually in the present. The future is the continuing summation of all our past actions and reactions, for there is only the moment in which we live. The eternal now is the only consciousness we have when living in the higher states of mind. A concept of this must begin working through your conscious and subconscious mind so that the subconscious will be well schooled when the intuitive nature awakens and you realize that there is no time, no past, no future—only the eternal now, which is a total of all the mind contains.

THE EIGHTEENTH APHORISM

When the conscious mind relies on its subconscious states to master the problem, having logically placed the problem before them, the result: no concern. Concern is a muddled understanding of the subconscious states of mind, filled with unreasonable doubts from the conscious mind.

The conscious mind has an intriguing way of holding up the progress of its subconscious. This is the result of mass thinking, fear, worry, doubt, lack of faith in oneself, and more than all, a lack of understanding of the workings of the mind. The conscious mind never lets the subconscious rest. It is always placing demands upon it. That is all right, because that is what the subconscious is for, but the demands must be placed in the right way. ¶It is impossible for the subconscious to handle two opposing thoughts at the same time. For instance, one thinks, "I shall do this if I can." Those are two opposite vibrations, and the poor subconscious doesn't know what to do. It should be impressed in a definite manner, for instance, with a statement, "I will do this," or "I can't do it." This is the only way you can keep your mind free from opposing thoughts. This is the beginning of thought control, and thought control is the greatest asset you can possibly have. ¶Concern is a state of mind caused by what I have just explained. It is really unnecessary, and an extra feeling that you can very well do without. To be free from concern is to have the power over your subconscious mind through the proper presentation of your thoughts. When impressing your subconscious, suppressed thoughts lurk in the subconscious, ready to spring out at a moment's notice, which if permitted, consume the entire mind. To avoid this, quiet the body, emotions and mind before giving a command to the subconscious mind.

THE NINETEENTH APHORISM

True happiness can never be found in the conscious mind or its subconscious states.

Happiness is not the first sign of awakening. It is only the first sign of a realization that there is something beyond the conscious and subconscious phases of the mind. When you think you are ready for a spiritual awakening, you have only realized that the awakening has already taken place in the subsuperconscious mind. It has not yet been able to manifest itself in the realms of the conscious and subconscious mind, because they are too possessed with material things and thoughts. It is impossible for your awakening to penetrate. So you live in the realm of desire, striving and hoping that the grace of God will descend upon you. ¶Instead, you must only wake up and release your mind from all worldly thoughts, feelings and desires long enough to unfold what is already within your subsuperconscious state of mind, locked up and waiting to be expressed. To do this, concentration is needed. Concentration brings light, or understanding, by holding the mind to one point. Then all material thoughts, feelings and desires fall away for the time and you are allowed to receive your rightful unfoldment. ¶This is not as hard as it seems. It does not require you to renounce the world. It only requires you to make an effort every day to concentrate the mind by first quieting the physical body and then the mind to free itself from all the thoughts of the day. Then hold the mind on one thing that is attractive to you for as long as you can. When it wanders, pull it back until the light of understanding begins to appear. You will be amazed at the results in a very short time. True happiness will then be yours, released from the subsuperconscious state of your own mind.

THE TWENTIETH APHORISM

The seed of desire is a false concept in relation to corresponding objects. The conscious mind throws into its subconscious a series of erroneous thoughts based upon a false concept. This creates a deep-rooted desire or complex. Single out the seed of desire by disregarding all other corresponding erroneous thoughts. Then destroy that seed through understanding its relation in itself and to all other corresponding thoughts. The deep-rooted desire or complex will then vanish.

All your conflicts in life are caused in this way. In tracing each major conflict back through the power of concentration, of which we shall learn more later, all seeds are gradually and systematically destroyed, giving you an intense release and a burst of light from within. ¶Get off to a good start now and congratulate yourself on the fact that you have at last found the key to remove all your suppressions, repressions, unqualified feelings and unfulfilled desires through the application of right thought. Concentration digs up the seed in this manner and brings it before the mind as a fact, not as an elusive remnant of fiction. ¶Call upon your inner intelligence to help you and guide your unfoldment from within. Show to your own mind the seed of desire, which may be far divorced form the desire itself. It may be so far removed you will wonder how it was ever connected and was able to create the desire in the first place. In this wondering, you begin the birth pains of understanding, and when the birth is complete through qualified thinking, the seed will vanish and the desire will resolve itself into the halls of memory. ¶Your major desires should be qualified first, then you can tackle the subtle ones. This law can be a tremendous help to you on your path of enlightenment, for the world is a place in which we learn. Therefore, all things of which we lack understanding represent a challenge to us, to qualify and resolve in our own consciousness.

THE APHORISMS THAT YOU HAVE JUST READ ARE SEEMINGLY UNRELATED, YET THERE IS A FINE CORD CONNECTING THEM. THEY MUST BE DIgested and then re-read for you to find this cord and follow it as it leads you deep into your own mind, freeing you from its bonds. We are free from what we understand, for it holds no mystery for us, no novelty, and is no longer intriguing.

There is a greater experience before you, beyond the mind which is yours to control, like the body and emotions which are yours to use as is your will. Even the will is yours to use in abundant or diminished amounts. Therefore, the real you is the consciousness deep within, above and around your tools for creative expression—namely, body, mind, emotions and will. In this consciousness of being ever conscious of being conscious, you must learn to live and from there radiate out from within the dynamic depths of your real Self.

You will experience the power to watch your conscious mind at work, for as pointed out previously, the conscious mind is but one-tenth of the whole mind, and as you progress on this journey of self-mastery, you will begin to learn about the subconscious mind, and how to use it and how it uses, helps or hinders you. The superconscious mind will become personified before you and will unfold its steady rays of all-seeing enlightenment through your subconscious, and directly through your conscious mind. You will learn to have inspiration at will, and to inspire others and to awaken and bring forth from them their inspiration and latent creative abilities.

Through the power of concentration, which will come easy to you when the body, mind and the emotions are dominated with your will, the doors to the subsuperconscious mind will swing wide, and you will view with interest findings that will remake your entire nature. As you progress with your study of self mastery, the importance of the transmutation of the creative forces will become apparent to you subconsciously as well as consciously, the complete knowledge of their uses and abuses and the advantages of their transmutation into higher forms of creative expression.

Take this section now and turn back the pages and reread with renewed interest the aphorisms and their explanations impressing each on your subconscious mind so that upon the third reading your superconscious intuition can give you an even deeper realization than is possible to transcribe through the means of writing. Then proceed and study Section Two of "Cognizantability," in which you will find the basic laws of transmutation.

Antaraṇasya Mūlavidhayaḥ

अन्तरणस्य मूलविधयः

Section Two

The Basic Laws of Transmutation

A VERY INTERESTING QUESTION COMES TO ALL OF US FROM TIME TO TIME, THAT IS: "WHY ARE WE WHAT WE ARE? WHY DO WE REACT as we do," etc? In the pages that follow, I elucidate the mind and give a few of the esoteric laws for the transmutation of the creative energy. It is very interesting to note that very little is known publicly and taught in schools regarding the transmutation of the sex force. Modern psychologists often speak of "sublimation," which is, of course, a step in the right direction towards transmutation, which elucidates your so-called problems to you, and your subconscious understanding of those problems does the same for others.

I would suggest that in reading the following laws of the mind that you concentrate on only one at a time until its meaning is made clear to you. This, as you may now think, will not be unduly difficult. In handling your study of "Cognizantability" in this manner, you will have great pleasure in the conscious elucidation of your own mind, which will, of course, lead to the subconscious transmutation of your creative energy, thus unfolding latent superconscious powers of which writers write, poets praise and saints pray for.

To give you an illustration of how your study will progress, I should like to give the finding of one of my students who found that concentration on any given thing for a length of time, as does prayer, calms the conscious mind, which is generally in a semi-confused state, when not entirely so. When this conscious state of mind is, to a certain extent, under your conscious control—and more so after you continue in this work—your subconscious mind, which never rests or sleeps, consciously takes hold of the situation concentrated upon and with the aid of the superconscious mind works out the thing concentrated upon. This appears perhaps to be rather a complex state of affairs. I can only suggest this: that if you don't thoroughly grasp it the first time, read it again. If not then, read it a third time, and by that time your superconscious mind will have had a chance to make the first reading of the data clear to your conscious mind. This sounds logical, doesn't it? You have only to try it to find that it works.

In these materialistic days of our modern civilization it is quite necessary for the layman to understand the laws of the mind in order to cope with the fast-moving world about him. Of course, psychologically we know that one of man's basic desires, whether he knows it or not, is to know himself.

The story of the transmutation of the creative forces is likened unto the boiling of water into steam to give a greater power. When we refer to transmutation, we do not mean to suppress, repress or inhibit; it is a natural law in the unfoldment of the spiritual being of man and should be understood as such. As man leaves his instinctive nature and unfolds spiritually, the forces of that nature must be brought under his conscious control. Much work in this direction is done under the guidance of the disciple's spiritual teacher, but the basic desire must be manifest in the disciple himself. The following laws give a brief summary of the basic psychology behind the unfoldment of the inner being, namely the transmutation process.

Sex plays an almost unduly time-consuming part in our lives today. It has been advertised, boasted about, displayed and enjoyed throughout the world. This treatise brings a new angle to sex that is as old as time, yet comparatively new to this century. The transmutation of the creative forces given here is the key to youth, happiness and creative living. Sex has been a problem to many, though a natural function in life. It plays a most important part in the unfoldment of one's inner nature to the realization of your real Self. Let your mind begin to intuit the sound fundamentals of an expanding consciousness backed by the creative forces of life itself.

The following aphorisms are the results of findings that have been lived rather than thought up. These are to be looked at intelligently, with an open mind, and to be put into practice as soon as understood. Taking into consideration the fact that this study is comparatively new, it has been advisable to tell in detail all the all about the mind and the body as it corresponds to the emotional and sexual nature. You will find your mind going along with these down-to-earth facts as you read this treatise. Looking into your own life, you find that you and you alone are responsible for your shortcomings and your successes. You have no one to praise but yourself, and no one to blame, for all is your own creation and your self-created universe; everything you placed into action you have reacted, enacted and reaped results. Take, for example, how you lived when you were a child, how free you were. Then, as you started to mature, society suppressed you, and through a series of these suppressions, a repression was formed deep within the subconscious mind, and the body changed as a result. Following the repression came desires that were completely unqualified. These desires shaped themselves into many forms: first in the form of sexual urges; second in the form of indulgences that were not in the least related to sex, but relieved the emotional nature enough so as to ease the pain of the repression that was beginning to burst loose. Sometimes it does break loose, creating havoc in one's life, but more often it remains tempered by enjoying releases through unrelated fields.

Read the aphorisms with an open mind. Do not try to understand them, agree or disagree with your findings until the second reading. Then your own nature will begin to give you clues as to how this wisdom relates to you; and you alone can apply it to your life, so that an abundance of creative power can be released within you through the transmutation of your sex energies.

CANTO FOUR

The Sexual Energies

THE TWENTY-FIRST APHORISM

Balance comes from understanding the effect of the emotional body upon the physical, and the physical body upon the emotional.

Balance as described here is related to the conscious and subconscious mind. It is a subsuperconscious feeling—which is true understanding bred of qualified thinking, seasoned with intuition—of balance between the physical body and the emotions. This only comes when the mind is tempered with enough creative power so that the will can dominate the emotions long enough to produce a subconscious knowing, which comes when the creative forces have been utilized in their higher forms by the will.

THE TWENTY-SECOND APHORISM

The conscious release of the creative forces through lower channels tends to slow down the physical and mental bodies leading to a conscious sleep. When carried to excess, this leads to their ultimate destruction.

All of the energy of the body becomes directed in the channel of sex when the consciousness coupled with the will to release or dissipate this energy is coordinated. The mentality then becomes slow and sluggish, as does the body, if carried to excess. A remedy to this is the reverse, and the mind will then become more awake than ever, as does the body.

THE TWENTY-THIRD APHORISM

Transmutation must be attained and maintained to build up a so-called bank account in the subconscious of the conscious mind, so that the desires, feelings and tendencies of the sub-subconscious can be automatically handled in the purification process.

The meaning of *transmutation* as used in this treatise is to transform, to change from a so-called gross form to a subtle form. This force that you possess is of the greatest value, and in its qualified, conscious control, without suppression, you can build a great reserve of power within your subconscious mind and the subtle forces of the body, so that when you begin the deeper studies of your consciousness, consciously cognizing your mind, this reserve force will lend itself in giving you stability, concentration and power to break through the thin veil that leads us to identify ourselves with that which we have created.

THE TWENTY-FOURTH APHORISM

Sublimation is the working of the sex energies either mentally (on the conscious/intellectual plane) or through physical exercise. Transmutation is the permanent change of one form to another.

To sublimate the sexual energies, regular habit patterns, physical exercise, intellectual development and the deliberate control over the lower emotions must happen before true transmutation, which is changing the form of gross energies into refined energies, or lifting the gross *prāṇas* from the lower *chakras* into the higher *chakras*. A moment of anger, misunderstanding (nonacceptance of the law of *karma*, a moment of forgetfulness), could plummet the higher energies into the lower *chakras* below the *mūlādhāra*, stopping the transmutation process. The sublimation of the vital forces is called *sādhana* in the Hindu vernacular.

THE TWENTY-FIFTH APHORISM

To consciously understand the functions of the physical body as against an educated subconscious knowing of the emotional unit, coupled with a subsuperconscious cognition of the mind as an object, is the secret of transmutation, the essence of *rāja yoga.*

The aphorism explains itself in the clearest terms. It may have to be thought over to become fully qualified in your subconscious. The word *yoga* mentioned herein is the Hindu word meaning "to yoke," to join two objects together, namely the conscious and the superconscious mind, creating a vacuum so that the consciousness can expand beyond the mind. This is attained through transmutation.

THE TWENTY-SIXTH APHORISM

The creative or sex energy, with its desires resulting in passions, must first be regulated, then consciously totally suppressed. The faculties of thinking will then be stimulated enough to consciously understand its causes and effects. This develops willpower, leading the Ego from concentration into meditation, then to contemplation. After this, the passionate nature can be controlled and will be depolarized. The mind and physique will have undergone a change. Then, only then, will transmutation commence.

Here again we have an aphorism that is self-explanatory, but for the fact that when you begin to transmute your energies, you will have to begin by putting your mind at ease, so that the mind will not be at cross purposes with itself, torn between the desire to disagree out of habit and the desire to transmute born from unqualified intellect. ¶Before transmutation really gets under way, we must suppress the sexual nature enough so that the "old habit mind" lets us freely begin to understand all our repressions, desires and feelings in regard to sex. After thus suppressing, understanding takes the place of repression. The vibrations of the body become refined, the subsuperconscious mind consciously works through the subconscious, and it becomes easy to transmute the creative forces without suppression and use them through higher channels. Those who practice transmutation awaken many latent talents from within, artistically and otherwise. It becomes easy for them to create and express themselves, as they are automatically in tune with the essence of creative energy.

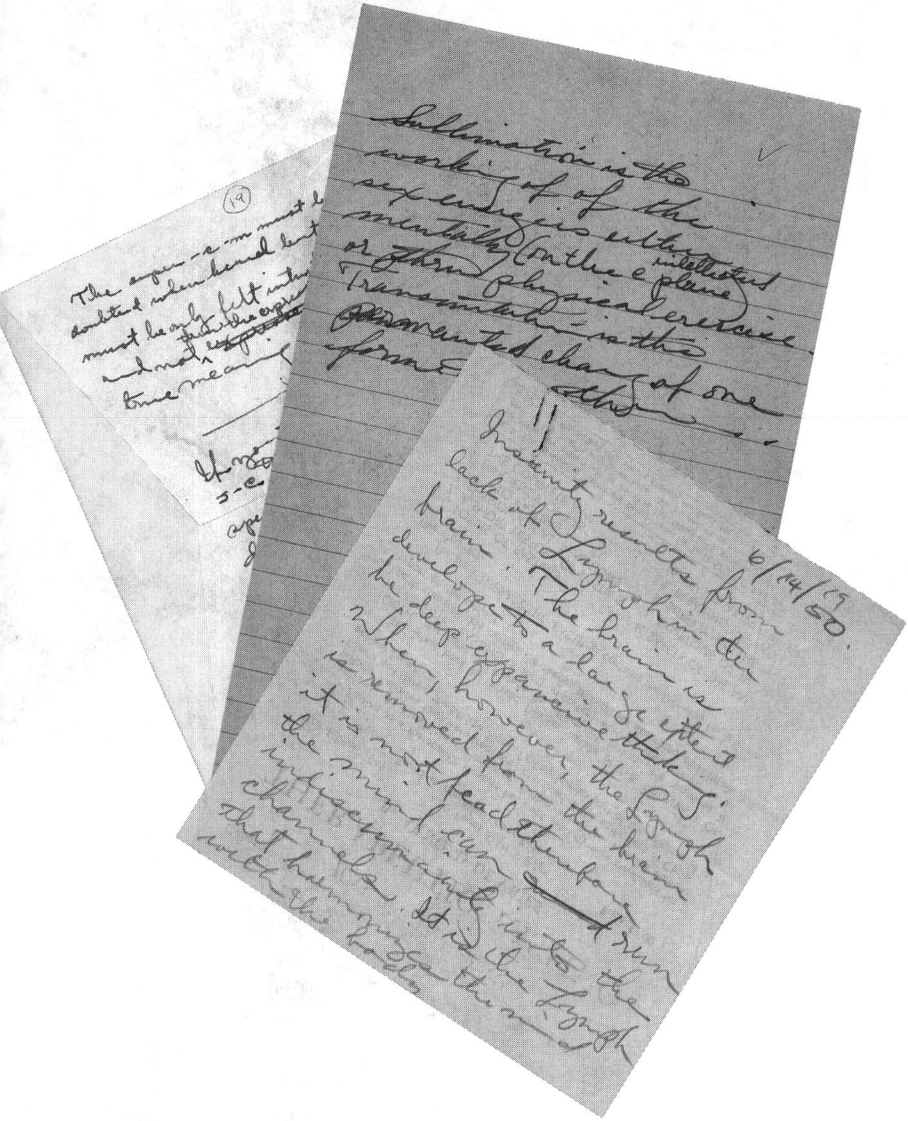

Sublimation is the working of of the sex energies either mentally (on the intellectual plane) or through physical exercise. Transmutation is the permanented change of one form ... other ...

11

6/14/50.

Insanity results from lack of Lymph in the brain. The brain is developed to a large extent by deep expensive thinking. When, however, the Lymph is removed from the brain it is not fed therefore, and run the mind can ... indiscriminately into the channels. It is the Lymph that harmonizes the mind with the body.

CANTO FIVE

Control of Speech

THE TWENTY-SEVENTH APHORISM

When transmutation of the intellect is observed—which is bringing the superconscious through the subconscious, consciously—subconscious transmutation is well on its way. This is not the end. This is only the beginning!

Before the actual transmutation of the sexual fluid becomes conscious, the subconscious mind must be thoroughly schooled in the laws of transmutation—schooled by the inner knowing born from the superconscious mind. For this, a qualified teacher is needed. The *guru*, the dispeller of darkness, gives the keys when the pupil is ready to unlock the final doors to his unfoldment. However, after the pupil has done his part, he will always meet his spiritual teacher. For each step that the sincere disciple takes toward his spiritual teacher, his spiritual teacher takes nine steps toward him.

THE TWENTY-EIGHTH APHORISM

The use and abuse of the sexual nature causes physical and emotional upheavals. Speaking without due consideration and discrimination causes intellectual and psychic upheavals. Therefore, the control of speech is the second step in the transmutation of the creative forces.

Speech is the second step in the transmutation process. To speak is to create, as to think is to create. Both go hand in hand. As a child is to man and woman, so is word to thought. Hence the control of the mind and tongue is of the greatest importance in the transmutation process.

THE TWENTY-NINTH APHORISM

Excessive talk overloads the subconscious mind, thus making it extremely difficult for the superconscious to express itself.

You know what it is to have a basement full of things you have no use for. This basement may easily be compared to your subconscious mind. Thoughts and words can be compared to things. In your basement you have a furnace that supplies heat to the entire house. Your furnace can be compared to your superconscious mind. If your basement is too congested, you may not be able to get to the furnace to light it and heat your home. So it is within the storehouse of your subconscious. Silence lends itself to understanding. It allows you to perceive, then cognize, for is it not true that we talk excessively in our effort to understand what we are talking about?

THE THIRTIETH APHORISM

Observation is the first faculty of the awakening of the superconscious regions. This observation is cultivated by abstinence from excessive talk.

This aphorism is self-explanatory, for we can plainly see that—in recognizing the fact that we have created our surroundings, and everything that happens to us, by our thoughts and desires of the past—it takes the observation of our creations to bring us to the point where we can reconcile them with the thoughts and desires that created them.

THE THIRTY-FIRST APHORISM

Continuous observation will become paramount through the conscious mind when transmutation is practiced. With the control of the speech, the forces will continue to be transmuted.

Observation brings us close to seeing forms as they are in relation to other objects. In this I am suggesting the mind and thought as form or objects. When observation is practiced, we lend our lower nature willingly to the great all-knowing superconscious mind and blend our Ego into the essence of time and space, thus bringing forth understanding beyond the realms of reason. Continued observation unfolds perceptive meditation upon what we observe, and perception unfolds the power to cognize. Cognition is the result of perfect subconscious concentration.

THE THIRTY-SECOND APHORISM

Transmutation brings the superconscious mind close to the conscious plane through the subconscious of the conscious mind. Then a conscious understanding of the subconscious mind as a unit is acquired.

All the forces of the body having been centered within, without suppression, allows the real self of man to unfold from within freely. When time stops, and space is no more, the consciousness comes into focus. Then the being comprehends the secrets behind the laws of transmutation of the creative forces into their highest forms of expression.

THE THIRTY-THIRD APHORISM

The final goal of transmutation is to actually have the creative cells ever reproducing, consciously absorbed by the blood stream. They then feed the brain and stimulate the mind. This results in a consciously conscious comprehension of the function of every current in the body as well as every thought wave, their actions and reactions. When this occurs as a physical process coupled with well-qualified understanding, your results will be unshakable and real.

There is not too much I can add here except that when the fluids are transmuted, it gives added food and energy to the physical body as well as stability to the emotional body. Through the transmutation process you will be able to control the emotional body, understand it and use it freely as a vehicle to work out the effects of past causes. ¶When the realization of the Self, *samādhi*, is experienced, all the teachings herein will be clearly understood. The consciousness will reside in the inner being, which knows nothing of the instinctive and intellectual natures, yet it cognizes all form. You will have that peace which surpasses all understanding and be able to look within and without simultaneously. The grand fulfillment of this incarnation awaits your command over your instinctive and intellectual natures.

Our men and women of the New Age, which is just dawning on this Earth, will understand the laws of truth written between the lines of this treatise as if they had always known them. They will lend their life willingly to the awakening of their Inner Self into the realization of their true Self, from whatever faith or creed they may be found. For Truth as it is knows no creed, knows no reason, knows no person. It is only known by the knower, and the laws given him in these few pages are designed to bring forth knowers—those who know that they know, not from intellectually remembering the words of others and re-creating them as their own, but from their own experience. Give yourself the benefit of believing in yourself as a great and wonderful object of creation, with the power to create, and let these teachings unfold within you as a bud unfolds into a flower.

"The Body and Transmutation"
Book II.
4/16/1950.

For Healing:

The sub-super-conscious mind works upon the subconscious of the conscious, however, full physical expression will not be the result as the "sub" of the subconscious will lock the inhibition or physical defect—until this "~~sub~~ creation" is released no healing can result.

Sākshiyātrā

साक्षियात्रा

Section Three

Journey of Awareness

THE FOLLOWING APHORISMS WERE BROUGHT TO THE CONSCIOUS PLANE AT THE SAME TIME AS THE APHORISMS IN SECTIONS ONE AND TWO but were never published until now, forty years after their revelation from the inner sky. It was in the winter of 1989 that I brought them forth from our archives and dictated commentaries. They are now made available to you on the vibration which you have helped create, that of the dawning New Age as the Kali Yuga's darkness wanes into the faint light of the dawn of the Sat Yuga.

Many marvelous unfoldments await you within these pages. Take each aphorism separately, think about it, concentrate on it, put it in the subconscious mind so the deeper understanding of it will unfold from within you. You, too, are a superconscious being. To acknowledge this is to invite its happening.

We know too little and too much at the same time. Yes, we all do, and this is the big problem with a capital B. This can be solved through drawing upon latent intelligence, as I did. My higher mind was the teacher of my lower mind. Was this an easy thing to accomplish? No, it was not. But all learning takes patience, takes times, takes dedication and, most importantly, takes the undivided interest of the student. In my case the teacher and the student were one and the same person. How do you figure this? Well, perhaps in this next section of "Cognizantability"—the ability to cognize, or to look deep into and understand—more insights will come to you so that you, too, will be able to unfold latent knowledge you did not know that you knew. Read on and enjoy the wonderful you inside of you recognizing these truths.

CANTO SIX

Perceptions on Understanding Ego

THE THIRTY-FOURTH APHORISM

The subconscious mind is externally portrayed in the world of form. Through so-called past incarnations, the subconscious mind has been created. To be unable to control what has been created in the external world, therefore, is due to insufficient transmutation of intellectual forces. Continued practice of concentration and meditation is the remedy here.

This aphorism speaks of the *prārabdha karmas* that manifest first in the subconscious mind through the subsuperconscious mind. It is in the subsuperconscious mind that they are carried from life to life. Once they become alive within the subconscious, they manifest themselves in one's life through other people in incidences. This is why a mystical person will ignore situations and even people, because they do not want to become a victim or a channel or a tool of another. A mystical person protects himself against that contingency, and thus avoids, or ignores, situations or people. So, as the *prārabdha karmas* manifest themselves through the subconscious mind from the subsuperconscious (they are lodged in the subsuperconscious), when they begin to sprout, they sprout through the subconscious and finally manifest in the conscious mind, generally through other people or group situations. ¶In this aphorism, "so-called incarnations" means that they are not regarded as past. They are ever-present in the current lifetime. We see them as past only in that we know that we did not manifest the particular *karma* or experiential pattern in this particular lifetime, so obviously it had to be another lifetime.

THE THIRTY-FIFTH APHORISM

The conscious mind is a cross-section between the instinctive and intellectual aspects. It is the point of balance between the real and the unreal, and hence the statement: "Lead us from the unreal to the real, from darkness to light, from death to immortality."

The conscious mind is the balancing agent of consciousness between the external and the internal. It has the power of the objective and subjective thinking, as well as observation, memory, reason, and therefore it, meaning the conscious mind, must be kept healthy, like the physical body. This is why right thought, right speech, right action, and the means of right action—*yamas* and *niyamas*—must be learned as a balancing agent. Further aphorisms state that the conscious mind when over-extended in externalities, into wrong speech, wrong thought and wrong action becomes insanity in its natural state. The conscious mind is the balance point between the unreal and the real. It is like a mirror, a two-way mirror. In and of itself it's almost nonexistent, yet it is the consciousness between the physical universe and the nonphysical universe. A two-way mirror is a mirror in which spectators on one side see through and those on the other side only see the mirror.

THE THIRTY-SIXTH APHORISM

When you have an egregious nature or uncomfortable feeling, it is only the cross-section between the superconscious mind and the conscious mind, because the conscious mind does not want to accept or does not want to believe what it formerly has been led to believe. But the superconscious mind lays down the law to the conscious mind from what has gone before, which will repeat in the future from little things you have observed, which will be magnified.

ability to ignore its own faults and to cover up the subconscious mind itself. People often know their base nature, be it greed or avarice. They are aware of their fears, worries and doubts, but would never admit them to anyone. The external mind, which we call the conscious mind, has the inbred deceitful ability to shield these very faults from one's own self. This goes on and on and on until the superconsciousness within manages to create a conscience in the individual. The conscience monitors the interrelated activities of the conscious and subconscious mind.

THE THIRTY-SEVENTH APHORISM

Nonreaction—one must look behind the situation. For instance, the cause is far different than the effect, and when the cause is known, the situation can be duly handled and mastered, for there will be no reaction to it.

In a state of meditation it is possible to view the mind as a series of experiences, reactions and seeds to new experiences that may be planted or destroyed at the hand of the observing Ego in this state of meditation. ¶Experience involves more than one conscious and subconscious state of mind; it encompasses many. Many can be helped or hurt by a sense experience held in the mind of one individual. Reactions are lifted through understanding, and understanding gives the wisdom of avoidance of future experiences of like nature. Understanding does not, however, conquer the subsubconscious minds of "others" involved in the same experience or happening or touched by it. Hence, "crumbs" of reaction still linger in the subsubconscious mind only to retrace through memory the experience from time to time; a lingering shadow hangs over the part of the mind left injured when it should have been healed into education. ¶How does this last healing process take place? Easy, though most difficult to the unawakened. Each experience of the past involuntarily remembered must be traced into the subconscious mind of one still reacting to the same experience and, while thus meditating in his subconscious, realize it as experience there. In other words, become conscious of your soul, or become superconscious in the subconscious mind of all those, one after another, who associated with you as you transgressed through an experience while you, too, were in lower states of mind, and you will calm the waves of worry into the calm of wisdom, not only for yourself but for all those *karmically* connected to you, associated by reaction through the years. ¶This can be done with the living or the so-called dead, for those in a reincarnated state have still two reactions, parts of which you carry and can be cleared by you. So, this is an important part of the play in the lower states of mind and can be mastered by one initiated into *rāja yoga*, stable in meditation and pure in heart. ¶This is the mystical life, the basis for soothsaying, fortune-telling, psychometry, psychology, crystal-gazing, astrology, numerology and more. The situation herein discussed means the collective *karmas* of one or more people in relation to oneself. When the *karmas* manifest, we see the effect of previous *karmas*. We do not want to psychoanalyze our subconscious mind as to how we had created this situation, or the subconscious cause for it, because the cause is not known within the subconscious mind. The cause occurred with the collective group in a past life. When the cause is intuited, emotions quiet, and the effects can be handled rationally and without emotion. Causes of these kinds of *karmic* situations when intuited are not always known, because the intuition does not always channel its knowledge through the thinking mind. But when the premonition, or the intuition is felt to be correct, the external mind and emotions will stop reacting to the situation because the cause is intuitively known. The intuition, which is the soul's mind, will give direct cognition as to how to quickly handle and dispatch the matter.

THE THIRTY-EIGHTH APHORISM

When forces are generated by karmic links, they, passing through the physical body, change any animate or inanimate object directly contacting that form. The physical body becomes a sensitive transmitter of forces, either positive or negative—reacting to neither when the mind taps superconscious regions.

The *karmic* link is what draws and holds two or more people together. It is created by their actions toward each other in past lives carried over as their *prārabdha karmas* in this life. Through that link, forces pass. These forces are energy, or *prāṇa.* They pass through the physical body, changing animate and inanimate objects. Remember, they, these forces, are set in motion in past lives. They can turn a building into a pleasant home, or the same building into a chaotic place, depending on the *karmas* involved. The physical body, the sensitive transmitter of these *karmic/prāṇic* forces, can be invigorated by them or become diseased. Forbearance is the answer here for overactive positive conditions or unbearable negative conditions. Forbearance is lifting one's awareness into the superconscious regions above the pairs of opposites. Only here will some rest be experienced. This is why compatibility in marriage and business relationships should be scrupulously observed, because there are *karmas* that can be avoided through one of the two kinds of wisdom, the wise and the otherwise.

THE THIRTY-NINTH APHORISM

Hypnosis tends to weaken the conscious mind of the victim, depleting the willpower through the subconscious mind. *Self-hypnosis,* a term widely used in Western thought, is a positive state when brought about naturally, without previous conditioning through hypnotic therapy, likened to meditation, of merely "cutting off" the conscious mind to view subconscious states through the subsuperconscious mind.

It has always been the dedicated aim of the Nandinātha Sampradāya's teaching and training to create an individual capable of and able to stand on his own two feet, loyal to his God, Gods and *guru* and the society in which he lives, but incapable of being influenced by anything or anyone other than his own superconsciousness, intuiting the direction of knowledge from God, Gods and *guru.* Jñānaguru Śiva Yogaswāmī always spoke of his inner orders, but they did not conflict with his service to community, relationship with other *gurus* and *swāmīs,* but rather enhanced that service. This mid-century European-derived dominance of one mind over another, which could be called hierarchical ignorance, breeds weakness, dependency in the individuals. Therefore, hypnosis, prying into another's life—while the subject, lying on his back like an animal in submission, with its four legs up—benefits the gathering of knowledge by the hypnotist rather than the patient, known here as "the victim." ¶True, society is built on the rule of the stronger minds over weaker minds. Even our *Holy Kural* states that if a country cannot control its people, it is the duty of the neighboring larger country to intervene. Mothers and fathers control their children. Employers control, guide, employees. In principle, the kings, the lawmakers, the counsels control the population to guide them to a better life. But the big question is, do they drug them, do they hypnotize them to effect this control? No, it is normally done quite openly. Everyone concerned is totally conscious. Free will abides. Whereas, in hypnotism, the hypnotist comes between the individual and God and the Gods. He is victimizing and playing God to an unsuspecting, not-totally-conscious subject. This, in turn, creates a subconscious pattern for the victim, to be subconsciously open, naively subconsciously open and vulnerable, to respond to suggestions by stronger minds, whoever they might be, in the future. His discriminating faculties no longer exist because of the hypnotic experiences. Self-hypnosis is quite a different matter.

THE FORTIETH APHORISM

Reactions from strong stimulants will release some minds from inhibitions. However, as they throw the mind into unnatural states, to others they may prove unnatural in themselves, as their seeds are pleasure.

Stimulants such as coffee, tea and alcohol release the subconscious and subsuperconscious states of mind within the individual. Diaphragmatic breathing, *yoga* practice, performs the same function if performed under proper conditions. One should be wary of releasing the conscious mind through stimulants of any kind. If the subconscious is overburdened, it may not produce positive results. This is because the external mind, which we call the conscious mind, acting like a barrier, protects one from himself. Some things are better forgotten than to again be revealed. However, if the subconscious is clear, these same strong stimulants can put to rest the conscious mind, and great subsuperconscious and superconscious revelations can be unfolded.

THE FORTY-FIRST APHORISM

When deep in the study of philosophy, should the consciousness make a sudden jump to external lines of thought, apparent superstition may result. As cycles repeat themselves, this too will pass away.

Superstition is a mixture of belief and doubt. When a belief has been corrupted by a reasonable doubt, consciousness is lowered into the *chakra* of fear. Therefore, it is very important to open and close a philosophical session, *saṅga* discussion or even some casual discussion with a beginning and ending blessing, preferably in Sanskṛit, to seal the happening and its outcome within the inner mind. In such discussions, new knowledge often comes from the superconscious for a new way of looking at and understanding a philosophical precept. It would take much time to prove the theories and mold them into the subconscious mind. Should this new information go into the subconscious mind abruptly, it may conflict with something that is already there, and all people are in fear of abrupt change. Fear and misunderstood concepts and phenomena make up what we call superstition. Superstition is hazardous and impedes the powers that amplify spiritual unfoldment on the path.

THE FORTY-SECOND APHORISM

Reason from the conscious mind, with the subconscious desire that the end in view will ratify some instinctive or mental craving, leads to destruction.

Often we can talk ourselves into many things which normally we would not be inclined to actually give ourselves permission to do. But the powers of self-gratification, the mental and physical cravings eager to be fulfilled, lead us to formulating plans based on questionable spiritual principles calculated to fulfill these desires. The self-destruction mentioned here is obviously the destruction of the spiritual nature, for the deviation from the path of *dharma* builds the lower nature. Personal, selfish gratifications are one of the gardens of discovery, an unending maze, a side-path off the path of San Mārga. ¶We must remember that reason is only a tool; when guided by the instinctive forces, it can have complicated results. When guided by the subsuperconscious forces, either from within one's own awakened mind or that of another, it is life-giving and also has beneficial results. Therefore, we must be well aware of what we talk ourselves into through reason.

THE FORTY-THIRD APHORISM

A line of reason from the conscious mind, placed before one living in superconscious states, will not be in harmony with the latter. When the same data is placed on the subsuperconscious mind of the former at a later time, it will intuitively be presented in a harmonious fashion, agreeable to the latter.

Those *gurus* living within the subsuperconscious area of the mind all of the time are beyond reason, not swayed by reason, when it comes from the reasoning mind. All reason, and the outcome of reasoning, must be placed at the Feet of the Deity, Lord Śiva, to ascertain the real motive of the desired outcome, be it instinctive gratification, intellectual ratification, or fulfillment for all. Unselfish gratification is acceptable to God and the Gods. Therefore, if the reasoning is from the purified intellect, the unselfish outcome will be listened to, absorbed and accepted and amplified by those beings living in the subsuperconscious state. We must be careful of what we say to the wise, lest we be deemed a fool, no matter how eloquently we present the arguments.

THE FORTY-FOURTH APHORISM

To be controlled by *karma* is to be governed by the instinctive planes of being. To control *karma* is to transmute the energies; this *karma* will then not willfully be controlled, but will be understood and not reacted to.

Those who think themselves controlled by *karma* are living in the instinctive plane. To control and understand this *karma*, nonreaction must be mastered through mind control. ¶Here we explain these *asuric chakras* below the *mūlādhāra.* Those living in the Narakaloka dualize themselves victim to anything that happens to them in their confused state. They struggle for help, and then anger at those who endeavor to help them. *Karma* is and remains in ignorance to these souls until they effect some personal controls over their lives and sexual energies. This is called *sādhana.* Those who perform *sādhana* slowly lift themselves into the *mūlādhāra chakra* through purifying thought, awakening compassion, which quells anger, awakening personal spiritual security, which quells jealousy, gaining philosophical confidence in the rightness of the universe, which quells fear. All this produces nonreaction. They and they alone are taught the mysteries of creation by Lord Gaṇeśa Himself, for they lift consciousness into the *mūlādhāra chakra* and see the rightness of the rightness manifest as each action produces an energy flow which returns. Then and only then will they understand. The concerted effort of *sādhana* is the only salvation. No person can be their savior. The *gurus*, the *swāmīs*, the *pandits,* the elders can but encourage repetitive efforts which result in lifting the soul from darkness into light. Those who think themselves controlled by *karma* live in darkness. The others live in light. Thus we pray: "Lead us from the unreal to the real, from darkness to light, from death to immortality," out of the Narakaloka to the Devaloka. *Karma*, of course, we know as a force emitted from ourself and received back generally through others at a later time. When we are governed by the instinctive mind, we have no understanding of how *karma* exactly works. Often we do not admit to its existence. Transmuting the instinctive energies into the higher *chakras* enables us to control *karma* or slow it down and understand its component parts. ¶*Karmas* are never willfully controlled, suppressed, shot at, destroyed before they attack you. *Karmas* are the life of the person and all persons on this planet. The interaction of *karma* is what we know of as human existence. The understanding of this magnificent cosmic law automatically ceases the emotional reaction, hence there is a seeming control of the *karma*, be it good, bad or mixed, a seeming or indirect or subtle control.

THE FORTY-FIFTH APHORISM

The Ego must learn to live within the laws of things and forms; not in things or for forms. This is nonreaction.

This is definitely a Nandinātha Sampradāya aphorism. Nāthas traditionally have endeavored to fit in to the countries, communities in which they live and the families in which they are born. They are law-abiding citizens within the context of where they find themselves. These advanced souls slowly change the existing environment in which they find themselves, as they are guided by a higher law. They do not succumb to the temptation of things, nor are they overpowered by the charm of forms. This is because they are spiritually unfolded within the *anāhata chakra*, filled and thrilled with the love of Lord Śiva and see Him in all manifest and unmanifest creation. This is truly nonreaction—so this aphorism states. Yes, it is true, the Ego must learn to live within the law of things or form, not within things or for forms. This is the liberation sought for on the path. The enlightened person living on the planet suffers the great acceptance of things as they are. No longer, through his ignorance, does he feel a need to be manipulative. *Sufferance* means acceptance, tolerance and a complete joyousness at seeing the Perfect ever interrelating in trillions of perfect ways.

THE FORTY-SIXTH APHORISM

The Ego passes through the stages of the conscious mind, then through the subconscious spheres into the subsuperconscious regions, until total superconsciousness prevails. Little of this, if any, is retained by the conscious mind. In continuation, the Ego passes back through the subsuperconscious and subconscious-conscious realms into the conscious plane. There it consciously views the conscious mind. As a result, the physical body dissolves into the nothingness of the mind's creation.

This aphorism is the path, the path that all of us are on, have been on, and those to follow will be on. It is a complete concept of this path. Study it, meditate upon it, derive from it what you can.

THE FORTY-SEVENTH APHORISM

When the superconscious pushes the desired knowledge through the subconscious, that is as close as the superconscious can come to time and space.

The subconscious mind is a repository of remembered experiences. This is to say that as an experience of any kind passes into it through the conscious mind, it is remembered simultaneously. It is also a repository of unremembered experiences, for the superconscious mind forces knowledge yet to be known into the subconscious. It is remembered there, but the conscious mind is not even aware that this process is occurring, let alone being aware of any new input. Slowly the knowledge infiltrates consciousness, and then is redeposited in the subconscious as remembered knowledge. The closeness of the superconscious to the external world of time and space is through the subconscious and or intuitive flashes penetrating the conscious mind. The superconscious knows about time and space, but is not in time and space as are the other four states of mind.

THE FORTY-EIGHTH APHORISM

Attachment is of the reasoning plane. Therefore, all attachments must be given up subconsciously, through understanding, before the Ego can go beyond the conscious mind. The conscious mind can be controlled through concentration, which leads into meditation (after the physical body has been stilled). This then unfolds into a state of contemplation, and finally the Self, spirit, Truth, or *samādhi,* is realized.

This aphorism means we must have faith in the future, faith in ourselves, faith in others. To truly give up attachment, we must be confident in our own personal powers of creation, lest we always be hanging onto the past—things, people and the ideas within it. The future is to be remembered and created just the way the divine forces working through us, from Lord Śiva Himself to the physical plane, will it to be. For nothing can happen but through His grace. Lord Gaṇeśa has opened the door for this knowledge to bloom. We in turn must unreservedly prostrate ourselves in complete abandon before the Supreme God of all the Gods in order to, as the aphorism states, unfold into states of contemplation, and finally the "Self—spirit, truth or *samādhi*—is realized," our true eternal Śivaness.

THE FORTY-NINTH APHORISM

You can't go into anything with freedom when you need it. You must be desireless and observe.

We must also have desirelessness, even for the realization of the Self itself, in order to freely proceed and attain the goal. The realization of the Self must never be to us a need to get away from something, an avoidance, a departure from or a means to become better than others. Now we can see that desire is the barrier to freedom, physically, mentally and emotionally. To give up desire is very difficult. Only when one is secure in the highest of attainments do many of the desires vanish. Desire is connected to the *āṇava mala,* which is the last fetter to be conquered before *mukti* is finally attained. *Māyā* can be understood and dealt with. All *karmas* can be unwound. *Āṇava mala* has encased within it the power to create new *karmas* through desire and regenerate the veiling ignorance of *māyā.*

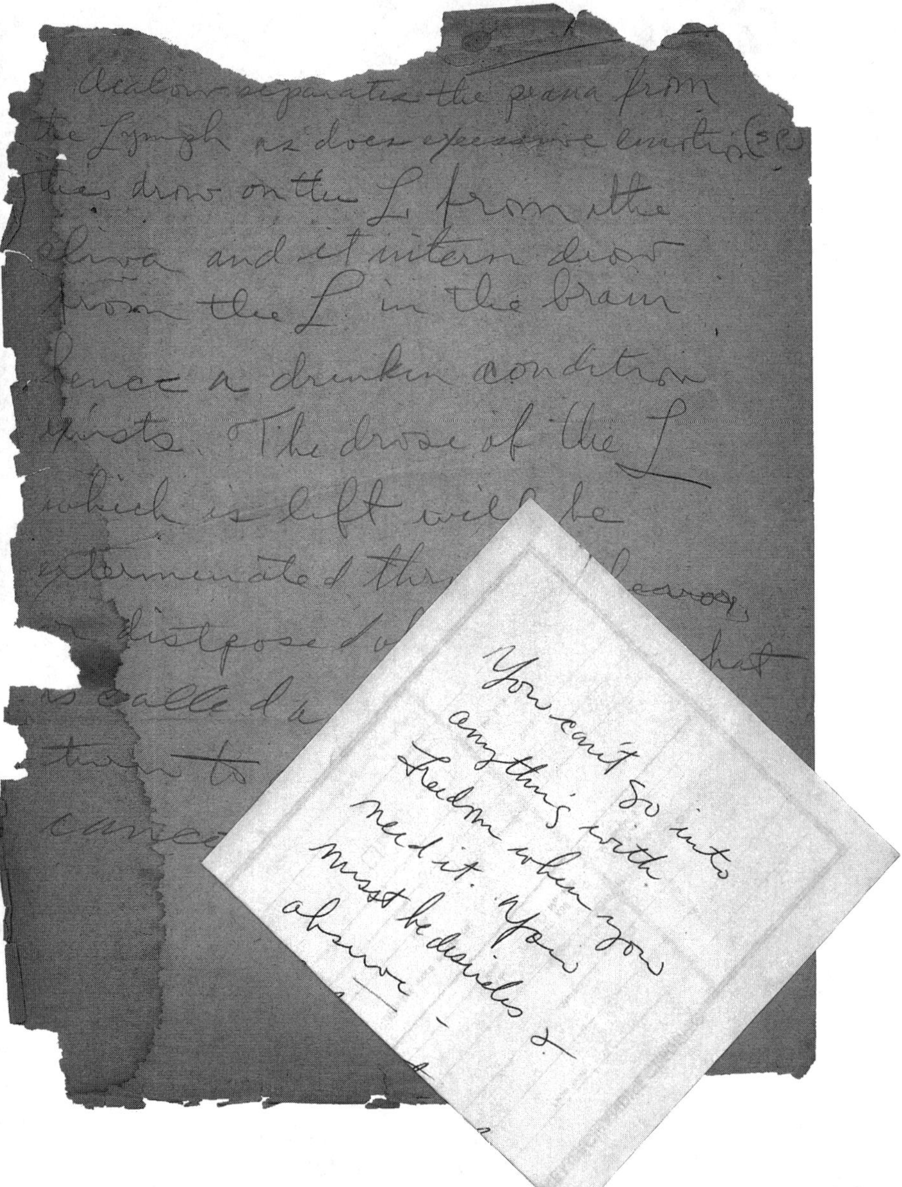

Alcohol separates the prana from the Lymph as does excessive emotion (58) this draw on the L from the saliva and it in turn draw from the L in the brain hence a drunken condition exists. The dross of the L which is left will be exterminated thr[illegible] leaves, or dispose [illegible] what is called a [illegible] turn to [illegible] cancer

You can't go into anything with freedom when you need it. You must be disciples & observe

CANTO SEVEN

Sleep and Dreams

THE FIFTIETH APHORISM

Sleep is a cleanser for the subconscious mind. By the use of willpower this can be done slowly or quickly.

When you sleep, you are cleaning out the subconscious mind and educating it to face the experiences that you must go through as you evolve. This is done automatically, but you can help it by the use of your will. Everyone has willpower, but few know that they have any more than a certain amount. It is really unfair to tell them they have unlimited powers, because they have not the consciousness of how to awaken them, and it only leads to a subconscious frustration unless you give the key along with the statement. This is the key, and when you practice it you will realize that you are not a mere man in a physical body. You are a being that has unlimited power within: the power to acquire, to give, to understand, to love, to remember, to be magnetic and to be happy. This power is yours. It is locked up within you, only to be realized through the conscious use of the will. The will is a thing, just like your body, your mind and emotions when you learn to separate and control them. The will you can also control, once you locate it through feeling. This feeling you must search yourself for and try to locate where it is, and trace it to what it controls and weigh it as to how much you use to accomplish different missions. You do this through concentration—just plain thinking, coupled with feeling. ¶This is your birthright, your heritage. When you grasp this will from within, your consciousness will unfold before your vision. And during sleep you will speed up the process of purification and build strength daily until you fall into a conscious sleep.

THE FIFTY-FIRST APHORISM

When the Ego functions in subconscious or subsubconscious dream states, situations are created. These situations remembered while in a conscious state, termed awake, will create on the conscious plane similar happenings.

Here we have a manifestation of the subsubconscious mind in the dream. It is apparent that we dream things that we could not have possibly thought up. Such dreams are a conglomeration of seemingly unrelated happenings that pass through the mind. The unrelated happenings do, however, re-impress the subsubconscious state of mind if remembered, and in turn impress the subconscious state, and similar happenings are created in our everyday life. This, perhaps, is hard to believe, but as we think back over our lives, we can pick instances where this rings true. ¶To change the picture, use the power of the subconscious mind to clear this subsubconscious state of mind and release within you the full, abundant life you were born to live. When using the subconscious mind in manifesting control over this situation, take into consideration that it is not able to eradicate the vibration. During sleep your subconscious will make it possible for you to continue working out the rate of vibration created while in the dream state and remembered while awake. ¶Simply tell your subconscious, when you are in the process of remembering a dream, to work out the remaining particles of that experience during sleep rather than recreating it on the physical plane.

THE FIFTY-SECOND APHORISM

Thoughts created at the time of intense concentration remain vibrating in the ether. When the Ego enters the etheric or astral plane in sleep, this powerful thought vibration generated while in the conscious mind draws the Ego to the spot of creation; then the Ego re-experiences the activities first concentrated upon. Another mind concentrated upon the same thought at the same time will intensify the above-stated situation.

It is in this way that two, three or more people can go into the same area of the astral plane and experience, learn from great teachers there. This is because they have shared the same thought, intensified it; the thought itself draws them in their astral body to the desired destination. Should the amplification of thought occur idly, similar results will happen. These are often called nightmares, disturbed sleep or fantasy. Yes, it is true that intense concentration does impact the lower astral world. Therefore, we must be aware that dreams of this nature are not prophetic, but self-created during normal daily life, or even within a state of meditation itself, when one is intensely concentrated upon a certain subject or a variety of subjects. ¶The dream has become a part of the intense concentration, and if you become conscious of it later, it is as much in your conscious mind as it was to begin with when it rose to manifestation. There are some of these playback creations that we want to have manifest in the material world, and others we don't. Therefore, when you find a playback happening within your dreams you wish to manifest, then intensely concentrate on it the following day. If you do not want it to manifest, endeavor to forget it as soon as possible. Tell no one, looking at it as a passing fantasy that never happened.

THE FIFTY-THIRD APHORISM

Upon passing into a state of sleep, the body's five positive currents are systematically depolarized; this allows the Ego to pass from the physical plane into the subsuperconscious regions. When the body is fully recuperated, the currents are again polarized, thus pulling the Ego back into the physical body, hence the conscious plane.

The conscious plane, when in a physical body, is always home base. The five currents hold individual awareness, which in this aphorism is referred to as the Ego in the conscious plane or conscious mind. Therefore, individual awareness can soar into the subsuperconscious regions and entertain great input, knowledge, direction for one's future, understanding of the *karmas* that have been gone through, as well as creativity that can later be manifest on the conscious plane. But as the aphorism says, once the body is fully recuperated from a state of sleep, individual awareness is now again aware of the conscious plane, which is the external world. All of the subsuperconscious input from the various regions is not forgotten, but is not remembered, and will slowly infiltrate from the subsuperconscious to the subconscious to the conscious mind and manifest in the conscious plane or conscious mind intelligence at a much later time. ¶The aphorism states that "the body's five positive currents are systematically depolarized." This implies that they can be depolarized in an unsystematic way. To have them systematically depolarized, *prāṇayama*, *haṭha yoga* and *japa* should precede the state of sleep. It also implies that the state of sleep is a state of deep meditation for the unfolded person. This does not happen for everyone. ¶This happens for the one who prepares himself to go into that kind of deep sleep, who is in a state in which the five currents can be systematically depolarized. The five currents are the five winds of the body. ¶*Depolarized* means that they all rest. It's like *neka-*

shum. When you are doing *nekashum,* you are withdrawing all the five winds into *simshumbese,* the center of your being. *Depolarizing* means to bring together that which is naturally apart. In the Shum language this is called *nekashum.* The energy of these five functions would be drawn into the *sushumṇā* current and enliven *kuṇḍalinī* activity somewhat, just enough for individual awareness to flow into subsuperconscious inner worlds of creative intelligence, absorbing all the knowledge which they at that time could contain. This then is held as a deposit, along with other intelligence experienced within the subsuperconscious mind, slowly infiltrating through the subconscious to the conscious mind.

THE FIFTY-FOURTH APHORISM

When the Ego "wakes up" from sleep, the physical body should be immediately put into action. To go back into the state of sleep immediately after naturally becoming conscious causes the five positive currents to be unconventionally depolarized—the Ego passes into the subsubconscious regions.

The mystical edicts have always been, "Wake up, get up." Any time during the night the mystic wakens, he sits up, stands up immediately, bringing himself totally into the conscious mind, turns on the light, moves the body, divorces individual awareness, his Ego, from whatever had been experienced during sleep. Then, as a conscious being, fully aware of head, arms, legs and the functions of the physical body, he puts the body to sleep again, to systematically depolarize and go back into the inner state he was drawn away from for one reason or another. The aphorism explains the penalties for neglecting this personal discipline, and, I might add, they double in effects once the discipline is known, because you know you should do something and you don't do it; that amount of extra energy will add in unconventionally depolarizing the currents. This means that some of the five currents give way half way and others will give way fully, and—as they merge together during this time into individual awareness—will conjure up the sub of the subconscious mind, give it strength and power to manifest at a later time. The sub of the subconscious mind should not be conjured up in this way, lest the manifestations not be welcome in the experiential pattern of the individual's life. There are other *sādhanas* to handle the sub of the subconscious mind. ¶It should be embarrassing to any devout Śaivite, especially one who has been initiated, to not wake up with "Aum Namaḥ Śivāya" in the mind. Traditional practices of basic *japa* are to fall asleep chanting "Aum Namaḥ Śivāya" and wake up starting off on the same syllable one left off on when going to sleep. Therefore, to quickly heal the embarrassment, the devotee should, upon awakening, mentally or verbally say, "Aum Namaḥ Śivāya," or "Śivāya Namaḥ Aum," bringing the mind back to normal consciousness. ¶In a state of sleep, one must know that he himself behaves as he would in an awakened, conscious state. The mystic knows there is no state of unconsciousness, and that the same laws apply, the *yamas, niyamas* and *pañcha nitya karmas,* whether one is awake or asleep. Whatever one does, even in a dream—lying, cheating or stealing, deceiving, coercing or mutilating—is a cause of *karmas* or forces to be re-experienced, re-enacted at a later time. Right thought, right speech, right action must hold through daily life and dream life. Those who do not have proper dreams, or who have violent dreams, should never be taught meditation, outside of group meditation, lest the power of meditation itself manifest their hidden unruly nature. ¶The *guru,* having all-pervasive consciousness, which is superconsciousness, is simultaneously within the subsuperconscious of all *śishyas* at every given moment or every space of time—in their waking states, in their dream states, guiding, loving and protecting.

BOOK REVIEW

"COGNIZANTABILITY"

SAN FRANCISCO SUNDAY CHRONICLE THIS WORLD, November 16, 1958

New Books on Yoga---A Philosophical; Historical Collection

By Curt Gentry

TO MANY people the word "Yoga" brings a mental picture of an inverted Clifton Webb. As booksellers have discovered over the past several years, however, it also means a constantly expanding collection of titles requested by an increasingly large audience. Surely this is in part (like the "discovery" of Zen Buddhism) related to the current mode for things Eastern, in part to widespread interest in a unique system of physical culture. But to a number of individuals it is something more, closer to the real meaning of the term—a valid path to achieving effective union of the physical, mental, and spiritual qualities of man. A summary of new books on the subject indicates the diversity of Yogas available:

"Yoga and Long Life," by Yogi Gupta (Dodd, Mead & Co.; $5), deals with Hatha Yoga, the best known and most basic of the Yogas. It teaches physical fitness and rhythmic regulation of the breath through the practice of *asanas* or bodily postures. Gupta's book contains many instructive photographs, as well as a general text that is an adequate introduction to the higher forms of Yoga.

The highest of these, Raja Yoga, the science of mind, is the subject of **"Cognizantability"** by Sri Subramuniya (Aquaria Publications, 3575 Sacramento St.; $3). In what at first glance appears to be a deceptively simple book of aphorisms and their explanations, the author discusses the five states of mind and their interrelation. The true depth of the book is apparent upon application. The Subramuniya Yoga Order, which has a branch in San Francisco, conducts regular classes in the study of this book. Containing much information not often available in book form—usually given only to the yogic initiate by his *guru* (teacher or "dispeller of darkness") — "Cognizantability" is recommended for persons seeking a practical guide to self-realization.

"Hinduism: Its Meaning for the Liberation of the Spirit," by Swami Nikhilananda, (Harper's World Perspective Series; $4), is a general survey of Hindu beliefs and customs, Included are chapters on major Yogas: Bhakti (Love); Karma (Action); Jnana (Philosophy); and Raja. Of primary interest is Nikhilananda's relating these beliefs to modern philosophical and religious thought.

CANTO EIGHT

Chakras

THE FIFTY-FIFTH APHORISM

To cognize the states of mind in relation to the physical body, it is necessary to understand the nervous system and the forces operating through it.

The mind flows through the physical body, influencing its every action. The physical body, in turn, influences the mind. Conscious awareness of the sympathetic and central nerve system is essential to progress on the path of *rāja yoga.*

THE FIFTY-SIXTH APHORISM

There are two nervous structures: the cerebral spine (brain and spinal cord), and the sympathetic or ganglionic. The sympathetic consists of a series of distinct nerve centers or ganglia, extending on each side of the spinal column from the head to the sacral plexus.

Rāja yoga practices demand a complete understanding of all that this aphorism refers to. There are many fine treatises on these subjects, but true insight comes from one's own chosen *guru.* The *guru* gives forth to the *śishya* what the *śishya* needs to know, when the knowing is needed to be known. Mystical knowledge comes at odd moments, in mysterious ways. Keep a watchful ear and an open mind in the *guru's* presence, for he speaks to your spiritual unfoldment, not to your external mind. It is essential to have an awakened *guru* for *rāja yoga* to begin, to continue and end in the result of *jñāna* in the individual. The *guru* takes away, closes the door forever on, the lower nature of anger, jealousy, resentment, fear, worries and doubts, allowing the soul in its natural state to soar.

THE FIFTY-SEVENTH APHORISM

The ganglia are called in Sanskṛit *chakras,* or "disks." About forty-nine have been counted, of which there are seven principal ones.

The nerve ganglia of the physical body on the astral plane are colorful spinning disks. Those below the *mūlādhara* spin from right to left, and the seven major ones, from the *mūlādhara* up to the *sahasrāra,* spin clockwise. The *rāja yogī,* looking within himself, through his third eye, down through the physical body, sees these disks, stacked one on top of another like phonograph records. They are not spinning out in front of him like airplane propellers, as often depicted by artists' conceptual illustrations.

THE FIFTY-EIGHTH APHORISM

The seven principal *chakras* are:

1)	**sacral ganglion**	***mūlādhara***
2)	**prostatic ganglion**	***svādhishṭhana***
3)	**epigastric ganglion**	***maṇipūra***
4)	**cardiac ganglion**	***anāhata***
5)	**pharyngeal ganglion**	***viśuddha***
6)	**pineal ganglion**	***ājñā***
7)	**pituitary ganglion**	***sahasrāra***

These *chakras* are the *chakras* of light. The seven below the *mūlādhāra,* of the 21, are the *chakras* of darkness. Again, a *rāja yoga guru* is essential to maintain consciousness in the *chakras* of light. Hence the invocations, "Lead us from the unreal to the real, from darkness to light, from death to immortality," and "Awake, arise and stop not until the goal is reached."

THE FIFTY-NINTH APHORISM

These *chakras* are guided in their unfoldment by the sympathetic system's three principal channels, called in Sanskṛit, *nāḍīs,* meaning tubes: 1) *sushumṇā* passes from the base of the spine to the pituitary through the center of the spinal cord; 3) *piṅgalā,* corresponding to the right sympathetic; 3) *iḍā,* corresponding to the left sympathetic.

These are very important channels of consciousness and must be balanced at all times—*iḍā-piṅgalā, yin-yang,* feminine-masculine, moon and sun, intuitive-intellectual, left brain-right brain, passive-aggressive—for a constant intuiting of the divine twenty-four hours a day. Regular *sādhana* balances these forces, *iḍā* and *piṅgalā,* harmonizes the entire nerve system, stimulating the intuitive, creative area of the mind.

THE SIXTIETH APHORISM

The *kuṇḍalinī* does not begin its activity through the *sushumṇā* until the *iḍā* (negative) and *piṅgalā* (positive) have preceded it by forming a positive and negative current along the spinal cord powerful enough to awaken the sixth *chakra*—*ajña.* The first *chakra* then awakens in its entirety as the *kuṇḍalinī* force is drawn through the *sushumṇā,* stimulating each *chakra* in turn, concluding with the unfoldment of the *sahasrara* center in the brain.

The *iḍā* and *piṅgalā* currents, through *rāja yoga* practice, begin a circular flow around the *sushumṇā,* the *piṅgalā* flowing up and *iḍā* flowing down, creating an electronic force field strong enough to stabilize the *sushumṇā,* to sustain the power of cosmic fire as the *kuṇḍalinī* uncoils and rises from the *mūlādhāra chakra* to its *ajña* destination. The seals are broken, irreparably broken, as consciousness journeys up the spine within the *sushumṇā* tube.

CANTO NINE

Mantras

THE SIXTY-FIRST APHORISM

Some languages in the Far East are created according to the natural expressions of the different stages of the mind in viewing their own creations; these languages are created to present mental pictures of things to be expressed. They can be understood when listening from superconscious states, even should the listener not consciously comprehend the language.

These mystical languages are said to be created by the Gods, and insofar as they are existing today, performing the same works as intended, the effects of the sound, meaning and knowledge are combined as one. Other languages have evolved out of other languages, and still other languages were created by ethnic, tribal groups. But the few that exist that were created by the Gods, like affirmations, create mental pictures and effect desired results, or undesired results, as the case may be. An awakened clairvoyant, clairaudient person listening from a high superconscious state can watch the pictures that a conversation is creating, similar to viewing a television screen with a dialogue going on in a language that he cannot consciously understand. ¶I remember once, when I was 23 years of age or so, listening to a group of people speaking in the Tamil language while I was in meditation. I saw a beautiful stream of water flowing by me like on television, and to my amazement later I found that they had been speaking about an irrigation channel. Subsequently I have had similar experiences. Therefore, somehow the vibration of the sounds creates mental pictures. ¶These *mantra* languages have persisted in their purity generation after generation. Though the meanings may have changed in certain words, the sounds have not. For instance, in ancient Tamil and modern Tamil, the sounds are the same. The meanings of the words may be more than slightly different, but the mental pictures that the arrangements of sounds produce would be similar century after century. In man-created alphabets, even the sounds of the alphabets change from century to century.

THE SIXTY-SECOND APHORISM

All superconscious languages can be spoken and/or comprehended superconsciously when the esoteric science of language is understood.

This aphorism was given in the early fifties, and it is very interesting that Shum, the language of meditation came superconsciously in the late sixties, almost twenty years later. Since Rahu has an eighteen-year cycle, this might be tied in somehow to this planet. The Shum language was created, taught and spoken and remained within a small group of people. Thirty years from its conception, in the late nineties, we began to bring it forward for the devotees in its fullness. This thirty-year history of the Shum-Tyaef language is an indication that it is a part of the fabric of all peoples of our planet.

THE SIXTY-THIRD APHORISM

The essence of language, resulting from superconscious expression, can be summed up in one word, namely the Sanskṛit word *mantra,* meaning "incantation."

Superconscious languages when spoken call forth *devas* within the inner worlds that surround the group that they are listening to. These *devas,* some of them disincarnate beings living close to the Earth on the astral plane, help to fulfill the wishes of the individuals who are having the conversation. ¶These *devas* are very alert to all conversations of all people who speak the same language. Some languages pierce into the Third World, others the Second. Man-made languages, or languages that change their sounds from century to century, totally localize to the area of consciousness they are spoken in. They don't penetrate the inner worlds. This is because they are not *mantra* languages, and speaking them is not an incantation.

THE SIXTY-FOURTH APHORISM

***Mantras* chanted in languages other than those of superconscious origins tap only the subconscious of the conscious mind in a form of auto-suggestion. *Mantras* of a superconscious origin awaken the subsuperconscious states of mind.**

This aphorism explains itself extremely well. The only other comment to be made would be that every seeker on the path of spiritual unfoldment should acquaint himself with a superconscious language and learn at least one or two hundred words and some phrases, so that in his private thoughts or with other devotees these words can be interspersed with the other language he is speaking. Sanskṛit, Pali, Tamil and other sacred languages penetrate the Devaloka and the Śivaloka, allowing the great souls there to get the gist of the conversations going on. The tones of the language also play an important part in bringing the devotee's awareness into an inner state of mind, be it the subconscious or the subsuperconscious.

THE SIXTY-FIFTH APHORISM

Use of *mantras* awakens various brain cells so that the Ego may vibrate superconsciously. They are the subtlest superconscious thoughts before the Ego enters fully into a superconscious state.

We can clearly see that *mantras* or affirmations chanted in languages created by the conscious mind would not produce the outcome this aphorism is indicating. But *mantras* created through the superconscious languages would definitely open the inner doors to supreme higher consciousness. ¶After one realizes Paraśiva, the Self-God within, the aftermath of realization is that sound is the first ever-emanating vibration out of that great depth of timeless, formless, spacelessness. These sounds are the first manifestations of form. These sounds captured by superconscious beings blended together create this high breed of language. Sanskṛit, for instance, is the perfect and foremost sacred language and benefits the devotee who chants it even if he does not know the meaning.

THE SIXTY-SIXTH APHORISM

The *mantras*, like a medicine, need not be understood by the conscious mind as to composition or literal meaning. Their own meaning will be made clear when practiced with faith and concentration at auspicious times.

The new knowledge we have obtained here, locked into words, is auspicious time. Some times are better than others to lift individual awareness into superconscious states. When these times are known, they can be used to great advantage. These tones emanating from the Self, when pronounced properly, lead one into the knowledge as to how to merge back into the Self. This knowledge unfolds from within as these great *mantras* are incantated, such as "Aum

Namaḥ Śivāya," which will finally awaken the experience of Śiva's perfect universe. Everything is in perfect harmony, law and order. ¶*Mantras* are given by a *guru* and this is important, because his *śākti* gives the first impetus to proceed. It is not the same as when taken from a book, because the thrust is not there. It must come from a *guru*. The proper *mantra* will be given for the next awakening in the sequence of awakenings. These *mantras* are definitely like medicines. Reading the label will not have any effect on the healing process of the medicine. The healing of the medicine works whether or not we consciously comprehend it. Some *mantras* are so old, their meaning has been lost eons ago, but they produce the same results within the individuals who pronounce them properly, and this, therefore, is the meaning.

THE SIXTY-SEVENTH APHORISM

***Mantras* intensify the five states of the mind, separating them to be viewed consciously, and their corresponding centers in the physique and brain. Before practice begins, precaution must be taken that physical and mental cleanliness is made manifest.**

The repetition of a *mantra*, especially if given by a *guru*, is a journey to a distant place. Consciousness is altered. And it must be performed at an auspicious time. Preparation must be made, bathing, cleaning oneself properly, then performed in a room which is prepared for this purpose. We are taking a journey; the room, the body and the exact time of starting are the conveyance. ¶Certain *mantras*, like "Aum Namaḥ Śivāya," bring knowledge of the five *chakras*—the *mūlādhāra* to the *viśuddha*—the five states of mind, the five elements (earth, water, fire, air and *ākāśa*). The constant repetition separates these all out and blends them all together one at a time in different patterns, bringing great new knowledge to the aspirant. ¶If precaution is not taken, or the *mantra* is chanted at an inauspicious time, in a place that is not sanctified, and the chanter's body has not been cleansed, the *mantra* will work as it should, no problem here. But the person who is performing the incantations will be be easily seen, due to the power of the *mantra*, by *asuric* forces, who will come and attach themselves to him, disturb him. In a clean and perfect place, under sanctified conditions the incantation will attract *devonic* forces who will, in turn, help him on the path to his eventual enlightenment. For finding out perfect times, you can refer to the *pañchāṅgam*, the sacred Hindu lunar calendar.

THE SIXTY-EIGHTH APHORISM

The practice of *mantras* will harmonize the physical body with the mental body, through the five great somatic currents, which in turn harmonize the five states of the mind while unfolding the seven *chakras*.

All this and more, too, these great *mantras* will do. Initiated Śaivites are permitted to chant the Namaḥ Śivāya *mantra*. This *mantra* is found in the exact middle of the *Vedas*. This *mantra* is the one that this aphorism addresses. ¶It refers to the five states of mind, the five currents and the *chakras*. The five states of mind are conscious, subconscious, subsubconscious, subsuperconscious and superconscious. The five somatic currents are *prāṇa*, outgoing breath; *apāṇa*, incoming breath; *vyāṇa*, retained breath; *udāṇa*, ascending breath; and *samāṇa*, equalizing breath.

THE SIXTY-NINTH APHORISM

It is said that the faithful practice of certain *mantras* alone will bring material wealth and abundance. This practice, however, only aids in transmuting the creative energies, thus calming the conscious mind, strengthening concentration and giving

unlimited vitality so that full use can be made of all states of mind consciously to attract material abundance.

Attracting material abundance is important and does come in many ways, but for these low-level *mantras* to be fully efficacious they should not be used unless the practitioner has been initiated into performing the high-level *mantras* as well, lest the use of the wealth and abundance go to unholy activities, and finally great loss be the corresponding result. ¶*Mantras* do produce, but to keep what has been produced by these low-level *mantras,* one must be a high-level person.

THE SEVENTIETH APHORISM

To aid in the depolarization and transmutation of creative forces, certain *mantras* are chanted. These logically concentrate the conscious mind, harmonize its subconscious and magnetize the brain. This draws the creative forces from the instinctive to the intellectual and superconscious regions.

Mantras, or incantations, are a study in themselves, however it is possible to explain the use of one of these *mantras* that will do the most in the depolarization and transmutation process. This *mantra* harmonizes the physical body with the mental and spiritual forces. Sound *A* (pronounced AH), and center the sound in the solar plexus region of the body. Next intone *U* (pronounced OO), and center this sound through the throat area. After that, intone *M* (pronounced MMM), sending this vibration through the cranium by placing the front teeth tightly together. First chant them separately, then blend the sounds together, forming *AUM.* This *mantra* is the essence of sound itself. All sounds blended together intone *AUM.* Listen to the sum total of all the noises of a big city, and you will hear the *AUM* as in a sea shell or the ocean waves. This is only the manifestation of creation from the creative power. As you intone these sounds you are releasing your creative energy into your creative centers in the brain. Then they are allowed to pour forth back through your mental, emotional and physical body to create a new world for you.

THE SEVENTY-FIRST APHORISM

The letters *A-U-M,* when correctly chanted, transmute the instinctive to the intellectual and the instinctive-intellectual to the superconscious. Direct cognition will then be attained.

The mantra *Aum* is the universal *mantra* which can be performed safely by the initiated and the uninitiated alike, under any condition, in any circumstance, whether the body is clean or dirty. It will heighten consciousness by harmonizing the physical with the mental and spiritual when chanted correctly. The Aum *mantra* will lead you to the *guru,* and when cognition has been attained, upliftment of consciousness to the fourth *chakra,* Śaiva *dīkshā,* or initiation into deeper *mantras,* would be the next unfoldment on the path to enlightenment.

THE SEVENTY-SECOND APHORISM

The *A-U-M* harmonizes the physical body with the mind and the mind with the intuitive nature.

Here again we can see the great benefits of the *mantra Aum.* It in itself is the ultimate psychiatrist. It in itself is the sound of the universe, the sound of a city in action, the sound at birth, the sound at death. Listen to the sounds anyplace, anywhere blended together and you will hear the Aum. While listening, mentally say the sound Aum and feel body, mind and the Godness within you blending as one.

THE SEVENTY-THIRD APHORISM

The *Aum* placed before or after a word adds power and concentrated forces to the word.

When you were encouraging someone and are saying those encouraging uplifting words, think "Aum." The vibration that you will create by doing this within yourself goes to him, adds power to your words and uplifts him as it is uplifting you.

THE SEVENTY-FOURTH APHORISM

The *Aum* projected through thought after or before a spoken word adds concentrated force to the spoken word.

You can project Aum mentally to a loved one in a far-off place. Each of the intonations has a color. Those colors blended together make one complete thought form which travels faster than the speed of life.

THE SEVENTY-FIFTH APHORISM

As there are five principal states of the mind, there are five types of *mantras*: 1) the *mantra* uttered with the voice; 2) the *mantra* uttered with the voice and projected from the mind; 3) the *mantra* projected from the mind; 4) the consciousness of the *mantra* being projected; 5) the *mantra* uttered without the utterance, physical or mental.

This last explanation to the five types of *mantras* is the most interesting. To try to understand more deeply, the *jīvanmukta,* who has attained ultimate realization, is an incantation of *mantras* within himself, as all of the *chakras* are functioning simultaneously one with another and giving forth these holy sounds. Being in the presence of a soul of this caliber, also seeing a soul of these attainments, would alter the life of the individual permanently. This is why Hindus value *darshan,* the sight of the realized soul, and value even more the sight of a realized soul while being in the aura of that soul. Nothing is expected of him but this; no lectures, no questions answered. All questions a thousand people might have would be answered within their own minds through his *darshan.* Life-changing directions and the altering of experiences yet to come would happen by being within or close to his aura or physical presence. The other four are progressive steps through the subtlety of the power of the *mantra.* To come to the feet of a truly awakened soul, the mantra *Aum* chanted verbally, projected with the mind, chanted silently and projected with the mind while holding the consciousness of it's being projected, can lead the sincere seeker to a soul of this caliber.

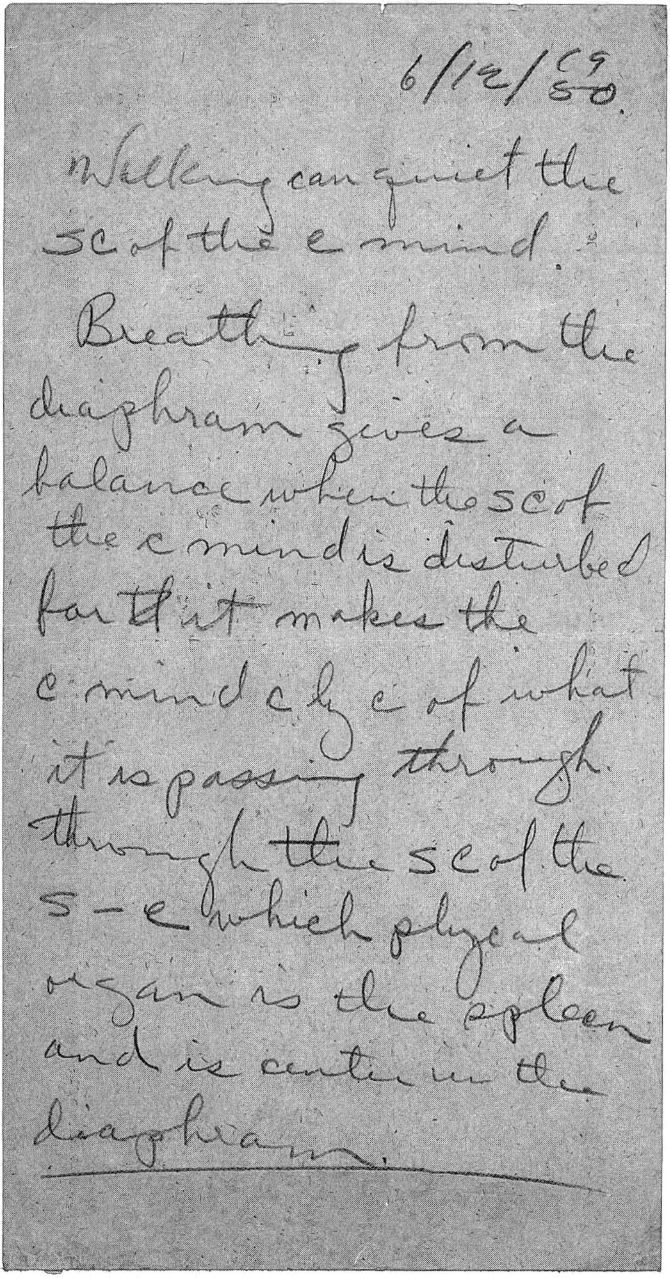

6/12/69 80.

Walking can quiet the sc of the c mind.

Breathing from the diaphram gives a balance when the sc of the c mind is disturbed for ~~tl it~~ makes the c mind c by c of what it is passing ~~through~~ through ~~the~~ sc of the s-c which physical organ is the spleen and is center in the diaphram.

CANTO TEN

Esoteric Theories

THE SEVENTY-SIXTH APHORISM

Esoteric teachings are to place the mind in correct channels after transmutation is well on its way—until then they would only register as excess intellectual knowledge in the subconscious of the conscious mind. A certain amount of superconscious awakening is necessary to cognize the esoteric modes of thought.

This is a frank statement. It tells us that a *guru* educating his *chela* should not allow books, discussions or knowledge beyond the point of his immediate spiritual unfoldment to enter his mind. No matter how deep, no matter how perfect the knowledge, it would serve to clutter the mind, thus retarding the progress. Rather, daily *sādhana*, the practice of *mantra yoga*, wrenches consciousness from the instinctive-intellectual areas of the mind, and the other forms of *rāja yoga* to be practiced during these early stages correctly channel the life force into the *sushumṇā* current within the spine. When all the inner currents are well established and direct experience occurs, then esoteric, written teachings may be read, but only to verify the experience experienced by the experiencer.

THE SEVENTY-SEVENTH APHORISM

When the conscious mind becomes balanced through the practice of nonreaction, the other states of mind elucidate, unravel, themselves before it, through the subsuperconscious mind. This is the nature of the mind—it is also called spiritual evolution.

Through the constant practice of *rāja yoga*, within an *ashram* under the watchful eye of an established *guru*, the conscious mind of the *chela* becomes balanced, because the *iḍā* and *piṅgalā* currents themselves become balanced. The *sushumṇā* current becomes prominent. This *rāja yoga* practice is in itself a fine art, but must be performed under direction and within the proper environment for positive results to be attained.

THE SEVENTY-EIGHTH APHORISM

The laws of the mind come superconsciously; they pass through the conscious plane and are registered in the subconscious of the conscious mind. Later they are comprehended subconsciously, then put into practical usage consciously.

In true spiritual unfoldment, knowledge is obtained from within oneself without being pre-programmed through lectures, books or promises. The adept performs his practices. The discovered knowledge is the result. Results properly obtained, are then verified by scripture and his *guru*. Direct experience is the only profound teacher.

THE SEVENTY-NINTH APHORISM

To bring forth a law of the mind or the solution of a problem, three facts or points must be had about the subject in question. Concentrate on each point individually, then meditate upon them collectively. The superconscious, through the subconscious, then will give the law or solution. To hold the law or solution consciously, the three points, which are of the conscious mind and its subconscious, must be remembered in their original logical order.

Here we are speaking about *samyama*—thought, meaning and knowledge combined as one. When combined as one, it lifts up the lid of the third eye. What is hidden behind the veil of ignorance is seen. Concentration is an art that once attained leads naturally into meditation, contemplation and *samādhi*. The three-point concentration spoken of in this aphorism releases the whole of the external from its internal counterpart of the *yogī's* awareness. A deep *yoga* law is discussed here.

THE EIGHTIETH APHORISM

A conscious mind trained by another mind teaching from superconscious states is able to consciously retain its own conscious expressions.

A *satguru* who teaches through his superconscious expression or through his silence not only teaches the *chela* within his immediate vicinity, but all *chelas* anywhere in the world who have received *dīkshā* from the *guru*. There is no space or time that divides the audience chamber in which the *guru* sits when the superconsciousness speaks out or is in silence. A *guru's dīkshā*, initiation, is sought for and valued because of the in-flow of knowledge, sustenance, security and sustaining grace which comes as a result from the *guru*, wherever the *guru* might be.

THE EIGHTY-FIRST APHORISM

The superconscious mind can only cognize what the lower states of mind place before it, or what it has placed before itself through the lower states of mind due to some previous cause. This is why the Ego must return to the conscious plane after living in superconscious thought—for all thought is in time and space and is stimulated through the effort of the will, though the superconscious mind is the essence of time and space. Spirit—truth—is beyond this object, the mind.

The superconscious being does not always reside in a superconscious state, though once awakened into permanent superconsciousness, his awareness has free flow through all states of mind and is held intact by the true Self, realized beyond all states of mind. Therefore, the adept living in superconscious states can function quite easily in the conscious mind.

THE EIGHTY-SECOND APHORISM

The deep thinkers of the Far East only have to deal with the instinctive plane. From there they can cut themselves off and become superconscious beings.

Children are taught likes and dislikes by their parents; mainly they learn this through observation. Later, when able to communicate, their parents teach them whom to love and hate, whom to look up to and whom to look down upon. When an Asian family recognizes Divinity in the child, they strive to live a religious life, setting the highest standards for him to grow up within. He is spared much of which would be taught if he were an ordinary person. Therefore, when spiritually alive, he is free from the world, having never entered it.

THE EIGHTY-THIRD APHORISM

Deep thinkers of the West have to deal with the instinctive and intellectual planes. While the beings of the Far East can cut off the instinctive without comprehension, the beings of the West must thoroughly comprehend the instinctive/intellectual before passing into higher superconscious planes.

This is because Western thought has no eternal truths as final goals, and the obvious and apparent become burdensome to the mind and, even more so, a barrier when the path of spiritual unfoldment is undertaken. Because the Western people are more analytical when it comes to everything in the outside world, a long preliminary process of trying to understand the instinctive nature and the lower intellectual mind usually occurs before the matter is finally put to rest and the fullness of the higher *chakras* catches hold.

THE EIGHTY-FOURTH APHORISM

The subsuperconscious mind has all the answers. But when the subsubconscious mind is mentally overly congested, the thoughts cannot be passed through. The subsuperconscious mind lies in silent knowing.

This means that everyone is a complete whole, with all five states of mind functioning at every point in time. However, when the sub of the subconscious mind totally takes over consciousness, and one becomes a victim of his past, be it positive, negative or mixed, any new input from the superconscious through the subconscious is totally blocked. The superconscious and the small part of the subconscious that it has deposited knowledge within remain waiting for a chance to complete the cycle. This means the answers are always there within everyone. This is why desirelessness, renunciation, giving up the past, are important tenets to be followed for spiritual unfoldment.

THE EIGHTY-FIFTH APHORISM

The subconscious mind can only know or put in order what you have already put into it or absorbed from the conscious plane. That is why you have to come back to the conscious plane to accumulate various pieces of information and facts so that when you go back into superconscious realms, the subsuperconscious mind can reorganize that.

If life is not working out well for you, then it is because the subconscious mind, which governs the fundamental patterns of life, has not been properly, sufficiently impressed.

The aphorism says we must then return to some conscious effort to correct the situation, such as affirmation, visualization. To do this, the problem within the subconscious mind must be brought consciously before the vision, as this new information is being added to it. The subconscious then will take all this and rearrange it according to the *karmas* of the individual.

THE EIGHTY-SIXTH APHORISM

They say that the superconscious mind is all-knowing, all pervading, knows past, present and future. However, the superconscious mind can only know what the lower states of mind put before it for comprehension and elucidation. The superconscious mind is beyond. It can elucidate and predict the future by happenings of the past, blended with the solidarity of character.

Yes, the superconscious mind is the restful fullness, an allness, a completion. It is the magical corrective mirror. One looks into it and sees his face as it really is. Putting thoughts forward, they come back unaltered but with insightful solutions attached. This peaceful fullness, all-pervasive knowing, reflects as a mirror the right knowledge when questions are asked of it. It is the venerable conscience within all humans and all living creatures. The allness of everything is the completion of everything. This means that every atom has everything within it that ever existed and will ever exist.

THE EIGHTY-SEVENTH APHORISM

Willfulness stems from the emotional body.

When our emotions are not under control, neither is our willpower. Uncontrolled emotions lead us into lower consciousness. Controlled emotions lead us to higher consciousness. Willpower is essential to advancement on the spiritual path.

THE EIGHTY-EIGHTH APHORISM

The deep thinkers in the Far East have previously passed through the instinctive/intellectual stages of the mind, unconscious through what they were passing. They must return, however, and function fully conscious of each state in which they find themselves. This is termed "Truth in action."

In Asia many decades ago, all learning occurred through the process of memory. Much of this is true even today. People are taught what to think, not encouraged to think about what they should be thinking. Learning by rote is not a part of Western education, where children are taught to make decisions at a very young age for themselves and others and learn by their own mistakes. Therefore, it is only the most enlightened persons who are able to return back into their intellectual structure, think and decide for themselves. They become the leaders and advisors of those who are not allowed to think for themselves.

THE EIGHTY-NINTH APHORISM

Those who hermit themselves away from the external world of things, repulsed by the instinctive plane, having previously so suffered through it, are the ones who create a God separate from themselves to depend on and worship. When they realize their true nature, they may function without negative reaction in all states of consciousness.

This refers to self-appointed *yogīs*, uninitiated, not *dharmically* under the guidance of any *guru* or elder within the community, but apart from the community itself. Having had a few instinctive experiences which they abhor, they retreat to *sādhana*, to God and themselves, in dualistic apartness. The two of them, they and their God, leave society. This particular God that they have conjured up within their own mind, they depend on, they worship. This dualistic dependency is the total sum of their so-called *yoga*. However, when they realize their true nature and learn to accept *advaitic* union with the Supreme, the great transformation occurs and true *rāja yoga* begins.

THE NINETIETH APHORISM

Walking can quiet the subconscious of the conscious mind. Breathing from the diaphragm gives a balance when the subconscious of the conscious mind is disturbed, for this makes the conscious mind consciously conscious of what is passing through the subconscious of the superconscious, which physical organ is the spleen and is centered in the diaphragm.

This aphorism tells us that walking and diaphragmatic breathing are very essential for advancement on the spiritual path, and harmonizing all of the currents of the inner and outer bodies and the various states of the mind itself. The spleen is a physical organ. The spleen is also a psychic center, connecting the subconscious with the superconscious. It is a little-known small *chakra*.

THE NINETY-FIRST APHORISM

The mind uses the brain; the brain sends messages to the various nerve centers which appear to be miniature brains. The solar plexus is their focal point, hence the solar plexus is called the seat of emotion. When the breath (breath is life) is sent down into the lower regions of the lungs or diaphragm, the solar plexus pours energy, *prāṇa*, into the smaller nerve centers all over the body. These external nerve centers or brains thus receiving their energy subconsciously think. These nerve centers are externally represented as people or animals. The internal nerve centers, however, are represented externally by astral and higher mental plane beings, when seen, termed visions.

This aphorism is complete within itself and is telling us that the physical body is the all that is objective and subjective. "I am that, I am. All that is is within me. I am the Self all souls are seeking." But to realize this and get the "I am" out of the way, it is very necessary to understand how the energies work throughout the physical body, and this is only a small part of the understanding to be understood.

THE NINETY-SECOND APHORISM

The solar plexus holds the sub of the subconscious mind, but when awakened, it is the sub of the superconscious mind.

The solar plexus is often called the sun center. It is the great balancer of all bodily functions. It contains the fire within the body. When the *manipūra chakra* sleeps, the sub of the subconscious begins to build. The individuals in this state appear to have no will of their own, nor would they dare to even think they could think for themselves. But when the *manipūra chakra* begins to unfold, individual willpower asserts itself—this is not without its problems—and if the individual is a spiritual person, the subsuperconscious mind begins to work through this *chakra*, healing the past.

THE NINETY-THIRD APHORISM

The lymph system is the external manifestation of the nerve forces. The ganglia are the way-house for the nerves. They register the nerve impulse which collects the lymph. This is carried by the blood.

This aphorism explains how the *chakras*, ganglia, are the way-house of the nerves, or where the nerves rest or are activated. It also tells us that the lymphatic system is the external manifestation on the physical plane in which the astral nerve energy is contained and flows through. The ganglia, or the *chakras*, compute or register all nerve impulses, collect and redistribute the lymph which is carried to various parts of the body through the blood.

THE NINETY-FOURTH APHORISM

Lymph is the manifestation of *prāṇa*. Thought, or thought forms, are the products of the lymph.

Here we learn that lymph is the physical manifestation of *prāṇic* energies. Thoughts, which create forms with various shapes, colors and sounds, are not only created by this *prāṇa*, they draw on the vital forces of the lymph itself. In those who think a lot, vitality is often depleted. Thought, *prāṇa* and lymph are the vital forces which create the *karmas* which eventually return to us through others.

THE NINETY-FIFTH APHORISM

The blood is the carrier for the lymph. The heart is the organ for the blood. The diaphragm is the organ for the lymph. The lymph carries the nerve force—negative chyme and positive chyle. Milk carries the lymph from the cow.

Here we learn that *prāṇa* derived from milk carries lymph from the cow, as well as the cow's mood. Hindus worship the cow, sing to the cow, endeavor to lift up the cow, so that the mood of the cow is the highest it can manifest. The mood, the *prāṇa*, the lymph go into the milk and uplift those who drink it.

THE NINETY-SIXTH APHORISM

The spleen is the placenta that nourishes the solar body. The reason why one must keep the body seventy-two hours after death is for the spleen to form the aura around the astral body to give it strength to soar to higher spheres.

Here we learn that the astral body needs help after death, at least for seventy-two hours. It draws upon the spleen of its former body, now decaying. Cremation should occur after this process has ended. The process is that the *astral* body draws all of the energies of the physical body into itself. Transmutation is occurring of the physical, emotional, as well as the energies of all of the physical organs, reconstructing the astral body. This is the slow death experience. Immediate cremation is under another law, and more time is needed for the astral body to reconstruct itself within its world. This expedient way is universally an accepted practice as is no formal funeral for still-borns or infants. Buried bodies remain Earth-bound. Entombment is an acceptable practice reserved for *satgurus*, saints or *swāmīs* who so choose, and whose bodies are then preserved in salt-filled crypts.

THE NINETY-SEVENTH APHORISM

Insanity results from lack of lymph in the brain. The organ of the mind, namely the brain, is developed to a large extent by deep, expansive thinking. When, however, the lymph and *prāṇa* (the controlling elements) are removed from the brain, the mind can run without discrimination through its various accustomed channels. It is the lymph and *prāṇa* which harmonize the mind with the body.

Some people think that the physical body contains an astral body, and the astral body contains the soul. But here we find that the soul, working through the astral body, lives in a physical body, and for it to function properly, all the elements within that vehicle must be working properly. In the Glossary we are noting scientific explanations of lymph and spleen, as well as the Vedic explanation of the word *prāṇa.* Study these carefully for deeper understanding of this aphorism and all related aphorisms that mention lymph, spleen and *prāṇa.* We call attention here to the import of the words, "the organ of the mind." This indicates that the mind itself is a perfect, complete entity unto itself, but if its organ, the brain, is deficient, communication to the external world might be limited or void.

THE NINETY-EIGHTH APHORISM

Discrimination is the result of an abundance of lymph in the brain through transmutation of the vital forces.

The vital sexual forces when transmuted feed the brain, but first all of the *chakras* leading up to the brain; and not only discrimination, which is depth of perception, is enhanced, but many other soul qualities as well, such as expanding consciousness, seeing through and into inner worlds and more.

THE NINETY-NINTH APHORISM

The sex function draws off lymph from the spleen. When done to excess it draws off the lymph from the heart as well. The cells of the heart are broken down and when replenishing themselves build massively back (as do the muscles develop while lifting weights). The system is accelerated to the height of emotion when the sex function or perverted states thereof accrue. However, the physique is unable to attain normalcy, as the life force of the body, namely the lymph, has been exhausted. Only after the lymph again is carried by the blood in abundance can the physique come back to normalcy. However, during the interval, complications can and are created, such as enlarging of the heart, weakening of the lungs, cancer, diseases of membranous kinds, etc.

This aphorism was spoken in the 1950s in a very clear and explicit way. Knowledge of lymph, ductless glands and soforth should be in the forefront of one's mind to understand it. It seems complete within itself, and those who have this kind of background knowledge may gain some insights. These aphorisms on lymph, normal sex and the height of emotion from perverted sex indicate the dangers of excessiveness. This excessiveness draws upon the vital forces to such an extent, they are not available, not there, to respond to various germ, virus, disease attacks that would normally be warded off by the proper functioning in a healthy condition. This shows that the lymph system and immunity are similar if not one and the same. ¶Note: while in states of meditation, the body and emotions are dismantled but can quickly attain a normal state due to the fact that there is an abundance of lymph surging through the blood and carrying calmed and controlled nerve force through the ductless glands and the sympathetic nervous system.

THE TIME HAS COME TO ACTUALLY MERGE INTO THE DIVINE, RISE INTO THE HIGHEST REALIZATION AND FLOW INDIVIDUAL AWARENESS INTO realms beyond the beyond. The time has come to advise you to take yourself more seriously than you have ever done before. You are a divine being headed toward a divine destination. The experience of life is your schooling. In looking back through the pages of "Cognizantability," you may see a conundrum, an aphorism or a commentary that you do not or have not immediately understood. If so, then read and reread it and carefully place it in your subconscious mind. Truly, amazingly, your superconscious will have clear cognition for you in an hour, a day or two. You then can claim the ability to cognize, or cognizantability. You, too, will begin to become your own teacher. After all, in the world today people learn very little in a lifetime. Great effort is there but accomplishments are few. For true learning is transformation. Transformation is spirituality in action. The higher Ego implants its revealed knowledge into the lower ego, and when this happens transformation takes place. How does one know when he has been transformed? Well, he does not act in response the same way as before. His emotional nature is controlled by his inner knowing. His intellect is controlled by his awakened abilities to learn from within and verify this knowledge through the faculty of reason. His instinctive nature is harnessed through understanding and applying the laws of transmutation of the creative forces rather than senselessly dissipating them away. Yes, transformation is what all persons are born to achieve. True realization brings transformation. We become different than before.

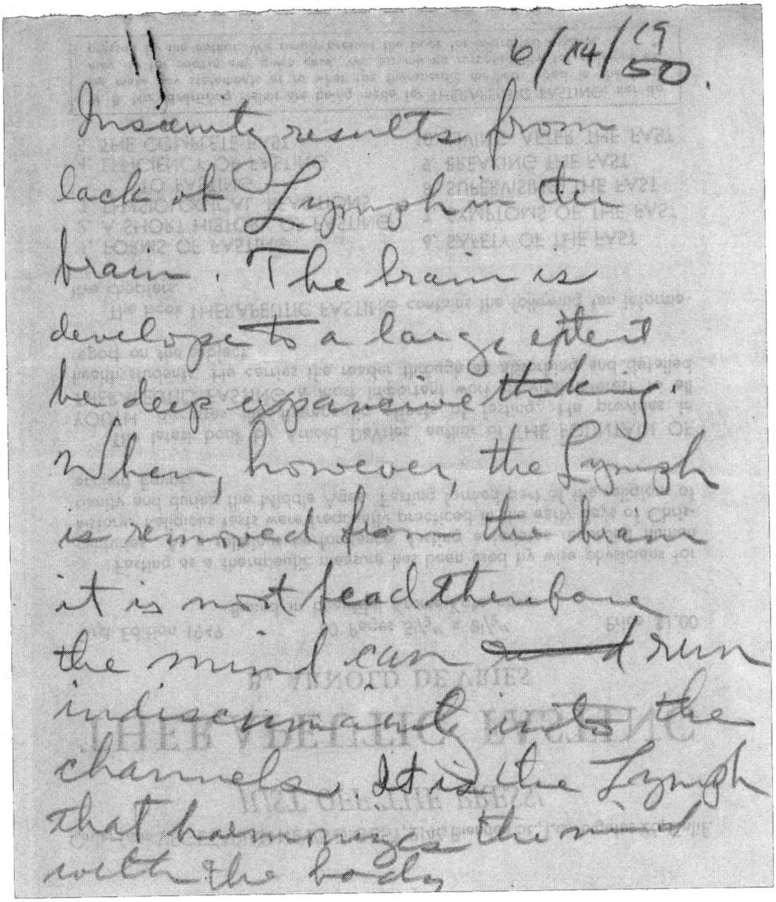

11 6/14/19 50.

Insanity results from lack of Lymph in the brain. The brain is developed to a large extent by deep expansive thinking. When, however, the Lymph is removed from the brain it is not fed therefore the mind can ~~and~~ run indiscriminately into the channels. It is the Lymph that harmonizes the mind with the body

Upagranthāḥ

उपग्रन्थाः

Resources

Eka Eva Antimanirṇayaḥ Sambhavaḥ

एक एव अन्तिमनिर्णयः सम्भवः

There Can Be Only One Final Conclusion

In the primal play of the Lord were souls, *jīvas*, created. Enveloped in mighty *malas* were they. Discarding them, they realized the Self and sought the feet of their ancient Lord. Thus, they became Śiva, with no more births to be.

TIRUMANTIRAM 2369

There Can Be Only One Final Conclusion

THE HISTORY OF RELIGIOUS DEBATE IN INDIA HAS NO PARALLEL IN THE WORLD. THROUGH THE CENTURIES, DEFENDERS OF OPPOSING PHILosophical viewpoints honed their positions and arguments to a steely, razor edge. From time to time entire populations were convinced or even compelled to change their faith, as when King Aśoka, born into the Brahmanical tradition, converted to Buddhism around 258 BCE and zealously promoted it from Afghanistan to Sri Lanka. Obviously, religious debate can have far-reaching effects, and such disputes are not merely the stuff of history, they are quite alive today. This Resource chronicles a controversial exchange which took place in India, Sri Lanka, Malaysia, Singapore, Mauritius, U.K. and the United States in the mid-1980s between two schools of Śaiva Siddhānta, the world's largest Śaivite denomination. On one side are the monistic theists who stress the ultimate oneness of man and God, and on the other stand the pluralistic theists who hold that God, soul and world are eternally separate. Here are the positions of two radically different views of man's relationship with God Śiva. The debate is a living expression of the classical discussion about the Divine, one that is common to every religious tradition and one that every seeker will benefit from exploring.

Visions of Truth: Dualism and Nondualism

Śaiva Siddhānta, the final conclusions of the awakened soul, who soars in superconsciousness above the mountaintop, diffuses through our minds as the distilled essence of the *Vedas, Śaiva Āgamas, Tirumurai* and most especially the great *Tirumantiram.* Śaiva Siddhānta is deeply rooted in these scriptures and surges forth as a giant banyan of their expression. These are our scriptures, and within our scriptures are found both the essential oneness of monism and the evolutionary two-ness of theism. Therefore the *ṛishis* of the *Upanishads*, the *siddhas* of the *Āgamas*, our Śaivite Saints and our Śiva Yogaswāmī Paramparā of the Nandinātha Sampradāya have always taught monistic theism so you, too, can awaken the natural perceptions of your own soul.

From this mountaintop perspective, we can observe, appreciate, understand and be lovingly tolerant of all theological paths to God Śiva. This is because we are seeing the outer and inner worlds from our soul's perspective.

However, when people see the outer and inner worlds from intellectual states of mind, perceiving a concrete reality of you and I and God and world eternally separate, with no union of being, there is a tendency to defend their theology and wage an intellectual war with other theologies. Their intellect is rigid and intolerant, quite the opposite of the soul's natural state of mind. There is no need for seekers to participate in these kinds of battles. What is important is for each of you to follow the path of our Śaivite saints and *siddhas*. It is a path more of love than of learning, more of tolerance than of entanglement. Our sages and seers have made themselves sufficiently clear. They need no interpolations.

Let us stand together, united in the knowledge of monistic theism as taught by our Nayanar saints and the enlightened savants of the *Vedas* and *Āgamas*. Let us remain high-minded in our thoughts and actions. People, who are always at one stage or another on the great San Mārga, will at some point lash out and attack you. This is predictable and natural. Set a fine example of tolerance and understanding in your community. Always hold the mountaintop perspective.

Remember, from the very beginning of man's encounter with Reality, in both the East and the West, discussions have persisted between those who see the world as one and those who see it as made up of two or more. Devotees sometimes ask which is right, monism (also known as *advaita,* or non-dualism) or dualism, *dvaita.* Both are indeed valid and to be found within the *Vedas,* the *Tirumurai* and other scriptures. To the awakened mind, both are right. The view which integrates both is most advanced, definitely more enlightened and in keeping with the wide tolerance within Hinduism. We recently heard a physicist say that his mentor, Werner Heisenberg, observed that there are two kinds of truth—shallow truth and deep truth. Shallow truth is one whose opposite is false. Deep truth is truth whose opposite may be perceived as an integral part of its own validity. That wise observation of the physical universe also applies to our spiritual knowledge. The deeper mystics do not draw a square to exclude, deny and condemn views which oppose their own. Instead, they draw a wide circle that embraces the entirety of the vast mystery of Śiva's creation.

There are various stages of realization on the path to Lord Śiva's holy feet. The world and God and soul look a little different from each stage. It really all depends on the window we are looking out of, the *chakra* in which we are functioning. Thus, in exploring monism and dualism one must keep an open mind. This will bring the realization that the view called monistic theism is the summation of them both and is the highest realization, the ancient philosophy that is indigenous to man, preceding even the Vedic era. What, then, is monistic theism? It is the belief in God, but God not separate from man. It is external worship of Śiva which is then internalized into realization of one's own Śivaness. It is a *bhakti,* experiential, yogically transforming philosophy.

The dualistic or pluralistic conception appears true from one perspective, but it is only a slice of the whole. It is not the whole. Regarded most simply, pluralism came as the philosophical conclusion or realization of *siddhas* and saints within the *charyā* and *kriyā pādas,* while monism joined with theism is the overwhelming vision within the *yoga* and *jñāna pādas*. Here is another way to explain the same thing. Visualize a mountain and the path leading to its icy summit. As the climber traverses the lower ranges, he sees the meadows, the passes, the giant boulders. This we can liken to theism, the natural dual state where God and man are different.

Reaching the summit, the climber sees that the many parts are actually a one mountain. This is likened to pure monism. Unfortunately, many pure monists, reaching the summit, teach a denial of the foothills they themselves climbed on the way to their monistic platform. However, by going a little higher, lifting the consciousness into the space above the topmost peak of the mountain, the entire truth is known. The bottom and the top are viewed as a one whole, just as theism and monism are understood and accepted by the awakened soul. The knower and the known become one.

Pluralistic Śaiva Siddhāntins make the part into the whole, tending to deny, redefine and modify the monism taught by the Śaiva saints and proclaimed in the *Vedas* and *Āgamas*. To know the final conclusions, to comprehend the monistic theism of Śaiva Siddhānta, they must go a little farther, do more *sādhana*, in order to see these truths from a higher plane of consciousness. As Ṛishi Tirumular admonishes, "Siddhānta without Vedānta is the common Śaiva's lot." Vedānta is and always has been the final conclusion of the *Vedas*, but it really, esoterically, means that these conclusion are the results of the realization of thousands. When *yogic* realization, and transformation because of it, is not present, it is said to become "the path of words." However, the basic understanding of Vedānta naturally leads into Siddhānta, once understanding matures into directing the force of desire into realization of the Self. Here we have the happy and necessary blend of Vedānta and Siddhānta as a way of life and spiritual practice.

My *satguru*, Śiva Yogaswāmī, asked me which of these

schools of thought was the right one. I told him that both were right in their own way. It all depends on whether you are on top of the mountain looking down or at the bottom of it looking up. He smiled and nodded.

Jñānaguru Yogaswāmī taught that monistic theism is the highest vision of truth. For pluralists to deny the *Vedas* is to deny Vedānta, and that is to deny Truth itself. For Vedāntists to deny the reality of God and creation is to deny Siddhānta, and that also is a denial of Eternal Truth. We cannot find a more shallow course of action than to declare the enlightened postulations of the illumined saints as superficial affirmations or as mad ravings, which a pluralist *pandit* once told me they were.

It is argued—as an issue involving Tamil nationalism within their state, Tamil Nadu, in India—that embracing monism may divide the Tamil people. This is indefensible. Monistic theism is the soul of Śaivism, and therefore it is the soul of the Tamil people. It is monistic theism that will unite all the Tamils the world over in a one unanimity of belief, worship and understanding.

It is also contended that by preserving pluralism as a unique feature of Tamil Śaivism, the Tamil identity is being preserved. This is a very narrow view. It only preserves a partial understanding of Truth and denies the Tamil people their rightful heritage of the fullness and richness of Sanātana Dharma. Dravidian history reveals that a united people are those who all worship the same Supreme God in the same way, pledging their allegiance to the fullness of the eternal truths discovered by their saints and sages. Thus, each one is strong in his or her *dharma* with developed qualities of leadership, compassion, insight, cooperation and fortitude. Thus, each one awakens the burning zeal of *sādhana* to personally experience these inner Truths.

The results of this unity are great civilizations like the Indus Valley, the Chola Empire and the Vijayanagar Empire.

But today we find the Tamils a people fractioned among themselves, divided into a multiplicity of "-isms." The more religious have escaped into the heights of Siddhānta-Vedānta. The more intellectual or Western-educated are ensnared in arguments and Western rationales or have wandered off into Buddhism and Christianity.

Monistic theism, that all-embracing and ancient path which is common among all Śaivite sects, is the solution to international unity among the Tamil people in the twenty-first century as it was 5,000 years ago, for its theology closes the door to conversion and puts the heart and mind at peace. Furthermore, it is this mountaintop view of reality which alone can free the soul from the cycles of birth and death, joy and sorrow. In this age of enlightenment, religion and the knowledge of Truth that it holds must be unquestionably easy to understand and universally available to all who seek refuge at Lord Śiva's holy feet.

The purpose of this Resource Section is to present the monistic Śaiva Siddhānta philosophy—sometimes known as Advaita Siddhānta or Advaita Īśvaravāda—and to juxtapose it briefly with pluralistic Śaiva Siddhānta or Dvaita Siddhānta. This comparison is important because the pluralistic teachings are widespread, so much so that many authoritative texts proclaim Śaiva Siddhānta to be wholly pluralistic and completely overlook the monistic school, which is actually far older, but less well known. Between these two schools there continues a philosophical debate that has persisted for twenty centuries and more about whether God and soul are ultimately one or two.

I first became aware of this ongoing debate in 1948 while living and performing *sādhana,* living in little mud huts with cow dung floors, in Jaffna, Sri Lanka, prior to my initiation from my *satguru,* Śiva Yogaswāmī. I learned that various pluralist adherents in the area were not pleased with this modern mystic's monistic statements and conclusions. In my life, the issue again came into prominence in the early '80s after my recognition by the world community of Śaivites as Guru Mahāsannidhānam of Kauai Aadheenam and Jagadāchārya of the Nātha Sampradāya's Kailāsa Paramparā. By that time, our small but dynamic Śaivite Hindu church had distributed thousands of copies of our Hindu Catechism, *Dancing with Śiva,* boldly proclaiming the monistic truths of the Kailāsa Paramparā and bravely claiming the term *Śaiva Siddhānta* as our own. This did not go unnoticed by pluralist scholars and *pandits* who for generations had faced little opposition to their claim that *Śaiva Siddhānta* is pluralistic by definition.

Letters poured into our temple at Kauai Aadheenam in Hawaii, objecting to our philosophical position and urging us to give up the appellation *Śaiva Siddhānta,* or to convert to the pluralistic view. We did not budge, arguing that, indeed, *Śaiva Siddhānta* is the perfect name for our teachings. In response, we reiterated our philosophical position clearly and compared it with the pluralist views, citing scriptural sources in a formal document called "Monism and Pluralism in Śaiva Siddhānta." And, in an inspired talk distributed throughout the world, I asserted, "There can be only one final conclusion, and that is monistic theism." To the pluralists, it appeared we had thrown down the gauntlet. The debate was on.

Once a relatively muted village affair, this age-old feud quickly escalated into a heated international debate among eight great monasteries in South India and Sri Lanka, of *saṅgas* in South Africa, Mauritius, Malaysia and England, and of philosophers, *pandits,* attorneys, judges and politicians from nearly every continent of the world. But for the first time, perhaps, the issue was faced with the goal of reaching a final resolution. Follow this debate, not as an exercise but as a way to deepen your own understanding of the ultimate things of life, of your own relationship with the universe around you, your own path toward merging in Śiva.

Monism and Pluralism in Śaiva Siddhānta

JUST AS THERE ARE THREE ORTHODOX SCHOOLS OF THOUGHT WITHIN THE VEDĀNTA PHILOSOPHY (NONDUALISM, QUALIFIED NONDUALISM and dualism), there are two within Śaiva Siddhānta (monism and pluralism). Both are orthodox and essential to Śaiva Siddhānta. Each is strengthened and clarified by the existence of the other. Śaivism would be less complete, less philosophically rich, without one or the other.

Religion may be simply defined as man's knowledge of himself, of the world in which he finds himself and of the Truth or Reality or God which transcends both. When properly understood, religion does not divide man from man, making this one a faithless sinner and that one a worthy recipient of Divine Grace. Purely known and practiced, religion is leading man, all men, to enlightenment and liberation. But religion is not always purely known—and even less often purely practiced—which gives rise to differences.

Differences in religion, arising as they do out of a variety of racial, cultural and individual experience, are to be expected and appreciated. They provide a fortress against philosophical monotony and spiritual stagnation. Though there are many who seek to convert the rest of the world to their own creed, the wise are tolerant of the beliefs of others and refuse to promote universal uniformity in cultural, intellectual or spiritual spheres.

Though their numbers are dwindling, there are still those who, in an effort to reconcile the differences between religions, claim that all religions are one. We commend the effort and all efforts which bring men into mutual understanding, which soften religious tensions, conflict and animosity. However, to simply say that they are all one and the same is simplistic. It is not true. All religions are not the same. To pretend that their differences are insignificant or nonexistent will not resolve those differences. Understanding is the only permanent resolution, and that comes through an open-minded and courageous study of the unique strengths and weaknesses inherent in each. This is the spirit in which we undertake this assessment of two philosophical schools that worship a one God, Śiva, and together comprise the religious tradition known as Śaiva Siddhānta.

1. The Need for Harmonious Coexistence

Śaivism is the world's most ancient religion, and its most comprehensive exposition is found in Śaiva Siddhānta, which can be roughly translated as the "Final Conclusions of the Śaiva Dharma." Śaivism—and most especially the traditions and philosophy expressed in Śaiva Siddhānta—is, we are convinced, the religion of the future, more suited than any other to a technological age, fully in harmony with science and more able to provide for mankind's resurgent demands for direct spiritual awakening and enlightened living than any other religion on the planet. The oldest faith has survived an age of reason, with its prophets of agnosticism, to become the newest faith in an age where mystical values are again appreciated.

2. Crucial Differences between Monism and Pluralism

Stated most simply, the monistic school holds that God Śiva created everything by emanation from Himself, the world, all things in the world and all souls, and that each soul is ultimately destined to merge in *advaitic* union with Him, just as a river merges into the sea. On the other hand, the pluralistic school postulates that God Śiva did not create the world or souls, but that they have eternally existed just as He has, and that the ultimate destiny of the soul is not *advaitic* union in God Śiva but nondual association with Him in eternal blessedness or bliss, just as salt dissolved in water.

In one view there is manifestation from Śiva in the beginning and merging back into Śiva in the end, and only the Supreme God, Śiva, is eternal and uncreated. In the second view there is no beginning for the soul, but eternal coexistence of the soul with Śiva from the *kevala* state, which goes back to the absolutely primordial time, to the *śuddha* state, which extends forever into the future. In the monistic view, God Śiva is everything; even this physical universe is a part of Him, though He transcends it as well. In the pluralistic view , God Śiva animates and guides the universe, but it is not a part of Him. The crux of the difference, then, is whether there is one eternal reality in the universe or three, whether the soul is eternally separate or is, in essence, one with Śiva.

3. Points of Agreement

It should be made clear that these are not diametrically opposing philosophies. They share more in common than they disagree about. In fact, between these two schools there is 95 percent agreement and only 5 percent dissidence. Both are committed to the importance of temple worship, to love of God Śiva, who is both immanent and transcendent, and of the Gods, Gaṇeśa and Muruga. They share the same scriptures and saints, a deep devotion to the *saṅga* of fellow Sivathondars, a belief in *karma* and reincarnation, a firm faith in the need to live a virtuous life and to perform *sādhana* and *yoga,* a veneration of the *satguru* and his necessary role in the spiritual illumination of the soul, which, they concur, moves progressively through the stages of *charyā, kriyā, yoga* and *jñāna.* They both argue vehemently against the Advaita Vedānta view of *māyā* as mere illusion, insisting that this world has a divine purpose—the evolution of the soul—and that, even though it is only relatively real, it is certainly not unreal. They do not agree with the Advaita Vedānta conception of the ultimate unreality of the soul, or of the Vedāntin's relegation of the mystical science of temple worship to a kindergarten for young souls. Again and again on a hundred issues they find themselves in harmony.

We now begin our comparison of these two schools of Śaiva Siddhānta, first with a restatement of their philosophical conclusions. Next a point-counterpoint of their most important beliefs is presented, followed by four major pluralistic arguments with monistic rejoinders.

4. Monistic Siddhānta in a Nutshell

God Śiva created and is constantly creating, preserving and reabsorbing all things, emanating from Himself the individual soul of man, all the worlds and their contents. He is the Beginning and the End, the Author of Existence. He is both material and efficient cause, and thus His act of manifestation may be likened to sparks issuing forth from a fire or fruits emerging from a tree. The individual soul—which is an effulgent being, a body of light—is created, evolves as a separate being and ultimately merges in undifferentiated union and oneness with God Śiva, which oneness may be called identity. The essence of the soul, which is Satchidānanda and Paraśiva, is eternal and uncreated, does not evolve but is forever perfect. This essence of the soul is not different from Śiva. The world and the soul are, in truth, but various forms of Śiva Himself, yet He also transcends His creation and is not limited by it. Also, the world and the soul cannot stand independent of God, a fact which makes it clear that they are evolutes and not eternal entities. When world and soul are absorbed in His Divine Form at the time of *mahāpralaya*—the end of a cosmic creational cycle—all three *malas (āṇava, karma* and *māyā)* are removed through His grace, and the soul's individual existence ceases, losing its separateness through union and fulfillment in Śiva. After *mahāpralaya,* Śiva alone exists until creation issues forth from Him in yet another cosmic cycle.

5. Pluralistic Siddhānta in a Nutshell

God Śiva did not create all things. Rather, there are three eternal and coexistent entities—God, soul and world. When we speak of creation of the world and all things in the world, we must understand that the primordial material of creation always existed and that God Śiva merely fashions it into its myriad forms, just as a potter shapes a multitude of pots from a pre-existing clay, but does not also create the clay. Thus, God Śiva is the efficient cause of the universe, but He is not the material cause, which is *māyā,* eternal and uncreated. The soul, too, exists from eternity, and God Śiva fashions the various bodies needed for its evolution and provides the faculties of perception, discrimination, and so forth. The ultimate destiny of the soul is to reach the feet of God Śiva and enjoy nondual (but not *advaitic* in the sense of oneness or identity) union in Him which may be thought of as eternally blissful beatitude and nearness in which the soul rests in union with Him, as salt dissolved in water, while yet retaining its individuality. At the time of *mahāpralaya,* it is not only God Śiva which exists; rather, the world and an infinity of souls are drawn near God Śiva. They retain their own individual and separate existence, whether real or potential, awaiting another cycle of cosmic creation.

6. Purport

Our tradition supports wholeheartedly the first of the above conclusions and believes it to be the pure, original and highest conclusion of Śaiva Siddhānta. The monistic interpretation is, after all, the view of creation and union described in the *Vedas* and *Śaiva Āgamas.* It is the conclusion of our Paramaguru Śiva Yogaswāmī, of my own personal realizations, and of every single one of my *sannyāsins* of the Śaiva Siddhānta Yoga Order. It is the postulation of the Nayanars of Śaiva Samāyām as expounded in their 18,400 hymns of *Tirumurai.* And, undeniably, it is the clear teaching of the peerless Ṛishi Tirumular in his *Tirumantiram,* the first and foremost scripture on Śaiva Siddhānta. Furthermore, it is the realization of hundreds of sages, saints and *satgurus* throughout the history of the Śaiva Neri, including Vasugupta, founder of Kashmīr Śaivism; Śrīkaṇṭha, founder of Śiva Advaita; and Basavaṇṇa, founder of Vīra Śaivism.

7. Definitions of Monism and Pluralism

Webster's Dictionary defines *monism* as "the doctrine that there is only one ultimate substance or principle, that reality is an organic whole without independent parts." This is the opposite of *dualism:* "the theory that the world is ultimately composed of, or explicable in terms of, two basic entities, ...the doctrine that there are two mutually antagonistic principles in the universe, good and evil." *Pluralism* is defined as "the theory that reality is composed of a multiplicity of ultimate beings, principles or substances."

8. The Importance of these Subtle Issues

Of course, these are all subtle distinctions which may not seem to relate to one's daily religious experience. Thus, we may be inclined to dismiss such issues as of concern only to theologians, *satgurus, swāmīs, yogīs* and philosophers. Yet, they are the very crux of religion and cannot be regarded as unimportant. They affect every Śaivite, for they define two distinct perceptions of the nature of the soul (and therefore of ourselves), of the world and of God Śiva. They offer a spiritual goal which is either to merge fully and forever in Him (a state which transcends even states of bliss) or to remain eternally separated from God (though such separation is seen positively as endless bliss, which cannot be derogated). One view is unity in identity in which the embodied soul, *jīva,* actually is and becomes Śiva; the other is unity in duality, two in one (two because the third entity, the world, or *pāśa,* does not ever, even partly, merge with God), in which the soul enjoys proximity with God Śiva but remains forever an individual soul.

9. Monism of the *Tirumantiram* versus Pluralism of the *Meykandar Śāstras*

To understand the doctrines of the two schools of Śaiva Siddhānta, we must consider briefly the contents of two important texts: *Tirumantiram* and *Meykandar Śāstras.* Tirumular was a *siddha,* a realized master and perfect *yogī* who composed over 3,000 mystic verses to delineate the path of enlightenment and the nature of the reality he had himself realized. These profound and sometimes difficult verses comprise the tenth of the *Tirumurai,* one of the primary scriptures of Śaiva Siddhānta. It is, in fact, the oldest (ca 100 BCE), most mystical and most comprehensive of all the *Tirumurai* and the first instance in history where the term *Śaiva Siddhānta* is recorded.

The *Meykandar Śāstras* are fourteen Tamil treatises written over a long period during the Middle Ages by six authors. In sum, they are scholarly texts presenting in detail the metaphysics of pluralism and refutations of other systems of thought. The fourth of these is *Śivajñānabodham,* composed by Saint Meykandar around 1200 CE, thirteen centuries after the *Tirumantiram.* It is considered by most Siddhāntins as the authoritative summation of pluralistic Śaiva Siddhānta philosophy, containing in forty lines all that is amplified in the larger commentaries and texts that comprise the balance of the *Meykandar Śāstras.*

Saint Meykandar's twelve verses, called *sūtras,* comprise the entire text of *Śivajñānabodham*—meaning "Knowledge of Śiva Realization" or "Compendium of Śiva Knowledge." In its aphoristic brevity, this digest may be likened to the philosophical equivalent of Einstein's cryptic equation, $E=MC^2$. This text, which may well be the shortest scripture ever written, is considered by many to be his only work, though others contend that he also composed his own commentaries on the verses.

Are there, in fact, any differences between Tirumular's *Tirumantiram* and Meykandar's *Śivajñānabodham?* Yes and no. Here, in sum, is our judgment: Meykandar himself composed his twelve *sūtras* in full accord with Tirumular's *Tirumantiram,* and there is not a single word or concept in *Śivajñānabodham* that is in conflict with *Tirumantiram,* though we find the relationship of the latter to the former as that of the whole to the part. This conclusion is founded on several of the more respected translations found in English.

Here we make a critical distinction between Meykandar's twelve renowned verses and the volumes, the virtual libraries, of commentary and interpretation which have arisen in explanation of his simple stanzas. There are a few who will argue that Meykandar himself was the author of the first of these commentaries, but we are persuaded, as are several authorities who have studied the matter, that this is not true. In keeping with the long-standing tradition of the philosophical poets, he wrote only the verses and none of the commentaries.

While the verses of *Śivajñānabodham* are themselves in consonance with *Tirumantiram,* the commentaries, being the balance of the *Meykandar Śāstras,* are not. Commentators and scholars who followed Meykandar interpreted his work (and the *Tirumantiram)* as pluralistic, setting into motion roughly 800 years ago the present-day pluralistic school, a school that has played a major, even dominant political, part in the modern history of Śaiva Siddhānta. Pluralists rightly place the beginning of their school at the time of the *Meykandar Śāstras.* What they do not often reveal is that Śaiva Siddhānta in its monistic form existed long before.

An analysis of the history of the times suggests that the founding fathers of pluralistic Śaiva Siddhānta were—as so often happens in particular historic circumstances—responding to powerful and compelling movements which were then in the ascendency. These included an aggressive Christian theology, the potent Vedāntic teachings of Adi Śaṅkara and Madhva's dualistic Vaishṇavite school—which were dominant forces in India during those formative centuries. The conclusions found in the *Meykandar Śāstras* are very close to the dualistic theism found in the Judaic-Christian-Islamic faiths and in Vaishṇavism. Thus, they are far removed from the monism which has been the basis of Śaivite Hinduism from its inception. We regret that because of this affinity between Christian dogma and the pluralistic school, whenever a Śaiva Siddhāntin wishes to give pride of position to his religion he calls upon the Catholic priests and Protestant ministers who freely proclaim the merits of pluralistic Śaiva Siddhānta. That, in itself, should be sufficient warning to Śaiva Siddhāntins that pluralism has diverged from the true Śaiva path, which is as far distinct from Judaic-Christian-Islamic theology as day is from night. It is Śaivites, not leaders of the Abrahamic religions, who should be called upon to espouse the greatness of our faith.

The differences between these two bodies of scripture must be emphasized. The *Tirumantiram* was written by Ṛishi Tirumular, a *siddha,* a perfect master. In contrast, the *Meykandar Śāstras* were authored by scholars and intellectual giants—though Meykandar himself was a notable exception. Whereas Tirumular spoke from his own direct, inner knowing of reality, attained through *sādhana* and *yoga,* writers of the *Meykandar Śāstras* took another approach, working through inference and reason, assembling, collating and synthesizing the existing tenets of Śaiva Siddhānta of their day. Whereas Tirumular lived before the dawn of the Common Era, authors of the *Meykandar Śāstras* lived thirteen centuries later, during the Middle Ages. Whereas the *Tirumantiram* is a primary scripture (the tenth of the twelve *Tirumurai),* the *Meykandar Śāstras* are a secondary scripture, not included in the *Tirumurai.* Whereas Tirumular is one of the 63 canonized Śaiva Saints, called Nayanars, Meykandar and his commentators are not. Thus, we have two forces: one spiritual and the other theological or philosophical; one intuitive, the other intellectual and political; one founded on enlightenment and the other based on exceptional mentality.

Few Śaivites have deeply studied *Śivajñānabodham* and fewer still are familiar with the contents of *Tirumantiram.* So, it is not surprising that they have assumed—wrongly—that the conclusions of the *Meykandar Śāstras* are in agreement with the *Tirumantiram.* A few know of the monistic school which defends creation and a complete merger, but they often do not know that this is the original Śaiva Siddhānta of Ṛishi Tirumular and before. Rather, they think of it as a renegade philosophy so similar to the postulations of Vedānta that it probably had its source in that tradition. This, of course, is not so.

10. Two Views of Creation

Again and again in several countries, I have been asked, is it the teaching of Śaiva Siddhānta that God Śiva created the world and the individual soul? Yes, most certainly. Ṛishi Tirumular is unequivocal on this point, stating time and again in his *Tirumantiram* that God Śiva has created everything from Himself in a process of emanation.

The word *create* poses certain problems, for it is commonly used in conjunction with the Abrahamic (Judaic-Christian-Islamic) concept of something being called into existence which did not previously exist. This is not our meaning of the word. Nor should we limit the word to only mean "to effect," as some are inclined to do. The English word, of ultimately Latin origin, derives from the verb "to grow or cause to grow." We use the word *create* in the specific sense of manifestation, of one thing growing out of or being produced or made from another. Thus, when we use the word *create,* it can always be assumed that we mean "to emanate," "to manifest" or "to become." The Sanskṛit word for creation is *sṛishṭi,* meaning "to emit," "to let loose," which corresponds closely to the definition of creation as found in the *Tirumantiram.* Tirumular employs the Tamil word *padai.*

Here are a number of the relevant verses from the *Tirumantiram* which demonstrate Tirumular's doctrine. We quote more than a few because there are some *pandits* who hold that Tirumular does not speak of Śiva's emanational creation, wrongly assuming he concurs with the view that God's only creative act is to reshape existing matter.

> Of yore He created worlds seven. Of yore He created celestials countless. Of yore He created souls without number. Of yore He created all—Himself, as Primal Param, uncreated (446).
>
> In the Primal Play of the Lord were souls *(jīvas)* created; enveloped in mighty *malas* were they. Discarding them, they realized the Self, and sought the feet of their ancient Lord. Thus they Śiva became, with no more births to be (2369).
>
> All worlds by vast oceans He girt, my Lord, filled pervasively, in omniscience, overseeing all. Of yore He created all, entirely, and stood diffusing His golden hue in worlds everywhere (3007).
>
> The Supreme is one, Absolute, without lapse, in descent thereof, Brahmā and Vishṇu becoming. Thus, He, the One into many ranked, by conscious choice a Self-deduction made (111).
>
> Sadāśiva, the He-She, creates universes all. He has five sons, the Holy One who creates universes all, Himself as the lotus-seated Brahmā, the Creator, became (386).
>
> With Hara who spewed out the seven worlds, with Brahmā, the four-headed Maker, the Primal One, the Lord of Celestial Beings, created, of yore, this vast universe (389).
>
> Death and birth the Holy One ordains; and in the hour when by His thought He commences the Act of Creation, He fills and pervades the eight directions, He, the Compassionate One (393).
>
> Out of *içcha,* of the three *śaktis,* arose *māyā;* And *māyā* in union with *bindu* yielded the rest of the three *māyās (śuddha,*

aśuddha and *prakṛiti).* And *nāda* was of Para born; and all this is the creative play of Paraśiva, the Ultimate (399).

The One alone created the worlds seven. The One alone spanned the worlds seven. The One alone survived the worlds seven. The One alone pervaded body and life (404).

One clay, many the receptacles,
one God pervades all species (440).

From end to end of this cosmic universe, there is nothing but the Bejeweled Lady. It is all but Śakti and Śiva (1210).

In union that knows no separateness, verily,
God is the Beginning and End of All (1570).

The Paraparam that is the End and the Beginning, Immanent,
He expanded thus. As Cause and Effect, too, He is (1927).

Vaikharī and the rest of sounds, *māyā* and the rest of
impurities, *purusha* and the rest of *tattvas* illusory—all
these, acting on *śaktis jñāna* and *kriyā,* the Lord
true from time immemorial made (2007).

If the cardinal directions are all Śiva, why speak of someone
else, O you men? All smoke emanates from fire.
All creation arises from our Primal Lord (3010).

To all who take the time to read these verses with care, Ṛishi Tirumular's message resounds again and again: God Śiva created everything of Himself, and everything includes the soul, *māyā* that is the substratum of this universe, the *tattvas* which constitute all forms, even the celestial Gods. And He Himself is His creation, both material and efficient cause. Tirumular speaks of Śiva as material cause:

He is the *tattvas* and their Lord (2795).
He is the First Being, the effort and the end of effort, too (11).

The hoary scriptures say the expanding space is His body (2463).

Holding the worlds apart, as the heavens high He spreads,
Himself the scorching fire, the sun and moon (10).

He is the master mahout of all *jīvas;*
He is *jīvas* themselves, too (3039).

> Water, earth, sky, fire and wind, the spark of light within the body—all these He is. He is Paraparam, He is Śiva, our Lord. He is the walking *jīva* here below. Deathless He is (3045).

Here again Tirumular is clear that God Śiva is both Creator and created, both material and efficient cause, the goal and the path, seeker and sought.

This is not the teaching of the Meykandar school, which asserts that *māyā* exists forever, without creation, as does the soul, and that God Śiva is the efficient cause but not the material cause of the universe. On this essential point the *Meykandar Śāstras* differ from all other scriptures of Śaiva Siddhānta, including *Tirumantiram,* the *Vedas,* their *Upanishads,* the *Tirumurai* and other Śaivite holy texts, which repeatedly affirm Śiva as material cause of the universe, saying that from Śiva arises all this universe, sentient and insentient. Here are a few examples from Śaivite scriptures of the emanational creation which is Śaivism's traditional philosophical view:

> He is the one God, the Creator. He enters into all wombs. The One Absolute, impersonal Existence, together with His inscrutable *māyā,* appears as the Divine Lord, endowed with manifold glories. With His Divine power He holds dominion over all the worlds. At the periods of creation and dissolution of the universe He alone exists. Those who realize Him become immortal. The Lord is One without a second. Within man He dwells, and within all other beings. He projects the universe, maintains it, and withdraws it into Himself *(Śvetāśvatara Upanishad* 3.1-2 UPP).

> Brahman is that from which all beings are born,
> that by which they live, that into which, when departing,
> they enter *(Taittirīya Upanishad* 3.1.1-6 UPH).

> As the sea issues forth foam, waves and bubbles which
> subside into it, the Absolute Spirit is the substratum
> whence arises the world animate and inanimate
> and thither it tends *(Mapadian* 151).

> He reflected, may I become many *(Taittirīya Upanishad* 2.6 UPR).

> Brahmā became the visible and the invisible.
> (*Taittirīya Upanishad* 2.6 UPH)

> It is likened to the sparks which issue from a fire.
> *(Bṛihadāraṇyaka Upanishad* 2.1.20 UPR)

> As a spider sends forth and withdraws its web, as hair grows from the body of a living person, so from the Imperishable arises this universe *(Muṇḍaka Upanishad* 1.1.7 UPR).

> He is all this world of the moving and the nonmoving. Whatever is, is He alone *(Panskara-Bhashya).*

> The *Raurava Āgama* describes creation as a spark of fire or light issuing forth from the third eye of the Creator.

11. What Do the Nayanars Teach?

The 63 Nayanars, Śaivite saints, represent a fundamental source of spiritual insight, knowledge and authority for Śaiva Siddhānta, both in the example of their lives and in their sacred writings. No Siddhāntin will gainsay their teachings, and thus it is important to know their views on the subject at hand. Ṛishi Tirumular and the other Nayanars (as well as in the *Vedas* and *Upanishads)* overwhelmingly express monistic Śaiva Siddhānta. Tirunavukarasu, Saint Appar, has spoken of the emanation of Śiva thus:

> Thou became the flesh! Thou became the life! Thou became the awareness within it! Thou became everything else. He is Himself He. He also becomes me (*Saint Appar).*

> He is the fruit, the juice and even the taster thereof;
> the "Thou" and the "I" *(Appar's Nindra Tiruttandakam* 6.94.5).

> He is the knower; He is the revealer; He is the knowledge; He is even the known; He is also this vast world, the sky and so on.
> (*Karaikkalammaiyar* 20)

There are literally thousands of testimonies in the *Tirumurai* and other Śaiva literature that Lord Śiva is everything, that He became everything. These scriptural verses cannot be simply denied or explained away. They represent clear and holy teachings of monistic theism by the foremost of Śaiva Saints.

12. Saint Tayumanavar on Emanational Creation

Śiva is universally lauded as the Creator, but then some claim He actually does not have that power, or they redefine it. If we say that Śiva did not create (or emanate) the world and the soul, then we deny Him one of the five powers, that of Creation, and thereby diminish His grcatness, limit the Unlimited, restrict the Unbounded, restrain the Omnipotent. For most Śaivites He is Creator, Preserver and Destroyer—which means nothing more and nothing less than He has created everything. We cannot say he created the world and not the soul. And if we try to say He created neither, then we say He created nothing and does not have the power of Creation. Scriptures are clear and unambiguous on this point—Śiva did create all things. It must follow that He created both soul and world, preserves them by His Grace and will ultimately withdraw them back to Himself. Saint Tayumanavar wrote of creation as emanation, and a few verses from his sacred hymns are extracted below.

> In the final dissolution all that was visible vanished, and what resulted was *mukti* of blemishless bliss; and so the functions of creation and preservation, along with *māyā,* ceased to exist; but who was it that stood with the garland of radiant-eyed white skulls stretching along His Hands and Feet? (15.3 HT).

> Alone, by Thyself, Thou arose in the Vast Expanse
> and danced in the arena of the Void (20.6 HT).

> Thou created the sky and the other elements,
> Thou preserves them and dissolves them (20.8).

13. From the Illumined Teachings of the Modern Siddha Satguru Śiva Yogaswāmī

Śaivite saints and *satgurus* have always stressed monism, never its opposite. In recent times, the greatest *siddha* in Sri Lanka was Śiva Yogaswāmī (1872-1964) of Columbuthurai. He was a *yogī* and mystic who awakened knowledge, who realized Śiva himself through great *sādhana* and *tapas.* He is considered among the greatest of modern sages, a true *jīvanmukta* of the highest order and the spiritual guide for Śaivites throughout Sri Lanka and South India for many decades. He taught again and again, in person and in his published *Natchintanai,* that Śiva is both Creator and creation, never speaking of a state in which the soul remains eternally separate from its Creator. Here are a few relevant quotes from his teachings. (The numbers following the verses denote page numbers in the English edition.)

> Can you not perceive that it is That
> which has become both heaven and earth? (38).

> He has become the sun and moon.
> He has become the constellations of the stars.
> *Mantra* and *tantra* has He become.
> He has become the medicine and those who swallow it.
> He has become the Gods, Indra and all the rest.
> He has Himself become the universe entire.
> The soul and body, too, has He become (144; 219).

> All things are of Śiva made, my treasure (81).

> Earth and water, air and light and space—
> He has all these become (104).

> You and I, he and it, fire and ether,
> ghosts and devils, other beings and Gods—
> upon examination will all appear as He (123).

> All is the work of Śiva. All is the form of Śiva.
> He is everything (127).

> The Unique One by sacrifice has All become (138).

He is body, He is life, He is I, He is you (141).

Before the body falls, revere the God
who both the One and many has become (202).

The universe of things that move and do not move
is all His form. The universe of things that move
and do not move is He (222).

There is nothing else but That! (234).

All is Śiva. Father and mother are Śiva.
All the Gods are Śiva. The whole universe is Śiva (237).

Thus resound the *Natchintanai* verses of my *satguru,* affirming the monism of Ṛishi Tirumular.

14. Monism in the Meykandar Sūtras

What did Meykandar himself have to say about monism and creation? A careful analysis has shown us that he does not disagree with Tirumular. We adduce here the famous twelve *sūtras* as translated by Kavi Yogi Shuddhānanda Bharati, *The Revelations of Saint Meykandar,* a translation chosen for its simplicity, not necessarily its scholarship.

1. *He, she and it*—these are the three terms in which the cosmic entity is spoken of. This cosmos undergoes three changes—birth, growth and death—triple functions. It appears, stays and disappears; but it reappears by dint of the ego-consciousness which binds it. He who ends it, is its origin. He, Hara, is the Supreme Master: so say the seers of knowledge.

2. He is one with souls; yet He is Himself unattached, beyond all. He is identified with His willpower, His knowledge-force in inseparable union. Through this force, He pervades all and submits souls to birth and death, allowing them to eat the fruits of their dual acts [good and bad deeds].

3. Because it says: "The body is the mechanism of nature. A soul dwells in its core." For it responds, "Yes" or "No." It asserts, "This is my body." It feels the five sensations. It is conscious in

dreams. It does not hunger, or eat or act in deep sleep. It knows when taught.

4. The soul is none of the *antaḥkaraṇas* [the inner faculties or senses]. The soul does not feel shrouded by egoism. It is cognizant only in conjunction with the Inner Instruments, just as the king knows the state of affairs through his ministers. Similar is the relation of the soul with the five planes of experience, too.

5. The senses perceive and carry impressions of external objects to the mind. But they cannot know themselves, nor do they know the soul. The soul perceives through the senses and the mind. But similarly, it cannot know itself or God. It is the Divine Grace that activates it, just like a magnet activates iron.

6. If [God] is knowable, then He is nonreal; if unknowable, He does not exist. Therefore, the wise of the world say that He is neither of the two, but the Supreme Reality, both knowable and unknowable. [This version is from Mariasusai Dhavamony's *Love of God According to Śaiva Siddhānta,* who renders this *sūtra* and the next more adequately.]

7. Before Being, all things are nonexistent; hence, Being does not know [nonbeing]; nonbeing does not exist, so it cannot know [Being]. Therefore, that which knows both [Being and nonbeing] is the soul, which is neither Being nor nonbeing. [Dhavamony.]

8. When the soul is sufficiently advanced in *tapasya* (spiritual discipline), the Supreme Lord comes in the form of a divine master. He instructs the soul: "O Soul, thou hast fallen into the hands of the hunters [the senses]; growing up among them, thou hast forgotten the Lord, who is thy very core. Awake!" The soul wakes up to Reality, renounces all attachments to the senses. It devotes itself unreservedly and uniquely to Hara and attains His Blessed Feet." (It is interesting that Dhavamony translates the latter part of this *sūtra* as "the soul leaves its association with the senses and being not other [than Him] reaches God's Feet.")

9. The Lord cannot be seen by carnal eyes, by the senses. The eye of knowledge must open. Thought must fix in it. Bondage of

the lower nature must be left off as a mirage. Then the soul finds shelter in God. To attain this blissful state, the soul should meditate upon the *mantra* Namaḥ Śivāya.

10. Śiva is one with the soul. The soul must merge its individuality, become one with Him and do His Will; then there shall be no stain of *māyā* and *karma* left in its immaculate self.

11. The soul sees and enables the eye to see. Even so, Hara sees, knows and enables the soul to see and know. The soul, by ceaseless devotion (love), attains the feet of Hara.

12. The three-fold impurities prevent the soul from attaining the virtuous, puissant feet of Hara. After washing off their stains, the liberated soul should keep the company of devotees, full of devotion, devoid of delusion and worship the forms and images in temples as Hara Himself. (Dhavamony gives us a more accurate final sentence here: "Let the soul, purified from the darkness of impurity, worship as Hara Himself the form of those who abound in love [devotees of Śiva] and [the form in] the temple.")

The whole concept of Realistic Pluralism is said to be derived from the writings of Saint Meykandar in *Śivajñānabodham.* However, there is no such teaching in these twelve respected verses. This is a startling fact to many, but it is undeniably true. In fact, in the first verse Meykandar states that all things—which he calls "he, she and it"—undergo the three processes (creation, preservation and dissolution). He also states that Śiva is Himself the end and the source of existence. We find no mention whatsoever in *Śivajñānabodham* for a pluralistic interpretation of Śaiva Siddhānta. That came later, from commentaries made on *Śivajñānabodham.* These twelve terse verses are the whole of Saint Meykandar's teachings as written by him. There is not a word here which defines and defends pluralism (the eternal separation of God, souls and world), but there is much which affirms that God and the soul are not different. Meykandar speaks of God, the Creator, as Beginning and End. Nowhere does he tell us that souls coexist from eternity with God, that there were three things in the beginning and will be three in the end. Rather, he clearly states that there is one Beginning, God; there is one End, God. Nor does he speak of an eternal, uncreated world. God both created in the beginning and will reabsorb in the end, he assures us.

We fully accept the views set forth by Saint Meykandar in his *Śivajñānabodham*, which we find consistent with Tirumular's *Tirumantiram.* However, we do not concur with the pluralistic postulations and interpretations found in other commentaries and other parts of the *Meykandar Śāstras.* Wherever the monism found in *Tirumurai* is contradicted in the *Meykandar Śāstras,* it is the *Tirumurai* which we follow.

15. Definitions of *Creation*

The use of the word *creation* might well make one conclude that Śiva is "making or bringing into existence something out of nothing." That, to be sure, is the Judaic-Christian-Western notion of God's creative act. But in the *Vedas,* their *Upanishads,* the *Tirumurai* and the *Āgamas,* we find creation to be from and of God Himself. The technical term for this in English is *emanation.* The *Oxford* definition is: "The process of flowing forth, issuing or proceeding from anything as a source. Often applied to the origination of created beings from God; chiefly with reference to the theories that regard either the universe as a whole, or the spiritual part of it, as deriving its existence from the essence of God, and not from an act of creation out of nothing." In his *Dictionary of Philosophy and Religion: Eastern and Western Thought* Dr. William L. Reese defines the word *emanation* thus: "From the Latin *e* ("from") and *mano* ("flow"). Emanation is the doctrine of the production of the world as due to the overflowing superabundance of the Divine. An alternative to the doctrine of creation.... A similar idea is present in Hindu philosophy as well."

16. Answers to Four Arguments against Monism & Creation

We present now four arguments which the Meykandar commentators have used for hundreds of years to support pluralism, and provide the monistic response and elucidation after each. From these four arguments one can gain a full and concise knowledge of the differences of the two schools.

PLURALISTIC ARGUMENT ONE:
"WHY GOD IS NOT THE CREATOR"

If you speak of a creation, then we must ask, "Why did God create?" There can be no reason that a perfect God would create either the soul or the world. All reasons for creation—whether it be some divine desire to enjoy creation, a demonstration of His glory, a necessity to create or merely a playful sport—make the Creator less than complete, less than self-sufficient, less than perfect. Therefore, there could not have been a creation, and it follows that the world and the soul must have always existed.

MONISTIC RESPONSE TO ARGUMENT ONE

The question arises from the second-*chakra* consciousness of logic, but the answer exists in the sixth-*chakra* consciousness of divine sight. We can never find an entirely adequate reason for creation, any more than a firefly can comprehend the incredible effulgence of a supernova. It is simply God Śiva's nature to create; it is one of His five powers, along with preservation, dissolution, concealing grace and revealing grace. There really is no reason. He creates worlds as naturally as we create thoughts. Is there a reason that we create our thoughts and feelings? Not really. It is simply how we are. It is our nature to do so. We require no reason and no reason can be found, for it is a fact that lies beyond reason. Similarly, God's nature is to create, and no reason can explain or limit His actions. Creation is, in fact, part of His Perfection. To find no reason for the creation and then to conclude that it never happens is like the firefly who, not being able to understand the stars above, concludes that stars do not exist. The argument that creation somehow limits God is unfounded, for only through His creation do we come to know His uncreated Being.

PLURALISTIC ARGUMENT TWO: "AN IMPERFECT WORLD CANNOT BE CREATED BY A PERFECT GOD"

The world is full of sorrow, injustice, evil, disease, death and all manner of imperfection. The soul, too, is tainted with the imperfections of ignorance and limitation. Neither the world nor the soul could possibly be the creation of a perfect God, for imperfection cannot arise out of perfection. If God had created the world or the soul, surely He would have made them perfect and there would be no evil. To say that the world, with its obvious faults, is manifested from God is to malign Him. The only satisfactory explanation to this problem of evil is to assume that the world always existed and that the soul has been immersed in darkness and bondage beginninglessly. Furthermore, if God had created souls, they would all be equal, all alike, for He would not have shown preferences, denying to some what He granted to others. But we observe that souls are different. Therefore, God did not create the world or the soul.

MONISTIC RESPONSE TO ARGUMENT TWO

Of course, it cannot be said that Perfection, if It were so inclined, could not give rise to something less than perfect, for that would limit Divine Power, implying that It was not all-powerful, making It less than perfect. So, a Perfect Being could create an imperfect world. The argument is flawed in that it denies the Vedic view that Śiva created the cosmic law of *karma,* and each soul, not God, is responsible for its actions and thus its differences and inequalities. And, of course, such inequity is a natural feature of the on-going creation, the fact that some souls are young and inexperienced, others old, mature and nearing their merger.

Our deeper response to the argument is that this world is, in fact, perfect, and not, as pluralists assume, imperfect. The world and the soul are God Śiva's divine and flawless creation. It is superficial to say that sorrow and death are evil, that only joy and life are good. That is an incomplete view of the pairs of opposites which, taken together, comprise a perfect whole. Life is precious, indeed possible, because of death. Light depends for its existence on darkness, and joy on sorrow.

Here again we encounter in pluralistic Śaiva Siddhānta the subtle influences of Judaic-Christian-Islamic dogma. The Abrahamic theologians saw a world in which there was good and bad, and were unwilling to make their God responsible for both. They therefore posited the ultimate dualism in which all that is good, true and beautiful is created by a benevolent God, and all that is evil, false and ugly is the handiwork of a malevolent Satan. The Meykandar pluralists, likewise convinced that there was something imperfect in the world, created a similar theology, with the difference that, instead of postulating a malevolent being to account for the ostensible defects, proposed that the world and the soul always existed, without creation. God was thus exonerated, and the apparent imperfection was, to them, explained and understood. However, this view has an inherent flaw which even the pluralists admit, for it limits the unlimited, it compromises the omnipotence of our great God Śiva, implying that He is not everything, that He did not create everything, that there are other and independent entities, separate realities over which He has dominion but which have their own eternal individuality, too.

The only way to assure the unconditional omnipotence of God is to admit that He is the Creator of all, the Beginning and the End, as Tirumular states so many times, and as Meykandar himself also says. To see evil in the world, as pluralists do, and to explain its existence by saying that God is not responsible because it always existed is not a satisfactory or acceptable answer. To assume that the soul and the world are somehow inherently corrupt, and to propose beginningless darkness (called *āṇava)* as the explanation, is itself a dark view of existence.

The view of Śuddha Śaiva Siddhānta as expressed by Saint Tirumular, the Śaiva Nayanars and Śiva Yogaswāmī is that this world is, when viewed from superconsciousness, perfect and that God Śiva has purposefully created each thing and its opposite: good and bad, beauty and deformity, light and darkness, joy and sorrow, life and death. Jñānaguru Yogaswāmī taught us that "There is not even one evil thing in the world." He urged us to "See God everywhere," not just in the obviously good. "Sarvam Śivamayam," the *satguru* observed. From our ordinary consciousness, this may be difficult to understand, especially when we personally are confronted with disease, death, violence, poverty and all forms of misery. It is these sets of opposites, of joys and sorrows, that provide the means for the growth and maturation of the soul, that make us to seek beyond the world of duality, that purify and evolve each soul and bring it to Śiva's holy feet. From the enlightened summit reached by the *siddhas,* all is seen as necessary and good, all is seen as God Himself. If it is true that the world is perfect, as our scriptures and *siddhas* say, then a perfect world has issued from a perfect Creator and the argument is answered.

PLURALISTIC ARGUMENT THREE:
"WHY SOULS EXIST FOREVER"

If there is a beginning, then there must be an end. But modern laws of physics tell us that energy and matter are neither created nor destroyed, they simply change form.

Creation implies that something arises from nothing; and destruction implies that something becomes nothing. But this is absurd and irrational. To think of the immortal soul as undergoing a birth and death is absurd. Why would a benevolent God bring a soul into existence only to lead it, ultimately, to destruction, to nonexistence? Obviously, He would not. We must, therefore, conclude that the soul is eternal and uncreated.

MONISTIC RESPONSE TO ARGUMENT THREE

This argument assumes a form of creation which, like that of the Abrahamic faiths—Judaism, Christianity and Islam—is analogous to a potter who fashions a pot. As the pluralists conceive of creation, God Śiva fashions already existing matter into various forms. God is the potter (called the efficient cause, or the maker). By means of a wheel (called the instrumental cause, thought of as God's power, or Śakti), He molds from already-existing clay (called the material cause and thought of as primordial matter, or *māyā)* a pot (the effect of these three causes). If we hold such a view of the creative act, then naturally the destructive act is abhorrent, for it merely is the ruination of the pot or its return to formless clay. Every Śaiva Siddhāntin is taught that the soul never dies, is never destroyed, so we are almost lured into accepting this argument to preserve our very existence.

But there is another, and more traditionally Hindu, understanding, of God Śiva's creation. Creation of the soul is like a wave arising from the ocean. In this analogy, the wave has a beginning, an evolution and an end. Does something arise out of nothing? No, water arises out of water. Does that water cease to exist when it returns to the vast ocean? No, it merges back into the ocean. It ceases to be a distinct wave and it becomes one with the ocean. That merging is fulfillment, not destruction. So, while the pluralists argue that destruction cannot apply to the soul, because that leads to nothing, to nonexistence, the monists answer that union in God is the ultimate blessing, the finite returning to the Infinite, the most glorious goal imaginable, the consummate condition. The soul arises from Śiva, evolves through many births and ultimately merges back in Him. Is it destroyed in that merging? No, it is made complete and perfect. It becomes Śiva. "Jīva becomes Śiva."

PLURALISTIC ARGUMENT FOUR:
"CONCERNING GOD AND THE SOUL"

Śiva pervades the soul, yet the soul is different from God Śiva. Being different, it does not wholly merge in Him at the end of its evolution. Rather, it reaches His holy feet, and becomes one with Him in every way except in the performance of the five powers, which are reserved for God alone. The individual soul never attains to the powers of creation, preservation, destruction, concealing and revealing. To say that the soul is God is an impertinent presumption. Look at this helpless creature, unable to control his own mind and body, ignorant of what will happen even an hour from now, powerlessly caught in the tides of fate, limited in a thousand ways, yet here he is claiming that he is God, the Supreme Being! What folly to claim that the soul is equal to Śiva! It is God Śiva who, by His limitless will, power and knowledge, does everything. The ultimate destiny of the soul, therefore, is to attain God's grace and live in perfect love and blessedness forever at His feet. We call this union *advaita,* but that does not mean oneness, it means not twoness. It is one and yet not one, like salt dissolved into water, like a flower and its fragrance. It is not two; neither is it perfectly one. This is the true meaning of *advaita.* To us, *advaita* means that the soul and God are not separate, but are inseparably united, even as salt is contained in the sea, and the fragrance in the flower. The salt cannot be the sea. The fragrance cannot become the flower. They have their individual existence, and yet they are one in proximity. Even so, the purified soul is embraced by the love of Śiva, and in that embrace, God and soul become one. Nevertheless, the soul remains soul, and God remains God. This is the true meaning of *advaita.*

MONISTIC RESPONSE TO ARGUMENT FOUR

While the pluralists maintain separateness, the monists proclaim oneness. The ultimate end of the soul is, of course, determined in the beginning. If the soul is a spark from Śiva, as the *Raurava Āgama* says, then it is natural that it returns to Śiva, like a drop emerging from the ocean and then once again merging its elements into that ocean. If the soul is separate at the outset, then it must be separate in the end. So here again we confront the issue of whether or not Śiva is the material cause of the world and the soul. However, it is most interesting to note that many pluralistic Śaiva Siddhāntins who hold intransigently to the uncreated beginning of the soul, nevertheless concur that the soul does merge fully and inseparably in God Śiva in the end.

As to the five powers, Ṛishi Tirumular states that the soul attains them in its ultimate evolution, not as an individual separate from God, but by merging in God wholly. The pluralist school assumes that attainment of these five powers somehow threatens the sovereignty of God Śiva. This would, of course, be true if there were still two entities, God and soul, in which case there would arise two Supreme Beings, then three and so on. But Ṛishi Tirumular makes it clear that the soul attains the five powers by becoming one with Śiva, as a drop returned to the ocean shares in the ocean's majestic powers, not by becoming another competing ocean, but by the fact of its union.

What is the teaching of Tirumular on the matter of the soul's ultimate destiny? He teaches of a complete and irrevocable union of the soul in God Śiva, a union which is identity. He speaks of oneness, not of "not twoness." His conclusions are powerful and compelling, and they are clearly not in accord with the pluralism that postulates eternal distinctions between God and soul. Here are a few verses from the *Tirumantiram* which reflect the *siddha's* teachings and remind us of the original doctrine of Śaiva Siddhānta:

> The tiny atom, swimming in the vast universe,
> merges in the Vast—no separate existence knows. So also
> the spirit's plastic stress, sweeping through all bodies at the
> sight of His holy feet, discovers its ancient home (137).
>
> Ridding themselves entirely of *āṇava,* and losing all
> consciousness of *jīva* memory, they become *bindu* and *nāda,*
> the highest heavenly goal of oneness with Śiva *tattva* (500).
>
> None know where the Lord resides. To them who seek Him,
> He resides eternally within. When you see the Lord, He and
> you become one (766).
>
> They tarry not in the pure *māyā* spheres of Śiva *tattvas.*
> There they but attain the status of the Gods. But that as a
> springboard their soul reaches farther out into Śiva Himself
> and merging in His union, Self effacing, they become
> Immaculate Śiva, they, forsooth, as Śuddha Śaivas (1440).
>
> Thus they say: By devotion the *jīva* first sojourns the
> Lord's world; then comes to dwell in the Lord's proximity.
> Further on, it receives the Lord's grace, and in the end
> attains *jñāna* in Śivohamic I-and-You Union.
> *Jīva* shall himself Śiva become (1469).
>
> Merged in one with Śakti and Śiva, as cool waters into
> the wavy sea, and realizing Truth of the Holy Word that is
> ambrosia sweet, the *jīva* reaches the shore beyond
> that indeed defies speech (2511).
>
> Be unto the river that into the wavy ocean merges (2513).
>
> Even as a shadow disappears with the body,
> even as a bubble returns into water,
> even as a flame of camphor leaves no trace,
> so it is when *jīva* into Param unites (2587).

> When body and Śiva, as unbroken, unite in *yoga*, then shall
> the grace of Śiva-Śakti be. Then does *jīva* become Param.
> *Jīva* that leaves this body then becomes all-pervasive.
> Without beginning or end, it merges forever in Śiva (2588).

Again and again, Ṛishi Tirumular tells us that *jīva* becomes Śiva, and that this union is of the nature of total oneness, without separation. It is water poured into water, the river flowing back into the sea. How does Satguru Śiva Yogaswāmī view the ultimate destiny of the soul? Is it the soul's coming close to Śiva in bliss, enjoying God's nearness forever in a Śaivite heaven, like the Vaishṇava Vaikuṇtha? Or is it a complete union in which the individual soul loses its individuality and merges wholly in the Divine? These are Satguru Śiva Yogaswāmī's teachings:

> By what does the eye see? That is the *ātma* (soul) or God.
> You are the sole emperor of the universe (18).

> What is my real nature? I am the Immortal One (20).

> "*Jīva* is Śiva," Chellappan declared.
> (See: 30, 45, 77, 93, 107, 125, 166, 181, 187, 218, etc.)

> "Aham Brahmasmi (I am God, Brahman)"—
> make this your daily practice (38, 133, 185).

> "I am He," you must affirm and meditate each day (106).

> The whole world has evolved from One.
> The whole world is sustained by One.
> The whole world will merge into One.
> That One is my support—Śivāyave! (163).

> By meditating on One, that One did I become (224).
> We are That. We do not become That.
> (*Testament of Truth*, p. 405).

> See that all is He and He alone (7).

> You are the Paramātma (12).

17. The Soul: Was It Created, or Does It Exist Eternally?

We do not teach and have never taught that the soul is not eternal and immortal. In fact, the immortality of the soul is an important teaching in our Hindu Catechism, *Dancing with Śiva*. It is the innermost essence of the soul that possesses this immortality and not the separate and outer individuality, which is created, evolved and, ultimately, merges in Śiva as water merges in water, as milk in milk.

As for the core of the soul (by which is meant Satchidānanda and Paraśiva), it is ever uncreated. This is true not because it has separate existence from Śiva, but because the essence of the soul is nondifferent from Śiva. It is Śiva with respect to the above two perfections, but not in Śiva's third perfection, as Maheśvara, Creator or Personal Lord.

That the soul as an individual and independent entity, or being, has a beginning and an end should not be understood to mean that it is ultimately destroyed or eliminated. Such an annihilative concept is alien to Śaivism. Rather, the soul is fulfilled, made perfect and brought into supernal grace when it merges ultimately in Śiva.

When the soul merges in Śiva, when *āṇava mala,* which separates it and gives it limited and separate identity, is completely removed, there is no ruination or loss, except the loss of separateness and beclouding *malas.* Quite the opposite; there is grace and union, there is return to Śiva's Perfect Being. The ego could construe this end of individual existence as something terrible, but that would be to misapprehend the greatest reward there is—perfect union in Śiva from which the soul was brought forth.

18. The Crucial Question: Is Monism Adverse to Pluralism?

The question of the creation of the soul is not the real issue. The more fundamental issue is monism versus pluralism. This issue may be described by another question: Is God Śiva everything, is this universe, including all souls, in Him and of Him, or is it distinct from Him? Is there more than one eternal Reality? Monistic theists hold that God Śiva is everything, the only eternal Reality. The universe and the soul are also Śiva. Monists contend, then, that the soul's individuality is Śiva, but it is only a part of His Wholeness (which part, being of the nature of manifest creation, relates to His perfection in form—Maheśvara), while its essence is identical with His two innermost perfections—Satchidānanda and Paraśiva. It is this identity which the mature *yogī* realizes in his contemplative, superconscious states.

Clearly Satchidānanda and Paraśiva are not created, and do not perish, as all created things must. What is created is the individuality of the soul, which we term the soul body. That individualness—which is the subtle, conscious, unique entity, endowed with the powers of *içchā*, *kriyā* and *jñāna*: desire-love, action-will and awareness-wisdom—is created, and it *does* perish, in Śiva, when *āṇava mala* is removed through His Grace. If *āṇava mala* is removed, then separateness no longer exists and the soul merges in Śiva wholly and irrevocably.

19. Vedānta Is the Fruit of the Siddhānta Tree

One of the fears of the Śaiva Siddhāntins of the Meykandar school is that an acceptance of an ultimate identity between God and soul (monism) will be tantamount to adopting the Vedāntin's philosophy, and in fact much of their arguments as stated above are a refutation of Vedānta. This is certainly not the case. Siddhānta and Vedānta are not two irreconcilable views. Tayumanavar sang, "Vedānta is the fruit on the tree of Siddhānta." Ṛishi Tirumular called that Siddhānta which does not accord with Vedānta "the common Śaiva's lot." And Śiva Yogaswāmī taught us again and again that "Śiva is the God of Vedānta and of illustrious Siddhānta" (166) and "Vedānta and Siddhānta we do not see as different" (41, 64, 87, 133, 187).

Monistic Śaiva Siddhāntins accept both Siddhānta and Vedānta. More precisely, they realize that Vedānta is the summit of the vast mountain of Siddhānta—monistic Siddhānta is the whole and Vedānta is the part, but the highest part of that whole. Here we speak of Vedānta not as the denial of all but the Absolute, not as the modern interpretation which makes everything, including the soul and its evolution, an illusion, but we speak of the original and pristine Vedānta of the *Upanishads.* No Siddhāntin need ever deny the Truths of Vedānta, for they are the jewels which adorn the Siddhānta religion.

But what is the monistic Siddhāntin's answer to the charge that to proclaim the soul as equal to God is the height of egotistical ignorance? He answers by saying that the essence of the soul, which is Satchidānanda and Paraśiva, is not different from God. That is not to say that there are two things and one is equally as majestic and supreme as the other, but that in their core they are the same. There is only one. So it is not a matter, at that depth of the soul, of the soul's crying out, "I am equal to You!" Rather, it is a realization that, "I am not apart from You. You and I are one!" This is not the ego speaking. It is a realization at the core of Being, and it really has nothing to do with the individual soul. It is the soul perceiving its Soul.

At its core, the soul is uncreated, eternal, for Satchidānanda and Paraśiva are uncreated and eternal and the soul and God Śiva share these two perfections deep within.

That is how the soul is the same as God Śiva. But monistic Siddhāntins also believe the soul is different from God. This difference exists with respect to the soul's individuality, not its essence. The body of the soul, which is composed of pure light, is created, and it is limited. It is not Omnipotent or Omnipresent at its inception. Rather, it is limited and individual, but not imperfect. That is what makes for evolution. That is the whole purpose behind *saṁsāra,* behind the cycles of birth and death, which lead this individual soul body into maturity. Of course, the various faculties of mind, perception, discrimination, which are not the soul but which "surround" the soul, are even more limited, and it would be, as stated above, folly to equate these with God Śiva, to say they were the same as He. Ultimately, after many births and further evolution which follows earthly existence, this soul body does merge in God Śiva. Then, of course, it cannot even say "I am Śiva," for there is no "I" to make the claim. There is only Śiva.

Jñānaguru Yogaswāmī taught us, "When the *Vedas* and *Āgamas* all proclaim that the whole world is filled with God, and that there is nothing else, how can we say that the world exists and the body exists? Is there anything more worthy of reproach than to attribute an independent reality to them? Sages, too, have declared: 'Those who have become Your own are not other than You.' Thus, for several reasons of this kind, there is nothing other than God."

20. The Extinction of Separateness, or *Āṇava Mala*

Any discussion of monism and pluralism must eventually confront the issue of *āṇava. Āṇava* may be simply defined as "ignorance, the sense of separateness and ego." It is often thought of as darkness. In Śaiva Siddhānta, *āṇava* plays an important philosophical role as the root *mala*, the first and foremost shroud which "covers" the soul, which conceals God. It is also the last veil to be removed from the soul in its evolutionary progress.

For the monist, the removal of this *āṇava mala* is the point of merger in Śiva. In his *Tirumantiram*, Ṛishi Tirumular is clear that at the conclusion of the evolution of the soul, at the point of final merger, *viśvagrāsa*, all three *malas* are totally absorbed by the grace of Sadāśiva. However, the pluralists are not certain, or at least not consistent, in their view of the removal of *āṇava mala*. They contend that *karma* and *māyā* are destroyed fully, but *āṇava* is merely nullified or subdued, offering the analogy of seeds which have been fried. Such seeds exist, yet they no longer have the power of germination. By this view, God is able to destroy the lesser *malas* of *karma* and *māyā*, but He does not have the power to extirpate *āṇava*. The monist would object, pointing out that Śaivite scriptures and realized men state that *āṇava mala* is indeed destroyed by Śiva's grace. For the pluralist, it is absolutely imperative that *āṇava* be somehow preserved, for that is by definition the preservation of the separateness of God and soul.

What Ṛishi Tirumular, the Nayanar saints and our Śaiva Siddhānta scriptures tell us is this: even the most tenacious of the *malas*, *āṇava*, is completely annihilated in the presence of God Śiva. With the destruction of *āṇava* comes the total loss of separateness. When separateness is lost, then there is oneness, not "not-twoness." The conclusion is compelling and clear: *āṇava mala* does not shroud the soul forever; rather, it is removed by Śiva's Grace, as are the other two *malas*. With its removal comes one incontrovertible fact: monism.

Āṇava may be called "individuality" and likened to the "dropness" in the analogy of creation in which the soul is brought forth from God just as a drop of water from the ocean. The first result of the manifestation of the soul from Śiva is its separateness from Him, its individualness, its *āṇava;* and the last "impurity" to be removed is that same ego or separateness. When that is ultimately removed, as most Siddhāntins aver it is, then *jīva* becomes Śiva. That is the final conclusion of Śaiva Siddhānta. Saint Manikkavasagar states:

> Having lost our identity, we merge in Him
> and become Śiva ourselves. Purifying my soul,
> He took control of me by making me Śiva.
> Having destroyed all my three *malas*,
> He made me Śiva and took lordship over me.

21. Mahāpralaya: Another Dilemma for Pluralism

Mahāpralaya is accepted by Śaiva Siddhāntins of both schools as the ultimate state of existence. Whereas creation is Śiva's outbreath, absorption is His inbreath—though we much prefer to look upon that sacred indrawing as withdrawal or dissolution or resolution, rather than destruction which implies a ruinous act, which *mahāpralaya* is not. Both schools appear to agree that after *mahāpralaya* only Śiva exists. He alone is. One without a second.

This view of *mahāpralaya*, found in all our scriptures, raises certain difficulties for the Meykandar school. If only Śiva exists, then what has happened to the world? What has become of the soul? Tirumular says they both have returned to their source. They have become Śiva. There seems to be no official doctrine on this question as expressed by the Meykandar commentators. Unofficially, supporters of pluralism will say that the world and souls "are drawn to Śiva's Feet and remain there until the next cycle of cosmic creation, at which time they are issued forth again." When asked if the world then survives the dissolution, they respond, "Not actually. But the world and the soul are reduced to their seed form; they then exist not as a 'thing' but as a 'potential.' They are extremely close to Śiva, so close that, for all practical purposes and appearances, only Śiva exists, but actually all three entities are there, in Him retaining their separate existence."

What, then, happens to an individual soul that has evolved already to Śiva's Feet during the previous cosmic cycle? Does it evolve again? Does it manifest its potential and then remain at Śiva's Feet during the next cycle, while less-evolved souls are sent forth into the ocean of *māyā* and *karma?* How does the memory of previous existence, previous experience and lessons, survive the dissolution? Are those records somehow preserved while everything else is lost? These are difficult questions for pluralists, and the answers, we found, are not well defined in their own system.

A few will theorize that all souls must, at the end of their evolution, form a one enlightened soul which lives in communion with Śiva throughout eternity—thus losing their personal identity which would otherwise distinguish them from countless other unique souls. This is not the official Meykandar school view, but is mentioned in absence of a formal doctrine. Clearly, the doctrine that the soul is forever separate from Śiva is painfully dashed upon the rocks of *mahāpralaya*. Even Arulnandi, the most respected of Meykandar's commentators, admits to the completeness of *mahāpralaya* and thereby transcends pluralism when he writes in *Śivajñāna Siddhiar:*

> Only One remains at the end of time.
> If two others *(paśu-souls* and *pāśam-fetters)* also remained at their posts, Then it cannot be.

22. A Crucial Verse from *Tirumantiram*

Pluralists seeking to bring Ṛishi Tirumular to their side and being aware of his many bold statements of oneness of *jīva* and Śiva, declare, "The most fundamental verse in the *Tirumantiram* is verse 115." They offer the following translation:

> Of the three entities, Pati, *paśu* and *pāśam* (God, soul and bondage), just as Pati (is beginningless), so are *paśu* and *pāśam* also beginningless. If Pati gets near *paśu* and *pāśam*, which are not capable of affecting Pati, the *paśu* (or *paśutvam*) and the *pāśam* (bonds—*āṇava, karma, māyā)* will disappear.

If we take this verse as it is written, we find Tirumular telling mankind he has discovered that the soul and the world are beginningless, but that they end when they come into contact or proximity with Śiva. They disappear or merge in Him. Monists find that this verse coordinates perfectly with the monistic view that the essence of soul and world are as beginningless and eternal as Śiva Himself, while the individual soul body has both a beginning and an end.

Alas, pluralists say that what Tirumular said is one thing and what he meant is quite another. We are told that Tirumular indeed meant the fettered soul when he used the word *paśu* in the first half of verse 115, but "here in the latter half of this verse it is used in the sense of the fettered state. It is not the soul itself that disappears but its fettered state." If Tirumular had meant that it is not the soul that disappears, he would have said so. But he did not in this verse nor in any other verse in his treatise of 3,047 verses. Instead, he said the soul and the world both disappear when they near Śiva. He alone exists. Surprisingly, pluralists frequently refer to verse 115, since they believe it to support their interpretation; but in doing so they refer to and emphasize only the first two lines of the four-line verse. In those lines, Ṛishi Tirumular says that souls and world are beginningless, as is God. They don't go on and quote from lines three and four, because Tirumular immediately shatters all hope of an eternally separate soul and universe by telling us that soul and world completely disappear when they come into proximity with Pati or Śiva.

This verse gives a vivid example of what is termed a "dipolar" view of God, and reveals the limitations of both the strict monistic view (which must deny and reject the first half of Tirumular's esoteric verse) and the pluralist view (which must deny and reject the second half). Only monistic theism can fully encompass this mysterious and profound statement without contradiction or reservation.

One eminent South Indian pluralist, realizing the strength with which monism is present in the *Tirumantiram*, became disturbed and criticized his own most holy scripture. He proposed to "throw it away" since "it obviously is a polluted pond at which we cannot drink." This is an extreme reaction, but it shows the tendency of some to dismiss that which does not accord with their view. Yet, Tirumular's importance in Śaiva Siddhānta is unshakable. Kalaipulavar K.

Navaratnam writes, "Saint Tirumular may be said to be the father of Āgamic Śaivism in South India." Thiru A.V. Subramania Aiyar affirms, "Saint Tirumular is regarded as the foremost Teacher and Guru in the Tamil land, and Saint Tayumanavar, who styles him as Thava Rāja Yogi, traces his spiritual descent from him." Let Tirumular's own words be the final guide:

> The soul, which in its real condition was of the form of Śiva,
> was confined and conditioned by its original *āṇava mala.*
> When this *mala* ceased to obstruct the soul,
> the soul resumed its original form of Śiva.
>
> Out of the Void, a soul it sprang. To the Void it returns.
> Yet it shall not be Void again. In that Void, exhausted,
> it shall die. That is the fate of Hara and Brahmā, too,
> who do not survive the holocaust of *saṁhāra* (429).
>
> Of yore He created the worlds seven.
> Of yore He created celestials countless.
> Of yore He created souls *(jīva)* without number.
> Of yore He created all—
> Himself, as Primal Param, uncreated (446).

23. Jīva Is Śiva. Tat Tvam Asī.
Aham Brahmāsmi. Sarvam Śivamayam.

Again and again in Śaiva scripture and from the mouths of our *satgurus* we hear that "*Jīva* is Śiva," "I am That." It is a clear statement of *advaita,* of monism, of the identity of the soul with God. Not only have all Śaivite sects accepted this view, it is the conclusion of Śaṅkara, Vallabhāchārya, Rāmakṛishṇa, of Vivekānanda, Rāmaṇa Maharshi, Swāmī Śivānanda, Śiva Yogaswāmī, Ānandamāyī Mā, Rādhākṛishṇan, Swāmī Muktānanda and others. Are we to assume that all great souls in Hindu religious history were wrong? Were they deluded? Did they stray from the path and fall short of the goal? Each and every one of them? Certainly not! Their monistic realizations were in fact the revelation of Truth in

Śivajñāna. And it is that same revelation that is propounded today by my Śaiva Siddhānta Yoga Order as an essential and unquestionable facet of the monistic theism of Śaiva Siddhānta.

The uniqueness about Śaiva Siddhānta, for both pluralists and monists, is the intensity and the magic of temple worship—the *homas* and *pūjās,* the elaborate invocation of the Gods and God into the inner sanctum through which they bestow their grace upon waiting devotees. One step to the Gods brings them hastening nine steps toward the devotees. This—along with scriptures and the *gurus,* the stress on *yoga* and *sādhanas*—is part of the ninety-five percent of Śaiva Siddhānta to which monists and pluralists both agree. The crying need for worship is what the Vedāntists deny when they understand that this is not a need, because understanding Vedānta is their realization.

Many South Indian pluralistic Siddhāntins deny the great Upanishadic sayings, the *mahāvākya,* by basically ignoring all but the *Meykandar Śāstras,* which they take to be the most important and authoritative scriptures. Some will go so far as to say that all other references in scripture which do not accord with the *Meykandar Śāstras* are to be discarded or disregarded. In Thiru M. Arunachalam's book, *The Śaiva Āgamas,* he discusses and later condemns this kind of posturing, quoting a typical Śaiva Siddhāntin writer's posture on the *Vedas*: "The Śaiva Siddhāntin has to ignore... the part in the *Jñānakāṇḍa* dealing with the absolute identification of the *jīvātma* and the Paramātma. The other parts of the *Vedas* are to be fully adopted by the Śaiva Siddhāntin, just like the *Āgamas*."

24. Verses from the Āgamas

If we accept that the 28 *Śaiva Āgamas* are, as Pillay says, the scriptural basis of Śaiva Siddhānta, then we must inquire as to what the *Āgamas* have to tell us. Quoting from page 105 of *The Collected Works of Rāmaṇa Maharshi,* edited by Arthur Osborne: "The *Āgamas* are traditional Hindu scriptures regarded as no less authoritative and authentic than the *Vedas.* They are regarded as divinely revealed teachings and no human authorship is ascribed to them. Temple worship is mainly founded upon them. There are twenty-eight *Āgamas* that are accepted as authorities. From among them, *Sarvajñānottara* and *Devīkālottara* are outstanding as expressing the standpoint of pure Advaita or nonduality.... Both are instructions in the Path of Knowledge given by Lord Śiva." Mr. Osborne then quotes from the *Āgamas,* from which we adduce the following excerpts:

> I will tell you, O Guha, another method by means of which even the unqualified, impalpable, subtle and immanent Absolute can be clearly realized, by which realization the wise become themselves Śiva. This has not hitherto been expounded to any other. Now listen!
>
> I permeate all this—visible and invisible, mobile and immobile, I am surely the Lord of all and from me all shine forth.
>
> Giving up the separate identity of yourself as distinct from Śiva, meditate constantly on the nondual unity: 'I am He who is known as Śiva.' One who is established in the contemplation of nondual Unity will abide in the Self of everyone and realize the immanent, all-pervading One. There is no doubt of this.
>
> When a pot is moved from place to place, the space inside it appears to move, too, but the movement pertains to the pot and not to the space within. So it is with the soul which corresponds to the space in the pot. When the pot is broken, its inner space merges in the outer expanse; similarly with the death of the gross body the Spirit merges in the Absolute.

25. Our Points of Agreement Must Be Stressed

For the most part, monists and pluralists within Śaiva Siddhānta are of a one mind. Both value the Nayanars and their *Tirumurai.* Both revere as scriptures the *Vedas* and the *Śaiva*

Āgamas. Both follow the Tamil traditions. Both emphasize *charyā, kriyā, yoga* and *jñāna.* Both practice the orthodox *sādhanas* and worship Gaṇeśa, Muruga and Śiva, urging the importance of temple worship and ritual for the benefit of the individual soul and of humanity at large. Both believe in *karma* and reincarnation. Both boldly deny the unreality of the world postulated in Māyāvāda Vedānta and accept *māyā* as Śiva's Grace in form rather than mere deluding appearance. To the Siddhāntin, the world is Śivamaya ("made of Śiva"), His gift to mankind. While the Vedāntins hold that it is nothing but *māyā* (by which is meant mere illusion) and the greatest obstacle to Brahmavidyā, we Siddhāntins see this world as Śiva's gracious way of leading us to union with Him. Thus, it is not the obstacle to Self Realization, but the means for it. Both pluralists and monists within Śaiva Siddhānta place the *satguru* at the highest pinnacle, but reject the Vaishṇavite concept that God incarnates as a man. Both love Śiva Peruman and consider Him our Supreme God. Clearly, pluralists and monists agree on ninety-five percent of what constitutes Śaiva Siddhānta. We can never forget that. Thiru A.P.C. Veerabhagu, an eminent South Indian Siddhāntin, a pluralist, called for our working together and lucidly summarized our essential points of agreement as "*guru, liṅgam, saṅgam* and *valipadu* (temple worship)." This, he said, is the essence of Śaiva Siddhānta as found in ancient Tamil literature.

26. An Unfortunate Image that Must Be Changed

It is sad but true that when a fine soul, raised in the pluralistic school of Śaiva Siddhānta, reaches toward the greater heights of spiritual *sādhana* and personal experience of Truth or God through *yoga* and meditation, he cannot find within his native Siddhānta a sufficiently profound pathway that satisfies and fulfills his spiritual yearnings, and he is therefore not infrequently inclined to leave the South and find spiritual solace and direction in the North of India. There, more often than not, he eventually adopts a Vedāntic view of God and man. Why? Because in Vedānta he finds the deepest of all human philosophical conclusions—monism. By this process, Śaiva Siddhānta is losing *swāmīs* to the Vedānta school, and suffering from a spiritual "brain drain."

This is unnecessary, for Siddhānta has always provided a monistic path which embraced Vedānta. Śaiva Siddhāntins everywhere can be proud that the highest teachings of monism were propounded by Ṛishi Tirumular eight hundred years before Ādi Śaṅkara was even born. The monistic truths (but not the pantheistic denial of relative existence or individual souls) found in the school of Advaita Vedānta were expounded by our own *siddhas* and Nayanars long ago. They taught this, and more. In fact, Tirumular, in order to distinguish his monistic theism from the pluralistic theism of others, coined the term *Śuddha* (pure) *Śaiva Siddhānta* to describe the teachings of his *Tirumantiram.*

In my considered opinion, the pluralist practitioners, heavy with the weight of book knowledge, refuse in many cases to listen to the inquiring minds of their youth, who then feel, quite naturally, that their religion is bigoted, intolerant, suffocating, unreceptive to their bright and eager desire to perform *yogic sādhanas* to know about God and His greatness. They are hushed and stifled and even beaten if they offer any "unorthodox" ideas or challenge the accepted creed, and soon they learn simply not to ask, for it just gets them in trouble. Or worse, when answers are offered, they are couched in arcane terminology which does not clarify but further confounds and confuses them. No wonder suicide is highly rated as a form of escape by youth.

The fear of parents' thrashing makes them fear God, as parents are the first *guru.* Naturally, *swāmīs* are to be feared next, as are the Catholic priests and nuns who beat them as a form of discipline with little mercy in schools. This is totally

Abrahamic in context—the fear of God, the beating of children, the denial of questioning. It is certainly not the free-flowing, inquiring, examinating, self-effacing monistic Śaiva approach taught in traditional *gurukulams* in ancient times. So explained Swami Gautamānanda, president of the the Rāmakṛishṇa Mission in Chennai, where *ahiṁsā,* nonhurtfulness of any kind, mentally, emotionally or physically, was the protocol.

Youth are often told, "You just can't understand Śaiva Siddhānta unless you know classical Tamil." Imagine if a young Christian were told he couldn't comprehend his religion unless he studied Aramaic, the language which Jesus spoke, or the ancient Hebrew and Greek in which their Bible was originally written! Christianity would soon wither and perish from the Earth. The fundamentals of Śaiva Siddhānta should be easily taught to the youth in any language to give them a foundation for living, to be practiced in confidence and without intimidation.

Not a single one of our Nayanars was a Tamil *pandit* or scholar, but will anyone claim they did not understand Siddhānta? No, religion is not learned in libraries or universities, but in transforming personal experience, in temples and caves and *satsaṅga.* It is learned in the silence of meditation and contemplation, in the rigors of *sādhana* and *yoga,* practices which are universal, transcending all cultural and linguistic barriers.

Tens of millions of Śaiva Siddhāntins have a direct and simple approach to their religion. They love Śiva Peruman. They worship Śiva Peruman. They serve and meditate upon and speak sweetly of Śiva Peruman and of His devotees. They know that Śiva is found in the heart, not in books, and they seek Him there. That is the vigorous and living faith of Śaiva Siddhānta, the San Mārga, the true path to God Śiva's Feet.

Vedānta captured the respect and imagination of the world and became immensely popular by offering its own positive, intelligent, well-crafted and pragmatic approach for seekers in the East and the West. Monistic Siddhānta is, we are convinced, more enlightened, more positive, more intelligent, more practical. It has a great future. But to live in the future, it must come out of the past.

That is one reason we have worked so hard for over half a century to give Siddhānta a fresh, new, bright, attractive modern-English thrust, availing ourselves of technological means of propagation. Most have applauded the effort; a few have requested that we continue introducing Śaiva Siddhānta to the international community.

27. Back to the Mountaintop

Asked by sincere devotees about how to understand the two schools, I once answered: Both are right. However, one is more advanced, more enlightened. But that does not make the other wrong. It all depends on whether you are on the top looking down or on the bottom looking up. One view is for the intellectual, the other is for the *ṛishi.* The intellectual will see it only one way; he will then discard the other view as wrong. The *ṛishi* can see it both ways, yet he knows that the monistic view is the higher realization. It all depends on where you are in your spiritual unfoldment. This is the merger of Vedānta and Siddhānta. You see, there are stages of realization and the world and God and soul look a little different from each stage. The dualistic or pluralistic conception is true, but it is a slice. It is not the whole thing. Some Śaiva Siddhāntins want to make the part into the whole, want to make one stopover of the soul's journey to God into the final destination. Again we say, to know the final conclusion of Siddhānta they must go a little farther, do a little more *sādhana* and see these truths from a higher plane of consciousness. The acceptance of both gives strength; the rejection of one or the other drains your energies, limits your comprehension of these great truths. If you understand this, it will make you strong. It will make your religion strong.

The debate, rekindled by our statement that there can be only one final conclusion, was resolved in the understanding that within Śaiva Siddhānta there is one final conclusion for pluralists and one final conclusion for monistic theists. This occurred in February of 1984 at the South Indian monastery of Śrīla-Śrī Shaṇmuga Desika Gñānasambandha Paramāchārya Swāmīgal, 26th Guru Mahāsannidhānam of the Dharmapura Aadheenam, at a meeting of professors, advocates, theologians, academicians and *pandits* on the issue. The resolution came when His Holiness, presiding over the meeting, effectively declared that all who follow the Meykandar philosophy are indeed pluralists when he had prepared for publication two books written by the late Śaiva Siddhānta scholar, V. K. Palasuntharam: 1) *Souls Are Beginningless,* and 2) *There Has Always Been Only a Pluralistic Śaiva Siddhānta Philosophy.*

Heretofore the Meykandar exponents had been equivocal in this area, considering themselves sort of *dvaitic* and sort of *advaitic,* and redefining the word *advaita* (which means "not dual") to allow for two things to exist in the state of oneness. Through His Holiness, the followers of the Meykandar lineage had formally, publicly declared themselves pluralists, and thus acknowledged their difference with the monistic school in Śaiva Siddhānta.

At the same time, as a result of two sometimes-heated debates at national and international levels and numerous formal papers, now the pluralistic school, which had been the popular view for centuries, heartfully and in loving trust accepted what had been the ever-present monistic Śaiva Siddhānta position. Thus the spirit of Sanātana Dharma that is modern Hinduism bound the monistic school and the pluralistic school into a productive, working partnership for the good of all, working together in the great Hindu renaissance, which is surging forward as a result of the global Hindu diaspora, and spawning an indomitable Hindu front.

We are happy to say that peace, tolerance, forbearance and mutual respect now exist between these two schools. We feel that the foundation for this coexistence of love and trust was made on January 30, 1981, when we met with His Holiness for the first time. I was on a holy pilgrimage to Śaivism's most sacred sites with my entourage of forty Eastern and Western devotees when messengers from His Holiness invited us to visit his ancient monastery. Together we sat in the inner chambers of his palatial spiritual refuge, built by *mahārājas* in the sixteenth century. It was quite a spectacle—Eastern *pandits* with their *guru*, and Western mystics with theirs, discussing the philosophical enigmas that have perplexed the mind of man from the dawn of history. Through our translators, we spoke of God, of the soul and the world, and of the dire need for Śaivite schools in South India, and around the world, to pass this great knowledge on to the next generation.

After our lively discussion, a special lunch was served. Later, one of our *swāmīs* casually inquired of His Holiness about his large golden earrings, wondering where such a pair might be obtained for myself. Without hesitation, the *guru* summoned an aide and whispered some instructions. Moments later, a pair of earrings identical to those he was wearing were placed in his hands. His Holiness indicated that these were for me. Joyfully shrugging off our objections that he was being too generous, he immediately set about placing them in my ears with his own hands, enlarging the existing holes to accept these massive gold rings which are the traditional insignia of a *paramāchārya guru mahāsannidhānam aadheenakarthar.* Then he presented new orange *kavi* cloth to me and to my *swāmīs* accompanying me.

We gratefully accepted the Sannidhānam's unexpected and generous gift as a gesture of goodwill to help us on our way of spreading the message of Śaiva Siddhānta. Perhaps even more importantly, it was to us a sign of cooperative efforts between two great monasteries, one firmly teaching pluralistic Śaiva Siddhānta in the East, and the other boldly promulgating monistic Śaiva Siddhānta in the West. We thought to ourself that all that transpired after this would be for the best. To the onlooking *pandits,* this presentation of the *āchārya* earrings meant that all knowledgeable Hindus would know that the Guru Mahāsannidhānam of Dharmapura Aadheenam and the Guru Mahāsannidhānam of Kauai Aadheenam would work together for the future of Śaiva Siddhānta. Later the same day, Mahāsannidhānam asked us to address several thousand people who were seated in the giant inner hall overlooking the large temple tank. We spoke of the greatness of Śaivism and Śaiva Siddhānta and the effects of its spreading into the Western world. The day culminated when His Holiness handed me an ornate silver casket, in which was kept a precious scroll honoring our work in spreading Śaiva Siddhānta.

Later, after being engraved with words of acknowledgement, the casket was officially presented to me at the 1,000-pillared hall in Chidambaram Temple just before the sacred Bharata Natyam performance by premier dancer Kumari Swarnamukhi, a state treasure of Tamil Nadu. This was the first dance performance within the temple's precincts in over fifty years since the British outlawed the dancing of Devadāsis in temples. More than 15,000 devotees were packed into the viewing area while 300,000 more, we were told, filled the 35-acre temple complex. The entire city of Chidambaram came forward, as well as neighboring villages, for this historic presentation of all 108 Tāṇḍava poses, a magnificent event, held on the temple's most popular evening, establishing once and for all that, yes, dance could again be held in Chidambaram. This tradition, once banned, now continues at Śiva's most hallowed sanctuary.

Śaivadarśanaṁ Santaparamparāścha

शैवदर्शनं सन्तपरम्पराश्च

Śaivite Hinduism And Holy Lineages

The acts of *kriyā* lead to Śiva *tattva*. The practice of prolonged *yoga* leads to divine grace and knowledge. Contemplation of Lord's form in *charyā* confers blessings many. In *jñāna* is comprehended all cosmic creation at once.

TIRUMANTIRAM 2189

Śaivite Hinduism And Holy Lineages

God Śiva is among the most mysterious, complex, compassionate and profound conceptions of the one Supreme Being to be found in the religions of mankind. He is Creator, Preserver and Destroyer of all existence, the Cosmic Dancer who animates the universe from within. He is pure love, light, energy and consciousness. He is the timeless, formless and spaceless Absolute Reality, Paraśiva. Those who worship the great God Śiva are Śaivites, and their religion is called Śaivite Hinduism. Śaivism represents roughly half, perhaps somewhat more, of Hinduism's one billion members. It shares far more common ground than differences with other Hindu denominations. Still, it is distinct. Unlike the second major Hindu faith, Vaishṇavism (which is strongly dualistic), Śaivism adds a meditative or *yogic* emphasis to a *bhakti* path. For Śaivites, God and soul are essentially one. Unlike Advaita Vedānta, Śaivism is strongly devotional and theistic, believing in a one true God who is Personal Lord and Creator. The term "monistic theism" defines the essential resolution of duality and nonduality which typifies Śaivism's philosophical stance.

Scholars tell us that Śaivite Hinduism is mankind's oldest religion, the venerable Sanātana Dharma. They have traced its roots back 6-8,000 years and more to the advanced Indus Valley civilization. A better-preserved history of Śaivism lies in the ruins of Dholavira, in Gujarat state, where another Indian civilization of about the same antiquity is coming to light in 1998. Yet, sacred writings and legend tell us that there never was a time on the Earth when Śaivism did not exist. Ten of the eleven great religions existing today have a beginning in history, a birth date before which they did not exist. All other religions and faiths were founded by men. Not Śaivism. It had no beginning. It can have no end.

Through history Śaivism has given rise to other faiths, such as Buddhism, Sikhism and Jainism, as well as to a multitude of sects within Hinduism itself. This oldest of religions is also among the largest. One out of every six people on the Earth is a Hindu, and recent studies show that Hinduism is among the fastest-growing faiths on thc planct.

It is neither antiquity nor size which make Śaivism great. The real grandeur derives from a sweet tolerance for the views of others coupled with these: a practical culture, an emphasis on personal spiritual effort and experience, the perception that God is everywhere present—and therefore no aspect of life may be divided from religion—and a joyous devotion to the one Supreme God who all people worship and Śaivism knows as Śiva, "the Auspicious One," and the knowledge that Truth lies within man himself.

Each Śaivite is unique, yet all seek the same things in life: to be happy and secure, to be loved and appreciated, to be creative and useful. Śaivite Hinduism has an established culture which fulfills these essential human wants and helps us to understand the world and our place in it. To all devotees it gives guidance in the qualities of character which are so necessary in spiritual life—patience, compassion for others, broadmindedness, humility, self-confidence, industriousness and devotion.

Śaivism centers around the home and the temple. Family life is very strong, and precious. Daily devotional services are conducted in the home shrine room. The massive and architecturally priceless temples—and a million other temples and shrines throughout the world—provide daily worship services and sacraments for life's passages. Śaivite worship is more individual than congregational, each approaching God directly. Yet during holy days the temple precincts resound with the genial voices of devotees gathered to sing God Śiva's praises.

Śaivism's Six Schools

In the search for peace, enlightenment and liberation, no path is more tolerant, more mystical, more widespread or more ancient than Śaivite Hinduism. Through history Śaivism has developed six major traditions: Śaiva Siddhānta, Pāśupata Śaivism, Kashmīr Śaivism, Vīra Śaivism, Siddha Siddhānta and Śiva Advaita. Within Śaivism, *Merging with Śiva* embodies and reflects the mystical teachings of Śaiva Siddhānta, particularly the monistic teachings of the Nandinātha Sampradāya.

Śaiva Siddhānta

Śaiva Siddhānta is the oldest, most vigorous and extensively practiced Śaivite Hindu school today, encompassing hundreds of millions of devotees, thousands of active temples and dozens of living monastic and ascetic traditions. Śaiva Siddhānta once enjoyed a glorious presence as an all-India denomination. That has passed, and today it is found primarily within the South Indian Tamil traditions. The term *Śaiva Siddhānta* means "the final, or established, conclusions of Śaivism." It is the formalized theology of the divine revelations contained in the twenty-eight *Śaiva Āgamas.*

The first known *guru* of the Śuddha, "pure," Śaiva Siddhānta tradition was Mahāṛishi Nandinātha of Kashmīr (ca 250 BCE), recorded in Pāṇinī's book of grammar as the teacher of *ṛishis* Patañjali, Vyāghrapāda and Vasishṭha. The only surviving written work of Mahāṛishi Nandinātha are twenty-six Sanskṛit verses, called the *Nandikeśvara Kāśikā,* in which he carried forward the ancient teachings. Because of his monistic approach, Nandinātha is often considered by scholars as an exponent of the Advaita school.

The next prominent *guru* on record is Ṛishi Tirumular,

a *siddha* in the line of Nandinātha, who came from the Valley of Kashmīr to South India to propound the sacred teachings of the twenty-eight *Śaiva Āgamas.* In his profound work, the *Tirumantiram,* "Holy Incantation," Tirumular for the first time put the vast writings of the *Āgamas* and the Śuddha Siddhānta philosophy into the sweet Tamil language. Ṛishi Tirumular, like his *satguru,* Mahāṛishi Nandinātha, propounds a Vedic monistic theism in which Śiva is both material and efficient cause, immanent and transcendent. Śiva creates souls and world through emanation from Himself, ultimately reabsorbing them in His oceanic Being, as water flows into water, fire into fire, ether into ether. The *Tirumantiram* unfolds the way of Siddhānta as a progressive, four-fold path of *charyā,* virtuous and moral living; *kriyā,* temple worship; and *yoga*—internalized worship and union with Paraśiva through the grace of the living *satguru*—which leads to the state of *jñāna* and liberation. After liberation, the soul body continues to evolve until it fully merges with God—*jīva* becomes Śiva, a union called *viśvagrāsa.*

Tirumular's Śuddha Śaiva Siddhānta shares common distant roots with Mahāsiddhayogī Gorakshanātha's Siddha Siddhānta, in that both are Nātha teaching lineages. Tirumular's lineage is known as the Nandinātha Sampradāya. Gorakshanātha's is called the Ādinātha Sampradāya.

Śaiva Siddhānta flowered in South India as a forceful *bhakti* movement infused with insights on *siddha yoga.* During the seventh to ninth centuries, saints Sambandar, Appar and Sundarar pilgrimaged from temple to temple, singing soulfully of Śiva's greatness. They were instrumental in successfully defending Śaivism against the threats of Buddhism and Jainism. Soon thereafter, a king's Prime Minister, Manikkavasagar, renounced a world of wealth and fame to seek and serve supreme God Śiva. His heart-melting verses, called *Tiruvasagam,* are full of visionary experience, divine love and urgent striving for Truth. The songs of these four saints are part of a compendium called the *Tirumurai*, which along with the *Vedas* and *Śaiva Āgamas* form the scriptural basis of Śaiva Siddhānta in Tamil Nadu, India, and Sri Lanka to this very day.

Besides the saints, philosophers and ascetics, there were innumerable *siddhas*, "accomplished ones," God-intoxicated men who roamed their way through the centuries as saints, *gurus*, as inspired devotees or even despised outcastes. Śaiva Siddhānta makes a special claim on them, but their presence and revelation cut across all schools, philosophies and lineages to keep the true spirit of Śiva present on Earth. These *siddhas* provided the central source of power to spur the religion from age to age. The well-known names include Sage Agastya, Bhogar Ṛishi, Tirumular and Gorakshanātha. They are revered by the Siddha Siddhāntins, Kashmīr Śaivites and even by the Nepalese branches of Buddhism.

In Central India, Śaiva Siddhānta of the Sanskṛit tradition was first institutionalized by Guhāvāsī Siddha (ca 675). The third successor in his line, Rudraśambhu, also known as Āmardaka Tīrthanātha, founded the Āmardaka monastic order (ca 775) in Andhra Pradesh. From this time, three monastic orders arose that were instrumental in Śaiva Siddhānta's diffusion throughout India. Along with the Āmardaka Order (centered in one of Śaivism's holiest cities, Ujjain) were the Mattamayūra Order, in the capital of the Chālukya dynasty, near the Punjab, and the Madhumateya Order of Central India. Each of these developed numerous sub-orders, as the Siddhānta monastics, full of missionary spirit, used the influence of royal patrons to propagate the teachings in neighboring kingdoms, particularly in South India. From Mattamayūra, they established monasteries in Maharashtra, Karnataka, Andhra and Kerala (ca 800).

Of the many *gurus* and *āchāryas* that followed, spreading Siddhānta through the whole of India, two *siddhas*, Sadyojyoti and Bṛihaspati of Central India (ca 850), are credited with the systematization of the theology in Sanskṛit. Sadyojyoti, initiated by the Kashmīr *guru* Ugrajyoti, propounded the Siddhānta philosophical views as found in the *Raurava Āgama.* He was succeeded by Rāmakaṇṭha I, Śrīkaṇṭha, Nārāyaṇakaṇṭha and Rāmakaṇṭha II, each of whom wrote numerous treatises on Śaiva Siddhānta.

Later, King Bhoja Paramāra of Gujarat (ca 1018) condensed the massive body of Siddhānta scriptural texts that preceded him into a one concise metaphysical treatise called *Tattva Prakāśa,* considered a foremost Sanskṛit scripture on Śaiva Siddhānta. Affirming the monistic view of Śaiva Siddhānta was Śrīkumāra (ca 1056), stating in his commentary, Tatparyadīpikā, on Bhoja Paramāra's works, that Pati, *paśu* and *pāśa* are ultimately one, and that revelation declares that Śiva is one. He is the essence of everything. Śrīkumāra maintained that Śiva is both the efficient and the material cause of the universe.

Śaiva Siddhānta was readily accepted wherever it spread in India and continued to blossom until the Islamic invasions, which virtually annihilated all traces of Siddhānta from North and Central India, limiting its open practice to the southern areas of the subcontinent.

It was in the twelfth century that Aghoraśiva took up the task of amalgamating the Sanskṛit Siddhānta tradition of the North with the southern Tamil Siddhānta. As the head of a branch monastery of the Āmardaka Order in Chidambaram, Aghoraśiva gave a unique slant to Śaiva Siddhānta theology, paving the way for a new pluralistic school. In strongly refuting any monist interpretations of Siddhānta, Aghoraśiva brought a dramatic change in the understanding of the Godhead by wrongly classifying the first five principles, or *tattvas*—Nāda, Bindu, Sadāśiva, Īśvara and Śuddhavidyā—into the category of *pāśa* (bonds), stating they were effects of a cause and inherently unconscious substances. This was clearly a departure from the traditional monistic teaching in which these five were part of the divine nature of God. Aghoraśiva thus inaugurated a new pluralistic Siddhānta, divergent from the original monistic Śaiva Siddhānta of the Himālayas.

Despite Aghoraśiva's pluralistic viewpoint of Śaiva Siddhānta, he was successful in preserving the invaluable Sanskṛitic rituals of the ancient Āgamic tradition through his writings. To this day, Aghoraśiva's Siddhānta philosophy is followed by almost all of the hereditary Śivāchārya temple priests, and his *Paddhati* texts on the *Āgamas* have become the standard *pūjā* manuals. His *Kriyākramadyotikā* is a vast work covering nearly all aspects of Śaiva Siddhānta ritual, including *dīkshā, saṁskāras, ātmārtha pūjā* and installation of icons of Deities.

In the thirteenth century, another important development occurred in Śaiva Siddhānta when Meykandar wrote the twelve-verse *Śivajñānabodham.* This and subsequent works by other writers laid the foundation of the Meykandar Sampradāya, which propounds a pluralistic realism wherein God, souls and world are coexistent and without beginning. Śiva is efficient but not material cause. They view the soul's merging in Śiva as salt in water, an eternal oneness that is also twoness. This school's literature has so dominated scholarship that Śaiva Siddhānta is often erroneously identified as exclusively pluralistic. In truth, there are two interpretations, one monistic and another dualistic, of which the former is the original Vedic philosophical premise found in pre-Meykandar scriptures, including the *Upanishads.*

Śaiva Siddhānta is rich in its temple traditions, religious festivals, sacred arts, spiritual culture, priestly clans, monastic orders and *guru*-disciple lineages. All these still thrive. Today Śaiva Siddhānta is most prominent among sixty million Tamil Śaivites who live mostly in South India and Sri Lanka. Here and elsewhere in the world, prominent Siddhānta societies, temples and monasteries abound.

The Nātha Sampradāya

Sampradāya is the strength and structure of Hinduism. It can be understood in two ways. First, it refers to an oral tradition of teaching—such as a *guru* of an established lineage verbally passing on eternal truths to his *śishya,* like a mother imparting knowledge to her daughter, or a father to his son. During these intimate moments when deep personal knowledge is transferred, a combination of meaning, experience and knowledge of realizations passes from teacher to pupil through the action of *sampradāya.* Second, *sampradāya* refers to an established historical lineage, a living stream of tradition or theology within Hinduism.

Nātha means lord or master, one who has mastered the intricacies of his inner bodies. Through history, Nāthas have been wielders of *siddhis* or powers of the soul, knowers of Śiva and masters of the esoteric knowledge of the universe. Nātha *siddhas* delve deep into the mind, invoking Śiva's grace, controlling the *kuṇḍalinī śākti* that is Śiva as the core power of being. The lotus-like *chakras* uncurl their petals as the spiritual forces are awakened within their inner being through extreme *tapas.* They come face to face with the Supreme God, Śiva.

Merging with Śiva embodies the teachings of the ancient Nandinātha Sampradāya. The Nātha lineage first historically appears with Satguru Nandinātha and his great *siddha* disciples, including Sundaranātha, known as Tirumular in South India. The Nātha teachings are articulated in his *Tirumantiram* which expounds the most comprehensive path of Śaiva Dharma.

The Nātha Sampradāya is the mystical fountainhead of Śaivism. The divine messages of the Eternal Truths and how to succeed on the path to enlightenment are locked within the Nātha tradition. From times and civilizations lost to history, the Nātha *gurus* worshiped with full heart and mind the Lord of Lords, Śiva, and in *yogic* contemplation experienced their identity in His Beingness. All that we know as Śaivism today—Āgamic temple worship, including *homa*-fire sacrifice; *sannyāsa, sādhana, tapas*, the *yoga/tantra* science and the ultimate Śaivite monistic theism theology—was carried forward by the Himālayan orders of the Nātha Sampradāya. In recent times one line of the Nātha Sampradāya has been passed on through the Śiva Yogaswāmī Guru Paramparā.

While a *sampradāya* is a living teaching tradition, *paramparā* denotes a succession of a certain line of *gurus*. Through one or more *paramparā*, the *sampradāya* is carried forward generation after generation.

In the twentieth century, now going into the twenty-first, the Ādinātha and Nandinātha lineages of the Nātha Sampradāya are both vibrant and vital, sharing a common ground of Śaiva Nātha theology, principles, *sādhanas* and many scriptures—including the *Vedas, Āgamas* and Patañjali's *Yoga Sūtras*. In addition, historical, societal and geographical forces over the past 1,000 years have shaped cultural differences between these two Nātha schools. It is important to note the differences because much of what is written or discussed today by scholars about the Nāthas is drawn from the northern Gorakshanātha line and lifestyle, while most of South India and Sri Lanka follow the Tirumular line. Some of these differences are as follows:

1. The foremost exposition of the Nandinātha lineage is the *Tirumantiram* (ca 200 BCE), while that of the Ādinātha lineage is Gorakshanātha's later *Siddha Siddhānta Paddhati* (tenth century).
2. The pre-eminent expositor of the Nandināthas is Tirumular, and that of the Ādināthas is Gorakshanātha.
3. The canons of the Nandināthas are written predominantly in the Tamil language, while those of the Ādināthas are in Sanskṛit.
4. The Nandinātha lineage is most influential in the South of India, while the Ādinātha lineage is most

prominent in the North of India.
5. The philosophy of the Nandinātha lineage is known as Śaiva Siddhānta, while that of the Ādinātha lineage is known as Siddha Siddhānta.

The Nandinātha Sampradāya's Belief Patterns

1. On the Nature of God: The Nandinātha Sampradāya is a mystical lineage that places great stress on direct and personal experience of God, on seeing God everywhere and in everyone, on knowing God within oneself. This is achieved through nonintellectual spiritual disciplines called *sādhana*—a term which in its fullest sense embodies *kuṇḍalinī yoga*, profound esoteric practices, intense introspective meditation and worship—through purificatory effort, mind-transforming austerities, egoless service and, most importantly, through the bountiful grace of the living *satguru*. Following such a path, the Nāthas have always come to know God, in ancient days and modern.

Enlightened sages of the Nātha Sampradāya teach that God is Śiva, the transcendent/immanent Supreme Being. Śiva is transcendent as unmanifest Paraśiva, the ineffable That which lies beyond time, form and space. Śiva is immanent as Satchidānanda, the substratum or primal substance and pure consciousness flowing through all form. And Śiva is also immanent as Maheśvara, the Primal Soul, who performs the five divine actions of creation, preservation, destruction, veiling and revealing. Though Śiva is a singular and sacred mystery, the Nāthas understand Him through these three perfections.

The one central teaching of the Nāthas is this: Śiva is All, and all is Śiva. This potent monism nonetheless acknowledges God's creation of world and souls, not as a dark or dreamlike existence, but as a real, purposeful, necessary and joyous one. However, God alone is Absolute, Eternal and Unchanging Reality. The creation—or more precisely, emanation—is relative, temporal and subject to change.

For the Nāthas, Vishṇu, Brahmā and Rudra are not separate Gods existing and acting apart from Lord Śiva. They are Śiva. Vishṇu names His sustaining, perpetuating power. Brahmā is none other than His creative power. And *Rudra* denotes His destructive or absorbing power. Likewise, Śaktī is not just a divine consort, as often represented, but is His manifest power. Śiva and Śaktī are the one unmanifest/manifest Reality.

In addition, Nāthas worship the Mahādevas Gaṇeśa and Kārttikeya (known as Murugan in the South) and revere all the 330 million Gods of Śaivism as separate but inseparable from Śiva, believing that they, like all souls, are created by Śiva and yet are wholly pervaded by Him. Thus, for the Nāthas there are many Gods and there is but one Supreme God, Śiva, whose holy names include Brahmā, Vishṇu, Rudra, Śaktī and more.

Regarding the notion of *avatāra,* that God takes birth upon the Earth as a savior, Nāthas hold that God Śiva does not incarnate to save mankind. He *is* mankind as well as the perfect and purposeful universe in which mankind matures spiritually. Having created all, consciously knowing all, lovingly guiding all, fully encompassing all, there is no "other" for Śiva, no need therefore to rectify a process already made perfect by Him.

2. On the Nature of the Soul: Each individual soul is born of God's Being, is of God, and is eventually absorbed, by Śiva's grace, back into Himself. The soul's journey through existence is its maturing from a germ or seed state to its fully unfolded innate Divinity. Each soul is, in its innermost essence, Paraśiva and Satchidānanda, eternal and uncreated. However, the individual soul body is created as an extension of God Śiva Himself in the image and likeness of His own Primal Soul form, differing only in its maturity. Over vast periods of time and through countless experiences, the soul body matures through experiencing self-created *karma.* Finally the soul seeks and realizes its identity as Śiva. Through grace "*jīva* becomes Śiva."

A three-fold bondage, called *pāśa,* both aids and hinders the soul's knowing of its oneness with God Śiva. *Pāśa* is comprised of *āṇava, karma* and *māyā. Āṇava* is the individuating veil of duality, source of ignorance which separates the soul from Śiva. *Māyā* is the principle of matter. *Karma* is the cause-and-effect principle governing *māyā.* Experienced subjectively by the soul, it is the result of its own deeds, both "good" and "bad."

For the Nātha, the soul always stands apart from the three bondages of its evolutionary progress into final merger. The Nāthas, through divine revelation and mastery of the many *yogas,* have realized it to be untarnished, unfettered, unmarred—only shrouded, or covered, by *āṇava, karma* and *māyā* temporarily. The soul's spiritual progress is along a successive path of *charyā, kriyā, yoga* and *jñāna.* This process is as natural and as beautiful as a lotus' blossoming. By following this path, the soul's identity with Śiva can be and will be fully realized when the seeming triple bondage of *āṇava, karma* and *māyā* is removed through Śiva's Grace.

Moksha—also called *kaivālya,* perfect inner freedom—is the soul's release from *saṁsāra,* the cycle of birth and death, attained after dynamic and personal *yogic* realization of Paraśiva and resolution of all seed *karmas.* Having known the Absolute, there is no fuller realization, no greater knowing, no higher "experience." Even when God Realization is attained, the soul body continues to evolve in this and other worlds until it merges with the Primal Soul as a drop of water merges with its source, the ocean.

The soul progresses through three stages *(avasthai)* of existence. These are *kevala avasthai, sakala avasthai* and *śuddha avasthai.* During *kevala avasthai* the soul is likened to a seed hidden in the ground or a spark of the Divine hidden in a cloud of unknowning called *āṇava,* the primal fetter of individuality, the first aspect of the Lord's *tirodhāna śakti,* or concealing grace. The *sakala avasthai,* the next stage in the soul's journey, is the period of bodily existence, the cyclic evolution through transmigration from body to body, under the additional powers of *māya* and *karma,* the second and third aspects of the Lord's *tirodhāna śakti.*

The journey through *sakala avasthai* is viewed in three stages. The first is called *irul,* "darkness," where the soul's impetus is toward *pāśa-jñānam,* knowledge and experience of the world. The next period is *marul,* "confusion," where the soul begins to take account of its situation and finds itself caught between the world and God, not knowing which way to turn. This is also called *paśu-jñānam,* the soul seeking to know its true nature. The last period is *arul,* "grace," when the soul yearns for the grace of God. Now it has begun its true religious evolution with the constant aid of the Lord.

How does *arul,* grace, set in? During the time of *paśu-jñānam,* the soul comes to find that if he performs good and virtuous deeds, life always seems to take a positive turn. Whereas in negative, unvirtuous acts he slowly becomes lost in a foreboding abyss of confusion. Thus, in faith, he turns toward the good and holy. A balance emerges in his life. This balance is called *iruvinaioppu.* The pleasures and pains in life no longer raise him to the sky, then crash him to the ground. He has found a peaceful center from where life can be lived in refined composure. Not that he has, all of a sudden, found perfect and final peace, but he has experienced a balanced state and now seeks to attain perfectly to it. Trials still come and go as his *karmic* patterns ebb and flow.

Whether he is conscious of it or not, what is occurring is that he is bringing the three *malas* under control. *Māyā* is less and less and enchanting temptress. *Karma* no longer controls his state of mind, tormenting him through battering experiences. And *āṇava,* his self-centered nature, is easing its hold, allowing him to feel a more universal compasion in life. This grows into a state called *malaparipakam,* the ripening of the *malas.*

This will allow, at the right moment in his life, *arul* to set in. This is known as the descent of grace, or *śaktinipāta.* The internal descent is recognized as a tremendous yearning for Śiva. More and more, he wants to devote himself to all that is spiritual and holy. The outer descent of grace is the appearance of a *satguru.* There is no question as to who he is, for he sheds the same clear, spiritual vibration as that unknown something the soul feels emanating from his deepest self. It is when the soul has reached *malaparipakam* that the Lord's *tirodhāna* function, or concealing grace, has accomplished its work. Now His concealing grace gives way to *anugraha,* revealing grace, and the descent of grace, *śaktinipāta,* occurs.

The religious path progresses through four stages: *charyā, kriyā, yoga* and *jñāna.* In *charyā* the main emphasis is complete refinement of virtuous qualities. Certain simple religious practices are enjoined, but we can go no farther till becoming a living exemplar of virtue. In *kriyā,* temple worship and the awakening of true *bhakti* occur. In *yoga,* mystic union with the Lord is sought through disciplined yogic *sādhanas* under the *guru's* guidance. The *jñāna* stage begins the *śuddha avasthai* and is the fruit of the previous three stages. It is vital to note that for the Śaiva Siddhāntin all three stages remain experientially active in the daily life of the *yogin.*

All of this—the three *avasthais;* the four *mārgas* as both progressive and perpetually upheld stages; the importance of *guru, liṅgam, saṅgam* and *valipadu;* the three-fold descent of Siva's grace; and the oneness of God and soul—distinguishes the Tamil religion from all other Indian traditions. Most important is that Śiva is the motivator in this tradition. It is His Will that allows the devoted to progress from one *avasthai* to another, one *mārga* into the next, until He, of His own volition, absorbs each soul back into Himself. For each step the soul takes toward Śiva, Śiva takes nine toward the devotee. Thus, merging with Śiva completes the cycle so clearly articulated in Tamil Śaivism.

In the *śuddha avasthai* the *yogi* has attained *samādhi* and lives with an inner realization that sets him apart from all other men. But the *jñāna* stage is not a relaxing or ending of spiritual endeavor. It is the beginning of even deeper self-transformation. The *jñānī* must now seek what is called *sāyujya samādhi,* perpetual immersion in Satchidānanda. Prior to this, he is not yet matured in his realization. He may go into *samādhi,* but comes out into his "same old self," though, of course, not losing his anchor, which he has set firmly in the Absolute. Now he must infuse his entire being with the spiritual force and power that he has recognized and attained to through *samādhi.* Slowly the dichotomy between the transcendent Absolute and the external world of form becomes less and less apparent, until he becomes as Śiva Himself—a divine being living in a constant state of *sāyujya samādhi,* transcendent-immanent realization of the Self flowing through all form. He is transformed from what he was to a recognizably different being. This is the joyous *sādhana* of *śuddha avasthai,* by which the *yogin* becomes the *jñānī,* a venerable *jīvanmukta,* able to set new patterns of evolution, uplift consciousness and radiate life-changing blessings.

3. On the Nature of the World: The Nātha Sampradāya understands and perceives the world as a manifest expression of God Śiva Himself. He is Creator and creation. While God is Absolute Reality and unchanging, the world is relatively real and subject to constant change. That does not mean that the world is illusion, ignorant seeming or nonexistence. It is important to note that *māyā* for the Nātha is not understood as the Smārtas' classic misapprehension of a rope as a snake. Rather, it is Śiva manifest. Seen thusly, the nature of the world is duality. It contains each thing and its opposite, joy and sorrow, love and hate. Therefore, in the Nātha view, there is no intrinsic evil. The entire range of human expression—whether intellectual achievement, social and cultural interaction, creative and psychological states of mind, instinctive desires or lofty *yogic* cognitions within the *chakra-nāḍī* network of man's inner nerve system—is but pure experience, powerful living lessons by which the soul learns, matures and progresses nearer to God. Experience is governed by *karma* and the divine laws of *dharma*, softened through God's grace.

This Nātha view of *māyā* also differs from the pluralistic Meykandar conception, which holds that *āṇava*, *karma* and *māyā* (as well as the soul) are separate from God, uncreated and eternally coexistent with Him. Under the pluralistic view, God is not both Creator and creation. Instead, He creates by "fashioning" already existing *māyā*, or matter, into the world. He does not create or destroy *māyā* itself.

In simple summary, it can be said that *māyā* is the classroom, *karma* the teacher and *āṇava* the student's ignorance. *Māyā* may be understood as that which is in the process of creation, preservation and destruction. Śiva emanates *māyā* and is the *māyā* He emanates.

4. Paths of Attainment: The Nātha path leads naturally and inevitably through *charyā*, *kriyā*, *yoga* and *jñāna*. *Charyā* is service and living everyday life according to traditional religious principles of conduct in order to purify oneself. *Kriyā* is the regular practice of temple worship, both internal and external, through which understanding, closeness and love for God Śiva deepen. As expounded in Patañjali's eight-limbed *(ashṭāṅga) yoga*, the *yoga mārga* is internalized worship which leads to union with God. It is the regular practice of meditation under the guidance and grace of a *satguru* through which the realizations of Satchidānanda and Paraśiva are attained. *Jñāna* is divine wisdom emanating from the maturely enlightened soul. It is immersion of the mind in the blessed realization of God, while living out earthly *karmas.* For these highest spiritual attainments, *sādhana, brahmacharya, kuṇḍalinī yoga* and renunciation of the world are required.

These four *mārgas* are not distinct approaches to Lord Śiva, but progressive stages of a one path. Each builds upon but does not exclude the other. For the Nātha, *jñāna* is not an intellectual amassing of knowledge, beliefs and attitudes, but a state attained only after God Realization. The Nātha Sampradāya insists on the necessity of the illumined *satguru* who alone brings the *śishya* to face and conquer the lower mind. He is the master who knows the Self and can therefore guide the disciple to the higher Self. The *guru* is a source of grace that sustains the *śishya's* personal *sādhana* as the spiritual forces unfold from within. For Nāthas the repetition of the sacred Pañchākshara Mantra, Namaḥ Śivāya, is the key to the awakening of Śivaness within each and every devotee on the path to Lord Śiva's holy feet.

5. Scripture and Religious Perspective: The primary scriptural authority of the Nandinātha Sampradāya's Kailāsa Paramparā derives from the *Vedas* and *Āgamas,* the *Tirumantiram, Tirukural, Natchintanai* of Jñānaguru Yogaswāmī, the *Tirumurai* and, last but not least, the teachings of Satguru Sivaya Subramuniyaswami, including *Loving Gaṇeśa, Dancing with Śiva, Living with Śiva, Merging with Śiva, Lemurian Scrolls* and the *Maṭhavāsi Śāstras.*

The Nātha Sampradāya teaches that Śaivism is the oldest religion in the world, the eternal faith or Sanātana Dharma, the precursor of the many-faceted religion now termed "Hinduism." Within Hinduism today, there are four main denominations: Śaivism, Vaishṇavism, Śāktism and Smārtism. But since long ago Sanātana Dharma has been none other than Śaivism. Though the beliefs of Śaivism and of other religions are diverse and different, the devout Śaivite respects and encourages all who worship God and tries never to criticize or interfere with anyone's faith or belief. He follows that single most fundamental practice: seeing Śiva everywhere and in everyone.

My *satguru,* Jñānaguru Yogaswāmī, was a great *siddha,* a master and a knower of God. He would say, "Liberation is within you." He would order his seekers to "See God in everything. You are in God. God is within you. To realize the Supreme Being within you, you must have a strong body and a pure mind." He was a powerful mystic from Sri Lanka, near India—perhaps the greatest to live in this century—and his words drove deeply into the hearts of all who heard them. "God is in everyone. See Him there. God is overwhelmingly present everywhere. Regard everything as a manifestation of God, and you will realize the Truth," were his words. Simple words for a simple truth, but very, very difficult to practice.

It takes much meditation to find God Śiva in all things, through all things. In this striving, regular daily disciplines must be faithfully adhered to in order to "See God Śiva everywhere and in everyone," a saying rendered in Sanskṛit as "Sarvasmin Sarvatra cha Śivadarśanam," सर्वस्मिन् सर्वत्र च शिवदर्शनम्. He is there, as the Soul of each soul. You can open your inner eye and see Him in others, see Him in the world, as the world. Little by little discipline yourself to meditate at the same time each day. Meditate. Discover the silent center of yourself, then go deep within, to the core of your real Being. Slowly the purity comes. Slowly the awakening comes.

Ākāśarāganideśanam

आकाशरागनिदेशनम्

Key to the Astral Colors

Central, East, South, North and West, these are the five faces of Sadāśiva. The central face is of crystal hue, the eastward face is crimson unto *kumkum*, the southward face is dark unto thick pitch, the northward face is red unto *aratham* flower, the westward face is white unto milky hue. Thus did He reveal unto me, His humble servant.

TIRUMANTIRAM 1735

Key to the Astral Colors

NOW I WOULD LIKE TO SHARE WITH YOU SOME KEY EXCERPTS FROM A RARE AND MOST WONDERFUL BOOK IN OUR LIBRARY THAT, AS FAR as we know, is not in print anymore and not easily available elsewhere. It is but one of many such books written by mystics in the first half of this century, when Indian *ṛishis*—wonderful, spiritually endowed clairvoyants and clairaudients—came to America. One would come and depart, and then another. They taught *prāṇāyāma,* demonstrated levitation (Mahāyogī Harirāma was noted for this), spoke of astral travel, discussed the *chakras* and appeared in the dreams of their newly found devotees. These highly-trained *kuṇḍalinī* Hindu missionaries from the spiritual land called India charmed American seekers with their unheard of insights. One example we would like to share now is by Swāmī Pañchadāsi Mahārāj, who explained the meanings of the colors of the human aura in his little book, *The Human Aura,* published in Illinois in 1912 by the Yoga Publication Society. We have published the full text, including chapters on thought forms and psychic protection, on our web site: *www.hindu.org.* His profound and exacting contribution to the West helped lay the foundation of modern metaphysics and furthered the ongoing Hindu renaissance. In recent times, this spiritual movement has been monitored by our informal international group of ministers and missionaries, the Satya Saṅga, over four hundred *āchāryas, swāmīs, yogīs* and *sādhus,* and recorded in our monthly magazine, HINDUISM TODAY, since 1979. There are well over three million such renunciate souls, dedicated to promoting Sanātana Dharma in today's world. They, like their predecessors, work tirelessly to uplift humanity by living and sharing these eternal truths.

Excerpts from *The Human Aura* By Swāmī Pañchadāsi

The term astral, so frequently employed by all occultists, is difficult to explain or define except to those who have pursued a regular course of study in occult science. For the purpose of the present consideration, it is enough to say that over and above the ordinary physical sense plane there is another and more subtle plane, known as the astral plane. Every human being possesses the innate and inherent faculty of sensing the things of this astral plane, by means of an extension or enlargement of the powers of the ordinary senses, so to speak. But in the majority of persons in the present stage of development, these astral senses are lying dormant, and only here and there do we find individuals who are able to sense on the astral plane, although in the course of evolution the entire race will be able to do so, of course. The colors of the human aura, which arise from the various mental and emotional states, belong to the phenomena of the astral plane and hence bear the name of "the astral colors." Belonging to the astral plane, and not to the ordinary physical plane, they are perceived only by the senses functioning on the astral plane, and are invisible to the ordinary physical plane sight. But to those who have developed the astral sight, or clairvoyance, these colors are as real as are the ordinary colors to the average person, and their phenomena have been as carefully recorded by occult science as have the physical plane colors by physical science. The fact that to the ordinary physical senses they are invisible does not render them any the less real. Remember, in this connection, that to the blind man our physical colors do not exist. And, for that matter, the ordinary colors do not exist to "color-blind" persons. The ordinary physical plane person is simply "color blind" to the astral colors—that's all.

On the astral plane each shade of mental or emotional

state has its corresponding astral color, the latter manifesting when the form appears. It follows then, of course, that when once the occultist has the key to this color correspondence, and thus is able to perceive the astral colors by means of his astral vision, he also is able to read the mental and emotional states of any person within the range of his vision, as easily as you are now reading the printed words of this book.

Before proceeding to a consideration of the list of astral colors in the human aura, I wish to call your attention to a slight variation in the case of the *prāṇa*-aura. I have stated that the *prāṇa*-aura is colorless, like a diamond or clear water. This is true in the average case, but in the case of a person of very strong physical vitality or virility, the *prāṇa*-aura takes on, at times, a faint warm pink tinge, which is really a reflection from the red astral color, the meaning of which color you shall now learn.

Like their physical plane counterparts, all the astral colors are formed from three primary colors, namely (1) red; (2) blue and (3) yellow. From these three primary colors, all other colors are formed. Following the primary colors, we find what are known as the secondary colors, namely: (1) green, derived from a combination of yellow and blue; (2) orange, formed from a combination of yellow and red and (3) purple, formed from a combination of red and blue. Further combinations produce the other colors, as for instance, green and purple form olive; orange and purple form russet; green and orange form citrine.

Black is called an absence of color, while white is really a harmonious blending of all colors, strange as this may appear to one who has not studied the subject. The blending of the primary colors in varied proportions produce what is known as the "hues" of color. Adding white to the hues, we obtain "tints," while mixing black produces "shades." Strictly speaking, black and white are known as "neutral" colors.

Now for the meaning of the astral colors—that is, the explanation of the mental or emotional state represented by each. I ask that the student familiarize himself with the meaning of the primary colors and their combinations. A clear understanding of the key of the astral colors is often an aid in the development of astral sight.

KEY TO THE ASTRAL COLORS

Red

Red represents the physical phase of mentality. That is to say, it stands for that part of the mental activities which are concerned with physical life. It is manifested by the vitality of the body, and in other hues, tints and shades, is manifested by passions, anger, physical cravings, etc. I shall describe the various forms of Red manifestation a little later on.

Blue

Blue represents the religious, or spiritual, phase of mentality. That is to say, it stands for that part of the mental activities which are concerned with high ideals, altruism, devotion, reverence, veneration, etc. It is manifested, in its various hues, tints and shades, by all forms of religious feeling and emotion, high and low, as we shall see as we proceed.

Yellow

Yellow represents the intellectual phase of mentality. That is to say, it stands for that part of the mental activities which are concerned with reasoning, analysis, judgment, logical processes, induction, deduction, synthesis, etc. In its various hues, tints and shades, it is manifested by the various forms of intellectual activity, high and low, as we shall see as we proceed.

White

White stands for what occultists know as Pure Spirit, which is a very different thing from the religious emotion of "spirituality," and which really is the essence of the ALL that really is. Pure Spirit is the positive pole of Being. We shall see the part played by it in the astral colors, as we proceed.

Black

Black stands for the negative pole of Being—the very negation of Pure Spirit, and opposing it in every way. We shall see the part played by it in the astral colors as we proceed.

The various combinations of the three astral primary colors are formed in connection with Black and White as well as by the blending of the three themselves. These combinations, of course, result from the shades of mental and emotional activity manifested by the individuality, of which they are the reflection and the key.

The combinations and blending of the astral colors, however, are numberless, and present an almost infinite variety. Not only is the blending caused by the mixing of the colors themselves, in connection with black and white, but in many cases the body of one color is found to be streaked, striped, dotted or clouded by other colors. At times there is perceived the mixture of two antagonistic color streams fighting against each other before blending. Again we see the effect of one color neutralizing another.

In some cases great black clouds obscure the bright colors beneath and then darken the fierce glow of color, just as is often witnessed in the case of a physical conflagration. Again, we find great flashes of bright yellow or red flaring across the field of the aura, showing agitation or the conflict of intellect and passion.

The average student who has not developed the astral vision is inclined to imagine that the astral colors in the human aura present the appearance of an egg-shaped rainbow or spectrum, or something of that sort. But this is a great mistake. In the first place, the astral colors are seldom at rest, for all mental and emotional activity is the result of vibration, change and rhythmic motion. Consequently, the colors of the aura present a kaleidoscopic appearance of constant change of color, shape and grouping—a great electrical display, so to speak, constantly shifting, changing and blending.

Great tongues of flamelike emanations project themselves beyond the border of the aura under strong feeling or excitement, and great vibratory whirls and swirls are manifested. The sight is most fascinating, although somewhat terrifying at first. Nature is wise in bestowing the gift of astral vision only gradually and by almost imperceptible stages of advance. There are many unpleasant, as well as pleasant, sights on the astral plane.

Remembering always the significance of the three primary colors on the astral plane, let us consider the meaning of the combinations, shades, hues and tints of these colors.

The Red Group

In this group of astral colors seen in the human aura we find strongly in evidence the clear bright red shade, similar to that of fresh, pure arterial blood as it leaves the heart, filled with pure material freshly oxygenated. This shade in the aura indicates health, life-force, vigor, virility, etc., in pure and untainted form. The aura of a healthy, strong child shows this shade of color very plainly and strongly.

Strong, pure natural emotions, such as friendship, love of companionship, love of physical exercise, healthy clean sports, etc., are manifested by a clear, clean shade of red. When these feelings become tainted with selfishness, low motives, etc., the shade grows darker and duller. Love of low companionship, unclean sports or selfish games, etc., produce an unpleasant, muddy red shade.

A shade of red very near to crimson is the astral color of love, but the tint and shade varies greatly according to the nature of this form of emotional feeling. A very high form of love, which seeks the good of the loved one, rather than the satisfaction of oneself, manifests as a beautiful rose tint—one of the most pleasing of the astral tints, by the way. Descending in the scale, we find the crimson shade becoming darker and duller, until we descend to the plane of impure, sensual, coarse passion, which is manifested by an ugly, dull, muddy crimson of a repulsive appearance, suggesting blood mixed with dirty earth or barnyard soil.

A peculiar series of red shades are those manifesting anger in its various forms, from the vivid scarlet flashes of anger color, arising from what may be called "righteous indignation," down the scale to the ugly flashes of deep, dull red, betokening rage and uncontrolled passion. The red of anger generally shows itself in flashes, or great leaping flames, often accompanied by a black background, in the case of malicious hate, or by a dirty, greenish background when the rage arises from jealousy, or envy. The color of avarice is a very ugly combination of dull, dark red, and a dirty, ugly green. If persons could see their own astral colors accompanying these undesirable mental states, the sight would perhaps so disgust them with such states as to work a cure. At any rate, they are most disgusting and repulsive to the occultist who beholds them in the human aura, and he often wonders why they do not sicken the person manifesting them—they often do just this thing, to tell the truth.

The Yellow Group

In this group of astral colors seen in the human aura we find as many varieties as we do in the red group. Yellow, denoting intellect, has many degrees of shade and tint, and many degrees of clearness.

An interesting shade in this group is that of orange,

which represents different forms of "pride of intellect," intellectual ambition, love of mastery by will, etc. The greater degree of red in the astral orange color, the greater the connection with the physical or animal nature. Pride and love of power over others have much red in its astral color, while love of intellectual mastery has much less red in its composition.

Pure intellectual attainment, and the love of the same, is manifested by a beautiful clear golden yellow. Great teachers often have this so strongly in evidence that at times their students have glimpses of a golden "halo" around the head of the teacher. Teachers of great spirituality have this "nimbus" of golden yellow, with a border of beautiful blue tint, strongly in evidence.

The paintings of the great spiritual teachers of the race usually have this radiance pictured as a "halo," showing a recognition of the phenomenon on the part of the great artists. Hoffman's celebrated painting of the Christ in the Garden of Gethsemane shows this nimbus so accurately depicted that the occultist is convinced that this artist must have actually witnessed a similar scene in the astral light, so true to the astral facts are its details. The images of the Buddha also show this radiance.

The rich golden shades of intellectual yellow are comparatively rare, a sickly lemon color being the only indication of intellectual power and found in the aura of the great run of persons. To the sight of the occultist, employing his power of astral vision, a crowd of persons will manifest here and there, at widely separated points, the bright golden yellow of the true intellect, appearing like scattered lighted candles among a multitude of faintly burning matches.

The Green Group

This is a peculiar group, consisting as of course it does of various combinations of blues and yellows, tinted and shaded by white or black. Even skilled occultists find it very difficult to account for the fact of certain green shades arising from the spiritual blue and the intellectual yellow. This is one of the most obscure points in the whole subject of the astral colors, and none but the most advanced occultists are able to explain the "why" in some instances. To those who are fond of analysis of this kind, I will drop the following hint, which may help them out in the matter, viz. The key is found in the fact that green lies in the center of the astral spectrum, and is a balance between the two extremes, and is also influenced by these two extremes in a startling manner.

A certain restful green denotes love of nature, out of door life, travel in the country, etc., and also, slightly differing in tint, the love of home scenes, etc. Again, a clear, beautiful, lighter tint of green indicates what may be called sympathy, altruistic emotion, charity, etc. Again, illustrating variety in this group of astral colors, another shade of green shows intellectual tolerance of the views of others. Growing duller, this indicates tact, diplomacy, ability to handle human nature, and descending another degree or so blends into insincerity, shiftiness, untruth, etc. There is an ugly slate-colored green indicating low, tricky deceit—this is a very common shade in the colors of the average aura, I am sorry to say. Finally, a particularly ugly, muddy, murky green indicates jealousy and kindred feelings, envious malice, etc.

The Blue Group

This interesting group of astral colors represents the varying forms and degrees of religious emotion, "spirituality," etc. The highest form of spiritual, religious feeling and thought is represented by a beautiful, rich, clear violet tint, while the lower and more gross phases of religious emotion and thought are represented by the darker and duller hues, tints, and shades until a deep, dark indigo is reached, so dark that it can scarcely be distinguished from a bluish black. This latter color, as might be expected, indicates a low superstitious form of religion, scarcely worthy of the latter name. Religion, we must remember, has its low places as well as its heights—its garden grows the rarest flowers, and at the same time the vilest weeds.

High spiritual feelings—true spiritual unfoldment—are indicated by a wonderfully clear light blue, of an unusual tint, something akin to the clear light blue of the sky on a cool autumn afternoon, just before sunset. Even when we witness an approach to this color in nature, we are inspired by an uplifting feeling as if we were in the presence of higher things, so true is the intuition regarding these things.

Morality, of a high degree, is indicated by a series of beautiful shades of blue, always of a clear inspiring tint. Religious feeling ruled by fear is indicated by a shade of bluish gray. Purple denotes a love of form and ceremony, particularly those connected with religious offices or regal grandeur of a solemn kind. Purple, naturally, was chosen as the royal color in the olden days.

The Brown Group

The brown group of astral colors represents desire for gain and accumulation, ranging from the clear brown of industrious accumulation, to the murky dull browns of miserliness, greed and avarice. There is a great range in this group of brown shades, as may be imagined.

The Gray Group

The group of grays represents a negative group of thought and emotions. Gray represents fear, depression, lack of courage, negativity, etc. This is an undesirable and unpleasant group.

Black

Black, in the astral colors, stands for hatred, malice, revenge and "devilishness" generally. It shades the brighter colors into their lower aspects, and robs them of their beauty. It stands for hate—also for gloom, depression, pessimism, etc.

White

White is the astral color of Pure Spirit, as we have seen, and its presence raises the degree of the other colors, and renders them clearer. In fact, the perception of the highest degree of Being known to the most advanced occultist is manifested to the highest adepts and masters in the form of "The Great White Light," which transcends any light ever witnessed by the sight of man on either physical or astral plane—for it belongs to a plane higher than either, and is absolute, rather than a relative, white. The presence of white among the astral colors of the human aura, betokens a high degree of spiritual attainment and unfoldment, and when seen permeating the entire aura it is one of the signs of the master—the token of adeptship.

Sannyāsi Gītā

संन्यासिगीता

Song of the Sannyāsin

Beyond birth and death, reached by renunciate *tapas* is He, my Lord of resplendent glory! Sing His praise! Incessant pray! The Heaven's Lord shall show you the Dharma's Land.

TIRUMANTIRAM 1614

Song of the Sannyāsin

INTRODUCING THE *SONG OF THE SANNYĀSIN* IS NOT ALL THAT EASY TO DO, BUT I SHALL GIVE IT A TRY BY FIRST SAYING THAT RENUNCIATION OF the world is not for everyone, but it is for many. For instance, if two thirds of the people on this planet were the spiritual leaders and had nothing on their mind but to spread the *dharma* of right thought, right speech and right action, would we have a most wonderful world or not? It truly would be a global village, a haven, a wonderland. But during this *yuga,* it may not be possible because younger souls inhabit the planet in abundance, and their only method of discipline among themselves is with the hatchet, the whip and harsh, insulting words. In this way they accrue much *karma* to be worked out in another birth. This makes a lot of sense, for if they did not make new *karma* they would not reincarnate and never become older souls. It is the tragedies, the hurts, the fears, the arguments that remain unresolved, that goad the young souls onward. They learn by their own mistakes, but very slowly, taking the lessons out of their experiences and always blaming on others what has happened to them. This and most of the above is how we come to distinguish an old soul from one in the intermediate grade and those who are unverified. ¶The intermediate souls struggle with their emotions; they hurt themselves more than others. Misunderstanding is not their enemy. It is their teacher of new discoverings. Theirs is the never-ending search. Theirs is the never-ending not being able to reach the end of their search. Unlike the young souls, their desires are well-defined. Unlike the young souls, their intellection has some development, maybe not keen but usable. For them, religion is an acceptable solution. They are not superstitious, meaning believing in what they do not understand, as are the young souls. They must be satisfied with adequate reasons of why, how and what the future holds. The intermediate souls all have to learn not to drag the past through life with them in the form of resentment, unforgivingness through unforgetability. This one lesson and this alone distinguishes them from their older examples. But they do look to the older souls for help and for solace, seeking to hold their hand, lean on their shoulder and share with them some of their experiential burdens.

Sannyāsa is for the older souls. These forgiving, intelligent beings rely on their memories of their past when they were young souls. They rely on their memories of the past when they were intermediate souls. They rely on their superconscious abilities to look through and see into every situation, happening, of past, present and future. Their test, and their supreme test, is to balance their inner and their outer life. So, they renounce the world, and in their renouncing, the world they renounced renounces them. Their humanness is still there, their striving is still there and their seeking elucidation is still there. But what is not there is the sense of their small self. The sense of the little I'go. The sense of "me and mine" is replaced by "us" and "ours."

Not all old souls are ready for the holy orders of *sannyāsa*, but some of them are, and these rare few have special qualities. Loyalty to their lineage is one of the most important, and another is love in their will. This means that they do make happenings happen in the external world. They do effect change, but they do not claim reward or recognition. They do not sulk if appreciation is not forthcoming. They move on, ever impelled by their spirituality, that ever-moving force of inspiration that does good rather than harm, that ever-moving spiritual force that quells the external ego and gives credit to others. That rewarding ability to see into the future, prepare for it and to guide others into it is theirs to develop.

Young souls merge with each other. Intermediate souls merge with projects and learning new things, merging with the mind and the intellect. Older souls, seeking the Self beyond, merge with the Spirit and with things spiritual. For them, a pure and nearly perfect life calls. They intuitively know that the profound merger of *jīva* in Śiva is no easy task, to be accomplished in a weekend seminar or *yoga* class. So they go farther, they renounce, they take up the ideals of the four *Vedas*—not to parrot them, but to live them, just as did the *ṛishis* of yore. That leads to the path of the renouncer, to the *sannyāsin,* in the Indian tradition.

Though you may not formally renounce the world, you can benefit your search immensely by knowing how the great ones live and respond to life. You can find ways in the midst of your life to follow their example.

Realize that the *sannyāsins,* the *sādhus* and the host of nameless mendicants from the traditional orders of Hinduism (there are estimated to be three million) do have built within them the spiritual, social, cultural structure that has survived siege and pestilence within the countries they serve. But most importantly, they have survived the siege of their lower self, the pestilence of their own mind, and risen above to the heights. This book, *Merging with Śiva,* contains within it the wisdom which, once read and understood, becomes knowledge to make the conquest of all conquests, the victory over the instinctive-intellectual mind and all that it contains. All this and more is summed up so eloquently in the "Song of the *Sannyāsin,*" a stirring poem by Śrīla Śrī Swāmī Vivekānanda Mahārāj (1863-1902), composed in July, 1885, at Thousand Island Park, New York. Live it, just live it, and try to fulfill in your life these high ideals. Proceed with confidence, for merger with Śiva is assured and certain. That's the way it is, and that is the way it is. Aum.

Song of the Sannyāsin

Wake up the note! the song that had its birth
Far off, where worldly taint could never reach,
In mountain caves and glades of forest deep,
Whose calm no sigh for lust or wealth or fame
Could ever dare to break; where rolled the stream
Of knowledge, truth, and bliss that follows both.
Sing high that note, *sannyāsin* bold! Say,
"Om Tat Sat, Om!"

Strike off thy fetters! bonds that bind thee down,
Of shining gold, or darker, baser ore—
Love, hate; good, bad; and all the dual throng.
Know slave is slave, caressed or whipped, not free;
For fetters, though of gold, are not less strong to bind.
Then off with them, *sannyāsin* bold! Say,
"Om Tat Sat, Om!"

Let darkness go; the will-o'-the-wisp that leads
With blinking light to pile more gloom on gloom.
This thirst for life forever quench; it drags
From birth to death, and death to birth, the soul.
He conquers all who conquers self.
Know this and never yield, *sannyāsin* bold! Say,
"Om Tat Sat, Om!"

"Who sows must reap," they say, "and cause must bring
The sure effect: good, good; bad, bad; and none
Escapes the law. But whoso wears a form
Must wear the chain." Too true; but far beyond
Both name and form is *ātman,* ever free.
Know thou art That, *sannyāsin* bold! Say,
"Om Tat Sat, Om!"

They know not truth who dream such vacant dreams
As father, mother, children, wife and friend.
The sexless Self—whose father He? whose child?
Whose friend, whose foe, is He who is but One?
The Self is all in all—none else exists;
And thou art That, *sannyāsin* bold! Say,
"Om Tat Sat, Om!"

There is but One: the Free, the Knower, Self,
Without a name, without a form or stain.
In Him is *māyā*, dreaming all this dream.
The Witness, He appears as nature, soul.
Know thou art That, *sannyāsin* bold! Say,
"Om Tat Sat, Om!"

Where seekest thou? That freedom, friend, this world
Nor that can give. In books and temples, vain
Thy search. Thine only is the hand that holds
The rope that drags thee on. Then cease lament.
Let go thy hold, *sannyāsin* bold! Say,
"Om Tat Sat, Om!"

Say, "Peace to all. From me no danger be
To aught that lives. In those that dwell on high,
In those that lowly creep—I am the Self in all!
All life, both here and there, do I renounce,
All heavens and earths and hells, all hopes and fears."
Thus cut thy bonds, *sannyāsin* bold! Say,
"Om Tat Sat, Om!"

Heed then no more how body lives or goes.
Its task is done: let *karma* float it down.
Let one put garlands on, another kick
This frame: say naught. No praise or blame can be
Where praiser, praised, and blamer, blamed, are one.
Thus be thou calm, *sannyāsin* bold! Say,
"Om Tat Sat, Om!"

Truth never comes where lust and fame and greed
Of gain reside. No man who thinks of woman
As his wife can ever perfect be;
Nor he who owns the least of things, nor he
Whom anger Chains, can ever pass through *māyā's* gates.
So, give these up, *sannyāsin* bold! Say,
"Om Tat Sat, Om!"

Have thou no home. What home can hold thee, friend?
The sky thy roof, the grass thy bed, and food
What chance may bring—well cooked or ill, judge not.
No food or drink can taint that noble Self
Which knows Itself. Like rolling river free
Thou ever be, *sannyāsin* bold! Say,
"Om Tat Sat, Om!"

Few only know the truth. The rest will hate
And laugh at thee, great one; but pay no heed.
Go thou, the free, from place to place, and help
Them out of darkness, *māyā's* veil. Without
The fear of pain or search for pleasure, go
Beyond them both, *sannyāsin* bold! Say,
"Om Tat Sat, Om!"

Thus day by day, till *karma's* power's spent,
Release the soul forever. No more is birth,
Nor I, nor thou, nor God, nor man. The "I"
Has All become, the All is "I" and Bliss.
Know thou art That, *sannyāsin* bold! Say,
"Om Tat Sat, Om!"

"Song of the *Sannyāsin*" by Swāmī Vivekānanda is quoted, with written permission, from *Inspired Talks, My Master and Other Writings;* copyright 1958 by Swāmī Nikhilānanda, trustee of the estate of Swāmī Vivekānanda; published by the Rāmakṛishṇa-Vivekānanda Center of New York. Remarkably, the handwritten original was discovered (long after his passing in 1902) hidden in a wall during the 1943 restoration of a retreat where Swāmijī had spent the summer and given *darshan* and discourses to Western seekers.

Chitrāṇi
चित्राणि

Charts

Those who receive Śiva's grace are liberated from the ego-binding impurity called *āṇava.* Transcending the states of *bindu*–light and *nāda*–sound, they become as Prāṇava Aum and merge in pure Śiva. Verily, this is the pristine state.

TIRUMANTIRAM 2233

Charts

THREE CHARTS ARE GIVEN ON THE FOLLOWING PAGES. THE FIRST SHOWS HINDU COSMOLOGY, CORRELATING THE VARIOUS DIVISIONS AND CATEGORIES OF MANIfestation, as well as the bodies, sheaths, *chakras* and states of consciousness of the soul. It is organized with the highest consciousness, or subtlest level of manifestation, at the top, and the lowest, or grossest at the bottom. In studying the chart, it is important to remember that each level includes within itself all the levels above it. Thus, the element earth, the grossest or outermost aspect of manifestation, contains all the *tattvas* above it on the chart. They are its inner structure. Similarly, the soul encased in a physical body also has all the sheaths named above—*prāṇic,* instinctive-intellectual, cognitive and causal.

Here, now, is a brief description of the major parts of the cosmology chart.

lokas (3 worlds & 14 planes): These are the classical divisions of consciousness, traditionally numbering 14, as listed. A simpler breakdown shows in column one the three *lokas:* causal, subtle and gross. The 14 planes correspond directly to the *chakras,* psychic force centers within the inner bodies of the soul, also listed in column two. The 14 *chakras* are "doorways" within man to each of the 14 planes.

kalā (5 spheres): The center of the chart lists the five *kalās*—vast divisions of consciousness or "dimensions" of the mind. Note that the five states of mind—superconscious, subsuperconscious, conscious, subconscious and subsubconscious—are also listed in this column.

tattva (36 evolutes): The 36 *tattvas,* listed to the right of the *kalās,* are the basic "building blocks" of the universe, successively grosser evolutes of consciousness. These are in three groups, as shown.

kośa & śarīra (3 bodies & 5 sheaths): The sheaths or bodies of the soul are given in the two right-hand columns. Note the correlation of these and the worlds by reading across the chart to the left to the two columns named "three worlds," and "14 planes."

On the second chart, the 14 *chakras* and their attributes are listed, and on the third, a complete list of all 36 *tattvas* is given. For more insights on the subjects in the chart, please refer to the glossary.

ॐ Vedic-Āgamic Cosmology

३ लोक **3 WORLDS**		१४ लोक **14 PLANES**		५ लोक **5 SPHERES**
3rd World, Śivaloka, "plane of God," and the Gods, or Kāraṇaloka, the "causal plane"		**7. Satyaloka,** "plane of reality," also called Brahmaloka, ***sahasrāra chakra***		**5. Śāntyatītakalā** Śivānanda, superconsciousness expanded into endless inner space.
		6. Tapoloka, "plane of austerity," ***ājñā chakra***		**4. Śāntikalā** *kāraṇa chitta,* superconscious forms made of inner sounds and colors
		5. Janaloka, "creative plane"		
		viśuddha chakra		**• LIBERATED SOULS •**
2nd World, Antarloka, subtle, or astral plane	higher astral plane	**4. Maharloka,** "plane of greatness," ***anāhata chakra***	Devaloka	**• BOUND SOULS •** **3. Vidyākalā** *anukāraṇa chitta,* • subsuperconscious awareness of forms in their totality in progressive states of manifestation • subsuperconscious cognition of the interrelated forces of the spiritual and magnetic energies
		maṇipūra chakra		
cycle of reincarnation, *saṁsāra* ↑↓	mid-astral	**3. Svarloka,** "celestial plane"		**2. Pratishṭhākalā** *buddhi chitta and manas chitta,* realm of intellect and instinct
	lower astral	**2. Bhuvarloka,** "plane of atmosphere," ***svādhishṭhāna chakra*** — Pitṛiloka, "world of ancestors"	Pitṛiloka	
		Pretaloka, "world of the departed," earth-bound souls	Pretaloka	**1. Nivṛittikalā** *jāgrat chitta, saṁskāra chitta* and *vāsanā chitta*—the conscious, subconscious and subsubconscious mind, the interrelated magnetic forces between people, people and their possessions
1st World, Bhūloka		**1. Bhūloka,** "earth plane," ***mūlādhāra chakra***		
Antarloka's netherworld, Naraka	sub-astral	**Naraka (7 hellish planes of lower consciousness,** descending order): -1) Put *(atala chakra),* -2) Avīchi *(vitalā chakra),* -3) Saṁhāta *(sutala chakra),* -4) Tāmisra *(talātala chakra),* -5) Ṛijīsha *(rasātala chakra),* -6) Kuḍmala *(mahātala chakra),* -7) Kākola *(pātāla chakra)*		

ब्रह्माण्ड The Inner and Outer Universe

<table>
<tr><th>Paraśiva (atattva, “beyond existence”)
३६ तत्त्व 36 EVOLUTES</th><th colspan="2">३ शरीर
3 BODIES</th><th>५ कोश
5 SHEATHS</th></tr>
<tr><td>śuddha māyā: pure spiritual energy
1) Śiva tattva: Parāśakti-nāda, Satchidānanda, pure consciousness
2) Śakti tattva: Parameśvara-bindu, Personal God</td><td colspan="3">viśvagrāsa: final merger of the golden ānandamaya kośa—svarṇaśarīra—in Parameśvara</td></tr>
<tr><td>3) Sadāśiva tattva: power of revealment
4) Īśvāra tattva: power of concealment
5) Śuddhavidyā tattva: dharma, pure knowing, the powers of dissolution, preservation and creation—Rudra, Vishṇu and Brahmā</td><td colspan="3">kāraṇa śarīra, “causal body” or ānandamaya kośa, “sheath of bliss” —the body of the soul, also called the actinic causal body</td></tr>
<tr><td>śuddhāśuddha māyā: spiritual-magnetic energy
6) māyā tattva: mirific energy
7) kāla tattva: time
8) niyati tattva: karma
9) kalā tattva: creativity, aptitude
10) vidyā tattva: knowledge
11) rāga tattva: attachment, desire
12) purusha tattva: shrouded soul</td><td rowspan="3">sūkshma śarīra “subtle body,” also called the astral body</td><td>refined astral body</td><td>vijñānamaya kośa “sheath of cognition,” the mental or actinodic causal sheath</td></tr>
<tr><td>aśuddha māyā: magnetic-gross energy
13) prakṛiti tattva: primal nature
14–16) antaḥkaraṇa: mental faculties
17–21) jñānendriyas: organs of perception
22–26) karmendriyas: organs of action
27–31) tanmātras: elements of perception
32–35) ākāśa tattva (ether), vāyu tattva (air), tejas tattva (fire), āpas tattva (water)</td><td rowspan="2">gross astral body</td><td>manomaya kośa intellectual (odic-causal sheath) and instinctive (odic-astral sheath)</td></tr>
<tr><td></td><td>prāṇamaya kośa “sheath of vitality,” which enlivens the physical body</td></tr>
<tr><td>36) pṛithivī tattva: earth</td><td colspan="3">sthūla śarīra, “gross body,” or annamaya kośa, “food-made sheath” —the physical body, or odic body</td></tr>
</table>

The *chakras* are nerve plexuses or centers of force and consciousness located within the inner bodies of man. In the physical body there are corresponding nerve plexuses, ganglia and glands. The seven principal *chakras* can be seen psychically as colorful, multi-petalled wheels or lotuses situated along the spinal cord. The seven lower *chakras*, barely visible, exist below the spine.

7 Sahasrāra
6 Ājñā
5 Viśuddha
4 Anāhata
3 Maṇipūra
2 Svādhishṭāna
1 Mūlādhāra

---

1 Atala
2 Vitala
3 Sutala
4 Talātala
5 Rasātala
6 Mahātala
7 Pātāla

ART BY A. MANIVEL OF CHENNAI, INDIA;
TEXT FROM HINDUISM TODAY, JULY, 1998

Seven Chakras Above: The most subtle of the *chakras* lie above and within the crown *chakra* at the top of the head. Buddhist literature cites thirty-two *chakras* above. Āgamic Hindu tradition delineates seven levels of the rarified dimensions of *paranādā,* the first *tattva* and the highest stratum of sound. They are: *vyāpinī, vyomāṅga, anantā, anāthā, anāśṛitā, samanā* and *unmanā.* The higher *chakras* have been experienced by a rare few as a conglomerate of *nāḍīs,* spiritual nerve currents, which when stimulated and developed by many *samādhi* experiences, slowly descend into the mental and astral bodies, effecting a permanent transformation of the entire being.

7. Sahasrāra सहस्रार Illumination, Godliness. The spiritual mountaintop, pinnacle of light, energy and consciousness. Aham Brahmasmi, "I am That," is unveiled. Here liberated ones abide in communion with the Self. Meaning: "thousand-petaled." Location: top of the cranium. Deity: Śiva. Śakti: Nirvāṇaśākti. Color: gold. Petals: 1,008. Plexus: pituitary. Plane: Satyaloka.

6. Ājñā आज्ञा Divine sight. Sensitives and clairvoyants reside in the pastel petals of this refined realm, with access to many levels of superconsciousness and inner worlds of light. Meaning: "command." Location: between the brows. Deity: Ardhanārīśvara. Śakti: Hākinī. Color: lavender. Vehicle: swan. Petals: two. Plexus: cavernous. Plane: Tapoloka.

5. Viśuddha विशुद्ध Divine love. Here, limitless love wells up, a vision of all souls as brothers and sisters and all things as sacred. Selfless souls, exceptional artists and mystical poets reside here. Meaning: "purity." Location: throat. Deity: Sadāśiva. Śakti: Śākinī. Color: smokey purple-blue. Vehicle: peacock. Petals: sixteen. Plexus: pharyngeal. Element: ether. Plane: Janaloka.

4. Anāhata अनाहत Direct cognition. Those who reach this realm, with their delicate, penetrating insight into many fields of activity and knowing, are mankind's guides, counselors, mentors and problem solvers. Meaning: "unsullied." Location: heart. Deity: Īśvara. Śakti: Kākinī. Color: smokey green. Vehicle: deer. Petals: twelve. Plexus: cardiac. Element: air. Plane: Maharloka.

3. Maṇipūra मणिपूर Willpower. This is the hub of willpower. Accomplished men and women perform at high levels mentally and physically when living in this center of energy, discipline and endurance. Meaning: "Jewelled city." Location: solar plexus. Deity: Mahārudra Śiva. Śakti: Lākinī. Color: yellow-amber. Vehicle: ram. Petals: ten. Plexus: epigastric or solar. Element: fire. Plane: Maharloka-Svarloka.

2. Svādhishṭhāna स्वाधिष्ठान Reason. Home of intellect. Educated people work through this center of logic and analysis. Great minds have mastered it. It is the *pandit's* dwelling place and the pragmatist's refuge. Meaning: "one's own place." Location: lower abdomen. Deity: Vishṇu. Śakti: Śākinī. Color: reddish orange. Vehicle: crocodile. Petals: six. Plexus: prostatic. Element: Water. Plane: Bhuvarloka.

1. Mūlādhāra मूलाधार Memory-time-space. The abode of memory, the foundation of all human knowledge, this center is also the seat of our basic instincts of survival, sexuality and others. Meaning: "foundation." Location: base of spine. Deity: Gaṇeśa and Brahmā. Śakti: Ḍākinī. Color: red. Vehicle: elephant. Petals: four. Plexus: sacral or pelvic. Element: Earth. Plane: Bhūloka.

Seven Chakras below the Mūlādhāra

1. Atala अतल Fear and lust. As awareness slips below the *mūlādhāra* into fear, indecision stymies ambition and a licentious lifestyle dulls the *prāṇic* sheath. Meaning: "without bottom." Plane: Put.

2. Vitala वितल Raging anger. Dark red-black streaks emblazen the aura when awareness enters this furnace of instinctive fire and then injures others. Meaning: "region of the lost." Plane: Avīchi.

3. Sutala सुतल Retaliatory jealousy. Wanting what others have and preoccupation with what one is not gnaws at the mind, instilling ill-will. Meaning: "great lower region." Plane: Saṁhāta.

4. Talātala तलातल Prolonged confusion. Perversions replace natural joys. Negative *karmas* compound and stiffen the flow of awareness. Reason warps. Meaning: "under the bottom level." Plane: Tāmisra.

5. Rasātala रसातल Selfishness. An imprisoning veil of "me" and "mine" blinds the natural instinct to care for others. Every action is for personal gain. Meaning: "lower region of moisture." Plane: Ṛijīsha.

6. Mahātala महातल Consciencelessness. Blindness to higher impulses prevails. Guilt, compunction, even fear, are foreign. Criminality is life. Meaning: "greatest lower region." Plane: Kuḍmala.

7. Pātāla पाताल Malice and murder. A virtual hell of hate, hurting, killing for its own sake without remorse. Reason rarely reaches this region. Meaning: "lower region of wickedness." Plane: Kākola.

21 Chakras

Seven Upper Chakras: The most subtle of the 21 *chakras* lie above and within the crown *chakra* at the top of the head. Āgamic Hindu tradition delineates seven levels of *paranāda*, the first *tattva* and the highest stratum of sound.

Name	Location/ Plexus	Attribute	Motor Organ	Endocrine Gland	Color/ Metal
7) ***sahasrāra***	crown of head/ pituitary	illumination		pituitary	gold
6) ***ājñā***	third eye/ cavernous	divine sight		pineal	lavendar/ silver
5) ***viśuddha***	throat/ pharyngeal	divine love	mouth	thyroid, parathyroid	smokey purple-blue/ mercury
4) ***anāhata***	heart/ cardiac	direct cognition	hand	thymus	smokey green/ copper
3) ***maṇipūra***	solar	willpower	feet	pancreas	yellow-amber/ iron
2) ***svādhish-ṭhāna***	navel/ hypogastric	reason	genitals	ovaries, testicles	reddish orange/ tin
1) ***mūlādhāra***	base of spine/ sacral, pelvic	memory, time, space	anus	adrenals	red
1) ***atala***	hips	fear, lust			
2) ***vitala***	thighs	raging anger			
3) ***sutala***	knees	retaliatory jealousy			
4) ***talātala***	calves	prolonged confusion			
5) ***rasātala***	ankles	selfishness			
6) ***mahātala***	feet	absence of conscience			
7) ***pātāla***	soles of feet	malice, murder			

Force Centers of Consciousness

They are: *vyāpinī, vyomāṅga, anantā, anāthā, anāśṛitā, samanā* and *unmanā,* experienced by a rare few as a conglomerate of *nāḍīs,* spiritual nerve currents, stimulated and developed by many *samādhi* experiences.

Deity/ Śakti	Vehicle	Plane	Planet	Element/ Sense	Petals	Letter*
Śiva/ Nirvāṇaśakti		Satyaloka	Neptune	Śūnya (void)	1008	
Ardha-nārīśvara/ Hākinī	swan	Tapoloka	Uranus	*mahā-tattva/* intuition	2	Aum
Sadāśiva/ Śākinī	peacock	Janaloka	Saturn	ether/ hearing	16	Ham/ Ya
Īśvara/ Kākinī	deer	Maharloka	Jupiter	air/ touch	12	Yam/ Vā
Mahārudra/ Lākinī	ram	Svarloka	Mars	fire/ sight	10	Ram/ Śi
Vishṇu/ Śākinī	crocodile	Bhuvarloka	Venus	water/ taste	6	Vam/ Ma
Gaṇeśa & Brahmā/ Dākinī	elephant	Bhūloka	Mercury	earth/ smell	4	Lam/ Na
		Put				
		Avīchi				
		Saṁhāta				
		Tāmisra				
		Ṛijīsha				
		Kuḍmala				
		Kākola				

*The first letter is the *bīja mantra* associated with the *chakra;* the second is the syllable of the Pañchākshara Mantra associated with the *chakra.*

The 36 Tattvas: Categories of Existence

Atattva: Paraśiva (Śivaliṅga, Absolute Reality), beyond all categories

5 ŚUDDHA TATTVAS
Actinic or Pure Spiritual Energy

1) *Śiva tattva:* Parāśakti-Nāda (Satchidānanda, pure consciousness)
2) *Śakti tattva:* Parameśvara-Bindu (Naṭarāja, Personal God), energy, light and love
3) *Sadāśiva tattva:* the power of revealment (Sadāśiva)
4) *Īśvāra tattva:* the power of concealment (Maheśvara)
5) *Śuddhavidyā tattva: dharma,* pure knowing, the powers of dissolution (Rudra), preservation (Vishṇu) and creation (Brahmā)

7 ŚUDDHĀŚUDDHA TATTVAS
Actinodic or Spiritual-Magnetic Energy

6) *māyā tattva:* mirific energy
7) *kāla tattva:* time
8) *niyati tattva: karma*
9) *kalā tattva:* creativity, aptitude
10) *vidyā tattva:* knowledge
11) *rāga tattva:* attachment, desire
12) *purusha tattva:* the soul shrouded by the above five *tattvas*

ĀŚUDDHA TATTVAS
Odic or Gross-Magnetic Energy

13) *prakṛiti tattva:* primal nature
14) *buddhi tattva:* intellect
15) *ahaṁkāra tattva:* external ego
16) *manas tattva:* instinctive mind
17) *śrotra tattva:* hearing (ears)
18) *tvak tattva:* touching (skin)
19) *chakshu tattva:* seeing (eyes)
20) *rasanā tattva:* tasting (tongue)
21) *ghrāṇa tattva:* smelling (nose)
22) *vāk tattva:* speech (voice)
23) *pāṇi tattva:* grasping (hands)
24) *pāda tattva:* walking (feet)
25) *pāyu tattva:* excretion (anus)
26) *upastha tattva:* procreation (genitals)
27) *śabdha tattva:* sound
28) *sparśa tattva:* feel/palpation
29) *rūpa tattva:* form
30) *rasa tattva:* taste
31) *gandha tattva:* odor
32) *ākāśa tattva:* ether
33) *vāyu tattva:* air
34) *tejas tattva:* fire
35) *āpas tattva:* water
36) *pṛithivī tattva:* earth

Conclusion

Nirvahaṇam

निर्वहणम्

THE END OF THIS BOOK, *MERGING WITH ŚIVA,* IS THE BEGINNING, AS THE BEGINNING WAS THE END. THE CONUNDRUMS OF CYCLES CONTINUE until *viśvagrāsa,* full merger of the soul in God, happens. *Viśvagrāsa* is not an experience; it is a permanent happening, as are birth and death, but even more permanent than both, for there is no singular experience that occurs after *viśvagrāsa* except, of course, constant unrelenting creation, preservation and dissolution, all occurring simultaneously. Merging with Śiva is the inevitable destination and conclusion of the evolution of all souls. As all water returns back to the ocean, all captured air when released finally returns to the sky, as all organic matter returns to earth, and as all fire merges into fire, all *ākāśa,* both inner space and outer space, merge together and become the grand relative reality, stemming from the Absolute Reality—so will it be for you, as the physical body is needed no more, as the astral body is needed no more, as the *prāṇic* body holding both together is needed no more, as the mental body is needed no more, and lastly as the ever-watching, all-knowing, self-contained soul body is needed no more. Where else to go but into the all of the All, the Self, Śiva? For you, then, merging with Śiva has become a conclusive reality. ¶Even at the beginning stages, merging with the Divine within oneself requires a great deal of resolve and commitment. This is called *saṅkalpa,* the preparation for the final merger with Śiva, which takes lifetimes. First, we must dance with Śiva, meaning accept consciously, subconsciously, subsubconsciously and subsuperconsciously the

Advaita Īśvaravāda philosophy, or outlook on life, and live by its tenets. This is the *charyā pāda*, not to be ignored. To do otherwise would be merely following a path of words, not the experiential path of living according to the wisdom of this profound Śaiva Siddhānta perspective. Then, before we can really, fully experience merger, which is well explained in this book, it is absolutely necessary that living with Śiva be perfected in every department of life, physically, emotionally, intellectually and culturally. This is the *kriyā pāda,* also not to be ignored. This means molding one's life according to the culture of Hindu Dharma so that the physical, emotional and mental bodies are all in perfect synchronicity with the great, Divine, master plan, the ultimate computer program of Śiva's perfect universe.

So, now we are aware of the path toward *viśvagrāsa,* final, irrevocable merger of the soul with Śiva, the Lord of Lords, God of Gods, above all, in all, below all, on all sides of all and within all—and all of the many prior levels of merging with the Divine.

The first two books of the trilogy, *Dancing with Śiva* and *Living with Śiva,* are the preparation that make merging with Śiva, even in the beginning stages, a reality in one's life. It is a progressive path. The first book is the foundation and the ground floor, the second is the upper stories, the third forms the penthouse at the top. To get to the penthouse takes time and effort, and so a secure foundation of *sādhana* is the necessary prerequisite. First dance, learn and become transfixed with the philosophy, then live the culture and obey its protocols, then all will become clear from the inside out. If you do, your life will be a model for all to follow. There is no doubt about it. Without such preparation, this book is, to the seeker, merely another path of metaphysical words—words that are inspiring, to be sure, but may easily be forgotten when other metaphysical instruction comes along.

The trilogy of *Dancing, Living, Merging with Śiva*—

which took many, many lives to experience before recording in this life—is my heritage and my legacy. They are now your inheritance, dear seeker, a most precious inheritance. Read them well. Read them often. Read them all. Live them fully. Live them fully. Experience the truths herein for yourself, step by step, and be transformed, never to be the same again.

Self Realization

Man came from God, evolves in God and ultimately merges into God. Thus, whether you fully know it or not, you are the story of God. Your life is the story of evolution. Now, in this book, that story becomes more conscious and purposeful than ever before.

Inwardly, people intuit that they are special, as indeed they are. They know, perhaps not consciously, but still they know deep down, that there is a profound meaning to life, a profound purpose for being here. The rare few find this purpose consciously and begin to pursue life as a great spiritual adventure. You may be one of these fortunate souls, these old souls, for whom the *yogas* here are familiar, for whom the inner light and sounds are like old friends, for whom the world's material opportunities are like the sand that could never quell the hunger of the famished villager. You may well be such an old soul, on a journey within. If so, this book will perhaps change your life forever. Certainly the spiritual experiences in it changed mine!

There is nothing more wonderful than knowledge about oneself that improves self-image. Everyone almost everywhere has this foremost on his agenda. But, still, there are those who are content to remain forever as they have been schooled to be. This division between those who are on the spiritual path of enlightenment and those who are not has existed for as long as I remember, and have been told much longer.

How do we know when someone is "on the path" or not? Well, there are signposts, and the biggest and most obvious is this one: people on the spiritual path will not argue. They will accept, meditate and draw their own conclusions. It now is obvious that those not on the path, when faced with challenging concepts, which can only be proven by personal realization and transformation, will endeavor to argue them out of their existence. These are those who resist selfless service of any kind of a spontaneous nature, always harboring an excuse of why they cannot and how they can't.

Realization is a signpost of finality. The question is often asked, "How do we know we have realized something?" The answer is easy: you just know, for realization is deeper than belief. Beliefs can be changed more easily than not. Realization is much deeper than faith. That can be taken away, too. But personal realization, especially of the spiritual kind, becomes stronger as the years pass by and is the foundation for personal transformation. It is some of these spiritual realizations that *Merging with Śiva* has just explained in utmost detail.

This Self of which we speak is subtle and elusive. To the ordinary man it is a fiction. To him, sex, money, food and clothes are more real. To him, the ego is a reality that cannot be transcended. To him, the ineffable Absolute Truth in all men, which is the Source of all things, is a fiction, a silliness, no more or perhaps even less real than an animated story by Disney or a special-effects film by Spielberg.

But to those who know this Truth, It is the All in all. It is the essence of life and love. The heart itself, with its every beat, sleeping and waking, touches instantaneously into this Self and thus continues its life-giving work. Thought and feeling could not be if the Self were not. Nor the senses, nor the stars, nor time and space. It is there, underlying all, sustaining all, giving existence to all, silently and without notice.

In fact, this Self is so subtle as to be hidden from all but the most awakened. How can it remain so unknown? Simplicity is the answer. The Self is so simple, so uncomplicated, that the ramified external mind overlooks it. From birth to death and back to birth, we live in the ocean of Being and see only the fishes of objective perception. We neglect to notice that these swim in the ocean of Being. When man comes to a point, as he must, when the things of this world possess less attraction for him than the path toward merging with Śiva, then only will he begin to detach himself enough to see the obvious, the Ocean of Śivaness that lies on every side, inside, outside, above and below. Then only will the merging we speak of here become meaningful to him. Then only will he be able to simplify his life and his thinking, his very perceptions, his hour-to-hour way of looking at things, enough to quiet the mind, for this Self can only be known in a quieted consciousness. Not even a thought can remain. Not a feeling. Not a hope or a question. One must be very pure for this realization to come, very pure indeed. The Self reveals itself, by the *satguru's* unique grace, to a mind that has, in a mystical but very pragmatic manner, eliminated itself. "You must die before you die," my *satguru,* Śiva Yogaswāmī, said. That is all that needs to be said.

Merging with Śiva—what is done by the soul is what is done: being and becoming. The soul establishes its identity and strengthens each *chakra,* from the soles of the feet to the top of the head and the seven above, through the stages of its evolution, referred to as three *avasthais.* All souls are in the process of evolution toward merging with Śiva, and that is the conclusive conclusion of this book.

Sanskṛit Pronunciation

Ucchāraṇa Vyākhyā

उच्चारण व्याख्या

VOWELS
Vowels marked like ā are sounded twice as long as the short vowels. The four dipthongs, e, ai, o, au, are always sounded long, but never marked as such.

अ a as in about
आ ा ā ...tar, father
इ ि i ...fill, lily
ई ी ī ...machine
उ ु u ...full, bush
ऊ ू ū ...allude
ऋ ृ ṛi ...merrily
ॠ ॄ ṛī ...marine
ऌ ॢ lṛi ...revelry
ए े e ...prey
ऐ ै ai ...aisle
ओ ो o ...go, stone
औ ौ au ...*Haus*

GUTTURAL CONSONANTS
Sounded in the throat.

क् k ...kite, seek
ख् kh ...inkhorn
ग् g ...gamble
घ् gh ...loghouse
ङ् ṅ ...sing

PALATAL CONSONANTS
Sounded at the roof of the mouth.

च् ch ...church
छ् çh ...mu*ch h*arm
ज् j ...jump
झ् jh ...he*dg*ehog
ञ् ñ ...hinge

CEREBRAL CONSONANTS
Pronounced with the tongue turned up and back against the roof of the mouth. These are also known as retroflex.

ट् ṭ ...true
ठ् ṭh ...nuthook
ड् ḍ ...drum
ढ् ḍh ...redhaired
ण् ṇ ...none

DENTAL CONSONANTS
Sounded with the tip of the tongue at the back of the upper front teeth.

त् t ...tub
थ् th ...anthill
द् d ...dot
ध् dh ...adhere
न् n ...not

LABIAL CONSONANTS
Sounded at the lips.

प् p ...pot
फ् ph ...path
ब् b ...bear
भ् bh ...abhor
म् m ...map

SEMIVOWELS

य् y ...yet (palatal)
र् ् r ...road (cereb.)
ल् l ...lull (dental)
व् v ...voice (labial),

but more like *w* when following a consonant, as in the word *s<u>w</u>āmī.*

ह् h ...hear (guttural)

SIBILANTS

श् ś ...sure (palatal)
ष् sh ...shut (cerebral)
स् s ...saint (dental)

ANUSVĀRA
The dot over Devanāgarī letters represents the nasal of the type of letter it precedes; e.g.: अंग = *aṅga.* It is transliterated as ṁ or as the actual nasal (ṅ, ñ, n, ṇ, m). At the end of words it is sometimes म् *(m).*

VISĀRGA (ः) ḥ
Pronounced like *huh* (with a short, stopping sound), or *hih,* after i, ī and e.

ASPIRATES
The *h* following a consonant indicates aspiration, the addition of air. Thus, *th* should not be confused with *th* in the word *then.*

SPECIAL CHARACTERS

ज्ञ् jñ ...a nasalized sound, like *gya* or *jya.*

क्ष् = क्+ ष् ksh

CONVENTIONS

1. As a rule, the root forms of Sanskṛit words are used (without case endings).
2. च्छ is transliterated as cçh, and च्च as cch.
3. Geographical names, e.g., *Himalaya,* are marked with diacriticals only as main lexicon entries.
4. Diacritical marks are not used for Tamil words.

Glossary

Śabda Kośa

शब्दकोश

aadheenakarthar: The *aadheenam* head, or pontiff, also called the *Guru Mahāsannidhānam.* See: *aadheenam, monastery.*

aadheenam: ஆதீனம் Endowment, foundation, institution, establishment, estate, property. A Śaivite Hindu monastery and temple complex in the South Indian Śaiva Siddhānta tradition. Also known as *maṭha* or *pīṭha,* as in Kailāsa Pīṭha. The *aadheenam* head, or pontiff, is called the *Guru Mahāsannidhānam* or *aadheenakarthar.* See: *monastery.*

abhor: To regard with horror; reject or shun.

Absolute: Lower case (absolute): real, not dependent on anything else, not relative. Upper case (Absolute): Ultimate Reality, the unmanifest, unchanging and transcendent Paraśiva—utterly nonrelational to even the most subtle level of consciousness. It is the Self God, the essence of man's soul. See: *Paraśiva.*

abstinence: Voluntary restraint from something believed to be undesirable or harmful.

abyss: A bottomless pit. The dark states of consciousness into which one may fall as a result of serious misbehavior; the seven *chakras* (psychic centers), or *talas* (realms of consciousness), below the *mūlādhāra chakra,* which is located at the base of the spine. See: *chakra, naraka, loka.*

accrue: Increase, accumulate.

actinic force: Spiritual, creating light. Adjective derived from the Greek *aktis,* "ray." Of or pertaining to consciousness in its pure, unadulterated state. Describes the extremely rareified superconscious realm of pure *bindu,* of quantum strings, the substratum of consciousness, *śuddha māyā,* from which light first originates. Actinic force is the superconscious mind and not a force which comes from the superconcious mind. Commonly known as life, spirit, it can be seen as the light in man's eyes; it is the force that leaves man when he leaves his odic physical body behind. It is not opposite to odic force, it is different than odic force as light is different than water but shines through it. Actinic force flows freely through odic force. The substantive form *actinism* is defined in the *Oxford English Dictionary* as:

"1) the radiation of heat or light, or that branch of philosophy that treats of it; 2) that property or force in the sun's rays by which chemical changes are produced, as in photography." See: *actinodic, kośa, odic, tattva.*

actinic prāṇa: Actinic force, spiritual energy, of which one manifestation is the dynamic force of the spiritual will, or *ātma śakti,* soul force. See: *actinic force, odic force, odic prāṇa, willpower.*

actinodic: Spiritual-magnetic. Describes consciousness within *śuddhāśuddha māyā,* which is a mixture of odic and actinic force, the spectrum of the *anāhata chakra,* and to a certain degree the *viśuddha chakra.* See: *actinic force, odic force, tattva.*

acumen: Keenness of intellect, judgment or insight.

adept: A highly skilled person; expert. *Adeptship* is such a condition.

adharma: अधर्म Negative, opposite of *dharma.* Thoughts, words or deeds that transgress divine law. Unrighteousness, irreligiousness; demerit. See: *dharma, sin.*

Ādinātha Sampradāya: आदिनाथसंप्रदाय See: *Nātha Sampradāya.*

admonition: Advice or warning.

adrenaline: A hormone released into the bloodstream in response to physical or mental stress, as from fear or injury. It initiates many bodily responses, including the stimulation of heart action and an increase in blood pressure, metabolic rate and blood glucose concentration.

adulate: To praise, revere or admire greatly, even uncritically and to excess.

adultery: Sexual intercourse between a married man or a woman who is not one's own wife or husband. Adultery is spoken of in Hindu *śāstras* as a serious breach of *dharma.* See: *sexuality.*

advaita: अद्वैत "Non dual; not twofold." Nonduality or monism. The philosophical doctrine that Ultimate Reality consists of a one principal substance, or God. Opposite of *dvaita,* dualism. See: *dvaita-advaita, Vedānta.*

Advaita Īśvaravāda: अद्वैत ईश्वरवाद "Nondual and Personal-God-as-Ruler doctrine." The Sanskṛit equivalent of *monistic theism.* A general term that describes the philosophy of the *Vedas* and *Śaiva Āgamas,* which posits simultaneously the ultimate oneness of all things and the reality of the personal Deity. See: *Advaita, Advaita Siddhānta, monistic theism.*

Advaita Siddhānta: अद्वैत सिद्धान्त "Nondual ultimate conclusions." Śaivite philosophy codified in the *Āgamas* which has at its core the nondual (*advaitic*) identity of God, soul and world. This monistic-theistic philosophy, unlike the Śaṅkara, or Smārta view, holds that *māyā* (the principle of manifestation) is not an obstacle to God Realization, but God's own power and presence guiding the soul's evolution to perfection. While Advaita Vedānta stresses *Upanishadic* philosophy, Advaita Siddhānta adds to this a strong emphasis on internal and external worship, *yoga sādhanas* and *tapas. Advaita Siddhānta* is a term used in South India to distinguish Tirumūlar's school from the pluralistic Siddhānta of Meykandar and Aghoraśiva. This unified Vedic-Āgamic doctrine is also known as *Śuddha Śaiva Siddhānta.* It is the philosophy on which this text is based. See: *Advaita Īśvaravāda, dvaita-advaita, monistic theism, Śaiva Siddhānta.*

Advaita Vedānta: अद्वैत वेदान्त "Nondual end (or essence) of the *Vedas.*" Names the monistic schools, most prominently that of Śaṅkara, that arose from the *Upanishads* and related texts. See: *advaita, Vedānta.*

aegis: Protection; sponsorship; patronage.

affectionate detachment: The power and wisdom of love born of understanding. Not becoming engrossed in the problems or negative attachments of others. As opposed to "running away" from the world or being insensitively aloof, affectionate detachment allows for more genuine, wholesome relationships with people and things.

affirmation: *Dṛidhavāchana* ("firm statement"). A positive declaration or assertion. A statement repeated regularly while concentrating on the meaning and mental images invoked, often used to attain a desired result.

afterlife: A life that follows death.

aftermath: Results, consequences or repercussions following an experience.

Āgama: आगम The tradition that has "come down." An enormous collection of Sanskṛit scriptures which, along with the *Vedas,* are revered as *śruti* (revealed scripture). Datinguncertain. The *Āgamas* are the primary source and authority for ritual, *yoga* and temple construction. See: *Śaiva Āgamas, śruti.*

Agastya: अगस्त्य One of 18 celebrated Śaiva *siddhas* (adepts), and reputed as the first grammarian of the Tamil language. See: *siddha.*

Aghoraśiva: अघोरशिव A Śaivite philosopher of South India who in the 12th century founded a Siddhānta school emphasizing dualistic passages of the *Āgamas* and other early texts. The later Meykandar pluralistic philosophy is based partly on Aghoraśiva's teachings. See: *dvaita-advaita, dvaita Siddhānta, Śaiva Siddhānta.*

agni: अग्नि "Fire." 1) One of the five elements, *pañchabhūta.* 2) God of the element fire, invoked through Vedic ritual known as *yajña, agnikāraka, homa* and *havana.* See: *havana, homa, yajña.*

ahaṁkāra: अहंकार "I-maker." Personal ego. The mental faculty of individuation; sense of duality and separateness from others. Sense of I-ness, "me" and "mine." *Ahaṁkāra* is characterized by the sense of I-ness, sense of mine-ness, identifying with the body, planning for one's own happiness, brooding over sorrow, and possessiveness. See: *āṇava, ego, mind.*

ahiṁsā: अहिंसा "Noninjury," nonviolence or nonhurtfulness. Refraining from causing harm to others, physically, mentally or emotionally. *Ahiṁsā* is the first and most important of the *yamas* (restraints). It is the cardinal virtue upon which all others depend. See: *yama-niyama.*

AIDS: *Acquired Immune Deficiency Syndrome.* An immune-system disease in which the body's resistance to certain infections and cancers is lowered.

ājñā chakra: आज्ञाचक्र "Command wheel." The third-eye center. See: *chakra.*

ākāśa: आकाश "Space." The sky. Free, open space. Ether, the fifth and most subtle of the five elements—earth, air, fire, water and ether. Empirically, the rareified space or ethereal fluid plasma that pervades the universes, inner and outer. Esoterically, mind, the superconscious strata holding all that potentially or actually exists, wherein all transactions are recorded and can be read by clairvoyants. It is through psychic entry into this transcendental *ākāśa* that cosmic knowledge is gathered, and the entire circle of time—past, present and future—can be known. See: *mind (universal).*

allegiance: Loyalty, as to a leader, lineage, cause or country.

aloha: "Love," traditional greeting and farewell in Hawaiian. In sound it curiously coincides with the Sanskṛit *a-loha,* "not iron" or "soft," though most probably is unrelated.

altruism: Unselfish concern for the well-being of others; selflessness.

altruistic: Unselfish. Showing more concern for others than oneself.

amalgamate: To combine and make into a whole.

Āmardaka Order: आमर्दक An order of *Śaiva sannyāsins* founded by Āmardaka Tīrthanātha in Andhra Pradesh (ca 775).

Āmardaka Tīrthanātha: आमर्दक तीर्थनाथ See: *Āmardaka Order.*

amass: To gather together; accumulate; pile up.

ambrosia: The food of the Gods which confers immortality, same as Sanskṛit *amṛita.* See: *amṛita.*

amends: Recompensation, making up for injury or loss caused to another. This is done through sincere apology, expressing regrets, contrition, public penance, such as *kavadi,* and ample gifts. See: *penance.*

amorphous: Of no definite shape or configuration. See: *formless.*

amṛita: अमृत "Immortality." Literally, "deathless," "without death" *(mṛita).* The nectar of divine bliss which flows down from the *sahasrāra chakra* when one enters very deep states of meditation.***anāhata chakra:*** अनाहतचक्र "Wheel of unstruck [sound]." The heart center. See: *chakra.*

analogy: An explanation or illustration made by comparing one thing with another, similar in some but not all respects.

ānanda: आनन्द "Bliss." The pure joy—ecstasy or enstasy—of God-consciousness or spiritual experience. See: *God Realization, Satchidānanda.*

ānandamaya kośa: आनन्दमयकोश "Bliss body." The body of the soul, which ultimately merges with Śiva. See: *soul, kośa.*

Ānandamayī Ma: (1857-1920) God-intoxicated *yoginī* and mystic Bengali saint. Her spirit lives on in devotees.

anantā: अनन्ता "Endless, infinite." The third of the seven *chakras,* or *nāḍi* conglomerates, above and within the *sahasrāra chakra.* See: *chakras above sahasrāra.*

anāśṛitā: अनाश्रृता "Independent." The fifth of the seven *chakras,* or *nāḍi* conglomerates, above and within the *sahasrāra chakra.* See: *chakras above sahasrāra.*

anāthā: अनाथा Having "no master." The fourth of the seven *chakras,* or *nāḍi* conglomerates, above and within the *sahasrāra chakra.* See: *chakras above sahasrāra.*

āṇava: आणव "Fragment; atom; minuteness, individuality." The veiling power that provides individualness, or individual ego, to each soul, making the soul seem separate and distinct from God and the universe. See: *āṇava mala, evolution of the soul, grace, mala, soul.*

āṇava mala: आणवमल "Impurity of smallness; finitizing principle." The fetter or individualizing veil of duality that enshrouds the soul. It is the source of finitude and ignorance, the most basic of the three bonds *(āṇava, karma, māyā)* which temporarily limit the soul. The presence of *āṇava mala* is what causes the misapprehension about the nature of God, soul and world, the notion of being separate and distinct from God and the universe. See: *āṇava, evolution of the soul, grace, mala, soul.*

āṇava mārga: आणवमार्ग "Path of ignorance." The path of egoity, separateness, self-indulgence, self-interest and selfishness. See: *āṇava mala.*

Anbe Sivamayam Satyame Parasivaṁ: அன்பே சிவமயம சத்தியமே பரசிவம் Tamil for "God Śiva is Immanent Love and Transcendent Reality." The affirmation of faith which capsulizes the entire creed of monistic Śaiva Siddhānta. In Sanskṛit it is *Premaiva Śivamāyā, Satyam eva Paraśivaḥ.*

anchorite: "Hermit." A monk or aspirant who lives alone and apart from society, as contrasted with *cenobite,* a member of a religious order living in a monastery or convent. See: *monk.*

animate-inanimate: From Latin *animatus,* "made alive, filled with breath." These terms indicate the two poles of manifest existence, that which has movement and life (most expressly animals and other "living" beings) and that which is devoid of movement (such as minerals and, to a lesser degree, plants). From a deeper view, however, all existence is alive with movement and possessed of the potent, divine energy of the cosmos.

annamaya kośa: अन्नमयकोश "Food sheath." The physical body. See: *kośa.*

antagonism: Opposition, hostility.

Antarloka: अन्तर्लोक "Inner World." The astral plane, or Second World. See: *astral plane.*

anugraha śakti: अनुग्रहशक्ति "Graceful or favoring power." Revealing grace. God Śiva's power of illumination, through which the soul is freed from the bonds of *āṇava, karma* and *māyā* and ultimately attains liberation, *moksha.* Specifically, *anugraha* descends on the soul as *śaktipāta,* the *dīkshā* (initiation) from a *satguru. Anugraha* is a key concept in Śaiva Siddhānta. It comes when *āṇava mala,* the shell of finitude which surrounds the soul, reaches a state of ripeness, *malaparipāka.* See: *āṇava, grace, Naṭarāja, śaktipāta.*

anukāraṇa chitta: अनुकारणचित्त Subsuperconscious mind; the superconscious mind working through the conscious and subconscious states, which brings forth intuition, clarity and insight. See: *mind (five states).*

Aśoka: The greatest Mauryan Emperor (ca 273-232 BCE), grandson of Chandragupta. In his 40-year reign, Buddhism became a world power. The *Rock and Pillar Edicts* preserve his work and teachings.

apāṇa: अपाण "Incoming breath." One of the body's five somatic currents of vital energy, or *prāṇa.* See: *prāṇa.*

apex: Highest point, peak, summit.

apex of creation: The highest or initial movement in the mind that will eventually manifest a creation. The quantum level of manifestation. See: *microcosm-macrocosm, quantum, tattva.*

aphorism: A terse and well-qualified, easy-to-remember statement of a truth placed in the subconscious mind.

Appar: அப்பர் "Father." Endearing name for Tirunavukarasu (ca 700), one of four Tamil saints, Samayāchāryas, who reconverted errant Śaivites who had embraced Jainism. See: *Nayanar, Śaiva Siddhānta.*

apparition: A ghost or being in its astral body visible to human eyes.

apsarā: अप्सरा Female Second World beings, nymphs, the counterpart to astral male lovers called Gandharvas in the *Vedas.* See: *gandharvas.*

arahat: (Pali) "Worthy one." (Sanskṛit: *arhat*) See: *nirvāṇī and upadeśī.*

archangel: A high-ranking angel or *deva.* See: *Mahādeva, deva.*

ardha-Hindu: अर्धहिन्दु "Half-Hindu." A devotee who has adopted Hindu belief and culture to a great extent but has not formally entered the religion through ceremony and taking a Hindu first and last name. See: *Hindu.*

arduous: Strenuous, laborious. Difficult to climb, do or accomplish.

Arjuna: अर्जुन A hero of the *Mahābhārata* and central figure of the *Bhagavad Gītā.* See: *Bhagavad Gītā.*

artha: अर्थ "Goal" or "purpose;" "wealth, property, money."

arul: அருள் "Grace." The third of the three stages of the *sakala avasthai* when the soul yearns for the grace of God, *śaktinipāta.* At this stage the soul seeks *pati-jñānam,* knowledge of God. See: Pati-*jñānam, sakala avasthā, śaktinipāta.*

āsana: आसन "Seat; posture." In *haṭha yoga* any of numerous poses prescribed to balance and tune up the subtle energies of mind and body for meditation and to promote health and longevity. See: *haṭha yoga, rāja yoga, yoga.*

ascendency: Superiority or decisive advantage; domination.

ascertain: To discover with certainty by experimentation or examination.

ascetic: A person who leads a life of contemplation and rigorous self-denial, shunning comforts and pleasures for religious purposes. See: *monk.*

ascribe: To assign something to; attribute.

ashram (āśrama): आश्रम "Place of striving." From *śram,* "to exert energy." Hermitage; order of the life. Holy sanctuary; the residence and teaching center of a *sādhu,* saint, *swāmī,* ascetic or *guru;* often includes lodging for students. Also names life's four stages. See: *āśrama dharma, sādhana.*

ashṭāṅga praṇāma: अष्टाङ्गप्रणाम "Eight-limbed salutation." See: *prostration.*

ashṭāṅga yoga: अष्टाङ्गयोग "Eight-limbed union." The classical *rāja yoga* system of eight progressive stages or steps as described in numerous Hindu scriptures including various *Upanishads*, the *Tirumantiram* by Saint Tirumūlar and the *Yoga Sutras* of Sage Patañjali. The eight limbs are: restraints (*yama*), observances (*niyama*), postures (*āsana*), breath control (*prāṇāyāma*), sense withdrawal (*pratyāhāra*), concentration (*dhāraṇā*), meditation (*dhyāna*) and contemplation (*samādhi*). See: *rāja yoga, yoga, yama-niyama, āsana, prāṇāyāma, pratyāhāra, dhāraṇā, dhyāna, samādhi.*

aspirant: A person who strives for some high achievement.

aspiration: A desire for some high achievement.

āśrama dharma: आश्रमधर्म "Laws of life development." Meritorious way of life appropriate to each of its four successive stages *(āśramas)*, observing which one lives in harmony with nature and life, allowing the body, emotions and mind to develop and undergo their natural cycles in a most positive way. The four stages are: —**1)** ***brahmacharya:*** Studentship, from age 12 to 24. —**2)** ***gṛihastha:*** Householder, from 24 to 48. —**3)** ***vānaprastha:*** Elder advisor, from 48 to 72. —**4)** ***sannyāsa:*** Religious solitary, from 72 onward. See: *dharma, gṛihastha dharma, sannyāsa dharma.*

assertion: Something declared or stated positively.

assimilation: Making one's own or similar to something else. Incorporation and absorption as into the mind.

astral body: The subtle, nonphysical body *(sūkshma śarīra)* in which the soul functions in the astral plane, the inner world also called Antarloka. The astral body includes the *prāṇic* sheath *(prāṇamaya kośa)*, the instinctive-intellectual sheath *(manomaya kośa)* and the cognitive sheath *(vijñānamaya kośa)*—with the *prāṇic* sheath discarded at the death of the physical body.

astral entity: Any being in the astral plane. See: *astral plane.*

astral plane: The subtle world, or Antarloka, spanning the spectrum of consciousness from the *viśuddha chakra* in the throat to the *pātāla chakra* in the soles of the feet. The astral plane includes: 1) the higher astral plane, ***Maharloka,*** "plane of balance;" 2) mid-astral plane, ***Svarloka,*** "celestial plane;" 3) lower astral plane, ***Bhuvarloka,*** "plane of atmosphere," a counterpart or subtle duplicate of the physical plane (consisting of the Pitṛiloka and Pretaloka); and 4) the sub-astral plane, ***Naraka,*** consisting of seven hellish realms corresponding to the seven *chakras* below the base of the spine. In the astral plane, the soul is enshrouded in the astral body, called *sūkshma śarīra.* See: *Antarloka, astral body, loka, Naraka, three worlds.*

astral school: A meeting place in the Antarloka where inner-plane masters teach devotees in their astral bodies during sleep. See: *astral plane.*

astral shell: The odic astral form which a soul leaves behind in the astral plane when it enters into a new physical birth. The astral shell soon disintegrates as creative forces generate a new physical and astral body.

astrology: Science of celestial influences. See: *jyotisha.*

aśuddha māyā: **अशुद्धमाया** "World of impurity." The realm of the physical and lower astral planes. See: *māyā.*

asura: **असुर** "Evil spirit; demon." (Opposite of *sura:* "deva; God.") A being of the lower astral plane, Naraka. *Asuras* can and do interact with the physical plane, causing major and minor problems in people's lives. *Asuras* do evolve and do not remain permanently in this state. See: *Naraka.*

asura loka: **असुरलोक** Another name for Naraka. A general term for the inner worlds of *asuric*/demonic energies. See: *asura, Naraka.*

asuric: Of the nature of an *asura,* "not spiritual."

asylum: A place of any refuge, often an institution for people with serious mental or emotional problems.

atala: **अतल** "Bottomless region." The first *chakra* below the *mūlādhāra,* at the hip level. Region of fear and lust. See: *chakra, loka, Naraka.*

Atharva Veda: **अथर्ववेद्** From Atharva, the name of the *ṛishi* said to have compiled this fourth *Veda.* See: *Veda.*

atheism: The rejection of all religion or religious belief, or simply the belief that God or Gods do not exist. See: *materialism.*

ātman: **आत्मन्** "The soul; the breath; the principle of life and sensation." The soul in its entirety—as the soul body *(ānandamaya kośa)* and its essence (Parāśakti and Paraśiva). One of Hinduism's most fundamental tenets is that we are the *ātman,* not the physical body, emotions, external mind or personality. In Hindu scriptures, *ātman* sometimes refers to the ego-personality, and its meaning must be determined according to context. The *Ātma Upanishad* (1–3) describes *ātman,* or *purusha,* as threefold: *bāhyātman,* the outer or physical person; *antarātman,* the inner person, excluding the physical form, who perceives, thinks and cognizes; and Paramātman, the transcendent Self God within. See: *Paramātman, kośa, soul.*

ātmārtha pūjā: **आत्मार्थपूजा** "Personal worship rite." Home *pūjā*—Sanskṛit liturgy performed in the home shrine. See: *pūjā.*

attachments: That which one holds onto or clings to with the energy of possessiveness, which is a natural function of the inner and outer ego of an individual. As one unfolds through the *chakras,* the force of attachment naturally diminishes through *sādhana, tapas* and the grace of the *guru.*

attainment: Acquisition, achievement or realization through effort. Spiritual accomplishment. Śaiva Siddhānta notes four primary levels of attainment: *sālokya* (sharing God's world, the goal of *charyā), sāmīpya* (nearness to God, the goal of *kriyā*), *sārūpya* (likeness to God, the goal of *yoga)* and *sāyujya* (union with God, the state of *jñāna).* See: *God Realization, pāda, Self Realization, siddha yoga, siddhi.*

attention: Focusing of the mental powers upon an object.

Aum: ॐ or **ओम्** Often spelled *Om.* The mystic syllable of Hinduism, placed at the beginning of most sacred writings. As a *mantra,* it is pronounced *aw* (as in *law*), *oo* (as in *zoo*), *mm.* Aum represents the Divine, and is associated with Lord Gaṇeśa, for its initial sound "aa," vibrates within the *mūlādhāra,* the *chakra* at the base of the spine upon which this God sits. The second sound of this *mantra,* "oo," vibrates within the throat and chest *chakras,* the realm of Lord Murugan, or Kumāra. The third sound, "mm," vibrates within the cranial *chakras, ājñā* and *sahasrāra,* where the Supreme God reigns.

aura: The luminous colorful field of subtle energy radiating within and around the human body, extending out from three to seven feet. The colors of the aura change constantly according to the ebb and flow of one's state of consciousness, thoughts, moods and emotions. Higher, benevolent feelings create bright pastels; base, negative feelings are darker in color. The aura consists of three aspects, the *prāṇa-aura,* the outer aura and the inner aura. The *prāṇa-aura* is the reflection of the physical body, the life force. The outer aura extends beyond the physical body and changes continuously, reflecting the individual's moment-to-moment panorama of thought and emotion. See: *prāṇa-aura.*

auric circle: An energy shell around the aura itself that acts as a shelter or shield against psychic influences.

auspicious: *Maṅgala.* Favorable, of good omen, foreboding well. One of the central concepts in Hindu life. Astrology defines a method for determining times that are favorable for various human endeavors. See: *jyotisha.*

austerity: Self-denial and discipline, physical or mental, performed for various reasons including acquiring powers *(siddhis),* attaining grace, conquering the instinctive nature and burning the seeds of past *karmas.* Ranging from simple deprivations, such as foregoing a meal, to severe disciplines, called *tapas,* such as always standing, never sitting or lying down, even for sleep. See: *penance, tapas.*

autonomous: Not controlled by or reliant upon other forces; independent.

autopsy: "Own viewing." The examination and dissection of a dead body to determine the cause of death, extent of disease, etc.

avail: To be of use or advantage toward completing an end.

avarice: Uncontrolled desire for wealth.

avasthā: अवस्था (Tamil: *avasthai.*) "Condition or state" of consciousness or experience. 1) Any of three stages of the soul's evolution from the point of its creation to final merger in the Primal Soul. 2) The states of consciousness as discussed in the *Māṇḍūkya Upanishad: jāgrat* (or *vaiśvānara),* "wakefulness;" *svapna* (or *taijasa),* "dreaming;" *sushupti,* "deep sleep;" and *turīya,* "the fourth," a state of superconsciousness. A fifth state, "beyond *turīya,*" is *turīyātīta.* See: *kevala avasthā, sakala avasthā, śuddha avasthā.*

avatāra: अवतार "Descent." A God born in a human (or animal) body. A central concept of Śāktism, Smārtism and Vaishṇavism. See: *incarnation, Ishṭa Devatā.*

avidyā: अविद्या Spiritual "ignorance." Wrongful understanding of the nature of reality. Mistaking the impermanent for the everlasting.

awareness: *Sākshin,* or *chit.* Individual consciousness, perception, knowing; the witness of perception, the "inner eye of the soul." The soul's ability to sense, see or know and to be conscious of this knowing. When awareness is indrawn *(pratyak chetana),* various states of *samādhi* may occur. Awareness is known in the Āgamas as *chitśakti,* the "power of awareness," the inner self and eternal witness. See: *consciousness, sākshin.*

axiom: A rule or maxim that is universally accepted as true; a fundamental principle or truth.

āyurveda: आयुर्वेद "Science of life," "science of longevity." A holistic system of medicine and health native to ancient India. The aims of *āyurveda* are *āyus,* "long life," and *ārogya,* "diseaselessness," which facilitate progress toward ultimate spiritual goals. Health is achieved by balancing energies (especially the *doshas,* bodily humors) at all levels of being.

Ayyappan: ஐயப்பன் The popular God of a recently formed sect that focuses on pilgrimage to the top of Sabarimalai, a sacred hill in Kerala, where He is said to appear at night as a divine light. Ayyappan is revered as a son of Vishṇu and Śiva (Hari-Hara *putra).* His *vāhana* is the tiger.

balk: To stop abruptly and refuse to go on.

ballast: A stabilizing weight, usually on a boat.

bane: Deadly harm, misfortune. A cause of death, destruction, or ruin.

Banyan tree: *Ficus indicus* (*vaṭa* in Sanskṛit), symbolizes Hinduism, which branches out in all directions, draws from many roots, spreads shade far and wide, yet stems from one great trunk. Śiva as Silent Sage sits beneath it.

bardo: A Tibetan term for an intermediate state between death and further destiny of the soul.

Basavaṇṇa: बसवण्ण A 12th-century philosopher, poet and prime minister who reformed and revived Vīra Śaivism in Karnataka. See: *Vīra Śaivism.*

bask: To enjoy pleasant warmth, sunshine, praise or blessing.

beatitude: Supreme blessedness or happiness.

beclouding: Darkening as if with clouds; obscuring.

bedrock: Solid rock beneath the soil. Firm foundation.

behoove: To be necessary, proper or befitting.

Being: Upper case: God's essential divine nature—Pure Consciousness, Absolute Reality and Primal Soul (God's nature as a divine Person). Lower case: the essential nature of a person, that within which never changes; existence. See: *Śiva.*

benign: Good, kindly, doing no harm. See: *ahiṁsā.*

bereft: Deprived of something.

beseech (besought): To ask of someone earnestly; solicit with fervor; beg.

bestow: To offer graciously as a gift.

betoken: To indicate, show; offer as a sign of the future; symbolize.

Bhagavad Gītā: भगवद् गीता "Song of the Lord." One of the most popular of Hindu writings, a conversation between Lord Kṛishṇa and Arjuna on the brink of the great battle at Kurukshetra. In this central episode of the epic *Mahābhārata* (part of the Sixth Book), Kṛishṇa illumines the warrior-prince Arjuna on *yoga,* asceticism, *dharma* and the manifold spiritual path. See: *Mahābhārata.*

bhakta: भक्त (Tamil: *Bhaktar.*) "Devotee." A worshiper. One who is surrendered to the Divine. See: *bhakti, bhakti yoga, devotee, guru bhakti.*

bhakti: भक्ति "Devotion." Surrender to God, Gods or *guru. Bhakti* extends from the simplest expression of devotion to the ego-decimating principle of *prapatti,* which is total surrender. *Bhakti* is the foundation of all sects of Hinduism, as well as *yoga* schools throughout the world. See: *bhakti yoga, darśana, prapatti, prasāda, yajña.*

bhakti yoga: भक्तियोग "Union through devotion." *Bhakti yoga* is the practice of devotional disciplines, worship, prayer, chanting and singing with the aim of awakening love in the heart and opening oneself to God's grace. *Bhakti* may be directed toward God, Gods or one's spiritual preceptor. *Bhakti yoga* is embodied in Patañjali's *Yoga Darśana* in the second limb, *niyamas* (observances), as devotion (Īśvarapraṇidhāna). See: *prapatti, yajña.*

Bhārata Nātyam: பரதநாட்டியம் One of the ancient dance forms of India dating back to the second century BCE. This dance type originated in the Hindu temples of Southern India and is one of the most graceful and sophisticated dance styles.

Bhogabhūmi: भोगभूमि "Land of pleasure," referring to the world.

Bhogar Ṛishi: போகர் ரிஷி One of the 18 *siddhas* of Śaiva tradition, an alchemist and *tantrika yogī,* associated with the Murugan temple in Palani Hills, South India. Chinese historical records suggest that he came from China. See: *siddha, siddhi, tantric.*

Bhojadeva Paramāra: भोजदेव परमार Śaivite king, poet, artist and theologian of Gujarat (1018-1060). Author of *Tattvaprakāśa.* Renowned for establishing a systematic, monistic Śaiva Siddhānta. See: *Tātparyadīpikā.*

bhukti: "Worldly enjoyment."

Big Bang: A theory on the origins of the cosmos holding that the universe—time, space and matter—originated approximately 20 billion years ago from the explosive expansion of a "singularity."

bīja mantra: बीजमन्त्र "Seed syllable." A Sanskṛit sound associated with a specific Deity used for invocation during mystic rites.

bindu: बिन्दु "A drop, small particle, dot." 1) The seed or source of creation. In the 36 *tattvas,* the nucleus or first particle of transcendent light, technically called Parābindu, corresponding to the Śakti *tattva.* See: *tattva.*

biophysics: The science of relating physics to biological processes and phenomena.

boddhisattva: बोद्धिसत्त्व See: *nirvāṇī and upadeśī.*

boon: *Varadāna.* A welcome blessing, a gracious benefit received. An unexpected gift or bonus. See: *grace.*

bounteous: Generously and copiously giving. Bountiful.

Brahmā: ब्रह्मा The name of God in His aspect of Creator. Śaivites consider Brahmā, Vishṇu and Rudra to be three of five aspects of Śiva. Smārtas group Brahmā, Vishṇu and Śiva as a Holy Trinity in which Śiva is the Destroyer. See: *Brahman, Parameśvara.*

brahmachārī: ब्रह्मचारी An unmarried male spiritual aspirant who practices continence, observes religious disciplines, including *sādhana,* devotion and service and who may be under simple vows. Names also a young man in the student stage, age 12-24, or until marriage. See: *āśrama dharma, monk.*

brahmacharya: ब्रह्मचर्य See: *yama-niyama.*

brahmachāriṇī: ब्रह्मचारिणी Feminine counterpart of *brahmachārī.*

Brahmadhvara: ब्रह्मध्वर The door to the seven *chakras* and the *Narakaloka* just below the *mūlādhāra.* In order for the higher *chakras* to come into power, this door must be shut, making it impossible for fears, hatreds, angers and jealousies to arise. *Sādhana* and right thought, word and deed are among the aids in this accomplishment. See: *Naraka, yoni.*

Brahmaloka: ब्रह्मलक The realm of *sahasrāra chakra,* it is the highest of the seven upper worlds. See: *sahasrāra chakra.*

Brahman: ब्रह्मन् "Supreme Being; Expansive Spirit." From the root *bṛih,* "to grow, increase, expand." Name of God or Supreme Deity in the *Vedas,* where He is described as 1) the Transcendent Absolute, 2) the all-pervading energy and 3) the Supreme Lord or Primal Soul. These three correspond to Śiva in His three perfections. Thus, Śaivites know Brahman and Śiva to be one and the same God: ***—Nirguṇa Brahman,*** God "without qualities" (*guṇa),* i.e., formless, Absolute Reality, Parabrahman, or Paraśiva—totally transcending *guṇa* (quality), manifest existence and even Parāśakti, all of which exhibit perceivable qualities; ***—Saguṇa Brahman,*** God "with qualities;" Śiva in His perfections of Parāśakti and Parameśvara—God as superconscious, omnipresent, all-knowing, all-loving and all-powerful. The term Brahman is not to be confused with 1) *Brahmā,* the Creator God; 2) *Brāhmaṇa,* Vedic texts, nor with 3) *brāhmaṇa,* Hindu priest caste (English spelling: *brāhmin*). See: *Parāśakti, Paraśiva.*

Brahmarandhra: ब्रह्मरन्ध्र See: *door of Brahman.*

Brahmavidyā: ब्रह्मविद्या "Knowledge or realization of God."

brāhmin (brāhmaṇa): ब्राह्मण "Mature or evolved soul." The class of pious souls of exceptional learning. From *Brāhman,* "growth, expansion, evolution, development, swelling of the spirit or soul."

brāhminical tradition: The hereditary religious practices of the Vedic *brāhmins,* such as reciting *mantras,* and personal rules for daily living.

brethren: Older plural of brother; often used for brothers in religion.

Bṛihadāraṇyaka Upanishad: **बृहदारण्यक उपनिषद्** One of the major *Upanishads,* part of the *Śatapatha Brāhmaṇa* of the *Yajur Veda.* Ascribed to Sage Yājñavalkya, it teaches modes of worship, meditation and the identity of the individual self with the Supreme Self. See: *Upanishad.*

Bṛihaspati: **बृहस्पति** "Lord of Prayer." Vedic preceptor of the Gods and Lord of the Word, sometimes identified with Lord Gaṇeśa. Also the name of a great exponent of Śaiva Siddhānta (ca 900).*Gaṇeśa.*

Buddha: **बुद्ध** "The Enlightened." Usually the title of Siddhārtha Gautama (ca 624–544 BCE), a prince born of the Śākya clan—a Śaivite Hindu tribe that occupied Northeastern India on the Nepalese border. He renounced the world and became a monk. After enlightenment he preached the doctrines upon which his followers later founded Buddhism. See: *Buddhism.*

buddhi chitta: **बुद्धिचित्त** "Intellectual mind." See: *intellectual mind.*

Buddhism: The religion based on the teachings of Siddhārtha Gautama, known as the Buddha (ca 624–544 BCE). He refuted the idea of man's having an immortal soul and did not preach of any Supreme Deity. Instead he taught that man should seek to overcome greed, hatred and delusion and attain enlightenment through realizing the Four Noble Truths and following the Eightfold Path. Prominent among its holy books is the *Dhammapada.* Buddhism arose out of Hinduism as an inspired reform movement which rejected the caste system and the sanctity of the *Vedas.* It is thus classed as *nāstika,* "unbelieving," and outside of Hinduism. Buddhism eventually migrated out of India, the country of its origin, and now enjoys a following of over 350 million, mostly in Asia. See: *Buddha.*

Buddhist: Relating to Buddhism, the religion based on the teachings of Siddhārtha Gautama, known as the Buddha. See: *Buddhism.*

buoyant, buoyed: Light, weightless; elated, happy, optimistic.

caliber: Quality, station or ability of a person.

canalize: To provide an outlet or channel for.

cancer: Disease characterized by the uncontrolled growth of cells in the body.

cardiac: Near, or relating to the heart.

cardinal: Of primary importance; paramount.

Catholicism: The faith, doctrine, system, and practice of the Catholic Church; a major Christian denomination.

causal body: *Kāraṇa śarīra,* the inmost body; the soul form, also called *ānandamaya kośa,* "bliss sheath," and actinic causal body. See: *kośa, soul.*

causal mind: *Kāraṇa chitta.* Superconscious mind. See: *mind (five states).*

causal plane: Highest plane of existence, Śivaloka. See: *loka.*

cause: *Kāraṇa.* Anything which produces an effect, a result. —**efficient cause:** *(nimitta kāraṇa)* That which directly produces the effect; that which conceives, makes, shapes, etc., such as the potter who fashions a clay pot, or God who creates the world. —**material cause:** *(upādāna kāraṇa)* The matter from which the effect is formed, as the clay which is shaped into a pot, or God as primal substance becoming the world. —**instrumental cause:** *(sahakāri kāraṇa)* That which serves as a means, mechanism or tool in producing the effect, such as the potter's wheel, necessary for making a pot, or God's generative Śakti. See: *māyā, tattva.*

cauterize: To burn or sear so as to remove unwanted tissue, or to seal a wound.

cavernous plexus: The region where the brain stem enters the skull from the spine, associated with the pineal gland and the *ājnā chakra.*

celestial: "Of the sky or heavens." Of or relating to the heavenly regions or beings. Highly refined, divine.

celibacy: Complete sexual abstinence. Also the state of a person who has vowed to remain unmarried. Celibacy is abstinence from the eight degrees of sexual activity: fantasy *(smaraṇa)*, glorification *(kīrtana)*, flirtation *(keli)*, glances *(prekshaṇa)*, secret talk *(guhya bhāshana)*, longing *(kāma saṁkalpa)*, rendezvous *(adhyavāsāya)* and intercourse *(kriyā nivṛitti)*. See: *brahmachārī, ojas, tejas, transmutation, yama-niyama.*

cenobite: A member of a monastery community.

cerebral: Relating to the brain.

ceremony: From the Latin *caerimonia,* "awe; reverent rite." A formal rite established by custom or authority as proper to special occasions.

chaitanya: चैतन्य "Spirit, consciousness," especially "higher consciousness;" "Supreme Being."A widely used term, often preceded by modifiers, e.g., *sākshī chaitanya,* "witness consciousness," or *bhakti chaitanya,* "devotional consciousness," or Śivachaitanya, "God consciousness." See: *chitta, consciousness, mind (five states), Śiva consciousness.*

chakra: चक्र "Wheel." Any of the nerve plexes or centers of force and consciousness located within the inner bodies of man. In the physical body there are corresponding nerve plexuses, ganglia and glands. The seven principal *chakras* can be seen psychically as colorful, multi-petaled wheels or lotuses. They are situated along the spinal cord from the base to the cranial chamber. The seven principle chakras, from lowest to highest, are: 1) ***mūlādhāra*** (base of spine): memory, time and space; 2) ***svādhishṭhāna*** (below navel): reason; 3) ***maṇipūra*** (solar plexus): willpower; 4) ***anāhata*** (heart center): direct cognition; 5) ***viśuddha*** (throat): divine love; 6) ***ājñā*** (third eye): divine sight; 7) ***sahasrāra*** (crown of head): illumination, Godliness.

Additionally, seven *chakras,* barely visible, exist below the spine. They are seats of instinctive consciousness, the origin of jealousy, hatred, envy, guilt, sorrow, etc. They constitute the lower or hellish world, called *Naraka* or *pātāla.* From highest to lowest they are 1) ***atala*** (hips): fear and lust; 2) ***vi-***

tala (thighs): raging anger; 3) ***sutala*** (knees): retaliatory jealousy; 4) ***talātala*** (calves): prolonged mental confusion; 5) ***rasātala*** (ankles): selfishness; 6) ***mahātala*** (feet): absence of conscience; 7) ***pātāla*** (located in the soles of the feet): murder and malice.

Seven *chakras,* or conglomerates of *nāḍīs,* exist within and above the *sahasrāra,* as the seven levels of the rarified dimensions of *paranāda,* the first *tattva* and the highest stratum of sound. From lowest to highest they are: 1) ***vyāpinī:*** "all-pervasive;" 2) ***vyomāṅga:*** "space-bodied;" 3) ***anantā:*** "infinity;" 4) ***anāthā:*** having "no master;" 5) ***anāśṛitā:*** "independent;" 6) ***samanā:*** "uniform, synchronous;" 7) ***unmanā:*** "ecstatic, trans-mental." See: *chakras above sahasrāra, Naraka* (also: *individual chakra entries).*

chakras above sahasrāra: The most subtle of the *chakras* exist above and within the crown *chakra* at the top of the head. Buddhist literature cites thirty-two *chakras* above. Āgamic Hindu tradition delineates seven levels of the rarified dimensions of *paranāda,* the first *tattva* and the highest stratum of sound. They are: *vyāpinī, vyomāṅga, anantā, anāthā, anāśṛitā, samanā,* and *unmanā.* These higher centers of consciousness have been experienced by a rare few as a conglomerate of *nāḍīs,* spiritual nerve currents. See: *Vyāpinī, Vyomāṅga, Anantā, Anāthā, Anāśṛitā, Samanā, Unmanā.*

chalice: An ornate cup or goblet.

Chālukya: चालुक्य Indian dynasty (450–1189) in the Punjab area.

Çhāndogya Upanishad: छान्दोग्य उपनिषद् One of the major *Upanishads,* it consists of eight chapters of the *Çhāndogya Brāhmaṇa* of the *Sāma Veda.* It teaches the origin and significance of *Aum,* the importance of the *Sāma Veda,* the Self, meditation and life after death. See: *Upanishad.*

Chandra: चन्द्र "The moon." Of central importance in Hindu astrology and in the calculation of the festival calendar. Considered the ruler of emotion.

chaos: Great disorder and confusion.

charyā mārga: चर्यामार्ग See: *charyā pāda.*

charyā pāda: चर्यापाद "Conduct stage." Stage of service and character building. See: *pāda, Śaiva Siddhānta, Śaivism.*

chelā: चेला "Disciple." (Hindi.) A disciple of a *guru;* synonym for Sanskṛit *śishya.* The feminine equivalent is *chelinā* or *chelī.*

Chellappan: Another name for Chellappaswāmī. See: *Chellappaswāmī.*

Chellappaswāmī: செல்லப்பாசுவாமி "Wealthy father." Reclusive *siddha* and 160th *satguru* (1840-1915) of the Nandinātha Sampradāya's Kailāsa Paramparā. Lived on Sri Lanka's Jaffna peninsula near Nallur Kandaswāmī Temple in a small hut where today there is a small *samādhi* shrine. Among his disciples was Sage Yogaswāmī, whom he trained intensely for five years and initiated as his successor. See: *Kailāsa Paramparā, Nātha Sampradāya.*

Chettiar: செட்டியார் The name of the merchant caste of South India and Sri Lanka.

Chidambaram: சிதம்பரம் "Hall of Consciousness." A very famous South

Indian Śiva Naṭarāja temple. See: *Naṭarāja.*

chit: चित् "Consciousness," or "awareness." Philosophically, "pure awareness; transcendent consciousness," as in *Sat-chit-ānanda.* In mundane usage, *chit* means "perception; consciousness." See: *awareness, chitta, consciousness, mind (universal), sākshin.*

chitta: चित्त "Mind; consciousness." Mind-stuff. On the personal level, it is that in which mental impressions and experiences are recorded. Seat of the conscious, subconscious and superconscious states. See: *awareness, consciousness, mind (individual), mind (universal), sākshin.*

Christ: See: *Jesus Christ.*

Christian: A follower of the religion based on the life and teachings of Jesus Christ. The second of the three Abrahamic religions, Judaism, Christianity and Islam.

Christian-Judaic: See: *Judaic-Christian.*

chronicle: A detailed, narrative report.

chyle: A milky fluid comprised of lymph and emulsified fat extracted from chyme during digestion and passed to the bloodstream through the thoracic duct.

chyme: The thick semifluid mass of partly digested food that is passed from the stomach to the duodenum.

citrine: A yellow-orange crystal; a light to moderate olive color.

clairaudience: "Clear-hearing." Psychic or divine hearing, *divyaśravana.* The ability to hear the inner currents of the nervous system, the *Aum* and other mystic tones. Hearing in one's mind the words of inner-plane beings or earthly beings not physically present. Also, hearing the *nādanāḍī śakti* through the day or while in meditation. See: *clairvoyance, extrasensory, ESP, nāda, nādanāḍī śakti.*

clairvoyance: "Clear-seeing." Psychic or divine sight, *divyadṛishṭi.* The ability to look into the inner worlds and see auras, *chakras, nāḍīs,* thought forms, non-physical people and subtle forces. See: *ākāśa, extrasensory, ESP, clairaudience.*

clear white light: See: *light.*

cliché: A much overused expression.

cloistered: Secluded, as in a monastery.

coexistent: Exist together in the same place or time.

cognition: Knowing; perception. Knowledge reached through intuitive, superconscious faculties rather than through intellect alone.

cognitive body: *Vijñānamaya kośa.* The most refined sheath of the astral, or subtle, body *(sūkshma śarīra).* It is the sheath of higher thought and cognition. See: *astral body, kośa.*

cognizant: Informed or aware of something.

cognizantability: The ability to perceive or become aware of knowledge through observation. A term coined by Satguru Sivaya Subramuniyaswami in 1950.

cognize: To take notice of something.

cohesive: Clinging together; not disintegrating.

component: An element; one of the parts constituting a whole.

comprehend: Understand; grasp.

comprehensive: Including much or all.

conceit: A regarding of oneself with often excessive favor. A high opinion of one's own abilities or worth. Also egoism or vanity.

conceive: To form or develop an idea, thought, belief or attitude.

concentration: Uninterrupted and sustained attention. See: *rāja yoga.*

concept: An idea or thought, especially a generalized or abstract idea.

conception: Power to imagine, conceive or create. Moment when a pregnancy is begun, a new earthly body generated. **—the point of conception; the apex of creation:** The simple instant that precedes any creative impulse and is therefore the source and summit of the powers of creation or manifestation. To become conscious of the point of conception is a great *siddhi.*

conclave: A secret or confidential meeting.

condemnation: To disapprove of strongly; severe reproof; strong censure.

confession: An admission, acknowledgement; as of guilt or wrongdoing.

confine(s): Boundary, limits, border. To restrict or keep within limits.

congeal: To solidify by or as if by freezing. To coagulate, jell.

congested: Overcrowded, overfilled, clogged.

conglomerate: A group of things put together.

conjure: Bring to mind, call up or evoke.

connotation: An idea or meaning suggested by or associated with a word or thing.

conscience: The inner sense of right and wrong, sometimes called "the knowing voice of the soul." However, the conscience is affected by the individual's training and belief patterns, and is therefore not necessarily a perfect reflection of *dharma.* It is the subconscious of the person—the sum total of past impressions and training—that defines the credal structure and colors the conscience and either clearly reflects or distorts superconscious wisdom. See: *creed, dharma, mind (individual).*

conscious mind: The external, everyday state of consciousness. See: *mind.*

consciousness: *Chitta* or *chaitanya.* 1) A synonym for mind-stuff, *chitta;* or 2) the condition or power of perception, awareness, apprehension. There are myriad of gradations of consciousness, from the simple sentience of inanimate matter to the consciousness of basic life forms, to the higher consciousness of human embodiment, to omniscient states of superconsciousness, leading to immersion in the One universal consciousness, Parāśakti. In "Cognizantability," written 50 years ago, when the word *consciousness* was used it referred to man's individual awareness in most cases, whereas later in Gurudeva's teachings he tended to use the word *awareness* to mean the same thing, and to refer to *consciousness* as a part of the intelligence within all living things. All-pervasive consciousness always means Satchidānanda. One needs to know the context and time of the *upadeśa* to make these subtle distinctions. Individual awareness is used to name the souls awareness that flows unattached through all states of mind. See: *awareness, chitta, chaitanya, jāgrat, sushupti, svapna, turīya, mind* (all entries).

constituent: An element, piece, part or component.

construe: Explain the meaning of; interpret in a certain way.

contemplation: Religious or mystical absorption beyond meditation. See: *rāja yoga, samādhi.*

contention: Striving in controversy or debate.

contentious: Likely to cause or involving intense debate; quarrelsome.

continuum: A continuous whole, quantity, or series; something whose parts cannot be separated or separately discerned.

conundrum: A paradoxical problem, riddle or mystery.

conveyance: A transfer of something; a vehicle.

cope: To contend with on equal terms. To face or deal with difficulties.

corollary: A natural consequence of effect.

cosmic: Universal; vast. Of, or relating to, the cosmos or entire universe.

Cosmic Soul: Purusha or Parameśvara. Primal Soul. The Universal Being; Personal God. See: *Parameśvara, Primal Soul, purusha, Śiva.*

cranial *chakras:* The *ājñā,* or third-eye center, and the *sahasrāra,* at the top of the head near the pineal and pituitary glands. See: *chakra.*

cranium: The skull.

cranny: A small space, interstice, *nook and cranny.*

creation: The act of creating, especially bringing the world into ordered existence. Also, all of created existence, the cosmos. Creation, according to the monistic-theistic view, is an emanation or extension of God, the Creator. It is Himself in another form, and not inherently something other than Him. See: *cause, damaru, tattva.*

Creator: He who brings about creation. Śiva as one of His five powers. See: *creation, Naṭarāja, Parameśvara.*

creed: *Śraddhādhāraṇā.* An authoritative formulation of the beliefs of a religion. See: *conscience.*

cremation: *Dahana.* Burning of the dead. Cremation is the traditional manner of disposing of bodily remains, having the positive effect of releasing the soul most quickly from any lingering attachment to the earth plane. Note that the remains of enlightened masters are sometimes buried or sealed in a special tomb called a *samādhi.* This is done in acknowledgement of the extraordinary attainment of such a soul, whose very body, having become holy, is revered as a sacred presence, *sānnidhya,* and which not infrequently becomes the spiritual seed of a temple or place of pilgrimage. See: *death, reincarnation.*

crescendo: A gradual increase of force or intensity.
crevice: A narrow opening or crack.
crimson: A deep to vivid purplish red.
crown *chakra:* *Sahasrāra chakra.* The thousand-petaled cranial center of divine consciousness. See: *chakra, sahasrāra chakra.*
crux: The essential, deciding or difficult point. Latin "cross." Originally a mark indicating a difficult textual problem in books.
crypt: An underground vault or chamber, often used as a burial place.
crystal: A mineral, especially a transparent form of quartz, having a crystalline structure.
crystal-gazing: An occult practice for divining the future by gazing into a crystal ball.
crystallize: To take on a definite, precise, and usually permanent form.
culminate: To bring to the highest point, to the greatest intensity, or to completion.
cumbersome: Difficult to handle due to weight or bulk.
cybernetics: The theoretical study of communication and control processes in biological, mechanical, and electronic systems, especially the comparison of these processes in biological and artificial systems.
cynical: Scornful of the motives or integrity of someone.

dakshiṇā: दक्षिणा A fee or gift to a priest given at the completion of any rite; also given to *gurus* as a token of appreciation for their spiritual blessings.
damaru: दमरु The thin-waisted rattle drum of Śiva. It is the symbol of Divine Creation, which begins with the soundless sound, *paranāda,* whence arises the mantra *Aum.* See: *Naṭarāja, Śiva, Aum.*
darshan (darśana): दर्शन "Vision, sight." Seeing the Divine. Beholding, with inner or outer vision, a temple image, Deity, holy person or place, with the desire to inwardly contact and receive the grace and blessings of the venerated being or beings. Even beholding a photograph in the proper spirit is a form of *darśana.* Not only does the devotee seek to see the Divine, but to be seen as well, to stand humbly in the awakened gaze of the holy one, even if for an instant, such as in a crowded temple when thousands of worshipers file quickly past the enshrined Lord. Gods and *gurus* are thus said to "give" *darśana,* and devotees "take" *darśana,* with the eyes being the mystic locus through which energy is exchanged. This direct and personal two-sided apprehension is a central and highly sought-after experience of Hindu faith. Also: "point of view," doctrine or philosophy.
dauntless: Not intimidated or discouraged; fearless.
death: The soul's detaching itself from the physical body and continuing on in the subtle body *(sūkshma śarīra)* with the same desires, aspirations and

occupations as when it lived in a physical body. See: *reincarnation, videhamukti.*

deceit (deception): The act of representing as true what is known to be false. A dishonest action.

decipher: To read or interpret ambiguous, obscure, or illegible matter.

deduction: The drawing of a conclusion by reasoning; the act of deducing.

defabricate: Take apart; disassemble.

defee: (Shum) The space aspect of the mind. The perspective of space travel, *devas* and Gods; inner communication. Pronounced *dee-fee.* See: *Shum, Shum perspectives.*

Deity: "God." Often the image or *mūrti* installed in a temple or the Mahādeva the *mūrti* represents. See: *pūjā.*

delineate: To mark or trace out the boundaries of a thing, concept, etc.

delinquent: Failing to do what law or duty requires.

delude: To deceive as by false promises or misleadings.

delusion: *Moha.* False belief, misconception.

demon: See: *asura.*

denote: To indicate, signify or refer to.

depolarize: To eliminate or counteract the polarization of.

derogate: To take away.

Destroyer: Epithet of God Śiva in His aspect of Rudra. See: *Naṭarāja.*

deterrent: Something that prevents or discourages action; frightens away.

detractor: One who takes away from the positive qualities of a group.

deva: देव "Shining one." A being living in the higher astral plane, in a subtle, nonphysical body. *Deva* is also used in scripture to mean "God" or "Deity." See: *Mahādeva.*

Devaloka: देवलोक "Plane of radiant beings." A synonym of Maharloka, the higher astral plane, realm of *anāhata chakra.* See: *loka.*

Devī: देवी "Goddess." A name of Śakti, used especially in Śāktism. See: *Śakti, Śāktism.*

Devīkālottara Āgama: देवीकालोत्तर आगम One recension (version) of the *Sārdha Triśati Kālottara Āgama,* a subsidiary text of *Vātula Āgama.* Also known as *Skanda Kālottara.* Its 350 verses are in the form of a dialog between Kārttikeya and Śiva and deal with esoterics of *mantras,* initiations, right knowledge, faith and worship of Śiva. See: *Śaiva Āgamas.*

devonic: Angelic, heavenly, spiritual. Of the nature of the higher worlds, in tune with the refined energies of the higher *chakras* or centers of consciousness. Of or relating to the *devas.* Implies that something is divinely guided. See: *deva.*

devotee: A person strongly dedicated to something or someone, such as to a God or a *guru.* The term *disciple* implies an even deeper commitment. See: *bhakta, bhakti, guru bhakti.*

devout: Strongly attached to religion or religious obligations. See: *bhakti.*

dhāraṇā: धारणा "Concentration." From *dhṛi,* "to hold." See: *meditation, rāja yoga.*

dharma: धर्म From *dhṛi,* "to sustain; carry, hold." Hence *dharma* is "that which contains or upholds the cosmos." *Dharma* is a complex and comprehensive term with many meanings, including: divine law, ethics, religion, rights, duties, responsibilities and obligations, virtue, justice and truth. Essentially, *dharma* is the orderly fulfillment of an inherent nature or destiny. Relating to the soul, it is the mode of conduct most conducive to spiritual advancement, the right and righteous path.

Dharmapura Aadheenam: தருமபுர ஆதீனம் A monastery and spiritual center in South India, established in the 16th century by Śrī Guru Jñānasambandhar. This *aadheenam* preaches pluralistic Siddhānta, as opposed to monistic Siddhānta or monistic theism. See: *aadheenam.*

dhyāna: ध्यान "Meditation." See: *internalized worship, meditation, rāja yoga.*

diabolical: Very wicked or cruel; devilish.

diametrically: Exactly opposite; contrary.

diaphragm: A muscular partition between the abdomen and chest cavity, instrumental in breathing.

diaphragmatic breathing: Deep regulated breathing from the diaphragm, at the solar plexus region, as opposed to the upper chest.

dīkshā: दीक्षा "Initiation." Solemn induction by which one is entered into a new realm of spiritual awareness and practice by a teacher or preceptor through the transmission of blessings. Denotes initial or deepened connection with the teacher and his lineage and is usually accompanied by ceremony. Initiation, revered as a moment of awakening, may be conferred by a touch, a word, a look or a thought. See: *grace, śaktipāta.*

diligent: Painstaking, steady in effort, marked by perseverance.

diplomacy: Tact and skill in dealing with people.

dipolar: Relating to two poles instead of only one. A philosophy is said to be dipolar when it embraces both of two contradictory (or apparently contradictory) propositions, concepts, tendencies, etc. Instead of saying "it is either this or that," a dipolar position says "it is both this and that." See: *dvaita-advaita.*

discern: To distinguish, discriminate and make balanced judgments.

discrimination: *Viveka.* Act or ability to distinguish or perceive differences. In spirituality, the ability to distinguish between right and wrong, real and apparent, eternal and transient, as in the Upanishadic maxim, *Neti, neti,* "It is not this, it is not that." See: *conscience.*

disdain: Regard or treat as beneath one's dignity, as being unworthy.

disincarnate: Having no physical body; of the astral plane; astral beings. See: *astral body, astral plane.*

dispatch: To send off promptly, especially on an errand. To finish quickly.

dispel: To scatter. To rid one's mind of. To drive away or off.

dissertation A lengthy, thorough, formal treatment of a subject in writing or speech; a thesis.

dissidence: Disagreement; dissent.

dissipate: Here, to let loose more than often the vital sexual energies, which must be transmuted in order to make progress in spiritual life. Dissipation occurs through excessive talk, and through loss of the vital fluids, such as through masturbation or excessive intercourse only for pleasure, with no intention of conceiving a child. In one explanation of ancient India's caste system, strength—mental, emotional and physical as well as spiritual—is directly related to the frequency of orgasms. A sudra (laborer), releases his sexual energies daily and thus drains his brain. The *vaiśya* (businessman) has sex weekly, as his energies are caught up in the mental activities of his business. The *kshatriya* (politician, defender of the country), engaged in statesmanship, martial arts, horsemanship, developing mind and body, expends his energies but monthly. The *brāhmin* (priestly caste) has sexual union yearly, and only for the creation of a child. His energies are transmuted in his Sanskṛit chanting, daily rituals and high-minded activities of all kind to uplift humanity. Thus, dissipation is on many levels and creates many kinds of people, according to the four levels of consciousness. See: *ojas, tejas, yoni, actinic, actinodic, odic, transmutation.*

dissolution: Dissolving or breaking up into parts. An alternative term for destruction. See: *mahāpralaya, Naṭarāja.*

distort: To twist out of shape. To misrepresent.

divest: To strip of, deprive or rid of something.

Divine: Godlike; supremely good or beautiful.

Divinity: A God, or Deity. Also the spirituality or holiness that pervades the universe and is most easily felt in the presence of a holy man or in a temple.

DNA: *Deoxyribonucleic Acid.* A nucleic acid that carries the genetic information in the cell. DNA consists of two long chains of nucleotides twisted into a double helix. The sequence of nucleotides determines individual hereditary characteristics.

dogma: An authoritative principle, belief, or statement of ideas or opinion, especially one considered to be absolutely true.

dominion: Rulership; domain; sway.

door of *Brahman*: *Brahmarandhra;* also called *nirvāna chakra.* A subtle aperture in the crown of the head, the opening of *sushumṇā nāḍī* through which *kuṇḍalinī* enters in ultimate Self Realization, and the spirit escapes at death. Only the spirits of the truly pure leave the body in this way. *Saṁsārīs* take a downward course. See: *jñāna, kuṇḍalinī, videhamukti.*

doordarshan: (***dūrdarśana*** **दूर्दशन**) "Vision from afar." Hindi for television.

dosha: **दोष** "Bodily humor; individual constitution." Three bodily humors, which according to *āyurveda* regulate the body, govern its proper functioning and determine its unique constitution. These are *vāta,* the air humor;

pitta, the fire humor; and *kapha,* the water humor. *Vāta* humor is metabolic, nerve energy. *Pitta* is the catabolic, fire energy. *Kapha* is the anabolic, nutritive energy. The three *doshas (tridosha)* also give rise to the various emotions and correspond to the three *guṇas,* "qualities:" *sattva* (quiescence—*vāta*), *rajas* (activity—*pitta*) and *tamas* (inertia—*kapha*). See: *āyurveda, kapha, pitta, vāta.*

Dravidian: The term used here to name the monastic communities of the Dvāpara and Kali Yugas. In modern times it refers to the various Caucasoid peoples of southern India and northern Sri Lanka. From the Sanskṛit *Drāviḍa,* of which it is believed the original form was *Dramid* (or *Dramil*), which meant "sweet" or "good natured," and is the source of the word *Tamil,* naming the Dravidian people of South India and Sri Lanka and their language.

dreamologist: One who studies and interprets dreams, a coined word.

dross: Rubbish, waste matter; useless byproduct.

Druidism: Beliefs of members of an order of priests in ancient Gaul and Britain who appear in Welsh and Irish legend as prophets and sorcerers.

dual: Having or composed of two parts or kinds.

dualism: See: *dvaita-advaita.*

duality: A state or condition of being dual.

ductless glands: The endocrine glands which release hormones to regulate many functions of the body.

Dvaita Siddhānta: द्वैतसिद्धान्त "Dualistic final conclusions." Schools of Śaiva Siddhānta that postulate God, soul and world are three eternally distinct and separate realities. See: *Pati-paśu-pāśa, Śaiva Siddhānta.*

dvaita-advaita: द्वैत अद्वैत "Dual-nondual; twoness-not twoness." Among the most important categories in the classification of Hindu philosophies. *Dvaita* and *advaita* define two ends of a vast spectrum. ***—dvaita:*** The doctrine of dualism, according to which reality is ultimately composed of two irreducible principles, entities, truths, etc. God and soul, for example, are seen as eternally separate. **—dualistic:** Of or relating to dualism, concepts, writings, theories which treat dualities (good-and-evil, high-and-low, them-and-us) as fixed, rather than transcendable. **—pluralism:** A form of non-monism which emphasizes three or more eternally separate realities, e.g., God, soul and world. ***—advaita:*** The doctrine of nondualism or monism, that reality is ultimately composed of one whole principle, substance or God, with no independent parts. In essence, all is God. **—monistic theism:** A dipolar view which encompasses both monism and dualism. See: *dipolar, monistic theism, pluralistic realism.*

ebb: A period of flow back, decline, or recession.

eccentric: Different from the recognized norm; unusual; queer.

ecstasy (ecstatic): State of being overtaken by emotion such as joy or wonder. Literally, "standing outside (oneself)." See: *enstasy, rāja yoga, samādhi.*

edict: A formal command by an authority.

efficacious: Producing or capable of producing the desired effect.

efficient cause: *Nimitta kāraṇa.* That which directly produces the effect; that which conceives, makes, shapes, etc. See: *cause.*

effulgent: Bright, radiant; emitting its own light.

ego: The external personality or sense of "I" and "mine." Broadly, individual identity. In Śaiva Siddhānta and other schools, the ego is equated with the *tattva* of *ahaṁkāra,* "I-maker," which bestows the sense of I-ness, individuality and separateness from God. See: *ahaṁkāra, āṇava mala.*

egocentric: Placing one's own ego in the center of all values and experiences.

egoism: The doctrine that morality is based of self-interest.

egoity: *Ahaṁkāra.* Self-interest, selfishness See: *āṇava mala, mind (individual), ahaṁkāra.*

egotist: One who is selfish, conceited or boastful.

egregious: Bad or offensive. Standing out of the norm.

Egyptian: Of or relating to Egypt, its people, culture or language.

elation: Exultant joy, high spirits, gladness.

eloquent: Fluent, forceful, graceful and persuasive speech or writing.

elucidate: Explain, clarify or make clear.

elucidation: A clear or plain explanation; clarification.

elusive: Tending to escape one's grasp or understanding. Hard to capture.

emanation: "Flowing out from." *Ābhāsa.* Shining forth from a source, emission or issuing from. A monistic doctrine of creation whereby God issues forth manifestation like rays from the sun or sparks from a fire.

emancipator: That which, or one who, liberates.

embalming: The process of treating a dead body with various chemicals to prevent it from decaying rapidly. See: *cremation.*

embellishment: A decoration; beautification.

eminent: High; above others in stature, rank or achievement. Renowned or distinguished; prominent, conspicuous. Not to be confused with: 1) *imminent,* about to happen; 2) *emanate,* to issue from; 3) *immanent,* inherent or indwelling.

emit: To send out matter, energy or light.

emkaef: (Shum) No awareness, state beyond that of singular awareness. Not a word for Self Realization, but the entry into that non-experience. Pronounced *eem-kaw-eef.* See: *Shum.*

emote: To express emotion.

emotional body: See: *manomaya kośa.*
emulate: To imitate. To attempt to equal or surpass someone, generally by copying his ways, talents or successes.
en masse: In a mass; as a whole; all together; in great numbers.
encase: To cover completely; to enclose; to envelope.
encasement: A covering or enclosure; an envelopment.
encompass: To surround or encircle; to include.
encumber: To put burden as with a heavy load.
encumbrance: A burden or impediment.
endearment: An expression of affection.
endocrine: Of or relating to endocrine glands (the "ductless glands") or the hormones secreted by them.
enlightened: Having attained enlightenment, Self Realization. A *jñānī* or *jīvanmukta.* See: *jīvanmukta, jñāna, Self Realization.*
enlightenment: For Śaiva monists, Self Realization, *samādhi* without seed *(nirvikalpa samādhi);* the ultimate attainment, sometimes referred to as Paramātma *darśana,* or as *ātma darśana,* "Self vision" (a term which appears in Patañjali's *Yoga Sūtras).* Enlightenment is the experience-nonexperience resulting in the realization of one's transcendent Self—Paraśiva—which exists beyond time, form and space. Each tradition has its own understanding of enlightenment, often indicated by unique terms. See: *enstasy, God Realization, kuṇḍalinī, nirvikalpa samādhi, Self Realization.*
enmesh: To entange or catch, as if in a net.
enstasy: A term coined in 1969 by Mircea Eliade to contrast the Eastern view of bliss as "standing inside oneself" (enstasy) with the Western view as ecstasy, "standing outside oneself." A word chosen as the English equivalent of *samādhi.* See: *ecstasy, samādhi, rāja yoga.*
ensuing: Following as a result of something.
enthrall: To hold in a spell; captivate; fascinate.
eon: Also aeon. An indefinitely long period of time; an age.
epigastric: The upper middle region of the abdomen.
epistle: A formal letter.
equivocal: Uncertain; undecided; doubtful.
eradicate: To "root out," destroy, get rid of.
err: To make a mistake or an error.
errant: Straying from the proper course; distracted.
erratic: Having no fixed course; without direction or consistency.
erroneous: Containing or based on error; wrong.
erroneously: Adverb form of *erroneous,* containing or deriving from error; mistaken.
erudite: Possessing wide knowledge; learned, scholarly.
escalate: To increase, enlarge, or intensify.
eschew: To shun, avoid, stay away from.

esoteric: Hard to understand or secret. Teaching intended for a chosen few, as an inner group of initiates. Abtruse or private.

ESP: "Extra Sensory Perception." Communication or perception by means other than physical. See: *clairvoyance, clairaudience, extrasensory.*

essence (essential): The most important, ultimate, real and unchanging nature of a thing or being. **—essence of the soul:** See: *ātman, soul.*

eternity: Time without beginning or end.

ether: *Ākāśa.* Space, the most subtle of the five elements. See: *ākāśa, tattva.*

ethereal: Highly refined, light, invisible.

etheric: Having to do with ether or space.

ethics: The code or system of morals of a nation, people, philosophy, religion, etc. See: *dharma, yama-niyama.*

ethnic: Pertaining to, or designating a large group or groups of people with the same culture, race, religion, or national heritage.

etymology: The science of the origin of words and their signification. The history of a word. See: *Sanskṛit.*

evanescent: Vanishing, or likely to vanish like vapor.

eve: Evening; the day or night before something.

evil: That which is bad, morally wrong, causing misery. See: *hell, karma.*

evolution of the soul: *Adhyātma prasāra.* In Śaiva Siddhānta, the soul's evolution is a progressive unfoldment, growth and maturing toward its inherent, divine destiny, which is complete merger with Śiva. This occurs in three stages, or *avasthas.* In its essence, each soul is ever perfect. But as an individual soul body emanated by God Śiva, it is like a small seed yet to develop. As an acorn needs to be planted in the dark underground to grow into a mighty oak tree, so must the soul unfold out of the darkness of the *malas* to full maturity and realization of its innate oneness with God. The soul is not created at the moment of conception of a physical body. Rather, it is created in the Śivaloka. It evolves by taking on denser and denser sheaths—cognitive, instinctive-intellectual and *prāṇic*—until finally it takes birth in physical form in the Bhūloka. Then it experiences many lives, maturing through the reincarnation process. Thus, from birth to birth, souls learn and mature. Evolution is the result of experience and the lessons derived from it. There are young souls just beginning to evolve, and old souls nearing the end of their earthly sojourn. In Śaiva Siddhānta, evolution is understood as the removal of fetters which comes as a natural unfoldment, realization and expression of one's true, self-effulgent nature. This ripening or dropping away of the soul's bonds *(mala)* is called *malaparipāka.* The realization of the soul nature is termed *svānubhuti* (experience of the Self). Self Realization leads to *moksha,* liberation from the three *malas* and the reincarnation cycles. Then evolution continues in the celestial worlds until the soul finally merges fully and indistinguishably into Supreme God Śiva, the Primal Soul, Parameśvara. In his *Tirumantiram,* Ṛishi Tirumular

calls this merger *viśvagrāsa,* "total absorption." See: *mala, moksha, reincarnation, saṁsāra, viśvagrāsa.*
ewe: A female sheep.
exalt: To praise highly or honor.
exhalation: Letting air out, especially from the lungs.
exhilaration: The state of being stimulated, refreshed or extremely happy.
exiled: Forceably sent out of one's native country.
existence: "Coming or standing forth." Being; reality; that which is.
existentialism: A philosophy that emphasizes the uniqueness and isolation of the individual experience in a hostile or indifferent universe, regards human existence as unexplainable, and stresses freedom of choice and responsibility for the consequences of one's acts.
existentialist: Pertaining to, or believing in *existentialism.*
experience: From the Latin *experior,* "to prove; put to the test." Living through an event; personal involvement. In Sanskṛit, *anubhava.*
explicitly: Openly stated with nothing hidden or implied.
expound: To explain or clarify, point by point.
exquisite: Elaborate, delicate or beautiful.
extol: "Raise up;" "lift up." To praise highly.
extraneous: Not pertinent; placed outside; superfluous.
extrasensory: Beyond the normal senses, especially psychic perception such as seeing or hearing at a distance. See: *clairvoyance, clairaudience, ESP.*
extroverted: Interested in things outside of one's self.
exuberant: Full of unrestrained enthusiasm or joy.

façade: A front (of a building). Often a deceptive, artificial appearance.
facet: One of numerous aspects of a subject, concept or idea.
facial: Having to do with the face.
facile: Done with little effort, easy.
fad: A fashion followed with great enthusiasm for a short period of time.
fallacious: Containing or based on a false concept.
fallacy: An understanding that is not correct; a misconception.
falter: To be unsteady in purpose or action; waver.
fanatical: Excessively or irrationally devoted to a cause; overly zealous.
fathom: To ascertain the depth of; to get to the bottom; to understand.
ferret: To uncover or understand by searching.
fervent: Showing a great watmth of feeling; ardent; passionate.
fervor: Intense warmth of emotion.
fetters: A chain or shackle for the ankles or feet. Something that serves to restrict; a restraint. In Saiva Siddhanta philosophy, specifically a translation

of *paśa,* the triple bonds of *āṇava, karma* and *māyā.* See: *āṇava, karma, māyā.*

feud: A bitter, often prolonged quarrel or state of enmity.

finicky: Too careful about particulars. Fussy; fastidious; difficult to please.

finite: Having an ending.

First World: The physical universe, called Bhūloka, of gross or material substance in which phenomena are perceived by the five senses. See: *loka.*

fizzle: To fail or end weakly (colloquial).

flamboyant: Elaborately colored; showy; outrageous

fluctuate: To flow, move, change back and forth.

fluent: Flowing easily and smoothly, especially of speaking and writing.

flux: Continuous flowing movement or change.

foible: A minor weakness or character flaw.

forbearance: Self-control; responding with patience and compassion, especially under provocation. Endurance; tolerance. See: *yama-niyama.*

force field: A region of space through which a force, for example, an electric current, is operative. Here the term is used in reference to psychic energies, both positive and negative, that are generated by the emotions, the mind, the higher or lower *chakras* or emanate from the inner higher or lower worlds. Positive psychic force fields, such as those surrounding and protecting a temple, an *ashram* or harmonious home, are built up by worship, invoking of the Deities, *sādhana, tapas* and disciplined living, attracting divine spirits, or *devas.* Negative force fields, such as found in the worst areas of a city or within an inharmonious home, are built up by anger, violence, lust and outbursts of such lower emotions, attracting evil spirits, or *asuras.* See: *odic, actinic, prāṇa.*

foreboding: A sense of impending danger or evil.

forged: Given form or shape (originally of metal by heating and hammering).

formless: Philosophically, *atattva,* beyond the realm of form or substance. Used in attempting to describe the wondersome, indescribable Absolute, which is "timeless, formless and spaceless." God Śiva has form and is formless. He is the immanent Pure Consciousness or pure form. He is the Personal Lord manifesting as innumerable forms; and He is the impersonal, transcendent Absolute beyond all form. Thus we know Śiva in three perfections, two of form and one formless. See: *Paraśiva, Satchidānanda.*

forsake: To give up, or renounce; abandon.

forsooth: In truth; indeed.

frank: Open, undisguised.

fretful: Irritated, disturbed, worried or troubled.

fringe: A decorative border or edging, or something that resembles such a border.

fruition: The bearing of fruit. The coming to fulfillment of something that has been awaited or worked for.

gait: A particular manner of walking.

gamut: A complete musical scale. Hence a complete range, spread or extent of anything.

Gaṇapati: **गणपति** "Leader of the *gaṇas.*" A surname of *Gaṇeśa.*

gaṇa(s): **गण** "Throng, troop; retinue; a body of followers or attendants." A retinue of demigods—God Śiva's attendants, devonic helpers under the supervision of Lord Gaṇeśa. See: *Gaṇapati, Gaṇeśa.*

gandharvas: **गन्धर्व** Astral male lovers, counterparts to the female *apsarā,* mentioned in the *Vedas.* See: *apsarā.*

Gaṇeśa: **गणेश** "Lord of Categories." (From *gaṇ,* "to count or reckon," and *Īśa,* "lord.") Or: "Lord of attendants *(gaṇa),*" synonymous with *Gaṇapati.* Gaṇeśa is a Mahādeva, the beloved elephant-faced Deity honored by Hindus of every sect. He is the Lord of Obstacles (Vighneśvara), revered for His great wisdom and invoked first before any undertaking, for He knows all intricacies of each soul's *karma* and the perfect path of *dharma* that makes action successful. He sits on the *mūlādhāra chakra* and is easy of access. See: *gaṇa, Gaṇapati, Mahādeva.*

Gaṅgā sādhana: **गंगासाधन** A practice for unburdening the mind, performed by releasing the energy of unwanted thoughts. An internal cleansing *sādhana* of sitting quietly by a river or stream and listening to the Aum sound as the water flows over the rocks. When a thought arises, it is mentally placed into a leaf held in the right hand, then gently tossed into the water. Then a flower is offered to thank the water for carrying away the thought. This is a subconscious cleansing process of letting go of hurts, anger, problems or whatever it is that rises in the mind to disturb the meditation.

Ganges *(Gaṅgā):* **गंगा** India's most sacred river, 1,557 miles long, arising in the Himalayas above Haridwar under the name Bhagīratha, and being named Gaṅgā after joining the Alakanada (where the Sarasvatī is said to join them underground). It flows southeast across the densely populated Gangetic plain, joining its sister Yamunā (or Jumnā) at Prayaga (Allahabad) and ending at the Bay of Bengal.

ganglia: Groups of nerve cells that form a nerve center outside of the brain or spinal cord. A center of power, activity, or energy. (Singular: ganglion). *See chakra.*

ganglionic: Referring to the ganglion.

Garuḍa: **गरुड** The king of birds. The celestial vehicle (*vāhana*) of Lord Vishṇu.

gauntlet: A medieval knight's glove thrown down in a challenge, as to a fight. Hence "throwing down the gauntlet" means to challenge or provoke.

Gāyatrī Mantra: **गायत्रीमन्त्र** 1) Famous Vedic *mantra* used in *pūjā* and personal chanting. *Om [bhūr bhuvaḥ svaḥ] tatsavitur vareṇyam, bhargo* *devasya dhīmahi, dhiyo yo naḥ prachodayāt.* "[O Divine Beings of all three worlds,] we meditate upon the glorious splendor of the Vivifier divine. May He illumine our minds."

genial: Having a pleasant, easy-going or friendly disposition or manner.

gestation: The period of time between conception and birth; pregnancy.

girt: To gird, surround.

gist: The central idea; the essence.

glorify: To give glory, honor, or high praise to; exalt.

God Realization: Direct and personal experience of the Divine within oneself. It can refer to either 1) *savikalpa samādhi* ("enstasy with form") in its various levels, from the experience of inner light to the realization of Satchidānanda, the pure consciousness or primal substance flowing through all form, or 2) *nirvikalpa samādhi* ("enstasy without form"), union with the transcendent Absolute, Paraśiva, the Self God, beyond time, form and space. In *Merging with Śiva,* the expression *God Realization* is used to name both of the above *samādhis,* whereas *Self Realization* refers only to *nirvikalpa samādhi.* See: *rāja yoga, samādhi, Self Realization.*

Gods: Mahādevas, "great beings of light." In *Dancing with Śiva,* the plural of *God* refers to extremely advanced beings existing in their self-effulgent soul bodies in the causal plane. The meaning of *Gods* is best seen in the phrase, "God and the Gods," referring to the Supreme God—Śiva—and the Mahādevas who are His creation. See: *Mahādeva.*

***Gorakhnāth Śaivism** (Gorakshanātha Śaivism):* गोरक्षनाथशैव One of the six schools of Śaivism, also called Siddha Siddhānta. See: *Siddha Siddhānta, siddha yoga.*

Gorakshanātha: गोरक्षनाथ Renowned *siddha yoga* master of the Ādinātha Sampradāya (ca 950). Expounder and foremost *guru* of Siddha Siddhānta Śaivism. He traveled and extolled the greatness of Śiva throughout North India and Nepal where he and his *guru,* Matsyendranātha, are still highly revered. See: *haṭha yoga, Siddha Siddhānta, Siddha Siddhānta Paddhati.*

gorgeous: Dazzlingly beautiful or magnificent.

grace: "Benevolence, love, giving," from the Latin *gratia,* "favor," "goodwill." God's power of revealment, *anugraha śakti* ("kindness, showing favor"), by which souls are awakened to their true, Divine nature. Grace in the unripe stages of the spiritual journey is experienced by the devotee as receiving gifts or boons, often unbidden, from God. The mature soul finds himself surrounded by grace. He sees all of God's actions as grace, whether they be seemingly pleasant and helpful or not. See: *prapatti, śaktipāta.*

grandeur: Greatness, magnificence; of lofty character; sublime nobility.

gratification: Indulging in what is desired.

grating: Irritating or annoying.

graven image: Sculpted or carved statue of God or a God, a negative term from the English Bible translation.

gṛihastha: गृहस्थ "Householder." Family man or woman. Family of a married couple and other relatives. Pertaining to family life. The purely masculine form of the word is *gṛihasthin,* and the feminine *gṛihasthī. Gṛihasthī* also names the home itself. See: *āśrama dharma, gṛihastha dharma.*

gṛihastha āśrama: गृहस्थ आश्रम "Householder stage." See: *āśrama dharma.*

gṛihastha dharma: गृहस्थधर्म "Householder law." The virtues and ideals of family life. See: *āśrama dharma.*

Grim Reaper: Personification of death in Western tradition, a hooded, black-robed skeleton figure carrying a scythe to cut down lives.

gross: Dense, coarse, unrefined, crude; carnal, sensual; lacking sensitivity.

Guhāvāsī Siddha: गुहावासीसिद्ध A *guru* of central India (ca 675) credited with the re-founding of Śaiva Siddhānta in that area, based fully in Sanskṛit. *Guhāvāsī*—literally "cave-dweller; he who is hidden," or "mysterious"—is also an epithet of Lord Śiva.

guile: Treacherous cunning; crafty deceit.

gulika kāla: गुलिक्काल An auspicious period of time. It changes according to the day of the week in the *pañchaṅga* calendar.

guru: गुरु "Weighty one," indicating an authority of great knowledge or skill. A title for a teacher or guide in any subject, such as music, dance, sculpture, but especially religion. See: *guru-śishya system, satguru.*

guru bhakti: गुरुभक्ति Devotion to the teacher. The attitude of humility, love and ideation held by a student in any field of study. In the spiritual realm, the devotee strives to see the *guru* as his higher Self. By attuning himself to the *satguru's* inner nature and wisdom, the disciple slowly transforms his own nature to ultimately attain the same peace and enlightenment his *guru* has achieved. *Guru bhakti* is expressed through serving the *guru,* meditating on his form, working closely with his mind and obeying his instructions. See: *guru, satguru, guru-śishya system, Kulārṇava Tantra.*

Guru Mahāsannidhānam: गुरु महासन्निधानम् Spiritual head of a traditional aadheenam. See: *aadheenakartar.*

guru paramparā: गुरुपरंपरा "Preceptorial succession" (literally, "from one teacher to another"). A line of spiritual *gurus* in authentic succession of initiation; the chain of mystical power and authorized continuity, passed from *guru* to *guru.* See: *sampradāya.*

Guru Pūrṇimā: गुरु पूर्णिमा Occurring on the full moon of July, Guru Pūrṇimā is for devotees a day of rededication to all that the *guru* represents. It is occasioned by *pādapūjā*—ritual worship of the *guru's* sandals, which represent his holy feet. See: *guru-śishya system.*

Gurudeva: गुरुदेव "Divine" or "radiant preceptor." An affectionate, respectful title for the *guru.* See: *guru.*

guru-śishya system: गुरुशिष्य "Master-disciple" system. An important educational system of Hinduism whereby the teacher conveys his knowledge and tradition to a student. Such knowledge, whether it be Vedic-Āgamic art, architecture or spirituality, is imparted through the developing relationship between *guru* and disciple. See: *guru, guru bhakti, satguru.*

gust: A short but strong blast of wind; an outburst.

hallowed: Sanctified; consecrated. Highly venerated; sacrosanct.

halo: A luminous ring or disk of light surrounding the heads of great spiritual teachers. An aura. See: *aura.*

hamper: To prevent progress, or free movement.

Hanumān: हनुमान् (Hindi) "Large jawed." The powerful monkey God-King of the epic, *Rāmāyaṇa,* and the central figure in the famous drama, *Hanumān-Nāṭaka.* The perfect devoted servant to his master, Rāma, this popular Deity is the epitome of *dasya bhakti.*

haphazard: Dependent on mere chance; casual.

Happy Hunting Ground: In the Native American beliefs, the place where the deceased go after death.

harken: To listen attentively; give heed.

harmonize: To bring about agreement or harmony.

hasten: To move or act swiftly. Cause to hurry, speed up.

hasty: Done or made too quickly to be accurate or wise; rash.

haṭha yoga: हठयोग "Forceful yoga." *Haṭha yoga* is a system of physical and mental exercise developed in ancient times as a means of rejuvenation by *ṛishis* and *tapasvins* who meditated for long hours, and used today in preparing the body and mind for meditation. In the West, *haṭha yoga* has been superficially adopted as a health-promoting, limbering, stress-reducing form of exercise, often included in aerobic routines. Esoterically, *ha* and *ṭha,* respectively, indicate the microcosmic sun *(ha)* and moon *(ṭha),* which symbolize the masculine current, *piṅgalā nāḍī,* and feminine current, *iḍā nāḍī,* in the human body. See: *āsana, kuṇḍalinī, nāḍī, yoga, rāja yoga.*

havana: हवन "Fire pit for sacred offering; making oblations through fire." Same as *homa. Havis* and *havya* name the offerings. See: *homa, yājñā.*

haven: A harbor. Metaphorically a place of rest or refuge; a sanctuary.

havoc: Widespread distruction, disorder, or chaos.

hazy: Cloudy. Not clearly defined; unclear or vague.

heart chakra: *Anāhata chakra.* Center of direct cognition. See: *chakra.*

heaven: The celestial spheres, including the causal plane and the higher realms of the subtle plane, where souls rest and learn between births, and mature souls continue to evolve after *moksha. Heaven* is often used by translators as an equivalent to the Sanskṛit *Svarga.* See: *loka.*

heed: To pay close attention to; take careful notice of.

heinous: Grossly wicked or reprehensible; abominable.

hell: *Naraka.* An unhappy, mentally and emotionally congested, distressful area of consciousness. Hell is a state of mind that can be experienced on the physical plane or in the sub-astral plane (Naraka) after death of the physical body. It is accompanied by the tormented emotions of hatred, remorse, resentment, fear, jealousy and self-condemnation. However, in the Hindu view, the hellish experience is not permanent, but a temporary condition of one's own making. See: *asura, loka, Naraka.*

hence: "From here." For this reason; therefore.

herald: One that gives an announcement or indication of something to come; a harbinger.

heritage: A tradition passed down from preceding generations as an inheritance.

hermit: One withdrawn from society, living a solitary life; an anchorite.

hierarchy: A group of beings arranged in order of rank or class; as a hierarchy of God, Gods and *devas.*

higher-nature, lower nature: Expressions indicating man's refined, soulful qualities on the one hand, and his base, instinctive qualities on the other. See: *kośa, mind (five states), soul.*

Himalayan Academy: An educational and publishing institution of Śaiva Siddhānta Church founded by Satguru Sivaya Subramuniyaswami in 1957. The Academy's objective is to spread the teachings of Sanātana Dharma through travel-study programs, *The Master Course,* books and other publications—particularly the monthly magazine HINDUISM TODAY and *Dancing with Śiva, Hinduism's Contemporary Catechism*—as a public service to Hindus worldwide. See: *Hinduism Today, Subramuniyaswami.*

Himālayas: हिमालय "Abode of snow." The mountain system extending along the India-Tibet border and through Pakistan, Nepal and Bhutan.

hiṁsā: हिंसा "Injury;" "harm;" "hurt." Injuriousness, hostility—mental, verbal or physical. See: *ahiṁsā.*

Hindu: हिन्दु A follower of, or relating to, Hinduism. Generally, one is understood to be a Hindu by being born into a Hindu family and practicing the faith, or by professing oneself a Hindu. Acceptance into the fold is recognized through the name-giving sacrament, a temple ceremony called *nāmakaraṇa saṁskāra,* given to born Hindus shortly after birth, and to Hindus by choice who have proven their sincerity and been accepted by a Hindu community. Full conversion is completed through disavowal of previous religious affiliations and legal change of name. While traditions vary greatly, all Hindus rely on the *Vedas* as scriptural authority and generally attest to the following nine principles: 1) There exists a one, all-pervasive Supreme Being who is both immanent and transcendent, both creator and unmanifest Reality. 2) The universe undergoes endless cycles of creation, preservation and dissolution. 3) All souls are evolving toward God and will ultimately find *moksha:* spiritual knowledge and liberation from the cycle of rebirth. Not a single soul will be eternally deprived of this destiny. 4)

Karma is the law of cause and effect by which each individual creates his own destiny by his thoughts, words and deeds. 5) The soul reincarnates, evolving through many births until all *karmas* have been resolved. 6) Divine beings exist in unseen worlds, and temple worship, rituals, sacraments, as well as personal devotionals, create a communion with these *devas* and Gods. 7) A spiritually awakened master or *satguru* is essential to know the transcendent Absolute, as are personal discipline, good conduct, purification, self-inquiry and meditation. 8) All life is sacred, to be loved and revered, and therefore one should practice *ahiṁsā,* nonviolence. 9) No particular religion teaches the only and exclusive way to salvation above all others. Rather, all genuine religious paths are facets of God's pure love and light, deserving tolerance and understanding. See: *Hinduism.*

Hindu solidarity: Hindu unity in diversity. A major contemporary theme according to which Hindu denominations are mutually supportive and work together in harmony, while taking care not to obscure or lessen their distinctions or unique virtues. The underlying belief is that Hinduism will be strong if each of its sects, and lineages is vibrant. See: *Hinduism.*

Hinduism (Hindu Dharma): हिन्दुधर्म India's indigenous religious and cultural system, followed today by nearly one billion adherents, mostly in India, but with large diaspora in many other countries. Also called Sanātana Dharma (Eternal religion) and Vaidika Dharma (Religion of the *Vedas.*) Hinduism is the world's most ancient religion and encompasses a broad spectrum of philosophies ranging from pluralistic theism to absolute monism. It is a family of myriad faiths with four primary denominations: Śaivism, Vaishṇavism, Śāktism and Smārtism. These four hold such divergent beliefs that each is a complete and independent religion. Yet, they share a vast heritage of culture and belief—*karma, dharma,* reincarnation, all-pervasive Divinity, temple worship, sacraments, manifold Deities, the *guru-śishya* tradition and a reliance on the *Vedas* as scriptural authority. From the rich soil of Hinduism long ago sprang various other traditions. Among these were Jainism, Buddhism and Sikhism, which rejected the *Vedas* and thus emerged as completely distinct religions, dissociated from Hinduism, while still sharing many philosophical insights and cultural values with their parent faith. See: *Hindu.*

Hinduism Today: The Hindu family magazine founded by Satguru Sivaya Subramuniyaswami in 1979, issued monthly by Himalayan Academy to affirm Sanātana Dharma and record the modern history of a billion-strong global religion in renaissance, reaching 150,000 readers in over 100 countries. See: *Himalayan Academy.*

hitherto: Until this time.

hoary: So old as to inspire veneration; ancient.

holy ash: See: *vibhūti.*

holy feet: The feet of God, a God, *satguru* or any holy person, often represented by venerable sandals, called *śrī pādukā* in Sanskṛit and *tiruvadi* in Tamil. The feet of a divinity are considered especially precious as they represent the point of contact of the Divine and the physical, and are thus revered as the source of grace. The sandals or feet of the *guru* are the object of worship on his *jayantī* (birthday), on Guru Pūrṇimā and other special occasions. See: *satguru.*

Holy Kural: See: *Tirukural.*

holy orders: A divine ordination or covenant, conferring religious authority. Vows that members of a religious body make, especially a monastic body or order, such as the vows (holy orders of renunciation) made by a *sannyāsin* at the time of his initiation *(sannyāsa dīkshā),* which establish a covenant with the ancient holy order of *sannyāsa.* See: *sannyāsa dīkshā.*

homa: होम "Fire-offering." A sacred ceremony in which the Gods are offered oblations through the medium of fire in a sanctified fire pit, *homakuṇḍa,* usually made of earthen bricks. *Homa* rites are enjoined in the *Vedas, Āgamas* and *Dharma* and *Gṛihya Śāstras.* See: *agni, havana, yajña.*

hopper: One who moves quickly from one thing to the next.

horrendous: Dreadful.

horrific: Terrifying, causing horror.

hospice: An institution that provides shelter and care to the terminally ill.

hover: To float or be suspended in the air.

hub: Center of a wheel. Center of interest, importance or activity.

hued: Having specific color.

humanitarian: One devoted to the promotion of human welfare.

humiliate: To hurt the pride or dignity of by causing to appear foolish or unworthy.

humility: Modesty in behavior, attitude, or spirit; not arrogant or prideful.

hummingbird: A small bird that beats its wings very rapidly, enabling it to hover in one place.

humorously: Said or done in a laughable, amusing or funny way.

hunch: An intuitive feeling.

hybrid: Something of mixed origin, such as a hybid plant whose parent stock were not genetically identical.

hymns: Songs of praise to God, Gods or guru.

hypnosis: A sleeplike state, usually induced by another person, in which the subject may experience heightened suggestibility, forgotten or suppressed memories, and hallucinations.

hypocrisy: Professing beliefs, feelings, or virtues that one does not hold or possess; false pretensions.

hypogastric: *Hypogastrium.* Lowest of the abdomen's three median regions.

hypothalamus: The part of the brain that regulates bodily temperature, certain metabolic processes, and other autonomic activities.

hypothesis: Something taken to be true for the purpose of argument or investigation; an assumption.

hysteria: Excessive or uncontrollable emotion, such as fear or panic.

icçhā śakti: इच्छाशक्ति "Desire; will."

iḍā nāḍī: इडानाडी "Soothing channel." The feminine psychic current flowing along the spine. See: *kuṇḍalinī, nāḍī, odic, piṅgalā.*

identifications: People, places, things (such as the body and the individual mind) or positions with which one may identify oneself. See: *ahaṁkāra.*

ideology: A set of doctrines or beliefs that form the basis of a system of thought, often used to mean narrow-minded or uncritical adherence to such a system.

illimitable: Impossible to limit or circumscribe; endless.

illustrious: Very luminous or bright; distinguished, famous; outstanding.

immaculate: Free from stain or blemish; pure.

immanent: Indwelling; inherent and operating within. Relating to God, the term *immanent* means present in all things and throughout the universe, not aloof or distant. Not to be confused with *imminent,* about to happen; *emanate,* to issue from; *eminent,* high in rank.

immemorial (from time immemorial): From a time so distant that it extends beyond history or human memory.

imminent: Threatening to happen without delay; impending.

impasse: A dead end; a point of no progress; stalemate. A difficulty with no solution.

impede: To obstruct or delay progress; make difficult to accomplish. (Noun: *impediment*).

impediment: That which "holds the feet." Hindrance; obstacle. Anything that inhibits or slows progress.

impervious: Incapable of being affected or penetrated.

impetus: A push that stimulates activity. Driving force; motive, incentive.

implant: To establish securely, as in the mind or consciousness; instill.

imposing: Forcing (oneself, for example) on another or others. Impressive, admirable by virtue of size, or power.

impregnate: To saturate or fill; permeate. Make pregnant.

impulse: A sudden wish or urge that prompts an unplanned act or feeling.

impurity: A state of immorality, pollution or sin. Uncleanliness.

inadequacy: Feeling of failure, as in not being able to meet a need.

inanimate: See: *animate-inanimate.*

inaugurated: Begun, especially officially or formally.

inauspicious: Not favorable. Not a good time to perform certain actions or undertake projects. Ill-omened.

inbred: Fixed in the character or disposition as if inherited by birth; deep-seated.

incantate: To chant, repeat or recite *mantras.* See: *japa*

incantation: *Japa* or *Mantraprayoga.* The chanting of prayers, verses or formulas for magical or mystical purposes. Also such chants *(mantra). Vaśakriyā* is the subduing or bewitching by charms, incantation or drugs. Incantation for malevolent purposes (black magic) is called *abhichāra.* See: *mantra.*

incarcerate: To put into jail. To shut in; confine.

incarnation: From *incarnate,* "made flesh." The soul's taking on a human body. **—divine incarnation:** The concept of *avatāra.* The Supreme Being's (or other Mahādeva's) taking of human birth, generally to reestablish *dharma.* This doctrine is important to several Hindu sects, notably Vaishṇavism, but not held by most Śaivites. See: *avatāra, Vaishṇavism.*

incessant: Continuing without interruption.

incomprehensible: Difficult or impossible to understand.

inconspicuous: Not readily noticeable; transparent; insignificant.

indelible: Impossible to remove, erase, or wash away; permanent.

indigenous: Intrinsic; innate; native.

indigo: A dark blue to grayish purple blue color.

indistinct: Not clearly or shaply defined, vague; difficult to understand.

individual soul: A term used to describe the soul's nature as a unique entity, emanated by God Śiva (the Primal Soul), as a being which is evolving and not yet one with God. See: *ātman, essence, kośa, Parameśvara, soul.*

individuality: Quality that makes one person or soul other than, or different from, another. See: *ahaṁkāra, āṇava mala, ego, soul.*

indoctrinate: To imbue with a partisan or ideological point of view.

indomitable: Not easily discouraged, defeated or subdued. Unconquerable.

Indra: **इन्द्र्** "Ruler." Vedic God of rain and thunder, warrior king of the *devas.*

induction: Deriving general principles from particular facts or instances.

indulgence: Yielding to the desires and whims of, especially to an excessive degree. To allow (oneself) unrestrained gratification.

Indus Valley: Region on the Indus River, now in Pakistan, where in 1924 archeologists discovered the remains of a high civilization which flourished between 5000 and 1000 BCE. There, a "seal" was found with the effigy of Śiva as Paśupati, "Lord of animals," seated in a *yogic* posture. See: *Śaivism.*

ineffable: Not amenable or possible to be spoken of, described or expressed.

I-ness: The conceiving of oneself as an "I," or ego, which Hinduism considers a state to be transcended. See: *āṇava mala, mind (individual).*

inevitable: Imposible to avoid or prevent. Predictable.

inexplicable: Impossible to explain or account for; inexcusable.

infatuation: The magnetic condition of being captured by a foolish or shallow love or affection.

inference: Deriving logical conclusions from premises assumed to be true.

inferiority complex: A persistent sense of inadequacy or a tendency to self-depreciation.

infidel: One who has no religious beliefs, or who rejects a particular religion.

infiltrate: To gradually penetrate so as to counteract or seize control from within.

infinitesimal: Infinitely small; too small to be measured.

influx: A flowing in. Mass arrival or incoming.

infuse: To transmit a quality, idea, knowledge, etc., as if by pouring. To impart, fill or inspire.

inherent (to inhere in): Inborn. Existing in someone or something as an essential or inseparable quality. **—inherent sin:** See: *sin.*

inherit: To receive from an ancestor, as property, title, etc.—or to reap from our own actions: "...seed *karmas* we inherit from this and past lives."

inhibit: To hold back, restrain, prohibit or forbid. To suppress.

initiation (to initiate): Entering into; admission as a member. In Hinduism, initiation from a qualified preceptor is considered invaluable for spiritual progress. See: *dīkshā, śaktipāta, sannyāsa dīkshā.*

inkling: A slight hint or indication.

innate: Naturally inborn; not acquired. That which belongs to the inherent nature or constitution of a being or thing.

inner advancement (or unfoldment): Progress of an individual at the soul level rather than in external life.

inner bodies: The subtle bodies of man within the physical body.

inner light: A moonlight-like glow that can be seen inside the head or throughout the body when the *vṛittis,* mental fluctuations, have been sufficiently quieted. To be able to see and bask in the inner light is a milestone on the path. See: *vṛitti.*

inner mind: The mind in its deeper, intuitive functions and capacities—the subsuperconscious and superconscious.

inner planes: Inner worlds or regions of existence.

inner sky: The area of the mind which is clear inner space, free of mental images, feelings, identifications, etc. Tranquility itself. The superconscious mind, Satchidānanda. See: *ākāśa.*

inner universes (or worlds): The astral and causal worlds. See: *kośa.*

innerversity: Learning from within. A word coined by Sivaya Subramuniyaswami which indicates turning inward, through *yoga* concentration and meditation, to the vast superconscious state of mind; whence knowledge can be unfolded.

inordinate: Exceeding reasonable limits; immoderate.

inroad: An advance, an encroachment, an incursion.

inrush: A sudden rushing in; an influx.

inscrutable: Difficult to understand or fathom.

insignia: Plural of the Latin *insigne.* Signs or symbols of identity, rank or office, such as a badge, staff or emblem.

instinctive: "Natural" or "innate." From the Latin *instinctus,* participle of *instingere,* "impelling," pricking," "instigating." The drives and impulses that order the animal world and the physical and lower *astral* aspects of humans—for example, self-preservation, procreation, hunger and thirst, as well as the emotions of greed, hatred, anger, fear, lust and jealousy. See: *manas, mind (individual), mind (three phases), yama-niyama.*

instinctive mind: *Manas chitta.* The lower mind, which controls the basic faculties of perception, movement, as well as ordinary thought and emotion. *Manas chitta* is of the *manomaya kośa.* See: *manas, manomaya kośa, yama-niyama, mind (individual), mind (three phases).*

instinctive-intellectual mind: The mind in ordinary consciousness, when actions are based either upon instinctive emotional desires and fears or intellectual concepts and reason. See: *manomaya kośa, astral body, instinctive mind, kośa, odic force, soul, subtle body, vāsanā.*

insure: To make certain, sure, or secure.

intact: Remaining sound, entire, or uninjured; not impaired in any way.

intangible: Incapable of being perceived ("touched") by the senses.

intellect: The power to reason or understand; power of thought; mental acumen. See: *buddhi chitta, intellectual mind, mind (individual), mind (three phases).*

intellectual mind: *Buddhi chitta.* The faculty of reason and logical thinking. It is the source of discriminating thought, rather than the ordinary, impulsive thought processes of the lower or instinctive mind, called *manas chitta. Buddhi chitta* is of the *manomaya kośa.* See: *buddhi chitta, mind.*

interface: A point at which independent systems (as in the physical and astral worlds) or diverse groups interact.

interim: A time in between one event and another.

interlaced: Interwoven; connected intricately.

interlude: A period of time between two events.

intermingle: To mix or become mixed together.

internalize: To take something inside of oneself.

internalized worship: *Yoga.* Worship or contact with God and Gods via meditation and contemplation rather than through external ritual. This is the *yogī*'s path, preceded by the *charyā* and *kriyā pādas.* See: *meditation, yoga.*

interrogation: Examine by formally or officially questioning.

intimacy: Privacy, essential, innermost quality.

intone: To speak with a singing tone or with a particular intonation.

intransigently: Refusing to moderate a position, especially an extreme position; uncompromising.

intrigue: A secret plot or scheme. To excite interest or curiosity.

intrinsic: Inward; essential; inherent. Belonging to the real nature of a being or thing.

introspection: "Looking inside." Examining one's own thoughts, feelings and sensations.

introversion: Turning within. Directing one's interest, mind or attention upon oneself.

intrusion: The act of entering without permission.

intuit: To know or sense without resorting to rational processes.

intuition (to intuit): Direct understanding or cognition, which bypasses the process of reason. Intuition is a far superior source of knowing than reason, but it does not contradict reason. See: *cognition, mind (five states).*

invariably: Consistently, constantly, unchangingly.

invigorate: To give strength, life or energy.

irresistible: Impossible to resist. Having an overpowering appeal.

irreverent: Disrespectful. Critical of what is generally accepted or respected.

irrevocably: In a manner not to be retracted, revoked or taken back.

irul: இருள் "Darkness." The first of three stages of the *sakala avasthai* where the soul's impetus is toward *pāśa-jñānam,* knowledge and experience of the world. See: *pāśa-jñānam, sakala avasthā.*

iruvinaioppu: இருவினையொப்பு "Balance." The balance which emerges in the life of a soul in the stage of *marul,* or *paśu-jñānam,* the second stage of the *sakala avasthai,* when the soul turns toward the good and holy, becomes centered within himself, unaffected by the ups and downs in life. See: *marul, paśu-jñānam, sakala avasthā.*

Ishṭa Devatā: इष्टदेवता "Cherished" or "chosen Deity." The Deity that is the object of one's special pious attention. *Ishṭa Devatā* is a concept common to all Hindu sects. See: *Śakti, Śiva.*

Ishṭa Mārga Saṁskara: इष्टमार्ग संस्कार "Path-choosing rite." A temple ceremony held around age 18 in which a young man voices his decision to either enter the *gṛihāstha āśrama* and accept the *dharma* of the householder, or in rare cases follow the *dharma* of the renunciate, beginning training as a monastic in preparation for taking holy orders of *sannyāsa.* See: *holy orders, sannyāsa, sannyāsa dharma, sannyāsin.*

Islam: The religion founded by Prophet Muhammed in Arabia about 625 CE. Islam connotes submission to Allah, the name for God in this religion. Adherents, known as Muslims, follow the "Five Pillars" enjoined in their scripture, the *Koran:* faith in Allah, praying five times daily facing Mecca, giving of alms, fasting during the month of Ramadan, and pilgrimage. One of the fastest growing religions, Islam has over one billion followers, mostly in the Middle East, Pakistan, Africa, Indonesia, China, Russia and neighboring countries.

Īśvara: ईश्वर "Highest Lord." Supreme or Personal God. See: *Parameśvara.*

Itihāsa: इतिहास "So it was." Epic history, particularly the *Rāmāyaṇa* and *Mahābhārata* (of which the famed *Bhagavad Gītā* is a part). This term sometimes refers to the *Purāṇas,* especially the *Skānda Purāṇa* and the *Bhāgavata*

Purāṇa (or *Śrīmad Bhāgavatam*). See: *Mahābhārata, Rāmāyaṇa, Smṛiti.*

itinerant: Traveling from place to place, with no permanent home. Wandering. See: *monk, sādhu, vairāgya.*

Jagadāchārya: जगदाचार्य "World teacher."

jāgrat: जाग्रत् "Wakefulness." The state of mind in which the senses are turned outward. Conscious mind. One of four states of consciousness, *avasthās,* described in the *Māṇḍūkya Upanishad.* See: *avasthā, consciousness.*

jagrat chitta: "Wakeful consciousness." The conscious mind.

Jainism: ***(Jaina)*** जैन An ancient non-Vedic religion of India made prominent by the teachings of Mahāvīra ("Great Hero"), ca 500 BCE. The Jain *Āgamas* teach reverence for all life, vegetarianism and strict renunciation for ascetics. Jains focus great emphasis on the fact that all souls may attain liberation, each by own effort. Their great historic saints, called Tīrthaṅkaras ("Ford-Crossers"), are objects of worship, of whom Mahāvīra was the 24th and last. Jains number about six million today, living mostly in India.

japa: जप "Recitation." Practice of concentrated repetition of a *mantra,* often while counting the repetitions on a *mālā* or strand of beads. It may be done silently or aloud. Sometimes known as *mantra yoga.* A major *sādhana* in Hindu spiritual practice, from the simple utterance of a few names of God to extraordinary feats of repeating sacred syllables millions of times for years on end. See: *amṛita, mantra, yama-niyama, yoga.*

jarred: Irritated, clashing, quarrelling, discordant.

Jehovah: Christian vocalization of Yahweh, Hebrew name for God.

jerk: A sudden quick thrust, push, pull or throw.

Jesus Christ: A teacher and prophet in the first century of this era whose teachings are the basis of Christianity.

Jew: An adherent of Judaism, or descendant of such adherents. See: *Judaism.*

jīva: जीव "Living, existing." From *jīv,* "to live." The individual soul, *ātman,* bound by the three *malas (āṇava, karma* and *māyā).* The individuated self *(jīva-ātman)* as opposed to the transcendental Self *(parama ātman).* The *jīvanmukta* is one who is "liberated while living." See: *ātman, evolution of the soul, jīvanmukta, purusha, soul.*

jīvanmukta: जीवन्मुक्त "Liberated soul." One who has attained *nirvikalpa samādhi*—the realization of the Self, Paraśiva—and is liberated from rebirth while living in a human body. (Contrasted with *videhamukta,* one liberated at the point of death.) This attainment is the culmination of lifetimes of intense striving, *sādhana* and *tapas,* requiring total renunciation, *sannyāsa* (death to the external world, denoted in the conducting of one's own funeral rites), in the current incarnation. While completing life in the physical body, the *jīvanmukta* enjoys the ability to re-enter *nirvikalpa samā-*

dhi again and again. See: *jīvanmukti, jñāna, kaivalya, moksha, Self Realization, Śivasāyujya, videhamukti.*

jīvanmukti: जीवन्मुक्ति "Liberation while living." The state of the *jīvanmukta.* Contrasted with *videhamukti,* liberation at the point of death. See: *death, jīvanmukta, moksha, reincarnation, videhamukti.*

jñāna : ज्ञान "Knowledge; wisdom." (Tamil: *jñānam*) The matured state of the soul. It is the wisdom that comes as an aftermath of the *kuṇḍalinī* breaking through the door of *Brahman* into the realization of Paraśiva, Absolute Reality. The repeated *samādhis* of Paraśiva ever deepen this flow of divine knowing which establishes the knower in an extraordinary point of reference, totally different from those who have not attained this enlightenment. *Jñāna* is sometimes misunderstood as book knowledge, as a maturity or awakening that comes from simply understanding a complex philosophical system or systems. Those who define *jñāna* in this way deny that the path is a progression of *charyā-kriyā-yoga-jñāna* or of *karma-bhakti-rāja-jñāna.* Rather, they say that one can choose one's own path, and that each leads to the ultimate goal. See: *God Realization, door of Brahman, Self Realization, samādhi.*

jñāna mārga: ज्ञानमार्ग See: *jñāna pāda.*

jñāna pāda: ज्ञानपाद "Stage of wisdom." According to the Śaiva Siddhānta *ṛishis, jñāna* is the last of the four successive *pādas* (stages) of spiritual unfoldment. It is the culmination of the third stage, the *yoga pāda.* Also names the knowledge section of each *Āgama.* See: *jñāna, pāda.*

jñāna śakti: ज्ञानशक्ति "Power of wisdom." One of Śiva's three primary *śaktis.* Also a name for Lord Kārttikeya's *vel.* See: *Kārttikeya, Śakti, triśūla.*

jñāna yoga: ज्ञानयोग "Union of knowledge." Describes the esoteric spiritual practices of the fully enlightened being, or *jñānī.* An alternative meaning, popularized by Swāmī Vivekānanda, is the quest for cognition through intellectual religious study, as one of four alternate paths to truth, the other three being *bhakti yoga, karma yoga* and *rāja yoga.* See: *jñāna, yoga.*

jñānī: ज्ञानी "Sage." One who possesses *jñāna.* See: *jīvanmukta, jñāna.*

jot: To make a brief note.

Judaic-Christian: Concerned with two of the three religions descended from Abraham, Judaism and Christianty, especially in the sense of their shared beliefs.

Judaism: The religion of over 12 million adherents worldwide (over half in the United States), first of the Abrahamic faiths, founded about 3,700 years ago in Canaan (now Israel) by Abraham, who started the lineage, and in Egypt by Moses, who emancipated the enslaved Jewish tribes. Its major scripture is the *Torah.*

judicious: Having or showing sound judgment; prudent.

jyotisha: ज्योतिष From *jyoti,* "light." "The science of the lights (or stars)." Hindu astrology, the knowledge and practice of analyzing events and circumstances, delineating character and determining auspicious moments, according to the positions and movements of heavenly bodies. In calculating horoscopes, *jyotisha* uses the sidereal (fixed-star) system, whereas Western astrology uses the tropical (fixed-date) method.

kaef: (Shum) The state of awareness being aware of itself. Pronounced *kaw-eef.* See: *Shum.*

Kailāsa: कैलास "Crystalline" or "Abode of bliss." The four-faced Himalayan peak in Western Tibet; the earthly abode of Lord Śiva. Associated with Mount Meru, the legendary center of the universe, it is an important pilgrimage destination for all Hindus, as well as for Tibetan Buddhists. Kailāsa is represented in Śāktism by a certain three-dimensional form of the *Śrī Chakra yantra* (also called *kailāsa chakra).*

Kailāsa Paramparā: कैलासपरंपरा A spiritual lineage of 162 *siddhas,* a major stream of the Nandinātha Sampradāya, proponents of the ancient philosophy of monistic Śaiva Siddhānta. The first of these masters that history recalls was Maharishi Nandinātha (or Nandikeśvara) 2,250 years ago, *satguru* to the great Tirumular, ca 200 BCE, and seven other disciples (as stated in the *Tirumantiram).* The lineage continued down the centuries and is alive today—the first recent *siddha* is known as the "Ṛishi from the Himālayas," so named because he descended from those holy mountains. In South India, he initiated Kadaitswāmī (ca 1810–1875), who in turn initiated Chellappaswāmī (1840–1915). Chellappan passed the mantle of authority to sage Yogaswāmī (1872–1964), who in 1949 initiated the present *satguru,* Sivaya Subramuniyaswami. See: *Nātha Sampradāya, Patañjali, Tirumular, Vyāghrapāda, Yogaswāmī.*

kaivalya: कैवल्य "Absolute oneness, aloneness; perfect detachment, freedom." Liberation. Kaivalya is the term used by Patañjali and others in the yoga tradition to name the goal and fulfillment of yoga, the state of complete detachment from transmigration. It is virtually synonymous with moksha. Kaivalya is the perfectly transcendent state, the highest condition resulting from the ultimate realization. It is defined uniquely according to each philosophical school, depending on its beliefs regarding the nature of the soul. See: *moksha, Śivasāyujya, jñāna.*

kaleidoscope: A tube-like instrument that shows a constantly changing show of colors and lights. Anything so changeable.

Kālī: काली "Black" Goddess. A form of Śakti in Her fierce aspect worshiped by various sects within Śāktism. She is dark, nude, primordial and fiercely powerful, as of a naked energy untamed. But from the perspective of devotees, She is the incomparable protectress, champion of *sādhana* and mother of liberation. The Goddess Durgā, seated on a tiger, has similar characteristics and is often identified with Kālī. See: *Śakti, Śāktism.*

Kali Yuga: कलियुग "Dark Age." The Kali Yuga is the last age in the repetitive cycle of four phases of time the universe passes through. It is comparable to the darkest part of the night, as the forces of ignorance are in full power and many subtle faculties of the soul are obscured. See: *mahāpralaya, yuga.*

kapha: कफ "Biological water." One of the three bodily humors, called *dosha, kapha* is known as the water humor. Principle of cohesion. *Kapha* gives bodily structure and stability, lubricates, heals and bestows immunity. See: *āyurveda, dosha.*

Karaikkalammaiyar: காரைக்காலம்மையார் The 23rd of the 63 canonized saints of Tamil Śaivism. Great mystic, poet and *yoginī,* she composed important hymns, which are part of *Tirumurai.*

karma: कर्म "Action," "deed." One of the most important principles in Hindu thought, *karma* refers to 1) any act or deed; 2) the principle of cause and effect; 3) a consequence or "fruit of action" *(karmaphala)* or "after effect" *(uttaraphala),* which sooner or later returns upon the doer. What we sow, we shall reap in this or future lives. Selfish, hateful acts *(pāpakarma* or *kukarma)* will bring suffering. Benevolent actions *(puṇyakarma* or *sukarma)* will bring loving reactions. *Karma* is threefold: *sañchita, prārabdha* and *kriyamāna.* **—*sañchita karma:*** "Accumulated actions." The sum of all *karmas* of this life and past lives. **—*prārabdha karma:*** "Actions begun; set in motion." That portion of *sañchita karma* that is bearing fruit and shaping the events and conditions of the current life, including the nature of one's bodies, personal tendencies and associations. **—*kriyamāna karma:*** "Being made." The *karma* being created and added to *sañchita* in this life by one's thoughts, words and actions, or in the inner worlds between lives. *Kriyamāna karma* is also called *āgāmi,* "coming, arriving," and *vartamāna,* "current, revolving, set in motion." While some *kriyamāna karmas* bear fruit in the current life, others are stored for future births. See: *āṇava, fate, mala, māyā, moksha, pāśa, sin, soul.*

karma mārga: कर्ममार्ग "Path of action-reaction." A coined word describing the worldly condition of souls totally enmeshed in the actions and reactions of the past, making new *karmas* so swiftly that little true personal identity is experienced. See: *āṇava mārga, pāda.*

karma yoga: कर्मयोग "Union through action." Selfless service. See: *yoga.*

Kārttikeya: कार्त्तिकेय Child of the Pleiades, from *Kṛittikā,* "Pleiades." Second son of Śiva, brother of Gaṇeśa. A great Mahādeva worshiped in all parts of India and the world. Also known as Muruga, Kumāra, Skanda, Shaṇmukhanātha, Subramaṇya and more, He is the God who guides that part of evolution which is religion, the transformation of the instinctive into a divine wisdom through the practice of yoga. See: *Muruga, Pleiades, Veda.*

Kashmīr Śaivism: कश्मीरशैव In this mildly theistic and intensely monistic school founded by Vasugupta around 850, Śiva is immanent and transcendent. Purification and *yoga* are strongly emphasized. Kashmīr Śaivism offers an extremely rich and detailed understanding of the human psyche, and a clear and distinct path of *kuṇḍalinī-siddha yoga* to the goal of Self Realization. The Kashmīr Śaivite is not so much concerned with worshiping a personal God as he is with attaining the transcendental state of Śiva consciousness. While the number of Kashmīr Śaivite formal followers is uncertain, the school continues to exert an important influence in India. See: *Śaivism.*

Kauai: Northernmost of the Hawaiian islands; 553 sq. mi., pop. 50,000.

Kauai Aadheenam: Monastery-temple complex founded by Sivaya Subramuniyaswami in 1970; international headquarters of Śaiva Siddhānta Church.

kaula: कौल "Of or related to *kula,*" a *tantric* teaching. *Kaula* also names the liberated soul in Śākta traditions, one to whom wood and gold, life and death are the same.

kavi: காவி "Ocher-saffron color." A Tamil word for the color taken on by robes of *sādhus* who sit, meditate or live on the banks of the Ganges. Hence the color of the *sannyāsin's* robes. The Sanskṛit equivalent is *kāshāya.*

kevala avasthā: केवल अवस्था "Stage of oneness, aloneness." (Tamil: *avasthai.)* In Śaiva Siddhānta, the first of three stages of the soul's evolution, a state beginning with its emanation or spawning by Lord Śiva as an etheric form unaware of itself, a spark of the Divine shrouded in a cloud of darkness known as *āṇava.* Here the soul is likened to seed hidden in the ground, yet to germinate and unfold its potential. See: *āṇava, avasthā, evolution of the soul, sakala avasthā, soul, śuddha avasthā.*

knack: A specific talent of cleverly doing something difficult or hard to teach.

konrai: கொன்றை The Golden Shower tree, *Cassia fistula*; symbol of Śiva's cascading, abundant, golden grace.

kośa: कोश "Sheath; vessel, container; layer." Philosophically, five sheaths through which the soul functions simultaneously in the various planes or levels of existence. They are sometimes compared to the layers of an onion. The *kośas,* in order of increasing subtlety, are as follows. ***—annamaya kośa:*** "Sheath composed of food." The physical or odic body, coarsest of sheaths in comparison to the faculties of the soul, yet indispensable for evolution and Self Realization, because only within it can all fourteen *chakras* fully function. See: *chakra.* ***—prāṇamaya kośa:*** "Sheath composed of *prāṇa* (vital force)." Also known as the *prāṇic* or health body, or the etheric body or etheric double, it coexists within the physical body as its source of life, breath and vitality, and is its connection with the astral body. *Prāṇa* moves in the *prāṇamaya kośa* as five primary currents or *vayus,* "vital airs or winds." *Prāṇamaya kośa* disintegrates at death along with the physical body. See: *prāṇa.* ***—manomaya kośa:*** "Mind-formed sheath." The lower astral body, from *manas,* "thought, will, wish." The instinctive-intellectual sheath of ordinary thought, desire and emotion. It is the seat of the *indriyas,* sensory and motor organs, respectively called *jñānendriyas* and *karmendriyas*. The *manomaya kośa* takes form as the physical body develops and is discarded in the inner worlds before rebirth. It is understood in two layers: 1) the odic-causal sheath *(buddhi)* and 2) the odic-astral sheath *(manas)*. See: *indriya, manas.* **—*vijñānamaya kośa:*** "Sheath of cognition." The mental or cognitive-intuitive sheath, also called the actinodic sheath. It is the vehicle of higher thought, *vijñāna*—understanding, knowing, direct cognition, wisdom, intuition and creativity. **—*ānandamaya kośa:*** "Body of bliss." The intuitive-superconscious sheath or actinic-causal body. This inmost soul form *(svarūpa)* is the ultimate foundation of all life, intelligence and higher faculties. Its essence is Parāśakti (Pure Consciousness) and Paraśiva (the Absolute). See: *actinic, actinodic, manomaya kośa, odic, soul, subtle body.*

Kṛishṇa: कृष्ण "Black." Also compared to *kṛishṭiḥ,* "drawing, attracting." One of the most popular Gods of the Hindu pantheon. He is worshiped by Vaishṇavas as the eighth *avatāra* incarnation of Vishṇu. He is best known as the Supreme Personage celebrated in the *Mahābhārata,* and specifically in the *Bhagavad Gītā.* For Gauḍīya Vaishṇavism, Kṛishṇa is the Godhead.

kriyā: क्रिया "Action." In a general sense, *kriyā* can refer to doing of any kind. Specifically, it names religious action, especially rites or ceremonies. In *yoga* terminology, *kriyā* names involuntary physical movements caused by the arousal of the *kuṇḍalinī.* See: *pāda.*

kriyā mārga: क्रियामार्ग See *kriyā pāda.*

kriyā pāda: क्रियापाद "Stage of religious action; worship." The stage of worship and devotion, second of four progressive stages of maturation on the Śaiva Siddhānta path of attainment. See: *pāda.*

kriyā śakti: क्रियाशक्ति "Action power." The universal force of doing. See: *Śakti, Triśūla.*

Kriyākramadyotikā: क्रियाक्रमद्योतिका A manual by Aghoraśiva (ca 1050) detailing Āgamic Śaiva ritual. It is used widely by South Indian priests today.

kriyamāna karma: क्रियमानकर्म "Actions being made." See: *karma.*

kukarma: कुकर्म "Unwholesome acts," or the fruit therefrom. See: *karma.*

kulachāra: कुलचार "The divine way of life;" the state of *jīvanmukti,* "Liberation while living" in Śāktism. It is attained through *sādhana* and grace.

kulaguru: कुलगुरु "Family preceptor" or "teacher." The *kulaguru* guides the joint and extended family, particularly through the heads of families, and provides spiritual education. He may or may not be a *satguru.*

kuṇḍalinī: कुण्डलिनी "She who is coiled; serpent power." The primordial cosmic energy in every individual which, at first, lies coiled like a serpent at the base of the spine and eventually, through the practice of *yoga,* rises up the *sushumṇā nāḍī.* As it rises, the *kuṇḍalinī* awakens each successive *chakra. Nirvikalpa samādhi,* enlightenment, comes as it pierces through the door of Brahman at the core of the *sahasrāra* and enters it. *Kuṇḍalinī śakti* then returns to rest in any one of the seven *chakras.* Śivasāyujya is complete when the *kuṇḍalinī* arrives back in the *sahasrāra* and remains coiled in this crown *chakra.* See: *chakra, door of Brahman, samādhi, nāḍī, tantra.*

kuṇḍalinī śākti: कुण्डलिनीशक्ति The pure (neither masculine nor feminine) force that flows through the *sushumṇā nāḍī.* See: *kuṇḍalinī, sushumṇā nāḍī.*

kuṅkuma: कुंकुम "Saffron; red." (Tamil: *kumkum*) The red powder, made of turmeric and lime, worn by Hindus as the *pottu* or *bindu,* dot, at the point of the third eye on the forehead. Names the saffron plant, *Crocus sativus,* and its pollen. See: *ājñā chakra.*

Kural: குறள் See: *Tirukural.*

labyrinth: Something highly intricate or convoluted in character, composition, or construction. A maze.

Lakshmī: लक्ष्मी "Mark or sign," often of success or prosperity. Śakti, the Universal Mother, as Goddess of wealth. The mythological consort of Vishṇu. Usually depicted on a lotus flower. Prayers are offered to Lakshmī for wealth, beauty and peace. See: *Śakti.*

lament: To express grief for or mourn.

lapse: To fall (or slip) down, away, or back. To cease or become forfeit or void by default.

larceny: Stealing personal property; theft.

latent: Present but hidden or potential; not evident or active.

laud: To praise. To sing, chant or speak the qualities or glories of.

layman: A man who is not a cleric or monastic.

ledger: A book in which monetary transactions are posted in the form of debits and credits.

lest: For fear that a thing might happen.

lethargy: A state of sluggishness, inactivity and apathy.

levitation: The power or ability to float in the air or to cause objects to do so at will.

liberal: Free; broad-minded; tolerant; unconfined; generous.

liberation: *Moksha,* release from the bonds of *pāśa,* after which the soul is liberated from *saṁsāra* (the round of births and deaths). In Śaiva Siddhānta, *pāśa* is the three-fold bondage of *āṇava, karma* and *māyā,* which limit and confine the soul to the reincarnational cycle so that it may evolve. *Moksha* is freedom from the fettering power of these bonds, which do not cease to exist, but no longer have the power to fetter or bind the soul. See: *mala, jīvanmukti, moksha, pāśa, reincarnation, satguru, Self Realization, soul.*

light: In an ordinary sense, a form of energy which makes physical objects visible to the eye. In a religious-mystical sense, light also illumines inner objects (i.e., mental images). **—inner light:** light perceived inside the head and body, of which there are varying intensities. When the *karmas* have been sufficiently quieted, the meditator can see and enjoy inner light independently of mental images. **—moon-like inner light:** Inner light perceived at a first level of intensity, glowing softly, much like the moon. The meditator's first experience of it is an important milestone in unfoldment. **—clear white light:** Inner light at a high level of intensity, very clear and pure. When experienced fully, it is seen to be permeating all of existence, the universal substance of all form, inner and outer, pure consciousness, Satchidānanda. This experience, repeated at regular intervals, can yield "a knowing greater than you could acquire at any university or institute of higher learning." See: *Śiva consciousness, tattva.*

limber: Bending or flexing readily; pliable.

lineage: A direct line of ancestors and descendants or predecessors and successors.

linger: To be slow in leaving, especially out of reluctance; tarry. To persist.

liturgy: The proper, prescribed forms of ritual.

loka: लोक "World, habitat, realm, or plane of existence." From *loc,* "to shine, be bright, visible." See: *three worlds.*

lore: Accumulated facts, traditions, or beliefs about a particular subject.

lotus flower: An aquatic plant *(Nelumbo nucifera)* native to southern Asia and Australia, having large leaves, fragrant, pinkish flowers, a broad, rounded, perforated seedpod, and fleshy rhizomes.

lotus pose: *Padmāsana.* The most famous of *haṭha yoga* poses and the optimum position for meditation. The legs are crossed, turning the soles of the feet up, which then resemble a lotus flower. See: *āsana, haṭha yoga, padmāsana.*

lucid: Clear; easily understood; intelligible.

luminaries: An object, such as a celestial body, that gives light.

luminous: Letting out light, especially of its own creation.

lurk: To wait unobserved or unsuspected in order to harm or attack.

lust: Intense desire or craving, especially sexual.

lymph: A clear, yellowish fluid of the body containing white blood cells and circulating throughout the lymphatic system. Among its functions, it removes bacteria and certain proteins from tissues, and transports fat from the small intestine. In *āyurveda,* lymph is part of *rasa,* the first of the human body's seven *dhātus* (constituants; tissues), each of which is transformed into the next: 1) *rasa* (which includes plasma, lymph, serum, cytoplasm and chyle); 2) *rakta* (red blood cells, blood tissue—the oxygen carrying unit); 3) *mamsa* (muscle tissue); 4) *meda* (adipose tissue—subcutaneous fat and sweat); 5) *asthi* (bone tissue); 6) *maija* (nerve tissue and bone marrow) and; 7) *shura* (reproductive tissue, semen). See: *āyurveda, ojas, tejas, transmutation.*

macrocosm: "Great world" or "universe." See: *microcosm-macrocosm, three worlds.*

Madhumateya: **मधुमतेय** A Śaiva Siddhānta monastic order founded by Pavanaśiva, preceptor of the Kalachuri kings of Central India.

Mādhva: **माध्व** South Indian Vaishṇava saint (1197–1278) who expounded a purely dualistic (pluralistic) Vedānta in which there is an essential and eternal distinction between God, soul and world, and between all beings and things. He is also one of the few Hindus to have taught the existence of an eternal hell where lost souls would be condemned to suffer forever. See: *dvaita-advaita, Vedānta.*

maestro: A master, especially in art or music (Originally Italian).

magnanimous: Courageously noble in mind and heart. Generous in forgiving. Eschewing resentment or revenge; unselfish.

magnetized: Having been made magnetic. As certain physical elements are magnetized with *actinodic* power within a shrine through the chanting of *mantras* and by various other means.

mahā: **महा** An adjective or prefix meaning "great."

Mahābhārata: **महाभारत** "Great Epic of India." The world's longest epic poem. It revolves around the conflict between two royal families, those of the Pāṇḍavas and Kauravas, and their great battle of Kurukshetra near modern Delhi in approximately 1424 BCE. The *Mahābhārata* is revered as scripture by Vaishṇavites and Smārtas. See: *Bhagavad Gītā, Itihāsa.*

Mahādeva: **महादेव** "Great shining one;" "God." Referring either to God Śiva or any of the highly evolved beings who live in the Śivaloka in their natural, effulgent soul bodies. God Śiva in His perfection as Primal Soul is one of the Mahādevas, yet He is unique and incomparable in that He alone is uncreated, the Father-Mother and Destiny of all other Mahādevas. He is called Parameśvara, "Supreme God." He is the Primal Soul, whereas the other Gods are individual souls. It is said in scripture that there are 330 million Gods. See: *Gods, Parameśvara, Śiva, deva.*

mahāpralaya: **महाप्रलय** "Great dissolution." Total annihilation of the universe at the end of a *mahākalpa.* It is the absorption of all existence, including time, space and individual consciousness, all the *lokas* and their inhabitants into God Śiva, as the water of a river returns to its source, the sea. Then Śiva alone exists in His three perfections, until He again emantes creation. During this incredibly vast period there are many partial dissolutions, *pralayas,* when either the Bhūloka or the Bhūloka and the Antarloka are destroyed. See: *yuga.*

Maharishi Nandinātha: **महर्षि नन्दिनाथ** (ca 250 BCE) The first *siddha satguru* of the major stream of the Nandinātha Sampradāya, the *Kailāsa Paramparā,* recorded in Pāṇini's book of grammar as the teacher of *ṛishis* Patañjali, Vyāghrapāda and Vasishṭha. Among its representatives today is Satguru Sivaya

Subramuniyaswami. See: *Kailāsa Paramparā, Nātha Sampradāya.*

Maharshi (Maharishi): महर्षि "Great seer." Title for the greatest and most influential of *siddhas.*

mahāsamādhi: महासमाधि "Great enstasy." The death, or quitting off of the physical body, of a great soul, an event occasioned by tremendous blessings. Also names the shrine in which the remains of a great soul are entombed. See: *cremation, death.*

mahātala: महातल Sixth netherworld. Region of consciencelessness. See: *chakra.*

mahāvākya: महावाक्य "Great saying." A profound aphorism from scripture or a holy person. Most famous are four Upanishad proclamations: *Prajanam Brahma* ("Pure consciousness is God"–*Aitareya U.), Aham Brahmāsmi* ("I am God"—*Bṛihadāraṇyaka U.), Tat tvam asi* ("Thou art That"—*Çhandogya U.)* and *Ayam ātma Brahma* ("The soul is God"—*Māṇḍūkya U.).*

Maheśvara: महेश्वर "Great Lord." In Śaiva Siddhānta, the name of Śiva's energy of veiling grace, one of five aspects of Parameśvara, the Primal Soul. *Maheśvara* is also a popular epithet for Lord Śiva as Primal Soul and personal Lord. See: *Naṭarāja, Parameśvara.*

mahout: The keeper or driver of an elephant.

mala: मल "Impurity." An important term in Śaivism referring to three bonds, called *pāśa—āṇava, karma,* and *māyā*—which limit the soul, preventing it from knowing its true, divine nature. See: *āṇava, karma, liberation, māyā, pāśa.*

malaparipakam: மலபரிபாகம் "Ripening of bonds." The state attained after the three *malas, āṇava, karma* and *māyā,* are brought under control during *marul,* the second stage of the *sakala avasthai.* At this time, the Lord's concealing grace, *tirodhāna śakti,* has accomplished its work, giving way to *anugraha,* His revealing grace, leading to the descent of grace, *śaktinipāta.* See: *āṇava, anugraha, karma, malas, marul, māyā, sakala avasthā, śaktinipāta, tirodhāna śakti.*

mālā: माला "Garland." A strand of beads for holy recitation, *japa,* usually made of *rudrāksha, tulasī,* sandalwood or crystal. Also a flower garland.

malevolent: Motivated by ill will, wishing harm to others; malicious. Exercising an evil or harmful influence.

malice: Ill will; desire or intent to do harm to another, generally without conscience. See: *mahātala.*

malign: To make evil, harmful, and often untrue statements about.

malleable: Pliable; amenable to be adjusted to changing circumstances; adaptable.

mana: The Polynesian word for *pranic śākti.* Supernatural or divine power, miraculous power, believed to reside in a person or thing.

manana: मनन "Thinking; deep reflection."

manas: मनस् "Mind; understanding." The lower or instinctive mind, seat of desire and governor of sensory and motor organs, called *indriyas. Manas* is termed the undisciplined, empirical mind. *Manas* is characterized by desire, determination, doubt, faith, lack of faith, steadfastness, lack of steadfastness, shame, intellection and fear. It is a faculty of *manomaya kośa,* the lower astral or instinctive-intellectual sheath. See: *awareness, instinctive mind, manomaya kośa, mind (individual).*

manas chakra: मनसचक्र The mature *sahasrāra chakra* at the top of the head. It attains this level after many experiences of Self Realizations when the *kuṇḍalinī* force coils itself at the top of the head. This then becomes the *muladhara chakra* of this golden soul body. See: *chakras, svarṇaśarīra, viśvagrāsa, ānandamaya kośa.*

manas chitta: मनस् चित्त "Instinctive mind." See: *manas, manomaya kośa, instinctive mind.*

manifest: To show or reveal. Perceivable or knowable, therefore having form. The opposite of unmanifest or transcendent. See: *formless, tattva.*

Manikkavasagar: மாணிக்கவாசகர் "He of ruby-like utterances." Tamil saint who contributed to the medieval Śaivite renaissance (ca 850). He gave up his position as Prime Minister to follow a renunciate life. His poetic *Tiruvasagam,* "Holy utterances"—a major Śaiva Siddhānta scripture (part of the eighth *Tirumurai)* and a jewel of Tamil literature—express his aspirations, trials and *yogic* realizations. See: *Tirumurai, Tiruvasagam.*

manipulate: To influence or manage shrewdly or deviously. To handle, maneuver or move.

maṇipūra chakra: मणिपूरचक्र "Wheel of the jewelled city." Solar-plexus center of willpower. See: *chakra.*

mannequin: A life-size full or partial model (figure) of the human body.

manomaya kośa: मनोमयकोश See: *kośa.*

mantra: मन्त्र "Mystic formula." A sound, syllable, word or phrase endowed with special power, usually drawn from scripture. *Mantras* are chanted loudly during *pūjā* to invoke the Gods and establish a force field. Certain *mantras* are repeated softly or mentally for *japa,* the subtle tones quieting the mind, harmonizing the inner bodies and stimulating latent spiritual qualities. Hinduism's universal *mantra* is Aum. To be truly efficacious, such *mantras* must be bestowed by the preceptor during initiation. See: *Aum, incantation, japa, pūjā, yajña.*

mārga: मार्ग "Path; way." From *mārg,* "to seek." See: *pāda.*

mārgī: मार्गी A "follower" on a specific path or *mārga.* See: *pāda.*

Mariyamman: மாரியம்மன் "Smallpox Goddess," known commonly as Amman, protectress from plagues. See: *Śakti, Śāktism.*

Markanduswāmī: மார்க்கண்டுசுவாமி A disciple of Satguru Yogaswāmī who passed his later years as a white robed *sādhu.* He lived an austere life and hardly spoke but to pronounce the words and sayings of his *guru.*

martyrdom: Extreme suffering, especially inflicted for a cause.

marul: மருள் "Confusion." The second of the three stages of the *sakala avasthai* when the soul is "caught" between the world and God and begins to seek knowledge of its own true nature, *paśu-jñānam.* See: *paśu-jñānam, sakala avasthā.*

masturbation: Manipulating one's own genitals, or the genitals of another, for sexual gratification. See: *celibacy, dissipation, ojas, tejas, transmutation.*

materialism (materialistic): The doctrine that matter is the only reality, that all life, thought and feelings are but the effects of movements of matter, and that there exist no worlds but the physical. Materialists usually hold that there is no God—a cosmic, material, prime mover perhaps, but no personal God. An Indian school of thought which propounded this view were the Chārvāka. See: *atheism, Chārvāka, nāstika, worldly.*

maṭha: मठ "Monastery." See: *monastery.*

maṭhavāsi: मठवासि "Monastic; monastery dweller." See: *monk.*

Mattamayūra Order: मत्तमयूर A Śaiva Siddhānta monastic order founded by Purandara (successor to Rudraśambhu), centered in the Punjab. Members of this order served as advisors to the king.

mauna: मौन The discipline of remaining silent.

maya: मय "Consisting of; made of," as in *manomaya,* "made of mind." See: *manomaya kośa.*

māyā: माया "Artfulness," "illusion," "phantom" or "mirific energy." The substance emanated from Śiva through which the world of form is manifested. Hence all creation is also termed *māyā.* It is the cosmic creative force, the principle of manifestation, ever in the process of creation, preservation and dissolution. *Māyā* is a key concept in Hinduism, originally meaning "supernatural power; God's mirific energy." See: *loka, mala, mind (universal), tattva, world.*

māyā mārga: मायामार्ग "Path of worldliness." The soul engrossed in the ignorance of the world and the fulfillment of instinctive and intellectual impulses. See: *pāda.*

meander: To wander aimlessly and idly without fixed direction.

meditation: *Dhyāna.* Sustained concentration. Meditation describes a quiet, alert, powerfully concentrated state wherein new knowledge and insights are awakened from within as awareness focuses one-pointedly on an object or specific line of thought. See: *internalized worship, rāja yoga, Satchidānanda.*

medley: A jumbled or mixed assortment; a mixture.

mendicant: A beggar; a wandering monk, or *sādhu,* who lives on alms. See: *sādhu.*

mental body (sheath): The higher-mind layer of the subtle or astral body in which the soul functions in Maharloka of the Antarloka or subtle plane. In Sanskṛit, the mental body is *vijñānamaya kośa,* "sheath of cognition." See:

intellectual mind, kośa, subtle body.

mental plane: Names the refined strata of the subtle world. Here the soul is shrouded in the mental or cognitive sheath, called *vijñānamaya kośa.* See: *vijñānamaya kośa.*

merge: To lose distinctness or identity by being sunk in, immersed or absorbed. To unite or become one with something larger.

mesh: A net or network. Something that snares or entraps.

metabolism: The physical and chemical processes within a living cell or organism necessary for the maintenance of life.

metamorphosis: Complete transformation, as in a caterpillar's becoming a butterfly. See: *kuṇḍalinī, reincarnation.*

metaphysics: The philosophy that examines the nature of reality, especially those aspects of reality beyond the realm of physical perception, or impossible to investigate by intellectual scientific study.

methodical: Proceeding in regular, systematic order.

methodology: Means, technique, or procedure; working method.

Meykandar: மெய்கண்டார் "Truth seer." The 13th-century Tamil theologian, author (or translator from the *Raurava Āgama*) of the *Śivajñānabodham.* Founder of the Meykandar Sampradāya of pluralistic Śaiva Siddhānta. See: *Śaiva Siddhānta, Śivajñānabodham.*

microcosm-macrocosm: "Little world" or "miniature universe" as compared with "great world." *Microcosm* refers to the internal source of something larger or more external (macrocosm). In Hindu cosmology, the outer world is a macrocosm of the inner world, which is its microcosm and is mystically larger and more complex than the physical universe and functions at a higher rate of vibration and even a different rate of time. The microcosm precedes the macrocosm. Thus, the guiding principle of the Bhūloka comes from the Antarloka and Śivaloka. Consciousness precedes physical form. In the *tantric* tradition, the body of man is viewed as a microcosm of the entire divine creation. "Microcosm-macrocosm" is embodied in the terms *piṇḍa* and *aṇḍa.* See: *apex of creation, quantum, tattva, tantra.*

militate: To work (mostly) against. To oppose, operate or "fight" for or against.

mind (five states): A view of the mind in five parts. **—conscious mind:** *Jāgrat chitta* ("wakeful consciousness"). The ordinary, waking, thinking state of mind in which the majority of people function most of the day. **—subconscious mind:** *Saṁskāra chitta* ("impression mind"). The part of mind "beneath" the conscious mind, the storehouse or recorder of all experience (whether remembered consciously or not)—the holder of past impressions, reactions and desires. Also, the seat of involuntary physiological processes. **—subsubconscious mind:** *Vāsanā chitta* ("mind of subliminal traits"). The area of the subconscious mind formed when two thoughts or experiences of the same rate of intensity are sent into the subconscious at different times and, intermingling, give rise to a new and totally different rate of vibration. This subconscious formation later causes the external mind to react to situations according to these accumulated vibrations, be they positive, negative or mixed. **—superconscious mind:** *Kāraṇa chitta.* The mind of light, the all-knowing intelligence of the soul. The Sanskṛit term is *turīya,* "the fourth," meaning the condition beyond the states of wakefulness *(jāgrat),* "dream" *(svapna),* and "deep sleep" *(sushupti).* At its deepest level, the superconscious is Parāśakti, or Satchidānanda, the Divine Mind of God Śiva. In Sanskṛit, there are numerous terms for the various levels and states of superconsciousness. Specific superconscious states such as: *viśvachaitanya* ("universal consciousness"), *advaita chaitanya* ("nondual consciousness"), *adhyātma chetanā* ("spiritual consciousness"). **—subsuperconscious mind:** *Anukāraṇa chitta.* The superconscious mind working through the conscious and subconscious states, which brings forth intuition, clarity and insight. See: *chitta, consciousness, saṁskāra, Satchidānanda, vāsanā.*

mind (individual): At the microcosmic level of individual souls, mind is consciousness and its faculties of memory, desire, thought and cognition. Individual mind is *chitta* (mind, consciousness) and its three-fold expression is called *antaḥkaraṇa,* "inner faculty" composed of: 1) *buddhi* ("intellect, reason, logic," higher mind); 2) *ahaṁkāra* ("I-maker," egoity); 3) *manas* ("lower mind," instinctive-intellectual mind, the seat of desire). From the perspective of the 36 *tattvas* (categories of existence), each of these is a *tattva* which evolves out of the one before it. Thus, from *buddhi* comes *ahaṁkāra* and then *manas. Manas, buddhi* and *ahaṁkāra* are faculties of the *manomaya kośa* (astral or instinctive-intellectual sheath). *Anukāraṇa chitta,* subsuperconsciousness, the knowing mind, is the mind-state of the *vijñānamaya kośa* (mental or intuitive-cognitive sheath). The aspect of mind corresponding directly to the *ānandamaya kośa* (causal body) is *kāraṇa chitta,* superconsciousness. See: *ahaṁkāra, buddhi, chitta, manas, mind (universal).*

mind (three phases): A perspective of mind as instinctive, intellectual and superconscious. **—instinctive mind.** *Manas chitta,* the seat of desire and governor of sensory and motor organs. **—intellectual mind.** *Buddhi chitta,* the faculty of thought and intelligence. **—superconscious mind:** *Kāraṇa chitta,* the stratum of intuition, benevolence and spiritual sustenance. Its most refined essence is Parāsakti, or Satchidānanda, all-knowing, omnipresent consciousness, the One transcendental, self-luminous, divine mind common to all souls. See: *awareness, consciousness, mind (five states).*

mind (universal): In the most profound sense, mind is the sum of all things, all energies and manifestations, all forms, subtle and gross, sacred and mundane. It is the inner and outer cosmos. Mind is *māyā.* It is the material matrix. It is everything but That, the Self within, Paraśiva, which is timeless, formless, causeless, spaceless, known by the knower only after Self Realization. The Self is the indescribable, unnameable, Ultimate Reality.

Mind in its subtlest form is undifferentiated Pure Consciousness, primal substance (called Parāśakti or Satchidānanda), out of which emerge the myriad forms of existence, both psychic and material. See: *chitta, consciousness, māyā, tattva, world.*

mirth: Gaiety, fun, amusement, especially expressed with laughter.

misapprehension: Incorrect apprehension; misunderstanding.

miserliness: The quality of being stingy, selfish, especially with money.

misfit: A person unable to adjust to social environment or disturbingly different from others in his place and group.

mishmash: A collection of confused or unrelated things.

moksha: मोक्ष "Liberation." Release from transmigration, *saṁsāra,* the round of births and deaths, which occurs after *karma* has been resolved and *nirvikalpa samādhi*—realization of the Self, Paraśiva—has been attained. Same as *mukti.* See: *jīvanmukta, kaivalya, kuṇḍalinī, nirvikalpa samādhi, Paraśiva, rāja yoga, videhamukti.*

molten: Made liquid by heat; melted.

monastery: "Place of solitariness." *Maṭha.* The age-old tradition, carried forward from Lemurian times into the Hindu culture of India, a sacred residence where those of the same gender live under strict vows and work out their birth *karmas* in community toward realization of the Self. In monasteries, dedicated to transmutation of the sexual energies, celibacy is strictly upheld and there is no fraternizing with the opposite sex. The purpose of the monastery is to create an environment in which the monastic can balance the male and female energies *(piṅgala* and *iḍā)* within himself so that he lives in the spiritual, or *sushumṇā,* energy, which cannot be maintained in close association with the opposite sex. The monastic, whether a monk or a nun, is in a sense neither male nor female, but a pure soul being. See: *āśrama, monk, nāḍī.*

monastic: A monk or nun (based on the Greek *monos,* "alone"). A man or woman who has withdrawn from the world and lives an austere, religious life, either alone or with others in a monastery. (Not to be confused with *monistic,* having to do with the doctrine of monism.) A monastery-dweller is a *maṭhavāsi,* and *sādhu* is a rough equivalent for mendicant. See: *monk, sannyāsin.*

monism: "Doctrine of oneness." 1) The philosophical view that there is only one ultimate substance or principle. 2) The view that reality is a unified whole without independent parts. See: *dvaita-advaita, pluralism.*

monistic theism: Advaita Īśvaravāda. Monism is the doctrine that reality is a one whole or existence without independent parts. Theism is the belief that God exists as a real, conscious, personal Supreme Being. Monistic theism is the dipolar doctrine, also called panentheism, that embraces both monism and theism, two perspectives ordinarily considered contradictory or mutually exclusive, since theism implies dualism. Monistic theism simultaneously accepts that God has a personal form, that He creates, pervades and *is* all that exists—and that He ultimately transcends all existence and that the soul is, in essence, one with God. Advaita Siddhānta (monistic Śaiva Siddhānta, or Advaita Īśvaravāda Śaiva Siddhānta) is a specific form of monistic theism. See: *advaita, Advaita Īśvaravāda, Advaita Siddhānta, dvaita-advaita.*

monk: A celibate man wholly dedicated to religious life, either cenobitic (residing with others in a monastery) or anchoritic (living alone, as a hermit or mendicant). Literally, "one who lives alone" (from the Greek *monos,* "alone"). A synonym for *monastic.* Its feminine counterpart is *nun.* See: *monastic, sannyāsin.*

montage: A single pictorial composition made by juxtaposing or superimposing many pictures or designs.

moolef: (Shum) The perspective of the mind in its intellectual, philosophical state. Pronounced *moo-leef.* See: *Shum, Shum perspectives.*

morass: Something that hinders, engulfs, or overwhelms.

mortal: Subject to death. Opposite of *immortal.* See: *amṛita, death.*

mortician: An undertaker who arranges for the burial or cremation of the dead and assists at the funeral rites.

mortification: Discipline of the body and the appetites by self-denial or voluntary privation.

mṛidaṅga: मृदङ्ग (Tamil: *mṛidaṅgam*) A South Indian concert drum, barrel-shaped and two-headed.

mukti: मुक्ति "Release." A synonym for *moksha.* See: *moksha.*

mūla: मूल "Root." The root, base or basis of anything, as in *mūlādhāra chakra.* Foundational, original or causal, as in *mūlagrantha,* "original text."

mūla mantra: मूलमन्त्र "Root mystic formula." See: *Aum.*

mūlādhāra chakra: मूलाधारचक्र "Root-support wheel." Four-petaled psychic center at the base of the spine; governs memory. See: *chakra.*

mull: To go over extensively in the mind; ponder; to "ruminate" (colloquial).

multiplicity: The state of being various; a large number.

multitude: A very large number of things or people.

mummify: To prepare a dead body for a long preservation by excisions, chemical and embalming agents and drying.

Muṇḍaka Upanishad: मुण्डक उपनिषद् Belongs to the *Atharva Veda* and teaches the difference between the intellectual study of the *Vedas* and their supplementary texts and the intuitive knowledge by which God is known.

mundane: Worldly, especially as distinguished from heavenly or spiritual. Ordinary. From Latin *mundus* "world;" *mundanus* "worldly."

murky: Dark, gloomy, obscure or clouded.

Muruga (Murugan): முருகன் "Beautiful one," a favorite name of Kārttikeya among the Tamils of South India, Sri Lanka and elsewhere. See: *Kārttikeya.*

muse: To be absorbed in one's thoughts. Contemplate.

mutilating: Disfiguring or damaging irreparably by cutting off a limb or part of a person or animal.

myriad: Constituting a very large, indefinite number; innumerable.

mystic: One who understands religious mysteries or occult rites and practices. Inspiring a sense of mystery and wonder.

mysticism: Spirituality; the pursuit of direct spiritual or religious experience. Spiritual discipline aimed at union or communion with Ultimate Reality or God through deep meditation or trance-like contemplation. From the Greek *mystikos,* "of mysteries." Characterized by the belief that Truth transcends intellectual processes and must be attained through transcendent means. See: *clairaudience, clairvoyance, psychic, trance.*

nāda: नाद् "Sound; tone, vibration." Metaphysically, the mystic sounds of the Eternal, of which the highest is the transcendent or Soundless Sound, Paranāda, the first vibration from which creation emanates. Paranāda is so pure and subtle that it cannot be identified to the denser regions of the mind. From Paranāda comes Praṇava, Aum, and further evolutes of *nāda.* These are experienced by the meditator as the *nādanāḍī śakti,* "the energy current of sound," heard pulsing through the nerve system as a constant high-pitched *hum,* much like a *tambura,* an electrical transformer, a swarm of bees or a *śruti* box. Listening to the inner sounds is a contemplative practice, called *nāda upāsanā,* "worship through sound," *nāda anusandhāna,* "cultivation of inner sound," or *nāda yoga.* The subtle variations of the *nādanāḍī śakti* represent the psychic wavelengths of established *guru* lineages of many Indian religions. *Nāda* also refers to other psychic sounds heard during deep meditation, including those resembling various musical instruments. Most commonly, *nāda* refers to ordinary sound. See: *Aum, nāḍī.*

nādanāḍī śakti: नादनाडीशक्ति "Energy current of sound." See: *nāda.*

nāḍī: नाडी "Conduit." A nerve fiber or energy channel of the subtle (inner) bodies of man. It is said there are 72,000. These interconnect the *chakras.* The three main *nāḍīs* are named *iḍā, piṅgalā* and *sushumṇā.* ***—iḍā:*** Also known as *chandra* ("moon") *nāḍī,* it is pink in color and flows downward, ending on the left side of the body. This current is feminine in nature and is the channel of physical-emotional energy. ***—piṅgaḷā:*** Also known as *sūrya* ("sun") *nāḍī,* it is blue in color and flows upward, ending on the right side of the body. This current is masculine in nature and is the channel of intellectual-mental energy. ***—sushumṇā:*** The major nerve current which passes through the spinal column from the *mūlādhāra chakra* at the base to the *sahasrāra* at the crown of the head. It is the channel of *kuṇḍalinī.* Through *yoga,* the *kuṇḍalinī* energy lying dormant in the *mūlādhāra* is awakened and made to rise up this channel through each *chakra* to the *sa-*

hasrāra chakra. See: *chakra, kuṇḍalinī, rāja yoga.*

nāgasvara: नागस्वर "Snake tone." A double-reed woodwind musical instrument about three feet long, similar to an oboe, but more shrill and piercing. Common in South India, played at Hindu *pūjās* and processions with the *tavil,* a large drum.

naively: Lacking critical ability or analytical insight; not subtle or learned. Simple and gullible.

nakshatra: नक्षत्र "Star cluster." Central to astrological determinations, the *nakshatras* are 27 star-clusters, constellations arranged along the ecliptic, or path of the sun. An individual's *nakshatra,* or birth star, is the constellation the moon was aligned with at the time of birth. See: *jyotisha.*

Namaḥ Śivāya: नमः शिवाय "Adoration (homage) to Śiva." The supreme *mantra* of Śaivism, known as the *Pañchākshara,* or "five syllables." *Na* is the Lord's veiling grace; *Ma* is the world; *Śi* is Śiva; *Vā* is His revealing grace; *Ya* is the soul. The syllables also represent the physical body: *Na* the legs, *Ma* the stomach, *Śi* the shoulders, *Vā* the mouth and *Ya* the eyes. Embodying the essence of Śaiva Siddhānta, it is found in the center of the central *Veda* (the *Yajur*). ¶In a second rendering, Na-Ma Śi-Vā-Ya corresponds to *Śiva's* five actions, reflected in the symbolism of Lord Naṭarāja as follows. *Na* represents *saṁhāra,* destruction or dissolution, corresponding to the hand which which holds a blazing flame. *Ma* stands for His concealing grace, *tirodhāna śakti,* symbolized by Lord Naṭarāja's planted foot. *Vā* indicates revealing grace, *anugraha śakti,* by which souls return to Him, reflected in the left front hand in the elephant trunk pose, *gajahasta,* pointing to His left foot, source of revealing grace. *Śi* stands for *sṛishṭi,* creation, and Śiva's back right hand holding the drum. *Ya* stands for Śiva's power of *stithi,* preservation and protection, shown in His hand gesturing *abhaya,* "fear not." ¶Na-Ma Śi-Vā-Ya also stands for the five elements: *Na* as earth; *Ma,* water; *Śi,* fire; *Vā,* air; and *Ya, ākāśa.* See: *mantra, japa.*

namaskāra: नमस्कार "Reverent salutations." Traditional Hindu verbal greeting and *mudrā* where the palms are joined together and held before the heart or raised to the level of the forehead. The *mudrā* is also called *añjali.* It is a devotional gesture made equally before a temple Deity, holy person, friend or momentary acquaintance.

Namo Myoho Renge Kyo: "Glory to the marvelous *Lotus Sūtra.*" A foremost Japanese Nichiren Buddhist *mantra.*

Nandi: नन्दि "The joyful." A white bull with a black tail, the *vāhana,* or mount, of Lord Śiva, symbol of the powerful instinctive force tamed by Him. Nandi is the perfect devotee, the soul of man, kneeling humbly before God Śiva, ever concentrated on Him. The ideal and goal of the Śiva *bhakta* is to behold Śiva in everything.

Nandikeśvara Kāśikā: नन्दिकेश्वरकाशिका The only surviving work of Nandikeśvara (ca 250 BCE). Its 26 verses are the earliest extant exposition of advaitic Śaivism, aside from the *Śaiva Āgamas.*

Nandinātha: नन्दिनाथ A synonym of *Nandikeśvara.* See: *Kailāsa Paramparā.*

Nandinātha Sampradāya: नन्दिनाथसंप्रदाय See: *Nātha Sampradāya.*

Naraka: नरक Abode of darkness. Literally, "pertaining to man." The nether worlds. Equivalent to the Western term *hell,* a gross region of the Antarloka. Naraka is a congested, distressful area where demonic beings and young souls may sojourn until they resolve the darksome *karmas* they have created. Here beings suffer the consequences of their own misdeeds in previous lives. *Naraka* is understood as having seven regions, called *tala,* corresponding to the states of consciousness of the seven lower *chakras.* They are described as places of torment, pain, darkness, confusion and disease, but none are the places where souls reside forever. Hinduism has no such concept as eternal hell. See: *asura, hell, loka* (also, *individual tala entries).*

Nārāyaṇakaṇṭha: नारायणकण्ठ Great exponent of Śaiva Siddhānta (ca 1050).

Naṭarāja: नटराज "King of Dance," or "King of Dancers." God as the Cosmic Dancer. Perhaps Hinduism's richest and most eloquent symbol, Naṭarāja represents Śiva, the Primal Soul, Parameśvara, as the power, energy and life of all that exists. This is Śiva's intricate state of Being in Manifestation. The dance of Śiva as Naṭeśa, Lord of Dancers, is the rhythmic movement of the entire cosmos. All that is, whether sentient or insentient, pulsates in His body, and He within it. Both male and female elements are depicted in this icon—as also shown in Ardhanārīśvara, the "half-female God," symbol of the inseparable nature of Śiva-Śakti. See: *Parāśakti Parameśvara, Parāśakti, Paraśiva, Sadāśiva.*

Natchintanai: நற்சிந்தனை The collected songs of Sage Yogaswāmī (1872–1964) of Jaffna, Sri Lanka, extolling the power of the *satguru,* worship of Lord Śiva, the path of *dharma* and the attainment of Self Realization. See: *Kailāsa Paramparā.*

Nātha: नाथ "Master, lord; adept." Names an ancient Himalayan tradition of Śaiva-yoga mysticism, whose first historically known exponent was Nandikeśvara (ca 250 BCE). *Nātha*—Self-Realized adept—designates the extraordinary ascetic masters of this school. Through their practice of *siddha yoga* they have attained tremendous powers, *siddhis,* and are sometimes called *siddha yogīs* (accomplished or fully enlightened ones). The words of such beings naturally penetrate deeply into the psyche of their devotees, causing mystical awakenings. Like all *tantrics,* Nāthas have refused to recognize caste distinctions in spiritual pursuits. Their *satgurus* initiate from the lowest to the highest, according to spiritual worthiness. *Nātha* also refers to any follower of the Nātha tradition. The *Nāthas* are considered the source of *haṭha* as well as *rāja yoga.* See: *Kailāsa Paramparā, Nātha Sampradāya, siddha yoga.*

Nātha Sampradāya: नाथसंप्रदाय "Traditional doctrine of the masters." *Sampradāya* means a living stream of tradition or theology. Nātha

Sampradāya is a philosophical and *yogic* tradition of Śaivism whose origins are unknown. This oldest of Śaivite *sampradāyas* existing today consists of two major streams: the Nandinātha and the Ādinātha. The Nandinātha Sampradāya has had as exponents Mahāṛishi Nandinātha and his disciples: Patañjali (author of the *Yoga Sūtras)* and Tirumūlar (author of *Tirumantiram).* Among its representatives today are the successive *siddhars* of the Kailāsa Paramparā. The Ādinātha lineage's known exponents are Mahāṛishi Ādinātha, Matsyendranātha and Gorakshanātha, who founded a well-known order of *yogīs.* See: *Kailāsa Paramparā, Nātha, Śaivism, sampradāya.*

Nayanar: நாயனார் "Teacher." The honorific title of the 63 canonized Tamil saints of South India, as documented in the *Periyapurāṇam* by Sekkilar (ca 1140). All but a few were householders, recognized as outstanding exemplars of devotion to Lord Śiva. Several contributed to the Śaiva Siddhānta scriptural compendium called *Tirumurai.*

near-death: Drawing very near the point of death, without actually dying.

negative attachment: A fear, worry or doubt about the future or a lingering regret about the past that keeps one from "flowing with the river of life," living fully in the moment as an independent, spiritual being, facing each experience in the light of understanding.

nekashum: (Shum) Withdrawing all the physical/astral energies into the spinal current. Pronounced *nee-kaw-shoom.* See: *Shum.*

neri: நெறி "Path."

nerves: Cordlike bundles of fibers made up of neurons through which impulses pass between the brain, central nervous system and other parts of the body. Here also names the fibrous network of inner bodies.

nervous system: The system of the brain, spinal cord, nerves, ganglia and parts of the receptor and effector organs that regulates the body's responses to internal and external stimuli.

neuroses: A mental or emotional disorder with symptoms such as insecurity, anxiety, depression and irrational fears.

neutralize: To counteract and affect or make useless; to balance.

neutron star: A star which has collapsed in on itself and is extremely dense. A neutron star the size of an orange would weigh more than the Earth.

nightingale: A European songbird vocal at night.

nightmare: A dream arousing feelings of intense fear, horror and distress.

nimbus: A radiant light surrounding a person or thing; an aura.

Nirguṇa Brahman: निर्गुणब्रह्मन् "God without qualities." See: *Brahman.*

nirvāṇa: निर्वाण "Extinction." In Buddhism it is the indescribable ultimate attainment or disinterested wisdom and compassion. In Hinduism it is the emancipation from ignorance and the end of all attachment. Also an ideal condition of rest, harmony, stability, or joy.

nirvāṇī* and *upadeśī: निर्वाणी उपदेशी *Nirvāṇī* means "extinguished one," and *upadeśī* means "teacher." In general, *nirvāṇi* refers to a liberated soul, or to a certain class of monk. *Upadeśī* refers to a teacher, generally a renunciate. In *Dancing with Śiva,* these two terms have special meaning, similar to the Buddhist *arhat* and *bodhisattva,* naming the two earthly modes of the realized, liberated soul. After full illumination, the *jīvanmukta* has the choice to return to the world to help others along the path. This is the way of the *upadeśī* (akin to *bodhisattva),* exemplified by the benevolent *satguru* who leads seekers to the goal of God Realization. He may found and direct institutions and monastic lineages. The *nirvāṇī* (akin to *arhat)* abides at the pinnacle of consciousness, shunning all worldly involvement. He is typified by the silent ascetic, the reclusive sage. See: *satguru, viśvagrāsa.*

nirvikalpa samādhi: निर्विकल्पसमाधि "Undifferentiated trance, enstasy *(samādhi)* without form or seed." The realization of the Self, Paraśiva, a state of oneness beyond all change or diversity; beyond time, form and space. The prefix *vi-* connotes "change, differentiation." *Kalpa* means "order, arrangement; a period of time." Thus *vikalpa* means "diversity, thought; difference of perception, distinction." *Nir* means "without." See: *enstasy, rāja yoga, samādhi, Self Realization.*

niyama: नियम "Restraint." See: *yama-niyama.*

nondualism: "Not two." Refers to monistic philosophy. See: *advaita, monism, monistic theism, Vedānta.*

nonsectarian: Not limited to or associated with a particular religious denomination.

nook: A hidden or secluded spot. Here it refers to areas of the mind.

nostalgia: A longing for past events, people or things; homesickness.

nuances: Subtle or slight degrees of difference, as in meaning, feeling, or tone. In this text, refers to shades of the mind and thought.

nucleus: A central part with other parts grouped around it; a core.

nullify: To make invalid or useless.

numerology: The study of the hidden meanings of numbers and how they influence human life.

oblation: An offering or sacrifice ceremoniously given to a God or *guru.* See: *yajña.*

oblige: To constrain, make indebted or grateful.

obscuration: Same as obscuring grace. See: *grace, Naṭarāja.*

obscure: Dark, hidden; not noticed or seen. Not clearly understood or explained; vague.

obscuring grace: See: *grace, Naṭarāja.*

observation: The act of being aware, recording or noting things.

obstinate: Overly determined to have one's own way. Stubborn.

obstruction: An obstacle; something that prevents a desired result.

occult: Hidden, or kept secret; revealed only after initiation. See: *mysticism.*

occultism: The study of, and attempted control over, the supernatural.

odic force: Spiritually magnetic—of or pertaining to consciousness within *aśuddha māyā,* the realm of the physical and lower astral planes. Odic force in its rareified state is *prakṛiti,* the primary gross energy of nature, manifesting in the three *guṇas: sattva, rajas* and *tamas.* All matter, earth, air, fire and water, as well as thought, are odic force. It is the force of attraction and repulsion between people, people and their things, and manifests as masculine (aggressive) and feminine (passive), arising from the *piṅgalā* and *iḍā* currents. These two currents *(nāḍī)* are found within the spine of the subtle body. Odic force is a magnetic, sticky, binding substance that people seek to develop when they want to bind themselves together, such as in partnerships, marriage, *guru-śishya* relationships and friendships. It, of itself, is stagnant and unflowing. Odic energy is the combined emanation of the *prāṇamaya* and *annamaya kośas.* See: *actinic, kośa, subtle body, tattva.*

odic prāṇa: Physical vitality. During the process of making the mind return to an object or subject of concentration, odic as well as actinic *prāṇa* is forced through the subtle nerve currents, causing them to grow strong so that concentration becomes effortless as the subconscious responds to the conscious-mind concentration efforts, causing a new process called meditation to occur. See: *actinic force, actinic prāṇa, odic force, willpower.*

officiate: Performing duties and responsibilities of an officer or priest.

offset: Made up for, compensated for, counterbalanced by.

offshoot: Something that branches out or derives its existence or origin from a particular source.

ojas: ओजस् "Vigor, force, strength, vitality." In *āyurveda,* the underlying life-sap or fluid-essence of the *dhatus,* the seven tissue systems of the body—plasma, blood, muscle, fat, bone, nerves and reproductive tissue. *Ojas* pervades every part of the body and underlies all physical capacities. It is not a physical substance, but exists on a subtle level. *Ojas* is depleted by excessive sex, drugs, talking, loud music, emotional burnout and insufficient rest. Signs of diminished *ojas* are fear, worry, sensory organ pain, poor complexion, cheerlessness, harshness, emaciation, immune system disorders and easily contracting of diseases (all the symptoms of the modern disease AIDS). Conservation of the vital sexual fluids increases the store of *ojas,* strengthens the immune system and enhances health and the quality of one's consciousness. *Ojas* is depleted at the time of ejaculation in men, and during orgasm and menstruation in women. After 30 days of complete sexual abstinence, sperm is transmuted into *ojas.* This abundance of *ojas* rises to the brain and becomes centered in the head *chakras,* where it is expressed as spiritual and intellectual power. Such an individual develops a radiance, called *tejas.* In the realized being, the energy of *ojas* is transmuted to Absolute Consciousness as *kuṇḍalinī śakti.* See: *āyurveda, lymph, tejas, transmutation, yoni.*

old soul: One who has reincarnated many times, experienced much and is therefore further along the path. Old souls may be recognized by their qualities of compassion, self-effacement and wisdom. See: *evolution of the soul, soul.*

Om: ओम् "Yes, verily." The most sacred *mantra* of Hinduism. An alternate transliteration of *Aum* (the sounds A and U blend to become O). See: *Aum.*

omen: A sign that predicts good or evil.

ominous: Foreboding; frightening, sinister.

omnipotent: All-powerful. Able to do anything.

omnipresent: Present everywhere and in all things.

omniscient: Possessing infinite knowledge, all-knowing.

oneness: Quality or state of being one. Unity, identity, especially in spite of appearances to the contrary—e.g., the oneness of soul and God. See: *monism.*

onerous: Burdensome; weighing heavily.

opalescent (opaline): Exhibiting the appearance like that of an opal; having rainbow-like colors.)

opinionated knowledge: A faculty of memory stored in the memory gridwork of the subconscious mind which provides a platform for the intellect, developing an ego. Knowledge gained through the study, hearing and quoting of opinions of others. Looking at the world through the eyes of others. See: *ego, intellect, subconscious mind.*

ordain (ordination): To confer the duties and responsibilities, authority and spiritual power of a religious office, such as priest, minister or *satguru,* through religious ceremony or mystical initiation. See: *dīkshā.*

orthodox: "Of right (correct) opinion." Conforming to established doctrines or beliefs. Opposite of *heterodox,* "different opinion."

overt: Open and observable to anyone; not covert, unconcealed.

overtone: *Harmonic.* A tone in the harmonic series of overtones produced by a fundamental tone.

pāda: पाद् "The foot" (of men and animals); quarter-part, section; stage; path. Names the major sections of the Āgamic texts and the corresponding stages of practice and unfoldment on the path to *moksha.* According to Śaiva Siddhānta, there are four *pādas,* which are successive and cumulative; i.e. in accomplishing each one the soul prepares itself for the next. (In Tamil, Śaiva Siddhānta is also known as *Nalu-pāda,* "four-stage," *Śaivam*). ***—charyā pāda*** (or ***mārga):*** "Good conduct stage." The first stage where one learns to live righteously, serve selflessly, performing *karma yoga.* It is also known as *dāsa mārga,* "servitor's path," a time when the aspirant relates to God as a servant to a master. Traditional acts of *charyā* include cleaning the temple, lighting lamps and collecting flowers for worship. Worship at this stage is mostly external. ***—kriyā pāda*** (or ***mārga):*** "Religious action; worship stage." Stage of *bhakti yoga,* of cultivating devotion through performing *pūjā* and regular daily *sādhana.* It is also known as the *satputra mārga,* "true son's way," as the soul now relates to God as a son to his father. A central practice of the *kriyā pāda* is performing daily *pūjā.* ***—yoga pāda*** (or ***mārga):*** Having matured in the *charyā* and *kriyā pādas,* the soul now turns to internalized worship and *rāja yoga* under the guidance of a *satguru.* It is a time of *sādhana* and serious striving when realization of the Self is the goal. It is the *sakhā mārga,* "way of the friend," for now God is looked upon as an intimate friend. ***—jñāna pāda*** (or ***mārga):*** "Stage of wisdom." Once the soul has attained Realization, it is henceforth a wise one, who lives out the life of the body, shedding blessings on mankind. This stage is also called the San Mārga, "true path," on which God is our dearest beloved. The *Tirumantiram* describes the fulfillment of each stage as follows. In *charyā,* the soul forges a kindred tie in "God's world" *(sālokya).* In *kriyā* it attains "nearness" *(sāmīpya)* to Him. In *yoga* it attains "likeness" *(sārūpya)* with Him. In *jñāna* the soul enjoys the ultimate bliss of identity *(sāyujya)* with Śiva. See: *jñāna, nirvāṇī and upadeśī.*

paddhati: **पद्धति** "Foot-path; track; guideline." The name of a class of expository writings, e.g., Gorakshanātha's *Siddha Siddhānta Paddhati,* and the many *paddhatis* that are guidebooks for ritual temple rites. There are *paddhatis* for the *Vedas* and for the *Āgamas.*

padma: **पद्म** The lotus flower, *Nelumbo nucifera,* symbol of spiritual development and the *chakras.* Because it grows out of mud and rises to perfect purity and glory, it is an apt representation of spiritual unfoldment.

padmāsana: **पद्मासन** "Lotus posture." The most famous *haṭha yoga āsana,* the optimum pose for sustained meditation. The legs are crossed, the soles of the feet upward, resembling a lotus flower. In this pose the intellectual-emotional energies are balanced and quieted. See: *lotus pose, rāja yoga, yoga.*

pale: To decrease in importance. Low intensity variation of a color, whitish.

Pali: Ancient Indian language; a scriptural medium of Hinayāna Buddhism.

palmist: One who analyzes a person's character and predict his future by interpreting the lines of the palm of his hand.

panacea: A supposed single remedy for all diseases or discomforts; cure-all.

pañcha nitya karma(s): **पञ्चनित्यकर्म** "Five constant duties." A traditional regimen of religious practice for Hindus: 1) *dharma* (virtuous living), 2) *upāsanā* (worship), 3) *utsava* (holy days), 4) *tīrthayātrā* (pilgrimage) and 5) *saṁskāras* (sacraments.) See: *dharma, saṁskāra, tīrthayātrā.*

Pañchākshara Mantra: **पञ्चाक्षरमन्त्र** "Five-lettered chant." Śaivism's most sacred *mantra.* See: *Namaḥ Śivāya.*

pañchāṅga: **पञ्चांग** "Five limbs, or parts." (Tamil: *pañchāṅgam*) The name of the traditional Hindu almanac, so named because of its five basic elements—*tithi, nakshatra, kāraṇa, yoga* and *vara* (or *vasara).* It provides information about unseen astrological factors, which influence the subtle environment. *Pañchāṅgams* are used to determine the optimum times for all activities.

pandit (paṇḍita): पण्डित A Hindu religious scholar or theologian, a man well versed in philosophy, liturgy, religious law and sacred science.

Pāṇini: पाणिनि Author of the *Ashṭādhyāyī*, systematizing Sanskṛit grammar in 4,000 rules. (Dating uncertain: 4th century BCE, or later according to Western scholars.)

panorama: An unbroken view of the whole of a surrounding area.

pantheon: All the Gods of a religion together.

pāpa: पाप "Wickedness; sin, crime." 1) Bad or evil. 2) Wrongful action. 3) Demerit earned through wrongdoing. Pāpa includes all forms of wrongdoing, from the simplest infraction to the most heinous crime, such as premeditated murder. Each act of *pāpa* carries its karmic consequence, *karmaphala,* "fruit of action," for which scriptures delineate specific penance for expiation. *Pāpa* is the opposite of *puṇya* (merit, virtue). See: *aura, evil, karma, penance, puṇya, sin.*

paper dragon: An artificially apparent but unreal threat or problem.

para: पर "Supreme; beyond." As a first member in compounds this preposition denotes the highest dimension of whatever it precedes—as in *Paraśiva* or *Parabrahman.* (Sometimes *parā,* as in Parāśakti.)

paradox: "Contrary to opinion," belief or expectation. An apparent contradiction according to conventional logic and reason.

Param: பரம் "The Supreme," i.e., God, in Tamil.

paramaguru: परमगुरु "Senior (superior) preceptor." The *guru* of a disciple's *guru.*

Paramātman: परमात्मन् "Supreme Self," or "transcendent soul." Paraśiva, Absolute Reality, the one transcendent Self of every soul. Contrasted with *ātman,* which includes all three aspects of the soul: *Paraśiva, Parāśakti* and *ānandamaya kośa.* See: *ātman, kośa, soul.*

Parameśvara: परमेश्वर "Supreme Lord or Ruler." God Śiva in the third perfection as Supreme Mahādeva, Śiva-Śakti, mother of the universe. In this perfection as Personal, father-mother God, Śiva is a person—who has a body, with head, arms and legs, etc.—who acts, wills, blesses, gives *darśana,* guides, creates, preserves, reabsorbs, obscures and enlightens. In Truth, it is Śiva-Śakti who does all. The term *Primal Soul,* Paramapurusha, designates Parameśvara as the original, uncreated soul, the creator of all other souls. Parameśvara has many other names and epithets, including those denoting the five divine actions—Sadāśiva, the revealer; Maheśvara, the obscurer; Brahmā, the creator; Vishṇu the preserver; and Rudra the destroyer. See: *Naṭarāja, Sadāśiva.*

paramount: Most important, highest.

paramparā: परंपरा "Uninterrupted succession." A lineage. See: *guru param-*

parā.

paranāda: परनाद "Beyond sound, tone or vibration." Metaphysically, the highest mystic sounds of the Eternal, the transcendent or Soundless Sound, the first vibration from which creation emanates. From Paranāda comes Praṇava, Aum, and further evolutes of *nāda.* See: *Aum, nāda.*

paranoiac: Having extreme fear or distrust of others.

Paraparam: பராபரம் "The Ultimate; Beyond the beyond."

Parāśakti: पराशक्ति "Supreme power; primal energy." God Śiva's second perfection, which is impersonal, immanent, and with form—the all-pervasive, Pure Consciousness and Primal Substance of all that exists. There are many other descriptive names for Parāśakti—Satchidānanda ("existence-consciousness-bliss"), light, silence, divine mind, superconsciousness and more. Parāśakti can be experienced by the diligent *yogī* or meditator as a merging in, or identification with, the underlying oneness flowing through all form. The experience is called *savikalpa samādhi.* See: *rāja yoga, Śakti, Satchidānanda, tattva.*

Paraśiva: परशिव "Transcendent Śiva." The Self God, Śiva in His first perfection, Absolute Reality. God Śiva as *That* which is beyond the grasp of consciousness, transcends time, form and space and defies description. To merge with Him in mystic union is the goal of all incarnated souls, the reason for their living on this planet, and the deepest meaning of their experiences. Attainment of this is called Self Realization or *nirvikalpa samādhi.* See: *samādhi, Śiva.*

pareschatology: Study of the details of the life between births.

pāśa: पाश "Tether; noose." (Tamil: *pāśam*) The whole of existence, manifest and unmanifest. That which binds or limits the soul and keeps it (for a time) from manifesting its full potential. *Pāśa* consists of the soul's threefold bondage of *āṇava, karma* and *māyā.* See: *liberation, mala, Pati-paśu-pāśa.*

pāśa-jñānam: பாசஞானம் "Knowledge of the world." That which is sought for by the soul in the first stage of the *sakala avasthai,* known as *irul.* See: *irul, sakala avasthā.*

passeth: Old English for *surpasses.*

passion: A powerful emotion, including strong sexual desire, or lust.

passive: Submitting to circumstances without objection or resistance.

paśu: पशु "Cow, cattle, kine; fettered individual." Refers to animals or beasts, including man. In philosophy, the soul. Śiva as Lord of Creatures is called Paśupati. See: *pāśa, Pati-paśu-pāśa.*

paśu-jñānam: பசுஞானம் "Soul-knowledge." The object of seeking in the second stage of the *sakala avasthai,* called *marul.* See: *marul, sakala avasthā.*

Pāśupata Śaivism: पाशुपतशैव Monistic and theistic, this school of Śaivism reveres Śiva as Supreme Cause and Personal Ruler of soul and world, denoted in His form as Paśupati, "Lord of Souls." This school centers around the ascetic path, emphasizing *sādhana,* detachment from the world and the quest for "internal *kuṇḍalinī* grace." The *Kāravaṇa Māhātmya* recounts the birth of Lakulīśa (ca 200 CE), a principal Pāśupata *guru,* and refers to the temple of Somanātha as one of the most important Pāśupata centers. Lakulīśa propounded a Śaiva monism, though indications are that Pāśupata philosophy was previously dualistic, with Śiva as efficient cause of the universe but not material cause. It is thought to be the source of various ascetic streams, including the Kāpālikas and the Kālāmukhas. This school is represented today in the broad *sādhu* tradition, and numerous Pāśupata sites of worship are scattered across India. See: *Śaivism.*

pātāla: पाताल "Fallen" or "sinful region." The seventh *chakra* below the *mūlādhāra,* centered in the soles of the feet. Corresponds to the seventh and lowest astral netherworld beneath the earth's surface, called Kākola ("black poison") or Pātāla. This is the realm in which misguided souls indulge in destruction for the sake of destruction, of torture, and of murder for the sake of murder. *Pātāla* also names the netherworld in general, and is a synonym for *Naraka.* See: *chakra, loka, Naraka.*

Patañjali: पतञ्जलि A Śaivite Nātha *siddha* (ca 200 BCE) who codified the ancient *yoga* philosophy which outlines the path to enlightenment through purification, control and transcendence of the mind. One of the six classical philosophical systems *(darśanas)* of Hinduism, known as Yoga Darśana. His great work, the *Yoga Sūtras,* comprises some 200 aphorisms delineating *ashṭāṅga* (eight-limbed), *rāja* (kingly) or *siddha* (perfection) *yoga.* Still today it is the foremost text on meditative *yoga.* Different from the namesake grammarian. See: *rāja yoga, yoga.*

Pati: पति "Master; lord; owner." An appellation of God Śiva indicating His commanding relationship with souls as caring ruler and helpful guide. In Śaiva Siddhānta the title is part of the analogy of cowherd *(pati),* cows *(paśu,* souls) and the tether *(pāśa—āṇava, karma* and *māyā)* by which cows are tied. See: *Pati-paśu-pāśa, Śiva.*

Pati-jñānam: பதிஞானம் "Knowledge of God," sought for by the soul in the third stage of the *sakala avasthai,* called *arul.* See: *arul, sakala avasthā, śaktinipāta.*

Pati-paśu-pāśa: पति पशु पाश Literally: "Master, cow and tether." These are the three primary elements *(padārtha,* or *tattvatrayī)* of Śaiva Siddhānta philosophy: God, soul and world—Divinity, man and cosmos—seen as a mystically and intricately interrelated unity. Pati is God, envisioned as a cowherd. *Paśu* is the soul, envisioned as a cow. *Pāśa* is the all-important force or fetter by which God brings souls along the path to Truth. The various schools of Hinduism define the rapport among the three in varying ways. For pluralistic Śaiva Siddhāntins they are three beginningless verities, self-existent, eternal entities. For monistic Śaiva Siddhāntins, *paśu* and *pāśa* are the emanational creation of Pati, Lord Śiva, and He alone is eternal reality. See: *pāśa, Śaiva Siddhānta, soul.*

pelvic: In the area of the pelvis, or hips.

penance: *Prāyaśchitta.* Atonement, expiation. An act of devotion *(bhakti),* austerity *(tapas)* or discipline *(sukṛitya)* undertaken to soften or nullify the anticipated reaction to a past action. Penance is uncomfortable *karma* inflicted upon oneself to mitigate one's *karmic* burden caused by wrongful actions *(kukarma).* It includes such acts as prostrating 108 times, fasting, self-denial, or carrying *kavadi (public penance),* as well as more extreme austerities, or *tapas.* Penance is often suggested by spiritual leaders and elders. See: *evil, prāyaśchitta, sin, tapas.*

pendulum: A suspended object that swings back and forth.

penicillin: A widely used antibiotic drug used to fight infection.

penthouse: A snug top floor office or apartment.

perennial: Lasting from year to year.

perfections: Qualities, aspects, nature or dimensions that are perfect. God Śiva's three perfections are Paraśiva (Absolute Reality), Parāśakti (Pure Consciousness) and Parameśvara (Primal Soul). Though spoken of as three-fold for the sake of understanding, God Śiva ever remains a one transcendent-immanent Being. See: *Parameśvara, Parāśakti, Paraśiva, Śiva.*

perfectionist: A person who does everything to a very high standard.

permeate: Pervade, penetrate throughout.

perpetuate: To prolong the existence of.

perplex: To confuse or puzzle.

perseverance: Steady adherance to a specific course of action.

personae: Masks or different personalities or attributes.

personality: The pattern of collective character, behavioral, temperamental, emotional, and mental traits of a person.

personification: Something that is an example of a certain quality or idea.

pervade: To permeate or be present throughout.

pessimism: The tendency to stress the negative.

Pharaoh: A king of ancient Egypt.

pharyngeal: Located near the throat.

phenomenon: Any fact, circumstance or experience. Especially an unusual occurrence, a marvel. Plural: phenomena.

phonograph: A machine that reproduces sound by means of a pin in contact with a grooved spinning disk, called a phonograph record.

phosphorescent: Emitting of light without burning, or burning slowly, giving off negligible heat.

physique: The build and appearance of the physical body.

pictorial: Composed of or represented by pictures.

pilgrimage: *Tīrthayātrā,* one of the five sacred duties *(pañcha nitya karmas)* of the Hindu is to journey periodically to one of the innumerable holy spots in India or other countries. Preceded by fasting and continence, it is a time of austerity and purification, when all worldly concerns are set aside and God becomes one's singular focus. Streams of devout pilgrims are received daily at the many ancient holy sites *(tīrthas)* in India, and tens of thousands at festival times. See: *pañcha nitya karma.*

pineal gland: A small gland located at the roof of the thalamic region of the brain, scientifically little understood but related to sexual maturation and sleep cycles. Of considerable importance esoterically as the reception point for external psychic contacts, consciousness expansion and as the terminal of the awakened kundalini flame. Masculine, or *iḍā,* in nature.

piṅgalā: पिंगला "Tawny channel." The masculine psychic current flowing along the spine. See: *kuṇḍalinī, nāḍī, rāja yoga.*

pinnacle: The culminating or highest point; apex.

pitta: पित्त "Bile; fire." One of the three bodily humors, called *doshas, pitta* is known as the fire humor. It is the *āyurvedic* principle of bodily heat-energy. *Pitta dosha* governs nutritional absorption, body temperature and intelligence. See: *āyurveda, dosha.*

pituitary gland: Small gland in the brain at the ventral surface of the hypothalamus regulating major life functions including growth, sexual activity, metabolism and coordinating endocrine secretions of other glands. Esoterically, the gland is feminine, *piṅgalā,* in nature, and the storehouse of spiritual forces associated with the *ājñā chakra.* See: *chakra, piṅgalā.*

placenta: An organ that develops in female mammals during pregnancy, for the nourishment of the fetus.

plasma: The clear, fluid portion of blood, lymph, or intramuscular fluid in which cells are suspended. An electrically neutral, highly ionized gas composed of ions, electrons, and neutral particles. It is a phase of matter distinct from solids, liquids, and normal gases.

plateau: A stable level, period or state.

plausible: Seemingly valid, likely or acceptable; possible.

Pleiades: A cluster of stars in the Taurus constellation, six of which are now visible from Earth. This group of stars is known in Sanskṛit as Kṛittikā, an important *nakshatra* for Lord Kārttikeya and believed to be this Deity's place of origin before He came to the star system of Earth. See: *Kārttikeya.*

plexus: A structure consisting of interwoven parts; a network. Especially of nerves, blood vessels, or lymphatic nodes.

plummet: To fall, drop, plunge abruptly.

pluralism (pluralistic): Doctrine that holds existence to be composed of three or more distinct and irreducible components, such as God, souls and world. See: *dvaita-advaita.*

pluralistic realism: A term for pluralism used by various schools including Meykandar Śaiva Siddhānta, emphasizing that the components of existence are absolutely real in themselves and not creations of consciousness or God.

point blank: Straightforward; blunt.

polarize: To turn, grow, think, feel in a certain way as a result of attraction or repulsion. Here: to consciously align individual spiritual forces with the higher cosmic forces, also to attract and sustain the presence of divine beings.

pornography: Writings, pictures, etc., intended to excite sexual sensations.

postulate: An assumption of a basic principle. To claim, demand or assume as self-evident.

prabhāmaṇḍala: प्रभामण्डल "Luminous circle," or *dīptachakra.* The ring of fire in which Śiva dances is the hall of consciousness, *chitsabhā;* in other words, the light-filled heart of man, the central chamber of the manifest cosmos. Also another name for the human aura.

practitioner: One who practices something.

pragmatic: Practical. Concerned with application, not theory or speculation.

prakṛiti: प्रकृति "Primary matter; nature." See: *odic, purusha, tattva.*

prāṇa: प्राण Vital energy or life principle. Literally, "vital air," from the root *praṇ,* "to breathe." The interrelated odic and actinic forces. The sum total of all energy and forces. *Prāṇa* in the human body moves in the *prāṇamaya kośa* as five primary life currents known as *vāyus,* "vital airs or winds." These are *prāṇa* (outgoing breath), *apāṇa* (incoming breath), *vyāṇa* (retained breath), *udāṇa* (ascending breath) and *samāṇa* (equalizing breath). Each governs crucial bodily functions, and all bodily energies are modifications of these. Usually *prāṇa* refers to the life principle, but sometimes denotes energy, power or the animating force of the cosmos. See: *apāṇam, kośa, tattva.*

prāṇa-aura: The phase of the human aura, *prabhāmaṇḍala,* closely bound to the physical body, comprised of the radiation of physical and mental life force from a living thing. Visible to the human eye yet colorless, its form and density indicate health and vitality. Energy from the *prāṇa-aura* is left behind for some time after the departure of a living being from one place to another, and is connected with certain physical emissions such as scent, etc. See: *aura, prāṇa.*

prāṇamaya kośa: प्राणमयकोश "Life-energy sheath." See: *kośa, prāṇa.*

prāṇāyāma: प्राणायाम "Breath control." See: *rāja yoga.*

prāṇic body: The subtle, life-giving sheath called *prāṇamaya kośa.* See: *kośa.*

***prāṇic* sheath:** See: *prāṇamaya kośa.*

praṇipāta: प्रणिपात "Falling down in obeisance." Prostration before God, Gods and *guru,* full body, face down, arms and hands outstretched. See: *prostration.*

prapatti: प्रपत्ति "Throwing oneself down." *Bhakti*—total, unconditional submission to God, often coupled with the attitude of personal helplessness, self-effacement and resignation. See: *bhakti, grace, pāda.*

prārabdha karma: प्रारब्धकर्म "Action that has been unleashed or aroused." See: *karma.*

prasāda: प्रसाद "Clarity, brightness; grace." 1) The virtue of serenity and graciousness. 2) Food offered to the Deity or the *guru,* or the blessed remnants of such food. 3) Any propitiatory offering. See: *sacrament, Vīra Śaivism.*

prate: To talk idly or to little purpose.

prattle: To talk or chatter idly or meaninglessly.

Pratyabhijñā: प्रत्यभिज्ञा "Recognition or recollection," from "knowledge" *(jñāna)* which "faces" *(abhi)* the knower and toward which he eventually "turns" *(prati).* A concept of Kashmīr Śaivism which denotes the devotee's recognition, as a result of the *guru's* grace, of the Truth that ever was—that Śiva is indeed everywhere, and the soul is already united with Him.

pratyāhāra: प्रत्याहार "Withdrawal." The drawing in of forces. In *yoga,* the withdrawal from external consciousness. (Also a synonym for *pralaya.)* See: *rāja yoga, mahāpralaya, meditation.*

prāyaśchitta: प्रायश्चित्त "Predominant thought or aim." Penance. Acts of atonement. See: *penance.*

precarious: Depending on will and power of another. Dangerously lacking in security or stability.

precept: A commandment meant as a rule of action or conduct.

preceptor: Highly respected teacher and head of a spiritual order and clan; the equivalent of the word *satguru.*

precinct: An enclosed or delimited area. Also the grounds surrounding a religious edifice.

precincts: A place or an enclosure marked off by definite limits, such as walls.

precipice: A high cliff. A hazardous situation.

precognition: Clairvoyant knowledge of something before it happens.

prejudice: Irrational suspicion or hatred of a particular group, race, or religion.

premonition: A feeling that something is about to occur.

Pretaloka: प्रेतलोक "World of the departed." The realm of the earth-bound souls. This lower region of Bhuvarloka is an astral duplicate of the physical world. See: *loka.*

Primal Soul: The uncreated, original, perfect soul—Śiva Parameśvara—who emanates from Himself the inner and outer universes and an infinite plurality of individual souls whose essence is identical with His essence. God in His personal aspect as Lord and Creator, depicted in many forms: Naṭarāja by Śaivites, Vishṇu by Vaishṇavites, Devī by Śāktas. See: *Naṭarāja, Parameśvara.*

Primal Substance: The fundamental energy and rarified form from which the manifest world in its infinite diversity is derived. See: *Parāśakti.*

procrastination: Postponing or needless delaying.

procreation: The process of begetting offspring.

prominence: The quality of being noticeable or conspicuous.

prominent: Foremost; obvious.

promiscuity: Engaging in sex indiscriminantly or with many partners.

promulgate: To make something known publicly.
prone: Tending or inclined toward.
prophetic: Fortelling future events.
prostatic: Relating to or near the prostate gland.
prostitute: A person who solicits and accepts payment for sexual acts.
prostrate: Lying face down, as in submission or adoration. See: *praṇipāta.*
prostration: *praṇāma:* प्रणाम "Obeisance; bowing down." Reverent salutation in which the head or body is bowed. ***—ashṭāṅga praṇāma:*** "Eight-limbed obeisance." The full body form for men, in which the hands, chest, forehead, knees and feet touch the ground. (Same as *śashṭāṅga praṇāma.*) — ***pañchāṅga praṇāma:*** "Five-limbed obeisance." The woman's form of prostration, in which the hands, head and legs touch the ground (with the ankles crossed, right over the left). A more exacting term for prostration is *praṇipāta,* "falling down in obeisance." See: *bhakti, namaskāra, prapatti.*
pry: To look into or snoop in an unwanted manner.
psalm: A sacred hymn, song or poem.
psyche: The soul.
psychiatrist: A medical specialist who treats mental and emotional disorders.
psychic: "Of the psyche or soul." Sensitive to spiritual processes and energies. Inwardly or intuitively aware of nonphysical realities; able to use powers such as clairvoyance, clairaudience and precognition. Nonphysical, subtle; pertaining to the deeper aspects of man. See: *mysticism, odic.*
Psychism: See: *ocultism.*
psychoanalyze: To interpret mental and emotional processes as results of unconscious impulses, repressed experiences and conflicts, etc.
psychologist: A person schooled in understanding of mental and emotional processes and behavior and treating disorders according to one or another of the various modern theories of human behavior.
psychological moment: A moment when the mind and emotions are especially open and receptive.
psychology: The intellectual study of mental processes and behavior. The emotional and behavioral characteristics of an individual, or an activity.
psychometry: The ability of one's nervous system or psychic faculty to register and interpret vibrations from objects.
puissant: Powerful; mighty.
pūjā: पूजा "Worship, adoration." An Āgamic rite of worship performed in the home, temple or shrine, to the *mūrti, śrī pādukā,* or other consecrated object, or to a person, such as the *satguru.* Its inner purpose is to purify the atmosphere around the object worshiped, establish a connection with the inner worlds and invoke the presence of God, Gods or one's *guru.* See: *yajña.*
pujārī: पुजारी "Worshiper." A general term for Hindu temple priests, as well as anyone performing *pūjā. Pujārī* (sometimes *pūjārī)* is the Hindi form of the Sanskṛit *pūjaka; pūsārī* in Tamil. *Archaka* is another term for the offi-

ciant priest used in the southern tradition. *Purohita* is a Smārta *brāhmin* priest who specializes in domestic rites. See: *pūjā.*

pungent: Producing a sharp sensation of taste or smell; stimulating.

puṇya: पुण्य "Holy; virtuous; auspicious." 1) Good or righteous. 2) Meritorious action. 3) Merit earned through right thought, word and action. *Puṇya* includes all forms of doing good, from the simplest helpful deed to a lifetime of conscientious beneficence. Each act of *puṇya* carries its *karmic* consequence, *karmaphala,* "fruit of action"—the positive reward of actions, words and deeds that are in keeping with *dharma.* (Opposite of *pāpa.)* See: *aura, karma, pāpa, penance.*

Purāṇa: पुराण "Ancient lore." Hindu folk narratives containing ethical and cosmological teachings relative to Gods, man and the world. They revolve around five subjects: primary creation, secondary creation, genealogy, cycles of time and history. There are 18 major *Purāṇas* designated as Śaiva, Vaishṇava or Śākta.

Purāṇic: Relating to the *Purāṇas.* See: *Purāṇa.*

pure consciousness: See: *Parāśakti, Satchidānanda, tattva.*

purport: The importance or significance of something spoken or written.

purusha: पुरुष "The spirit that dwells in the body/in the universe." Person; spirit; man. Metaphysically, the soul, neither male nor female. Also used in Yoga and Sāṅkhya for the transcendent Self. A synonym for *ātman. Purusha* can also refer to the Supreme Being or Soul, as it sometimes does in the *Upanishads.* See: *karma, penance.*

purusha dharma: पुरुषधर्म "A man's code of duty and conduct." See: *dharma.*

quantum: Quantity or amount. In science's quantum theory: a fixed basic unit, usually of energy. **—quantum particles of light:** Light understood not as a continuum, but as traveling bundles each of a same intensity. Deeper still, these particles originate and resolve themselves in a one divine energy. **—at the quantum level (of the mind):** Deep within the mind, at a subtle energy level. See: *apex of creation, microcosm-macrocosm, tattva.*

quell: To put an end to, subdue or make quiet.

quiescence: The state of being quiet, still or inactive.

quiescent: Remaining quiet, still, or calm; inactive.

radiance: The quality of giving out light or energy.

radiant: Filled with light, bright.

radiate: To send out rays or waves.

rāja yoga: राजयोग "King of *yogas.*" Also known as *ashṭāṅga yoga,* "eight-limbed *yoga.*" The classical *yoga* system of eight progressive stages to Illumination as described in various *yoga Upanishads,* the *Tirumantiram* and, most notably, in the *Yoga Sūtras* of Patañjali. The eight limbs are: 1) ***—yama:*** "Restraint." Virtuous and moral living, which brings purity of mind, freedom from anger, jealousy and subconscious confusion which would inhibit the process of meditation. 2) ***—niyama:*** "Observance." Religious practices which cultivate the qualities of the higher nature, such as devotion, cognition, humility and contentment—inducing the refinement of nature and control of mind needed to concentrate and ultimately plunge into *samādhi.* 3) ***—āsana:*** "Seat" or "posture." A sound body is needed for success in meditation. This is attained through *haṭha yoga,* the postures of which balance the energies of mind and body, promoting health and serenity, e.g., *padmāsana,* the "lotus pose," for meditation. 4) ***—prāṇāyāma:*** "Mastering life force." Breath control, which quiets the *chitta* and balances *iḍā* and *piṅgalā.* Science of controlling *prāṇa* through breathing techniques in which lengths of inhalation, retention and exhalation are modulated. *Prāṇāyāma* prepares the mind for deep meditation. 5) ***—pratyāhāra:*** "Withdrawal." The practice of withdrawing consciousness from the physical senses first, such as not hearing noise while meditating, then progressively receding from emotions, intellect and eventually from individual consciousness itself in order to merge into the Universal. 6) ***—dhāraṇā:*** "Concentration." Focusing the mind on a single object or line of thought, not allowing it to wander. The guiding of the flow of consciousness. When concentration is sustained long and deeply enough, meditation naturally follows. 7) ***—dhyāna:*** "Meditation." A quiet, alert, powerfully concentrated state wherein new knowledge and insight pour into the field of consciousness. This state is possible once the subconscious mind has been cleared or quieted. 8) ***—samādhi:*** "Enstasy," which means "standing within one's self." "Sameness, contemplation." The state of true *yoga,* in which the meditator and the object of meditation are one. See: *āsana, enlightenment, enstasy, samādhi, yoga.*

rajas: रजस् "Passion; activity."

Rāma: राम Venerated hero of the *Rāmāyaṇa* epic, and one of the two most popular incarnations of Vishṇu, along with Kṛishṇa. His worship is almost universal among Vaishṇavas, and extensive among Smārtas and other liberal Hindus. He was a great worshiper of Śiva, and a Śiva temple, called Rāmeśvaram, was built in his name at the southern tip of India.

Rāmakaṇṭha I: रामकण्ठ A great exponent of Śaiva Siddhānta, ca 950. In the lineage of Aghoraśiva.

Rāmakaṇṭha II: रामकण्ठ Great exponent of Śaiva Siddhānta, ca 1150. Aghoraśiva's teacher.

Rāmakṛishṇa: रामकृष्ण (1836–1886) One of the great saints and mystics of modern Hinduism, and a proponent of monistic theism—fervent devotee of Mother Kālī and staunch monist who taught oneness and the pursuit of *nirvikalpa samādhi,* realization of the Absolute. He was *guru* to the great

Swāmī Vivekānanda (1863–1902), who internationalized Hindu thought and philosophy.

Ramana Maharshi: ரமண மகரிஷி (1879-1950) Hindu Advaita renunciate renaissance saint of Tiruvannamalai, South India.

ramifications: All the resulting effects and consequences of something.

ramify: To create more effects and consequences that tend to complicate.

rampant: Unchecked; unrestrained.

rapport: Relationship, especially of trust and understanding.

rapturous: Filled with great joy; ecstatic.

rareified : Made thin or less dense; purified or refined.

rasātala: रसातल "Subterranean region." The fifth *chakra* below the *mūlādhāra,* centered in the ankles. Corresponds to the fifth astral netherworld beneath the earth's surface, called Ṛijīsha ("expelled") or Rasātala. Region of selfishness, self-centeredness and possessiveness. *Rasā* means "earth, soil; moisture." See: *chakra, loka, Naraka.*

ratification: Official or formal approval, giving sanction to.

rationales: Fundamental principles and reasons, especially in the sense of providing a plausible basis for a way of thinking or acting.

rationalize: To devise self-satisfying but often incorrect reasons for one's behavior, way of thinking, reactions, etc.

Raurava Āgama: रौरव आगम Among the 28 *Śaiva Siddhānta Āgamas,* this scripture was conveyed by Lord Śiva to sage Ruru (hence the name). Its extensive *kriyā pāda* section details the structure of the Śiva temple and its annexes.

reabsorption (reabsorb): Taking in again, as is water squeezed from and then drawn back into a sponge. See: *mahāpralaya.*

reaction: A response to an action.

realm: A kingdom, region, area or sphere. See: *loka.*

reams: A very great amount. Originally a certain (large) quantity of paper.

receptacle: A container.

recess: A receding hollow or secluded place.

reckless: Careless, disregarding the consequences of actions.

reconcile: To settle or resolve, as a dispute. To make consistent or compatible, e.g., two conflicting ideas.

reconciliation: Harmonization of quarrels or mending of differences.

recuperate: To return to health or strength; recover.

redolent: Having or giving off fragrance.

re-enact: To enact or perform again.

regimen: A regulated lifestyle system, such as diet, exercise, training, to achieve a beneficial effect.

regress: To go back; return to a previous, usually worse state.

Reiki: A spiritual healing practice of laying on of hands, first popular in Japan.

reincarnate: To take birth in another body, having lived and died before.

reincarnation: "Re-entering the flesh." *Punarjanma;* metempsychosis. The process wherein souls take on a physical body through the birth process. The cycle of reincarnation ends when *karma* has been resolved and the Self God (Paraśiva) has been realized. This condition of release is called *moksha.* Then the soul continues to evolve and mature, but without the need to return to physical existence. See: *evolution of the soul, karma, moksha, saṁsāra, soul.*

relative: Quality or object which is meaningful only in relation to something else. Not absolute.

relative reality: *Māyā.* That which is ever changing and changeable. Describes the nature of manifest existence, indicating that it is not an illusion but is also not Absolute Reality, which is eternal and unchanging. See: *absolute, māyā.*

relegate: To assign to an obscure position or class.

religion: From Latin *religare,* "to bind back." Any system of belief in and worship of superhuman beings or powers and/or of a Supreme Being or Power. Religion is a structured vehicle for soul advancement which often includes theology, scripture, spiritual and moral practices, priesthood and liturgy. See: *Hinduism.*

religionist: A member of a particular religion, or one who is excessively religious.

remnant: Something left over; a surviving trace or vestige.

remorse: Deep, painful regret or guilt over a wrong one has done. Moral anguish. See: *penance.*

remote: Distant, secluded; hidden away or difficult to reach.

renaissance: "Rebirth" or "new birth." A renewal, revival or reawakening.

render: To cause to become.

renunciation: See: *sannyāsa, tyāga.*

repercussion: The often indirect result or consequence of an action.

replenish: To fill up or cause to be full again.

repose: To rest peacefully.

repository: A place where things may be put or stored for safekeeping.

repressions: Experiences, desires or inner conflicts residing in the subconscious mind and hidden from the conscious mind. Suppressed desires.

reprieve: To postpone or cancel.

repulse: To drive away, spurn.

resent (resentment): A feeling of ill-will, indignation or hostility from a sense of having been wronged.

residue: Remainder. That which is left over after a process.

retaliate: To pay back an injury like for like, to get even.

retard: To slow, delay or impede progress.

retroactive: Applying back or operating prior to a particular time.

retrofit: To fit new parts, terms or ideas to a pre-existing system.

retrospect: A looking back on; thinking about the past.
retrospection: The looking back or contemplating on past actions or events.
reverberation: A resounding or repeated result or consequence, like an echo.
revere: To respect with love and devotion.
reverie: A state of abstract musing. Here, an intense and blissful state.
righteous indignation: A standing up for *dharma,* a show of angry displeasure on personal moral or religious principles, accompanied in its lower forms by a vain sense of superiority.
ṛishi: ऋषि "Seer." A term for an enlightened being, emphasizing psychic perception and visionary wisdom. In the Vedic age, *ṛishis* lived in forest or mountain retreats, either alone or with disciples. These *ṛishis* were great souls who were the inspired conveyers of the *Vedas.* Seven outstanding *ṛishis* (the *sapta-ṛishis)* mentioned in the *Ṛig Veda* are said to still guide mankind from the inner worlds.
rite (or ritual): A religious ceremony. See: *sacrament, saṁskāra.*
rites of passage: Sacraments marking crucial stages of life. See: *saṁskāra.*
ritual: A religious ceremony conducted according to some prescribed order.
rival: A competitor, someone coveting same or better accomplishment or position.
roam: To move about constantly far and wide with no permanent destination or plan.
rote: "Learning by rote" is a method of teaching where students memorize statements on a subject, but are not encouraged to do further analysis.
Rudra: रुद्र "Controller of terrific powers;" or "red, shining one." The name of Śiva as the God of dissolution, the universal force of reabsorption. *Rudra-Śiva* is revered both as the "terrifying one" and the "lord of tears," for He wields and controls the terrific powers which may cause lamentation among humans. See: *Naṭarāja, Śiva.*
Rudraśambhu: रुद्रशम्भु Principal *guru* in the Āmardaka order of Śaiva monastics, about 775 in Ujjain, one of Śaivism's holiest cities. The sect served as advisors to the king until Muslim conquest around 1300.
russet: A moderate to strong brown.

śabda kośa: शब्दकोश "Sheath of sounds, or words." Vocabulary; a dictionary or glossary of terms.
sacral: Near the sacrum, a triangular bone made up of five fused vertebrae and forming the bottom section of the pelvis.
sacrament: 1) Holy rite, especially one solemnized in a formal, consecrated manner which is a bonding between the recipient and God, Gods or *guru.* This includes rites of passage *(saṁskāra),* ceremonies sanctifying crucial events or stages of life. 2) *Prasāda.* Sacred substances, grace-filled gifts, blessed in sacred ceremony or by a

holy person. See: *prasāda, saṁskāra.*

sacrifice: *Yajña.* 1) Giving offerings to a Deity as an expression of homage and devotion. 2) Giving up something, often one's own possession, advantage or preference, to serve a higher purpose. The literal meaning of *sacrifice* is "to make sacred," implying an act of worship. It is the most common translation of the term *yajña,* from the verb *yuj,* "to worship." In Hinduism, all of life is a sacrifice—called *jīvayajña,* a giving of oneself—through which comes true spiritual fulfillment. *Tyāga,* the power of detachment, is an essential quality of true sacrifice. See: *tyāga, yajña.*

sacrosanct: Sacred and secure from intrusion.

Sadāśiva: सदाशिव "Ever-auspicious." A name of the Primal Soul, Śiva, a synonym for Parameśvara, which is expressed in the physical being of the *satguru. Sadāśiva* especially denotes the power of revealing grace, *anugraha śakti,* the third *tattva,* after which emerge Śiva's other four divine powers. This five-fold manifestation or expression of God's activity in the cosmos is represented in Hindu *mantras,* literature and art as the five-faced Sadāśivamūrti. See: *Parameśvara, tattva.*

sādhaka: साधक "Accomplished one; a devotee who performs *sādhana.*" A serious aspirant who has undertaken spiritual disciplines, is usually celibate and under the guidance of a *guru.* He wears white and may be under vows, but is not a *sannyāsin.* See: *sādhana.*

sādhana: साधन "Effective means of attainment." Religious or spiritual disciplines, such as *pūjā, yoga,* meditation, *japa,* fasting and austerity. The effect of *sādhana* is the building of willpower, faith and confidence in oneself and in God, Gods and *guru. Sādhana* harnesses and transmutes the instinctive-intellectual nature, allowing progressive spiritual unfoldment into the superconscious realizations and innate abilities of the soul. See: *pāda, rāja yoga, sādhana mārga, spiritual unfoldment.*

sādhana mārga: साधनमार्ग "The way of *sādhana.*" A phrase used by Sage Yogaswāmī to name his prescription for seekers of Truth—a path of intense effort, spiritual discipline and consistent inner transformation, as opposed to theoretical and intellectual learning. See: *mysticism, pāda, sādhana, spiritual unfoldment.*

sādhu: साधु "Virtuous one; straight, unerring." A holy man dedicated to the search for God. A *sādhu* may or may not be a *yogī* or a *sannyāsin,* or be connected in any way with a *guru* or legitimate lineage. *Sādhus* usually have no fixed abode and travel unattached from place to place, often living on alms. The feminine form is *sādhvī.*

Sadyojyoti: सद्योज्योति Sadyojyoti, along with Bṛihaspati of Central India (ca 850), is credited with the systematization of Śaiva Siddhānta in Sanskṛit.

saffron: An orange yellow, traditional color of the Hindu monk, said to originate from the mud of the Gaṅgā discoloring their white robes.

sagacious: Keen-minded, discerning, prudent, wise.

sage: A person respected for his spiritual wisdom and judgement.

Saguṇa Brahman: **सगुणब्रह्मन्** "God with qualities." The Personal Lord. See: *Brahman, Parameśvara.*

sahasra lekhana sādhana: **सहस्रलेखनसाधन** "Thousand-times writing discipline." The spiritual practice of writing a sacred *mantra* 1,008 times.

sahasradala padma: **सहस्रदलपद्म** "Thousand-petaled lotus." Another name for the *sahasrāra*, or crown, *chakra.* See: *sahasrāra chakra, chakra.*

sahasrāra chakra: **सहस्रारचक्र** "Thousand-spoked wheel." The cranial psychic force center. See: *chakra.*

Śaiva: **शैव** Of or relating to Śaivism or its adherents, of whom there are about 400 million in the world today. Same as *Śaivite.* See: *Śaivism.*

Śaiva Āgamas: **शैव आगम** The sectarian revealed scriptures of the *Śaivas.* Strongly theistic, they identify Śiva as the Supreme Lord, immanent and transcendent. They fall in two main divisions: the 64 *Kashmīr Śaiva Āgamas* and the 28 *Śaiva Siddhānta Āgamas.* The latter group are the fundamental sectarian scriptures of Śaiva Siddhānta. The *Śaiva Āgama* scriptures, above all else, are the connecting strand through all the schools of Śaivism. The *Āgamas* themselves express that they are entirely consistent with the teachings of the *Veda,* that they contain the essence of the *Veda,* and must be studied with the same high degree of devotion. See: *Āgama, Vedas.*

Śaiva Dharma: **शैव धर्म** Another name for Śaivism. See: *Śaivism.*

Śaiva Neri: **சைவநெறி** "Śaiva path." Tamil term for Śaivism. See: *Śaivism.*

Śaiva Samayam: **சைவ சமயம** "Śaivite religion." See: *Saivism.*

Śaiva Siddhānta: **शैवसिद्धान्त** "Final conclusions of Śaivism." The most widespread and influential Śaivite school today, predominant especially among the Tamil people in Sri Lanka and South India. It is the formalized theology of the divine revelations contained in the twenty-eight *Śaiva Āgamas.* Other sacred scriptures include the *Tirumantiram* and the voluminous collection of devotional hymns, the *Tirumurai,* and the masterpiece on ethics and statecraft, the *Tirukural.* For Śaiva Siddhāntins, Śiva is the totality of all, understood in three perfections: Parameśvara (the Personal Creator Lord), Parāśakti (the substratum of form) and Paraśiva (Absolute Reality which transcends all). Souls and world are identical in essence with Śiva, yet also differ in that they are evolving. A pluralistic stream arose in the Middle Ages from the teachings of Aghoraśiva and Meykandar. For Aghoraśiva's school (ca 1150) Śiva is not the material cause of the universe, and the soul attains perfect "sameness" with Śiva upon liberation. Meykandar's (ca 1250) pluralistic school denies that souls ever attain perfect sameness or unity with Śiva. See: *Śaivism.*

Śaiva Siddhānta Church: "Church of God Śiva's Revealed Truth," founded in 1949 by Satguru Sivaya Subramuniyaswami.

Śaivism (Śaiva): **शैव** The religion followed by those who worship Śiva as supreme God. Oldest of the four sects of Hinduism. The earliest historical evidence of Śaivism is from the 8,000-year-old Indus Valley civilization in the form of the famous seal of Śiva as Lord Paśupati, seated in a *yogic* pose. There are many schools of Śaivism, six of which are Śaiva Śiddhānta, Pāśupata Śaivism, Kashmīr Śaivism, Vīra Śaivism, Siddha Siddhānta and Śiva Advaita. They are based firmly on the *Vedas* and *Śaiva Āgamas*, and thus have much in common, including the following principal doctrines: 1) the five powers of Śiva—creation, preservation, destruction, revealing and concealing grace; 2) The three categories: Pati, *paśu* and *pāśa* ("God, souls and bonds"); 3) the three bonds: *āṇava, karma* and *māyā;* 4) the three-fold power of Śiva: *icçhā śakti, kriyā śakti* and *jñāna śakti;* 5) the thirty-six *tattvas,* or categories of existence; 6) the need for initiation from a *satguru;* 7) the power of *mantra;* 8) the four *pādas* (stages): *charyā* (selfless service), *kriyā* (devotion), *yoga* (meditation), and *jñāna* (illumination); 9) the belief in the Pañchākshara as the foremost *mantra,* and in *rudrāksha* and *vibhūti* as sacred aids to faith; 10) the beliefs in *satguru* (preceptor), Śivaliṅga (object of worship) and *saṅgama* (company of holy persons). See: *Śaivism.*

Śaivite (Śaiva): शैव Of or relating to Śaivism. See: *Śaivism.*

sakala avasthā: सकल अवस्था "Stage of embodied being." (Tamil: *avasthai.)* In Śaiva Siddhānta, the second of three stages of the soul's evolution, when it is engaged in the world through the senses as it first develops a mental, then emotional and astral body, and finally a physical body, entering the cycles of birth, death and rebirth under the veiling powers of *karma* and *māya.* Progress through *sakala avasthā* is measured in three stages: 1) *irul,* "darkness;" when the impetus is toward *pāśa,* knowledge and experience of the world *(pāśa-jñānam)*; 2) *marul,* "confusion;" caught between the world and God, the soul begins to turn within for knowledge of its own nature *(paśu-jñānam)*; and 3) *arul,* "grace," when the soul seeks to know God (Pati-*jñānam*); and receive His grace. See: *avasthā, evolution of the soul, kevala avasthā, śuddha avasthā.*

Śaṅkara, Ādi: शङ्कर One of Hinduism's most extraordinary monks (788-820) and pre-eminent *guru* of the Smārta Sampradāya. He is noted for his monistic philosophy of Advaita Vedānta and his many scriptural commentaries. See: *Advaita Siddhānta, Vedānta.*

sākshin: साक्षिन् "Ocular witness." Awareness, the witness consciousness of the soul. Known as *nef* in the mystical Nātha language of Shum. See: *awareness, consciousness (individual), chit, Shum, soul.*

Śakti: शक्ति "Power, energy." The active power or manifest energy of Śiva that pervades all of existence. Its most refined aspect is Parāśakti, or Satchidānanda, the pure consciousness and primal substratum of all form. In Śaiva Siddhānta, Śiva is All, and His divine energy, Śakti, is inseparable from Him. Śakti is most easily experienced by devotees as the sublime, bliss-inducing energy that emanates from a holy person or sanctified Hindu temple. See: *kuṇḍalinī, Parāśakti, Śāktism.*

śaktinipāta: शक्तिनिपात "Descent of grace," occuring during the advanced stage of the soul's evolution called *arul,* at the end of the *sakala avasthai. Śaktinipāta* is two-fold: the internal descent is recognized as a tremendous yearning for Śiva; the outer descent of grace is the appearance of a *satguru.* At this stage, the devotee increasingly wants to devote himself to all that is spiritual and holy. Same as *śaktipāta.* See: *arul, grace, sakala avasthā, śaktipāta.*

śaktipāta: शक्तिपात "Descent of grace." *Guru dīkshā,* initiation from the preceptor; particularly the first initiation, which awakens the *kuṇḍalinī* and launches the process of spiritual unfoldment. See: *dīkshā, grace, kuṇḍalinī.*

Śāktism (Śākta): शाक्त "Doctrine of power." The religion followed by those who worship the Supreme as the Divine Mother—Śakti or Devī—in Her many forms, both gentle and fierce. Śāktism is one of the four primary sects of Hinduism. Śāktism's first historical signs are thousands of female statuettes dated ca 5500 BCE recovered at the Mehrgarh village in India. In philosophy and practice, Śāktism greatly resembles Śaivism, both faiths promulgating, for example, the same ultimate goals of *advaitic* union with Śiva and *moksha.* But Śāktas worship Śakti as the Supreme Being exclusively, as the dynamic aspect of Divinity, while Śiva is considered solely transcendent and is not worshiped. There are many forms of Śāktism, with endless varieties of practices which seek to capture divine energy or power for spiritual transformation. See: *Kālī, Śakti, tantric.*

sālokya: सालोक्य "Sharing the world," of God. The first of four progressive attainments of the soul in Śaiva Siddhānta. It comes as the fulfillment of religious duty well performed. See: *attainment.*

samādhi: समाधि From verb-root with prepositional prefixes samādhā "to hold together completely." "Enstasy," which means "standing within one's Self." "Sameness; contemplation; union, wholeness; completion, accomplishment." *Samādhi* is the state of true *yoga,* in which the meditator and the object of meditation are one. *Samādhi* is of two levels. The first is *savikalpa samādhi* ("enstasy with form" or "seed"), identification or oneness with the essence of an object. Its highest form is the realization of the primal substratum or pure consciousness, Satchidānanda. The second is *nirvikalpa samādhi* ("enstasy without form" or "seed"), identification with the Self, in which all modes of consciousness are transcended and Absolute Reality, Paraśiva, beyond time, form and space, is experienced. This brings in its aftermath a complete transformation of consciousness. Note that *samādhi* differs from *samyama.* See: *enstasy, kuṇḍalinī, Paraśiva, rāja yoga, samyama, Satchidānanda, Self Realization, trance.*

samāna: समान "Equalizing breath." One of the body's five somatic currents of vital energy, or *prāṇa.* See: *prāṇa.*

samanā: समना "Uniform; synchronous." The sixth of the seven *chakras,* or *nāḍi* conglomerates, above and within the *sahasrāra chakra.* See: *chakras* *above sahasrāra.*

samayam: சமயம் "Religion."

sāmīpya: सामीप्य "Nearness" to God. The second of four progressive attainments of the soul in Śaiva Siddhānta. It is the fruition of religious worship and surrender. See: *attainment.*

sampradāya: संप्रदाय "Traditional doctrine of knowledge." A living stream of tradition or theology within Hinduism, passed on by oral training and initiation. The term derives from the noun *samprada,* meaning "gift, grant, bestowing or conferring; handing down by tradition; bequeathing." See: *paramparā.*

saṁsāra: संसार "Flow." The phenomenal world. Transmigratory existence, fraught with impermanence and change. The cycle of birth, death and rebirth; the total pattern of successive earthly lives experienced by a soul. A term similar to *punarjanma* (reincarnation), but with broader connotations. See: *evolution of the soul, karma, punarjanma, reincarnation.*

saṁskāra: संस्कार "Impression, activator; sanctification, preparation." 1) The imprints left on the subconscious mind by experience (from this or previous lives), which then color all of life, one's nature, responses, states of mind, etc. 2) A sacrament or rite done to mark a significant transition of life, such as name-giving, first feeding, commencement of learning, coming of age and marriage. See: *mind (five states), sacrament.*

saṁskāra chitta: संस्कारचित्त The subconscious mind, holder of past impressions, reactions and desires. Also, the seat of the involuntary physiological processes. See: *mind (five states).*

Samyama: सम्यम the continuous meditation on a single subject or mystic key (such as a *chakra*) to gain revelation on a particular subject or area of consciousness. As explained by Patañjali, *samyama* consists of *dhāranā, dhyāna* and *samādhi.* See: *dhāraṇa, dhyāna, samādhi.*

samyama: सम्यम "Constraint." Continuous meditation on a single concept to gain revelation on a particular subject or area of consciousness. As explained by Sage Patañjali, *samyama* consists of *dhāranā, dhyāna* and *samādhi.* See: *rāja yoga.*

San Mārga: सन्मार्ग "True path." The straight spiritual path leading to the ultimate goal, Self Realization, without detouring into unnecessary psychic exploration or pointless development of *siddhis.* A *San Mārgī* is a person "on the path," as opposed to a *saṁsārī,* one engrossed in worldliness. *San Mārga* also names the *jñāna pāda.* See: *pāda, sādhana mārga.*

San Mārga Sanctuary: A meditation *tīrtha* at the foot of the extinct volcano, Mount Waialeale, on Hawaii's Garden Island, Kauai.

Sanātana Dharma: सनातनधर्म "Eternal religion" or "Everlasting path." It is a traditional designation for the Hindu religion. See: *Hinduism.*

sañchita karma: सञ्चितकर्म "Accumulated action." The accumulated consequence of an individual's actions in this and past lives. See: *karma.*

sanctify: To make sacred or holy.

sanction: Authoritative permission or approval.

sanctum sanctorum: "Holy of holies." *Garbhagṛiha.* The most sacred part of a temple, usually a cave-like stone chamber, in which the main icon is installed. See: *temple.*

saṅga: सङ्ग "Association; fellowship." (Tamil: *Saṅgam*) Coming together in a group, especially for religious purposes.

sanitarium: A place for the treatment of serious, chronic diseases.

saṅkalpa: संकल्प "Will; purpose; determination." A solemn vow or declaration of purpose to perform any ritual observance. Most commonly, *saṅkalpa* names the mental and verbal preparation made by a temple priest as he begins rites of worship. During the *saṅkalpa,* he proclaims to the three worlds what he is about to do. He summond the name of the Deity, and announces the present time and place according to precise astrological notations and the type of the ritual he is about to perform. Once the *saṅkalpa* is made, he is bound to complete the ceremony. See: *pūjā.*

Śaṅkara: शङ्कर "Conferring happiness; propitious." An epithet of Śiva.

sannyāsa: संन्यास "Renunciation." "Throwing down" or "abandoning." *Sannyāsa* is the repudiation of the *dharma,* including the obligations and duties, of the householder and the assumption of the even more demanding *dharma* of the renunciate. See: *sannyāsa dharma, sannyāsa dīkshā, videhamukti.*

sannyāsa dharma: संन्यासधर्म "Renunciate virtue." The life, way and traditions of those who have irrevocably renounced prerogatives and obligations of the householder, including personal property, wealth, ambitions, social position and family ties, in favor of the full-time monastic quest for divine awakening, Self Realization and spiritual upliftment of humanity. See: *sannyāsa, sannyāsa dīkshā, sannyāsin, videhamukti.*

sannyāsa dīkshā: संन्यासदीक्षा "Renunciate initiation." This *dīkshā* is a formal rite, or less often an informal blessing, ushering the devotee into renunciate monasticism, binding him for life to certain vows which include chastity, poverty and obedience, and directing him on the path to Self Realization. See: *sannyāsa dharma, videhamukti.*

sannyāsin: संन्यासिन् "Renouncer." One who has taken *sannyāsa dīkshā.* A Hindu monk, *swāmī,* and one of a world brotherhood (or holy order) of *sannyāsins.* Some are wanderers and others live in monasteries. See: *sannyāsa, sannyāsa dharma, sannyāsa dīkshā, swāmī.*

Sanskṛit: संस्कृत "Refined; perfected." The classical sacerdotal language of ancient India, considered a pure vehicle for communication with the celestial worlds. It is the primary language in which Hindu scriptures are written, including the *Vedas* and *Āgamas.* Employed today as a liturgical, literary and scholarly language, but no longer used as a spoken vernacular.

śānti: शान्ति "Peace."

sapphire: A clear, hard gemstone that is usually blue.

sapta ṛishis: **सप्तऋषि** Seven inner-plane masters who help guide the *karmas* of mankind.

Sarasvatī: **सरस्वती** "The flowing one." Also spelled Saraswati. Śakti, the Universal Mother; Goddess of the arts and learning, mythological consort of the God Brahmā. Sarasvatī, the river Goddess, is usually depicted wearing a white *sārī* and holding a *vīna,* sitting upon a swan or lotus flower. Prayers are offered to her for refinements of art, culture and learning. See: *Śakti.*

Śaravaṇabhava: **शरवणभव** "Thicket of reeds." The *mantra* which calls upon Lord Kārttikeya, son of God Śiva and guardian of the spiritual quest, who arose from the sacred lake of primal consciousness. Its mirror-like surface symbolizes a quieted, peaceful mind. This *mantra* is prescribed for Śaivites not yet initiated by a *satguru* into the divine Pañchākshara Mantra, *Namaḥ Śivaya.* See: *Kārttikeya, Pañchākshara Mantra.*

sārī: **सारी** (Hindi: **साड़ी**) The traditional outer garment of a Hindu woman, consisting of a long, unstitched piece of cloth, usually colorful cotton or silk, wrapped around the body, forming an ankle-length skirt, and around the bosom and over the shoulder.

sārūpya: **सारूप्य** "Likeness" to God. The third of the four progressive attainments of the soul in Śaiva Siddhānta. It is the cultimination of the *yoga pāda.* See: *attainment.*

Sarvajñānottara Āgama: **सर्वज्ञानोत्तर आगम** This work is not among the traditional list of *Āgamas* and subsidiary scriptures. But it is thought to be a second version of *Kalajñām,* a subsidiary tract to *Vātula Āgama.* The extant sections deal with right knowledge.

Sarvam Śivamayam: "All is Śiva." One of the four great sayings capsulizing the message of Sage Siva Yogaswami.

śāstra: **शास्त्र** "Sacred script; teaching." 1) Any religious or philosophical treatise, or body of writings. 2) A department of knowledge, a science.

sat: **सत्** "True, existing, good; reality, existence, truth." See: *Satchidānanda.*

Sat Yuga (Satya Yuga): **सत् युग** "Age of Truth," also called Kṛitā, "accomplished, good, cultivated, kind action; the winning die cast of four dots." The first in the repetitive cycle of *yugas,* lasting 1,728,000 years, representing the brightest time, when the full light of the Central Sun permeates Earth. See: *yuga.*

Satchidānanda (Sachchidānanda): **सच्चिदानन्द** "Existence-consciousness-bliss." A synonym for *Parāśakti.* Lord Śiva's Divine Mind and simultaneously the pure superconscious mind of each individual soul. Perfect love and omniscient, omnipotent consciousness, the fountainhead of all existence, yet containing and permeating all existence. Also called pure consciousness, pure form, substratum of existence, and more. One of the goals of the meditator or *yogī* is to experience the natural state of the mind, Satchidānanda, subduing the *vṛittis* through *yogic* practices. See: *Parāśakti,* *tattva.*

satguru (sadguru): सद्गुरु "True weighty one." A spiritual preceptor of the highest attainment and authority—one who has realized the ultimate Truth, Paraśiva, through *nirvikalpa samādhi*—a *jīvanmukta* able to lead others securely along the spiritual path. He is always a *sannyāsin,* an unmarried renunciate. All Hindu denominations teach that the grace and guidance of a living *satguru* is a necessity for Self Realization. He is recognized and revered as the embodiment of God, Sadāśiva, the source of grace and of liberation. See: *guru bhakti, guru, guru-śishya system.*

satsaṅga: सत्संग Gathering in the company of good souls.

sattva guṇa: सत्त्वगुण "Perfection of Being." The quality of goodness or purity.

sattvic: Of, or relating to the *sattva guṇa,* the quality of goodness or purity.

savant: A learned person; a scholar.

savikalpa samādhi: सविकल्पसमाधि "Enstasy with form" or "seed." See: *rāja yoga, samādhi.*

savior: A person or God who saves another from harm or loss, especially by divine intervention or grace without any effort on the beneficiary's part.

sāyujya: सायुज्य "Union" with God. The highest of the four attainments of the soul in Śaiva Siddhanta. The state of *jñāna.* See: *attainment, Śivasāyujya, viśvagrāsa.*

scarlet: A strong to vivid red or reddish orange.

schism: A separation, a break into factions.

scintillating: Sparkling or shining.

scribe: A person who writes things down, especially as dictated by another or copied.

scripture (scriptural): "A writing." A sacred text or holy book(s) authoritative for a given sect or religion. See: *śāstra, smṛiti, śruti.*

scrutinize: Examine or inspect in detail and with great care.

scrutiny: Close, careful examination or study.

Second World: The astral or subtle plane. Here the soul continues its activities in the astral body during sleep and after the physical body dies. It is the in-between world which includes the Devaloka and the Narakaloka. The Second world exists "within" the First World or physical plane. See: *loka.*

secretion: The process in which a gland, tissue, etc., produces a moist substance, such as bile, pancreatic juice or perspiration. Also refers to the substances thus produced.

sect: A group of adherents who form a smaller asociation withing a larger (often religious) body. A religious denomination.

sectarian: Narrow adherence to the beliefs of a specific sect, especially in the sense that all other sects are incorrect or incomplete.

secular: Not sacred or religious; temporal or worldly.

sedentary: Accustomed to sitting. Here, inclined toward intellectual study rather than actual practice.

seed experience: Impression in the subconscious mind made by the original experience of a particular type or range of experience. The single vibration stored in the subconscious mind to which other vibrations in a similar frequency range will be added to construct the sub of the subconscious mind. The seed experience is the experience which must be cognized for all subsequent experiences (subconscious dross) of similar vibration to release their hold on the awareness of the individual.

seed *karma:* Dormant or *anārabdha karma.* All past actions which have not yet sprouted. See: *karma.*

seer: A wise person who sees beyond the limits of ordinary perception.

Self Realization: Direct knowing of the Self God, Paraśiva. Self Realization is known in Sanskṛit as *nirvikalpa samādhi;* "enstasy without form or seed;" the ultimate spiritual attainment (also called *asamprajñata samādhi).* Esoterically, this state is attained when the mystic *kuṇḍalinī* force pierces through the *sahasrāra chakra* at the crown of the head. This transcendence of all modes of human consciousness brings the realization or "nonexperience" of That which exists beyond the mind, beyond time, form and space. But even to assign a name to Paraśiva, or to its realization is to name that which cannot be named. In fact, it is "experienced" only in its aftermath as a change in perspective, a permanent transformation, and as an intuitive familiarity with the Truth that surpasses understanding. See: *enstasy, God Realization, liberation, kuṇḍalinī, Paraśiva, rāja yoga, samādhi.*

Self (Self God): God Śiva's perfection of Absolute Reality, Paraśiva—That which abides at the core of every soul. See: *Paramātman, Paraśiva.*

self-aggrandizement: Enhancement or exaggeration one's own importance.

self-effacement: Modest, retiring behavior; giving all credit to God, preceptor and other persons and not accepting praise for one's accomplishments.

self-effulgent: Shining brilliantly by itself.

self-gratification: Satisfying one's own desires.

self-hypnosis: The process of putting oneself in a sleeplike state in which the subconscious mind becomes accessable.

self-impose: Deciding to do something to oneself.

self-indulgent: Satisfying one's own appetites and desires.

self-luminous: Producing its own light; radiating light.

self-mastery: Full command of one's mind and emotions.

semblance: An outward and superficial appearance or resemblance.

sensuous: Of, or related to the senses, especially the pleasures of the senses.

sentries: Guards.

sevā: सेवा "Service." *Karma yoga.* An integral part of the spiritual path, where the aspirant strives to serve without thought of reward or personal gain. The central practice of the *charyā pāda.* See: *yoga.*

sexuality: Hinduism has a healthy, unrepressed outlook on human sexuality, and sexual pleasure is part of *kāma,* one of the four legitimate goals of life.

On matters such as birth control, sterilization, masturbation, homosexuality, bisexuality, petting and polygamy, Hindu scripture is tolerantly silent, neither calling them sins nor encouraging their practice, neither condemning nor condoning. The two important exceptions to this understanding view of sexual experience are adultery and abortion, both of which are considered to carry heavy *karmic* implications for this and future births. See: *celibacy, dissipation, odic force, ojas, tejas, transmutation, yoni.*

shamanism (shamanic): From the Sanskṛit *śramaṇa,* "ascetic," akin to *śram,* meaning "to exert." Generally refers to any religion based on the belief that good or evil spirits can be influenced by priests, or shamans. Descriptive of many of the world's tribal, indigenous faiths. See: *Śāktism.*

sheath: A covering or receptacle, such as the husk surrounding a grain of rice. In Sanskṛit, it is *kośa,* philosophically the bodily envelopes of the soul. See: *kośa, soul, subtle body.*

shiftiness: Dishonesty, evasiveness, deceitfulness.

Shinto: The indigenous religion of Japan.

Shum: A Nātha mystical language of meditation revealed in Switzerland in 1968 by Sivaya Subramuniyaswami. Its primary alphabet looks like this:

Shum perspectives: The four perspectives of the mind: —***moolef:*** intellectual/philosophical; —***shumef:*** individual awareness; —***simnef:*** scientific/intellectual; —***defee:*** space travel, *devas* and Gods, inner communication. See: *defee, moolef, shumef, simnef.*

shumef: (Shum) The perspective of the mind as a solid and individual awareness traveling from one area of the mind to another. Pronounced *shoom-eef.* See: *Shum, Shum perspectives.*

Shum-Tyaef: Pronounced *shoom-tyay-eef.* See: *Shum.*

shun: To keep away from, ignore or avoid scrupulously or consistently.

siddha: **सिद्ध** A "perfected one" or accomplished *yogī,* a person of great spiritual attainment or powers. See: *siddhi, siddha yoga.*

Siddha Siddhānta: **सिद्धसिद्धान्त** Siddha Siddhānta, also called Gorakhnātha Śaivism, is generally considered to have evolved in the lineage of the earlier ascetic orders of India. Its most well-known preceptor was Gorakshanātha (ca 1000) a disciple of Matsyendranātha, patron saint of Nepal, revered by certain esoteric Buddhist schools as well as by Hindus. The school systematized and developed the practice of *haṭha yoga* to a remarkable degree. Indeed, nearly all of what is today taught about *haṭha yoga* comes from this school. Siddha Siddhānta theology embraces both transcendent Śiva (being) and immanent Śiva (becoming). Śiva is both the efficient and material cause of the universe. Devotion is expressed through temple worship and pilgrimage, with the central focus on internal worship and *kuṇḍalinī yoga,* with the goal of realizing Parāsamvid, the supreme transcendent state of Śiva. Today there are perhaps 750,000 adherents of Siddha Siddhānta Śaivism, who are often understood as Śāktas or *advaita tantrics*. The school fans out through India, but is most prominent in North India and Nepal. Devotees are called *yogīs*, and stress is placed on world renunciation—even for householders. This sect is also most commonly known as Nātha, the Gorakshapantha and Siddha Yogī Sampradāya. Other names include Ādinātha Sampradāya, Nāthamaṭha and Siddhamārga. See: *Gorakshanātha*.

Siddha Siddhānta Paddhati: **सिद्धसिद्धान्तपद्धति** "Tracks on the doctrines of the adepts." A text of 353 highly mystical verses, ascribed to Gorakshanātha, dealing with the esoteric nature of the inner bodies and the soul's union with Supreme Reality. See: *Gorakshanātha, Siddha Siddhānta.*

siddha yoga: **सिद्धयोग** "*Yoga* of perfected attainment," or "of supernatural powers." 1) A term used in the *Tirumantiram* and other Śaiva scriptures to describe the *yoga* which is the way of life of adepts after attaining of Paraśiva. *Siddha yoga* involves the development of magical or mystical powers, or *siddhis*, such as the eight classical powers. It is a highly advanced *yoga* which seeks profound transformation of body, mind and emotions and the ability to live in a flawless state of God Consciousness. 2) The highly accomplished practices of certain alchemists.

siddhānta: **सिद्धान्त** "Final attainments" or "conclusions." Siddhānta refers to ultimate understanding arrived at in any given field of knowledge.

siddhānta śravaṇa (or śrāvaṇa): **सिद्धान्तश्रवण** "Scriptural audition." See: *yama-niyama.*

siddhi: **सिद्धि** "Power, accomplishment; perfection." Extraordinary powers of the soul, developed through consistent meditation and deliberate, often uncomfortable and grueling *tapas*, or awakened naturally through spiritual maturity and *yogic sādhana*. Through the repeated experience of Self Realization, *siddhis* naturally unfold according to the needs of the individual. Before Self Realization, the use or development of *siddhis* is among the greatest obstacles on the path because it cultivates *ahaṁkāra*, "I-ness" (egoity), and militates against the attainment of *prapatti*, complete submission to the will of God, Gods and *guru*. See: *ahaṁkāra, prapatti, siddha yoga.*

Sikhism: "Discipleship." Religion of nine million members founded in India about 500 years ago by the saint Guru Nānak. A reformist faith which rejects idolatry and the caste system, its holy book is the *Ādi Granth*, and main holy center is the Golden Temple of Amritsar.

silver cord: The astral substance which connects the physical body to the astral body which is disconnected at the time of death of the physical body.

simile: A figure of speech in which two unlike things are compared, often in a phrase introduced by "like" or "as."

simnef: (Shum) The perspective of the mind in its scientific, intellectual state.

Pronounced *sim-neef.* See: *Shum, Shum perspectives.*

simshumbese: (Shum) To become aware of the power within the spine. Pronounced *sim-shoom-bee-see.* See: *Shum.*

sin: Intentional transgression of divine law. Akin to the Latin *sons,* "guilty." Hinduism does not view sin as a crime against God, but as an act against *dharma*—moral order—and one's own self. See: *karma.*

śishya: शिष्य "A pupil" or "disciple," especially one who has proven himself and has formally been accepted by a *guru.*

sitār: सितार् A lutelike stringed Indian instrument with a long, fretted neck, and a resonating gourd or gourds.

Śiva: शिव The "Auspicious," "Gracious," or "Kindly one." Supreme Being of the Śaivite religion. God Śiva is All and in all, simultaneously the creator and the creation, both immanent and transcendent. As personal Deity, He is Creator, Preserver and Destroyer. He is a one Being, perhaps best understood in three perfections: Parameśvara (Primal Soul), Parāśakti (Pure Consciousness) and Paraśiva (Absolute Reality). See: *prapatti, Parameśvara, Parāśakti, Paraśiva, Naṭarāja, Sadāśiva, Śaivism, Satchidānanda.*

Śiva Advaita: शिवाद्वैत Also called Śiva Viśishṭādvaita, or Śaivite "qualified nondualism," Śiva Advaita is the philosophy of Śrīkaṇṭha (ca 1050) as expounded in his commentary on the *Brahma Sūtras* (ca 500-200 BCE). Patterned after the Vaishṇavite Viśishṭādvaita of Rāmānuja, this philosophy was later amplified by Appaya Dīkshita. Brahman, or Śiva, is transcendent and the efficient and material cause of the world and souls. Souls are not identical with Him and never merge in Him, even after liberation. As a school Śiva Advaita remained exclusively intellectual, never enjoying a following of practitioners. Purification, devotion and meditation upon Śiva as the Self—the *ākāśa* within the heart—define the path. Meditation is directed to the Self, Śiva, the One Existence that evolved into all form. Liberation depends on grace, not deeds. See: *Śaivism, Śrīkaṇṭha.*

***Śiva* consciousness:** Śivachaitanya. A broad term naming the experience or state of being conscious of Śiva in a multitude of ways. See: *jñāna, mind (five states), Śivasāyujya.*

Śivāchārya: शिवाचार्य The hereditary priests of the Śaiva Siddhānta tradition. The title of Ādiśaiva Brāhmins. An Ādiśaiva priest who has received the necessary training and *dīkshās* to perform public Śiva temple rites known as Āgamic *nitya parārtha pūjā.* A fully qualified Śivāchārya is also known as *archaka. Śivāchārya,* too, names the family clan of this priestly tradition. See: *brāhmin.*

Śivajñānabodham: शिवज्ञानबोधम् "Memorandum on Śiva Realization." A digest authored (or, some believe, a portion of the *Raurava Āgama* translated into Tamil) by Meykandar, ca 1300, consisting of 12 *sūtras* describing the relationship between God, soul and world. The Meykandar Sampradāya revere it as their primary philosophical text, and consider it a pluralistic exposition. For others, it is monistic in character, the pluralistic interpretation viewed as introduced by later commentators. Connected with this important text is an acute commentary on each of the 12 *sūtras.* See: *Meykandar.*

Śivaliṅga: शिवलिङ्ग "Mark," "Token" or "Sign of Śiva." The most prevalent emblem of Śiva, found in virtually all Śiva temples. A rounded, elliptical, aniconic image, usually set on a circular base, or *pīṭha.* The Śivaliṅga is the simplest and most ancient symbol of Śiva, especially of Paraśiva, God beyond all forms and qualities. The *pīṭha* represents Parāśakti, the manifesting power of God. Liṅgas are usually of stone (either carved or naturally existing, *svayambhū,* such as shaped by a swift-flowing river), but may also be of metal, precious gems, crystal, wood, earth or transitory materials such as ice. See: *Śaivism.*

Śivaloka: शिवलोक "Realm of Śiva." See: *loka.*

Śivamaya: शिवमय "Formed, made, consisting of" or "full of Śiva." A part of the Śaivite affirmation of faith denoting that all of existence—all worlds, all beings, all of manifestation, that which undergoes creation, preservation and destruction, all dualities and paradoxes—consists of and is pervaded by Śiva. An important concept of monistic Śaivism. See: *world, tattva.*

Śivaness: Quality of being Śiva or like Śiva, especially sharing in His divine state of consciousness. See: *Śiva consciousness, Śivasāyujya.*

Sivaperuman: சிவபெருமான் "Śiva, the Great One." See: *Śiva.*

Śiva-Śakti: शिवशक्ति Father-Mother God, both immanent and transcendent. A name for God Śiva encompassing His unmanifest Being and manifest energy. See: *Parameśvara, Primal Soul, Śiva.*

Śivasambandha: सिवसंबन्ध "Bound together in love of Śiva." The underlying unity and harmony among devotees of Śiva, irrespective of caste or creed.

Śivasāyujya: शिवसायुज्य "Intimate union with Śiva." Becoming one with God. The state of perpetual Śiva consciousness; simultaneous perception of the inner and the outer. A permanent state of oneness with Śiva, even in the midst of ordinary activities, a plateau reached or aftermath of repeated Self Realization experiences. Esoterically, it dawns when the *kuṇḍalinī* resides coiled in the *sahasrāra chakra.* See: *jīvanmukti, kaivalya, kuṇḍalinī, moksha, sahasrāra chakra.*

sivathondar: சிவதொண்டர் "Servant of Śiva." Conveys the same mystic meaning as Sivanadiyar, denoting a devotee who regularly performs actions dedicated to God Śiva; selfless work in service to others. See: *karma yoga, sivathondu.*

Sivathondu: சிவதொண்டு "Service to Śiva." Akin to the concept of *karma yoga.* See: *karma yoga.*

Śivāya Namaḥ: शिवाय नमः "Adoration to Śiva." Alternate form of *Namaḥ Śivāya.* See: *Namaḥ Śivāya.*

Sivayave: சிவாயவே "Śiva is also that." A phrase in Tamil that implies an obvious truth.

Śivohamic: Anglicized adjective from the great saying, *Śivoham*, meaning "I am That; I am Śiva," carrying the spirit of the underlying unity of God and the soul.
skepticism: A doubting or questioning state of mind, especially when one feels no absolute truth or knowledge is even possible.
śloka: श्लोक A verse, phrase, proverb or hymn of praise, usually composed in a specified meter. Especially a verse of two lines, each of sixteen syllables. *Śloka* is the primary verse form of the Sanskṛit epics, *Rāmāyaṇa* and *Mahābhārata.*
slough: To shed an outer layer of something.
sluggish: Lacking alertness, vigor or energy.
smog: A form of polluted air.
smolder: Fire or slight smoke without flame. To exist in a supressed state.
smṛiti: स्मृति That which is "remembered;" the tradition. Hinduism's nonrevealed, secondary but deeply revered scriptures, derived from man's insight and experience. *Smṛiti* speaks of secular matters—science, law, history, agriculture, etc.—as well as spiritual lore, ranging from day-to-day rules and regulations to superconscious outpourings. From the vast body of sacred literature, *śāstra,* each sect and school claims its own preferred texts as secondary scripture, e.g., the *Rāmāyaṇa* of Vaishṇavism and Smārtism, or the *Tirumurai* of Śaiva Siddhānta. Thus, the selection of *smṛiti* varies widely from one sect and lineage to another. See: *Mahābhārata, Tirumurai.*
sojourn: To reside temporarily in a place.
solace: A source of comfort or consolation.
solar plexus: A major physical and psychic nerve center of the body, located physically at the base of the sternum.
solemn: Ceremoniously observed or performed according to ritual or tradition. Formal, serious, inspiring feelings of awe. **—solemnize:** To consecrate with formal ceremony. See: *sacrament, saṁskāra.*
somatic: Relating to the body. The *somatic currents* are the five forms of breath beginning with *prāṇa,* the outgoing breath. See: *prāṇa.*
soothsaying: The art of foretelling events.
sophisticated: Technically advanced, elaborated, complex, artful, "smart."
soul: The real being of man, as distinguished from body, mind and emotions. The soul—known as *ātman* or *purusha*—is the sum of its two aspects, the form or body of the soul and the essence of the soul (though many texts use the word *soul* to refer to the essence only). **—essence or nucleus of the soul:** Man's innermost and unchanging being—Pure Consciousness *(Parāśakti* or *Satchidānanda)* and Absolute Reality *(Paraśiva)*. This essence was never created, does not change or evolve and is eternally identical with God Śiva's perfections of Parāśakti and Paraśiva.
soul body: *ānandamaya kośa* ("sheath of bliss"), also referred to as the "causal body" *(kāraṇa śarīra),* "innermost sheath" and "body of light."

Body of the soul, or *soul body,* names the soul's manifest nature as an individual being—an effulgent, human-like form composed of light (quantums). It is the emanational creation of God Śiva, destined to one day merge back into Him. During its evolution, the soul functions through four types of outer sheaths that envelope the soul form—mental, instinctive-intellectual, vital and physical—and employs the mental faculties of *manas, buddhi* and *ahaṁkāra,* as well as the five agents of perception *(jñānendriyas),* and five agents of action *(karmendriyas).* The "soul body" is not a body in sense of a case, a vessel, vehicle or enclosure for something else. The soul body is the soul itself—a radiant, self-effulgent, human-like, super-intelligent being. Its very composition is Satchidānanda in various subtle levels of manifestation. It is the finest of subatomic forms, on the quantum level. The soul form evolves as its consciousness evolves, becoming more and more refined until finally it is the same intensity or refinement as the Primal Soul, Parameśvara. See: *ātman, evolution of the soul, indriya, kośa, Parāśakti, Paraśiva, purusha, quantum, Satchidānanda, spiritual unfoldment.*

Soundless Sound: Paranāda. See: *nāda.*

spasmodic: Seizing on intermittently.

spinal: Relating to, or situated near the spine or spinal cord.

spinster: A single woman, specifically one who has not married by the normal age either by choice or circumstances.

spiritual unfoldment: *Adhyātma vikāsa.* The unfoldment of the spirit, the inherent, divine soul of man. The very gradual expansion of consciousness as *kuṇḍalinī śakti* slowly rises through the *sushumṇā.* The term *spiritual unfoldment* indicates this slow, imperceptible process, likened to a lotus flower's emerging from bud to effulgent beauty. Contrasted with *development,* which implies intellectual study; or *growth,* which implies character building and *sādhana.* Sound intellect and good character are the foundation for spiritual unfoldment, but they are not the unfoldment itself. When philosophical training and *sādhana* is complete, the *kuṇḍalinī* rises safely and imperceptively, without jerks, twitches, tears or hot flashes. Brings greater willpower, compassion and perceptive qualities.

spleen: A large organ near the stomach which stores and filters blood. Psychically the physical and astral spleen connect the subconscious with the superconscious, carrying negative vibrations out of the body and bringing positive solar rays in. The spleen is unique in that it is so large yet the body can live without it, unlike, for example, the liver. Other glands of the body take over the spleen's physical functions, while the spleen's astral double continues its psychic functions.

sporadic: Scattered. Happening from time to time irregularly and infrequently.

Śrī Chakra: श्रीचक्र The most well known *yantra* and a central image in Śākta worship. Consisting of nine interlocking triangles, it is the design of Śiva-

Śakti's multidimensional manifestations.

Śrī Rudram: श्रीरुद्रम् "(Canticle) to the Wielder of Awesome Powers." Pre-eminent Vedic hymn to Lord Śiva as the God of dissolution, chanted daily in Śiva temples throughout India. It is in this long prayer, located in the *Yajur Veda, Taittirīya Saṁhitā,* in the middle of the first three *Vedas,* that the Śaivite *mantra* Namaḥ Śivāya first appears.

Śrīkaṇṭha: श्रीकण्ठ A saint and philosopher (ca 1050) who promoted a Śaivite theology which embraced monism and dualism. Founder of the Śaiva school called Śiva Advaita, or Śiva Viśishṭādvaita, teaching a "Śaivite qualified nondualism," resembling Rāmānuja's Vaishṇavite Viśishṭādvaita. He was also known as Nīlakaṇṭha Śivāchārya. See: *Śiva Advaita.*

Śrīkumāra: श्रीकुमार Monistic Śaiva Siddhānta philosopher (ca 1050) who refuted the Śaṅkaran Vedānta doctrine of *māyā* as illusion and expounded that Śiva is both material cause *(upādāna kāraṇa)* and efficient cause *(nimitta kāraṇa).*

sṛishṭi: creation, or emanation, represented by Śiva's upper right hand and the *ḍamaru* (drum), upon which he beats Paranāda, the Primal Sound from which issue forth the rhythms and cycles of creation;

śruti: श्रुति That which is "heard." Hinduism's revealed scriptures, of supreme theological authority and spiritual value. They are timeless teachings transmitted to *ṛishis,* or seers, directly by God thousands of years ago. *Śruti* is thus said to be *apaurusheya,* "impersonal," or rather "suprahuman." *Śruti* consists of the *Vedas* and the *Āgamas,* preserved through oral tradition and eventually written down in Sanskṛit. Among the many sacred books of the Hindus, these two bodies of knowledge are held in the highest esteem. See: *Āgama, smṛiti, Veda.*

stagnant: Stationery. Not developing or progressing.

stamina: Physical or mental endurance; strength.

stampede: The sudden "headless" rush of a crowd of people or animals.

stereotype: Conventional and oversimplified idea or opinion.

sthūla: स्थूल "Gross; physical." See: *vāk.*

stimulants: Drugs that temporarily arouse or accelerate physiological or organic activity. Certain drugs are capable of stimulating psychic experiences, often with unpleasant consequences.

stimulus: Incentive, something that rouses to action.

stratum: A section or layer of something.

strī dharma: स्त्रीधर्म "Womanly conduct." See: *dharma.*

stuffy: Lacking sufficient air flow or ventilation.

subatomic: Of the inner parts of atoms; anything smaller than an atom.

subconscious mind: *Saṁskāra chitta.* See: *conscience, mind (five states).*

sublimate: To cause an instinctual impulse to manifest itself in a higher expression rather than a lower form. Coined after the property of some substances to transform themselves directly from a solid to a gas without becoming liquid. See: *ojas, tejas, transmutation, yoni.*

sublime: Exalted, noble, grand. Inspiring awe or reverence.

subliminal: Below the threshold of consciousness or apprehension, such as an attitude of which one is not aware. Subconscious. See: *mind (five states).*

submission: Yielding to the power of another. Compliance; meekness.

Subramuniyaswami: சுப்பிரமுனியசுவாமி Current and 162nd *satguru* (1927–) of the Nandinātha Sampradāya's Kailāsa Paramparā. He was ordained Sivaya Subramuniyaswami by Sage Yogaswāmī on the full-moon day of May 12, 1949, in Jaffna, Sri Lanka, at 6:21 PM. This was just days after he had attained *nirvikalpa samādhi* in the caves of Jalani. The name *Subramuniya* is a Tamil spelling of the Sanskṛit *Śubhramunya* (not to be confused with *Subramaṇya).* It is formed from *śubhra* meaning "light; intuition," and *muni,* "silent sage." *Ya* means "restraint; religious meditation." Thus, *Subramuniya* means a self-restrained soul who remains silent or, when he speaks, speaks out from intuition.

subside: To become less active or less intense. To abate.

substance: Essence; real nature; matter; material possessions.

substratum: "Layer underneath." In philosophy, the substance or underlying force which is the foundation of any and all manifestation: Satchidānanda. See: *Parāśakti, Satchidānanda, tattva.*

subsubconscious mind: *Vāsanā chitta* ("mind of subliminal traits"). The area of the subconscious mind formed when two thoughts or experiences of the same rate of intensity are sent into the subconscious at different times and, intermingling, give rise to a new and totally different rate of vibration. This subconscious formation later causes the external mind to react to situations according to these accumulated vibrations, be they positive, negative or mixed.

subsuperconscious mind: *Anukāraṇa chitta.* See: *mind, tattvas.*

subtle: So slight as to be difficult to detect; elusive; delicate. Not obvious.

subtle body: *Sūkshma śarīra,* the nonphysical, astral body or vehicle in which the soul encases itself to function in the Antarloka, or subtle world. The subtle body includes the *prāṇamaya, manomaya* and *vijñānamaya kośas* if the soul is physically embodied. It consists of only *manomaya* and *vijñānamaya* after death, when *prāṇamaya kośa* disintegrates. And it consists of only *vijñānamaya kośa* when *manomaya kośa* is dropped off just before rebirth or when higher evolutionary planes are entered. Also part of the subtle body are the *antaḥkaraṇa* (mental faculty: intellect, instinct and ego—*buddhi, manas* and *ahaṁkāra),* the five *jñānendriyas* (agents of perception: hearing, touch, sight, taste and smell); *and* the five *karmendriyas* (agents of action: speech, grasping, movement, excretion and generation). See: *jīva, kośa.*

succumb: To give in to an overpowering force; give up, yield, surrender.

śuddha: शुद्ध "Pure."

śuddha avasthā: शुद्ध अवस्था "Stage of purity." (Tamil: *avasthai.)* In Śaiva Siddhānta, the last of three stages of evolution, in which the soul is immersed in Śiva. Self Realization having been attained, the mental body is purified and thus reflects the divine soul nature, Śiva's nature, more than in the *kevala* or *sakala* state. Now the soul continues to unfold through the stages of realization, and ultimately merges back into its source, the Primal Soul. See: *avasthā, evolution of the soul, kevala avasthā, sakala avasthā, viśvagrāsa.*

Śuddha Śaiva Siddhānta: शुद्धशैवसिद्धान्त "Pure Śaiva Siddhānta," a term first used by Tirumular in the *Tirumantiram* to describe his monistic Śaiva Siddhānta and distinguish it from pluralistic Siddhānta and other forms of Siddhānta that do not encompass the ultimate monism of Vedānta.

Śuddhavidyā: शुद्धविद्या "Pure Knowledge." The fifth *tattva* in the Śaiva Siddhānta system. See: *tattva.*

sukarma: सुकर्म See: *karma.*

sulk: To withdraw into silent resentment or ill humor.

summation: Adding up to a total, summing up. Reaching a high point.

Sundaranāthar: சுந்தரநாதர் Original name of Nātha Siddha Tirumular before he trekked to South India from the Himalayas. See: *Tirumular.*

śūnya: शून्य "The void, the distinctionless absolute."

superconscious mind: *Kāraṇa chitta.* See: *mind (five states), mind (three phases), Satchidānanda, tattva.*

superficial: Shallow; on the surface; not substantial.

supernatural: Beyond or transcending the natural laws of the physical cosmos. Of or relating to an order of existence beyond the visible universe, referring to events, agencies or knowledge superseding or mystically explaining the laws of nature. See: mysticism, shamanism.

supersede: To cause to be set aside, especially to displace as inferior.

superstition: A belief or practice not supported by experience or reason.

supplicate (supplication): To ask for, beg humbly. To earnestly pray for.

suppressed: Subdued; ended forcibly. Kept from being revealed; inhibited. Deliberately excluded from the mind, such as with unacceptable desires or thoughts.

suppression: Desires, thoughts or memories consciously excluded from the mind. Related to repression, in which similar desires, etc., are excluded, but on a completely subconscious level.

supreme: Highest in rank, power, authority.

Supreme God: Highest God, the source or creator of all other Gods, beings and all manifestation.

Sūrya: सूर्य "Sun." One of the principal Divinities of the *Vedas,* also prominent in the epics and *Purāṇas.* Śaivites revere Sūrya, the Sun God each morning as Śiva Sūrya. Smārtas and Vaishṇavas revere the golden orb as Sūrya Nārāyaṇa.

sushumṇā nāḍī: सुषुम्णानाडी "Most gracious channel." Central psychic nerve current within the spinal column. See: *kuṇḍalinī, nāḍī, samādhi.*

sushupti: सुषुप्ति "Deep sleep." A state more refined than the ordinary dream state, the perceptions of which are often too subtle to be remembered upon awakening. This is the state of visionary dreams. One of the four *avasthās* described in the *Māṇḍūkya Upanishad.* See: *consciousness.*

sutala: सुतल "Great abyss." Region of obsessive jealousy and retaliation. The third *chakra* below the *mūlādhāra,* centered in the knees. Corresponds to the third astral netherworld beneath the earth's surface, called Saṁhāta ("abandoned") or Sutala. See: *chakra, hell, loka, Naraka.*

svādhishṭhāna: स्वाधिष्ठान "One's own base." See: *chakra.*

svapna: स्वप्न Sanskṛit word for dream, second of the four states of consciousness, waking, dreaming, deep sleep and "the fourth." See: *avasthā.*

svarṇaśarīra: स्वर्णशरीर The golden actinic body formed after many experiences of Self Realization. See: *viśvagrāsa, ānandamaya kośa.*

svarṇaśarīra viśvagrāsa: स्वर्णशरीरविश्वग्रास The final merging with Śiva where there exists no Soul, only Śiva. See: *viśvagrāsa.*

Śvetāśvatara Upanishad: श्वेताश्वतर उपनिषद् An *Upanishad* of the *Yajur Veda* that emphasizes theism—personal God and devotion—and at the same time monism—the unity of God, soul and world. It is valued as a major *Upanishad,* among the greatest panentheist writings, especially precious to Śaivite schools. See: *Upanishad, Veda.*

swāmī: स्वामी "Lord; owner; self-possessed." He who knows or is master of himself. A respectful title for a Hindu monk, usually a *sannyāsin,* an initiated, orange-robed renunciate, dedicated wholly to religious life. As a sign of respect, the term *swāmī* is sometimes applied more broadly to include non-monastics dedicated to spiritual work. See: *monk, sannyāsa dharma, sannyāsin.*

symbolism: The representation of one thing by something else. For example, the *ḍamaru,* drum, is a symbol of creation.

sympathetic nervous system: The part of the autonomic nervous system originating in the thoracic and lumbar regions of the spinal cord that in general inhibits or opposes the physiological effects of the parasympathetic nervous system, as in tending to reduce digestive secretions, speeding up the heart, and contracting blood vessels.

symptomatic: Characteristic of a disease or a condition.

syndrome: Symptoms occuring together and characterizing a certain disease or condition.

synonymous: Having the same or similar meaning.

synopsis: A brief outline or summary. Presentation in one review.

synthesis: Here: the application of reason to reach a particular conclusion from general concepts; also the combination of ideas to form a new idea.

syphon: To draw off of, take away or channel from.

tackle: To take on and wrestle with.

tact: Sensitivity to what is proper in dealing with others, including the ability to speak or act without offending.

tainted: Sullied, spoiled or stained. Morally corrupt or depraved.

Taittirīya Upanishad: तैत्तिरीय उपनिषद् Belongs to the *Taittirīya Brāhmaṇa* of the *Yajur Veda* and is divided into three sections called *valli(s)*. The first deals with phonetics and pronunciation, the second and third with Brahman and the attainment of bliss.

tala: तल "Plane or world; level; base, bottom; abyss." Root of the name of the seven realms of lower consciousness centered in the seven *chakras* below the *mūlādhāra*. See: *chakra, hell, loka, Naraka.*

talātala chakra: तलातल "Lower region." The fourth *chakra* below the *mūlādhāra*, centered in the calves. Region of chronic mental confusion and unreasonable stubbornness. Corresponds to the fourth astral netherworld beneath the earth's surface, called Tāmisra ("darkness") or Talātala. This state of consciousness is born of the sole motivation of self-preservation. See: *chakra, loka, Naraka.*

tamas(ic): तमस् "Force of inertia." *Tamas* is the most crude of the three gunas or fundamental cosmic qualities of nature as described in the Samkhya system of philosophy—*tamas* (inertia), *rajas* (activity) and *sattva* (illumination, purity). The *tamaguna* is the quality of denseness, inertia, contraction, resistance and dissolution.

taṁbūrā: तंबूरा (Hindi) A long-necked, four-stringed fretless lute that provides a drone accompaniment for a singer or instrumentalist.

Tamil: தமிழ் The ancient Dravidian language of the Tamils, a Caucasoid people of South India and Northern Sri Lanka, now living throughout the world. The official language of the state of Tamil Nadu, India.

Tamil Nadu: தமிழ் நாடு State in South India, 50,000 square miles, population 55 million. Land of countless holy scriptures, saints, sages and over 40,000 magnificent temples, including Chidambaram, Madurai, Palani Hills and Rāmeśvaram.

tāṇḍava: ताण्डव "Exuberant dance." Any vigorous dance sequence performed by a male dancer. There are many forms of *tāṇḍava.* Its prototype is Śiva's dance of bliss, *ānanda tāṇḍava.* The much softer feminine dance is called *lāsya,* from *lasa,* "lively." Dance in general is *nartana.* See: *Naṭarāja.*

tangent: Irrelevant sidetrack.

tangible: Something palpable or concrete.

tangled: Mixed together in a confused mass.

tantra: तन्त्र "Loom, methodology." 1) Most generally, a synonym for *śāstra,* "scripture." 2) A synonym for the Āgamic texts, especially those of the Śākta faith, a class of Hindu scripture providing detailed instruction on all aspects of religion, mystic knowledge and science. The *tantras* are also associated with the Śaiva tradition. 3) A specific method, technique or spiritual practice within the Śaiva and Śākta traditions. For example, *prāṇāyāma* is a *tantra*. *Tantra* generally involves a reversal of the normal flow of energies. See: *kuṇḍalinī, sushumṇā nāḍī.*

tantric (tāntrika): तान्त्रिक Adjectival to qualify practices prescribed in the Tantra traditions. Also to name a follower of any of the *tantric* traditions. See: *tantra.*

tapas: तपस् Also *tapasya.* Literally, "burning, heat, ardor." State of accelerated unfoldment and working with the forces through spiritual practices. A state of humble submission to the divine forces and surrender to the processes of inner purification which occur almost automatically at certain stages. In the monastery *tapas* is administered and guided by the guru. Denotes religious austerity, severe meditation, penance, bodily mortification, special observances; connotes spiritual purification and transformation as a "fiery process" which "burns up" impurities, ego, illusions and past karmas that obstruct God Realization.

tapasvin: तपस्विन् One who performs *tapas* or is in the state of *tapas.*

tarry: To be slow to move on. To prolong a temporary stay.

Tātparyadīpikā: तात्पर्यदीपिका A commentary by Śrīkumāra (ca 1100) on the *Tattvaprakāśa* of Śrī Bhojadeva Paramāra (1018–1060), a philosopher-king in Central India who expounded Śaiva Siddhānta. Śrīkumāra upheld the monistic basis of Bhojadeva's work, while later commentator Aghoraśiva reinterpreted it in dualistic terms. See: *Aghoraśiva, Śaiva Siddhānta.*

tattva: तत्त्व "That-ness" or "essential nature." *Tattvas* are the primary principles, elements, states or categories of existence, the building blocks of the universe. Lord Śiva constantly creates, sustains the form of and absorbs back into Himself His creations. *Ṛishis* describe this emanational process as the unfoldment of *tattvas,* stages or evolutes of manifestation, descending from subtle to gross. At *mahāpralaya,* cosmic dissolution, they enfold into their respective sources, with only the first two *tattvas* surviving the great dissolution. The first and subtlest form—the pure consciousness and source of all other evolutes of manifestation—is called Śiva *tattva,* or Parāśakti-*nāda.* But beyond Śiva *tattva* lies Paraśiva—the utterly transcendent, Absolute Reality, called *attava.* That is Śiva's first perfection. The Sāṅkhya system discusses 25 *tattvas.* Śaivism recognizes these same 25 plus 11 beyond them, making 36 *tattvas* in all. See: Resource 5, Charts, for full listing.

Tattva Prakāśa: तत्त्वप्रकाश "Illumination of the categories." Text of 76 verses by the philosopher-king Bhoja Paramāra which systematized and consolidated monistic Śaiva Siddhānta in the 11th century.

taut: Pulled or drawn tight.

Tayumanavar: தாயுமானவர் A Tamil Śaivayogī, devotional mystic and poet saint (ca 17th century) whose writings are a harmonious blend of philosophy and devotion. In his poem "Chinmayānanda Guru," Tayumanavar places himself in the lineage of Ṛishi Tirumular. See: *Tirumular.*

tejas: तेजस् "Brilliance, fire, splendor." Heat or fire, one of the five elements—earth, water, fire, air, ether. *Tejas* also names the glow of *tapas* in the shining expression of the *tapasvin. Tejas* is increased through *brahmacharya,* control of the sexual energies by lifting the heat into the higher *chakras.* See: *brahmacharya, ojas, tapas, transmutation, yoni.*

temple: An edifice in a consecrated place dedicated to, the worship of God or Gods. Hindus revere their temples as sacred, magical places in which the three worlds most consciously commune—structures especially built and consecrated to channel the subtle spiritual energies of inner-world beings. The temple's psychic atmosphere is maintained through regular worship ceremonies *(pūjā)* invoking the Deity, who uses His installed image *(mūrti)* as a temporary body to bless those living on the earth plane. In Hinduism, the temple is the hub of virtually all aspects of social and religious life. It may be referred to by the Sanskṛit terms *mandira, devālaya* (or Śivālaya, a Śiva temple), as well as by vernacular terms such as *koyil* (Tamil). See: *pilgrimage.*

temporal: Referring to time; subject to time. Passing, existing only for a time.

temptation: Something tempting, enticing or alluring.

temptress: An alluring, enchanting woman.

tenacious: Holding firmly, not easily letting go. Firm in purpose.

tenet: A principle, doctrine, or belief held as a truth, as by a group.

tenuous: Long and thin; slender.

tenure: The length of time during which something is held or done.

thalamic: Pertaining to the thalamus, a large ovoid mass of gray matter situated in the front part of the forebrain that relays sensory impulses to the cerebral cortex. The pineal gland sits atop the thalamus.

That: When capitalized, this simple demonstrative pronoun refers uniquely to the Ultimate, Indescribable or Nameless Absolute. The Self God, Paraśiva. It is the English equivalent of *Tat,* as in, *Tat tvam asi,* "You are That!"

theistic: The belief that God exists as a real, conscious, personal Supreme Being, creator and ruler of the universe. May also include belief in the Gods.

theology: The study of religious doctrines, specifically of the nature of God, soul and world. —**theologians:** Those who study, are expert in or formulate theology.

Theosophy: The philosophy of an esoteric religious sect, the Theosophical Society, founded in 1875 by Russian mystic Madame Blavatsky, incorporating aspects of Buddhism and Hinduism. It has greatly influenced all modern metaphysical movements.

Third World: Śivaloka, "Realm of Śiva." The spiritual realm or causal plane of existence wherein Māhadevas and highly evolved souls live in their own self-effulgent forms. See: *Śivaloka, three worlds, loka.*

thither: Toward that place; there. Farther.

thought form: Manifestations of astral matter, or odic force, created within the aura of a person, which travel through astral space, or odic force fields, from one destination to another. They have the power to create, preserve, protect and destroy. They can also be seen, just as auras can be seen. A series of thought forms compose the intellect. See: *astral plane, aura, odic force, intellect.*

three worlds: The three worlds of existence, *triloka,* are the primary hierarchical divisions of the cosmos. 1) Bhūloka: "Earth world," the physical plane. 2) Antarloka: "Inner" or "in-between world," the subtle or astral plane. 3) Śivaloka: "World of Śiva," and of the Gods and highly evolved souls; the causal plane, also called Kāraṇaloka. See: *chakra, loka, Naraka, tattva.*

thyroid: A gland located in the throat which regulates physical growth and other vital functions. Psychically, it assists in the formation of habits and in maintaining mental balance. Regarded as the connecting link between spirit and personality, it has a tremendous influence over the nervous system and the emotions. It is associated with the *viśuddha chakra.*

timeless: Outside the condition of time, or not measurable in terms of time.

tinge: To imbue a little with color.

tirodhāna śakti: तिरोधानशक्ति "Concealing power." Veiling grace, or God's power to obscure the soul's divine nature. *Tirodhāna śakti* is the particular energy of Śiva that binds the three bonds of *āṇava, karma, māyā* to the soul. It is a purposeful limiting of consciousness to give the opportunity to the soul to grow and mature through experience of the world. See: *evolution of the soul, grace.*

tīrthayātrā: तीर्थयात्रा "Journey to a holy place." Pilgrimage. See: *pilgrimage.*

tiru: திரு "Sacred; holy." The exact Tamil rendition of *śrī.* Feminine equivalent is *tirumati.*

Tirukural: திருக்குறள் "Holy couplets." A treasury of Hindu ethical insight and a literary masterpiece of the Tamil language, written by Śaiva Saint Tiruvalluvar (ca 200 BCE) near Chennai. See: *Tiruvalluvar.*

Tirumantiram: திருமந்திரம் "Holy incantation." The Nandinātha Sampradāya's oldest Tamil scripture; written ca 200 BCE by Ṛishi Tirumular. It is the earliest of the *Tirumurai,* and a vast storehouse of esoteric *yogic* and *tantric* knowledge. It contains the mystical essence of *rāja yoga* and *siddha yoga,* and the fundamental doctrines of the 28 *Śaiva Siddhānta Āgamas,* which in turn are the heritage of the ancient pre-historic traditions of Śaivism. See: *Tirumurai, Tirumular.*

Tirumular: திருமூலர் An illustrious *siddha yogī* and *ṛishi* of the Nandinātha Sampradāya's Kailāsa Paramparā who came from the Himalayas (ca 200 BCE) to Tamil Nadu to compose the *Tirumantiram.* In this scripture he recorded the tenets of Śaivism in concise and precise verse form, based upon his own realizations and the supreme authority of the *Śaiva Āgamas* and the *Vedas*. Tirumular was a disciple of Mahāṛishi Nandinātha. See: *Tirumantiram, Kailāsa Paramparā, Vedānta.*

Tirumurai: **திருமுறை** "Holy script." A twelve-book collection of hymns and writings of South Indian Śaivite saints, compiled by Saint Nambiyandar Nambi (ca 1000).

Tirunavukarasu: **திருநாவுக்கரசு** See: *Appar.*

Tiruvalluvar: **திருவள்ளுவர்** "Holy weaver." Tamil weaver and householder saint (ca 200 BCE) who wrote the classic Śaivite ethical scripture Tirukural. He lived with his wife, Vasuki, famed for her remarkable loyalty and virtues, near modern-day Chennai. There a memorial park, the Valluvar Kottam, enshrining his extraordinary verses in marble. See: *Tirukural.*

Tiruvasagam: **திருவாசகம்** "Holy Utterances." The lyrical Tamil scripture by Saint Manikkavasagar (ca 850). Considered one of the most profound and beautiful devotional works in the Tamil language, it discusses every phase of the spiritual path from doubt and anguish to perfect faith in God Śiva, from earthly experience to the *guru-disciple* relationship and freedom from rebirth. See: *Manikkavasagar, Tirumurai.*

tithe (tithing): In Sanskṛit *daśamāṁśa*, or *makimai* in the Tamil tradition. The spiritual discipline, often a *vrata*, of giving one tenth of one's gainful and gifted income to a religious organization of one's choice, thus sustaining spiritual education and upliftment on earth. Tithing is given not as an offering, but as "God's money."

trance: In spiritualism, trance describes the phenomenon in which the medium leaves the physical body, and a disincarnate being enters or takes control of the body, often giving forth verbal messages to others in attendance, as in a seance. See: *samādhi.*

tranquil: Quiet, peaceful.

transcend: To go beyond one's limitations, e.g., "to transcend one's ego." Philosophically, to go beyond the limits of this world, or more profoundly, beyond time, form and space into the Absolute, the Self God.

transcendent: Surpassing the limits of experience or manifest form. In Śaiva Siddhānta, a quality of God Śiva as Absolute Reality, Paraśiva, the Self. Distinguished from immanent. See: *Paraśiva.*

transcribe: To make a full written copy.

transference: Passing something from one place (or state) to another.

transform: To change markedly.

transgress: To overstep or break a law or ethical principle.

transition: Passing from one state, condition or place to another. A synonym of death which implies, more correctly, continuity of the individual rather than his annihilation. See: death.

translucent: Transmitting light but causing sufficient diffusion to prevent perception of distinct images.

transmigration: Reincarnation, the repeated rebirth of the soul in a succession of human bodies.

transmitter: Here, something that transmits or sends psychic vibrations.

transmutation: Change from one form to another. Here, changing or transforming the sexual/instinctive energies into intellectual and spiritual ones. *Transmutation* means to reverse the forces that constantly flow from the *sahasrāra* downward into the *mūlādhāra.* It is lifting the force of sexual impulses that would tend to manifest in visualization, longing for affection and sensual feelings, often leading to masturbation and loss of the sacred fluids. One exception for both men and women is the occurrence of wet dreams, for here the astral, psychic vitality of the actinodic into the actinic energies rises as the odic fluids are released. However, night emissions are to be controlled and may be minimized or eliminated by taking only liquid or light foods in the evening. ¶Swāmī Śivānanda discusses wet dreams in his *Yoga Lessons for Children,* chapter 36 on Brahmacharya. He states, "Many young boys and men suffer from wet dreams. Srī Aurobindo states that an occurrence once a week is normal. To have it more frequently indicates indulgence in sex thoughts." Sivananda advises a *sattvic* diet, rising early (as wet dreams usually occur in the last quarter of the night), cold showers, *haṭha yoga,* fresh fruit and raw foods, not going to bed right after a heavy meal. He says, "The actual essence does not come out during wet dreams. It is only the watery prostatic juice with a little semen. When nocturnal emission takes place, the mind which was working in the inner astral body suddenly enters the physical body vehemently in an agitated condition. That is the reason why emission takes place suddenly." He concludes, "Do not get depressed or anxious. It is best not to give too much importance to these dreams. Forget them, then they will not trouble you." ¶Monks enhance transmutation by not eating after high noon, not viewing pornography, not mentally conjuring up sexually stimulating images, never joking or talking about sexuality and, of course, not flirting or interacting sensually with women or men. If sexual energies are aroused or one has erred from his disciplines, he performs the appropriate penance (such as fasting) or *tantra* (such as *prāṇāyāma*) to correct the matter. The *Tirumantiram* (verse 1948) states, "If the sacred seed is retained, life does not ebb; great strength, energy, intelligence and alertness: all these are attained." See: *actinic, celibacy, odic, ojas, tejas, yoni.*

traumatic: In psychology, a great emotional disturbance that leaves a lasting effect on the person.

traverse: To travel or pass across, over, or through. To move to and fro over; cross and recross.

treasure-trove: A discovery of great value.

treatise: An article or book which systematically discusses a subject.

triple bondage: See: *mala, pāśa.*

Triśūla: त्रिशूल A three-pronged spear or trident wielded by Lord Śiva and certain Śaivite ascetics. Symbolizes God's three fundamental *śaktis* or powers—*icçhā* (desire, will, love), *kriyā* (action) and *jñāna* (wisdom).

Truth: When capitalized, ultimate knowing which is unchanging. Lower case (truth): honesty, integrity; virtue.

tumult: Noise, uproar, disturbance; agitation, confusion.

turbulent: Violently agitated. Marked by turmoil or wildly irregular motions.

turīya: तुरीय "The fourth." The superconscious state beyond waking, dreaming and deep sleep. One of the four states of consciousness, *avasthās,* described in the *Māṇḍūkya Upanishad.* See: *consciousness.*

turmeric: A plant of India, *Curcuma longa,* of the ginger family whose powdered rhyzome is a prized seasoning and yellow dye. It has rich *āyurvedic* properties, is used in holy ritual and serves also to make *kuṅkuma.*

turmoil: Extreme commotion, uproar, confusion.

twitch: A sudden involuntary movement.

tyāga: त्याग "Letting go, detachment, renunciation." Described in the *Bhagavad Gītā* as the basic principle of *karma yoga,* detachment from the fruits of one's actions. See: *sannyāsa.*

ubiquitous: Being or seeming to be everywhere at the same time.

udāna: उदान "Ascending breath." One of the body's five somatic currents of vital energy, or *prāṇa.* See: *prāṇa.*

Ugrajyoti: उग्रज्योति Kashmīri *guru* of Sadyojyoti, proponent of Siddhānta philosophical views. See: *Sadyojyoti.*

ultimate: Final, last. —**Ultimate Reality:** Final, highest Truth. God Śiva's Absolute Reality, Paraśiva.

umbilical cord: The cord connecting a fetus to its mother or a like source of support or sustenance.

unambiguous: Clear, doubtless, certain.

unbearable: Intolerable due to being unpleasant, distasteful or painful.

unbidden: Not invited, asked, or requested.

uncanny: Extraordinary, as if of supernatural origin.

uncomely: Unattractive, ugly, unpleasant.

unconscious: Lacking conscious awareness, thought or control.

unconventional: Out of the ordinary, not normal.

undertaker: One who handles funerals as a profession.

undue: Exceeding what is appropriate or normal; excessive.

unduly: Excessively; immoderately, exceeding normal bounds.

unencumbered: Without a heavy load or burden. Unhindered in an action.

unequivocal: Admitting of no doubt or misunderstanding; clear and unambiguous.

unfathomable: Impossible to ascertain its depth, to get to the bottom.

Difficult or impossible to understand or measure.

unfettered: Free of bonds or restrictions.

unfold: To open gradually, especially in stages. See: *spiritual unfoldment.*

unholy: Wicked; immoral.

unmanā: **उन्मना** "Ecstatic; trans-mental." The seventh and highest of the seven *chakras,* or *nāḍi* conglomerates, above and within the *sahasrāra chakra.* See: *chakras above sahasrāra.*

unmanifest: Not evident or perceivable. Philosophically, akin to *transcendent.* Śiva is unmanifest in His formless perfection, Paraśiva. See: *formless.*

unravel: To undo, to separate, disentangle something entangled.

untimely: Occurring or done at an inappropriate time; inopportune.

unwavering: Not hesitating or having any doubt or indecision; of firm mind.

upadeśa: **उपदेश** "Advice; religious instruction." Often given in question-and-answer form from *guru* to disciple. The *satguru's* spiritual discourses.

upadeśī: **उपदेशी** A liberated soul who chooses to teach, actively helping others to the goal of liberation. Contrasted with *nirvāṇī.* See: *nirvāṇī and upadeśī, satguru.*

Upanishad: **उपनिषद्** "Sitting near devotedly." The fourth and final portion of the *Vedas,* expounding the secret, philosophical meaning of the Vedic hymns. The *Upanishads* are a collection of profound texts which are the source of Vedānta and have dominated Indian thought for thousands of years. They are philosophical chronicles of *ṛishis* expounding the nature of God, soul and cosmos, exquisite renderings of the deepest Hindu thought. See: *śruti, Veda, Vedānta.*

utterance: Something said, a verbal statement; expression.

vacillation: Indecisiveness, constantly changing from one focus of attention to another.

vacuum: A state of emptiness; a void.

vaikharī vāk: **वैखरी वाक्** "The faculty of speech." See: *vāk.*

Vaikuṇṭha: **वैकुण्ठ** "Vishṇu's heaven." See: *Vaishṇavism.*

vairāgya: **वैराग्य** "Dispassion; aversion." Freedom from passion. Distaste or disgust for worldliness because of spiritual awakening and the constant renunciation of obstacles on the path to liberation. See: *sannyāsa.*

Vaishṇavism (Vaishṇava): **वैष्णव** One of the four major religions, or denominations of Hinduism, representing roughly half of the world's one billion Hindus. It gravitates around the worship of Lord Vishṇu as Personal God, His incarnations and their consorts. The doctrine of *avatāra* (He who descends), especially important to Vaishṇavism, teaches that whenever *adharma* gains ascendency in the world, God takes a human birth to reestablish "the way." The most renowned *avatāras* were Rāma and Kṛishṇa.

Vaishṇavism stresses the personal aspect of God over the impersonal, and *bhakti* (devotion) as the true path to salvation. The goal of Vaishṇavism is the attainment of *mukti*, defined as blissful union with God's body, the loving recognition that the soul is a part of Him, and eternal nearness to Him in Vaikuṇṭha, heaven.

vāk: वाक् "Speech." Theologically, it is through the supreme Vāk (or Paravāk), the "Primal Word" of the *Vedas*, and its various aspects, that creation issues forth.

valipadu: வழிபாடு Ritualistic temple worship. See: *pūjā*

Vallabhāchārya: वल्लभाचार्य "Beloved." Vaishṇava saint (ca 1475-1530) whose panentheistic Śuddha Advaita (pure nondualism) philosophy became the essential teaching of the nonascetic Vaishṇava sect that bears his name. The sect is strongest in Gujarat. See: *Vedānta.*

valor: Marked courage or bravery.

Vārāṇasī: वाराणसी Also known as Kāśī or Banāras. One of the most holy of Śaivite cities, and among the oldest cities in the world. Located in North India on the Ganges River. Hindus consider it highly sanctifying to die in Kāśī, revering it as a gateway to *moksha.*

vāsanā: वासना "Abode." Subconscious inclinations. From *vās,* "dwelling, residue, remainder." The subliminal inclinations and habit patterns which, as driving forces, color and motivate one's attitudes and future actions. *Vāsanās* are the conglomerate results of subconscious impressions *(saṁskāras)* created through experience. *Saṁskāras,* experiential impressions, combine in the subconscious to form *vāsanās,* which thereafter contribute to mental fluctuations, called *vṛitti.* The most complex and emotionally charged *vāsanās* are found in the dimension of mind called the sub-subconscious, or *vāsanā chitta.* See: *saṁskāra, mind (five states), vāsanā daha tantra, vṛitti.*

vāsanā chitta: वासनाचित्त "Mind of subliminal traits." The subsubconscious state of mind. See: *mind (five states).*

vāsanā daha tantra: वासनादहतन्त्र "Purification of the subconscious by fire." *Daha* means burning, *tantra* is a method, and *vāsanās* are deep-seated subconscious traits or tendencies that shape one's attitudes and motivations. *Vāsanās* can be ether positive or negative. One of the best methods for resolving difficulties in life, of dissolving troublesome *vāsanās,* the *vāsanā daha tantra* is the practice of burning confessions, or even long letters to loved ones or acquaintances, describing pains, expressing confusions and registering grievances and long-felt hurts. Writing down problems and burning them in any ordinary fire brings them from the subconscious into the external mind, releasing the supressed emotion as the fire consumes the paper. This is a magical healing process. See: *vāsanā.*

Vasishṭha: वसिष्ठ Disciple of Maharishi Nandikeśvara (Nandinātha) (ca 250 BCE) along with Patañjali and Vyāghrapāda (as recorded in Pāṇini's book of grammar). Also the name of several other famous sages, including the *ṛishi* attributed with composing the hymns of the *Ṛig Veda's* seventh *maṇḍala*, another who plays a central role in the epics and certain *Purāṇas* and *Upanishads*, and a third famous sage who expounds the ancient *yogic* wisdom to Lord Rāma in the 29,000-verse *Yoga Vāsishṭha*.

Vasugupta: वसुगुप्त Celebrated preceptor (ca 800) whose finding of the *Śiva Sūtras* catalyzed the reemergence of the ancient Kashmīr Śaiva tradition. It is said that he discovered the 77 *sūtras* carved in a rock on Mahādeva mountain after a visionary dream in which Lord Śiva told him of their location. The sacred rock, named Śaṅkarpal, is revered to this day. See: *Kashmīr Śaivism*.

vāta: वात "Fluctuation." *Vāyu*, "wind, air-ether." One of the three bodily humors, called *dosha*, *vāta* is known as the air humor. Principle of circulation in the body. *Vāta dosha* governs such functions as breathing and movement of the muscles and tissues. See: *āyurveda, dosha*.

Veda: वेद् "Wisdom." Sagely revelations which comprise Hinduism's most authoritative scripture. They, along with the *Āgamas*, are *śruti*, that which is "heard." The *Vedas* are a body of dozens of holy texts known collectively as the *Veda*, or as the four *Vedas: Ṛig, Yajur, Sāma* and *Atharva*. In all they include over 100,000 verses, as well as additional prose. The knowledge imparted by the *Vedas* is highly mystical or superconscious rather than intellectual. Each *Veda* has four sections: *Saṁhitās* (hymn collections), *Brāhmaṇas* (priestly manuals), *Āraṇyakas* (forest treatises) and *Upanishads* (enlightened discourses). The *Saṁhitās* and *Brāhmaṇas* (together known as the *karmakāṇḍa*, "ritual section") detail a transcendent-immanent Supreme-Being cosmology and a system of worship through fire ceremony and chanting to establish communication with the Gods. The *Āraṇyakas* and *Upanishads* (the *jñānakāṇḍa*, "knowledge section") outline the soul's evolutionary journey, providing *yogic*-philosophic training and propounding a lofty, nondual realization as the destiny of all souls. The oldest portions of the *Vedas* are thought by some to date back as far as 6,000 BCE, written down in Sanskṛit in the last few millennia, making them the world's most ancient scriptures. See: *śruti, Upanishad*.

Vedānta: वेदान्त "Ultimate wisdom" or "final conclusions of the *Vedas*." Vedānta is the system of thought embodied in the *Upanishads* (ca 1500-600 BCE), which give forth the ultimate conclusions of the *Vedas*. Through history there developed numerous Vedānta schools, ranging from pure dualism to absolute monism. The first and original school is Advaita Īśvaravāda, "monistic theism" or panentheism, exemplified in the Vedānta-Siddhānta of Ṛishi Tirumular (ca 250 BCE) of the Nandinātha Sampradāya in his *Tirumantiram*, which is a perfect summation of both the *Vedas* and the *Āgamas*. See: *dvaita-advaita, monistic theism*.

Vedic-Āgamic: Simultaneously drawing from and complying with both of

Hinduism's revealed scriptures *(śruti)*, *Vedas* and *Āgamas*, which represent two complimentary, intertwining streams of history and tradition. The difference between Siddhānta and Vedānta is traditionally described in the way that while the *Vedas* represent man looking for God, the *Āgamas* hold the perspective of God looking to help man. This is reflected in the fact that while the *Vedas* are voiced by *ṛishis*, God or the Goddess is the bestower of truth in the *Āgama* texts. See: *grace, śruti.*

vegetarian: *Śakāhāra.* Of a diet which excludes meat, fish, fowl and eggs. Vegetarianism is a principle of health and environmental ethics that has been a keystone of Indian life for thousands of years. Vegetarian foods include grains, fruits, vegetables, legumes and dairy products. Natural, fresh foods, locally grown, without insecticides or chemical fertilizers, are preferred. The following foods are minimized: frozen and canned foods, highly processed foods, such as white rice, white sugar and white flour; and "junk" foods and beverages (those with abundant chemical additives, such as artificial sweeteners, colorings, flavorings and preservatives). See: *yama-niyama.*

vehemently: Characterized by intensity of emotion or conviction.

veil: A piece of cloth used to conceal. To cover or hide.

veiling grace: *Tirobhāva śakti.* The divine power that limits the soul's perception by binding or attaching the soul to the bonds of *āṇava, karma,* and *māyā*— enabling it to grow and evolve as an individual being. See: *grace.*

venerable: Deserving respect by virtue of age, dignity, character or position.

veneration: Sincere respect or reverence.

Venus: The second planet from the Sun, associated with the second *chakra.*

viable: Capable of success, practicable, able to thrive.

vibhūti: विभूति "Prevalent," "prepotent." Holy ash, prepared by burning cow dung along with other precious substances, milk, *ghee,* honey, etc. It symbolizes purity and is one of the main sacraments given at *pūjā* in all Śaivite temples and shrines. Śaivites wear three stripes on the brow as a distinct sectarian mark, as do many Smārtas.

vibration: A distinctive emotional aura or atmosphere that can be instinctively sensed or experienced.

vicarious: Felt as if one were feeling or taking part in the experiences of another.

videhamukti: विदेहमुक्ति "Disembodied liberation." Release from reincarnation through *nirvikalpa samādhi*—the realization of the Self, Paraśiva—at the point of death. Blessed are those who are aware that departure, *mahāsamādhi,* is drawing near. They settle all affairs, make amends and intensify personal *sādhana.* They seek the silver channel of *sushumṇā* which guides *kuṇḍalinī* through the door of *Brahman* into the beyond of the beyond. They seek total renunciation as the day of transition looms strongly in their consciousness. Those who know that Lord Yama is ready to receive them, seek to merge with Śiva. They seek *nirvikalpa samādhi* as the body and earthly life fall away. Those who succeed are the *videhamuktas,* honored as among those who will never be reborn. Hindu tradition allows for vows of renunciation, called *ātura sannyāsa dīkshā,* to be taken and the orange robe donned by the worthy *sādhaka* or householder in the days prior to death. See: *jīvanmukti, kaivalya, moksha, Paraśiva, Self Realization.*

vidyā: विद्या "Knowledge, learning, science." The power of understanding gained through study and meditation. Contrasted with *avidyā,* ignorance.

Vijayanagar: विजयनगर् "City of Victory." Vast and opulent city and last Indian empire, centered in present-day Karnataka state, which extended as far as Malaysia, Indonesia and the Philippines. It flourished from 1336 until the Empire was defeated and the city razed by Muslim armies.

vijñānamaya kośa: विज्ञानमयकोश "Sheath of cognition." The soul's mental or cognitive-intuitive sheath, also called the actinodic sheath. See: *kośa, mental body, soul.*

vilayam: विलयम् "Dissolution, liquefaction, disappearance." See: *viśvagrāsa.*

vim: Spirited force, energy or vigor.

vīṇā: वीणा Large South Indian popular musical instrument usually having seven strings and two calabash gourd as resonance boxes.

Vīra Śaivism (Śaiva): वीरशैव "Heroic Śaivism." Made prominent by Basavaṇṇa in the 12th century. Also called Liṅgāyat Śaivism. Followers, called Liṅgāyats, Liṅgavantas or Śivaśaraṇās, always wear a Śivaliṅga on their person. Vīra Śaivites are proudly egalitarian and emphasize the personal relationship with Śiva, rather than temple worship. Today Vīra Śaivism is a vibrant faith, particularly strong in its religious homeland of Karnataka, South Central India. By rejecting the *Vedas,* they continue to stand outside mainstream Hinduism, but in their profound love of Śiva and acceptance of certain *Śaiva Āgamas,* as well as the main truths of the Vedic wisdom, they have identified themselves as a unique Śaiva sect. Though they have established their faith as a distinct and independent religion in Indian courts of law, they are still widely embraced as devout brothers and sisters of the Hindu *dharma.* See: *Śaivism.*

virility: Manliness; masculine strength, spirit or power.

Vishṇu: विष्णु "All-pervasive." Supreme Deity of the Vaishṇavite religion. God as personal Lord and Creator, the All-Loving Divine Personality, who periodically incarnates and lives a fully human life to re-establish *dharma* whenever necessary. In Śaivism, Vishṇu is Śiva's aspect as Preserver. See: *Vaishṇavism.*

vista: A broad mental or physical view.

visualize (visualization): To imagine, create, mental images. Exercising the power of thought to plan for and shape the future.

viśuddha chakra: विशुद्धचक्र "Wheel of purity." The fifth *chakra.* Center of divine love. See: *chakra.*

viśvagrāsa: विश्वग्रास "Total absorption." The final merger, or absorption, of the soul in Śiva, by His grace, at the fulfillment of its evolution. It is the ultimate union of the individual soul body with the body of Śiva—Parameśvara—within the Śivaloka, from whence the soul first emanated. This occurs at the end of the soul's evolution, after the four outer sheaths—*annamaya kośa, prāṇamaya kośa, manomaya kośa* and *vijñāmaya kośa*—have been discarded. Finally, *ānandamaya kośa,* the soul form itself, merges in the Primal Soul. Individuality is lost as the soul becomes Śiva, the Creator, Preserver, Destroyer, Veiler and Revealer. Individual identity expands into universality. Having previously merged in Paraśiva and Parāśakti in states of *samādhi,* the soul now fully merges into Parameśvara and is one with all three of Śiva's perfections. *Jīva* has totally become Śiva—not a new and independent Śiva, as might be construed, for there is and can only be one Supreme God Śiva. This fulfilled merger can happen at the moment the physical body is abandoned, or after eons of time following further unfoldment of the higher *chakras* in the inner worlds—all depending on the maturity, ripeness and intentions of the soul, by which is meant the advanced soul's choice to be either an *upadeśī* or a *nirvāṇī.* See: *ātman, evolution of the soul, nirvāṇī and upadeśī, samādhi, soul.*

Viśvaguru: विश्वगुरु "World as teacher." The playful personification of the world as the *guru* of those with no *guru,* headmaster of the school of hard knocks, where students are left to their own devices and learn by their own mistakes rather than by following a traditional teacher.

vital: Relating to life or living. Also used in the sense of essential to continued existence or effectiveness.

vital forces: The life-giving energies in the physical body.

vitala: वितल "Region of negation." Region of raging anger and viciousness. The second *chakra* below the *mūlādhāra,* centered in the thighs. Corresponds to the second astral netherworld beneath the earth's surface, called Avīchi ("joyless") or Vitala. See: *chakra, loka, Naraka.*

Vivekānanda, Swāmī: विवेकानन्द Disciple of Śrī Rāmakṛishṇa who was overtaken by an ardent love of Hinduism and a missionary zeal that drove him onward. He passed into *mahāsamādhi* at the age of 39 (1863–1902).

vivid: Very clear, distinct or brilliant.

viz.: That is; namely. Used to introduce examples, lists or items.

voilà: An (originally French) exclamation of satisfaction or mild boast with a thing shown or accomplished.

volition: Will, faculty of choosing.

vortex: A place or situation regarded as drawing into its center all that surrounds it. Plural: *vortices.*

vrata: व्रत "Vow, religious oath." Often a vow to perform certain disciplines over a period of time, such as penance, fasting, specific *mantra* repetitions, worship or meditation. *Vratas* extend from the simplest personal promise to irrevocable vows made before God, Gods, *guru* and community. See: *sannyāsa dīksha.*

vrātyastoma: व्रात्यस्तोम "Vow pronouncement." The traditional purification rite, outlined in the *Taṇḍya Brāhmaṇa,* to welcome back into a Hindu community those who have become impure. It is performed for Hindus returning to India from abroad and for those who have embraced other faiths.

vṛitti: वृत्ति "Whirlpool, vortex." In *yoga* psychology, names the fluctuations of consciousness, the waves of mental activities *(chitta vṛitti)* of thought and perception. A statement from Patañjali's *Yoga Sūtras* (1.2) reads, "*Yoga* is the restraint *(nirodha)* of mental activity *(chitta vṛitti).*" In general use, *vṛitti* means: 1) course of action, mode of life; conduct, behavior; way in which something is done; 2) mode of being, nature, kind, character. See: *mind (individual), rāja yoga.*

Vyāghrapāda: व्याघ्रपाद "Tiger feet." Famous Nandinātha Sampradāya *siddha* (ca 200 BCE), trained under Maharishi Nandinātha, was a brother disciple of *ṛishis* Tirumular and Patañjali. He pilgrimaged south from Kashmir, settling at Tamil Nadu's Chidambaram Śiva Temple to practice *yoga.* See: *Kailāsa Paramparā.*

vyāna: व्यान "Retained breath." One of the body's five somatic currents of vital energy, or *prāṇa.* See: *prāṇa.*

vyāpinī: व्यापिनी "All-pervasive." The first of the seven *chakras,* or *nāḍi* conglomerates, above and within the *sahasrāra chakra.* See: *chakras above sahasrāra.*

vyomāṅga: व्योमांग "Space-bodied." The second of the seven *chakras,* or *nāḍi* conglomerates, above and within the *sahasrāra chakra.* See: *chakras above sahasrāra.*

waft: To float easily and gently, as on air.

wallow: To roll around clumsily and happily as a pig does in mud.

wane: To decrease, diminish.

ward off: To turn aside, prevent, avert.

waver: To vacillate, showing doubt or indecision. Characteristic of not being firm-minded. To be unsure of oneself.

wealth: *Artha.* Abundance; material affluence.

wellspring: A source, fountainhead.

whence: From where. Whence does it come? Where does it come from?

wherein: In what way; in which location.

willful: Said or done on purpose; deliberate.

will-o'-the-wisp: A phosphorescent light that hovers over swampy ground at night, possibly caused by spontaneous combustion of gases emitted by rotting organic matter. Something that misleads or deludes; an illusion.

willpower: The strength of will to carry out one's decisions, wishes or plans.

woeful: Sad, pitiful, full of sorrow and misery. —**woeful birth:** An unfavorable birth; a life of difficulties resulting from negative *karmas* accrued in previous lives.

world: In Hindu theology, *world* refers to 1) ***loka:*** a particular region of consciousness or plane of existence. 2) ***māyā:*** The whole of manifest existence; the phenomenal universe, or cosmos. In this sense it transcends the limitations of physical reality, and can include emotional, mental and spiritual, physical realms of existence, depending on its use. Also denoted by the terms *prakṛiti* and Brahmāṇḍa. 3) ***pāśa:*** In Śaivism, the term *world* is often used to translate the term *pāśa* in the Āgamic triad of fundamentals—Pati, *paśu, pāśa,* "God, soul, world." It is thus defined as the "fetter" *(pāśa)* that binds the soul, veiling its true nature and enabling it to grow and evolve through experience as an individual being. In this sense, the world, or *pāśa,* is three-fold, comprising *āṇava* (the force of individuation), *karma* (the principle of cause and effect) and *māyā* (manifestation, the principle of matter, Śiva's mirific energy, the sixth *tattva).* See: *microcosm-macrocosm, Śivamaya, tattva.*

worldly: Materialistic, unspiritual. Devoted to or concerned with the affairs or pleasures of the world, especially excessive concern to the exclusion of religious thought and life. Connoting ways born of the lower *chakras:* jealousy, greed, selfishness, anger, guile, etc.

wrenches: To twist, pull, yank or jerk in order to set something free.

yajña: यज्ञ "Worship; sacrifice." One of the most central Hindu concepts—sacrifice and surrender through acts of worship, inner and outer. See: *agni, havana, homa.*

Yama: यम "The restrainer." Hindu God of death; oversees the processes of death transition, guiding the soul out of its present physical body. See: *death.*

yama: यम "Reining in, restraint." See: *yama-niyama.*

yama-niyama: यम नियम The first two of the eight limbs of *rāja yoga,* constituting Hinduism's fundamental ethical codes, the *yamas* and *niyamas* are the essential foundation for all spiritual progress. The *yamas* are the ethical restraints; the *niyamas* are the religious practices. Here are the ten traditional *yamas* and ten *niyamas.* —***yamas:*** 1) ***ahiṁsā:*** "Noninjury." 2) ***satya:*** "Truthfulness." 3) ***asteya:*** "Nonstealing." 4) ***brahmacharya:*** "Divine conduct." 5) ***kshamā:*** "Patience." 6) ***dhṛiti:*** "Steadfastness." 7) ***dayā:*** "Compassion." 8) ***ārjava:*** "Honesty, straightforwardness." 9) ***mitāhāra:*** "Moderate appetite." 10) ***śaucha:*** "Purity." —***niyamas:*** 1) ***hrī:*** "Remorse." 2) ***santosha:*** "Contentment." 3) ***dāna:*** "Giving." 4) ***āstikya:*** "Faith." 5) **Īśvara-pūjana:** "Worship of the Lord." 6) ***siddhānta śravaṇa:*** "Scriptural audition." 7) ***mati:*** "Cognition." 8) ***vrata:*** "Sacred vows." 9) ***japa:*** "Recitation." 10) ***tapas:*** "Austerity." See: *rāja yoga.*

yantra: यन्त्र "Vessel; container." A mystic diagram composed of geometric and alphabetic designs—usually etched on small plates of gold, silver or copper. Sometimes rendered in three dimensions in stone or metal. The purpose of a *yantra* is to focus spiritual and mental energies according to a computer-like *yantric* pattern, be it for health, wealth, childbearing or the invoking of one God or another. It is usually installed near or under the temple Deity. Psychically seen, the temple *yantra* is a magnificent three-dimensional edifice of light and sound in which the *devas* work. On the astral plane, it is much larger than the temple itself.

Yin-yang: A Chinese philosophical concept of two polar energies that, by their interaction, are the cause of the universe. It is a symbol of the balance of opposites, feminine, masculine, dark, light, etc.

yoga: योग "Union." From *yuj,* "to yoke, harness, unite." The philosophy, process, disciplines and practices whose purpose is the yoking of individual consciousness with transcendent or divine consciousness. One of the six *darśanas,* or systems, of orthodox Hindu philosophy. *Yoga* was codified by Patañjali in his *Yoga Sūtras* (ca 200 BCE) as the eight limbs *(ashṭāṅga)* of *rāja yoga.* It is essentially a one system, but historically, parts of *rāja yoga* have been developed and emphasized as *yogas* in themselves. Prominent among the many forms of *yoga* are *haṭha yoga* (emphasizing bodily perfection in preparation for meditation), *kriyā yoga* (emphasizing breath control), as well as *karma yoga* (selfless service) and *bhakti yoga* (devotional practices) which could be regarded as an expression of *rāja yoga's* first two limbs *(yama* and *niyama).* See: *austerity, bhakti yoga, haṭha yoga, jīvanmukta, rāja yoga, siddha yoga.*

yoga break: Taking time out during one's work routine to lie on the floor in the corpse pose, relaxing all tensions and stress for five minutes, a practice made famous by Indra Devi in the 1950s and '60s.

yoga mārga: योगमार्ग See: *yoga pāda.*

yoga pāda: योगपाद् The third of the successive stages in spiritual unfoldment in Śaiva Siddhānta, wherein the goal is Self Realization. See: *pāda, yoga.*

Yoga Sūtras: योगसूत्र The great work by Śaivite Nātha *siddha* Patañjali (ca 200 BCE), comprising some 200 aphorisms delineating *ashṭāṅga* (eight-limbed), *rāja* (kingly) or *siddha* (perfection) *yoga.* Still today, it is the foremost text on meditative *yoga.* See: *Kailāsa Paramparā, rāja yoga, yoga.*

yoga tapas: योगतपस् "Fiery union." Relentless, sustained *yoga* practice that awakens the fiery *kuṇḍalinī,* bringing the transforming heat of *tapas* and ultimately the repeated experience of the Self God, leading to *jñāna,* the wisdom state. See: *Advaita Siddhānta, austerity, jīvanmukta, karma, jñāna, penance, siddhi, tapas, yama, yoga.*

Yoganāthan: யோகநாதன் The boyhood name of Satguru Śiva Yogaswāmī.

Yogaswāmī: யோகசுவாமி "Master of *yoga*." Sri Lanka's most renowned contemporary spiritual master (1872[8]1964), a Sivajñāni and Nātha *siddhar* revered by both Hindus and Buddhists. He was trained in and practiced *kuṇḍalinī yoga* under the guidance of Satguru Chellappaswami, from whom he received *guru dīkshā*. Sage Yogaswāmī was in turn the *satguru* of Sivaya Subramuniyaswami, current preceptor of the Nātha Sampradāya's Kailāsa Paramparā. Yogaswāmī conveyed his teachings in hundreds of songs, called *Natchintanai*, "good thoughts," urging seekers to follow *dharma* and realize God within. See: *Kailāsa Paramparā*.

yogī: योगी One who practices *yoga*, especially *kuṇḍalinī* or *rāja yoga*. (Hindu and modern Indian vernaculars. Sanskṛit: *yogin*.)

yoginī: योगिनी Feminine counterpart of *yogī*.

yoke: To join securely as if with a yoke; bind: partners who were yoked together for life. To force into heavy labor, bondage, or subjugation.

yoking: Joining securely or closely uniting.

yoni: योनि "Source, origin; womb." In certain *tantric* sects the Śivaliṅga is worshiped as a phallic symbol, and the base of the *liṅga* as a vulva, or *yoni*. While the *liṅga* represents the unmanifest or static Absolute of Śiva, the *yoni* represents the dynamic, creative energy of Śakti, the womb of the universe. Metaphysically, in men and women, the *yoni* is the area between the anus and genitals. It is the lower counterpart to the door of Brahman in the cranium. It corresponds to Brahmadvara, the psychic passageway to the lower *chakras*. Likewise, it serves as the highest point of those who live totally in these counter-clockwise-spinning *chakras*. See: *brahmacharya, brahmadvara, door of Brahman, Naraka, ojas, tantra, tejas, transmutation, Śivaliṅga*.

yore: Of yore: a long time ago, in a distant past. See: *Śivaliṅga, tantric*.

young soul: A soul who has gone through only a few births, and is thus inexperienced or immature. See: *soul*.

yo-yo: A toy consisting of a string attached to a round device, that when thrown, comes back.

yuga: युग "Aeon," "age." One of four ages which chart the duration of the world according to Hindu thought. They are: Satya (or Kṛita), Tretā, Dvāpara and Kali. In the first period, *dharma* reigns supreme, but as the ages revolve, virtue diminishes and ignorance and injustice increases. At the end of the Kali Yuga, in which we are now, the cycle begins again with a new Satya Yuga. See: *mahāpralaya*.

zealously: Filled with or motivated by zeal; fervor; eagerness.

zenith: Highest point; apex; summit.

Index

Anukramaṇikā

अनुक्रमणिका

ling, 958; depends on evolution, 282; dreams and, 553; explains inequities, 1038; facing, 572; giving and, 263; going to seed, 527; good and bad, 580; *guru* guides, 578; *guru* sharing, 579; hastened, 706; helping others,' 832; high-pitched sound "eee", 577; inhibiting life's goal, 5; intensified by meditation, 305; interraction hastens, 628; keeps us from knowing, 5; leg story, 576; like writing on water, 577; *mārga*, 323, 332; meditation and, 594; meditation intensifies, 572; *moksha* and, xviii; neglect of family duties, 814; non-acceptance of law, 934; others' experiences, 575; patterns changed by *darshan*, 276; penance resolves, 291; planetary changes, 579; *prārabdha* and the subconscious, 949; *prārabdha* germinating, 816; protection from, 751; resolution and *moksha*, xxv; resolved, *charyā-kriyā*, 878; resolving in meditation, 164; resolving internally, 574; *sakala avasthai*, 1079; *satguru*'s guiding, 578; spiritual teacher, 573; status at *mahāpralaya*, 1051; subduing, 730; sudden death and, 842; supreme judge and jury, 853; temple alleviating, 746; three categories of, 581; transferable, 576; ultimate healing of, xxix; under control, 1079; understanding, 959; working out in dreams, 560; world binding, 755; worship keeps current, 293; "the teacher", 1082

Karma *yoga:* anger remedy, 686; art of giving, 473; character flaws and, 344; patterns explained, 874

Karmic: cycle, at end of, 317; links, changing an object, 953

Kārttikeya: Nātha worship, 1077

Kashmīr Śaivism: views of liberation, xxiv

Kauai Aadheenam: bond with Dharmapura, 1063; seasons at, xv

Kaula: Śākta Hinduism, xxiii

Kavi: Dharmapura gift, 1062; saffron robes, 636

Kevala avasthai: fear in the, 793; not inwardly directed, 795; stage of soul development, 1078

Kevala state: beginning of, 793-794; pluralistic view, 1019

Key: astral, Resource 1087-1099

Kilinochi; Sri Lanka, chariots, xxxiv:

Killing; *Bhagavad Gītā*, xxx: lower chakras and, 688

Kindergarten; Vedāntic view of temple worship, 1019:

Knees: center of pride, 813

Knowing: all is within you, 21; all-pervasive, 994; is within, vii, 17, 19, 21, 23, 25, 27, 29, 157, 192, 451; that is known, 799; within oneself, 158

Knowledge: about oneself, 1127; best is experiential, 549; fourth merger with Śiva, xxviii; from meditation, 705; latent, 947; of the *jñānī*, 762; opinionated, 498, 905; right thought and, 318

Konrai: blooms, 269

Kośa: aspects of man, 488; Charts Resource, 1113; five-fold in *viśvagrāsa*, xxix

Kremlin: Aum in, xxxiv

Kṛishṇa: morals, xxx

Kriyā: bhakti yoga, 304; correct meaning, 758; defined, 1082; *pāda*, *avasthais*, 1080; patterns defined, 874-875

Kriyākramadyotikā: Aghoraśiva, 1073

Kriyamāna: category of *karma*, 581

Kshamā: yama, defined, 208

definition of inner, 211-212; experience of clear white, 84; external world disappears, 123; finding at top of head, 808; first attainment, 503; first step to here and now, 249; from pure consciousness, 775; golden yellow, *sushumṇā*, 610; great white, transcends all light, 1099; in darkened room, 447; inner, mind casts shadows over, 133; intense bursts of, 107-108; moonlike, 110; of understanding, 133, 211, 395, 412, 477, 909, 922; of your True Being, 781; pink, *iḍā*, 610; seeing within, 20; shadows and, 115; that lights thoughts, xxviii, 14; think you're seeing, 135; *Tirumantiram*, Subconscious, 391; tunnel of, 850; turning on, 351; viewing experiences in, 394; see also *Clear white light*

Lineage: sound and, 704

Liṅgam: importance of, 1080

Lions: roar like, xii; three, 377

Living with Śiva: prelude to *Merging with Śiva*, xvi; preparation for merging, 1126; Śiva, scriptural canon, 1083

Living with others: 629

Lizard chirp: signs and, 868

Lokas: asura, 307; Charts Resource, 1113; lower *chakras* and, 310, 679

Loose ends: cause rebirth, 400

Lord Muruga: *chakras* and, 312; see *Murugan*

Lotus flower: mind depicted as, 198; soul stands on, 109, 795; of the mind, 871; see *Awareness* as a, 35

Lotus pose: conquers *iḍā*, 606, 607

Lotus of the heart: *anāhata chakra*, 666; analogy of the heart, 121; analogy to *avastais*, 795; analogy to *chakras*, 660; analogy to man, 36; constant presence, 123; diamond in, 127; feeling the, 122; inspired talk, 119-128

Love: affectionate detachment is greatest, 49; astral color, 1095; auric colors, 509; *chakra* of divine, 667; conquers all, 254; divine, *viśuddha chakra*, 1117; for the Gods, 280, 293; Gods, 299; heart of the mind, 253; melts odic forces, 258; odic, 492; of everyone, 404; religion of, Hinduism, 279; removes barriers, 314; source of understanding, 139; the inner self, 259; *Tirumantiram*, total surrender, 301; trust and, xxviii, 326

Lovers: astral, 548

Loving Gaṇeśa: scriptural canon, 1083

Lower nature: dealing with positively, 767

Loyalty: to the *satguru*, 737

Lungs: weakening due to lack of lymph, 1001

Lust: as a way of life, 847; *atala chakra*, 1119; instinctive force, 366; renunciate and, 1109; *talātala chakra*, 687; *Tirumantiram* verse, 377; *yama*, defined, 208

Lying: *yama*, defined, 208

Lymph: abundance of, 1000; insanity, 1000; manifestation of *prāṇa*, 998; sex and, 1001; system, external nerve force, 998

Machine gun *japa:* 354

Macrocosm: microcosm within, 296, 679; *pūjā* and, 297; Śivaloka or Third World, 297

Madhumateya: Order, 1071

Madhva: influence on Meykandar's

xvii, 1074-1076; order, xiv
Nandinātha Sampradāya: Ādināthas and, 1075; aim of, 954; beliefs detailed, 1082; beliefs regarding God, 1076-1077; beliefs regarding the soul, 1078; described, xvii; *nāda*, 704
Narakaloka: living in the, 958; see also *Asuras*
Natchintanai: scriptural authority, 1083; teachings on creation, 1032
Nātha: beliefs regarding God, 1076-1077; beliefs, soul and world, 1078; beliefs, world, 1082; endeavored to fit in, 959; lineage, 1074-1075; path defined, 1082-1083; schools, comparison, 1075-1076; *siddhas*, 1074
Nātha Sampradāya: beliefs regarding the world, 1081-1082; fountainhead, 1074
Nationalism: Tamil, 1013
Nature: awaken higher, 9; deal positively with lower, 9; love of, astral color, 1097; Śivanāda found in, xxviii
Navaratnam, Tiru K.: quote on Tirumular, 1054
Nayanars: did so much wrong, 15; greatness, 13; Jainism and, 1070; survived with love of Śiva, 15; were not *pandits*, 1059
Naṭarāja: author's introduction to, xxx; cosmic dance, lxv
Near-death experience: escapism and, 850; Self Realization, 881
Need: freedom and, 962
Nekashum: withdrawing five winds, 969
Nerve: centers, represented by people, 997; plexus, *mūlādhāra chakra*, 661; system atomic psychic sounds, 108; system energizing, 128, 599
Nerve currents: 6,000 miles, 622; *chakras* and, 660; explained, 501; feeling, 598; finding at top of head, 811; *haṭha yoga*, 476
Nervous: difficulties, meditation aids, 163; system, grows through understanding, 140; system, understanding the, 973; two structures, 973
Nervousness: conscious mind, 904; holding to river bank, 54; subconscious overloaded, 100; *yoga* break, 142
Nether poles, 310:
Neuroses: subconscious overloaded, 100
Neurosis: conscious mind, 904
Neutralizing: astral colors, 1093
Neutron star: emanations, 790; Self as like, 789
New Age: men and women of, 942; *viśuddha chakra*, 672
Nightmares: causes, 545; children, 545; neither good nor bad, 197; not prophetic, 967; plagued by, 711
Nine: ways of merger, xxvii
Nine steps: God's, devotee's one, 1055; law of *guru*, 684; Śiva takes, 764; Śiva toward devotee, 1081
Nirguṇa: Brahman, *Vedas* on, 865; Saguṇa and, 864
Nirvāṇa: revelation and, 896
Nirvāṇī: arahat, 856; choosing to be a, xix; duties of, 615; role and attitudes, 857
Nirvikalpa samādhi: ājñā chakra and, 669; choice after, 615; complete renunciation, 504; death after, 828; do it again, 804; first breakthrough into, 803; *kuṇḍalinī* and, 613; laws of, 805; like cut glass, 881; multiple times, 616; Paraśiva, 774; physical body required, 834; Siddhānta summary, xxv; strengthening nerve fibers, 109; when bonds released, xviii; years after, 503

Scriptural Bibliography

Śāstrīya Sandarbhagranthasūchi

शास्त्रीय सन्दर्भग्रन्थसूची

The sourcebooks from which were drawn the scriptural quotations used in *Merging with Śiva,* as notated in "Verses from Scripture" and elsewhere.

ABBREVIATION EDITOR-TRANSLATOR SCRIPTURE PUBLISHER

AT: Karaikkalammaiyar, *The Arputat Tiruvantati* (Pondicherry, Institut Francais d'Indologie, 1956)

BO: Based on translation from…

EH: Karan Singh, *Essays on Hinduism* (Delhi, Ratna Sagar Ltd., 1990)

HT: Dr. B. Naṭarājan, *The Hymns of Saint Tayumanavar* (Kauai Aadheenam, Hawaii. Typescript)

MC: Chinmayānanda, Swāmī, *Mundakopanishad* (Madras: The Chinmaya Publications Trust, 1967)

NT: The Sivathondan Society, *Natchintanai, Songs and Sayings of Yogaswami* (Jaffna, The Sivathondan Society, 1974)

RM: Arthur Osborne, ed., *The Collected Works of Ramana Maharshi* (London, Rider, 1959)

SY: Ratna Chelliah Navaratnam, *Saint Yogaswami and the Testament of Truth* (Columbuturai, Thiru Kasipillai Navaratnam, 1972)

TM: Dr. B. Naṭarājan et al., *Tirumantiram, Holy Utterances of Saint Tirumular* (Hawaii, Saiva Siddhanta Church, 1982)

UPH: Hume, Robert E., *Thirteen Principal Upanishads* (Madras: Oxford University Press, second edition, 1958)

UPM: Mascaro Juan, *The Upanishads* (Baltimore: Penguin Books Inc., 1965)

UPP: Prabhavānanda, Swāmī; and Manchester, Frederick, *The Upanishads, Breath of the Eternal* (Hollywood: Vedanta Press, 1971)

UPR: Rādhākṛishṇan, S., *The Principal Upanishads* (New York: Harper and Brothers, 1953)

VE: Panikkar, Raimond, *The Vedic Experience* (Delhi: Motilal Banarsidass, 1989).

YM: Danielou, Alain, *Yoga: The Method of Re-Integration* (New York: University Books, 1955)

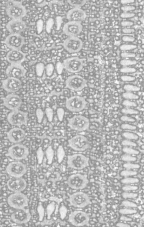

Index of Inspired Talks

Preraka Vārtānukramaṇī

प्रेरक वार्तानुक्रमणी

The Self God
An inspired talk given by Gurudeva at the San Francisco Sacramento Street Temple to a small group of *karma yoga* initiates on October 3, 1959, just before flying to the Hawaiian island of Oahu for the first time. In the original recording we can still hear the waterfall splashing on the altar which held many candles, respresentating our many Gods and saints. In this temple, the now famous Swāmī Chinmayananda, just beginning his Hindu renaissance career, gave one of his earliest lectures.

1: How to Realize God
An inspired talk given at Kauai Aadheenam, January 1, 1984, in which he answers a disciple's questions about God Realization. The section at the very end of this chapter is Gurudeva speaking on the Śaiva Saints in the Kadavul Hindu Temple after a procession following his *pāda pūjā* during Satguru Pūrṇimā, July 7, 1998, at the headquarters established in 1970, originally named Śivāshram. Here many *swāmīs, gurus, pandits* and *sādhus* visit through the year, creating very special occasions.

2-3: All Knowing Is Within You & What Is the Meaning of Life?
Drawn from the 1970 Audio Cassette Edition of *The Master Course,* recorded in the Guru Pīṭham (the seat of spiritual power from which the Satguru presides) at Kauai Aadheenam. About thirty Himalayan Academy students had come to the Garden Island of Kauai to be with Gurudeva. He gave dozens of recorded talks during this Innersearch Travel-Study Program, sharing about his spiritual path, his teachers and more.

4: The River of Life
An inspired talk given in 1957 at Gurudeva's first temple on Sutter Street in San Francisco (where he had the vision of Śiva dancing above his head). "The River of Life" was a central lesson in the *World Fellowship of Yoga* Correspondence Course, 1960. It was also published in 1972 as one of six books in the Pathfinder's Library series. At this temple, the eminent Swāmī Vishṇudevānanda gave one of his first talks in America, accompanied by Swāmī Rādhā, who later founded an *ashram* in Canada. The title of his talk was "Bhakti Yoga."

5-7: The Story of Awareness, Wisdom's Path & Willpower
Drawn from Gurudeva's 12-hour 1970 Audio Cassette Edition of *The Master Course* and earlier manuscripts.

8: The Clear White Light
Handwritten by Gurudeva during hours of seclusion on August 13, 1967, at Carl Jung's lakeside Casa Eranos villa on Lago Maggiore during the 1967 Innersearch Travel/Study Program in Ascona, Switzerland. It was at this same chalet on the large lake connecting Switzerland and Italy that Gurudeva reavealed Shum, the language of meditation, the following year.

9: Lotus of the Heart
An inspired talk given in 1972 and published by Comstock House as one of the six books in the On the Path series.

10: From Darkness to Light
An inspired talk given in the San Francisco Temple on Sacramento Street in 1965, where Gurudeva gave weekly Sunday sermons without fail for seventeen years. Saturday and Sunday's lessons comprise "The Yoga Break," first published in 1964. His Holiness Bhaktivedānta Prabhupāda was among the august speakers at this temple during his very early years of ministry.

11: The Power of Affirmation
An inspiring inspired talk given in 1958 in San Francisco and published in the *World Fellowship of Yoga* Correspondence Course, 1960; the 1967 *Master Course* and, in 1972, as part of the Pathfinder's Library series.

12: Beginning to Meditate
Compiled from "The Intensity of Meditation," an inspired talk published in 1965, and "Beginning to Meditate," given at his San Francisco Temple, the first Hindu temple in America, October 19, 1970 (beginning with Wednesday's lesson, third paragraph). Sunday's lesson is an *upadeśa* from the 1970s.

13: Five Steps to Enlightenment
Drawn from the 1970 Audio Cassette Edition of *The Master Course.*

14: Life, the Great Experience
An inspired talk given in 1957 at the Sutter Street Temple in San Francisco, which Gurudeva established at age 30. It served as his teaching center for the first year before he purchased the Sacramento Street property.

15: Facing Life's Tests
An early inspired talk drawn from *The Master Course,* 1967 edition, assembled by the monks of the Subramuniya Yoga Order at Gurudeva's Mountain Desert Monastery in Virginia City, Nevada, along with "Changing Your Circumstances," an inspired talk given in San Francisco in 1964 (beginning with Saturday's lesson).

16: I'm All Right, Right Now
Questions and answers recorded October, 1972, and subsequently published as part of the Pathfinder's Library series.

17: The Eternal Now
An inspired talk given at the San Francisco Temple in 1961. Saturday's and Sunday's lessons are drawn from *upadeśas* given in the early 1970s.

18: Love Is the Sum of the Law
Compiled from a lesson of the same name in *The Master Course*, 1967, and from "The Yoga Called Bhakti," published in *The Lotus of the Heart*, 1972 (beginning with Wednesday's lesson), and concluding with excerpts from "Bhakti Yoga," a talk given in the late '50s.

19-20: Love of the Gods & The Esoterics of Worship
An inspired talk given in the Kadavul Hindu Temple, on the Garden Island of Kauai, on October 11, 1978. Governor Arioshi later placed in the state archives acknowledgement of this first Hindu Temple in Hawaii.

21: Total Surrender
A series of *upadeśas* given in Hawaii, August, 1990, at Gurudeva's afternoon editing sessions which he has faithfully held each day from 1975 onward.

22: The Path of Egoity
A series of afternoon *upadeśas* given in Hawaii, December, 1989.

23: The Yoga of Incantation
A series of six afternoon *upadeśas* given in Hawaii, August 12-17, 1990.

24-29: The Universe of the Mind & chapters on the five states of mind
Drawn from *The Master Course*, 1967, as well as from the 1970 Audio Cassette Edition, and subsequent *upadeśas*, including a series of talks on the sub of the subconscious mind given in 1990.

30: The Nature of Thought
Compiled from two unpublished talks giving in Hawaii in the 1970s: "The Nature of Thought" and "Be a Witness."

31-32: The Physical and Prāṇic Bodies & The Astral Body
From "Man, His Seven Aspects," published in the *World Fellowship of Yoga* Correspondence Course, 1960 and *The Master Course*, 1967.

33-34: The Human Aura & Colors' Magic
Drawn from the *World Fellowship of Yoga* Correspondence Course, *The Master Course* and a series of *upadeśas* given during the 1986 Mauritius Innersearch Program of Himalayan Academy

35: Sleep and Dreams
A series of afternoon *upadeshas* given by Gurudeva in Hawaii, on May 9,

21,27-31, and June 4,5 & 8, 1990.

36: Karma, the Natural Law
Drawn from *The Master Course*, 1967 edition, and from *upadeśas* on *karma* given in the 1970s and the 1990s.

37: The Fine Art of Meditation
Questions and answers recorded in Gurudeva's San Francisco Hindu Temple on the evening of November 5, 1972, for a "Meeting of the Ways" radio program, and published as part of the Pathfinder's Library series.

38: Powers of the Spine
Drawn from the *The Master Course*, 1967 and 1970 editions.

39-40: Renunciate Life and the Two Paths & Men and Women Are Not the Same
From "The Two Paths," from the early 1970s a manuscript based on "Man's Key to a Woman's Mind," composed in the early '60s.

41-42: Spinning Wheels of Consciousness & Evolution of Consciousness
Drawn from *The Master Course*, 1967 and 1970 editions, and from *upadeśas* given at Kauai Aadheenam, July-August, 1989.

43: Force Fields and Psychic Protection
Drawn from the 1970 Audio Cassette Edition of *The Master Course*, along with *upadeshas* psychic protection given in the early '90s, and two unpublished manuscripts dictated on Kauai in the early 1970s: and "Sensitivity" (beginning at Friday's lesson, ¶2) and "Force Fields" (from Saturday, ¶2); (

44-45: Darshan, Grace of the Guru & Spiritual Training
An *upadeśa* entitled "Darshan," given at the Maharaja's Lake Palace in Udaipur, India, to 72 pilgrims who joined Gurudeva on a three-month Indian Odyssey, the largest tour group at that time to enter India. "Darshan" was partially published as *The Search Is Within*, in the On the Path Series, 1972. Chapter 45 concludes with an *upadeśa* on *bhakti* given in Hawaii, 1990.

46: Jñānīs and the Path They Teach
An *upadeśa* given at Kauai Aadheenam in February, 1984, published in HINDUISM TODAY that same year.

47: The Two Perfections of Our Soul
An inspired talk given to his Śaiva Swāmī Saṅgam at Kauai Aadheenam on May 18, 1981. Thursday's lesson begins "On the Brink of the Absolute," August 28, 1960, followed by "Everything Is Within You," 1959, both given at the San Francisco Hindu Temple.

48: Soul, Self and Samādhi
A short afternoon *upadeśa* comparing the Self to a neutron star, given in Hawaii on October 13, 1990; followed by (in Tuesday's lesson onward) an

upadeśa on the nature of the soul, *circa* 1975.

49: The Responsibility of Enlightenment
A talk originally entitled "Samādhi," given at Gurudeva's Mountain Desert Monastery in Virginia City Nevada in 1967, followed by "The Responsibility of Enlightenment" given in Hawaii on July 16, 1990 (beginning in Saturday's lesson, paragraph 3), with other discourses.

50: Reincarnation
From the 1958 and 1967 *Master Course* and subsequent *upadeśas.*

51: Death and Dying
A series of five afternoon *upadeśas* given in Hawaii, August 8, 16, 23, September 6 & 9, and October 2, 1989.

52: Final Conclusions for All Mankind
An inspired talk given October 10, 1978, in Hawaii. Gurudeva dictated the final day of study, "Eternal Questions" at the monastery's Hale Makai seaside retreat in Kapaa on June 13, 1998.

Part Four: Cognizantability
Aphorisms brought through from the inner skys in 1950 in Oakland, California, during the year following Gurudeva's first breakthrough into Self Realization. The commentaries came seven years later, in 1957, in Denver, Colorado. Sections One and Two of *Cognizantability* were first published in 1958 in book form and in the *World Fellowship of Yoga* Correspondence Course, 1960, and in 1970 as *Raja Yoga.* Section Three, "Journey of Awareness," consists of unpublished aphorisms also brought through in 1950 to which Gurudeva dictated commentaries on November 29, December 7 *&* 12, 1989, and January 1, 8-9, 1990, on Kauai.

Resource One: There Can Be Only One Final Conclusion
From *Śaivite Controversy, Monism and Pluralism in Śaiva Siddhānta,* 1991, comprising three documents: 1) a paper entitled "There Can Be Only One Final Conclusion," written in August of 1981 by Gurudeva and his Śaiva Swāmī Saṅgam of Kauai Aadheenam and sent to Śaivite scholars, authorities and monasteries throughout the world, critically comparing the two schools of Śaiva Siddhanta—and later updated for submission to the delegates of the First International Seminar on Śaiva Siddhānta, May 11-13, 1984, at Dharmapura Aadheenam, South India; 2) "Response to the Pamphlet 'Souls Are Beginningless,' " from Kauai Aadheenam, following a closed-door session on Monism and Pluralism in Kuala Lumpur, July 14, 1983—part of a conference, at which Gurudeva was the primary speaker, convened to discuss the issues raised in the monograph "There Can Be Only One Final Conclusion," and 3) "Visions of Truth: Dualism and Nondualism," an inspired talk Gurudeva gave to devotees in Mauritius in the summer of 1984.

Colophon

Antyavachana

अन्त्यवचन

M*ERGING WITH ŚIVA: HINDUISM'S CONTEMPORARY METAPHYSICS* IS THE CULMINATION OF FIFTY YEARS OF TEACHING. IT *WAS* DRAWN together by Gurudeva in unfailing daily afternoon editing sessions from January, 1997, to November, 1998. This third book in the *Dancing, Living* and *Merging with Śiva* trilogy was designed and illustrated by the *āchāryas* and *swāmīs* of the Śaiva Siddhānta Yoga Order at Kauai's Hindu Monastery on the Garden Island of Kauai. It was edited and assembled in Quark XPress on a network of Power Macintosh G3 computers. The text is 12.5-point Minion on 15-point linespacing. Sanskṛit and Tamil fonts include those by Ecological Linguistics, Brahmi Type and Srikrishna Patil. Pages were output to film by BookCrafters in Chelsea, Michigan, and printed by offset press on 40# Finche Opaque paper.

The cover art is a watercolor by Tiru S. Rajam, 79, of Chennai, India, commissioned for this book in 1997. The Deity paintings on the title page and after the introduction are by the same artist, a venerable national treasure of South India, musical composer and traditional Tamil Śaivite artist whose work is permanently exhibited in the British Museum in London. The vivid oil portrait of Gurudeva on the back cover and the Gaṇeśa on page ii were gifts by India's renowned artist and national treasure, Sri Indra Sharma, 73, during his sojourn on Kauai in late 1997. He was also commissioned to execute the portrait of Jñānaguru Yogaswāmī on page iv, a likeness described to be "just like he looked," said Śrila Śrī Śivaratnapūri Tiruchiswāmīgal of Bangalore, who knew him well. The elegant and philosophically rich paintings that initiate each chapter are the work of Tiru A. Manivel, 56, commissioned in 1998. The computer graphic patterns were done by a gifted soul of our *sannyāsin* order. Assistance in indexing and the glossary was provided by Śivanadiyar Jivananda and Selvan Jnanadeva Shanmuganatha. Gurudeva enjoyed painting with *vibhūti* on black paper the art that appears on the title page of each chapter. A few of Gurudeva's original handwritten aphorisms and commentaries from the 1950s appear on the pages of "Cognizantability."

For the transliteration, or spelling, of Sanskṛit words we chose the system used by Monier Williams (1819-1899) in his Sanskṛit dictionaries. It seemed more natural to us than the system now used in academic texts. Denoting the *ch* sound and the *sh* sound are two of the main differences. In the academic system, the *ch* sound (as in *chakra)* is spelled with a simple *c.* We chose *ch* instead, because in English the *c* is always sounded as *c* as in *count*, or *c* as in *cinder*, never as a *ch* sound, as in *charm.* We also sought a system that does not require a change in spellings when diacriticals are dropped off. That's why we also chose to not use the dot under the *s* for ष, and instead use *sh*, and to put an *i* after *ṛ*, as in *ṛishi.* A chart of pronunciation is found on page 1130.

Assistance in Sanskṛit translation was provided by Dr. Swamy Satyam, with Sanskṛit proofreading by Dr. P. Jayaraman, Executive Director, Bharatiya Vidya Bhavan, Woodside, New York, and Georg Feuerstein, Ph.D., Director, Yoga Research Center, Lower Lake, California. Proofreading of the entire book was completed and by Vayudeva and his wife Peshala Varadan of Rockville, Maryland.

Finally, we give our "mahalo nui loa" (that's our Hawaiian-style "thank you") to devotees worldwide who supported this first edition with *pūjās* and prayers, and to all the insightful souls who tirelessly penned reviews and comments so thoughtfully. Thank you, thank you, thank you.

About the Author

Once in a while on this Earth there arises a soul who, by living his tradition rightly and wholly, perfects his path and becomes a light to the world. Satguru Sivaya Subramuniyaswami is such a being, a living example of awakening and wisdom, a leader recognized worldwide as one of Hinduism's foremost ministers. In 1947, as a young man of 20, he journeyed to India and Sri Lanka and was two years later initiated into *sannyāsa* by the renowned *siddha yogī* and worshiper of Śiva, Jñānaguru Yogaswāmī of Sri Lanka, regarded as one of the 20th century's most remarkable mystics. For over four decades Subramuniyaswami, affectionately known as Gurudeva, has taught Hinduism to Hindus and seekers from all faiths. He is the 162nd successor of the Nandinātha Kailāsa lineage and *satguru* of Kauai Aadheenam, a 51-acre temple-monastery complex on Hawaii's Garden Island of Kauai. From this verdant Polynesian *āśramā* on a river bank near the foot of an extinct volcano, he and his monastics live their cherished vision, following a contemplative and joyous existence, building a jewel-like white granite Śiva temple, meditating together in the hours before dawn, then working, when rainbows fill the sky, to promote the *dharma* together through Śaiva Siddhānta Church, Himalayan Academy and Hindu Heritage Endowment. Gurudeva is known as one of the strictest *gurus* in the world. His Church nurtures its membership and local missions on five continents and serves, personally and through books and courses, the community of Hindus of all sects. Its mission is to protect, preserve and promote the Śaivite Hindu religion as expressed through three pillars: temples, *satgurus* and scripture. Its congregation is a disciplined, global fellowship of family initiates, monastics and students who are taught to follow the *sādhana mārga*, the path of inner effort, yogic striving and personal transformation. Gurudeva is the recognized hereditary *guru* of 2.5 million Sri Lankan Hindus. His is a Jaffna-Tamil-based organization which has branched out from the Śrī Subramuniya Ashram in Alaveddy to meet the needs of the growing Hindu diaspora of this century. He has established a branch monastery on the island of Mauritius and gently oversees more than 40 temples worldwide. Missionaries and teachers within the family membership provide counseling and classes in Śaivism for children, youth and adults. HINDUISM TODAY is the influential, award-winning, international monthly magazine founded by Gurudeva in 1979. It is a public service of his monastic order, created to strengthen all Hindu traditions by uplifting and informing followers of *dharma* everywhere. Gurudeva is author of more than 30 books unfolding unique and practical insights on Hindu metaphysics, mysticism and *yoga.* His *Master Course* lessons on Śaivism, taught in many schools, are preserving the teachings among thousands of youths. Hindu Heritage Endowment is the public service trust founded by Gurudeva in 1995. It seeks to establish and maintain permanent sources of income for Hindu institutions worldwide. In 1986, New Delhi's World Religious Parliament named Gurudeva one of five modern-day Jagadāchāryas, world teachers, for his international efforts in promoting a Hindu renaissance. Then in 1995 it bestowed on him the title of Dharmachakra for his remarkable publications. The Global Forum of Spiritual and Parliamentary Leaders for Human Survival chose Subramuniyaswami as a Hindu representative at its unique conferences. Thus, at Oxford in 1988, Moscow in 1990 and Rio de Janiero in 1992, he joined religious, political and scientific leaders from all countries to discuss privately, for the first time, the future of human life on this planet. At Chicago's historic centenary Parliament of the World's Religions in September, 1993, Subramuniyaswami was elected one of three presidents to represent Hinduism at the prestigious Presidents' Assembly, a core group of 25 men and women voicing the needs of world faiths. In 1996 Gurudeva upgraded the newspaper HINDUISM TODAY to a magazine, a quantum leap that placed it on newsstands everywhere. In 1997 he responded to President Clinton's call for religious opinions on the ethics of cloning and spearheaded the 125th anniversary of Satguru Yogaswāmī and his golden icon's diaspora pilgrimage to Sri Lanka. Recently Gurudeva has been a key member of Vision Kauai, a small group of inspirers (including the Mayor and former Mayor, business and education leaders and local Hawaiians) that meets to fashion the island's future based on spiritual values. If you ask people who know Gurudeva what is so special about him, they may point to his incredible power to inspire others toward God, to change their lives in ways that are otherwise impossible, to be a light on their path toward God, a father and mother to all who draw near.

You can visit Gurudeva's home page on the Web: www.hindu.org/gurudeva/ and hear his daily voice message at www.hindu.org/today/

There are a few unusual men who have had enough of the world and choose to dance, live and merge with Śiva as Hindu monks.

These rare souls follow the path of the traditional Hindu monastic, vowed to poverty, humility, obedience, purity and confidence. They pursue the disciplines of *charyā, kriyā, yoga* and *jñāna* that lead to Self Realization. Knowing God is their only goal in life. They live with others like themselves in monasteries apart from the world to worship, meditate, serve and realize the truth of thc *Vedas* and *Āgamas.*

Guided by Satguru Sivaya Subramuniyaswami and headquartered at Kauai Aadheenam in Hawaii, USA, the Śaiva Siddhānta Yoga Order is among the world's foremost traditional Hindu monastic orders, accepting candidates from every nation on Earth. Young men considering life's renunciate path who strongly believe they have found their spiritual master in Gurudeva are encouraged to write to him, sharing their personal history, spiritual aspirations, thoughts and experiences. Holy orders of *sannyāsa* may be conferred in Gurudeva's order after ten to twelve years of training.

Satguru Sivaya Subramuniyaswami
Guru Mahāsannidhānam, Kauai Aadheenam
107 Kaholalele Road, Kapaa, Hawaii 96746-9304 USA

Hail, O sannyāsin, love's embodiment! Does any power exist apart from love? Diffuse thyself throughout the happy world. Let painful māyā cease and never return. Day and night give praise unto the Lord. Pour forth a stream of songs to melt the very stones. Attain the sight where night is not, nor day. See Śiva everywhere and rest in bliss. Live without interest in worldly gain. Here, as thou hast ever been, remain.

YOGASWĀMĪ'S NATCHINTANAI 228

The Mini-Mela Giftshop

For all our books, visit www.hindu.org/mini-mela/

Dancing with Śiva

Hinduism's Contemporary Catechism
By Satguru Sivaya Subramuniyaswami

This remarkable 1,008-page sourcebook covers every subject, answers every question and quenches the thirst of the soul for knowledge of God and the Self. Clearly written and lavishly illustrated, expertly woven with 600 verses from the *Vedas, Āgamas* and other holy texts, 165 South Indian paintings, 40 original graphics, a 40-page timeline of India's history and a 190-page lexicon of English, Sanskṛit and Tamil. A spiritual gem and great value at twice the price. "The most comprehensive and sensitive introduction to the living spiritual tradition of Hinduism ...a feast for the heart and the mind (Georg Feuerstein)." Fifth edition, 1997, 8½" x 5½", softcover (ISBN 0-945497-97-0), $29.85.

Living with Śiva

Hinduism's Contemporary Culture
By Satguru Sivaya Subramuniyaswami

Hindu culture is nowhere illumined better than in this priceless collection of Gurudeva's honest, unflinching thoughts on every aspect of human life. And at its core are 365 spiritual rules for the lion-hearted, verses on how Hindus approach God, family life, sex, relationships, money, food, health, social protocol, worship and more. This book proclaims and clearly explains the ancient wisdom of how followers of Sanātana Dharma lived and interrelated with one another in the days when love and peace, respect and wisdom prevailed, and it shows how that spiritual life can and should be lived today. Second edition, 1999, 8½" x 5½", 1008 pages, beautifully illustrated with original paintings, softcover (ISBN 0-945497-99-7), $29.85. **Available September 1999.**

Loving Gaṇeśa

Hinduism's Endearing Elephant-Faced God
By Satguru Sivaya Subramuniyaswami

It began September 21, 1995, when an image of Gaṇeśa in a New Delhi temple began sipping milk, a modern miracle soon witnessed by millions, in temples, shrines and homes worldwide. How timely that, just days before, Satguru Sivaya Subramuniyaswami had finished the 800-page sourcebook *Loving Gaṇeśa.* The book is simple, deep and practical, teaching how Gaṇeśa's grace can be attained by devotion, song, prayer and meditation. "Lord Gaṇeśa comes to life through the pages of this inspired masterpiece. Loving Gaṇeśa makes approaching Ganesh easy and inspiring (The Mystic Trader)." First Edition, 1996, 8½" x 5½", 794 pages, beautifully illustrated with classical Rajput paintings, softcover (ISBN 0-945497-64-4), $24.85.

The Master Course

Level One,
Śaivite Hindu Religion

What every Hindu parent needs: intelligent, nonviolent, traditional texts for their kids—an authentic, illustrated, seven-book series called *The Master Course,* teaching philosophy, culture and family life. Based on the holy *Vedas,* the world's oldest scripture, this course is the loving work of Sivaya Subramuniyaswami. An excellent resource for educators and parents, it explains the "why" of each belief and practice in simple terms in three languages. Prominent leaders of all sects have given enthusiastic endorsements. "A commendable, systematically conceived course useful to one and all with special significance to fortunate children who shall be led on the right path (Sri Sri Sri Tiruchi Mahaswamigal, Bangalore, India)." Book One (5- to 7-year-old level) is available in a Hindi-Tamil-English edition. Softcover, 8½" x 5½", 170 pages, $12.95. Book Two (6- to 8-year-old level), English-Tamil-Malay, 196 pages, $12.95.

The Vedic Experience

Back when we were gathering Vedic verses for *Dancing with Śiva*, we could hardly believe our eyes when we came upon this brilliant anthology from the Vedic *Saṁhitās, Brāhmaṇas, Āraṇyakas* and *Upanishads* and other scriptures. This Vedic epiphany tells the story of the universal rhythms of nature, history and humanity. The translation and abundant commentary are the work of renaissance thinker Raimon Panikkar—the fruit of twelve years of daily *sādhana* in Varanasi between 1964 and 1976 while he lived above a Śiva temple on the Holy Gaṅga. He considers it perhaps his most significant literary contribution. This classic makes the *Vedas* available to all. Motilal Banarsidass, Delhi, 1977, smythe-sewn and case bound, cloth cover, 8½" x 5½", 1,000 pages, $41.

Hinduism Today

The International Monthly Magazine

Since 1979 Hinduism Today has been the foremost news magazine on Sanātana Dharma worldwide. For Hindus and non-Hindus alike, it covers the life, experience and ways of a faith in renaissance in communities from New Delhi to New York, from Moscow to Durban. Coverage includes religion, controversy, yoga, vegetarianism, meditation, nonviolence, environmental ethics, pilgrimage, interfaith harmony, family life, and more. Reporting from the spectrum of Hindu lineages, leaders and personalities, it is clear, articulate and stunning in full-color photos and art. Educational posters, humor, cartoons, sections on health, astrology and insightful commentary bring classical culture and contemporary wisdom to your fingertips each month. And yes, the author of this book is founder and publisher of this global magazine. US3.95; CAN$4.95 • ISSN 0896-0801; UPC: 0-74470-12134-3. See order form for subscription rates.

Lemurian Scrolls

Angelic Prophecies Revealing Human Origins
By Satguru Sivaya Subramuniyaswami

Enliven your spiritual quest with this clairvoyant revelation of mankind's journey to Earth millions of years ago from the Pleiades and other planets to further the soul's unfoldment. Learn about the ensuing challenges and experiences faced in evolving from spiritual bodies of light into human form and the profound practices followed and awakenings achieved in ancient Lemuria. These angelic prophecies, read by Sivaya Subramuniyaswami from *ākāśic* records written two million years ago, will overwhelm you with a sense of your divine origin, purpose and destiny and motivate a profound rededication to your spiritual quest. An extraordinary metaphysical book which answers the great questions: Who am I? Where did I come from? Where am I going? First Edition, 1998, 7" x 10", 400 pages, beautifully illustrated with original drawings, smythe-sewn and case bound with printed color cover (ISBN 0-945497-70-9), $29.85.

Monks' Cookbook

Vegetarian Recipes from Kauai's Hindu Monastery, Sivaya Subramuniyaswami

South Indian ashrams serve the finest cruelty-free meals enjoyed anywhere, and Kauai's Hindu Monastery carries on the 6,000-year-old tradition. They believe good food is mankind's best medicine, and there is an energy in their culinary contemplations, called *prāṇa,* that nourishes body and soul alike. Now the monks have shared their secret collection of recipes, gathered over the years and perfected in the Islands made famous by, wouldn't you know, Captain Cook! Enhance all your meals with this cornucopia of Jaffna-style and Indian dishes from around the world for daily meals and elaborate festivals. Also included is a 30-page ready reference on the unique *āyurvedic* qualities of a vast variety of spices, grains, fruits and vegetables. First Edition, 1997, 8½" x 11", 104 pages, lightly illustrated, durable paper, maroon spiral binding, softcover (ISBN 0-945497-71-7), $16.95.

Order Form

☐ Please send me free literature.

☐ I consider myself a devotee of Satguru Sivaya Subramuniyaswami. I kindly request to receive my first *sādhana* (spiritual discipline).

☐ I wish to subscribe to HINDUISM TODAY.

☐ 1 year, $39 ☐ 2 years, $74 ☐ Lifetime, $600

I would like to order:

☐ *Dancing with Śiva*, $29.85 ☐ *Living with Śiva*, $29.85 ☐ *Loving Ganeśa*, $24.95

☐ *Śaivite Hindu Religion:* Book 1 (ages 5-7), $12.95; ☐ Book 2 (ages 6-8), $12.95

☐ *Vedic Experience*, $41 ☐ *Monks' Cookbook*, $16.95 ☐ *Lemurian Scrolls*, $29.85

Prices are in U.S. currency. Add 20% for postage and handling in USA and foreign, $1.50 minimum. Foreign orders are shipped sea mail unless otherwise specified and postage is paid. For foreign airmail, add 50% of the merchandise total for postage.

☐ My payment is enclosed. Charge to: ☐ MasterCard ☐ Visa ☐ Amex

Card number: ____________________

Expiration, month: ________ year: ________ Total of purchase: ____________

Name on card: [PLEASE PRINT] ____________________

Signature: ____________________

Address: [PLEASE PRINT] ____________________

____

____

Phone: ____________________ Fax: ____________________

E-mail: ____________________

Mail, phone, fax or e-mail orders to:

Himalayan Academy Publications, Kauai's Hindu Monastery, 107 Kaholalele Road, Kapaa, Hawaii 96746-9304 USA. Phone (US only): 1-800-890-1008; outside US: 1-808-822-7032 ext. 238; Fax: 1-808-822-4351; E-mail: books@hindu.org; World Wide Web: www.hindu.org/mini-mela/

Also available through the following. (Write or call for prices.)

Sanāthana Dharma Publications, Bukit Panjang Post Office, P. O. Box 246, Singapore 916809. Phone: 65-362-0010; Fax: 65-442-3452; E-mail: sanatana@mbox4singnet.com.sg

Śaiva Siddhanta Church of Mauritius, La Pointe, Rivière du Rempart, Mauritius, Indian Ocean. Phone: 230-412-7682; Fax: 230-412-7177.

Iraivan Temple Carving Site, P.O. Box No. 4083, Vijayanagar Main, Bangalore, 560 040. Phone: 91-80-839-7118; Fax: 91-80-839-7119; E-mail: jiva@giasbg01.vsnl.net.in

Om Vishwa Guru Deep Hindu Mandir, Europe: Phone/Fax: 361-3143504; E-mail: ervin@mail.matav.hu

Merging with Siva is a splendidly written compendium of aphorisms and commentaries for daily practice that gives Saiva practitioners a lucid and simple method for inner transformation. Satguru Sivaya Subramuniyaswami's clear articulation demonstrates a wisdom and a love of Saivism that is uplifting and heartening. His true spiritual depth shines through in this work which will be treasured by all readers who seek clarity, insight and a tool with which to merge in the Divine.

Swami Chetanananda Saraswati, Spiritual Head of Nityananda Institute; Portland, Oregon

There are so many important things in *Merging with Siva.* My favorites: "The Story of Awareness." Philosophies are to be experienced step by step. Get acquainted with yourself as Being Awareness! Say to yourself, "I am not the body... I am not the emotions... I am not the thinking mind... I am Pure Awareness!" "The Search is Within." Each of the 36 contemporary dharmic principles opened up doors for me. Instead of paying attention to my real purposes in this life. Spreading my energy in too many directions. Try to save "the world" plus all of my relatives, friends, students and clients. This book has given me the knowledge and energy to move further onto my spiritual path.

Patricia-Rochelle Diegel, Ph.D, well known teacher, intuitive healer and consultant on past lives, the human aura and numerology; Las Vegas, Nevada

Merging with Siva demonstrates the good news that sacred scriptures continue to be written for the benefit of spiritual seekers. At the heart of this monumental work are ninety-nine mystical aphorisms together with their commentaries. In the manner of the ancient Vedic seers, both aphorisms and commentaries spontaneously formulated themselves in Satguru Sivaya Subramuniyaswami's *yoga*-trained mind many years ago. Building on this revealed wisdom, *Merging with Siva* expounds in easily assimilated form the highest aspect of the Saiva Siddhanta path to liberation, which is *jnana yoga*. It consists in recognizing who you truly are—not this limited body-mind but the eternal, blissful Self that is seamlessly merged with Siva. For this recognition to be possible, you must first transmute your body and mind into a pure vessel through diligent *yoga* practice. This book discloses many secrets about the actual path and the subtle energetic system whose workings must be understood to achieve success in the noble endeavor of self-purification and self-transmutation. This magnificent volume is an empowered communication about wisdom and love, which are the two wings by which the human spirit can raise itself above primal ignorance *(avidya)* and its many baneful byproducts. There is not a page in this scripture that does not contain profound insights or helpful words of encouragement. *Merging with Siva* is not merely an indispensable sourcebook for practitioners of Saiva Siddhanta, its timeless wisdom also speaks to spiritual seekers within other traditions. May it open the eyes and hearts of countless individuals.

Georg Feuerstein, Ph.D., Director of the Yoga Research Center; author of thirty books, including *The Yoga Tradition, The Shambhala Encyclopedia of Yoga,* and *Tantra: The Path of Ecstasy;* Lower Lake, California

The masterpiece book by Satguru Sivaya Subramuniyaswami is really a panacea to all Hindus all over the world. "Religion is realization, it is being and becoming." –Swami Vivekananda. The world is torn in several directions. Many people are deeply engrossed in worldly pursuits. This book is going to heal many a wound of many people across the universe.

H.H. Swami Chidrupananda, Sri Ramakrishna Sarada Sevashram; Point Pedro, Jaffna, Sri Lanka

Going through some of the chapters of this book, I see that the book is an outcome of the author's life-long dedicated study and spiritual practice. I am sure *Merging with Siva* will be found a source of Siva's grace by every devotee of Siva.

H.H. Swami Dayananda Saraswati, Founder and Spiritual Head, Arsha Vidya Gurukulam, Pennsylvania; Swami Dayananda Ashram, Rishikesh; Arsha Vidya Ashram Gurukulam; Coimbatore, India

Merging with Siva is a monumental work, a veritable course book of *yogic* development in the broadest sense of the term. It maps out all the domains of consciousness and shows us how to develop them in a systematic and harmonious manner. It unfolds the keys to our various bodies, *koshas* and *chakras* and how to purify and transform them for the ultimate goal of liberation. Through this complexity the book keeps to a simple, practical language that is accessible to any sincere devotee and helpful on a daily basis in everything that we do. ¶Such a book is quite unique in an age in which this deeper knowledge, if it is given at all, comes out only in fragments. *Yogic* knowledge in the West has recently been subject to various distortions, getting reduced to physical postures, divorced from any sense of renunciation, caught up in the illusions of the astral plane, and disconnected from its genuine religious and spiritual base. Satguru Sivaya Subramuniyaswami shows what the complete and authentic *yoga* is, shining his vast light upon the great mountains and seas of inner experience, connecting us with the vast wisdom of the *rishis* of old. ¶*Merging with Siva*

is an elixir that can cure all the ills of the soul. The book is one of the most important *sadhana* manuals available and will be welcomed by all those who wish to really connect to their higher Self and experience the Infinite.

Dr. David Frawley, O.M.D., Vedacharya; Director of the American Institute of Vedic Studies; author of *Yoga and Ayurveda: Self-Healing and Self-Realization;* co-author of *The Yoga of Herbs,* Santa Fe, New Mexico

In truth, man receives what he is ready to receive at the precise time he is ready to receive it. And it is now, at the time of the release of this great work that the serious researcher can discern how so many of the great schools of thought dealing with spirituality and metaphysics have been leading up to the central themes so beautifully illustrated here. Appropriately enough, it is released now, at the time of the millenium, when many spiritual paths have been trod, and countless books have been penned and read, all leading to the basic realization that Self Realization is the only realization that truly matters. It would seem that the countless paths of spirituality with which we are acquainted, especially in the West, have all been ramifications, offshoots at best, of what here is so clearly described, and which are the basic tenets of Hinduism. Looking into the future, it is to be seen that coming generations will consider this book a landmark, a condensation of what so many books had been trying to convey by supplying bits and pieces of the Truth as they could. And yet it has always been from the East that Western Metaphysics has derived its greatest inspirations, and indeed its very existence. Just as Paramahansa Yogananda's *Autobiography of a Yogi* first brought the concept of Self Realization as the ultimate goal of the spiritual path to the attention of a whole generation of Truth-seekers in the West, so also does this book, *Merging with Siva,* outline that goal and the means to achieve it. It has been said that all things return to the Source, and so it is that in this book Sivaya Subramuniyaswami has brought us back Home again to that Source which we all have been seeking, and which is and always has been, the Self God.

Arthur Pacheco, well-known counselor, healer, astrologer, theosophist, occultist, medium and parapsychologist, lecturer on psychic development, cosmic laws, mediumship and astrology; Honolulu, Hawaii

We find in *Merging with Siva* the teachings of a respected spiritual guide, based on his studies, experiments and experiences in the path of spiritual quest, extending for half a century. ¶Saiva Siddhanta is one of the important schools of philosophy in Hinduism, and the author of the present book is an eminent modern exponent of the same, engaged also in the task of bringing together the Hindus scattered all over outside India, and trying to harmonize their thought and practices. ¶The book deals with holy life, the theme is Siva-oriented and maintains a high level. The language is clear and forceful, the fine printing makes it easy on the eyes. It is bound to attract and also benefit various seekers. ¶Happily the accent is on earnest practice and personal experience, rather than intellectual or sentimental satisfaction. While many may be drawn to reading the book, only those who take to earnest practice will get the true benefit in life. Only those who are earnest about leading a holy life can test the teachings given and testify to their validity in life.

H.H. Swami Sastrananda, senior monk of the Ramakrishna Order, Vivekananda Ashrama; Bangalore, India

Book is too poor a word for this great work by H. H. Sivaya Subramuniyaswami. Such an immense compendium of spiritual knowledge is even more than a "treasury," it is an entire cosmos: an ordered world where the spiritual seeker can be at home and will find that everything connects to everything else in a vast, harmonious whole. In this cosmos the seeker's path to the ultimate Goal is clearly charted. ¶The realities pictured here could be described as concentric circles. At the center is the individual seeker, and his or her inner and outer life. The outer life expands to the family, the religious community, the lineage of Saiva Siddhanta epitomized by monistic theism, the Hindu world at large, our whole planet Earth, and beyond to the infinite universe with its many worlds and dimensions. The evolutionary dynamic of these realities and their different levels of consciousness are elucidated by Satguru Sivaya Subramuniyaswami forcefully and practically, yet with all their subtlety, and often with sweetness and humor. The reader will always feel the voice of the Master speaking intimately and directly to him or her, telling the seeker that this is your experience, this is your truth, this is your path. Here we find psychology, ethics, history, theology, esoteric teachings and mystical utterances all arrayed so that everything we need to learn and apply is easily accessible. ¶There is no way to single out parts of the book that are most important or better than others, since *Merging with Siva* is one organic whole. But as each of us has personal responses to every teaching, I will say that I was deeply compelled by the extraordinary revelation of "The Self God," which has pride of place in this voluminous work. I also take as especially useful for Western seekers these points: devotion is the indispensable preparation and foundation for all other spiritual practices, and formal worship can be a highly effective way to cultivate a bumper crop of devotion. The surrounding culture and community of a practitioner play a huge part in spiritual progress. In this progress knowledge of the "esoteric" (secret) or "occult" (hidden) is not some strange or forbidden realm, but a natural and inevitable stage in a continuous process of spiritual development. Talk of esoteric matters, however, means almost nothing to those who have no direct experience of them, and so it is actually counterproductive to try to learn about them by reading! The purpose of books is not, in this case, to provide information; the opposite is true: for one who already has knowledge, writings by others confirm it. This is a bracing and timely caution to countless seekers who indulge in mental preoccupation with the occult, or seek experiences outside their natural progression. All the knowledge and instruction that is needed as one embarks on the journey is given with clarity and luminosity in *Merging with Siva*. ¶Satguru Sivaya Subramuniyaswami brings down from intuitive planes beyond the mind a wealth of spiritual truth, and makes these riches usable by the seeker at whatever stage he or she may be, from the absolute beginner considering how to enter the path to the advanced meditator. It is his synthesis of *yoga*, and will prove to be a classic not only for disciples of Saiva Siddhanta and all Siva-lovers, but for all Hindus and indeed all spiritual seekers. Our hearts' deepest gratitude is due for this beautiful, illumining and nourishing gift to humanity.

Dr. Kusumita P. Pedersen, Chair of the Department of Religious Studies, St. Francis College, former Executive Director of the Project on Religion and Human Rights; Brooklyn, New York

Merging with Siva is a monumental work. Its 365 lessons are not mere random thoughts. They are the manifestations of what H.H. Gurudeva has himself realized through life long *sadhana* of this life and his past lives with his Guru's grace. ¶The book is most relevent today when the world is being shattered by terrorism, violence, loss of moral and ethical values in personal life, conduct and behavior. *Merging with Siva* would motivate and provoke everyone to think why a person is born, what is or what ought to be the mission of life, how to purify the self by inner devotion, dignity of thought and love toward others. Life is precious. It is a means to achieving realization of the Self within, realization of the Lord, Siva. This is not a myth or pure imagination. It is realizable. Saints and sages have realized it and that is why they advocate for it. *Merging with Siva* shall guide and give light to all truth seekers.

H.H. Sri Sri Swami Pragyanand, Founder/Patron of Sai Pragya Dham, Pragya Mission International, Pragya Mitra Pariwar and Pragya Yoga Foundation, New Delhi, India; Vishwa Mata Gayatri Trust, Delhi, India

Merging with Siva is the last book in a trilogy. Dancing *(charya)*, and Living *(kriya)* automatically lead to Merging *(yoga)*. Instead of calling it *jnanapada*, I would like to call it *layapada*, because *laya* or merging is the ultimate goal of which *jnana* is the first step. It is an excellent book – "a complete study for a lifetime, or two or more." Here is a book for training the soul, the eternal traveler. It fulfills the desire of the Great Child of Siva "to build a bridge between the East and West,... and roar like a lion around the world." Yes, the Jagadacharya has, sometimes, roared like a lion giving a stern warning to those who are commercializing *yoga* and other valuable gifts of *rishis* and making them very cheap. His roar, however, is a vibrant mixture of courage, bravery, straightforwardness, frankness, truthfulness, pain, sympathy, love and sweetness. The book is based on the experiences of the sweet-hearted author who wants to communicate the message of Siva in simplest terms, as a kind father wants to explain the subtlest things of philosophy to his innocent, but devoted, children. I can realize his merciful soul peeping through the words and sentences. One can easily feel him and Him joined in the *yoga* of love and *bhakti* and that is why the sentences touch the heart of a reader. No doubt these words have come out from his "inner sky," that It is Siva Himself speaking through the best conductor. "You do not have to be a saint, sage, philosopher or anything but an ordinary person to experience inner light. This experience makes you an extraordinary person." How soothing, encouraging and inspiring these words are! This is what we need today, especially for our youth, and that is the specialty of this great book. ¶The presentation and editing of the book is marvelous. The drawings, titles and sub-titles with Sanskrit translations, the headings at the start of paragraphs, the simple messages for different days of the year focusing mainly on improving the practical life and the final conclusion along with "Astral Colors" and the "Song of the Sannyasin" have infused *prana* into the book and I hope that the book will enliven and enlighten humanity through all generations to come. "Go thou, the free, from place to place, and help them out of darkness."

Dr. Swamy Satyam, Vice Chancellor of the Vedic University of America; author of over 20 books on Vedic *dharma*; Castro Valley, California

For someone who must constantly read a considerable amount of Hinduism professionally, this book possesses three particular virtues: its Saiva dimension, its autobiographical dimension and its philosophical dimension. ¶Any study of Hinduism from within it must be situated somewhere in it (as distinct from the Archimedian point that the academic is perpetually seeking outside it). This book is situated solidly in the Saiva tradition. Many studies of Hinduism, consciously or unconsciously, tend to possess a Vaishnava orientation. This book complements these other studies of Hinduism in a fulfilling way. ¶The author does not hesitate to speak in the first person. This is refreshing, for religious experience underlies religion. This constitutes the second of the two meta-messages of the book: that religion is locational, and that it is personal. ¶The author tries to come to terms with a central issue of not just Hindu but perhaps all philosophy—that of identity and difference—through a discussion of the issue in a Saiva context. This is done in a way which is almost emotionally moving it its rational elegance. ¶The inclusion of Swami Vivekananda's "Song of the Sannyasin" is a specially wonderful gift to the reader, like the author's introduction and Resource entitled "There Can Be Only One Final Conclusion." The perusal of this book can also only lead to one final conclusion: that Hindus, too, have been to the mountaintop, that they too have seen the promised land, and that they have also seen that there are many paths leading to the promised land.

Arvind Sharma, Birks Professor of Comparative Religion in the Faculty of Religious Studies at McGill University; Montreal, Canada

In *Merging with Siva, Hinduism's Contemporary Metaphysics* the relentless crusader in the global Renaissance movement of Hinduism, H.H. Satguru Sivaya Subramuniyaswami, shares his most precious spiritual insights with the whole human family. This book offers much more than illuminating reading. Daily practice of its lessons has the power to elevate each reader to the heights of perfection which are already there, embedded in the soul. Subramuniyaswamiji distills the most ancient religion in simple language, making it available and understandable to seekers of all faiths. He transcends the limitations of dogma. *Merging with Siva, Hinduism's Contemporary Metaphysics* is a powerful treasure. It flows with living revelation from the heart of one who has spent his entire life practicing what he teaches, into the heart of every sincere reader. May Lord Siva inspire one and all for the widest circulation possible of this incredible book on the science of life. Om Shanti.

H.H. Srimat Shuddhananda Brahmachari, Founder of the Lokenath Divine Life Mission, India, and Lokenath Divine Life Fellowship, USA

The new book, *Merging with Siva,* has much information and inspiration to offer to spiritual seekers around the world. H.H. Satguru Sivaya Subramuniyaswami has once more given a great gift to humanity: to Hindus, to know their heritage better and to non-Hindus, to appreciate the glory of the great Sanatana Dharma. The voluminous work has rich theories and concrete practices. Based on his own personal experiences, on authentic texts of Hinduism in general and of the Nandinatha Sampradaya (tradition) in particular, the guidance here boosts the morale of any devotee on the path. May Lord Siva bless every reader with great spiritual progress!

H.H. Swami Tejomayananda, Spiritual Head of Chinmaya Mission, Central Chinmaya Mission Trust, Sandeepany Sadhanalaya; Mumbai, India

I find the lessons to be simple to use and filled with Divine light and grace. Pujya Swamiji's *Merging with Siva* is divinely inspired and an imperative lesson book for all in quest of a conscious life and inner freedom. This book provides the clear and trenchant means to help spiritual aspirants walk the path of simplicity and consciousness by adhering to and following Hindu Dharma.

Brahmacharini Maya Tiwari, Founder of the Wise Earth School of Ayurveda; author of *Migrant Spirit: Recovering Our Ancestral Memories;* Asheville, North Carolina

To even try in some way to give a definition of the great work of Satguru Sivaya Subramuniyaswami is a harder task than climbing Mount Kailasha. It's with great wonder and respect that we admire the effects of his magnificent work which nowadays is of extreme importance for the diffusion and the coming together of Hindu culture and religion, and of Saiva Siddhanta in particular. His work is indeed concrete and not simply abstract. His deep knowledge and realization can be perceived in all his works, in his words and actions. Satguru Sivaya Subramuniyaswami is a true blessing for the whole of humanity and above all, for the Hindu world which has welcomed in its heart such a great soul. *Merging with Siva* is an extraordinary guide in every aspect of Hindu spirituality and its omniscient metaphysics. In this book, as in his life, Gurudeva takes the devotee's hand and guides him to the highest peaks of realization. *Merging with Siva* is a work of fundamental importance and is essential for every devotee. Each written word is a flow of blessings for all of us. May everyone take delight in the joy of reading it. Om Tat Sat.

H.H. Svami Yogananda Giri, Spiritual Head of Gitananda Ashram; Carcare, Italy

Packed with gems of wisdom, if this book were a jewel it would be a crown. The pages of *Merging with Siva* unfold with practical application of the divine inspiration of ancient sages and seers. Satguru Sivaya Subramuniyaswami gives in concise detail methods of *yoga* and meditation understood by saints but rarely explained. The friendly and engaging text is useful for the novice as well as advanced practitioner. One can read the book from front to back, back to front or opened and read in sections. There is so much content in these pages, that any one of the week-long lessons can be a sublime *sadhana*.

Sri Shambhavananda Yogi, Founder and President of Shoshoni Yoga Retreat and Shambhava School of Yoga with centers in the US, UK and Australia; author of *Spontaneous Recognition;* El Dorado Springs, Colorado